# Applying the Arm's Length Principle to Intra-group Financial Transactions

# Applying the Arm's Length Principle to Intra-group Financial Transactions

Edited by

Robert Danon
Vikram Chand
Guglielmo Maisto
Amanda Pletz

Wolters Kluwer

*Published by:*
Kluwer Law International B.V.
PO Box 316
2400 AH Alphen aan den Rijn
The Netherlands
E-mail: lrs-sales@wolterskluwer.com
Website: www.wolterskluwer.com/en/solutions/kluwerlawinternational

*Sold and distributed by:*
Wolters Kluwer Legal & Regulatory U.S.
920 Links Avenue
Landisville, PA 17538
United States of America
E-mail: customer.service@wolterskluwer.com

ISBN 978-94-035-4023-8

e-Book: ISBN 978-94-035-4035-1
web-PDF: ISBN 978-94-035-4040-5

# Editors

**Robert Danon** is a full Professor of Law and heads the Tax Policy Center of the University of Lausanne. He also serves as the chairman of the Permanent Scientific Committee (PSC) of the International Fiscal Association (IFA). Next to his academic duties, Professor Danon is a founding partner of Danon, an independent tax firm. At the international level, his practice focuses on dispute resolution (including investment treaty arbitration), tax treaties and transfer pricing. He frequently acts as a consultant or expert witness in high-profile international investment arbitration cases or litigation procedures. He also advises governments and has testified before parliamentary committees in relation to international tax reforms.

**Vikram Chand** is a Professor of Law at the University of Lausanne (UNIL), Switzerland. He currently also serves as the Program Director of the Executive Program in Transfer Pricing offered by UNIL, the Managing Editor of the Kluwer International Tax Law Blog, the International Tax Training expert for several tax administrations and the co-founder of the International Tax Law Research and Policy Network. He is also an independent tax practitioner and government advisor. His core areas of research expertise relate to the Application of the Arm's Length Principle to various Intra Group Transactions in various industries, Tax Treaty Law and Interpretation, International Tax Avoidance, Taxation of the Digital Economy (Pillar II and Pillar I) as well as Tax Controversy Management.

**Guglielmo Maisto** is the founder of Maisto e Associati, a tier-1 tax law firm with offices in Milan, Rome and London and a Professor of international and comparative tax law at the Università Cattolica di Piacenza. He is Vice-President of the International Fiscal Association (IFA), Chair of the European Region and President of the Italian Branch of the same organization. He is a member of the Board of Trustees of the International Bureau of Fiscal Documentation ( IBFD) in Amsterdam and of the Board of the American Chamber of Commerce in Italy, among others. He is a member of several law societies and on the editorial board of various Italian and foreign tax legal journals.

**Amanda Pletz** brings 20 years of experience in applying economic analyses to transfer pricing and international tax matters, focusing on litigation, regulation, pricing, and valuation. Her expertise spans various industries, including amongst other private banking, asset management, fintech, private equity, real estate, insurance, trading, and banking sectors. Ms Pletz advises on capital structure, cash pooling, loan pricing, hybrid instruments, guarantees, captive insurance arrangements, leasing, and other asset valuations. She has authored expert reports for global tax audits, facilitated negotiations for advanced pricing agreements (APAs) with European tax authorities, and provided support in litigation and arbitration cases involving guarantees, valuations, financing arrangements, and state aid. Ms Pletz has been repeatedly recognized as a Global Elite Thought Leader by Who's Who Legal for her expertise in transfer pricing.

# Contributors

**Rachit Agarwal** has practised transfer pricing in India and the Netherlands before joining DLA Piper in the UK. He advises multinationals on intra-group financing arrangements, achieving optimum operating model design, developing risk mitigation processes with a view on audit defence and valuing IP and other assets. His main focus area is intra-group financing covering cash pools, loan portfolio valuations, debt pricing, guarantee fees pricing, debt capacity review, derivatives analysis, designing and defending group financing policies. He is an instructor for transfer pricing courses at IBFD and Lausanne University and has conducted training sessions for tax authorities from Estonia, Hong Kong, Saudi Arabia, Uganda, and Tanzania.

**Denis Amici** is an Italian Chartered Accountant and Auditor dealing with transfer pricing and related international tax matters, such as attribution of profits to permanent establishments, business model restructurings and intragroup arrangements. He graduated *summa cum laude* in Economics at LUISS University – Rome in 2002. After the first transfer pricing experience gained in the Big Four, he deepened his tax background in a small firm and then moved into the banking sector. He completed the Executive Program in Transfer Pricing at the University of Lausanne in 2019 and he has been practising at Bacciardi Partners Law Firm (Pesaro, Italy) since 2020.

**Melanie Appuhn-Schneider** is a Transfer Pricing Director at WTS, a multinational tax consultancy firm, and currently serves as Co-Leader of the WTS Global Transfer Pricing Services practice. Melanie has been advising MNEs on a broad range of transfer pricing aspects for more than 15 years with a focus on economic and financial transfer pricing issues. She is a frequent speaker at international conferences and is part of the visiting faculty of the Executive Program in Transfer Pricing at the University of Lausanne. Melanie joined WTS in 2016 and previously worked at an international law firm for 10 years. She holds a BA and MA in Economics.

**Ulf Andresen** is a partner in DLA Piper's Frankfurt office. He is a German-certified tax advisor and an Australian Chartered Accountant. He advises multinational groups of companies and family-owned businesses in international tax and transfer pricing matters. He graduated from the European Business School in 1995, and his doctoral dissertation received an honourable mention at the 2000 I.F.A. Congress in Munich. He has spent 24 years of his career in two Big Four firms, 16 years thereof as a partner, and focuses on controversial matters at the law firm he joined with a team in 2019.

**Anwesha Bandyopadhyay** is a Chartered Accountant associated with Vispi. T. Patel & Associates, in the field of tax, transfer pricing and litigation services.

**Sven-Eric Bärsch** is a Tax Partner of Flick Gocke Schaumburg (Tax and Germany) and is based in Frankfurt. He has broad experience in European tax planning and handling tax controversies, defending international tax and transfer pricing strategies through all phases of tax audits, and obtaining greater legal certainty from tax authorities, especially relating to tax rulings, competent authority procedures (MAPs) and bilateral APAs. His track record includes assisting on numerous complex tax disputes and litigation on behalf of multinational corporations operating and investing in Germany and Europe across a broad spectrum of sectors for more than ten years. Mr Bärsch has a PhD in international business taxation and is an adjunct professor/lecturer at the Business School of the University of Mannheim, where he teaches a course in international business taxation.

**Danny Beeton** is of counsel, transfer pricing at the Luxembourg law firm Arendt & Medernach and a Director of the transfer pricing advisory firm Beeton Consulting Limited. He was previously a tax partner and head of transfer pricing at the accounting firm Grant Thornton, head of transfer pricing economics at the law firm Freshfields Bruckhaus Deringer and managing director of transfer pricing at the valuations consultancy Duff & Phelps. Danny's directory listings have included World TP Guide ('Highly Regarded'). His publications include the regular 'Transfer Pricing Cases of the Year' reviews in the Tax Management International Journal.

**Mark Berenblut** is an experienced expert providing expert reports and testimony for complex matters involving economic damage quantum, insolvency and restructuring, financial investigation, white-collar crime, intellectual property, securities, and business valuation. Mark is recognized as a leading expert witness in arbitration by Who's Who Legal: Arbitration where peers and clients describe him as 'a seasoned professional', 'very knowledgeable, thorough and diligent both in his written work and his oral testimony'. Mark is a graduate of The London School of Economics, a former managing partner of both a US venture capital investment fund and a bioscience fund and co-author/author of two books: *The Litigator's Guide to Expert Witnesses* and *Proving Economic Loss*.

**Ronald Bernstein** is a Principal in NERA's global transfer pricing practice and is based in Berlin. He has worked for clients from various industries to provide rigorous analysis of value chains and operating models, structuring of supply chains, valuation of intangibles, financial modelling, and business restructuring projects, including post-merger integrations. Prior to joining NERA, Dr Bernstein worked for a Big Four firm for approximately nine years. During this time, he also worked as an external contractor for one of the firm's major clients in the transportation sector, where he gathered valuable industry experience.

**Simon Bowden** is an Of Counsel in the Australian tax team of international law firm Jones Day. Simon practices in the area of tax advisory and dispute resolution, with a particular focus on transfer pricing, anti-avoidance and international tax issues. He has extensive experience in advising clients on cross-border issues, responding to audits, managing dispute processes, and providing strategic advice, across a range of industries from energy and resources, to financing, to consumer goods.

**Alessandro Bucchieri** is Head of Tax Affairs of Enel Group, one of the largest multinational utilities in Europe operating in more than 30 countries worldwide. Degree in Economics and Business from the University of Rome 'La Sapienza', Alessandro is qualified as a certified public accountant in Italy and a member of the Italian Institute of Auditors. He started his career working as a consultant at Arthur Andersen and Deloitte. In recent years, he has been very active in promoting the adoption by large multinationals of a responsible and transparent approach to taxation within associations such as the European Business Tax Forum and B-Team.

**Andreas Bullen** is a tax partner at Wiersholm law firm in Oslo and advises on tax treaty law, transfer pricing, corporate tax law, EU/EEA tax law, tax procedural law, tax payment law and tax litigation. Andreas Bullen wrote a doctoral thesis at the University of Oslo titled *Arm's length transaction structures*, which was awarded the Mitchell B. Carroll Prize by IFA and the European Academic Tax Thesis Award by the European Commission and the European Association of Tax Law Professors. Andreas Bullen has also written the book *EU, EEA and Tax* and a number of articles on domestic and international tax law.

**Natassia Burkhalter-Martinez** is the head of the Transfer Pricing section at the Swiss Federal Tax Administration (SFTA) which she created from scratch. Her work focuses on unilateral APA and TP audits. Natassia and her team also support the cantonal tax authorities in their TP issues. Previously, Natassia worked as Policy Advisor at the State Secretariat for International Financial Matters, where she worked on BEPS and represented Switzerland at the OECD. She holds a PhD and an LLM in International Tax Law. She is also co-director of the Executive Program in Transfer Pricing of the University of Lausanne and the author of several publications in international and Swiss tax law. She is a frequent speaker at conferences in Switzerland and abroad.

**Chloe Burnett SC** is a barrister specializing in tax law with chambers in Sydney, Australia. She received her LLM from New York University (International Tax Program, 2005) and has lectured part-time at the University of Sydney since 2006. She appears in and advises on tax controversies of all varieties and takes a particular interest in international tax matters. She is the Vice-President of the Australian Branch of IFA and was Chair of the Recent Developments Panel at the 2018 to 2020 IFA Congresses.

**Mukesh Butani** is the founder and managing partner of BMR Legal, a law firm specializing in the areas of corporate international tax, transfer pricing, GST, Customs and International trade law, with expertise in litigation services, controversy management, strategic transaction advisory and tax policy. With specialization in domestic corporate international tax and transfer pricing, Mukesh has over three decades of experience in advising multinationals and Indian conglomerates on a wide range of matters relating to FDI policy, business re-organizations, cross-border tax structuring, tax controversy and regulatory policy. He is an acknowledged expert in the area of international tax policy, controversy and advocacy and has to his credit several landmark judicial pronouncements and depositions before expert committees. He has been deposed as an expert witness on contentious cross-border tax treaties and TP matters in foreign jurisdictions. He acts as an expert in issuing opinions, giving depositions, witness statements, examinations & cross-examination before appellate/arbitration forums.

**Richard Collier** is an Associate Fellow at the University of Oxford Said Business School, a Research Fellow at the University of Amsterdam Centre of Transfer Pricing and a door tenant at Field Court Tax Chambers, London. He specializes in international tax treaties, transfer pricing and financial instruments. Richard worked at the OECD in the role of head of the transfer pricing, treaties, and financial transactions team from May 2019 and from 2020 as a Senior Tax Advisor until May 2021. Richard has degrees in Philosophy and Law and completed academic research in international taxation at the University of Cambridge (LLM) and the University of London (PhD). He qualified as a barrister and chartered accountant.

**Bernardo Danesi** is a London-based economist who advises multinational companies on their intra-group cross-border transactions, assisting in the implementation of optimal pricing policies. Mr Danesi has been involved in a wide range of transfer pricing cases related to the financial services industry, including fund fee pricing, intercompany financing, and guarantee fee pricing. Furthermore, he has contributed to the delineation of value chain analyses for clients in a variety of sectors, including shipping and logistics, financial services, eyewear, and art auction houses. He has also worked on several disputes in the context of state aid claims and tax settlements.

**Meindert de Vreeze** is the Group International Treasurer with Publicis Groupe, one of the world's largest communication groups, since 2016. He is responsible for the group's global treasury operations including cash management, investments and hedging. Prior to this, he worked with General Electric for 4 years as Director of intercompany Funding EMEA based in Ireland, and 13 years with LeasePlan as Director Structured Finance & Securitisation, International Funding Manager, and Finance Manager based in Ireland, the Netherlands, and Brazil. He holds a Master's in Business Economics from the University of Groningen, the Netherlands and is a Chartered Financial Analyst (CFA).

**Georg Dettmann** is a Senior Economist in the transfer pricing team of Copenhagen Economics in Stockholm, Sweden. Georg is dealing with transfer pricing aspects both in a professional and an academic context. He has extensive experience in advising international corporations, financial institutions, energy companies and businesses at the forefront of the digital economy across Europe, the Americas, Asia and Africa. He regularly provides support on the transfer pricing aspects of financial services and the valuation of intellectual property. Georg's recent professional work includes the structuring of transfer pricing insurances, the valuation of intellectual property for IT companies and the provision of transfer pricing support for asset management companies. One of the focus points of his work is providing transfer pricing expertise in litigation cases. Prior to joining Copenhagen Economics, Georg worked as a Principal at NERA Economic Consulting.

**Robin Deutsch** is a Partner at Oliver Wyman, a global management consulting firm, based in New York. He has over a decade of experience advising primarily financial institutions on their strategic priorities, including those in their risk management and treasury functions. Robin is a trusted advisor to senior industry leaders across three continents and has executed complex consulting engagements for over 15 years. He began his career in London, after his graduation with First Class distinction from the University of Warwick.

**Xaver Ditz** studied economics in Mannheim and Hamburg (1999 Diplom-Kaufmann, 2003 Dr rer. pol.). He has been a partner with Flick Gocke Schaumburg in Bonn since 2005. Xaver is a professor at Trier University, lectures at the universities of Zurich and Lausanne, and at the German Federal Financial Academy. He co-edits commentaries on double tax treaty law, handbooks on transfer pricing and permanent establishment taxation, and journals such as 'Internationale Steuerrundschau' and 'International Transfer Pricing Journal'. Xaver is a board member of the German branch of the International Fiscal Association (IFA), and a member of the tax committee at the International Chamber of Commerce and the 'Außensteuerrecht des Instituts der Wirtschaftsprüfer e.V.'. He is a board member of TAXAND and chairman of the 'Fachinstitut der Steuerberater e.V.'.

**Craig Elliffe** is a Professor of Taxation and Law at the University of Auckland, Faculty of Law. Before taking a chair, he was a tax partner at major accounting and law firms for 23 years. His research areas are particularly in tax avoidance, international tax and corporate tax. He is the Director of the University of Auckland's Master of Taxation Studies programme. Craig is a member of the Tax Advisory Group of Chartered Accountants ANZ and was a member of the Permanent Scientific Committee of IFA and the New Zealand Government's Tax Working Group (2018-2019). He is the author of a number of journal articles in publications such as the *British Tax Review*, *Canadian Tax Journal*, *Australian Tax Forum*, and the *World Tax Journal* and has authored the JF

Northey prize-winning book *International and Cross-Border Taxation in New Zealand* published by Thomson Reuters (2015 and 2018), and *Taxing the Digital Economy: Theory, Policy and Practice*, Cambridge University Press (2021).

**Daniel F. Gibson, FCAS, MAAA** is a Partner at Oliver Wyman Actuarial Consulting, Inc., Dan leads its North American Property and Casualty Practice. A Fellow of the Casualty Actuarial Society and a Member of the American Academy of Actuaries, Dan has over 20 years of experience – over 15 in consulting and 5 with a Bermuda-based mutual and reinsurance company. Dan lives in Houston, Texas with his wife, Jennifer, and three boys, Caleb, Ethan, and Aaron. As a family, they serve locally and globally through their charities and support each other in the academic, musical, and athletic endeavours they all enjoy.

**Andrea Grainger** is the Global Head of Transfer Pricing at Swiss Re, one of the world's largest reinsurers. Based in Zürich, Switzerland, she has specialized in insurance tax and transfer pricing since 2002. Before joining Swiss Re in 2017, she held roles in EY, KPMG, and two European insurance groups in London and Edinburgh. She is a Chartered Tax Adviser in the UK and holds a Law degree from Duke University. Andrea started her career as US Navy Lawyer before moving to the UK and requalifying in tax.

**Alexander Haller** is a certified tax advisor in Munich, Germany. He has been a director at WTS, a multinational tax consultancy firm, since 2015. Before, he worked at an international law firm. After having completed his studies in business administration and tax laws, Alexander started his career in the tax department of a German multinational chemical company. His practice focuses on international corporate taxation and tax litigation.

**Stephen Hawkes** spent his career working within various elements of the Insurance Industry. Most recently, he worked for Marsh within the Captive Solutions segment, leading the International Advisory practice, and providing risk financing advice to a wide range of commercial organizations. Before taking on this role, Stephen managed Marsh's Captive management business in Guernsey. Stephen has worked in the insurance industry since 1978 across a range of disciplines such as Marine, Property and Casualty, Financial Lines and Risk Consulting as well as secondments out to clients to see the challenges of delivering practical solutions to risk financing challenges. Stephen retired from Marsh at the end of 2022.

**Zachary Held** is a director in the Kroll Transfer Pricing practice, based in New York. He has extensive experience performing transfer pricing, valuation and general economic consulting services to multinationals, funds and non-profit organizations. He specializes in assisting clients with compliance and documentation around the use of intercompany debt, including debt characterization analyses and arm's-length interest rate benchmarking studies. Zachary received a BBA with concentrations in finance and analytic consulting from Emory University's Goizueta Business School and is a Chartered Financial Analyst (CFA) charter holder from the CFA Institute.

**Michael Hewson** has over 17 years of experience in transfer pricing (TP) in Africa. He is the founder and director of Graphene Economics, a specialist economics advisory firm focussing on TP across the continent. Under his leadership, the Graphene Economics team was awarded the International Tax Review TP Firm of the Year award for South Africa in 2021. Michael has lectured or presented on the topic of TP in a number of countries including Ghana, Kenya, South Africa, Tanzania, the UAE, the UK and Zimbabwe. He is a member of Transfer Pricing Economists for Development, a Paris-based NPO, as well as the subcommittees of both SAICA and SAIT.

**Andrew Hickman** was Head of Transfer Pricing at the OECD between 2014 and 2016 and responsible for the G20-mandated BEPS outputs including the 2017 revisions to the OECD Transfer Pricing Guidelines. Involved in transfer pricing for over thirty years, Andrew was a tax partner with KPMG in London and before that an official with the UK tax authority. Andrew now operates as an independent consultant and works on matters that he finds interesting, including disputes, arbitration and research, and has contributed to the work of the UN subcommittee on transfer pricing. He holds a doctorate from the University of Oxford and is a research fellow at the Centre for Transfer Pricing and Income Allocation, part of the University of Amsterdam.

**Thomas Hug** is a Swiss Certified Tax Expert and Deputy Head Group Tax at Bank Julius Baer & Co. Ltd., Zurich, one of the world's largest pure private banking groups. Thomas' responsibilities include among others the bank's transfer pricing policy and the implementation of Pillar II. Prior to joining the bank, Thomas was a senior manager at PwC Switzerland. Thomas is an examiner for the Swiss Certified Tax Expert examinations, regularly publishes journal papers and speaks at national and international tax seminars. Thomas is co-author of the first comprehensive book on transfer pricing law in Switzerland.

**Diana Kabir** specializes in providing functional and economic analysis to multinational clients, with a focus on the financial services sector and the application of the OECD TP Guidelines. Her experience encompasses a variety of industries including pharmaceutical, E-commerce and energy. Diana has also provided planning and documentation support for large multinational companies, given guidance to clients contemplating a bilateral APA in Australia and analysed and documented the arm's length remuneration and interest rates for large multinationals. Her experience allows her to create bespoke economic solutions to their problems and ensure all supporting analyses and documentation meet local requirements.

**Michael Kobetsky** is an Honorary Professor at the ANU College of Law, Australian National University. He is a Fellow at the Tax and Transfer Policy Institute at the Crawford School of Public Policy, Australian National University. Professor Kobetsky is an Honorary Principal Fellow at the Melbourne Law School, University of Melbourne. Professor Kobetsky is a member of the United Nations Sub-Committee on Transfer Pricing (since 2010) and the United Nations Sub-Committee on Extractive Industries (since 2014). Professor Kobetsky has worked as a consultant for the United Nations, OECD, IMF, World Bank, Asian Development Bank, USAID, GIZ, and the IBFD.

**Adam Kosmala** graduated with honours from the Warsaw School of Economics, the leading business school in Poland. Afterwards, he spent two years as a researcher and then joined a tax department of a Big Four consulting company. He was involved in all types of advisory projects, from transfer pricing compliance to planning, Advance Pricing Agreement negotiations and audit support. He also led an excellence centre providing methodological support to other teams. Currently, he is a transfer pricing manager in a commodity trading firm.

**Seema Kejriwal** specializes in corporate international tax and transfer pricing, with nearly two decades of experience in advising Fortune 500 multinationals and large Indian business houses on a wide range of international tax and transfer pricing matters. Seema is a Commerce graduate from the University of Mumbai and is a qualified Chartered Accountant. She has worked with Big 4 firms and was seconded to the US transfer pricing practice of the firm. Besides her contributions to public policy initiatives of the firm, she regularly speaks at global seminars and contributes to research papers and columns on tax and transfer pricing policy which find mention in leading academic publications, such as IBFD, Kluwers, Bloomberg, Tax Notes, etc.

**Gary Lambert** has more than 30 years of experience in finance, with expertise in derivatives, structured products and hedge funds, covering markets, structuring and pricing, trading and execution. Mr Lambert acts as a financial expert in financial disputes, government enforcement actions, and in financial services transfer pricing.

**Benjamin Lancaster** is an Of Counsel in the Australian tax team of international law firm Jones Day. Benjamin predominately practices in the area of tax dispute resolution, with a particular focus on transfer pricing, anti-avoidance and other international tax issues. He has extensive experience in responding to audits, managing objection processes, providing strategic advice, and conducting tax litigation.

**Andrea Lee** was born in the Czech Republic. She studied at the University of Economics in Prague and Postgraduate of International Tax Law in Vienna, Austria. During her studies, she started working in consulting industry (M&A and international tax). During her consulting career, she lived and worked in Prague and Vienna, Shanghai (China), HCMC (Vietnam), Melbourne (Australia) and Brussels (Belgium). Over the course of time, she started to specialize in transfer pricing. In September 2014, after nearly 15 years in the consulting industry, Andrea decided to follow her passion for financial transactions and went into the banking industry. Currently, Andrea is working for Raiffeisen Bank Group.

**Emmanuel Llinares**, Chair of NERA's Transfer Pricing Practice, is an economist specializing in transaction pricing, asset and business valuations, and intellectual property analyses in an international tax context. He has over 20 years of experience in advising multinational companies and their legal advisors on defining and implementing their intra-group pricing policies and valuing assets. He has assisted them in the context of various re-structuring, pricing design, and negotiations with tax authorities. He has also provided economic analyses in the context of tax and IP-related litigations including the preparation of expert reports.

**Céline Martin**, Tax Advisor in Zurich (Switzerland) and Expert judge at the Administrative Court of the Canton of Aargau. She is an attorney at law and economist with a qualification as a Swiss-certified tax expert and has also completed the Executive Program in Transfer Pricing at the University of Lausanne. She regularly advises domestic and international clients in transfer pricing matters and has long-standing experience in tax procedures.

**Sandra Martinho Fernandes** is an Associate Director, Domiciliation and International Taxation at the European Bank for Reconstruction and Development (EBRD) in London. Sandra is an experienced international tax professional with more than 15 years' experience. Prior to joining EBRD, Sandra worked as a tax lawyer for several law firms in Porto and Luxembourg, as a tax integrity expert at the European Investment Bank in Luxembourg, and as a research fellow at the IBFD in Amsterdam. In 2018, Sandra obtained her Doctor of Laws (PhD) from KU Leuven. She regularly publishes articles and speaks at international tax conferences.

**Aurelio Massimiano** is partner of Maisto e Associati. His areas of expertise comprise transfer pricing and international tax with a special focus on Advance Pricing Agreement (APA) and competent authorities procedures. Aurelio has developed a large experience in transfer pricing in the asset management industry and the luxury industry. He is a member of the board of the Italian Branch of the International Fiscal Association. He often speaks at tax conferences and lectures on international tax matters for specialization courses at the university level and for various other organizations. He obtained an LLM in International Tax Law at the University of Leiden, The Netherlands.

**Timothy McKenna** is an Associate Director in NERA's Securities Practice. His areas of expertise include asset valuation, market structure, and forecasting. He has consulted on valuation, market manipulation, and related topics for corporate and governmental clients. He has led engagements related to the value of credit guarantees and the impact of subsidies on the cost of debt for US governmental agencies. Mr McKenna received his BA in economics from the University of Chicago, his MA in economics from the University of Pennsylvania, and his MBA from New York University's Stern School of Business, where he specialized in accounting and finance.

**Ralph Meghames** provides best-in-class advice in valuation, intellectual property and transfer pricing matters. His work spans a plethora of industries for which he has provided economic expertise in the context of advisory services as well as in disputes, litigation, and international arbitration. He has extensive experience designing and implementing complex systems and models driving the allocation of profits within multinational companies. He is also a frequent lecturer at Paris Dauphine University and at the Vienna University of Economics and Business. Mr Meghames is recognized as a leading corporate tax expert by Who's Who Legal.

**Jérôme Monsenego** is a full professor of international tax law at Stockholm University, a research fellow at the Amsterdam Centre for Transfer Pricing and Income Allocation, and Chairman of IFA Sweden. He served as Visiting Professor at Université Paris 1 Panthéon-Sorbonne (2022-2023), Università degli Studi di Torino (2021-2022) and Meiji University (2019). He has been advising Governments on several legislative projects and regularly intervenes as an expert before courts. He worked as an international tax advisor at PwC in Paris and Stockholm between 2003 and 2015.

**Aitor Navarro**, LLM, is Senior Research Fellow at the Max Planck Institute for Tax Law and Public Finance (Munich, Germany). He specializes in corporate taxation as well as in European Union and international tax law.

**Eugene Ng** is an economist who is experienced in servicing entities in the public and private sectors by providing economic expertise in the context of advisory services, disputes, and international arbitrations. He works with a diverse array of clients spanning multiple industries, including financials and fintech, aerospace, energy, real estate and hospitality. Mr Ng is involved in projects involving asset valuation, including enterprise and equity valuation; company restructuring; the pricing of complex financial securities, transactions and services; and the quantification of damages in commercial disputes. He also has experience in designing models for the allocation of profits within multi-jurisdictional organizations.

**Marta Pankiv** is a senior director, head of group tax and transfer pricing, at a tech company with dual headquarters in the USA and Austria and has nearly two decades of international tax experience including in leadership roles in-house and at PwC. She holds an LLM in International Tax Law and PhD in International Business Taxation from Vienna University (WU). Dr Pankiv is also a guest lecturer at the University of Lausanne and a regular speaker at tax conferences. Her book on transfer pricing published by IBFD was cited in the 2018 decision of the Tax Court of Canada.

**Vispi T. Patel** founded the firm Vispi T. Patel & Associates, Chartered Accountants. He is a Fellow member of the Institute of Chartered Accountants of India, has expertise in the areas of Transfer Pricing, International Tax and litigation, and experience spanning over 38 years in the profession.

**Rani Aldridge Peffer** has been employed by Procter & Gamble for over two decades and is currently a Senior Director and CFO Circle Expert in the Global Treasury organization. She has expertise in external and intra-group financing activities, including cash pooling operations, and she has been inducted into Procter & Gamble's CFO Circle program as recognition of mastery in the Global Treasury Capital Markets area. Rani holds a Bachelor of Science in Accounting and Economics and a Master of

Business Administration in Finance from the University of Kentucky, and she is also a Certified Public Accountant and Certified Management Accountant.

**Stefanie Perrella** is a managing director, the Global Head of Transfer Pricing, and the New York Office Leader for Kroll. Stefanie is a trained Economist and has been providing strategic advice on complex pricing and valuation questions for her clients for more than a decade. She is a thought leader on transfer pricing for financial services clients as well as establishing best practices for assessing intercompany debt and other financing arrangements for the firm's top clients across a wide spectrum of industries.

**Fabian Peters** is an economic and financial consultant who provides advice to law firms, international corporations, and medium-sized enterprises. He has worked on a variety of cases related to arbitration, litigation, and transfer pricing. Fabian's expertise includes the assessment of lost profits and additional costs in commercial disputes before ICC tribunals in relation to pharmaceutical products and construction delays. Fabian has also valued intangible assets, financial instruments and businesses across industries, to determine arm's length royalties, interest rates and other transfer prices in tax litigation, corporate restructuring and state aid contexts.

**Thomas Petrakos** is a manager at Embridge Economics and specialized in transfer pricing aspects of financing and asset management-related transactions. Thomas holds a Master's in Finance from the University of Amsterdam and a Bachelor's in Public Administration from Panteion University, Athens, Greece. In addition, Thomas has accomplished the Executive Program in Transfer Pricing ("EPTP") from the Tax Policy Center of the University of Lausanne, Switzerland. In 2021, Thomas has written an article relating to financial transactions which was published in the International Transfer Pricing Journal. Thomas joined Embridge Economics in 2017.

**Serena Picariello** is a Transfer Pricing Manager at Deloitte Luxembourg, specializing in the financial services sector and financial transactions. She advises many of the key players in the asset management industry and the banking and insurance sectors. Serena holds an MSc in Management and Accounting from the University of Siena (Italy), an MSc in Management from EBS Universität für Wirtschaft und Recht (Germany), and an LLM in International Tax from the Institute for Austrian and International Tax Law - WU (Austria). Additionally, she completed an Executive Program in Transfer Pricing from HEC Lausanne (Switzerland). Serena regularly presents at tax conferences and contributes to technical publications.

**Daniel Prates** serves as Tax Official at the Brazilian Revenue Service. He has more than 17 years of combined practical experience both in private and public sectors and has 3 advanced law degrees with a specialization in International Law (JD from USP, post-graduation and LLM from IBDT-SP).

**Dan Pybus** is a Partner based in the PwC London office. He has worked in transfer pricing for the last fifteen years, leading operational transformations, policy redesigns, multiple APAs and tax audits, and global documentation projects and has specific industry specialisms in the automotive, consumer products, entertainment, media, digital and technology industries. Within PwC, Dan is the leader of the UK Technology, Media and Telecoms TP industry segment and the EMEA leader for the Global Financial Transactions TP network.

**Serena Picariello** is a Transfer Pricing Senior Manager at Deloitte Luxembourg, specializing in the financial services sector and financial transactions. She advises many of the key players in the asset management industry and the banking and insurance sectors. Serena holds an MSc in Management and Accounting from the University of Siena (Italy), an MSc in Management from EBS Universität für Wirtschaft und Recht (Germany), and an LLM in International Tax from the Institute for Austrian and International Tax Law – WU (Austria). Additionally, she completed an Executive Program in Transfer Pricing from HEC Lausanne (Switzerland). Serena regularly presents at tax conferences and contributes to technical publications.

**Kinha Romanovska** is a research associate at the Tax Policy Center of the University of Lausanne. She is also a PhD candidate, and her main area of research is international tax competition and global minimum taxation. She combines academic research with practical experience working as a tax lawyer with individual and corporate clients, advising on international tax matters and dealing with complex multi-jurisdictional asset allocation. She has been recognized as a leading lawyer by Legal 500 and Chambers legal rankings. She is a member of the Bar in Poland.

**Luís Eduardo Schoueri** is a Full Professor of Tax Law at the University of São Paulo and Vice President of the Brazilian Institute for Tax Law. He was the Hauser Global Professor of Law at the New York University (2016/1) and Professor-in-Residence at the International Bureau of Fiscal Documentation (2017-2018). Luís Schoueri has also been a tax lawyer for more than 30 years, acting as a tax consultant as well as in litigation procedures before Brazilian courts. He is a senior partner at Lacaz Martins, Pereira Neto, Gurevich & Schoueri Law Firm.

**Jonathan Schwarz** is an English, Irish and Canadian Barrister and a South African Advocate. His practice focuses on international tax disputes as counsel and as an expert and advises on solving cross-border tax problems. He is a visiting Professor at King's College London where he is Programme Director of the LLM (International Tax Law). He is the author of *Schwarz on Tax Treaties* and *Booth and Schwarz: Residence, Domicile and UK Taxation* among other publications. He has been listed as a leading tax Barrister by reference to international transactions and particular expertise in transfer pricing. In the Chambers Guide, he is commended for his 'encyclopaedic knowledge of double tax treaties' and described as 'clearly amongst the best international tax barristers'. In Who's Who Legal UK Bar, he is lauded for his 'brilliant' handling of cross-border tax problems. He has served as First Vice President and on the Permanent Scientific Committee of the International Fiscal Association.

**Emilia Siravo** is the Head of Intagroup Reinsurance Process and Management at Swiss Re. Based in Zürich, Switzerland, Emilia is specialized in pricing global intragroup reinsurance transactions. Emilia recently completed the Executive Program in Transfer Pricing at the University of Lausanne. In addition, she holds a Master's in Education from the New School University, and a Bachelor's in Economics from the Wharton School of Business, along with several professional certifications including the: ARe, CPCU, CELTA I, CELTA III and SVEB.

**Niraja Srinivasan** assists law firms, multinational companies, and tax authorities with expert economic analysis to resolve transfer pricing disputes in matters involving intellectual property and arm's length compensation for global value generation. She brings a unique perspective to her solutions by leveraging 25 years of corporate and consulting leadership experience at Dell Technologies, GE, and other firms. She teaches at the Texas A&M University School of Law and Chairs the American Bar Association Tax Section's Transfer Pricing Committee. She is a frequent speaker at conferences and has published extensively on taxation and transfer pricing in the digital economy.

**Paul Sutton** is a corporate lawyer who specialises in intercompany agreements and legal structures for multinational groups. He is the author of 'Intercompany Agreements for Transfer Pricing Compliance – A Practical Guide', and the co-founder of corporate law firm LCN Legal. Paul regularly writes and speaks on the subject of the legal implementation of transfer pricing and works alongside leading transfer pricing professionals globally, helping to make sure that the transfer pricing policies of the groups concerned have legal substance and are implemented through appropriate intercompany agreements – which are kept up-to-date and tax audit-ready.

**Louise Sykes** is Head of Transfer Pricing at a major global property and casualty insurer. She previously worked in the banking and technology sectors and holds a degree in history from the University of Oxford. Any views expressed in this work are entirely her own.

**Niv Tadmore** is a partner at Jones Day and leads the Australian tax practice of the firm. The key focus of the practice is the resolution of tax disputes, mainly representing multinationals in respect of international tax and transfer pricing matters. Niv is the chair of the global IFA Supervisory Board and a member of the NYU Tax Council and the Melbourne University Advisory Board.

**Alessandro Turina** is a senior research associate within the Academic Department of the International Bureau of Fiscal Documentation (Amsterdam), managing editor of International Tax Studies and scientific coordinator of the Observatory on the Protection of Taxpayers' Rights. He currently holds teaching positions at Bocconi University (Milan) and at the University of Fribourg (Fribourg, Switzerland). He has been a post-doctoral research fellow at the Tax Policy Center of the University of Lausanne and a visiting lecturer at the University of Florida Levin College of Law.

**Benedetta Veneziano** is since 2019, an International Tax Specialist of Enel S.p.A. Degree in Business Administration from the University of Rome's 'Link Campus', Benedetta is qualified as a certified public accountant in Italy. She started her career working as a Transfer Pricing consultant at PwC TLS Associazione Professionale di Avvocati e Commercialisti.

**Camille Vilaseca** is a PhD candidate and teaching and research associate at the University of Lausanne, Switzerland. Her main areas of research and expertise involve transfer pricing, the digitalization of the economy and Pillar I. She is currently writing her PhD thesis on profit allocation of multinational enterprise groups, which includes an analysis of the ALP and Pillar I Amount A. Previously, she completed an LLM in International Tax at the University of Melbourne, Australia, and worked for Caterpillar in Geneva, Switzerland, as a graduate intern in the area of transfer pricing.

**Rhea Wadia** is associated with Vispi. T. Patel & Associates in the field of tax and transfer pricing.

**Scott Wilkie** is a Distinguished Professor of Practice at Osgoode Hall Law School, York University and a retired partner of a major Canadian law firm. Widely published, he teaches and writes broadly about taxation, notably international taxation and tax policy. He is a former vice-chair of the Permanent Scientific Committee of the International Fiscal Association, served as president of the Canadian branch of the International Fiscal Association, and is a past chair of the Canadian Tax Foundation.

# Summary of Contents

# Table of Contents

# List of Figures

# List of Tables

# List of Abbreviations

| | |
|---|---|
| AE | Associated Enterprise |
| AFR | Applicable Federal Rates |
| ALM | Asset and Liability Management |
| ALP | Arm's Length Principle |
| AOA | Authorised OECD Approach |
| APA | Advanced Pricing Agreement |
| APR | Annual Percentage Rate |
| APY | Annual Percentage Yield |
| ATAD | Anti-Tax Avoidance Directive |
| ATO | Australian Tax Office |
| BEPS | [OECD's Action Plan on] Base Erosion and Profit Shifting |
| BRICS | Brazil, Russia, India, China, South Africa |
| CAPEX | Capital Expenditure |
| CAPHL | Chevron Australia Holdings Pty Ltd |
| CAPM | Capital Asset Pricing Model |
| CCD | Compulsorily Convertible Debentures |
| CCS | Cross Currency Swap |
| CDS | Credit Default Swap |
| CeFi | Centralised Finance |
| CEN | Capital Export Neutrality |
| CESA | Cameco Swiss Branch |
| CEL | Cameco Swiss Subsidiary |
| CFC | Chevron Texaco Funding Corporation |
| CFC | Controlled Foreign Company |
| CFCA | Canadian Federal Court of Appeals |
| CFO | Chief Financial Officer |

| | |
|---|---|
| CIN | Capital Import Neutrality |
| CJEU | Court of Justice of the European Union |
| CMA | Common Monetary Area |
| CMF | Committee on Financial Markets |
| CPM | Cash Pool Masters |
| CPP | Cash Pool Participants |
| CRA | Canadian Revenue Agency |
| CTC | Canadian Tax Court |
| CUP | Comparable Uncontrolled Price |
| CVX | Chevron Corporation |
| DAPE | Dependent Agent Permanent Establishment |
| DCM | Debt Capital Markets |
| DeFi | Decentralised Finance |
| DEMPE | Development, Enhancement, Maintenance, Protection and Exploitation. |
| DIS | Decision Impact Statement |
| DSO | Days Sales Outstanding |
| DTC | Direct Taxes Code |
| EBIT | Earning Before Interest and Taxation |
| EBITDA | Earnings Before Interest, Taxes, Depreciation and Amortisation |
| ECB | European Central Bank |
| ECJ | European Court of Justice |
| EEA | European Economic Area |
| EMEA | Europe, Middle East and Africa |
| ERC-20 | Ethereum Request for Comments 20 |
| ERD Test | Expected Reinsurance Deficit Test |
| ERP | Equity Risk Premium |
| ESG | Environmental Social Governance |
| ESTR | Euro Short Term Rate |
| ETH | Ethereum |
| EURIBOR | Euro Interbank Offered Rate |
| FAR | Functional, Asset and Risk |
| FCA | Financial Conduct Authority |
| FFD | Fully Fledged Distributor |
| FFS | Fix Floating Swap |
| FFT | Fiat Finance and Trade |
| FMCG | Fast Moving Consumer Goods |
| FNA | Farmers of North America |
| FTA | Forum on Tax Administration |
| FX | Foreign Exchange |

| | |
|---|---|
| FY | Financial Year |
| GAAR | General Anti Avoidance Rule |
| GILTI | Global Intangible Low-Taxed Income |
| GLoBE | Global Anti-Base Erosion [rules] |
| HMRC | HM Revenue and Customs |
| IBAR | Inter Bank Average Rate |
| IBOR | Inter-Bank Offered Rate |
| IFA | The International Fiscal Association |
| IFRS | International Financial Reporting Standard |
| IIR | Income Inclusion Rule |
| IMF | International Monetary Fund |
| IP | Intellectual Property |
| IPO | Initial Public Offering |
| IPRG | Federal Act on Private International Law |
| IRC | Internal Revenue Code |
| IT | Information Technology |
| ITA | Income Tax Act (Canada) |
| ITAT | Income Tax Appellate Tribunal |
| JIBAR | Johannesburg Interbank Average Rate |
| JV | Joint Venture |
| LIBOR | London Interbank Offered Rate |
| LOESS | Locally Estimated Scatterplot Smoothing |
| LRD | Limited Risk Distributor |
| LTC | Loan to Cost |
| LTV | Loan to Value |
| MAP | Mutual Agreement Procedure |
| MEUR | Million Euro |
| MC | Model Convention |
| MLI | Multilateral Instrument |
| MNE | Multinational Enterprise |
| Nat Cat | Natural Catastrophe |
| NDR | Non-domestic Rates |
| NIBOR | Norwegian Interbank Offered Rate |
| OCD | Optionally Convertible Debentures |
| OECD | Organisation for Economic Co-operation and Development |
| ORAs | Options Realistically Available |
| P&C | Property and Casualty |
| PCC | Protected Cell Company |
| PCG | Practical Compliance Guideline |
| PE | Permanent Establishment |

| | |
|---|---|
| PoS | Proof of Stake |
| PoW | Proof of Work |
| PSI | Perfect Sneakers Inc. |
| PSM | Profit Split Method |
| PV | Present Value |
| RAO | Regulatory Activities Order |
| RBI | Reserve Bank of India |
| RCF | Revolving Credit Facility |
| REIT | Real Estate Investment Trusts |
| RMS | Revenue Management System |
| RoL | Rates-on-Line |
| RSA | Receivables Sales Arrangement |
| RWA | Risk Weighted Assets |
| SACR | Czech Supreme Administrative Court |
| SAI | Singtel Australia Investment |
| SARB | South African Reserve Bank |
| SARON | Swiss Average Rate Overnight |
| SARS | South African Revenue Service |
| SBI | State Bank of India |
| SFTA | Swiss Federal Tax Administration |
| SMEs | Small and Medium-sized Enterprises |
| SOFR | Secured Overnight Financing Rate |
| SONIA | Secured Overnight Index Average |
| StaaS | Staking-as-a-service |
| STAI | Singapore Telecom Australia Investments |
| TC | Thin Capitalisation |
| TFEU | Treaty on the Functioning of the European Union |
| TIOPA | Taxation International and Other Provisions |
| TNMM | Transactional Net Margin Method |
| TP | Transfer Pricing |
| TPG | Transfer Pricing Guidance |
| TVaR | Tail-Value-at-Risk |
| UN | United Nations |
| UTPR | Undertaxed Payments Rule |
| VaR | Value-at-Risk |
| WACC | Weighted Average Cost of Capital |
| WHO | World Health Organisation |
| WOS | Wholly Owned Subsidiary |
| WOSDS | Wholly Owned Step-Down Subsidiaries |
| YTM | Yield to Maturity |

| | |
|---|---|
| YTRM | Yield to Remaining Maturity |
| YTW | Yield to Worst |
| ZBA | Zero Balance Agreement |

# Part I Introduction: Applying the ALP to Intra-group Financial Transactions

CHAPTER 1

# Introduction

*Vikram Chand & Amanda Pletz*[*]

## I WHY THIS BOOK?

Intercompany financing arrangements play a fundamental role in any business or multinational's value-creation process. More specifically, businesses spend a significant amount of time deciding on optimal capital structures that are conducive to growth over the long run. Where a business is in its development, industry or objectives can lead to varying decisions on what is deemed as optimal with respect to amount, type, and ideal terms associated with debt or equity-type financing.[1]

The financial services sector and the credit markets continuously evolve with new financing options coming to market. An example of this is the increase in subordinated debt and alternative lending, such as streaming or royalty-based finance or other forms of mezzanine financing that grew in prevalence after the financial crisis in 2008.[2] The open banking legislation and crypto markets fuel the diverse range of financing options available to market participants.[3]

These trends coupled with the increasing complexity in the financial markets, the COVID-19 crisis (which has left a large hole in the pocket of many governments), and

* The views and opinions set forth herein are the personal views or opinions of the authors; they do not necessarily reflect the views or opinions of the organization with which the authors are associated.

1. A. Damodaran, *Corporate Finance: Theory and Practice*, 2nd ed., Wiley, 2003, pp. 537-541.
2. 'New Approaches to SME and Entrepreneurship Financing: Broadening the Range of Instruments', OECD Report, 2015, pp. 63-71.
3. 'Financial Services Unchained: The Ongoing Rise of Open Financial Data', McKinsey & Company Insights, 11 July 2021, https://www.mckinsey.com/industries/financial-services/our-insights/financial-services-unchained-the-ongoing-rise-of-open-financial-data; and 'Future of Finance, Review on the Outlook for the UK Financial System: What It Means for the Bank of England', Bank of England Report, June 2019, https://www.bankofengland.co.uk/-/media/boe/files/report/2019/future-of-finance-report.

other political pressures have resulted in financing arrangements being subject to more scrutiny. The number of dispute cases involving some sort of financing has increased significantly in recent years, not only in the context of applying the arm's-length principle (ALP) and transfer pricing rules but also in the broader anti-avoidance context. Some cases are the GE Capital Canada case, the Australian Chevron- and Singtel case, the UK Blackrock case, and the Fiat case of the European Court of Justice (ECJ).[4]

In response to the increased scrutiny and complexity in the transfer pricing area, in February 2020, the Organisation for Economic Co-operation and Development (OECD) released the first-ever draft guidance focused on how to address transfer pricing issues of financial transactions.[5] The draft guidance was subsequently adopted as part of the OECD Transfer Pricing Guidelines 2022.[6] The United Nations also introduced some key guidance on transfer pricing issues for financing arrangements.[7]

The released guidance provided a framework of certain considerations when addressing transfer pricing issues for financing transactions. On the one hand, the current guidance has created a more level playing field for taxpayers and tax authorities alike, by creating a homogeneous outline of aspects to consider when analysing financing arrangements.

On the other hand, as with all types of guidance, this high-level outline can also create issues with interpretation that can lead to more controversy. The controversy would also increase if countries adopted diverging approaches towards interpreting this guidance.

Against this background, the main purpose of this book is to provide insights into several practical and policy-related issues by focusing mainly on the transfer pricing aspects of intragroup financial transactions. The book also provides insights into the applicability of the broader anti-avoidance and dispute management landscape to intragroup financial transactions. The book is loaded with practical examples and case studies that cover legal and economic aspects.

The book has 55 chapters written by leading global transfer pricing and international tax experts (more than 50 experts) who hail from different countries and are currently working either in academia, tax administrations, multinational enterprises (MNEs), and consulting or law firms.

---

4. *General Electric Capital Canada Inc. v. Her Majesty the Queen*, Tax Court of Canada, 2009, 563; *Chevron Australia Holding Pty Ltd v. Commissioner of Tax*, FCAFC 62, 2017, Income Tax Assessment Act 1997, Division 820; *Singapore Telecom Australia Investment Pty Ltd v. Commissioner of Taxation*, Federal Court of Australia 1597, 2021 (Australia); The Commissioners for Her Majesty's Revenue and Customs (HMRC) and Blackrock Holdco 5 LLC, UK Upper Tribunal reference code UKUT00199 (TCC), 2022 (UK); Joined Cases C-885/19 P and C-898/19 P, *Fiat Chrysler Finance Europe v. Commission*, European Court of Justice, November 2022.
5. OECD, *Transfer Pricing Guidance on Financial Transactions: Inclusive Framework on BEPS Actions 4, 8-10*, OECD (2020).
6. OECD, *Transfer Pricing Guidelines for Multinational Enterprises and Tax Administrations 2022*, OECD (2022).
7. UN, *Practical Manual on Transfer Pricing for Developing Countries*, United Nations (2021).

## II HOW IS THE BOOK STRUCTURED?

The book is divided into nine parts and is structured as follows.

**– The Interaction Between the Selected Anti-Avoidance Rules and Transfer Pricing Rules with a Focus on Financing**

Part II focuses on the interaction of selected national anti-avoidance rules and transfer pricing rules with a focus on financing. The national rules covered are shams, general anti-abuse rules (GAARs), controlled foreign company (CFC) rules as well as other interest limitations (including Base Erosion and Profit Shifting (BEPS) Action 4 rules). Several interesting questions are raised, for instance, the order of the rules to be followed when analysing a case dealing with financial transactions and the resulting ramifications. In addition, tax treaty issues are considered, such as whether tax treaties restrict recharacterization of intragroup financial transactions carried out through domestic anti-avoidance measures.

**– ALP Framework for Financial Transactions: A Transactional Approach**

Part III of the book follows a transactional approach and offers insights on credit ratings and the application of ALP and transfer pricing rules to intercompany loans, guarantees, and cash pooling. Indeed, these latter transactions are analysed not only from an accurate delineation or recognition standpoint but also from a comparability standpoint.

For credit ratings, topics covered include how credit ratings are determined and the various issues surrounding implicit support. In particular, the book provides a toolset that includes how to perform a shadow credit rating analysis using publicly available methodologies from rating agencies such as Moody's, Fitch, or S&P, plus considerations for implicit support and the implication that this may have on the stand-alone credit rating of an affiliate under various scenarios.

On intercompany loans, insights are offered as to whether Article 9(1) of the OECD Model Convention authorizes recharacterizing loan arrangements. Additionally, realistically available options for loans are analysed. Thereafter, various approaches to price intercompany loans, including data considerations such as bond or loan transactional data, are outlined. The loan section considers the pertinence of different approaches under varying terms and conditions. Several practical examples pertain to fixed-rate loan transactions, floating-rate loan transactions, convertible bonds, the build-up approach and cost of funds approach, loans in the real estate sector, and the cryptocurrency industry. Case law emerging on some of these matters is extensively discussed from a German and Australian perspective. Finally, this section provides insight into the appropriate clauses to be inserted in contracts, the implications of safe harbours by governments, and the impact of crisis situations such as COVID-19 on transfer pricing of intercompany financial transactions and comparability considerations.

For guarantees, the contributors take a deep dive into the various transfer pricing challenges that arise when analysing intragroup financial guarantees. In addition to the delineation of the transaction and challenges relating to realistically available options, the book covers the practical application (through case studies) of the comparable uncontrolled price method by using data such as credit default swaps, the yield or market approach, and the actuarial approach to price guarantees. A chapter is dedicated to transfer pricing aspects of performance guarantees.

With respect to cash pooling, several issues are demonstrated through concrete case studies. Issues discussed with respect to physical and notional arrangements include the appropriate characterization of the cash pool leader and options available to the MNE, the allocation of appropriate rewards to the cash pool leader, and cash pool participants and challenges surrounding cash pool guarantees.

**– ALP Framework for Treasury Activities**

Part IV of the book begins by providing a general overview of how treasury operations can be structured in a group and the decision-making process often involved in providing related-party funding. The form of a treasury company (centralized versus decentralized), the functions undertaken, and the risks assumed can drive its return. In this context, the contributors consider specific issues related to allocation of risk and returns from a general standpoint and from a treasury entity's perspective. This section provides practical insights into the concepts of control over risk, financial capacity to bear the risks, and the extent to which such returns may need to be shared with other parties in the group.

A function that the treasury may undertake on behalf of group entities in particular is hedging. Treasury companies may hedge financial risks to which their MNE is exposed to avoid potential losses outside the risk appetite of the firm. The contributing authors provide an in-depth look at the fundamentals of financial risk management and how hedges offset or mitigate these risks, profit versus cost orientation, and transfer pricing considerations.

**– ALP Framework for Other Types of Activities**

Part V of the book contributes guidance on other transactions that are more and more observed in MNEs. In particular, the authors provide in-depth analyses of how to apply the ALP to factoring and captive insurance transactions.

In the case of factoring, characterizing and benchmarking a factoring transaction are complex tasks for several reasons. Transactions are often multilayered, entail significant credit risk, and have varying terms and conditions. Data available to benchmark these transactions are often scarce, thereby creating the need for other types of build-up approaches to derive the ALP. The McKesson case exemplifies several of these difficulties when dealing with factoring transactions.[8] In addition to appropriately delineating the transactions, the case demonstrates the importance of using accurate assumptions in such models. The contributors provide a practical example using the actuarial approach to derive the ALP for factoring transactions.

Understanding the type of captive company (including the benefits achieved) is a key starting point when considering transfer pricing of captive insurance companies.

8. *McKesson Canada Corporation v. The Queen*, TCC 404, 2013, para. 22.

A captive insurance transaction requires an initial assessment as to whether the captive is genuinely undertaking insurance/reinsurance business. For this assessment, the OECD Transfer Pricing guidelines list hallmarks to be met in part or in full. This book provides some practical examples and considerations when analysing an insurance transaction to establish whether the hallmarks have been met and whether risk controls are exercised by the captive, including its financial capacity to act as an insurer. Once a transaction has been determined to be one of genuine insurance, different approaches (including the comparable uncontrolled price, actuarial method, and transaction net margin method) can be relied on to determine the arm's-length nature of the transaction. This section provides practical examples, including data considerations on how to apply the methods.

**– Special Considerations for Transactions with Permanent Establishments**

Part VI of the book deals with financial transactions carried out by a permanent establishment (PE). Currently, profits are allocated to a PE based on either the arm's-length standard or a formulary standard. This choice depends on the domestic law and tax treaty in force. Assuming that the ALP approach is followed, the authorized OECD approach (AOA) comes into play. The contributors provide practical insights on how profits can be allocated to PEs that undertake treasury activities. Moreover, insights are offered on recognition of financial dealings between a head office and a PE. Several case studies and practical examples illustrate potential solutions for these issues.

**– The EU Perspective**

Part VII deals with a selected European Union (EU) issue, that is, state aid and its interaction with transfer pricing rules. The contributor takes a deep dive into the Fiat case and the ECJ judgement. One of the ECJ's key observations is that the reference system for state aid analysis can only be based on domestic law. It could well be possible that many EU countries could incorporate the OECD Guidelines into their national law. If they do so, the OECD Transfer Pricing guidelines and Chapter 10 would be relevant for any state aid analysis that deals with intercompany financial transactions.

**– Dispute Resolution under the OECD, UN and EU Framework**

Part VIII of the book deals with treaty-based dispute resolution tools to intragroup financial transactions. In this regard, the authors offer insights on various issues that could be analysed under mutual agreement and arbitration procedures. The chapters provide the OECD, UN, and EU perspectives (EU Dispute Resolution Directive and EU Arbitration) on these matters.

**– A Developing Countries Perspective on Financial Transactions: Selected Issues**

Finally, Part IX of the book provides a developing country's perspective on financial transactions. This section offers information on the Brazilian, Indian, and South African perspectives.

# Part II The Interaction Between Selected Anti-Avoidance Rules and Transfer Pricing Rules with a Focus on Financing

CHAPTER 2

# Do Tax Treaties Restrict Adjustments Made to Related Party Loans When the Tax Administration Applies the Sham Doctrine (Including Court-Based Rules) or Domestic GAARs?

*Vikram Chand & Craig Elliffe**

## I INTRODUCTION

In many countries, borrowings by related borrowers have been attacked by tax administrations under the (i) domestic sham/simulation doctrines or Courts have developed flexible facts and circumstances rules to characterize a financial instrument (such as United States (US) Courts) or (ii) general anti-avoidance rules. The rules could disregard/restructure the transaction (wholly or partly) as actually entered/structured by the taxpayer. The question analyzed in this section is to what extent can tax treaty provisions prevent such re-characterizations given the fact that tax treaties, in general, restrict national law? In this regard, it should be noted that this chapter will not deal with situations when re-characterizations are carried out through domestic transfer pricing rules or fixed ratio rules as an analysis of those issues is made in other chapters in this book.

* The views and opinions set forth herein are the personal views or opinions of the authors; they do not necessarily reflect the views or opinions of the organization with which the authors are associated.

## II DO TAX TREATIES RESTRICT ADJUSTMENTS MADE PURSUANT TO THE SHAM DOCTRINE (OR COURT-BASED RULES) WITH RESPECT TO RELATED PARTY LOANS?

At the outset, we would like to state that tax treaties do not create taxing rights. This means that tax authorities are not allowed to adjust the structure of the transaction unless it is authorized by domestic law.[1] At the same time, tax treaties (including Article 9) could restrict the application of national law.[2]

In order to get into the transfer pricing analysis, we need to first, determine the facts of the controlled transaction. Thus, as a first step, we need to establish the facts of the transaction or determine the controlled transaction that needs to be priced[3]. In other words, as provided by Article 9, identifying the "conditions ... made or imposed between two associated enterprises in their commercial or financial relations." With respect to the first step, the question arises as to whether Article 9 restricts the application of national law measures which, when applicable, could look beyond the arrangements as structured/executed by taxpayers and identify "commercial or financial relations" based on real facts or underlying reality or actual conduct?

Naturally, tax law (including transfer pricing rules), should apply to real facts of a case. Accordingly, tax treaties (including Article 9) do not per se restrict the application of domestic fact-finding rules or Court developed doctrines which characterize a financial instrument as a loan or equity contribution.[4] In this regard, the sham doctrine as well as other Court based approaches stand out as important doctrines since a reference to them has been made in various versions of the Organisation for Economic Co-operation and Development Transfer Pricing (OECD TP) Guidelines.

For instance, it should be noted that the OECD's 1979 transfer pricing report (issued on March 12, 1979)[5] contained a chapter dedicated to intercompany loans (Part 5). In general, it was recognized that *prior to undertaking a transfer pricing analysis* it is important to determine whether or not a financial instrument is a debt or equity. In this regard, paragraphs 185-191 discuss the various approaches adopted by States. In paragraph 186, it is remarked that Courts in one Country (most likely the US), adopted a "*fairly flexible approach*" which examines the circumstances of each individual case. The most important factors seem: "(1) whether there is an unconditional written promise to pay a fixed amount of principal at a fixed maturity date; whether the loan is subordinated to the rights of other creditors; the ratio of debt to equity of the company(2); whether the debt is convertible into stock or shares of the issuing company; whether the shareholders of the company hold the alleged debt instruments

1. Andreas Bullen, *Arm's Length Transaction Structures: Recognizing and Restructuring Controlled Transactions in Transfer Pricing* (IBFD Doctoral Series, 2011), pp. 75-56.
2. *Ibid.*, pp. 68-74.
3. OECD, *OECD Transfer Pricing Guidelines for Multinational Enterprises and Tax Administrations 2022* (OECD Publishing, 2022), para. 1.33.
4. Bullen, *supra* n. 1, pp. 146-147. Also *see* Chand Vikram and Elliffe Craig, *The Interaction of Domestic Anti-Avoidance Rules with Tax Treaties in the Post-BEPS and Digitalized World*, 74 Bull. Intl. Taxn. 4/5, (2020), pp. 304-307.
5. *See* Jeff Borghino, *Debt vs. Equity in the Tax Court, The Tax Adviser* (February 1, 2013), available at https://www.thetaxadviser.com/issues/2013/feb/clinic-story-01.html.

pro rata in relation to their shareholdings; the rights of the holders in the event of a default in the payment of interest (3); whether the parties 'intended' to create a debtor-creditor relationship or not." Paragraph 187 then discusses the approach of a country which adopted a "somewhat flexible approach" based on facts and circumstances as well as different ratios for different sectors in which the borrower operates (the approach seems to be the Swiss approach). Thereafter, paragraph 188 discusses a pragmatic approach adopted by another country. According to this approach, "all circumstances of a particular case would be considered to determine whether an alleged loan is to be regarded as 'hidden capital' contribution … . In practice, it seems to happen rarely that a financial transaction, which is treated as a loan under civil law, would be considered as capital for taxation purposes."

On the other hand, while the report recognizes the use of debt-equity ratios by various countries (paragraph 191) it recommended that such ratios should not be given considerable weight on a standalone basis. Rather the report suggests that countries should adopt a flexible approach even though it could be difficult to implement this approach.

Although the 1979 guidelines used the phrase "underlying reality" on several occasions to determine the controlled transaction (paragraphs 89, 113 and 170), a reference to a "*sham*" was made in the next version of the guidelines. The 1995 OECD Guidelines in paragraph 1.28 stated that the roles and responsibilities of the parties to a transaction should be determined on the basis of written contracts. This said, the guidelines also provide that it is "important to examine whether the conduct of the parties conforms to the terms of the contract or whether the parties' conduct indicates that the contractual terms have not been followed *or are a sham*. In such cases, further analysis is required to determine the true terms of the transaction."

The discussion made in the 1995 guidelines with respect to "*sham*" was repeated in the 2010 OECD TP Guidelines in Chapter I in paragraph 1.53.

The 2017 OECD TP Guidelines which were updated as a result of Base Erosion and Profit Shifting (BEPS) Actions 8-10, in paragraph 1.45 provide that "if the characteristics of the transaction that are economically relevant are inconsistent with the written contract between the associated enterprises, the actual transaction should generally be delineated for purposes of the transfer pricing analysis in accordance with the characteristics of the transaction reflected in the conduct of the parties."[6] Additionally, in paragraph 1.46 it is stated that "It is, therefore, particularly important in considering the commercial or financial relations between associated enterprises to examine whether the arrangements reflected in the actual conduct of the parties substantially conform to the terms of any written contract, *or whether the associated enterprises' actual conduct indicates that the contractual terms have not been followed, do not reflect a complete picture of the transactions, have been incorrectly characterised or labelled by the enterprises, or are a sham.* Where conduct is not fully consistent with economically significant contractual terms, further analysis is required to identify the actual transaction. Where there are material differences between contractual terms and

6. OECD TPG 2022, *supra* n. 3, para. 1.45.

the conduct of the associated enterprises in their relations with one another, the functions they actually perform, the assets they actually use, and the risks they actually assume, considered in the context of the contractual terms, *should ultimately determine the factual substance and accurately delineate the actual transaction.*" Preference for factual substance is also highlighted in paragraph 1.120.

Moreover, the 2022 OECD TP Guidelines in paragraph 10.8 states that while it is recognized that transfer pricing rules could be used to accurately delineate the intercompany loan, "it is acknowledged that other approaches may be taken to address the issue of the balance of debt and equity funding of an entity *under domestic legislation* before pricing the interest on the debt so determined. These approaches may include a multi-factor analysis of the characteristics of the instrument and the issuer."

Also, it should be noted that recently the OECD launched a paper which proposed changes to the Commentary on Article 9(1).[7] The draft paper states in new paragraph 3 that "in considering whether an interest payment can be regarded as an arm's length amount, a State will typically examine the terms and conditions of the loan such as the rate of interest. *It may also need to examine, based on the facts and circumstances, whether a purported loan should be regarded as a loan or as another kind of transaction, in particular a contribution to equity capital. The State making a determination as to the extent to which the purported loan is regarded as a loan will do so taking into account factors discussed in its domestic laws (including judicial doctrine),* or in the OECD Transfer Pricing Guidelines."

Based on the above discussion on the various versions of the OECD transfer pricing guidelines, one may thus state that tax treaties do not restrict the application of the sham doctrine or Court developed doctrines to the extent they are used to determine the "real" amount of debt among associated enterprises.

In this regard, it is worthwhile to note that the US regulations, which were published in 1994, made a reference to the concept of bonafied indebtedness[8] on several occasions with respect to intercompany loans. Essentially, §1.482-2(a)(1)(ii)(B) states that the US transfer pricing rules would apply to only bonafied indebtedness and will not apply "*to payments with* respect to all or a portion of such alleged indebtedness where in fact all or a portion of an alleged indebtedness is a contribution to the capital of a corporation or a distribution by a corporation with respect to its shares" ... "Payments made with respect to alleged indebtedness (including alleged stated interest thereon) shall be treated *according to their substance. See* §1.482-2(a)(3)(i)." The regulations state that in order to determine the substance "*all the relevant facts and circumstances shall be considered and* ***any law*** *or* ***rule of law (assignment of income, step transaction, etc.***) *may apply.* Only the rate of interest with respect to the stated principal amount of the bona fide indebtedness (within the meaning of paragraph (a)(1) of this section), if any, shall be subject to adjustment under section 482, paragraph (a) of this section, and any other Internal Revenue Code section." Thus, it seems that in a US context, national law rules or judicial doctrines can

7. OECD, *Public Consultation: Proposed Changes to Commentaries in the OECD Model Tax Convention on Article 9 and on Related Articles* (OECD, May 28-29, 2021), p. 6.
8. The 1994 US regulations are available at https://www.irs.gov/pub/irs-apa/482_regs.pdf.

be used to fix the amount of debt which then needs to be priced for transfer pricing purposes.

Also, the Dutch practice on intercompany loans needs to be highlighted here. In general, from a Dutch perspective, loans are generally recognized under civil law relations, i.e., the form-over-substance approach. However, depending on the situation and under established case law, loans are considered to be equity when the facts and circumstances indicate that (i) the loan is essentially a disguised capital contribution; (ii) the loan gives the lender a right to participate in the borrowers business (profit-participating loan) or; (iii) when the receivable arising from the loan has no or little value since the outset (loan without any repayment clauses).[9]

New Zealand practice, consistent with the general principles of the common law recognizes the legal form of intercompany loans.[10] So the starting point is a form-over-substance approach. Domestic law in New Zealand recognizes that a loan might constitute a sham in law in accordance with the principles outlined in the famous judgment of Lord Diplock in *Snook v. London & West Riding Investments Ltd.*[11] This means that a sham might arise in two situations. First, where the documentation does not reflect the real agreement made between the parties (and never did). Second, where the documentation reflects the parties' intentions, but in reality, the parties agree to depart from its terms while allowing third parties to believe that the arrangement is that documented. It is recognized that sham is a difficult concept to establish evidentially in litigation because it is a serious allegation and the standard of proof reflects the gravity of the claim.[12] This has meant that the concept of sham is seldom argued in tax avoidance cases in New Zealand over the last couple of decades. The tax avoidance law under the general anti-avoidance provisions being more than equal to the task of dealing with overly egregious tax-motivated planning. Under New Zealand domestic law, if the contract is held to be a sham, the actual intentions of the parties must be ascertained and the consequences of those actual legal rights and obligations respected under the tax law.[13]

Our analysis is also confirmed by the OECD Commentary on Article 1. The following example is discussed in paragraph 75 of Article 1 "assume, for example, that

---

9. For instance, *see* Jaap Reyneveld & Mark Bonekamp, *Non Business Motivated Loans: Considerations from an Economic Perspective*, 19 International Transfer Pricing Journal 227 (2012), pp. 227-228; Arco C.P. Bobeldijk & Rick van der Velden, *The "Non-businesslike Loan": A New Doctrine for the Tax Treatment of Equity and Debt Capital in the Netherlands*, 43 Intertax 276 (2015), pp. 277-278; *see also*, Michel van der Breggen, *Netherlands in Transfer Pricing and Intra Group Financing* (IBFD, 2nd ed., 2021), pp. 667-669.
10. Acknowledging that specific tax rules in common law jurisdictions might provide for special features of debt/equity characterization, such as those found in the Australian provisions (Division 974 of the Income Tax Assessment Act 1997).
11. *Snook v. London & West Riding Investments Ltd* [1967] 2 QB 786, at 802, where Diplock LJ stated "I apprehend that, if it [sham] has any meaning in law, it means acts done or documents executed by the parties to the 'sham' which are intended by them to give to 3rd parties or to the court the appearance of creating between the parties legal rights and obligations different from the actual legal rights and obligations (if any) which the parties intend to create."
12. *See* the comments in the New Zealand Court of Appeal decision *Regal Castings Ltd v. Lightbody* (2007) 2 NZTR 17-025 at para. [55].
13. *Buckley v. Young Ltd v C of IR* (1978) 3 NZTC 61,271 at 61,280 (New Zealand).

the domestic law of State A provides for the taxation of gains derived from the alienation of shares of a domestic company in which the alienator holds more than 25 per cent of the capital if that alienator was a resident of State A for at least seven of the 10 years preceding the alienation. In year 2, an individual who was a resident of State A for the previous 10 years becomes a resident of State B. Shortly after becoming a resident of State B, the individual sells the totality of the shares of a small company that he previously established in State A. The facts reveal, however, that all the elements *of the sale were finalised in* year 1, that an interest-free 'loan' corresponding to the sale price was made by the purchaser to the seller at that time, that the purchaser cancelled the loan when the shares were sold to the purchaser in year 2 and that the purchaser exercised de facto control of the company from year 1. Although the gain from the sale of the shares might otherwise fall under paragraph 5 of Article 13 of the State A-State B treaty, the circumstances of the transfer of the shares are such that the alienation in year 2 constitutes a sham within the meaning given to that term by the courts of State A. In that case, to the extent that the sham transaction doctrine developed by the courts of State A does not conflict with the rules of interpretation of treaties, it will be possible to apply that doctrine when interpreting paragraph 5 of Article 13 of the State A State B treaty, which will allow State A to tax the relevant gain under its domestic law rule."[14] In the example, the facts, which were determined by invoking the sham doctrine, reveal that the taxpayer made the gain on sale of shares in year 1 as opposed to year 2. In year 1, the taxpayer was still a resident of State A. Therefore, applying the treaty from State A's perspective, the provisions of Article 13(5) will not prevent State A from levying its tax. We cannot disagree with these statements as the sham transaction doctrine in this case ascertains the real facts to which a domestic and treaty rule will both apply.

This said, we have the following general remarks. First, it should be noted that in some countries (e.g., the UK,[15] Canada[16] and New Zealand) there is a high degree of convergence with respect to understanding the sham/simulation concept, in particular, with respect to the presence of an element of "*falsity*" or "*deceit*" or "*lies.*" Moreover, even though several commonalities exist among countries with respect to understanding the meaning of these concepts, there is no common universal definition of sham (or simulation). Second, the issue is the same with respect to Court developed doctrines for intercompany loans. Although there could be a high degree of convergence in the criteria outlined by Courts in different countries, there could also be differences. Thus, there is a strong possibility that the same financial/loan transaction could be treated as a debt in one country and as a capital contribution by another based on domestic law rules or doctrines. This is clearly not satisfactory for taxpayers who could be exposed to double taxation due to differences in characterization of financial instruments by different States. Thus, from a policy standpoint, it would be desirable

14. OECD, *Model Tax Convention on Income and on Capital: Commentary on Article 1* (OECD Publishing, 2017), para. 75.
15. *Snook v. London & West Riding Investments Ltd, supra* n. 11, p. 528.
16. For example, *see Lee v. The Queen*, 2018 TCC 230 (Canada), paras. 48-73 and *Cameco Corporation v. The Queen*, 2018 TCC 195, paras. 582-670.

if the OECD could possibly consider developing a list of criteria for characterization of instruments as debt or equity. In this regard, the work done in the context of the Commentary on Article 10 in paragraph 25 can be used as a starting point. This would indeed mitigate the risk of double taxation (and probably to some extent double nontaxation).

## III DO TAX TREATIES RESTRICT ADJUSTMENTS MADE PURSUANT TO STATUTORY GAARS WITH RESPECT TO RELATED PARTY LOANS?

### 1 The Issues

The issues that we seek to examine are quite complex. Assume a State applies a domestic statutory general anti-avoidance rules (GAAR) and (i) re-characterizes the loan instrument concluded by related parties into equity with the effect that the initial interest payment on the loan is denied as a deduction. At the same time, the tax administration re-classifies the denied interest as dividends on which they then seek to levy dividend withholding taxes; or (ii) or the tax administration, without re-characterizing the instrument, simply denies the deduction of interest and re-classifies the denied amount as dividends and imposes withholding taxes on these dividends. We assume for the purpose of our discussion that the withholding tax on dividends is higher than withholding taxes on interest. We assume that the withholding tax on dividends is 10% whereas on interest it is 5% according to the treaty.

The question under both situations is whether the provisions of tax treaties can restrict the State applying the GAAR from applying the "effect" of its domestic rule. In this regard, the treaty provisions that we will analyze are Articles 9(1), 10(3) and 11(3). Moreover, we will also comment on whether or not the taxpayer has access to Article 25(1).

With respect to Article 9(1), the issue is whether this provision could be invoked with the effect that the State applying the GAAR is restricted to only making arm's length adjustments. With respect to the distributive rules on dividends and interest, the question arises as to whether this re-characterized or "deemed dividend" is governed by the definition of dividends or interest as defined in Article 10(3) or Article 11(3) respectively? Finally, whether the taxpayer can obtain access to a Mutual Agreement Procedure (MAP) when a domestic GAAR applies? We will analyze these three issues separately after providing a brief introduction to GAARs.

### 2 How Are Domestic Statutory GAARs Structured?

In general, it should be noted that national statutory GAARs are used to achieve one or more of the following objectives: to target transactions that comply with a direct interpretation of the legislation but which generate tax advantages the State considers to be against the intention/purpose of the law; to apply an economic substance or business purpose test to determine whether a transaction is lawful or; to define the features of an artificial scheme, transaction or arrangement that has been designed to extract a tax advantage or apply an economic substance or business purpose test to determine if a transaction is bona fide. Although it is generally accepted that statutory GAARs apply to tax avoidance and not to tax mitigation, drawing the line between the two is often contentious and problematic.

Although a comparative analysis of such national rules is beyond the scope of this contribution, a high-level analysis of the statutory GAAR regimes of common law or civil law States indicates that there are several commonalities within the GAAR models used even though the rules are structured differently. In general, the GAAR provisions have some common design features which require a combination of the following features in order to be triggered: (i) a "transaction" or "arrangement" needs to be identified; (ii) the "tax benefit" or "tax advantage" from the transaction/arrangement needs to be identified/quantified; (iii) it has to be proven that the "transaction" or "arrangement" satisfies the purpose test, in the sense that, a main purpose (or one of the main purpose) of entering into the "transaction" or "arrangement" was to obtain a "tax benefit" or "tax advantage" or the "transaction" or "arrangement" was undertaken for other than bonafide purposes; and (iv) the "transaction" or "arrangement" is "impermissible" or "abusive" of a tax provision. No consistency exists with respect to which party bears the burden of proof in regard to establishing whether the statutory GAAR is triggered. Sometimes it falls exclusively on the taxpayer or tax authorities and sometimes it is shared.

If triggered, the GAAR provisions can have far-reaching effects, which may lead to cancelation of the "tax benefit" or "tax advantage" associated with the "transaction" or "arrangement." There is no global consistency in the form the counteraction takes. For instance, tax authorities could deny tax benefits associated with the transaction; re-characterize an item of income; re-determine a taxpayer to whom income is allocated or deny deductions.

## 3 Does Article 9(1) Restrict Adjustments Made under GAARs up to the Arm's Length Standard?

In order to discuss the concrete application of GAARs in the context of loans, the Expert Committee report (2012) on General Anti-Avoidance Rules[17] in India contains an interesting example. In that example, a foreign company (X Ltd—which we assume is an associated enterprise) grants a loan to an Indian company and the agreement provides that the latter shall pay interest at the following rate: "Rate of interest = (Annual Profit of the Indco/Loan amount) × 100." Essentially, as the interest in linked exclusively to the profits of the borrower the report states this "is a case where the form of the arrangement is to show Indco has received a debt from X Ltd. but in substance there is high likelihood that it is equity investment, as the rate of interest is directly based on the rate of return, or profit of Indco. Thus, it could be viewed as an

17. *See* Expert Committee (India), *Final Report on General Anti-Avoidance Rules (GAAR) in Income-tax Act, 1961* (2012), pp. 65-69 available at https://dea.gov.in/sites/default/files/report_gaar_itact1961.pdf.

arrangement *whose main purpose is to obtain a tax benefit by claiming actual dividend payment as interest payment. The tainted element here is the abnormal manner in which such a transaction is being carried out which would not be so in case of a bonafide transaction (loan). Hence, GAAR provisions would be invoked in the case of Indco to treat the arrangement as an impermissible avoidance arrangement. Consequently, in the case of Indco, the loan by X Ltd. would be treated as equity for tax purposes; interest payment would not be allowed as deduction as this would be re-characterized as dividend ... .*"

Building on these facts, assume that the loan amount from X Ltd was USD 1,000. Also, assume that the profit that the Indian Company makes in year 1 is 400. Applying the formula in the intercompany agreement, the Indian Company claims a tax deduction of USD 40 as interest (400 × (100/1,000) which is equal to USD 40). However, during the course of the trial and based on reports filed by expert witnesses it is determined that the amount that an independent lender would have lent to the Indian Company based on the Indian company's current financial status, the commercial project for which the loan was entered into as well as the future financial projections as a result of executing the project is USD 800. Moreover, the arm's length interest rate on such a loan would have been 2% (USD 16). Nevertheless, the tax administration invokes the GAAR (as discussed above) and re-characterizes the entire funding as equity funding and the interest of USD 40 as dividends and they seek to apply the dividend withholding tax rate on this payment (10%).

The question that we then seek to analyze here is whether Article 9(1) could oblige the tax administration to permit a deduction of up to USD 16 (the arm's length amount).

Ideally, the tax administration should apply national transfer pricing rules to resolve the case before invoking the GAAR as a specific rule should prevail over a general rule. By doing so, the loan amount and interest rate could be re-determined up to an arm's length level. As discussed in another chapter in this book (Chapter 10), Article 9(1) would indeed permit these adjustments under the broad notions of accurate delineation of the transaction as well as through the application of the commercial irrationality exception. However, it could well be possible that in many countries, national transfer pricing rules only authorize pricing adjustments and not loan amount-related adjustments. Thus, these jurisdictions could invoke statutory GAARs (or other anti-tax avoidance doctrines).

In this regard, questions on interaction of domestic thin capitalization rules (including domestic GAARs) with Article 9 were analyzed by the OECD in its 1986 report on thin capitalization.[18]

As a start, it should be noted that the Report discusses the approaches adopted by countries in their domestic law to deal with problems arising from thin capitalization. These approaches are broadly divided in the Report between those that are based on the application of general rules and those that involve the use of fixed/arbitrary ratios.

18. OECD, *Thin Capitalization Report* (OECD Publishing, 1986). The report is available at https://read.oecd-ilibrary.org/taxation/model-tax-convention-on-income-and-on-capital-2014-full-version/r-4-thin-capitalisation_9789264239081-97-en#page1.

To elaborate, under the former approach, a country looks at all facts and circumstances, i.e., the terms and nature of a contribution and the circumstances in which it has been made to determine whether the contribution is debt or equity. Such facts and circumstances can be ascertained pursuant to (i) particular national rules or (ii) either general anti-abuse rules (such as statutory GAARs, abuse of law, substance over form, etc.) or (iii) pursuant to domestic TP rules which use the arm's length standard.[19] In general, from a tax policy standpoint, the report proposes countries adopt a flexible approach as opposed to focusing on standard fixed debt-equity ratios. The approach seems similar to the flexible approach which was discussed in previous versions of the TP guidelines (in particular, the 1979 version).

The report concludes that a thin capitalization rule that is based on a pure fixed ratio approach and which applies *among associated enterprises*[20] can be considered to be contrary to Article 9 as it does not respect the arm's length standard.[21] This is because such rules cannot be regarded as complying with the arm's length standard as they could lead to the adjustment of profits to an amount exceeding the arm's length amount. The 1986 Thin Capitalization (TC) Report, nevertheless, provides that if a domestic thin capitalization rule uses a combination approach, i.e., it provides a fixed ratio as a safe haven rule and gives the taxpayer (borrower) the option of demonstrating that such a ratio is an arm's length ratio, then such a rule can be considered to be compatible with Article 9.[22]

On the other hand, the 1986 TC Report provides that domestic thin capitalization rules which ascertain all facts and circumstances and rely on evidence of transactions between independent persons are compatible with the provisions of Article 9.[23]

Interestingly the 1986 TC Report, after discussing the general impact of Article 9 on thin capitalization rules, *leaves open the question of whether domestic thin capitalization rules which re-characterize interest to dividends pursuant to domestic GAARs need to be tested against Article 9.*[24]

Similar to the 1986 TC report, the current Commentary on Article 1[25] implicitly states that thin capitalization rules that are based on fixed debt/equity ratios could trigger a conflict with tax treaty provisions. Moreover, the commentary on Article 9(1)[26] states "the Article does not prevent the application of *national rules on thin capitalisation* insofar as their effect is to assimilate the profits of the borrower to an amount corresponding to the profits which would have accrued in an arm's length situation." It seems that the "*national rules*" discussed here seem to be specific thin capitalization rules which apply only to associated enterprises. However, in our case, the denial of a deduction takes place through a general rule, that is, a statutory GAAR.

19. *Ibid.*, para. 25(i).
20. *Ibid.*, para. 25(ii).
21. *Ibid.*, para. 79.
22. Luc De Broe, *International Tax Planning and Prevention of Abuse* (IBFD Doctoral Series, 2008), p. 509.
23. OECD, Thin Capitalization Report 1986, *supra* n. 18, para. 78.
24. *Ibid.*, para. 80.
25. OECD Model 2017: Commentary on Article 1, *supra* n. 14, paras. 72 and 74.
26. OECD, *Model Tax Convention on Income and on Capital: Commentary on Article 9* (OECD Publishing, 2017), para. 3.

So the question (to repeat) is whether a denial of deduction that takes place *through a general rule needs* to be tested with Article 9(1).

To reiterate, Article 9 deals with adjustments to profits that may be made for tax purposes where transactions between associated enterprises are made on non-arm's length conditions. Article 9(1) of the OECD Model, in its various versions, allows the tax authorities of a state to adjust the profits of the enterprises resident in that state if, as a result of the special relations between that enterprise and other *associated enterprises* resident in another State, the profits of the first enterprise have been diverted to the other associated enterprises, due to the fact that they operate with each other on a non-arm's length basis. Where the tax authorities have adjusted the profits, Article 9(2) of the OECD Model is aimed at eliminating the economic double taxation that may arise pursuant to Article 9(1). Clearly, several commentators are of the opinion that Article 9(1) is restrictive in nature,[27,28] that is, it restricts national law rules whereas others (a minority) support an "illustrative" view.[29] But what does Article 9(1) exactly restrict?

It is clear that national rules, which serve as allocation norms (profit allocation norms), need to be tested with Article 9(1).[30] Article 9 restricts national allocation norms if they apply beyond the boundaries of the arm's length principle (ALP) (for example, a national formulary norm).[31] Also, it is clear from the developments to the OECD Commentary that Article 9(1) would restrict a State from applying its national thin capitalization rules among related parties which are based on arbitrary formulas up to the arm's length standard. However, it is less clear whether adjustments made under national GAAR rules can be restricted up to the arm's length standard pursuant to Article 9(1).[32] Arguments for and against are discussed hereafter.

First, arguably, the historical development of Article 9 indicates that it has an anti-avoidance flavour in the sense of combating tax avoidance among associated enterprises.[33,34,35,36] In light of this, one may argue that all national anti-abuse rules need to be tested with Article 9.

27. Bullen, *supra* n. 1, pp. 68-74. *See also* VIKRAM CHAND & GIOVANNI LEMBO, *Intangible-Related Profit Allocation Within MNEs Based on Key DEMPE Functions: Selected Issues and Interaction with Pillar One and Pillar Two of the Digital Debate,* 3 Intl. Tax Stud. 1 (2020), p. 14; GEORG KOFLER & ISABEL VERLINDEN, *Unlimited Adjustments: Some Reflections on Transfer Pricing, General Anti-Avoidance and Controlled Foreign Company Rules, and the "Saving Clause,"* 74 Bull. Intl. Taxn. 269 (2020), section 3.2 (and all references therein).
28. JENS WITTENDORF, *The Transactional Ghost of Article 9(1) of the OECD Model,* 63 Bull. Intl. Taxn. 107, (2009), section 5.2.1.
29. For recent support of this view, *see* BRIAN J. ARNOLD, *The Relationship Between Restrictions on the Deduction of Interest under Canadian Law and Canadian Tax Treaties,* 67 Canadian Tax Journal/Revue fiscale canadienne 1051 (2019), p. 1074.
30. *See also* CHAND & LEMBO, *supra* n. 27, pp. 14-23.
31. WITTENDORF, *supra* n. 28, at section 5.2.1.
32. *See.* DE BROE, *supra* n. 22, pp. 639-641. On this point, also *see* CHAND & LEMBO, *supra* n. 27, p. 23.
33. LUÍS EDUARDO SCHOUERI, *Arm's Length: Beyond the Guidelines of the OECD,* 69 Bull. Intl. Taxn. 690 (2015), pp. 690 et seq.
34. RICHARD COLLIER & JOSEPH L. ANDRUS, *Transfer Pricing and the Arm's Length Principle after BEPS* (Oxford University Press, 2017), Chs 1 and 2.
35. KOFLER & VERLINDEN, *supra* n. 27, sections 2.1 and 2.6.
36. LIOUBOV POGORELOVA, *Transfer Pricing and Anti-abuse Rules,* 37 Intertax 683 (2018), pp. 688-691.

Second, it is clear that Article 9(2) aims at avoiding economic double taxation.[37] Economic double taxation, in the classical sense, arises when two different persons are taxable in respect of the same income or capital.[38] As domestic statutory GAARs, similar to transfer pricing rules, could possibly lead to economic double taxation among related parties they fall within the testing scope of Article 9. For example, the payment is taxable in the hands of the recipient but not deductible in the hands of the payor because of the re-classification.

Third, some have even argued that the ALP is customary international law which applies to all transactions between related parties. Thus, they would argue that states need to adhere to the principle whenever they deal with associated enterprises (even though this may not be the predominant view among scholars).[39]

Fourth, the European Court of Justice (ECJ) regularly uses the principle of proportionality to check whether national direct tax legislation is proportional in the sense that the ECJ analyzes whether the national rule is suitable for the attainment of the objective it pursues and the rule does not go beyond what is necessary for attainment of the objective. Although European Union (EU)-specific, the application of this principle from a reasonable standpoint would mean that States need to adhere to the ALP with respect to profit adjustments when dealing with associated enterprises.

In this regard, in the *Test claimants'* judgment, the ECJ held that the UK thin capitalization rules were indeed suitable for the attainment of the objective of preventing profit shifting to low-tax countries through base-eroding interest payments.[40] Furthermore, when analyzing whether the UK thin capitalization rules went beyond the objective they pursued, the ECJ held that such domestic rules are

---

37. OECD Model 2017: Commentary on Article 9, *supra* n. 26, paras. 5, 6.1 and 10; OECD, *Model Tax Convention on Income and on Capital: Commentary on Article 25* (OECD Publishing, 2017), paras. 10-12; and De Broe, *supra* n. 22, section 6.2.1.1.
38. OECD, *Model Tax Convention on Income and on Capital: Commentary on Article 23* (OECD Publishing, 2017), para. 2.
39. Some scholars support this view. For example, *see* Reuven S. Avi Yonah, *Altera, the Arm's Length Standard, and Customary International Tax Law*, 38 MJIL Opinio Juris 1 (2018). One could argue that this development is to some extent reflected in the recent decision of the General Court in the *Apple* case with respect to the OECD Transfer Pricing Guidelines and the Authorized OECD Approach; *see* IE: EGC, July 15, 2020, *Ireland and Others v. Commission*, Cases T-778/16 and T-892/16, Case Law IBFD. On the other hand, it should be noted that some other commentators have expressed justifiable doubt as to whether the standards of customary international law are met. For example, *see* Lepard Brian, *International Rules on Allocating Income for Tax Purposes*, in *Customary International Law: A New Theory with Practical Applications (ASIL Studies in International Legal Theory)* (2010), pp. 297-305. Also *see*, Braumann Céline, *Taxes and Custom: Tax Treaties as Evidence for Customary International Law*, 23 J. Intl. Econ. L. 767-769 (2020). Moreover, as the ECJ ruled in the *Fiat* case, though "a certain consensus in the field of international taxation that transactions between economically linked companies, in particular intra-group transactions, must be assessed for tax purposes as if they had been concluded between economically independent companies" reference must only be made to national provisions that are relevant for the purposes of analysing whether particular transactions must be examined in the light of the ALP. *See Fiat Chrysler Finance Europe v. Commission Case* C-885/19 P (Joined Cases C-885/19 P, C-898/19 P), ECJ, at [96]. available at https://curia.europa.eu/juris/document/document.jsf?text=&docid=267888&pageIndex=0&doclang=en&mode=lst&dir=&occ=first&part=1&cid=280485.
40. ECJ: *Test Claimants in the Thin Cap Group Litigation v. Commissioners of Inland Revenue*, Case No. C-524/04, March 13, 2007, paras. 76-77.

proportional if such rules adhere to the arm's length standard, that is, they do not adjust the profits of the borrower beyond that mandated by the arm's length standard.[41] It is stated in paragraph 83 that "In order for such legislation to remain compatible with the principle of proportionality, it is necessary, in the second place, that, where the consideration of those elements leads to the conclusion that the transaction in question represents a purely artificial arrangement without any underlying commercial justification, the re-characterisation of interest paid as a distribution is limited to the proportion of that interest which exceeds what would have been agreed had the relationship between the parties or between those parties and a third party been one at arm's length." Similar conclusions with respect to limiting adjustments to arm's length adjustments were reached in the *Lammers & Van Cleef*,[42] *Itelcar*[43] and the *SGI*[44] judgment.

Keeping the above in mind, assuming our issue is a treaty issue, one may argue that the principle of proportionality should also be used in the tax treaty interpretation process. Essentially, this principle would fit into Article 31(3)(c) of the Vienna Convention of the Law of Treaties (VCLT) which provides that "any relevant rules of international law applicable in the relations between the parties" need to be taken into account.[45] The relevant rules of international law could either be general principles of law or principles that stem from other treaties (including EU Treaties). As the principle of proportionality would represent a relevant rule of international law this could then possibly mean that it would warrant that profit adjustments are made only up to the arm's length standard. Of course, this matter needs to be investigated further, assuming the issue at stake becomes a treaty issue.

The consequence of the above arguments is that if all the conditions to apply the national GAARs are triggered then the counteraction measure by tax administration should be reasonable and proportional, in other words, at arm's length. This seems to have been upheld recently in an Argentinean case wherein the Supreme Court held that the GAAR provisions could not be used to re-characterize debt to equity when the terms and conditions of the loan are at arm's length (although it is not entirely clear).[46] Thus, if the tax administrations make income/profit allocations beyond the ALP then taxation of the amount beyond the ALP is prohibited by Article 9(1). In our case study, this would mean that the country applying the GAAR can only deny the deduction for

41. *Ibid.*, paras. 80-83.
42. ECJ: *Lammers & Van Cleeff NV v. Belgische Staat*, Case No. C-105/07, January 17, 2008, paras. 28-29.
43. ECJ: *Itelcar—Automóveis de Aluguer Lda v. Fazenda Pública*, Case No. C-282/12, October 3, 2013, paras. 37-38.
44. ECJ: *Société de Gestion Industrielle (SGI) v. Belgian State*, Case No. C-311/08, January 21, 2010, paras. 71-72.
45. *See* Robert Danon & Sebastian Wuschka, *International Investment Agreements and the International Tax System: The Potential of Complementarity and Harmonious Interpretation*, 75 Bull. Intl. Taxn. 11/12 (2022), section 4.
46. Mirna S. Screpante, *Argentinian Supreme Court's Landmark Decision in Intercompany Loans in Times of Economic Downturn*, 28 Intl. Transfer Pricing J. 49 (2021).

the non-arms length amount. This means that USD 16 needs to be allowed as a deduction.[47]

However, one may argue that effect of national GAARs does not need to be tested with Article 9(1). This is because such national rules are general rules and are applicable across the board in the sense that they apply to related and unrelated relations.

Also, these rules can be used to fix the amount of debt which then needs to be priced. As highlighted before, the OECD launched a paper which proposed changes to the Commentary on Article 9(1).[48] The draft paper states in new paragraph 3 that a State "may also need to examine, based on the facts and circumstances, whether a purported loan should be regarded as a loan or as another kind of transaction, in particular a contribution to equity capital. *The State making a determination as to the extent to which the purported loan is regarded as a loan will do so taking into account factors discussed in its domestic laws (including judicial doctrine).*"

One could also draw a link with the recent developments around BEPS Action 4[49] which provides recommendations in designing domestic law rules to prevent base erosion through the use of (excess) interest expenses.[50] Essentially, a fixed ratio rule is recommended to restrict interest deductions. In particular, the rule restricts the interest payment of an entity of a multinational enterprise (MNE) group to a percentage of that entity's earnings before interest, taxes, depreciation and amortization (EBITDA)[51] (payment made to both related and unrelated parties). The recommendation leaves open the possibility for states to choose a percentage between 10% and 30% based on certain parameters. Furthermore, the report recommends countries incorporate a group ratio rule alongside the fixed ratio rule. This approach would enable entities with net interest expense above a country's fixed ratio rule to deduct interest up to the level of the net interest/EBITDA ratio of its worldwide group[52] (subject to certain conditions).

With respect to interaction of such domestic rules with Article 9(1),[53,54] the OECD proposes other changes. Paragraph 3 of the Commentary, which dealt with the

47. For another analysis, *see* De Broe, *supra* n. 22, p. 509.
48. *See* OECD Public Consultation—Proposed changes to commentaries in the OECD Model Tax Convention on Article 9 and on related articles, *supra* n. 7, p. 6.
49. OECD, *Limiting Base Erosion Involving Interest Deductions and Other Financial Payments, Action 4—2015 Final Report* (OECD/G20 Base Erosion and Profit Shifting Project, OECD Publishing, 2015).
50. For a discussion on these rules, *see* Craig Elliffe, *Interest Deductibility: Evaluating the Advantage of Earnings Stripping Regimes in Preventing Thin Capitalisation*, II New Zealand Law Review 257 (2017).
51. OECD, Action 4 Final Report, *supra* n. 48, paras. 18-20.
52. *Ibid.*, paras. 22-32.
53. In this regard, it should be noted that some commentators have argued that BEPS Action 4 rules (comprehensive interest barriers) conflict with the ALP contained in Article 9(1) when applied to payments between separate related companies (also Article 7(2) when applied to PEs). This is mainly because the rules lead to an unequitable inter-nation tax base allocation (as payor countries can deny a deduction for arm's length expenses) and also lead to economic double taxation. *See* Sandra Martinho Fernandes, *International Double Taxation of Interest* (IBFD Doctoral Series, 2019), section 4.4.2.2.

interaction of national thin capitalization rules with tax treaties, is going to be replaced with new wording. As discussed previously, the old wording, in paragraphs 3a and 3c explicitly provided that article 9, in some situations, could prevent the application of national thin capitalization rules. Proposed new paragraph 3.1 states that: Once the profits of the two enterprises have been allocated in accordance with the ALP, "it is for the domestic law of each Contracting State to determine whether and how such profits should be taxed, as long as there is conformity with the requirements of other provisions of the Convention. *Article 9 does not deal with the issue of whether expenses are deductible when computing the taxable income of either enterprise. The* ***conditions for the deductibility of expenses are a matter to be determined by domestic law, subject to the provisions of the Convention*** *and, in particular, paragraph 4 of Article 24. Paragraph 30 of the Commentary on Article 7 makes an equivalent statement for the application of Article 7.*[55] *Examples of domestic rules that can deny a deduction for expenses include ...* ***interest such as those recommended in the final report on Action 4 of the OECD/G20 BEPS Project.*** [Emphasis added.] These statements could imply that even if arm's length allocations are made, the national law of the State of the borrower could restrict deductions through other domestic rules (comprehensive interest barriers or even general anti-avoidance rules).

Thus, one may argue that national transfer pricing rules and Article 9 only deal with ensuring an arm's length allocation of income and expenses (and, as a consequence, profits) among associated enterprises. Once these items are allocated to a state, then that state is free to determine, under its general tax rules, the tax treatment of those items (e.g., restrict a deduction). Indeed, a state may apply a general interest limitation rule, which targets BEPS, to an arm's length interest expense that has been allocated to it. Thus, by applying an interest limitation rule, a state seeks to deny a deduction of an arm's length interest expense that has been allocated to it. This line of reasoning can also be considered for GAARs which are general rules. Once again, Article 9 deals with ensuring an arm's length allocation of income and expenses (and, as a consequence, profits) among associated enterprises. Once these items are allocated to a state, then that state is free to determine, under its general tax rules, the tax

54. In this regard, some have argued that the German interest barrier rule conflicts with Article 9 as they disallow deductions only to entities (payors) that belong to an MNE group, even though, the denial applies to all interest payments made by these entities including third-party interest. *See* Andreas Fross, *Earnings Stripping and Thin Cap Rules: Maintaining an Arm' s Length Distance*, 53 Eur. Taxn. 507 (2013), pp. 514-515 (also *see* the sources mentioned therein).

55. OECD, *Model Tax Convention on Income and on Capital: Commentary on Article 7* (OECD Publishing, 2017), para. 30. The commentary states: "Paragraph 2 determines the profits that are attributable to a permanent establishment for the purposes of the rule in paragraph 1 that allocates taxing rights on these profits. Once the profits that are attributable to a permanent establishment have been determined in accordance with paragraph 2 of Article 7, it is for the domestic law of each Contracting State to determine whether and how such profits should be taxed as long as there is conformity with the requirements of paragraph 2 and the other provisions of the Convention. *Paragraph 2 does not deal with the issue of whether expenses are deductible when computing the taxable income of the enterprise in either Contracting State. The conditions for the deductibility of expenses are a matter to be determined by domestic law, subject to the provisions of the Convention and, in particular, paragraph 3 of Article 24 (see paragraphs 33 and 34 below)*" [emphasis added].

treatment of those items (e.g., restrict a deduction). Indeed, a state may apply a national GAAR and if the conditions to invoke it are satisfied then it seems unlikely that Article 9(1) can act as a restriction.

In our case study, this would mean that the country applying the GAAR can deny the entire interest payment as a deduction (USD 40).

Weighing in these arguments for and against, we arrive at the following conclusions. One may argue that the GAAR, or indeed a national rule which applies across the board and prevents an interest deduction, can operate notwithstanding the arm's length requirement of Article 9. There are several reasons for this. First, as indicated in the paragraphs above, there is a clear statement in the OECD Commentary that the ALP in Article 9 is consistent with the disallowance of interest deductions under domestic law. This is justified from the perspective of the domestic law affecting the quantum of the deduction and not the allocation of profits on an arm's length basis. This is perhaps a matter of semantics as the consequence of the interest expense disallowance under domestic law is a non-arm's length pricing outcome. The relationship between domestic law and public international law (treaties) is redefined by the OECD Commentary on the basis that this is not an allocation of taxing rights per se, but a quantification of profits (or more accurately allowable deductions). The fundamental difference is that the double tax agreement determines matters of which country gets to tax the profits, but the domestic law decides how to do so and how much. This is an approach to interpretation used by Courts in monist jurisdictions to coordinate treaty obligations and domestic law. In the Dutch Supreme Court, the question of the legitimacy of an exit tax (which deemed a disposal of emigration) was challenged as being contrary to the treaty obligations in Article 13.[56] The Dutch Supreme Court held that the treaty established that the Netherlands had the right to tax the economic appreciation or gain up until the time of the change in residency and that it was also open to them to determine a mechanism for the deemed realization just prior to emigration. The exit tax on the holding of substantial shareholdings in Dutch companies resulted in the domestic law definitions determining the taxation consequences. The domestic law did so, however, in accordance with the taxing rights allocated under the tax treaties.[57]

Such non-derogation of the domestic law is obviously problematic to the ALP, but we need to recognize that there is increasing skepticism from countries that transfer pricing can provide the right answer in all circumstances. A number of countries will not put up with it being used as a justification for abuse. The OECD Secretariat's Proposal on Pillar One suggested, in the context of far-reaching international reform on the digital economy, that:[58] "While there seems to be adherence among Inclusive Framework members to the principle that routine transactions can normally be priced

---

56. HR February 20, 2009, 42 701, BNB 2009/260 (tax treaty with Belgium); HR February 20, 2009, 43 760, BNB 2009/261 (tax treaty with U.S.); HR February 20, 2009, 07/12314, BNB 2009/262 (tax treaty with U.K.).
57. For a description of this approach to interpretation *see* Craig Elliffe, *Preventing Unacceptable Tax Treaty Overrides*, 2022 B.T.R (2022), pp. 38-63 para. 4.2.
58. OECD, *Public Consultation Document - Secretariat Proposal for a "Unified Approach" Under Pillar One* (OECD, October-November 2019), p. 6, para. [17].

at arm's length, there are increasing doubts that the arm's-length principle can be relied on to give an appropriate result in all cases (such as, for example, cases involving non-routine profits from intangibles). Moreover, there seems to be an argument that the arm's-length principle is becoming an increasing source of complexity and that simplification would be desirable to contain the increasing administration and compliance costs of trying to apply it."

A court will examine the chronology of events including the Commentary in place at the time the treaty was concluded. In the case of Alta Energy, the Crown "relies on revisions to the Commentaries on the OECD Model Treaty that were published in 2003 and 2017, several years after Canada and Luxembourg negotiated the Treaty."[59] As a result, the majority in the Canadian Supreme Court did not place much weight on the revised OECD Commentary. Côté J., delivering the majority judgment, held as follows:[60] "[42] In this case, I am of the view that the 2003 and 2017 Commentaries do not reflect the intentions of the drafters of the Treaty. The extensive revisions made to the Commentaries in 2003 purported to clarify the relationship between tax treaties and domestic anti-avoidance rules, and, in particular, one of the revisions was made to include the prevention of tax avoidance as a purpose of such treaties. The changes were not mere clarifications and have been described as being "created out of thin air by the OECD in 2003" and as "a significant change in the stated attitude of the OECD to the relationship between tax treaties and tax avoidance."[61]

This suggests that the role of the OECD Commentary as an interpretative aid is more nuanced and that the OECD Commentary in place when the treaty was negotiated will also be considered.

Apart from the OECD Commentary's observation that there really is no conflict with the ALP and thus only a domestic law quantification of profits (or deductions) exercise, the relationship between treaties and domestic law might be viewed through one lens as one of the areas where treaties are overridden by domestic law. Controversial though this is, there are some areas where the supremacy of the treaty is threatened: the role of controlled foreign company legislation, the general anti-avoidance rule, and thin capitalization or interest allocation rules. All of these areas focus on anti-tax planning and avoidance and are designed to protect the tax base of the country enacting them. The Commentary of the OECD Model makes a special case for the unfettered role of these domestic anti-avoidance regimes vis-à-vis the tax treaty network. As domestic rules are designed to prevent abuse, the argument is that when they conflict with treaties, the treaty must be interpreted in light of their object and purpose.[62] The Committee of Fiscal Affairs identifies these objects and purposes as primarily "the avoidance of double taxation *and the prevention of fiscal evasion* but

59. *Canada v. Alta Energy Luxembourg S.A.R.L.*, 2021 SCC 49, at [39].
60. *Ibid.*, at [42], per Côté J., (on behalf of the majority, Abella/Moldaver/Karakatsanis/Côté/Brown/Kasirer JJ).
61. Brian J. Arnold, *Tax Treaties and Tax Avoidance: The 2003 Revisions to the Commentary to the OECD Model*, 58 Bull. Intl. Taxn. 244 (2004), at pp. 249 and 260.
62. UN, Vienna Convention on the Law of Treaties, May 23, 1969, United Nations, Treaty Series, vol. 1155, Article 31(1).

also have the objective of allocating tax revenues equitably between the two Contracting States."[63] (Emphasis added). Rules that are designed to prevent fiscal abuse and evasion, even domestic rules, therefore receive a special carve out and preservation against the supremacy of treaties in the eyes of Working Party 1.

By resorting to this line of reasoning we would most likely arrive at an unreasonable outcome for the taxpayer when GAARs are used. In other words, Article 9(1) may not act as a restriction when a GAAR is applied and the interest deduction is denied for the local taxpayer. Indeed, it seems that the question would be outside the scope of a tax treaty. Thus, we would recommend national policymakers ensure that when GAARs are used to challenge related party transactions, the counteraction is made up to the arm's length standard and not beyond it.[64]

## 4 Does the Re-characterized Income Fit in Article 10 or Article 11?

If the domestic anti-avoidance rule re-characterizes the instrument from loan to equity (not for private or commercial law but only for tax law purposes) by using domestic anti-avoidance rules and the interest as dividends for the purpose of national law then the question is whether this re-characterized amount is governed by Article 10 or Article 11? The question is important because the withholding tax on dividends (10%) is higher than the withholding tax on interest (5%). Put differently, the OECD Commentary since 2003 provides that the provisions of a tax treaty will be applied only after a domestic anti-avoidance rule re-characterizes an item of income[65]. It states "other forms of abuse of tax treaties ... and of possible ways to deal with them, including 'substance-over-form,' 'economic substance' and general anti-abuse rules have also been analysed, particularly as concerns the question of whether these rules conflict with tax treaties ... ." In response, it is stated in paragraph 22.1 "to the extent that the application of the rules referred to in paragraph 22 results in a recharacterisation of income ..., the provisions of the Convention will be applied taking into account these changes."[66] The question in our case is which provisions?

One may directly argue that Article 10 of the OECD Model is applicable. This is because the domestic law of the State applying the GAAR treats the payment as dividends.

On the other hand, one may directly argue that a proper treaty analysis needs to be done. Article 10(3) of the OECD Model defines "dividends." The definition is divided into three parts, i.e., dividend includes (i) income from shares, jouissance shares or jouissance rights, mining shares, founder's shares (ii) income from other rights, not being debt claims, participating in profits and (iii) income from other corporate rights

63. OECD Legal Instruments, "Recommendation of the Council concerning Tax Treaty Override," OECD/Legal/0253, (Adopted on October 2, 1989), para. 19(a).
64. One of the authors to this contribution is inclined to move in this direction.
65. *See also*, OECD, *Preventing the Granting of Treaty Benefits in Inappropriate Circumstances, Action 6—2015 Final Report* (OECD/G20 Base Erosion and Profit Shifting Project, OECD Publishing, 2015), para. 59. In para. 59 *see* para. 26.6.
66. OECD, *Model Tax Convention on Income and on Capital: Commentary on Article 1* (OECD Publishing, 2003), para. 22.1.

which is subject to the same taxation treatment as income from shares by the laws of the State of residence of the distributing company. The wording of Article 10(3) lays out a precise relationship between the three parts of the definition. First, the use of the expression "other rights, not being debt claims, participating in profits" in (ii) implies that the examples enumerated in (i) cannot be debt claims participating in profits and that such limitation is not applicable to (iii). Second, the expression "*other corporate rights*" provided in (iii) makes clear that all the rights covered by the three parts of the definition must be "*corporate rights.*" Lastly, recourse to domestic law applies only to (iii).

Conversely, Article 11(3) defines "*interest*"[67] in an exhaustive manner to include income from debt claims of every kind, whether or not secured by a mortgage and whether or not carrying a right to participate in profits. It should be noted that Article 10(3) excludes "*debt claims*" from the definition of dividends (only in relation to the first and second parts) whereas Article 11(3) includes "*debt claims whether or not they have a right to participate in the debtors profits*" within the definition of interest. However, Article 10(3) (last part) could be interpreted to include income from "*debt claims*" as dividends only if the domestic law of the State of residence of the distributing company assimilates such income from debt claims as income from "*corporate rights.*" Consequently, the question arises: what is a "*corporate right?*"

The term "*corporate rights*" is not defined in the OECD Model. Accordingly, reference has to be made to the domestic law of the State applying the treaty pursuant to Article 3(2) in order to ascertain the meaning of this term, unless a specific meaning is agreed to in an interpretative MAP or the context requires otherwise. In our view, the term "*corporate rights*" should be interpreted autonomously in its "*context*" in the way that the owner of the right bears risks which are similar to that of a shareholder, i.e., the term should cover all those rights that carry title not only to a share in current profits but also to at least a share in the liquidation proceeds of the company. This approach seems to have been accepted by the Czech Supreme Administrative Court (SACR) in the *2004 AAA* case.[68] The SACR did not accept the domestic law definition of dividends because the loans provided to the Czech borrower did not constitute corporate rights within the meaning of the "*Dividend*" Article. According to the Court, the term "*corporate rights*" means rights to participate in profits, control and liquidation proceeds of the borrower.

In this regard, the OECD Commentary states in paragraph 25 that "Article 10 deals not only with dividends as such but also with interest on loans insofar as the *lender effectively shares the risks run by the company, i.e. when repayment depends*

67. Article 10(3) of the OECD Model provides that "The term 'interest' as used in this Article means income from debt-claims of every kind, whether or not secured by mortgage and whether or not carrying a right to participate in the debtor's profits, and in particular, income from government securities and income from bonds or debentures, including premiums and prizes attaching to such securities, bonds or debentures. Penalty charges for late payment shall not be regarded as interest for the purpose of this Article." The provision has not changed since the 1977 OECD Model and it appears in the same format in the 2017 OECD Model.
68. SACR: *AAA v. Financial Directorate*, (269) j 2Afs 108/2004-106, 8 ITLR 178, February 10, 2005, pp. 178-205. The author relied on the unofficial translation to analyze this case. In the author's view the unofficial translation was not accurate.

*largely on the success or otherwise of the enterprise's business. Articles 10 and 11 do not therefore prevent the treatment* ***of this type of interest*** *as dividends under the national rules on thin capitalisation applied in the borrower's country.*" This view is based on the discussion made in the 1986 TC report in paragraphs 56-60.

In our case study, one may argue that the lender does not bear such shareholder risks because the re-characterization achieved through applying the domestic anti-avoidance rule does not entitle the lender to a return on corporate rights (as tax law does not give a right to the lender to participate in current or liquidation proceeds of the company making the distribution). Therefore, one may argue that the re-classified amount will fall under the definition of "*interest*" in Article 11(3) even though the domestic law treats it as dividends. This would mean that the entire USD 40 would fall under Article 11.

If this is the case, one may still raise the question as to whether Article 11(6) applies. The provision states that "Where, by reason of a special relationship between the payer and the beneficial owner or between both of them and some other person, *the amount of the interest,* ***having regard to the debt-claim for which it is paid,*** *exceeds the amount which would have been agreed upon by the payer and the beneficial owner in the absence of such relationship, the provisions of this Article shall apply only to the last-mentioned amount. In such case, the excess part of the payments shall remain taxable according to the laws of each Contracting State, due regard being had to the other provisions of this Convention.*"

Essentially, the question is whether the lower withholding tax rate on interest (5%) should be extended to the entire payment (USD 40) or only up to the arm's length amount (USD 16) or another amount.

Indeed, one may argue that Article 11 benefits should only be extended to USD 16 as that amount reflects an arm's length amount (based on the 1st sentence of this provision). In this sense, Article 9 and Article 11(6) coincide. One may also argue that the excess amount (USD 40 - USD 16 = USD 24) is then taxable according to the national law "due regard being had to the other provisions of this Convention." The question is which distributive rule would govern this payment? Is it Article 7 or Article 21? Article 10 seems to be out because we already argued that the payment would fit into Article 11.

Indeed, Article 11(6) raises several challenging questions the analysis of which is beyond the scope of this contribution. The difficulties in interpreting this provision are also recognized in the commentary which ultimately provides that countries could resort to the MAP procedure to resolve double taxation issues.[69]

## 5 Does the Taxpayer Have a Right to Invoke the MAP under Article 25 to Resolve Any Double Taxation?

Article 25(1) provides that taxpayers can access the MAP when "taxation not in accordance with the provisions of this Convention" is detected.

69. *See* OECD Model 2017: Commentary on Article 11, *supra* n. 37, paras. 35-36.

If one goes ahead with the argument that Article 9(1) cannot restrict the effect of the domestic GAAR then the entire issue becomes a domestic law issue and there is no treaty issue at stake.

This said, if a State re-characterizes the excess interest as dividends and applies the tax rates mentioned in Article 10 (to the extent they are higher than the rates mentioned in Article 11 or the other distributive rules) then a treaty conflict could be detected. As a result, thin capitalization situations could lead to taxation not in accordance with the provisions of the Convention and the taxpayer should, in principle, have access to MAPs.

In this regard, paragraph 9 to the Commentary on Article 25 states "In practice, the procedure applies to cases—by far the most numerous—where the measure in question leads to double taxation which is the specific purpose of the Convention to avoid. Among the most common cases, mention must be made of the following: ...—cases of application of legislation to deal with thin capitalisation when the State of the debtor company has treated interest as dividends, *insofar as such treatment is based on clauses of a convention corresponding for example to Article 9 or paragraph 6 of Article 11.*" One may raise a question as to whether the reference to Article 9 in this paragraph means that access to a MAP is given only in situations when interest is treated as dividends when Article 9 applies or can it also be given when this article does not apply and the GAAR applies?

With respect to the latter, the question is whether contracting states may block access to the MAP for the taxpayer based on the consideration that the double taxation would be triggered through the application of a general anti-avoidance rule. In this regard, Spanish case law indicates that access to the MAP was denied by the tax administrations on grounds of tax avoidance, an orientation which appears to have recently been upheld by the Spanish Supreme Court.[70]

On the other hand, while the 2017 version of the Commentary of Article 25 recognizes that: "Some States may deny the taxpayer the ability to initiate the mutual agreement procedure under paragraph 1 of Article 25 in cases where the transactions to which the request relates are regarded as abusive," it nevertheless provides: "[...] In the absence of a special provision, there is no general rule denying perceived abusive situations going to the mutual agreement procedure, however. The simple fact that a charge of tax is made under an *avoidance provision of domestic law* should not be a

70. *See* Tribunal Supremo, decision of September 22, 2021, *SGL Carbon Holding*, ECLI: ES:TS:2021:3572 (Spain); for a critical assessment of the decision, *see* Aitor Navarro, *Spanish Supreme Court denies Access to MAP in domestic GAAR Cases*, MNE Tax (November 2, 2021), available at https://mnetax.com/spanish-supreme-court-denies-access-to-map-in-domestic-gaar-tax-case-46099. Lower courts on the other hand had set forth different arguments and raised different conclusions on analogous issues, *see* Audiencia Nacional, Case 171/2017 of March 28, 2017 and Case 232/2015 of the Spanish National Court of April 17, 2017 (Spain). The Spanish Courts, however, determined that in the event of economic double taxation, domestic law cannot be invoked in rejecting an application to initiate a MAP, even when domestic GAAR legislation has been used to question the transactions undertaken by the taxpayer.

reason to deny access to mutual agreement."[71] Thus, we would be inclined to argue that taxpayers should indeed have the right to access MAPs in such situations even though the practice adopted in various countries indicates that such a procedure cannot be invoked when transactions are challenged under statutory GAARs.

Indeed, many States preserve the application of their GAARs to override their treaties either under their domestic law[72] or under tax treaty provisions themselves,[73] meaning that taxpayers may find no real benefit in invoking MAP processes.

In any case, double taxation arising from invoking a domestic GAAR should nevertheless be dealt with in the MAP provided by Article 25(3) of the OECD Model. Indeed, the competent authorities are also entitled to consult each other to eliminate double taxation in cases not provided for in the OECD Model.

## IV CONCLUSION

This chapter first, attempted to analyze whether tax treaties (in particular, Article 9.1) restrict adjustments made to related party loans through the domestic sham doctrine or domestic fact-finding rules or Court developed doctrines. In this regard, we are inclined to argue that tax law should apply to real facts of a case. Accordingly, tax treaties (including Article 9) do not per se restrict the application of outcomes under such rules.

The second issue is related to outcomes under statutory GAARs. The first question was whether Article 9(1) restricts adjustments made to related party loan transactions pursuant to statutory GAARs up to arm's length outcomes. Arguments for and against were detailed. One could indeed argue that, most likely, Article 9(1) does not restrict the effects of national GAARs. This said, at least within the EU, we believe that the proportionality principle could possibly restrict the counteraction up to the arm's length standard. This would be the case when facts and circumstances statutory GAARs are used and the tax administrations have broad powers to enforce a counteraction. More broadly, one may also raise the question as to whether any provisions of Bilateral Investment Treaties, for instance, the Fair and Equitable Treatment (FET) Standard could restrict national GAARs. Of course, the question merits further research, especially, with respect to the exact avenue through which the proportionality principle could apply.

The second question, assuming a re-characterization is made, is whether the re-characterized amount falls within the definition of "*dividends*" or "*interest*" for the purpose of tax treaties. One may indeed argue that the re-classified amount will fall under the definition of "*interest*" in Article 11(3) even though the domestic law treats it as dividends. A related question would then be if treaty benefits (Article 11 benefits) are required to be provided for the entire payment or a part of it, that is, the arm's length amount. Our view on this was outlined.

---

71. *See* OECD Model 2017: Commentary on Article 25, *supra* n. 37, para. 26.
72. The United Kingdom, Australia, Canada and New Zealand for example.
73. Article 11 of the Multilateral Convention to Implement Tax Treaty Related Measures to Prevent Base Erosion and Profit Shifting (the MLI).

The third question was whether taxpayers can access MAPs. In this regard, we would be inclined to state that taxpayers should indeed have the right to access MAPs in such thin capitalization situations even though the practice adopted in various countries indicates that such a procedure cannot be invoked when transactions are challenged under statutory GAARs.

CHAPTER 3

# The Interaction Between CFC Rules and TP Rules with a Focus on Financing

*Aurelio Massimiano & Kinha Romanovska*[*]

## I SCOPE OF CFC RULES AND TP RULES

### 1 Origin and Interaction

#### *A The US and Subpart F*

The history of interaction of Controlled Foreign Company (CFC) regulations with Transfer Pricing (TP) regulations is rather symptomatic. Both regimes, originating from the United States (US) income tax system, spread across the world in the second half of the twentieth century.[1]

In 1917, when US corporations already used TP manipulation to avoid or reduce taxes, the US War Revenue Act of 1917 empowered the Commissioner of Internal Revenue to require related corporations to file consolidated returns 'whenever necessary to more equitably determine the invested capital or taxable income'.[2] In 1921, this principle was transformed into law and authorised a Commissioner to consolidate the

* The views and opinions set forth herein are the personal views or opinions of the authors; they do not necessarily reflect views or opinions of the organisation with which the authors are associated.

1. FILIP MAJDOWSKI & KATARZYNA BRONZEWSKA, *Revolutionary Changes to the Arm's Length Principle under the OECD BEPS Project: Have CFC Rules Become Redundant?*, Intertax (2018) 46/3, p. 214; *See also* REUVEN S. AVI-YONAH, *Constructive Unilateralism: US Leadership and International Taxation*, University of Michigan Public Law Research Paper (2015), 463, 13 June (10 June 2022): https://ssrn.com/abstract=2622868 or http://dx.doi.org/10.2139/ssrn.2622868.
2. REUVEN S. AVI-YONAH, *The Rise and Fall of Arm's Length: A Study in the Evolution of U.S. International Taxation*, University of Michigan, Law & Economics Working Papers, Law & Economics Working Papers Law & Economics Working Papers Archive: 2003-2009 (2017), 10 June 2022: https://papers.ssrn.com/sol3/papers.cfm?abstract_id=1017524.

accounts of affiliated corporations 'for the purpose of making an accurate distribution or apportionment of gains, profits, income, deductions, or capital between or among such related trades or business'. Seven years later, in 1928, section 45 of the Internal Revenue Code (IRC) was introduced (the earliest predecessor of section 482), which replaced the consolidation regime.[3] Enacted '*in order to prevent evasion of taxes or clearly to reflect the income of any of such trades or businesses*', section 45 authorised a Commissioner to '*distribute, apportion, or allocate gross income or deductions between or among such trades or businesses, if he determines that such distribution, apportionment, or allocation is necessary*'. To specify the meaning of 'clearly reflect the income', in 1935, the regulations under section 45 of the Code, introduced the arm's length standard for the first time. However, the regulations lacked any explanation as to the methods that should be used to arrive at an arm's length price. To fill a regulatory vacuum, courts took on considerable discretion to obtain arm's length outcomes.[4] Such a state of affairs continued until 1968 when regulations under section 482[5] of the Code established rules for applying the arm's length principle to specific types of transactions.[6]

Although primitive and with no guidance as to the application of an arm's length principle, TP rules had already been in the US legal framework for a decade when the issue of avoiding taxes by US corporations through deferral of tax liability was attracting greater attention. This problem was addressed in 1961 by President John F. Kennedy in his speech to Congress, who said that '[...] more and more enterprises organised abroad by American firms have arranged their corporate structures aided by artificial arrangements between parent and subsidiary regarding intercompany pricing, the transfer of patent licensing rights, the shifting of management fees, and similar practices [...] in order to reduce sharply or eliminate completely their tax liabilities both at home and abroad'.[7]

As rightly pointed out by Professor Mitchell Kane with respect to this presidential statement of 1961, the issue of intercompany pricing and shifting of management fees were essentially about benefits that can be captured by related parties relative to unrelated ones, which he described as the 'milking' problem. The reference to the transfer of patent licensing rights is a different problem that could involve abusive pricing but not the only one. The main issue here was a deferral of tax that a company could achieve if it could make a tax-free outgoing transfer of intangible property to a foreign entity. The reference point in this case is not the unrelated party but the unincorporated foreign branch, which would not benefit from any deferral. This is what the author identified as the basic problem of 'parking'.[8]

3. R. Avi-Yonah, *supra* n. 2, p. 3.
4. Mitchel A. Kane, *Milking Versus Parking: Transfer Pricing and CFC Rules under the Internal Revenue Code*, Tax L. Rev. 66/487, (2013), 10 June 2022: https://www.law.nyu.edu/sites/default/files/ECM_PRO_073859.pdf, p. 5.
5. *Ibid.*
6. Avi-Yonah, *supra* n. 2, p. 8.
7. J.F. Kennedy, Special Message to the Congress on Taxation, 1961, available at: http://www.taxhistory.org/thp/readings.nsf/ArtWeb/2B727964C0A28BE5852571690051FD23?OpenDocment.
8. Kane, *supra* n. 4, p. 6.

In light of the above, the enactment of CFC rules in Subpart F by the Revenue Act of 1962, which was based on President Kennedy's proposal, was viewed as counteracting what was perceived to be an ineffective regime under section 482, providing historical evidence that the CFC rules have always been understood to function as a backstop to the TP rules.[9]

The relations between TP and CFC rules, as demonstrated by Professor Kane, can be observed based on their scope. Where CFC rules would have resulted in current inclusion of all income earned through controlled foreign subsidiaries, then pricing issues and the need for TP rules would disappear completely, as any advantage from profit shifting in the first instance would be immediately reversed through the full current inclusion result. In such a case, CFC rules would operate as 'a bludgeon that flattens the entire TP problem out of existence'.[10] In contrast, where CFC rules allow for tax deferral of an active income and apply exclusively to passive income, the CFC provisions can still act as a backstop, opening a gateway to possible interaction between two regimes.

With regard to CFC rules, it must be noted that the US tax reform of 2017 has limited the exclusion of active income by introducing a tax on global intangible low-taxed income (GILTI) within Subpart F.[11] Designed to protect the tax base from the possible migration from the US to low-tax countries that could occur as a side effect of a participation exemption regime enacted by the same reform, GILTI requires the US shareholders of CFCs to determine a current tax inclusion on their pro-rata portion of the foreign income derived by CFCs from business activities conducted in foreign countries.[12] It must be noted that it is not required that the income captured by GILTI in fact constitutes intangible income or be derived from intangible property. GILTI is rather a measure of CFC income that is deemed to exceed a routine rate of return on tangible assets.[13] Thus, the GILTI targets both passive and active income of a CFC and subjects it to tax in the US.

The question that arises is: how do these changes to Subpart F and the effect of GILTI impact the further need for TP rules? In other words, do CFC rules still serve as a 'backstop' to TP rules or perhaps they have become redundant? In the authors' opinion, despite the enactment of the GILTI regime, which leads to the almost full inclusion of a CFC's income, TP rules are still an important instrument to combat tax avoidance that can be used in the instances where CFC rules are circumvented. Moreover, considering that the primary purpose of TP rules is not to tackle tax avoidance, but to align primary taxing rights with value creation, they have their own independent role in the international tax framework. Thus, CFC regimes even with a full inclusion system do not eliminate the need for TP rules.

---

9. *Ibid.*, p. 5.
10. *Ibid.*, p. 6.
11. US: Internal Revenue Code § 951A, enacted by Public Law 115-97, 22 December 2017.
12. Carlos Perez-Gautrin, *US Tax Cuts and Jobs Act: Part 1 – Global Intangible Low-Taxed Income (GILTI)*, Bull. Int'l Tax'n (2019), p. 36.
13. John G. Rienstra, *Pillar Two from the US Perspective, Global Minimum Taxation? An Analysis of the Global Anti-Base Erosion Initiative* (Andreas Perdelwitz and Alessandro Turina eds), IBFD Tax Research Series (2021), 4, p. 317.

### B The OECD and BEPS Action 3

The issue of CFC rules was addressed by one of the actions of the Base Erosion and Profit Shift (BEPS) Action Plan, namely, BEPS Action 3, which developed a set of recommendations in respect of the design and application of effective CFC rules. Generally, the view of the Organisation for Economic Co-operation and Development (OECD) as regards the interaction of TP and CFC rules is that the latter do not complement TP rules and their reference as a 'backstop' to TP rules is delusive.[14] It is indicated that high tax rates applied under CFC rules may eliminate some incentives for TP manipulations, however, it is not their main purpose, but a mere coincidental outcome. The BEPS Action 3 report indicated that although CFC rules, in some cases, may target the same income as TP rules, it is unlikely that either CFC rules or TP rules in practice eliminate the need for the other set of rules.[15] The position of the OECD is that the need for both sets of rules is justified by a number of reasons:

- *Different design of CFC legislation*, which may have a different impact on the incentives for multinational groups to shift profits through TP schemes. As mentioned above, only CFC rules with a full-inclusion system are efficient enough to be a 'backstop' to TP rules, since a high tax rate of a controlling parent applied to all income of a controlled subsidiary removes the benefit to them of engaging in TP manipulation.[16] A partial-inclusion system, which often excludes an active income, captures TP schemes haphazardly, thus, it is not able to catch all income that is undertaxed.
- As *CFC rules restore only the taxation right of a parent's jurisdiction*, they would not be able to restore the taxing rights of all the states involved in the foreign-to-foreign base erosion cases.[17]
- Multinational groups will still benefit from profit shifting where a *parent is subject to a lower tax rate than its subsidiaries*.[18]
- CFC rules can be avoided by setting up structures with parent companies *resident in jurisdictions without CFC rules or with low tax rates with access to the same capital markets*. TP rules, in contrast, can be applied by all countries where economic activity takes place to protect their own tax bases.[19]
- As *CFC rules, even with full inclusion of income, are limited to parents and their controlled subsidiaries rather than sibling enterprises or other related parties* that do not have control over each other, TP rules are still needed to capture transactions which go beyond parent-subsidiary relations.[20]
- *TP rules alone are not able to capture all the income that would be targeted by CFC rules*. To prevent the erosion of domestic tax bases, *TP rules focus on*

14. OECD, *Public Discussion Draft, BEPS Action 3: Strengthening CFC Rules* (12 May 2015), para. 21.
15. *Ibid.*, para. 22.
16. *Ibid.*, para. 23.
17. *Ibid.*, para. 24.
18. *Ibid.*, para. 25.
19. *Ibid.*, para. 26.
20. *Ibid.*, para. 27.

*individual transactions between related parties, whereas CFC rules focus on profit earned by a controlled party from transactions with a variety of counterparties*. Thus, the overlap between these two rules is not exact, and not all profit earned by foreign subsidiaries that would be captured by CFC rules would be captured by TP rules.[21]

- While TP rules are not intended to address the profit shifting to low-tax jurisdictions - their main purpose is to align primary taxing rights with value creation - CFC rules, as deterrent measures, would discourage multinationals from shifting profits to foreign subsidiaries in low-tax jurisdictions, and therefore, complement TP rules as a backstop.[22]
- Both CFC rules and TP rules provide tax administrations with two different enforcement tools to combat BEPS practices.[23]

## 2 Scope of CFC Rules

Though varying in some of their aspects, the common principle of CFC rules all over the world is to tax the income of controlled foreign subsidiaries in the hands of resident shareholders. As described above, initially enacted as an instrument against deferral of tax liability, CFC rules are currently used to protect revenue by ensuring profits remain within the tax base of the parent or, in the case of CFC regimes that also target the stripping of third countries' bases ('foreign-to-foreign stripping'), other group companies, typically by preventing taxpayers from shifting income into controlled subsidiaries.[24] In other words, CFC rules are aimed to discourage and prevent shifting of income either from the parent jurisdiction, or from the parent and other jurisdiction, to a low-tax jurisdiction of a controlled subsidiary by restoring taxing right of a parent jurisdiction.

The feature of a 'control' in terms of a CFC can vary among different jurisdictions, which typically refers to a legal,[25] economic[26] or de facto control test.[27] As regards the level of control, it is set on more than 50% ownership of legal or economic interest in a controlled entity.[28] A different approach can be found in the US, according to which the interests, of all residents, in the CFC are aggregated so long as each interest is higher

21. *Ibid.*, para. 28.
22. *Ibid.*
23. *Ibid.*
24. OECD, *Designing Effective Controlled Foreign Company Rules, Action 3 – 2015 Final Report* (2015), OECD Publishing, p. 13.
25. *Ibid.*, p. 24, refers to a resident's holding of share capital to determine the percentage of voting rights held in a subsidiary.
26. Focuses on rights to the profits, as well as capital and assets of a company in certain circumstances such as dissolution or liquidation.
27. Looks at similar factors to those considered by many countries when considering where a company is resident for tax purposes, for example, at one who takes the top-level decisions regarding the affairs of the foreign company or who has the ability to direct or influence its day-to-day activities.
28. Yariv Brauner & Christine A. Davis, *Controlled Foreign Company Legislation in the United States*, in *Controlled Foreign Company Legislation* (Georg Kofler et al. eds, WU Institute for Austrian and International Tax Law European and International Tax Law and Policy Series, 2020) p. 836.

than 10%. A foreign company is a CFC if it is owned more than 50% by US people who each own at least 10%.

Depending on the design, CFC rules result in taxation at the level of a parent company of some (partial inclusion) or all (full inclusion) of the income of some or all of their foreign subsidiaries. To ensure the balance between taxing foreign income, in terms of capital export neutrality and capital import neutrality, and to maintain competitiveness, CFC regulations usually adapt the form of partial inclusion and apply to a 'passive', exempting an 'active' income that, to some extent, can be regarded as an indicator of economic activity in the foreign subsidiary and has not been, or is less likely to have been, shifted from the parent company.[29]

In the European Union (EU), Anti-Tax Avoidance Directive (ATAD) provides for two alternative implementation options of a CFC regime.[30] Under the first one, the taxpayer must include, in the tax base, certain specified types of income of the CFC ('categorical approach').[31] According to the second option, the taxpayer includes, in the tax base, income of the CFC arising from non-genuine arrangements which have been put in place for the essential purpose of obtaining a tax advantage ('transactional approach').[32]

It must be underlined that application of CFC rules in the EU has been restricted as a result of case law, according to which CFC rules of member states which apply to cross-border transactions and are justified by the prevention of tax avoidance must 'specifically target wholly artificial arrangements which do not reflect economic reality and whose only purpose would be to obtain a tax advantage'. [33]

To reflect the limitations set forth by the case law, the ATAD Directive adopts a carve-out for substantive economic activity[34] (in case of categorical approach) and it targets only non-genuine arrangements that have been put in place for the essential purpose of obtaining a tax advantage (for the 'transactional' approach). The carve-out for a substantive economic activity may not be applicable to a CFC that is resident or situated in a third country that is not a party to the European Economic Area (EEA). Thus, member states are free to tax under their CFC regimes low-tax income generated by subsidiaries resident in a third state even if it is derived from the substantive

29. OECD, *Discussion Draft, BEPS Action 3, supra* n. 14, p. 9.
30. ATAD Directive, *infra* n. 70, Article 7(2).
31. *Ibid.* The non-distributed income of the entity or the income of the permanent establishment which is derived from the following categories: (i) interest or any other income generated by financial assets; (ii) royalties or any other income generated from intellectual property; (iii) dividends and income from the disposal of shares; (iv) income from financial leasing; (v) income from insurance, banking and other financial activities; (vi) income from invoicing companies that earn sales and services income from goods and services purchased from and sold to associated enterprises, and add no or little economic value.
32. *Ibid.* An arrangement or a series thereof shall be regarded as 'non-genuine' to the extent that the entity or permanent establishment would not own the assets or would not have undertaken the risks which generate all, or part of, its income if it were not controlled by a company where the significant people functions, which are relevant to those assets and risks, are carried out and are instrumental in generating the controlled company's income.
33. Case C-196/04, *Cadbury Schweppes plc and Cadbury Schweppes Overseas Ltd v. Commissioners of Inland Revenue*; Case C-282/12, *Itelcar – Automóveis de Aluguer Lda. v. Fazenda Pública.*
34. An activity supported by staff, equipment, assets, and premises, as evidenced by relevant facts and circumstances.

activity.[35] For instance, such an approach was adopted by Polish,[36] German[37] and Portuguese[38] regulations that grant the substance carve-out only if a CFC is based inside the EU or in the EEA. In contrast, Austrian[39] and Croatian[40] CFC legislation applies the substance carve-out also to third countries and, thus, there is no differentiation between EEA and third states. On a side note, it is indicated that the fact that the ATAD Directive permits application of CFC rules to third countries without any carve-out for genuine business activities could be regarded as an unjustified restriction on free movement of capital.[41]

A separate comment should be made in relation to the US CFC regulations and already discussed in section A.1 GILTI tax. As mentioned, GILTI was introduced in 2017 as the amendment to Subpart F of the IRC which contains CFC provisions. GILTI applies in addition to the other CFC rules of Subpart F that remain in force, which means that the former does not substitute or replace the latter. Despite the unfortunate name, i.e., 'GILTI', gross income for the purposes of GILTI applies to types of revenue that can go far beyond what common sense would suggest is 'global intangible income'. This means that gross income for GILTI expands to encompass foreign income derived not only from the licensing of intangibles but also from the sale of goods, service fees and interest income.[42] Thus, the application of GILTI extends also to income which can be categorised as 'active' from the perspective of CFC regulations.

## 3 Scope of TP Rules

The fundamental role of TP rules is the allocation of tax base between jurisdictions in accordance with Article 9 of tax treaties concluded on the basis of the OECD Model Convention. Such a purpose is apparent taking into account that TP rules apply also in cases of transactions taking place between entities all located in high-tax jurisdictions. Nevertheless, TP rules could help to prevent price manipulation between related

35. For instance, this approach was adopted in Poland, where CFC rules allow to tax passive income of a CFC resident in a third state regardless of the 'substance' of its activity.
36. PL: Ustawa z dn. 15 lutego 2992 r. o podatku dochodowym od osób prawnych (ze zm.) [Corporate Income Tax Act as amended].
37. Jochen Gerbracht, *Controlled Foreign Company Legislation in Germany*, in *Controlled Foreign Company Legislation* (Georg Kofler et al. eds, WU Institute for Austrian and International Tax Law European and International Tax Law and Policy Series, 2020) p. 299.
38. Ricardo da Palma Borges & Marta Carmo, *Controlled Foreign Company Legislation in Portugal*, in *Controlled Foreign Company Legislation* (Georg Kofler et al. eds, WU Institute for Austrian and International Tax Law European and International Tax Law and Policy Series, 2020) p. 581.
39. Martin Klokar & Mario Riedl, *Controlled Foreign Company Legislation in Austria*, in *Controlled Foreign Company Legislation* (Georg Kofler et al. eds, WU Institute for Austrian and International Tax Law European and International Tax Law and Policy Series, 2020) p. 84.
40. Nevia Čičin-Šain & Stjepan Gadžo, *Controlled Foreign Company Legislation in Croatia*, in *Controlled Foreign Company Legislation* (Georg Kofler et al. eds, WU Institute for Austrian and International Tax Law European and International Tax Law and Policy Series, 2020) pp. 186-187.
41. Robert J. Danon, *EU Fiscal Protectionism versus Free Movement of Capital: The Case of the ATAD CFC Categorical Model*, in *European Tax Integration: Law, Policy and Politics* (Pasquale Pistone ed., IBFD, 2018).
42. *See* Gautrin, *supra* n. 12, p. 42.

enterprises which is one of the most common tax avoidance techniques.[43] In the cross-border context, 'transfer mispricing' could allow profits to be shifted from a high-tax jurisdiction of one related enterprise to the jurisdiction of another where these profits are subject to low taxation or no taxation at all. TP rules are intended to adjust the taxable profits of such related enterprises also in order to eliminate distortions arising whenever the prices or other conditions of transactions between them differ from what they would have been if these enterprises had been unrelated.[44] It is achieved by the arm's length principle which seeks to determine whether transactions between related taxpayers reflect their 'true' tax liability by comparing them to similar transactions between unrelated taxpayers dealing at arm's length.[45]

According to the OECD TP Guidelines (2022), the determination if an arrangement is at arm's length requires a comparison of the related party transactions with comparable uncontrolled transactions.[46] There are two key stages of such an analysis. The first one is an identification of the commercial or financial relations between related parties and the conditions and economically relevant circumstances attached to those relations in order to accurately delineate a controlled transaction. The second stage is to undertake a comparability analysis to compare the controlled transactions with uncontrolled transactions.[47]

An accurate delineation of the actual transaction requires a functional analysis to be conducted. In the context of financial transactions, the analysis seeks to identify the functions performed, the assets used, and the risks assumed by the parties to controlled transactions.[48] In the case of an intra-group loan, the relevant economic characteristics of the borrowing entity need to be established, in particular, a credit rating evaluation of the borrowing entity. Further, an arm's length interest rate needs to be determined. The arm's length interest rate consists of a base rate (risk-free rate) that is determined on the basis of currency and maturity and a credit spread that is determined on the basis of the risks undertaken by the lender with respect to the lending transaction.[49]

The OECD TP Guidelines (2022) indicate that the risk should be allocated to the entity which has control and the financial capacity to assume the risk associated with the financial asset.[50] To allocate the risks, a functional analysis requires the identification and consideration of risks assumed by each party of a transaction, since the actual assumption of risks would influence the prices and other conditions of transactions between the associated enterprises.[51]

In particular, it is necessary to determine how the associated enterprises that are parties to the transaction operate in relation to assumption and management of the

43. *See* Avi-Yonah, *supra* n. 2, p. 2.
44. OECD, *Discussion Draft, BEPS Action 3, supra* n. 14, para. 21.
45. Avi-Yonah, *supra* n. 2, p. 1.
46. OECD TP Guidelines (2022), *infra* n. 50, para. 1.33.
47. *See* Vikram Chand, *Transfer Pricing Aspects of Intra-Group Loans in Light of the Base Erosion and Profit Shifting Action Plan*, Intertax 44/12 (2016).
48. OECD TP Guidelines (2022), *infra* n. 50, para. 10.23.
49. Chand, *supra* n. 47, p. 889.
50. OECD, *OECD Transfer Pricing Guidelines for Multinational Enterprises and Tax Administrations 2022* (OECD Publishing, 2022) ('OECD TP Guidelines (2022)'), para. 1.103.
51. *Ibid.*, para. 1.56.

specific, economically significant risks, and in particular which enterprise or enterprises perform control functions and risk mitigation functions, which enterprise or enterprises encounter upside or downside consequences of risk outcomes, and which enterprise or enterprises have the financial capacity to assume the risk.[52] The OECD TP Guidelines (2022) propose a six-step analysis to assess a risk in a controlled transaction, in order to accurately delineate the actual transaction with respect to that risk. It requires the following steps to be undertaken:[53]

| | |
|---|---|
| Step 1 | Identification of economically significant risks. |
| Step 2 | Determination of how specific, economically significant risks are contractually assumed by each of the parties under the terms of the transaction. |
| Step 3 | Determination of how parties to the transaction operate in relation to *assumption and management* of the specific, economically significant *risks*, and in particular which party performs *control functions and risk mitigation functions*, which party encounters upside or downside consequences of risk outcomes, and which has the *financial capacity to assume the risk* |
| Step 4 | Interpretation of the information obtained under Steps 2-3 and determination if the contractual assumption of risk is consistent with the conduct of parties and other facts of the case by analysing (i) whether the parties follow the contractual terms and (ii) whether the party assuming risk exercises control over the risk and has the financial capacity to assume the risk. |
| Step 5 | Where the party assuming risk under steps 1-4 does not control the risk or does not have the financial capacity to assume the risk, then return must be allocated to the party that controls the risk and has the financial capacity to bear the risk. |
| Step 6 | The actual transaction, as accurately delineated, should be priced taking into account the financial and other consequences of risk assumption, as appropriately allocated, and appropriately compensating risk management functions. |

The term 'risk management', which should be differentiated from 'an assumption of a risk'[54], is used to refer to the function of assessing and responding to risk associated with commercial activity. Risk management comprises three elements:

(i) the capability to make decisions to take on, lay off, or decline a risk-bearing opportunity, together with the actual performance of that decision-making function;

52. *Ibid.*, para. 1.60.
53. Chand, *supra* n. 47, p. 896. *See also* OECD TP Guidelines (2022), *supra* n. 50, paras 1.56-1.60.
54. OECD TP Guidelines (2022), *supra* n. 50: Risk assumption means taking on the upside and downside consequences of the and other consequences if the risk materialises. A party performing part of the risk management functions may not assume the risk that is the subject of its management activity but may be hired to perform risk mitigation functions under the direction of the risk-assuming party. For example, the day-to-day mitigation of product recall risk may be outsourced to a party performing monitoring of quality control over a specific manufacturing process according to the specifications of the party assuming the risk.

(ii) the capability to make decisions on whether and how to respond to the risks associated with the opportunity, together with the actual performance of that decision-making function; and
(iii) the capability to mitigate risk, in other words, the capability to take measures that affect risk outcomes, together with the actual performance of such risk mitigation.[55]

It must be noted that the OECD TP Guidelines (2022) explicitly state neither a mere formalising of the outcome of decision-making in the form of, for example, meetings organised for formal approval of decisions that were made in other locations, minutes of a board meeting and signing of the documents relating to the decision, nor the setting of the policy environment relevant for the risk, qualifies as the exercise of a decision-making function sufficient to demonstrate control over a risk.[56] Persons responsible for and actually performing decision-making functions should possess the relevant competences and experience in the area of the particular risk for which the decision is being made and should be capable of understanding the risk based on a relevant analysis of the information required for assessing the foreseeable downside and upside risk outcomes of such a decision and its impact on business.[57]

Financial capacity to assume risk should be understood as access to funding to take on the risk or to lay off the risk, to pay for risk mitigation functions and to bear the consequences of the risk if the risk materialises.[58] Access to funding by the party assuming the risk takes into account the available assets and the options realistically available to access additional liquidity, if needed, to cover the costs anticipated to arise should the risk materialise.

Control over risk involves the first two elements of risk management referred to above, i.e.:

(i) the capability to make decisions to take on, lay off, or decline a risk-bearing opportunity, together with the actual performance of that decision-making function; and
(ii) the capability to make decisions on whether and how to respond to the risks associated with the opportunity, together with the actual performance of that decision-making function.[59]

The day-to-day mitigation is not necessary to demonstrate a control over risks and might be outsourced. However, in this case, control over risk would involve a capability to manage and supervise the outsourced activities.[60]

55. OECD TP Guidelines (2022), *supra* n. 50, para. 1.61.
56. *Ibid.*, para. 1.66.
57. *Ibid.*, para. 1.66.
58. *Ibid.*, para. 1.64.
59. *Ibid.*, para. 1.65.
60. *Ibid.*

## II IS THERE A NEED FOR BOTH RULES?

### 1 Cases of Application of CFC Rules Which May Be Tackled with the TP Rules

To demonstrate a situation where CFC and TP rules may lead to very close outcomes, the following example can be analysed (*see* Figure 3.1).

#### *A Facts*

- Parent Co is a company located in an EU high-tax country that has incorporated a fully controlled subsidiary CFC in an EU low-tax country.
- CFC owns two subsidiaries, Sub Co 1 and Sub Co 2, both resident for tax purposes in high-tax countries with no withholding tax and inefficient thin capitalisation rules.
- The CFC neither owns nor rents office premises; it only uses the address of a fiduciary company for registration purposes and as a 'letter box', nor it employs any personnel.
- The CFC has a minimum statutory capital and is predominately funded through debt.
- The main activity of the CFC is to finance activities of other entities within a group.
- The CFC is formally managed by one local director acting as a fiduciary and director resident in the State of a Parent Co who travels every year to the State of the CFC in order to approve and formalise the funding decisions, which are based on the analysis received by the finance team of the Parent Co which has appropriately qualified and experienced personnel in place and principally performs the loan creation and loan management activities.
- The CFC rules of the State of Parent Co exclude 'passive' income from substantiative economic activities conducted only within the EU.[61]

61. CFC rules adopt a 'categorical' approach and carve-out in line with Article 7(2)a of ATAD.

*Figure 3.1 Transactional Flow Chart: Example 1*

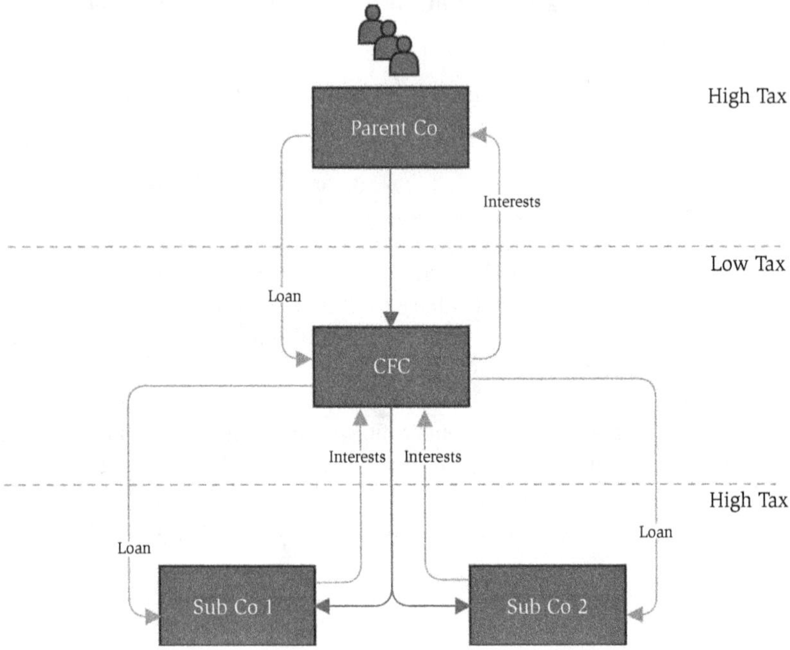


### B TP Approach

The TP analysis has to take into account the outcomes of the BEPS Report Actions 8-10 and subsequent amendments of the OECD TP Guidance (2017), which deny allocation of any excess profits to capital-rich entities without any other relevant economic activities ('cash boxes') and obligate to allocate to such entities the profits equivalent to no more than a risk-free return.[62] This means that if a related party does not have the financial capacity to bear the financial risks associated with its funding activities and it does not have control over these risks (e.g., because it just provides the money when it is asked to do so, without any assessment of whether the party receiving the money is creditworthy), then it should not be allocated the profits associated with the financial risks and should be entitled to no more than a risk-free return,[63] or less if, for example,

62. OECD, *Aligning Transfer Pricing Outcomes with Value Creation, Actions 8-10 – 2015 Final Reports, OECD/G20 Base Erosion and Profit Shifting Project* (OECD Publishing, 2015) ('BEPS Actions 8-10 Final Report'), p. 11.
63. OECD, *Transfer Pricing Guidance on Financial Transactions: Inclusive Framework on BEPS Actions 4, 8-10* (OECD, 2020), para. 1.109: A risk-free rate of return is the hypothetical return which would be expected on an investment with no risk of loss. Ultimately, there is no investment with zero risk, and the reliability of available proxies for approximating a risk-free rate of return will depend on prevailing facts and circumstances.

the transaction is not commercially rational and therefore the guidance on non-recognition applies.[64] The risk will be allocated to the enterprise which has control and the financial capacity to assume the risk associated with the financial asset.[65]

Considering the above, the functional analysis provides evidence that the CFC neither has the financial capacity to assume the risk nor does it have the capability and authority to control the risk associated with the loans granted to Sub Co 1 and Sub Co 2.

First of all, as the CFC is mainly financed by the parent through the debt, it is questionable whether it has proper access to funding to take on the risk or to lay off the risk, to pay for the risk mitigation and to bear the consequences of the risk once it has materialised. Therefore, one may argue that it has no financial capacity to bear the risk.

Second, the CFC does not have the decision-making capability to take on, lay off, or decline the financing opportunity, or the capability to make decisions on whether and how to respond to the risks associated with such financing. These functions are performed by Parent Co which has a properly qualified and experienced financial team of experts.

Moreover, the CFC does not perform functions which could allow it to evaluate the financing opportunity to consider the appropriate risk premium and other issues to determine the appropriate pricing of the financing opportunity and to evaluate the appropriate protection of its financial investment. It is Parent Co that is responsible for and, in fact, performs these functions.

Considering the above, the CFC would not be entitled to any more than a risk-free return as an appropriate measure of the profits it is entitled to retain since it lacks the capability to control the risk associated with loan transactions with Sub 1 and Sub 2. The risk should be allocated to Parent Co which has control and the financial capacity to assume the risk associated with the financial asset.

### *C CFC Approach*

As regards the applicability of CFC rules in the above example, the passive income accumulated in the CFC that lacks any substantial activity falls within the scope of CFC rules of a state of Parent Co and, therefore, is subject to tax in its hands. The Facts of the example clearly indicate that the CFC has no staff, equipment, assets or premises necessary to conduct business. Thus, no arguments can be put forward to justify the application of potential carve-out for substantive economic activity that is available under CFC rules of the State of Parent Co.

Consequently, low-taxed profits of a CFC equal to risk-free returns will be taxed in the state of Parent Co at the domestic (high) tax rate. This approach is in accordance with the view adopted by the OECD in BEPS Actions 8-10 Report, that CFC regulations may have a subsidiary role in relation to TP regulations applicable to the so-called

64. BEPS Actions 8-10 Final Report, *supra* n. 62.
65. *Ibid.*, paras 1.85, 1.103.

over-capitalised companies with no-significant activities that, for example, provide financing (cash-boxes companies).[66]

However, the effect of CFC rules is far greater than 'grasping' the profits, which from Parent's Co perspective remain undertaxed after the application of TP rules. This is because CFC rules are designed as a determent measure aimed to discourage multinational groups from engaging in pricing manipulation and, consequently, to neutralise potential tax benefits of tax planning structures, as presented in the example.

## 2 Cases of Application of CFC That Cannot Be Tackled with the Application of the TP Rules

In the contrast to the above example, there may be cases that can be approached only by the application of CFC rules. These may be presented by the following example (*see* Figure 3.2).

### *A Facts*

- The Parent Co is a company located in an EU high-tax country and it incorporated a fully controlled subsidiary CFC in a *non-EU low-tax country*.
- The CFC has two subsidiaries Sub Co 1 and Sub Co 2, which are both resident for tax purposes in high-tax countries with no withholding tax and inefficient thin capitalisation rules.
- The CFC rents office premises in the State of its residence.
- The CFC is funded through capital contributions.
- The main activity of the CFC is to finance activities of other entities within a group.
- The CFC is managed by resident directors, who are supported by a local finance team, which includes appropriately qualified and experienced personnel that perform the loan creation and loan management activities.
- CFC rules of the State of Parent Co exclude 'passive' income from substantiative economic activities conducted only within the EU.[67]

66. BEPS Actions 8-10 Final Report, *supra* n. 62, p. 11. *See also* MAJDOWSKI & BRONZEWSKA, *supra* n. 1.
67. CFC rules adopt a 'categorical' approach and carve-out in line with Article 7(2)a of ATAD Directive.

*Figure 3.2 Transactional Flow Chart: Example 2*

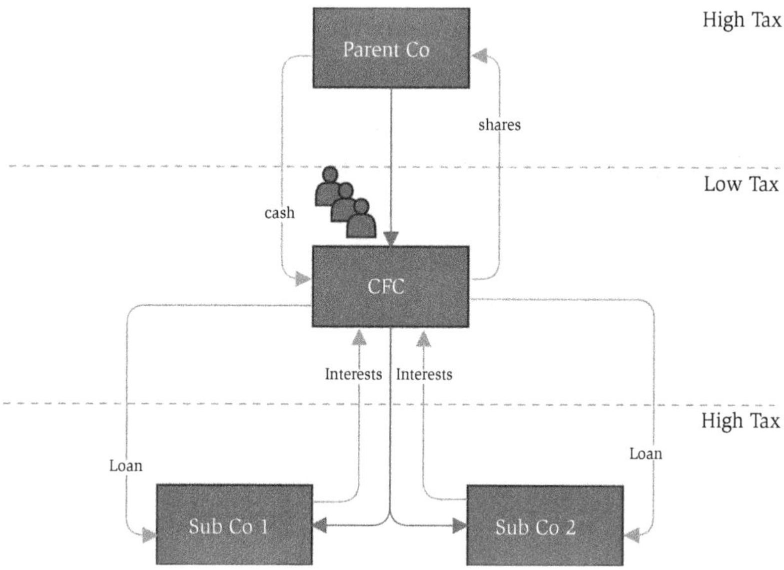


### B TP Approach

In light of the above, the TP analysis in this example is straightforward. The CFC has a financial capacity to bear the financial risks associated with loan agreements with Sub Co 1 and Sub Co 2 and it does perform control over these risks – all decision-making functions with respect to: (i) taking on, laying off or declining financial risks, and (ii) deciding on whether and how to respond to the various financial risks associated with the decision-making opportunity, are performed by a local financial team. Therefore, the CFC should be allocated the entire financing return associated with the loans to Sub Co 1 and Sub Co 2. Consequently, according to TP rules, all profits of the CFC will be taxed at a low rate in its jurisdiction.

### C CFC Approach

The facts presented in the example provide solid evidence that the CFC performs substantiative economic activities in the States of its residence. Specifically, the CFC employs adequate staff (directors and local finance team) and has access to the office premises where it performs loan creation and loan management activities.

The tax implications in a State of Parent Co depend on the existence and design of carve-out for substantiative economic activities available under CFC legislation. Considering that according to the assumptions made in the example, CFC rules of the state of Parent Co do not provide an exclusion for substantial activities outside the EU, all income of a CFC that is located in a third state will be subject to tax at the level of

Parent Co. Thus, in this situation, CFC rules will be capable of 'grasping' all low-taxed income that under TP rules was allocated to a low-tax state of a CFC. If, however, the carve-out was available, then the effects of the application of CFC rules would correspond to TP outcomes and all income of CFCs would be subject to low tax only in the State of its residence.

## III DOUBLE TAXATION DERIVING FROM THE APPLICATION OF CFC AND TP RULES AND POSSIBLE RESOLUTION MECHANISMS

### 1 Possible Double Taxation

The final report on BEPS Action 3 acknowledges that application of CFC rules could trigger double taxation mainly for three reasons: (i) the attributed CFC income is also subject to foreign corporate taxes in the State of residence or in the source countries of the income; (ii) CFC rules are applied in more than one jurisdiction on the same CFC income; and (iii) CFC actually distributes dividends out of income that has already been attributed to its resident shareholders under CFC rules.[68] The report provides recommendations for eliminating double taxation in the above circumstances, consisting of cases (i) and (ii) in allowing a tax credit for taxes actually paid by the CFC in other jurisdictions, and for case (iii) in exempting dividends (or capital gains on disposition of shares) if the income of the CFC has previously been taxed in the State of residence of the parent company.[69] Such recommendations have been addressed by most CFC legislation, including Article 8 of the EU ATAD Directive,[70] whereby a tax credit should be granted in taxing the income of CFC in the state of the shareholder[71] and any amount previously taxed in application of the CFC rules should not be taxed at the moment of distribution of dividend by the CFC.[72]

However, the report on BEPS on Action 3 acknowledges that double taxation could also arise in other situations, 'for instance where there has been a transfer pricing adjustment between two jurisdictions and a CFC charge arises in a third jurisdiction'.[73]

The case could be illustrated by the following example (*see* Figure 3.3).

68. OECD, BEPS Action 3-2015 Final Report, *supra* n. 24, para. 122.
69. *Ibid.*, para. 123.
70. Council Directive (EU) 2016/1164 of 12 July 2016 laying down rules against tax avoidance practices that directly affect the functioning of the internal market, OJ L 193 (2016) ('ATAD Directive').
71. *Ibid.*, Article 8(7) which provides that 'the Member State of the taxpayer shall allow a deduction of the tax paid by the entity or permanent establishment from the tax liability of the taxpayer in its state of tax residence or location. The deduction shall be calculated in accordance with national law'.
72. ATAD Directive, *supra* n. 70, Article 8(5) which provides that 'where the entity distributes profits to the taxpayer, and those distributed profits are included in the taxable income of the taxpayer, the amounts of income previously included in the tax base pursuant to Article 7 shall be deducted from the tax base when calculating the amount of tax due on the distributed profits, in order to ensure there is no double taxation'.
73. OECD, BEPS Action 3-2015 Final Report, *supra* n. 24, para. 122.

### *A* *Facts*

- Parent Co is a company located in a high-tax EU country and it incorporated a fully controlled subsidiary CFC in a low-tax EU country.
- The CFC neither owns nor rents office premises; it only uses the address of a fiduciary company for registration purposes and as a 'letter-box', nor does it employ any personnel.
- The activity is conducted by the personnel of Parent Co on the basis of a service agreement between the CFC and Parent Co.
- The CFC's primary purpose is to finance activities of other entities within a group, i.e., Sub Co residents for tax purposes in a high-tax country.
- The funds used by the CFC are borrowed from a third-party bank.
- Parent Co taxes the profit of the CFC in the year of production (FY X) for the amount resulting from the financial statement of the CFC (equal to 100).
- In FY X + 3, Sub Co receives a TP assessment referred to FY X challenging the amount of the deduction of the interest paid to the CFC, from 1,000 to 900.

*Figure 3.3 Transactional Flow Chart: Example 3*

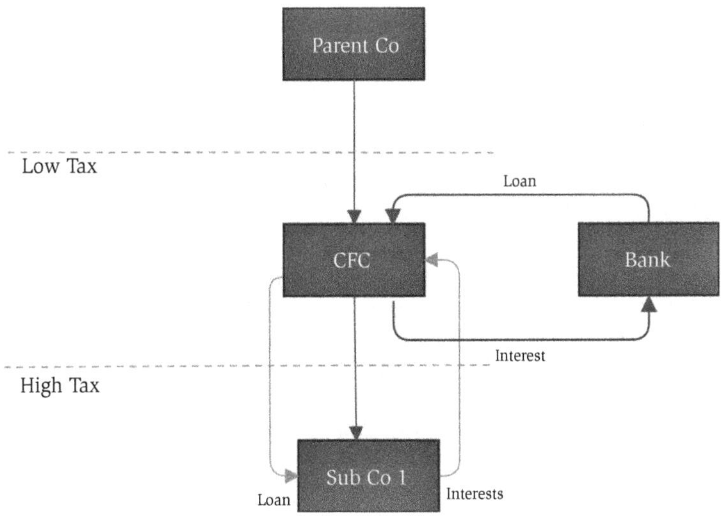


### *B* *Double Taxation*

In the situation at stake, the TP claim from Sub Co tax authorities triggers economic double taxation, being the 100 of income adjusted already taxed in the State of Parent Co in FY X in application of the CFC rules.

With reference to such a situation, the report on BEPS on Action 3 only indicates that 'it is left to individual jurisdictions to address other situations giving rise to double taxation, but the overall recommendation for this building block is to design CFC rules to ensure that they do not lead to double taxation'.[74] EU ATAD Directive does not provide any rule for eliminating double taxation in case of TP adjustment on the income of CFC. It is therefore necessary to investigate if in the case at stake, in the lack of internal rules for eliminating double taxation, competent authorities' procedure under relevant tax treaty, or Arbitration Convention or Dispute resolution directive could be initiated.

## 2 MAP under Tax Treaty

The analysis of the applicability of Article 25 of the OECD Model Convention,[75] should start by enquiring about the possible applicability of the relevant tax treaty. In particular, in the case at stake, the double taxation derives from the taxation of the income of the CFC both in the State of Parent Co ('State P') and in the State of Sub Co ('State S'). Therefore, it is necessary to investigate the applicability of the Treaty between P and S.

As Parent Co is a resident of State P, and Sub Co 1 resident of State S, they could, in theory, invoke the application of P-S tax treaty. Nevertheless, for activating Mutual Agreement Procedure (MAP) under Article 25 it is necessary to demonstrate that the action of one or both of the contracting States results in taxation not in accordance with the provision of the convention.[76]

It is therefore necessary to analyse if the taxation of State S and State P is in breach of Article 9 of the P-S Treaty. The applicability of such provision requires the existence of two related enterprises of the contracting States, being taxed on the same income. According to Article 3 of the OECD Model Convention, the term enterprise of a contracting state means 'the enterprise carried on by a resident of a contracting state'. It is therefore clear that Article 9 is not applicable in the case at stake, namely, the transaction between the CFC (resident in a State other than State P) and Sub Co, resident in State S.

The lack of the breach of a provision of P-S Treaty leads to the consequence of non-applicability of Article 25(1) of the treaty itself.[77,78] It has been observed by authoritative scholars[79] that tax treaties do not attempt to avoid double taxation in general, but only within their scope. This means that cases of double taxation not covered by the scope of the treaty have to be accepted. Cases of so-called economic double taxation, for example, are not solved by the tax treaty. The only restriction is

74. OECD, BEPS Action 3-2015 Final Report, *supra* n. 24, para. 123.
75. OECD, *Model Tax Convention on Income and on Capital* (OECD, 2017), Article 25.
76. *See* Annika Soom, *Double Taxation Resulting from the ATAD: Is There Relief?*, Intertax 48/3 (2020), pp. 273-285.
77. *See ibid.*
78. The opposite view, *see* Blazej Kuzniacki, *The Need to Avoid Double Economic Taxation Triggered by CFC Rules under Tax Treaties, and the Way to Achieve It*, Intertax, 43/12 (2015) pp. 758-772.
79. Michael Lang, *The Application of the OECD Model Tax Convention to Partnerships: A Critical Analysis of the Report Prepared by the OECD Committee on Fiscal Affairs*, 29 (Vienna, 2000).

based on Article 9 OECD Model Convention, which provides that profits resulting out of conditions made or imposed between associated enterprises may only be adjusted on an arm's length basis. This means that the OECD Model Convention does not prevent the contracting partners from allocating the income to different taxpayers in other situations not covered by the Article 9 OECD Model Convention.[80] The case at stake is clearly a case of economic double taxation not covered by Article 9 of the Treaty, and therefore out of the scope of the treaty itself.

It should be noted that according to Article 25(3), the last paragraph of the OECD Model Convention, Competent Authorities may also consult together for elimination of double taxation in cases not provided for in the convention. Such provision could therefore be invoked for eliminating double taxation in the case at stake.[81] Nevertheless, the application of such a provision does not entail an arbitration phase, therefore if the two tax authorities do not reach an agreement or do not open the MAP, the double taxation will remain.[82]

For sake of completeness, a possible alternative for eliminating double taxation would be to start a MAP under the treaty between the CFC and Sub Co, if any, that is, without any doubt, applicable. Once the income of the CFC is redetermined as a result of the MAP, it should be verified on the basis of the internal CFC rules of Parent Co jurisdiction if an amended tax return could be filed for redetermining the income of the CFC.[83]

## 3 Applicability of Arbitration Convention

The scope of Arbitration Convention[84] is to eliminate double taxation within the EU deriving from adjustment of profit between associated enterprises. According to Article 1, the Convention shall apply where, for the purposes of taxation, profits which are

80. *See ibid.*; and more recently, Michael Lang & Claus Staringer, *General Report: Qualification of Taxable Entities and Treaty Protection*, (99b) Cahiers de droit fiscal international 42 (IFA Congress in Mumbai, 2014).
81. Pitambar Das, *Corresponding Adjustment and Its Interaction with the Mutual Agreement Procedure under Article 25 of the OECD Model*, International Transfer Pricing Journal (2019).
82. *See* Roland Ismer, *Article 25. Mutual Agreement Procedure*, in *Klaus Vogel on Double Taxation Conventions* (Ekkehart Reimer & Alexander Rust eds, Kluwer Law International BV, 2022), pp. 2064-2068; J. Scott Wilkie, *Article 25: Mutual Agreement Procedure*, Global Tax Treaty Commentaries, Global Topics IBFD (Last Reviewed: 29 September 2021), para. 4.2; Heinz Jirousek & Annika Streicher, *Mutual Agreement Procedures and the Implementation of Mutual Agreements in Domestic Law*, in *Tax Treaties and Procedural Law* (Michael Lang et al. eds, IBFD, 2020), pp. 168 ff.; John Francis Avery Jones et al., *The Legal Nature of The Mutual Agreement Procedure under the OECD Model Convention*, British Tax Review, No. 6 (1979) pp. 13-20 and No. 1 (1980) pp. 346-353.
83. This solution is not feasible to the extent that the book values are the basis for redetermining the income of CFC in Parent Co jurisdiction, considering that the MAP does not imply a rewriting of financial statement.
84. Convention of 20 August 1990, on the elimination of double taxation in connection with the adjustment of profits of associated enterprises, 90/463/EEC.

included in the profits of an enterprise of a Contracting State are also included or are also likely to be included in the profits of an enterprise of another Contracting State on the grounds that the arm's length principle, as set out in Article 4, has not been observed. In particular, according to Article 4, where conditions are made or imposed between two associated enterprises[85] 'in their commercial or financial relations which differ from those which would be made between independent enterprises, then any profits which would, but for those conditions, have accrued to one of the enterprises, but, by reason of those conditions, have not so accrued, may be included in the profits of that enterprise and taxed accordingly'.

Moving to the example above, to the extent Parent Co and Sub Co are resident within the EU, the Arbitration Convention seems at first glance to be applicable. Indeed, the profit of the CFC is included in the profit of the two EU resident enterprises (Parent Co and Sub Co). Nevertheless, Article 4 requires for applying the Arbitration Convention that the 'conditions are made or imposed between the two enterprises [NDR of the Contracting States] in *their commercial or financial relations*' (emphasis added) differ from the one that would be agreed upon at arm's length between independent parties. In the case at stake, Parent Co and Sub Co do not have commercial or financial relations that are instead in place between the CFC and Sub Co. This argument should lead to the non-applicability of the Arbitration Convention.

It should be noted that the Arbitration Convention does not eliminate all the cases of economic double taxation within the EU. For example, the convention does not apply in the case of TP adjustment between the European permanent establishment (PE) of a non-EU resident enterprise and an EU resident enterprise.[86]

## 4 Applicability of Dispute Resolution Directive

According to Article 1, the Dispute Resolution Directive[87] lays down rules on a mechanism to resolve disputes between Member States when those disputes arise from the interpretation and application of agreements and conventions that provide for the elimination of double taxation of income and, where applicable, capital.

Having concluded in the previous paragraphs that the double taxation in the case at stake is not covered either by a double tax treaty or Arbitration convention, the Dispute Resolution Directive cannot be invoked to resolve the case.[88]

---

85. *Ibid.*, Article 4, para. 2.
86. *See* Harm Mark Pit, *Dispute Resolution in the EU* (IBFD, 2018), pp. 340-344; M.L.B. Van der Lande, *Het Arbitrageverdrag*, Handboek Internationaal Belastingrecht (Delwel, 1997), para. 1.1.6; Ben J.M. Terra & Peter J. Wattel, *European Tax Law* (Kluwer Law International, 2012), p. 720.
87. Council Directive (EU) 2017/1852 of 10 October 2017 on tax dispute resolution mechanisms in the European Union, OJ L 265.
88. As to the possible inclusion in the scope of the Dispute Resolution Directive of mutual agreements concluded pursuant to Article 25(3) OECD MC, *See* Guglielmo Maisto, *Oggetto e ambito della Direttiva*, Capitolo V, in L. Del Federico, *La risoluzione delle controversie fiscali internazionali nell'Unione Europea* (Pacini Editore, 2021), p. 105; Moris Lehner, *Neue Regelungsebenen und Kompetenze im Internationalen Steuerrecht* in *IStR* (2019), p. 283.

## IV CONCLUSION

During recent decades, both TP and CFC rules underwent a notable transformation. Although initially introduced as a backstop to the TP rules, CFC rules have gained more importance as a measure that eliminates incentives to manipulate transaction prices.

The interaction of these rules depends on the design of CFC legislation adopted across different states, in particular, its applicability to all or passive income only and existence of carve-outs for substantive activities. Where a CFC does not perform significant functions in a group of related companies/has no minimum substance, TP rules tax only the part of the CFC's profits allowing to 'park' profits equal to risk-free return in low-tax jurisdictions, whereas the effect of CFC rules extends also on profit that TP rules attribute to such jurisdiction. In this case, CFC rules effectively operate as a 'backstop' to TP rules. If, however, a CFC performs significant functions/has minimum substance and CFC legislation of a state of a parent does not exclude profits derived by CFC from substantive activities, then such profits while being entirely allocated to a CFC under TP rules and subject to a low level of tax can be brought into charge by the state of a parent and taxed accordingly under its CFC regime. Thus, CFC rules tackle cases of low taxation of profits while TP rules do not.

In certain situations, the application of both rules can lead to economic double taxation. Specifically, it is the case when there is a TP adjustment between two states and a CFC charge arises in a third jurisdiction. Neither BEPS Action 3 nor OECD TP Guidelines (2022) provides guidance on how to deal with the issue of double taxation in this instance.

The first and most obvious instrument to consider is MAP stipulated in Article 25 of the OECD Model Convention. Generally, tax treaties do not solve issues of economic double taxation, except for certain cases falling within Article 9 and Article 25 (3) of the OECD Model Convention. Nonetheless, the discussed case of economic double taxation is not covered by Article 9, and therefore out of the scope of the treaty itself. Article 25 (3) could be possibly applicable, however, to a limited extent, as it does not provide for the arbitration phase. As a result, if the two tax authorities do not reach an agreement or do not open the MAP, double taxation will remain.

For the reasons indicated before, to solve the issue of economic taxation at stake, it is also not possible to evoke either provision of the Arbitration Convention or Dispute resolution Directive. Hence, theoretically, TP and CFC rules may interact in a way that leads to economic double taxation with no legal instrument for solving it.

CHAPTER 4

# The Interaction of Interest Limitation Rules, Thin Cap Rules, ALP-Based Rules and the Pillar Two UTPR: What Comes First?

*Chloe Burnett SC*[*]

## I INTRODUCTION

Multinationals' cross-border interest deductions come under attack from all angles. The debtor's jurisdiction, concerned about base erosion, is likely to have erected interest limitation, thin capitalisation and/or transfer pricing rules, plus there are many other specific interest limitation rules around the world. At the same time, low-tax outcomes in the creditor's jurisdiction may be reversed under Controlled Foreign Company (CFC), hybrid mismatch, fat capitalisation, transfer pricing or minimum tax rules such as the Two Pillar GloBE proposal currently before the international community.

Nonetheless, these are some of the largest financial flows around the world. Cross-border related party debt finance of multinational enterprises (MNEs) is necessary and ubiquitous. The metaphor of an unstoppable force meeting an immovable object is usually given as an example of a paradox. But in this area of public finance, the immovable object of cross-border interest-bearing debt and the unstoppable force of ever-expanding tax rules are constantly coming together. It falls to tax professionals to reconcile the clashes.

* The views and opinions set forth herein are the personal views or opinions of the authors; they do not necessarily reflect the views or opinions of the organisation with which the authors are associated.

This chapter considers the interaction between three major (and often overlapping) regimes adopted by many countries: interest limitation rules, thin capitalisation rules and arms-length-price (ALP) based transfer pricing rules. It also considers the undertaxed payments rule (UTPR) as part of the Pillar Two GloBE proposal. This rule will deny deductions not only in respect of interest – it applies across the board – but it is relevant to this discussion as it is a further layer of potential deduction disallowance with which MNEs will soon have to contend.

What comes first? It depends on whether this is a legal, practical or normative question. Legally, the transfer pricing rules precede the thin capitalisation, interest limitation and pending UTPR rules in most jurisdictions where these regimes are in force. Practically, as they are simpler than transfer pricing to apply and administer, it is rather the interest limitation or thin capitalisation rules that are likely to be the de facto primary rule. Normatively, there is a trade-off between the principled and multilateral (but cumbersome and poorly targeted) transfer pricing rules and the rough but relatively simple approach of interest limitation and thin capitalisation rules. For large MNEs, the proposed UTPR would operate after all of these rules, as a further layer of deduction disallowance to the extent that the minimum tax threshold of 15% per jurisdiction is not cleared.

The conclusion of this chapter is that traditional ALP-based transfer pricing is poorly adapted to the internal financing of MNEs and that fixed ratio interest limitation and thin capitalisation rules can be improved by the use of group ratio alternatives, safe harbours and predictable calculations (of which the UTPR is an example, albeit the calculation is complex), double taxation relief and dispute resolution.

## II THE OVERLAPPING REGIMES

Before seeking to resolve the overlaps, this chapter describes the respective regimes of ALP-based transfer pricing rules, thin capitalisation rules, interest limitation rules and the UTPR. Because they are also relevant to this ensemble of rules, debt/equity rules are described as well. Not described are all of the other domestic rules by which countries limit and regulate the taxation of interest in their jurisdiction.

Overlaps exist because the various regimes have been introduced at different points in time, and legislatures have been reluctant to 'turn off' one set of rules where another applies, for fear of missing out on revenue or facilitating avoidance. There is also something of a 'silo' effect – those responsible for drafting or administering one of the regimes are often not the people responsible for the other regime.

Transfer pricing rules are longstanding in many jurisdictions. However, there was relatively little certainty or guidance about how they should apply to finance transactions until recently.[1] Thin capitalisation rules were introduced in waves in the last few decades, usually applying a fixed ratio of debt to equity (whether as a safe

1. OECD, *Transfer Pricing Guidance on Financial Transactions* (OECD Publishing, February 2020); before this publication the topic had not been substantively addressed by the OECD since 1979: OECD, *Report of the OECD Committee of Fiscal Affairs on Transfer Pricing and Multinationals* (OECD Publications, 1979).

harbour or an absolute limit). These attacked interest stripping base erosion in a simpler but more blunt fashion than transfer pricing rules. Interest barrier rules are the latest wave of rules to find favour, and at the same time, the international transfer pricing guidance for financial transactions has developed markedly.[2] The recent guidance, discussed in more detail below, suggests that transfer pricing rules can do some of the work of thin capitalisation/interest barrier rules, by a different mechanism - a conclusion with which not all jurisdictions agree.

Lastly, this paper describes the UTPR within the proposed Pillar Two GloBE regime currently before the international community.[3] If implemented as expected from 2023 onward, it will provide a further potential layer of interest deduction disallowance, even if all the other regimes described in this paper have been complied with.

The overlaps, thus, are a function of history, of caution on the part of legislatures, and of the layering of multilateral common rules on top of heterogeneous domestic approaches.

## 1 Debt/Equity Rules

A prerequisite for characterising (and deducting) payments as interest, in most jurisdictions, is that they be payments on a debt instrument.

Many tax systems simply take the instrument as they find it. Debt or equity characterisation is a matter of legal form, or of other legal rules independent of the tax system. In other jurisdictions, however, there are rules which determine, or at least have the capacity to influence, debt or equity characterisation for the purposes of the tax system. Those rules will logically 'come first', given 'debt' is usually a precondition for interest deductibility. The rules for debt/equity characterisation may apply to all instruments, or they may be exceptional anti-abuse rules. An example of the latter is the 'sham' doctrine, which can operate where the parties to a transaction intended it to have a different legal character (e.g., equity) from how it is documented (e.g., as a debt).[4]

Two examples of countries with detailed tax regimes for distinguishing debt and equity are the United States and Australia, but their approaches couldn't be more different. In the United States, the characterisation of a funding instrument as debt or equity has long been a matter of 'judge-made' law, with a long line of cases distilling around 14 factors which can point toward one conclusion or the other, with their

2. OECD, *Transfer Pricing Guidance on Financial Transactions* (OECD Publishing, February 2020).
3. OECD, *Tax Challenges Arising from the Digitalisation of the Economy: Global Anti-Base Erosion Model Rules (Pillar Two)* (OECD Publishing, December 2021).
4. *See, e.g.*, the doctrine of *schijnleningen* (sham loans) in the Netherlands: e.g., *Rechtbank Haarlem* 21 January 2011, No. 09/3391, NTFR 2011/1548; *see also* Edwin Simpson & Miranda Stewart, *Sham Transactions* (Oxford University Press, 2013).

balancing and trading-off a matter for the court's discretion and judgment.[5] The factors include stated intent to repay, extent of shareholder control, dividend history, whether the terms resemble traditional debt terms, accounting treatment, repayment history and source, participation in management and adequacy of capitalisation. Australia has adopted the opposite approach, with a statutory 'bright line' test which allocates an instrument to either debt or equity according to mathematics.[6] Specifically, if the term is 10 years or less, the instrument is debt if the debtor has a non-contingent obligation to repay the creditor at least the amount advanced; if the term exceeds 10 years, the comparison is done in present value terms using a minimum rate of return equal to 75% of an arm's-length interest rate. It is predictable, sometimes arbitrary, and often produces hybrid outcomes.

It is not the purpose of this paper to survey different debt/equity rules around the world.[7] But their presence is important to note in a consideration of the ordering dilemmas which arise between interest barriers, thin capitalisation and transfer pricing rules. Usually, those rules operate after the instrument has been characterised, so specific debt/equity rules, if they exist, will generally 'come first' in this ordering exercise.

A question which arises is whether transfer pricing rules can also do the work of characterising an instrument as debt or equity; this is discussed below in the transfer pricing section. A further question is whether they can or should do this even in jurisdictions which already have specific debt-equity rules. This is explored further below in the discussion of the interactions.

## 2 Interest Limitation Rules

These are rules which prevent MNEs from deducting interest to the extent that it exceeds a certain proportion of the MNE's earnings in that jurisdiction. It is an 'income statement' or 'profit and loss' approach, as opposed to the 'balance sheet' approach of traditional thin capitalisation rules. They are also referred to as 'interest barrier' rules.

In 2015, the Organisation for Economic Co-operation and Development (OECD) recommended such a rule, and it has been adopted by at least 27 countries to date.[8]

5. *See, e.g.*, *Illinois Tool Works Inc v. Commissioner* 116 TCM (CCH) 124 (2018) (United States Tax Court, 6 August 2018); *Hewlett-Packard Co v. Commissioner* No 14-73047 (9th Circuit, 2017); *NA General Partnership v. Commissioner* TC Memo 2012-172 (United States Tax Court, 2012) (Scottish Power case).
6. Division 974, Income Tax Assessment Act 1997 (Australia).
7. As to which, *see* International Fiscal Association, 'The debt-equity conundrum', Cahiers de Droit Fiscal International, vol. 97b, Kluwer 2012; Patricia Brown & Machiel Lambooij, 'Consequences of an Arbitrary Distinction – The Debt-Equity Conundrum' (2012) 66 Bulletin for International Taxation 9; Christian Kahlenberg & Agnieszka Kopec, 'Hybrid Mismatch Arrangements – A Myth or a Problem That Still Exists?' (2016) 8 World Tax Journal 1; Wolfgang Schön 'The Distinct Equity of the Debt Equity Distinction' (2012) 66 Bulletin for International Taxation 9.
8. As of 2019, it had been adopted or was in the process of adoption by Argentina, Belgium, Bulgaria, the Czech Republic, Denmark, Finland, France, Germany, Hungary, Iceland, India, Italy, Japan, Luxembourg, Malta, the Netherlands, Norway, Peru, Poland, Portugal, the Republic of Korea, the Republic of Srpska, Spain, Sweden, the United Kingdom and the United States: *See* J. Gadwood & P. Morton, Interest deductibility: the implementation of BEPS Action 4, (2019) 104a Cahiers de

The OECD's Action 4 Final Report was published in October 2015 and updated to its final form in 2016.[9] It was not a compulsory 'minimum standard' model but a 'best practice recommendation' for adoption into domestic law. The Action 4 Final Report commenced by describing the perceived problem in the following way:[10]

> multinational groups may achieve favourable tax results by adjusting the amount of debt in a group entity. The influence of tax rules on the location of debt within multinational groups has been established in a number of academic studies and it is well known that groups can easily multiply the level of debt at the level of individual group entities via intragroup financing. Financial instruments can also be used to make payments which are economically equivalent to interest but have a different legal form, therefore escaping restrictions on the deductibility of interest. Base Erosion and Profit Shifting (BEPS) risks in this area may arise in three basic scenarios:
>
> - Groups placing higher levels of third-party debt in high-tax countries.
> - Groups using intragroup loans to generate interest deductions in excess of the group's actual third party interest expense.
> - Groups using third party or intragroup financing to fund the generation of tax exempt income.

The OECD's recommended solution was a fixed ratio interest limitation rule, which cuts off an MNE's interest deductions in the debtor jurisdiction if they reach more than a fixed percentage (most countries use 30%) of the MNE's earnings before interest, taxes, depreciation and amortisation (EBITDA) in that jurisdiction.[11] The OECD stated that either EBITDA or Earnings Before Interests and Taxes (EBIT) could be used in this context; it noted that EBITDA is more commonly used and excludes the two largest non-cash costs in a typical profit and loss statement (depreciation and amortisation), giving a reflection of the sources from which to pay cash interest, although EBITDA could favour entities with high fixed asset investments by excluding those outgoings entirely from the ratio.[12]

The OECD defined a 'corridor' of 10% to 30%, and where in that range the limit is set is a matter for the country to determine. This is appropriate, not least because interest rates can vary considerably by currency. The percentage can also be varied

Droit Fiscal International (SDU Fiscale, Netherlands, 2019) (some countries' rules pre-dated Action 4). Further countries legislating or considering the measures from 2019 onwards include Canada, Ireland and South Africa. In several of these countries, the interest limitation ratio (based on a percentage of Earnings Before Interest and Taxes (EBIT) or EBITDA) applies alongside a balance sheet thin capitalisation ratio (that is, debt on which interest is deductible is limited to a certain percentage of the company's equity or assets) as well.

9. OECD, *BEPS Action 4: Limiting Base Erosion Involving Interest Deductions and Other Financial Payments: 2016 Updated Report* (OECD 2017) (Action 4 Final Report).
10. OECD, *BEPS Action 4: Limiting Base Erosion Involving Interest Deductions and Other Financial Payments: 2016 Updated Report* (OECD 2017), p. 13.
11. EBITDA is the most common, although not universal, denominator. It is notable that the United States interest limitation rule currently uses EBITDA but is changing to EBIT for tax years commencing rom 1 January 2022, without any projected change to the level at which the ratio is set (30%).
12. OECD, *BEPS Action 4: Limiting Base Erosion Involving Interest Deductions and Other Financial Payments:* 2016 Updated Report (OECD 2017), p. 48.

over time, as leverage and interest rates rise and fall, both cyclically and in response to shocks. For example, the COVID-19 pandemic has seen the further reduction of already very low interest rates, but at the same time an increase in leverage and, in many (but not all) sectors, increased incidence of losses.[13]

It is a blunt instrument. This is because 30% (or another fixed percentage on the 'corridor') will rarely reflect the amount of interest being paid to third parties, or on an arm's-length basis, or some other normative definition of appropriate interest deductions. It will only do so by coincidence. However, this arbitrariness was considered a suitable price to pay for the relative simplicity and predictability of a fixed ratio.

The OECD recommended an alternative 'group ratio' rule, which is more tailored to the MNE in question, and accordingly less arbitrary, but involves further calculations.[14] It is best illustrated with a simple example. If the worldwide MNE group as a whole outlays, say 45% of its (third party) EBITDA as interest payments to (third party) lenders, then the group ratio rule provides that the MNE's presence in each jurisdiction should be able to deduct interest, whether intragroup or third party, of up to 45% of the EBITDA in that jurisdiction. Another option offered is a similar group ratio calculation but based on a balance sheet ratio; this is also referred to as an 'equity escape' rule.

## 3 Thin Capitalisation Rules

The term 'thin capitalisation rules' is used in this chapter to refer to a rule where interest is limited based on a ratio of debt to equity; that is, a balance sheet ratio. The rule typically denies interest deductions on so much of the debt that exceeds the ratio.

This was traditionally the more popular type of rule, but interest limitation rules have outshone it in the last few years, following the Action 4 Final Report. However, a number of countries still have thin capitalisation rules instead of interest limitation rules.[15] Many countries have both, either together or as alternatives.

The Action 4 Final Report acknowledged that balance sheet ratio rules have some advantages, in that they are easier to administer and less volatile than EBITDA ratios. It also noted their disadvantages: they are susceptible to manipulation through asset revaluations and can be unsuitable for companies whose value is attributable to off-balance-sheet factors.

Another disadvantage of balance sheet ratios is that they leave open the question of the interest rate to a greater degree than earnings ratios. That is, an earnings-based limit will cap the amount of interest expense, no matter what interest rate is charged,

13. For example, the 2021 Canadian Budget proposal for introducing a rule similar to the Action 4 recommendation proposes that the rate be set at 40% for the first year (calendar 2023), reducing to 30% thereafter.
14. OECD, *BEPS Action 4: Limiting Base Erosion Involving Interest Deductions and Other Financial Payments: 2016 Updated Report* (OECD 2017), Chapter 7.
15. For example (as of 2019, at least), Australia, China, Colombia, Brazil, Mexico, New Zealand, Russia, Slovenia, Switzerland, Taiwan and Turkey. As at 2022, the Australian Treasury is consulting with a view to introducing a 30% of EBITDA interest barrier rule and further tightening the thin capitalisation regime: https://treasury.gov.au/sites/default/files/2022-08/c2022-297736-cp.pdf.

whereas a balance sheet limit will cap the amount of debt but leave open the capacity for base erosion through excessive interest rates and in any event place more reliance on the resource-intensive transfer pricing process.

The Action 4 Final Report favoured an earnings-based ratio but stated that countries may use a balance-sheet-based ratio as part of their group-wide ratio alternative, which is useful, particularly where the group has negative EBITDA. It also stated that 'exceptionally' countries can use a balance sheet approach in their main rule for well-capitalised groups with high levels of tangible assets.

Nonetheless, as noted above, a significant number of countries continue to use balance sheet-based thin capitalisation rules as their main or only interest limitation rule, and not merely for well-capitalised groups with high levels of tangible assets or in exceptional circumstances.

An interesting ordering question arises where the country's debt to equity ratio is a 'safe harbour'; that is, interest will be deductible on debt up to that ratio without need for evidence that it is an arm's-length amount of debt. How is that to be reconciled with transfer pricing rules? This is addressed below in the discussion of interactions. In short, it is often a compromise. In Australia, the compromise has been struck in the following way: the transfer pricing rules apply first to determine the amount of debt which the company could have at arm's length. The arm's-length interest rate that applies to that amount is then determined. The thin capitalisation safe harbour (currently 1.5 to 1) is then applied: the rate determined under transfer pricing is applied to the safe harbour quantum of debt.[16] For example, if the company's arm's-length debt limit is USD 100, on which arm's-length interest would be 6%, but it has issued debt at the maximum safe harbour debt amount of USD 150 (a ratio of 1.5 to 1 debt to equity), the company can deduct interest of 6% on the full USD 150 of debt.

## 4 ALP-Based Transfer Pricing Rules

Transfer pricing rules are longstanding in many jurisdictions and are provided for in most tax treaties as well. They are rules of general application. They are not targeted at financial transactions, but in principle, they apply to related party financial transactions of any type.

However, for decades there was an absence of international guidance on the transfer pricing of financial transactions. The OECD's Transfer Pricing Guidance on Financial Transactions, published in its final form in February 2020[17] and incorporated as Chapter X of the OECD Transfer Pricing Guidelines in January 2022 (2022 OECD Financial Transactions Chapter)[18] was the first major multilateral document on the subject since 1979.[19] Forty-one years is a long time. The time elapsed partially explains

16. Sections 815-25 and 815-140 of the Income Tax Assessment Act 1997 (Australia).
17. OECD, *Transfer Pricing Guidance on Financial Transactions* (OECD Publishing, February 2020).
18. OECD, *Transfer Pricing Guidelines for Multinational Enterprises and Tax Administrations* (OECD Publishing, January 2022), Chapter X.
19. OECD, *Report of the OECD Committee of Fiscal Affairs on Transfer Pricing and Multinationals* (OECD Publications, 1979), Chapter V.

why so many other interest limitation rules have proliferated around the world in recent decades.

The 2022 OECD Financial Transactions Chapter deals with a number of topics. Germane to this chapter are three of them:

(a) determination of whether a purported loan should be regarded as a loan;
(b) accurate delineation of financial transactions – with the potential to 'recharacterise' terms of the financing agreement, e.g., as to quantum of debt, covenants and security (or lack thereof); and
(c) determining the arm's-length interest rate on an intercompany loan using a credit rating agency approach, including notching for implicit support.

These are considered in turn.

### *A Delineation as Debt or Equity*

The determination of whether a purported loan should be regarded as a loan appears to be a kind of debt/equity rule, embedded within the transfer pricing rules. It is discussed in paragraphs 10.4 to 10.13 of the 2022 OECD Financial Transactions Chapter, which picks up the short reference in the Commentary on Article 9 of the OECD Model Convention to the capacity for transfer pricing rules to determine whether a loan can be regarded as a loan or instead as a contribution to equity (paragraph 3(b)) and develops the topic. In 2021, the OECD published a draft revised commentary to Article 9, which proposes to reiterate even more clearly that Article 9 can be used to recharacterise debt as equity, consistently with the 2020 Guidance.[20]

The 2022 OECD Financial Transactions Chapter suggests the following factors are relevant in this transfer pricing delineation exercise: the presence or absence of a fixed repayment date; the obligation to pay interest; the right to enforce payment of principal and interest; the status of the funder in comparison to regular corporate creditors; the existence of financial covenants and security; the source of interest payments; the ability of the recipient of the funds to obtain loans from unrelated lending institutions; the extent to which the advance is used to acquire capital assets; and the failure of the purported debtor to repay on the due date or to seek a postponement.[21]

These are very similar to the tests used by some countries in their debt/equity rules. In relation to this overlap, the 2022 OECD Financial Transactions Chapter states:

> 10.8 Although this guidance reflects an approach of accurate delineation of the actual transaction in accordance with Chapter I to determine the amount of debt to be priced, it is acknowledged that other approaches may be taken to address the issue of the balance of debt and equity funding of an entity *under domestic legislation* before pricing the interest on the debt so determined. *These approaches*

20. OECD Publishing, Proposed Changes to Commentaries in the OECD Model Tax Convention on Article 9 and on Related Articles (29 March-28 May 2021).
21. OECD, *Transfer Pricing Guidelines for Multinational Enterprises and Tax Administrations* (OECD Publishing, January 2022), Chapter X, para. 10.12.

> *may include a multi-factor analysis of the characteristics of the instrument and the issuer.*
>
> 10.9. Accordingly, this guidance is not intended to prevent countries from implementing approaches to address the balance of debt and equity funding of an entity and interest deductibility under domestic legislation, nor does it seek to mandate accurate delineation under Chapter I as the only approach for determining whether purported debt should be respected as debt.

There is no other reference to thin capitalisation, interest barrier or debt/equity rules in the 2022 OECD Financial Transactions Chapter. This is a bit surprising, given that the OECD had only recently published the large body of work on Action 4 of the BEPS project. It may be an example of the somewhat 'siloed' approach that can prevail in this area.

## *B Quantum of Debt and Other Recharacterisation*

Even if a purported debt is respected as debt, the 2022 OECD Financial Transactions Chapter contemplates that it still needs to be in an *amount* which can be justified on an arm's-length basis. It states in paragraph 10.19:

> From the borrower's perspective, the options realistically available will include broader considerations than the entity's ability to service its debt, for example, the funds it actually needs to meet its operational requirements. In some instances, although an entity may have the capacity to borrow and service an additional amount of debt, it may choose not to do so to avoid placing negative pressure on its credit rating and increasing its cost of capital, and jeopardising its access to capital markets and its market reputation.

This suggests that transfer pricing rules may be used to recharacterise a debt of a certain amount into a debt of a lesser amount, if the options realistically available at arm's length do not include such a large indebtedness. Again, there is some overlap, this time with the objectives of thin capitalisation rules. It is odd that there is no reference at this point, or elsewhere in the 2022 OECD Financial Transactions Chapter, to thin capitalisation rules, interest limitation rules or the work done under BEPS Action 4 more generally.

The 2022 OECD Financial Transactions Chapter also averts the potential to assimilate loans which are unsecured and lack covenants to arm's-length loans which are secured and have maintenance covenants. It reasons that between related parties there is often no need to explicitly include security and covenants in the loan agreement because it is there de facto, through the control of the MNE group: paragraphs 10.56, 10.86.[22]

There is an acknowledgement in the 2022 OECD Financial Transactions Chapter that 'jurisdictions may have different views on the application of Article 9 to determine the balance of debt and equity funding of an entity within an MNE group': paragraph

22. *See also Chevron Australia Holdings Pty Ltd v. Commissioner of Taxation* (2017) 251 FCR 40 (Full Court of the Federal Court of Australia) at paras 38, 54 and 55.

10.10. Indeed, case law in countries such as Finland, India and Sweden has held that transfer pricing can only adjust the interest rate on a loan, not the amount of the loan.[23] In such countries, it is only thin capitalisation rules (if they exist) or other specific rules which can recharacterise the transaction for tax purposes, if recharacterisation is possible at all.

A further complication is that there are often two sources of transfer pricing law – domestic legislation and the equivalent treaty article to Article 9. Domestic legislation is often worded differently from Article 9, and may not pick up all of the concepts from the OECD Transfer Pricing Guidelines or like publications. Sometimes domestic transfer pricing law is narrower, for example, being clearly restricted to re-pricing the given transaction rather than recharactersing it, or using only the comparable uncontrolled transactions method as opposed to other OECD methods.[24] Domestic courts sometimes have to grapple with whether their task is to apply the treaty or the domestic law, and the constitutional position varies amongst countries.[25]

### C Arm's-Length Interest Rates

The 2022 OECD Financial Transactions Chapter states that all economically relevant characteristics of an intragroup loan or debt are important to determining the arm's-length interest rate. It suggests that the lender will carry out a 'thorough credit assessment' of the potential borrower, as well as an analysis of the wider economic conditions that prevail and are likely in future: paragraph 10.54. The credit rating, which a rating agency such as Standard & Poor's or Moody's would hypothetically give the borrower, can be estimated, in order to find potential comparables.

Estimating a credit rating is a far-reaching and fact-intensive examination of every aspect of the business and financing of the subsidiary, the MNE group, the industry sector and macroeconomic factors. It also involves subjectivity – even the rating agencies acknowledge that credit rating is as much an art as it is a science, and rating agencies will often disagree on the rating to apply to a particular issuer or issue.

The concept of 'implicit support' – the creditworthiness benefit, which a subsidiary gains from being a member of an MNE, also known as passive association or group affiliation – is acknowledged in the 2022 OECD Financial Transactions Chapter. That is, the 'orphan theory', where the borrower is assumed not to have any parent company or be a member of any MNE group, is rejected.[26] Where the subsidiary is of high

23. *See also* Gregorio Piran & Matteo Piva, 'A Conundrum Within the Conundrum: The Requalification of Loans as Equity under the OECD Guidance on Financial Transactions' (2020) 60 European Taxation 8.
24. *See, e.g., Commissioner of Taxation v. SNF (Australia) Pty Ltd* (2011) 193 FCR 149 (Full Court of the Federal Court of Australia) at paras 116 to 118.
25. *See, e.g.,* Javier Céron & Claudia Méndez, Country Report (Chile), Interest deductibility: the implementation of BEPS Action 4, Vol 104a (2019) *Cahiers de Droit Fiscal International* (SDU Fiscale, Netherlands, 2019), at p. 225; *Chevron Australia Holdings Pty Ltd v. Commissioner of Taxation (No 4)* (2015) 102 ATR 13 (Federal Court of Australia) at paras 50-61.
26. For further discussion, comparison and critique of implicit support and the orphan theory, *see* Jens Wittendorff, 'Transfer Pricing Oddity: The OECD's New Guidelines on Financial Transactions' (2020) 99(6) Tax Notes International 723-739.

strategic importance to the MNE, its credit rating may be the same as or close to that of the parent, whereas a less important subsidiary may have a rating closer to its hypothetical stand-alone rating, or some notches upwards from this. The rating agencies have processes for 'notching'. A notch is a single credit rating increment, e.g., the difference between ratings of A and A+ is one notch. Sometimes, although not frequently, there is instead a 'negative halo effect', where the subsidiary's creditworthiness would be higher were it not for the rest of the MNE group. Again, this depends on the specific factual circumstances of the entities. Notching is a very subjective exercise and rating agencies will often disagree on the extent of notching.

Some jurisdictions publish fixed 'arm's-length' interest rates, either as an absolute cap or as a safe harbour. In Brazil, interest paid to foreign related parties is not deductible if it exceeds the Libor rate for a six-month period or the rate for Brazilian sovereign bonds plus a spread established by the Ministry of Finance (in 2019 it was 3.5% per year).[27] In the United States, there is a safe harbour for related party loans in US dollars, applicable to MNEs outside the banking and financial industries. The rate is 100% to 130% of the applicable federal rate, which is set monthly by the Treasury, on the date that the loan was issued.[28]

## *D ALP-Based Thin Capitalisation Rules*

In this chapter, the term 'ALP-based rules' usually refers to transfer pricing rules. However, it is important to note that ALP-based rules can also include variations on the thin capitalisation and interest barrier rules described above, where the MNE is not limited to the fixed ratio if they can prove that their interest expense or quantum of debt is at a level which can be justified on arm's-length principles.

In some countries, such as the United Kingdom and South Africa, the thin capitalisation rule was for many years part of the transfer pricing rules. That is, it was clearly acknowledged that the transfer pricing rules can adjust the amount of debt on which interest is deductible, and there was no fixed ratio thin capitalisation rule. The MNE had to show for each loan that the amount of debt was an arm's-length amount. Both countries are now in the process of implementing an interest barrier rule along the lines of the Action 4 recommendation.

In some countries, an arm's-length alternative sits alongside a fixed ratio thin capitalisation rule. In Australia, the thin capitalisation fixed ratio (presently 1.5 to 1) can be exceeded by a company if it can prove that its quantum of debt is a quantum that

27. Carlos Adolfo Teixeira Duarte, Country Report (Brazil), Interest Deductibility: The Implementation of BEPS Action 4, Vol. 104a (2019) *Cahiers de Droit Fiscal International* (SDU Fiscale, Netherlands, 2019), at p. 158.
28. Lauren Ann Ross, Country Report (United States), Interest Deductibility: The Implementation of BEPS Action 4, Vol. 104a (2019) *Cahiers de Droit Fiscal International* (SDU Fiscale, Netherlands, 2019), at p. 729.

would reasonably be expected to be advanced by unrelated lenders.[29] This 'arm's-length debt test' rule sits outside Australia's transfer pricing rules and while the concepts are similar, the mechanisms are not identical.

The OECD in the Action 4 Final Report declared that ALP-based rules:

> are not considered to be best practices in tackling base erosion and profit shifting involving interest and payments economically equivalent to interest.[30]

This is a striking statement from the body which has been safeguarding the arm's-length principle for many decades. The fact that the United Kingdom and South Africa are adopting the Action 4 recommendation in place of their ALP-based rules suggests that the statement is having an impact.

However, just four years after this OECD statement, the OECD issued its 2020 Guidance on Financial Transactions, which was subsequently incorporated as the 2022 OECD Financial Transactions Chapter. That Chapter clearly states that a company's capital structure is something that can be adjusted under ALP-based transfer pricing rules, although noting that not all countries take this approach: paragraph 10.10. The obvious dilemma of how to reconcile that proposition with Action 4's disavowal of ALP-based rules was simply not addressed.

The surface answer is that Action 4 was concerned with base erosion whereas the 2022 OECD Financial Transactions Chapter is about the ALP and applies to all related party transactions. But that is not a very satisfying explanation, because interest barrier rules arising from Action 4 also apply widely to all transactions – they do not require base erosion or a tax avoidance purpose, they simply cut off interest deductions above the relevant fixed limit.

A better explanation may be that an 'arm's-length' amount of debt or interest can be a high amount of debt or interest, which leaves too much room for base erosion. The arm's-length capital structures of MNE groups vary considerably, and an MNE has no single ideal capital structure.[31] Even within one industry, some groups are more leveraged than others. An ALP-based approach to leverage will permit MNEs to establish related party leverage that is within the arm's-length 'range', and that range will often be large.[32] The MNE can establish related party gearing at the top end of that range and still justify it on ALP principles. In turn, high amounts of gearing usually lead to higher interest rates (as an independent lender would require more compensation for the risk to its capital occasioned by the high indebtedness). A race to the top of the range is a form of 'race to the bottom'. It seems from the Action 4 Final Report that the OECD did not want the ALP principle to be used in this way. It may be that this issue

29. Sections 820-105 and 820-215 of the Income Tax Assessment Act 1997; *see also* Taxation Ruling TR 2020/4 and Practical Compliance Guideline 2020/7 (Australia).
30. OECD, *BEPS Action 4: Limiting Base Erosion Involving Interest Deductions and Other Financial Payments: 2016 Updated Report* (OECD 2017), at para. 15.
31. Franco Modigliani & Merton Miller, *Corporate Income Taxes and the Cost of Capital: A Correction* (1963) 53(3) American Economics Review 443; Stewart Myers, *The Capital Structure Puzzle* (1984) 39(3) Journal of Finance.
32. Chloe Burnett, Intra-group Debt at the Crossroads: Stand-Alone Versus Worldwide Approach" (2014) 6 World Tax Journal 1.

didn't need to be addressed in the 2022 OECD Financial Transactions Chapter because, by 2022, so many countries were already using an Action 4-type rule as a ceiling on interest deductions.

## 5 UTPR

The 137 or so members of the Inclusive Framework on BEPS are presently working on the 'two pillar' solution to the tax challenges of the digitalisation of the economy, with 'practical implementation' contemplated by 2024.[33] The Pillar Two GloBE model rules were published in December 2021.[34] The GloBE is essentially a top-up tax which aims to ensure corporate tax is paid by reference to each jurisdiction in which the MNE operates, at a level of at least 15%. The GloBE only applies to MNE groups with revenue in excess of 750 Euros and with cross-border operations.

The GloBE has a primary income inclusion rule (IIR) for the ultimate parent entity, plus the UTPR, which acts as a backstop for cases where the parent entity's jurisdiction has not implemented the GloBE. The total IIR or UTPR is calculated similarly but imposed on different parts of the MNE. The UTPR is imposed by denying deductions (or making similar adjustments) to members of the MNE resident in jurisdictions which have implemented the GloBE. It is calculated by reference to the extent to which the tax paid by the MNE in a jurisdiction falls short of the minimum tax rate of 15% and is apportioned (according to employees and tangible assets) across the jurisdictions in which the MNE is present, and which have implemented the UTPR. The UTPR and the IIR operate a bit like CFC rules or anti-hybrid rules, where tax is payable to a country on account of a *different* country's low tax burden and acts to neutralise the attractiveness of zero-tax or very low-tax regimes. The model rules published by the OECD in December 2021 set out complex but essentially quantitative calculations. The model rules flag the future development of optional safe harbours.

GloBE only applies to large MNEs, and only where the minimum tax rate has not been cleared. But where it does apply, it will apply after the other rules described above (interest barrier, transfer pricing, thin capitalisation, etc.), to the extent that the jurisdictions in question have those rules. This is because GloBE applies in a mathematical and formulaic way, upon an accounting income base and without regard to traditional qualitative principles like the ALP or the tax law characterisation of receipts and outgoings.

## 6 Interactions: What Comes First?

What comes first? It depends on whether this is a legal question, a practical question, or a policy question. Each of these layers is unpeeled below.

33. Van Leeuwen, *Push for Global Tax Deal Has Slowed, Mathias Cormann Admits*, Australian Financial Review (25 May 2022).
34. OECD, *Tax Challenges Arising from the Digitalisation of the Economy: Global Anti-Base Erosion Model Rules (Pillar Two)* (OECD Publishing, December 2021); *see also* the Commentary thereto published by the OECD on 14 March 2022.

### A Legally, Transfer Pricing Rules Usually Precede Interest Barrier and Thin Capitalisation Rules

In relation to rules to restrict interest deductions, the General Reporters of the 'Interest deductibility: the implementation of BEPS Action 4' Topic at the 2019 International Fiscal Association (IFA) Congress stated:

> Most jurisdictions have several rules which apply simultaneously and the interaction between them is frequently unclear.[35]

This is certainly true. However, a survey of the jurisdictions indicates that the most common ordering of priority, in countries having two or more of the below sets of rules, is the following:

(a) debt/equity rules (including sham or like rules); then
(b) transfer pricing (ALP) rules; then
(c) interest barrier/thin capitalisation rules;[36] then
(d) GloBE IIR or UTPR, if applicable.

Legally, there is some logic in this ordering. Interest is usually only deductible if it is a payment on a debt, so debt/equity rules apply in the first instance to answer that threshold question. Next come transfer pricing rules. One reason they usually apply before interest barrier/thin capitalisation rules is because transfer pricing rules apply on a transaction-by-transaction basis. By contrast, interest barrier/thin capitalisation rules usually apply to the aggregation of the interest or debt of the entity or group of MNE entities in the jurisdiction. So they will apply at the end, to cap off any further interest, even if the debt/equity and transfer pricing rules have been complied with for each and every instrument and transaction within the aggregation. Thus, interest barrier/thin capitalisation rules apply last and can prevail over the transfer pricing outcomes. If and when it is implemented, the GloBE will apply last of all, because it operates mathematically and regardless of traditional arm's length or other characterisation principles.

The ordering described in the previous paragraph is not uniform. For example, in Korea, the provisions adopted based on the Action 4 Final Report stand prior to the provision on the adjustment to the arm's-length interest rate in accordance with the transfer pricing rules.[37] In countries with a safe harbour in their thin capitalisation

35. J. Gadwood & P. Morton, Interest Deductibility: The Implementation of BEPS Action 4, Vol. 104a (2019) *Cahiers de Droit Fiscal International* (SDU Fiscale, Netherlands, 2019).
36. In countries having both interest barrier and thin capitalisation rules, it is necessary to look at the detail of the legislation to see whether *both* thresholds need to be cleared for interest to be deductible or whether it suffices that *either* the interest barrier or thin capitalisation ratio is satisfied.
37. Jaeho Lee & Seung-Yeong Jeong, Country Report (Republic of Korea), Interest Deductibility: The Implementation of BEPS Action 4, Vol. 104a (2019) *Cahiers de Droit Fiscal International* (SDU Fiscale, Netherlands, 2019), at pp. 435-436.

rules, some mediation is required with transfer pricing. As noted above, in Australia this has taken the form of a fiction – permitting interest deductions at the arm's-length rate (i.e., the rate that would apply to the, lower, arm's-length amount of debt) multiplied by the actual amount of debt as long as that debt is below the safe harbour limit (currently a debt-to-equity ratio of 1.5 to 1).[38]

Although debt/equity rules logically come first, that does not mean that debt, so characterised, is immune from recharacterisation as equity under transfer pricing or other rules. In Australia, for example, the tax authority takes the view that the transfer pricing rules take priority over the debt/equity rules, despite Australia's notably rigid and deterministic debt/equity regime.[39] The policy merits of this can be debated, but the position is certainly open given the way the legislation is structured. The result is that the debt/equity rules operate first, in that debt characterisation is a prerequisite for interest deductions, but an amount can lose its debt character under transfer pricing if, at arm's length, the debt amount would be less. That is, meeting the debt/equity test for debt is a necessary but not sufficient condition for interest deductibility – the thin capitalisation and transfer pricing rules can still deny interest deductions.

For example, an Australian company may issue 15-year related party debt in a quantum which is high, but just below Australia's thin capitalisation safe harbour debt/equity ratio. This may be a large amount of debt relative to average debt levels in that particular industry or sector, with the result that the interest rate applied by the parties is relatively high. The arrangement would not fall foul of the thin capitalisation rules because it is (just) within the safe harbour. It would also be respected as debt under the debt/equity rules because the high interest rate would clear the present value calculation threshold in those rules. However, the Australian tax authority has, in this guidance, made it clear that it may still use the transfer pricing rules to adjust the quantum of debt if it considers that the amount of debt is more than this subsidiary could bear on an arm's-length basis. In turn, that quantum would be used only to work out the arm's-length rate, which would then be applied to the actual debt issued, in order to respect (if only partially) the safe harbour – see the example at the end of section C, above.

Like so much in tax law, debt/equity characterisation does not work the opposite way, even where symmetry would be coherent. That is, amounts which are equity under the debt/equity rules do not generate deductions merely because at arm's length, the company would have *more* debt. This is because the transfer pricing rules (the primary adjustment rules, that is) only operate to reduce deductions or increase assessable income.

38. Sections 815-25 and 815-140 of the Income Tax Assessment Act 1997 (Australia); as noted above, the Australian Treasury is currently consulting about a move to an EBITDA-based interest barrier rule.
39. Taxation Determination TD 2019/10 (Australia).

## B Practically, Interest Barrier and Thin Capitalisation Rules Are Often the First and Only Rules Applied

At a practical level, because interest barriers and thin capitalisation rules are simpler to apply than transfer pricing rules, they are the de facto primary rules. That is, most MNEs will not have all (or any) of their financing transactions subject to long and complex transfer pricing audits. But whether their leverage or interest expense complies with the thin capitalisation/interest barrier rule is something that can be tested relatively simply based on financial statements.

This creates an incentive for MNEs to not 'waste' deductible interest 'capacity'. If its aim is to maximise deduction capacity under interest barrier and transfer pricing rules, an MNE might be expected to set its related party leverage at a relatively high level – but not higher than the debt capacity it can justify on arm's-length terms. This relatively high level of debt would in turn, under arm's-length principles, usually justify a relatively high interest rate. The total interest may be subject to capping under the interest barrier rule (most typically at the level of 30% of EBITDA), but at least all of the 30% capacity will have been utilised. However, too much engineering may attract anti-abuse rules, such as General Anti Avoidance Rules (GAARs).

## C Policy Considerations

From a policy perspective, a trade-off is apparent. It is the familiar trade-off between principled but complex rules, on the one hand, and simpler (or more predictable) but rougher rules, on the other.

Transfer pricing rules based on the ALP have the benefit of being principled and multilateral. They take a fine-grained, transaction-by-transaction approach and use the arm's-length principle as their yardstick. They are manifest in the longstanding network of tax treaties, so they benefit from mechanisms for double tax relief and dispute resolution as well as the body of thought contained in the OECD Transfer Pricing Guidelines and similar publications.

However, transfer pricing rules are cumbersome to apply. The 2020 Guidance endorses the process of estimating what would be the debtor's credit rating if the debt was at arm's length and also estimating the rating agency's 'notching' process for the debtor's relationship to its MNE group. As noted above, both of these are very fact-intensive processes. They also involve subjectivity and scope for disputation. The recent trend, exemplified by the Two Pillars project in particular, has been for formulaic calculations (albeit complex ones) to supplant traditional 'facts and circumstances' ALP-based rules. In the author's view, this is a significant shift and one which is not likely to change direction in the foreseeable future.

Further, transfer pricing is not targeted at interest stripping in particular. For example, transfer pricing rules will often respect an MNE strategy of using high levels of intragroup debt with the creditor subsidiary in a low-tax jurisdiction and the debtor subsidiary in a high-debt jurisdiction (noting that this strategy is becoming less viable as various other anti-BEPS measures develop). As long as the leverage is an amount which can be justified on arm's-length terms (which is frequently possible, given the large range of arm's-length leverage ratios even in one industry sector), transfer pricing rules will not intervene. Not only that, they will often require, then, that a relatively high interest rate be applied, in light of the high leverage which, at arm's length, tends to make the debtor less creditworthy.

Thus, many countries use thin capitalisation and/or interest barrier rules, plus there is the pending GloBE proposal under which the UTPR can further reduce deductions, and as noted above the usual practice is for them to apply after the transfer pricing rules.

However, the policy logic of how these rules interact is not perfect. It does not seem intuitively right that all of an MNE's related party finance transactions could satisfy the ALP under the rigorous, fact-heavy transfer pricing rules, and yet the interest barrier, thin capitalisation rule or UTPR could nonetheless operate to deny interest deductions. But this is what happens under the usual ordering.

A further disconnect occurs where the thin capitalisation/interest barrier rule involves a safe harbour, under which taxpayers are guaranteed a certain tax treatment. The objective of safe harbour rules is certainty and administrability (for both taxpayers and tax administrations). These are desirable features. If transfer pricing rules always precede thin capitalisation/interest barrier rules, this could obviously cut off access to the safe harbour. Some jurisdictions have grappled with this. The Australian approach of having transfer pricing determine the rate based on an (often lower) arm's-length amount of debt and then applying that rate to the actual debt amount so long as it is within the safe harbour limit,[40] is one way of striking the compromise (see example above at the end of section C), but it is not particularly elegant. The question of how the UTPR will fit together with the safe harbours that exist under some states' thin capitalisation and interest barrier rules has not yet been resolved.

## III CONCLUSION

It is clear from the above that while transfer pricing comes first in terms of the conceptual legal principles in many countries, as a matter of practical administration, interest barriers and thin capitalisation rules based on fixed ratios are becoming the dominant regime for managing interest deductions.

The question 'what comes first' also invokes normative considerations. How *should* the rules in this area apply? Interest limitations and transfer pricing of debt is a complicated area. The laws described above clearly involve a trade-off: ease of administration versus principled complexity.

The view of the author is that traditional ALP-based transfer pricing does not work well for all cases of related party financing transactions. The compliance burden and uncertainty burden which they place on MNEs and tax authorities alike is very heavy. Superficially, transfer pricing of debt should be simple – millions of arm's-length financing transactions take place every year and are available on the public

40. Sections 815-25 and 815-140 of the Income Tax Assessment Act 1997 (Australia).

record or in databases. However, in practice the scope for disagreement about the correct arm's-length interest rate – and other terms such as quantum, security, covenants and the like – is large.[41]

One of the reasons for this is a comparability problem. Most debt transfer pricing cases involve a subsidiary of the MNE borrowing from another entity in the MNE group, without a guarantee from the MNE parent or asset-rich financing subsidiary. By contrast, for their arm's-length borrowings, for amounts of any substance, most MNEs choose to borrow either at the parent level or through a subsidiary which is explicitly guaranteed by the parent or another asset-rich part of the MNE.[42] This gives the MNE the lowest cost of debt, all other things being equal. Of course, this is not universal and there are reasons why MNEs sometimes borrow at arm's length through unguaranteed subsidiaries, although this is not common for large amounts. The dearth of implicit support notching examples (apart from those occasioned by a takeover) in credit rating publications exemplifies this.

Another reason is subjectivity. Even professional credit rating agencies frequently disagree about the creditworthiness of a given business. Creditworthiness assessment involves a prediction about how a large number of different variables will interact in the future, and the future is inherently uncertain.

Ultimately, there may be a conceptual problem. Related party debt within an MNE is often, economically, a close substitute for equity funding.[43] Equity funding is the very thing that – inherently – cannot be subjected to a transfer pricing analysis. It may be that this proximity explains why there are so many challenges in practice in transfer pricing debt.

These problems have been recognised with the emergence of interest limitation rules as a form of de facto primary rule. This is consistent with the trend towards fixed ratios and objective (if complex) calculation formulae, which is further illustrated by the 15% accounting-based GloBE Pillar Two model rules. But fixed ratio rules also have their problems. Chief amongst them is the arbitrariness of the fixed rate, as well as the difficulties involved in coordinating double tax relief.

In relation to interest deductions, a better solution would be for fixed-rate interest limitation rules to be accompanied by a group ratio alternative, as suggested in the

41. *See* Graeme Cooper & Richard Vann, 'Transfer Pricing Money *bis*' in Georg Kofler, Ruth Mason & Alexander Rust, *Thinker, Teacher, Traveler: Reimagining International Tax: Essays in Honor of H. David Rosenbloom* (IBFD, 2021) at pp. 163-164; Thomas Petrakos, Vikram Chand & Amanda Pletz, *Interest Rate Benchmarking for Transfer Pricing Purposes: A Comparison Between the Loan and the Bond Approach* (2021) 28(4) International Transfer Pricing Journal 242-255.

42. Bhagwan Chowdhry & Vikram Nanda, *Financing of Multinational Subsidiaries: Parent Debt vs. External Debt* (1994) 1 Journal of Corporate Finance 259-281; Pascal Janssens et al., *The End of Intra-Group Financing… or Not Just Yet* (2015) 55 European Taxation 281 ('assuming that groups acting rationally from a commercial perspective centralise their financing in the entity that is the most efficient').

43. Gary Hufbauer & Arial Assa, *US Taxation of Foreign Income* (Peterson Institute for International Economics 2007), p. 159; David Rosenbloom, *Banes of an Income Tax: Legal Fictions, Elections, Hypothetical Determinations, Related Party Debt* (2004) 26 Sydney Law Review 35; David Southern, Country Report (United Kingdom) The Debt-Equity Conundrum, Vol. 97b (2012) *Cahiers de Droit Fiscal International* (Kluwer, 2012), 764; Chloe Burnett, *Intra-group Debt at the Crossroads: Stand-Alone Versus Worldwide Approach* (2014) 6 World Tax Journal 1.

Action 4 Final Report.[44] This is tailored to the MNE in question and is less arbitrary. The capacity for an MNE to justify interest, for a particular transaction, above the limit implied by the interest barrier could be retained for exceptional or unusual transactions, for example where the borrowing subsidiary is notably different from the MNE parent or group or where capital flows are restricted by domestic law. Safe harbour interest rates are also desirable, to reduce the compliance and uncertainty burden.

Lastly, the strict demarcation that has historically existed between transfer pricing on the one hand, and interest barrier/thin capitalisation rules on the other, ought to be reduced. In particular, interest barriers and thin capitalisation rules (and the pending Pillar Two GloBE regime)[45] would ideally become subject to expanded treaty mechanisms for double tax relief in terms of secondary adjustments, the mutual agreement procedure and mandatory binding arbitration.

44. OECD, *BEPS Action 4: Limiting Base Erosion Involving Interest Deductions and Other Financial Payments: 2016 Updated Report* (OECD 2017), Chapter 7.

45. Vikram Chand, Alessandro Turina & Kinha Romanovska, 'Tax Treaty Obstacles in Implementing the Pillar Two Global Minimum Tax Rules and a Possible Solution for Eliminating the various challenges', Working Paper, available on SSRN.

CHAPTER 5

# Critical Assessment of Interest Limitation Rules: Global Perspective

*Sandra Martinho Fernandes*[*]

## I INTRODUCTION

The unequal taxation of interest and dividends has been a common characteristic of the majority of corporate income tax systems for almost a century. While interest is deductible from the taxable income of an enterprise, dividends are non-deductible. The non-deductibility of dividends results in economic double taxation as there is a concurrent taxation of the company's profits in the hands of the company and of the dividends in the hands of the shareholders, whereas, as a general rule, there is no economic double taxation of interest as the interest payment is fully deductible in the hands of the payer and the interest income is fully subject to tax in the hands of the recipient. This problem is the so-called debt-equity bias.

Against this background, it has been considered that the problem of economic double taxation of dividends should be addressed either by means of applying the exemption or the credit method (i.e., granting an indirect tax credit) in order to tackle the debt bias of the corporate tax systems. Such an approach has indeed been implemented through the introduction of the so-called participation exemption regimes in the domestic tax regimes of different countries, by agreeing on the relief for the economic double taxation of dividends under double tax treaties and at European Union (EU) level through the adoption of the EU Parent-Subsidiary Directive.[1]

* The views and opinions set forth herein are the personal views or opinions of the authors; they do not necessarily reflect the views or opinions of the organization with which the authors are associated.

1. Council Directive (EU) 2011/96 of 30 November 2011 on the common system of taxation applicable in the case of parent companies and subsidiaries of different member states, as amended, OJ L 345, 29.12.2011.

However, even if full relief were granted to solve the issue of economic double taxation of dividends so that both interest and dividends (i.e., the returns on debt and equity capital) would not trigger any economic double taxation, the tax consequences of financing an entity with debt or equity capital are still not the same. The main reason for this is that the international allocation of taxing rights in relation to the returns on debt and equity capital is not the same. Accordingly, the country that will tax the dividends (i.e., the return on equity capital) is the source country (i.e., dividends are taxable in the hands of the payer and exempt or granted a full indirect tax credit in the hands of the recipient), whereas the country that will tax the interest paid (i.e., the return on debt capital) is the residence country of the recipient (i.e., interest payments are deductible in the hands of the payer and interest income is taxable in the hands of the recipient). In basic terms, everything being equal,[2] in a cross-border scenario asymmetric taxing rights are allocated to the source country or to the residence country depending on the way in which the investor chooses to finance its investment with equity or debt capital.

Notwithstanding the fact that most of the corporate taxation regimes do provide relief to economic double taxation of dividends, the debt-equity bias of the current corporate tax systems could also be further addressed via an allowance for corporate equity or notional interest deduction systems.[3]

Indeed, as rightly pointed out by Piltz in 1996 in the International Fiscal Association (IFA) General Report:

> [w]ith equity financing, the source country receives the lion's share of the taxes, whereas with debt financing, the bulk of tax revenue goes to the shareholder's country of residence. In this respect, it is of little importance whether a DTC stipulates the credit method or the exemption method for dividends. Debt financing only offers a significant tax advantage for subsidiary companies and shareholders taken together if the shareholder pays no taxes on the income received, e.g. because he benefits from tax exemption, is making losses or is a resident in a

2. In practice, in a cross-border scenario, there will always be differences between the tax system of the country of the payer and of the recipient of interest or dividends, such as the tax rate, loss carry forward rules, scope of the participation exemption, etc. On the other hand, there may be tax differences between the payer and the recipient as one may be in a profit-making position and the other in a loss-making position (or vice versa), or one may be a fully exempt entity and the other a fully taxable entity. As a result of such differences, i.e., the specific tax features and situation of the payer and recipient, debt financing may become more interesting than equity financing (or the other way round).
3. In this respect, it is interesting to note that the Communication on Business Taxation for the twenty-first century, which was released on 18 May 2021, included the announcement of the introduction of a legislative proposal for a Debt-Equity Bias Reduction Allowance (DEBRA) as part of the EU tax policy agenda and vision for the future. *See* https://ec.europa.eu/taxation_customs/system/files/2021-05/communication_on_business_taxation_for_the_21st_century.pdf. Subsequently, on 15 June 2021, the European Commission published the impact assessment for DEBRA, noting that further rules are needed to mitigate the tax induced debt-equity bias and noting that six Member States (Belgium, Cyprus, Italy, Malta, Poland and Portugal) have already introduced such kind of measures. The latter measures differ in policy design but all provide for a tax allowance on equity in order to reduce the debt-equity bias. *See* https://ec.europa.eu/info/law/better-regulation/have-your-say/initiatives/12995-Debt-equity-bias-reduction-allowance-DEBRA-_en.

> non-tax or a low-tax country. *Consequently, thin capitalization regulations are aimed at protecting the tax revenue of the source country* [emphasis added].[4]

It follows from the above that in a cross-border scenario the debt-equity bias and the asymmetric allocation of taxing rights in relation to dividends and interest can clearly influence the decision of, *inter alia*, the shareholder, manager or director to finance the company with debt instead of equity capital. As a result, in order to protect their tax revenues and avoid the erosion of their tax base, the majority of the countries have adopted rules that target thinly capitalized companies, i.e., companies whose financing sources are mainly debt instead of equity financing instruments.

The measures drafted by the different countries against thin capitalization are diverse but used to operate mainly through general legal rules and principles, e.g., general anti-avoidance rules, the substance-over-form principle, or through specific, technical, thin capitalization rules. These rules generally refer to an international standard – the arm's length principle (ALP) – to determine whether the quantum of loans provided and the interest rate agreed between related parties are consistent with what unrelated parties would have agreed upon under conditions of free and fair competition. The main purpose of thin capitalization rules is to prevent multinational enterprises (MNEs), often on the basis of presumptions, from shifting their profits from one jurisdiction to another by the use of excessive debt financing. Therefore, these rules initially targeted cross-border intra-group financing and not domestic intra-group financing.

Yet, in a globalized world, the financing of MNEs has become a worldwide problem due to the strong concern that MNEs can plan their worldwide leverage to minimize their overall tax liability. This concern has highlighted the risk of base erosion and profit shifting (BEPS) through the use of excessive interest expenses.

In order to address this growing concern, in 2013, when the Organisation for Economic Co-operation and Development (OECD) launched its work on BEPS plan, one of the issues considered was the need to reinforce measures to tackle BEPS through the deduction of interest and other financial payments. This matter was considered under BEPS Action 4, which made recommendations to limit base erosion through the use of interest expense to achieve excessive interest deductions or to finance the production of exempt or deferred income (hereinafter referred to as the 'BEPS Action 4 Rules'). Pursuant to the 2015 final report on BEPS Action 4 and the updated report thereon released in December 2016, the recommended approach by the OECD regarding the limitation of interest deductions and other financial payments, i.e., the BEPS Action 4 Rules, is as follows:

> a fixed ratio rule which limits an entity's net deductions for interest and payments economically equivalent to interest to a percentage of its earnings before interest, taxes, depreciation and amortization (EBITDA). As a minimum, this should apply to entities in multinational groups. ... The approach can be supplemented by a

4. Detlev J. Piltz, *General Report on International Aspects of Thin Capitalization*, IFA Cahiers de droit fiscal international, vol. 81b (Kluwer Law International 1996), at p. 97.

worldwide group ratio rule which allows an entity to exceed this limit in certain circumstances.[5]

Building on the BEPS Action 4 Rules, the European Commission submitted in January 2016 an anti-tax avoidance package, which included a proposal for a Council Directive proposing rules against tax avoidance practices that directly affect the functioning of the internal market. The Anti-Tax Avoidance Directive (ATAD) proposal included, among other measures to tackle BEPS, an interest limitation rule mirroring the recommended BEPS Action 4 Rules. On 12 July 2016, the EU Council approved the proposed ATAD, as amended throughout its legislative process, which basically reflects a part of the aforementioned January 2016 proposals submitted by the European Commission to strengthen the rules against corporate tax avoidance.[6] The ATAD includes a specific provision to deal with the limitation of the tax-deductibility of interest and similar financial payments by corporate taxpayers, i.e., Article 4 of the ATAD (hereinafter referred to as the 'ATAD's Article 4'). As we will see later in this chapter, the ATAD's Article 4 is loosely similar to the recommended BEPS Action 4 Rules.

Under the veil of merely broadening the scope of traditional thin capitalization rules, or of becoming comprehensive, the new interest limitation rules set under the BEPS Action 4 Rules or ATAD's Article 4 in fact represent a conceptual change from traditional thin capitalization rules. In addition, in a cross-border context, the new interest limitation rules create international economic double taxation of interest because the non-deductible interest is taxed in the source country of the interest payment (or country of residence of the borrowing company) and in the country of residence of the recipient of the interest income. It is not expected that the latter will give relief to this economic double taxation of interest since the amount of interest that is non-deductible at source is not defined in accordance with traditionally accepted international tax practices and principles. As a result of the non-deduction of interest payments at source, the source country also seems to regain some taxing powers, albeit creating international economic double taxation of interest.

In fact, the new interest limitation rules seem to constitute an attempt to address the problem that the tax jurisdiction is exercised on the concept of net income determined on the basis of the separate enterprise method (as opposed to the formulary apportionment method). With respect to interest, this means that in a globalized

5. OECD, *Limiting Base Erosion Involving Interest Deductions and Other Financial Payments, Action 4 – 2015 Final Report*, OECD/G20 Base Erosion and Profit Shifting Project (OECD Publishing 2015) (cit. BEPS Action 4 Final Report) at p. 11; and OECD, *Limiting Base Erosion Involving Interest Deductions and Other Financial Payments, Action 4 – 2016 Update: Inclusive Framework on BEPS*, OECD/G20 Base Erosion and Profit Shifting Project (OECD Publishing 2017), p. 13 (cit. BEPS Action 4 Updated Report) (hereinafter referred to as 'BEPS Action 4 Final Report and BEPS Action 4'. Updated Report will be referred together as the 'BEPS Action 4 Reports').

6. Council Directive (EU) 2016/1164 of 12 July 2016 laying down rules against tax avoidance practices that directly affect the functioning of the internal market, OJ L 193 19.7.2016 (ATAD). The ATAD comprises the following measures against tax avoidance and base erosion practices: the interest limitation rule, exit taxation rules, the general anti-abuse rule, the controlled foreign company rule and rules on hybrid mismatches. Subject to certain exceptions, the Member States had until 31 December 2018 to transpose the ATAD into domestic law.

context, the financing method determines the revenue which the jurisdiction can tax, i.e., the decision to locate the lender and the borrower in country A or B will automatically determine the profits which each jurisdiction can tax.

In order to submit a critical assessment of these interest limitation rules, the author will start by making a separate recap on the scope and main features of the BEPS Action 4 Rules and ATAD's Article 4 in the next section of this chapter (Part II). Subsequently, the author will elaborate on the reasons why the interest limitation rules, all of which are inspired or based on the BEPS Action 4 Rules or ATAD's Article 4, should be critically reviewed (Part III). The author will then conclude with some final remarks on the last section of this chapter (Part IV).

## II INTEREST LIMITATION RULES: BEPS ACTION 4 RULES[7] AND ATAD'S ARTICLE 4[8]

### 1 Subjective Scope

#### *A BEPS Action 4 Rules*

As regards the subjective scope of the BEPS Action 4 Rules, the latter should apply, as a minimum, to all entities which are part of a multinational group and may be

7. For an overview of the evolution of thin capitalization rules and for an in-depth analysis of the BEPS Action 4 Rules, *see*, in particular, PILTZ, *supra* n. 4, at pp. 83-139; PASCAL HINNY, *General Report on New Tendencies in Tax Treatment of Cross-Border Interest of Corporations*, IFA Cahiers de Droit Fiscal International, vol. 93b (IFA 2008), at pp. 15-52; PATRICIA BROWN, *General Report on the Debt-Equity Conundrum*, IFA Cahiers de Droit Fiscal International, vol. 97b, subject 2 (Sdu Uitgevers, cop. 2012); and JAMES GADWOOD & PAUL MORTON, *General Report on Interest Deductibility: The Implementation of BEPS Action 4*, IFA Cahiers de Droit Fiscal International, vol. 104a (IFA 2019), at pp. 15-46. *See also* SANDRA M. FERNANDES, *International Double Taxation of Interest*, IBFD Doctoral Series Book (IBFD 2019) at sections 2.2., 3.2.5, and 3.3 and references referred therein.
8. For an in-depth and critical analysis of the ATAD and ATAD's Article 4, *see*, in particular, ADAM ZALASINSKI, *EU Report on Interest Deductibility: The Implementation of BEPS Action 4*, IFA Cahiers de Droit Fiscal International, vol. 104a (IFA 2019), at pp. 49-64; ALOYS RIGAUT, *Anti-Tax Avoidance Directive (2016/1164): New EU Policy Horizons*, 56 European Taxation 11, pp. 497-505 (2016); AITOR NAVARRO, LEOPOLDO PARADA & PALOMA SCHWARZ, *The Proposal for an EU Anti-Avoidance Directive: Some Preliminary Thoughts*, 25 EC Tax Review 3, pp. 117-131 (2016); ANA PAULA DOURADO, *The EU Anti-Tax Avoidance Package: Moving Ahead of BEPS?*, 44 EC Tax Review 6/7, pp. 440-446 (2016); ANA PAULA DOURADO, *The Interest Limitation Rule in the Anti-Tax Avoidance Directive (ATAD) and the Net Taxation Principle*, 26 EC Tax Review 3, pp. 112-121 (2017); DANIEL GUTMANN ET AL., *The Impact of the ATAD on Domestic Systems: A Comparative Survey*, 57 European Taxation 1, pp. 2-20 (2017); GIANLUIGI BIZIOLI, *Taking EU Fundamental Freedoms Seriously Does the Anti-Tax Avoidance Directive Take Precedence over the Single Market?*, 26 EC Tax Review 3, pp. 167-175 (2017); GUGLIELMO GINEVRA, *The EU Anti-Tax Avoidance Directive and the Base Erosion and Profit Shifting (BEPS) Action Plan: Necessity and Adequacy of the Measures at EU Level*, 45 Intertax 2, pp. 120-137 (2017); MICHAEL TELL, *Interest Limitation Rules in the Post-BEPS Era*, 45 Intertax 11, pp. 750-763 (2017); PETER VAN OS, *Interest Limitation under the Adopted Anti-Tax Avoidance Directive and Proportionality*, 25 EC Tax Review 4, pp. 184-198 (2016); and STEFFEN LAMPERT, MEICKMANN TILL & MARIA REINERT, *Article 4 of the EU Anti-Tax Avoidance Directive in Light of the Questionable Constitutionality of the German 'Interest Barrier' Rule*, 56 European Taxation 8, pp. 323-327 (2016). *See also* SANDRA M. FERNANDES, *supra* n. 7, at sections 2.2, 3.2.6, and 3.3 and references referred therein.

expanded to include entities of a domestic group and/or standalone entities which are not part of a group.[9] In order to ensure a level playing field between domestic and foreign multinational groups, BEPS Action 4 Rules should apply to both of such groups, without making any distinction.[10]

As a result, one of the key definitions for the purpose of applying the BEPS Action 4 Rules is the definition of a multinational group (or MNE).[11] In a nutshell, BEPS Action 4 Rules should be applied to any subsidiaries and/or permanent establishments (PEs) which are controlled by the same foreign entity and which are carrying out their business activities in more than one country.

Notwithstanding the above, as explained in the BEPS Action 4 Reports, there might be situations warranting the application of BEPS Action 4 Rules to standalone entities held by complex holding structures because the 'level of base erosion and profit shifting risk may be similar to that posed by a group structure'.[12]

In the same vein, the BEPS Action 4 Reports also propose to tailor the BEPS Action 4 Rules in such a way as to provide certain exemptions to entities or projects posing low BEPS risks or to facilitate the practical implementation of the rules, such as the possibility of providing for certain *de minimis* monetary thresholds, to apply these rules at a group level (instead of to each group entity separately) or to apply these rules or to exclude certain entities carrying out public-benefit projects.[13]

As a result, it follows from the above that the determination of the subjective scope (i.e., the inclusion and/or exclusion of entities) of the BEPS Action 4 Rules is clearly guided by the main policy goal of the rules, i.e., to address the BEPS issue resulting from the use of interest deductions and other financial payments.

Finally, the proposed BEPS Action 4 Rules do not apply to any entities acting in the banking and insurance sectors as the latter warrant a different set of 'suitable and specific rules that address BEPS risks in these sectors',[14] which was done in the updated report on BEPS Action 4 released by the end of 2016.[15] The study of these specific rules does not fall within the scope of this chapter.

---

9. BEPS Action 4 Final Report, *supra* n. 5 at p. 33, paras 43-44; and BEPS Action 4 Updated Report, *supra* n. 5 at p. 37, paras 43-44.
10. Of particular importance in this respect are the EU treaty freedoms and the prohibition of discrimination of an EU group vis-à-vis a purely domestic group, *see* BEPS Action 4 Final Report, *supra* n. 5 at p. 34, paras 49-51; and BEPS Action 4 Updated Report, *supra* n. 5 at p. 38, paras 49-51, as well as Annex A and Annex I.A. to the relevant reports concerning the EU law issues.
11. The proposed definition of this key term in the BEPS Action 4 Reports reads as follows: 'An entity is part of a group if the entity is directly or indirectly controlled by a company, or the entity is a company which directly or indirectly controls one or more other entities. A group is a multinational group where it operates in more than one jurisdiction, including through a permanent establishment', *see* BEPS Action 4 Final Report, *supra* n. 5 at p. 33, para. 45; and BEPS Action 4 Updated Report, *supra* n. 5 at p. 37, para. 45.
12. BEPS Action 4 Final Report, *supra* n. 5 at p. 34, para. 52; and BEPS Action 4 Updated Report, *supra* n. 5 at p. 38, para. 52.
13. BEPS Action 4 Final Report, *supra* n. 5 at pp. 33-35 and 39-41, paras 47-51, 54-56 and 64-70; and BEPS Action 4 Updated Report, *supra* n. 5 at pp. 37-39 and 43-44, paras 47-51, 54-56 and 64-70.
14. BEPS Action 4 Final Report, *supra* n. 5 at p. 12.
15. The approaches to addressing BEPS involving interest in the banking and insurance sectors are carried out in Part III of the BEPS Action 4 Updated Report.

### B *ATAD's Article 4*

The ATAD applies to all taxpayers that are subject to corporate income tax in one or more Member States, including entities resident for tax purposes in a third country and having PEs in one or more Member States.[16] As a general rule, the interest limitation rules provided by ATAD's Article 4 apply separately to each and every taxpayer within the scope of the ATAD.

That said, the ATAD does allow for certain exceptions to this general rule, all of which are in line with similar derogations provided by the BEPS Action 4 Rules.

Firstly, in certain circumstances, ATAD's Article 4 may be applied at a group level (when domestic rules allow for group taxation regimes), instead of to each group entity separately.[17]

Secondly, as per Article 4(3)(a) of the ATAD, the Member States may introduce a *de minimis* monetary threshold whereby any corporate taxpayer whose exceeding borrowing costs for any given year would not exceed EUR 3 million would de facto not be subject to (or impacted by) these rules. As pointed out in the eighth recital of the ATAD, the purpose of this *de minimis* monetary threshold is to 'reduce the administrative and compliance burden of the rules without significantly diminishing their tax effect'.

Thirdly, as per Article 4(3)(b) of the ATAD, the Member States may, on a discretionary and optional basis, decide to exclude standalone entities from the scope of ATAD's Article 4.[18] As explained in the 8th recital of the ATAD, the possible exclusion of standalone entities from the scope of ATAD's Article 4 is justified because, in the absence of intra-group debt arrangements, the risks of tax avoidance are limited '[s]ince BEPS in principle takes place through excessive interest payments among entities which are associate enterprises'. Notwithstanding that, ATAD's Article 4 has decided to cover and restrict the tax-deductibility of interest payments made to related and unrelated parties (without providing any exception in the case of limited or nil tax avoidance risks in light of the type of lender).

Fourthly, pursuant to Article 4(7) of the ATAD, the Member States may also exclude, if they so wish, regulated financial undertakings from the scope of ATAD's Article 4. As explained in the ninth recital of the ATAD, even though in principle regulated financial undertakings, i.e., financial institutions and insurance undertakings, should also be subject to interest limitation rules, it was advisable to exclude them from the scope of the ATAD at that point in time. The reason being that such entities 'present special features which call for a more customised approach' and there is no definite or conclusive international agreement on the specific rules that should apply to them.[19]

---

16. *See* Article 1 ATAD.
17. *See* Article 4(1)(a) and (b) ATAD.
18. The term standalone entity is defined in the last paragraph of Article 4(3)(b) ATAD and reads as follows: 'a standalone entity means a taxpayer that is not part of a consolidated group for financial accounting purposes and has no associated enterprise or permanent establishment'.
19. For completeness, it is noted that while the position taken in the ATAD to exclude regulated financial undertakings is fully compliant with the conclusions drawn by the OECD in the BEPS

## 2 Objective Scope

### *A BEPS Action 4 Rules*

The BEPS Action 4 Rules should apply to interest and payments economically equivalent to interest paid to related and unrelated parties.[20] Yet, the exact definition of interest or of payments economically equivalent to interest is a matter to be addressed and determined by each jurisdiction in their domestic tax laws, instead of by the BEPS Action 4 Reports.

That said, the BEPS Action 4 Reports do nonetheless advise countries to ensure that the definitions of those terms are sufficiently broad so as to include, at least, '(i) interest on all forms of debt; (ii) payments economically equivalent to interest; and (iii) expenses incurred in connection with the raising of finance'.[21] In this respect, the BEPS Action 4 Reports do include a list of certain payments or items that should normally be expected to be included within the scope of the BEPS Action 4 Rules,[22] such as payments under profit-participating loans, imputed interest on instruments such as convertible bonds and zero-coupon bonds and amounts due under alternative financing arrangements, and another list with certain payments or items that should be excluded from the scope of the rules,[23] e.g., forex gains or losses which are not connected with the raising of finance, royalties and operating leasing payments.

Furthermore, the BEPS Action 4 Rules apply and limit interest expenses and similar financial payments paid to any parties (i.e., third parties, related parties and group entities) after offsetting interest income.[24] In other words, this means that the recommended BEPS Action 4 Rules are an interest limitation rule that applies and restricts the tax-deductibility of the net interest expense (instead of the gross interest expense) of an entity in any given year.

### *B ATAD's Article 4*

Like the BEPS Action 4 Rules, ATAD's Article 4 provides for a mechanical rule limiting the tax-deductibility of the exceeding borrowing costs (or net interest expenses, instead of gross interest expenses) incurred by a taxpayer. As a result, the definition of the

Action 4 Final Report released in 2015, since then the OECD has released the BEPS Action 4 Updated Report in 2016 which includes a proposal for specific interest limitation rules for regulated financial undertakings, which arguably could have been taken into account by the ATAD too.

20. BEPS Action 4 Final Report, *supra* n. 5 at p. 47, para. 85; and BEPS Action 4 Updated Report, *supra* n. 5 at p. 51, para. 85.
21. BEPS Action 4 Final Report, *supra* n. 5 at p. 29, para. 36; and BEPS Action 4 Updated Report, *supra* n. 5 at p. 33, para. 36.
22. BEPS Action 4 Final Report, *supra* n. 5 at p. 30, para. 36; and BEPS Action 4 Updated Report, *supra* n. 5 at p. 34, para. 36.
23. BEPS Action 4 Final Report, *supra* n. 5 at p. 30, para. 39; and BEPS Action 4 Updated Report, *supra* n. 5 at p. 34, para. 39.
24. BEPS Action 4 Final Report, *supra* n. 5 at pp. 38-39, paras 60-63; and BEPS Action 4 Updated Report, *supra* n. 5 at pp. 42-43, paras 60-63.

terms borrowing costs and exceeding borrowing costs are key to determining the objective scope of ATAD's Article 4.

Borrowing costs are defined in Article 2(1) of the ATAD in a very broad manner and cover, *inter alia*, any interest expenses on all forms of debt, other costs economically equivalent to interest and expenses incurred in connection with the raising of finance (as defined in national law), as well as payments under profit-participating loans, imputed and notional interest on certain financial instruments and derivatives, as well as amounts due under alternative financing arrangements or financial lease payments, forex gains or losses connected with the raising of finance and, in general, any kinds of fees connected with the borrowing of funds.[25]

Exceeding borrowing costs are defined in the ATAD as 'the amount by which the deductible borrowing costs of a taxpayer exceed taxable interest revenues and other economically equivalent taxable revenues that the taxpayer receives according to national law'.[26]

It should be noted, however, that the ATAD still grants some limited possibilities for the Member States to make some exclusions to this wide objective scope of ATAD's Article 4, if they so wish. First, Article 4(4)(a) of the ATAD allows Member States to introduce a grandfathering clause whereby any exceeding borrowing costs incurred on loans which were concluded before 17 June 2016 would fall outside the scope of the ATAD and therefore remain fully deductible. Noting that, in case of any subsequent change to such loans, the grandfathering clause would only apply to the original terms and conditions of the relevant loan.[27] Second, in accordance with Article 4(4)(b) of the ATAD, the Member States may exclude exceeding borrowing costs incurred on loans used to fund a long-term public infrastructure project where the project operator, borrowing costs, assets and income are all in the Union (and provided such exclusion is compliant with other EU rules, like state aid rules). The justification brought forward by the ATAD to justify this exclusion is the fact that such long-term public infrastructure projects present nil or limited BEPS risks.[28]

## 3 Thresholds/Ratios

### *A BEPS Action 4 Rules*

The BEPS Action 4 Rules propose a fixed earnings ratio rule according to which any entity falling within the scope of such rules should only be allowed to deduct its net interest expenses and similar financial payments up to a certain threshold, i.e., a fixed

25. The definition of the term borrowing costs under the ATAD is clearly inspired by and is very much aligned with the proposed definition of the term interest expenses provided under the OECD BEPS Action 4 Reports, *see supra* section II.A.
26. *See* Article 2(2) ATAD.
27. *See* the fourth sentence of the 8th recital of the ATAD.
28. *See*, for more details, the last two sentences of the 8th recital of the ATAD.

earnings ratio determined by each country implementing the rules within a 10% to 30% corridor.[29]

Now, the next question is how each jurisdiction should determine its own earnings ratio benchmark within the allowed corridor, as it is quite a wide one.[30] In that respect, the BEPS Action 4 Reports provide jurisdictions with a list of different factors, such as the average earnings before interest and taxes (EBIT) and earnings before interest, taxes, depreciation and amortization (EBITDA) figures for the major sectors in the country's economy.[31]

In addition, the BEPS Action 4 Reports, also allow the jurisdictions, if they so wish, to combine the fixed earnings ratio rule with a group ratio rule on the basis of the earnings of the group or of the value of the assets of the group.[32]

The recommended BEPS Action 4 Rules therefore work by reference to a fixed earnings ratio rule and require the following three-step process:

> Firstly, calculating the appropriate measure of EBITDA; secondly, applying the statutory benchmark fixed ratio to an entity's EBITDA to determine the maximum deductible interest expense; and thirdly, comparing this with the actual interest expense of the entity.[33]

As to the definition of earnings for the purpose of the BEPS Action 4 Rules, it is clarified that it should either correspond to the amount of the EBIT (earnings before interest and taxes) or of the EBITDA (earnings before interest, taxes, depreciation and amortization) of an entity, corrected in both cases by excluding all the non-taxable income received by the same entity in the same financial year, such as branch profits, dividend income and income from foreign real estate. The same correction is applied in case an assets-based rule would be available, by excluding from the relevant assets the computation of any assets producing tax-exempt income.

### *B ATAD's Article 4*

As per Article 4(1) of the ATAD 'exceeding borrowing costs shall be deductible in the tax period in which they are incurred only up to 30% of the taxpayer's earnings before interest, tax, depreciation and amortisation (EBITDA)'. Thus, ATAD's Article 4 works by reference to the same kind of simple and objective cap on interest deductibility, as the one recommended by BEPS Action 4 Rules.

---

29. BEPS Action 4 Final Report, *supra* n. 5 at pp. 25-26, paras 23-24; and BEPS Action 4 Updated Report, *supra* n. 5 at pp. 29-30, paras 23-24.
30. The 10% to 30% corridor proposed by the OECD may be revised in future, but that has not yet happened so far, *see* BEPS Action 4 Final Report, *supra* n. 5 at p. 50, para. 97; and BEPS Action 4 Updated Report, *supra* n. 5 at pp. 53-54, para. 97.
31. The factors are listed in Chapter 6 of the relevant BEPS Action 4 Final Report, as well as in Chapter 6 of the BEPS Action 4 Updated Report.
32. BEPS Action 4 Final Report, *supra* n. 5 at pp. 25-26, paras 22-24; pp. 45-46, paras 81-84; and BEPS Action 4 Updated Report, *supra* n. 5 at pp. 29-30, paras 22-24; pp. 49-50, paras 81-84.
33. BEPS Action 4 Final Report, *supra* n. 5 at pp. 47-48, para. 88; and BEPS Action 4 Updated Report, *supra* n. 5 at pp. 51-52, para. 88.

With respect to the computation of the EBITDA for the purposes of applying ATAD's Article 4, this Directive clarifies that tax-exempt income shall be excluded from the EBITDA of a taxpayer[34] because 'only taxable income should be taken into account in determining how much interest may be deducted'[35] for tax purposes.

In addition, ATAD's Article 4, like the BEPS Action 4 Rules, also allows for some flexibility to the Member States, if they so wish, by providing some group ratio rules. First, the equity escape rule whereby ATAD's Article 4 would not apply if the taxpayer can demonstrate that the ratio of its equity to its total assets is either equal to or lower than (by not more than 2 percentage points) the equivalent ratio of the worldwide group.[36] Second, an earnings-based worldwide group ratio rule whereby a taxpayer is allowed to deduct its exceeding borrowing costs up to the level of the net interest/EBITDA ratio of the worldwide group to which it belongs.[37]

## 4 Consequences

### *A BEPS Action 4 Rules*

Any net interest expenses and similar net financial payments exceeding the said fixed earnings ratio (or other allowed ratios, like the assets or group ratio, if implemented by the countries) would be permanently disallowed. This means that such excessive net interest amount would be added back to the accounting result and taxable income for the year of the relevant entity, which would therefore be taxed in the hands of the debtor at the applicable standard rate.

As a result, the outcome of the proposed BEPS Action 4 Rules would be to create economic double taxation of interest on a world scale because a certain portion of the interest expenses would no longer be tax-deductible in the hands of the debtor, while the corresponding interest income would normally be taxed in the hands of the creditor.

While the BEPS Action 4 Reports also point out that double taxation of interest may arise as a result of the implementation of the proposed BEPS Action 4 Rules, the same report has decided to address the issue mildly by outlining a couple of mechanisms that countries could implement at their own discretion to correct (up to a certain extent) the outcome of the said rules. These reports suggest that countries may, if they so wish, implement adjustments to the issue of double taxation created by BEPS Action 4 Rules, such as by allowing: (i) carry forward disallowed interest expense, (ii) carry forward disallowed interest expense and unused interest capacity and (iii) carry

34. Article 4(2) ATAD. The same idea is expressed in the 6th recital of the ATAD by noting that '[t]ax exempt revenues should not be set off against deductible borrowing costs'.
35. *See* 6th recital of the ATAD.
36. *See* Article 4(5)(a) ATAD.
37. *See* Article 4(5)(b) ATAD.

forward and carry back disallowed interest expense.[38] Arguably, all these mechanisms would be crucial to an entity in a loss-making position so that it could carry forward its disallowed interest expense and offset it against the profit of future periods.[39] Yet, the introduction of measures to mitigate the economic double taxation of interest remains a discretionary exercise and, in addition, that such mitigating measures, even when implemented, may still be limited by the countries implementing them in terms of time and/or value.[40]

In addition to the above-mentioned mitigating measures, the BEPS Action 4 Reports have also outlined that the fixed earnings ratio itself could also be corrected by the countries, at their full discretion, in order to reduce the impact of non-deductibility of interest of an entity resulting from the short-term volatility of its earnings. In order to address this earnings volatility issue, it is suggested in the relevant reports the benchmarking of an entity's average economic activity over a certain period of time (instead of measuring its economic activity in a single year).[41] In addition, groups in different economic sectors may have different levels of leverage or that groups may intrinsically have different leverage and risk profiles.[42] In this respect, the BEPS Action 4 Rules suggest that countries could, if they so wish, correct or, at least, mitigate such distortion by combining the mandatory earnings fixed ratio rule with a group ratio rule.[43]

It follows from the above that the proposed BEPS Action 4 Rules did not include any mandatory mechanisms or measures to address the shortcomings of the proposed earnings ratio or to address the issue of double taxation, leaving it at the full discretion of the countries to implement any of the proposed optional measures to mitigate the non-deductibility of interest and related economic double taxation of interest that may arise as the result of such rules.

By restricting the deduction of the net interest expense of any entity up to a fixed proportion of its EBITDA, the final outcome of the BEPS Action 4 Rules is that such rules will ensure that a portion of the entity's adjusted profit (i.e., the profit or loss of the year increased or decreased, respectively, by the amount of non-deductible interest) is effectively subject to tax in that country.[44]

38. BEPS Action 4 Final Report, *supra* n. 5 at p. 68, para. 161; and BEPS Action 4 Updated Report, *supra* n. 5 at p. 72, para. 161.
39. BEPS Action 4 Final Report, *supra* n. 5 at p. 44, para. 77; and BEPS Action 4 Updated Report, *supra* n. 5 at p. 48, para. 77.
40. BEPS Action 4 Final Report, *supra* n. 5 at p. 69, para. 165; and BEPS Action 4 Updated Report, *supra* n. 5 at p. 73, para. 165.
41. BEPS Action 4 Final Report, *supra* n. 5 at pp. 67-68, paras 156-158; and BEPS Action 4 Updated Report, *supra* n. 5 at p. 71, paras 156-158.
42. BEPS Action 4 Final Report, *supra* n. 5 at p. 57, para. 115; and BEPS Action 4 Updated Report, *supra* n. 5 at p. 61, para. 115.
43. In such a case, only net interest expenses which would exceed both the benchmark fixed earnings ratio and the ratio of its group would be disallowed. *See* BEPS Action 4 Final Report, *supra* n. 5 at pp. 25, 57 and 67, and paras 22, 115-117 and 155; and BEPS Action 4 Updated Report, *supra* n. 5 at pp. 29-30, 61 and 71, and paras 22-23,115-117 and 155.
44. BEPS Action 4 Final Report, *supra* n. 5 at p. 47, para. 85; and BEPS Action 4 Updated Report, *supra* n. 5 at p. 51, para. 85.

### B ATAD's Article 4

The practical effect of transposing ATAD's Article 4 into the Member States' domestic tax laws is that the exceeding borrowing costs[45] incurred by any corporate taxpayer of a Member State on intra-group and third-party loans are only deductible for tax purposes up to 30% of the relevant taxpayer's EBITDA unless one of the group escape clauses allows the tax deductibility of a higher amount. Any exceeding borrowing costs above the said 30% EBITDA cap or above the amount allowed under any of the group escape clauses (if at all implemented by any of the Member States) would not be deductible for tax purposes in the hands of the relevant corporate taxpayer and would therefore be added back to its taxable income and subject to tax at the applicable standard rate.

Thus, in practice, this means that ATAD's Article 4 does not provide for any allowance to deduct any exceeding borrowing costs above the 30% EBITDA threshold in cases where the taxpayer would provide evidence that the net interest expenses were incurred for sound business reasons, do not concern artificial arrangements and were agreed at arm's length. Thus, the presumption of avoidance or use of excessive or artificial debt structures set by ATAD's Article 4 cannot be reversed in any way or form by the corporate taxpayer.

The next question addressed by ATAD's Article 4 was whether the disallowance of the tax deductibility of the amount exceeding borrowing costs of a taxpayer above the EBITDA cap or group escape clauses is permanently disallowed for tax purposes (or not). In this respect, the ATAD has opted to defer to the Member States on decisions relating to the implementation of such measures.

Pursuant to Article 4(6) of the ATAD, each Member State may (on a fully discretionary basis) implement ATAD's Article 4 in such a way as to give any corporate taxpayer one (or more) of the following rights:

(a) to carry forward indefinitely the amount of exceeding borrowing costs that cannot be deducted for tax purposes in any given tax year;[46] or
(b) to carry forward indefinitely, as well as to carry back for a maximum of three years, the amount of exceeding borrowing costs that cannot be deducted for tax purposes in any given tax year;[47] or
(c) to carry forward indefinitely the amount of exceeding borrowing costs that cannot be deducted for tax purposes in any given tax year, as well as to carry forward any unused interest capacity for a maximum of five years.[48]

The discretionary options proposed by ATAD's Article 4 to be implemented by the Member States (if they so wish) are in line with the mechanisms outlined by the

45. That is, the amount by which tax-deductible interest and similar financial payments incurred by a taxpayer in any given year exceed the taxable interest and similar financial revenues derived for the same tax year. *See supra* section II.2.B.
46. Article 4(6)(a) ATAD.
47. Article 4(6)(b) ATAD.
48. Article 4(6)(c) ATAD.

OECD under the BEPS Action 4 Reports in order to ensure a balanced application of the interest limitation rules over a number of years, as well as to reduce the effect of incidental fluctuations in the taxpayer's EBITDA and amount of net interest expense.[49]

Turning now to the issue of economic double taxation of interest resulting from the application of ATAD's Article 4, as a certain portion of interest expenses would not be deductible in the hands of the debtor, while the corresponding interest income would normally be taxed in the hands of the creditor. It should be noted that ATAD's Article 4 does not address this issue at all. This is particularly striking as the fifth recital of the ATAD clearly states that each of the rules proposed under the ATAD 'should not only aim to counter tax avoidance practices but also avoid creating other obstacles, such as double taxation'.

On the basis of the above, it seems fair to conclude that even though the ATAD does not include any specific provision to deal with the issue of double taxation arising from the application of its rules, such as the ones provided under ATAD's Article 4, it still lays down an important general principle in accordance with which whenever double taxation arises as a result of its application, EU corporate taxpayers should receive relief for the tax triggered in the other country. Yet, as this matter was not dealt with in the legal provisions of the ATAD itself, none of the Member States has considered this principle when transposing the ATAD into their domestic tax laws. That said, one can arguably submit that there is still room for this matter to be subject to a legal dispute in the future. Notably, the affected taxpayer could bring forward the content of the fifth recital of the ATAD, which provides that:

> it is necessary to lay down rules against the erosion of tax bases in the internal market and the shifting of profits out of the internal market. Rules in the following areas are necessary in order to contribute to achieving that objective: limitations to the deductibility of interest [...]. Where the application of those rules [such as the application of the interest limitation rule set under ATAD's Article 4] gives rise to double taxation, taxpayers should receive relief through a deduction for the tax paid in another Member State or third country, as the case may be.

## III CRITICAL ASSESSMENT OF THE BEPS ACTION 4 RULES AND ATAD'S ARTICLE 4

### 1 Were BEPS Action 4 Rules the Right Tool to Tackle the Identified Issues?

One of the focus points of the BEPS work carried out by the OECD was the possibility of MNEs using interest expenses to erode the tax base. In particular, the OECD identified three basic scenarios where the risks related to the deductibility of interest by MNEs may arise: (i) by allocating third-party debt to high-tax countries, (ii) by using intra-group loans to generate more interest expenses than the MNE's actual third-party

49. *See supra* section II.4.A regarding the BEPS Action 4 Rules.

interest expenses, and (iii) by using third-party or intra-group financing to fund tax-exempt assets.

Against this background, as noted above, the main goal of the BEPS Action 4 Reports was to make 'recommendations regarding best practices in the design of rules to prevent base erosion through the use of interest expense'.[50]

Now, the real question is whether the above-described BEPS Action 4 Rules[51] actually address the main risk scenarios submitted in the BEPS Action 4 Reports. In the author's view, this question should be answered in the negative for the main reasons outlined hereunder.

Firstly, the BEPS Action 4 Rules do not address the risk of MNEs allocating third-party debt to high-tax countries. This risk can still be achieved under the proposed rules. In order to illustrate this statement, let's consider the following example:

- Company A is subject to corporate income tax in country A at the rate of 25%. This company has received shareholder loans from its parent Company B in the amount of 100 million, yielding interest at the rate of 3.5% per annum, generating therefore an annual interest expense of 3.5 million. Company A has not received any interest income and its EBITDA for the same financial year is 12 million (after excluding from its earnings the amount of exempt income received of 3 million). Thus, assuming a 30% EBITDA fixed ratio rule, company A would continue to be able to deduct its full amount of net interest expenses of 3.5 million. Thus, BEPS Action 4 Rules would not impact the tax position of Company A.
- Company B is subject to corporate income tax in country B at the rate of 9% (thus, a considerably lower rate than in country A of 25%). Company B has received 50 million of equity from its shareholders and a third-party loan in the amount of 50 million at the rate of 2%. Company B has on-lent 100 million to Company A at the rate of 3.5%, retaining therefore a margin on these intra-group financing activities of 1.5% per annum. Company B is also not affected by the BEPS Action 4 Rules since it has a positive net interest position, i.e., the amount of interest income exceeds its interest expenses.

Second, BEPS Action 4 Rules have also not been tailored to address the possibility of MNEs eroding the tax base by using intra-group loans to generate more interest expenses than the MNE's actual third-party interest expenses. This can be illustrated by considering the same example depicted above. In our example, the amount of intra-group loans of 100 million generates more interest expenses than the MNE's actual third-party interest expenses due on the third-party loan in the amount of 50 million. Thus, by considering the above-mentioned example, one needs to conclude that these rules were designed in a way that defeats their main goals. Indeed, in order

50. BEPS Action 4 Final Report, *supra* n. 5 at p. 11; and BEPS Action 4 Updated Report, *supra* n. 5 at p. 13.
51. *See supra* II.1.A-II.4.A.

to tackle the issue of artificial 'intra-group' loans exceeding the MNE's third-party loans and related expenses, the rules should have been designed differently.

Notably, a worldwide group ratio rule could have been used as a starting point to decide whether an MNE would be subject (or not) to the BEPS Action 4 Rules or otherwise as a mandatory threshold provided by such rules. In this way, only when it would have been established that MNEs were eroding the tax base by using intra-group loans to generate more interest expenses than the MNE's actual third-party interest expenses, BEPS Action 4 Rules would kick in. Instead of making MNEs subject to such EBITDA fixed ratio, which could, at the countries' discretion, be supplemented by a worldwide group ratio rule allowing an entity to exceed this limit in certain circumstances. Similarly, if the MNE would be using intra-group loans to generate more interest expenses than the MNE's actual third-party interest expenses, BEPS Action 4 Rules should also kick in to restrict the tax-deductibility of such excessive interest expenses. On this basis, had BEPS Action 4 Rules remained consistent with its initial goals, they should have been designed differently so as to always capture a situation whereby intra-group loans would be used to generate more interest expenses than the MNE's actual third-party interest expenses. Likewise, if intra-group loans would instead not be used to generate more interest expenses than the MNE's actual third-party interest expenses, the MNE should not be affected by BEPS Action 4 Rules.

Thirdly, the use of third-party or intra-group financing to fund tax-exempt assets continues to be allowed under BEPS Action 4 Rules. While it is true that the mechanics of these rules do target this concern by excluding tax-exempt income or assets from the earnings or assets thresholds, BEPS Action 4 Rules, as such, do not prevent this issue. In other words, a company can still continue to use third-party or intra-group financing to fund tax-exempt assets, albeit subject to BEPS Action 4 Rules. As shown in the above-mentioned example, the fact that Company A uses expenses to finance tax-exempt assets, had no impact on its position under BEPS Action 4 Rules.

Again, the reason why BEPS Action 4 Rules fail to address the issue of using third-party or intra-group financing to fund tax-exempt assets is simply because these rules were actually not adequately targeted to address it. Yet, there were simple and straightforward rules that could have been implemented instead. Namely, by introducing interest recapture rules whereby interest expenses in connection with tax-exempt income would not be tax-deductible.[52]

It follows from the above analysis, that the recommended BEPS Action 4 Rules fail to address the three basic scenarios identified by the OECD in the BEPS Action 4 Reports where the risks related to the deductibility of interest by MNEs may arise. One

52. For example, Luxembourg has a recapture system according to which (i) any expenses incurred in connection with tax-exempt income are not deductible for tax purposes in that financial year and (ii) any capital gains realised will become taxable up to the amount of the aggregate expenses and write-downs in relation to the tax-exempt assets which were deducted for tax purposes during the year of realization of the exempt capital gain and in the previous years. In the same vein, some countries also have depreciation recapture rules whereby the realized gain from the disposal of an asset must be compared with the accumulated depreciation on the same asset since its acquisition. By doing so, the tax authorities can recapture the amount of depreciation of an asset which has been used to reduce the amount of taxes due on ordinary taxable income for the previous financial years of the same taxpayer.

may wonder why the OECD has in any case proposed such rules in the way it did. The rules could have easily been further refined in order to be better fit-for-purpose, by having gateway tests, simultaneous application of earnings and assets thresholds or interest recapture rules.

## 2 Was ATAD's Article 4 the Right Tool to Tackle the Identified Issues?

In accordance with the European Commission, the proposed interest limitation rules under ATAD's Article 4 were needed to counteract the so-called low-tax loans or to discourage artificial debt arrangements designed to minimize taxes. The so-called low-tax loans are perceived to be an artificial debt arrangement whereby the lender is located in a low-tax country so that the interest income triggers low or no tax, and the debtor is located in a high-tax country where it deducts its financing costs for tax purposes.[53]

Thus, it follows from the above that the goal of ATAD's Article 4 is to reduce the 'incentive to shift profits out of the State of origin to low or no tax jurisdictions'[54] by generally restricting the amount of net interest that can be deducted by any taxpayer. In light of the goal of the proposed ATAD's Article 4, the next question that one has to ask is whether the design and drafting of such proposed rules are in line with and proportional to their goal. For the same reasons, as the ones explained above in relation to the BEPS Action Rules,[55] this question should be answered in the negative.

Indeed, if one has a closer look at the scope of the said rules, one has to conclude that, similarly to the BEPS Action 4 Rules, ATAD's Article 4 is not a measure that actually counteracts 'low tax loans' or tackles artificial debt arrangements. The said rules are a revenue-raising measure simply disallowing the deductibility of any net interest and similar financial payments in the hands of the payer exceeding a certain threshold, regardless of whether: (i) the interest income is taxed at a high or low rate in the hands of the recipient or (ii) the relevant interest payment is a genuine payment and it is compliant with the ALP (or not).

ATAD's Article 4[56] works by reference to the net financing expenses of a company, which means that, provided that the financing costs of a certain taxpayer do not exceed its financing income, the rules will not kick in. In practice, this means that

---

53. *See, inter alia,* the justifications submitted by the European Commission for the need to enact interest deductibility rules under the European Commission's staff working document, *see* European Commission, Commission Staff Working Document accompanying the document Communication from the Commission to the European Parliament and the Council - Anti-Tax Avoidance Package: Next Steps towards delivering effective taxation and greater tax transparency in the EU SWD/2016/06 final (2016), https://eur-lex.europa.eu/legal-content/EN/TXT/?uri=CELEX:52016SC0006, at p. 26. *See also* the illustrative picture describing ATAD's Article 4, named as 'The Low Tax Loans: Interest Limitation Rules', *see* EU Tax & Customs, *Exit taxation, hybrid mismatches and interest limitation rules are part of the adopted #ATAD. #ECOFIN #FairTaxation,* Twitter (12 July 2016), https://twitter.com/eu_taxud/status/75282964961761 2800 (*see* photo 3).
54. European Commission, *supra* n. 53 at p. 26.
55. *See supra* explaining why the BEPS Action 4 Rules do not actually address the issue of the use of excessive debt financing granted to borrowers in high-tax countries.
56. For a detailed analysis of ATAD's Article 4, *see supra* II.1.B-II.4.B.

the rules, in fact, do not prevent, as initially intended, the situation whereby the borrower obtains tax relief for his financing costs in a high-tax jurisdiction and the lender is taxed at a low rate (or not taxed at all) on the interest income as it is located in a low-tax country. By way of example, if the treasury company of the group is located in a low-tax jurisdiction and the intra-group borrower is located in a high-tax jurisdiction, contrary to what one would have expected this potential tax avoidance arrangement through 'low-tax loans' is not mandatorily captured nor prevented by ATAD's Article 4. The reason for that is that ATAD's Article 4 does not link the allowance of the tax deductibility of the financing expenses with the tax treatment of the interest income in the hands of the recipient, as they should arguably have done in order to adequately target the identified problem of 'low tax loans' justifying the introduction of ATAD's Article 4. For the application of the 30% EBITDA threshold provided by ATAD's Article 4, it is immaterial whether any practice of 'low tax loans' is actually put in place by the taxpayer (or not) as these are mechanical and blind rules.

On this basis, it seems reasonable to conclude that ATAD's Article 4 simply implemented (or replicated) the BEPS Action 4 Rules without any critical assessment being made. In particular, no critical assessment was made on whether such interest limitation rules were fit-for-purpose and proportional to address the issue of debt shifting by MNEs 'whereby they obtain tax relief for excessive financing costs in high tax jurisdictions, while the interest income is shifted towards low or no tax jurisdictions'.[57] As a result, the proposed rules under ATAD's Article 4 do not address the issue, which was proposed to be addressed by these rules, and are also not proportional, as they are purely mechanical and blind rules.

## 3 Earnings: Is It an Objective Measure of an Entity's Economic Activity?

The OECD stated (and repeated it throughout the relevant reports) that BEPS Action 4 Rules should be endorsed because such rules restrict the 'ability of an entity to deduct interest expense based on an *objective measure* of its economic activity [author's emphasis]'.[58] However, the BEPS Action 4 Reports also admit that the same rules are also a '*blunt tool* which does not take into account the fact that groups operating in different sectors may require different amounts of leverage, and even within a sector some groups are more highly leveraged for non-tax reasons [author's emphasis]'.[59] In addition, earnings are also a quite volatile benchmark against which economic activity

57. *See* European Commission, *supra* n. 53 at p. 26 describing the objectives and features of the 'low tax loans: interest limitation rules' proposed under ATAD's Article 4.
58. BEPS Action 4 Final Report, *supra* n. 5 at p. 43, para. 72; and BEPS Action 4 Updated Report, *supra* n. 5 at p. 47, para. 72.
59. BEPS Action 4 Final Report, *supra* n. 5 at p. 26, para. 24; and BEPS Action 4 Updated Report, *supra* n. 5 at p. 30, para. 24. The same idea is repeated later in the relevant BEPS Action 4 Reports, *see* BEPS Action 4 Final Report, *supra* n. 5 at p. 47, para. 86; and BEPS Action 4 Updated Report, *supra* n. 5 at p. 51, para. 86.

can be measured.[60] With respect to the volatility of the earnings ratio proposed under the BEPS Action 4 Rules, it is interesting to point out some recent findings of the New Zealand authorities. On the basis of New Zealand's statistical data,[61] the aforesaid authorities have noted the difficulties for corporate taxpayers in anticipating the level of net interest expenses that may be deducted for tax purposes from year to year, which of course raises the issue of tax uncertainty brought by BEPS Action 4 Rules, but also the issue of the tax fairness of such rules.

Thus, this begs the question of why has then the OECD decided to endorse the BEPS Action 4 Rules on the basis of an earnings ratio. A careful review of the BEPS Action 4 Reports suggests that this proposal seems to be purely driven by pragmatic and simple reasons.

As remarked in the BEPS Action 4 Reports, the use of earnings-based rules presents several advantages (but also drawbacks, which will be discussed thereafter). The first one, as submitted by the OECD, is that a 'clear correlation between earnings and taxable income'[62] should be expected and that the earnings, as such, ought to be a 'useful indicator of an entity's ability to meet its obligations to pay interest'.[63] As a result, the earnings are considered in the relevant BEPS Action 4 Reports as the right benchmark to use in measuring the amount of debt an entity is able to borrow from related and unrelated parties. The second advantage is that earnings-based rules are more difficult to circumvent with tax planning strategies.[64] The reason for that is that it is only through the increase of its earnings (and therefore of its taxable income in a certain country) that an entity may increase its net interest deductions.[65]

Thus, as noted in the BEPS Action 4 Reports, the rules proposed thereunder ensure 'that an entity's net interest deductions are directly linked to the taxable income generated by its economic activities'.[66] In practice, this statement seems to suggest, that by implementing BEPS Action 4 Rules countries would be able to align interest deductions with taxable economic activity. The reason for that, as outlined by the OECD, is that 'measuring economic activity using earnings should be the most effective way to ensure that the ability to deduct net interest expense is matched with the activities that generate taxable income and drive value creation'.[67]

60. For more details, *see* the relevant BEPS Action 4 Reports discussing the downside of an earnings ratio and the recourse to the group ratio rule as an optional cap for the purposes of implementing the BEPS Action 4 Rules into domestic law. *See* BEPS Action 4 Final Report, *supra* n. 5 at pp. 43-45, paras 76 and 79; and BEPS Action 4 Updated Report, *supra* n. 5 at pp. 47-48, paras 76 and 79.
61. *See* New Zealand, Minister of Finance and Minister of Revenue, BEPS - Strengthening our interest limitation rules: a Government discussion document (3 March 2017), https://taxpolicy.ird.govt.nz/en/publications/2017/2017-dd-beps-interest-limitation, at Chapter 2, p. 6, n. 7.
62. BEPS Action 4 Final Report, *supra* n. 5 at p. 43, para. 73; and BEPS Action 4 Updated Report, *supra* n. 5 at p. 47, para. 73.
63. *Ibid.*
64. BEPS Action 4 Final Report, *supra* n. 5 at p. 43, para. 74; and BEPS Action 4 Updated Report, *supra* n. 5 at p. 47, para. 74.
65. *Ibid.*
66. BEPS Action 4 Final Report, *supra* n. 5 at p. 12; and BEPS Action 4 Updated Report, *supra* n. 5 at p. 14.
67. BEPS Action 4 Final Report, *supra* n. 5 at p. 43, para. 73; and BEPS Action 4 Updated Report, *supra* n. 5 at p. 47, para. 73.

From the perspective of the author, by proposing the implementation of the BEPS Action 4 Rules, OECD took a quite ground-breaking position because by doing so it clearly endorsed the idea that earnings should be used as the preferred proxy or measure to address artificial practices and profit shifting, at least, in the field of deduction of (net) interest expenses.

Moreover, the OECD by recommending the BEPS Action 4 Rules indirectly rejects the application of the long-standing ALP and of a full benchmarking analysis of the entity by reference to its functions, assets and risks to determine the amount of debt an entity is able to borrow or to attribute the fair/ arm's length amount of profits of the different entities of an MNE.

Similarly, the OECD also acknowledges that using earnings as a measure of the economic activity of an entity has also drawbacks. Notably, regarding the volatility of earnings and the difficulties of a group to compute up front the amount of net interest expenses that each group entity would be allowed to deduct, the proposed BEPS Action 4 Rules do not include any measures to address it. Instead, it is up to the countries to implement such rules to consider drafting such rules so as to allow the use of average earnings over a number of financial periods as the benchmark (instead of an annual earnings period benchmark) or by permitting the entity to carry forward disallowed interest expense and unused capacity to deduct interest.[68] The latter mechanism would be crucial to an entity in a loss-making position so that it could carry forward its disallowed interest expense and offset it against the profit of future periods.[69] Despite the importance of this issue, the BEPS Action 4 Rules have decided to leave it to the discretion of the countries to implement (or not) such corrections to the new proposed rules.[70]

Another disadvantage of an earnings fixed ratio is that it does not take into account the fact that groups in different economic sectors may have different levels of leverage or that groups may intrinsically have different leverage and risk profiles.[71] In order to address that issue, the BEPS Action 4 Rules proposed that countries could combine the mandatory earnings fixed ratio rule with an optional group ratio rule.[72] Again, even though the OECD acknowledges certain deficiencies or risks with the proposed BEPS Action 4 Rules, any mechanisms to correct the result of such rules remain fully optional and thus at the countries' full discretion to implement them (or not).

68. BEPS Action 4 Final Report, *supra* n. 5 at pp. 43-44, para. 76; and BEPS Action 4 Updated Report, *supra* n. 5 at pp. 47-48, para. 76.
69. BEPS Action 4 Final Report, *supra* n. 5 at p. 44, para. 77; and BEPS Action 4 Updated Report, *supra* n. 5 at p. 48, para. 77.
70. BEPS Action 4 Final Report, *supra* n. 5 at pp. 67-68, paras 156-158 and 161; and BEPS Action 4 Updated Report, *supra* n. 5 at pp. 71-72, paras 156-158 and 161.
71. BEPS Action 4 Final Report, *supra* n. 5 at p. 57, para. 115; and BEPS Action 4 Updated Report, *supra* n. 5 at p. 61, para. 115.
72. BEPS Action 4 Final Report, *supra* n. 5 at p. 25, para. 22 and p. 57, para. 115; and BEPS Action 4 Updated Report, *supra* n. 5 at pp. 29-30, paras 22-23 and p. 61, para. 115. For completeness, it is noted that the detailed guidance on the elements of design and operation of the optional group ratio rule was only included in the BEPS Action 4 Updated Report.

Similarly, and even more surprisingly, ATAD's Article 4 has also decided not to fix some of these shortcomings, when trying to develop a common standard and 'minimum level of protection for national corporate tax systems against tax avoidance practices across the Union'[73] under the ATAD. By way of example, Member States may freely decide to implement (or not to implement) group escape clauses, which can allow the tax deductibility of interest up to the relevant group ratio (instead of up to the 30% EBITDA threshold), or to provide/not provide for a *de minimis* threshold to apply these rules, or to exclude/not to exclude certain taxpayers or certain loans. Thus, the next question that one may ask is what should be considered the minimum level of protection in this regard. After all, each of these possibilities will only be available to taxpayers doing business in a Member State that has implemented such optional clauses. Furthermore, no critical assessment was done in the ATAD on whether the relatively straightforward rule recommended by BEPS Action 4 Rules was the right minimum level of protection to be implemented at the EU level and whether such rules really ensure that an entity's interest deductions are directly linked to its economic activity (or not).

Against this background, it is fair to conclude that earnings are indeed a pragmatic and easy way to measure an entity's economic activity, but they are also a 'blunt tool'[74] that the OECD BEPS Action 4 Reports should have corrected or recalibrated before recommending it under the BEPS Action 4 Rules. Likewise, the EU has also missed the opportunity of recalibrating BEPS Action 4 Rules when it implemented them in the ATAD's Article 4.

## 4 Dismissal of the Long-Standing ALP by BEPS Action 4 Rules and ATAD's Article 4: Was It Justified?

At the outset, it is important to recall that the overarching aim of the proposed BEPS Action 4 Rules is of 'aligning interest deductions with taxable economic activity'.[75] Thus, the main rationale of the proposed BEPS Action 4 Rules is to ensure, in as much as possible,[76] that a 'portion of an entity's profits remains subject to tax'[77] in that country, as clearly stated in the BEPS Action 4 Reports.

73. *See* 3rd recital of the ATAD. The same recital also clarifies that there is a need 'to coordinate the responses of Member States in implementing the outputs of the 15 OECD Action Items against BEPS with the aim to improve the effectiveness of the internal market as a whole in tackling tax avoidance practices'.
74. BEPS Action 4 Final Report, *supra* n. 5 at p. 26, para. 24; and BEPS Action 4 Updated Report, *supra* n. 5 at p. 30, para. 24.
75. BEPS Action 4 Final Report, *supra* n. 5 at p. 18, para. 8; and BEPS Action 4 Updated Report, *supra* n. 5 at p. 22, para. 8.
76. It is quite clear that if the corporate taxpayer is in a tax-loss making position, it can still remain in a tax-loss position after the application of the BEPS Action 4 Rules. However, the amount of its tax losses, which would normally be carried forward to offset its future taxable profits, would have nonetheless been decreased as a result of the application of the said rules.
77. BEPS Action 4 Final Report, *supra* n. 5 at p. 47, para. 85; and BEPS Action 4 Updated Report, *supra* n. 5 at p. 51, para. 85.

In other words, one of the main goals of the BEPS Action 4 Rules is therefore to, in as much as possible, ensure a minimum effective taxation of business profits in the source country that was allegedly being abusively eroded by tax-deductible interest payments.[78]

This begs the question of why BEPS Action 4 Rules dismissed the long-standing ALP when their goal is also to function as a new allocation of taxing rights rule by 'ensuring that a portion of an entity's profit remains subject to tax in a country'.[79] A detailed analysis of the BEPS Action 4 Reports suggests that the choice made by the OECD was mainly driven by pragmatic reasons.

First, the arm's length tests (as well as withholding taxes) were deliberately not scrutinized in (and were even excluded from the scope of) the consultation process carried out under the BEPS Action 4 Reports.[80] Second, the application of arm's length test rules to limit the deductibility of interest payments, as such, would be burdensome to apply and may still prove ineffective.[81] Third, the application of arm's length test rules is focused on the particular commercial circumstances of an entity which is very time-consuming for the taxpayer and for the tax administration and does not ensure the required upfront security and certainty, despite its advantage of recognizing that entities may have different levels of interest expense depending on their circumstances and would normally not distort genuine commercial behaviour.[82] Fourth, the arm's length test rules do not prevent an entity from claiming deductions on interest expenses which are economically linked with exempt assets or exempt streams of income, which, as noted earlier, is a specific risk and concern outlined in the BEPS Action 4 Reports.

Likewise, ATAD's Article 4, building on BEPS Action 4 Rules, also dismissed the ALP without further consideration. In particular, it should be recalled here that previously, in June 2010, the EU Council adopted a resolution on the coordination of the Member State's tax policies with regard to anti-abuse provisions where it was, e.g., reaffirmed that thin capitalization rules need to be compliant with the ALP.[83] In this respect, it is quite interesting to note that the non-exhaustive list of indicators suggesting an artificial transfer of profits (through the use of excessive debt financing) already included at the time the same caps and thresholds as the ones provided under BEPS Action 4 Rules and ATAD's Article 4. Namely, (i) capping (in principle) net

78. As clearly outlined in the BEPS Action 4 Reports, 'the premise underlying the fixed ratio rule is that an entity should be able to deduct interest expense up to a specified proportion of EBITDA, ensuring that a portion of an entity's profit remains subject to tax in a country', *see* BEPS Action 4 Final Report, *supra* n. 5 at p. 47, para. 85; and BEPS Action 4 Updated Report, *supra* n. 5 at p. 51, para. 85.
79. *Ibid.*
80. *See* OECD, Public Discussion Draft BEPS Action 4: Interest Deductions and Other Financial Payments, OECD/G20 Base Erosion and Profit Shifting Project (18 December 2014), https://www.oecd.org/ctp/aggressive/discussion-draft-action-4-interest-deductions.pdf, at p. 13, paras 21-22.
81. *Ibid.*
82. *Ibid. See also* BEPS Action 4 Final Report, *supra* n. 5 at p. 19, para. 12; and BEPS Action 4 Updated Report, *supra* n. 5 at p. 24, para. 12.
83. *See* Council Resolution of 8 June 2010 on coordination of the Controlled Foreign Corporation (CFC) and thin capitalization rules within the European Union, OJ C 156, 16.6.2010.

interest above a certain earnings threshold and (ii) a comparison of the debt-to-equity ratio of the company with the debt-to-equity ratio of the group.[84]

Thus, even though the application of the ALP to thin capitalization rules was undoubtedly endorsed by the EU Council in 2010, the latter was also not immune to the evolution of thin capitalization rules into broader interest limitation rules, which had already started before the BEPS Action 4 Rules were recommended by the OECD. Yet, pursuant to this EU Council's Resolution, there is no direct linkage between exceeding such indicators and the definite conclusion of the existence of an artificial transfer of profits through the use of excessive debt financing (or thin capitalization). This therefore means that, in 2010, the EU taxpayer still retained the right to show that its debt financing structure, if deemed excessive under thin capitalization rules, could in fact still be justified by valid commercial reasons and should therefore be considered at arm's length.[85] Unfortunately, six years later, this was not the path followed by ATAD's Article 4, which simply replicated the BEPS Action 4 Rules without any further thought being given to the previous EU framework regulating this matter.

Considering that the ALP is a long-standing international tax principle and standard, in the author's view, dismissing it for purely pragmatic reasons does not seem to be justified.

## 5 Interaction of Article 9 of the OECD Model Convention and BEPS Action 4 Rules

As regards the interaction of thin capitalization and interest limitation rules, such as the ones recommended by BEPS Action 4 Rules, with Article 9(1), it should be noted that quite recently the OECD launched a paper which proposes changes to the OECD Commentary on Article 9.[86] The proposed changes build on and also cross-refer to the previous work of the OECD on financial transactions, whose findings were also

84. *See* section B of the relevant Council Resolution, *supra* n. 83, which provides that:

> With respect to Thin Capitalization rules, which will respect the arm's length principle, the assessment will be on a case-by-case basis. A non-exhaustive list of indicators suggesting an artificial transfer of profits includes in particular the following:
>
> a. the level of debt to equity is excessive;
> b. the amount of net interest paid by the company goes beyond a certain threshold of the earnings before interest and taxes (EBIT) or of the earnings before interest, taxes, depreciation and amortization (EBITDA);
> c. a comparison between the equity percentage of the company to that of the group worldwide appears to prove that the debt is excessive.

85. *See* the relevant Council Resolution, *supra* n. 83, which states that: 'thin capitalisation rules which observe the arm's-length principle are capable of preventing tax avoidance, or maintaining the balanced allocation of taxing powers, or both' and that 'thin capitalisation rules can usefully comprise "safe harbour" criteria beyond which the possibility of abuse is highest so long as the taxpayer is allowed to produce evidence of the contrary'.
86. *See* OECD, *Proposed Changes to Commentaries in the OECD Model Tax Convention on Article 9 and on related Articles* (29 March 2021), https://www.oecd.org/tax/treaties/public-consultation-document-proposed-changes-to-commentaries-in-oecd-mtc-on-article-9.pdf, at p. 6.

included in the 2022 update to the OECD Transfer Pricing Guidelines.[87] In this respect, the proposed revised OECD Commentary on Article 9 states that 'in order to ensure the elimination of double taxation, the arm's length principle and the guidance on its interpretation in the OECD Transfer Pricing Guidelines should be followed in any re-writing of accounts'.[88]

Subsequently, the newly proposed paragraph 3 of the commentary on Article 9 no longer makes reference to thin capitalization rules, but rather focuses on the arm's length adjustments allowed under Article 9, such as examining the terms and conditions of the loan such as the rate of interest or whether a purported loan should be regarded as a loan or as another kind of transaction, in particular a contribution to equity capital.[89]

Furthermore, the new commentary on Article 9 also discusses the relationship between BEPS Action 4 Rules and this article in the new proposed paragraph 3.1, which reads as follows:

> Once the profits of the two enterprises have been allocated in accordance with the arm's length principle, it is for the domestic law of each Contracting State to determine whether and how such profits should be taxed, as long as there is conformity with the requirements of other provisions of the Convention. Article 9 does not deal with the issue of whether expenses are deductible when computing the taxable income of either enterprise. The conditions for the deductibility of expenses are a matter to be determined by domestic law, subject to the provisions of the Convention and, in particular, paragraph 4 of Article 24. Paragraph 30 of the Commentary on Article 7 makes an equivalent statement for the application of Article 7. Examples of domestic rules that can deny a deduction for expenses include certain rules on entertainment expenses and on interest such as those recommended in the final report on Action 4 of the OECD/G20 Base Erosion and Profit Shifting (BEPS) Project.[90]

Thus, despite the clear correlation between BEPS Action 4 Rules and ensuring certain minimum taxation in the source country clearly stated in the BEPS Action 4 Reports, the OECD now submits a different view. Instead, the OECD now states that BEPS Action 4 Rules should be considered as a general rule concerning the determination of taxable profits, which may include rules denying a deduction for interest

---

87. *See* OECD, *Transfer Pricing Guidance on Financial Transactions: Inclusive Framework on BEPS Actions 4, 8-10* (11 February 2020), https://www.oecd.org/tax/beps/transfer-pricing-guidance-on-financial-transactions-inclusive-framework-on-beps-actions-4-8-10.pdf. Subsequently, these findings were included in the recent update to the OECD Transfer Pricing Guidelines, *see* paras 10.4-10.13 of the OECD, *OECD Transfer Pricing Guidelines for Multinational Enterprises and Tax Administrations 2022* (OECD Publishing, 2022) (cit. OECD TP Guidelines). Notably, interest limitation rules, like the ones proposed by the BEPS Action 4 Rules, were not considered to be within the scope of those OECD publications, *see* para. 10.9 of the aforesaid OECD publications. By contrast, the issue of qualification of the financial instrument as debt or equity has been dealt with in those publications, i.e., whether a prima facie loan can be regarded as a loan for tax purposes or whether it should be considered as some other kind of capital contribution, such as a contribution to equity capital.
88. *See* OECD, *supra* n. 86 at p. 5, new para. 2.
89. *See ibid.*, new para. 3. and OECD TP Guidelines, *supra* n. 87, paras 10.4-10.13.
90. *See* OECD, *supra* n. 86 at p. 6, new para. 3.1. and, in the same vein (albeit in a briefly manner), OECD TP Guidelines, *supra* n. 87, para. 10.9.

expenses. The author does not consider this position to be appropriate for the reasons outlined hereunder.

As noted above,[91] the aim of the BEPS Action 4 Rules is not to restrict the deductibility of interest payments as such, but instead to prevent an MNE from discretionarily allocating the interest expenses within the group in such a way as to select the country where the deductibility of interest expenses will actually be incurred. Thus, the goal of these rules is to prevent an MNE from electing, or being able to manipulate, the country where the interest payments of the group entities will be tax-deductible. As clearly stated in the BEPS Action 4 Reports, the main premise underpinning BEPS Action 4 Rules is to ensure 'that a portion of an entity's profit remains subject to tax in a country'.[92]

Similarly, the goal of thin capitalization rules is also to prevent MNEs from taking advantage of the differential tax treatment of debt and equity in order to minimize the taxable income beyond a permissible level. As rightly pointed out by Australia's future tax system review panel in 2010:

> The thin capitalisation rules can be seen as placing a limit on the degree to which the normal, risk-adjusted, return from an investment in Australia can be excluded from Australian tax (by being characterised as a return on debt) and the extent to which it is taxable (as the return on equity). ... thin capitalisation and transfer pricing rules should continue to be used as mechanisms to *ensure that what is judged to be the appropriate level of tax is collected from investments in Australia* [emphasis added].[93]

Against this background, in the author's view, BEPS Action 4 Rules should instead be considered as an anti-abuse rule which tries to reallocate taxing rights, just like thin capitalization or fat capitalization rules try to do too, instead of being a general rule for the determination of the taxable profits, like the OECD and some commentators tend to consider.[94,95] Like other commentators noted, BEPS Action 4 Rules target the 'strategic allocation of interest expenditure within corporate groups'[96] and 'are apparently more directed toward issues about the location of the interest expense, rather

91. *See supra* II.1.A-II.4.A and III.3.
92. BEPS Action 4 Final Report, *supra* n. 5 at p. 47, para. 85; and BEPS Action 4 Updated Report, *supra* n. 5 at p. 51, para. 85.
93. *See* Review Panel of Australia's Future Tax System, Australia's future tax system, *Report to the Treasurer, Part Two Detailed Analysis*, Vol. 1 (Commonwealth of Australia 2010), https://treasury.gov.au/sites/default/files/2019-10/afts_final_report_part_2_vol_1_consolidated.pdf, at pp. 179-180.
94. *See also* Fernandes, *supra* n. 7, at sections 4.4.2.2, and 5.2-5.4 (especially section 5.2.2 and references referred therein).
95. For a recent support of the OECD's position, *see*, for all, Vikram Chand, Alessandro Turina & Kinha Romanovska, *Tax Treaty Obstacles in Implementing the Pillar Two Global Minimum Tax Rules and a Possible Solution for Eliminating the Various Challenges*, 14 World Tax Journal 1, pp. 3-50 (2022) considering that the BEPS Action 4 Rules 'do not seem to conflict with article 9 as they are a general rule for the determination of the taxable profit of the payor. The fact that the rule applies only to a payor (who is a part of the MNE group) does not change this conclusion as it applies to all interest payments made by such a payor' at p. 23 (which is based on the authors' previous analysis at pp. 21-23 and references referred therein).
96. Hugh J. Ault & Brian J. Arnold, *Comparative Income Taxation: A Structural Analysis*, 3rd revised edition (Kluwer Law International 2010), at p. 510.

than denying the interest completely'.[97] This statement can also be further substantiated by the main reasons outlined hereunder. That said, there is quite an important difference between thin capitalization rules and BEPS Action 4 Rules. The former build on and work by reference to the ALP, whereas the latter do not work by reference to the ALP, but instead rely on mechanical thresholds.[98]

Firstly, as a general rule, BEPS Action 4 Rules are not applicable to all taxpayers operating in a certain country. Instead, these rules clearly target specific entities (either PEs and/or subsidiaries of non-resident entities) which belong to an MNE. In other words, to fall within the scope of the BEPS Action 4 Rules, the relevant taxpayer has to belong to a group of companies or MNE, instead of being a standalone group.

As clearly stated in the BEPS Action 4 Reports, BEPS Action 4 Rules may still be applied to standalone entities only when additional risk factors are identified, such as the fact that such standalone entities are held through complex holding structures. The reason being that only in this specific situation, it can be fairly assumed that the 'level of base erosion and profit shifting risk may be similar to that posed by a group structure'.[99]

In a similar vein, ATAD's Article 4 also provides for the exclusion of low-risk entities from the scope of these rules if the Member States so wish.[100] As explained in the eighth recital of the ATAD, the possible exclusion of standalone entities from the scope of ATAD's Article 4 is justified because, in the absence of intra-group debt arrangements, the risks of tax avoidance are fairly limited.[101]

Secondly, BEPS Action 4 Rules only restrict the deductibility of net interest expenses, i.e., deductible interest expenses on funds borrowed minus interest income received on amounts lent by the relevant taxpayer. Arguably, a general rule for the determination of taxable income, as well as an overall limitation of the deductibility of interest expenses for tax purposes, should be applicable to gross or total (instead of net)

97. Graham S. Cooper, *Theories of Modern Tax Reformers*, 15 The Tax Specialist 1 (2011), at p. 12.
98. In this respect, it is interesting to note that, in accordance with the ATAD, the European Commission Services deemed, e.g., the Slovenia thin capitalization rules as being equally effective to ATAD's Article 4. The Slovenian thin capitalization rules only apply to interest on loans from shareholders holding directly or indirectly at any time during the tax year at least 25% of the capital or voting rights of the Slovenian taxpayer. These rules also rely on debt-to-equity ratio and the ALP, instead of covering both intra-group and third-party debt or relying on mechanical thresholds. On this basis, Slovenia has not yet implemented ATAD's Article 4. As such, Slovenia may continue to apply its thin capitalization rules for intra-group loans inly until 1 January 2024 at the latest, after which it must transpose the ATAD provision into its legislation. This is also an additional argument to make the case that thin capitalization rules and interest limitation rules target the exact same issue and have therefore the same exact nature, albeit by reference to different mechanics and thresholds.
99. BEPS Action 4 Final Report, *supra* n. 5 at p. 34, para. 52; and BEPS Action 4 Updated Report, *supra* n. 5 at p. 38, para. 52.
100. *See* last paragraph of Article 4(3) ATAD and, for more details, on this point *see supra* II.1.A.
101. With respect to the exclusion of standalone entities, it is interesting to note that the 8th recital of the ATAD clearly states that it is appropriate and justified to exclude them from the scope of ATAD's Article 4 because of the limited risks of tax avoidance by such entities '[s]ince BEPS in principle takes place through excessive interest payments among entities which are associate enterprises'. Yet, that said, this statement is at odds with the objective scope of the relevant rules which cover and restrict the interest deductibility of any related- and unrelated-party debt exceeding a certain cap (without any exception in the case of limited or nil tax avoidance risks).

interest expenses. In other words, for the purpose of computing the taxable income of a taxpayer, it should be immaterial whether the allowable deductible interest expenses are offset by the same amount of interest income (or not). As a matter of fact, for the determination of net income the deduction of all genuine business expenses is normally allowed. This is, unlike the functioning of the BEPS Action 4 Rules, it is generally not required for the deduction of business expenses for tax purposes that such expenses are wholly or partially compensated by positive income. If that were to be the case, a company could never be in a tax-loss position as the deductibility of its expenses would be permissible in so far as such expenses would be covered by positive income only. In fact, the underlying reasoning for BEPS Action 4 Rules to exclusively target and cap net interest expenses is that only in that case scenario is there a tangible and real fear from the relevant country that the location of interest expenses within the MNE has been manipulated and that, as a consequence, the taxable base in that country might have been (or be at risk of being) excessively eroded.

Thirdly, one also needs to consider the key role attributed to the comparison of the level of debt of the group in a certain country with the worldwide level of debt of the same group. The worldwide gearing debt amount works both as a leverage threshold, above which the deductibility of net interest payments may be restricted, and as an escape clause as it shows the consistency of the leverage of the domestic entity with the leverage of the worldwide group. Hence, it is exactly this domestic-worldwide group leverage consistency that provides evidence of the non-existence of planning and manipulation of the allocation of interest expenses across the different countries where the MNE operates. Conversely, the discrepancy between the domestic-worldwide group leverage is deemed to provide sufficient evidence of planning and manipulation of the allocation of interest expenses across the different countries where the MNE operates.

In contrast, if the BEPS Action 4 Rules were indeed a general rule on the determination of taxable income, one would expect that the worldwide gearing debt amount would not be taken into account as it would constitute an irrelevant factor for these purposes. Doing otherwise would mean that the computation of the taxable income would no longer be an objective exercise nor determined on the basis of the accounts of the relevant taxpayer. In fact, the outcome of the computation of the taxable income of two entities under the exact same facts and circumstances would vary depending on the amount of leverage of the group to which each entity belonged. From a tax policy standpoint, such an outcome in the determination of the taxable income would normally not be acceptable because of its absolute arbitrariness and randomness. By contrast, the domestic-worldwide leverage ratio seems to be a conceivable and acceptable factor to be taken into account among other factors in order to ascertain whether the debt-to-equity ratio of an entity is at arm's length or even to determine the arm's length debt-to-equity ratio of an entity.[102,103]

102. By way of example, the capital structure of the enterprise is a factor to be taken into account to determine the capital structure of a PE under the thin capitalization approach proposed by the OECD under the Authorised OECD Approach (AOA), *see* OECD, *2010 Report on the Attribution*

## 6 BEPS Action 4 Rules and ATAD's Article 4: Unsolved Economic Double Taxation of Interest

Any interest paid on the excessive debt, i.e., above the stipulated legal threshold by the BEPS Action 4 Rules or ATAD's Article 4, will be disallowed as a deductible interest payment for tax purposes in the hands of the debtor. As a result, the interest paid on the excessive amount of debt will be added back to the taxable income of the taxpayer in the relevant year and taxed at the standard corporate income tax rate in the hands of the debtor.[104] In addition, none of these rules recharacterizes the non-deductible interest as a dividend payment.

The BEPS Action 4 Rules or ATAD's Article 4 do not include any mandatory mechanism to address the issue of economic double taxation as well, but instead prefer to simply describe and discuss possible mechanisms or optional rules to the Member States (in the case of ATAD's Article 4) to minimize the negative effects of the volatility of the entity's earnings over a certain period of time (i.e., carry back and/or carry forward of disallowed interest expense and/or carry forward of unused interest capacity), leaving it to the countries or the Member States to decide at their own full discretion whether to include such mechanisms (or not) when implementing the relevant rules.

Despite the importance of the problem of economic double taxation of interest, the OECD decided to take the position that the introduction of the aforementioned measures remains at the full discretion of the countries, which may opt to implement them (or not) or to implement them subject to certain limitations.[105] This position is particularly striking, considering that the aim set by the OECD for the BEPS project

*of Profits to Permanent Establishments* (22 July 2010), https://www.oecd.org/ctp/transfer-pricing/45689524.pdf at Part I, para. 130. The same OECD report also discusses an important matter regarding a situation where a PE would be entirely funded by third-party debt clearly stating that adjustment to the PE's capital structure 'would be consistent with Article 7 to make such an adjustment, given that the PE when hypothesised as a separate and independent enterprise would have free capital as discussed earlier in the Report' (*see* Part I, para. 167; followed by an explanation in the following paragraph of how such adjustment could be done).

103. Similarly, as noted above, the EU Council's Resolution of 8 June 2010, *supra* n. 83, included as relevant indicators for the purposes of determining whether, on a case-by case basis, a company is thinly capitalized, which should remain in compliance with the ALP, the comparison of the debt-to-equity of a taxpayer to the debt-to-equity ratio of the group and having an amount of net interest expenses above a certain EBIT/EBITDA threshold. However, subsequently, both the OECD and the EU have recommended the introduction of or have adopted interest limitation rules under BEPS Action 4 and ATAD's Article 4, respectively, which work by reference to blind mechanical caps without any reliance on the ALP.

104. With respect to this, it is worth noting that the first paragraph of the OECD Commentary on Article 11 states that 'unlike dividends, interest does not suffer economic double taxation, that is, it is not taxed both in the hands of the debtor and in the hands of the creditor'. Against the back of the BEPS Action 4 Rules and ATAD's Article 4, it is now time to reconsider this statement as well as to address the new issue of economic double taxation of interest by means of non-deduction of interest in the hands of the debtor brought by these rules.

105. BEPS Action 4 Final Report, *supra* n. 5 at p. 68, paras 159 and 161 and p. 69, para. 165; and BEPS Action 4 Updated Report, *supra* n. 5 at p. 72, paras 159 and 161 and p. 73, para. 165.

would be to propose new rules to address BEPS, such as the BEPS Action 4 Rules, but such new rules 'should not result in double taxation'.[106]

The same narrative was conveyed under ATAD's Article 4. As per the fifth recital to the ATAD:

> Where the application of those rules gives rise to double taxation, taxpayers should receive relief through a deduction for the tax paid in another Member State or third country, as the case may be. Thus, the rules should not only aim to counter tax avoidance practices but also avoid creating other obstacles to the market, such as double taxation.

Yet, ATAD's Article 4 is completely mute in relation to the issue of economic double taxation so created and on the solution to address such issue. In compliance with the relevant recitals to the ATAD, one would have expected the EU legislator to assess the practical result of each of the newly proposed anti-avoidance rules, as well as to present solutions for any double taxation created by such new rules. Unfortunately, this was not the path followed by the EU legislator in the ATAD's Article 4.[107]

On this basis, it is not expected that the creditor's country of residence will provide relief for the economic double taxation of the interest disallowed in accordance with the BEPS Action 4 Rules or ATAD's Article 4. The reason being that these rules do not rely on the ALP. Thus, while the application of BEPS Action 4 Rules or ATAD's Article 4 leads to economic double taxation of interest, no definite and mandatory solution is provided by any of these rules.

## IV CONCLUDING REMARKS

The fear of base erosion through the use of excessive intra-group debt financing has led different countries to introduce so-called thin capitalization rules. In the last couple of years, many countries, as well as international organizations such as the OECD and the EU, have been taking the view that due to their narrow scope, the thin capitalization rules do not properly prevent the use of excessive leveraging by MNEs.

Against this background, certain countries have replaced and entirely substituted traditional intra-group thin capitalization rules with comprehensive interest limitation rules. These new rules have also been endorsed by the OECD under BEPS Action 4 and adopted by the EU under the ATAD (ATAD's Article 4). In a nutshell, the latter are domestic protective measures which limit the total amount of related- and/or unrelated-party debt capital with which an entity may be funded, by reference to an asset ratio and/or earnings cap and/or the worldwide asset debt ratio of the group to which the entity belongs.

In a cross-border scenario, these interest limitation rules led to a new kind of economic double taxation of interest whereby interest is taxed in the hands of the

106. *See* back cover page of the BEPS Action 4 Final Report and back cover page of the BEPS Action 4 Updated Report.
107. For an earlier discussion of this important issue, *see also* the comments made *supra* in section II.4.B.

debtor by means of non-deduction of the interest payment for tax purposes, and in the hands of the related or unrelated party creditor who will be taxed on the full amount of the interest income received. It is not expected that the residence country of the creditor/the recipient of income will be prepared to address this new kind of economic double taxation of interest.

Against this background, it is time for BEPS Action 4 Rules and ATAD's Article 4 to be revisited. These rules should either be revamped or, at least, be recalibrated in order to include an antidote for the economic double taxation created by these rules. This could be achieved by the simultaneous application of an earnings and debt threshold, instead of just an earnings threshold. In addition, a mandatory escape clause should always be provided whenever the leverage of the company is consistent with the worldwide leverage of the group and/ or does not exceed the third-party debt received by the same group. Finally, recourse of the taxpayer to the ALP should also be considered.

Finally, looking ahead, as BEPS Pillar Two takes shape and its roll-out starts to be considered, including its transposition at the EU level, one needs to start considering the consistency of all these different new rules. BEPS Pillar Two (also referred to as the '*Global Anti-Base Erosion*' or '*GloBE*' proposal) calls for the development of a coordinated set of rules to address ongoing risks from structures that allow MNEs to shift profit to jurisdictions where they are subject to no or very low taxation. Does it make sense for BEPS Action 4 Rules and ATAD's Article 4 to coexist with Pillar Two Rules or should they be revamped accordingly? In other words, should BEPS Action 4 Rules and ATAD's Article 4 be redesigned so as to be consistent with the new Pillar Two Rules? For instance, one option could be to consider that BEPS Action 4 Rules and ATAD's Article 4 would apply to gross interest payments (instead of net interest payments), which could only be tax-deductible if the corresponding interest income had attracted sufficient taxation in the hands of the recipient. Conversely, the gross interest payment would not be tax-deductible if the corresponding interest income had not attracted sufficient taxation in the hands of the recipient. In addition, traditional thin capitalization rules would deal with the issue of the use of excessive debt financing by MNEs.

While time will tell whether BEPS Action 4 Rules and ATAD's Article 4 will be reconsidered (or not), it is important for the OECD and the EU to consider the consistency of all the different rules and their compliance costs as well as to ensure that any new rules do not create double taxation. Unsolved economic double taxation has a serious impact on businesses and therefore needs to be addressed.

# PART III ALP Framework for Financial Transactions: A Transactional Approach

## A Credit Ratings/Default Risk: Considerations

CHAPTER 6

# Shadow Credit Ratings for Intercompany Transactions

*Georg Dettmann & Diana Kabir*[*]

## I INTRODUCTION

In the context of intercompany financing transactions, assessing the borrowing company's creditworthiness is a critical step for deriving a suitable interest rate.

A shadow credit rating is in fact a necessary comparability criterion when evaluating comparable market prices for financial transactions. In particular, for determining the appropriate conditions for an intragroup loan, it is necessary to analyse the conditions under which a comparable company would take out a loan on the open market. To do this, the creditworthiness of the company receiving the loan must be determined. If there is already a publicly available rating, this can be used.[1] If no credit rating is available for the receiving company, a so-called shadow rating is first created (shadow credit rating).

This chapter provides an introduction to shadow credit ratings and methods for how to approximate this rating in an intercompany context. We determine a standalone credit rating for a subsidiary, including considerations for implicit support, instrument rating, and country risk and their effects on the final credit rating.

Using the method described in this chapter, an assessment of creditworthiness can be estimated which then forms the basis of the rest of the analysis in the determination of an arm's-length interest rate on intragroup loans.

---

* The views and opinions set forth herein are the personal views or opinions of the authors; they do not necessarily reflect the views or opinions of the organization with which the authors are associated.

1. If a group rating is already established and publicly available, it can be relied on, as long as the group guarantees the amounts loaned to the respective subsidiary.

## II BACKGROUND ON CURRENT GUIDANCE

Intragroup financial transactions have become an important transfer pricing topic in recent years. Besides the different national laws that govern various jurisdictions, the Organisation for Economic Co-operation and Development (OECD) has issued overarching guidance on the treatment of financial transactions in an intercompany context. In addition to the 2017 Transfer Pricing Guidelines (TPGs),[2] the OECD issued its specific Transfer Pricing Guidance on Financial Transactions in 2020,[3] which reflected the increased importance of the topic. For the first time, the OECD has provided a more coherent framework for analysing the commercial and financial relations amongst related parties in a financial transaction. In January 2022, the OECD published the 2022 edition of the OECD Transfer Pricing Guidelines for Multinational Enterprises and Tax Administrations,[4] which consolidates the changes to the 2017 edition of the Transfer Pricing Guidelines (resulting from, e.g., the Transfer Pricing Guidelines on Financial Transactions from 2020) into a single publication.

In its approach, the OECD emphasizes the need for an analytical framework to effectively document financial transactions. For using credit ratings in a context of, say, intercompany loans, the OECD stipulates an elaborate framework. The OECD defines credit ratings as follows:[5]

> The credit rating of an MNE or MNE group (usually referred to as the 'issuer credit rating') is an opinion about its general creditworthiness. Such an opinion is usually premised on the MNE or MNE group's capacity and willingness to meet its financial obligations in accordance with the terms of those obligations. The credit rating [...] is effectively a form of relative ranking of the creditworthiness in comparison to other borrowers. In general, a lower credit rating will indicate a greater risk of default and be expected to result in a higher rate of return for lenders.

With regard to credit ratings in the context of intercompany transactions, the OECD further stipulates:[6]

> Where an MNE has a publicly available credit rating published by an independent credit rating agency, that rating may be informative for an arm's length analysis of the MNE's controlled financing transactions. However, in most cases, publicly available credit ratings are only available for the MNE group. An approach often used for a specific MNE is to *apply quantitative and qualitative analyses* [emphasis added] of the individual characteristics of the MNE using *publicly available financial tools or independent credit rating agencies' methodologies* [emphasis

2. OECD, *OECD Transfer Pricing Guidelines for Multinational Enterprises and Tax Administrations*, OECD (July 2017), http://dx.doi.org/10.1787/tpg-2017-en.
3. OECD, *Transfer Pricing Guidance on Financial Transactions: Inclusive Framework on BEPS: Actions 4, 8–10*, OECD (February 2020). www.oecd.org/tax/beps/transfer-pricing-guidance-on-financial-transactions-inclusive-framework-on-beps-actions-4-8-10.htm.
4. OECD (2022), OECD Transfer Pricing Guidelines for Multinational Enterprises and Tax Administrations 2022, OECD Publishing, Paris, https://doi.org/10.1787/0e655865-en.
5. OECD Transfer Pricing Guidelines for Multinational Enterprises and Tax Administrations 2022, para. 10.64.
6. *Ibid.*, para. 10.71. Emphasis added.

> added] to seek to replicate the process used to determine the credit rating of the MNE group. This approach also involves taking into account improvements in creditworthiness that the specific MNE would be assumed to receive as a result of being part of the MNE group.

In the absence of a publicly available credit rating, the OECD thus recommends either relying on available rating tools or deducting a rating by mimicking the methodologies used by the relevant independent rating agencies. The use of the rating tools, however, encompasses certain challenges, as acknowledged by the OECD:

> The credit rating methodology used in publicly available financial tools may differ significantly in certain respects from the credit rating methodologies applied by independent credit rating agencies to determine official credit ratings and the impact of any such differences should be carefully considered. For instance, publicly available tools generally use only a limited sample of quantitative data to determine a credit rating.[7]

The lack of qualitative factors in the rating tools may have an effect on their reliability. Some countries (e.g., Germany) may therefore deny the applicability of ratings derived from such tools for intercompany loan transactions.[8] The OECD recommends deriving a credit rating following the methodology of an independent rating agency and applying qualitative and quantitative factors:

> For these reasons, the reliability of credit rating results derived from the use of publicly available financial tools may be improved to the extent the analysis can reproducibly demonstrate consistency of ratings using such tools with those provided by independent credit rating agencies.[9]

For intercompany transactions (which applies to intercompany loans), the OECD recommends conducting and documenting a rating for the transacting entities that relies on qualitative and quantitative measures and follows a methodology similar to those used by the main rating agencies (in the absence of a publicly available rating).

The remainder of this chapter provides a brief introduction on finding the most relevant rating methodology in line with the OECD requirements and can thus be applied in the context of intercompany loan transactions. This initial example of establishing a rating follows a methodology published by Moody's and will be referred to as a shadow credit rating assessment.[10] This rating will apply both qualitative and quantitative factors that will jointly compose the final rating.

7. OECD Transfer Pricing Guidelines for Multinational Enterprises and Tax Administrations 2022, para. 10.73.
8. Münster Fiscal Court, Case 13 K 4037/13 K, F, *German Tax Authority v. X Sub GmbH* [2016].
9. OECD Transfer Pricing Guidelines for Multinational Enterprises and Tax Administrations 2022, para. 10.74.
10. Moody's Investor Services, *Approach for REITs and Other Commercial Property Firms*, Moody's (July 2021). The analysis is based on author interpretations of the rating methods and the rating agencies may have diverging interpretations of such methods.

## III CONDUCTING A SHADOW CREDIT RATING ASSESSMENT

Using a methodology comparable to that of the major rating agencies (Moody's, Standard & Poor's Global Ratings, Fitch Ratings), the creditworthiness of a company (typically the borrower) is categorized in an intercompany loan framework. By means of various factors, both qualitative and quantitative, creditworthiness is determined on a scale between Aaa (debtor with the highest creditworthiness) and C (payment default).[11] These ratings can be transformed into a numeric value using the conversion table determined by Moody's.

Above all, the most appropriate methodology must be selected, otherwise, there is a risk that the qualitative and quantitative factors will not apply to the borrower and will result in a skewed shadow credit rating that does not reflect the facts and circumstances.

### 1 Choosing an Appropriate Credit Rating Methodology

It is important that the shadow rating is adapted to the characteristics of the respective company. Depending on the type and business area of the company, such a rating is based on different factors. For each case, the methodology needs to specifically apply to the characteristics of the entity for which the credit rating is established, that is, banking entities need to be evaluated with a methodology tailored to the characteristics of banks, retailers with a methodology for retail companies, and so on. As an initial stylized example, we use Moody's *Investor Services Approach for REITs and Other Commercial Property Firms* (published July 2021) for this section of the chapter.[12] A more detailed step-by-step example follows in the case study.

Rating methods and risk matrices are updated continuously as the market changes. Thus, to simulate a current rating for the entity, it is important to use rating methodologies that are relevant at the time of the analysis and for the sector under review.[13] If the analysis is to be done for a past point in time, the methodology would need to be based on what was available at that time.

Before applying a method, careful consideration should also be given to how the subfactors are calculated. Differing assumptions can influence financial calculations and results, thereby affecting the final rating. Furthermore, as highlighted in the OECD Guidance, 'the credit rating derived in light of such intra-group transactions may not be reliable,'[14] since related parties' financials can be influenced by the non-arm's-length nature of other transactions. Thus, it is key to ensure the arm's-length nature of these transactions before performing the credit assessment.

---

11. The scale shown here is equivalent to the one used in the selected Moody's methodology. Other rating agencies may use diverging scales that generally would be based on the same principles.
12. REITs operate as companies that own, operate, or finance real estate assets to produce income.
13. OECD Transfer Pricing Guidelines for Multinational Enterprises and Tax Administrations 2022, s. B3.
14. *Ibid.*, para. 10.75.

With the correct methodology selected, we take a closer look at the qualitative and quantitative factors in the methodology and how they are analysed.

## 2 Quantitative Rating Factors

The quantitative factors are essentially key figures that are mostly calculated from the annual financial statements of the companies or other financial documents (management accounts, interim reports, etc.). Typically, these are assessments of the size and success of a company (evidenced through sales and profit) or debt sustainability (e.g., interest coverage).

For example, the partial factor of debt sustainability should be explained as part of a rating. In the example under consideration for real estate investment trusts (REITs), this factor is weighted 10% in its contribution to the final shadow credit rating. It is calculated as the ratio of the company's net debt to the profit for the financial year (net debt/EBITDA) (earnings before interest, taxes, depreciation, and amortization). Depending on the result derived from applying this ratio, the corresponding credit rating is mapped for this subfactor in line with Table 6.1. A lower debt/profit ratio correlates with a higher credit rating for this subfactor. Table 6.1 summarises the assessments to be applied to this subfactor.[15]

*Table 6.1 Net Debt/EBITDA Mapping*

| | *Aaa* | *Aa* | *A* | *Baa* | *Ba* | *B* | *Caa* | *Ca* |
|---|---|---|---|---|---|---|---|---|
| Net debt/EBITDA ratio | < 2.0 × | < 3.5 × | < 4.0 × | < 6.0 × | < 8.0 × | < 10.0 × | < 13.0 × | > 13.0 × |

*Example 1*: A company reports an annual EBITDA of EUR 1 million. As reported on the balance sheet, the company has a net debt of EUR 7 million. This results in a factor of 7 ×, which in turn corresponds to a partial rating of Ba. Key figures are determined for all quantitative subfactors, from which the respective sub-rating is derived.

Table 6.6 at the end of this section provides an overview of all the subfactors relevant to this credit rating methodology, which ultimately make up the overall rating. Further quantitative factors in the REIT example considered here are gross assets, unencumbered assets/gross assets, total debt + preferred stock/gross assets, net debt/EBITDA, secured debt/gross assets, and fixed-charge coverage.

## 3 Qualitative Rating Factors

Insight into qualitative criteria can typically be obtained as part of the factual review conducted on the group. A thorough analysis of the value chain, functions, assets, risk,

15. Moody's Investor Services, *Approach for REITs and Other Commercial Property Firms*.

and industry will generally provide a suitable level of information for determining the qualitative factors for the borrower. Some common factors that appear in methodologies (although they can differ in wording) include market positioning, governance approach, and the company's financial policy.

One qualitative factor in the REIT methodology is a company's liquidity and access to the capital market. Better access to (additional) financing would, as expected, lead to a better partial rating. Table 6.2 summarizes the (abbreviated) qualitative assessments and the corresponding ratings for the liquidity and access to financing subfactor.[16]

16. *Ibid.*

*Table 6.2 Liquidity and Access to Capital Mapping*

| | *Aaa* | *Aa* | *A* | *Baa* | *Ba* | *B* | *Caa* | *Ca* |
|---|---|---|---|---|---|---|---|---|
| Liquidity and access to capital | Extremely high levels of internal liquidity and committed bank facilities, unparalleled access to private and public capital, with no need for external funding for at least two years | Substantial internal liquidity and committed bank facilities, superior access to private and public capital, with no need for external funding for at least one year | Considerable internal liquidity and committed bank facilities, excellent access to private and public capital, with minimal reliance on external funding to cover one year of debt maturities and cash needs | Sufficient internal liquidity and committed bank facilities, good access to private and public capital, with some reliance on external funding to cover one year of debt maturities and cash needs | Adequate internal liquidity and committed bank facilities, moderate access to many sources of capital, with some reliance on external funding to cover one year of debt maturities and cash needs | Insufficient internal liquidity and committed bank facilities, sporadic access to many sources of capital, must rely on external funding to cover one year of debt maturities and cash needs | Insufficient internal liquidity and committed bank facilities, limited access to capital, or must rely on external funding to cover one year of debt maturities and cash needs, access to which is uncertain | Insufficient internal liquidity and committed bank facilities, no access to capital, or must rely on external funding to cover one year of debt maturities and cash needs, access to which is unlikely or doubtful |

*Example 2*: The information received from a company's finance department shows that the related entity in question (verifiable) has substantial internal liquidity and superior refinancing options. It has already demonstrated this through equity and debt financing. In this case, a rating of Aa might be appropriate for this subfactor. This subfactor in turn contributes 15.00% to the overall rating.

More qualitative factors in the REIT example considered here are: market positioning and asset quality and operating environment.

The OECD points out there is a tendency to rely more on quantitative inputs at the expense of qualitative factors. However, qualitative factors can have a significant influence on the final rating.[17] For example, the REIT methodology includes a relatively high number of qualitative factors (making up 40% of the final shadow rating). Other methodologies can be substantially less affected by the qualitative factors (e.g., insurance brokers and service companies, 0% where there are no qualitative factors for consideration). Because their influence can differ quite substantially between various methodologies and to be able to document the qualitative with solid evidence, it is critical that the more correct methodology is selected and applied.

## 4 Final Rating Assessment

The overall rating is ultimately derived from the weighted mean of all quantitative and qualitative (partial) factors. For each subfactor, the outcomes are matched to a broad rating category (Aaa, Aa, A, Baa, Ba, B, Caa, or Ca), the so-called alpha categories, and to a numeric score.

The qualitative factors are scored, based on their description and the scale shown in Table 6.3.

*Table 6.3 Alpha-Numeric Scoreboard for Qualitative Factors*

| *Alpha Categories* | *Aaa* | *Aa* | *A* | *Baa* | *Ba* | *B* | *Caa* | *Ca* |
|---|---|---|---|---|---|---|---|---|
| Numeric score | 1 | 3 | 6 | 9 | 12 | 15 | 18 | 20 |

*Source*: Moody's Investor Services, *Approach for REITs and Other Commercial Property Firms*, Moody's (July 2021).

*Example 3*: The Aa score that results from the estimation of the liquidity and access to capital subfactor outlined in Example 2 would translate into a numerical score of 3 for this qualitative subfactor. This contributes to the final numerical score of the rating.

The quantitative factors, on the contrary, are scored on a linear continuum, based on the scale shown in Table 6.4.

17. OECD Transfer Pricing Guidelines for Multinational Enterprises and Tax Administrations 2022, para. 10.73.

*Table 6.4 Alpha-Numeric Scoreboard for Quantitative Factors*

| *Alpha Categories* | *Aaa* | *Aa* | *A* | *Baa* | *Ba* | *B* | *Caa* | *Ca* |
|---|---|---|---|---|---|---|---|---|
| Numeric score | 0.5–1.5 | 1.5–4.5 | 4.5–7.5 | 7.5–10.5 | 10.5–13.5 | 13.5–16.5 | 16.5–19.5 | 19.5–20.5 |

*Source*: Moody's Investor Services, *Approach for REITs and Other Commercial Property Firms*, Moody's (July 2021).

For each subfactor, the value derived is translated into a numerical score by using linear interpolation based on the value's position in the scoreboard range. This numerical score can also be a fraction. In a purely theoretical example, if the range corresponding to the Baa alpha category for some subfactor was from 50 × to 100 × (with 100 × being the more favourable outcome), Table 6.4 tells us this translates into a numeric score between 7.5 and 10.5. Should the analysis derive a value of 99 × for the respective company in this subfactor, the corresponding numeric score would be close to 7.5 and far from 10.5.

*Example 4*: In Example 1, we have seen that the net debt/EBITDA value was 7 × , resulting in a subfactor rating of Ba. Table 6.1 showed that the Ba score for this subfactor is from 6 × to 8 × . A value of 7 × is thus right in the middle of the Ba range of values. Applying linear interpolation, the corresponding numerical score should be the straight average of the numerical rating for the range for Ba. It should thus be 12.0, the average of 10.5 and 13.5 (*see* Table 6.4).

From the numerical values of all qualitative and quantitative subfactor ratings, a weighted average can be calculated, applying the respective weighting that is given for each subfactor to the numerical outcome. The resulting total numerical score (or aggregated numeric score) is mapped back into a final shadow credit rating outcome by applying Table 6.5.

*Table 6.5 Scoreboard for Determining Final Shadow Credit Rating*

| *Scoreboard-Indicated Outcome* | *Aggregated Numeric Score* |
|---|---|
| AAA | $x \leq 1.5$ |
| Aa1 | $1.5 \leq x \leq 2.5$ |
| Aa2 | $2.5 \leq x \leq 3.5$ |
| Aa3 | $3.5 \leq x \leq 4.5$ |
| A1 | $4.5 \leq x \leq 5.5$ |
| A2 | $5.5 \leq x \leq 6.5$ |
| A3 | $6.5 \leq x \leq 7.5$ |
| Baa1 | $7.5 \leq x \leq 8.5$ |
| Baa2 | $8.5 \leq x \leq 9.5$ |
| Baa3 | $9.5 \leq x \leq 10.5$ |
| Ba1 | $10.5 \leq x \leq 11.5$ |

| *Scoreboard-Indicated Outcome* | *Aggregated Numeric Score* |
|---|---|
| Ba2 | $11.5 \leq x \leq 12.5$ |
| Ba3 | $12.5 \leq x \leq 13.5$ |
| B1 | $13.5 \leq x \leq 14.5$ |
| B2 | $14.5 \leq x \leq 15.5$ |
| B3 | $15.5 \leq x \leq 16.5$ |
| Caa1 | $16.5 \leq x \leq 17.5$ |
| Caa2 | $17.5 \leq x \leq 18.5$ |
| Caa3 | $18.5 \leq x \leq 19.5$ |
| Ca | $19.5 \leq x \leq 20.5$ |
| C | $x \geq 20.5$ |

*Source*: Moody's Investor Services, *Approach for REITs and Other Commercial Property Firms*, Moody's (July 2021).

Finally, Table 6.6 shows in a stylized manner how the composition of the rating at the example for an investment company in the real estate sector (REIT) can be done, applying all of the above.

*Table 6.6 Example of a Shadow Credit Rating Calculation for REIT or Other Commercial Real Estate Firm*

| *Weight (%)* | | *Sub-rating* | *Weighted Numeric Rating* |
|---|---|---|---|
| **5.00** | **Scale** | **Aa** | **3.0** |
| 5.00 | Gross assets | Aa | 3.0 |
| **25.00** | **Business profile** | **Aa** | **4.2** |
| 15.00 | Market positioning and asset quality | Aa | 3.0 |
| 10.00 | Operating environment | A | 6.0 |
| **25.00** | **Liquidity and access to capital** | **A** | **5.4** |
| 15.00 | Liquidity and access to capital | Aa | 3 |
| 10.00 | Unencumbered assets/gross assets | Baa | 9 |
| **45.00** | **Leverage and coverage** | **Ba** | **11.8** |
| 15.00 | Total debt + preferred stock/gross assets | Ba | 10.5 |
| 10.00 | Net debt/EBITDA | Ba | 12.0 |
| 10.00 | Secured debt/gross assets | Ba | 12.0 |
| 10.00 | Fixed-charge coverage | B | 13.5 |
| 100 | Total numeric value | | 7.9 |
| | Final shadow credit rating | | Baa1 |

*Source*: Moody's Investor Services, *Approach for REITs and Other Commercial Property Firms*, Moody's (July 2021) and authors' own estimation.

In the example considered here, the overall rating is Baa1, derived from a total numeric value of 7.9 (applying Table 6.5).

It should be noted that the rating that is derived in the above steps is the rating for an entity ('issuer rating'). If the Shadow Credit Rating analysis intends to provide a rating for a financial instrument, this rating would need to be further adjusted to reflect the risks inherent to the financial instrument ('instrument rating').[18]

When relying on an issuer rating, the rating may still need to be adjusted further, based on the exact circumstances of what the rating is used for and the position of the rated company in the group as a whole. If the rating is used as the basis for a loan benchmarking, which is common, reasons for an adjustment calculation may be needed to account for existing structural subordination of the loan under consideration, the increased risk depending on the jurisdiction in which the loan takes place, or the existence of some level of implicit group backing available to the borrowing company. The next sections will discuss these notions in more detail.

## IV CONSIDERATIONS THAT MAY IMPACT STANDALONE RATING

### 1 Group Support, Explicit and Implicit Guarantees

When determining the creditworthiness of a subsidiary, international tax authorities regularly question the extent to which the group as a whole explicitly or implicitly provides a guarantee to its subsidiary. If there is an (explicit) guarantee, an appropriate remuneration for these internal group guarantees would have to be determined. A distinction must be made between contractually agreed explicit guarantees, which must be assessed economically and for which an appropriate fee must be determined, and an implicit backing. In the latter case, market participants would assume that if the subsidiary found itself in financial difficulties, the group would intervene to provide support even if there was no obligation to do so (group backing).

The OECD states in its 2022 guidance that 'The effect of potential group support on the credit rating of an entity and any effect on that entity's ability to borrow or the interest rate paid on those borrowings would not require any payment or comparability adjustment.'[19] This implies that such implicit backing by the group does not require any remuneration. However, different opinions have been presented that suggest this depends on the specific facts and circumstances of the case. An implicit guarantee is not to be remunerated if it is in the interests of the shareholder of the subsidiary, that is, the head company (shareholder reasons). In this case, the group backing is in the interest of the group itself; accordingly, the group or another group company would not insist on remuneration but act out of its own economic interest.[20]

18. *See, e.g.*: Updated Summary Guidance for Notching Bonds, Preferred Stocks and Hybrid Securities of Corporate Issuers. Moody's Investor Services, March 2007.
19. OECD Transfer Pricing Guidelines for Multinational Enterprises and Tax Administrations 2022, para. 10.77.
20. 'Grundsätze für die Prüfung der Einkunftsabgrenzung bei international verbundenen Unternehmen (1983)', para. 4.4.1f.

On the other hand, if the guarantee provides a clear benefit to the receiving company (business reason), this form of guarantee is to be paid for by the receiving company, provided that such a payment would also have been agreed to amongst external third parties. For determining the corresponding remuneration, the same methods can be used as that for determining a fee for an explicit guarantee.

This also applies if there is already an explicit guarantee. In this case, only the part of the explicit guarantee should be reimbursed that is not already covered by the implicit guarantee, provided that this guarantee is based on the interests of the receiving company (business reasons). This question should be explained in detail as part of the transfer pricing documentation.

Shareholder reasons exist due to the strategic importance of a subsidiary, for example. Likewise, damage to the reputation of the whole group can be caused by a possible bankruptcy of a foreign subsidiary. In this situation, the shareholders have clear incentives to avert this bankruptcy. The group's backing would not have to be remunerated.

If the group company examined is economically important for other individual group entities, for example, in the context of supply chains or networks (this could be in the automotive and logistics industries), these other companies would have to assume these risks and guarantees.

Whilst the OECD assumes that there always is some degree of corporate backing,[21] there is also the opinion that various criteria must be used to check whether such an implicit backing can be expected.[22] The major rating agencies provide criteria that can be used to determine the degree of group support. For this purpose, one might consider the importance of the corresponding company for opening up a certain market or the extent to which the company under consideration manufactures preliminary products that are indispensable for the production chain. As described, reputation considerations are also taken into account. For example, it is relevant whether the subsidiary operates under the same name as the group as a whole. It should also be considered whether the respective group of companies has a history of letting subsidiaries default. This could be considered an indication of limited implicit support in that group.

Depending on the assumed degree of implicit backing, the rating of the receiving company can therefore increase (or decrease) by one or two notches, or be equal to or even better than the rating of the whole group.[23] For this reason, a credit rating for the entire group should be created in the same way as the one described already if this does not already exist or is not available.

21. OECD Transfer Pricing Guidelines for Multinational Enterprises and Tax Administrations 2022, para. 10.78.
22. *Ibid.*, s. I.D.8.
23. Amongst the three big rating agencies, S&P Global Ratings assumes that the rating of an affiliated subsidiary (taking on the loan) can never be better than that of the total group or the head company. Fitch Ratings and Moody's do not make this assumption. Moody's Investor Service, *Assessing Affiliate Support in the Absence of a Guarantee*, Moody's (2021); Fitch, *Parent and Subsidiary Rating Linkage*, Fitch (2021); S&P Global Ratings, *General Criteria, Group Rating Methodology*, S&P (2013).

## 2 Country Risk

Sovereign ceilings are another factor that can influence entities' creditworthiness. Sovereign or country ratings are produced by the common ratings agencies, which independently consider various political and economic factors to assess the risk level when investing in a particular country's debt. In circumstances where an entity operates in an industry that is not amongst the country's main economic drivers, it is unlikely that the entity would default if the sovereign state were to default.[24]

It is crucial to understand how the broader macroeconomic environment can also affect a company's credit rating, and the concept of country risk captures conditions or events outside of the control of the borrower that can make the event of non-payment more likely. Third-party lenders would assess the risk level associated with the jurisdiction in where the borrower is located because this can affect the terms and conditions offered by the lender and thus would change the arm's-length conditions. For example, a country may restrict the movement of funds in and out, which could hinder the ability to make offshore payments. Some corporate ratings therefore already include aspects of a country rating, e.g., in the form of a macro-level indicator capturing the strength of a country's institutions and government.[25] Any effect that can cause repayment delays or loan defaults needs to be considered. Whether to account for country risk is ultimately a case-to-case consideration.[26] In the case where an entity is rated higher than the sovereign rating, it would mean the entity can service its own debt even in extremely dire circumstances such as inflation and fiscal crises.

## 3 Subordination

Intragroup loans are often subordinated relative to external creditors (whereby the latter is treated as priority debt). This results in a structural disadvantage for creditors within the group. This in turn may result in a need for a pricing adjustment, which can lead to a downgrade of up to two notches in the credit rating. Standard & Poor's writes about this: 'When priority debt and other liabilities amount to 30% of the assets, lower-priority debt is substantially disadvantaged and is, therefore, differentiated by two notches.'[27]

The corresponding adjustment normally leads to a higher interest rate, which compensates the internal creditor for the structural disadvantage compared with external creditors.

The issue rating may differ from the issuer rating, as it measures the default risk associated with a specific financial obligation or a specific class of financial obligations for an issuer. Typically, the more junior or subordinated a financial instrument is, the

24. S&P Global Ratings, *Ratings above the Sovereign – Corporate and Government Ratings: Methodology and Assumptions*, S&P (19 November 2013), 4.
25. For example, Moody's Investor Services, *Finance Companies Methodology* (November 2019). https://ratings.moodys.com/api/rmc-documents/65543
26. In some cases, accounting for country risk might result in a higher entity credit rating of two to four notches above the sovereign rating. S&P, *Ratings above the Sovereign*, 4.
27. S&P Global Ratings, *Corporate Ratings Criteria*, 35.

riskier the instrument will be, and thus the lower the rating of that instrument compared with the assessed credit rating of the borrowing entity. For example, an issuer rating of BBB+ would apply to senior unsecured debt. The issuer rating for the same issuer for subordinated debt may well be BBB or lower depending on the debt mix already relied on.[28]

Whilst the above sections predominately focused on the theoretical aspects and legal considerations with regard to Shadow Credit Ratings, the next section contains a case study on a borrowing entity and how its respective Shadow Credit Rating can be derived. The case study provides a practical example and goes through the steps necessary to establish a Shadow Credit rating.

## V CASE STUDY

Here we take a closer look into applying the facts and circumstances to a borrowing entity and how a shadow credit rating can be established. Before any sort of analysis can begin, a thorough understanding of the parties involved is required. This is defining the function, asset, and risk profile of the borrower and lender and the key terms and conditions of the transaction. this information is key for constructing a shadow credit rating reflective of the borrower's circumstances.

### 1 Facts of the Case

A multinational group is in the retail business operating numerous brick-and-mortar stores across Europe. The group is headquartered in the United Kingdom (UKHeadCo) and has many affiliates in Europe. The treasury company managing the group's liquidity is also based in the UK and is a wholly owned subsidiary of UKHeadCo. The group treasury activities are centralized, thereby managing the group liquidity and funding requirements. As part of its treasury role, affiliates can get loans from the treasury entity when necessary. For the purpose of this case study, the two United Kingdom (UK) entities will jointly be referred to as UKCo, because the treasury entity, in substance, operates as an extension of UKHeadCo.

### 2 Profile of the Entities

UKCo can be described as an in-house bank containing all the necessary functions, reserves, and substances to manage risk and issue financing. The OECD also stipulates that in expected arm's-length conditions, a lender must have the financial capacity to

28. The latest information from Moody's Investors Services on the issue is *Moody's Proposes Update to Notching Corporate Instrument Ratings Based on Differences in Security and Priority of Claim* (14 July 2017). https://www.moodys.com/research/Moodys-Proposes-Update-to-Notching-Corporate-Instrument-Ratings-Based-on--PBC_1044134.

assume the risk.[29] Given the functional, asset, and risk profile, a routine remuneration is not sufficient to compensate the treasury function for the services provided.[30]

UKCo manages and optimizes liquidity across the group, procures capital on the financial markets, and ensures that all operating entities have adequate resources to meet their goals. The extent to which local entities require capital is determined locally, and an application or business plan is put forward to the treasury team for assessment. As a result, the treasury entity, together with UKHeadCo, is charged with managing and mitigating most of the group's financial risks (e.g., credit risk, foreign exchange risk) and bears the majority of financial risks with regard to unrelated party funding and credit risk in relation to the borrowing entity.

UKCo is responsible for determining the product offerings and product mixes in the various operating regions with some input from local entities. UKCo has its own range of items that it designs and produces. It gives its affiliates standard marketing materials to ensure consistent messaging and branding with some local adaptation. UKCo also centralizes procurement services to manage costs and increase efficiency.

UKCo has affiliates in Germany. The German operations are a sizable portion of the group's total business operations, accounting for roughly 30% of the group's revenue. However, it does not use the group's name and branding because it joined the group through a recent acquisition. The main operating entity (GermanCo) operates and manages the stores across the country. It localizes the marketing materials to attach its brand and logo and will procure some products directly from the market to meet its customers' tastes and preferences.

To modernize the operations across Germany and bring it more in line with the group's style, GermanCo put forward its business plan, outlining the expected costs and timeline for using the funds. By considering all the factors, UKCo (acting as the lender) provides GermanCo (the borrower) a midterm loan of three years for EUR 200 million.

29. OECD Transfer Pricing Guidelines for Multinational Enterprises and Tax Administrations 2022, para. 10.25.
30. As stated in the OECD guidance, understanding the functional, asset, and risk profile of the lender and the extent to which the lender has the necessary functions and processes in place to decide whether and under which terms to advance funds. This would 'typically include an analysis and evaluation of the risks inherent in the loan, the capability to commit capital of the business to the investment, determining the terms of the loan and organising and documenting the loan', amongst other considerations. OECD Transfer Pricing Guidelines for Multinational Enterprises and Tax Administrations 2022, para. 10.24.

## 3 Group Value Chain

The main value drivers of the group are shown in Figure 6.1.

*Figure 6.1 Case Study: Industry Value Chain*

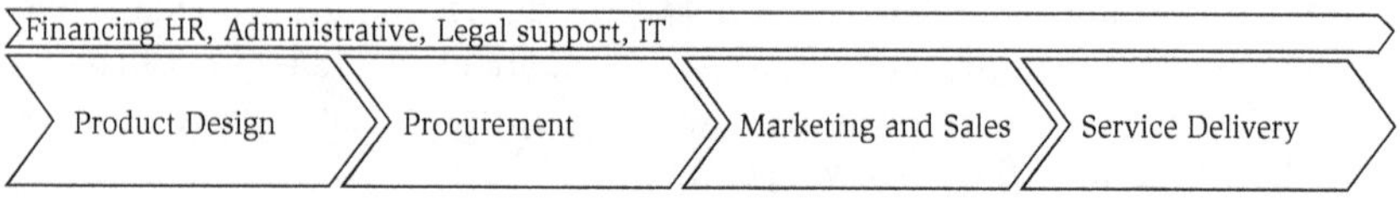


UKCo is responsible for the first two value drivers (Product Design and Procurement), and most support services, whilst GermanCo is responsible for the latter two (Marketing and Sales and Service Delivery). Due to the need of having localized products available, GermanCo may perform some activities independently of UKCo to obtain and sell such products. To a large extent, the strategy for the local market is managed locally. It is crucial to understand the borrower's contribution to value creation because this provides insight into the group's overall business strategy and the potentially realistically available options when it comes to funding available to the borrower.[31]

## 4 Choosing the Appropriate Methodology

For this case study, the Business and Consumer Service Industry Rating Methodology, published by Moody's Investor Services in October 2016, was selected. This rating methodology remains the agency's most recent version.[32]

This methodology relies on five broad factors and eight subfactors, displayed in Table 6.7, along with their weightings. These factors are specific to each sector methodology, and although there may be some partial overlap between specific sector methodologies, the weightings will ultimately be different between different sectors.

*Table 6.7 Business and Consumer Services Industry Rating Methodology Criteria and Weightings*

| *Factors* | *Factor Weight (%)* | *Subfactors* | *Subfactor Weight (%)* |
|---|---|---|---|
| Scale | 20 | | |
| | | Revenues | 20 |
| Business profile | 20 | | |

31. *Ibid.*, s. B.3.5.
32. It should be noted that this case study reflects author interpretations of the methodology and may not be fully aligned with interpretations of Moody's.

| Factors | Factor Weight (%) | Subfactors | Subfactor Weight (%) |
|---|---|---|---|
| | | Demand characteristics | 15 |
| | | Competitive profile | 5 |
| Profitability | 10 | | |
| | | Earnings before interest, taxes, and amortization (EBITA) margin | 10 |
| Leverage and coverage | 40 | | |
| | | Debt/EBITDA | 15 |
| | | EBITA/interest | 15 |
| | | Retained Cash Flow (RCF)/net debt | 10 |
| Financial policy | 10 | | |
| | | Financial policy | 10 |

*Source*: Moody's Investor Services, *Business and Consumer Service Rating Methodology*, Moody's (3 October 2016).

The factors in this methodology are quantitative, except for business profile and financial policy. Furthermore, this methodology requires past and forecasted data. Moody's leaves the raters with the final choice of the chosen time period to be evaluated.[33] This is done to reflect possible differences in the material situations of different companies. Often a one-year period is sufficient to estimate the shadow credit rating of a firm in this sector.

In this methodology, the mapping table slightly differs (yet immaterially) from that shown in Table 6.5 because the conversion to a credit rating decreases to the lowest rating of Ca, and therefore a C rating is not possible. However, all the incremental values remain the same.

## 5 Determining the Shadow Credit Rating

It is not feasible to demonstrate the calculation of every subfactor in Table 6.7 given the extent of the analysis required. However, we use the same approach for this credit rating methodology as outlined in section 3 by calculating a numerical value (e.g., ratio) for the quantitative factors, reviewing the possible options for each qualitative factor, and deciding which scenario best fits the circumstances of the entity being rated.

33. Moody's Investor Services, *Business and Consumer Service Rating Methodology*, Moody's (3 October 2016), 3.

This analysis is conducted for all subfactors to determine the implied rating and assign a numerical value to each factor. Table 6.3 is referred to in this case, and under this methodology, there is one scorecard that applies to all qualitative and quantitative factors. The results is shown for all factors in Table 6.8.

*Table 6.8 Shadow Credit Rating Scores Calculation for GermanCo*

| *Weight (%)* | | *Sub-rating* | *Weighted Numeric Rating* |
|---|---|---|---|
| **20.00** | **Scale** | | |
| 20.00 | Revenue | B | 15.00 |
| **20.00** | **Business profile** | | |
| 15.00 | Demand characteristics | Baa | 9.00 |
| 5.00 | Competitive profile | B | 15.00 |
| **10.00** | **Profitability** | | |
| 10.00 | EBITA margin | B | 15.00 |
| **40.00** | **Leverage and coverage** | | |
| 15.00 | Debt/EBITA | Ba | 12.00 |
| 15.00 | EBITA/interest | Ba | 12.00 |
| 10.00 | RCF/net debt | Baa | 9.00 |
| **10.00** | **Financial policy** | | |
| 10.00 | Financial policy | Baa | 9.00 |
| 100 | Total numeric value | | 12.00 |
| | Final shadow credit rating | | Ba2 |

The final score is calculated by estimating the weighted average of all factors (i.e., multiplying the weights in the first column and the numeric rating). Based on this approach, GermanCo received an aggregate numeric rating of 12.00, which corresponds to Ba2 using Moody's rating system (BB using the S&P rating system). The derivation of the final shadow credit rating is done by reference to Table 6.5.

This shadow rating is a standalone rating and does not consider any positive or negative factors that GermanCo may be exposed to by operating as part of the group. Thus, although it is a starting point for calculating default risk, further consideration is required. One would expect to take into account the level of implicit support, but for the purpose of this example, implicit support is not further considered.

We may consider the present level of sovereign risk. In this case, the loan is extended to an affiliate in the German jurisdiction. Given the political and financial (and thus overall) stability of this market, we do not anticipate an adjustment being needed to account for sovereign risk.

Subsequently, the issuance of the new loan can be re-evaluated in line with the borrower's current debt obligations to determine whether it is subordinated and how this can affect the shadow credit rating. For example, if there are already substantial loans in place, some with external creditors that will take precedence in the event of limited finances, then S&P considers that there may be a lowering of the shadow credit rating by up to two notches. Applying this would result in an issuance rating of B1.

## VI CONCLUSION

This chapter outlines the application of Shadow Credit Ratings in a Transfer Pricing context. Shadow Credit Ratings are an important tool for the application of the arm's-length principle on financing transactions. A shadow credit rating is in fact a comparability criterion when evaluating comparable market prices for financial transactions. In particular, when determining the appropriate conditions for an intragroup loan, it is necessary to analyse the conditions under which a comparable company would take out a loan on the open market. To do this, the creditworthiness of the company receiving the loan must be determined.

It is important that the shadow rating is adapted to the characteristics of the respective company. Depending on the type and business area of the company, such a rating is based on different factors. For each case, the methodology needs to specifically apply to the characteristics of the entity for which the credit rating is established.

In addition to the rating, other factors might need to be analysed. This chapter therefore also discusses notions of implicit support, country risk and subordination. Finally, the chapter provides a case study that provides a practical example and goes through the steps necessary to establish a Shadow Credit rating.

The above chapter thus provides a coherent framework for the application of Shadow Credit Ratings in a Transfer Pricing context. The methods applied form an economically reasonable assessment of the arm's-length principle.

CHAPTER 7

# The Issue of Implicit Support and Implications for a Transfer Pricing Analysis

*Andrea Lee, Amanda Pletz & Ronald Bernstein*[*]

Implicit support is an assumption by the lender that in the event of the borrower's financial difficulties, another company in the group (usually the parent company) will step in and support the borrower to ensure fulfillment of its liabilities *without* any binding contractual support commitments in place. Implicit support is not to be mixed up with a guarantee, which is a commitment of financial support accompanied by a legally binding agreement. With implicit support, there is no written commitment of a guarantor; there is purely an expectation from the lender. This expectation may or may not be based on past experience or events that are typical for the particular industry. A perfect example is the banking industry where the good name of a bank is so crucial for its success and stability, it is highly unlikely that a parent company of a banking group would allow any of its subsidiaries to default on its obligations. There is a general assumption that the implicit support in the banking industry is one of the strongest.

Implicit support does not have to come only from within a group. Similar support can be provided (and thus expected) by market participants from the government and its institutions. This may be relevant for essential services like utilities.

In international tax and transfer pricing, the notion of implicit support has been a widely discussed topic for more than a decade. This followed a number of high-profile disputes that revealed complexities in the concept. The notion of implicit support was already acknowledged in previous versions of the Organisation for Economic Co-operation and Development (OECD) guidance, for example, the 2010 OECD Transfer Pricing Guidelines paragraph 7.13, referencing the incidental benefit of being part of a wider group:

* The views and opinions set forth herein are the personal views or opinions of the authors; they do not necessarily reflect the views or opinions of the organization with which the authors are associated.

> Similarly, an associated enterprise should not be considered to receive an intra-group service when it obtains incidental benefits attributable solely to its being part of a larger concern, and not to any specific activity being performed. For example, no service would be received where an associated enterprise by reason of its affiliation alone has a credit rating higher than it would if it were unaffiliated, but an intra-group service would usually exist where the higher credit rating was due to a guarantee by another group member, or where the enterprise benefitted from the group's reputation deriving from global marketing and public relations campaigns.[1]

The dispute cases that occurred merely highlighted the importance of implicit support and the role it may play in the cost of funding. The result is that the issue of implicit support has been high on the OECD's agenda under the Base Erosion and Profit Shifting initiative first launched in 2013.

## I THE OECD ON THE NOTION OF IMPLICIT SUPPORT

The OECD first explicitly referred to the implications of implicit support linked to funding as part of its Actions 8-10. This in turn led to revisions to the existing OECD Guidance with the elaboration of multinational enterprise (MNE) group synergies:

> P is the parent company of an MNE group engaging in a financial services business. The strength of the group's consolidated balance sheet makes it possible for P to maintain an AAA credit rating on a consistent basis. S is a member of the MNE group engaged in providing the same type of financial services as other group members and does so on a large scale in an important market. On a stand-alone basis, however, the strength of S's balance sheet would support a credit rating of only Baa. Nevertheless, because of S's membership in the P group, large independent lenders are willing to lend to it at interest rates that would be charged to independent borrowers with an A rating, i.e. a lower interest rate than would be charged if S were an independent entity with its same balance sheet, but a higher interest rate than would be available to the parent company of the MNE group.[2]

The OECD further expanded on this concept in its Chapter X of the Transfer Pricing Guidance on Financial Transactions, where it provides more insight on the topic under the section "Effect of Group Membership." In this section, the OECD highlights that:

> Implicit support from the group may affect the credit rating of the borrower or the rating of any debt which it issues. The relative status of an entity within the group may help determine what impact that potential group support has on the credit rating of a debt issuer. Entities of an MNE group will be more or less likely to receive group support according to the relative importance of the entity to the MNE group as a whole and the linkages between the entity and the rest of the MNE group, either in its current form or in terms of future strategy.[3]

1. OECD Transfer Pricing Guidelines 2010, "Chapter VII: Intragroup Services," p. 209, para. 7.13.
2. OECD Transfer Pricing Guidelines 2022, "Chapter I: Arm's Length Principle," p. 88, para. 1.184.
3. OECD Transfer Pricing Guidance 2022, Transfer Pricing Aspects of Financial Transactions, para. 10.78, p. 419.

In the context of this discussion, the OECD acknowledges that the effect of implicit support will vary based on the facts and circumstances of the case. It further acknowledges that an assessment of implicit support is a matter of judgment.[4]

Similarly to the OECD, the United Nations chapter on financing highlights that implicit support may affect the stand-alone credit rating of an entity and that such an assessment is subject to interpretation.[5] The UN paper continues to outline a basic framework that can be used to evaluate implicit support that is based on S&P Global Ratings methodology. One area where the UN and OECD differ is that the UN chapter highlights that implicit support can lead to a negative adjustment, whereas the OECD is silent on this issue.[6,7]

## II IMPLICIT SUPPORT IN CASE LAW

Although this chapter is not intended to consider case law on implicit support and financing in great depth, we believe that it is necessary to understand some of the complexities on the topic when looking at case law. Two well-publicized cases where the notion of implicit support was analyzed include the GE Capital Canada case in 2010 and the Chevron Australia case in 2015.

### 1 GE Capital Canada

The GE Capital Canada case in the Canadian tax courts led to a ground-breaking decision in relation to implicit support. The Canadian court issued its final decision in December 2009, and it was the first clear decision regarding the implication of implicit support of its kind.

The case involved a United States (US) parent company (General Electric Company, GEUS) and its indirectly wholly owned Canadian subsidiary (General Electric Capital Canada Inc., GEC). The underlying audit issue was regarding a fee for a guarantee provided by GEUS to GEC for third-party financing secured by the latter. The agreed guarantee fee was set at 100 basis points (1 %) per year. The Canadian tax authorities argued that a third party would not be willing to pay any fee as there was no service or benefit provided.

The Canadian authorities argued that GEC's credit rating should be the same as the credit rating of GEUS based on the affiliation to the group. In other words, the Canadian tax authority argued that implicit support has the same strength to lift a borrower's rating to the level of the group as an explicit (legally binding) guarantee. It

4. *Ibid.*, para. 10.80, p. 419.
5. *United Nations: Practical Manual on Transfer Pricing for Developing Countries* (2021), para. 9.11.2, p. 347.
6. *United Nations: Practical Manual*, para. 9.8.12, p. 370.
7. A negative adjustment means that implicit support can also lead to a notching downward of the stand-alone rating.

is important to add that the rating difference between GEUS and GEC as a stand-alone entity was 12-13 notches.[8]

The judge accepted a witness argument that implicit support can lead to an uplift in creditworthiness, but in the case at hand for only two to three notches, this conclusion was applied accordingly. The final conclusion was that implicit support for GEC caused an uplift from the stand-alone rating by three notches (paragraph 301) and, thus, a guarantee fee would have been due in an unrelated party circumstance.[9]

## 2 Chevron Australia

Chevron Australia was decided by the Federal Court of Australia in October 2015. Central to the proceeding was a credit facility provided by Chevron Australia from its U.S. resident subsidiary.

The discussion evolved mainly around two points. First, would an independent enterprise have borrowed the funds in Australian dollars (as Chevron did), despite the fact that the USD-based interest rates were substantially lower at the time? Second, what should have been the arm's length pricing of the loan under consideration of implicit support, among other aspects?

In the Chevron case, the Australian judge did not see implicit support as having much of an influence on the rating and consequently on the pricing. In the end, the judge concluded that "implicit credit support had very little, if any, impact on pricing by a lender in the real world."[10]

Even though this conclusion may sound very different compared with the GE Capital case, one needs to keep in mind that implicit support is one of many elements that have an influence on the credit rating, and credit rating is one of many elements that influence the pricing of the loan. More important, credit rating and pricing by financial institutions are done differently from one institution to another.

## 3 Other Cases

The most recent case that discusses implicit support is between Singapore Telecom Australia Investments PTY Ltd. and the Australian government from December 2021.[11] The interesting discussion regarding implicit support starts from paragraph 196 of the court decision, with two interesting aspects worth mentioning. One is whether the

8. *Canada v. General Electric Capital Canada Inc.*, 2011 DTC 5011 [at 5558], 2010 FCA 344, para. 27: https://taxinterpretations.com/content/354681.
9. *General Capital Canada Inc. v. Her Majesty the Queen*; Dockets 2006-1385(IT)G and 2006-1386(IT)G; appeal from December 4, 2009.
10. *Chevron Australia Holdings Pty Ltd v. Commissioner of Taxation* (No 4) [2015] FCA 1092, para. 606: https://www.judgments.fedcourt.gov.au/judgments/Judgments/fca/single/2015/2015fca1092.
11. *Singapore Telecom Australia Investments Pty Ltd v. Commissioner of Taxation* [2021] FCA 1597, file no. VID 1231, 2019.

correct starting point should be top-down (in this specific case leading to six to eight notches up) or bottom-up (leading to two to three notches up). The judge confirmed that bottom-up is the more appropriate approach because it is more cautious, that is, there must be clear indications that in case of borrower distress, the parent would provide all necessary support.

The second point is related to the first one. In paragraph 326 of the court decision, there is a notable observation that the main reason the external funding is usually taken up by the parent company and provided as an intra-group loan to its subsidiaries is that the parent will usually be able to secure the funding at a (much) better rate than its subsidiaries. "It's because the market really doesn't have a lot of faith in that implicit support in terms of lowering the risk that they are facing, and if they were, they would be borrowing on the subs[12] name without any explicit support."

## III IMPLICATION OF IMPLICIT SUPPORT

As mentioned, the implication of implicit support is that the lender assumes a better credit rating of the borrower than what it would have been on a stand-alone basis. This potentially means that the borrower can obtain better pricing (a lower interest rate) on its loans or a larger amount than what it would have if it was not part of the group. The obvious difficulties in an intercompany scenario are whether implicit support is real, how big is the impact on the borrower's credit rating and thus on the pricing of the loan, and whether there is any effect on the "silent guarantor."[13]

Many discussions on the topic revolve around the extent to which implicit support truly features when third parties (such as banks, rating agencies, or insurance companies) consider applications for funding or insurance products (such as credit insurance). In other words, to what extent does one really need to evaluate implicit support and its role in funding?

Although there may be some perceptions that MNEs may not let an affiliate fail, the rating agencies take the view that a group's willingness to support an affiliate in financial distress will likely depend on the affiliate's strategic importance, legal arrangements, and operational ties and on the parent's overall financial position. Thus, in certain situations, MNEs might not necessarily provide support to a failing subsidiary. This can be demonstrated by empirical evidence. Table 7.1 presents a few examples from 2012 to 2021, across different industries, where parent companies allowed their affiliates to fail.[14]

12. Subs is referencing Subsidiary.
13. Silent Guarantor refers to an entity that provides an implicit guarantee regardless of any contractual arrangements.
14. Because we were not able to identify any disclosure rules for companies to make such information available to the press, this list should be only viewed as a small sample rather than an indication of the number of multinationals allowing subsidiaries to fail.

*Table 7.1 Parent Companies Allowing Affiliates to Fail from 2012 to 2021*

| *Year* | *Parent* | *Subsidiary* | *Reason for Failure* |
|---|---|---|---|
| 2012 | Dynegy Inc. (energy) | Dynegy Holdings (energy) | Falling electricity prices and debt that surpassed USD 5 billion the year before bankruptcy |
| 2013 | FCC Group (construction) | Alpine Holding GmbH (construction) | Insufficient liquidity due to costly expansion in Eastern Europe, unsuccessful in selling energy and engineering units to raise necessary cash |
| 2013 | Suntech Power Holdings Co. (photovoltaics) | Wuxi Suntech Power Holdings Co. (photovoltaics) | Default on its US bonds and following insolvency |
| 2017 | Toshiba Corp. (electronics) | Westinghouse Electric Co. (nuclear energy) | Massive losses related to nuclear projects in the US, owing to factors such as cost overruns, delays, stricter safety regulations |
| 2017 | Insel Air (aviation) | Insel Air Aruba (aviation) | Rapidly accumulated debt, no stabilization plan, cost-cutting measures, and no efforts to start generating income |
| 2017 | Takata Corp. (automotive) | TK Holdings (automotive) | Large recall of airbags: contractual indemnity, reimbursements, and contribution claims |
| 2018 | Anhui Liuguo Chemical Co. (chemicals) | Jiangxi Liuguo Chemical Co. (chemicals) | Long-term deficit |
| 2020 | Norwegian Air (aviation) | Subsidiaries in Denmark and Norway (aviation) | Cash flow problems due to coronavirus pandemic |
| 2021 | Johnson & Johnson (pharmaceuticals) | LTL Management LLC (pharmaceuticals) | Defense strategy from 28,900 pending lawsuits accusing a product of causing ovarian cancer and other physical injuries |

*Source*: Factiva News Search.

## 1 Rating Agencies Approaches

When evaluating implicit support for transfer pricing purposes, practitioners and tax authorities typically need to rely on methodologies and approaches disclosed by rating agencies and financial institutions. We describe in more detail some of the key considerations and viewpoints as described by the rating agencies. In general, the rating agencies use the term "parent rating" rather than "group rating." However, as described in the chapter on financial sector view, in cases where parent rating and group rating are not the same, the group rating should be taken into consideration for potential notching up of the subsidiary.

### *A Moody's Investor Services (Moody's)*

According to Moody's, the likelihood of providing support is based on both the willingness and the ability to do so.[15] Within those two headings, Moody's analyzes several distinct aspects.

#### *a Willingness to Provide Support*

Moody's takes into account the percentage of ownership, the subsidiary's financial track record, operational integration, strategic alignment, market confidence, the role of financial and other regulators, and other incentives or barriers to support. Regulatory considerations are particularly important for financial institutions.

Moody's acknowledged examples of parent companies that have decided to let their subsidiaries default despite having publicly articulated their strategic nature as well as the promise of ongoing support.[16] More specifically, a parent company might not support its financially distressed subsidiaries if such support compromises its ability to maximize shareholder value.

#### *b Ability to Provide Support*

The ability to provide support considers the parent credit rating, the links between the parent's and the subsidiary's financial conditions, and the relative magnitude and timing of all such expected investments.

Although some of the factors used to measure the ability to provide support may arguably be less important when analysing implicit support more broadly, it is nonetheless a fundamental analysis for pricing certain financial instruments. This is particularly the case for financial guarantees, where a parent's financial ability to provide support in a situation where a subsidiary may be in financial distress is a key driver of the economic benefit to the entity being guaranteed.

Moody's makes a broad distinction regarding typical characteristics of supported and supporting entities that would likely lead to different levels of willingness to support and rating uplift or credit drag. In one extreme, such characteristics might lead

15. "Assessing Affiliate Support in the Absence of a Guarantee (Cross-Sector Rating Methodology)," Moody's Investor Service, July 19, 2021. https://www.moodys.com/research/Assessing-Affiliate-Support-in-the-Absence-of-a-Guarantee--PBC_1269284
16. "Rating Non-Guaranteed Subsidiaries: Credit Considerations in Assigning Subsidiary Ratings in The Absence of Legally Binding Parent Support," Moody's Investors Service, 2003, p. 3.

to the affiliate receiving no support at all (implying no credit rating uplift), and in the other extreme, the characteristics might lead to the affiliate receiving such a high extent of support that its rating would be lifted up to (or close to) the rating of the supporter. In a middle scenario, Moody's considers characteristics that might lead to limited support and a credit rating uplift of two notches.[17]

### *B* *Standard & Poor Global Ratings*

Standard & Poor Global Ratings (S&P) states that a weak subsidiary owned by a strong parent will usually (but not always) enjoy a stronger rating.[18] The effect of support between the rating equalization to the group rating to the total absence of help depends on the evidence of support, analyzed through the economic incentive of the parent to provide support (among other factors). S&P therefore stipulates that the gap between the subsidiary's stand-alone rating and that of its parent is a function of their perceived relationship: "the greater the integration, the greater the potential for parent or sponsor support."[19] This relationship can narrow the gap between the rating levels of the parent and the subsidiary.

S&P highlights that there is not one single factor determining the relationship, but several factors taken together. These factors to a varying degree are comparable to those used by the other rating agencies and include, for example, the strategic importance (including its role in the supply chain), whether the subsidiary operates under the same name as the parent (reputational risks), the financial capacity to provide support or whether the parent firm has a track record of supporting subsidiaries in distressed financial situations.[20] Moreover, in a recent publication, S&P details how one can assess the relationship of a subsidiary's credit rating based on how strategic the subsidiary is in the MNE. In case a subsidiary is integral to the group's strategy and identity, S&P recommends using the same rating as the group. On the opposite side of the spectrum, if a subsidiary holds little or no strategic value to the group, the recommendation is to use the stand-alone rating. Table 7.2 summarizes the S&P framework.[21]

17. "Assessing Affiliate Support in the Absence of a Guarantee (Cross-Sector Rating Methodology)," Moody's Investor Service, July 19, 2021 https://www.moodys.com/research/Assessing-Affiliate-Support-in-the-Absence-of-a-Guarantee--PBC_1269284.
18. S&P Global Ratings, *Corporate Ratings Criteria* (2001), p. 100, http://regulationbodyofknowledge.org/wp-content/uploads/2013/03/StandardAndPoors_Corporate_Ratings_Criteria.pdf (accessed June 18, 2019).
19. *Ibid.*
20. For S&P Global Ratings and Fitch Ratings, "strategic importance" refers to linked lines of business. .
21. S&P Global Ratings, *General Criteria: Group Rating Methodology*, July 1, 2019, pp. 4, 5.

*Table 7.2 S&P Global Ratings Framework for Rating a Subsidiary in a Group*

| *Subsidiary Strategic Status Within the Group* | *Definition* | *Potential Credit Rating* |
|---|---|---|
| Core | Integral to the group's current identity and future strategy. The rest of the group is likely to support these entities under any foreseeable circumstances. | Group credit profile (GCP). |
| Highly strategic | Almost integral to the group's current identity and future strategy. The rest of the group is likely to support these group members under almost all foreseeable circumstances. | One notch lower than the GCP, unless the Stand-Alone Credit Profile (SACP) on that entity is equal to or higher than the GCP. In such cases, the potential credit rating is equal to the GCP. |
| Strategically important | Less integral to the group than "highly strategic" group members. The rest of the group is likely to provide support in most foreseeable circumstances. However, some factors raise doubts about the extent of group support. | Three notches above SACP. This is subject to a cap of one notch below the GCP unless the SACP is at least equal to the GCP, in which case the potential issuer credit rating (ICR) is equal to the GCP. |
| Moderately strategic | Not important enough to warrant support from the rest of the group in some foreseeable circumstances. Nevertheless, there is potential for some support from the group. | One notch above SACP. This is subject to a cap of one notch below the GCP unless the SACP is at least equal to the GCP, in which case, the potential ICR is equal to the GCP. |
| Nonstrategic | No strategic importance to the group. | SACP is capped at the GCP. |

*Source:* Standard & Poor's.

By the nature of these factors, an assessment will always be subjective. Considering these factors together will provide a picture that leads to some assessment of the degree to which implicit support can be assumed. Depending on the assumed degree of implicit support, the borrowing entity's rating may be raised to a better rating (notching), typically by one or two incremental steps.[22]

22. Amongst the three major rating agencies, S&P assumes that the rating of the borrowing entity cannot be better than the one of the entire group or the parent company, respectively. Fitch and Moody's do not apply that restriction. *See* Fitch Ratings, *Parent and Subsidiary Linkage Rating Criteria* (December 1, 2021) and Standard & Poor's, *General Criteria: Group Rating*.

### C Fitch Ratings

Fitch Ratings (Fitch) recommends a three-step approach using a decision flow diagram to determine the credit rating of a subsidiary. This includes establishing if a parent and subsidiary relationship exists. If this is the case, a stand-alone credit profile should be derived for the parent and the subsidiary, as well as the consolidated credit profile. Implicit support is determined by the strength of the relationship by considering various factors.[23] The Fitch methodology outlines different approaches depending on whether the parent is stronger rated to the subsidiary or the other way around. If the parent is rated higher, the factors considered are the legal incentive, the strategic incentive, and the operational incentive. However, if the subsidiary is rated higher, the factors are legal ring-fencing and access and control. Compared with the other two rating agencies, Fitch provides a systematic framework of subfactors to consider, including elements like guarantees and cross-defaults in the context of legal incentives. The factors and sub-factors would lead to a notching adjustment to the stand-alone rating that can be up or down.

## 2 Financial Sector View

A significant portion of transfer pricing analysis focuses on identifying comparable data for transactions between uncontrolled parties. In terms of identifying comparable financial transactions, the most obvious options would be loans provided by banks to third parties and the issuance of bonds.

In terms of comparability to intragroup transactions, there is an obvious difference between funding provided by a bank and funding provided by a related party in a nonfinancial industry: the business purpose of a bank is to make a profit from the financial services it provides to its clients. Compared with other corporations, banks generally have easier access to funding. At the same time, banks have higher costs relating to back-office activities because they are required to comply with financial regulations that other corporations do not have. For corporations outside of the financial industry, the provision of an intragroup loan is a secondary transaction, with the purpose of enabling the borrower to perform its main business purpose.

Let's assume that a bank loan is a comparable transaction. How do banks deal with the topic of rating and implicit support in particular? Banks rate their customers to comply with banking regulations and to price the loans properly. What is often not known (at least not among transfer pricing practitioners) is the fact that most banks develop their own rating models using historical customer data (including default rates). This leads to every bank having its own rating model based on different data, possibly leading to different rating results for the same customer at different banks.

Implicit support in banking rating models in the European Union is not specifically regulated. In the European Banking Authority Guidelines, we can find a single

23. Fitch Ratings, *Parent and Subsidiary Linkage Rating Criteria* (December 1, 2021): https://www.fitchratings.com/research/corporate-finance/parent-subsidiary-linkage-rating-criteria-01-12-2021

reference: "The rating of a such third party being taken into account as an indication of an override of the assignment of the relevant obligor to a grade or pool."[24] Therefore, banks may or may not reflect implicit support in their rating models, and their approach is usually based on their historical customer data. The outcome may differ from bank to bank, and country to country, depending on the situation in the market.

Based on observations in the Austrian market, we can conclude that implicit support is considered in the corporate rating models and is referred to as group/parental support. The effect on ratings is usually around one to three notches. In some specific cases, as also described in the S&P methodology, it can lead to an upgrade equal to the group rating. It is important to mention that in the banking industry, such group support can also have a negative impact. This may be the case when the parent company or another core subsidiary is in financial difficulty, and it may be expected that to save itself or the subsidiary, it may liquidate the borrower's assets.

Another point worth mentioning is that even though implicit support is often referred to as parental support, the applicable rating is the group rating. In the majority of cases, the group rating and parent rating will be the same, but they may differ depending on the structure of the group.

Having established that banks may consider implicit support, the question remains what the implications for the pricing of the loans would be. Banks base their ratings on financial data (objective values) as well as on soft facts (subjective values). Implicit support is one of many elements of the latter, and as such may have relatively limited influence on the overall rating itself.

Once a rating has been established, for the subsequent pricing of the loan, banks consider other elements of the loan, not limited to the currency of the loan, maturity, fixation, reference rate, and collaterals. Moreover, the relationship with the customer might be considered. For example, it might be a long-standing customer with many other products, and the loan may be secondary. In a different scenario, the bank might be trying to pitch for a new customer and attract it with low-interest rates. Last, every bank has its own pricing model (so-called fund transfer pricing), which considers internal costs and the (potential) funding cost of the bank.

In summary, banks may consider implicit support (group support) with often limited impact of one to three notches going either direction (positive or negative) on the entity credit rating. In the scheme of all things, implicit support may more generally have a limited effect on pricing, unless it is one of the rare cases where the group support is so strong that it leads to an equalization (or close to it) of the borrower's rating. In addition, as most banks develop their own rating models and have different pricing models, a customer with the same rating by different banks may receive different pricing for a loan. The reverse is also true: a customer can be rated differently by two banks, and the pricing of the loan may be the same or similar.

24. European Banking Authority, EBA/GL/2017/16; "Guidelines on PD Estimation, LGD Estimation and the Treatment of Defaulted Exposure," para. 62(b).

## IV PRACTICAL EXAMPLE CONSIDERING IMPLICIT SUPPORT

Implicit support is presented in the OECD transfer pricing guidelines as an example of the synergies inherent in large groups and should be accounted for in transfer pricing analyses.[25] In reality, it is not straightforward to determine a highly accurate credit rating that the market recognizes for a subsidiary company. As described, varying approaches and implications are observed when studying different financial services market participants. All three major rating agencies provide descriptions on how they consider implicit support. On the other hand, the approach of banks is not publicly available, and the applicable regulations (at least in the European Union) are very limited, not only allowing but expecting banks to apply an approach based on their historical data and regional specifics.

Regardless of the level of implicit support, the effect it has on the stand-alone rating can vary with different methods, and to a certain extent it is a subjective opinion of the person who is determining the rating. It is crucial to document the applied methodology and approach and justify in detail any specific adjustments.

As a practical example, let us consider the following fact pattern:

- A multinational group operates in the fast-moving consumer goods (FMCG) industry.
- The group set-up is such that the parent company (HoldCo) functions as a holding and financing and investment company. All products are produced centrally by one fully owned production company (ProdCo), which then sells the products across the world using fully fledged distribution subsidiaries.
- The largest distribution entity is the Chinese fully owned subsidiary, which has been active in the Chinese market for over 20 years, uses the same name and logo as the group, and is responsible for 40% of the overall group sales. It has a stand-alone rating of A–.
- The remaining part of the products are distributed by 35 (fully owned) subsidiaries, where the majority has no group branding.
- The group performs very well. The annual profit and the free cash flow are centralized at the level of HoldCo, which invests it in the financial market.
- HoldCo's rating is AA–, which is due to its strong financial position with limited liabilities.
- ProdCo has a stand-alone rating of A. It has a large balance sheet with substantial assets, such as the factory and raw materials and goods. However, it also has historical loans that were used to build up the operation. The loans were provided externally and by HoldCo.
- The stand-alone rating of the other subsidiaries—fully fledged distributors (FFDCos)—varies between A– and BBB–.

25. *See* OECD Transfer Pricing Guidelines 2022, "Chapter I: Arm's Length Principle," p. 8892, para. 1.184.

Against this fact pattern, questions arise about whether the group rating is the same as the HoldCo's rating, and the effect of implicit support on ProdCo and the FFDCos.

Considering the substantial assets that ProdCo holds and that it is solely responsible for the production function in the group, which through a value chain analysis has been determined to be a key value-added function, it seems obvious that it has a strong and (within the group) irreplaceable position. The situation of the individual FFDCos, however, would have to be assessed based on their size and relative importance, given their respective markets.

The following sections discuss the possible effect that implicit support might have based on the different methodologies of Moody's, S&P, and Fitch.

## 1 The Moody's Approach

According to Moody's, the likelihood of providing support is based on both the willingness and the ability to provide support. Tables 7.3 and 7.4 explain these criteria. We try to apply Moody's approach to assess whether the group is likely to support the borrower. Typically, the insight required for this assessment is obtained from the factual review, including the value chain, functional, asset and risk, and industry analyses.

*Table 7.3 Moody's: Willingness to Provide Support*

| *Factor* | *Assessment* |
|---|---|
| Percentage of ownership | Each entity is a wholly owned subsidiary of the group. This may lead to a potential notching adjustment for implicit support, subject to an evaluation of other factors. Other factors, such as an integrated management structure or an analysis on how subsidiaries are organized and managed, also need to be considered. |
| Subsidiary's financial track record | The stand-alone ratings (without consideration of implicit support) in the case study vary between A and BBB–, with each entity's financial performance and financial needs determined by local market factors and wider group strategy. An analysis of each subsidiary's track record and the group investments into a subsidiary is typically needed. Let's assume that apart from the Chinese entity, which accounts for 40% of group revenues with a long and established financial track record, all the other FFDCo entities have stable but variable financial track records over time; some markets are financially more important and established compared with others. |

| *Factor* | *Assessment* |
|---|---|
| Reputational considerations | Reputational considerations are of utmost importance, especially in the context of financial institutions. For nonfinancial institutions where reputational damage of default in one market may influence credit terms or a group's operations in other markets, a parent entity or group may well be more willing to provide support.<br>Assume that there are some financial risks arising from reputational damage because the Chinese distributor uses the same branding as the group. These risks would be largely limited to the Chinese market only, and branding in this specific FMCG industry has limited importance. In this context, no adjustment for reputational considerations would necessarily be needed. |
| Operational integration | Operational integration refers to the extent to which there may be management overlap, entities being functionally dependent on other entities, legal connections, etc. The higher the degree of operational adjustment, the larger the potential notching adjustment that may be appropriate.<br>Based on the functional asset and risk analysis, ProdCo was determined to be the only production company in the group supplying all the distribution entities. The value chain analysis revealed that ProdCo is crucial for the existence of the group. Furthermore, the group has a centralized treasury that mostly funded the production company activities, and let's assume some centralized procurement and other support activities were also available to all entities in the group. Assume there is limited shared management with HoldCo, and each market is managed largely independently, following group guidelines determined by central management. Given the varying levels of operational integration, a notching adjustment may be justifiable for most of the group entities but may be limited across markets, functions, and entities. |
| Strategic alignment | Strategic alignment is fundamental factor when it comes to implicit support. A value chain analysis often provides significant insight into the extent of strategic importance of a business unit, function, or entity to the group as a whole or the parent. The more important a function, entity, or business unit is to the group's central strategy, potentially the more likely a parent company would be willing to step in. It should be noted that the strategic positioning and alignment of a group, business unit, or entity may change over time.<br>The Chinese distributor represents a sizable proportion of the group's revenues. ProdCo is crucial for the existence of the group and its products. However, even in this scenario, outsourcing the production function may be a feasible option. |

| Factor | Assessment |
| --- | --- |
| | Therefore, in both cases, one could expect that the parent company would support these subsidiaries because of their strategic importance in the context of the overall value creation, to the extent that the parent believes there to be economic or shareholder value to do so. The other FFDCos' importance to the group varies depending on the market, size, and management strategy. |
| Role of financial and other regulators | This factor is of key importance for financial services companies, utilities, etc. A group may choose to protect its financially regulated entities to preserve the group's reputation. A regulator may impose criteria to provide support.<br>In the case study, it is not relevant in this sector. |
| Other incentives or barriers to support | Some industry- or company-specific factors (such as keep-well agreements, integrated or shared management teams, and cross-default or legal arrangements) may also affect the extent to which a subsidiary may be supported. A detailed functional, asset, and risk analysis and value chain analysis will reveal factors that may influence a group's willingness to support.<br>Let's assume that no specific factors could be identified in our case study. |

*Source:* "Assessing Affiliate Support in the Absence of a Guarantee (Cross-Sector Rating Methodology)," Moody's Investor Service, July 19, 2021.

*Table 7.4 Moody's: Ability to Provide Support*

| Factor | Reasoning |
| --- | --- |
| Parent credit rating | In the case study, the group has continuously been AA– rated and is operating in a stable industry. This is an investment grade rating, which is evidence of the strong financial capabilities of the group. Other considerations may entail the extent to which changes in markets may influence group performance and overall rating. A group may be willing to support an entity that is a greater driver of the group rating compared with entities that are not. The opposite may also be true in that if an entity were to default and if the group is unable to financially support it due to the default being too large, the group may not be in a financial position to provide the support and thus may not have any choice but to allow the default to occur. |
| Links between parent's and subsidiary's financial conditions | The Chinese distributor and ProdCo are crucial for the group in our case study and would potentially heavily influence the overall group performance. Because there is only one key value-adding production company, the whole group fully depends on it, including the extent to which its products can be produced in a cost-effective manner. |

| *Factor* | *Reasoning* |
|---|---|
| | As the Chinese distributor provides 40% of the group's overall profits, any inability to perform its activities may have an adverse effect on the overall financial stability of the group.<br>Both entities can be argued to be influencing the group's overall financial performance and are sizable. Although this feature may impose that the group be more willing to provide support due to the financial link, this can also lead to a situation wherein it is not financially feasible for a parent entity to support either entity. Thus, due to the linkage, a parent may choose to outsource production activities or divest the Chinese entity to protect the wider business as a going concern. |
| Relative magnitude and timing of any investments | Typically, when there are frequent investments into a particular entity it may suggest that the entity or business is a strategic focus area to the group and more important compared with other affiliates.<br>In the case study, we assume that no such investments are made. |

Among the factors mentioned in the tables, the links between the parent's and the subsidiary's financial conditions are probably the most relevant. Moody's states that "the amount of 'lift' that the jointly supported obligation can achieve relative to the stronger obligor's rating will depend on two factors: the rating of the weaker obligor and the correlation between default events for the two obligors."[26]

In the case study, ProdCo and the Chinese FFDCo have investment grade ratings (A and A–), thus the risk of financial difficulties is generally limited. HoldCo is a cash-rich company with a strong balance sheet that would allow it to provide support to a certain extent. Here it would be important to analyze the financials in further detail—size of the loan, period, size of the balance sheet, cash availability, and so on. Let's assume that the loans provided to the subsidiaries would not represent a financial risk to HoldCo.

In summary, we established that outside of large crisis-like events, the group is capable of supporting the Chinese distributor and ProdCo.

## 2 The S&P Approach

S&P stipulates that the gap between the subsidiary's stand-alone rating and the parent's is a function of the subsidiary's status in the group. In a recent publication, S&P details how one can assess the relationship of a subsidiary's credit rating based on how strategic the subsidiary's role is in the group. If a subsidiary is integral to the group's

26. Moody's Investor Services, Special Comment, "The Incorporation of Joint-Default Analysis into Moody's Corporate, Financial and Government Rating Methodologies," February 2005, p. 2.

strategy and identity, S&P recommends using the same rating as the group. On the opposite side of the spectrum, if a subsidiary holds little or no strategic value to the group, the recommendation is to use the stand-alone rating.

Evaluating a subsidiary's strategic role requires a thorough investigation of the facts of the case. S&P considers many factors: strategic importance, parent's credit rating, shared name (reputation), magnitude of the investment, domicile location, and general capacity to sustain the subsidiary should it become insolvent. In addition, S&P considers some other factors, such as the group's ownership structure, the public stance of the management, the nature of the reporting lines, and the group's track record in similar circumstances.

S&P does not offer an analytical framework to weigh these factors. The final notching decision is in the hands of the analyst. To this end, the rating agency notes that "there is an element of subjectivity in assessing most of these factors, as well as the overall conclusion regarding the relationship."[27]

In the case study, the Chinese distributor and ProdCo were deemed to be strategic for the group, so S&P recommends using a stand-alone credit rating and applying a notch-up adjustment as appropriate.

## 3 The Fitch Approach

Fitch recommends a three-step approach for determining the credit rating of a subsidiary. These include determining if a parent and subsidiary relationship exists and, if so, deriving stand-alone credit ratings for them. Implicit support is determined by the strength of the relationship (*see* Table 7.5). The methodology outlines a difference in approach depending on whether the parent is rated stronger than the subsidiary or the other way around. As mentioned, if the parent is higher rated, the factors are the legal incentive, the strategic incentive, and the operational incentive. If the subsidiary is higher rated, the factors considered are legal ring-fencing and access and control.[28] While the other rating agencies do not explicitly include guarantees and cross-defaults in their descriptions of assessing implicit support, the remainder of the factors is similar to those considered by Moody's. Specifically, the evaluation should devote adequate attention to the strategic and operational factors in the group.

27. S&P Global Ratings, *Corporate Ratings Criteria* 2013, p. 102, https://regulationbodyofknowledge.org/wp-content/uploads/2013/03/StandardAndPoors_Corporate_Ratings_Criteria.pdf.
28. Fitch Ratings, *Parent and Subsidiary Rating Linkage Rating Criteria* (December 1, 2021): *https://www.fitchratings.com/research/corporate-finance/parent-subsidiary-linkage-rating-criteria-01-12-2021*

*Table 7.5 Fitch: Factors for Implicit Support*

| *Factor* | *Assessment* |
|---|---|
| **Legal incentive** | |
| Guarantees | In our case study, no explicit guarantees are in place, and hence no rating adjustment would be needed for this factor. However, if a guarantee were to be in place, it would create a legal incentive for support to be provided and for which an adjustment to the rating would have been needed. |
| Other legal ties/cross-defaults | Cross-default arrangements can indicate significant legal linkage across group entities and contribute to the extent of implicit support. In the case study, we assume there are no cross-defaults or other relevant legal ties in the parent-subsidiary relationship. Thus, no adjustment is needed. |
| **Strategic incentive** | |
| Financial contribution | The Chinese distributor represents a sizable proportion of the group's revenues. ProdCo is crucial for the existence of the group. In both cases, one could expect that the parent company will support the subsidiaries to some extent. |
| Competitive advantage | The Chinese distributor may offer a competitive advantage to the group given its size and track record. This may be true for other markets in which the group operate. That said, the competitive advantage may be very locally oriented. When considering ProdCo, products or processes may provide the group with a competitive advantage. Nonetheless, ProdCo's activities could be outsourced. Although both entities are important to the group and an adjustment is likely, the extent of this adjustment may vary. |
| Growth potential | Let us assume that both the Chinese distributor and ProdCo are likely to have good growth prospects. This factor may also be important for other markets, where the group is looking to strategically expand their presence. |
| **Operational incentive** | |
| Operational synergies | The Chinese distributor represents a sizable proportion of the group's revenues. ProdCo is crucial for the existence of the group and supplies all the group distribution entities. The group has a central treasury function, centralized procurement, and some centralized support services. One can expect that there may well be some parental support, especially in relation to the ProdCo and the Chinese distributor. |
| Management & brand overlap | There is limited central management control on production; HoldCo sets goals, but ProdCo management is largely independent. Due to the importance of the Chinese market, let's assume that one of three managing directors of the Chinese entity is also a managing director of HoldCo. |

For each path (i.e., stronger parent or stronger subsidiary), the Fitch methodology provides a matrix that recommends a notching relationship that depends on the outcome of the linkage factor assessment. For the case study, this would a require a judgement on the significance of each factor by differentiating between low, medium, and high relevance.

## 4 Case Study Conclusion

After reviewing the group's information in the frameworks offered by the rating agencies, we conclude that given the operational set-up, the following adjustments to the stand-alone rating of the individual subsidiaries due to implicit support can be justified:

(1) ProdCo: due to its crucial role in the group, the operational integration, and size of the balance sheet, it can be safely assumed that as long as the group is financially successful overall, HoldCo will provide all support needed to maintain production. Even though the function is strategic to the group, the production activity could be outsourced. Therefore, adjusting the stand-alone rating by one or two notches, rating at the level of the group or one notch just below may be justifiable (from A to AA–).

(2) Chinese FFDCo: because of the importance of the subsidiary, shared branding, operational integration, and substantial share of the group profitability, it can be safely assumed that in case of financial distress, the parent company would potentially step up and support the subsidiary and its own financial interest. Therefore, notching up from A– to A+ or A (one or two notches below the parent company) would be a reasonable adjustment. If one were to change the fact pattern to conclude that the group is focusing its investments in other markets instead, and thereby have limited the level of investment and importance it has dedicated to the Chinese FFDCo, the conclusion may change, for example, the rating change may be limited to a maximum of one notch. Similarly, if the amount of the loan was so substantial that potential fallout may cause financial difficulties to the overall group, it may be justifiable to keep the stand-alone rating.

(3) The remaining FFDCos would likely remain at their stand-alone rating or receive at most a one-notch adjustment. However, this would have to be determined based on the facts and circumstances of each entity.

It is important to note that in case of a rating being provided by all three agencies, it is not unlikely that they may come to different conclusions. The relative importance of a group entity can also change over time. For this reason, for the purposes of in-house transfer pricing assessment and documentation, it is crucial to consider the topic of implicit support in the context of the group's prevailing value chain at the time of the assessment. Further one should document each step including all considerations in detail while applying the specific facts and circumstances of the case at hand.

## V CONCLUSION

We may conclude the following:

- implicit support as such is an incidental benefit and does not have to be remunerated;
- the effect of implicit support on a credit rating has been acknowledged by the updated OECD guidelines; however, its exact effect remains unclear and subjective;
- all third-party market players, for example, rating agencies and financial institutions, have slightly different approaches to this topic;
- the exact effect of implicit support on loan pricing is unclear and, based on experience in the banking industry, often rather limited. This can be attributable to the strict regulatory environment and more cautious approach of the banks, compared with rating agencies.

From a transfer pricing perspective, implicit support will remain a subjective opinion with a potential for disputes with tax authorities. Because the relative importance of any group entity can change as the group business model and value chain evolves over time, the level of implicit support for any specific market, entity, or business area may change over time. Having formal, written documentation of a detailed fact pattern and rationalization based on the prevailing value chain and functional, asset, and risk analysis at issuance is a must.

CHAPTER 8

# Revisiting the GE Case: Key Lessons for the Current Transfer Pricing Landscape

*J. Scott Wilkie*[*]

## I WHAT IS 'THE GE CASE'?

### 1 The Circumstances in Brief

In 2009 and 2010, the Tax Court of Canada[1] (TCC) and the Federal Court of Appeal of Canada[2] (FCA), respectively, adjudicated whether and how a non-arm's-length guarantee should be compensated, considering Canada's relevant statutory versions of the 'arm's-length principle' (the 'principle' or 'ALP') in subsections 69(2) and 247(2) of the *Income Tax Act* (Canada)[3] (the 'Act'). Those provisions applied, respectively, to some of several taxation years of the Canadian taxpayer straddling the replacement in 1998 by section 247, Canada's prevailing transfer pricing 'rule', of the former similar 'rule' in subsections 69(2) and (3). Canada has long embraced the ALP as set out in the Transfer Pricing Guidelines (the "TPG" or 'Guidelines') of the Organisation for Economic Co-operation and Development (OECD), as an influence on that statutory manifestation in the Act of the ALP and a source of interpretation and administrative practice by the Canadian tax authorities, the Canada Revenue Agency (CRA). In the case, there was general agreement that for relevant purposes there was no material

* The views and opinions set forth herein are the personal views or opinions of the authors; they do not necessarily reflect the views or opinions of the organization with which the authors are associated.

1. *General Electric Canada Inc. v. The Queen*, 2009 TCC 563 (TCC).
2. *The Queen v. General Electric Canada Inc.*, 2010 FCA 344 (FCA).
3. *Income Tax Act*, RS.C. 1985, c. 1 (5th Supp) as amended.

difference between the original enactment of the ALP in subsections 69(2) and (3) and the successor section 247 of the Act.[4]

The Canadian taxpayer, General Electric Capital Canada Inc. ('GE Canada') was an indirect wholly owned subsidiary of General Electric Capital Services, Inc. (GECUS), a United States member of the General Electric corporate family of which both GE Canada and GECUS were members. Both GE Canada and GECUS conducted financial services businesses for a range of independent commercial customers. In GE Canada's case, this included equipment and real estate financing, vehicle leasing and management, distribution and financing of technology products, railcar financing, auto lease financing, trailer leasing and financing, and private label credit cards.[5] Effectively GE Canada and GECUS operated as near banks or industrial banks.

GE Canada relied on frequent substantial issuances of commercial paper and unsecured debentures guaranteed by GECUS to fund its Canadian financing business.[6] GECUS did not charge for the guarantee it had provided since 1988, until 1996 when it began to charge GE Canada a 1% guarantee fee on otherwise unchanged terms. At the time guarantee fees were assimilated to the treatment of interest for withholding tax purposes under subsection 214(15) of the Act and GE Canada had dutifully withheld, collected and remitted to the CRA withholding tax at the 10% rate called for by the Canada – United States Income Tax Convention as it then applied.[7] The intended consequence of GECUS's guarantee was the ability of GE Canada to borrow at significantly reduced interest rates that would have applied if only its own credit supported its debt. The commercial arrangements and their effectiveness according to their terms, but for the guaranteed fee in the years it was charged, were not remarkable.

## 2 The CRA's Assessing Action and Controversy

The CRA contended that GE Canada ought to have paid nothing for its affiliate's, GECUS's, guarantee in the years when the guaranteed fee was charged and paid. The tax authorities asserted that as a member of the GE corporate family, GE Canada benefited from 'implicit support' and had, in fact, not paid for that support for many years before 1996 when the guarantee fee was initiated. This implicit support, sometimes referred to as 'affiliation benefits' or the 'halo effect'[8], was simply, in the CRA's view an attribute of GE Canada's corporate personality on which lenders would rely with the same effect even absent an explicit guarantee. Consequently, the CRA

4. FCA, para. 12.
5. TCC, paras 15 and 16.
6. FCA, para. 8.
7. Presently and uniquely among Canada's tax treaties, the withholding tax rate on non-arm's-length interest and guaranteed fees (generally deemed under the Act to be interest) is now zero, which reflects the significance commercial connections of US and Canadian MNEs in each other's economic life. But these exceptions did not exist for the years in issue in the GE case.
8. *See, generally*, OECD, *Transfer Pricing Guidelines for Multinational Enterprises and Tax Administrations* (2022), particularly Chapter I, section D.8 and Chapter VII, para. 7.13, and, as an example of how the 'halo' description is sometimes used, Ernst & Young, EY Tax News Update U.S. Edition, 21 April 2020, 2020-1059 (https://taxnews.ey.com/news/2020-1059-oecds-transfer-pricing-guidance-on-financial-transactions-considerations-for-us-taxpayers).

denied GE Canada's deduction of the guarantee fee in computing its income, even though the fee did not lose its commercial existence of connotations for withholding tax purposes, and in addition assessed withholding tax on a deemed dividend shareholder benefit as a secondary adjustment. The result was elevated taxable income of GE Canada by the amount of the denied guarantee fee deductions, non-resident withholding tax that had in the ordinary course been remitted on the guarantee fee as it had been paid since the commercial nature of that arrangement as seen by the Act was unchanged, and additional withholding tax on the guarantee fee re-cast under the Act as a deemed dividend subject to a 5% withholding tax. In effect, the guarantee fee was subjected to a 15% withholding tax, despite the reduction of interest and dividend withholding tax under the Canada-United States tax treaty to 10% for interest and 5% (for direct dividends to substantial shareholders) respectively, and GE Canada faced an increased Canadian income tax liability for GE Canada.

Essentially, the CRA asserted that GE Canada and its lenders enjoyed no material benefit from the guarantee by GECUS, compensated or not to GECUS, and accordingly GE Canada ought not to have paid for it. In the CRA's view, 'GECUS would have supported the respondent [GE Canada] regardless of the guarantee ... .'[9] In part, the CRA grounded its position with reference to paragraph 7.13 of the OECD TPG, which remains unchanged though elaborated in other places[10] from the form in which it existed for this case, which, broadly, denies that the benefits associated merely with being a member of a corporate family, i.e., 'by reason of its affiliation alone', should be compensated unless in the case of a guarantee 'the higher credit rating [of the affiliate whose debt was guaranteed] were due to a guarantee by another group member ...'. The issue was joined by GE Canada which contended that 'the guarantee fee was *at least* commensurate with an arm's length price and that it had properly computed and remitted the exigible Part XIII [withholding] tax'. [Emphasis added].

## 3 The Issues

The GE case framed two fundamental issues, which have significance beyond the immediate practical question of what, if anything, should be paid for a financial guarantee and if anything, by what standard should the 'arm's-length charge' be determined. They penetrate the core of transfer pricing analysis.

'Who' is that taxpayer, that is, what are its characteristics that, once established, are the foil for a comparison with how transactions in an arm's-length situation would have been undertaken?

Is transfer pricing a search for the 'right price' or the value of the shared benefit arising from membership in a multinational corporate family and, consequently, the value of any enhanced or incremental benefit attributable to legal commitments undertaken contractually in favour of others who may enforce them?

9. FCA, para. 13.
10. TCC, para. 167. *See supra* n. 8 to consult relevant provisions of the TPG.

Percolating beneath these two transfer pricing questions in the case is a third question: Should transfer pricing analysis apply to the organizational and transactional events as taxpayers have constructed them, assuming that they abide by the intrinsic expectations of those arrangements in their conduct, or to an imagined alternative formulation that yields economically and apart from tax financially equivalent outcomes but with different tax consequences?

That last question spoken more 'technically' invokes a critical inquiry, mostly absent it seems, into present transfer pricing's willingness to operate outside of or beyond, or for that matter to discard the significance in a transfer pricing analysis of the private law and its constructions, indeed the law, as the starting point for any tax analysis in favour of 'recharacterization'.[11] This question invites inquiry about what the contemporary, but malleable even slippery notions of 'accurate delineation', 'commercial rationality', and 'value creation' mean if they are not merely clumsily descriptive of an evidence-based inquiry to determine as a constructive and not mechanical matter what the enforceable legal arrangements actually and at law undertaken by taxpayers are.[12]

---

11. Transfer pricing has been overcome by loose notions of transactional definition, all in one way or another, taking for granted that 'substance' is its goal. 'Substance' is not self-defining or self-evident; economics is not law even if industrial economics offers ways to better understand evidence about parties' dealings as they have configured their commercial relations otherwise as the law permits. Transfer pricing's deference to untethered notions of 'substance' is criticized in Scott Wilkie, *The Substance of 'Substance' – Substance Abuse? Law's Role in the Economics of Transfer Pricing – Competitor, Combatant or Collaborator?*, prepared for the 2022 WU Global Transfer Pricing Conference, 14-17 February 2022, Institute for Austrian and International Tax Law, www.wu.ac.at/taxlaw, Session 6, Transfer Pricing and Substance, now published in Transfer Pricing Developments Around the World 2022, Michael Lang and Raffaele Petruzzi Eds., *Recent Developments on Transfer Pricing and Substance*, (The Netherlands: Wolters Kluwer Kluwer Law International B.V., 2022), Ch. 6, 165-211.
12. These issues are usefully engaged by Professor Vikram Chand and Giovanni Dembo, in *Intangible-Related Profit Allocation within MNEs based on Key DEMPE Functions: Selected Issues and Interaction with Pillar One and Pillar Two of the Digital Debate*, (Amsterdam: International Bureau of Fiscal Documentation, International TAXS, 2020), notably section 3 Scope-Related Issue. This paper usefully engages a variety of different issues associated with 'intangibles', a notion that has dominated the OECD's approach to transfer pricing and international income allocation, via the BEPS and Pillars projects. But, in the financial context, there is less concern with 'intangible' manifestations of value in a descriptive sense because the law has a great deal to say about law-determined relationships that are not the creation of economics. Intangibles – oriented profit allocation, which itself is problematic for various reasons, ought not to be conflated with the law and finance of guarantees. Certainly, the commitments and obligations under a guarantee are 'intangible' in a sense, but in the sense primarily that the obligations and rights they reflect they are property (or not if the issue is implicit support although even this depiction may be considered to comport with a contract even if not written). The rights and obligations under a guarantee, under the laws of guarantee, property, and contract, are incorporeal property – the watchword being 'property' as a legal matter. A problematic aspect of the way in which the OECD from the outset of its review of 'intangibles' in the late 2000s has approached the subject of 'intangibles', is not focusing precisely on the fact that 'intangibles' – some manifestation of shared or residual value – are not typically property unless the law makes them so. In the case of guarantees, the law makes it so. There is an explicit arm's-length aspect that is controlling even when the guarantor and the guaranteed party are not at arm's length, and financial markets really do know how to price this risk because they do it in the ordinary course of typical financial relation. There is very little new or novel. The issue of implicit support is partly an issue of 'corporate genetics', as commented on elsewhere in this chapter, and partly

### A 'Affiliation Benefits', 'Implicit Support', the 'Halo Effect'[13]

First, as basic as it seems to say it this way, the foundational questions for transfer pricing were: 'who is the taxpayer', and what are its relevant characteristics?

The CRA contended that as a member of a corporate family, the taxpayer was the sum of its own immediate features plus its commercial pedigree as a group member, subsumed in the notion of 'affiliation'. This is as much as would be the case, for example, of a human being whose essence is found in her or his direct manifestation and personality but 'in the genes' too. So, in the CRA's view, the first step in a transfer pricing analysis is to determine all relevant characteristics of and influences on a taxpayer as others would see the taxpayer and evaluate the taxpayer in relation to their own commercial interests and conduct.

The taxpayer, on the other hand, rejected what amounted to the theory of 'corporate and commercial genetics', though not expressed that way nevertheless having that effect. The taxpayer effectively cast that perception of how the arm's-length standard should apply as a tautology – to determine an arm's-length outcome, first a non-arm's-length premise must be established. The taxpayer said no that the requisite analysis should proceed by reference to the standalone characteristics of the taxpayer, unadulterated by the implications of or any influence by group affiliation, by 'corporate and commercial genetics'.

### B The Arm's-Length Price

Second, on the assumption that the guarantee was worth something and accordingly compensable, by what standard, according to the ALP as engaged by the Act, should that compensation be determined? Is the quest to find the value of a benefit, or, otherwise, to determine 'a price', or is a price simply the outgrowth of the value of the benefit? The premise of these questions and indeed more generally transfer pricing's interest is that 'money', 'finance', and 'credit' are in the nature of 'things', whether products or the outcome of services provided, just as much as typical products and services. Accordingly, even though financial notions are often bedevilling for other reasons in a tax context, they are objects of taxation, effectively 'commodities', as much as more familiar tangible objects of taxation, to which transfer pricing notions can and ought to be applied in a customary way. Pointedly, transfer pricing should not have to reinvent itself to address financial transactions and the appropriate cost of credit, either for the provider or credit or the beneficiary of the provider's financial accommodation by way of a direct financing or indirect support by way of a guarantee

contractual even where the contractual arrangement is implied. In that event the dominant consideration is whether the implicit support is enforceable actually or constructively according to reasonable expectations that it is enforceable or in any event would be provided if called on in the same way as if it would be enforceable. Then the question is what that support is worth, and whether that value is degraded, but still extant, because support by (reasonable) implication than typical written contract, introduces a risk, though a risk that financial markets are capable of valuing, i.e., 'pricing'.

13. *See supra* n. 8.

to the beneficiary. The objectives and approaches of a suitable transfer pricing analysis need not and ought not to proceed differently simply because the transactional object is money or a monetary commitment.

## II A PAUSE TO CONSIDER WHAT *IS* THE CURRENT TRANSFER PRICING LANDSCAPE FOR WHICH THE GE CASE OFFERS LESSONS

### 1 Four Developments

What is the 'current transfer pricing landscape' that is meant to learn or have learned lessons from the GE case? What are its features and elements, and what is shaping the terrain of the ALP's landscape which we think makes the landscape 'current' and more fiscally verdant in relation to perceptions of its earlier features, sense and significance?

For this discussion, there are four notable 'developments', though how much they reflect changes to rather than a more cogent understanding of transfer pricing and a concomitant willingness to admit its persistent and unchanged undercurrents is debatable.

### 2 First Development

The first development, the bedrock of the current landscape, is the test of transfer pricing's purpose and analytics undertaken as part of the OECD – led Base Erosion and Profit Shifting (BEPS) project, notably as framed in the immediate respect by the 2015 Report on Actions 8-10 and continuing work led by the OECD to refine aspects of that Report's analysis and guidance. At least in so far as transfer pricing is concerned, this followed an earlier focused restatement of the TPG concerning 'intangibles' and the introduction into the TPG of specific guidance concerning 'business restructurings'. These bear marks of transfer pricing's usual but amplified insistence on economic determinism labelled 'economic substance' spoken in the language of 'contributions' made to 'value creation' (according to 'accurately delineated' and 'commercially rational' transactions as tax authorities would decide) as the means by which income arising within the legally fragmented organizational and transactional realities of internationally complex multinational enterprises (MNEs) should be parsed and allocated in ways that reflect the economic unity of MNEs. Despite, however, the sometimes slavish repetition of 'economic substance' as the hallmark of transfer pricing and analytical triumph of transfer pricing methodology in the service of the ALP, a careful study of the BEPS transfer pricing guidance reveals several essential features: the necessary role played by legal substance in the sense of an evidence based evaluation of whether members of MNEs reasonably conducted themselves as the intrinsic expectations of their organizational and transactional circumstances objectively would expect; the essence of transfer pricing as profit splitting despite, again slavishly, a continuing focus on methodological analysis as if transfer pricing methodology were the principle, and a guarded acceptance of formulary or fractional approaches to income allocation reflected in an understated and nuanced way by the advancement of DEMPE functions ('Development', 'Enhancement', 'Maintenance', 'Protection', and 'Exploitation') and allowing for the acceptability of 'outsourcing' of activities in the service of functions where those functions are conducted.

## 3 Second Development

The second development, the landscape's foliage and flora so to speak, with deep historical roots reaching right back to work undertaken under the auspices of the League of Nations in the 1930s[14] but more recently as a set of 'methodological' instructions to 1979, is a 'development' only in its most recent BEPS induced restatement in 2017. It is the expanse of transfer pricing guidance captured in the TPG from 1979 to the present, recalibrated in 2017 and again in 2022. The present transfer pricing guidance in the 2022 TPG, its essence in articulating the ALP cast in Article 9 of the OECD Model Tax Convention, is fundamentally unchanged from its first articulation as guidance in 1979, despite the most recent affection for notions of 'accurate delineation', 'commercial rationality', and 'value creation', as if they have objective significance as justifications for displacing what taxpayers actually do with what it may be imagined they could or ought to have done to achieve economically equivalent outcomes in different and more taxable ways.[15] A more refined perception of these notions, together with other outgrowths of what may be regarded as 'BEPS 1', is

14. For some of this history and its significance for the ongoing international conversation about transfer pricing and the recalibration of key jurisdictional tenets of international taxation, *see* J. Scott Wilkie, *The Way We Were? The Way We Must Be? The 'Arm's Length Principle' Sees Itself (for What It Is) in the 'Digital' Mirror*, Intertax, Volume 47, Issue 12, 2019, 1087-1102.
15. It is to be noted that the 2010 TPG, which preceded the present 2017 version, acknowledged more clearly in section D.2 of Chapter I that transfer pricing guidance and analysis applied to taxpayer's 'actual transactions' and only in 'exceptional cases' – cases I would say reflect of incompatibility of organizational and transactional mechanics, on the one hand, and an evidence-based determination of the legal significance of how taxpayers actually conducted themselves – should 'the tax administration ... disregard the actual transactions or substitute other transactions for them.' This is consistent with the how Canadian courts approach transfer pricing cases, proceeding on the basis of transactions undertaken by taxpayers as they have framed them using legal constructions provided pertinent evidence reveals that they actually conducted themselves accordingly, but also understanding that contracts do not have to be written to exist and an important part of a transfer pricing analysis is discovering whether within the arrangements as taxpayers have expressed them contractually or organizationally there are latent legal relations constituting contracts that are equally significant and authoritative needing to be examined independently and in context from a transfer pricing point of view. These notions arise from, for example, the Supreme Court of Canada's *GlaxoSmithKline* (*Canada v. GlaxoSmithKline Inc.*, 2012 SCC 52, [2012] 3 SCR 3) and the FCA's *Cameco* (*The Queen v. Cameco Corporation*, 2020 FCA 112 (FCA) cases cited below. For a more considered recent commentary about the *Cameco* case, *see* J. Scott Wilkie, *Transfer Pricing Rules Past Cameco and Digital Tax on Tech Giants*, IBFD International Transfer Pricing Journal, September/October, 2021, 307-319, and J. Scott Wilkie, *The Cameco Transfer Pricing Appeal Ends Today, Tax at Osgoode Hall Law School Conversations and Commentary on Tax Law*, https://tax.osgoode.yorku.ca/2021/02/the-cameco-transfer-pricing-appeal-ends-today-2/.

guidance to detect using evidence-based legal empiricism whether what taxpayers have apparently undertaken mechanically accords with the reasonable expectations of the legal formulations they employed in the commercial settings in which activities and responsibilities that define those formulations, as a legal matter, actually take place and even for so-called intangibles are observable. An over-arching influence on and of the TPG, more acutely detectable in light of the BEPS focus, is profit splitting within an MNE group assisted by the TPG and a constructive legal and commercial examination of the role and responsibilities of the fragmented legal elements of the economic unity that is the MNE. In other words, all elements of the MNE have the same 'corporate and commercial genes', even if they also have their separate existences and discrete manifestations transactionally. Transfer pricing analysis has always been fundamentally concerned with the functioning of the 'whole' commercial person and not merely the separate manipulation of its limbs and organs, even though the misconception of the ALP as being the methodologies offered as analytical devices to be used judiciously may have distorted the implications of transfer pricing analysis and regulation.

As an important aside and as relevant context, it is to be noted since the catalyst for these comments is a Canadian tax case, that the preeminence of the law and in particular the Act's statutory statement of the ALP has been reaffirmed a number of times by Canadian courts. They have said explicitly that though analytically helpful the OECD's guidance does not have the legal significance of the Act's provisions.[16]

## 4 Third Development

The third development, this landscape's fiscal fauna as it were, is the specific transfer pricing guidance for financial transactions published by the OECD in February 2020 which is now incorporated in the TPG (the 'February 2020 guidance').[17] Essentially, this guidance, which applies to all manner of financing, is an exposition on how to conduct the usual kind of functional analysis, but of financial transactions rather than other transfers of goods and services, in the fashion usually advocated for transfer pricing in deference to the ALP. That is, the only real difference is the object of the transactions, money. That is not insignificant, of course, because aside from the confusion in tax law that 'money' and 'currency' as transactional objects often occasions, there are unique features about how MNEs solicit and procure money for their enterprises that make transfer pricing analysis of money transactions difficult. Mostly, these challenges arise from the usual source of debate, what is an arm's-length equivalent transaction in circumstances where MNEs often 'face' financial markets as

16. *See* the *GlaxoSmithKline* and *Cameco* cases, for example, *supra* n. 15. *See also supra* n. 14.
17. OECD, *Transfer Pricing Guidance on Financial Transactions, Inclusive Framework on BEPS: Action 4, 8-10,* announced by the OECD on 11 February 2020 in *OECD releases Transfer Pricing Guidance on Financial Transactions*, now incorporated in the recently released 2022 edition of the TPG and contained in Chapter 1, section D.1.2 (particularly D.1.2.2.2) and Chapter X, as explained in this Report. For convenience and clarity in drawing attention to the unchanged substance and text of this guidance, this chapter refers to the OECD guidance or 2020 guidance or February 2020 guidance. The section and paragraph designations in the guidance carry over to the 2022 edition of the TPG.

a whole enterprise acting through a principal member with market status and credibility which then disburses market-raised funding throughout the MNE using internal transactions of a typical financial sort but which, it has been observed, in that situation where there are not adverse interests of the transacting parties for which the legal nature of the transactions is important and defining could just as readily have assumed any 'form'.[18]

More pointedly, an implicit thread of the February 2020 guidance, consistent with the underlying themes of BEPS and the renovated 2017 and 2022 TPG, is a careful movement to recognize that transfer pricing is, as Article 9 of the OECD Model Tax Convention says and implies, is directed to allocating collective profit among participating or contributing MNE members unadulterated by the exercise of common control in what would amount to a fiscally chauvinistic way. In other words, while respecting the legal fragmentation of MNEs organizationally and transactionally, evaluate jurisdictional attachments to and attractions of income on a constructively unitary basis.

A case in point, pertinent to these comments, is guarantees. Clearly, the objective of the supplementary OECD guidance is to determine the value of a guarantee and what should be paid for it. Striking to the heart of this guidance, the OECD advocates evaluating the benefit of a (contractual) guarantee in two stages.

First, determine the benefits that inevitably and incidentally arise from being an MNE group member, with reference to how external markets and transacting parties perceive a relevant taxpayer. In other words, identify the financial support reasonably expected of MNE group members in relation to each other, that arises from affiliation, that is implicit in the relationship, that is essentially costless. In this step, the implied credit of taxpayers beyond that if were standing alone is to be determined. For that, in line with historical and continuing guidance of the OECD in paragraph 7.13 of the TPG, which was considered in the GE case, nothing would be paid; this is the benefit that elevates the taxpayer-borrower's credit from BBB to A, in the examples offered in section D.3 of the February 2020 guidance.[19]

Next, assuming that the taxpayer benefits from an explicit guarantee being provided by another and likely superior MNE group member, determine with reference to financial market measures and expectations, i.e., what lenders would 'pay' for creditworthiness beyond that generated by the borrower's circumstances alone assuming some measure of implicit support. The calculus is clear: interest rates and other financing costs derive among other things importantly from an obligor's credit, and if

18. *See, e.g.*, H. DAVID ROSENBLOOM, *Address, Banes of an Income Tax: Legal Fictions, Elections, Hypothetical Determinations, Related Party Debt*, Sydney Law Review, Volume 26, 2004, 17-35.

19. *See supra* n. 16. The United Nations Transfer Pricing Manual published in 2020 addresses financial transactions and guarantees in much the same manner as the OECD February 2020 guidance which is now incorporated in the TPG. *See* United Nations Practical Manual on Transfer Pricing for Developing Countries (2021), ST/ESA/377 (New York: United Nations, 2021), for this discussion Chapter 9 and for guarantees section 9.13. The United Nations Manual includes useful examples of the kind of analysis involved although the principle applied in relation to transfer pricing guidance more generally is fundamentally the same as that reflected and grounded in the OECD TPG. Accordingly, this chapter focuses on the TPG; any nuances in the UN discussion would not change the comments here. For these comments it is convenient and not inaccurate to consider reference to the OECD guidance as also to the UN guidance.

a lower financing cost is to be offered, there is a quid pro quo for that forbearance that in present value terms provides alternative compensation to the financiers.

The OECD guidance offers various possible ways for conducting this market-oriented transfer pricing analysis, all consistent with the familiar comparison-based transfer pricing analysis that applies more easily when the object of the transfers is something other than money: the 'CUP method', 'yield approach', 'cost approach', 'valuation of expected loss approach', and 'capital support method' are all offered, though all of them, because of the unique but usually necessary circumstances of MNE financial transactions internally and with markets, suffer from the same sorts of objective limitations of comparison-based transfer pricing analysis as are encountered when the objects of transactions are not money.

There is an evident methodological deference to and preference for, however, the 'yield approach', which is how the applied guidance in the examples takes shape. This may follow the unique financial and legal nature of a guarantee. It should be but almost never is noted that, unlike most transfers to which transfer pricing guidance applies, guarantees are not bilateral transactions. They are trilateral. They manifest intersecting axes of financial and legal interest. For that reason, since the root of the arrangements – where the money and interest rate forbearance come from – lies in financial accommodations by non-MNE group members, fundamentally guarantees are arm's-length arrangements even though one of the axes involves, as in the GE case a support commitment of one group member in favour of another who pays for that support. That is, the determinants of the adjusted cost of money, i.e., interest and other financing charges, effectively 'prices' the value of a guarantee's benefit to disinterested third parties whose only concern is getting repaid with a fair return for the implied risk of the transaction which implied or implicit or affiliation benefit support only goes so far to ameliorate as may be objectively determined by the behaviour of financial markets.

More specifically, a guarantee is an enforceable contractual commitment by the guarantor to a third party, the price of which is determined with reference to the creditworthiness of a borrower, which benefits from the guarantee, and the creditworthiness of the guarantor which temporarily and on terms 'lends' or contributes its credit to the affiliated borrower for compensation. The lenders effectively pay the compensation for the guarantee to the borrower as reduced borrowing costs – interest and other financing charges; the borrower 'shares' that 'fee' – the market measure of the value of the guarantee or, put another way, the incremental benefit arising from it, by paying its affiliated guarantor some portion of that 'fee' or benefit, in other words for the contractual commitment between the borrower and the guarantor that is endorsed, also contractually, for the benefit of lenders as a directly (by them) enforceable obligation, to them, of the guarantor.

The compensation to the guarantor, a function of the benefit of the guarantee, theoretically could range up to the entire value of the benefit. If it were the entire value of the benefit, then the borrower would be indifferent about having the benefit of the guarantee; it could either pay the higher interest without the guarantee or the lower interest plus the (present value) of the interest rate difference which together result in the same or equivalent financing cost to the borrower as if there were no guarantee. In either case, the lenders are indifferent; the credit risk they take vis-á-vis the borrower is fully compensated by enforceable obligations that essentially leave them 'whole'. Accordingly, the intramural compensation paid by a borrower to its affiliate guarantor to purchase the benefit of the guarantor's incremental credit could conceivably reach the full value of the benefit, but that, likely, would undermine the 'commercial rationality' of the guarantee in the first place, and so would be expected to be less. The difference, that is part of the value of the guarantor's credit that is 'left in the transaction', has the economic flavour of a capital contribution or non-interest-bearing loan that is constructively extracted or repaid when the guarantee expires.

This way of looking at guarantees, which only implicitly the OECD guidance does, as complex multiparty arrangements with a fundamental arm's-length root, illustrates the chameleon-like nature of internal financial transactions within an MNE group the equivalent economic and financial significance of which can conceivably be replicated by different legal configurations, with different deduction and withholding tax consequences. It also provides an explanation as to why intuitively perhaps the transfer pricing analysis of guarantees would have the most confidence in the yield approach.

Notable in the February 2020 guidance on financial transactions is an evident though guarded respect for analysing MNEs as unities and in that connection recognizing what fashionably in transfer pricing descriptors is referred to as implicit support, affiliation benefits, or the halo effect. All of these phrases disguise the essential nature of transfer pricing analysis as profit splitting, with not only qualified deference but also scepticism about the fiscal significance of legal constructions by which the economic unity is fragmented. In that vein and consistent with more over-arching commentary in the TPG about factoring in the influence of group membership, the February 2020 guidance recognizes this 'wholistic' transfer pricing outlook when speaking about treasury functions including cash pooling generally and pointedly considering 'group membership' and the use of an MNE group's credit rating,[20] and specifically with respect to guarantees where the 'effect of group membership' deserves its own subsection.[21] The evaluation of affiliation here mirrors undercurrents of the historical and continuing qualification of affiliation benefits in paragraph 7.13 of the TPG, which in the 2017 TPG was supplemented by section D.8 in Chapter 1 dealing with 'MNE Group Synergies' informed be salient Example 1 and Example 2 in paragraphs 1.164 to 1.167 of Chapter 1, essentially an economical statement of what the February 2020 guidance, now incorporated in the 2022 TPG, built out considerably and more pedantically.

To summarize very briefly, the February 2020 guidance and accordingly the 2022 TPG in so far as it applies to guarantees recognizes the relevance and significance of implicit support or affiliation benefits as a point of departure for determining in a financial sense 'who' is the taxpayer and then recommends the most reliable evaluation of incremental contractual credit support using the yield method. It does this fully a decade after the GE case was decided, about which more below. It is also to be observed, again, that, in keeping with the sense of Article 9 of the OECD Model Tax

20. *See supra* n. 17, paras C.1.1.3, C.1.1.4, and C.1.1.6 in the February 2020 guidance.
21. *See supra* n. 17, para. D.1.2 in the February 2020 guidance.

Convention, the focus is on identifying the benefit of a guarantee and consequently what ought to be paid for it as a function of 'commercial and financial relation' as Article 9 speaks, and not on the application of methodological analysis for its own sake as if it were the ALP. And, aside from one elliptical reference to 'accurate delineation'[22] offering no analytical clarity or direction, the analysis proceeds by accepting the relevant transactions as taxpayers have arranged and expressed them in familiar legal ways. We will bear all of this in mind when we return to the GE case to consider what the courts decided and what lessons there are for the landscape to be learned from that case.

## 5 Fourth Development

The fourth development is encapsulated in the OECD Pillars One and Two outgrowths of BEPS, sometimes referred to as BEPS 2, most recently endorsed by the G20 Finance Ministers and Leaders on 8 and 30 October 2021, respectively. The Pillars provide the 'blue sky' above the terrain of the first three developments below it, completing the vista of the current transfer pricing landscape. These comments are not to assess the Pillars. But observations, consistent with the earlier landscape comments, are apposite.

First, particularly envisaged by Pillar One, there is a latent and even guarded willingness to overcome commercialized transfer pricing's enduring affection for typical transaction-based methodological analysis according to the TPG, in favour of some manifestation of formulary or fractional apportionment. This is in the spirit of what the ALP really means, as framed by Article 9 of the OECD Model Tax Convention.

While the catalyst for this epiphany is 'digital', effectively Pillar One, but Pillar Two also in a less direct and possibly more blunt way, reflects a willingness for international tax purposes to recognize that the fiscal significance of legal constructions that fragment economic unities may be debatable where the result is that economic actors in equivalent economic and business positions relative to the 'sources' of their income are treated differently for tax because of those legal constructions and the hoary attachment of jurisdictional notions in international tax to tangible or physical presence that is entirely otiose for the kind of business being conducted. In other words, the economic actor is the group, and the international tax exercise is to assign or allocate profit among group members in ways that reflect the necessary and extant income-earning connections to where income at least partly originates.

That is, affiliation is a hallmark of the commercial and tax personalities of MNEs – 'who' they are as tax subjects – and the time has come to resist vestigial and economically irrelevant associations that are fiscally debatable and, even, not necessary if the usual jurisdictional parameters are interpreted and applied descriptively in relation to the characteristics of businesses rather than prescriptively as if they mandated forms of business and kinds and degrees of business conduct that are arcane and even precious in contemporary economic circumstances.

22. *See supra* n. 17, in para. 10.169 of Chapter D of the February 2020 guidance.

Second, leaving aside the debate about what 'source' means, 'source' countries are entitled to tax a share of group income to a reasonable degree, as a function of its attachment to those 'sources' – jurisdictional sources that are established in relation to legal sources attendant on applicable private and public law constructions and the 'economics' of how an evidence-based analysis of the conduct of business reveals how the income was earned. This is a country-to-country rubric, as are most elements of international tax. This also reflects the essence of the BEPS Actions 8-10 recommendations, which essentially deal with the fiscal insignificance of some MNE group members whose contributions are considered to be marginal, not by 'lifting the corporate veil' or the like but by evaluating corporate groups effectively on a consolidated basis and leaving a modest low-risk return to group members with legal existence but little business or economic significance and so resulting in the material group income gravitating to those jurisdictions where, functionally, it could only have been 'earned' in any event.[23] The only question then is whether the assignment, apportionment, or allocation – all the same – of the income is to be accomplished qualitatively or quantitatively and if the latter, by what 'formula' or 'fractions'.

## III WHAT DID THE GE CASE COURTS DECIDE?

Getting to the point quickly, the TCC and the FCA of Canada, in 2009 and 2010, decided the following.

### 1 Affiliation Benefits, Implicit Support Matter

The 'who' of a transfer pricing analysis takes account of all the relevant functional and financial characteristics of a taxpayer embedded in its corporate family genetics because third-party observers of that business and financial personality would take account of those genetics:

> [54] The concept underlying subsection 69(2) and paragraphs 247(2)(a) and (c) is simple. The task in any given case is to ascertain the price that would have been paid in the same circumstances if the parties had been dealing at arm's length. *This involves taking into account all the circumstances which bear on the price whether they arise from the relationship or otherwise.*[24] [Emphasis added].

23. For discussion of this, *see also* WILKIE, *supra* n. 13 and SCOTT WILKIE, *New Rules of Engagement? Corporate Personality and the Allocation of 'International Income' and Taxing Right*, in Brian J. Arnold (ed.), *Tax Treaties after the BEPS Project: A Tribute to Jacques Sasseville* (Toronto: Canadian Tax Foundation, 2018), 349-371.
24. FCA, and *see also*, paras 21 (the Tax Court justice found that 'GECUS's [the guarantor] implicit support, which derives from the respondent [GE Canada, the borrower whose debt was guaranteed, and the taxpayer in this case] being a member of the GE family, was a relevant factor', 47, 48, 50, and 59. The Supreme Court of Canada determined in the *GlaxoSmithKline* transfer pricing case, *supra* n. 13, what the FCA determined and articulated at its stage of the appeal of that case, 'all relevant circumstances were to be taken into account'; the FCA went on to say in para. 59 of its reasons in the GE case, 'there is no doubt that the existence of the implicit guarantee is relevant to the inquiry and must be considered in identifying the arm's length price'. Note that the FCA in the *Cameco* case applied the same approach to perceiving the 'whole

## 2 The Value of the Benefit Is What Is to Be Measured: The 'Price' Follows from That

The Tax Court found, and the FCA agreed 'that what should be measured is the value of the benefit provided by the explicit guarantee'. By way of explanation, the FCA said:

> [60] There is equally *no merit* to the respondent's argument that the method used by the Tax Court Judge is flawed because it identifies the benefit which the explicit guarantee procured rather than the arm's length price which the respondent would have to pay for this guarantee. No doubt, *the method seeks to identify the benefit which the explicit guarantee provides. However, it necessarily follows that if the explicit guarantee provides no benefit, an arm's length person, standing in the shoes of the respondent, would not have paid anything towards it. The assessment of the benefit is but a means to ascertain whether a guarantee fee would have been paid by an arm's length party.*[25] [Emphasis added].

## 3 The Transfer Pricing Analysis Applies to the Transaction That Occurred

The Tax Court's first step was to identify the relevant transactions, as the FCA observed, by observing the transaction as configured by the taxpayer and evaluating the contributions made by it and the other relevant parties to it:

> [22] The Tax Court Judge then proceeded to the determination of the arm's-length price of the guarantee transaction. He noted that the first step is to properly identify the transaction at issue. In the case at bar, that entailed 'identifying the parties to the controlled transaction, the functions performed by each party and the risk assumed as part of the transaction' (Reasons at para. 232).

There was no question about recharacterizing, or in even more contemporary transfer pricing lexicon re-'delineating' the transaction:

> [52] It is important to note that the respondent [GE Canada, the taxpayer] *does not contend that the method adopted by the Tax Court Judge has the effect of re-casting the transaction in an impermissible way.* The method *identifies the transaction as it took place between the respondent and GECUS* and seeks to ascertain the benefit to the respondent by comparing, based on recognized rating criteria, the credit rating associated with the implicit support with that associated with the explicit support. The only question is whether implicit support is a factor that can be considered when applying subsection 69(2) and paragraphs 247(2)(a) and (c), given that it arises by reason of the non-arm's-length relationship.[26] [Emphasis added].
>
> [53] The Tax Court Judge answered this question in the affirmative. I can detect no error in this regard.

---

taxpayer' – 'who' it is, for a transfer pricing analysis, taking account of its corporate and commercial genes: *see* the FCA's decision in the *Cameco* case, in particular para. 61 and in this regard also paras 43, 44, and 55 of the FCA's decision, *supra* note 15.

25. FCA.
26. FCA.

The FCA's confirmation that it is a transaction as actually undertaken that grounds the transfer pricing analysis and not an imagined alternative is evident in the Court's rejection of an analytical expedient used by the Tax Court justice to imagine ('re-cast', or more provocatively recharacterize) the transaction as something it was not by imagining the state of affairs to be without an explicit guarantee of any kind, though this criticism of the Tax Court's approach in the FCA's view was inconsequential for the outcome. The Court said:

> [66] In so saying, the Tax Court Judge lost sight of the fact that the purpose of the yield approach which he adopted was to measure the benefit which the explicit guarantee brought to the respondent in comparison with implicit support. He could not re-cast the transaction on the basis that the explicit guarantee had, in fact, been removed and assess the impact of the removal.
>
> [67] That being said, I do not believe that this error would have altered the conclusion which the Tax Court Judge reached. ...[27]

The Court's deference to the private law configuration of the transaction, implicitly being satisfied that the parties conducted themselves accordingly as relevant evidence would have disclosed, is consistent with Canadian courts' insistence that 'recharacterization' is not contemplated by the Act's provisions dealing with transfer pricing, most recently articulated in the *Cameco* Corporation case and that as evidence discloses about the legally articulated commercial relations concerned, it is the transaction undertaken and configured by a taxpayer to which the Act applies and not some hypothetical or imagined alternate reality.[28] Correspondingly, it was said explicitly by the Cameco courts and by the Supreme Court of Canada in the GlaxoSmithKline case that as useful as analytic tools the TPG may be, the law is to be found in the Act; the TPG does not have the force of statutory law and cannot and cannot be inferred to supplement the Act of fill gaps or supply unlegislated standards or conditions.[29]

27. FCA.
28. *See* the TCC's decision in *Cameco Corporation v. The Queen*, 2018 TCC 195, notably paras 582-670 where the Court declined to ignore the transactions undertaken by the taxpayer which relevant evidence showed to have been implemented in accordance with their terms and specifically not a 'sham' and para. 696 in which the Court denies the existence of a 'recharacterization' aspect in section 247 of the Act, the prevailing Canadian statutory transfer pricing rule. It is noted that the Tax Court justice did refer to 'commercial rationality', but the context was an evidence-based evaluation of the legal significance of the private law formed transactions he was scrutinizing – that is, an analysis of their legal substance grounded in evidence, which is a legal analysis, not connoting an exercise in second guessing the business judgment of the taxpayer. It is also noted that the observations made in the *Cameco* case about 'recharacterization' not being a part of Canadian transfer pricing analysis (para. 696 of the TCC decision) were made in the context of section 247 of the Act, the prevailing statement of the ALP in the Act, while both the *GlaxoSmithKline* case (*supra* n. 13) and some two of the taxation years in the GE case were assessed according to section 247's precursors in subsections 69(2) and (3) of the Act, as the case may be. However, as both the CRA and GE Canada agreed in the GE case there was no material difference, at least for this case, in the different statutory statements of Canada's transfer pricing 'rule'. *See also* the FCA's decision in the *Cameco* case, *supra* n. 15.
29. *See* the TCC's *Cameco* decision in paras 697-699, *supra* n. 26, and the Supreme Court of Canada's reasons in para. 14 of its GlaxoSmithKline decision, *supra* n. 15.

### 4 The Yield Method Is the Most Reliable Approach to Measuring the Value/Price of a Guarantee

The Tax Court and the FCA applied the yield approach to measure the incremental benefit of the explicit guarantee provided by GECUS in favour of GE Canada's lenders. A three-step approach was applied: first, the standalone credit rating of GE Canada assuming a market-oriented measurement of implicit support was determined; then, the incremental value of the explicit guarantee, again applying credit market standards was determined; then it was determined whether the guarantee fee charged exceeded the market measurement of the incremental benefit of the explicit guarantee. In this case, it was determined that the incremental benefit was 1.83%; the guarantee fee charged was 1%, well within that parameter.[30] Consequently, according to credit market-determined standards and implicitly recognizing the perception and significance of a guarantee as outlined earlier in relation to the OECD's February 2020 guidance, the guarantee fee satisfied the expectations of the ALP as articulated in the Act's relevant provisions.

In coming to its application of the yield approach, the Tax Court considered and rejected as relatively less reliable the 'insurance-based model' and the 'credit swap method', both dealing with circumstances in which financial risk of one kind or another is priced and compensated. The FCA observed the intimate connection between this method to value the benefit of the explicit guarantee and the significance of 'implicit support' as an element of that analysis and the definition for transfer pricing purposes of the economic and financial personality of the tested taxpayer in relation to the transactions it undertook:

> [56] In the present case, it is common ground that in the context of the yield method, implicit support is a factor which an arm's length person would find relevant in pricing the guarantee. It follows that it had to be considered. *The suggestion that implicit support should be ignored would require the Court to turn a blind eye on a relevant fact and deprive the transfer pricing provisions of their intended effect.*[31] [Emphasis added].

## IV LESSONS FOR THE CURRENT TRANSFER PRICING LANDSCAPE FROM THE GE CASE?

It is irresistible to refer to the mid-1980s movie 'Back to the Future'[32] to infer what if any lessons there are remaining to learn from the GE case. In that movie, the lead character finds himself transported back in time and struggles to find the way back to his former present which had by misadventure become the future for him. His adventures in the past allowed him to modify the future to which he would return, to be a happier future for himself and his family and a close friend whose time travel invention had gone

30. FCA, para. 29.
31. FCA.
32. *Back to the Future*, in https://en.wikipedia.org/wiki/Back_to_the_Future.

awry. The story contemplates further time travel to the real future to protect that future from problems as they might otherwise occur.

This commentary transports us to the past of transfer pricing, the GE case, which given how much conversation there has been and continues to be about transfer pricing is a somewhat distant past, over a decade ago. We find ourselves in that distant past and contemplate a return to the future from that vantage, which is our present, and we imagine what that present bodes for our actual transfer pricing and more broadly international tax future.

It is to be noted, again, that the GE case was decided *over 10 years ago*, before BEPS, before Pillars, before the 2017 and 2022 restatements of the TPG, and before the specific February 2020 transfer pricing guidance for financial transactions now included in the 2022 TPG. All of that subsequent guidance is voluminous, in terms of words, compared to the much more economical reasons of the TCC and the FCA of Canada. Yet, the GE case *is* the 'current transfer pricing landscape' as a comparison of how that 'landscape' and the decision of the GE case, above reflect. It is not necessary to draw out and therefore repeat the earlier observations. The February 2020 guidance – why and how it is conceived, how it is organized and expressed, what the analytical and methodological recommendations are, what the examples are to focus and consolidate the significance and application of those recommendations – *is* the GE case.

Standing in the past as a then present, before any of the subsequent developments were even conceived, the GE case is the future as it has evolved to be, certainly for the transfer pricing of guarantees and as an over-arching and highly accurate influence more broadly on the transfer pricing of financial transactions as, for example, framed by the OECD's February 2020 guidance on the transfer pricing of financial transactions and related commentary in the TPG concerning group benefits and 'synergies'.

The GE case the present as we know it that was the future in 2009 and 2010 when the case was decided. The courts adopted a group outlook while respecting for tax purposes the legal significance of organizational and transactional formulations as the private law offers them to taxpayers and accessories to which, it is almost trite to say, tax law inevitably is. They were able to recognize that 'substance' is legal substance, which, in an evidence-based analysis that inherently is a legal analysis, is necessarily informed by what far too casually in transfer pricing is assumed to be 'economics'.

The courts understood that a transfer pricing exercise does not search for a disembodied 'right' or 'fair market value' price, but seeks to assess in a particular MNE context whether there is a benefit that is valuable, that engages 'value creation', and if so what a fair evaluation of that benefit is by evaluating, as Article 9 of the OECD Model Tax Convention requires to be assessed, whether distortions in the allocation of group profit among MNE members have arisen because affirmatively or incidentally the opportunities to avoid the objective implications of private law constructions because of the absence of genuine adverse counterparty interests have overcome what the commercial circumstances would consider reasonable. In explaining why all circumstances including 'implicit support' are relevant and so important to defining the financial personality of a tested taxpayer – discovering its corporate and commercial and therefore fiscal genes – and why the rest of the transfer pricing analysis depends so much on this, the FCA said:

> [55] This interpretation flows from the normal use of the words as well as the statutory objective which is to prevent the avoidance of tax resulting from price distortions which can arise in the context of non-arm's length relationships *by reason of the community of interest shared by related parties.* The *elimination of these distortions by reference to objective benchmarks is all that is required* to achieve the statutory objective. Otherwise, all the factors which an arm's length person in the same circumstances as the respondent would consider relevant should be taken into account.[33] [Emphasis added].

To say again, the GE case *is* the landscape – all of it – 10 years before its time, at least as a direct exposition of the underlying vestigial expectations of the ALP and the TPG as they have been available to be understood constructively. The examples offered by the OECD in section D.3 of chapter D of the OECD's February 2020 guidance *are* the GE case. The analysis undertaken by the OECD to get there *is* the analysis of the TCC and the FCA of Canada in the GE case.

The GE case is the schoolmaster for lessons that the transfer pricing landscape, it may boldly be said, must have learned from that case – but only a decade later, perhaps. Does the GE case have lessons 'for' the current pricing landscape? In a way, yes but those lessons evidently have been learned – again, the landscape, in the relevant respect anyway but arguably more, *is* the GE case.

## 1 Another Lesson?

International tax has a kaleidoscopic aspect. Twist the cylinder just a little bit, and the coloured tiles and the image they have depicted shift to reveal something else. The tiles are the same; the cylinder is intact; but the new image is different.

The GE case invites a 'thought experiment' that may offer insight into the ongoing conversation induced and framed by the Pillars.

Leaving aside that implication of Pillar Two as a prescriptive general anti-avoidance rule, which is fundamentally what it is, the Pillars seek to address the perceived inadequacy and vulnerability of typical notions of tax jurisdiction associated with gauging where business is carried on and what is a taxable business presence with which source country profits should be associated.[34] Essentially, at issue is how to tax

33. FCA.
34. The Pillars, as they have been heroically embraced by the OECD's Inclusive Framework and the G20, present as many, indeed many more, questions as answers as ostensible girders to support what amounts to a parallel universal multilateral corporate income tax 'system'. *See* J. Scott Wilkie, *Critical Questions to Ask about the Next Stage of the Erection of the Pillars – Moving From a Political 'Deal' to 'Enforceable Law'*, Tax Notes (pending, expected 22 November 2021). It is important in this context to realize an underlying direction in the Pillars, both Pillar One and Pillar Two, to simulate the unity of a MNE for transfer pricing regulation and the expectation in this regard and more generally that countries' tax rules will be institutionalize harmonized for in-scope taxpayers according to a common legislative template. These are dramatic ideas in international taxation although in some respects they reflect the essential 'truth' of transfer pricing that a MNE, expressed according to determinations exclusively within the control of

business profits of enterprises that in economic terms are just as present in a source country as similarly situated residents of that country. But they are 'excused' from paying tax on their business income because of a combination of two elements. First is the wooden construction of institutionalized international tax jurisdiction parameters as they are commonly understood as prescriptive depictions of how business must be conducted to be locally taxable rather than the descriptive manifestations of the intrinsic connotations of business as it may be conducted from time to time by non-residents in relation to similarly situated local residents. Second is the facility offered by private law constructions to fragment economic and business unities into pieces that can be moved around at will. The 'poster' example of the ability to be everywhere and nowhere at the same time is all manner of 'digital' – businesses that trade in 'digital products including services' or that adopt digital modalities to conduct more traditional trade in goods and services and therefore, not be stealth or connivance but according to the nature of their businesses, do not have as 'tangible' or observable business infrastructures elements what those businesses do not need or indeed use.

The complaint is that because of the absence of a typical taxable business presence in the source country, and, as far as the OECD is concerned (but not, interestingly, the United Nations via its Model Tax Convention, in which new Article 12B of offers a default withholding tax solution[35]), because withholding taxes have very little to offer, business income escapes source country taxation if earned without a personal presence of a taxpayer in the jurisdiction where at least partly income is generated.

Does a different kind of analysis of the GE case reveal anything? Recall that the case essentially concerns the measurement and taxation of the business income of GECUS, the guarantor, as a non-resident Canadian taxpayer. Because it engaged in a financial business, as did its Canadian affiliate, and because money even outside the current transfer pricing and Pillars maelstrom has always moved 'silently'[36] in defiance of jurisdictional markers more suitable to non-financial businesses, it is possible to

taxpayers as a constellation of legally distinct elements, is fundamentally an economic unity. This raises the very hard question about the fiscal significance of legal abstractions, on which the Pillars shine a very bright light given the implications associated with 'digital' of being able to conduct business without being present in market countries or for that matter producing countries in the traditional ways taken for granted as markers of normative jurisdiction to tax and the parsing and allocation of inter-nation taxing rights.

35. *See* new Article 12B, approve by the Committee of Experts on International Co-operation in Tax Matters for addition to the United Nations Model Tax Convention: https://www.un.org/development/desa/financing/sites/www.un.org.development.desa.financing/files/2021-09/Article%2012B%20and%20Commentary%20after%2022nd%20Session%20Meetings%2029%20April%202021.pdf. The Committee had engaged earlier work bearing on Article 12, which offers recommendations similar to what is formulated, now, in Article 12B; *see* J. Scott Wilkie, The character and purpose of Article 12 with reference to 'industrial, commercial and scientific equipment' and software payment-related issues, E/C.18/2015/CRP.6, Committee of Experts on International Co-operation in Tax Matters Eleventh Session Geneva, 19-23 October 2015 Agenda item 3 (a) (v) Article 12 (Royalties) a.) The meaning of 'industrial, commercial and scientific equipment' b.) Software payment-related issues.

36. Consider Part II of the OECD Authorised OECD Approach 'AOA') for measuring the attribution of profits to permanent establishments of Banks, https://www.oecd.org/ctp/transfer-pricing/45689524.pdf.

perceive GECUS as carrying on it financial business in the relevant respect 'in' Canada (the 'source' or market for the compensable financial service it provided, with as much local presence that this required, that is, none in a typical way) without actually being in Canada in the ways necessary to invoke the application of the Act as it would apply to a Canadian resident taxpayer in a similar situation, but nevertheless to earn its income in the same way and indeed with a Canadian origin, which is of course what happened in the case. Consider also that withholding taxes are in important respects proxy business income taxes that apply in circumstances where the non-resident income earner's present is not personal but 'virtual' in the form of its financial or other property used by residents who compensate the non-resident for the use by shifting some of their business income by way of deductible charges to the non-resident whose business income it is.

Now let us conduct a 'thought experiment' - admittedly imperfect and simple, but possibly revealing. Let us look at the circumstances of the GE case again, twisting the tax kaleidoscope ever so gently.

Assume that GECUS - not 'the' GECUS but a financial services business entity in the nature of a near bank which it is convenient in this example to refer to as GECUS - had conducted its business in Canada through a permanent establishment located in a Canadian province, exposing it to corporate income tax at the federal and provincial levels in much the same way as a similarly situated resident. Assume that the combined federal and provincial tax rate is 26.5%.

Assume that its profit after deducting 500 (likely, in the circumstances a quite modest assumption) of relevant other expenses but before deducting interest and other financing costs is 500, generated by one revenue stream of 1,000 from the hypothetical party we are calling for convenience in this example GE Canada. What we are calling GECUS for this experiment has many other transactions and therefore sources of income; we are simplifying. Assume that GECUS pays interest of 50 on third-party indebtedness it incurred to be able to conduct its financing business. The result is a taxable income of 450 and at a 26.5% tax rate, 119.5 of tax. What is its effective tax rate? 26.5%.

If the taxpayer had earned the same income (revenue less expenses) as a non-resident, with all other considerations being the same except that lacking a Canadian permanent establishment it did not pay Canadian corporate income tax, how much pseudo or proxy corporate tax would it have paid at the then applicable 10% gross basis withholding tax rate under the withholding tax regime in Part XIII of the Act modified by the Canada-United States tax treaty? It would have paid 100 - 10% of 1,000.

Expressed as an equivalent to the resident corporate net basis corporate income a taxpayer with a Canadian permanent establishment would have paid, recognizing that though not considered for withholding tax purposes still it would have incurred relevant expenses, it pays tax computed using the withholding tax rate and base at an effective comparative corporate income tax rate of 22% - 100 divided by 450. Interesting.

GECUS paid a 10% withholding tax on business income via the guarantee fee it received from GE Canada. To be the financial services business it was and to have the capital presence in financial markets it evidently needed and had, it is reasonable to assume that it undertook material leverage to earn its financial business income. It had expenses, possibly much more than the assumed 500, that the Canadian and it is common other withholding tax regimes do not consider in levying gross basis withholding tax.

Now, let us alter the experiment slightly, by adjusting for the fact that because the business of the hypothetical taxpayer is a financial business, the gearing or leverage of a financial business is often comparatively much higher than for a typical industrial business, possibly as the Act anticipates up to 20 times higher than 'regulatory capital' (equity) for banks. To make this simple, let us assume a four times debt multiple (of the debt that generated interest of 50 in the base example) but that everything else remains the same, resulting in enterprise interest charges of 200 – four times 50. The taxpayer's net income is now 300, and the tax it pays as an equivalent to a Canadian resident – that is, assuming a personal Canadian tax presence – is 79.5. That is, the tax Canada would have collected on a net basis.

Finally, let us return to the actual circumstances, that is, there is no personal Canadian tax presence because this business activity does not require one. As noted, the withholding tax regime does not take account of the costs of earning income, only the revenue. But, the expenses still are incurred, making tax at withholding tax rates materially higher as an effective income tax rate.[37] As a non-resident, but all else being the same, the hypothetical taxpayer's Canadian tax is still 100 (*greater* than the 79.5 it would be if taxable on a net basis), computed as 10% of 1,000, but its effective tax rate on a fully economic basis is 33.33% – 100 divided by 300. Effectively the Canadian withholding tax is equivalent on the assumptions made in this 'thought experiment' to Canadian corporate income at an effective tax rate far higher than what ordinarily applies when there would be a taxable local business presence. Indeed, there would be room, on reasonable assumptions, to reduce the withholding tax rate and still maintain a degree of equivalence with how a similarly situated Canadian resident taxpayer or non-resident taxpayer with a Canadian permanent establishment would have been taxed.

Does this tell us anything about whether the GE case was really or necessarily a transfer pricing case, having in mind what transfer pricing regulation seeks to control – that is, considering what Article 9 of the OECD Model Tax Convention means?

Does this tell us anything about the possible utility of withholding tax or, dare it be said 'digital services taxes' possibly in the image of the United Nations Model Tax Convention's recently minted Article 12B, as a means to impose a respectable pseudo or proxy business income tax using *familiar* 'income tax' machinery and administration?

Is this another lesson of the GE case, so far not instructed, that hence may be 'back to the future' but standing where we are and again thinking about the undercurrents of the GE case, might be said to be looking 'forward into the past'. Is there a lesson

37. This factor coupled with the propensity of non-resident financiers to be 'grossed up' for source withholding tax have typically been presented as arguments for getting rid of withholding tax on interest.

here for the turmoil attendant on the implication of the Pillars to create a parallel corporate tax universe?[38]

## V A CONCLUDING COMMENT

The objectives of transfer pricing analysis, the stresses from MNE arrangements enabled by private law constructions, and even descriptive responses to issues presented in the Pillars and underlying BEPS conversations, are all directed to ensuring an allocation of taxable business income among countries somehow connected to how it is earned, in relation to each other. Transfer pricing does not exist to tell economic actors how they ought to conduct business or how successful they ought to be doing it. Rather the 'discipline' of transfer pricing is to identify when common control is asserted for ulterior non-commercial purposes, as earlier expressed in a chauvinistic way relative to identifiable commercial conditions and justifiably relevant fiscal interests of countries. The courts who adjudicated the GE case understood that, and formulated their understanding in an outcome that, as it turns out, is not only a lesson for the future then was not imaginable in its current state but became that future conceptually and indeed in specific terms. It may be that the GE case is even still a source of more lessons for the present international tax conversation.

38. There may be an urge to imagine another lesson, possibly, namely that 'safe harbours' would be a useful way to introduce stability and predictability into transfer pricing analysis in the area of financial transactions generally and financial guarantees in particular. It might be imagined, on this basis, that some kind of formulaic 'splitting of the difference' would be applied to allocate the 'intangible' value of financial guarantees and to avoid uncertainty about possible ranges of the cost of capital underlying financial transactions. An undercurrent of the present comments, though, is that particularly in the financial services and instruments area, it is possible to rely on very objective and deeply informed financial markets to evaluate the cost of money, of capital, including implied financial obligations associated with notions of implicit support and the 'halo' effect. The GE case is a clear indication that though financial transactions comprise 'intangibles' those 'intangibles' have the status of property or are able readily to be evaluated in relation to well understood property notions relied on by financial markets. In this context, the particular but also discoverable features of affected taxpayers which are pertinent in any case, are discernible according to normative law and market-based financial analysis. In effect the formulaic implications of income apportionment within a MNE and among its legally distinct rudiments, is found in normative financial analysis that is readily able to price money as it is deployed in particular ways with varying participations on which others rely. Accordingly, it is not clear that safe harbours, in the sense of splitting the benefits of bargains that lack readily accessible objective reference points, would be a lesson from the GE case. The financial analysis in this case was very precise and grounded in relevant law and market- based financial theory, with the features of the taxpayer and its group in mind. It is not clear that a 'rougher' kind of transfer pricing justice would be helpful, even if as the Pillars discussions now embrace formulaic or fractional approaches otherwise have merit. As for the desirability of formulaic approach, *see* Wilkie, *supra* n. 13. A corollary of the comment in this note 38, is that there is less 'new' in the ongoing examination of financial transactions by the OECD and the UN than might be thought; the levers and devices of financial analysis in relation to relations that are well-defined legally offers the kind of objective and accessible analysis that the new guidance seems to crave and think needs to be created as new.

# B Intercompany Loans

CHAPTER 9

# Setting the Arm's Length Framework for Intercompany Loans

*Marta Pankiv*[*]

## I INTRODUCTION

As a rule, all loans between related parties must be priced at arm's length. In an attempt to comply with the rule, multinational companies replicate what third parties would do to determine an interest rate for a loan. A third-party lender prior to lending to a potential borrower first and foremost evaluates the financial standing of the borrower. If as a result of such evaluation a decision is made to lend, the next step is to agree on terms and conditions. Finally, the parties execute a loan agreement specifying among others the loan's principal amount, interest rate, frequency of payments and tenure. The entire process serves as a basis for pricing an intercompany loan.

## II ARM'S LENGTH FRAMEWORK FOR INTERCOMPANY LOANS

The framework for the arm's length pricing of intercompany loans has broadly been defined by the international guidelines issued by the Organisation for Economic Co-operation and Development (OECD)[1] and the United Nations (UN).[2] The guidelines disregard the practice of tax authorities of applying the statistical data as a reference for intercompany interest rates arguing that it does not take into account the commercial

* The views and opinions set forth herein are the personal views or opinions of the authors; they do not necessarily reflect the views or opinions of the organisation with which the authors are associated.

1. OECD, *Transfer Pricing Guidance on Financial Transactions: Inclusive Framework on BEPS Actions 4, 8-10* (Paris: OECD, 2020), https://www.oecd.org/tax/beps/transfer-pricing-guidance-on-financial-transactions-inclusive-framework-on-beps-actions-4-8-10.pdf [OECD, *OECD Guidance*].

and financial relations of the parties to a loan transaction. Similarly, the guidelines disregard the practice of certain taxpayers of collecting bank opinions from independent banks to support the arm's length nature of intercompany interest rates. The practice is considered to be contradictory to the very nature of the arm's length principle as such bank opinions do not reflect a comparison with third-party transactions. In all other respects, the OECD and the UN guidelines essentially encapsulate the market best practices for pricing a loan.

As with any other intercompany transaction, the assessment of the arm's length nature of an intercompany loan requires that the commercial and financial relations are properly identified, including the characteristics of a financial instrument, contractual terms of a loan transaction, functions, assets, and risks of the parties to the transaction, their economic circumstances as well as market conditions and business strategies. The pricing methodology is largely driven by business considerations and by taking into account all facts and circumstances at the time of a transaction. The key steps in the pricing process of intercompany loans can be summarised as follows:

- delineation of actual transaction;
- calculation of credit rating; and
- determination of the arm's length interest rate.

## 1 Loan Versus Equity

The first step in the pricing process of intercompany loans is to identify whether the total amount of funds transferred by one company to another within a multinational enterprise (MNE) group is actually a loan or whether it should be characterised as other kinds of payment, e.g., a capital contribution.[3] In such an assessment the following criteria are looked at: the company's ability to pay back the loan, which could be estimated based on a financial forecast; the form and purpose of financing; the availability of a written loan agreement and of the terms and conditions that would be typical for a third-party loan agreement.

The correct delineation of transaction as debt or equity depends on the exact facts and circumstances. For example, an MNE receives an advance of funds for a term of 10 years from a related party and based on its financial projections it is clear that it would

2. UN, *United Nations Practical Manual on Transfer Pricing for Developing Countries* (New York: United Nations, 2021), https://www.un.org/development/desa/financing/sites/www.un.org.development.desa.financing/files/2021-04/TP_2021_final_web%20%281%29.pdf, Chapter 9 [UN, *UN Guidance*].
3. Based on the Commentary on Article 9 of the OECD Model Tax Convention, the determination of a financial transaction as a loan or a contribution to equity should be defined by domestic laws or the OECD Transfer Pricing Guidelines. *See* OECD, *Public Consultation Document, Proposed Changes to Commentaries in the OECD Model Tax Convention on Article 9 and on Related Articles* (28 May 2021), https://www.oecd.org/tax/treaties/oecd-invites-public-input-on-proposed-changes-to-commentaries-in-the-oecd-model-tax-convention-on-article-9-and-on-related-articles.htm [OECD, *Proposed Commentary on Article 9*]; OECD, *OECD Transfer Pricing Guidelines for Multinational Enterprises and Tax Administrations 2022* (Paris: OECD, 2022), https://read.oecd-ilibrary.org/taxation/oecd-transfer-pricing-guidelines-for-multinational-enterprises-and-tax-administrations-2022_0e655865-en#page1 [OECD, *Transfer Pricing Guidelines 2022*].

not be able to repay a loan of a large amount. As such, the amount of the intercompany loan should be estimated based on the maximum amount an unrelated lender would be willing to lend and an unrelated borrower would be able to borrow in the given circumstances. If the advance exceeds such maximum amount, any excess should not be recognised as a loan, but as a capital contribution that would not bear any interest.[4]

Further consideration is the purpose of the intercompany loan. If a borrowing company intends to use the funds to cover its short-term working capital needs, it would be more appropriate to designate (delineate) such loan as a combination of short-term loans rather than a single long-term loan. In such a case an independent borrower would not be willing to sign up for a 10-year loan agreement but would instead be taking short-term loans as the need may be.[5] At the same time, a financial instrument that is defined as short-term in the intercompany agreement, but is constantly replaced with a new instrument, may be accurately delineated as a long-term instrument.[6]

If a borrowing company receives funds from a related party based on the loan agreement that does not include any maturity date, nor does it include any security clause, and the interest amount is contingent on certain levels of profits to be achieved by the borrower, it may indicate that the advance of funds is not per se a loan. In this case, the assumed loan has the characteristics of equity rather than debt and should not be delineated as a loan for transfer pricing purposes.

## 2 Terms and Conditions

If an advance of funds is delineated as a loan, the following factors will have an impact on the loan's interest rate and should be considered by related parties when drafting an intercompany loan agreement:

- Loan type: bullet loans, which are repaid at the end of the term, would normally require higher interest rates; revolving loans, which typically are a variable credit line, would in addition to higher than in other loans interest rates also have additional fees for the loan extension.
- Principal amount: generally, a higher principal amount is reflected in an increased interest rate that is explained by a higher default risk exposure.
- Grant date: interest rates may significantly fluctuate on capital markets over time; that is why it is important to establish the exact grant date of a loan for a correct assessment of its pricing.
- Loan term: the longer the term, the higher the interest rate. This factor is associated with the standard shape of a yield curve which is normally upward sloping, i.e., the interest rates are increasing with the increasing maturity. One of the theories explaining the upward-sloping shape of a yield curve is that the

4. OECD, *Transfer Pricing Guidelines 2022*, Chapter X, para. 10.12.
5. *Ibid.*, para. 10.37.
6. *Ibid.*, Chapter I, para. 1.113.

longer the maturity, the riskier the loan, and therefore a higher interest rate is expected to be charged.

- Borrower's credit rating: companies with a higher credit rating will normally be paying lower interest rates. The arm's length rate can be established based on either the credit rating of the borrower or the rating of the specific financial instruments.
- Floating and fixed rates: the floating rates consisting of a base rate and a spread are generally preferred by lenders as they are sensitive to market changes and are less risky than the fixed rates.
- Country risk: the risk is reflected in the premium that is calculated based on a number of macroeconomic factors, including volatile exchange rates and political instability. The country risk premium is higher in the developing markets than in the developed ones and may cap the credit ratings of local companies.
- Industry of the borrower: higher interest rates would be expected in riskier or more volatile industries such as construction, agriculture, and manufacturing, to name a few.
- Currency: the currency in which the loan is negotiated represents certain risks associated with foreign exchange markets; if the currency tends to devaluate, it will usually trigger higher interest rates.
- Senior and subordinated loans: the subordinated loans are paid after the senior loans are settled. A senior loan is considered unsubordinated debt and less risky than subordinated loan; lower interest rates are thus expected to be applied to this type of debt.
- Collaterals and guarantees: when additional collaterals or guarantees are part of a loan transaction, it would result in a reduction in the risk of default and lower interest rates.
- Covenants: the loan agreements between independent parties would generally include certain covenants, i.e., incurrence or maintenance covenants, to protect the lender and to limit its risk. If the covenants are absent[7] in the intercompany agreement, it would be appropriate to consider whether such covenants would have existed between unrelated parties and what impact they would have on the pricing of the loan.

Generally, such characteristics of a loan as a long maturity, no security, subordination or usage of the loan in risky arrangements would increase the interest rate to cover the risk for the lender, whereas strong collateral clauses and high-quality guarantees would lower the interest rate as the risk for the lender would be minimised.

7. The absence of covenants in the intercompany agreements may be explained by the fact that related parties would likely not experience information asymmetry. It is also less likely that an MNE group would be willing to take the same restrictive measures against the related party borrower as it would be the case if covenants were breached under a third-party loan agreement.

## 3 Perspectives of All Parties

When considering the commercial and financial relations between two related parties, as well as when analysing the economically relevant characteristics of an intercompany loan transaction, the perspectives of a lender and a borrower should be taken into account (although these perspectives may not always align). In addition, it would be necessary to analyse the transaction from a third-party perspective and to consider all options realistically available to each party. The key consideration for both lender and borrower would be a risk that each of them assumes in a loan transaction. The risks that would generally be considered in the transfer pricing analysis of an intercompany loan are credit risk, interest rate risk, liquidity risk, currency risk, industry risk and country risk.

From an independent lender perspective, the decision of whether to make a loan and on what terms, is based on the results of a robust credit risk assessment of a potential borrower. The assessment aims to identify the risks and establish the mechanism for monitoring and managing the risks. Although a related party lender may not need to go through the same information gathering and risk assessment process as independent lenders, it would still need to take into account the same commercial considerations that would be accounted for in a third-party arrangement, including the creditworthiness of a borrower and the economic circumstances of a loan transaction. This would be necessary to prove to the tax authorities that an intercompany loan is priced at arm's length.

From an independent borrower perspective, it is important to understand the overall cost it will incur to attract financing in the form of either debt or equity, or both. The cost of debt is relatively easy to calculate by adding up all company's loans and other debt financing such as credit card balances, then calculating the annual interest rate expense for each loan and credit card and adding them up, and finally dividing the total interest cost by the total debt to derive the cost of debt. The cost of equity represents the return that the market expects in exchange for owing an asset and assuming the risk associated with such ownership; it is usually estimated by using the capital asset pricing model (CAPM) where the cost of equity is equal to the risk-free rate of return plus a premium expected for risk. As such, prior to deciding on taking on a loan, an independent borrower would multiply the cost of debt and the cost of equity by the relevant weight of each component based on market value and add them up to determine the weighted average cost of capital (WACC). This would allow the borrower to make an informed decision with respect to the most cost-effective way of financing.

Even after a loan contract is signed, the options realistically available to the borrower and to the lender would be of relevance in case of changes in the financing costs on the market and the ability of the parties to renegotiate the terms of the loan on more favourable terms. It means that once an intercompany loan agreement is signed by both parties, it is not the end of the story. The market conditions should be constantly monitored, at least once a year, to evaluate if the option of refinancing would be more beneficial for the borrower. For example, the borrower should initiate a discussion with the lender to renegotiate the existing loan on better conditions, e.g., a lower interest rate, if the borrower is able to refinance the loan on better conditions with an unrelated party.

All the above-mentioned considerations in the pricing process of intercompany loans are essentially mirroring the behaviour of unrelated parties and their perspectives as a lender and a borrower. In addition to that, special rules have been introduced by the OECD targeting so-called cash box entities within an MNE group. If a lender does not exercise control over the risks associated with an advance of funds, nor does it have the financial capacity to assume the risks, such risks should be allocated to the entity exercising control and having the financial capacity to assume the risks.[8] The identification of how the risks are allocated in an intercompany loan transaction should be part of the transfer pricing analysis. However, such allocation may be seen as a deviation from the arm's length principle (as it is unlikely that an unrelated lender would not be able to exercise control over the risks with respect to the funds it provides) and can only be enforced through local laws or regulations.

For example, if one MNE company advances funds to another company of the same MNE group and it is evident that the lending company does not exercise control over the risks associated with the transferred funds, the company that exercises such control and has the financial capacity to assume such risks would be the parent company of the MNE group. The parent company will assume the risks associated with the financing, whereas the lending company will be entitled to no more than a risk-free return.[9] If a company that advances funds exercises control over the risks related to the financing, a risk-adjusted rate of return would be applied. In this situation, the difference between the financial risk assumed by the lending company and the operational risk assumed by the borrowing company should be considered. A risk-adjusted rate of return consists of a risk-free rate and a premium reflecting the risks assumed by the funder.[10]

To determine a risk-free return in a loan transaction, the cost of funding the borrowing company would normally be taken into account. In practice, the interest rate on certain government securities is used as a reference rate for a risk-free return because government securities are generally considered to not carry significant default risk. For example, the interest rates on government bonds with the same functional currency as that of a lender, similar maturity, and issued at a time close to the time of intra-group funding could be a reference for a risk-free return. The interbank rates, interest rate swap rates, or repurchase agreements of highly rated government-issued securities can also be used in the determination of a risk-free return. A risk-adjusted rate of return can be determined based on comparable uncontrolled transactions, bond issuances or loans, risk-free return with adding risk premium, or the cost of funds.[11]

8. OECD, *Transfer Pricing Guidelines 2022*, Chapter X, para. 10.25, Chapter I, para. 1.98.
9. *Ibid.*, Chapter I, section D.1.2.1.
10. *Ibid.*, para. 1.120.
11. *Ibid.*, paras 1.122-126.

## III CREDIT RATING CALCULATION

The credit rating of the borrower is a key determinant of the interest rate to be charged in a loan transaction. The determination of credit rating requires quantitative and qualitative analyses and should be thoroughly documented for transfer pricing purposes. The publicly available financial tools or methodologies of independent credit rating agencies can be used in such analyses to determine the credit rating of a specific company within an MNE group. However, the assessment of the credit rating by using publicly available financial tools may not be fully compliant with the arm's length principle (as it is not based on a direct comparison with transactions between unrelated parties) and therefore the accuracy of assessment depends on the accuracy of data inputted into such tools.

Moreover, the estimation of credit rating by means of financial tools may be focused more on quantitative inputs rather than qualitative ones and may not be a transparent process. More robust quantitative and qualitative analyses could instead be achieved by applying the official credit ratings of independent rating agencies, as they take into account both historic and forecasted entity performance, as well as such qualitative considerations as the characteristics of the company's management, the industry specifics, and the company's market share.

### 1 Rating and Scoring

The methodologies that are applied in the pricing of intercompany loans are developed by the largest credit rating agencies, i.e., Moody's, Standard and Poor's Global Ratings (S&P) and Fitch Ratings. All three agencies use the letter rating system ranging from A (excellent) to C and D (obligation in default). Borrowers with excellent credit rating would be expected to pay lower interest rates, whereas those with lower credit ratings would usually pay higher interest rates to cushion the higher risk assumed by lenders. As such, the borrower's credit rating is of particular importance in the transfer pricing analysis as it indicates with a high degree of reliability that an intercompany loan is priced at arm's length.

The credit rating of the rating agencies is usually available only for the parent company of an MNE group. Generally, it is assumed that the companies that are members of an MNE group tend to have a rating at or below the parent's rating. This is because the parent company would normally directly influence the equity position of the group members and their creditworthiness (except for special cases when it is the other way around and a group company may impact the rating of its parent). To derive the credit rating of an MNE group's company from the rating of its parent, a so-called notching adjustment is often applied in the transfer pricing analysis, depending on how important the borrowing company is for the group. For example, if the credit rating of the parent company is A3 on Moody's scale or A-on Fitch's and S&P's scales, then the borrower that is not considered a core company for the group, may be deemed to be two notches below the parent's rating and have a credit rating of Baa2 (Moody's) and BBB (Fitch/S&P) according to the rating methodologies.

As an alternative to adjusting the credit rating of the parent, it is possible to search for the borrower's loans with third parties to establish the credit rating of the borrower or to use the credit scoring approach. Credit scoring is used by lenders based on the probability of repayment and is usually applied to smaller businesses. Generally, the higher the score, the lower the interest rate. The credit score is based on the information available in the borrower's credit report, including the company's ownership, number of employees, sales data, historical business data, payment history and collections, industry, etc. However, credit scoring does not estimate the borrower's probability of default, it only assesses how risky the borrower is on a scale from the highest to the lowest. As such, the application of the methodologies of the credit rating agencies, including the notching adjustments, remains the most reliable approach to determine the credit rating of a borrower.

## 2 Implicit Support

The form of intercompany loan and its terms and conditions are informed by the funding policies of an MNE group as well as by the practices of the group management, including the interest rate and all relevant characteristics of the loan such as its type, term, currency, security, covenants, business strategy. In case the borrowing company of an MNE group experiences financial difficulties, the group may support such company to ensure it meets its financial obligations. An incidental benefit arising for the borrowing company solely by virtue of its affiliation with the group is called 'implicit support' or 'passive association'. Such support may affect the credit rating of the borrowing company or the rating of any debt that such company issues.

The assessment of the effect of implicit support is an indispensable part of the credit rating analysis. One of the considerations with respect to such assessment is how likely the borrowing company of an MNE group would receive the group support and how strong such support would be. It is assumed that a group company with stronger links and strategic importance to an MNE group would likely be supported by the group and would have its credit rating closely linked to the group's credit rating. In case there is no evidence of group support, it may be appropriate to analyse the borrowing company based on its stand-alone credit rating.

Another consideration in relation to implicit support is whether other group members would be impacted by the fact of supporting or not supporting the related party borrower. The answer would depend on the status of the borrowing company including such criteria as the regulatory requirements, its strategic importance and operational integration with the group. If the borrowing company is important to the group and the borrower's indicators of creditworthiness do not differ significantly from those of the group, then not only a stand-alone rating of a specific MNE company but also the credit rating of the entire MNE group should be taken into account in the transfer pricing analysis.

## IV DETERMINATION OF INTEREST RATE

The methods that have been used for decades to price intercompany loans are the following:

- the internal and external comparable uncontrolled price (CUP);
- the cost-of-funds approach;
- the credit default swaps (CDS); and
- the economic modelling.

In certain countries, in addition to the above-mentioned loan pricing methods, the so-called 'safe harbour' rules for intercompany interest rates have been introduced. The safe harbours rules, such as applicable federal rates (AFR)[12] in the United States, indicative margins in Singapore,[13] and annual official interest rates or margins in a number of other countries, have been issued to simplify the process of determining the arm's length interest rates.[14]

For example, the safe harbour rate could be applied by certain categories of taxpayers with respect to the loan principal amounts that are below certain thresholds and would in such a way exempt such taxpayers from the obligation to prove that the loan is priced at arm's length. However, such simplification measures or safe harbours should be considered together with the application of the arm's length principle in both domestic and international contexts as otherwise, they may lead to potential double taxation if not accepted by all parties to a loan transaction.

### 1 CUP Method

As soon as the terms and conditions are assessed and the credit rating of the borrower is determined, the next step in the transfer pricing analysis of intercompany loans is to look at the market yields on a third-party financial instrument with comparable features to benchmark a range of potential coupon rates. The benchmark of interest rates could be performed by using publicly available data on other loans. A range of the arm's length rates rather than a single rate would likely be the outcome of such benchmark. The search should not necessarily be restricted to a stand-alone entity, which is borrowing from an independent lender but could also include a member entity of a different MNE group borrowing from an independent lender, or a loan between the members of different MNE groups.

The benchmark of intercompany loans can also be performed based on alternative financial instruments such as bonds, deposits, convertible debentures, and commercial papers. However, certain comparability adjustments may be required to

12. *See* the U.S. Internal Revenue Code Treas. Reg. § 1.482 Regulations [US IRC Sec 482 Regs], https://www.irs.gov/pub/irs-apa/482_regs.pdf.
13. *See* the Inland Revenue Authority of Singapore's Transfer Pricing Guidelines (Sixth Edition), para. 15.50 [IRAS TPG], https://www.iras.gov.sg/media/docs/default-source/e-tax/etaxguide_cit_transfer-pricing-guidelines_6th.pdf?sfvrsn=26bfb1a6_9.
14. UN, *UN Guidance*, para. 9.11.1.

eliminate the material effects of differences between the tested intercompany loan and such alternative instruments, including their liquidity, maturity, and existence of collateral or currency. The most commonly used approaches in the benchmark analysis of intercompany loans are the following:

- the loan approach, i.e., the search for comparable loan transactions; and
- the bond approach, i.e., the search for comparable bonds.

The loan approach may be seen as more suitable for the pricing of intercompany loans as it compares the same instruments. In practice, however, the lack of third-party loan data and rather sophisticated loan arrangements that do not always allow to make appropriate comparability adjustments would give preference to the bond approach. In contrast to the loan approach, where private loan data is used, the bond approach is based on market conditions and could therefore provide more reliable results.[15]

In addition to the third-party loans and realistic alternatives serving as external CUPs, an internal CUP can also be used to benchmark the interest rate for a tested loan. In this case, appropriate adjustments to increase the comparability would be necessary. Such adjustments may be required in order to consider all relevant terms and conditions not included in the comparable data, e.g., the type of financial transaction, principal amount, tenure (maturity), type of interest rate, currency, embedded options, seniority, collaterals and guarantees.[16]

## 2 Cost of Funds

The cost-of-funds approach can be used to price intercompany loans in case no comparable uncontrolled transactions are identified. Such cost represents the amount spent by a lender to acquire funds for on-lending to a borrower. Based on this approach, an intercompany loan could be priced based on the lender's cost of funding, which increases with an increase in the absolute rate of interest on the market, and a profit margin, which includes the lender's incremental cost of the equity necessary to support the loan.

The cost-of-funds approach should be applied by considering the lender's cost of funds in comparison to the cost of funds of other lenders on the market. A third-party lender would aim to keep operating costs as low as possible to minimise the cost of acquiring funds for lending and to secure a higher margin on such lending. It is expected that a related party lender would not price its loan exclusively based on the

15. Thomas Petrakos, Vikram Chand & Amanda Pletz, *Interest Rate Benchmarking for Transfer Pricing Purposes: A Comparison Between the Loan and the Bond Approach*, 28 Int'l Transfer Pricing J. 4 (2021) [Petrakos, Chand & Pletz].
16. In order to support its rating, the borrower may be required to provide a guarantee from another party to the lender, whereas the lender would need to assess whether the guarantor would be able to step in and take on the borrower's liabilities in case of the latter's default or inability to meet its obligations. In order to consider a guarantee in setting or adjusting the terms and conditions of the intercompany loan, the lender would need to undertake the same steps in evaluating the guarantor as it undertakes in evaluating the borrower to assess if the guarantor would be able to meet its obligations in the event of the borrower's default.

cost of funds (as it could be too high if compared with a third-party lender that acquired such funds at a lower cost) but should also account for other factors to ensure the loan is priced at arm's length.[17]

From an arm's length perspective, the application of the cost-of-funds approach would be limited to the cases when the funds are received by an MNE group from a third-party lender and passed down the chain through affiliated companies of the group. In such cases, the affiliates in between perform only agency or intermediary functions, and their remuneration should not be calculated as a markup on the cost of funds but rather on the cost of their agency function.[18]

## 3 Credit Default Swaps

As a proxy for the risk premium on intercompany loans, in case of the absence of information regarding the underlying asset, the spreads of CDS can be used as a comparable transaction for intercompany loans.[19] CDS is a contract by which one party acquires from another party protection against the credit default of a so-called reference entity (a corporation or government); such reference entity is not a party to the CDS contract. CDS is similar to a guarantee, but unlike the latter, CDS is not necessarily limited to compensation upon actual default occurrence. A typical example of the use of CDS is when one party holds a loan from a third party and is seeking guarantee against the borrower's potential default. The loan holder may approach a second party using a CDS, under which the loan holder pays to the second party a swap spread periodically for the life of the loan, whereas the second party agrees to make predetermined payment to the loan holder in case the borrower defaults.[20]

The CDS implied spread of a reference entity is usually close to the credit spread on the bonds of similar maturity of the reference entity. The credit spread is the difference in yield between government bonds and other bond issuances of the same maturity measured in basis points. For example, a credit spread of 100 basis points is calculated as the difference between a 10-year government bond with a yield of 4% and a 10-year corporate bond with a yield of 5%. As such, the bond's and CDS's spreads are similar in level and reflect credit market and derivative market participants' respective perceptions of the debtor's creditworthiness.[21]

At the same time, in contrast to bonds, CDS are characterised by a high level of volatility. Considering that the value of CDS contracts is discontinuous because there is only a pay-out to CDS protection buyer in case of default prior to expiration of the CDS contract, the CDS market participants have incentives to trigger technical defaults before the expiration of a CDS contract or to avoid them until after the CDS contract

17. OECD, *Transfer Pricing Guidelines 2022*, Chapter X, para. 10.98.
18. *Ibid.*, para. 10.100.
19. *Ibid.*, para. 10.101.
20. Anuschka Bakker & Marc M. Levey, *Transfer Pricing and Intra-Group Financing* (IBFD 2012) [Bakker/Levey].
21. Robert K. Rasmussen & Michael Simkovic, *Bounties for Errors: Market Testing Contracts*, 10 Harv. Bus. L. Rev. 117, 130-131 (2020) [Rasmussen & Simkovic].

expires, depending on their position.[22] As such, the CDS spreads may indicate an elevated risk of default, as was the case in periods of financial crisis. In addition, the credit default spreads may reflect not only the risk of default but also such unrelated factors as the liquidity of CDS contracts or their volume. As a result, the same instrument may have different CDS spreads.[23] Therefore, the use of CDS to approximate the risk premium for intercompany loans would require a certain degree of caution.[24]

### 4 Economic Modelling

In addition to CDS, economic modelling can be used as an alternative approach to price an intercompany loan in the absence of reliable third-party comparables. The economic modelling allows constructing an interest rate that would approximate an arm's length interest rate and may involve the evaluation of other fees and charges as relevant to the loan.[25] The interest rate derived from such modelling is a combination of a risk-free interest rate and a risk premium. The significance of the premium depends on various aspects of the loan such as default and liquidity risks, inflation, and loan maturity. In addition to that, some models would also account for compensations of the lender's operational expenses.

However, the models do not represent real-life transactions and the comparability adjustments would likely be required to arrive at the arm's length rate. Although the models could be a useful alternative to price intercompany loans, their application is subject to the same constraints as other alternatives, such as the cost-of-funds approach. The lender cannot establish the interest rate based exclusively on its economic model but should also take into account the competitive market environment and establish its interest rate at the level that a third-party borrower would accept in comparable circumstances.

## V CONCLUSION

To pass the arm's length test, intercompany loans are expected to largely mirror third-party arrangements. Terms and conditions of a related party loan would generally be informed by the situation on financial markets. If an intercompany loan with a long-term maturity has a fixed interest rate that is higher than the rate that an independent borrower of similar creditworthiness would accept in comparable circumstances, it may be prudent to renegotiate such intercompany agreement and potentially switch to a floating interest rate. The floating rate would allow sharing of the risk between the lender and the borrower and could eliminate the need for refinancing that

22. RASMUSSEN & SIMKOVIC, *supra* n. 21, at 129.
23. OECD, *Transfer Pricing Guidelines 2022*, Chapter X, para. 10.102.
24. *Ibid.*, para. 10.103.
25. UN, *UN Guidance*, paras 9.12.2.9-9.12.2.10.

would otherwise be required from a third-party perspective. In times of financial instability, the contracting parties may need to revisit the existing loans as such loans may no longer be reflecting the market conditions and can potentially be challenged by tax authorities on the grounds of non-compliance with the arm's length principle.

# CHAPTER 10
# Accurate Delineation of Intercompany Loans

*Vikram Chand, Michael Kobetsky & Camille Vilaseca*[*]

## I INTRODUCTION

Over the past decade, tax authorities from several jurisdictions have significantly increased their focus on transfer pricing aspects of cross-border-related party financial transactions,[1] such as intra-group loans, financial guarantees[2] and cash pooling arrangements.[3] This attention is warranted as cross-border debt financing may result in Base Erosion and Profit Shifting.[4]

---

* The views and opinions set forth herein are the personal views or opinions of the authors; they do not necessarily reflect the views or opinions of the organization with which the authors are associated.

1. ANUSCHKA BAKKER, *Transfer Pricing and Intra Group Financing: Low-Hanging Fruit?* 15 Derivatives and Financial Instruments 27 (2013), 27; DAVIS LEDURE et al., *Financial Transactions in Today's World: Observations from a Transfer Pricing Perspective*, 38 Intertax 350, 350-352 (2010); CHLOE BURNETT, *Interest Deductibility: Implementation of Action 4 of the OECD/G20 Base Erosion and Profit Shifting Project and the Future of Transfer Pricing of Intra-Group Finance*, 73 Bulletin for International Taxation 325 (2019); GREGORIO PIRAN & MATTEO PIVA, *A Conundrum Within the Conundrum: The Requalification of Loans as Equity under the OECD Guidance on Financial Transactions*, 60 European Taxation. 357 (2020).
2. NATASSIA BURKHALTER-MARTINEZ, *Transfer Pricing Aspects of Intragroup Financial Guarantees in Light of the Recent OECD TP Guidance on Financial Transactions*, 2020/4 IFF Forum für Steuerrecht 347 (2020); VERA AVERYANOVA & JIGNA SAMPAT, *Transfer Pricing Aspects of Intra-Group Financial Guarantees in Light of the BEPS Action Plan*, 22 International Transfer Pricing Journal 361 (2015).
3. VIKRAM CHAND, *Transfer Pricing Aspects of Cash Pooling Arrangements in Light of the BEPS Action Plan*, 23 International Transfer Pricing Journal 38 (2016); ALEXANDER HALLER & VIKRAM CHAND, *Application of the Arm's Length Principle to Physical Cash Pooling Arrangements in Light of the OECD Discussion Draft on Financial Transactions*, 47 Intertax 349 (2019).
4. The following simplified example shows how debt can be shifted to reduce an MNE group tax liability. Co A is the parent entity of an MNE group. It maintains a wholly owned subsidiary Co

The increased transfer pricing scrutiny of financial transactions led to the publication by the Organisation for Economic Co-operation and Development (OECD) in 2020 of supplementary guidance on financial transactions.[5] The additional guidance was published in the 2022 consolidated version of the OECD Transfer Pricing Guidelines (TPG) under Chapter X but formed part of the OECD TPG from 2020.[6] Additionally, in 2021, the UN updated its Practical Manual on Transfer Pricing for Developing Countries to integrate a new chapter on financial transactions.[7]

Article 9 of the OECD Model[8] contains the arm's-length principle for pricing transactions between associated enterprises. From a transfer pricing perspective, intercompany loans among associated enterprises must comply with the arm's-length principle. It should be noted that Article 9(1) does not authorize States to make arm's-length transfer pricing adjustments (structural or price adjustments). The adjustment provisions must be in the domestic transfer pricing law of a State. Article 9(1) restricts the application of domestic transfer pricing law if they breach the arm's-length principle. This means that profits of associated enterprises can only be adjusted up to arm's-length conditions or an arm's-length profit.[9]

The purpose of this chapter is to consider when a purported intra-group loan satisfies the arm's-length principle. The chapter will consider the complexity involved in the accurate delineation of an intra-group loan agreement and the uncertainty that may arise for both taxpayers and tax authorities. The transfer pricing financing cases reflect the complexity of analysing intra-group loans. Meeting the arm's-length principle requires taxpayers to have documented analysis on the accurate delineation of the controlled loan transaction; and a robust comparability analysis of loans between independent parties in identical or similar circumstances. The accurate delineation of

B. Co A and Co B are respectively resident for tax purposes of Country A and Country B. Country A is a high-tax jurisdiction while Country B is a low tax jurisdiction. Specifically, Country B does not tax interest income from foreign sources. Co B could lend funds to Co A, although Co A does not need any advance of funds, and in exchange Co A would pay interest to Co B. The interests would not be taxed in Country B. Hence, unless Country A applies a withholding tax on interest pursuant to national tax law and tax treaties, Co B would be untaxed on the interest income. The intra-group loan would thus have allowed Co A to shift profits from Country A to Country B.

5. OECD, *Transfer Pricing Guidance on Financial Transactions: Inclusive Framework on BEPS Actions 4, 8-10* (OECD Publishing, 2020).
6. OECD, *Transfer Pricing Guidelines for Multinational Enterprises and Tax Administrations 2022 (OECD Guidelines)* (OECD Publishing, 2022).
7. UN, *Practical Manual on Transfer Pricing for Developing Countries* (United Nations New York, 2021).
8. OECD, *Model Tax Convention on Income and on Capital: Condensed Version*, Article 9 (OECD Publishing, 2017). Specifically, Article 9(1) allows tax authorities of a State to adjust the profits of the enterprises resident in that State, if as a result of the special relations between that enterprise and other associated enterprises resident in other States, the profits of the first enterprise have been diverted to the other associated enterprises, due to the fact that they operate with each other on a non-arm's length basis. Article 9(2) aims at eliminating the economic double taxation that may arise pursuant to Article 9(1). Similar provisions are found in the UN Model. *See also* UN Model, *supra* n. 7, Article 9.
9. Andreas Bullen, *Arm's Length Transaction Structures: Recognizing and Restructuring Controlled Transactions in Transfer Pricing*, 67-78 & 356-357 (IBFD Doctoral Series, 2011). On the other hand, another commentator argues that Article 9(1) does not authorize structural adjustments. *See* Jens Wittendorff, *The Transactional Ghost of Article 9(1) of the OECD Model*, 63 Bulletin International Taxation 108, 110-114 (2009).

a controlled transaction requires a thorough examination of the facts and circumstances of a purported intra-group loan, including the use of the funds by the borrower.

We initially consider the contentious issue of whether Article 9 of the OECD Model Convention (MC) permits re-characterization of funding transactions. We then analyse the situations in which an advance of funds may be delineated as a loan under an accurate delineation of the controlled transaction. Finally, the chapter examines the issue of whether a purported loan may be recognized and any consequent re-characterization under the commercial rationality exception in the OECD TPG. As the chapter is based on the OECD TPG and UN Practical Manual, the chapter commences with a consideration of the legal standing of these publications.

## II THE STANDING OF THE OECD TPG AND THE UN PRACTICAL MANUAL

### 1 Introduction

Base Erosion and Profit Shifting (BEPS) Actions 8-10 on transfer pricing and BEPS Action 14 on dispute resolution[10] have made the OECD TPG a key international tax document. The influence of the OECD TPG was also extended by the creation of the OECD/G20 Inclusive Framework on Base Erosion and Profit Shifting.[11]

Depending on the jurisdiction, the OECD TPG may have 'legal status'. First, the OECD recommendation requires OECD member countries and certain non-member countries to follow the OECD TPG. Second, the latter are asserted to be part of the Commentary on Article 9 in the OECD MC and may accordingly be used for tax treaty interpretation purposes by jurisdictions under the Vienna Convention on the Law of Treaties[12] (Vienna Convention). Third, some jurisdictions have prescribed that the OECD TPG are a guidance document for the interpretation of domestic transfer pricing provisions.[13] Finally, countries may expressly agree that Article 9 of a tax treaty is to be interpreted in accordance with the OECD TPG, especially, regarding dispute resolution matters. In contrast, the UN Transfer Pricing (TP) Manual is published by the UN

10. BEPS Action 14 deals with the resolution of disputes between countries. When countries that have agreed to have unresolved mutual agreement disputes finalized through arbitration under BEPS Action 14, the transfer pricing disputes will (mostly) be decided using the principles in the Guidelines.
11. The Inclusive Framework was established to allow jurisdictions and countries, including developing countries, to participate on an equal footing to implement the BEPS package of measures. The Inclusive Framework has 141 participating countries and jurisdictions. *See* the several Progress Reports of the Inclusive Framework on BEPS published by the OECD (2017, 2018, 2019, 2020, 2021, 2022).
12. UN, Vienna Convention on the Law of Treaties, 23 May 1969, United Nations, Treaty Series, vol. 1155.
13. Countries may prescribe that the domestic transfer pricing rules are to be interpreted in accordance with the United Nations Transfer Pricing Manual.

Committee of Experts on International Cooperation in Tax Matters[14] (United Nations Tax Committee) which is not an inter-government body.[15]

## 2 The OECD Transfer Pricing Recommendation

OECD member countries and certain non-member countries, called member and non-member adherents, are expected to follow the OECD TPG when reviewing transfer pricing cases:[16] 'The Recommendation on the Determination of Transfer Pricing between Associated Enterprises was adopted by the OECD Council on 13 July 1995 on the proposal of the Committee on Fiscal Affairs. This Recommendation recommends that Adherent's tax administrators follow the OECD Transfer Pricing Guidelines for Multinational Enterprises and Tax Administrations. The Guidelines provide guidance on the application of the "arm's-length principle", which is the international consensus on transfer pricing, i.e. on the valuation for tax purposes of cross-border transactions between associated enterprises.'[17]

On an independent basis, the Recommendation has no legal force.

## 3 The Vienna Convention on the Law of Treaties

It is claimed that the OECD TPG are incorporated by reference into the OECD Commentary on Article 9 and that the OECD TPG have treaty interpretation status under the Vienna Convention. Over 100 countries are parties to the Vienna Convention

14. UN, ECOSOC Tax Committee: About, https://www.un.org/development/desa/financing/what-we-do/ECOSOC/tax-committee/about.
15. Treaty countries may expressly agree to use the United Nations Transfer Pricing Manual as a guidance document for the interpretation of the associated enterprises article. Certain jurisdictions have prescribed that both the Guidelines and the United Nations Transfer Pricing Manual may be used as a guidance document.
16. OECD, *Recommendation of the Council on the Determination of Transfer Pricing between Associated Enterprises*, OECD/LEGAL/0279: The Recommendation of the Council on the Determination of Transfer Pricing between Associated Enterprises 'On the proposal of the Committee on Fiscal Affairs:

> I. RECOMMENDS that Members and non-Members adhering to this Recommendation (hereafter the "Adherents"):
> i) follow, when reviewing, and if necessary, adjusting transfer pricing between associated enterprises for the purposes of determining taxable income, the Guidelines – considering the whole of the Guidelines and the interaction of the different chapters – for arriving at arm's length pricing for transactions between associated enterprises;
> ii) encourage taxpayers to follow the Guidelines; to that effect Adherents should give the Guidelines publicity and have them translated, where necessary, into their national language(s);
> iii) develop further co-operation, on a bilateral or multilateral basis, in matters pertaining to transfer pricing.'

17. *Ibid.*, p. 3.

and it is regarded as reflecting customary international law in non-signatory countries.[18] The Vienna Convention contains a two-step process of treaty interpretation starting with the general rule on treaty interpretation in Article 31. Article 31(1) provides that a treaty should be interpreted: in good faith; in accordance with the ordinary meaning of the terms; in their context; and in light of its objects and purpose. The second step is contained in Article 32 on the supplementary means of interpretation. Article 32 provides authority for the use of supplementary material in interpreting treaties. Under Article 32 supplementary material may be used to confirm a meaning established under Article 31. Supplementary material may also be used if the meaning established under Article 31 results in a meaning that is ambiguous or leads to a result that is absurd. The consensus is that the Commentary may be used when interpreting the associated enterprises' article under either Article 31 or 32.[19] As claimed above, if the OECD TPG are part of the Commentary, then they may be used in treaty interpretation. This is the second basis on which the OECD TPG may be used in certain jurisdictions.[20]

## 4 The OECD TPG as a Guidance Document under Domestic Legislation

Finally, some countries provide that the OECD TPG are a guidance document for the application of domestic transfer pricing provisions. For instance, in Australia, the OECD TPG may be used as a guidance document for the transfer pricing rules. Under Australia's transfer pricing provisions, an entity's arm's-length conditions must be identified 'so as best to achieve consistency with the documents' prescribed.[21] Currently, the only prescribed document in Australian law is the OECD TPG as last amended on 19 May 2017.[22] The following changes to the OECD TPG published after May 2017 have not yet been prescribed: *Revised Guidance on the Transactional Profit Split Method* (2018),[23] *Guidance for Tax Administrations on the Application of the Approach to Hard-to-Value Intangibles* (2018)[24] and *Transfer Pricing Guidance on Financial Transactions* (2020).[25] These publications have been incorporated into the OECD TPG.[26] It is presumed that these three parts of the OECD TPG will be prescribed documents for Australian transfer pricing purposes as they were incorporated into the consolidated version of the OECD TPG in the 2022 update. The amendment may be

18. Jan Klabbers, *Virtuous Interpretation, in Treaty Interpretation and the Vienna Convention on the Law of Treaties: 30 Years on* (M. Fitzmaurice, A.O. Elias & P. Merkouris eds, Martinus Nijhoff Publishers 2010), p. 24.
19. David A. Ward et al., *The Interpretation of Income Tax Treaties with Particular Reference to the Commentaries on the OECD Model* (International Fiscal Association/IBFD 2005), p. 18.
20. Michael Kobetsky, *The Status of the OECD Transfer Pricing Guidelines in the Post-BEPS Dynamic*, 3 International Tax Studies 2 (2020).
21. Section 815-135 of the Income Tax Assessment Act 1997 (Australia).
22. *Ibid.*, section 815-135(2)(a).
23. OECD, *Revised Guidance on the Transactional Profit Split Method* (OECD Publishing, 2018).
24. OECD, *Guidance for Tax Administrations on the Application of the Approach to Hard-to-Value Intangibles* (OECD Publishing 2018).
25. OECD, Guidance on Financial Transactions, *supra* n. 5.
26. 'The current provisions of Section C of Part III, Chapter II of the OECD Transfer Pricing Guidelines for Multinational Enterprises and Tax Administrations are deleted in their entirety

made by a legislative amendment of the income tax law or a regulation. By February 2023, the 2022 update to the OECD TPG had not been prescribed. The Portuguese transfer pricing law constitutes another example. Indeed, in 2021, its domestic legislation was amended to require the guidance contained in the 2017 version of the OECD TPG to be followed.[27] The amendment specifically mentions the three amendments made to the OECD TPG since 2017.[28] The amendments were the first major update of the Portuguese transfer pricing rules in 20 years.[29] The United Kingdom (UK) transfer pricing provisions[30] prescribe that the provisions must be interpreted 'in such manner that best secures consistency' with, *inter alia*, the OECD TPG.[31] The 2022 update to the OECD TPG applies in the UK with effect for corporation tax purposes for tax periods commencing on or after 1 January 2023 and for income tax purposes, for the 2023-2024 tax year and subsequent tax years.[32]

## 5 Agreement by Treaty Countries to Use the OECD TPG

Some countries may specifically provide authority for the use of the OECD TPG in the interpretation of the associated enterprises article in tax treaties. Article 21 of the United States (US) Technical Explanation of the 2007 US-Canada protocol on compulsory arbitration specifically provides that an arbitration board may, *inter alia*, use the OECD TPG in resolving an arbitration case.

In making its determination, the arbitration board will apply the following authorities as necessary: (i) the provisions of the Convention, (ii) any agreed commentaries or explanation of the Contracting States concerning the Convention as amended, (iii) the laws of the Contracting States to the extent they are not inconsistent with each other, and (iv) any OECD Commentary, OECD TPG or Reports regarding relevant analogous portions of the OECD Model Tax Convention.[33]

---

and replaced by the following language.': OECD, *Revised Guidance on the Application of the Transactional Profit Split Method: Inclusive Framework on BEPS: Action 10* (OECD Publishing 2018),p. 11.

'The guidance for tax administration on the application of the HTVI [Hard-to-Value Intangibles] approach contained in this document has been incorporated into the Transfer Pricing Guidelines as an annex to Chapter VI.': OECD, Guidance on HTVI, *supra* n., p.8.

'Sections A to E of this report are added to the OECD Transfer Pricing Guidelines as Chapter X. Numbering and cross-references included in other parts of the OECD Transfer Pricing Guidelines will be amended as needed.': OECD, Guidance on Financial Transactions, *supra* n. 5, p. 4.

27. Ryan Finley, *Portugal Aligns Transfer Pricing Guidance with OECD Standards*, 104 Tax Notes International 1159-1160 (2021).
28. Ordinance N. 268/2021 (Portugal). Michael Kobetsky would like to thank Dr R.M. Correia da Cunha in translating the Ordinance into English.
29. Finley, *supra* n. 27.
30. Taxation (International and Other Provisions) Act 2010.
31. Section 164(1)(b) of the Taxation (International and Other Provisions) Act 2010.
32. The Taxation (International and Other Provisions) Act 2010 Transfer Pricing Guidelines Designation Order 2022.
33. Department of the Treasury Technical Explanation of the Protocol Done at Chelsea on 21 September 2007, Amending the Convention Between the United States of America and Canada

The Technical Explanation is a US document, but it has bilateral status as the Canadian government has agreed to its contents by stating that: 'The Technical Explanation is an official United States guide to the Protocol. The Government of Canada has reviewed this document and subscribes to its contents. In the view of both governments, this document accurately reflects the policies behind particular Protocol provisions, as well as understandings reached with respect to the application and interpretation of the Protocol and the Convention.'[34]

This type of agreement is given standing by the Vienna Convention. Article 31(2)(b) provides that any instrument made by the parties in connection with the conclusion of a treaty is treated as being part of the context of the treaty. The US Technical Explanation qualifies as part of the context of the US-Canada Protocol in this circumstance.

## 6 Status of the United Nations Practical Manual on Transfer Pricing

The Inclusive Framework seeks 'to combat BEPS and the ongoing development of consensus-based, anti-BEPS solutions to strengthen the international tax system.'[35] In contrast, the United Nations Tax Committee is a subsidiary body of the United Nations Economic and Social Council.[36] The United Nations Tax Committee comprises 25 members nominated by governments and appointed as experts by the United Nations Secretary-General for a term of four years.[37] The role of the United Nations Tax Committee is to provide guidance for governments, tax administrations and taxpayers 'to help strengthen tax systems, with a view to mobilizing financing for sustainable development'.[38] The members of the United Nations Tax Committee participate as experts and not as government representatives, consequently, governments are not bound by the Committee's publications, such as the UN TP Manual. To underscore this point, the Commentary to the UN MC does not provide countries with the capacity to record a reservation on treaty provisions or an observation in the Commentary. However, the OECD, as an intergovernmental body provides participating countries with capacity to make a reservation to a treaty provision and to record observations in the Commentary. The OECD TPG, as an OECD report, does not provide countries with the ability to record observations. While the UN TP Handbook is not an inter-government document, governments may choose to adopt the UN TP Manual as a guidance document in their domestic legislation.

---

with Respect to Taxes on Income and on Capital Done at Washington on 26 September 1980 as amended by the Protocols done on 14 June 1983, 28 March 1994, 17 March 1995, and 19 July 1997, p. 45.

34. *Ibid.*, p. 1.
35. Developing Countries and the OECD/G20 Inclusive Framework on BEPS, *OECD Report for the G20 Finance Ministers and Central Bank Governors* (OECD Publishing, 2021), pp. 12-13.
36. UN, ECOSOC Tax Committee, *supra* n. 14.
37. *Ibid.*
38. *Ibid.*

## III RE-CHARACTERIZING FINANCIAL TRANSACTIONS UNDER ARTICLE 9(1) OECD MC

We argue that if an intra-group cross-border financing arrangement may be adjusted under a jurisdiction's domestic transfer pricing law, Article 9(1) provides that the jurisdiction retains its authority to make transfer pricing adjustments to both the rate of interest and the amount of debt finance.[39] While this issue appears to be beyond doubt, commentators have claimed that Article 9(1) merely authorizes adjustments to the rate of interest, but not to the amount of debt financed. The authors will demonstrate that this is a narrow and outlier interpretation of Article 9(1) that conflicts with the OECD's statements since 1979 on the scope of Article 9(1).[40]

To reiterate, tax treaties do not create or expand taxing rights that are not contained in a jurisdiction's domestic law. Jurisdiction to tax must be based on domestic law and a tax treaty may confirm the taxing right, reduce the taxing right or eliminate the taxing right. A jurisdiction's domestic transfer pricing law will usually provide a tax authority with the power to make adjustments to an entity's intra-group financing arrangements. It is argued that if an intra-group cross-border financing arrangement may be altered under domestic law, Article 9(1) confirms the jurisdiction's capacity to re-characterize the loan component of an associated entity.[41] However, if the power given to a tax administration under domestic law is narrow and it does not permit re-characterizations, then it is futile to rely on Article 9(1). For example, this outcome was recently upheld in Finland regarding intra-group financing under the former Finnish transfer pricing provisions.[42] Indeed, Finnish Transfer Pricing legislation has been amended with effect from 1 January 2022 and section 31 of the Finnish Tax Procedure Code prescribes the non-recognition and re-characterization of a transaction, including re-characterization of loans.

The terms of Article 9(1) are: 'Where [...] conditions are made or imposed between the two enterprises in their commercial or financial relations which differ from those which would be made between independent enterprises, then any profits which would, but for those conditions, have accrued to one of the enterprises, but, by reason of those conditions, have not so accrued, may be included in the profits of that enterprise and taxed accordingly.'

We assert that in Article 9(1) the 'conditions' that 'are made or imposed ... in their commercial or financial relations' provide authority to make adjustments to both

39. Sham intra-group financing transactions would not be recognized for domestic law or tax treaty. The 2021 UN TP Manual defines a sham as 'something that appears genuine, but when looked at more closely lacks reality, and is not valid under many legal systems' (*supra* n. 7, para. 3.4.3.2).
40. OECD TPG 2022, *supra* n. 6, para. 10.4.
41. The domestic law must create the tax liability as tax treaties do not generally create tax liabilities. For a detailed discussion on whether or not Article 9(1) allows for a structural adjustments *see* Bullen, *supra* n. 9, 231-273.
42. Finland, Supreme Administrative Court cases 2014:119 and 2020:35, analysed in Merja Raunio & Matti Urpilainen, *Case SAC 2020:35 – Supreme Administrative Court Reasserts the Prohibition to Recharacterize Transactions, Now in a Case that Deals with Group Internal Financing*, 27 International Transfer Pricing Journal 379 (2020).

the interest rates and levels of debt finance. The OECD's statements on Article 9(1) confirm the broad interpretation of the provision. For instance, the Commentary on Article 9(1) unequivocally confirms that the provision allows adjustments to be made to the level of intra-group debt finance. It states 'b) the Article is relevant not only in determining whether the rate of interest provided for in a loan contract is an arm's-length rate, but also *whether a prima facie loan can be regarded as a loan or should be regarded as some other kind of payment*, in particular a contribution to equity capital'[43] (emphasis added).

The Commentary expressly provides that a tax authority may adjust an associated entity's profits if the entity's transactions fail to comply with the arm's-length principle.[44] In particular, the Commentary states that a tax authority can rewrite the accounts of the enterprises if, as a result of the special relations between the associated enterprises, the accounts do not show the true taxable profits arising in that State.[45] Additionally, the Commentary provides the qualification that a re-writing of the accounts is proscribed if the loan satisfies the arm's-length principle.[46]

The OECD's interpretation was originally stated in the Committee on Fiscal Affairs' Report on Thin Capitalisation and has been retained in the 1992,[47] 2003,[48] 2010[49] and 2017 versions of the Commentary.[50] Moreover, the position has also been expressed in the 1979 Transfer Pricing Report[51] and the subsequent OECD TPG (1995[52] and 2010[53] OECD TPG). Accordingly, Article 9(1) provides the power for a tax authority to make adjustments to an entity's interest expense and the amount of debt finance.

Our interpretation is supported by the proposed new paragraph 3 of Article 9 Commentary which states that: 'In considering whether an interest payment can be regarded as an arm's-length amount, a State will typically examine the terms and conditions of the loan such as the rate of interest. It may also need to examine, based on the facts and circumstances, whether a purported loan should be regarded as a loan or as another kind of transaction, in particular a contribution to equity capital. The State making a determination as to the extent to which the purported loan is regarded

43. OECD Model 2017, *supra* n. 8, Commentary on Article 9, para. 3.
44. *Ibid.*
45. *Ibid.*, para. 2.
46. *Ibid.*
47. OECD, *Model Tax Convention on Income and on Capital: Condensed Version September 1992*, Commentary on Article 9, para. 2(b) (OECD Publishing 1992).
48. OECD, *Model Tax Convention on Income and on Capital: Condensed Version 2003*, Commentary on Article 9, para. 3(b) (OECD Publishing 2003).
49. OECD, *Model Tax Convention on Income and on Capital: Condensed Version 2010*, Commentary on Article 9, para. 3(b) (OECD Publishing 2010).
50. OECD Model 2017, *supra* n. 8, Commentary on Article 9, para. 3(b).
51. OECD, *Transfer Pricing Guidelines for Multinational Enterprises and Tax Administrations 1979*, paras 15, 23, 24 (OECD Publishing 1979).
52. OECD, *Transfer Pricing Guidelines for Multinational Enterprises and Tax Administrations 1995*, para. 1.37 (OECD Publishing 1995).
53. OECD, *Transfer Pricing Guidelines for Multinational Enterprises and Tax Administrations 2010*, paras 1.65 to 1.69 (OECD Publishing 2010).

as a loan will do so taking into account factors discussed [...] in the OECD Transfer Pricing Guidelines.'[54]

Our interpretation is also supported by the decisions of selected Courts,[55] and the guidance issued by the tax authorities of certain jurisdictions on Article 9, e.g., the US[56] and South Africa.[57] Our interpretation is also consistent with commentators who argue that Article 9(1) is broad and covers situations where non-arm's length debt financing can be re-characterized as equity.[58]

However, the OECD's interpretation of Article 9(1) has been questioned by commentators using a narrow interpretation of the article.[59] For instance, a commentator claims that Article 9(1) can only be used to determine whether the interest rate charged on loans between associated enterprises is at arm's length or not and cannot be used to re-characterize debt to equity. The commentator's view is based on a strict literal interpretation of Article 9(1). Under this narrow interpretation, the term 'conditions [...] made or imposed' is restricted to the terms of the contract, such as security, subordination and other factors which have an impact on the interest rate, but not to the overall 'commercial or financial relations' between the associated enterprises.[60] In other words, the contractual form of the transaction as determined by the associated enterprises needs to be respected and Article 9(1) only allows adjustments to terms and conditions of transactions. The narrow interpretation seems to have been followed by courts, for example, in France.[61]

Nevertheless, the commentator's approach is not supported by the OECD's longstanding statements in the Commentary which reflects the views of OECD member countries and certain non-member countries (the non-member adherents). As stated

54. OECD, *Proposed Changes to Commentaries in the OECD Model Tax Convention on Article 9 and on Related Articles*, 5 (OECD Publishing, 2021).
55. *See, e.g.*, *Chevron Australia Holding Pty Ltd v. Commissioner of Tax* [2017] FCAFC 62, para. 82: 'The notion of conditions in Art 9 refers to the circumstances or environment that can be seen to operate between the two enterprises in their commercial or financial relations which are different to the circumstances or environment which would operate between independent enterprises. The word "conditions" is broad and flexible.' *See also*, decision of the German Bundesfinanzhof of 27 February 2019, I R 73/16 summarized and commented in Bob Michel, *Germany – Case I R 73/16, 27 February 2019 (Summary)*, IBFD (2019) and briefly mentioned in Hans van den Hurk, *Is the Interaction Between Chapter X of the OECD Transfer Pricing Guidelines and the EU Directive on Tax Dispute Resolution Mechanisms an Effective One?*, 29 International Transfer Pricing Journal 1, para. 3.1 (2022).
56. *See, e.g.*, IRS (USA), *United States Model Technical Explanation Accompanying the United States Model Income Tax Convention of November 15, 2006*, (2006), Article 9, para. 1.
57. *See* https://www.sars.gov.za/wp-content/uploads/Legal/Drafts/LAPD-LPrep-Draft-2022-04-Draft-IN-on-intragroup-loans-11-February-2022.pdf, section 5.2 and example 7 on p. 33.
58. For example, *see* Luc De Broe, *International Tax Planning and Prevention of Abuse*, 505 (IBFD Doctoral Series, 2008).
59. For example, *see* Georg Kofler, *Article 9: Associated Enterprises, B. Article 9(1) OECD and UN MC, in Klaus Vogel on Double Taxation Conventions*, para. 79.
60. Fred de Hosson & Geerten Michielse, *Treaty Aspects of the 'Thin Capitalization' Issue – A Review of the OECD Report*, 17 Intertax 476, 480 (1989); Wittendorff, *supra* n. 9, 115-120.
61. *See, e.g.*, France, Société Andritz, Conseil d'État, Section du Contentieux, 30/12/2003, 233894 : les stipulations de l'article 9 *ne sauraient toutefois avoir pour objet ou pour effet de permettre à ces Etats d'apprécier le caractère normal du choix arrêté par une entreprise de financer par l'octroi d'un prêt, de préférence à un apport de fonds propres, l'activité d'une autre entreprise qu'elle détient ou contrôle et d'en tirer, le cas échéant, de quelconques conséquences fiscales*.

above, under Article 32 of the Vienna Convention supplementary materials may be used to confirm an Article 9(1) interpretation or to resolve ambiguity resulting from an Article 31 interpretation of Article 9(1). Assuming that the OECD Commentary qualifies as supplementary material, then Article 9(1) clearly provides tax authorities with the power to adjust an entity's intra-group loan capital. Some jurisdictions may even conclude that the Commentary is part of the context under Article 31 of the Vienna Convention. Consequently, the Commentary may be considered when interpreting Article 9(1).

In summary, we assert that Article 9(1) provides tax authorities with the power to make adjustments to an entity's amount of debt finance under the commercial irrational exception if the domestic law provides the authority to make such adjustments.

## IV CAN AN ADVANCE OF FUNDS AS LOANS BE DELINEATED AS ANOTHER FINANCIAL ARRANGEMENT UNDER THE BROAD NOTION OF ACCURATE DELINEATION?

### 1 Overview

Preceding the analysis on whether a loan can be disregarded or substituted by tax authorities under the commercial irrationality exception, the controlled transaction needs to be accurately delineated in accordance with the 2022 OECD TPG. The accurate delineation determines whether the purported loan should be recognized as debt or equity for transfer pricing purposes.

For example, if a Parent Company, resident in Country A, has a wholly owned subsidiary, Subsidiary Company, in Country B and Parent Company lends funds to Subsidiary Company. Under the loan agreement, the subsidiary is only required to pay interest to its parent entity if the subsidiary makes profits and no repayment schedule for the principal amount is provided and the loan is unsecured. The central question is whether the accurate delineation of the loan results in the purported loan being characterized as equity or debt. In order to determine whether a third party would have entered into such arrangement, an accurate delineation of the intra-group loan, through a functional analysis, is required.

Overall, the OECD TPG offer details and practical examples on how to accurately delineate financial transactions and, particularly intercompany loans. The principles in section D.1 of Chapter I of the OECD TPG apply to any controlled transaction, including financial transactions. Therefore, the accurate delineation of an intercompany loan requires a multinational enterprise (MNE) or a tax authority, to 'identify the commercial or financial relations between the associated enterprises and the conditions and economically relevant circumstances attaching to those relations so that the controlled transaction is accurately delineated'.[62] While performing this task, 'both the lender's

62. OECD TPG 2022, *supra* n. 6, para. 1.33.

and borrower's perspectives should be taken into account, acknowledging that these perspectives may not align in every case'.[63]

According to the 2022 OECD TPG, the MNE is first required to perform a broad-based analysis of the industry sector in which the MNE group operates 'and of the factors affecting the performance of any business operating in that sector'.[64] To this end, the MNEs' financing and transfer pricing policies must be analysed to determine, for instance, which group entities or projects receive funding in priority and the group funding or treasury strategy, and whether it is consistent with the industry in which the group and company operate.[65] Next, the identification of the operations of the related entities of the MNE group and their commercial or financial relations is required. This step involves an understanding of the group's associated enterprises and how they interact with each other.

Finally, the economically relevant characteristics or comparability factors used to accurately delineate a purported intercompany loan are:

- the contractual terms of the loan;
- a functional analysis of both associated enterprises, i.e., the borrower and the lender;
- the characteristics of the intercompany loan;
- the economic circumstances of the associated enterprises and the market in which the parties operate; and
- the business strategies used by the parties.[66]

The economically relevant characteristics of a purported intra-group loan are critical in assessing whether the loan should be recognized for transfer pricing purposes by tax authorities.

In situations where the purported loan is delineated as another financial arrangement by tax authorities, the new structure should be consistent with the economically relevant characteristics mentioned above. The facts and circumstances should also guide the selection of potential replacement structures. Therefore, the accurate delineation of the intercompany loan is a crucial step in the recognition or non-recognition of a financial instrument.

## 2 General Overview of Economically Relevant Characteristics

### *A Contractual Terms*

A written agreement is usually created by both parties to explicitly describe the terms and conditions of the intragroup loan. Under the OECD TPG, the loan agreement is the starting point for the accurate delineation of a controlled transaction.

63. *Ibid.*, para. 10.51.
64. *Ibid.*, para. 1.34.
65. *Ibid.*, para. 10.16.
66. *Ibid.*, para. 1.36.

The UK HM Revenue and Customs (HMRC) has for instance published a Manual outlining the terms of a third-party loan agreement.[67] Such terms should also be reproduced in intra-group loan agreements which tend to lack details due to the close relationship between associated enterprises. The terms of a loan agreement should include the value of the loan; its purpose; its currency; the amount and timing of repayments; the interest rate, its calculation and when and how it is payable; securities provided/unsecured nature of the loan; default of payment and its consequences; the party bearing the costs; which party pays fees and when. It is also crucial to integrate into the agreement the list of participants to the loan, such as the lender, the borrower and the guarantor. Furthermore, a list of definitions should be provided, especially if there are financial covenants in the agreement. Finally, the agreement should also mention whether financial information is required to be provided and how often.[68] A detailed intra-group loan agreement will make it easier to accurately delineate the controlled transaction. Similar requirements are also listed in the UN Manual on Transfer Pricing.[69]

Nevertheless, 'between associated enterprises, the contractual arrangements may not always provide information in sufficient detail or may be inconsistent with the actual conduct of the parties or other facts and circumstances'.[70] Therefore, it may be necessary to refer to other documents and communications between the parties, such as board meeting minutes or internal management notes to determine the substance of the purported loan.

The terms of the loan should be aligned with the actual conduct of the parties. If the form and substance of the purported loan conflict, the substance as reflected in the conduct of the parties prevails. The actual conduct of the parties requires further analysis and can be supported by the other four categories of economically relevant characteristics of the controlled transaction. The actual conduct of the parties must be identified when no written agreement has been concluded by the associated enterprises.

### *B Functional Analysis*

A functional analysis is required to identify the functions performed, the assets used and the risks assumed by both parties to a controlled transaction, i.e., the borrower and the lender.

According to the OECD TPG, functions of the lender would generally include loan creation and loan management functions such as 'an analysis and evaluation of the risks inherent in the loan, the capability to commit capital of the business to the investment, determining the terms of the loan and organising and documenting the

67. HMRC (UK), *Thin capitalisation: practical guidance: third-party loan agreements: the general form of third-party loan agreements* (International Manual INTM522010, 2016).
68. *Ibid.*
69. UN TP Manual 2021, *supra* n. 7, para. 9.7.2.2.
70. OECD TPG 2022, *supra* n. 6, para. 10.22.

loan. This may also include any ongoing monitoring and periodic review of the loan'.[71] By contrast, the relevant functions of the borrower generally involve 'ensuring the availability of funds to repay the principal and the interest on the loan in due time; providing collateral, if needed; and monitoring and fulfilling any other obligation derived from the loan contract'.[72]

The OECD TPG does not explicitly refer to specific assets used by the borrower and the lender entering into an intercompany loan. Generally, according to the OECD TPG, the functional analysis should lead to the determination of the type and nature of assets used by both parties.

Regarding risks, the OECD TPG insists on the relevance and practical difficulties of identifying the risks assumed by the parties, and to this end, a detailed six-step process has been developed. Without getting into the details of each step, as a starting point, an identification of economically significant risks with specificity is required.[73] According to the OECD TPG, risks are defined 'as the effect of uncertainty on the objectives of the business'.[74] It also insists on the fact that such identification of risks should concern those assumed by both the lender and borrower. The risks relevant for delineating an intercompany loan, 'relate to repayment of the amount transferred, compensation expected for the use of that amount over time, and compensation for other associated risk factors'.[75] The UN TP Manual mentions other risks such as 'interest rate risk, reinvestment risk, call/prepayment risk, inflation (or purchasing power) risk, liquidity risk, exchange rate (or currency) risk, volatility risk, political or legal risk, event risk, sector risk and country risk'.[76]

If the lender does not control the key risks, e.g., default, credit risk, associated with the loan or does not have the financial capacity to assume the risks, the latter should be allocated to the associated enterprise that has control over them, and the financial capacity to assume the risks.[77] The OECD TPG provides the following example: 'consider a situation where Company A advances funds to Company B. Consider further that the accurate delineation of the actual transaction indicates that Company A does not exercise control functions related to the advance of funds but that Company P, the parent company of the MNE group, is exercising control over those risks, and has the financial capacity to assume such risks'.[78] In this case, the returns associated with the risks need to be allocated to the parent.

Additionally, the OECD TPG provides other examples of risk-free returns vis-à-vis subsidiary's funding activities for intangibles.[79] In one example, Shuyona is the parent company of an MNE group which initially owns the group's intangibles such as patents and other technology-related intangibles. The entity decides to sell those intangibles to

71. *Ibid.*, para. 10.24.
72. *Ibid.*, para. 10.26.
73. *Ibid.*, paras 1.71 to 1.76.
74. *Ibid.*, para. 1.71.
75. *Ibid.*, para. 10.52.
76. UN TP Manual 2021, *supra* n. 7, para. 9.12.1.3.
77. OECD TPG 2022, *supra* n. 6, para. 10.25.
78. *Ibid.*
79. *Ibid.*, Annex To Chapter VI: Examples On Intangibles, Example 16.

a newly established subsidiary, Company T, which is also a manufacturing entity. Simultaneously, Company T contractually agrees to bear the financial risk associated with possible failure of future R&D projects as well as agrees to assume the cost of all future R&D activity. However, Company T has no technical personnel capable of conducting or supervising the research activities and does not perform any key development, enhancement, maintenance, protection and exploitation (DEMPE) functions regarding the intangibles. Moreover, Company T does not control risks in relation to the acquisition of the intangibles or to their further development. In reality, Shuyona still supervises and controls the R&D activities in relation to the sale of the intangibles and hence performs the key DEMPE functions and controls the risks related to the intangibles. A thorough transfer pricing analysis reveals that Company T should be entitled to no more than a risk-free return for its funding activities because, although it contractually bears the risks related to the intangibles, in substance Company T does not exercise control over those risks.

The lender can mitigate its risks through covenants. The covenant, whether of incurrence or maintenance, will offer a higher degree of protection to the lender. The OECD TPG defines incurrence and maintenance covenants as: 'Incurrence covenants require or prohibit certain actions by the borrower without the consent of the lender.'[80] On the contrary, 'Maintenance covenants refer typically to financial indicators which have to be met at regular, predetermined intervals during the life of a covenanted loan.'[81] Risk can also be mitigated through the use of a financial guarantee[82] which 'provides for the guarantor to meet specified financial obligations in the event of a failure to do so by the guaranteed party'.[83] An intercompany loan may be guaranteed by an associated enterprise, such as the parent entity, or an external party (a bank) to support the borrower's credit rating. However, associated lenders and borrowers may choose not to include these terms in an intragroup loan. Thus, it is recommended that such terms, depending on the facts and circumstances, are included in intra-group loan agreements. In fact, such covenants were subject to significant consideration in the UK BlackRock Hold Co 5 LLC case.[84]

To summarize the facts of the case, the BlackRock group subsidiaries included LLC4, a US tax resident, LLC5, a UK tax resident, and LLC6, a US tax resident. LLC4 lent funds to LLC5 which in turn lent funds to LLC6 which purchased an independent business, Barclays Global Investors.[85] LLC5 was created and used as part of the acquisition structure. In this case, the Court had to address two issues. First, the 'transfer pricing issue' on whether an independent lender acting at arm's length would have made the same loans as the loans made by LLC4 to LLC5 used.[86] Second, the 'unallowable purpose issue' concerned whether there was a commercial purpose for

80. *Ibid.*, para. 10.84.
81. *Ibid.*, para. 10.85.
82. A full chapter of this book is dedicated to guarantees.
83. OECD TPG 2022, *supra* n. 6, para. 10.155.
84. *Blackrock Holdco 5 LLC v. HMRC* [2022], UKUT 00199 (TCC) (UK).
85. For a more detailed diagram on the group structure and acquisition structure, *see ibid.*, Appendix 1.
86. *Ibid.*, para. 4.

the loans or whether the purpose was to secure a tax advantage (or whether there were dual purposes).[87]

On appeal, the UK Upper Tribunal ruled in favour of the HMRC. On the 'transfer pricing issue', the Upper Tribunal concluded that 'the FTT[88] erred in law in permitting new third-party covenants absent from the actual transaction to be taken into account when considering whether an independent lender would make a $4 billion loan to LLC5. The FTT decided that such an independent lender would not have made a $4 billion loan to LLC5 without such covenants being in place and that important finding should itself have determined that there was no comparable arm's length transaction'.[89] On the second issue, although the conclusion on the 'transfer pricing issue' renders this issue immaterial to the outcome of the appeal,[90] the Upper Tribunal still dealt with the grounds raised by the parties. It agreed with the conclusion of the FTT that the loans made to LLC5 had both a commercial and an unallowable tax advantage.[91] However, it disagreed with the lower tribunal and ruled that all the debits arising from the loans made to LLC5 must be apportioned to the unallowable tax purpose, rather than to the commercial purpose, implying that these debits are not brought into account.[92]

Hence, in the BlackRock case, the Upper Tribunal recognised the importance of risks in transfer pricing and the impact of covenants on the risks assumed by an associated enterprise regarding intercompany loans. The introduction of covenants in a loan influences the transfer pricing analysis given it materially affects the relevant characteristics of the intragroup transaction.

### C The Characteristics of the Intercompany Loan

The characteristics of an intra-group loan are usually expressed in a written loan agreement, hence there is an apparent overlap between the terms and conditions in a loan agreement and the characteristics of the loan. As already discussed, a list of possible features and attributes of an intercompany loan includes 'the amount of the loan; its maturity; the schedule of repayment; the nature or purpose of the loan (trade credit, merger/acquisition, mortgage, etc.); level of seniority and subordination, geographical location of the borrower; currency; collateral provided; presence and quality of any guarantee; and whether the interest rate is fixed or floating'.[93]

87. *Ibid.*, para. 101.
88. The First-tier Tribunal (FTT).
89. *Blackrock v. HMRC, supra* n. 84, para. 76.
90. *Ibid.*, para. 102.
91. *Ibid.*, para. 200.
92. *Ibid.*, para. 199.
93. *Ibid.*, para. 10.29.

### D Economic Circumstances

In the case of intercompany loans, '[m]acroeconomic trends such as central bank lending rates or interbank reference rates, and financial market events like a credit crisis, can affect prices.'[94] and hence constitute the economic circumstances surrounding the controlled transactions. The OECD TPG also notes the importance of currency differences as economic circumstances which influence the price of the interest payment. Other economic factors 'such as growth rate, inflation rate, and the volatility of exchange rates, mean that otherwise similar financial instruments issued in different currencies may have different prices'.[95] Moreover, even though the currency used for the intercompany loan may be the lender's domestic currency or the borrower's domestic currency, 'prices for financial instruments in the same currency may vary across financial markets or countries due to regulations such as interest rate controls, exchange rate controls, foreign exchange restrictions and other legal and practical restrictions on financial market access'.[96] Similar criteria are listed in the UN TP Manual.[97]

### E Business Strategies

Finally, the business strategies pursued by both the lender and borrower must be analysed. In the case of financial transactions and intercompany loans, it is crucial to consider the borrower's and lender's financing strategies, especially, in light of their business models. Indeed, such strategies can have an impact on the structure of the examined intercompany loan and the day-to-day operations of the associated enterprises. The financing strategy can be inferred through the analysis of the intent of the parties regarding the loan and the participation in management and voting power by the lender.[98] Regarding business strategies, the OECD TPG provides the following example: 'independent lenders may be prepared to lend on terms and conditions to an enterprise undertaking a merger or acquisition which might otherwise not be acceptable to the lender for the same business if it were in a steady state'.[99]

### F Accurate Delineation of the Funding Arrangement in Light of the Above Economically Relevant Characteristics: Illustrations

As stated above, the economically relevant characteristics of the intercompany loan are critical to determining whether the purported loan should be recognized as a loan with alterations or whether it should not be recognized and consequently be characterized

94. OECD TPG 2022, *supra* n. 6, para. 10.32.
95. *Ibid.*, para. 10.33.
96. *Ibid.*
97. UN TP Manual 2021, *supra* n. 7, para. 9.7.2.2.
98. *Ibid.*, para. 9.7.2.2.
99. OECD TPG 2022, *supra* n. 6, para. 10.35.

into, for instance, equity. As a result, it is crucial to take into account both the lender's and borrower's perspectives.[100]

We will consider two types of transfer pricing adjustments of loans. The first type, which is more common, deals with the situation when an analysis of the economically relevant characteristics of the intercompany loan leads to the conclusion that a modification of the written terms and conditions of the loan is warranted. The substance of the loan requires that additional terms and conditions should be imputed or disregarded under the accurate delineation of the loan transaction which changes the interest rate. The second type deals with the situation when an analysis of the economically relevant characteristics of the intercompany loan leads to the conclusion that either part of the loan or the entire loan must be re-characterized as equity.

For the first type of adjustment, consider the following case which deals with an intra-group unsecured loan. Assume that a subsidiary, which has high-value moveable and immovable assets, borrows an advance of EUR 10 million from its parent entity. According to the written agreement, the subsidiary does not provide any security. As the loan is unsecured, accordingly the interest rate reflected in the agreement is high. Normally, independent parties dealing at arm's length with each other would agree on a security. The provision of a security would usually result in a lower interest rate. From the borrower's perspective, an independent borrower would probably not have entered into such arrangement due to the high interest rate. From the lender perspective, an independent lender would not have advanced such funds in the absence of securities. Therefore, under the accurate delineation of the transaction, a security clause could be included in the agreement. In practice, intra-group loans should be treated as being secured and consequently, the interest rate would be lower.

The UN TP Manual provides the following example on the loan currency for principal and interest: 'Borrowing Company, BCo, pays loan interest to Lending Company, LCo. BCo and LCo are associated enterprises. The loan agreement specifies that the advance is denominated in currency X. On further examination of the facts, it is found that the advance was made in currency Y, and regular interest payments have been made in currency Y computed on the outstanding balance expressed in currency Y.'[101] In this example, the actual conduct of the parties regarding the currency of the intragroup loan differs from the one agreed upon in the loan agreement. Therefore, the accurate delineation of the transaction leads to the conclusion that for transfer pricing purposes, the currency of the loan should be Y and not currency X. This adjustment may affect the interest rate.

Finally, we consider an example of loan maturity. Two scenarios are possible, it could occur that the accurate delineation of the loan leads to the conclusion that the loan maturity should be shortened, or that it should be extended. To illustrate the latter, suppose that Co A is the parent entity of an MNE group. In 2022, subsidiary Co B is created by Co A and Co A enters into a two-year loan agreement to lend Co B funds.

100. Vikram Chand, *Transfer Pricing Aspects of Inter Company Loans in Light of the BEPS Action Plan*, 44 Intertax 885, 888 (2016); Raffaele Petruzzi & Raphael Holzinger, *Accurate Delineation vs. Recognition of Intragroup Loans*, 98 International Tax Notes 1111, 1114 (2020).
101. UN TP Manual 2021, *supra* n. 7, para. 9.12.2.12.

However, during fiscal years 2022 and 2023, Co B used the advance of funds to finance fixed assets and it appears that it will not be able to repay the loan to Co A maturity. Due to the non-repayment, the two associated enterprises decide to extend the loan on the same terms for an additional period of two years. The accurate delineation of the actual transaction determines that the loan maturity should not be two years but should be longer, such as four years if the loan principal and interest is eventually repaid to Co A.[102]

We now move to the second type of transfer pricing adjustment. Consider the following example which deals with the debt service capacity of the borrower. Company A is the parent entity of an MNE group. It sets up a subsidiary, Sub Co, in Country B. In the first five years of its activity, Sub Co was profitable. As it wanted to expand its business, it borrowed funds from its parent entity in year six. Under the intercompany loan agreement, it was agreed that the loan will mature in three years, the interest rate is 6% and the loan was subordinated to external loans from other third-party lenders. However, as a result of a series of poor financial decisions, Sub Co was on the verge of bankruptcy in year eight and it was clear that it would be unable to repay the loan principal and interest to Co A. The company's standalone credit rating also dropped several notches to *C* based on S&P ratings and *Ca* based on Moody's. Due to reputational concerns, Co A decided to lend additional funds to its Sub Co to meet its working capital requirements, on the same terms and conditions as the first loan, despite Sub Co being unable to pay the principal and interest on the first loan. An objective analysis of Sub Co's current business operations and financial projections[103] leads to the conclusion that repayment of both loans is highly unlikely. In this case, one may argue that based on a debt service capacity analysis, the second loan needs to be partially or wholly characterized as equity as the borrower would be unable to repay the loan principal interest.

Additionally, as highlighted in the UN TP Manual, careful consideration should also be given to the entity's profile when an intra-group loan is provided.[104] Consider the following example: Company A, located in Country A, is the parent of an MNE. It sets up a limited risk distributor (LRD) Sub B, in Country B. Sub B buys products from the parent and agrees to pay the parent within 30 days from receipt of the order. Also, in general, it agrees with its clients that they can pay for the purchase within 30 days of delivery of the products. For one large global customer, Sub B, based on the decision made by the parent, allows this customer to pay Sub B within six months of delivery of the product. In order to pay Company A, Sub B borrows money from another related party, Sub C in Country C, and uses those funds to pay the purchase from Company A within 30 days of receipt of order. The interest on this short-term loan was 1% and the loan from Sub C was repaid after the large customer paid its invoice. This financing arrangement raises the question of whether Sub B should be allowed a deduction of the interest expense for tax purposes that as an LRD is insulated from financial and credit risks and the decision to extend favourable credit terms was made at the level of the

102. UN TP Manual 2021, *supra* n. 7, para. 9.12.2.11; OECD TPG 2022, *supra* n. 6, para. 10.37.
103. *See also*, OECD TPG 2022, *supra* n. 6, para. 10.13.
104. UN TP Manual 2021, *supra* n. 7, para. 9.12.3.

parent. It may be argued that the loan from Sub C and the associated funding costs should not be attributed to Sub B but rather to Company A for transfer pricing purposes. The decision to deviate from the standard financing practice for the products was made at the level of the parent (for a similar example on a factoring case, *see* Chapter 39).

## V CAN LOANS RECOGNIZED UNDER THE NOTION OF ACCURATE DELINEATION BE DISREGARDED/RE-CHARACTERIZED UNDER THE COMMERCIAL IRRATIONALITY EXCEPTION?

The 2010 version of the OECD TPG provided two exceptional situations where a loan could be disregarded: the economic substance exception and the commercial rationality exception. Since the 2017 version, the commercial rationality exception remains while the economic substance exception has been merged into the accurate delineation of the intra-group financing arrangement. The commercial rationality exception was described in the 1995 and 2010 versions of the OECD TPG as: 'The second circumstance arises where, while the form and substance of the transaction are the same, the arrangements made in relation to the transaction, viewed in their totality, differ from those which would have been adopted by independent enterprises behaving in a commercially rational manner and the actual structure practically impedes the tax administration from determining an appropriate transfer price.'[105] In such versions, the commercial rationality exception comprised two conditions commonly referred to as the commercial irrational requirement and the practical impediment requirement. The latter requirement was modified in the 2017 OECD TPG version.

Since 2017, the OECD TPG provide that a related party transaction can be disregarded and replaced with another arrangement if the related party arrangement, viewed holistically, differs from those which would have been adopted by independent enterprises behaving in '*a commercially rational manner*' thereby preventing the determination of a price that would be acceptable to both parties taking into account their respective perspectives and the options realistically available (ORA) to them.[106]

The test to ascertain the commercial rationality of an arrangement involves two steps. Under the first step, it must be determined whether the intra-group loan, differs from an arrangement that would have been entered into by independent parties behaving in a rational manner and in comparable circumstances. Under the second step, it must be determined whether the differences between the intra-group arrangement and an arrangement between independent parties would prevent the setting of a price that would be acceptable to both parties. The transfer pricing analysis must be based on the respective perspectives of both the lender and the borrower. Furthermore, the determination must be based on the ORA to both the lender and the borrower at the time of entering into the transaction.

105. OECD TPG 1995, *supra* n. 52, and OECD TPG 2010, *supra* n. 53, para. 1.37.
106. OECD TPG 2022, *supra* n. 6, para. 1.142.

For example, Company C has an overall arm's-length borrowing capacity of USD 1,000 at 3%. It has borrowed funds of up to USD 600 from a related party. Company C's unused arm's-length borrowing capacity is USD 400. Consequently, in order to maximize the amount of deductible interest available to it, the MNE Group decides to increase Company C's intra-group debt to achieve a level closer to the arm's-length amount even though there is no commercial purpose for the additional loan. Accordingly, Company C borrows USD 600 from a related party, Company B, at 3% and deposits the funds in a local bank account which generates an interest income of 1%. The principal reason for a loan is to generate an interest deduction (2% differential) which is deductible in Company C's country of residence for tax law purposes. This raises the issue of whether such an arrangement can be challenged under the transfer pricing rules.

Under the accurate delineation of the loan, the additional borrowing of USD 600 should not be classified as a loan. In general, a loan is given for a particular commercial purpose. However, in our case, the USD 600 was extended only to generate an interest deduction. Thus, one may argue that as the loan does not have any real commercial purpose, the advanced funds should not be delineated as debt. Even if the advance passes the delineation phase, it may be argued that it was given for general investment purposes or for making passive investments, but a tax authority may be able to apply the commercial rationality test.

It may be claimed that independent parties generally strive for profit maximization. This means that an independent lender and an independent borrower would enter into the transaction if both can expect an increase in their respective net profits, immediately or in the near future. However, in this example, the borrower will continue paying the interest without any possibility to increase its net profits currently or in the near future. Also, it is unlikely that an independent borrower would borrow money at a high interest rate to deposit the funds in a bank account which generates a net loss for Company C. Further, there are no genuine commercial reasons or purpose for which the funds are used except the fact that they are deposited in the bank account at a lower rate of interest. Also, from a lender's perspective, in open markets, commercial lenders usually lend funds only when the borrower carries out certain economic and commercial activities associated with those funds. Lenders do not lend if there is no commercial purpose to lend. Thus, it may be argued that the arrangement differs from an arrangement that would have been entered into by independent parties behaving in a rational manner and in comparable circumstances.

It may be argued that from the borrower's perspective, borrowing funds is not necessary as there is no commercial requirement for the loan principal. Also, the borrowing does not lead to any expected future net profits and is consequently irrational. A rational borrower would not have entered into the loan arrangement. As stated in the OECD TPG in Para 10.19, even though the borrower has the borrowing capacity, the latter would 'avoid placing negative pressure on its credit rating and increasing its cost of capital and jeopardising its access to capital markets and its market reputation'. From the lender's perspective, if it is unlikely to lend funds, a realistic option for the lender would be to contemplate other realistically available investment opportunities. Consequently, as there is no 'commercial rationale' for the additional funding, the advance of funds can simply be disregarded for transfer pricing purposes.

If the borrower can demonstrate the commercial rationality for the loan, such as for undertaking commercial activities, and establishes that comparable uncontrolled transactions are available, it may be argued that the transaction should not be disregarded or substituted.[107] This argument would be persuasive if the taxpayer can prove that independent parties are ready to enter into such transactions in comparable economic circumstances. Consequently, if it is established that the additional debt would have been entered into had the lender been an independent party then the interest payable on that debt should be deductible. Accordingly, the threshold for disregarding the transaction under the 'commercially rational' standard appears to be high.[108]

## VI CONCLUSION

The chapter has established that intra-group financing is a key area of transfer pricing to counter MNE groups engaging in base erosion and profit shifting. The potential for transfer pricing intra-group financing disputes was illustrated in the UK *BlackRock* case.[109] The inclusion of Chapter X in the OECD TPG was a significant development and the guidance in the chapter provides MNEs with the ability to prevent transfer financing disputes with tax authorities. The complexity and uncertainty involved in a transfer pricing analysis of intra-group financing were considered in the chapter. Consequently, MNEs should document and explain in detail their transfer pricing analysis conducted. The documentation should include a detailed loan agreement with appropriate terms, conditions, securities and covenants based on comparable uncontrolled loan agreements between independent parties in the same or similar circumstances. An intra-group loan agreement should be modified when necessary and the modifications should be supported with comprehensive documentation.

Article 9 MC OECD allows a State to make a transfer pricing adjustment to a loan arrangement between associated enterprises if it is not at arm's length. The chapter established that Article 9 provides that adjustments can be made to both the amount of a purported intra-group loan and the interest rates. It is important for jurisdictions to ensure that their domestic transfer pricing allows for both the amount of the loan and the cost of funds to be adjusted. This will ensure transfer pricing reciprocity between jurisdictions for intra-group loans. The chapter claimed that the accurate delineation of an intra-group loan requires, an objective understanding of the economically relevant characteristics of the intercompany loan. It is critical to determine whether the purported loan should be recognized as a loan and whether the terms and conditions of the purported loan agreement should be amended. Finally, in extreme cases, the

---

107. OECD TPG 2022, *supra* n. 6, para. 1.123.
108. Martijn de Lange, Paul Lankhorst & Rutger Hafkenscheid, *(Non-) Recognition of Transactions Between Associated Enterprises: On Behaving in a Commercially Rational Manner, Decision Making Traps and BEPS*, 22 International Transfer Pricing Journal 85, 88 (2015).
109. *Blackrock v. HMRC* (UK), *supra* n. 84.

loan should not be recognized for tax purposes because independent parties would not have created a loan in the same or similar circumstances and consequently the loan principal may be characterized as equity. Towards this end, after considering the economically relevant characteristics, several examples were considered. Finally, the chapter examined the circumstances in which the commercial rationality exception could possibly be invoked.

# CHAPTER 11
# Options Realistically Available Vis-à-Vis Loans

*Andreas Bullen*[*]

## I INTRODUCTION

When a multinational group needs external funding there are two different models in which to structure the funding. A first model is to obtain all external borrowing in a top group company (typically the ultimate parent company), which then funds other group companies with a mix of equity and intra-group loans. A second model is to allow each group company to obtain external funding in order to fund its own business activities. In practice it is difficult to strictly follow a single model and, we therefore often see a mix of the two approaches.

The first model will often be preferred as it generally will attract lower external borrowing costs at the group level than the second model, e.g., since the external lenders would have exclusive rights to the entire group's assets in the event of default, and not only to the single group company's assets. The first model also has significant administrative advantages since the group will have fewer external loan contracts to negotiate and follow up on, and intra-group loans and equity can be issued quickly from the top company when a subsidiary is in need of capital. As a result, many

* Mr Håkon Marius Mørch, also a lawyer at Wiersholm law firm, has made a significant contribution to the drafting and content of this chapter. The end result is very much the fruits of both his and my own efforts. The views and opinions set forth herein are the personal views or opinions of the authors; they do not necessarily reflect the views or opinions of the organisation with which the authors are associated.

multinational groups have adopted the first model. This leads to a large number of cross-border intra-group loans being issued. Transfer pricing issues related to intra-group loan transactions are therefore very common.

The first step of a transfer pricing analysis is to identify the actual transaction that has taken place between the associated enterprises by accurately delineating the controlled transaction.[1] With regard to capital transactions, a fundamental issue in the delineation process is to determine whether the capital contribution should be classified as a loan or as a contribution of equity.[2] Such classification under the delineation process is important because equity contributions fall outside of the scope of the arm's length principle in Article 9 of the Organisation for Economic Co-operation and Development (OECD) Model Tax Convention.[3] This is mainly based on the fact that equity contributions cannot be made, or entered into, between independent enterprises, and thus the conditions of an equity contribution cannot differ from those which would have been made between independent enterprises. The arm's length principle can thus not be applied in a meaningful manner to equity contributions. We will not go further into these classification issues in this chapter. Any reference to loans, loan agreements, etc., in this chapter, is a reference to a transaction that has been accurately delineated as a loan, i.e., typically a type of credit arrangement in which a sum of money is lent from one group company to another in exchange of interest and the future repayment of the principal amount.

If the capital contribution is classified as a loan, it will be necessary to accurately delineate the key terms and conditions of the loan agreement. '*Key*' terms and

1. *See, e.g.*, the OECD Guidelines para. 1.33: 'Application of the arm's length principle is based on a comparison of the conditions in a controlled transaction with the conditions that would have been made had the parties been independent and undertaking a comparable transaction under comparable circumstances. There are two key aspects in such an analysis: the first aspect is to identify the commercial or financial relations between the associated enterprises and the conditions and economically relevant circumstances attaching to those relations in order that the controlled transaction is accurately delineated.'
2. *See* OECD Guidelines paras 10.10-10.32 regarding the determination of whether a purported loan should be regarded as a loan.
3. This position is supported by the judgment from the Norwegian Supreme Court in *IKEA* (HR-2016-2165-A, para. 81), where the court stated that equity transactions fall outside the scope of the domestic Norwegian arm's length provision. The position is also supported by the fact that none of the transactions examined under the arm's length principle in the OECD Guidelines are equity transactions (such as equity capital contributions, equity capital reductions, dividends or intra-group contributions). *See also* Georg Kofler in Klaus Vogel, *Klaus Vogel on Double Taxation Conventions* (2015), p. 637 note 57 to Article 9 ('*The notion of "commercial and financial" relations* [in Article 9(1) of the OECD Model] is frequently contrasted with the effects of pure shareholder relations (e.g., in-kind dividend distributions, increases and decreases in share capital'); Richard S. Collier & Joseph L. Andrus, *Transfer Pricing and the Arm's Length Principle after BEPS*, 184-187 (2017), where the authors first conclude, in para. 5.77, with the following: 'Accordingly (...) ALP-based transfer pricing rules were, prior to BEPS, an ineffective tool for addressing concerns relating to excessive equity capital', before, secondly, stating in para. 6.40 that no definition of excessive capital nor any rules on the determination of an appropriate level of capital under the arm's length principle were established under the BEPS effort.

conditions mean terms and conditions having a significant impact on the arm's length interest rate. Depending on the circumstances, such key terms and conditions may include the amount of the loan, the seniority of the loan (subordinated or not?), securities, the term of the loan and default clauses.

The main topic of this chapter is the application of the so-called *realistically available options standard* (hereinafter 'the RAO standard'), used as a legal standard to disregard or restructure the intra-group loan. Such adjustments are referred to as *non-recognition* or *structural adjustments* for transfer pricing purposes. We will first provide an overview of the RAO standard and its relevance to the different steps of the analysis under the arm's length principle (section II). We will then give a brief overview of different steps of a non-recognition analysis (section III), before addressing the application of the RAO standard to selected key terms and conditions of intra-group loan agreements (section IV).

## II THE RAO STANDARD: AN OVERVIEW

### 1 Introduction

When considering whether to enter into a potential transaction, an independent enterprise will, more or less consciously, first identify the options that are realistically available to it, and then choose the option that all in all appears to be the most advantageous at the time of the decision. An independent enterprise would not be expected to enter into a transaction if another alternative seems clearly more attractive than the potential transaction. This concept is referred to as the RAO standard. In the OECD Guidelines, the RAO standard is articulated as follows in paragraph 1.38:

> Independent enterprises, when evaluating the terms of a potential transaction, will compare the transaction to the other *options realistically available* to them, and they will only enter into the transaction if they see no alternative that offers a *clearly more attractive opportunity* to meet their commercial objectives. In other words, independent enterprises would only enter into a transaction if it is not expected to make them worse off than their next best option. (Emphasis added)

Under the RAO standard, the examiner must thus perform an analysis of the taxpayer's realistically available options, and then compare the attractiveness of the actual transaction and the realistically available option(s), *see* section III below.

In the following subsections, we will address the relevance of the RAO standard to different steps of the analysis under the arm's length principle.

### 2 The RAO Standard Used for Non-recognition Purposes

The RAO standard is, first of all, relevant when determining whether the tax authorities are authorised to disregard or restructure the actual transaction, i.e., whether the tax authorities are authorised to undertake so-called *structural adjustments* of the controlled transaction. A structural adjustment will either (less commonly) imply that the controlled transaction is *disregarded* altogether or (more commonly) substituted with an alternative transaction. Typically, what is substituted is only one or a few key terms and conditions, deemed to have a significant impact on the transfer price.

The starting point for the assessment of whether the arm's length principle authorises structural adjustments is the so-called *as-structured principle*.[4] The as-structured principle provides that the arm's length principle, as a clear point of departure, should be applied to the controlled transaction the associated enterprises have actually undertaken, as it has been structured by them. The tax authorities can only disregard or restructure the controlled transaction in '*exceptional circumstances*'. Thus, the threshold for disregarding the actual structure of the transactions is high, *see* OECD Guidelines paragraph 1.141:

> *Every effort should be made to determine pricing for the actual transaction* as accurately delineated under the arm's length principle. (...) A tax administration should not disregard the actual transaction or substitute other transactions for it unless the *exceptional circumstances* described in the following paragraphs 1.142-1.145 apply.[5] (Emphasis added).

The tax authorities are only authorised to make exceptions from the as-structured principle if the strict conditions for making structural adjustments based on the so-called *rationality exception* have been met. These conditions are established in OECD Guidelines paragraph 1.142:

> The transaction as accurately delineated may be disregarded, and if appropriate, replaced by an alternative transaction, where the arrangements made in relation to the transaction, viewed in their totality, *differ from those which would have been adopted by independent enterprises behaving in a commercially rational manner in comparable circumstances, thereby preventing determination of a price* that would be acceptable to both of the parties taking into account their respective perspectives and the options *realistically available* to each of them at the time of entering into the transaction. (Emphasis added).

Hence, in order for the rationality exception to apply the arrangements made in connection with the controlled transaction must differ from those that would have been adopted by independent enterprises behaving in a commercially rational manner.

Further, in considering whether the conditions for applying the rationality exception are met the options realistically available to the relevant parties must be taken into account. The RAO standard is thus a crucial part of the assessment of

4. *See, e.g.*, David Francescucci & Demet Tepe, *Canada Revenue Agency Updates Guidelines on Referrals to Transfer Pricing Review Committee*, 13 International Transfer Pricing Journal (2006), p. 310; Andreas Bullen, *Arm's Length Transaction Structures* (2011), pp. 83-85.
5. *See also* similar wording in the United Nations Practical Manual on Transfer Pricing (2021), para. 3.3.2.2.

whether the tax authorities are authorised to undertake structural adjustments of a controlled transaction, in the sense that the standard operationalizes the conditions for undertaking structural adjustments.

## 3 The RAO Standard Used for Pricing Adjustments

The RAO standard is also relevant when considering *pricing* adjustments under the arm's length principle, i.e., for the assessment of whether a transfer price, e.g., an interest rate, is within the arm's length range.

The OECD Guidelines paragraph 1.38, where the RAO standard is formulated, further exemplifies the RAO standard by stating that an independent enterprise selling products would not be willing to accept a *price* if the enterprise knows that it can achieve a higher price from another party:

> For example, one enterprise is *unlikely to accept a price offered for its product* by an independent commercial enterprise if it knows that other potential customers are willing to *pay more* under similar conditions, or are willing to pay the same under more beneficial conditions. (Emphasis added).[6]

A higher price offer for the relevant products, all other things being equal, would be clearly more attractive for the selling enterprise. If such an option is realistically available, this clearly suggests that the transfer price is below arm's length.

In pricing cases, the most challenging issue, attracting the main focus, is the identification of the (price) options that were realistically available for the taxpayer at the time of the transaction, e.g., what interest rates the borrowing enterprise could have achieved in negotiations with unrelated lenders.

If it can be established that the borrower could have borrowed money from an independent enterprise at a lower interest rate than that agreed in the intra-group loan agreement, or in other words that such a lower interest rate was a realistically available option for the borrower, it is normally obvious that this option would have been clearly more attractive for the borrower. Analysing and comparing the levels of attractiveness of two prices, or interest rates, in isolation is rather straightforward. Since this second test under the RAO standard is normally not challenging in pricing cases, the RAO standard is often not explicitly invoked in such cases. This is different in cases regarding structural adjustments, where it is normally the second issue, i.e., comparing levels of attractiveness, which is the most challenging part.

6. *See also* the OECD Guidelines para. 1.40: 'All methods that apply the arm's length principle can be tied to the concept that independent enterprises consider the *options realistically available* to them and in comparing one option to another they consider any differences between the options that would significantly affect their value. For instance, before purchasing a product at a *given price*, independent enterprises normally would be expected to consider whether they could buy an equivalent product on otherwise comparable terms and conditions but at a *lower price* from another party.' (Emphasis added).

## 4 The RAO Standard Used for Delineation Purposes

As mentioned in section I above, the first step of a transfer pricing analysis is to accurately delineate the controlled transaction.[7] A question is whether the RAO standard is relevant to the delineation process.[8]

The delineation process is an analysis of the controlled transaction that has actually taken place. Such an analysis of the facts of the case, and the economically relevant characteristics of the relevant transaction, is not only necessary in transfer pricing cases, but also in other types of tax cases involving uncontrolled transactions. In order to apply any tax rule correctly to a transaction, the transaction must first be delineated.

The delineation process is, in our opinion, not an application of the arm's length principle, but rather a necessary initial step in order to be able to apply the arm's length principle.[9] Delineation aims at identifying which terms and conditions the associated enterprises have *actually* made or imposed, not whether these conditions differ from those that independent enterprises would have made.

In contrast, the RAO standard is at the heart of the arm's length principle. Application of the RAO standard, i.e., identification of realistically available options and comparing their attractiveness to the attractiveness of the transaction actually undertaken, is usually not relevant in cases involving uncontrolled transactions.

One might therefore say, that the RAO standard is not relevant for the delineation process, but accurately delineating the controlled transaction is relevant, and often also crucial, for the application of the arm's length principle and the RAO standard. As we see it, the application of the RAO standard is a *step* in the transfer pricing analysis subsequent to the delineation process. The RAO standard should therefore be applied *after*, and separately from, the delineation process.[10]

---

7. *See, e.g.*, the OECD Guidelines para. 1.33.
8. *See* examples from domestic law in the Netherlands and Australia further illustrating the somewhat blurred boundaries between the accurate delineation of the transaction and the application of the RAO standard described in VIKRAM CHAND & GIOVANNI LEMBO, *Intangible-Related Profit Allocation Within MNEs Based on Key DEMPE Functions: Selected Issues and Interaction with Pillar One and Pillar Two of the Digital Debate*, 6-2020 International Tax Studies (2020).
9. *See* AITOR NAVARRO, *Transactional Adjustments in Transfer Pricing* (2017) Chs 3 and 6.4 where it is similarly argued that the fact assessment stage is a step prior to the analysis of structural adjustments.
10. *See also* the OECD Guidelines para. 1.33 that states that the delineation process is distinct from the aspect of considering the pricing of the controlled transaction under the arm's length principle: 'This section of Chapter I provides guidance on identifying the commercial or financial relations between the associated enterprises and on accurately delineating the controlled transaction. This first aspect of the analysis is distinct from the second aspect of considering the pricing of that controlled transaction under the arm's length principle' and the OECD Guidelines para. 1.35 that states that it is vital to identify the economically relevant characteristics of the controlled transaction before making comparisons with uncontrolled transactions: 'The application of the arm's length principle depends on determining the conditions that independent parties would have agreed in comparable transactions in comparable circumstances. Before making comparisons with uncontrolled transactions, it is therefore vital to identify the economically relevant characteristics of the commercial or financial relations as expressed in the controlled transaction.'

As mentioned, and cited, in section II.1 above, the RAO standard is formulated in the OECD Guidelines, paragraph 1.38. Further from this paragraph it follows that when independent parties consider whether any of their realistically available options are clearly more attractive, they base these assessments on the economically relevant differences in the options' characteristics, e.g., the differences in the level of risk. Therefore, it is essential to identify the economically relevant characteristics of the actual transaction by accurately delineating the controlled transaction:

> Independent enterprises will generally take into account any *economically relevant differences between the options realistically available* to them (such as differences in the level of risk) when valuing those options. Therefore, identifying the economically relevant characteristics of the transaction is essential in accurately delineating the controlled transaction and in revealing the range of characteristics taken into account by the parties to the transaction in reaching the conclusion that there is no clearly more attractive opportunity realistically available to meet their commercial objectives than the transaction adopted.[11] (Emphasis added).

Hence, the economically relevant characteristics of the controlled transaction will be the factors that the analysis under the RAO standard should be based on, see our brief and general account for these analyses in section III below.

As an example, assume that the economically relevant characteristic of a controlled loan transaction, amongst others, is that the purpose of the intra-group loan is to finance the borrower's long-term investment in a large office building in which the borrower will establish its head office. This characteristic could quite significantly affect the application of the RAO standard, e.g., by serving as an argument in the assessment of whether it was a realistically available option, which was clearly more attractive for the borrower, to secure the intra-group loan by using the acquired real estate as collateral. The fact that the intra-group loan was meant to be long-term and that it would finance an asset that is particularly suitable to use as collateral may increase the level of attractiveness of the option of securing the loan. The accurate delineation of the controlled transaction, and thereby identifying the economically relevant characteristics, e.g., the purpose and the term of the intra-group loan, may thus be relevant, and also crucial, for the application of the RAO standard at a later stage.

In the OECD Guidelines paragraph 10.19, under the headline 'B.2. Identifying the commercial or financial relations' it is, e.g., stated that 'in considering the options realistically available' for each party to the controlled transaction, other investment opportunities may be contemplated:

> in the case of an entity that advances funds, *other investment opportunities may be contemplated*, taking account of the specific business objectives of the lender and the context in which the transaction takes place. From the borrower's perspective, the *options realistically available* will include broader considerations than the entity's ability to service its debt, for example, the funds it actually needs to meet its operational requirements. In some instances, although an entity may have the capacity to borrow and service an additional amount of debt, it may choose not to

11. OECD Guidelines para. 1.38.

> do so to avoid placing negative pressure on its credit rating and increasing its cost of capital, and jeopardising its access to capital markets and its market reputation (*see* comments upon 'The lender's and borrower's perspectives' in Section C.1.1.1 of this chapter). (*Emphasis* added).

When the title and statement are interpreted together, it could be understood so that the examiner should analyse the tested party's realistically available options as part of the delineation process, and, thus, that the RAO standard would be relevant for the delineation process. However, as we see it, it only follows from the OECD Guidelines that when applying the RAO standard (cf. the wording: '*in considering the options realistically available*') one needs to take into account, e.g., the parties' other investment opportunities. Thus, we do not interpret this to indicate that the RAO standard is actually directly relevant to the delineation process.

It is the controlled transaction actually undertaken that is subject to the delineation process. The relevant enterprise's realistically available options are, however, only hypothetical transaction alternatives which have not actually been undertaken. These hypothetical options are not, and cannot be, subject to the delineation process provided for in the OECD Guidelines. Therefore, the RAO standard, which entails analyses of hypothetical transactions, is not directly relevant to the delineation process.

## III THE NON-RECOGNITION ANALYSIS

### 1 Introduction

As mentioned in section II.2 above, the tax authorities are only authorised to undertake structural adjustments if the strict conditions for applying the rationality exception are met.[12] In order for the rationality exception to apply the arrangements made in connection with the controlled transaction must differ from those that would have been adopted by independent enterprises behaving in a commercially rational manner. To assess whether these conditions are met, the examiner must answer the following questions:

- Is it possible to identify transactions between independent enterprises that are comparable with the actual controlled transactions (the empirical arm's length test)?
- Did the taxpayer have other realistically available options than to enter into the controlled transaction actually undertaken (the hypothetical arm's length test part I)?
- Did any of the realistically available options (if any) seem clearly more attractive for the taxpayer than the controlled transaction actually undertaken (the hypothetical arm's length test part II)?

12. OECD Guidelines para. 1.142.

## 2 Empirical Arm's Length Test

The empirical arm's length test consists of examining whether it is possible to identify uncontrolled transactions that are comparable to the examined controlled transaction. If the empirical arm's length test is answered in the affirmative, the conditions for applying the rationality exception are not met, and the tax authorities are not authorised to disregard or restructure the controlled transaction.[13] If, however, comparable uncontrolled transactions cannot be identified, this will not as such mean that the conditions for applying the irrationality exception are met.[14] The consequence of a negative finding is *merely* that it is necessary to perform a hypothetical arm's length test.

## 3 Hypothetical Arm's Length Test: The RAO Standard

### *A Identification of Realistically Available Options*

When analysing whether the taxpayer had any realistically available options,[15] several factors should be taken into account.[16] First, in order for an option to be deemed a *realistically available* option, it must be sufficiently readily available at the time of the transaction. Options that are not readily available due to external factors, such as technological limitations, should not be deemed *realistically* available. However, even if the option was not readily available immediately at the time of the transaction, but was still fairly easily obtainable and thus not entirely unrealistic, it is debatable whether the option was sufficiently readily available to be deemed realistic.[17] As an example, some commentators have argued that a taxpayer's option of manufacturing a product itself should not be deemed sufficiently readily available if the taxpayer does

13. The OECD Guidelines para. 1.142: '*Where the same transaction can be seen between independent parties in comparable circumstances* (i.e. where all economically relevant characteristics are the same as those under which the tested transaction occurs other than that the parties are associated enterprises) *non-recognition would not apply*.' (Emphasis added).
14. The OECD Guidelines para. 1.142: 'Importantly, *the mere fact that the transaction may not be seen between independent parties does not mean that it should not be recognised*. Associated enterprises may have the ability to enter into a much greater variety of arrangements than can independent enterprises, and may conclude transactions of a specific nature that are not encountered, or are only very rarely encountered, between independent parties, and may do so for sound business reasons.' (Emphasis added). *See also* United Nations Practical Manual on Transfer Pricing for Developing Countries (2021) para. 8.1.3.6: 'However, the lack of reliable third-party data should not lead the tax authorities to automatically conclude that the business restructuring as a whole does not comply with the arm's length principle.'
15. Note also that a realistically available option may also be not to enter into the relevant transaction, *see, e.g.*, the United Nations Practical Manual on Transfer Pricing for Developing Countries (2021) para. 8.1.3.6: 'In certain cases, one realistically available option might be not to enter into a transaction in the event that it does not make commercial sense.'
16. *See* ANDREAS BULLEN, *Arm's Length Transaction Structures* (2011) for a further analysis of the below-listed factors, and of other general factors.
17. ANDREAS BULLEN, *Arm's Length Transaction Structures* (2011), pp. 551-553.

not possess the excess capacity,[18] and/or manufacturing intangibles,[19] necessary to manufacture the product. If the taxpayer however is fully capable of manufacturing the product itself, and it only requires that the taxpayer, e.g., acquires necessary, though easily obtainable, raw materials, it can be discussed if the option is sufficiently readily available.

Second, the option must be acceptable to the other party to the transaction. An option can only be considered *realistically* available to an associated enterprise under the RAO standard if the other enterprise(s) would have accepted the option had they been unrelated.[20]

Third, the taxpayer must have knowledge of the option. If it can be established that the taxpayer did not have knowledge about the relevant option at the time of the transaction, the option cannot be deemed a realistically available option.[21]

Fourth, the option cannot be illegal. If it can be established that the relevant option was illegal under the domestic law of at least one of the parties to the transaction, the option cannot be regarded as a realistically available.[22]

Fifth, the option cannot violate contractual obligations. Hence, if an option would imply that the taxpayer would breach an existing agreement with a third party the option should not be deemed realistically available. An example: Let us assume the taxpayer's parent company has obtained external borrowing from a third-party lender and agreed on a negative pledge insofar as concerns the subsidiary's assets. In this case, it would not be a realistically available option for the subsidiary to pledge its assets as security for an intra-group loan as this would involve breaking the parent company's loan agreement.

### B The Clearly-More-Attractive Test

After having established which options were realistically available to the taxpayer, the examiner must analyse whether one or several of the identified options were *clearly more attractive* for the taxpayer than the actual transaction.[23]

18. *See* Baker & McKenzie, The Baker & McKenzie North American Tax Practice Group, Intercompany Pricing Rules: Temporary and Proposed Section 482 Regulations (Chicago/Dallas/Juarez/Los Angeles/Miami/Mexico City/Monterrey/New York/Palo Alto/San Diego/San Francisco/Tijuana/Toronto/Washington) (1993), at I-17; Baker & McKenzie, The Baker & McKenzie North American Tax Practice Group, Intercompany Pricing: Guide to the New 1993 United States Rules (Deventer) (1993) at 21.
19. *See* Leonard Podolin, *AICPA Criticizes Transfer Pricing Regs for Departure from Arm's-Length Standard*, 92 TNI 31-49 (P.C.L., Online), 19. August (1992), section I.B.1.
20. *See* Andreas Bullen, Arm's Length Transaction Structures (2011), pp. 553-554; Chaid Dali-Ali & Simon Langlois, *OECD Discussion Draft on Business Restructurings: Is the OECD on the Right Track to Achieving Its Objectives?*, 17 Tax Management Transfer Pricing Report 543 (2008), p. 546; Jens Wittendorf, *The Transactional Ghost of Article 9(19) of the OECD Model*, 63 Bulletin for International Taxation 107 (2009), p. 128.
21. Andreas Bullen, *Arm's Length Transaction Structures* (2011), p. 554.
22. *Ibid.*, pp. 554-555.
23. *See, e.g.*, Aitor Navarro, *Transactional Adjustments in Transfer Pricing* (IBFD 2017) pp. 195-196.

The clearly-more-attractive test should be performed as a two-step process by first analysing the level of *attractiveness* of both the actual transaction and the relevant realistically available options, and then, secondly, comparing their levels of attractiveness.

The analysis of the options' levels of attractiveness should be based on an assessment of their *commercial* advantages and disadvantages for the enterprise, as opposed to other advantages and disadvantages (e.g., environmental, scientific or religious). This, e.g., follows from the wording of the OECD Guidelines paragraph 1.38 where it is stated that independent enterprises will only enter into a transaction if they see no other alternative that 'offers a clearly more attractive opportunity to *meet their commercial objectives*'[24] (emphasis added).

Normally, and broadly stated, an enterprise's commercial objective is to maximize its profits by increasing its gross income and/or by reducing costs. The analysis of the options' attractiveness should therefore normally be based on the options' abilities to contribute positively to the enterprise's net profits. Sometimes, an option's advantages and disadvantages can only be fully understood when analysing the option's attractiveness in a broad sense along with other related transactions. As a result, the options' profit-maximising abilities should therefore often be considered in a broad sense while taking into account that the relevant option may be part of a broader arrangement involving other transactions.[25]

This naturally also applies to intra-group loan agreements. For example, when considering whether it was a clearly more attractive option for a borrower to secure the intra-group loan by pledging some of its assets as collateral, it should also, e.g., take into account the implications of pledging the relevant assets as collateral for the borrower's overall financing, hereunder the borrower's possible subsequent loan transactions.[26]

24. *See also* OECD Guidelines para. 10.19: 'Independent enterprises, when considering whether to enter into a particular financial transaction, will consider all other *options realistically available* to them, and will only enter into the transaction if they see no alternative that offers a *clearly more attractive opportunity* to meet their commercial objectives (see paragraph 1.38 of Chapter I).' (Emphasis added).
25. *See* OECD Guidelines para. 1.38: '(...) In making such an assessment, it may be necessary or useful to assess the transaction in the context of a broader arrangement of transactions, since assessment of the options realistically available to third parties is not necessarily limited to the single transaction, but may take into account a broader arrangement of economically related transactions.' *See also* OECD Guidelines, Ch. X, para. 10.19: 'In considering the options realistically available, the perspective of each of the parties to the transaction must be considered. For instance, in the case of an entity that advances funds, other investment opportunities may be contemplated, taking account of the specific business objectives of the lender and the context in which the transaction takes place. *From the borrower's perspective, the options realistically available will include broader considerations than the entity's ability to service its debt*, for example, the funds it actually needs to meet its operational requirements. In some instances, although an entity may have the capacity to borrow and service an additional amount of debt, it may choose not to do so to avoid placing negative pressure on its credit rating and increasing its cost of capital, and jeopardising its access to capital markets and its market reputation (*see* comments upon "The lender's and borrower's perspectives" in section C.1.1.1 of this chapter).' (Emphasis added).
26. *See* OECD Guidelines para. 10.58: 'Borrowers seek to optimise their weighted average cost of capital and to have the right funding available to meet both short-term needs and long-term

After having analysed the attractiveness of the actual transaction and the relevant options, their levels of attractiveness must be compared. Pursuant to the wording of the OECD Guidelines, it is not sufficient that a realistically available option has a higher level of attractiveness. The option must have a significantly higher level of attractiveness, cf. the wording '*clearly* more attractive' (emphasis added),[27] in order for it to satisfy the *clearly-more-attractive test*. This requirement also serves as a reminder of the *as-structured principle* and the high threshold for undertaking structural adjustments, *see* section II.2 above.

As mentioned in section II.3 above, in pricing cases, the identification of realistically available options, e.g., what interest rates the taxpayer could have achieved in negotiations with unrelated lenders, is often the most challenging issue, while comparing the *attractiveness* of the realistically available interest rates with the actual interest rate is far easier. By contrast, in cases regarding structural adjustments, the most challenging part of the analysis under the RAO standard is normally to assess whether the realistically available options were clearly more attractive for the taxpayer. This is primarily due to the fact that the options' levels of attractiveness are often not easily convertible to a monetary (or another type of numeric) value, as opposed to, e.g., interest rates and prices which already are numeric values that can be easily compared to each other for the purpose of identifying the most attractive option. For example, it will often be far from obvious whether a termination period of three months, four months or six months would be most attractive to the taxpayer. In practice, comparing the relevant options' levels of attractiveness is a complex and difficult exercise. This is an important reason why structural adjustments may only be made in '*exceptional circumstances*'.[28]

## IV THE RAO STANDARD APPLIED TO NON-PRICE TERMS AND CONDITIONS OF INTRA-GROUP LOANS

### 1 Introduction

In this section, we will analyse selected key terms and conditions in intra-group loan agreements that could typically have a significant impact on the arm's length interest

objectives. When considering the options realistically available to it, an independent business seeking funding operating in its own commercial interests will seek the most cost effective solution, with regard to the business strategy it has adopted. For example in respect of collateral, in some circumstances, assuming that the business has suitable collateral to offer, this would usually be secured funding, ahead of unsecured funding, recognising that a business's collateral assets and its funding requirements may differ over time, e.g. because collateral is finite, the decision to pledge collateral on a particular borrowing precludes the borrower from pledging that same collateral on a subsequent borrowing. *Therefore, an MNE pledging collateral would take into account its options realistically available regarding its overall financing (e.g. possible subsequent loan transactions).*' (Emphasis added).

27. OECD Guidelines para. 1.38.
28. *See* the OECD Guidelines para. 1.141: 'A tax administration should not disregard the actual transaction or substitute other transactions for it unless the exceptional circumstances described in the following paragraphs 1.142-1.145 apply.'

rate. The purpose is to illustrate how the RAO standard should be applied to examine such terms and conditions and to address certain main issues that often arise. The section does not in any way purport to give an exhaustive account of these matters.

The analyses under the RAO standard could be performed either from the perspective of the lending enterprise or from the borrowing enterprise. The perspective would typically depend upon whether the examined taxpayer in a particular case is the lender or borrower. We have chosen to perform the analyses in this section from the borrowing enterprise's perspective, as we experience that this is the most practical perspective in these cases.

For the purpose of the below analysis, we presuppose that the outcome of the empirical arm's length test is negative, i.e., that it is not possible to identify comparably structured uncontrolled loans. The outcome of the case therefore depends on the outcome of the hypothetical arm's length test, which involves the application of the RAO standard.

## 2 The Amount of the Loan (Thin Capitalisation)

### *A The Condition and Its Price Relevance*

An important condition in all loan agreements is, of course, the condition governing the loan amount. The loan amount can often significantly affect the arm's length interest rate. Generally, one can say that the greater the loan amount, the higher the economic risk for the lender, and, thus, the higher the arm's length interest rate. However, as always, the significance of the condition for the arm's length interest rate would need to be assessed concretely, and in light of the other conditions in the loan agreement.

### *B Thin Capitalisation: An Overview*

The perhaps most practical example of a situation where the RAO standard is undertaken in the context of a controlled loan agreement is thin capitalisation. Thin capitalisation refers to a situation where an enterprise is capitalised with a high level of debt from a related party so that the loan exceeds the enterprise's borrowing capacity.

The reason why a multinational group may decide to thinly capitalise subsidiaries is normally due to the difference in tax treatment of equity and debt, combined with different tax levels in different jurisdictions or tax regimes. In many jurisdictions, interest payments are deductible for the debtor, whereas dividends are not. If the debtor is financed with a high share of intra-group debt, the debtor would incur a high deductible cost related to intra-group interest payments, and thus its tax base would be reduced while the related creditor's tax base would be increased. If the debtor is subject to taxation in a relatively high-tax regime, while the creditor is subject to taxation in a relatively low-tax regime, the group's total tax burden would be reduced as a result of this scheme.

The issue of thin capitalisation is not explicitly discussed in the new Chapter X of the OECD Guidelines: '*Transfer Pricing Aspects of Financial Transactions*'. A reason why the issue is not discussed in any detail could be that many countries have introduced domestic legislation (e.g., fixed debt-equity ratios) in order to counter thin capitalisation and that the issue therefore is less practical for many countries. Also, thin capitalisation raises several complex and controversial issues, and it might also be that the OECD Member countries could agree on more detailed guidance.

To prevent tax benefits created by thin capitalisation, many countries have also introduced rules in their domestic laws that limit the amount of interest that can be deducted when calculating the borrower's taxable profits. Such rules thus limit the practical need for applying the arm's length principle to situations of thin capitalisation. Nevertheless, the arm's length principle, and the RAO standard, can be used to counter thin capitalisation.[29]

### C *Delineation*

The condition governing the loan amount could be structured and phrased differently in different types of loan agreements, e.g., as a fixed amount, as a maximum limit to a credit facility or otherwise. The actual loan amount can also be identified by accurately delineating the controlled transaction otherwise than through the written agreement, e.g., by taking into account the conduct of the associated enterprises (e.g., actual capital transfers between the parties).[30]

In the following subsections, we will assume that the controlled transaction to be reviewed has been accurately delineated as a high-amount, intra-group loan and that the borrower's debt-equity ratio is very high. Assume for example that the amount of the loan is EUR 500 million, which provides the borrower with an equity ratio of 5%-10%. The parties have further agreed that the interest rate shall be the London Interbank Offered Rate (LIBOR) + 10% in order to reflect the large loan amount and the borrower's low equity ratio. The issue is whether the condition governing the amount of the loan could be subject to a structural adjustment based on the rationality exception and the RAO standard.

29. *See, e.g.*, OECD Commentaries Article 9 para. 3; OECD/G20 Base Erosion and Profit Shifting Project, Limiting Base Erosion Involving Interest Deductions and Other Financial Payments, ACTION 4: 2015 Final Report (2015), para. 11: 'Rules currently applied by countries fall into six broad groups, with some countries using a combined approach that includes more than one type of rule: 1. Arm's length tests, which compare the level of interest or debt in an entity with the position that would have existed had the entity been dealing entirely with third parties'; OECD Commentaries, Commentary on Article 9, paragraph 3: 'As discussed in the Committee on Fiscal Affairs' Report on "Thin Capitalisation", there is an interplay between tax treaties and domestic rules on thin capitalisation relevant to the scope of the Article. The Committee considers that: a) the Article does not prevent the application of national rules on thin capitalisation insofar as their effect is to assimilate the profits of the borrower to an amount corresponding to the profits which would have accrued in an arm's length situation.'
30. OECD Guidelines para. 1.43: 'Taken together, the analysis of economically relevant characteristics in all five categories provides evidence of the actual conduct of the associated enterprises. (...) If the contract neither explicitly nor implicitly (taking into account applicable principles of contract interpretation) addresses characteristics of the transaction that are economically relevant, then any information provided by the contract should be supplemented for purposes of the transfer pricing analysis by the evidence provided by identifying those characteristics.'

### D Realistically Available Options

When applying the RAO standard to the loan amount the first question is whether it was a realistically available option for the borrower to obtain a loan with the actually agreed amount, e.g., MEUR 500.

Normally, the first question is whether the taxpayer had any realistically available *options* at the time of the transaction. In this situation, however, the question is whether the *actual structure of the transaction*, more specifically the agreed loan amount, was a realistically available option for the borrower.

In cases of thin capitalisation, i.e., where the loan amount is higher than the amount the borrower could have borrowed from an unrelated lender, it would not be a realistically available option for the borrower to obtain the loan with the actually agreed amount. An unrelated party would not have agreed to provide the borrower with such a loan of, e.g., MEUR 500, as the lender's risk related to the loan is unreasonably high particularly given the borrower's low equity ratio (e.g., 5%-10%) as a result of the large loan amount.

Generally, one can say that the higher the loan amount, the higher the lender's risk and the higher the arm's length interest rate. However, when a potential loan, as a result of its amount, will make the borrower thinly capitalised, the loan amount is so significant that a higher interest rate cannot compensate for the risk involved for the lender, e.g., because the borrower would not be able to pay such a high-interest rate.

How to determine when a borrower should be deemed thinly capitalised, is a difficult issue that requires an in-depth analysis of the company's significant projected cash flows, risk factors and other concrete factual circumstances of the case. We will not discuss this issue further in this chapter.

### E Attractiveness

When it can be determined that the option of obtaining the intra-group loan was not a realistically available option for the borrower, there is initially no need to analyse and compare the attractiveness of the identified realistically available options.

### F The Structural Adjustment and the Price Adjustment

If it is established that an intra-group loan agreement shall be restructured by way of reducing the loan amount, a first issue is how much the loan shall be reduced. At least, it is necessary to reduce the loan amount so much that the remaining loan lies within the borrower's borrowing capacity. Which loan amount within the borrower's borrowing capacity shall be chosen, depends on a complex economic analysis, which will not be attempted here. The borrower will only be granted a deduction for interest on the part of the intra-group loan amount which is recognised.

Assume that the analysis shows that the borrower's maximum loan capacity, taking into account what would be an acceptable equity ratio, was at MEUR 300, and not MEUR 500. Further, the analysis shows that an unrelated borrower would likely have used its maximum loan capacity. In this example, the tax authorities could first, as a structural adjustment, reduce the loan amount down to MEUR 300.

Secondly, after having undertaken this structural adjustment, the tax authorities must determine an arm's length interest rate for an 'arm's length loan amount' of EUR 300. Assuming that a comparability analysis shows that in comparable uncontrolled loan transactions, with, e.g., similar loan amounts, the parties agree on interest rates in the range between LIBOR +2.5% and 3.0%, this would indicate that the arm's length interest rate for this loan should be somewhere within this range, perhaps LIBOR +2.75%. Hence, in our example, the loan amount would be reduced from MEUR 500 to MEUR 300, and the interest rate would be reduced from LIBOR +10% to LIBOR +2.75%. The reduction of the interest rate could, e.g., be due to the fact that the lender would assume lower risk if the loan amount is 'merely' MEUR 300 (as opposed to MEUR 500), translating into a lower arm's length interest margin.

### *G Secondary Adjustments*

The next question is how the *excessive capital transfer*, i.e., the difference between the actual loan amount and the adjusted loan amount (MEUR 200 in our example), shall be treated.

According to the OECD Guidelines, such a 'secondary adjustment' is ordinarily made by re-characterising the transfer of the excess loan amount to an equity transaction, typically an equity contribution.[31]

The re-characterisation of the excess loan amount through a secondary adjustment is not based on the arm's length principle. The arm's length principle, and the RAO standard, only provide a legal basis for, in cases of thin capitalisation, *reducing* the agreed loan amount by way of a primary adjustment, and do not provide a legal basis for performing the secondary adjustment. The legal basis for performing the secondary adjustment is rather the domestic laws of the state performing the secondary adjustment,[32] e.g., the domestic classification rules of that country.

---

31. *See* OECD Guidelines para. 4.68: '(…) To make the actual allocation of profits consistent with the primary transfer pricing adjustment, some jurisdictions having proposed a transfer pricing adjustment will assert under their domestic legislation a constructive transaction (a secondary transaction), whereby the excess profits resulting from a primary adjustment are treated as having been transferred in some other form and taxed accordingly. Ordinarily, the secondary transactions will take the form of constructive dividends, constructive equity contributions, or constructive loans.'.
32. *See*, e.g., the OECD Commentaries, Commentary on Article 9, para. 2: 'It is not the purpose of the paragraph to deal with what might be called "secondary adjustments". (…) It should be noted that nothing in paragraph 2 prevents such secondary adjustments from being made *where they are permitted under the domestic laws of Contracting States*' (Emphasis added); OECD Guidelines, Glossary: '*Secondary adjustment* – An adjustment that arises from imposing tax on a secondary transaction. *Secondary transaction* – A constructive transaction that some countries will assert under their domestic legislation after having proposed a primary adjustment in order to make the actual allocation of profits consistent with the primary adjustment. Secondary transactions may take the form of constructive dividends, constructive equity contributions, or

The above seems to have escaped the Swedish Administrative Supreme Court in its judgment in *Norsk Hydro Bensin.*[33] In this case, the Supreme Court concluded that the Swedish arm's length provision did not authorise re-characterisation of debt into equity in cases of thin capitalisation. The reasoning for this conclusion was that unrelated parties do not contribute capital in the form of equity, but only in the form of debt However, it would have been sufficient for Sweden to use its arm's length provision to reduce the amount of the intra-group loan. Sweden could have used other rules of its domestic law, perhaps domestic classification rules, to classify the excess part of the loan as something else, e.g., an equity contribution.

## 3 Level of Seniority and Subordination

### *A The Condition and Its Price Relevance*

Another type of condition that could affect the arm's length interest rate is the loan's level of seniority, i.e., the lender's ranking priority compared to other creditors.

Lenders of subordinated loans will have a more limited claim to the debtor's assets and must therefore accept that lenders of the more senior loans are repaid first if the borrower lacks liquidity to service all of its loans. Lenders of subordinated loans thus assume higher risk than the lenders of more senior loans.

Depending on the circumstances, the lender's priority may significantly affect the determination of an arm's length interest rate. Generally, one can say that the lower the priority, the higher the risk, and, thus, the higher the arm's length interest rate.[34] However, as always, the significance of the condition in question for the arm's length interest rate would need to be assessed concretely, and in light of the other conditions in the loan agreement.

constructive loans'; ROHATGI ROY, *Basic International Taxation* (2002), p. 402: 'Thin capitalisation adjustments may be both primary and secondary adjustments (*see* Glossary). "..." *Secondary adjustments are required to establish the situation exactly as it would have been if the transactions had been undertaken at an arm's length.* It involves further financial, legal, commercial and accounting adjustments. Therefore, the disallowed loan may be reclassified as equity and the excess interest deemed as a dividend payment or loan. *The OECD MC itself does not provide for secondary adjustments, but the Commentary mentions that secondary adjustments may be made under domestic law.* The tax treatment and the tax relief for the recharacterised payment would depend on the domestic laws of the two States and the tax treaty provisions. The lender State would be obliged to grant relief on the constructive dividend if the lender effectively shares the risks in the borrower company. If the source country reclassifies the interest payments as a dividend, Article 10(3) would also require the lender country to accept the source country definition of a dividend and grant relief under Article 23. Article 11 would continue to apply if the source country only disallows the interest expense.' (*Emphasis* added).

33. RÅ 1990 ref 34 *Norsk Hydro Bensin.*
34. *See* OECD Guidelines para. 10.90: 'Characteristics which will usually *increase the risk for the lender*, such as long maturity dates, absence of security, *subordination*, or application of the loan to a risky project, *will tend to increase the interest rate*' (Emphasis added).

### B Delineation

The intra-group agreement could explicitly specify that the controlled loan is subordinated to other loans. In the absence of such regulation, the controlled loan would, as a point of departure, not be deemed to be subordinated. However, applicable domestic background rules of law (e.g., insolvency law) may determine that in case of insolvency, the debtor would have to repay its liabilities towards unrelated parties before its intra-group liabilities.[35] Thus, even though a written intra-group loan agreement does not govern the controlled loan's priority, subordination could still be implied.

After accurately delineating the intra-group loan transaction the question is how the RAO standard would be applied to conditions governing ranking priority in intra-group loan agreements. Below, we will assume that the controlled transaction to be reviewed has been accurately delineated as a subordinated loan and that the issue is whether this particular condition could be subject to a structural adjustment based on the RAO standard.

### C Realistically Available Options

First, the question would be whether it was a realistically available option for the borrower to agree on another priority for the loan, i.e., to allow the lender a better priority. Normally, agreeing on another priority for a loan would be a realistically available option for the borrower. If, however, this is not practically possible since, e.g., domestic law provides that other liabilities shall be repaid first, or if the borrower has already agreed to give other unrelated lenders senior priority, the option of agreeing to another priority for the loan would not be realistically available.

### D Attractiveness

Secondly, if higher priority was a realistically available option, the question is whether this option was *clearly more attractive* for the borrower. This requires an analysis of the level of *attractiveness* of the actually agreed ranking priority, and of alternative (higher) ranking priority of the intra-group loan. Then, their levels of attractiveness must be compared.

These analyses must be based on broad assessments where all economically relevant circumstances are taken into account. An example is the judgment from the Norwegian Borgarting Court of Appeals in *Lyse Energi*.[36] In this case, the shareholders of a Norwegian power company had granted the company a *subordinated* loan of NOK 3 billion. The tax authorities argued that it was clear that an unrelated borrower would

35. *See* OECD Guidelines para. 10.61: 'The economic conditions of loans should also be viewed in the context of regulations that may affect the position of the parties. For example, *insolvency law in the jurisdiction of the borrower may provide that liabilities towards associated enterprises are subordinated to liabilities towards unrelated parties.*' (Emphasis added).
36. Utv. 2009 p. 210, *Lyse energi*.

not have agreed to *subordinate* the loan (due to the increased interest costs). The key issue was whether it was a clearly more attractive option to agree on a higher priority for the loan. The court conducted a broad and thorough assessment of the attractiveness of the relevant options, and e.g., emphasized the beneficial effects of subordinated loans, hereunder that additional borrowing became less expensive and could take place more quickly. The court concluded that the subordination of the loan could not be disregarded based on the Norwegian arm's length provision.

### E The Structural Adjustment and the Price Adjustment

If the conditions under the rationality exception and the RAO standard are met, and the tax authorities thus are authorised to undertake structural adjustments of the condition in the intra-group loan agreement governing the lender's ranking priority, the OECD Guidelines, paragraph 1.144, provides that the actual structure of the transaction should be replaced by an alternative transaction that comports as closely as possible with the actual controlled transaction:

> The structure that for transfer pricing purposes, replaces that actually adopted by the taxpayers should *comport as closely as possible with the facts of the actual transaction undertaken* whilst achieving a commercially rational expected result that would have enabled the parties to come to a price acceptable to both of them at the time the arrangement was entered into.[37] (Emphasis added).

Hence, the structural adjustment should not necessarily involve providing the lender with the best priority of all the borrower's creditors. The structural adjustment should only better the ranking priority enough so that the conditions under the RAO standard are not met. After having undertaken the structural adjustment, the tax authorities should assess and determine an arm's length interest rate on the restructured loan transaction.

### F Example

The above can be illustrated with the following example. Assume that the examined controlled transaction is a NOK 1 billion, subordinated loan. An analysis of the conditions under the RAO standard shows that it was commercially irrational to agree to make the loan subordinated in its entirety, but subordinating 25% of the loan can be seen as commercially rational, i.e., no other realistically available options seem clearly more attractive.

In this example, the tax authorities could restructure the transaction so that 75% of the loan is no longer subordinated. Further, as a result of the structural adjustment,

37. *See also* the OECD Guidelines para. 9.35: 'The structure that for transfer pricing purposes, replaces that actually adopted by the taxpayers should comport as closely as possible with the facts of the actual transaction undertaking whilst achieving a commercially rational expected result that would have enabled the parties to come to a price acceptable to both of them at the time the arrangement was entered into'; Aitor Navarro, *Transactional Adjustments in Transfer Pricing* (2017) p. 196.

the different parts of the loan should be assessed separately when subsequently determining the arm's length interest rates. The part of the loan that is recognised as being subordinated would have a higher interest rate than the part of the loan that has been restructured into a higher-priority loan.

## 4 Secured Versus Unsecured Intra-group Loans

### A *The Condition and Its Price Relevance*

Another type of condition that could significantly affect the arm's length interest rate is the condition determining whether or not the loan shall be secured, i.e., whether the loan shall be backed by some type of collateral. If the loan is secured, the lender can seize the collateral in case the borrower defaults on its interest payments or the repayment of principal amounts. This right for the lender in case of a default reduces the lender's risk, and thus generally implies a lower interest rate than if the loan is unsecured.

### B *Delineation*

In our experience, intra-group loan agreements are often silent on the issue of whether the loan is secured. If the agreement is silent, the loan must, as a point of departure, be deemed to be unsecured. The parties could however have agreed on securing the loan in other agreements or correspondence, etc. The actual conduct of the associated enterprises could also be a relevant factor when accurately delineating the transaction.[38] However, the mere fact that the borrower possesses assets that could in principle be used as collateral does not itself mean that the loan is secured. Security must be based on some form of agreement stating the nature of the security, etc.

For the purpose of the analysis in the following subsections, we will assume that the examined controlled transaction has been accurately delineated as an unsecured loan, and that the issue is whether this condition could be subject to a structural adjustment based on the rationality exception and the RAO standard.

### C *Realistically Available Options*

When applying the RAO standard, the first question would be whether it was a realistically available option for the borrower to provide securities for the intra-group loan.

38. OECD Guidelines para. 1.43: 'Taken together, the analysis of economically relevant characteristics in all five categories provides evidence of the actual conduct of the associated enterprises. (...) If the contract neither explicitly nor implicitly (taking into account applicable principles of contract interpretation) addresses characteristics of the transaction that are economically relevant, then any information provided by the contract should be supplemented for purposes of the transfer pricing analysis by the evidence provided by identifying those characteristics.'

Assets that have been offered as security for a loan cannot be used by their full value as collateral more than once. Consequently, if the borrower's assets already have been placed as collateral for other loans, they cannot be used as collateral for a new intra-group loan. In such cases, the option of securing the controlled loan with the relevant assets would not be a realistically available option.

As mentioned in section I above, many groups have a funding structure where all external borrowing is placed in a top group company, which then funds the subsidiaries with a mix of equity and intra-group loans. One of the factors that makes this model attractive is that it will generally attract relatively low external borrowing costs as the group's external lenders will have access to the entire group's assets in the event of a default, instead of only one single group company's assets. In order for this model to work, the subsidiaries of the group, implicitly or explicitly, must agree not to use their assets for security for other loans. In such cases, securing an intra-group loan would not be a realistically available option for the borrower, as this would involve breaking the parent company's loan agreement, and the subsidiary's agreement with the parent company.

### D Attractiveness

Secondly, if it was a realistically available option to secure the intra-group loan, the question is whether the option of securing the loan was *clearly more attractive* for the borrower. This requires an analysis of the level of *attractiveness* of securing and not securing the intra-group loan. Then, the options' levels of attractiveness must be compared.

From the lender's perspective, securing the loan would reduce its risk, but would also reduce the arm's length interest rate. The lender's potential profit from the loan transaction is reduced whereas the risk of incurring a loss is also reduced.

From the borrowing enterprise's perspective, securing the loan will generally reduce the arm's length interest rate and thereby its borrowing costs. However, the assets used as collateral for the intra-group loan cannot be used in full as collateral for additional loans from another lender, and the borrower may also be restricted from selling the assets. Consequently, the analysis should be based on a broad assessment of all factors that may be relevant to shed light on the attractiveness of the relevant options, hereunder the potential commercial disadvantages of using the assets as collateral.[39] Relevant factors may be the purpose of the loan, the borrower's creditworthiness, the types of assets that the borrower owns and that can be used as collateral and the type of loan, e.g., the loan amount and/or the term of the loan.

39. *See* the OECD Guidelines para. 10.58: 'Borrowers seek to optimise their weighted average cost of capital and to have the right funding available to meet both short-term needs and long-term objectives. When considering the options realistically available to it, an independent business seeking funding operating in its own commercial interests will seek the most cost effective solution, with regard to the business strategy it has adopted. For example in respect of collateral, in some circumstances, assuming that the business has suitable collateral to offer, this would usually be secured funding, ahead of unsecured funding, recognising that a business's collateral assets and its funding requirements may differ over time, e.g. *because collateral is finite, the*

As follows from the above, the outcome of the assessment is very much dependent on a number of economically relevant circumstances. Therefore, no general guidance on what should be the outcome of such assessments can be provided.

### E The Structural Adjustment and the Price Adjustment

As mentioned in section IV.3 above, if the conditions under the rationality exception and the RAO standard are met, and the tax authorities are therefore authorised to undertake structural adjustments, the actual structure of the transaction should be replaced by an alternative transaction that comports as closely as possible with the actual controlled transaction.[40]

If it is determined that securing the intra-group loan would be a realistically available option that was clearly more attractive for the borrower, the tax authorities are authorised to impute collateral for the loan. In this process, the tax authorities must determine which of the borrower's assets should be imputed as collateral, how many of the assets should be used as collateral, etc. In some cases, when the purpose of the loan solely was to acquire one valuable asset, e.g., real estate, the most sensible solution would be to place this asset as collateral for the loan. However, in other cases when the loan has several purposes the solution may be far less evident.

The above assessment should be based on a concrete assessment of several of the same factors as mentioned above, e.g., the purpose of the loan, the types of assets that the borrower owns, etc., but keeping in mind that the alternative transaction replacing the actual transaction should comport as closely as possible with the actual controlled transaction. The tax authorities should thus not, by its structural adjustment, place more assets as collateral for the loan than what is necessary in order to achieve a commercially rational expected result that would have enabled the associated enterprises to agree on an arm's length interest rate.

After having undertaken the structural adjustment, the tax authorities should assess and determine an arm's length interest rate on the restructured loan transaction. The imputed security would result in a lower arm's length interest rate than on an unsecured loan.

### F Example

The above can be illustrated with the following example. Assume that the related parties have agreed to an interest rate of the Norwegian Interbank Offered Rate (NIBOR) + 10% on the unsecured intra-group loan and that the tax authorities agree that this would be an arm's length interest rate on an unsecured loan. Further, assume that it is common ground in the industry, in which the examined taxpayer operates,

*decision to pledge collateral on a particular borrowing precludes the borrower from pledging that same collateral on a subsequent borrowing. Therefore, an MNE pledging collateral would take into account its options realistically available regarding its overall financing* (e.g. possible subsequent loan transactions).' (Emphasis added).

40. *See* the OECD Guidelines, para. 1.144.

that unsecured loans are priced at an additional 5% interest margin to NIBOR compared to the interest rate on secured loans.

In this example, assuming that the conditions under the RAO standard mentioned above are met, the tax authorities may, as a structural adjustment, impute certain of the borrower's assets as collateral for the loan. After having undertaken this structural adjustment, the tax authorities must determine an appropriate arm's length interest rate on the restructured loan transaction. In this example, the facts indicate that the agreed interest margin, following the structural adjustment, should be reduced by 5%. As a result, the agreed interest rate would be reduced from NIBOR +10% to NIBOR +5%.

## 5 The Duration of the Loan (Extreme Long-Term Loans)

### *A The Condition and Its Price Relevance*

Another type of condition that could significantly affect the arm's length interest rate is the condition governing the term (duration) of the loan or the loan's maturity date. The term of a loan can range from a few months to a number of years. A loan with a longer agreed term will generally carry a higher risk for the lender, than a short-term loan. Thus, viewed in isolation, the longer the term of the loan, the higher the arm's length interest rate.[41]

### *B Delineation*

Considering that the term (duration) of the loan or the maturity date is one of the key conditions in a loan agreement, it would be preferable that the term follows from the intra-group agreement (if any). For example, in a loan granted in December 2021, it could be determined that the term of the loan is five years, or that the maturity date is 31 December 2026.

If the term is not explicitly regulated in the intra-group agreement, the term would need to be determined based on a further analysis of the facts and circumstances of the case, and of the actual conduct of the associated enterprises.[42] Examples of the parties' actual conduct that could be relevant when accurately delineating the term of an intra-group loan are the use or purpose of the loan, e.g., if the loan is used to finance a short or a long-term investment, the term of other intra-group loans taken up by the borrower's and the actual time period in which the loan has been outstanding. If, as a

41. *See* OECD Guidelines para. 10.90: '(...) Characteristics which will usually *increase the risk for the lender*, such as *long maturity dates*, absence of security, *subordination*, or application of the loan to a risky project, *will tend to increase the interest rate*.' (Emphasis added).
42. OECD Guidelines para. 1.43: 'Taken together, the analysis of economically relevant characteristics in all five categories provides evidence of the actual conduct of the associated enterprises. (...) If the contract neither explicitly nor implicitly (taking into account applicable principles of contract interpretation) addresses characteristics of the transaction that are economically relevant, then any information provided by the contract should be supplemented for purposes of the transfer pricing analysis by the evidence provided by identifying those characteristics.'

result of the delineation process, it is determined that the loan has no maturity date, this would support the position that the capital contribution is not a loan, but an equity capital contribution.

As mentioned, the term of the loan may be explicitly governed by the written agreement. However, if the written agreement is inconsistent with the actual conduct of the parties the term of the loan should be accurately delineated in accordance with the conduct of the parties.[43] An example that is provided in Chapter X of the OECD Guidelines is where a financial instrument or a loan is short term under the written intra-group agreement but is consistently replaced with a new instrument. In such cases, depending on the facts and circumstances, the term of the loan may be accurately delineated as a longer-term loan.[44]

In our experience, the issue of applying the rationality exception and RAO standard to the term (duration) of the loan would typically arise if the loan is extremely long term. In the following subsections, we will therefore assume that the controlled transaction has been accurately delineated as an extremely long-term loan and that the issue is whether the term of the loan could be subject to a structural adjustment based on the RAO standard. Assume for example that the term of the intra-group loan is 30 years and that the parties have agreed that the interest rate shall be the Euro Interbank Offered Rate (EURIBOR) + 8% in order to reflect the length of the term.

### C Realistically Available Options

The first question would be whether it was a realistically available option for the borrower to agree on a shorter term than 30 years. Often, agreeing on a shorter term for the loan would be a realistically available option for the borrowing enterprise.

However, if the intra-group loan was established for the purpose of financing a specific project or investment, and shortening the term of the loan from 30 years would imply that the borrower's funding need would last longer than the term of the loan, the question could be raised whether it was a realistically available option for the borrower to agree on a shorter term for the loan than 30 years. However, as long as it is a realistically available option for the borrowing enterprise to obtain external financing as a replacement for its intra-group financing when the intra-group loan agreement reaches its maturity date, shortening the term of the intra-group loan would be a realistically available option.

43. OECD Guidelines para. 1.45: 'If the characteristics of the transaction that are economically relevant are *inconsistent with the written contract* between the associated enterprises, the actual transaction should generally be delineated for purposes of the transfer pricing analysis in accordance with *the characteristics of the transaction reflected in the conduct of the parties.*' (Emphasis added).
44. OECD Guidelines para. 1.113: 'The duration of the controlled investment should be determined as part of the process of accurate delineation of the actual transaction. For example, a financial instrument which is short-term under the written contractual terms between the parties but which is consistently replaced with a new instrument may, depending upon the exact facts and circumstances, be accurately delineated as a long-term investment.'

### D Attractiveness

Second, the question is whether one or several of the identified realistically available options, hereunder especially to shorten the term of the loan from 30 years, were *clearly more attractive* for the borrower. This requires an analysis of the level of *attractiveness* of the actually agreed term (30 years), and of the relevant realistically available options, i.e., the alternative of shortening the term. Then, the options' levels of attractiveness must be compared.

As also mentioned above, it is important to conduct a broad assessment of the commercial advantages and disadvantages of each option. Even though agreeing to a shorter term for the loan than 30 years, given the circumstances, could imply a lower interest rate, there could be other factors that support the decision of agreeing to a term of 30 years. Whether it would be clearly more attractive for the borrower to agree to reduce the term will, as always, depend upon the circumstances.

As mentioned above, if the intra-group loan was issued for the purpose of financing a specific project or investment and shortening the term of the loan would imply that the borrower's funding needs related to this project would last longer than the term of the loan, this would support the position that it would not be clearly more attractive for the borrower to reduce the term of the loan. Similarly, in the opposite situation, if the purpose of the loan implies that the borrower has a more time-limited funding need than 30 years, it would often be clearly more attractive for the borrower to shorten the term of the loan in order to make the loan's maturity date to correspond with the borrower's actual funding need.

An example of a case where the tax authorities had restructured the term of an intra-group loan is found in an unpublished, and confidential, administrative decision from the Norwegian tax authorities. In this case, the tax authorities had restructured the condition in the intra-group loan agreement, and adjusted the term downwards from 15 years to 5-7 years. The restructuring was, in short, based on the reasoning that no comparable uncontrolled loan transactions could be identified that had similarly long terms, and that it would be less attractive for the lender to issue the loan with such long maturity as the lender's risk would be unreasonably high. The taxpayer appealed the decision to the administrative appeal board and, e.g., argued that the borrower had a long-term need for financing so that a reduction of the term of the loan would lead to an unreasonably high refinancing and liquidity risk for the borrower. The taxpayer further argued that the lender had achieved external financing, with a significantly longer term than the intra-group loan, in order to provide the loan. Thus, the lender would have sufficient margins on its lending activity, even though the intra-group loan had a term of 15 years. The lender would therefore have agreed to a long term on the intra-group loan even if it had been an unrelated party. The tax authorities abandoned the argumentation before the appeal board decided the case.

### E The Structural Adjustment and the Price Adjustment

As mentioned above, if the conditions under the rationality exception and the RAO standard are met, and the tax authorities are therefore authorised to undertake structural adjustments, the actual structure of the transaction should be replaced by an alternative transaction that comports as closely as possible with the actual controlled transaction.[45] If it is determined that reducing the 30-year term of the intra-group loan would be a realistically available option that was clearly more attractive for the borrower, the tax authorities' structural adjustment should involve reducing the term of the intra-group loan, but only down to a level that is necessary in order to achieve a commercially rational expected result that would have enabled the associated enterprises to agree on an arm's length interest rate.

After having undertaken the structural adjustment, the tax authorities should determine an arm's length interest rate on a restructured loan transaction. Assuming that the analysis shows that it was a realistically available option that was clearly more attractive for the borrower to shorten the term of the loan from 30 years down to 15 years, the structural adjustment should not involve a further shortening of the agreed term. Further, after having undertaken this structural adjustment, the tax authorities should be able to determine an appropriate arm's length interest rate for the loan. Provided that a comparability analysis shows that comparable loan transactions entered into between unrelated parties with an agreed term of 15 years have interest rates in the range between EURIBOR +4% and +5%, this would indicate that the arm's length interest rate for this loan should be somewhere within this range.

## 6 Default Clauses

### A The Condition and Its Price Relevance

Another type of condition that could significantly affect the arm's length interest rate is conditions governing the parties' rights and responsibilities in case of default from the other party.

In theory, both parties to a loan agreement could be in default, but the most practical default situation is that the borrower breaches the agreement by making late or no payments of the principal amount and/or interest. Thus, below, this will be the type of situation referred to when referring to the default of a loan agreement.

Default clauses are very important in loan agreements in order to make sure that the other party actually fulfils its obligations under the agreement, or to make sure that the defaulting party compensate the other party for losses incurred as a result of the default.

45. *See* The OECD Guidelines, para. 1.144.

Since associated enterprises, however, normally do not have conflicting interests in the same manner as independent parties,[46] default clauses may not be as important in intra-group loan agreements as in agreements between independent parties.

However, if it is established that the intra-group loan contract does not provide for any remedies in a case of default, this would be a circumstance that generally would increase the creditor's risk, which in turn will imply a higher arm's length interest rate.

### *B Delineation*

Even though an intra-group contract does not explicitly regulate the situation where the borrower is in default the domestic laws applicable to the contract could have rules that provide for certain remedies if a party breaches the agreement. Such laws may also be mandatory, and thus apply even if the contract provides for another solution. Through the accurate delineation of the controlled loan transaction, it is thus important to assess whether the contract is governed by any domestic laws that supplement the conditions of the contract.

In the following subsections, we will assume that the examined controlled transaction has been accurately delineated as an intra-group loan with no remedies to the lender in case of the borrower's default, and that the issue is whether this part of the agreement could be subject to a structural adjustment based on the rationality exception and the RAO standard.

### *C Realistically Available Options*

The first question would be whether it was a realistically available option to regulate default situations differently in the agreement, i.e., to include a default clause providing the lender with an effective remedy in case of the borrower's default instead of explicitly or implicitly agreeing that the lender would have no such remedy. Normally, agreeing to such a default clause would be a realistically available option for the borrower.

### *D Attractiveness*

The second question would be whether the realistically available option of including a condition providing the lender with an effective remedy in case of the borrower's default, was *clearly more attractive* for the borrower. This requires an analysis of the level of *attractiveness* of the actually agreed default remedies (if any), and of the alternative (more extensive) default remedies. Then, the options' respective levels of attractiveness must be compared.

Since remedies in case of the borrower's default reduce the lender's risks related to receiving late payments and not receiving repayment, the inclusion of such remedies

46. *See* OECD Guidelines para. 1.2.

would normally reduce the arm's length interest rate. The regulations' implications on the interest rate should be taken into account when assessing the option's attractiveness for the borrower. However, if the lender is given far-reaching remedies, this may also be detrimental to the borrower. Again, a broad-based, overall assessment must be undertaken.

## E *The Structural Adjustment and the Price Adjustment*

As mentioned above, if the conditions under the RAO standard are met, and the tax authorities thus are authorised to undertake structural adjustments, the actual structure of the transaction should be replaced by an alternative transaction that comports as closely as possible with the actual controlled transaction.[47]

If it is determined that including a condition in the intra-group loan agreement providing the lender with remedies in case of the borrower's default would be a realistically available option that was clearly more attractive for the borrower, the tax authorities' structural adjustment should involve imputing such remedies into the intra-group loan. The tax authorities should, however, not include more far-reaching default clauses than necessary in order to achieve a commercially rational expected result that would have enabled the associated enterprises to agree on an arm's length interest rate.

After having undertaken the structural adjustment, the tax authorities should assess and determine an arm's length interest rate on the restructured loan transaction.

## F *Example*

The above can be illustrated by the following example. Assume that the intra-group loan agreement, as accurately delineated, includes a clause providing for a default interest rate in cases of the borrower's late payments, but no other default clauses are included in the agreement. There are, e.g., no clauses providing the lender with any remedies in case the borrower becomes financially distressed.

Further, assume that the parties have agreed to an interest rate of LIBOR +10%. A comparability analysis is performed, but no comparable loan agreements entered into between unrelated parties have been identified with the same regulations of default. However, the comparability analysis identifies several comparable loan agreements containing default clauses providing the lender with remedies in cases where the borrower becomes financially distressed. In these loan agreements, the interest rates lie in the range between NIBOR +2.5% and NIBOR +3%.

In this example, assuming that the conditions under the RAO standard mentioned above are met, the tax authorities may undertake a structural adjustment that involves including such a default regulation in the intra-group loan agreement. After having undertaken such a structural adjustment, the tax authorities should be able to determine an appropriate arm's length interest rate. In this example, the comparability

47. *See* The OECD Guidelines, para. 1.144.

analysis indicates that the interest rate should be somewhere in the range between NIBOR +2.5% and +3%.

## V SUMMARY

This chapter is dedicated to the topic of applying the rationality exception and the RAO standard to key terms that could significantly affect the arm's length interest rate on intra-group loan agreements. However, the vast majority of transfer pricing cases regarding intra-group loan transactions actually revolve around pricing adjustments, i.e., the issue of whether, and how, to adjust the interest rate, and not structural adjustments of other (non-price) conditions in the intra-group loan agreement.

This is most likely because the as-structured principle provides the starting point for the assessment and the clear main rule that the arm's length principle should be applied to the actual controlled loan transaction as it has been structured by the associated enterprises. The tax authorities are only authorised to disregard the transaction in 'exceptional circumstances', and the threshold for disregarding the actual structure of the transactions is therefore very high.[48] Further, as a result of the freedom of contract, one can find a large variety of all types of conditions in loan contracts between independent enterprises. Consequently, the *arm's length range* of non-price conditions is very broad.

Further, and with that said, in our experience, most cases regarding structural adjustments of intra-group loan agreements involve the issue of thin capitalisation, i.e., the issue of whether the condition in the loan agreement regulating the amount of the loan can be adjusted. Even though the introduction of domestic laws that limit the amount of interest that a borrower can deduct has led to a decrease in cases regarding thin capitalisation, this still seems as the most practical use of the rationality exception and the RAO standard to intra-group loan agreements.

48. *See* OECD Guidelines para. 1.141.

CHAPTER 12

# Data Available to Price Loans with a Focus on Loan and Bond Approach

*Thomas Petrakos*[*]

## I INTRODUCTION

According to the latest OECD Transfer Pricing Guidelines ('OECD TP Guidelines 2022'), the widespread existence of markets for borrowing and lending money and the frequency of such transactions between independent borrowers and lenders, coupled with the widespread availability of information and analysis of such markets makes it easier to apply the Comparable Uncontrolled Price (CUP) method when pricing an intercompany loan.[1] The CUP method is also treated in the United Nations Practical Manual on Transfer Pricing for Developing Countries as the most commonly used transfer pricing method when pricing intra-group loans.[2]

In the search for external CUPs, two approaches are commonly used, the loan approach, which utilises comparable loan transactions, and the bond approach, which utilises comparable bond transactions.[3] In this chapter, data on loan and bond transactions are analysed and compared to each other. The ultimate purpose of this analysis is to present the various aspects and characteristics of these two instruments

* The views and opinions set forth herein are the personal views or opinions of the authors; they do not necessarily reflect the views or opinions of the organization with which the authors are associated.

1. OECD TP Guidelines 2022, para. 10.90.
2. United Nations Practical Manual on Transfer Pricing for Developing Countries (2021), paras 9.10.1. & 9.12.2.4.
3. OECD TP Guidelines 2022, para. 10.93: 'Arm's length interest rates can also be based on the return of realistic alternative transactions with comparable economic characteristics. Depending on the facts and circumstances, realistic alternatives to intra-group loans could be, for instance, bond issuances, loans which are uncontrolled transactions, deposits, convertible debentures, commercial papers, etc.'

and discuss how they can be implemented in the context of pricing an intercompany loan. For the purpose of the analysis under this chapter, the databases that are used are LoanConnector[4] for the loan approach and EIKON[5] for the bond approach. It should be noted that there are also various other database sources with potentially more data on bonds or loans. However, such sources are not further discussed or analysed.

As initial remark, it should be noted that, in general, information on data about bond transactions is more abundant compared to information about loan transactions. Due to bonds trading on the capital market, bond data is readily available in public databases in terms of the number of records and data quality. The difference in data availability can be illustrated by the fact that the number of all corporate[6] loans issued globally within the period between September 2020 and September 2021 with available information on borrower's credit rating and pricing is 2,179 (hereafter referred to as 'the loans sample under review'), while the respective number of corporate bonds is 4,918 (hereafter referred to as 'the bonds sample under review').

This relative lack of data on debt instruments issued by rated issuers also exists when searching for transactions further back in the past. When looking at a five-year period (i.e., between September 2016 and September 2021), the number of all corporate loans issued globally with available information on borrower's credit rating and pricing is approximately 12,000, while the respective number of all corporate bonds is approximately 18,000.

This lack of data could be attributed to the fact that a company does not need to have a public rating through one of the credit rating agencies to access debt financing. Many lenders have their own credit models, which use in order to assign to the borrower their own 'private' rating. The details of such rating are typically not available. Only when a borrower has a history of lending in the capital markets or when it has to pay for a rating for regulatory purposes will it have a public rating via a credit rating agency.

Pricing an intercompany loan based on loans between third parties is potentially considered to be the most accurate approach from a transfer pricing perspective since it compares the same instrument. The arm's length interest rate for a tested loan can be benchmarked against publicly available data for other borrowers with the same credit rating for loans with sufficiently similar terms and conditions and other comparability factors.[7] From a database search criteria perspective, LoanConnector offers several search field criteria that can, theoretically, align all the possible terms and conditions of an intercompany loan agreement with the terms and conditions of the third-party transactions, including but not limited to type and purpose of loan, rank and seniority,

4. LoanConnector is a web-based loan information platform that contains deal terms and conditions for over 220,000 historical loan transactions from both primary and secondary loan markets around the world.
5. EIKON is an online platform for analysing financial markets. Through EIKON's open technology platform, apps can be used to access financial data. The apps are tailored to specific asset classes, financial markets and/or datasets. EIKON contains 2,000 contributing sources, 99% coverage of global market cap, 3.3 million transactions and 65 years of information.
6. Excluding governmental institutions, banks, and non-banks financials.
7. OECD TP Guidelines 2022, para. 10.91.

term, type of collateral and financial covenants. However, from a data availability and fee transparency perspective, this is not always the case, since information on all the possible terms and conditions are not disclosed or are not readily available often making it challenging to use such data for transfer pricing analyses.

The bond approach uses bond transactions and compares the yield to remaining maturity (YTRM) of the bond with the interest rate of the intercompany loan transaction. Bond transactions are to a large extent comparable to loan transactions. Instead of referring to lenders and borrowers, the bond market refers to bond issuers (borrowers) and bond holders (lenders). Similar to loans, bond issuers obtain an amount that has to be fully repaid at a certain moment in time and pay a compensation for this amount, in the form of coupon payments. Although the compensation is a combination of the bond's face value and the bond's coupon rate, the YTRM reflects the overall return of the bondholder, expressed as an annual rate. In other words, the YTRM is the total rate of return (i.e., total interest rate) that investors would earn.[8] The YTRM can be considered a reliable measure of calculating the return of a bond since it takes into account the time value of money by accounting for the present value of a bond's future coupon payments.[9]

The next paragraphs present the most important comparability factors and characteristics that should be considered when pricing an intercompany loan and set various considerations and interpretations regarding the available data in relation to those factors as well as the potential benefits and drawbacks stemming from the use of the two approaches.

According to Organisation for Economic Co-operation and Development (OECD), those characteristics may include but are not limited to, the amount of the loan, its maturity, the schedule of repayment, the nature or purpose of the loan, level of seniority and subordination, geographical location of the borrower, currency, collateral provided, presence and quality of any guarantee and whether the interest rate is fixed or floating.[10] In general, characteristics which will usually increase the risk for the lender, such as long maturity dates, absence of security, subordination, or application of the loan to a risky project, will tend to increase the interest rate. Characteristics which limit the lender's risk, such as strong collateral, a high-quality guarantee, or restrictions on future behaviour of the borrower, will tend to result in a lower interest rate.[11]

In summary, the following factors are discussed:

(1) borrower's credit rating;
(2) principal amount;
(3) maturity/term;
(4) repayment type;

8. P. Veronesi, Fixed Income Securities: Valuation, Risk and Risk Management, pp. 47-49, (Wiley 2010).
9. In other words, the YTRM is the discount rate that equates the net present value of a bond's future coupon payment to the bond's price.
10. OECD TP Guidelines 2022, para. 10.29.
11. *Ibid.*, para. 10.90.

(5) purpose of the loan;
(6) seniority;
(7) borrower's location;
(8) issuance currency;
(9) security;
(10) type of interest rate; and
(11) other considerations.

## II LOAN CHARACTERISTICS

### 1 Credit Rating of Borrower

The creditworthiness of the borrower is one of the main factors that independent lenders take into account when determining an interest rate to charge. Credit ratings can serve as a useful measure of creditworthiness and therefore help to identify potential comparables or to apply economic models in the context of related party transactions.[12] The credit rating of a company is effectively a form of relative ranking of the creditworthiness (or default risk) in comparison to other borrowers. In general, a lower credit rating will indicate a greater risk of default and be expected to result in a higher rate of return for lenders.[13]

Not all loan transactions include information on borrower's credit ratings. When looking at all the corporate loans issued globally within the period from September 2020 to September 2021 that have information on pricing, only 22.5% include information on borrower's credit ratings. Taking into account that the search is performed at the tranche level and not at the deal level (a deal may include several tranches with different terms and conditions), it may be the case that there are multiple observations (i.e., tranches) that have been issued by the same borrower in the context of a wider deal. This brings the amount of unique rated borrowers to 911 within the last year. Figure 12.1 illustrates the number of borrowers per credit rating range.

12. *Ibid.*, para. 10.62.
13. *Ibid.*, para. 10.64.

*Figure 12.1 Number of Rated Borrowers Per Credit Rating Range*

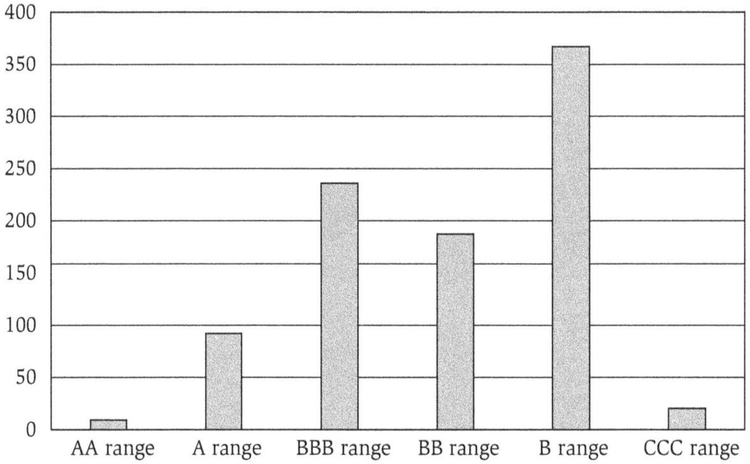


Of the rated borrowers, 1.0% have a credit rating between AA- and AA+, 10.1% between A- and A+, 25.9% between BBB- and BBB+, 20.5% between BB- and BB+, 40.3% between B- and B+ and 2.2% between CCC- and CCC+.[14] Interestingly, the amount of borrowers in the non-investment grade area (between CCC- and BB+) is almost double the amount of borrowers in the investment grade area (between BBB- and AA+). This difference could be explained by the fact that companies with poor ratings do not have easy access to public bond market and more commonly will have to rely on the private loan market for their financing needs. This argument is also consistent with the renegotiation and liquidation hypothesis, which argues that borrowers with high probability of default, as reflected in a low credit rating, in the foreseeable future are inclined to rely on private banks for their financing needs since it is more challenging for them to effectively negotiate the terms and conditions of debt arrangements with thousands of bondholders compared to a single bank or a limited number of banks.[15]

Similar to loans, not all bonds include information on credit ratings. When looking at all the corporate bonds issued globally within the period from September 2020 to September 2021 that have information on pricing, 40.4% include information on borrower's credit ratings. The percentage of bond transactions involving rated issuers is significantly higher than the respective loan transactions. This could be explained by the fact that to get access to the public financing markets, a company needs in most cases a public credit rating.

14. For simplicity purposes, credit ratings provided by Moody's and Fitch have been converted to the equivalent S&P credit rating.
15. M. Berlin & J. Loeys, Bond *Covenants and Delegated Monitoring*. Journal of Finance Volume 43, 397-412 (1988).

Of the bonds with rated issuers, several involve the same issuer. This brings the amount of unique rated bond issuers to 1,540 within the database. Figure 12.2 illustrates the number of borrowers per credit rating.

*Figure 12.2 Number of Rated Bond Issuers Per Credit Rating Range*

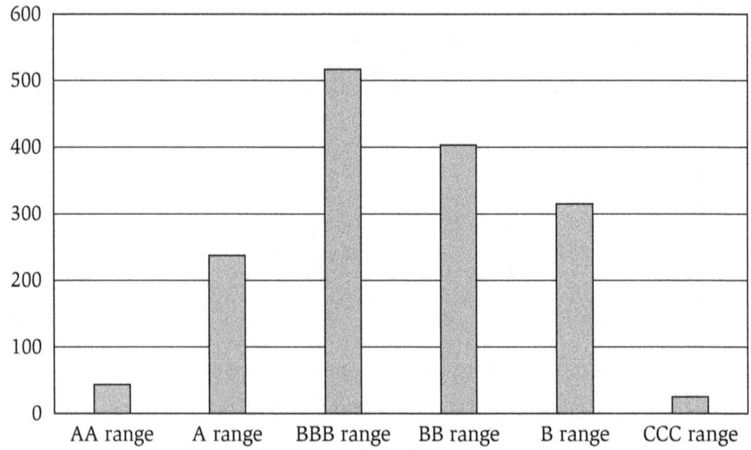


Of the rated bond issuers, 2.8% have a credit rating between AA- and AA+, 15.4% between A- and A+, 33.6% between BBB- and BBB+, 26.2% between BB- and BB+, 20.5% between B- and B+ and 1.6% between CCC- and CCC+. In the bond sample, the split between investment-graded and non-investment-graded issuers is almost equal (52% versus 48%). When looking at the individual ranges, the highest concentration is observed in the BBB credit rating range, followed by the BB range. Similar to loans, the lowest amount of observations involves the highest (AA) credit rating and the lowest (CCC) credit rating. First, the lack of observation relates to the fact that there are not that many AA-rated companies worldwide, and, second to the fact that AA-rated companies rarely need external debt financing. For the latter, the lack of observation relates to the fact that CCC-rated companies do not have the ability to issue public debt, and even if they have, they find it challenging to issue public debt against a reasonable yield.

Overall, the data support the theory that, in general, the funding options of the riskiest firms, as reflected by the CCC credit rating range, are more limited to equity or other alternative lending options, such as distressed debt, mezzanine financing, convertibles and other hybrid lending. On the contrary, safer firms, as reflected by the B and BB credit rating ranges, are more inclined to take out bank loans and the investment grade firms, as reflected by the credit rating ranges above BBB, turn to the capital market for their financing needs.[16] While this is a general theory, it could well be possible that there could be exceptions to it.

From a transfer pricing perspective, the above results indicate that benchmarking intercompany loans in the CCC credit rating range may be challenging due to the insufficient number of observations in this credit rating range both for loan and bond transactions. This lack of sufficient transactions typically forces the transfer pricing practitioners to expand the scope of the analysis by broadening other search criteria, such as geographic location or industry, which weakens the comparability, and/or to perform comparability adjustments, for instance, by adding a premium for the increased risk, which results in an indirect determination of an arm's length interest rate.

## 2 Principal Amount

The issuance amount is another parameter that should be examined when analysing an intercompany loan,[17] since loan size may affect the interest rate for reasons relating primarily to liquidity. Small issues may garner less focus from institutional investors, and this lack of demand may result in a higher cost to borrowers.

There are many cases where a benchmarking analysis is required for intercompany loans that involve relatively small amounts. In these cases, benchmarking the interest rate using the bond approach may not be appropriate, since bond issuances typically involve relatively large amounts. When looking at the EUR-denominated corporate bonds issued during the examination period, only 10 bonds (0.9% of the sample) have a principal amount of less than EUR 100 million. The outcome is similar for the USD-denominated bonds of the sample, out of which only 4.9% have a principal amount of less than USD 100 million. This lack of data in bond transactions involving small amounts is also present when expanding the period to five years. Of the USD-denominated bonds with information on YTRM and issuer's credit rating, 3.6% involves amounts less than USD 100 million and of the EUR-denominated bonds with information on YTRM and issuer's credit rating, 3.6% involves amounts of less than EUR 100 million.

The above results are in line with the flotation cost theory, which argues that issuing public debt requires significant costs, hence issuing a small amount will not be efficient from a cost perspective.[18] Therefore, in the majority of cases, companies choose to issue bonds only for considerable amounts.

16. P. Bolton & X. Freixas, *Equity, Bonds, and Bank Debt: Capital Structure and Financial Market Equilibrium under Asymmetric Information*, Journal of Political Economy, volume 108, issue 2, 324-351 (2000).
17. OECD TP Guidelines 2022, para. 10.29.
18. J. Houston & C. James, *Bank Information Monopolies and the Mix of Private and Public Debt Claims*, The Journal of Finance, Volume 51, Issue 5 (1996), S. Krishnaswami, P.A. Spindt & V. Subramaniam, *Information Asymmetry, Monitoring, and the Placement Structure of Corporate Debt*, 51 Journal of Financial Economics 3 (1999) and D.J. Denis & V. Mihov, *The Choice among Bank Debt, Non-bank Private Debt, and Public Debt: Evidence from New Corporate Borrowings*, Journal of Financial Economics, Volume 70, Issue 1, pp. 3-28 (2003).

Taking the above arguments into account, one would expect that, in theory, data on loan transactions with small amounts would be more abundant in public loan databases compared to bonds. When looking at the EUR-denominated loans issued during the examination period, 11.5% have a principal amount of less than EUR 100 million. The outcome is similar for the USD-denominated loans of the sample, out of which, 10.0% have a principal amount of less than USD 100 million. When widening the examination period to five years, the results are similar: of the loans issued in EUR, 13.9% have a nominal amount of less than EUR 100 million, while of the loans issued in USD, and 12.9% have a nominal amount of less than USD 100 million.

The available data suggests that the proportion of loans with small amounts is indeed (somewhat) greater than the respective proportion of bonds, in line with the existing theories and the arguments presented above. However, this proportion would have been significantly greater if the majority of the loan transactions in the public loan databases would relate to bilateral agreements rather than syndicated ones, which, by definition, involve considerable amounts. The syndicated transactions topic is covered in detail later in this chapter.

The impact of the size of the loan amount on the quantum of interest rate is difficult to be assessed and quantified due to the lack of observations in small amounts. As a result of this lack of observations, addressing comparability issues that may arise and performing the necessary comparability adjustments may be challenging.

## 3 Term

Another important consideration when pricing an intercompany loan is the term of the loan. Typically, long-term loans have higher interest rates than short-term loans due to the increased credit risk incurred by the lender arising from the borrower's increased probability of default in the long run.

To see whether the above argument is valid, two similar searches were performed, one for loans and one for bonds.

The following criteria were applied:

(1) borrower's industry: All corporates excluding financials;
(2) borrower's credit rating: Between S&P's BBB– and BBB+ or Moody's or Fitch equivalent;
(3) tranche active date: Between September 2016 and September 2021;
(4) seniority: Senior;
(5) loan purpose: General purposes
(6) currency: USD;
(7) base rate: Libor.

The following criteria were applied:

(1) security status: Only active bonds;
(2) issuer's industry: All corporates excluding financials;

(3) issuer's credit rating: Between S&P's BBB- and BBB+ or Moody's or Fitch equivalent;
(4) issuance date: Between September 2016 and September 2021;
(5) seniority: Senior unsecured;
(6) currency: USD.

Table 12.1 provides the results of the analysis.

*Table 12.1 Interquartile Ranges of Loan Spread and YTRM for Various Terms*

| *Term to Maturity* | *Short Term - -< =2 Years* | *Mid-term - >2 and < =5 Years* | *Long Term - - >5 Years* |
|---|---|---|---|
| Interquartile range | | Loan spread (bps) | |
| Lower Q. | 75 | 105 | 110 |
| Median | 110 | 125 | 140 |
| Upper Q. | 140 | 150 | 175 |
| Observations | 187 | 249 | 61 |
| Interquartile range | | Bond YTRM (bps) | |
| Lower Q. | 70 | 131 | 237 |
| Median | 89 | 159 | 287 |
| Upper Q. | 124 | 195 | 330 |
| Observations | 348 | 743 | 2,582 |

*Sources*: LoanConnector for the loan spread and EIKON for the YTRM

Table 12.1 shows that, especially for bonds, as the remaining term till maturity increases, the compensation for credit risk increases. This effect is also present in loans but it is more limited.

Another interesting result relates to the amount of observations for the long-term instruments. When looking at the sample of loans, the amount of long-term loans is the smallest, while in the sample of bonds, it is the largest. This indicates, that the bond approach may be more appropriate when pricing an intercompany loan with a long term.

## 4 Repayment Type

In general, there are three types of loan repayments: revolving repayment, bullet repayment and term amortization. A revolving loan facility provides the borrower with the ability to draw down and repay various amounts at his discretion. A bullet loan is fully repaid in one instalment at the end of the term of the loan. Lastly, a term loan is repaid in fixed, predetermined instalments during its term.

The repayment type is a search field that is available for loans. However, this information is not disclosed for all loan transactions. Table 12.2 presents the various repayment types of all the loan transactions with information on pricing and borrower's credit rating for two different time periods.

*Table 12.2 Distribution of Loan Transactions Per Type of Repayment*

| *Repayment Type* | *Last 1 Year (%)* | *Last 5 Years (%)* |
|---|---|---|
| Revolving | 41.6 | 42.3 |
| Term Amortization | 8.9 | 9.4 |
| Bullet | 2.2 | 3.2 |
| Other | 0.0 | 0.0 |
| No information | 47.4 | 44.9 |
| Total | 100.0 | 100.0 |

*Source*: LoanConnector.

As can be seen from the table, for both samples, almost half of the transactions do not include information on the repayment type. Of the transactions with information on repayment type, revolving loan facilities get the lion's share, with 41.6% in the one-year sample and 42.3% in the five-year sample. This mainly relates to the fact that the vast majority of the loan transactions in LoanConnector are syndicated, which, typically are revolving facilities.

This relative lack of information on the type of repayment should be considered when pricing an intercompany loan since the type of repayment plays an important role in the determination of the interest rate that should be applied in a loan agreement.[19] For instance, a term loan is expected to have a lower interest rate than a bullet loan. This is due to the fact that the principal of a term loan is being gradually repaid in fixed predetermined instalments while the principal of a bullet loan is fully repaid at the maturity date. As a result of the gradual decrease of the outstanding loan amount, the risk for the lender decreases during the term of the loan, and therefore, a lower interest rate is typically applied.

To see whether the above assumption is valid, two searches were performed, one representative for the low-grade credit ratings, assuming a credit rating range of B, and one for the investment grade credit ratings, assuming a credit rating range of BBB. The following criteria were applied:

(1) borrower's industry: All corporates excluding financials;[20]
(2) tranche active date: Between September 2011 and September 2021;
(3) seniority: Senior;
(4) collateral: Secured for the B rating and unsecured for the BBB rating;
(5) currency: USD;
(6) tranche amount: Less than USD 1 billion;

19. OECD TP Guidelines 2022, para. 10.29.
20. The search excludes banks and non-bank financial companies.

(7) tranche tenor: Long-term loans, with a term greater than or equal to five years; and
(8) base rate: London Interbank Offered Rate (LIBOR).[21]

Table 12.3 provides the results of the analysis.

*Table 12.3 Loan Spreads for Bullet and Term Loans Across Two Credit Ratings*

| *Interquartile Range* | *From B– to B+* | | *From BBB– to BBB+* | |
|---|---|---|---|---|
| | *Bullet* | *Amortization* | *Bullet* | *Amortization* |
| Lower Q. | 475 | 325 | 119 | 125 |
| Median | 775 | 400 | 150 | 138 |
| Upper Q. | 863 | 500 | 170 | 150 |
| Observations | 52 | 605 | 92 | 56 |

*Source*: LoanConnector.

For the loans issued both by borrowers with B credit rating and BBB credit rating, the argument that the term loans bear lower interest rates than the bullet loans is supported by the results. This outcome is much more profound for borrowers with poor credit ratings. In addition, Table 12.4 shows that the number of term loans within the B credit rating is significantly higher than the respective bullet loans. This can be attributed to the inherent higher-risk nature of a bullet loan in combination with the already high-risk profile of a B-rated borrower, which makes bullet loans much less attractive to lenders.

## 5 Purpose of Loan

A notable advantage of the loan approach compared to the bond approach is that it offers the possibility to search for loans with a purpose similar to the intercompany loan in scope since information related to this field is more easily accessible for loans rather than bonds.

21. LIBOR has historically been one of the main interest rate benchmarks used in financial markets. It determines interest rates for financial contracts around the world. Since the global financial crisis in 2008-2009, activity in the markets that LIBOR measures has reduced. The low volume of underlying transactions means that LIBOR is no longer sustainable. In line with announcements from the Financial Conduct Authority (FCA), publication of 24 of the 35 LIBOR settings ceased from 1 January 2022. Six GBP and JPY LIBOR settings will continue for the duration of 2022 on a 'synthetic' basis. Five USD LIBOR settings will continue to be calculated using panel bank submissions until mid-2023, although its use for new business will be restricted from end-2021, with limited exceptions. Risk-free rates, which are robust alternatives to LIBOR, are already available. These include Secured Overnight Funding Rate (SOFR) and the Sterling Overnight Index Average (SONIA) benchmark. *See* Bank of England, Transition from LIBOR to risk-free rates (4 January 2022), available at https://www.bankofengland.co.uk/markets/transition-to-sterling-risk-free-rates-from-libor.

The purpose or nature of the loan (financing project, working capital, acquisition) is an important parameter that should be examined when pricing an intercompany loan[22] since it has direct impact on the quantum of the applied interest rate. In general, according to the finance theory, third-party lenders would offer more favourable terms and conditions where they deem the cash flows to be more stable and thereby have less risk of default. Similarly, OECD acknowledges that third-party lenders would typically offer more favourable terms and conditions in cases where the loan will be used for an investment with high expected returns.[23]

Table 12.4 presents the distribution of loan transactions with information on pricing and borrower's credit rating across the various loan purposes for two different time periods.

*Table 12.4 Distribution of Loan Transactions Per Purpose*

| *Loan Purpose* | *Last 1 Year (%)* | *Last 5 Years (%)* |
|---|---|---|
| Dividend Recapitalization | 2.5 | 2.6 |
| General Purpose | 65.0 | 67.7 |
| Exit financing | 0.6 | 0.3 |
| Spinoff | 0.7 | 0.7 |
| Acquisition | 5.6 | 4.5 |
| Takeover | 7.2 | 7.8 |
| General Purpose/Refinance | 5.4 | 4.7 |
| Leveraged Buyout | 5.0 | 4.5 |
| Working capital | 1.4 | 1.6 |
| Commercial paper backup | 0.0 | 0.0 |
| Sponsored Buyout | 4.6 | 3.1 |
| Dividend or Distribution to Shareholders | 0.3 | 0.2 |
| Stock Repurchase | 0.1 | 0.1 |
| Capital expenditure | 0.4 | 0.5 |
| Recapitalization | 0.2 | 0.1 |
| Merger | 0.8 | 0.9 |
| Debtor-in-possession | 0.0 | 0.0 |
| Real estate loan | 0.2 | 0.1 |
| Pre-Export | 0.0 | 0.1 |
| Project Finance | 0.0 | 0.1 |
| Aircraft & Ship Finance | 0.0 | 0.0 |
| Infrastructure | 0.0 | 0.0 |

22. OECD TP Guidelines 2022, para. 10.29.
23. OECD, Public Discussion Draft – BEPS Actions 8-10 – Financial Transactions (2018), para. 34 [hereinafter Discussion Draft 2018].

| *Loan Purpose* | *Last 1 Year (%)* | *Last 5 Years (%)* |
|---|---|---|
| Initial Public Offering (IPO) Related Financing | 0.0 | 0.1 |
| Restructuring | 0.0 | 0.0 |
| Ship Finance | 0.0 | 0.1 |
| General Purpose/Stock Repurchase | 0.0 | 0.0 |
| Other | 0.0 | 0.0 |
| Total | 100.0 | 100.0 |

*Source*: LoanConnector.

As it can be seen in Table 12.4, the majority of the loans in both sample are provided for general corporate purposes, followed by loans financing various forms of acquisitions, including takeovers, leveraged and sponsored buyouts. There is also a limited amount of loans that relate to very specific purposes such as exit financing and commercial paper backup or specific industries such as real estate, shipping and aerospace and defence.

Overall, the majority of loans can theoretically be grouped into four broad categories based on their purpose:

(1) loans financing operations: This group includes loans for general purposes, working capital, project finance and capital expenditure as well as industry-specific loans;
(2) loans financing shares: This group includes loans for acquisition, merger, takeover, leveraged and sponsored buyouts and repurchase;
(3) loans financing dividends: This group includes loans for distribution to shareholders and dividend recapitalization; and
(4) loans used for repayment of existing debt: Repayment of existing debt is not an available option under the loan purpose search field criterion in LoanConnector.

To identify and examine potential differences in the spread between the four groups of loans, a search across various credit rating ranges was performed using the following criteria:

(1) borrower's industry: All corporates excluding financials;
(2) tranche active date: Between September 2016 and September 2021;
(3) tranche type: All revolving loan facilities;
(4) seniority: Senior;
(5) currency: USD;
(6) base rate: Libor.

Table 12.5 provides the results of the analysis.

*Table 12.5 Loans Spread for the Three Broad Groups of Loan Purposes Across Various Credit Rating Ranges*

| From B– to B+ | Financing Operations | Financing Shares | Financing Dividends |
|---|---|---|---|
| Lower Q. | 200 | 275 | 325 |
| Median | 275 | 350 | 375 |
| Upper Q. | 350 | 400 | 450 |
| Observations | 1,181 | 398 | 49 |
| **From BB– to BB+** | **Financing Operations** | **Finaning Shares** | **Financing Dividends** |
| Lower Q. | 150 | 150 | 325 |
| Median | 175 | 200 | 375 |
| Upper Q. | 200 | 250 | 375 |
| Observations | 1,031 | 88 | 5 |
| **From BBB– to BBB+** | **Financing Operations** | **Financing Shares** | **Financing Dividends** |
| Lower Q. | 102 | 113 | n.a. |
| Median | 113 | 130 | 200 |
| Upper Q. | 125 | 165 | n.a. |
| Observations | 1,095 | 42 | 1 |

*Source*: LoanConnector.

The data indicate that, for all credit rating ranges, the median spread of the loans issued for the purpose of financing shares is higher than the spread of the loans issued for the purpose of financing operations, suggesting an increased risk profile. Regarding the loans directly financing dividend distribution, and taking into account the amount of observations per credit rating range, meaningful results can only be derived from the B credit rating range, whereby the median spread of those loans is the greatest. The data suggest that this group of loans may have the highest risk profile.

When looking at the bonds sample under review, 39.2% of the bond transactions do not include information on loan purpose ('use of proceeds'). Despite this relative lack of data on this parameter, the bond approach could be considered in the case where the intercompany loan in scope is provided for the purpose of repayment of existing debt since such type of purpose is available for bonds (10.6% of the bonds sample under review are issued for the purpose of repayment of existing debt).

## 6 Seniority

Seniority or ranking is another important factor that needs to be considered when pricing an intercompany loan.[24] A loan can be ranked as senior, subordinated or

24. OECD TP Guidelines 2022, para. 10.29.

mezzanine. Senior loans are debt obligations that a company must settle first if it goes out of business. Subordinated debt refers to forms of debt issued with a lower priority for repayment than the senior debt claims in the case of default. Therefore, subordinated loans tend to be riskier for lenders, and thus carry higher interest rates compared to senior debt issued from the same borrower.

In general, data for detailed subordinated loans tends to be less readily available for transfer pricing purposes. When looking at the loans sample under review, there is not even one subordinated loan included in the sample. After expanding the examination period to five years, there is only one subordinated loan transaction with information on pricing and borrower's credit rating. Even when dropping the credit rating criterion, there are less than 20 subordinated loan transactions during the last five years. The lack of data availability on subordinated debt is also present in the bond market. Of the bonds from the sample under review, only 2% is subordinated. Similarly, when broadening the examination period to five years, only 1% involves subordinated bond transactions.

This lack of data on subordinated transactions makes the direct determination of an arm's length interest rate challenging, especially under the loan approach. Under the bond approach, however, and despite the relative lack of data on subordinated bonds, an arm's length rate may be indirectly derived based on available data on senior bond transactions. This indirect calculation in essence entails modelling what the rate would have been by analysing comparability differences and adjusting for those differences accordingly. In their most common variation, such economic models calculate an interest rate through a combination of a risk-free interest rate and a number of premiums associated with different aspects of the loan, for example, differences in default risk, liquidity risk, expected inflation or maturity.[25]

The reliability of economic models' outcomes depends upon the parameters factored into the specific model and the underlying assumptions adopted. In evaluating the reliability of economic models as an approach to pricing intra-group loans, it is important to note that economic models' outcomes do not represent actual transactions between independent parties and that, therefore, comparability adjustments would be likely required.[26]

Similar to subordinated transactions, information on mezzanine transactions are scarce in public databases. Mezzanine loans reflect deeply subordinated debt that represents a claim on a company's assets which is senior only to that of the common shares. Mezzanine loans are the riskiest, and therefore, the most expensive way of debt financing, since in the event of default of the borrower, the mezzanine loan is less likely to be repaid in full as it ranks below all other debt obligations.

25. *Ibid.*, para. 10.105.
26. *Ibid.*, para. 10.106.

## 7 Geographic Location

Another comparability factor that should be considered when analysing an intercompany loan is the geographic location of the borrower[27] since local regulations and the market conditions prevailing in a specific geographic region may have a direct impact on the prices of financial instruments issued by companies in that region.[28]

Table 12.6 illustrates the allocation of the transactions included in the loans sample under review and the bonds sample under review per borrower's geographic region.

*Table 12.6 Allocation of Loan and Bond Transactions Per Region*

| *Region* | *Loans (%)* | *Bonds (%)* |
|---|---|---|
| US/Canada | 88.0 | 46.8 |
| Western Europe | 7.4 | 15.1 |
| Eastern Europe/Russia | 0.2 | 1.1 |
| Asia Pacific | 3.4 | 34.3 |
| Latin America/Caribbean | 1.0 | 1.6 |
| Africa | 0.0 | 0.2 |
| Middle East | 0.0 | 0.8 |
| Total | 100 | 100 |

*Sources*: LoanConnector for the loan transactions and EIKON for the bond transactions.

With regard to loans, the coverage of loan transactions in regions other than the US–Canada is considerably limited. When looking at the loans sample under review, 88.0% relates to borrowers from the US–Canada region, while only 165 7.6% relates to borrowers from the wider European region and 4.4% relates to borrowers from the rest of the world. As a result, it may be challenging to directly benchmark a European intercompany loan with sufficiently comparable European third-party loan transactions without making appropriate comparability adjustments to account for the different regions.[29]

The geographic coverage of bond transactions is more dispersed. Although also in this sample the majority of the bonds (52.7%) are issued from issuers located in the US–Canada, there is relatively a sufficient number of observations for other regions: 16.2% relates to issuers from the wider European region and 34.3% relate to issuers from the Asia/Pacific region. However, the number of transactions initiated in regions other than the US–Canada, Europe and Asia–Pacific is limited (2.6%). Therefore, it

27. *Ibid.*, paras 10.29 & 10.31.
28. *Ibid.*, para. 10.29.
29. *Ibid.*, para. 1.40: 'Where there are differences between the situations being compared that could materially affect the comparison, comparability adjustments must be made, where possible, to improve the reliability of the comparison.' *See also* para. 10.20.

may also be necessary to perform comparability adjustments when examining inter-company loans issued in these regions.

An example of comparability adjustment in such cases is the addition of a country risk premium (or discount, depending on the location of the borrower and the location of the comparable companies). A country risk premium is typically applied when the borrower is located in a country where such a premium is justified (i.e., emerging or frontier economies). To determine an arm's length country risk premium, reference could be made to country credit default swap (CDS) rates. A CDS is a swap designed to transfer credit exposure of fixed-income products between two or more parties. It can be compared to an insurance as it provides the buyer of the contract, who often owns the underlying credit, with protection against default, a credit rating downgrade, or another negative 'credit event'. For the determination of an appropriate country risk premium, a comparison between the CDS rate of the borrower's country with the CDS rate of the countries of the borrowers in the selected comparable transactions. The difference is considered to reflect a country-specific risk premium.

## 8 Issuance Currency

Currency differences also play an important role when performing a comparability analysis. Economic factors such as growth rate, inflation rate, and the volatility of exchange rates, mean that otherwise similar financial instruments issued in different currencies may have different prices. Moreover, prices for financial instruments in the same currency may vary across financial markets or countries due to regulations such as interest rate controls, exchange rate controls, foreign exchange restrictions and other legal and practical restrictions on financial market access.[30] In general, loans issued in weak or unstable currencies that fluctuate significantly entail higher foreign currency exchange risks for both the lender and the borrower.

Table 12.7 provides an overview of the number of loan and bond transactions per currency.

*Table 12.7 Allocation of Loan and Bond Transactions Per Currency*

| *Issuance Currency* | *Loans (%)* | *Bonds (%)* |
|---|---|---|
| US Dollar | 90.6 | 52.7 |
| Euro | 5.6 | 10.6 |
| Indian Rupee | – | 0.2 |
| Thai Baht | – | 0.2 |
| Japanese Yen | 0.3 | 3.5 |
| Russian Ruble | – | 0.6 |
| Chinese Yuan | 0.1 | 18.2 |

30. *Ibid.*, para. 10.33.

| *Issuance Currency* | *Loans (%)* | *Bonds (%)* |
|---|---|---|
| Australian Dollar | 0.4 | 0.7 |
| Canadian Dollar | 0.9 | 3.0 |
| British Pound | 1.0 | 0.9 |
| Turkish Lira | – | 0.1 |
| Singapore Dollar | – | 0.1 |
| Swedish Krona | – | 2.6 |
| Norwegian Krone | – | 0.6 |
| Hong Kong Dollar | 1.0 | 0.2 |
| Indonesian Rupiah | – | 0.8 |
| New Zealand Dollar | 0.1 | 0.1 |
| Taiwanese Dollar | – | 1.0 |
| Mexican Peso | – | 0.1 |
| Mexican Unidad d'Inversion | – | 0.0 |
| South Korean Won | – | 3.4 |
| Swiss Franc | – | 0.3 |
| Israeli New Sheqel | – | 0.0 |
| Malaysian Ringgit | – | 0.1 |
| Hungarian Forint | – | 0.0 |
| Polish Zloty | – | 0.1 |
| South African Rand | – | 0.1 |
| Total | 100 | 100 |

*Sources*: LoanConnector for the loan transactions and EIKON for the bond transactions.

As can be seen from Table 12.7, the bonds sample under review includes transactions issued in 27 different currencies worldwide. During the examination period (September 2020 and September 2021), 52.7% of the bonds with information on YTRM and issuer's credit rating were issued in USD, 10.6% in EUR, 3.5% in JPY, 18.2% in CNY, 3.0% in CAD, 2.6% in SEK and 33.4% in KRW. Although for some of the remaining currencies, the number of transactions is limited to less than 10, the coverage of several different currencies is an advantage that cannot be ignored. Especially when compared to the respective coverage of loan transactions, whereby only 10 different currencies are included in the sample, out of which, the vast majority of the sample (90.6%) is USD-denominated loans, while only 5.6% have been issued in EUR and 3.8% have been issued in other currencies, including, among some others, CAD and GBP. This relative lack of data, especially in EUR loan transactions, may deem the bond approach to be more appropriate when analysing an intercompany loan denominated in EUR.

## 9 Secured Versus Unsecured

Another important factor when analysing an intercompany loan is whether it is secured by collateral or not[31] since the presence of collateral has direct impact on the quantum of the applied interest rate. In the case of a loan granted by the parent entity of a multinational enterprise (MNE) group to a subsidiary, the parent already has control and ownership of the subsidiary, which would make the granting of security less relevant to its risk analysis as a lender. Therefore, in evaluating the pricing of a loan between associated enterprises it is important to consider that the absence of contractual rights over the assets of the borrowing entity does not necessarily reflect the economic reality of the risk inherent in the loan. If the assets of the business are not already pledged as security elsewhere, it will be appropriate to consider under Chapter I analysis whether those assets are available to act as collateral for the otherwise unsecured intercompany loan and the consequential impact upon the pricing of the loan.[32]

Factors other than the existence of non-already-pledged collateral that should be considered before treating an unsecured intercompany loan as secured are regulatory constraints, such as minority shareholder protection rights and bankruptcy rules. For instance, if the subsidiary faces bankruptcy, there might be debt claims that have to be paid before the debt claim of the parent company. Hence, if the parent company has no explicit/contractual security (as the security is only deemed to exist for transfer pricing purposes), it might not recover any portion of the loan, especially if the deemed security is not recognized under the insolvency law of the particular country.[33]

In terms of third-party transactions, whether a loan/bond is secured or unsecured, is information that is always readily available for every transaction. Figures 12.3 and 12.4 illustrate the number of secured and unsecured loans and bonds, respectively, per credit rating.

31. *Ibid.*, para. 10.29.
32. *Ibid.*, para. 10.56.
33. A. Sulejmani, *Pricing Intercompany Financial Transactions: Loans, Guarantees and Cash-Pooling Arrangements*, International Transfer Pricing Journal, Volume 26, Issue 6 (2019).

*Figure 12.3 Number of Secured and Unsecured Loans Per Credit Rating*

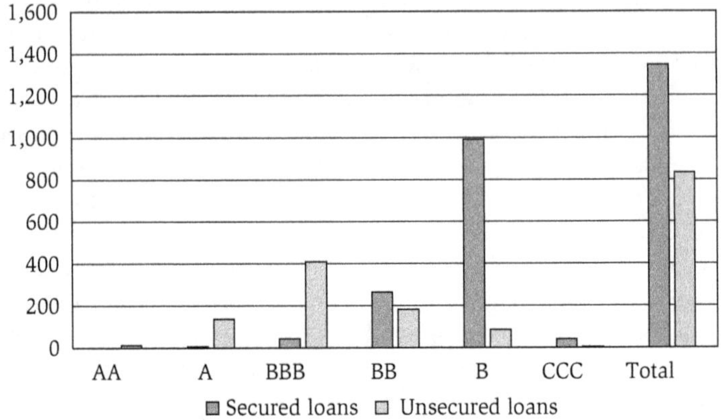


*Figure 12.4 Number of Secured and Unsecured Bonds Per Credit Rating*

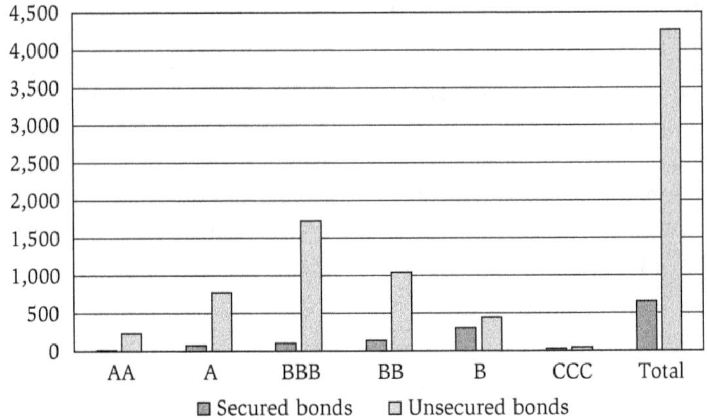


The analysis reveals that debt issuance between third parties is not always collateralized. When looking at the loans, there is a clear indication that the lower the credit rating, the greater the amount of secured loans relative to unsecured and vice versa. In the bond sample, there is no such obvious trend. However, when looking at the proportion of the secured bonds per credit rating, it also increases while moving towards the low credit ratings.[34] This relates to the fact that the credit rating of a borrower affects the likelihood of a loan being securitized.[35]

34. The increase in the proportion of secured debt.
35. T.D. Nadauld, *Did Securitization Affect the Cost of Corporate Debt?*, Journal of Financial Economics, Volume 105, Issue 2, 332-352 (2012).

A loan or bond provided to/by a/an borrower/issuer with a poor credit rating is perceived by independent lenders as an investment with a high-risk profile. As a result, the lender will most highly require a security, in the form of collateral, in order to mitigate the high risk. In other words, the probability (or necessity) of collateralization increases very strongly with the probability of default and with a reduction in creditworthiness, respectively.[36] From the borrower's perspective, a low-rated borrower may have no option but to pledge an asset as collateral in order to get affordable financing. On the other hand, companies with higher credit quality find secured credit less attractive. Such companies prefer, but also have the ability, not to provide collateral. Instead, they conserve it in order to have the flexibility to use it when it is truly needed, for example when unexpected adverse shocks hit.[37]

One example of a troubled firm that benefited from spare/unused collateral is Carnival Corporation, which operates cruise lines. Carnival had an investment grade rating before the pandemic hit, but was bleeding USD 1 billion of cash a month as cruise bookings fell off a cliff. A downgrade was imminent as the pandemic's consequences became apparent, and indeed Carnival was downgraded in June 2020 below investment grade and fell a few further notches subsequently. However, in April 2020, it managed a sale of USD 4 billion of bonds, backed by USD 28 billion of its ships. The Financial Times wrote, 'Carnival had so much freedom to pledge its assets because its investment-grade rating meant it was previously able to borrow freely on an unsecured basis.' Carnival has managed to avoid bankruptcy, in large part because of its unused collateral.[38]

The data both on loans and bonds as well as the example mentioned above illustrate that collateral is especially relevant for loans with relatively high risk. For loans with low risk, collateral is less relevant. In all cases, when assessing the impact of collateral, the interaction with other existing debt and the availability of collateral should be considered.

## 10 Type of Interest Rate[39]

An interest rate can be either fixed or floating. When pricing an intercompany loan with a floating interest rate, the loan approach may provide an abundance of potentially comparable transactions, as the vast majority of the loan transactions have floating rates. This is illustrated in Table 12.8.

36. F. Ebeling, N. Nolden & G. Schneider, *Are Bonds Suitable to Determine Arm's Length Interest Rates of Intercompany Loans and Do Intercompany Loans Have to Be Collateralized ? – An Empirical Investigation*, International Transfer Pricing Journal, Volume 28, Issue 6 (2021).
37. E. Benmelech, N. Kumar & E. Rajan, *The Decline of Secured Debt*, NBER Working Paper Series, Working Paper 26637 (2020).
38. E. Benmelech, N. Kumar & E. Rajan, *The Secured Credit Premium and the Issuance of Secured Debt*, NBER Working Paper Series, Working Paper 26799 (2021).
39. OECD TP Guidelines 2022, para. 10.29.

*Table 12.8 Fixed Versus Floating Interest Rates*

| *Base Rate* | *Share (Rounded) (%)* |
|---|---|
| LIBOR | 92.1 |
| Euribor | 5.3 |
| Other base rates | 2.4 |
| Fixed Rate | 0.2 |
| Total | 100.0 |

*Source*: LoanConnector.

Table 12.8 shows that the vast majority of the loans (92.1 %) have Libor as base rate, followed by loans with Euribor as base rate (5.3 %). This relates to the fact that the USD-denominated loan transactions dominate in the sample. It should be noted that Libor can be in various currencies other than USD, such as GBP and CAD. However, loan transactions with Libor as base rate issued in currencies other than USD are limited in the sample, representing only 2 % of the total amount of Libor transactions.

Notably, only 0.2 % of the loan transactions have a fixed rate. This could be explained that, from a lender's perspective, floating rates are perceived as less risky since they are changing in line with the prevailing market conditions. From a borrower's perspective, fixed rates are preferable since they provide more certainty. The borrower has locked in a specific rate which pays during the whole term loan. As a result, the borrower is not impacted by movements of interest rates (either positively or negatively).

An intercompany loan with a floating rate could also be benchmarked under the bond approach. However, in this case, an additional step of analysis is required, as the YTRM reflects the total rate of return (i.e., interest rate) of the bond, which combines compensation for both market and credit risk. To estimate the credit spread, the corresponding maturity money market rate should be deducted from the YTRM. Finally, the base rate should be added to the credit spread.

When pricing an intercompany loan with a fixed interest rate, the bond approach may be more appropriate due to the abundance of data and the fact that no further analysis to differentiate between the market risk and the credit risk component is required (assuming similar currencies, maturities, etc.).

## 11 Other Considerations

### *A Covenants*

The purpose of covenants in a loan agreement is generally to provide a degree of protection to the lender and so limit its risk, and therefore, it typically has the effect of reducing the interest rate, since it provides the lender with more security. Typically, and assuming all other factors that have an impact on the quantum of interest rate are similar, stricter covenants are accompanied by lower interest rates, while looser covenants are accompanied by higher interest rates.

Intra-group lenders may choose not to have covenants on loans to associated enterprises, partly because they are less likely to suffer information asymmetry and because it is less likely that one part of an MNE group would seek to take the same kind of action as an independent lender in the event of a covenant breach, nor would it usually seek to impose the same kind of restrictions. In the absence of covenants in any written agreement between the parties, it will be appropriate to consider whether there is, in practice, the equivalent of a maintenance covenant[40] between the parties and the consequential impact upon the pricing of the loan.[41]

Contrary to intra-group loan transactions, in reality, all the loan agreements concluded between unrelated parties include at least one covenant.[42] However, such information is not readily available in public loan databases. Of the loan transactions during the last five years with information on pricing and borrower's credit rating, 24.7% have information on financial covenants.

With regard to bonds, the covenant is a feature that is typically not common in bond issuances.[43] As a result, such information is not present in EIKON.

Quantifying the impact of a covenant in an intercompany loan may be challenging taking into account the very specific nature of each covenant and the relative lack of data on third-party loan transactions that include information on covenants. However, one could address the impact of the existence of a covenant by qualitatively assessing and analysing the specific characteristics of that covenant. As a next step, and assuming that the qualitative assessment indicates that the covenant in scope could indeed impact the quantum of the interest rate, one could for instance select a rate that is closer to the lower or the upper quartile of the median of the arm's length range, depending on the nature and the magnitude of the covenant as well as the characteristics of the comparable loan transactions.

### *B Issuer Versus Issuance Credit Rating*

According to the OECD TP Guidelines 2022, 'on prevailing facts and circumstances, and provided there is comparability between the third party debt issuance and the controlled transaction, when both an issuer and issue ratings are available, the issue rating of the particular debt issuance would be more appropriate to use to price the controlled financial transaction'.[44]

In most cases, the credit rating of a senior unsecured instrument should in most cases be in line with the overall credit rating of the issuer. There are some instances,

40. Maintenance covenant typically refers to financial indicators which have to be met at regular, predetermined intervals during the life of a covenanted loan.
41. OECD TP Guidelines 2022, paras 10.83-10.86.
42. M.R. Roberts & A. Sufi, *Control Rights and Capital Structure: An Empirical Investigation*, The Journal of Finance Volume 64, Issue 4, 1662 (2009).
43. C. Smith & J.B. Warner, *On Financial Contracting: An Analysis of Bond Covenants*, 7 Journal of Financial Economics 2, at pp. 117-161 (1979).
44. OECD TP Guidelines 2022, para. 10.83.

however, where the credit rating of an issued instrument may differ from the credit rating of the issuing company due to the fact that the credit risk of a financial instrument is linked to its specific features and not only to the risk profile of the borrowing company. [45] Those features include the level of seniority of the instrument and whether it is secured or not.[46]

Practical guidance on the rating of debt issuances is provided by Moody's,[47] according to which, for any given debt instrument, its rating should be measured relative to a baseline/reference rating of the issuer, which is typically based on senior unsecured financial obligations and contracts.[48] Consequently, in the case where an entity issues a senior secured debt instrument, the rating of that instrument should exceed the baseline rating of the issuing entity. Conversely, if the issuance relates to subordinated debt, the baseline credit rating should be notched downwards.

In terms of data availability, the use of the instrument's credit rating instead of the borrower's may result in more observations and more reliable results, especially in low credit ratings. The number of all active bond transactions with information on YTRM that are issued by corporate issuers (excluding financials) with a credit rating between CCC- and CCC+ is 329. The number of active bond transactions with information on YTRM that are themselves rated with a credit rating between CCC- and CCC+ is 795, which is more than double compared to the rated borrowers.

There are two reasons for this difference. First, an already overleveraged B-rated borrower with bad financial position that needs extra financing may not be able to raise more debt under terms and conditions that are representative of his credit rating. In order to get access to the financing, it may need to accept terms reflecting an even worse credit, for example, CCC in this case. Second, there may be unrated issuers or issuers whose credit rating has been withdrawn by the rating agencies but the credit rating of their instruments is still valid.

### C *Syndicated Loans*

One of the most notable disadvantages of the loan approach relates to the type of loan transactions included in the public databases. In reality, the vast majority of loan transactions are bilateral agreements that involve one borrower and one lender ('one to one'). This is not the case in the public loan databases whereby the vast majority of loan transactions with available data are syndicated loans,[49] which involve one borrower and various lenders ('one to many') (*see* Table 12.9).

45. *Ibid.*, para. 10.70.
46. *Ibid.*, para. 10.69.
47. Moody's Investors Service, Moody's Proposes Update to Notching Corporate Instrument Ratings Based on Differences in Security and Priority of Claim, July 2017.
48. Moody's Investors Service, Rating Symbols and Definitions, November 2021.
49. A typical syndicated loan is issued to a single borrower jointly by a group of lenders. These lenders are usually banks, but they can also include other financial institutions. Mandated by the borrower, a lead bank (or banks) promotes the loan to potential lenders that are interested in taking exposure in certain corporate borrowers. The lead arranger provides probable participants with a memorandum including borrower-specific information. Usually, each participant

*Table 12.9 Distribution of Loan Transactions Per Type of Loan*

| *Type of Loan* | *Last 1 Year (%)* | *Last 5 Years (%)* |
|---|---|---|
| Syndication | 88.0 | 90.3 |
| Club Deal | 10.0 | 8.2 |
| Bilateral | 0.7 | 0.7 |
| Other | 1.3 | 0.8 |
| Total | 100.0 | 100.0 |

*Source*: LoanConnector.

Table 12.9 shows that for both samples, the vast majority of the loans are syndicated (88.0% for the one-year period and 90.3% for the five-year period), followed by club deals, which are also a form of syndicated loans.

Benchmarking a bilateral intercompany loan with third-party syndicated loans may not be appropriate, since the spread of the syndicated loan will likely tend to be higher. Contrary to standard bilateral bank loan agreements, whereby the spread is determined based on the borrower's creditworthiness and other characteristics, in a syndicated loan, the spread may also incorporate a form of an additional premium,[50] which is not related to borrower's specific characteristics but compensates the participating banks for the adverse selection[51] and moral hazard risks[52] they incur.

## D Early Repayment Clauses

Early repayment is a common feature in all loan agreements. Early repayment can be either subject to penalty (call protected) or free from penalty (freely callable) based on the initial agreement between the two parties.[53] According to the OECD, 'commercial and industrial loans at banks tend to be freely callable';[54] in other words, no prepayment penalties exist. In addition, according to Practical Law Finance, 'many

funds the loan at identical conditions and is responsible for its particular share of the loan; it therefore has no legal responsibility for other participants' shares. Overall, syndicated loans lie somewhere between relationship (i.e. private) loans and public debt, where the lead bank may have some form of relationship with the borrower. *Source*: Y. Altunbas, A. Kara & D. Marqués-Ibáñez, *Large Debt Financing: Syndicated Loans Versus Corporate Bonds*, The European Journal of Finance, Volume 16, Issue 5 (2010).

50. V. Ivashina, *Asymmetric Information Effects on Loan Spreads*, Journal of Financial Economics, Volume 92, Issue 2, 300-319 (2009).
51. When participating in a syndicated loan, participant banks are highly dependent upon the information with regard to the borrower that is provided to them by the lead bank. This heavy reliance on the lead bank creates an adverse selection problem since the lead bank is incentivized to syndicate 'bad or risky' loans.
52. The moral hazard risk arises from the fact that after the lead bank sells parts of the loan to the participants, its motivation to effectively continue monitoring is declined.
53. Practical Law UK Practice Note, Corporate Loan Facilities, 1-107-4985, 6 (2016).
54. S.A. Lumpkin, *OECD, Financial Market Trends, The Integration of the Corporate Bond and Commercial Loan Markets* (2003).

loan agreements permit the borrower to voluntarily prepay all or part of the loans at any time without any premium or penalty'.[55] However, in some cases, there are specific conditions in which a prepayment penalty may apply. These include for example the type of lender and its own objectives or the type of deal. Typically, a prepayment fee is a feature generally associated with institutional term loans. This fee is seen mainly in weak markets as an inducement to institutional investors, such as Hedge funds.[56]

The early repayment clause in the majority of the cases is either not visible in the public loan databases or not available at all. Therefore, when there is a need to price such a feature, for intercompany loan transactions with an embedded early repayment option, the use of the loan approach may be challenging. The use of the bond approach can on the other hand be very useful in this case, as one of the main characteristics of many bonds is that they are callable; that is, they include provisions that allow the issuer to call, or prepay, the bond upon its discretion prior to maturity. When looking at the bonds sample under review, 61.4% are callable bonds.

The right to repay earlier the principal amount is an option often reserved by the bond issuers in order to preserve financial flexibility and to allow for opportunistic refinancing should interest rates drop. Since this option has the potential to lower the return to investors, investors will generally demand a higher yield on a callable bond compared to an equivalent non-callable bond to compensate for this risk, irrespective of the credit risk profile.

To check whether this argument is valid, two searches for callable and non-callable corporate bonds with similar terms and conditions were performed, one for EUR-denominated bonds and one for USD-denominated bonds. The following search criteria were applied:

(1) security status: Only active bonds;
(2) issuer's industry: All corporates excluding financials;
(3) remaining term to maturity: Between one and three years from the pricing date (i.e., 1 September 2021);
(4) seniority: Senior unsecured; and
(5) coupon type: Plain vanilla fixed coupon.[57]

Table 12.10 provides the results of the analysis.

55. Practical Law Practice Note, What's Market: Loan Prepayment Provisions, 0-501-5459, 6 (2016).
56. Standard & Poor's Global Ratings, *European Guide to the Loan Market* (4th edition), 20 (2010).
57. A bond may include several features and additional options, such as zero coupon or conversion to shares, that have impact on its yield. By only selecting plain vanilla fixed coupon bonds, which are considered the most straightforward and simple bonds, the likelihood the sample includes bonds with embedded features and options is minimized.

*Table 12.10 Interquartile Ranges of YTRM of Callable and Non-callable Bonds for Two Different Risk Categories and Currencies*

| *Bond Rating* | *Investment Grade* | | | |
|---|---|---|---|---|
| *Currency* | *EUR* | | *USD* | |
| YTRM (bps) | Callable | Non-Callable | Callable | Non-Callable |
| Lower | -5 | -23 | 92 | 73 |
| Median | 7 | -10 | 115 | 103 |
| Upper | 25 | 9 | 140 | 145 |
| Transactions | 235 | 201 | 773 | 598 |
| Bond rating | High yield | | | |
| Currency | EUR | | USD | |
| YTRM (bps) | Callable | Non-Callable | Callable | Non-Callable |
| Lower | 97 | 59 | 285 | 234 |
| Median | 182 | 92 | 541 | 344 |
| Upper | 409 | 228 | 958 | 904 |
| Transactions | 56 | 15 | 237 | 133 |

*Source*: EIKON.

As illustrated in Table 12.10, all quartiles (with exception of one) of both investment grade and high yield bonds and for both currencies are greater in callable bonds compared to non-callable ones.

### E *Duplicate Transactions*

One potential issue that may arise when using the bond approach is the existence of 'duplicate' transactions. For example, two or more bonds issued by the same issuer that have the same start date, currency, principal amount, coupon rate and maturity date should be treated as duplicates. Bonds are sometimes issued on various exchanges, for example in the United States and the Eurozone. Although they are considered separate transactions from a legal/exchange perspective, they are similar from an economic perspective and therefore they should be removed from the sample in order not to double count, which would result in distortion of the range.

## III CONCLUSION

There are various approaches to analyse and price an intercompany loan that can lead to a wide range of different results. The selection of the most appropriate approach should always be based on the prevailing facts and circumstances of each specific case and the availability of sufficient and reliable data. This chapter presented the two most commonly used approaches, namely the loan and the bond approach, and discussed the most important comparability factors and characteristics that should be considered when pricing an intercompany loan. In addition, various considerations and interpretations regarding the available data in relation to those characteristics as well as the potential advantages and disadvantages of the two approaches were discussed. From a comparability perspective, the loan approach could be perceived as more appropriate, since it compares the same instruments. However, from a practical standpoint, certain shortcomings of the loan approach, such as the relative lack of sufficient data on private loans, the timing differences in pricing and the complexity of loan transactions in terms of additional 'hidden' features that cannot be identified or filtered upon,[58] in combination with the abundance and quality of bonds data, have led transfer pricing practitioners to use more regularly the bond approach for transfer pricing analyses.

58. T. Petrakos, A. Pletz & V. Chad, *Interest Rate Benchmarking for Transfer Pricing Purposes: A Comparison Between the Loan and the Bond Approach*, International Transfer Pricing Journal, Volume 28, Issue 4 (2021).

CHAPTER 13

# Fixed Rate Loan Transactions: A Case Study

*Ralph Meghames, Bernardo Danesi, Diana Kabir & Amanda Pletz*[*]

## I INTRODUCTION

In its latest Transfer Pricing Guidelines[1] (also 'TPG' from here on out), the Organisation for Economic Co-operation and Development (OECD) highlighted the need for a comprehensive analysis of the commercial and financial relations among the parties involved in a loan transaction. It also recommended that such an analysis should consider the options realistically available to both the borrower and the lender in respect of a loan transaction.

As such, an analysis of loan transactions needs to be grounded in an appropriate analytical framework, especially with regard to the accurate delineation of the transaction(s). This means that a detailed analysis of the commercial and financial relations between parties is necessary – in particular, the functions performed, risks assumed, and assets owned. Another important point raised by the OECD is that it considers the actual conduct of the parties to the transaction to depict the relevant facts, as opposed to the terms of written agreements. In absence of such rigorous analysis, tax administrations may deny or adjust deductions associated with loan transactions or, in some cases, even requalify the entire transaction.

The analytical framework pertaining to intercompany financing transactions is identical to any other intercompany transaction falling under the arm's length principle. As such, the principles laid out in Chapters I-III of the OECD TPG are applied to

---

* The views and opinions set forth herein are the personal views or opinions of the authors; they do not necessarily reflect the views or opinions of the organisation with which the authors are associated.

1. OECD, *OECD Transfer Pricing Guidelines for Multinational Enterprises and Tax Administrations*, OECD (January 2022), https://doi.org/10.1787/0e655865-en.

ultimately assess the interest rate, fee or commission that remunerates lenders at arm's length.

The analytical framework starts with an understanding of the roles and responsibilities of the parties, in light of the functions they perform, risks they bear and assets they own as well as the value chain of the multinational enterprise (MNE). This is done in the specific context of the intercompany transaction under review.

At the same time, it is fundamental to thoroughly review the terms and conditions of the transaction. The terms and conditions play a critical role in determining what the arm's length remuneration for the parties involved would be, as many features in loan contracts can be associated with price premia or discounts. While some loan terms such as the maturity of the transaction, its currency, etc., are relatively straightforward to account for, some others require more attention. This is the case, for yield structures (e.g., fixed, floating, payment in kind), subordination, and prepayment terms, among others.

The next step to any financing transaction analysis is a credit assessment of the borrower, i.e., the assessment of an entity's ability to meet its financial obligations in full and on time. In practice, the credit rating assessment can be seen as one of the comparability factors to be considered in order to price the transaction.

It is only after carefully examining the facts and circumstances surrounding the transaction that choosing and applying the pricing methodology can be initiated. In line with both the OECD guidelines and the UN manual, [2] given the availability of information, the Comparable Uncontrolled Price (CUP) method is usually applied when evaluating intercompany loan arrangements.[3] In the remainder of this chapter, we show how the above-described analytical framework can be applied in the context of a fixed-rate loan transaction.

## II THE CASE STUDY

For the purpose of this case study, we consider the hypothetical situation of a United Kingdom (UK)-based industrial company ('the Group'), with the headquarters ('HeadCo') hosting intercompany treasury activities. HeadCo routinely provides financing to its subsidiaries worldwide, such as long-term loans.

Recently, to finance new research and development activities, the French affiliate ('FrenchCo') of the Group requested financing from HeadCo in the form of a 10-year intercompany fixed-rate loan. This comes in the context of the Group's and FrenchCo's strategy to diversify its activities and develop products with lower environmental impact.

2. Committee of Experts on International Cooperation in Tax Matters, *Update of the United Nations Practical Manual on Transfer Pricing for Developing Countries*, Chapter B.9 on Intra-group Financial Transactions, para. 3.2.5.
3. OECD, *OECD Transfer Pricing Guidelines for Multinational Enterprises and Tax Administrations*, OECD (January 2022), https://doi.org/10.1787/0e655865-en, para. 10.90.

## 1 Functional Analysis

A company's funding strategy is usually driven by what is deemed to be an appropriate capital structure for commercial purposes. Capital structure varies depending on, among others, the specific industry and competitive landscape, product life cycles, business strategies, transaction costs, etc. Hence the first step in addressing questions relating to financing, and in particular loans, is to analyse and understand what drives value in the Group, the role that financing plays in this process, and how the respective entities involved fit into the transaction. In this context, understanding the activities performed by the various entities and the risks assumed, as well as their ownership and usage of assets (both tangible and intangible) are essential. Furthermore, the regulatory environment in which an entity and/or the MNE operates should be considered. Certain regulatory guidelines may affect a borrower's preferences for certain types and levels of funding, thereby influencing the potential options a borrower may realistically consider, such as bank debt, market debt, mezzanine financing, or other hybrid forms of funding.

### *A The Value Chain of the Group*

In the case at hand, the success of market players of the industry in which the Group operates is determined by how well they satisfy their customers' frequently changing needs and how efficiently they can manufacture their products. An assumed description of the determined industry value chain is depicted in Figure 13.1.

*Figure 13.1 Industry Value Chain*

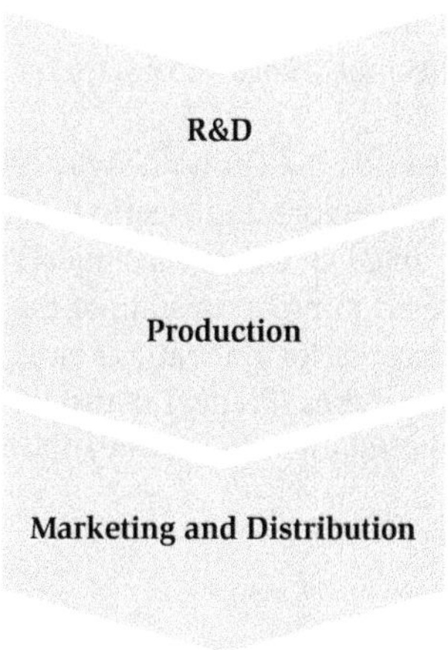


In this industry it is imperative for brands to differentiate themselves to attract customers. Research and Development (R&D) efforts are therefore essential to help marketers increase brand awareness, enhance products appeal, and draw the eye of discerning consumers with innovative production techniques.

Most products are commoditised and switching costs between suppliers tend to be low. In such contexts, production is a key function that allows the company to offer quality products and low prices through production costs reductions.

The group sells its solutions either directly to customers or rely on third-party distributors. In the former case, the Group generally provides a service that includes some level of customisation to the clients' needs. Ensuring high levels of customer services on an integrated basis is important in a cost-driven environment as it helps differentiate companies from one another.

### *B The Functions, Assets, and Risks of the Group*

#### *a The Functions*

The Group is generally organised into three segments. Each operating segment has its own sales and marketing staff located regionally. Large contracts may be centrally negotiated, but products are typically manufactured and distributed by the local manufacturing facilities, which are generally located in close proximity to the division's major customers, particularly when products are too costly and inefficient to ship. All production is scheduled to meet customer requirements based on estimates of product and quantity requirements agreed with each customer.

HeadCo is responsible for the main treasury activities of the Group throughout Europe. These functions include funding activities, cash pooling, foreign exchange risk and commodity risk management and management of intercompany guarantees. The Group treasurer and the financial analysis team are both hosted by HeadCo.

To assist with day-to-day operations and to provide funding for growth opportunities, HeadCo enters into various cross-border intra-group transactions with its affiliates. HeadCo also provides short-, medium-, and long-term intra-group funding to related entities. When subsidiaries need funds, they will file a request with HeadCo, who will assess their need on a case-by-case basis. Collating this information on a global basis, HeadCo uses this to anticipate the funds it requires from the external market and tends to use a mixture of bank loans and commercial paper to raise funds. HeadCo has relationships with a few key external banks and will borrow funds from the bank offering the most competitive rate at that time.

FrenchCo is the largest subsidiary that the Group has in Continental Europe and it operates as an important manufacturing and R&D hub for Europe. FrenchCo's activities include undertaking logistics and manufacturing for other countries in the area, and sales activities for the French and Belgian markets. FrenchCo is a well-established entity that was set up decades ago and has become a core subsidiary for the entire Group's operations.

As mentioned, FrenchCo has a dedicated R&D area that the Group heavily relies on to maintain its competitive advantage vis-à-vis its competitors and ensure that it is keeping up with technological advancements. Its well-trained and highly technical staff have a deep level of industry knowledge and are devoted to creating state-of-the-art products as well as improvements to manufacturing processes. Its innovations and best practices are shared with the Group's other manufacturing sites. FrenchCo also works with these entities to implement the changes making its role within the organisation key to the continued success of the Group.

#### *b Assets*

In respect of intangible assets utilised, an important one related to financing transactions is the know-how accumulated in the treasury team. The staff holding this knowledge are located in the UK and are employees of HeadCo. In addition, there are back and middle office staff supporting the front office employees in carrying out treasury functions. The necessary technology systems are in place to manage and execute such transactions and HeadCo has established relationships with external banks. As such, the front office employees are responsible for foreign exchange risk management, commodities hedging, and cash pooling. The back-office employees are responsible for controlling, confirming, and settling any executed transactions and maintaining consistency with the bank documentation. In short, the treasury department at HeadCo is developed and knowledgeable in all aspects related to financing transactions.

FrenchCo has a variety of tangible and intangible assets. Tangible assets include its office space, physical equipment and machinery to carry out the manufacturing of the goods. Intangible assets include specialised know-how regarding the technical manufacturing tools used, the technical skills for R&D as well as bespoke and ingrained knowledge of its markets. FrenchCo also owns the local trademarks in the markets in which it distributes the products. FrenchCo has sufficient assets on its balance sheet to carry debt.

### *c* *Risks*

The key risks HeadCo is exposed to in the loan agreements are described below.

**Strategic Risks: Market Risk**

Market factors such as future competition, market conditions and other regulatory and political factors can impact the credit quality of the borrower. In the context of a fixed-rate loan, any foreseeable interest rate increases due to market conditions or a reduction in credit rating of the borrower creates a risk for the lender who will bear the opportunity cost associated with the interest rate. However, if interest rates are expected to decline (or the credit quality of the borrower increase), then the lender is protected by avoiding a decrease in interest rate payments in line with the lower interest rate (or higher rating). In general, the market volatility of interest rates (or changes in credit standing) creates a non-negligible risk for the parties to the transaction.

**Financial Risks: Credit Risk**

Two main factors need to be considered when evaluating the credit risk of a borrower. These are (i) the borrower's likelihood of default and (ii) the potential loss suffered by the lender conditional on the borrower's default.

Taking the characteristics of the financing transactions into account, the repayment is dependent on the borrower's income. Thus, the repayments of the debt and debt interest are subject to the customers honouring their payments. In the event that customers default, the borrower is at risk of not being able to pay its full interest on debt obligations and principal payments on the debt.

FrenchCo's income is dependent on its own ability to service customers effectively and use its track record to attract new ones while managing its own risks. These risk factors may include operational risks stemming from potential issues with the manufacturing processes or compliance with consumer regulations, strategic risks related to investments made into unsuccessful new technologies, and counterparty risks, all of which may influence FrenchCo's ability to generate income and therefore the credit risk in the transaction at hand.

In summary, all of the above considerations, including the value chain and industry, the functional profile, as well as assets and risks influence the credit standing of a local company and the type (and amount) of funding that may be realistically available to it at any given point in time.

## 2 Analysis of the Terms of the Transaction

Companies can choose among a wider range of financing options which include several types of financial instruments with varying terms and conditions. Nevertheless, depending on facts and circumstances, only a subset of instruments or terms may be realistically available. The OECD guidelines note that a transaction is only entered into if it is the most appropriate and attractive option to meet its financial needs when compared to the other options realistically available.[4] Thus, in addition to the functional analysis described above, several aspects need to be considered, including its size, its purpose, its timing, as well as the structure of the balance sheet. All these factors (among others) would affect the type of funding that may be appropriate, as well as the applicable rate of the transaction.

In the case at hand, the terms of the transaction are as follows:

- Lender: Headquartered in the UK ('HeadCo')
- Borrower: FrenchCo ('FrenchCo')
- Notional amount and currency: EUR 300,000,000
- Issue date: 10 October 2020
- Repayment features: Interest accrues quarterly, but it is capitalised and paid yearly on coupon day.[5] Capital is repaid on maturity. Borrower can pre-pay at any time with no benefit nor penalty
- Maturity date: 10 years
- Interest rate: 3% fixed rate.

The level of funding a lender is willing to extend, and the terms associated with that funding, are partly (if not largely) driven by the lender's capability and willingness to take on risk. This can vary from lender to lender and between different types of funding arrangements.

An analysis of FrenchCo's balance sheet and external market options is appropriate to determine whether a similar transaction may be carried out in the open

4. OECD, *OECD Transfer Pricing Guidelines for Multinational Enterprises and Tax Administrations*, OECD (January 2022), https://doi.org/10.1787/0e655865-en., para. 10.19.
5. Over a fiscal year, three quarterly interest payments are capitalised. There is one interest payment yearly occurring on coupon day.

market. In other words, FrenchCo's debt and equity structure, and assets available will influence the funding options it realistically can access in the market.

## 3 Credit Risk Assessment

To determine the arm's length terms and conditions that will be associated with a loan transaction, it is critical to understand the level of default risk. Default risk is typically determined through a credit risk assessment.

As described, this assessment dictates an entity's ability to fully and timely satisfy its financial obligations (issuer rating). In open market transactions between two or more third parties, often a credit rating is required (either a standalone rating of the borrower or a Group credit rating) for each contracting party to the transaction and sometimes such ratings are made publicly available. However, in the context of intercompany financing transactions, such an analysis may not have been carried out previously.

In such instances, an analysis known as a shadow credit rating can be performed to estimate this level of default risk, relative to the borrower and the transaction itself. Credit rating methodologies published by credit rating agencies (e.g., S&P, Fitch, Moody's, etc.) can be applied to the borrowing entity to understand the level of default risk embedded in the transaction. This analysis includes an assessment of both quantitative and qualitative factors relative to the entity being assessed. Once a standalone credit rating has been produced, additional analyses may follow that can notch up or down the shadow credit rating by considering other factors such as implicit support, sovereign credit rating ceilings, and subordination of the financial instrument.

For the purpose of this case study, a credit rating for the entire Group had been performed by Moody's in early 2020 and was given as Ba2 (corresponding to BB in Fitch/S&P rating). A standalone shadow rating (before considering factors such as implicit support) of FrenchCo was determined to be Ba3. To establish the standalone credit rating for FrenchCo, we applied a similar methodology published by a major rating agency.

We also considered the implicit support of being a part of a larger group and its impact on the entity's credit rating. This review can be based on criteria listed by the global rating agencies. For example, S&P published a methodology dated July 2019, that describes the impact of implicit support on the standalone credit rating.[6] It is imperative to use the latest methodology available at the time of the transaction (in this case at the time of the loan issuance) so the analysis can be conducted to reflect the most recent data available and market conditions at that time.

In cases where a subsidiary holds strategic value for the group, S&P recommends 'notching up' the standalone credit rating of the subsidiary or potentially equating the subsidiary's credit rating to the group credit rating. On the opposite side of the

6. Standard & Poor's Global Ratings Global Market Intelligence, General Criteria: Group Rating Methodology, 1 July 2019.

spectrum, if a subsidiary holds no strategic value to the group, the recommendation is to use its standalone rating.

As previously described in the functions, assets, and risk analysis, FrenchCo is strategically important to the Group, due to its involvement in most R&D activities as well as designing the manufacturing process for all other plants within the MNE organisation. Based on this assessment, a one-notch adjustment would be warranted at a minimum, if not an equalisation of ratings with the Group rating. In our case, the Group credit rating is only one notch up from the standalone credit rating. As a result, we conclude that a Ba2 rating is appropriate for FrenchCo.

### A *Subordination*

In this context, it is useful to draw a distinction between issuer credit rating and instrument credit rating. The issuer credit rating is determined by carrying out the standalone credit rating and then adjusting this for implicit support. Once the issuer credit rating is assessed, one should consider the seniority of the loan issued and whether an adjustment to the issuer rating is required. Debt subordination impacts the likelihood of recovering borrowed funds in the case of borrower default. As a result, it should impact the rating of the debt itself. The diagram below shows a typical seniority structure for company liabilities or also referred to as a debt waterfall.

*Figure 13.2 Hierarchy of Debt Instruments*

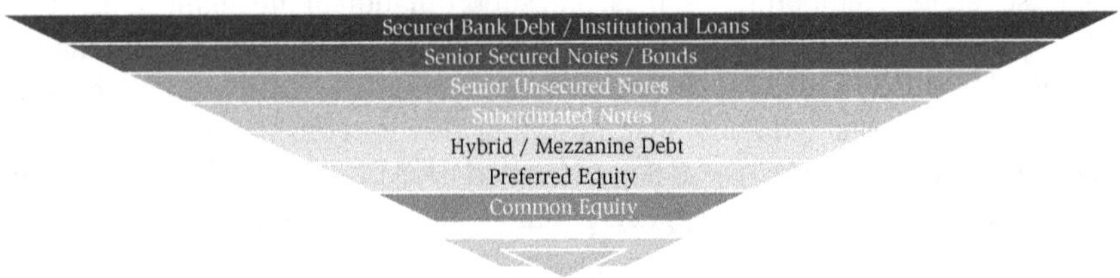


The issuer rating and the issue rating coincide in cases where the debt issued is senior unsecured (in most cases). In other words, a tranche of debt can remain unadjusted if it is senior unsecured. If the debt that is being analysed has a different level of seniority, an adjustment may be in order. Table 13.1 shows Moody's recommendations for notching debt on the basis of its seniority.

*Table 13.1 Moody's Notching Criteria Based on Seniority of Debt*[7]

| *Seniority* | *Notches* | *Additional Description* |
|---|---|---|
| Senior Secured Debt | +1 / +2 | Plus one notch for issuers rated Baa3 or higher. Plus one to two notches for issuers rated Ba1 or lower and reliable bankruptcy regime. |
| Senior Unsecured Debt | 0 | |
| Subordinated Debt | -1/-2 | For issuers rated Ba1 or lower, minus two notches if deeply subordinated and reliable bankruptcy regime. Otherwise, minus one notch. |
| Junior Subordinated Debt | -1/-2 | For issuers rated Ba1 or lower, minus two notches if deeply subordinated and reliable bankruptcy regime. Otherwise, minus one notch. |
| Preferred Stock | -2 | Minus two notches also applies to junior-most hybrid securities that may include both debt and equity characteristics. However, if a junior-most hybrid includes mandatory coupon skip triggers, then minus three notches. |

Following a review of the borrower's annual accounts for the year of the loan issuance, this showed FrenchCo had no other outstanding debt on the balance sheet. In addition, given the capital structure of the Group, the loan under review is not subordinated and therefore no adjustment needs to be made to the issuer credit rating, which coincides with the issue credit rating for this loan.

### *B Conclusion to the Credit Risk Assessment*

A review of the sovereign credit ratings of the UK and France also does not impact the credit rating established for FrenchCo and therefore no adjustment is necessary in this respect.

As a result, we estimate the credit rating that FrenchCo as well as its senior unsecured notes would obtain in the market to be Ba2. In this review, we evaluated public information about the Group in the form of a rating decision by Moody's, as well as issues of implicit support and subordination to obtain the final rating for the borrower of the loan transaction.

7. Moody's Investor Services, Notching Corporate Instrument Ratings Based on Differences in Security and Priority of Claim, Moody's, October 2017. https://www.moodys.com/researchandratings/research-type/methodologies-frameworks/-/003006/003006/-/-1/0/-/0/-/-/-/-/-/-/-/-/global/pdf/-/rra.

## 4 Pricing

### A *Method Selection*

When it comes to pricing a financial instrument, a major contributor in selecting which is the most appropriate transfer pricing method is data availability. As per the OECD Guidelines and given the usually greater access to data, it may be easier to apply the CUP method when evaluating loan arrangements in comparison to other transactions.[8] Nevertheless, in some instances, the combination of credit rating and maturity might render its application problematic, due to a lack of available market data. This more commonly occurs where the credit rating determined is below investment grade and/or the maturity of the tested transaction is not often seen in the open market (especially in Europe where transactions are more commonly private). This bears the question of the arm's length nature of the transaction as well as the options realistically available and will need to be considered in the analysis.

Under the CUP method, there are two possible applications, the internal CUP which considers transactions between the tested entity (or a group member of the tested entity) and a third party. The other option is the external CUP which relies entirely on market data conducted among third parties. The most common type of data relied upon for an external CUP is yield data which can be based on bond indices or portfolios of individual bonds. This type of data is available through platforms such as Bloomberg L.P. or FactSet. Alternatively, private loan data or syndicated loan data from alternate sources such as Thomson Reuters LoanConnector or S&P's Leveraged Commentary & Data can also be relied upon. While loan yields may be preferable to bond yields in terms of comparability, it is generally more difficult to source data regarding the former as most loan arrangements are not in the public domain or only limited information is available involving individual transactions.

Finally, credit default swaps can be a reliable source of comparable data. However, when available, its comparability hinges on the definition of a credit event, and how it compares to the terms and conditions regarding default in the tested transaction's loan documents.

Included in the analysis, adjustments may need to be performed to the data if there are material differences between the tested transaction and the market data used that could affect the interest rate that is charged. This could be a result of applying a country adjustment to account for differences in political and economic conditions, currency adjustments for using market data in a different currency to the tested transactions or to adjust for different/exotic features of the loan (e.g., prepayment options, fixed vis-à-vis floating interest rate, hybrid features, etc.)

8. OECD, *OECD Transfer Pricing Guidelines for Multinational Enterprises and Tax Administrations*, OECD (January 2022), https://doi.org/10.1787/0e655865-en Paragraph 10.90.

### B Sourcing of Data for Analysis

The first step is to find suitable CUP data to be used in the analysis. Based on this data and any potential adjustments, it aims to determine the range of arm's length interest rates that would apply to the loan being lent by HeadCo to FrenchCo based on the characteristics of the loan and the borrower.

As presented above, FrenchCo has a shadow credit rating (considering implicit support) of Ba2 (equivalent to BB in the S&P rating scale) at the time of the loan issuance. To estimate the arm's length interest rates, we use index data. Such data can be sourced from multiple data platforms such as Bloomberg L.P., EIKON, FactSet, etc.

The transaction under review is a 10-year fixed-rate loan in EUR. Therefore, the most comparable data would be EUR-based individual bond data or index data composed of 10-year instruments that are rated BB. However, upon performing the search for such data, we find little publicly available data for below investment grade bonds in Europe. United States (US)-based companies are more likely to rely on the public bond markets to raise debt compared to European companies which often use bank loans or private placements. As a result, the US market generally provides more data to carry out this type of analysis. We therefore search for US bond yield curves in comparable industry segments. Based on this search we obtained yield data for a 10-year BB-rated USD Index issued by industrial companies.[9]

For the above index (and subsequent fixed income indices sourced), the data analysed must refer to the same time periods. Therefore, we obtain the price data for the three months preceding the loan issuance date (i.e., 10 October 2020). We find that a three-month period of data provides enough data points to give an appropriate indication of market rates and conditions at the time of the transaction[10] whilst not being too wide whereby market conditions no longer reflect the time in which the loan was granted. The relevant period to rely upon would potentially be based on the prevailing market conditions at the transaction date and one may consider extending or reducing the time period based on the specific facts and circumstances.

### C Deriving a Comparable EUR Rate

From a theoretical point of view, the full interest rate charged captures the risk-free reference rate, which remunerates the time value of money as well as an additional margin (or spread) remunerating the lender for the credit risk that it bears and for its administrative functions related to the issuance of the loan. Therefore, as part of our analysis, the spread that we calculate using a BB-rated instrument needs to be added to the appropriate risk-free rate. An appropriate risk-free rate needs to match the currency and the maturity of the tested loan. In addition, the cost of debt in a certain country is heavily affected by the political and economic conditions in the market issuing said

9. It is advisable when sufficient data on individual bonds are available to rely on such data instead of broad-based indices. For the purpose of this article, we assume that such a review was conducted, and index data (and its constituents) was determined to be the most representative.
10. The mentioned databases offer daily end-of-day yield/price data for their fixed income indices.

debt. There are many factors that contribute to varying costs of debt across different countries/markets: the central bank's borrowing rates are the main factors, but general, political, and economic risks also play a large role. The data that we collected are US indices in USD for the same maturity and credit profile of the tested transaction. Therefore, two factors need to be considered:

- the risk-free rate of the transaction should reflect the French or, if appropriate, the European market;
- the differences with respect to the money market conditions and currency, i.e., differences in rates between USD and EUR, need to be accounted for.

### *a* *Risk-Free Rate Considerations Between the US and Europe*

To account for the various economic and political differences between a US-based transaction and a French transaction, we use government bonds as a proxy for risk-free rates. More specifically we estimate the USD and EUR risk-free rates using the yields of government bonds issued in those currencies and with the same maturity i.e., 10 years. Indices averaging out yields of government bonds can be sourced from the same platforms mentioned above. Thus, we replace the benchmark's US-based risk-free rate component with the EUR-sourced rates. It should be noted for the purpose of this illustration we have made the assumption that the European index is representative of the local French market.

Table 13.2 shows how we mathematically substitute risk-free rates to ensure comparability.

*Table 13.2 Replacing the Risk-Free Rate*

| *Instrument* | *Procedure Explanation* |
|---|---|
| Euro Govt 10-Year Yield | [1] |
| US Govt 10-Year Yield | [2] |
| **Risk-free rate adjustment from the US to Europe** | **[3] = [1]-[2]** |

### *b* *Determining the Impact of Differences in Currency*

The index selected is comparable in terms of its industry and credit rating to the tested loan. However, the index that we selected is denominated in USD, while the tested loan is denominated in EUR.

To account for specificities of the European or French Market one not only need to account for varying risk-free rates between the US and France but also differences in currency. The Currency adjustment considers the specificities of each currency, which may lead to potential differences in the way financial assets are priced in different currencies. To do this, we look at the difference between corporate bond yield spreads observed in EUR currency versus USD currency.

Although numerous methodologies can be relied upon including looking at currency swap transactions, a simplified approach to proxy such an adjustment and that we demonstrate consists of comparing available yield spreads for similar indices, ratings, and maturities between the two currencies. The closest rating for which similar comparable data in both currencies can be obtained should ideally rely upon this approach. The underlying assumption of this approach is that the currency adjustment is linear across all ratings. [11]

In practice, to estimate a currency adjustment, the following formula can be applied as an example.

*Currency Adjustment = (EUR BBB 10-year Index – EUR Government Bond Yield 10-year Index) – (USD Industrial BBB 10 year Index – US Government Bond Yield 1 Year Index)*

The formula above calculates the corporate credit spread for both the original currency of the comparable indices and the currency of the tested transaction, ultimately substituting the former for the latter.

To further illustrate this adjustment, Table 13.3 includes all the indices used and a step-by-step procedure to derive the adjusted rate. As mentioned above, these calculations are performed for each day in the 3-month date range.

*Table 13.3 Currency and Country Adjustment Summary*

| *Instrument* | *Procedure Explanation* |
|---|---|
| EUR BBB 10-Year | [1] |
| EUR Government Rate 10 Year | [2] |
| EUR Spread | [3] = [1]-[2] |
| USD BBB 10-Year | [4] |
| USD Government Rate 10 Year | [5] |
| USD Spread | [6] = [4]-[5] |
| **USD to EUR Currency Adjustment** | **[7] = [3]-[6]** |
| **Adjusted Rate** | **Europe Risk-Free rate adjusted yield + Currency Adjustment** |

This adjusted rate now reflects market conditions in the European market for a EUR-denominated instrument. As described for the purpose of illustration we have made some key assumptions that the European market data is representative of the

11. In other words, in our case study, we have used BBB indices as these are the closest available data to the credit rating of the tested transaction (BB). Under the above-mentioned assumption, i.e., that the credit spreads across currencies are linear across credit ratings. That is the spreads calculated for BBB transactions in both currencies are the same, or similar enough, to the BB credit spread we are trying to estimate.

French market. In practice, careful consideration should be applied to the comparability of the data, as well as any assumption made to arrive at the arm's length interest rate.

### D *Other Considerations*

As discussed earlier, there may be reasons why additional adjustments could be required to increase the comparability between the tested transaction and the comparables used.

#### a *Prepayments*

In this case, the loan extended to FrenchCo has no exotic features for which adjustments are necessary. Regarding the prepayment feature, it is common practice to include prepayment provisions in loan agreements, and in the majority of cases, such prepayment options are neither subject to penalty nor premium upon prepayment, nor does it have an impact on loan pricing.

Nevertheless. market evidence suggests that a small portion of loans are call protected (hence include some sort of penalty); the majority of such agreements are loans with institutional investors' participation or require specific conditions to be met before triggering the prepayment penalty. Only in rare cases do these loan agreements request unconditional penalties or premiums, and such agreements normally have substantially lower nominal agreement values than the tested loan agreement. Given the facts and circumstances of the tested loan transaction, no prepayment adjustment is needed.

#### b *Upfront Fees*

Also, no adjustment is required for the tested loan having a fixed-interest rate as we are not using other executed loans as comparables but index data instead. The comparable indices that we use to benchmark the loan also present their yields as 'all-in' fees which are composed of a risk-free reference rate plus a credit margin. As a result, the interest rates compiled are comparable in terms of rate composition.

#### c *Illiquidity*

The last adjustment that needs to be applied to obtain comparability between the comparables and the tested transaction is an illiquidity adjustment. The tested transaction is a private facility that cannot be traded as easily in the open market as a bond would. The illiquidity premium considered is specific to medium-term instruments

(5-10 years) with a credit rating of BB and is based on the closest available premia observed in the market; it corresponds to 127 bps.[12]

### E Arm's Length Interest Rate

Table 13.4 shows the estimated arm's length rate for the loan transaction. The data below is purely hypothetical for illustration purposes and was not sourced from any particular database.

*Table 13.4 Loan 4 Final Ranges*

| | *Rate after Risk-Free Rate and Currency Adjustment* | *Illiquidity Premium* | *Total Adjusted Rate* | *Tested Rate* |
|---|---|---|---|---|
| | [1] | [2] | [3] = [1] + [2] | [4] |
| | (%) | (%) | (%) | (%) |
| **Minimum** | **0.920** | 1.273 | **2.193** | **3.000** |
| Median | 2.199 | | 3.472 | |
| **Maximum** | **3.845** | | **5.118** | |

As noted from the above analysis the total adjusted yield ranges from 2.19% (the minimum) to 5.12% (the maximum) and a median of 3.47%. Given that bond data is traded data all market data relied upon is equally comparable. In addition, the data relied upon are indices which in itself is already a weighted average of the constituent bonds included in the index. For these reasons the entire range as opposed to the interquartile range can be relied upon as a benchmarking range. As such, the fixed-term interest rate of 3.0% is within the arm's length range.

## III CONCLUSION

In this article, we detail the analytical framework pertaining to intercompany financing transactions. We show how understanding the value chain and roles and responsibilities of the parties as well as the terms and conditions of the transaction play a critical part in determining what the arm's length remuneration for the borrower should be.

Also, we give a step-by-step method with which to analyse fixed-rate loan transactions. Nonetheless, this framework can be applied to any other type of financing transaction, having described how to account for the different loan characteristics that

12. Illiquidity and Credit Premia for IFRS 17 at End December 2018, Moody's Analytics, May 2019, p. 9. The document used data for investment grade instruments only. We estimated the expected illiquidity premium for BB instruments using a regression analysis.

may have an impact on the arm's length interest rate, such as subordination, currency, up-front fees, and other modalities.

Most importantly, understanding the purpose of the loan and the nature of the relationship between the parties is important to ensure effective delineation of the transaction.

CHAPTER 14

# Floating Rate Loan Transaction: A Case Study

*Stefanie Perrella & Zachary Held**

## I INTRODUCTION

This chapter is intended to describe, using an illustrative case study, important considerations when performing a transfer pricing analysis for an intercompany floating rate loan. In practice, the exact steps taken in performing the analysis will vary based on the facts and circumstances of the loan under review, including, notably, the applicable regulatory guidance based on the tax jurisdictions of the legal entities involved in the transaction. This case study will make a simplifying assumption that the analysis should adhere to the guidance from the Organisation for Economic Co-operation and Development (OECD) Transfer Pricing Guidelines for Multinational Enterprises and Tax Administrations (the "OECD Guidelines"), as it is the most widely relied upon source of guidance by taxing authorities worldwide (though specific interpretations of the less prescriptive sections of the guidance may vary). The OECD Guidelines are inclusive of the Transfer Pricing Guidance on Financial Transactions: Inclusive Framework on BEPS Actions 4, 8-10, (the "Financial Transactions Guidance") which were issued on February 12, 2020.[1]

The Financial Transactions Guidance in some ways reshaped the requirements for an intercompany loan analysis and as such taxpayers and practitioners have

* The views and opinions set forth herein are the personal views or opinions of the authors; they do not necessarily reflect the views or opinions of the organization with which the authors are associated.

1. The Financial Transactions Guidance which will be henceforth included in the OECD Guidelines as Chapter X and as additional language in Chapter I. As such, references to the OECD Guidelines generally are considered to be inclusive of the Financial Transactions Guidance.

adjusted their approaches for financial transactions transfer pricing accordingly. These components can be broadly categorized into the following requirements:

- identify the characteristics of the loan (including of the borrower);
- perform a functional analysis to understand the respective functions, risks, and assets of all parties to the intercompany loan;
- ensure the accurate delineation of the loan as debt; and
- establish an arm's-length range of pricing (e.g., interest rate and other fees, as appropriate).

The remainder of this case study will describe each of these considerations in detail.

## II IDENTIFY THE CHARACTERISTICS OF THE LOAN

The characteristics of the loan under review will have a material bearing on both the accurate delineation of the instrument as debt as well as the determination of an arm's-length rate of interest. Characteristics can refer to the terms of the loan as well as the characteristics of the borrower of the loan and the context of the decision to enter into the loan transaction.

### 1 The Terms of the Loan

The terms of the loan agreement can be crucial for assessing the accurate delineation of the loan as debt as well as the arm's-length interest rate for the loan. For example, the tenor of the loan is a key variable in benchmarking an arm's-length interest rate because, all else equal, in a normal interest rate environment, a loan with a longer time to maturity will generally command a higher interest rate to compensate for the increased default risk. Similarly, a contractual fixed maturity date is referenced in the OECD Guidelines as being a potentially useful characteristic for accurately delineating an instrument as debt for tax purposes.[2] *Table* 14.1 presents certain key terms for the hypothetical loan that will be reviewed as part of the case study, herein referred to as the "Subject Loan."

*Table 14.1 Characteristics of the Subject Loan*

| *Subject Loan* | |
|---|---|
| Borrower | BorrowCo (referred to as the "Borrower") |
| Lender | LendCo (referred to as the "Lender") |
| Issuance Date | December 15, 2021 |
| Tenor | Ten years |
| Currency Denomination | Euros |

2. Financial Transactions Guidance, para. 10.12.

| Subject Loan | |
|---|---|
| Principal Balance | EUR 350M |
| Interest Rate | Euribor[3] + 200 basis points ("bps") |
| Interest Payment Frequency | Quarterly |
| Principal Payment Structure | Non-amortizing |
| Collateralization | Unsecured |
| Seniority | This issuance ranks pari passu with any other intercompany debt |
| Prepayment terms | Pre-payable with make-whole provision |

Table 14.1 is just a subset of the most relevant loan characteristics for the purpose of this analysis. Other characteristics that could be important could include guarantees, covenants (particularly if there are covenants that significantly impact the perceived riskiness of an investment), conversion features, or any other characteristics that a lender would consider relevant for evaluating the Subject Loan as an investment option.

## 2 Description of the Borrower and Loan Purpose

Both the Borrower and the Lender are assumed to both be subsidiaries of a parent company referred to herein as the "Company." The Company designs, manufactures, markets, and distributes industrial electrical equipment for commercial use in an array of industries. The Company sells its products in the Americas, Europe, the Middle East and Africa, and throughout the Asia-Pacific region.

The Borrower is a holding company that was formed for the purpose of executing an acquisition. As such, though it will be exposed to the industry in which the Company operates, its own functions will be relatively limited. Upon execution of the acquisition, its consolidated financial results will include the results of the entity it is acquiring, which will be an operating company in a related service line to the Company's current primary service line and will gradually be integrated with the Company (the acquired company will be referred to herein as the "Target"). The Subject Loan itself was issued (along with equity) for the purpose of funding the acquisition.

3. Given the upcoming cessation of certain commonly used reference rates such as LIBOR, it could be helpful to include "fallback" language in all floating rate loan agreements that define alternative reference rates or other recourse in the case of cessation of the applied reference rates. European Central Bank (ECB) recommendations for Euribor fallback rates may be found here: https://www.ecb.europa.eu/pub/pdf/other/ecb.recommendationsEURIBORfallback triggereventsandESTR.202105~9e859b5aa7.en.pdf.

## 3 Credit Rating of the Borrower and Issuance

Interest rates are primarily derived such that they provide lenders adequate compensation for bearing the risks associated with the underlying instrument. Creditworthiness, a measure of either a borrower's or issuance's likelihood of default and the expected loss in default, is therefore a crucial metric in determining the interest rate an unrelated lender would require to consider a loan an attractive investment. As such, performing an analysis of the Borrower's creditworthiness and ideally, the associated instrument's creditworthiness as measured by their credit rating is an important step in benchmarking an arm's-length interest rate.

Third parties often use credit ratings designated by rating agencies (e.g., Standard & Poor's Global Ratings, Moody's, and Fitch Ratings) to assess the creditworthiness of a borrower and/or issuance.

The rating systems used by Moody's, S&P and Fitch are shown in Table 14.2.

*Table 14.2 Rating Systems*

| *Moody's* | *Standard & Poor's/Fitch* |
|---|---|
| Aaa | AAA |
| Aa1, Aa2, Aa3 | AA+, AA, AA– |
| A1, A2, A3 | A+, A, A– |
| Baa1, Baa2, Baa3 | BBB+, BBB, BBB– |
| Ba1, Ba2, Ba3 | BB+, BB, BB– |
| B1, B2, B3 | B+, B, B– |
| Caa1, Caa2, Caa3 | CCC+, CCC, CCC– |
| Ca | CC |
| C | C |

Subsidiaries, such as the Borrower, often do not have published stand-alone credit ratings. However, certain rating agencies publish models that can be used to estimate a stand-alone credit rating for the Borrower. These models are generally designed to examine an entity's characteristics and financial data and simulate a stand-alone credit rating that is close to the stand-alone rating that the rating agency would assign the Borrower if it were to perform a comprehensive credit rating analysis.

Given that financials are an important input for these credit rating models, it is necessary to identify the most relevant financials for credit rating purposes. Since the Borrower is a newly formed holding company that will not have any operations until the acquisition, performing the analysis based on historical financials is not possible. However, it is possible to perform the analysis based on projected financials, noting that such data is subject to assumptions (and possibly bias) and should therefore be tested for sensitivity. It is ideal to use financial information that was otherwise prepared for business purposes.

Applying the projected financial data for the Borrower for the four quarters following the acquisition, the credit model that was applied outputted a stand-alone (senior unsecured) credit rating of BB- on the S&P/Fitch scale, or Ba3 on the Moody's scale. This result was not found to be impacted by rerunning the analysis with more conservative revenue and income assumptions, aimed at testing the projections for sensitivity.

The OECD Guidelines note that credit ratings of borrowing subsidiaries may be impacted by the subsidiaries' membership in the broader multinational group, a concept commonly referred to as implicit support.[4] As such, in order to perform an analysis that satisfies taxing authorities that follow OECD Guidelines, it is necessary to consider whether such taxing authorities would consider implicit support to have an impact on the borrower credit rating. The precise impact that implicit support should have on a borrower credit rating is not explicitly prescribed in the OECD Guidelines, but rather is more generally described as being a facts-and-circumstances determination driven by the likelihood that a subsidiary would receive support from the parent company or broader multinational group in the case of distress, as evidenced by factors such as the amount of strategic, operational and legal ties between the parent and the subsidiary and the importance of the subsidiary to overall group operations.[5]

Depending on the impact of implicit support, the Borrower's credit rating could either be its estimated stand-alone credit rating (in this case BB–), the Company's public corporate credit rating (the Company has a recent public credit rating of A–), or something in between (e.g., adjusted upward from the stand-alone credit rating or downward from the group credit rating). In the absence of explicit guidance on determining the level of implicit support in the OECD Guidelines, documents published by credit rating agencies that provide guidance on analyzing the creditworthiness of subsidiary entities can be consulted. Specifically, these publications provide recommendations for how to rate subsidiaries of broader multinational groups with regard to their stand-alone and group ratings based on the specific characteristics of the subsidiaries. It is recommended to consult these publications in conjunction with the business to determine the appropriate characterization and again assess whether a sensitivity analysis is warranted.[6]

In this case, given that the Borrower is a newly formed legal entity that is not presently vital to the Company's operations and is acquiring a business that is not core to the Company's current offerings, it could be that the Company would provide very little, if any, support to the Borrower in the case of distress and therefore a stand-alone rating for the Borrower is appropriate. On the other hand, it could be considered that while not relevant to the Company's current offerings, the Borrower's acquired business does factor into the Company's future plans, and as such the guidance could suggest that the most appropriate credit rating would be one that was based primarily on that of the stand-alone Borrower but included a one notch "lift" for likely

4. OECD Guidelines, paras. 10.77-10.78.
5. *Ibid.*, paras. 10.78-10.80.
6. For some jurisdictions, it may be necessary to consider whether explicit support in the form of a binding parent company guarantee would reasonably be expected to have been provided under arm's-length conditions, the effect of which would be to increase the subsidiary's credit rating to that of the parent company. In this case, implicit support would be irrelevant.

nonbinding support from the Company. Therefore, for purposes of this chapter, we assume a credit rating of BB/Ba2 (i.e., one notch up from BB-/Ba3) to the Borrower.

Individual issuances may have credit ratings that can differ from the Borrower's credit rating to the extent the issuance has characteristics that either increase (e.g., security, guarantees) or decrease (e.g., subordination) its relative creditworthiness. The Subject Loan did not have any such characteristics; as such the issuance credit rating was also assumed to be BB/Ba2.

## III FUNCTIONAL ANALYSIS

Paragraph 10.23 of the OECD Guidelines states, "[i]n accurately delineating the actual financial transaction, a functional analysis is necessary. This analysis seeks to identify the functions performed, the assets used and the risks assumed by the parties to that controlled transaction." Though at arm's length, the functions undertaken by a borrower or a lender would not necessarily have bearing on the pricing of a financing instrument, under the OECD Guidelines the functions, risks, and assets of the borrower and lender are considered key inputs to whether a purported intercompany loan is accurately delineated as debt and to which entities within a company are entitled to interest income. To the latter point, the OECD Guidelines state that if a lender is not exercising control over the risks associated with the advance of funds or does not have the financial capacity to assume the risks, then the lender would be entitled to no more than a risk-free return.[7] More generally, a determination that the lender or the borrower in a transaction did not perform the functions that would be performed by a lender or a borrower operating at arm's length with respect to evaluating an investment decision can lead to reclassification of a purported loan.

With this guidance in mind, a functional analysis should clearly describe the functions that both the borrower and lender undertook in evaluating the Subject Loan as either a source of funds (for the lender) or use of funds (for the borrower). As such, the functional analysis may also be an appropriate place to discuss the borrower and lender's realistically available alternatives for sourcing or using funds, which is a necessary consideration for accurately delineating and pricing the intercompany loan. This section presents an illustrative functional analysis for the Borrower and the Lender with respect to the Subject Loan.

### 1 Lender Functions

The OECD Guidelines describe certain key functions that should be performed by a lender, stating "[f]or instance, in the case of an intra-group loan, the key functions performed by a lender to decide whether and under which terms to advance funds would typically include an analysis and evaluation of the risks inherent in the loan, the capability to commit capital of the business to the investment, determining the terms of the loan and organizing and documenting the loan. This may also include any ongoing

7. OECD Guidelines, para. 10.25.

monitoring and periodic review of the loan."[8] In doing so, the OECD Guidelines note that a lender operating at arm's length would consider the same commercial considerations and economic circumstances as would a lender in a loan between independent enterprises (though noting it will not necessarily do so at the same intensity as an independent lender, given that there is less informational asymmetry in the intercompany context).[9] The OECD Guidelines also note that independent enterprises, when considering whether to enter into a particular financial transaction, will consider all options realistically available to them, and will only enter into the transaction if they see no alternative that offers a clearly more attractive opportunity to meet their commercial objectives[.]"[10]

The Lender is a legal entity that primarily performs finance functions. The Lender has full-time employees that include several employees performing a treasury function, an accounting team, and a finance department. It has a board of directors that is majorly local residents that have to approve all loans with the materiality of the Subject Loan; as such, it can be considered to have decision-making power for its issuance of intercompany debt. The Lender also has possession and control over the capital that is being deployed and bears the full risk of the activities it performs, including interest rate and debt default risk of its debtors. These activities are not guaranteed by the parent company. As such, it performs evaluations of the reasonableness of intercompany lending arrangements.

In evaluating the Subject Loan from a perspective of a lender, the Lender first evaluated the creditworthiness of the Borrower (i.e., an analysis of risks inherent in the loan) and the compensation it would receive for bearing that risk (i.e., the interest rate). From the perspective of the Lender, it is notable that at arm's length, borrowers with equal or worse creditworthiness than that of the Subject Borrower are generally able to obtain funding on similar terms. The Borrower's credit rating is noted earlier as being BB/Ba2 and there is adequate evidence of commercial loans or bonds (including long-term loans or bonds) to borrowers with equal or worse credit ratings. Though such debt instruments carry additional risk compared to the Subject Loan, lenders and other-such investors operating at arm's length frequently willingly enter into riskier investments, provided that the potential return provides adequate compensation commensurate with the additional risks. Similarly, there exist loans and other investment vehicles on the market that would be viewed as less risky than the Subject Loan; however, these instruments would be expected to provide lenders or investors with a lower rate of return. Simply put, if a debt instrument is priced at arm's length, that means, by definition, that it is providing the Lender appropriate compensation for its level of risk, and that any other debt options available that offer either higher return or lower risk come with a tradeoff of higher risk or lower return, respectively. As such, no realistically available alternative debt instruments on the market should be thought of as objectively better for the Lender from a risk-return perspective, as the marketplace for debt instruments ensures that all loans are priced (by the market) to provide equally

8. *Ibid.*, para. 10.24.
9. *Ibid.*
10. *Ibid.*, para. 10.19.

appropriate return for each instrument's relative risk. As such, an analysis of realistic alternatives for the Lender is a matter of identifying the instrument that is appropriate for the Lender's specific goals (e.g., a manager of a high-yield debt fund would likely have a relatively high return profile and in turn a greater risk tolerance).

The Lender also evaluated its capacity to commit its own capital in the form of the Subject Loan and determined that it did have sufficient capital with which to make the investment in the Subject Loan. The Lender has procedures in place to monitor and periodically review the performance of the loan.

Given the analysis described in this section, it can reasonably be concluded that the Lender is adequately fulfilling the functions of a lender and may be accurately delineated as such.

## 2 Borrower Functions

Using a similar framework to consider the functions of the Borrower, the OECD Guidelines state, "[f]rom the perspective of the borrower, the relevant functions would usually refer to ensuring the availability of funds to repay the principal and the interest on the loan in due time; providing collateral, if needed; and monitoring and fulfilling any other obligation derived from the loan contract."[11]

The Borrower's availability of funds to repay the principal and interest of the loan is presented later in this chapter and demonstrates that the Borrower has adequate ability to make all payments required under the Subject Loan. The Borrower has no obligation to provide collateral under the Subject Loan. Finally, as noted, the Lender has procedures in place to ensure ongoing monitoring of the loan contract.

It is also necessary to consider whether the Borrower, if operating at arm's length, would have entered into the Subject Loan as structured and priced, given considerations such as the terms it could have gotten from independent lenders, its business needs and strategies, its financing policy, etc. The structure and amount of the Subject Loan were directly related to business needs (i.e., the acquisition of the Target).

In choosing to issue debt rather than equity, it is reasonable that a Borrower at arm's length would, all else equal, have a preference for non-dilutive forms of financing, provided that they have the means to service the debt (which as discussed the Borrower does). It is also worth noting that the Borrower will be issuing some equity in addition to the Subject Loan as part of its financing of the acquisition, but determined that a mix of debt and equity would be a more optimal capital structure. In choosing to enter into a ten-year intercompany loan, rather than, for example, a short-term lending instrument, the Borrower considered the fact that the loan will be financing an acquisition, and therefore will be deploying the cash from the loan immediately. Loans for acquisitions are often financed with longer-term instruments so that borrowers can outlay all or most of the cash balance immediately to fund the

11. *Ibid.*, para. 10.26.

acquisition and gradually accumulate the cash for repayment out of earnings over time.[12]

### 3 Risks

The Lender and Borrower both face risks pursuant to the Subject Loan.

From the Lender's perspective, serving as a lender is inherently a risk-bearing endeavor. The Lender temporarily advances its own funds in return for compensation (i.e., interest) and bears the risk that the Borrower will be unable to repay and that therefore the Lender will not recoup the funds it has advanced. The Lender does have bankruptcy protections in the loan agreement which partially mitigate the risks of the Subject Loan by creating a legally binding obligation for the Borrower to liquidate and take all steps available to repay the Subject Loan in the case of its insolvency. However, that does not guarantee that the Lender will be fully made whole in a bankruptcy scenario.

The Borrower also bears risks pursuant to the Subject Loan. Specifically, it bears the risk that in the case of extreme financial hardship will be unable to repay the Subject Loan and therefore will have to declare bankruptcy. It also bears the risk that the Subject Loan will create downward pressure on its creditworthiness and its ability to obtain future funding in the future.

As discussed in the overview of functions, both Borrower and Lender have considered these risks and nonetheless determined that the Subject Loan is a beneficial arrangement from both perspectives.

### 4 Assets

As they relate to the Subject Loan, the Lender's assets are primarily its reservoir of cash on which it may draw to make various investments such as the Subject Loan. The Borrower's assets following the Subject Loan and its use in executing the acquisition will be limited to the investment in the Target and the Target's cash-generating operations on which it may draw to service and repay the Subject Loan.

## IV ACCURATE DELINEATION OF THE SUBJECT LOAN

The OECD Guidelines contain an overview of the steps that need to be taken to accurately delineate a purported intercompany loan, *stating* "the purpose of this section is to provide guidance for countries that use the accurate delineation under Chapter I to determine whether a purported loan should be regarded as a loan for tax purposes (or should be regarded as some other kind of payment, in particular a contribution to equity capital)."[13]

12. It is also worth mentioning that many borrowers would choose to refinance rather than repay at maturity.
13. *Ibid.*, para. 10.10.

The OECD Guidelines do not provide explicit criteria for determining the accurate delineation of a purported loan. They do provide a list of factors that "may be useful indicators," including:

> the presence or absence of a fixed repayment date; the obligation to pay interest; the right to enforce payment of principal and interest; the status of the funder in comparison to regular corporate creditors; the existence of financial covenants and security; the source of interest payments; the ability of the recipient of the funds to obtain loans from unrelated lending institutions; the extent to which the advance is used to acquire capital assets; and the failure of the purported debtor to repay on the due date or to seek a postponement.[14]

Bearing in mind this list of factors, along with other considerations described throughout the OECD Guidelines, the considerations that may be used to accurately delineate a purported loan can be broadly divided into the following categories:

- the characteristics of the instrument;
- the borrower's ability to service the instrument;
- the borrower and lender's functions;
- whether the instrument as structured would have been agreed to at arm's length by both borrower and lender, given all realistic alternatives; and
- ongoing behavior of both borrower and lender (i.e., whether the loan agreement is followed in practice).

The Borrower and Lender's functions, as well as the manner in which, in conducting their respective functions, they each evaluated the appropriateness of the Subject Loan respective to reasonable alternatives, is addressed as part of the Functional Analysis. Ongoing behavior cannot be evaluated at this present state given that this case study assumes it is being written pursuant to the initial issuance of the Subject Loan (though it is worth noting the existence of internal measures to ensure the regular payment of intercompany interest). That said, it is important for purposes of accurate delineation that the substance of the loan agreement in practice match the contractual form. This section will therefore focus on an overview of the debt-like characteristics of the Subject Loan and the ability of the Borrower to bear the debt.

## 1 Characteristics Supporting Indebtedness

The list of factors that may be useful indicators of accurate delineation from the OECD Guidelines, paragraph 10.12 (quoted in full above) includes five characteristics that can generally be described as applying to the characteristics of the loan as articulated in a loan agreement. They are:

- the presence or absence of a fixed repayment date;
- the obligation to pay interest;
- the right to enforce payment of principal and interest;

14. *Ibid.*, para. 10.12.

- the status of the funder in comparison to regular corporate creditors; and
- the existence of financial covenants and security.

An accurate delineation analysis can consider the existence (or nonexistence) of these characteristics. For example, in considering the Subject Loan's accurate delineation, the following characteristics noted in the loan agreement are relevant:

- agreement is stated as being a "Term Loan Agreement";
- there is a fixed maturity date, given as ten years after the issuance date;
- there is an interest rate, stated as Euribor + 200 bps;
- there are additional details on making payments of interest, noting quarterly payment dates and the dates each quarter on which payments are due;
- there is a description of events of default, providing the lender with recourse in the case of overdue principal or interest, insolvency, or change of control;
- the Borrower is disallowed from taking on additional indebtedness without permission from the Lender; and
- the Lender is given information rights, meaning the Borrower is obligated to promptly provide the Lender with any business, financial, or corporate information as requested.

These facts generally reinforce debt characterization. Specifically, there is a legally binding agreement noting a fixed maturity date, the requirement to make interest payments, and the borrower's rights to monitor and enforce the loan agreement. The loan agreement does not comment directly on the Subject Loan's level of seniority; however, this fact is less relevant given that the Borrower will not have any other debt before entering into the Subject Loan and is disallowed from taking on additional indebtedness without the Lender's permission. The loan agreement also does not provide explicit covenants; however, covenants are less important in the intercompany context given that there is no informational asymmetry between borrower and lender as there is in the arm's-length context,[15] and especially in this case given the information rights provided in the loan agreement. Therefore, it is reasonable to conclude that based on the loan agreement, the Subject Loan has characteristics that are consistent with debt.

## 2 Debt Capacity Analysis

The OECD Guidelines recommend using the same considerations that an independent lender would use to assess the creditworthiness of the borrower, noting "[a] credit assessment will include understanding the business itself as well as the purpose of the loan, how it is to be structured and the source of its repayment which may include analysis of the borrower's cash flow forecasts and the strength of the borrower's balance sheet."[16] In that light, the OECD Guidelines note that a borrower's ability to

15. A fact acknowledged by the OECD Guidelines in para. 10.86.
16. OECD Guidelines, para. 10.54.

service and repay an intercompany loan could impact the accurate delineation of the purported loan.[17] Therefore, it can be instructive to perform a cash flow analysis and/or a financial ratio analysis to assess a borrower's expected ability to repay the subject debt. The following subsections will illustratively perform each of these analyses to assess the Borrower's ability to bear the Subject Loan.

## A *Cash Flow Analysis*

Using projections, one can assess the Borrower's expected ability to repay the Subject Loan by demonstrating that, based on its expected cash balance (and cash inflows) and its required debt servicing payments, the Borrower's cash balance at all times would be greater than their quarterly interest payments and principal balance due at maturity (i.e., starting principal plus interest accrued for the year).

Table 14.3 below presents a truncated version of a cash flow analysis for the Borrower. This was done based on projections, with a downward adjustment to test the projections for sensitivity. In this table, the starting cash balance is EUR 50 million, which the Company expects to be the cash remaining following the use of its funds on the acquisition of the Target. The remainder of the table shows the Borrower's projected free cash flows (exclusive of the Subject Loan), the impact of interest[18] and principal payments (less the tax savings[19] due to the deductibility of interest), and the resulting cash balance projections as of each year-end.[20]

*Table 14.3 Cash Flow Analysis (EUR, million)*

| *Year Following Issuance* | *Key* | *1.00* | *2.00* | *3.00* | *4.00* | *10.00* |
|---|---|---|---|---|---|---|
| Starting Cash Balance | [A] = Prior year [F] | 50.00 | 78.71 | 108.42 | 139.17 | 347.10 |
| Cash Flow from Operations | [B] | 33.40 | 34.40 | 35.43 | 36.50 | 43.58 |
| Loan Payment (Interest and Principal) | [C] | -7.00 | -7.00 | -7.00 | -7.00 | -357.00 |
| Tax Shield Savings from New Debt | [D] = - [C] * 33% | 2.31 | 2.31 | 2.31 | 2.31 | 2.31 |
| Adjusted Free Cash Flow | [E] = [B] + [C] + [D] | 28.71 | 29.71 | 30.74 | 31.81 | -311.11 |
| Ending Cash Balance | [F] = [A] + [E] | 78.71 | 108.42 | 139.17 | 170.97 | 35.99 |

17. *Ibid.*, para. 10.13.
18. Given that the loan has floating rate interest, the rate of Euribor + 200 basis points was estimated as 2.00%.
19. A tax rate of 33% is assumed.
20. Each quarterly interest payment is aggregated into one yearly payment for each year of the analysis.

As shown in Table 14.3, there will be sufficient cash to repay the principal at maturity. Further, it should be noted that having sufficient cash to repay the principal balance at maturity is not necessarily required to demonstrate a reasonable expectation of an ability to repay, given that a borrower at arm's length could choose instead to refinance. An analysis that was not performed for the Subject Loan but could be performed would be to assess the Borrower's projected financial standing as of maturity and demonstrate its expected ability to obtain debt financing with which to refinance its maturing obligations.

### *B* *Ratio Analysis*

Another means of testing the Borrower's capacity to bear the debt is looking at whether the Borrower's leverage and coverage ratios are in line with what a reasonable lender operating at arm's length would accept. The intent of this analysis is to demonstrate that at arm's length, borrowers with equal or worse credit profiles than that of the Borrower attained comparable issuances from third parties and that as a result, the Borrower's leverage is not unreasonable in light of third-party behavior. Simply comparing the Borrower's credit rating of BB to borrowers in the market that still manage to obtain debt financing does largely fulfil this requirement, but the ratio analysis provides a more comprehensive assessment.

For this analysis, a search such as the following could be performed:

- credit rating is less than BB (in order to isolate the lowest-rated companies that are able to obtain financing);
- offer date in last 12 months;
- maturity date is 10 years or greater into the future (since relying on observations for shorter-term loans would not be sufficient to conclude that lenders would be willing to lend for at least the tenor of the Subject Loan to similar- or worse-rated borrowers);
- security type or features do not materially differ from that of the Subject Loan in a way that would make it perceived as safer and/or more attractive than the Subject Loan (e.g., secured, guaranteed, convertible); and
- operates in a similar industry to that of the Company.

When performing this type of search for the Subject Loan, five companies were identified. Tables 14.4 and 14.5 display the ratio analysis conducted and compares them to the Borrowers' leverage and coverage ratios, based on its projected financial statements for the year following the acquisition.

Table 14.4 *Leverage Ratio Analysis*

| *Leverage Ratios* | *Market Equity/Total Capital* | *Book Equity/Total Capital* | *Net Debt/Total Assets* |
|---|---|---|---|
| Minimum | 0.52 | -0.12 | 0.48 |
| Lower Quartile | 0.58 | 0.12 | 0.52 |
| Median | 0.64 | 0.14 | 0.57 |
| Upper Quartile | 0.67 | 0.31 | 0.64 |
| Maximum | 0.69 | 0.34 | 0.71 |
| Weighted Average of Tested Borrower | 0.70<br>Above maximum | 0.14<br>Within interquartile range | 0.41<br>Below minimum |

Table 14.5 *Coverage Ratio Analysis*

| *Coverage Ratios* | *EBIT Interest Coverage* | *EBITDA Interest Coverage* | *Debt to EBIT* | *Debt to EBITDA* |
|---|---|---|---|---|
| Minimum | 1.30 | 1.92 | 4.17 | 3.32 |
| Lower Quartile | 1.69 | 3.57 | 5.02 | 4.28 |
| Median | 3.08 | 4.01 | 5.16 | 4.45 |
| Upper Quartile | 3.98 | 5.00 | 9.43 | 5.10 |
| Maximum | 4.80 | 5.63 | 12.10 | 6.39 |
| Weighted Average of Tested Borrower | 3.72<br>Within interquartile range | 5.48<br>Above upper quartile | 6.69<br>Within interquartile range | 4.56<br>Within interquartile range |

The leverage ratios displayed in Table 14.4 measure a company's leverage compared to its equity, assets, or total capital. The coverage ratios in Table 14.5 measure a company's ability to service its ongoing financial obligations. In the case of our tested Borrower, the metrics indicate that their ability to service the Subject Loan is consistent with comparable companies. The financial metrics in the tables show that the Borrower does not have financial ratios that appear significantly riskier or less favorable from the perspective of the lender than the majority of identified issuances, and in many cases appear more favorable than most. As such, the Borrower's leverage and interest payments are reasonable compared to third-party issuances and therefore not out of line with reasonable leverage seen in the marketplace, demonstrating that if the Borrower and Lender were unrelated, the Borrower would have been able to obtain similar funding from an unrelated third party.

Alternatively, observed debt covenants under commercial loan agreements entered into by the identified comparable companies, if published in their financial statements, can be used to assess the Borrower's capacity to meet its debt liabilities.

Although not considered for purposes of this case study, the commerciality of the Borrower's returns can also be tested by benchmarking the post-interest profitability (e.g., return on assets) and return on equity based on the identified independent comparable companies, or alternatively deriving an expected return on equity using the capital asset pricing model.

## V INTEREST RATE BENCHMARKING ANALYSIS

The arm's-length nature of intercompany transactions is typically determined under one of five standard methods. These five methods are generally accepted by taxing authorities globally and are specified in the OECD Guidelines. They include the following:

- Comparable uncontrolled price (CUP) method
- Resale price method (RPM)
- Cost plus method
- Transactional net margin method (TNMM)
- Profit split method.

However, the Financial Transactions Guidance provides a further discussion on methods that can be used for determining the arm's-length interest rate on intra-group loans, discussing the following five methods:

- CUP method
- Cost of funds
- Credit Default Swaps
- Economic Modeling
- Bank Opinions.

Where it is possible to identify comparable uncontrolled transactions, the OECD Transfer Pricing Guidelines state that the CUP method is the most direct and reliable way to apply the arm's-length principle, and is preferable over all other methods.[21] The Financial Transactions Guidance seems to extend this preference to financial transactions specifically, noting that the widespread availability of lending data may make it easier to apply the CUP to financial transactions than to other types of intercompany transactions.[22]

The Financial Transactions Guidance also discusses a cost-of-funds approach, which would reflect the borrowing costs incurred by the lender incurred in raising the funds to lend, plus expenses of arranging and servicing the loan, a risk premium, and a profit margin. However, the Financial Transactions Guidance describes the cost-of-funds approach as something that may be used as an alternative method for pricing loans in some circumstances and in the absence of comparable uncontrolled transactions.

21. OECD Guidelines, para. 2.14.
22. *Ibid.*, para. 10.89.

The Financial Transactions Guidance also raises several of these potential methods for purposes of raising concerns about their applicability or outright disqualifying them as appropriate methods. The OECD notes that a credit default swap approach should be used "In the absence of information regarding the underlying asset that could be used as a comparable transaction ..."[23] and notes that the credit default swaps could be subject to a high degree of volatility or situations where the same instrument has different credit default swap spreads due to factors unrelated to default risk.[24] Economic modeling is another approach the OECD discusses but notes such models' sensitivities to the reliability of user inputs and states that since such models are not representative of actual transactions, they should be viewed as a secondary approach in the absence of comparables for a CUP approach.[25] Finally, the Financial Transactions Guidance outright rejects bank opinions (i.e., letters from independent banks stating what they feel an appropriate interest rate would be) stating that "Such letters would therefore not generally be regarded as providing evidence of arm's length terms and conditions."[26]

Given the seeming preference for the CUP method in the OECD Guidelines (and specifically the Financial Transactions Guidance), the analysis should first assess whether an application of the CUP method is possible. The CUP method compares the price charged for property or services transferred in a controlled transaction to the price charged in a comparable uncontrolled transaction under similar circumstances. For the purposes of the CUP method, an uncontrolled transaction is considered comparable if one of the following conditions is met:

- none of the differences between the transactions being compared or between the enterprises involved in the transactions could materially affect the price in the open market; or
- adjustments can be made to eliminate the material effects of any such differences.[27]

A reliable CUP is often found when comparable transactions are internally generated ("internal CUP"), where one of the parties relevant to the analyzed intercompany transaction is involved in a similar transaction, under similar circumstances, with a third party. For the Subject Loan, this would require identifying a comparable loan transaction(s) entered into by the Borrower or one or more members of the Company (or related persons) under sufficiently similar circumstances, with an unrelated party(ies). For purposes of this case study, it is assumed that neither the Borrower nor the Lender (or related persons) has entered into any potentially comparable loan transactions with unrelated parties.

23. *Ibid.*, para. 10.101.
24. *Ibid.*, para. 10.102.
25. *Ibid.*, para. 10.106.
26. *Ibid.*, para. 10.108.
27. OECD Transfer Pricing Guidelines, para. 2.14.

Nevertheless, it is possible to obtain information on comparable transactions between external independent parties (external comparables), which allows for application of an external CUP analysis identifying comparable loan transactions with characteristics similar to the Subject Loan. Therefore, the CUP is selected as the most appropriate methodology with which to assess the arm's-length nature of the Subject Loan.

## 1 Search for Comparable Issuances

Comparable debt issuances can be identified by searching any number of readily available databases, such as Bloomberg Professional Service, Refinitiv Loan Connector DealScan, and S&P Capital IQ. The criteria applied when searching for comparable issuances will be crucial for finding the most broadly similar debt instruments in order to construct a range of arm's-length interest rates. Different (or multiple) databases may be more appropriate for different types of loans, so it can be helpful upfront to determine the most appropriate issuances to search for.

For the Subject Loan, the search was focused primarily on bond issuances given that (a) there is a greater amount of available information on bond issuances than on other types of debt (e.g., bond issuances are re-priced daily which corrects for differences in timing between issuance of the comparables and the Subject Loan, unlike private loans which are generally not re-priced) and b) bonds are characteristically similar to intercompany debt such as the Subject Loan in that they are often issued for longer tenors, are unsecured, etc. One consideration when using bonds is the relative liquidity of a bond versus the Subject Loan. In some cases, it may be appropriate to quantify this adjustment with an upward adjustment to the bond pricing to reflect the relative lack of liquidity of the Subject Loan relative to bond issuance, which would make the Subject Loan relatively riskier and therefore require additional compensation.

A common alternative (or corroborative) approach to a search for bonds when benchmarking floating rate issuances is a search for syndicated loans. Depending on the specific facts of the analysis, syndicated loans can be more (e.g., expressed as floating rate) or less (e.g., syndicated loans are often secured or guaranteed) comparable to an intercompany loan under review than bonds are, and as such in some instances can be more appropriate for benchmarking purposes and/or provide an additional source of potential comparable issuances. Relative liquidity and a potential adjustment may also be relevant for certain syndicated loan issuances relative to the Subject Loan too.

The approach taken will ultimately be guided by accepted best practices, tax authority preferences in the relevant tax jurisdictions, and availability of data and information.

For purposes of this case study, a bond search was applied, though some differences between bonds and the Subject Loan remain for which reliable adjustments may be made. Listed below are certain additional important characteristics considered in searching for comparable issuances.

### *A Currency*

The currency of the loan is Euros. As such, a search was undertaken for Euro-denominated issuances. However, there was insufficient data in the Euro-denominated market, especially when looking for comparables with contemporaneous re-pricing necessary for a date-specific Yield to Worst (YTW).

The USD-denominated corporate bond market is commonly regarded as the largest and most liquid bond market in the world. Therefore, the search was expanded to include USD-denominated issuances, noting that reliable adjustments for differences in currencies can be made (as will be discussed later).

### *B YTW Date*

YTW is the lowest potential yield that can be received by an investor on a bond without the issuer actually defaulting. A bond's YTW is calculated based on all possible call dates as it is assumed that a prepayment would occur if the bond has a call option and the issuer would be expected to be able to exercise the option and refinance for a lower rate. Therefore, YTW is the lowest of yield to maturity (YTM) or yield to call[28] if a bond contains prepayment provisions. A bond's YTW may equal its YTM (e.g., if there are no call options or if the call options would not be expected to lead to a lower yield) but it can never be higher.

A benefit of using YTW or YTM (as opposed to just the interest rate of debt) is that it reflects a contemporaneous re-pricing of issuances based on changes in market factors, borrower creditworthiness and other criteria that would impact the compensation an investor in the loans would expect. It also increases the number of potentially comparable issuances versus searching for comparable issuances with similar characteristics that were issued in a similar timeframe as the Subject Loan. A bond investor would be theoretically indifferent between a thirty-year bond issued ten years ago (i.e., twenty years until maturity) and a twenty-year bond issued today, provided that they were from the same borrower and were otherwise equivalent in every way. Therefore, YTW allows comparables to be included in a search regardless of issuance date and tenor at issuance, as long as the comparables have a time until the "YTW Date" (i.e., maturity or call date, depending on which one creates the "worst" outcome that creates the YTW observation) within the same timeframe as the Subject Loan. Therefore, it might be appropriate to review observations that had time until YTW dates between 8 and 12 years (creating a spread of long-term loans around the Subject Loan tenor of 10 years) to identify yields for issuances with similar characteristics as the Subject Loan.

Given that YTW and YTM are based on contemporaneous re-pricing of the loan, the YTW/YTM on a given issuance would be immediately impacted by new information about a specific loan or borrower and thus is reflective of all structural changes to a company's business between a loan's issuance date and the evaluation date. Credit

28. Yield to call is defined as the annual rate of return assuming the bond is redeemed by the issuer on a specific call date.

ratings can be slower to adjust to changes in businesses, which can create a situation where a YTW/YTM and a credit rating for a company may be misaligned if, for example, an event has occurred impacting the perceived creditworthiness of a company by the market that is reflected in its YTW/YTM but not yet reflected in its credit rating. As such, it is recommended to perform diligence on all comparable issuances to ensure the YTW/YTM is not being impacted by any recent events.

## 2 Industry

A determination of the impact of the borrower's industry on interest rate fluctuations comes with many competing considerations.

On one hand, industries are already accounted for when setting credit ratings (e.g., it is an input in the credit modeling tools). For example, if a borrower on the market has a similar financial profile to that of the borrower in the Subject Loan but is in a riskier industry such that a lender operating at arm's length would demand a higher interest rate, this could be reflected in the borrower in the riskier industry having a lower credit rating than the borrower in the Subject Loan. Separately, if certain industries lead companies therein to have a certain financial profile (e.g., manufacturers may have greater fixed asset intensity and operating leverage), this would be accounted for when using that borrower's financial profile to set a credit rating. As such, some would argue that as long as credit rating is included as a search criterion, there is no reason to separately exclude comparables on the basis of industry.

However, certain industry considerations are important to this analysis. Credit ratings tend to be "sticky," meaning that they tend not to change frequently over time; in many cases, borrower credit ratings are only updated after event-driven factors or when someone (such as the Borrower) specifically requests a new evaluation. As such, if borrowers become more or less risky due to an industry's normal movements along the business cycle, it may not be reflected in the credit rating observed for the industry, but could be reflected in market interest rate or yield movements (which could be adjusted daily). Further, interest rates and yields are primarily driven by supply and demand, and industries could have unique supply and demand considerations (e.g., a general sentiment among investors that it is favorable to be exposed to a certain industry) that would move prices for reasons that have nothing to do with creditworthiness.

It is also important to note that the definitions and characteristics of industries tend to be difficult to specify and are often not agreed upon across different sources. For example, an industry defined as "healthcare" in a database could include everything from healthcare service providers to medical device manufacturers to owners and operators of hospitals.

Given these considerations, it may be most appropriate to generally allow a broad range of industries to be brought into the search in order to get a larger set of comparables wherein systemic industry factors could be smoothed out, rather than relying on a specific industry screen that could not be performed reliably and would reduce the sample size of the observations (thus increasing the exposure to idiosyncratic characteristics). However, it may also be appropriate to make an exception and exclude borrowers operating in industries where any of the following are true:

- there is potential for significant relationships between the borrower/issuance and the government that might impact interest rates (e.g., infrastructure companies such as railroad manufacturers or operators, aerospace and defense, utilities);
- the financial profile of participants in the industry is materially different than that of the Borrower in a way that could impact the demand for issuances from this industry (e.g., pure service providers with no fixed assets); or
- the industry is one that is considered to have significant and unique risks that would cause interest rate fluctuations to materially differ from other industries (e.g., banking and finance or real estate).[29]

## 3 Credit Rating

In order to get balance achieving a broad enough set of comparable issuances while searching for comparable issuances with similar enough creditworthiness to that of the Subject Loan, it is reasonable to restrict the search to issuances one notch below (i.e., BB–) and one notch above (i.e., BB + ) the Borrower's credit rating of BB but within the same rating category as interest rates tend to vary more between categories than within categories.

## 4 Interest Rate Structure

The Subject Loan is noted as being a floating rate loan. A floating rate refers to an interest rate that is priced as the total of a spread and a reference rate, such as Euribor. Reference rates are expected to fluctuate regularly commensurate with movements in market interest rates, meaning that the interest rate on a floating rate loan will increase or decrease over time based on movements in the market. This can be contrasted with a fixed-rate loan, in which a single interest rate is locked in at issuance and will not change regardless of what movements there are in market interest rates. As such, payments on a fixed-rate loan will be more predictable but will have a greater likelihood of at times appearing incongruent with present market interest rates. Neither the borrower nor the lender can expect to be better off under a fixed or floating rate arrangement in all cases; if market interest rates increase during the tenor of a loan, the borrower will be better off than the lender under a fixed-rate arrangement (because the legacy fixed interest rate will be low compared to market rates), but in turn, the lender will be better off with a fixed rate if market interest rates decline (and they are then earning excess compensation).

29. For example, according to corporate yield curves sourced from S&P Capital IQ, the yield on 10-year, AAA-rated, USD bonds in the financial industry is 2.12 %, compared to 2.51 % for bonds with the same characteristics but categorized as nonfinancial (as of January 25, 2022).

Depending on the search criteria, it may not be possible to identify a sufficient number of comparable issuances that are similarly structured as floating rate loans. This is especially true for the search for bond issuances for purposes of benchmarking the Subject Loan, as bonds more commonly carry fixed interest rates and because the relevant metric, YTW, is analogous to a fixed (not a floating) interest rate. As such, it will necessary to make adjustments for this characteristic after identifying comparable issuances (similar to currency).

## 5 Summary

Using this guidance, the search below would be appropriate to identify comparable issuances:

- the issuance has a credit rating between BB– and BB + –;
- currency is US dollar or Euro;
- security type is a corporate bond;
- issuance has available descriptive and financial information, including a reported YTW greater than 0;
- maturity date or YTW date is between 8 and 12 years into the future; and
- industry Classification is not Energy, Real Estate, Financials, or Utilities.

The comparables identified from the search can then be manually screened for comparability characteristics such as the following:

- the borrower operates in an industry that exhibits any of the characteristics discussed above that would merit rejection;
- the borrower does not have sufficient descriptive or financial information for purposes of evaluating comparability; or
- the issuance was a duplicate offering.

After performing the screens, 13 issuances remained. These issuances were denominated in both USD and EUR and were structured as both fixed and floating rate issuances. In order to control for differences in currency with the Subject Loan, it was necessary to make adjustments to the USD-denominated bonds and account for the impact of the currency on interest rates. One approach for correcting for this is to perform a cross-currency swap (CCS), using a CCS tool provided by third parties (e.g., Bloomberg Swap Manager function) to control for material differences in the lending environments for USD-denominated and Euro-denominated loans. This is consistent with corporates fully hedging the foreign exchange risk associated with foreign currency loans using cross-currency interest rate swaps.

A CCS takes an interest rate in a starting currency and outputs the interest rate in a separate currency at which an investor would be theoretically indifferent between the investments in the two currencies. In this case, for each USD-denominated issuance inputted, the CCS outputs the Euro-equivalent rate. A CCS calculates equivalent rates based on market forward currency conversion rates, and specifically on the currency appreciation or depreciation that would occur if a borrower were to convert to a subject currency on the issuance date at the spot rate and convert back to the starting currency on the maturity date at the forward rate that could be locked in today.[30] In other words, the outputted Euro-equivalent rate is set such that a USD-denominated investor would receive equal returns if they were to receive the USD interest rate versus converting their currency into Euros, invest in the Euro-equivalent rate, and convert cash back to USD at the forward rate that can be locked in today.

One can similarly use third-party tools to perform a fixed-floating swap (FFS) which converts a fixed-rate issuance into the equivalent spread over a reference rate such as Euribor (or vice versa). Using this tool, it is possible to convert the fixed-rate issuances identified in the search into equivalent Euribor-based rates which would be more directly comparable to the Subject Loan. Alternatively, in the absence of such tools, users can approximate the fixed rate equivalent to a floating rate issuance using publicly available data on swap rates; for example, a user can deduct from a fixed rate the "swap rate" associated with the target reference rate and solve for the equivalent spread over that reference rate.

The information on the selected comparable issuances and their adjusted YTWs can be found in Table 14.6.

*Table 14.6 Comparable Loan Observations*[31]

| *Issuer* | *Time to Maturity (Years)* | *Currency* | *Yield* | *Euro-Equivalent Rate* | *Equivalent Spread over Euribor (bps)* |
|---|---|---|---|---|---|
| Company A | 9.70 | USD | 4.29% | 1.95% | 186.1 |
| Company B | 10.30 | USD | 5.11% | 2.66% | 256.9 |
| Company C | 11.69 | EUR | 2.30% | 2.30% | 206.00 |
| Company D | 8.04 | USD | 3.99% | 1.72% | 167.6 |
| Company E | 9.12 | EUR | 1.89% | 1.89% | 180.8 |
| Company F | 10.67 | EUR | 2.66% | 2.66% | 255.8 |
| Company G | 8.34 | USD | 4.65% | 2.54% | 250.7 |
| Company H | 11.99 | EUR | 2.41% | 2.41% | 217.00 |
| Company I | 10.01 | USD | 4.33% | 1.91% | 178.9 |
| Company J | 8.54 | USD | 5.21% | 4.04% | 289.6 |
| Company K | 9.33 | USD | 3.75% | 1.41% | 132.8 |
| Company L | 11.76 | EUR | 2.96% | 2.96% | 272.00 |
| Company M | 10.17 | USD | 4.74% | 2.29% | 219.9 |

Table 14.7 details the calculation of the arm's-length range using the accepted comparables' interest rates detailed above.

30. Gee Hee Hong et al., "IMF Working Paper: What to Deviations from Covered Interest Parity and Higher FX Hedging Costs Mean For Asia," International Monetary Fund, August 2019.
31. Each comparable's YTW is pulled as of February 6, 2020.

*Table 14.7 Construction of Arm's-Length Range (bps over Euribor)*

| | *Construction of Arm's-Length Range* |
|---|---|
| Minimum | 132.8 |
| Lower Quartile | 180.8 |
| Median | 217 |
| Upper Quartile | 255.8 |
| Maximum | 289.6 |

As seen in Table 14.7, the full range of adjusted rates for comparable issuances ranged from 132.8 to 289.6 bps over Euribor. Paragraph 3.57 of the OECD Guidelines notes that in situations where comparability defects may remain (as is the case in this analysis, given that any market issuance will have idiosyncratic factors affecting interest rates that cannot be completely adjusted for) but where the range includes a sizable number of observations, "... statistical tools that take account of central tendency to narrow the range (e.g., the interquartile range or other percentiles) might help enhance the reliability of the analysis."

As such the interquartile range of rates, which was a spread over Euribor of 180.8 bps to 255.8 bps, with a median of 217.0 bps was considered. A spread over Euribor within the interquartile range of results presented, such as the spread of 200.0 bps charged in the Subject Loan, would be arm's-length.

## 6 Additional Considerations

Though not ultimately relevant in this particular case study, there are several additional considerations which may be relevant when performing an interest rate benchmarking analysis for a floating rate loan.

### *A Additional Fees and Discounts*

In some cases, an interest rate might not make up the entirety of the compensation that a lender is expected to receive pursuant to a loan. In such cases, in order to apply a CUP method, it may be necessary to adjust the observed interest rates for this additional compensation or to benchmark all components of the compensation.

For example, it may be the case that a loan or bond was issued at a discount to its par value, meaning that the amount of cash that the lender provided to the borrower at issuance is less than the amount that they will be repaid at maturity. As such, in addition to the periodic interest that they will collect, the lender will also receive compensation in the form of appreciation of the loan value. If only the interest rate were considered in a benchmarking analysis, it would fail to include the totality of compensation that the lender is earning in return for issuing the funds and bearing risks. As such, it might make sense to calculate an "effective" interest rate that is inclusive of the total annualized return the lender expects to earn on the issuance and apply that figure for benchmarking purposes.[32]

Similarly, lenders may charge borrowers additional fees either upfront or over the course of the loan (e.g., a fee on the undrawn amount). For example, an origination fee is an upfront fee that a lender may charge a borrower in return for originating the loan. As with a discount, the interest rate applied for benchmarking purposes may need to be adjusted for the fees in order to ensure the analysis is considering the total compensation that the lender is earning for the loan.

### B *IBOR Transition*

Historically, floating rate issuances have often been priced using Interbank Offered Rates (IBORs) as the reference rates. IBORs are calculated based on rates submitted by a participating group of banks and are intended to represent the cost of short-term wholesale borrowing by large multinational banks. With certain IBORs set to cease after December 31, 2021, country-specific transition committees have been set up internationally to introduce their own local currency-denominated alternative reference rates for short-term lending.

New intercompany loans priced based on floating rates will have to be based on alternative reference rates; for most IBOR rates, there presently exist consensus replacement reference rates that may be used. For example, for USD London Interbank Offer Rate (LIBOR) the consensus alternative reference rate will be the Secured Overnight Financing Rate (SOFR), and as such new floating rate intercompany loans in the United States will commonly reference SOFR. Existing intercompany loans that are based on IBORs that are being phased out will need to be amended to reference these new alternative reference rates. Given the differences between the legacy reference rates and the new alternative reference rates (e.g., IBORs incorporate a credit spread whereas the new reference rates are generally based on a risk-free rate, meaning that the new reference rates will likely be lower than the old), spreads will likely have to be adjusted as well. At arm's length, the process of amending floating rate loans to reference replacement reference rates has generally been determined by contractual language in third-party agreements (e.g., fallback provisions) and/or case-by-case negotiations between the parties to the loan. There is also guidance published by data providers such as Bloomberg and ICE on appropriate adjustments to spreads for certain reference rate conversions.[33]

---

32. This particular consideration is not relevant for a bond search applying YTW, as YTW is already calculated using the "price" of the bond as of the evaluation date and therefore incorporates the appreciation of the lender or investor would earn on the difference between the price paid and the par value at maturity.
33. "IBOR Fallbacks." Bloomberg Professional Services. March 5, 2021: https://assets.bbhub.io/professional/sites/10/IBOR-Fallbacks-LIBOR-Cessation_Announcement_20210305.pdf.

## VI CONCLUSION

As noted in the introduction, the requirements to ensure an intercompany loan is in compliance with the OECD Guidelines can be broadly categorized into four primary categories:

(i) identify the characteristics of the loan (including the borrower);
(ii) perform a functional analysis to understand the respective functions, risks, and assets of all parties to the intercompany loan;
(iii) ensure the accurate delineation of the loan as debt; and
(iv) establish an arm's-length interest rate (or range of interest rates).

The intention of this case study was to describe how to fulfill each of these requirements.

First, one must identify the characteristics of the loan, including the characteristics of the borrower itself. Many of these characteristics can be found in the loan agreement, which will generally dictate the terms of the loan. In reviewing these loan terms, it is important to stay abreast of characteristics that could impact the characterization of the instrument as debt and/or would be a relevant consideration for the compensation a lender would require in return for issuing funds (i.e., the interest rate).

Second, one must perform a functional analysis to understand the respective functions, risks, and assets of all parties to the loans. As described during the case study, the OECD Guidelines suggest it may be appropriate to re-characterize a transaction and/or adjust or redirect interest payments depending on the respective functions of the Lender and Borrower.

Third, one must ensure the loan is accurately delineated as debt. This is most commonly thought of as ensuring a purported loan instrument is actually best characterized as debt, as opposed to another type of financing such as equity (for which, importantly, "interest" payments would not be tax deductible). Accurate delineation may be supported by demonstrating that the loan carries debt-like characteristics and by demonstrating that the borrower actually has the ability to bear the debt.

Finally, is the interest rate benchmarking analysis? In this instance, a search was performed for market issuances with comparable characteristics to that of the Subject Loan. Where there were material differences between the comparable issuances and the Subject Loan, such as the currency or whether the interest rate was fixed or floating, adjustments could be made to correct for these differences. The analysis demonstrated that the rate in the Subject Loan is arm's-length.

CHAPTER 15

# Different Benchmarking Approaches for Convertible Bonds

*Serena Picariello*[*]

## I INTRODUCTION

Companies have a wide range of alternatives when seeking sources of financing. When setting up an adequate capital structure, there are several options available within the equity-debt spectrum. For example, companies can use equity by issuing new shares of common stock or use debt in the form of loans or bonds. Generally, debt is considered safer than equity because it gives investors a steady regular cash flow. It is also more senior in liquidation claims and ensures principal protection since the principal will be returned upon maturity. On the other hand, the return on stocks mainly hangs on a company's performance, outlook and ability to generate cash flow. While the dividends may be unpredictable and irregular, the share price can greatly appreciate depending on company performance.

In order to obtain the best from both worlds (i.e., equity and debt) companies increasingly use "hybrid" securities as an alternative to traditional financial instruments, even in intra-group contexts. One of the best-known types of hybrid securities is the convertible bond. This financial instrument combines the features of corporate bonds (i.e., interest payments and the return of the principal at maturity) and equity (i.e., an option for the bond to be converted into a predetermined number of common stocks or equity shares).

Corporations have used convertible bonds to raise external capital for around 150 years. They were first issued in the nineteenth century when United States (US)

* The views and opinions set forth herein are the personal views or opinions of the authors; they do not necessarily reflect the views or opinions of the orhanization with which the authors are associated.

railroad companies needed capital to finance their business operations. As the US was a rapidly growing economy at that time, capital was not easy to obtain through issuing traditional financial instruments (e.g., shares or bonds).[1]

Due to the uncertainty and very low-interest rates of the current economic and financial environment, convertible bonds have proved attractive to companies and investors alike. The convertible bond market has significantly grown in the last decade, particularly in the US. Today, the convertibles market is dominated by US issuers (65%), followed by European issuers (22%) and other rapidly growing Asian countries.[2] In February 2021, the global convertible bond market reached a record-high volume of over USD 490 billion.[3]

Given this instrument's relevance to intra-group financing activities, this study aims to provide an overview of the key types of convertibles and their main features, as well as analyze the potentially available benchmarking approaches to determine an arm's length interest rate for these instruments.

## II CONVERTIBLE BONDS

A convertible bond is a fixed-interest bond that may give the subscriber a right or an obligation to convert it into equity of the issuer (i.e., the issuing company or its parent) when certain specified terms and conditions are fulfilled.[4] The conversion price (i.e., the price per share at which the bond may be converted to common stock) is set at the time of issuance, typically at a premium to the equity's market value at the time of issue.[5]

Convertible bonds have the following main features and elements:[6,7]

- *Interest rate*: convertible bonds carry an interest rate typically lower than plain vanilla bonds.[8]
- *Maturity*: as convertible bonds can have different maturities, the instruments on the market can range from short-term to perpetual convertible debt. Typically, convertible bonds are issued with a fixed maturity and/or repayment date.

1. Credit Swiss, *The case for convertible bonds* 20 (2021), https://www.credit-suisse.com/pwp/am/downloads/marketing/br_convertible_bonds_eng.pdf.
2. Refinitiv data as of 31 December 2020.
3. Credit Swiss, *supra* n. 1, p. 20.
4. IMF, *External Debt Statistics: Guide for Compilers and Users—Appendix 1. Special financial instruments and transactions: classifications*, Washington DC 224 (2003), https://www.imf.org/external/pubs/ft/eds/Eng/Guide/file6.pdf.
5. *Ibid.*
6. Jakob Bundgaard, *Convertible Debt Instruments in International Tax Law—Part 1*, 57 Eur. Taxn. 4 (IBFD ed. 2017), p. 138.
7. Pierre Vernimmen, *Corporate Finance: Theory and Practice*, Ch. 24, 433 (4th ed. Wiley 2014).
8. Convertible bonds are considered a cheaper source of financing for the issuer since they usually carry lower yields compared with vanilla comparable bonds, and investors benefit from the potential upside in the stock price without incurring the same risks as an equity investment.

- *Conversion right*: convertible bonds give their holder the right to convert them into equity under certain conditions.
- *Conversion period*: the bond indenture or issue contract specifies the period when the conversion right can be exercised. This could be (1) at a fixed date; (2) at one of several fixed conversion dates; or (3) during a conversion period that may begin on the issue date or later.
- *Conversion ratio:* the number of shares the bond may be converted into, is usually set at the time of issue but may vary from year to year.
- *Conversion premium:* the amount by which the conversion price (i.e., the price of the shares that the bonds can be converted into) exceeds the share's current market price.
- *Call option for the issuer*: an option of some convertible bonds that allows the issuer to buy them back at a predetermined price. This may be subject to "call protection," which prevents the holder from exercising the option for a certain period.

A variety of convertible bonds exists on the market, which can be grouped into the following main types:[9]

(1) *Vanilla optional convertibles:* these allow the investor to choose whether to hold the bond until maturity or convert it to the issuing company's shares. Generally, an investor would convert the bond into stock if the gain from selling the shares exceeds the bond's face value plus the present value of the total amount of remaining interest payments.
(2) *Mandatory convertibles:* these include terms that require mandatory or very likely conversion by the subscriber at a particular conversion ratio and price level. Mandatory convertible bonds are deemed closer to equity[10] than debt since repayment is in the form of shares; therefore, the "downside protection" is minimal.
(3) *Reverse convertibles:* these give the issuer (rather than the holder) the right to convert the bond to shares or keep the fixed-interest bonds until maturity.
(4) *Contingent convertibles (CoCos):* these are typically issued by banks or other regulated financial institutions to shore up their Tier 1 balance sheets. CoCos have features that help the issuing financial institution absorb a capital loss and optimize the capital adequacy position. They have a specific strike price that, once breached, can convert the bond into equity or stock at pre-negotiated terms.

As the convertible bonds market is growing quickly, multinational groups are increasingly making recourse to this type of financial instrument in intra-group

9. This study focuses on vanilla optional convertibles.
10. Furthermore, mandatory convertibles are, in many instances, treated as equity for accounting and rating agency purposes. For further details, *see* Jakob Bundgaard, *supra* n. 6, p. 139.

contexts. Therefore, it is important to understand the Transfer Pricing (TP) implications and challenges around the use of convertible bonds for intra-group financing activities.

## III APPLICATION OF OECD GUIDANCE TO CONVERTIBLE BONDS

The Organisation for Economic Co-operation and Development's (OECD) final report[11] on group financing, published on February 11, 2020, represented a turning point in the application of TP rules to financial transactions. The report was then incorporated as Chapter X of the latest OECD Transfer Pricing Guidelines (TPG). According to Chapter X's guidance, financial transactions should be addressed through a four-step analysis.[12]

The first two steps of the analysis leading to a correct application of the arm's length principle would focus on the accurate delineation and recognition of a transaction, while Step 3 and Step 4 focus on the pricing of the transaction. Since this report explores the different benchmarking approaches to pricing convertible bonds (i.e., Steps 3 and 4), it only provides an overview of the key considerations of Steps 1 and 2, mainly elaborating on the methodologies to determine an arm's length interest rate for convertible bonds.

### 1 Steps 1 and 2: Identifying the Commercial or Financial Relations and Recognizing the Accurately Delineated Transaction Undertaken

Chapter X stresses the importance of accurately delineating an advance of funds, representing the starting point of the TP analysis. It refers to the guidance in Chapters I-III of the OECD TPG,[13] in that accurately delineating a financial transaction (i.e., Step 1) should begin with a detailed identification of the transaction's economically relevant features, including an examination of the five comparability factors.[14] Furthermore, all other options realistically available to each party to the transaction must be considered. For example, in the case of convertible bonds, specific conditions can typically be observed for this instrument to be a realistic option. If these are not met, the parties may look at other investment opportunities.[15]

---

11. OECD, *Transfer Pricing Guidance on Financial Transactions: Inclusive Framework on BEPS: Action 4, 8-10.*
12. For further details on the four-step analysis, *see* R. Petruzzi et al., *Fundamentals of Transfer Pricing: A Practical Guide*, Ch. 1 (Lang/Cottani/Petruzzi/Storck eds., Wolter Kluwer 2019).
13. In section D, para. 1.36 of the 2022 OECD TPG, the OECD took the position that the accurate delineation of the actual transaction, or transactions between the associated enterprises, requires the analysis of the transaction's economically relevant characteristics, which are based on the five comparability factors.
14. Chapter X OECD TPG, para. 10.17.
15. The market has several hybrid instruments that could be a potential alternative to convertible bonds, e.g., bonds cum warrants. A warrant is a security allowing the holder to subscribe to another newly issued security (share, bond, or even another warrant) during a given period, in a proportion and at a price fixed in advance. For further details, *see* Pierre Vernimmen, *supra* n. 7, p. 248.

When considering the options realistically available, each party's perspective on the transaction (i.e., the issuer's and holder's perspective) must be considered[16] to understand whether there is an actual rationale behind its issuance.[17]

Convertible bonds offer the issuer two main potential advantages: lower yield and less restrictive covenants compared to a plain vanilla bond since the investor pays for the right to convert the instrument into the issuing firm's shares.[18] The decision to issue a convertible bond is generally sound when the firm expects that its business will be more stable than the market's assessed firm-specific volatility. This is because the issuer will be able to reduce its financing costs without needing to dilute[19] (at least initially) the equity base by issuing more equity shares, as the convertible's terms can postpone the possible issue of any new shares for several years.[20]

From the holder's perspective, convertible bonds can be a particularly attractive instrument if the holder faces constraints relating to equity risk. Since convertible bonds are debt instruments, they allow the constrained investor to assume more equity risk. They also ensure downside protection—if the underlying common stock's price declines in the market (i.e., due to an economic downturn), the bond will not be converted, and the holder will still be entitled to its return—while allowing holders to share in the potential benefits of common stock in a growing firm.[21]

Once the transaction is delineated under Step 1,[22] Step 2 of the analysis can begin, resulting in either the transaction's recognition or non-recognition. For the latter, the transaction could be disregarded or even replaced with another one.[23] In this respect, the OECD provides guidance on whether an intra-group loan should be regarded as a loan or "should be regarded as some other kind of payment, in particular a contribution

16. Chapter X OECD TPG, para. 10.19.
17. For example, if the convertible bond's holder is the sole shareholder of the issuing entity, there would not be a benefit for the holder in the exercise of its right to convert the instrument into shares.
18. Chris P. Dialynas & John C. Ritchie, *The Handbook of Fixed Income Securities*, Ch. 59, pp. 1375-1376, (7th ed., Fabozzi, McGraw-Hill 2005).
19. If the convertible bond is converted into equity, additional shares of stock will be issued. Hence, the exercise of the conversion could result in several downsides for the current shareholders (e.g., a reduction of the value of the existing shareholders' shares, reduction in their ownership proportion, diluted earnings per share, less voting power, etc.).
20. Patrick J. Brown, *An Introduction to the Bond Markets*, Ch. 4 69 (Wiley ed. 2006).
21. Chris P. Dialynas & John C. Ritchie, *supra* n. 18, p. 1377.
22. If as a result of the analysis, the features of the loan will be delineated differently from the one in the intra-group agreement, that delineation will not require any amendment to the contracts, since the accurately delineated characteristics will be taken into account for the pricing of the loan. For further details, *see* Raffaele Petruzzi & Raphael Holzinger, *Accurate Delineation vs. Recognition of Intragroup Loans*, Tax Notes (8 June 2020), https://www.taxnotes.com/tax-notes-international/transfer-pricing/accurate-delineation-vs-recognition-intragroup-loans/2020/06/08/2cjgw.
23. The issue of regarding a loan as a loan should be addressed using the recognition step, also confirmed by the 2010 OECD TPG. However, Chapter X does not seem to provide a clear-cut distinction in the analysis whether a loan should be treated as such or as equity differentiating between the two steps. In fact, some authors have argued that, regarding the two steps of the TP analysis, Chapter X has some pitfalls: (1) it focuses more on the delineation of the actual transaction rather than the recognition; (2) it first addresses recognition issues and then delineation issues; and (3) the wording of para. 10.10 and in paras. 10.12-10.13 mixes up the two concepts. For further details, *see* Raffaele Petruzzi & Raphael Holzinger, *supra* n. 22.

of equity capital."[24] The OECD also acknowledges that re-characterizing the loan based on the arm's length principle should not be the only approach for determining whether a purported debt should be respected as debt.

In fact, jurisdictions may have already implemented approaches to address the balance of debt and equity funding[25] under their general tax laws.[26] Furthermore, many countries have specific tax rules on how to classify and treat convertible bonds.[27] Although convertible bonds have equity-like features, this does not mean the instrument should be recognized and treated as an equity instrument. In fact, under Step 2, the focus shifts from the transaction's characteristics to the purpose of the involved parties in light of the overall commercial rationality of the accurately delineated loan.[28]

Should Steps 1 and 2 conclude that an unrelated party company would have been able to issue a convertible bond with features comparable to the instrument under analysis and that a third-party investor would have purchased a similar instrument, the convertible bond should be recognized as such and priced accordingly.

## 2 Steps 3 and 4: Selection and Application of the Most Appropriate TP Method

Once the accurately delineated transaction undertaken is recognized, the TP analysis focuses on the pricing. Determining an arm's length interest rate for convertible bonds can be challenging due to their unique contractual characteristics. Compared with standardized instruments, they are highly heterogeneous as they can contain specific tailor-made clauses. Given the array of terms and clauses used in convertible bond contracts, the selection and application of the comparable uncontrolled price (CUP) method—either internal or external—may not lead to comparable results, at least on a

24. Paragraphs 10.4-10.13 OECD TPG.
25. Paragraph 10.9 OECD TPG.
26. Regardless, the OECD's attempt to treat the debt/equity issue under the arm's length principle was rejected by several countries. In fact, supreme court decisions in many countries (e.g., France, Sweden, Germany and Finland, to name a few) have held that the arm's length principle does not authorize the recharacterization of loans into equity. In fact, in paras. 10.8-10.10 of Chapter X, it is acknowledged that other approaches may be taken to address the issue of the balance of debt and equity funding at a domestic level. For further details, *see* Jens Wittendorff, *Transfer Pricing Oddity: The OECD's New Guidelines on Financial Transactions*, Tax Notes (10 August 2020), https://www.taxnotes.com/tax-notes-international/transfer-pricing/transfer-pricing-oddity-oecds-new-guidelines-financial-transactions/2020/08/10/2crg1.
27. For a detailed comparative analysis of how different countries treat convertible bonds from a domestic tax law perspective, *see* Jakob Bundgaard, *Convertible Debt Instruments in International Tax Law—Part 1 & 2*, European Taxation 57(4-5) (IBFD ed. 2017).
28. As a general remark regarding the commercial rationality of these transactions, it is worth pointing out that convertible bonds are transactions also observable on the market between third parties. In fact, the global convertible bond market is growing at a fast pace; convertibles have become a global asset class and not only an instrument issued by small to medium-sized companies seeking growth with limited access to funds. For further details, *see* Credit Swiss, *supra* n. 1, p. 20.

standalone basis.[29,30] In fact, applying an external CUP by performing an external database search to select comparable instruments with similar features (e.g., bond with warrant or with call option) could result in inaccurate outcomes,[31] as the price of convertible bonds is driven by the value of the underlying assets (i.e., shares).

Furthermore, the application of other TP methods should be considered. If it is deemed that the TP methods could lead to unreliable results, the OECD acknowledges that other methodologies (e.g., economic models) can be relied upon to price intra-group loans. These models are detailed in the following paragraphs.

## IV BENCHMARKING APPROACHES

Generally, under the option pricing models, the valuation of a convertible bond must consider two components, i.e., the vanilla bond's price and the call option's price[32,33] and both the dilution effect of the new shares issued and the coupon payments saved as a result of the conversion. Since options derive their value from the underlying assets' value, and the cash flows depend on a specific event's occurrence, different option pricing models can be used to determine the value of the call options.[34]

Therefore, this report discusses several benchmarking approaches to illustrate potential alternatives[35] to determine an arm's length coupon for convertible bonds.

29. Although the CUP method should not be used in isolation to price convertible bonds, the report will present how a mixture of methods could be necessary to price these instruments. Hence the (external) CUP can be used as part of the economic analysis together with other methods to derive an arm's length interest rate for convertible bonds.
30. It is quite difficult to price convertible bonds through similarities with other convertibles, even ones issued by the same firm, since the convertible bond is issued at a specific point in time, with specified maturity, when a specific conjuncture is found.
31. For example, unlike a bond with attached equity warrants, a convertible bond is an indivisible product, i.e., the straight bond cannot be sold separately from the warrant.
32. An option is a contract between two sides, where one side gives the other side the right (but not the obligation) to buy from them (a call option) or to sell to them (a put option) an asset in exchange for the payment of a premium. For further details, *see* PIERRE VERNIMMEN, *supra* n. 7, p. 407.
33. As mentioned, a convertible bond is an indivisible product, since the vanilla bond cannot be sold separately from the call option. This is why the approach of considering the convertible bond's value as the sum of two segments (straight bond's value and option value) can have pitfalls. For further details, *see* PIERRE VERNIMMEN, *supra* n. 7, p. 435.
34. The value of an option depends on many different factors. The value of a call option increases as the value of the underlying asset increases. The volatility in the underlying asset's value also corresponds positively with the option's value, as high volatility increases the chance for high returns deriving from the option. The fewer restrictions imposed on the exercise of an option, the higher its value. In addition, the risk-free market interest rate needs to be considered for an option's value. Generally, a high-interest rate increases the value of a call option. However, given the current low level of interest rates, the effect is less strong. Moreover, the value of a call option decreases if dividends are distributed during the option's lifetime, as the holder only benefits from dividends after exercising the option. LISHANG JIANG & CANGUO LI, *Mathematical Modeling and Methods of Option Pricing*, Ch. 1 3 (World Scientific ed. 2005).
35. Although this report presents several alternative benchmarking approaches based on economic and financial models that can be used to determine an arm's length coupon rate, the author acknowledges there may be other alternative approaches to the ones presented.

## 1 Black-Scholes Model

One of the most common options pricing models is the Black-Scholes. In 1972, Fisher Black and Myron Scholes presented a model in a now-famous article for pricing European-style[36] options, based on a portfolio composed of the underlying asset and a certain number of options so that the portfolio is insensitive to fluctuations in the underlying asset's price. As such, it can only return the risk-free rate. The model calculates the underlying asset's possible prices at maturity as well as their respective probabilities of occurrence, based on the fundamental assumption that it is a random variable with a log-normal distribution.[37]

For a call option, the Black-Scholes formula can be broken down into two parts, as seen in Figure 15.1. The value of an option calculated with this model is given—in rough terms—by the difference between the stock price (i.e., V) and the time value of its strike price (i.e., the strike price needs to be discounted to the present value at an interest-free rate), also considering the relevant probabilities of occurrence.[38,39]

*Figure 15.1 Black-Scholes Formula*[40]

$$\text{Value of the call option} = N(d_1) \times V = N(d_2) \times K \times e^{-T \times r_F}$$

with

$$d_1 = \frac{\text{In}\left(\frac{V}{\text{K}}\right) + \left(r_F + \frac{\sigma^2}{2}\right) \times T}{\sigma \times \sqrt{T}} \text{ and } d_2 = d_1 - \sigma \times \sqrt{T}$$

The formula's key elements are:

- $V$, the current price of the underlying asset
- $N()$, a cumulative standard normal distribution (average 0, standard deviation 1)
- $K$, the option's strike price[41]

36. Options that can only be exercised on the expiry date are known as European options, and those that can be exercised any time before the expiry date are called American options. The terms "European" and "American" have no geographic relevance, since both styles of options can be used in any market. Bermudan options, which can be exercised on any set of specified dates, also exist. For further details, *see* Moorad Choudhry, *Fixed-Income Securities and Derivatives Handbook*, p. 161 (Wiley 2nd ed., Bloomberg Press, 2010).
37. Pierre Vernimmen, *supra* n. 7, p. 418.
38. N(d2) is the probability that the stock price will be at or above the strike price when the option expires (meaning the option will be exercised), while N(d1) is the future value of the stock if the stock price is above the strike price at expiration.
39. Nicolas Merlino, *Switzerland—Tax Treatment of Employee Stock Options*, 4 Finance and Capital Markets (formerly Derivatives & Financial Instruments) 3 (IBFD ed. 2002), p. 106.
40. Pierre Vernimmen, *supra* n. 7, p. 418.
41. The strike price is the price of the underlying asset at which the option is exercised. For example, a call option to buy ordinary shares of a listed company may have a strike price of USD 10,

- $r_F$, the continual annual risk-free rate
- $\sigma$, the standard deviation of the return on the underlying asset
- $T$, the time remaining until the option expires (in years).[42]

As a result, under a Black-Scholes-based pricing model, these variables affect the option's price. For example, compared to the stock price, there is an inverse relationship between the exercise price and the option price, because the farther that price is from the asset's present value, the fewer possibilities the option holder has to exercise. The option's duration or life also affects the pricing of the option since the option price rises as the maturity date is extended. Another key variable to consider with call options is volatility, since an option is exercised only when it is in the money, i.e., when the exercise price is less than the underlying asset's value. The higher the volatility (i.e., the higher the standard deviation of the return), the greater the differential can be between the value of the stock and the exercise price and, therefore, the more valuable the option becomes.[43]

The Black-Scholes model is neat and intuitive. Although the model was initially designed to price European-style options (i.e., an option that can only be exercised at maturity), one of its many advantages is that it can be easily modified to handle other option types.

Users of the Black-Scholes model should always keep in mind that it relies on several important assumptions. For example, apart from the underlying asset's price ($V$) and the time ($T$), all the model's variables are assumed to be constant, including, most crucially, the volatility variable. In addition, the following assumptions[44] are made:

- there are no transaction costs, and the market allows short-selling;
- trading is continuous;
- there are no dividend payouts throughout the option's life;[45]
- the interest rate during the option's life is known and constant;
- that market participants behave rationally; and
- there are no arbitrage opportunities in the market.

Despite these simplifying assumptions and the reliance on some proxies (e.g., the use of historical volatility) for the inputs, the Black-Scholes model has been de facto adopted by many market operators, with more complex models being derived from it to overcome these practical constraints or better customize the equation to the

meaning that the underlying stock can be bought at USD 10 a share by exercising the contract. For further details, *see* Moorad Choudhry, *supra* n. 36, p. 161.

42. Pierre Vernimmen, *supra* n. 7, p. 418.
43. Christopher J. Faiferlick et al., *Using Real Options to Transfer Price Research-Based Intangibles*, 7 Finance and Capital Markets (formerly Derivatives & Financial Instruments) 2, (IBFD ed. 2005), p. 46.
44. Pierre Vernimmen, *supra* n. 7, p. 419.
45. According to Merton's extension, the Black-Scholes formula may be adjusted to reflect the effects of dividend payments. *See* Robert C. Merton, *Theory of Rational Option Pricing*, 4 The Bell Journal of Economics and Management Science 1 (Spring, 1973), pp. 141-183.

underlying asset.[46] In fact, the Black-Scholes model can be considered the mainstream approach to price options and is often used to price convertible bonds.

## 2 Binomial Model

Another popular technique for pricing options is building a binomial tree, a diagram representing the different paths that may be followed by the stock price and the option value over an option's life.[47] Figure 15.2 is an example of a binomial tree, which consists of several "nodes" and "legs." Each leg represents a temporal interval over time, while the nodes represent the distribution of future values at each point in time. Each node is labeled as N and has a combination of L's and H's in subscript. The subscripts indicate whether the node is lower or higher on the tree relative to the other nodes.[48]

*Figure 15.2 Binomial Tree*[49]

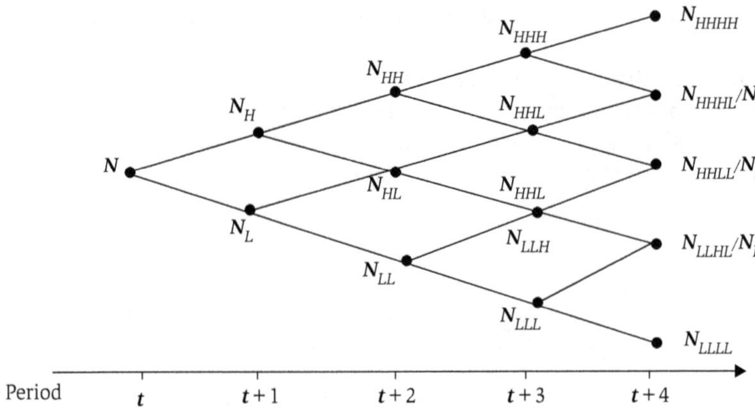


The binomial model is based on the assumption that the underlying asset's price follows a random walk. At each step in time, the price has a certain probability of moving up by a certain percentage (i.e., the "up" scenario, a higher node on the tree) and a certain probability of moving down by a certain percentage (i.e., the "down" scenario, a lower node). The binomial tree also assumes that the values evolve over time based on a log-normal random walk with a known (stationary) volatility.[50] Although a simplifying assumption often used to build the tree is to adopt 1-year

46. PIERRE VERNIMMEN, *supra* n. 7, p. 420.
47. JOHN C. HULL, *Options, Futures, and Other Derivatives*, Ch. 13, p. 274, (9th ed., Pearson, 2015).
48. CHRIS P. DIALYNAS & JOHN C. RITCHIE, *supra* n. 18, p. 852.
49. MOORAD CHOUDHRY, *supra* n. 36, p. 289.
50. *Ibid.*, p. 854.

intervals, binomial trees can be modeled with shorter time periods. In the limit, as the time step becomes smaller, this model is the same as the Black-Scholes.[51]

Based on this model's mechanics, the value of the option value at any node depends on the probability that the underlying asset's price will either decrease or increase at any given node. For example, let's assume that a stock, whose price is now USD 20, will be either USD 22 or USD 17 in 1 year. We want to value a European call option to buy the stock for USD 21 in 1 year. Therefore, the value of the option will be USD 1 if the stock price turns out to be USD 22, otherwise, it will be zero if the stock price turns out to be USD 17.[52]

A convertible bond's value is a function of several variables (e.g., the price of the convertible bond, price of the underlying equity, dividend yield on the underlying share, bond coupon, annualized share price volatility, etc.) that should be factored in the model. To illustrate this, the report will describe how this methodology can be used to value bond options (e.g., call options); however, it is also possible to value convertible bonds within this same framework by adding some additional inputs.[53]

For illustrative purposes, let's assume a callable four-year bond and a value at maturity of USD 100. The interest rate volatility is 10%, and we assume that rates at any point in time have the same probability of occurring (i.e., the probability is 50% on each leg).

To value this bond using a binomial tree, the following steps[54] need to be followed.

Step 1: Calibration of the Binomial Model

The binomial tree must be calibrated to match a particular term structure. This calibration boils down to the following steps:

(1) calculation of the relevant spot and forward rates for a known par value curve;
(2) building up the interest rate tree through backward induction by determining the rate at each node by using the assumed volatility and the interest rate previously determined; and
(3) calibration of the tree to ensure it is arbitrage-free (i.e., the value of a bond must be equal to its market price).

Now, let's assume that we determined the binomial interest tree shown in Figure 15.3.[55]

51. John C. Hull, *supra* n. 47, p. 274.
52. *Ibid.*
53. For a detailed example, Moorad Choudhry, *supra* n. 36, pp. 288-299.
54. The following example is based on the illustration presented in Chris P. Dialynas & John C. Ritchie, *supra* n. 18, pp. 856-865.
55. For a detailed explanation of how the binomial tree can be calibrated, *see* Moorad Choudhry, *supra* n. 36, pp. 288-299.

*Figure 15.3 Binomial Interest Rate Tree for Valuing Up to a Four-Year Bond for Issuer*[56]

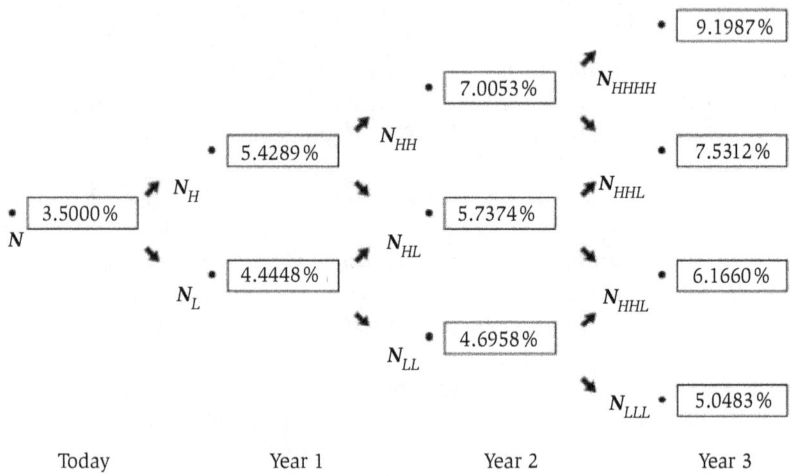


Once the tree is calibrated, bonds with embedded options—as well as option-free bonds—can be evaluated in the same way by using the binomial model, which is detailed further in the following steps.

Step 2: Determination of the Straight Bond's Value

First, a benchmark study is performed to determine an arm's length interest rate applicable to a plain vanilla bond, which has the same features as the callable bond but a conversion option. For this example, we assume that the interest rate determined through the economic analysis is equal to 7%.

Then, we need to determine the straight bond's value. We know that the four-year bond value at maturity is USD 100 plus USD 7 of coupon payment, i.e., USD 107, and we have to determine the value at $N_{HHH}$ and $N_{HHL}$ using the previously determined discount rates of the binomial tree, i.e., 9.1987% and 7.5312%, respectively. The value of the bond is:

- At $N_{HHH}$ equals to USD 97.99 (= USD 107/1.0919)
- At $N_{HHL}$ equals to USD 99.51 (= USD 107/1.0753)

The bond's value at $N_{HH}$ is given by the average value[57] of the bond at $N_{HHH}$ and $N_{HHL}$ plus the coupon, discounted by relative discount rates of the binomial tree. Therefore, the value of the bond at $N_{HH}$ is 98.82 (= [0.5(97.99 + 99.51) + 7]/1.7).

56. Chris P. Dialynas & John C. Ritchie, *supra* n. 18, p. 861.
57. We have assumed a 50% probability of occurring for each leg.

The same process is applied to calculate the tree's other nodes, the outcome of which is shown in Figure 15.4.

*Figure 15.4 Valuation of a Vanilla Bond*

**Vanilla bond**

| **Interest rate** | 7.00% | | | | |
|---|---|---|---|---|---|
| **Coupon(s)** | | 7 | 7 | 7 | 107 |
| **T** | **0** | **1** | **2** | **3** | **4** |
| | | | | 97,9866 | 107 |
| | | | 98,82343 | | |
| | | 101,56478 | | 99,50602 | 107 |
| | 106,4289 | | 101,3338 | | |
| | | 104,74295 | | 100,7856 | 107 |
| | | | 103,4633 | | |
| | | | | 101,8579 | 107 |

Step 3: Determination of the Value of the Bond with the Option

When determining the value of the bond with the option, the only difference is regarding specific considerations on how to adjust the cash flows on the tree. If there is a call option, the call will be made when the present value (PV) of the future cash flows is greater than the call price at the node where the decision to exercise is being made.

Therefore, the second tree refers to the first tree. But if the bond value for the corresponding node in the initial tree is such that the option is economical, the bond value in the second tree is replaced with the option strike price. This operation is performed at each node where the bond is eligible for call.[58]

Figure 15.5 shows how the previous tree was adjusted where the option was economical to determine the values at T = 0 of the bond.

58. If the option is not exercisable for a period of time, the model would simply not (re)assess the bond value at the nodes for which it is not exercisable. Tim Reichert et al., *How To Accurately Price and Design Intercompany Debt* (Economics Partners, LLC ed., White Paper Series, 2012), p. 22.

*Figure 15.5 Valuation of a Bond with the Call Option*

| | **Convertible bond** | | | | |
|---|---|---|---|---|---|
| **Interest rate** | 7.00% | | | | |
| **Coupon(s)** | | 7 | 7 | 7 | 107 |
| **T** | **0** | **1** | **2** | **3** | **4** |
| | | | | 97,9866 | 107 |
| | | | 98,82343 | | |
| | | 100 | | 99,50602 | 107 |
| | 103,3816 | | 100 | | |
| | | 100 | | 100 | 107 |
| | | | 100 | | |
| | | | | 100 | 107 |

Step 4: Determination of the Option Value

The option value is given by the difference between the values at T = 0 in the two interest rate trees.[59] Therefore, the call option value is 3.047 (= 106.429 - 103.382).

Step 5: Determination of the Interest Rate for the Convertible Bond

It is worth mentioning that, for the purposes of pricing an arm's length interest rate for the convertible bond, we are most likely not interested in the nominal value of the option, but rather the implications of the option to convert on the interest rate for the borrower. In the present example, we have identified the value of the bond with an embedded option compared with the value of a comparable plain vanilla bond. Therefore, to account for the conversion option, the convertible bond's interest rate would need to be adjusted downwards accordingly.

Finally, the coupon rate for the convertible bond will be priced as the coupon rate equalizing the net present value of the vanilla bond and the convertible bond to zero.

## 3 Monte Carlo Simulation

Another alternative to pricing a convertible bond is to build a forecast of the share price evolution using a Monte Carlo simulation.[60] This statistical tool uses a set of different

---

59. For an illustrative example of this methodology's implementation, please refer to TIM REICHERT ET AL., *supra* n. 58, p. 22.
60. The Monte Carlo method was developed in the late 1940s after World War II by Enrico Fermi, John von Neumann and Stanislaw Marcin Ulam. Its name was given by Nicholas Constantine Metropolis in reference to Monte Carlo's famous Casino, since chance and random outcomes are central to the modeling technique, similar to games like roulette, dice, and slot machines. *See* WILL KEATON, *Monte Carlo Simulation*, (October 4, 2021), https://www.investopedia.com/terms/m/montecarlosimulation.asp.

values for variables to determine a corresponding set of outcomes to estimate a distribution of possible outcomes.[61] This simulation method is widely used by TP and finance practitioners around the globe (mainly to evaluate derivative products), due to its relatively objective way of determining the statistical evolution of asset prices.

The key concept of a Monte Carlo simulation is that the probability of varying outcomes cannot be determined due to random variable interference. When a forecast or estimation faces significant uncertainty, the Monte Carlo simulation overcomes this issue by using multiple values within a confidence interval, rather than just replacing the uncertain variable with a single average number. In fact, a Monte Carlo simulation focuses on constantly repeating random samples to model the probability of different outcomes in a process to eliminate and/or minimize statistical deviations. It assigns a random value to the variable that cannot be easily predicted and/or estimated (i.e., the share price in the case at hand). This process is repeated several times, and the model assigns the variable in question with many different values to achieve multiple results.

The Monte Carlo simulation can be used to price convertible bonds by running different scenarios for the share price evolution. Since the option's price is closely connected to the issuer's share price (and linked to the risk of the underlying investment), this methodology can be used to forecast the share price evolution by:

(1) setting a starting value for the investment;
(2) identifying additional inputs: the relevant volatility rate (which can be retrieved from sources such as Bloomberg or Thomson Reuters databases) and a growth rate must be determined and factored into the model to simulate the share price's potential year-by-year changes until the convertible bond matures;[62] and
(3) elimination and/or minimization of standard deviation by using multiple values and/or iterations.

Through the Monte Carlo simulation, we can determine a forecasted share price value (i.e., the yearly underlying investment's value) for each year until maturity, which is a key element of an investor's optimal exercise strategy.

Let us assume we want to price a European-style convertible bond with a maturity T of two years and a redemption value of 100. For simplicity, the convertible bond in this example[63] is assumed to provide no coupon payments.

Step 1: Monte Carlo Simulation to Determine the Conversion Value at Maturity

The evaluation of the convertible bond is cash flow based and starts at the final exercise date, which is at maturity. At this time, the investor chooses to convert the convertible bond if the conversion value is higher than the redemption value. The conversion value

61. G. Deshpande, *The Transfer Pricing Aspects of Cross-Border Performance Guarantees*, 71(7) Bull. Intl. Taxn. 358 (IBFD ed. 2017).
62. Will Keaton, *supra* n. 60.
63. The example presented in this paragraph is based on the pricing model described in Christian Wilde & Axel H. Kind, *Pricing Convertible Bonds with Monte Carlo Simulation* (March 11, 2005), https://ssrn.com/abstract=676507 or http://dx.doi.org/10.2139/ssrn.676507.

at maturity can be determined by running a Monte Carlo simulation, which will provide us with a finite number of paths for our unknown variable (i.e., the conversion value at maturity).

Step 2: Identification of the Paths Where the Investor Would Exercise the Conversion Option

For illustration purposes, let us assume that the Monte Carlo simulation identified 10 paths for the conversion value shown in Table 15.1.

*Table 15.1 Potential Paths for the Conversion Values Based on the Monte Carlo Simulation*[64]

| *Path* | *Conversion Value at Maturity Based on the Monte Carlo Simulation* | *Investor's Optimal Exercise Strategy* | *Payoff* |
|---|---|---|---|
| 1 | 120 | Conversion | 120 |
| 2 | 95 | Redemption | 100 |
| 3 | 75 | Redemption | 100 |
| 4 | 135 | Conversion | 135 |
| 5 | 80 | Redemption | 100 |
| 6 | 140 | Conversion | 140 |
| 7 | 125 | Conversion | 125 |
| 8 | 85 | Redemption | 100 |
| 9 | 137 | Conversion | 137 |
| 10 | 97 | Redemption | 100 |

While in the second, third, fifth, eighth and tenth paths the investor will prefer to receive the redemption value (i.e., 100), they will decide to exercise the conversion option in the remaining paths.

Step 3: Determination of the Convertible Bond's Value at T = 0

To obtain the European-style equivalent price of this convertible bond, only the exercise decisions and the corresponding payoffs at maturity need to be considered. Therefore, the value of the convertible bond is determined by the average of all the corresponding discounted cash flows arising from each path.

Step 4: Determination of the Conversion Option

To determine the value of the conversion option, a benchmark study is performed to determine an arm's length interest rate applicable to a plain vanilla bond with the same features as the convertible bond (except the conversion option). Then, the conversion option is determined by comparing the situation when subscribing for the convertible bond with the situation to be faced when granting a vanilla bond at the market rates.

64. *Ibid.*

Based on the results from Step 3, it is possible to identify the difference between the net present value of the vanilla bond and the convertible bond, which will represent the value of the conversion option.

Step 5: Determination of the Interest Rate for the Convertible Bond

Finally, the convertible bond's annual coupon rate is determined, which is the interest rate that would leave no discrepancy between the two alternatives over the loan contract's horizon. In other words, the coupon rate for the convertible bond will be priced as the coupon rate equalizing the net present value of the vanilla bond and the convertible bond to zero.

## V COMPARISON OF THE DIFFERENT METHODOLOGIES

When evaluating the appropriate pricing for convertible bonds, it could be argued that recourse to OECD-recognized methods could result in unreliable outcomes, given the instrument's intrinsic characteristics posing several comparability issues. However, as previously discussed, several methodologies based on financial modeling and statistical techniques are available to practitioners for pricing convertible bonds. It should be noted that each methodology's appropriateness should be assessed on a case-by-case basis, as well as the instruments' specificities and the availability of relevant data to be factored into the respective model. Therefore, it is worth highlighting that not all the aforementioned methods will be applicable or appropriate in all cases since they present specific advantages and disadvantages.

In this respect, it is worth noting that option pricing models share some common limitations. In Chapter X, the OECD acknowledges that operators may rely on economic models to price intra-group loans, but states that the reliability of economic models' outcomes depends upon the parameters and underlying assumptions factored into the specific model. The key issue of these models is their reliance on specific critical assumptions and proxies that tax administrations can challenge, resulting in prolonged litigation.

It is also recognized that, while economic models can be useful tools in situations where reliable comparable uncontrolled transactions cannot be identified, their outcomes do not represent actual transactions between independent parties;[65] therefore, tax authorities could be inclined to challenge them. In fact, although they are widely used by market operators and valuators, they all have a relevant drawback in their application, i.e., they risk creating a "black-box effect." They require advanced financial and statistical skills to be applied properly, making their use unpractical and economically burdensome for small (and also medium) taxpayers.[66]

Table 15.2 summarizes the key advantages and disadvantages of each methodology.

65. OECD TPG, 10.106.
66. G. Deshpande, *supra* n. 61, p. 358.

*Table 15.2 Advantages and Disadvantages of the Pricing Methodologies Analyzed*

<table>
<tr><td></td><td colspan="3">Option Pricing</td></tr>
<tr><td></td><td>Black-Scholes Model</td><td>Binomial Model</td><td>Monte Carlo Simulation</td></tr>
<tr><td>Pros</td><td>- Accurate results/outcomes<br>- Very sophisticated methodology<br>- Mainstream approach for pricing convertible bonds</td><td>- Widely recognized methodology to value options as well as convertible bonds<br>- Fairly easy to model out mechanically</td><td>- Widely used method to determine the statistical evolution of asset prices<br>- Fairly easy to model out</td></tr>
<tr><td>Cons</td><td>- Reliance on underlying assumptions and proxies<br>- Complexity and risk of creating a black-box effect<br>- Requires several inputs to be factored into the model, which may not be available<br>- Complex to illustrate to tax administrations</td><td>- Reliance on underlying assumptions<br>- Risk of having an overly complex and impractical model to overcome the intrinsic limits of the methodology<br>- Complex to illustrate to tax administrations</td><td>- Reliance on underlying assumptions (e.g., it works on a normal distribution, but a skewed upward or downward distribution may apply)<br>- Complex to illustrate to tax administrations</td></tr>
</table>

## VI CONCLUSION

Benchmarking financial instruments like convertible bonds can be challenging, given the peculiar features of these types of instruments. Nevertheless, this study aimed to provide an overview of the different alternatives available to determine an arm's length interest rate for convertible bonds. As the different methodologies have certain advantages and drawbacks, TP practitioners should decide which one to apply on a case-by-case basis.

Furthermore, when analyzing a convertible bond for TP purposes, it is worth stressing that the focus of TP practitioners and tax authorities should not only be on the determination of an arm's length interest rate but primarily on an accurate delineation of the transaction and its recognition in line with the OECD's latest guidance in Chapter X of the TPG.

CHAPTER 16

# The Use of Other Methods for Loan Benchmarking: A Yield Build-Up Approach and Cost of Funds

*Eugene Ng, Gary Lambert & Amanda Pletz*[*]

The Organisation for Economic Co-operation and Development (OECD) Guidance and the UN Manual consider that given the availability of information, it may be easier to apply the Comparable Uncontrolled Price (CUP) method when evaluating financing arrangements compared to other transactions.[1] Although this may be the case, in some situations CUP data cannot be identified, and alternative approaches may be needed. In this context, the OECD highlights two alternative approaches that can be used if CUP market data (such as yield data or Credit Default Swap (CDS) data) are not generally available: the cost of funds approach and economic modelling.[2] We discuss these approaches in more detail.

* The views and opinions set forth herein are the personal views or opinions of the authors; they do not necessarily reflect the views or opinions of the law firm with which the authors are associated.

1. OECD, *Transfer Pricing Guidelines for Multinational Enterprises and Tax Administrations*, January 2022, para. 10.90, section C.1.2.1, available at: https://www.oecd.org/tax/transfer-pricing/oecd-transfer-pricing-guidelines-for-multinational-enterprises-and-tax-administrations-20769717.htm; Committee of Experts on International Cooperation in Tax Matters, *Update of the United Nations Practical Manual on Transfer Pricing for Developing Countries 2021*, part B, Chapter 3, para. 3.2. Available at: https://www.un.org/development/desa/financing/sites/www.un.org.development.desa.financing/files/2021-10/Transfer%20Pricing%20with%20new%20cover.pdf.
2. OECD, *Transfer Pricing Guidelines for Multinational Enterprises and Tax Administrations*, para. 10.97, section C.1.2.5.

## I COST OF FUNDS APPROACH: AN INTRODUCTION

Economic and financial theory indicates that the interest rate charged for a loan is a combination of (a) a risk-free rate;[3] (b) expected inflation;[4] and (c) the premiums associated with default,[5] liquidity,[6] and maturity.[7] These components compensate a lender for the risk it takes when providing financing over a specified period of time, including its cost of funds. In the case of banks and other financial intermediaries, the interest rate includes some element of functional compensation, typically relied on to cover a bank's operational expenses or payment and liquidity management.

Internal comparable uncontrolled price transactions, such as the average borrowing rate of a firm (cost of funds), can mask a wide range of factors that influence the interest rates paid by a firm. These can include currency, maturity, size, position in the capital structure, entity borrowing, and default risk. Unless both identified transactions – the tested transaction and the transactions relied on to apply an internal comparable uncontrolled price – are very similar (same currency, same maturity, same credit risk, timing, similar covenants, etc.), the interest rate on external debt should not necessarily be considered a viable comparable, unless appropriate adjustments can be performed.[8] In spite of its shortcomings, it may be possible in some circumstances to rely on a group's cost of funds to infer an appropriate arm's length interest rate.

Because the cost of funds reflects the lender's general borrowing costs, various adjustments must be applied to account for the specific characteristics of the tested loan. These may include (amongst other factors to consider) the following:

> A credit spread corresponding to the borrower's credit risk might have to be added. This is necessary because different entities in a group do not necessarily have the same creditworthiness, with the financing entity often being rated higher than the related parties.

3. This is a hypothetical rate typically reflecting the time value of money. As described in the OECD Guidance, the risk-free rate aims to capture a potential zero-risk investment, which may often be based on government-issued securities but can also be in reference to interest rate swap rates or interbank rates, to name a few. *See* OECD, *Transfer Pricing Guidelines for Multinational Enterprises and Tax Administrations*, January 2022, p. 67, para. 1.109.
4. The market has expectations of price increases (or declines); inflation expectations are therefore factored into interest rates.
5. A higher probability of default increases investment risk and thus increases the price necessary to bear such a risk (through higher interest rates). This default risk is estimated by considering potential losses of capital (expected loss) given default of the borrower.
6. Liquidity is defined as the ability to sell an asset on short notice, at a price that reflects the level at which the market as a whole values that asset at that time (efficient market). The inability to do so (or the partial ability to do so) might force a seller to concede to a discount when offloading the asset. Holding everything else constant, the holder of a less liquid security must be compensated for that potential scenario, and thus receive a higher interest rate than would have been prevalent had the security been fully negotiable at any time.
7. In general, investors need to be compensated for investing money for longer periods of time. This is true for normal economic environments where the interest rate curve is upward sloping – that is, where long-term rates are greater than shorter-term ones. In case of an interest rate curve inversion, the opposite is true.
8. OECD, *Transfer Pricing Guidelines for Multinational Enterprises and Tax Administrations*, para. 10.95.

Maturity adjustments may be relevant where there is a mismatch between the tenor of the evaluated loan and the lender's cost of funds. Group treasury companies may seek funding via capital markets, which may, for example, be longer-term transactions. Assuming the issuance dates coincide, and the cost of funds method can be relied on, it would be necessary to consider the difference in the maturity of the third-party lending relative to the related-party lending being provided.

Seniority and collateral adjustments may need to be considered because related-party debt can be subordinated to arrangements entered into by group treasury entities and third parties. Differences in collateral and seniority of the instruments and the effect this may have on the risk profiling of the transaction should be carefully considered and adjusted for.

Currency of the underlying transaction versus the third-party debt should be considered. Group treasury entities can often raise funds in a number of different currencies as they manage funding and liquidity globally for entities in multiple jurisdictions. Where there is a mismatch in currency denomination between the tested loan and lender's cost of funds, appropriate adjustments must be made to accurately account for the risks inherent in each local market.

Other factors, such as expenses related to loan arrangement and servicing, and a profit margin required by the lender, may need to be considered when relying on the cost-of-funds approach.[9] Third-party transactions may have a lower coupon attached, whilst additional return is captured via upfront fees. The cost of funds should reflect the full extent of the fees charged by a lender and not just the stated interest rate.

The timing of the issuance is a key driving factor of whether the cost-of-funds approach can be used. When the group treasury loan transactions' issuance date is vastly different compared to the related-party transactions, it becomes questionable to what extent such transactions would have occurred under similar market conditions. Cost of funds can change markedly from one period to the next. For this reason, careful consideration should be given to the effect that different dates of issuance would have had on third-party and related-party transaction yields.

## 1 Case Study: Cost of Funds Approach

Facts of the Case

A multinational company operates in the hospitality industry and is headquartered in the United Kingdom. The group's treasury entity, also based in the United Kingdom (UKFinco), predominantly raises funds in GBP and manages the group's liquidity and funding requirements centrally. UKFinco has extended an intercompany loan to a

9. *Ibid.*, para. 10.97.

subsidiary of the company in the Czech Republic (CzSubco) for general corporate expenditures.

Terms of the Transaction

> Notional amount CZK 145,000,000
> Issue date: 1 January 2019
> Repayment features: interest and capital at maturity
> Maturity date: 1 January 2020
> Interest rate: 3 % fixed
> Seniority: senior unsecured

Determining Creditworthiness of the Borrower

To price the loan to CzSubCo, a detailed value chain, functional, asset, and risk analysis needs to be conducted to fully understand the relational dynamics between the parties. More specifically, the transaction should be accurately delineated.[10] Then the economic analysis can be conducted considering the comparability factors that may affect the pricing of the transaction. These include, for example, the creditworthiness (default risk) of the borrower. To assess the default risk associated with CzSubCo, rating methods from major rating agencies can be relied on. Since CzSubCo is not rated by any of the major agencies, the authors derive its corporate entity letter rating by applying Moody's Investor Services Credit Rating Methodology, which in most cases gives the rating applicable to senior unsecured debt instruments. After considering the various quantitative and qualitative factors within the methodology and implications of implicit support and sovereign ratings, CzSubCo's alphanumeric credit rating was determined to be Baa2 (BBB on the Standard & Poor Global Ratings rating scale). UKFinco's shadow credit rating was also estimated to be Baa2, similar to the subsidiary.

Determining Applicable Loan Benchmarks

Having determined the alphanumeric credit rating for the Czech operating entity (and therefore the alphanumeric rating applicable to the senior unsecured instrument), we can estimate the expected yield of the loan by identifying comparable instruments on the market.

Given that data for lower-rated (BBB and lower) CZK-denominated debt instruments are generally sparse, comparable instruments with features sufficiently related to the tested loan could not be identified. However, UKFinco has entered into recent funding transactions with external counterparties, which can be used as a benchmark. More specifically, on analysing UKFinco's external funding transactions, we identified one bank loan with an issue date most contemporaneous with the tested loan. Although in some cases the weighted average cost of funding of a company may be relevant, the instances where this may occur are slim, especially for term loans and where representative adjustments can be done. In this example we consider only one

10. *Ibid.*, paras 1.51, 1.56, 1.139.

loan transaction entered into by the group finance company with third parties. A similar analysis could be completed on the average weighted cost of funding of a group.

As can be seen in Table 16.1, the loans have comparable terms, except for the currency and maturity. Adjustments would need to be performed for these features to ensure that the comparability criteria are met.

*Table 16.1 Comparison of Debt Features Based on Hypothetical Case Study*

| | *Tested Loan* | *Bank Loan: Comparable Transaction* |
|---|---|---|
| Maturity | 1 year | 5 years |
| Credit rating | Baa2 (BBB) | Baa2 (BBB) |
| Currency | CZK | GBP |
| Sector | Hospitality | Hospitality |
| Issue date | 1 January 2019 | 12 January 2019 |
| Interest rate | 3% | 4% |

Currency, Maturity Adjustments, and Yield Analysis

The GBP third-party loan has a different maturity from the tested transaction. To account for this, one can compare the effect on yields between different maturity instruments at a specific time, in particular on the transaction date. In this case, considering the maturity by using the difference between similar GBP bond yields of a one-year versus a five-year instrument, or similar maturity swap rates (depending on what is available) can provide a proxy for the effect that maturity may have on an instrument:

*Maturity Adjustment = GBP 5-Year Bond Yield or Swap Rate-GBP 1-Year Bond Yield or Swap Rate*

This type of data can typically be obtained from databases such as Bloomberg, Factset, and EIKON. For this purpose, we assume the effect of maturity to be from 1% to 1.5% based on a comparison between a one-year and five-year bond index.[11] In this instance, a three-month period from the date of the transaction and preceding the transaction has been relied upon. The relevant period will be based on the facts and circumstances of each individual case.

Having now determined the impact that maturity may have on the instrument, the next step will be to consider the impact of currency not only from an economic and money market perspective but also from a sovereign risk perspective. In the case at hand the loan is a fixed-rate loan. For this purpose, two aspects should be considered:

11. Short-term yields are lower than long-term yields in the economic environment at the time, so this adjustment will be subtracted.

(1) difference and its impact between the GBP risk-free rate or Government rate and the Czech Republic Risk-free rate or Government rate;
(2) difference in credit spreads (i.e., risk premium added to the risk-free rate) between GBP-denominated instruments versus CZK-denominated instruments. For the latter currency swaps or inferences comparing similar rated instruments credit spreads available in both currencies can be relied upon.

The yield of the tested loan can therefore be benchmarked using UKFinco cost of funds, accounting for the difference in maturity (in this case which would lead to a negative adjustment on the rate) and political, economic and money market risk factor (in this case which would lead to a positive adjustment):

*Tested Yield = GBP Bank Loan Yield – Maturity Adjustment + Considerations for political and Currency impact adjustment*

The range for the tested transaction is presented in Table 16.2. All data are hypothetical and do not reflect actual data as of the transaction date.

*Table 16.2 Yield Range for Hypothetical Case Study*

| | *Cost of Funds (Internal CUP or Cost of Funds)* | *Maturity Adjustment* | *Sovereign and Currency Risk Considerations* | *Total Adjusted Range* |
|---|---|---|---|---|
| | (1) | (2) | (3) | (4) = (1) - (2) + (3) |
| Upper bound | 4% | 1.00% | 0.80% | 3.80% |
| Median | 4% | 1.25% | 0.64% | 3.39% |
| Lower bound | 4% | 1.50% | 0.35% | 2.85% |
| Tested rate | | | | 3.00 % |

Concluding Remarks

We demonstrate using the cost of funds of the treasury entity as a benchmark to value an intercompany loan where external CUP data were not available. The credit ratings of both lender and borrower are similar, and the loans were issued at similar times, so the cost of funds data could be used effectively as a proxy for the tested yield following currency and maturity adjustments. The analyses shown here determined that UK-Finco applied an interest rate that is at arm's length for its internal funding arrangements.

## II ECONOMIC MODELLING INTRODUCTION

When using the CUP method, finding the appropriate data may be difficult because it needs to be sufficiently comparable to the transaction, or the required adjustments can be performed, which might not always be possible. This may be true where the credit rating of the transaction is very low, or the transaction occurs in a market where CUP data are scarce. Under such circumstances, one might resort to economic modelling to price intercompany loans. This approach estimates interest rates by creating a model that incorporates factors based on the underlying assumptions in accordance with economic theory.

## 1 Case Study: Economic Modelling Approach

Facts of the Case

A group operating in the food processing sector is headquartered in Italy (Euroheadco) and has affiliates across Europe. Our hypothetical case study centres on the valuation of an intercompany loan issued by Euroheadco to a European operating subsidiary (Eurofoodco). All data in this case example are hypothetical.

Terms of the Transaction

Notional amount: EUR 30,000,000
Issue date: 4 January 2018
Repayment features: interest annually; capital on maturity
Maturity date: 4 January 2023
Interest rate: 8% fixed
Seniority: senior secured (collateralized by the assets of the operating company)

Determining Creditworthiness of the Borrower

The interest rate or price of a debt instrument, such as the loan provided to Eurofoodco, depends on the creditworthiness of the borrower. The interest rate on the loan should therefore incorporate expected credit losses. By estimating the shadow credit rating of the obligor/borrower, one can derive the estimated expected credit losses and obtain the corresponding arm's length interest rate to apply to the loan.

Because Eurofoodco is not rated by any of the major credit rating agencies, we derive its corporate entity letter rating by applying Moody's Investor Services Credit Rating Methodology, which estimates the rating applicable to senior unsecured debt instruments. After considering the various quantitative and qualitative factors in the methodology, we determined Eurofoodco's numeric rating to be 16.94. This numeric rating equates to an alphanumeric credit rating of Caa1 (or CCC+ on the Standard & Poor's rating scale).

Adjusting Eurofoodco's Corporate Entity Letter Rating for Lien

The loan facility provided to Eurofoodco is a senior loan secured by company assets. Given the loan features and the fact that Moody's methodology applies to the issuer or senior unsecured debt rating, we have to adjust Eurofoodco's rating for lien of the instrument. In short, to impact the credit rating (and hence the correct interest rate on the loan) for lien, we calculate the effect of added recovery value associated with secured loans to the credit losses (which are now reduced) and infer a new and better credit rating, reflecting the improved security associated with a secured loan.

To start, we rely on corporate default and recovery rate statistics. Such data can be obtained from the major credit rating agencies such as Moody's, S&P Global Ratings and Fitch Ratings. For illustrative purposes, we relied solely on hypothetical datafor:

- annual credit losses for senior unsecured facilities by corporate entity letter rating;
- annual default rate by letter rating; and
- loan recovery rates by seniority.

Using a statistical tool referred to as regression analysis, we regress the annual credit losses[12] for unsecured obligations with the credit ratings (as defined by their numeric values).[13] *See* the grey line in Figure 16.1.

To find the lower credit losses linked to secured obligations, additional modelling is necessary because data available (equating credit losses to credit rating) are generally only available for unsecured obligations. On the other hand, recovery values for both secured and unsecured obligations are generally available. We can construct a synthetic data series equating credit losses to credit rating for secured obligations by integrating their improved recovery rates. Using the synthetic data series, we perform another regression of annual credit losses for secured obligations against credit ratings. *See* the black line in Figure 16.1.

In effect, we use the corporate entity letter rating of Eurofoodco of Caa1 (16.94) to find the associated annual credit loss for unsecured bonds of 3.83%. The corresponding annual credit loss for secured bonds given the corporate entity letter rating (applicable to Senior Unsecured bonds) is 2.94%. We use this last value to imply the equivalent corporate bond credit rating of B3 (16.16) from improved recovery values associated with senior secured obligations compared with senior unsecured obligations (and a decrease in expected credit losses from 3.83% to 2.94%).

12. Credit ratings represent a rank-ordering of creditworthiness or expected credit loss. Expected credit loss is a function of the probability of default and the expected severity of loss given a default. Mathematically, credit loss can be expressed as:

$$\textbf{Annual Credit Loss} \approx \textbf{Annual Default Rate} \times (1 - \textbf{Recovery Rate}).$$

*See* Moody's Rating System in Brief, available at https://www.moodys.com/sites/products/productattachments/moody%27s%20rating%20system.pdf.

13. This regression was done using hypothetical data (i.e., a data series equating credit losses to credit rating for unsecured obligations).

*Figure 16.1 Annual Credit Loss for Eurofoodco's Secured Obligations*

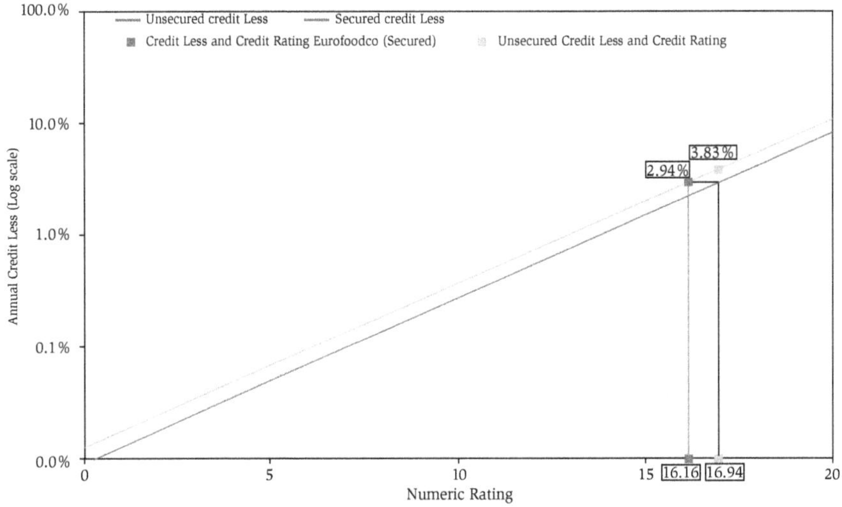


Our final result (one-notch upgrade in credit rating) is consistent with Moody's Senior Ratings Algorithm and Estimated Senior Ratings on Notching for Subordination guidelines,[14] where credit rating increases one notch for secured bonds if the corporate entity letter rating is Caa1.

*Table 16.3 Eurofoodco's Corporate Entity Letter Rating Adjusted for Lien*

| *Numeric Value* | *Letter Rating* | *Annual Credit Loss* |
|---|---|---|
| 16.16 | B3 | 2.94% |

Yield Analysis

Having determined the letter rating associated with the seniority of the senior secured instrument, we can estimate the expected yield of the debt facility. The yield analysis methodology we use involved the identification of comparable bond indices available on the market. Many financial market data providers (such as Bloomberg and IBOXX) derive such indices for several industries, maturity terms, and credit ratings. We considered the maturity, credit ratings, currencies, sector, and geographical area. This approach was used because insufficient information was available on individual bonds accessible.

Table 16.4 shows the comparable indices we selected given the characteristics of the senior secured loan. Because data were not available for credit ratings below BBB,

14. Moody's Investors Service, *Notching Corporate Instrument Ratings based on Differences in Security and Priority of Claim*, October 2017, available at https://www.moodys.com/credit-ratings-tab/Methodology/120500?orgname=VW-Credit-Inc-&rle=MIS.

we used bond indices with credit ratings of AA, A, and BBB[15] as a starting point to extrapolate the appropriate yield for the senior secured facility (B3 Moody's, B– S&P), assuming a linear relationship between credit loss and yield.[16] *See* equation (1):

$$\text{Yield} = \alpha + \beta \text{ Annual Credit Loss} + u_i \quad (1)$$

Specifically, we used daily data from the three-month period preceding the transaction to compute the intercept (α) and slope (β) by regressing the AA, A, and BBB yields against the annual credit losses associated with these ratings. We used this estimated linear relationship to predict yields for the senior secured liability with the corporate entity letter rating of B3, and an annual credit loss of 2.94%. In other words, for each day in the three-month period, we use that day's yield data for the AA, A, and BBB indices to extrapolate the corresponding B–/B3 yield, in effect constructing a synthetic data series of daily yields corresponding to an issuer with a B3 credit rating.

*Table 16.4 Comparable Indices to Eurofoodco's Senior Secured Liability (Hypothetical) Case Study*

| | *Senior Secured Liability* | *EUR Composite (BBB, A, and AA) Five-Year* |
|---|---|---|
| Maturity | 5 years | 5 years |
| Credit rating | B3 (B–) | Baa (BBB), A (A), and Aa (AA) |
| Currency | EUR | EUR |
| Sector | Food processing | Mix of several sectors, including food processing |
| Geographical area | Europe | Europe |

By calculating the interquartile range of the daily B–/B3 yields from our synthetic data series spanning three months before the transaction, we conclude (*see* Table 16.5) that the tested yield of 8.00% is within arm's length range.

*Table 16.5 Yield Range for Hypothetical Case Study*

| | |
|---|---|
| Upper Bound | 11.18% |
| Median | 9.03% |
| Lower Bound | 7.85% |
| Tested rate | 8.00 % |

15. These are Baa2, A2, and Aa2 under Moody's rating system.
16. All data relied on are hypothetical.

### Concluding Remarks on the Case Study

The case study provides a walkthrough on how to construct an economic model to estimate a range of interest rates when comparable uncontrolled price data may be difficult to source. This approach can easily be used to account for lien of the debt and thereby the relevant default risk. Following determination of default risk, a second economic model was constructed to estimate yields applicable to lower credit ratings where data were not available. This approach involved extrapolating yields from readily available indices using linear regression. The analyses shown here determined that Euroheadco applied an interest rate that is at arm's length for its internal funding arrangements.

## III CONCLUSION

The method for pricing a particular transaction depends on its underlying characteristics and data availability. When using the CUP method, challenges may arise because of lack of data or inability to perform the required adjustments. When considering the cost of funds approach, a decision must be made on whether the average cost of funds or a particular transaction will be used as the CUP. Care must be taken such that the relevant adjustments are correctly applied to align the lender's funding cost with the characteristics of the tested transaction. The market environment for funding at the applicable time must be considered when assessing whether a rate based on the lender's cost of funds is a realistic option for comparison.

Although the economic modelling approach can be relied on in most circumstances, it is rather academic (i.e., technical) and might be difficult to apply for market participants in practice. It is based on historical (default) probability and recovery rate data, and thus comparability to current market conditions might prove problematic, for which adjustments might have to be performed.

Nevertheless, both methods are welcome additions to the analyst's toolkit to test or determine the arm's length nature of the interest rate applied to tested transactions.

# CHAPTER 17
# Intercompany Loans for Real Estate Financing: A Case Study

*Danny Beeton*[*]

## I INTRODUCTION

When considering a related party loan to acquire a real estate asset, the considerations and the sources of information are quite specific to that context. The purpose of this chapter is therefore to work through the creation of a real estate lending transfer pricing study, at least in terms of sources and methods.

The structure of the chapter is as follows:

- methods for determining the arm's length amount of debt for a real estate borrower;
- methods for determining the credit rating of a real estate borrower;
- methods for determining the interest rate on a real estate loan;
- comparability adjustments to the interest rate for a real estate loan;
- conclusions.

## II ESTABLISHING THE ARM'S LENGTH AMOUNT OF DEBT

### 1 Overview

Compliance with the Arm's Length Principle of transfer pricing requires that a real estate loan should have terms and conditions that could have been agreed upon

* The views and opinions set forth herein are the personal views or opinions of the authors; they do not necessarily reflect the views or opinions of the organization with which the authors are associated.

between independent parties in the same situation, including the size of the loan. In the context of a real estate loan, the borrower's debt capacity will also be influenced by the features of the property or property construction/development project which the loan is to help finance and what is to be done with the property after it is acquired – for example, lenders allocate a lower debt capacity when the borrower intends to dispose of the property rather than let it, or where the property is expected to generate lower or more uncertain cash flows by reason of the nature of the tenants or the tenant contracts.

As for any loan, the amount of debt for a real estate loan is limited by two main considerations, namely the short-term ability to pay the interest on time and the longer-term ability to repay the principal. For example, the 'recommended' or 'best practice' approach of the Organisation for Economic Co-operation and Development (OECD)/G20 *BEPS Action 4 Final Report* is based on the ratio between an entity's net deductions for interest and payments economically equivalent to interest to a percentage of its earnings before interest, taxes, depreciation and amortization (EBITDA).[1] However, it also notes the 'thin capitalization' approach of linking interest deductibility to the debt/equity ratio.[2] This 'thin capitalization' approach is discussed as a way of attributing 'free' capital to a permanent establishment in the OECD's 2010 *Report on the Attribution of Profit to Permanent Establishments*.[3]

In the context of real estate loans, another approach used by lenders is to link the amount of a loan to the value of the property which the loan is to finance, either in its present form or after the improvement/repurposing works which the loan is also to finance. Where the project is more speculative, such as the acquisition of a brownfield site without planning permission for development, the borrower may instead link the size of the loan to the cost of the project.

A key difference between standard 'OECD' methods and the specialist real estate lender approach is that the former involve financial ratios which are usually calculated on the basis of a run of financial periods, whereas the Loan-to-Value (LTV) or Loan-to-Cost (LTC) calculations are based on the value or cost at a single point in time.

Another difference is that the LTV approach links the amount of borrowing to the Assets side of the Balance Sheet, and drills down into factors which influence the quality of the property asset in question. Thus, for example, the achievable LTV will be higher for better quality buildings in better locations with better occupancy rates, higher quality tenants and longer tenancy agreements with less generous break

1. OECD/G20, *Base Erosion and Profit Shifting Project: Limiting Base Erosion Involving Interest Deductions and the Financial Payments: Action 4: 2015 Final Report* (2015). *See*, for example, Executive Summary, p. 11, Introduction, p. 21, para. 18 and Chapter 1, pp. 23, 25.
2. *Ibid. See*, for example Introduction, p. 21, para. 17, which states that 'The majority of countries applying fixed ratio rules link interest deductibility to the level of equity in an entity, typically through thin capitalisation rules based on a debt/equity test.'
3. OECD, *Report on the Attribution of Profits to Permanent Establishments*, 23 July 2010. *See*, for example, paras 129-134.

clauses, and there could be different LTV ratios for the same property depending on its proposed use for residential, retail, office, warehouse or other accommodation, and whether it is to be sold or let, what stage of development/improvement it as at and whether there is already planning permission for any such work. These factors influence the prospective sale proceeds or size and stability of the letting income from the property, and as such, they affect the lender's risk in terms of repayment of the principal and the payment of interest when due.

Benchmarking of the maximum size of a real estate loan could therefore involve reference to evidence of arm's length LTV or LTC ratios, or even the more indirect approach of using published research on the relationship between LTV credit rating and limiting the loan size to the minimum implied credit rating which it is thought the borrower would want to maintain.

For example, consider a property developer which wished to acquire a property for office rental. Assume that it has good earnings to maintain a high Debt Service Coverage Ratio (DSCR) and is therefore focusing on the maximum LTV which would still leave it with its target minimum credit rating of BBB.

*Table 17.1 Illustrative Relationship Between LTVs and Corresponding Credit Ratings*

| *Rating Level* | *Average LTV Threshold (%)* |
|---|---|
| AAA | Around 40 |
| AA | Around 50 |
| A | Around 60 |
| BBB | Around 70 |
| BB | Around 80 |
| B | Around 90 |
| CCC | Around 95 |
| CC | Around 100 |
| C | Around 105 |

*Source*: Hypothetical figures to illustrate the relationship.

Table 17.1 indicates that if the cost of the acquisition or project is 100, then a maximum of 70 of this can be financed by debt and the rest by equity if the borrower wishes to maintain a minimum BBB rating. A tax administration might therefore argue that either because the borrower or its wider group has a stated BBB rating target, or because that is the average or lower bound assigned by rating agencies for companies in the borrower's industry, it would not be commercially rational for the borrower to take on debt of more than 70 and it should not be entitled to interest deductions for any borrowing above this level.

## 2 Use of 'Internal' Transactions to Determine the Maximum Amount of Debt

One way of determining the maximum amount of related party borrowing is to refer to similar transactions between unrelated parties.[4]

Given that fewer comparability adjustments are likely to be needed where loans to the same party from unrelated parties can be referred to, the financial covenant ratios in these 'internal comparable uncontrolled transactions' is a potential reference for determining the arm's length amount of debt. This is especially so in the case of real estate loans because a very common context for a real estate loan is that a special purpose vehicle company borrows from both a bank and a related party at the same time to help finance the same property acquisition or development project so that the loans are already comparable in some important aspects.

If some such internal benchmarks are available but are not being used, then this decision must at least be explained. Typically, this would be because some of the comparability adjustments cannot be made reliably or the cumulative effect of the adjustments would be very large, calling into question the initial comparability of the benchmark transactions. In particular, senior real estate loans between independent parties typically differ from related party real estate loans in the following ways:

- being secured on the property and senior to any other debt, and involving loan arrangement and administration fees;[5]
- involving tighter financial covenant ratios not directly related to the debt-to-equity ratio;
- not including the options to prepay (possibly without a penalty) or to roll up interest payments until the end of the loan agreement which often appears in related party loan agreements;
- being advanced on the assumption that planning permission has been secured (which is often not the case for speculative related party construction projects).

For a typical unsecured, subordinated related party loan with options, loose financial covenant ratios and no fees, the calculation of the size of each LTV comparability adjustment (some of which will be large) compared to a benchmark independent bank loan could be more problematic than when using 'external' transactions as benchmarks, so that it may be more reliable to undertake instead a search for initially more comparable external transactions which need fewer adjustments (e.g., loans which are unsecured and subordinated like the related party loan) instead of

4. For example, para. 10.20 of OECD, *Transfer Pricing Guidelines for Multinational Enterprises and Tax Administrations* (2022) states that 'In an ideal scenario, a comparability analysis would enable the identification of financial transactions between independent parties which match the tested transaction in all respects ... where differences exist ... it may be possible ... to make comparability adjustments.'
5. In addition, in most real estate loans from independent banks there is either a clause in the agreement or a separate intercreditor agreement covering the allowable seniority of any further liens of debt and in most cases the bank will dictate that all other property will be subordinated.

trying to make a series of large and debatable adjustments to debt-to-equity benchmarks obtained from internal transactions. However, it is also often the case that there are features specific to a property which are important, and which will have been taken into account in the 'internal' transaction, but will not have been a factor in a particular set of 'external' benchmarks.

The following examples illustrate situations when an internal transaction may or not provide a reliable benchmark for the arm's length debt capacity.

Example 1:

Suppose that company R owns company S and that company S wishes to acquire two identical properties, both valued at 100, in the same location and at the same time. For the first property, company R infuses 20 as equity and 80 as a senior secured loan to company S.

For the second property, an independent bank provides a senior secured loan of 100. Company S uses the full amount of this loan to buy the property so that the LTV is 100%.

In this example, the LTV for the second property could be used as an internal benchmark for the maximum LTV in the first transaction.

Example 2:

Suppose that company X owns company Y and that company Y wishes to acquire a property valued at 100. An independent bank provides a senior secured loan of 60. Company X proposes to infuse an amount of equity and provide a subordinated unsecured loan.

In this example, the LTV in the independent bank loan cannot be used as a benchmark for the maximum LTV in the loan from company X. This is because the loan from company X is a higher risk tranche of funding for which a higher interest rate will be charged to reflect this additional risk. Such loans are normal practice between independent parties in the real estate sector. A more reliable benchmark for the maximum LTV in the loan from company X may be obtained by reference to the LTV in comparable loan agreements between independent parties.

## 3 Use of 'External' Transactions to Determine the Maximum Amount of Debt: Loan Databases

If reliable internal transaction benchmarks are not reliable, then the next step should be to consider individual external transactions. Here the problem that often arises is that the credit rating of the borrower, after taking on the related party debt, is so poor that the set of relevant benchmarks in a loan database for that credit rating of borrower is very small, and therefore perhaps not representative. (This may be simply a reflection of the type of loans (often large and syndicated) which are publicly available to compilers of loan databases.) One solution might be to identify an arm's length range of debt-to-equity ratios for a better credit rating of real estate borrowers and then to adjust this range by the general difference between debt-to-equity ratios for all loans to borrowers of the lower and the higher credit rating respectively. However, the reliability of this comparability adjustment may be questioned.

## 4 Use of 'External' Transactions to Determine the Maximum Amount of Debt: Real Estate Lending Market Surveys

Another approach when a good set of comparable real estate loan agreements cannot be identified is to consult a survey of real estate loans. For example, the *UK Commercial Real Estate Lending Survey* is cited in HMRC's International Manual for its tax inspectors and is sometimes referred to in transfer pricing studies in other European jurisdictions (on the assumption of similarities between property markets).[6] Certain property advisory firms, real estate agents, accounting firms and rating agencies also publish lending market surveys for other jurisdictions and regions, for example, major cities across Europe. These surveys report the maximum LTV/LTC[7] ranges by property type, quality of property, quality of location and purpose of loan, sometimes in the form of grids showing the results for different combinations of these factors.[8]

Internal transactions and loan databases have the advantage that they involve individual transactions (i.e., loans) which can be examined and (hopefully) adjusted for any comparability differences. In contrast, loan surveys have the disadvantage that they are based on ranges which lenders have reported for various subsets of their loans so that the individual loans cannot be examined and adjusted for their exact comparability differences.

## 5 Use of 'External' Transactions to Determine the Maximum Amount of Debt: Databases of Financial Statements

Another approach when considering the arm's length amount of debt is to identify the range of debt-to-equity ratios which are reported in the financial statements of comparable companies (especially, ones in the same industry). This is similar to the 'Thin Capitalization' approach to allocating 'free capital' to a permanent establishment discussed in the OECD's *2010 Report on the Attribution of Profits to Permanent Establishments*.[9]

---

6. Cass Business School, City, University of London, *The UK Commercial Real Estate Lending Survey*. The information is collected and published twice yearly.
7. The LTV ratio is based on the fair market value of the (developed) property and tends to be more commonly used when evaluating financing for developed property. The LTC ratio is used in commercial real estate construction in the debt financing of a project, taking into account the cost of building or developing a property. *See*, for example, Mark Bonekamp & Neil Schaatsbergen, *Transfer Pricing Aspects of Real Estate Financing*, March/April 2020 International Transfer Pricing Journal 113 (2020).
8. *See*, for example, Moody's Investors Service, *Moody's Approach to Rating EMEA CMBS Transactions* (14 October 2020), KPMG, *Property Lending Barometer 2020* (2020), BCM Global, *Market Trend Analysis Issue 5* (March 2021).
9. *See* paras 129 to 134 and in particular the reference to 'The range of actual capital structures of independent host country enterprises carrying on the same or similar activities as the PE under the same or similar conditions … .'

This approach has the benefit of simplicity and verifiability (in that the tax administration is likely to have access to these financial statements), but it has several disadvantages, including the following:

- the information does not come from individual loans to each company but is, instead, the result of various loans advanced to it at different times in different market conditions and when its financial performance may have been different;
- the proportion of debt financing at the time of the individual loans will be changed by subsequent changes in the profitability of the borrower and hence in its retained earnings – that is, the debt-to-equity ratio in the latest financial statements of a company may have drifted away from the ratio when any of the earlier loans were advanced;
- if the chosen method is to use the debt-to-equity ratio as a measure of the arm's length LTV so as to benchmark an individual real estate loan, it is necessary to assume that all of the debt in a benchmark real estate company's balance sheet was incurred in order to fund the acquisition of real estate assets (i.e., that debt / (debt plus equity) = LTV). This will be truer for real estate businesses than for other borrowers, but even real estate businesses will have other reasons to borrow than to purchase a real estate asset.

More generally, the OECD's *2010 Report on the Attribution of Profits to Permanent Establishments* notes that:

> One concern with such an approach is what appears to be the wide range of debt-to-equity ratios observable at arm's length and whether, given the diverse range, it is possible to apply a thin capitalization approach outside the financial sector ... A critical issue is whether it is possible to take into account all the factors that underlie such different debt-to-equity ratios.[10]

## III TECHNIQUES FOR DETERMINING THE CREDIT RATING OF A REAL ESTATE BORROWER

A number of international transfer pricing cases have supported the position that a separate credit rating should be determined for a subsidiary, rather than making automatic reference to the credit rating of the shareholder. Only once this has been done should an adjustment be made for the credit rating improvement (if any) which an independent lender would have made for the implicit financial support of the shareholder for its subsidiary.[11] This view has also been adopted by the OECD's

10. *See* para. 132.
11. *See*, for example, Tax Court of Canada, *General Electric Capital Canada v. the Queen*, TCC 563 (2009), especially the Analysis section of the judgment beginning at p. 48 and in particular the sub-section 'Framework for the Determination of an Arm's Length Price' beginning at p. 62. Paragraph 235 refers to the importance of the standalone credit rating of the borrower and para. 274 also does this in the context of a two-stage approach in which an implicit support adjustment is a second stage; also Full Federal Court of Australia, *Chevron Australia Holdings Pty v.*

*Transfer Pricing Guidelines for Multinational Enterprises and Tax Administrations* (2022), *Chapter X*[12] and the United Nations' 2021 *Practical Manual on Transfer Pricing for Developing Countries.*[13]

In the context of asset-backed financing such as the acquisition of real estate, the relevance of credit rating of the shareholder is even less relevant, in that the financing is linked to the value of the asset.

The credit rating of a real estate borrower can be derived easily from the prospective LTV or LTC ratio, reading off a ratings agency's tables – for example, the Standard & Poor Global Ratings grid, while *Moody's Approach to Rating EMEA CMBS Transactions*[14] gives a Ba rating to loans with an LTV of 65%-75% and a DSCR of 1.2 or better.[15] Other Moody's methodologies such as the ones for Real Estate Investment Trusts and Residential Mortgage-Backed Securities may also be helpful for benchmarking certain real estate loans.

Similarly to non-real estate loans, a more detailed approach is to use a published methodology, requiring more comprehensive quantitative and qualitative information. Where a license to a ratings agency's model has been obtained, this information can be entered into the model online for a more exact and more clearly independent rating report.[16]

## IV INTEREST RATE BENCHMARKING FOR REAL ESTATE LOANS

### 1 Introduction

The Chapter X of the OECD *Transfer Pricing Guidelines for Multinational Enterprises and Tax Administrations (2022)* was the first substantive consideration by an international body of the implications of a number of international tax cases for the practical application of the OECD Transfer Pricing Guidelines to related party loans. It does not address real estate loans specifically but it does consider issues which are important to the determination of the arm's length interest rate in such loans in section C.1 ('Intra-group loans'), including the importance of the borrower's standalone credit rating, the potential adjustment for implicit group support, comparability adjustments (including special situations in which they should not, in fact, be made because, at arm's length, the borrower would have entered into a different loan), and the choice of benchmarking method. These issues are discussed in the remainder of this section.

*Commissioner of Taxation*, FCAFC 62 (2017), especially para. 124 on standalone creditworthiness and para. 130 on the necessity to consider the impact of group support.

12. *See*, for example, paras 10.71 and 10.78.
13. *See* section 9.8, 'Considering the Creditworthiness of Associated Enterprises', especially para. 9.8.6.
14. CMBS (Commercial Mortgage-Backed Securities).
15. *See* for example *Moody's Approach to Rating EMEA CMBS Transactions*. https://www.moodys.com/research/Moodys-Approach-to-Rating-EMEA-CMBS-Transactions--PBS_1264385.
16. *See*, for example, Moody's RiskCalc Model and Standard and Poor's Credit Model.

## 2 Use of 'Internal' Transactions to Determine the Arm's Length Interest Rate

Chapter X of the OECD *Transfer Pricing Guidelines for Multinational Enterprises and Tax Administrations (2022)* notes that:

> The widespread existence of markets for borrowing and lending money and the frequency of such transactions between independent borrowers and lenders, coupled with the widespread availability of information and analysis of loan markets may make it easier to apply the CUP method to financial transactions than may be the case for other types of transactions.[17]

However, it says nothing about the use of internal comparable uncontrolled prices (CUPs) such as senior bank loans. This is surprising given that, in the real estate context at least, some properties have very specific features and development projects in particular may have very uncertain returns (e.g., depending on whether planning permission has been obtained and what harmful substances may be found during the construction work on 'brownfield' sites). It may be difficult to find close external benchmarks for these transactions. Thus, even when ultimately focusing on external loan benchmarks, it is normal in real estate interest rate studies to also closely examine any potential internal comparable loan agreements, much more so than in other industries.

## 3 Use of 'External' Transactions to Determine the Arm's Length Interest Rate: Loan Databases

On the other hand, Chapter X of the OECD *Transfer Pricing Guidelines for Multinational Enterprises and Tax Administrations (2022)* is relatively enthusiastic about the use of market data for benchmarking interest rates, observing that:

> With the extent of competition often present within lending markets, it might be expected that, given the characteristics of the loan ... there would be a single rate at which the borrower could obtain funds and a single rate at which a lender could invest funds to obtain an appropriate reward. In practice, however, there is unlikely to be a single 'market rate' but a range of rates although competition between lenders and the availability of pricing information will tend to narrow the range.[18]

Arm's length interest rates can also be based on the return of realistic alternative transactions with comparable economic characteristics, such as bonds.[19] There is a range of proprietary databases with such information for use in an external CUP

17. Paragraph 10.90.
18. Paragraph 10.91.
19. For a comprehensive discussion of the pros and cons of using bond yields as benchmarks for an interest rate, *see* T. Petrakos, V. Chand & A. Pletz, *Interest Rate Benchmarking for Transfer Pricing Purposes: A Comparison Between the Loan and the Bond Approach*, 28 Intl. Transfer Pricing J. 4 (2021), Journal Articles & Opinion Pieces IBFD.

analysis.[20] These include loans to real estate industry borrowers, although details of the properties involved may not be available.

### 4 Use of 'External' Transactions to Determine the Arm's Length Interest Rate: Real Estate Lending Market Surveys

Real estate lending surveys report averages and ranges rather than individual transactions and provide less precise benchmarks for that reason. However, they are more precise than loan databases in that they provide great detail on the appropriate size of interest rate adjustments for property details and indeed the type of lender. In practice, they are therefore more commonly referred to in the real estate context than for other loans.

### 5 Use of 'External' Transactions to Determine the Arm's Length Interest Rate: Databases of Financial Statements

In a very high-level approach, taxpayers or advisers without access to benchmark loan transactions sometimes calculate the average interest rate paid by comparable companies by comparing the interest expense and debt figures in their financial statements. This may contribute to a wider analysis involving other methods but it is problematic by itself for a number of reasons – for example, the interest rates being paid by a comparable company now will reflect how long ago they entered into the loan agreements, on what terms, and (in the real estate context), the details of the properties which they acquired. These may be particular to each company. These problems are not considered by the OECD's *2010 Report on the Attribution of Profits to Permanent Establishments* in its discussion of the 'Thin Capitalization' approach to determining the arm's length debt-to-equity ratio for a permanent establishment by using sets of company financial statements, but they become important if these financial statements are to be used to benchmark an interest rate.

## V COMPARABILITY ADJUSTMENTS FOR REAL ESTATE LOANS AND HOW TO MAKE THEM

### 1 Comparability Adjustments in the Context of Real Estate Loans

The five OECD comparability factors apply to real estate loans just as they would to any other related party transaction. Some ways in which they could influence the interest rate on a real estate loan are shown in Table 17.2. (For a real estate lender, these features might more usually be grouped in a different way, e.g., the four factors of borrower, property portfolio, individual property and tenant.)

20. For example, Refinitiv's LoanConnector DealScan database (loans) and Refinitiv's EIKON database (bonds).

*Table 17.2 Examples of Comparability Adjustments in the Context of a Real Estate Loan*

| *OECD Comparability Factor* | *Examples in the Context of Real Estate Loans* |
|---|---|
| The contractual terms of the transaction | - Security over the property<br>- Seniority/subordination<br>- Separate arrangement, administration and commitment fees |
| The functional analysis | - Real estate industry know-how of borrower's management |
| The characteristics of the property of service provided | - Type of property (office, commercial, residential...)<br>- Diversity of property types in the portfolio (if applicable)<br>- Location of property (prime, secondary)<br>- Quality of the property (prime, secondary)[21]<br>- Quality of tenants, the remaining tenor of their tenancy agreements and their break clauses<br>- Phase of development of the property and percentage occupancy (if applicable)<br>- Planning permission (if relevant)<br>- Property to be sold or let |
| The economic circumstances of the persons and the market | - Purpose of the loan, e.g., a property acquisition or bridging finance[22] |
| The business strategies of the parties | - Synergy benefits (e.g., need to expand around current premises) |

*Source*: Analysis by the author.

These adjustments are considered further below.

## 2 The Contractual Terms of the Transaction

### *A Overview*

Lending surveys often present ranges of interest margins separately for senior and junior loans. A general adjustment can be calculated for the impact of subordination on

21. For example, this was determined to be a vitally important comparability factor which had not been adjusted for in the interest rate in the real estate lending case Administrative Court of Luxembourg, *Luxembourg v. Lender Societe*, 42083 (2019).
22. *See*, for example, BONEKAMP & SCHAATSBERGEN, 113.

the interest rate by comparing sets of relevant senior and subordinated loans in a database, but there are very few instances of otherwise similar senior and junior loans being advanced to the same borrower to allow a more precise comparison.

With regard to security, a number of international transfer pricing cases have considered the position that a shareholder loan cannot be assumed to be secured (in the absence of a security condition in the loan agreement) simply because the shareholder has control over the subsidiary and the asset is being purchased with the shareholder loan. For example, in the Government Court of Sweden, *Diligentia AB v. The Swedish Tax Agency*, 2483-2485-09, (2010), the court decided that a parent company does not need the security which a third party might require because it controls the subsidiary and has full information about its financial position, to the extent that a parent company loan can always be benchmarked against secured loans. (In this case, the loans had been borrowed to finance real estate investments.) By way of contrast, in the more recent Administrative Court of Luxembourg, *Luxembourg v. Lender Societe* (2019), it was not disputed that the shareholder real estate acquisition loan should be treated as an unsecured one. In the intervening 2017 decision in *Chevron Australia Holdings Pty v. Commissioner of Taxation*, it is stated that 'The evidence before, and found by, his Honour amply supported his Honour's prediction of the reasonable expectation of a borrowing ... being supported by security ... An objective of the group was to obtain the lowest cost of funding ....'[23] The first case cited concludes that the security was already implicit, the second did not accept this argument and the third concluded that the security was not implicit but an alternative, a secured loan could be imputed in place of the actual one and then priced.

Chapter X of the OECD *Transfer Pricing Guidelines for Tax Administrations and Multinational Enterprises* (2022) (partially) adopts the first and third perspectives. First, in paragraph 10.56 it is noted, from the lender's perspective, that:

> In the case of a loan from the parent entity of an MNE group to a subsidiary, the parent already has control and ownership of the subsidiary, which would make the granting of security less relevant to its risk analysis as a lender. Therefore, in evaluating the pricing of a loan between associated enterprises, it is important to consider the absence of contractual rights over the assets of the borrowing entity does not necessarily reflect the economic reality of the risk inherent in the loan. If the assets of the business are not already pledged as security elsewhere, it will be appropriate to consider under Chapter I analysis[24] whether those assets are available to act as collateral for the otherwise unsecured loan and the consequential impact upon the pricing of the loan.

Second, from the borrower's perspective, it is noted in paragraph 10.58 that they would seek to optimize their weighted average cost of capital and consider their 'options realistically available':

> in respect of collateral [security], in some circumstances, assuming that the business has suitable collateral to offer, this would usually be secured funding, ahead of unsecured funding ....

23. *See* para. 132.
24. In particular, section I.D.1 'Identifying the Commercial or Financial Relations'.

The following examples can help to illustrate these different positions.

### *B* *Example 1*

Company B is a subsidiary of Company A. Company B wishes to purchase a real estate property with a loan from Company A. The loan is not formally secured on the asset and there is no other loan which is secured on the asset. The interest rate on the loan is nevertheless set by reference to the arm's length rate of interest on comparable secured loans, on the basis that Company A has effective security because it can require Company B to sell the asset and dividend up the proceeds.

### *C* *Example 2*

Company D is a subsidiary of Company C. Company D wishes to purchase a real estate property with a loan from Company C. The loan is not formally secured on the asset and there is no other loan which is secured on the asset. The interest rate on the loan is set by reference to the arm's length rate of interest on comparable unsecured loans, on the basis that this respects the legal form of the loan agreement.

### *D* *Example 3*

Company F is a subsidiary of Company E. Company F wishes to purchase a real estate property with a loan from Company E. The loan is not formally secured on the asset and there is no other loan which is secured on the asset. The interest rate on the loan is nevertheless set by reference to the arm's length rate of interest on comparable secured loans, on the basis that the asset is available to act as security and offering the asset as security would have optimized Company F's weighted average cost of capital.

Chapter X of the OECD *Transfer Pricing Guidelines for Multinational Enterprises and Tax Administrations* (2022) authorizes the approach in Examples 1 and 3 unless it can be shown that the borrower is keeping the property available as potential security for a future third-party loan. However, it is possible that individual tax administrations may take contradictory positions on this issue.

## 3 The Functional Analysis

The relevant experience of the borrower's management team is an important qualitative factor which can be taken into account when using a rating agency's model to rate a borrower, alongside the financial forecasts.

## 4 The Characteristics of the Property or Service Provided

Lending surveys sometimes present ranges of interest margins separately by type of property, quality and phase of development. This is more difficult to identify when using individual loan agreements in a database.

The impact of planning permission on the interest rate can (for example) be observed from offers received from mezzanine lenders (or the indicative rates shown on their websites) with and without planning permission.[25]

### 5 The Economic Circumstances of the Persons and the Market

In the situation of borrowing to cover a cashflow problem, the correct benchmarking approach may not be to make a comparability adjustment to the interest rate on a normal term loan, but instead to refer to the (higher) interest rates on very short-term bridging loans.

For example, suppose that Company T wishes to acquire Property 2 and to finance this purchase with the sale of its existing Property 1. There will be a gap between selling Property 1 and the proceeds becoming available to buy Property 2. Company T therefore seeks a loan from its parent Company S for a period of two weeks in order to purchase Property 2. Shortly afterwards it will receive the payment from the sale of Property 1 and will repay Company T in full. This particular arrangement is so close to the conventional bridging loans between independent parties that Company S and Company T agree that the most comparable set of loan agreements for determining an arm's length interest rate would be bridging loans from independent lenders to borrowers with the same credit rating as company T, rather than arm's length loans for purchasing similar properties.

### 6 The Business Strategies of the Parties

The location of the property may be more attractive to the related party borrower than to any other prospective purchaser, for example, because of its proximity to its existing property which could allow it to expand its operations cost-effectively or to improve its offering by adding, for example, customer car parking facilities.

## VI CONCLUSIONS

The transfer pricing aspects of real estate loans are broadly similar to any other loan, i.e.: determine the maximum amount of debt, a credit rating for the borrower, the initial arm's length range of interest and any necessary comparability adjustments.

However, there are some important differences between transfer pricing for real estate loans compared to other loans, namely:

25. However, these offers can only provide indications of the size of comparability adjustments: para. 10.108 of the OECD *Transfer Pricing Guidelines for Multinational Enterprises and Tax Administrations* (2022) reminds us that 'such letters do not constitute an actual offer to lend. Before proceeding to make a loan, a commercial lender will undertake the relevant due diligence and approval processes that would precede a formal loan offer'.

- the maximum arm's length amount of borrowing is usually determined by the value of the asset being acquired with the loan, rather than the amount of the borrower's equity of profit;
- the calculation of the size of loan is based on the value of the property at a specific point in time, rather than the borrower's balance sheet of profit and loss account across a period of time;
- comparability adjustments are a more important issue for real estate loans because the features of the property being acquired are the focus of the comparability adjustments, rather than the terms and conditions of the loan agreement, and real estate assets differ across a range of important characteristics such as quality, location and type of use.

# CHAPTER 18
# Transfer Pricing Considerations for Intercompany Cryptocurrency

*Fabian A. Peters, Amanda Pletz & Mark L. Berenblut*[*]

## I INTRODUCTION

Intra-group financing transactions are an important element of transfer pricing. Determination of an appropriate arm's length/market return or interest on the transferred funds is a key component for such transactions.[1] Common methods to arrive at interest rates when looking at financing transactions denominated in fiat currency (e.g., USD, EUR, JPY, GBP) utilise external price comparisons with publicly traded bonds and other financial instruments. Such information is normally readily available from sources such as Bloomberg, FactSet, and EIKON. In cases where the identified instruments are not perfectly comparable to the tested instrument or transaction, adjustments are typically made to account for differences in, for example, maturities, (fiat) currencies, optionality, and subordination.

Recently, companies have started to hold cryptocurrencies alongside fiat currencies, whether for operational purposes such as global liquidity management or for investment. The rise in popularity of cryptocurrency stems, in part, from the ease and speed at which payments are transferred from one country to another. As a result a corresponding increase in the number of intercompany cryptocurrency transactions to be addressed from a transfer pricing perspective can be expected.

---

* The views and opinions set forth herein are the personal views or opinions of the authors; they do not necessarily reflect the views or opinions of the organization with which the authors are associated.

1. Other aspects such as national rules on the tax deductibility of interest on (intercompany) debt, the economic substance of the lender or cash pool master or the arm's length nature of other transaction terms (e.g., termination options) are not within the scope of this chapter.

Publicly available data on crypto bonds is limited or nonexistent[2] and common benchmarking approaches for intercompany transactions in fiat currencies cannot be applied to transactions denominated in cryptocurrencies. Fortunately within the expanding cryptocurrency market there are alternative ways to benchmark returns on cryptocurrencies. These include data from online exchanges, brokers and infrastructure providers publish data on corresponding yield conditions. Such data for transfer pricing needs to account for fundamental differences in risk and return profiles of the transactions.

We now discuss the risk-return trade-off of crypto-denominated transactions and consider information that may be relied upon for benchmarking and transfer pricing purposes.

## II CRYPTOCURRENCY MARKET

The valuation exercise for pricing any financing transaction requires an understanding the subject industry; the value chain; the functions, assets and risks of the transacting parties; and the reasons for the financing transaction (in crypto or fiat currency). Part of this analysis involves identifying the industry dynamics under which such transactions are executed, which not only influence the associated risks but also the options realistically available to holders of cryptocurrency, and the resulting choice of optimal pricing.

### 1 Cryptocurrency and Blockchain

Cryptocurrency can be defined as "any form of currency that only exists digitally, that usually has no central issuing or regulating authority but instead uses a decentralized system to record transactions and manage the issuance of new units, and that relies on cryptography to prevent counterfeiting and fraudulent transactions."[3]

The underlying cryptography technology is a blockchain. Blockchains are digital ledgers stored in multiple copies on multiple independent computers or nodes in decentralized networks. No single entity controls a ledger, and changes to ledgers can only be made if more than 50% of users in a blockchain network agree with the change. Credible entries to a ledger—such as transactions conducted in good faith by consenting traders— are validated automatically by the blockchain network algorithms and stored automatically on the nodes(*see* Figure 18.1). Non-credible attempts to change a ledger – such as attempts to record nonconsensual trades or transfers will be—rejected

2. A notable exception is a bitcoin denominated loan issue in 2019 by Argento Access, a Luxembourg-registered securitization. *See* https://www.whatinvestment.co.uk/bitcoin-bond-launched-for-digital-currency-fans-in-for-the-medium-term-2616425/.
3. Definition according to Merriam-Webster online dictionary. *See* https://www.merriam-webster.com/dictionary/cryptocurrency.

automatically using those algorithms. For this reason, blockchain ledgers cannot be easily duplicated or fraudulently manipulated.[4]

*Figure 18.1 Blockchain-Based Transactions*

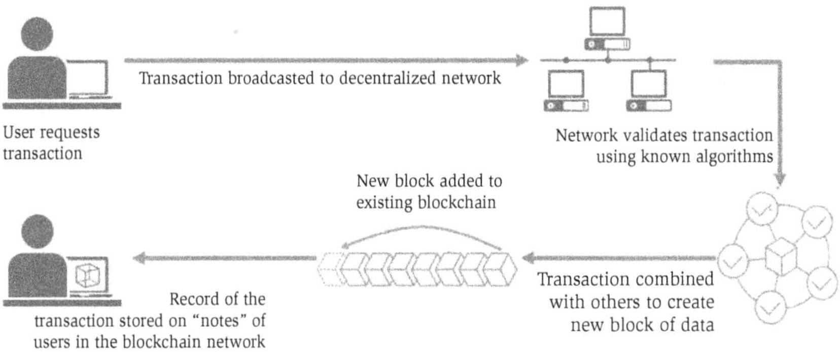


## 2 Consensus Mechanisms

The algorithms used to validate new transactions and add them to the blockchain are called "consensus mechanisms." To incentivize users in a blockchain network to participate in the validation, consensus mechanisms create or "mint" new crypto "tokens"/"coins"[5] on or in the underlying blockchain/cryptocurrency and distribute them as reward to the users that participate in the validation. Currently, there are two major consensus mechanisms:[6]

- *Proof of Work (PoW)* first pioneered by bitcoin and also used by Ethereum 1.0, among others, uses mining to achieve consensus. PoW blockchains are secured and verified by virtual "miners." The quickest miner to solve a mathematical operation updates the blockchain with the latest verified block of transactions and is rewarded by the network with a predetermined number of tokens.
- *Proof of Stake (PoS)* used by Ethereum 2.0 and other, generally newer, blockchains, use "staking" to achieve consensus. PoS blockchains are secured and verified by virtual validation stakes. The most invested "staker" or

4. *See* Max Luke et al., "Blockchains in Power Markets: Decentralized Disruption or Incremental Innovation?" and "Blockchain in Electricity: a Critical Review of Progress to Date," 2019, NERA Economic Consulting, https://www.nera.com/content/dam/nera/publications/2019/PUB_Blockchains_and_Power_Markets_0219.pdf.
5. Tokens and coins are digital assets in the crypto ecosystem. Unlike cryptocurrencies, which are native to a specific blockchain network, crypto tokens are created by platforms that build on top of other blockchains. *See* "Crypto: A New Asset Class?" in Top-of-Mind issue 98, May 21, 2021, published by Goldman Sachs Global Macro Research.
6. *See* ethereum.org., "Consensus mechanisms," 2022, https://ethereum.org/en/developers/docs/consensus-mechanisms.

"validator," that is, the one with the most or longest committed tokens staked in the blockchain updates the blockchain with the latest verified block of transactions and is rewarded by the network with a predetermined number of tokens.

## 3 Nodes and Entry Barriers

The blockchain software is run on nodes that transmit information across the blockchain network. Participating in a blockchain requires setting up and operating a node. Servers, computers, laptops or mobile phones with an IP address connected to the blockchain can function as nodes. The nodes are connected to the blockchain and constantly update each other with the latest information added to the blockchain. Different kinds of nodes function in the blockchain:[7]

- *Full nodes* maintain all the transaction records in the blockchain. An entire blockchain history can be stored with a single full node running it, but the more nodes in a blockchain, the more decentralized it becomes and thus more resilient to threats such as system failures or power outages. Full nodes can be broken down into different types of nodes depending on the underlying network and consensus mechanism.
- *Light nodes* have a similar purpose to full nodes; however, instead of holding a complete history of a blockchain, they only hold information about partial blockchain histories. They are typically downloaded wallets and are connected to full nodes to further validate information stored on the blockchain. As light nodes hold and process less data than full nodes, they require fewer resources and know-how to set up and run.

Setting up full nodes to become a miner in a PoW blockchain or a validator in a PoS blockchain network requires technical know-how. In the case of PoW or mining it also requires significant amounts of computing power and energy resources; in the case of PoS, it requires financial access to cryptocurrency assets/tokens that can be staked on the blockchain as validation capital.

## 4 Crypto Rewards and Transfer Pricing

Owners of excess crypto liquidity can choose different ways of earning crypto-denominated income that can be relevant for benchmarking and transfer pricing purposes. Only crypto staking and crypto lending are considered in this chapter, although other channels also exist:[8]

7. *See* Nodes.com, "Blockchain Nodes: How They Work (All Types Explained)," 2022, https://nodes.com/.
8. Crypto mining is not included here. In crypto mining, computing power, not liquidity, is exchanged for crypto-denominated income.

- *Crypto staking*: Crypto staking is unique to the cryptocurrency market. In crypto staking the currency owner locks up tokens on a node that can be used to validate new transaction blocks on the blockchain. In exchange, the staker can earn block rewards, that is, a share of new tokens created on the blockchain. Staking a cryptocurrency is directly linked to the PoS consensus mechanism and can only be executed on blockchains that use such a mechanism. As of March 2022, about USD 100 billion is locked in staking.[9] Crypto staking is discussed further in section 2 below.
- *Crypto lending*: Compared to crypto staking, crypto lending is more comparable to traditional lending in fiat terms. The currency lender or depositor provides tokens in exchange for interest paid by a borrower. In traditional (non-crypto) finance, lending is typically facilitated by centralized financial institutions such as banks. In the cryptocurrency space, lending and borrowing can be organized through centralized finance (CeFi) companies or crypto-banks. In the crypto space, there is also the alternative of decentralized finance (DeFi), which allows token owners to become lenders in a completely decentralized way.[10] Technologically, DeFi (crypto) lending is based on smart contracts, that is, programs that run on open blockchains, primarily Ethereum. Consequently, DeFi crypto lending yields can primarily be earned in Ethereum or in tokens that are somehow related to the Ethereum protocol. In quarter one of 2022, USD 50 billion is locked in DeFi lending.[11] Further details on crypto staking are provided in section III below.

The Organisation for Economic Co-operation and Development (OECD) Transfer Pricing Guidelines for Multinational Enterprises and Tax Administrations provide that the accurate delineation of intercompany financing transactions requires identification of the economically relevant characteristics of the transaction, including an examining the contractual terms of the transaction, the characteristics of the financial instruments, and the functions performed, assets used, and risks assumed by the transacting parties.[12]

We now turn to the technological features and risk and return drivers related to crypto staking and crypto lending. These are distinct for the particular income channels discussed. However, for purposes of a transfer pricing analysis, the different options need to be treated as interdependent. For intercompany crypto transactions, each income channel may represent available outside options that can cap the arm's length

9. According to Staking Rewards, a blockchain data tracking company, https://www.stakingrewards.com/.
10. In addition to DeFi lending, crypto asset owners can deposit their tokens in DeFi trading exchanges. Unlike CeFi exchanges, which execute trades via traditional buy/sell order books, decentralized exchanges (DEX) rely on prefunded "liquidity pools" to enable trades/currency exchanges. As a reward for funding providing liquidity to such pools, depositors are rewarded with trading fees and tokens. Earning crypto income by depositing tokens to DEX liquidity pools is often referred to as "crypto farming." The technical features, economic principles and risk and return drivers are similar to DeFi lending and not discussed separately in this chapter.
11. *See* https://www.bis.org/publ/bisbull57.pdf.
12. OECD (January 2022), Transfer Pricing Guidelines for Multinational Enterprises and Tax Administrations, OECD, Paris, para. 10.17.

yield accepted for entering a given intercompany crypto transaction.[13] In economic terms, the crypto staking and lending yields determine the opportunity costs of crypto-denominated intercompany transactions (and of one another).[14]

## III CRYPTO STAKING

Crypto staking is the process of keeping crypto assets locked on a node to validate transactions through the PoS consensus mechanism. Depending on their technical expertise and desire for involvement, crypto asset owners can decide to stake through different staking channels:

- *Private hardware wallets* such as Ledger, and Trezor. These are also used for storing cryptocurrencies.
- *Cryptocurrency exchanges* such as KuCoin, Coinbase, Binance, Kraken, and Poloniex. These are also used for trading cryptocurrencies.
- *Staking-as-a-service (STaaS) platforms and node-as-a-service providers*, for example, Figment Networks, Stake Fish, Staked, MyContainer, Validation Capital, and StackOfStake. These are dedicated primarily to staking.

A stake represents a voting right in a particular PoS network that is earned after purchasing a minimum number of coins. The more coins held, the more voting rights were obtained. Voting to validate transactions helps the underlying network operate efficiently and securely (*see* Figure 18.2). To incentivize this, a staking reward in the form of new tokens is paid out. PoS validators can earn new tokens as reward, and they can lose some of their stakes if their node goes offline or they validate a bad block of transactions ("slashing"). This results in the staked tokens also being collateral to disincentivize adverse behavior.[15]

13. *Ibid.*, para. 10.19.
14. The remainder of this chapter focuses on the economically relevant characteristics for benchmarking arm's length yields in cryptocurrency transactions when intercompany transferor and transferee have already been characterized for transfer pricing purposes. It does not explicitly address the functional characterization of the parties and the instrument for transfer pricing purposes. This fundamental exercise considers a case-dependent value chain analysis, including an analysis of the entities involved in the development, ownership, and exploitation of important intangibles,
15. *See* Binance Academy, "What Is Staking?," 2022, https://academy.binance.com/en/articles/what-is-staking.

*Figure 18.2 Private Crypto Staking (Without Intermediary)*

## 1 Risk and Expected Return

The use of crypto staking yields for benchmarking and transfer pricing purposes requires an understanding of the economically relevant characteristics and risk and return drivers of crypto staking. These drivers relate to the staking channel and degree of involvement chosen, and to the general user behaviour in the underlying blockchain:

- *Block rewards/yield*: When a validator successfully validates new blocks on the blockchain, it receives staking rewards in the form of tokens on the underlying blockchain. The most common return metric is the annual rate of return or annual percentage rate (APR) or annual percentage yield (APY), which represents the estimated annualized rate of return. Typically, this is expressed in real terms, that is, after adjusting for (projected) inflation of the underlying currency.
  The real APR/APY is primarily determined by the inflation and participation rates in the underlying blockchain network, and by the lock-up period for the staking:
- *Inflation*: The total inflation rate in a PoS network is directly and intrinsically linked to the staking returns used to incentivize validators in the network: total inflation in the network equals the maximum rewards available to incentivize validators. If 100% of the tokens in a network were staked, this would mean that there could be no positive staking yields in real terms, as the rewards earned would be completely offset by inflation/dilution (disregarding appreciation of the crypto value relative to other currencies).[16]
- *Participation*: In practice, stake rate or participation rate, that is, the percentage of staked tokens in overall existing tokens, is dynamic, but generally lower than 100%.[17] This means that inflation/dilution is spread amongst all tokens in the network, whilst nominal staking returns are earned only by those token

16. Nominal APY = tokens staked × (1 + inflation rate) / tokens staked. Real APY = tokens staked × (1 + inflation rate) / (1 + inflation rate) / tokens staked.
17. According to a study by Messari Hub, commissioned by Blockdaemon, and using data as of November 25, 2021, the majority of top PoS networks have > 50% staking participation. (Messari.io. "Crypto Research, Data, and Tools," 2022, https://messari.io/article/what-s-at-stake-in-staking-as-a-service.)

owners participating in the staking.[18] For this reason, there is an inverse relationship between participation rate and real staking yield in a network: when more stakers participate in the network, the real yield decreases, as staking rewards must be distributed to a larger group.

- *Lockup/maturity*: Staking is a commitment to the security of the underlying blockchain network. Therefore, some networks require assets to be locked up to prevent a collapse of the underlying network in situations where all stakers want to withdraw their assets at once. The lockup period, that is, the period required before a staker can unstake its assets, is unique to each network (and typically depends on the volatility of its tokens), but rarely exceeds two weeks. As a result, maturity risks are typically limited.

**Example:**
*How inflation, participation, and maturity drive staking yield*: At the beginning of the period, there are 100 tokens in a PoS blockchain. Of these tokens, 75 are locked as validation capital, while the other 25 tokens are not staked and are being used for running applications or making transactions on the network. This amounts to a participation rate of 75% at the beginning of the period. Assuming that 10 new tokens are minted during the maturity period; this yields a total nominal yield of 13% (10 new tokens/75 staked tokens) and a total inflation of 10% (10 new tokens/100 initial tokens) over the staking period. Given that the inflationary rewards are only distributed amongst holders who participated in the staking, their real yield amounts to approximately 3% ((1 + 13% nominal yield)/(1 + 10% inflation) – 1).[19]

- *Staking commissions*: Many token owners do not meet the entry barriers to operate as full validators. Such entry barriers include technical know-how, stable infrastructure, financial minimum number of tokens required,[20] and risk tolerance to operate as a full validator. These token owners can still stake/delegate their tokens on nodes that are run by other parties that provide STaaS. In return for taking care of the technical aspect and associated risks of the staking, STaaS providers take a percentage fee of the staking rewards earned.

  STaaS businesses can be classified as custodial or noncustodial:

- *Custodial*: The customer gives up custody over its tokens while they are being staked (*see* Figure 18.3). This is generally targeted towards retail users who want minimal involvement in the technical backend. It introduces additional

18. Real APY = tokens staked × (1 + inflation rate total) x inflation rate total / inflation rate unstaked tokens / tokens staked.
19. Calculated using the Fischer equation: Real APY = (1 + nominal APY) / (1 + inflation rate) – 1.
20. The financial minimum is defined in the protocol as set by the initiator of the network.

counterparty risk and requires trust in the STaaS provider's technical ability to operate and maintain the day-to-day validating node infrastructure or outsource this responsibility to yet another third party.[21] The (real) block rewards, net of the percentage commission to the custodial STaaS provider, are distributed to the stakers on a pro rata basis depending on the number of staked tokens by each contributor to the given node(s).[22]

*Figure 18.3 Crypto Staking via Custodial Intermediary*

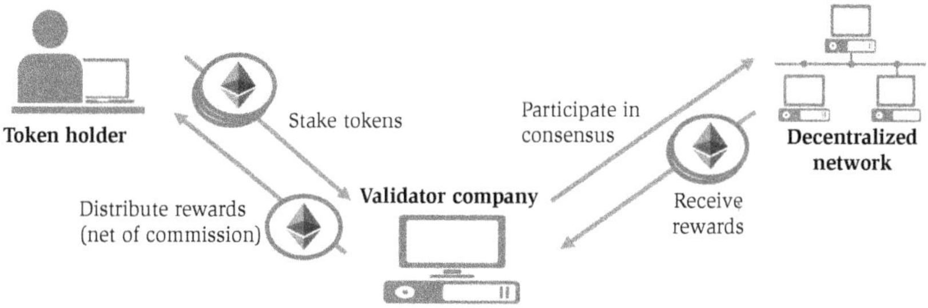


- *Noncustodial*: The customer "delegates" tokens but retains custody over them while they are being staked (*see* Figure 18.4). The process of delegation is built into the network. As a result, the underlying network can channel a delegator's share of rewards directly to the delegator, rather than leaving it up to the validator to distribute the rewards. This helps reduce some of the counterparty risk associated with the custodial STaaS business model.[23]

21. Some of the companies listed under STaaS platforms above, such as, Staked, also provide node-as-a-service (NaaS) to custodial crypto exchanges such as Coinbase or Kraken. In early 2021, NaaS provider Bison Trails was directly acquired by Coinbase for a reported price of USD 80 million. *See* https://messari.io/article/what-s-at-stake-in-staking-as-a-service.
22. Medium, "Introduction to Crypto Staking," https://medium.com/chorus-one/introduction-to-crypto-staking-ced72bc1756b.
23. Messari.io, "Crypto Research, Data, and Tools," 2022, https://messari.io/article/what-s-at-stake-in-staking-as-a-service.

*Figure 18.4 Crypto Staking via Noncustodial Intermediary*

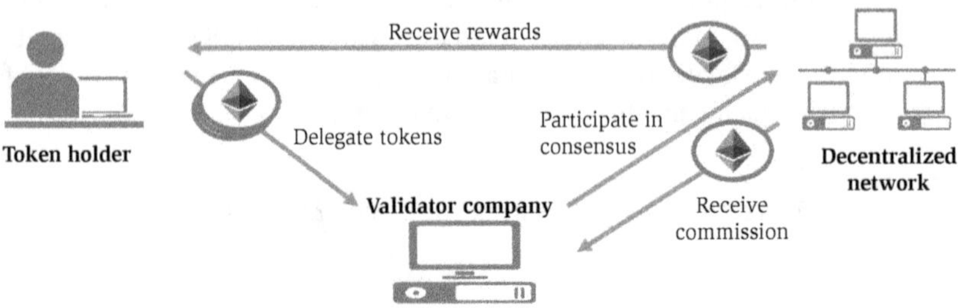


## 2 Data Availability for Benchmarking Purposes

The websites of cryptocurrency exchanges and StaaS providers generally present yield data that could be used for crypto yield benchmarking. However, the quoted yields are not contractually fixed in advance. They represent projections based on historical staking rewards and inflation rates and estimated future participation rates in the relevant networks. These yield quotes do not present actual comparable transactions. Referencing these yields as evidence for the arm's length rate of return for intercompany staking or other intercompany crypto transfers would represent a departure from an arm's length approach that requires comparison of *actual* transactions (in the same way that, according to the latest OECD transfer pricing guidance, "bank opinions"[24] do not serve as actual evidence for the arm's length rate of interest on an intra-group loan).[25]

Actual staking yield is a function of the actual number of transactions and associated inflation rate and the actual participation rate in the network. These are in turn governed by the underlying protocol/algorithm and ever-changing behavior of token holders. In the past, real staking yields, before commissions, have typically ranged between 10% and 15%.[26]

Stakers who cannot, or prefer not to, run a full validation node themselves can exchange certain technical risks associated with staking (e.g., slashing), for counterparty risk vis-à-vis an intermediary StaaS provider, especially when delegating tokens to a custodial StaaS provider. In that case, the real staking yield (net of fees) also depends on the commission rates charged by the StaaS provider. Commission rates are generally fixed in a range between 5% and 20% of the staking rewards earned.[27]

24. Bank opinions are one sided quote from a bank on a hypothetical transaction and are not considered as evidence of arm's length pricing in accordance with the OECD guidelines.
25. OECD (2022), Transfer Pricing Guidelines, OECD, Paris, para. 10.107.
26. These returns are often currency specific and can vary significantly from one currency to the next.
27. Messari.io, "Crypto Research, Data, and Tools." In the medium to long term, one may expect to see STaaS commission rates exhibit a similar pattern to consumer banking fees since about 2000. Increased competition from financial technology companies forced banks to offer lower and lower fees to retain their customers. Similarly, the growing number of STaaS solutions will put downward pressure on the commissions charged on customers' staking rewards.

## IV CRYPTO LENDING

Crypto lending is the lending of crypto assets to a borrower over a fixed or variable period of time in exchange for interest. Often, the term "crypto lending" includes crypto-secured cash lending, when the loan itself is denominated in fiat currency and the cryptocurrency is only used as collateral. In a broad sense of the term, interest in crypto lending can therefore be denominated in the same cryptocurrency, in another cryptocurrency, or in fiat currency. Asset owners can decide to lend through different lending channels:

- *Centralized finance (CeFi)*, for example, Binance, Block-Fi, Nexo, Celsius, and Gemini. These are dedicated businesses, banks, trading desks, exchanges, or platforms.
- *Decentralized finance (DeFi)*, for example, AAVE, Compound, Maker. These are protocols that rely on smart contracts (typically the Ethereum protocol).

### 1 Risk and Expected Return

The use of crypto lending yields for benchmarking and transfer pricing purposes requires an understanding of the economically relevant characteristics and risk and return drivers of crypto lending.

For an OECD-compliant transfer pricing analysis, these characteristics are different for CeFi and DeFi lending:

- *CeFi lending*: The mechanisms of many CeFi crypto businesses are similar to those of a traditional bank. In these cases, the CeFi company acts as a form of principal or depository institution (*see* Figure 18.5). However, as discussed below, there are differences with respect to the supply of liquidity that determine interest rates in cryptocurrencies as opposed to fiat money.

*Figure 18.5 Crypto Lending via CeFi Principal*

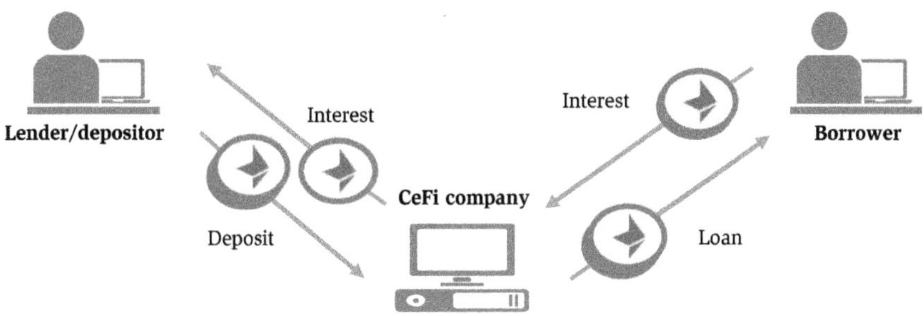


Economically relevant characteristics for CeFi crypto lending relate primarily to the following risk and return drivers:

- *Custody*: In CeFi crypto lending, the lender generally gives up custody of the tokens. This exposes the lender to counterparty risk vis-à-vis the CeFi lending company.
- *Counterparty*: When the CeFi company acts as principal, like a traditional bank, customers set up an account into which they deposit their tokens. They receive interest payments on this deposit at regular intervals, denominated in cryptocurrencies or fiat currencies. There are other arrangements in which the CeFi company only intermediates peer-to-peer loans between lenders and borrowers for an agent fee.[28] In those cases, the CeFi company is not the lending counterparty, but it may create counterparty risk related to the technical implementation of the intermediation/transfer.
- *Collateral*: In CeFi crypto lending, the borrower is generally not required to secure the loan. Similarly, deposits at the CeFi company are typically unsecured. As a result, the lender is exposed to borrower credit risk.
- *Lockup/maturity*: Depending on the model, coins that have been deposited may be taken out of the account prematurely. On other CeFi platforms that form lending pools with the deposited coins and lend them to borrowers, redemption may not be possible until the borrower(s) have repaid the loan, the pool is dissolved, and the lender(s) can withdraw the coins again. This means that there can be significant lockup periods.
- *Interest/yield*: When lending to a CeFi company that acts as a principal, the interest rate is set by that central authority and generally fixed. Variable interest rates are also possible but less common. The rates/rules can be set by the CeFi company, considering the maturity, the liquidity supplied and demanded by users of the CeFi crypto lending platform, and the underlying blockchain protocol. This is a key difference to traditional lending systems in fiat currencies, where liquidity and interest rates are determined through policy rates and associated interbank rates set by central banks, considering inflation and other macroeconomic parameters.
- *DeFi lending*: DeFi crypto lending differs from traditional lending and CeFi crypto lending in several key dimensions (*see* Figure 18.6).

28. *See* for example, Gemini's "Earn" program, https://www.gemini.com/earn.

*Figure 18.6 Crypto Lending via DeFi Protocol*

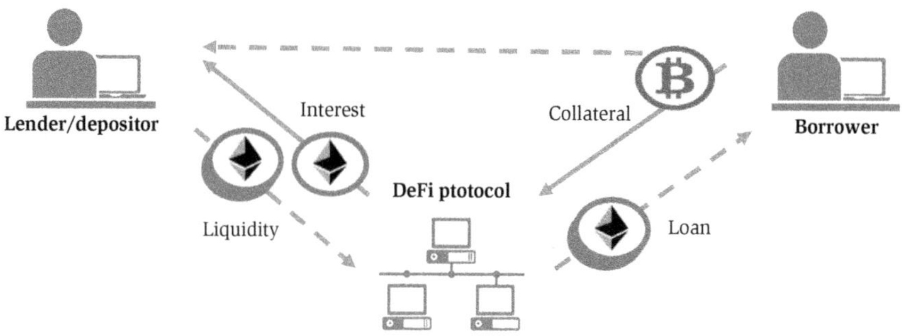


Economically relevant characteristics for DeFi crypto lending relate primarily to the following risk and return drivers:

- *Custody*: Unlike in CeFi crypto lending platforms, users of DeFi lending protocols do not transfer ownership of their tokens. To carry out the lending, lenders need to connect their wallets to the platform protocol. This can be more complicated and require more technical expertise than lending through a CeFi lending business as a central facilitator.
- *Counterparty*: Unlike in traditional finance or CeFi lending, where identity of the counterparty and/or central intermediary authority is known, DeFi lending counterparties are unknown. Funds are intermediated anonymously between users by programmed protocols. The role that an intermediary would play in traditional or centralized finance is replaced by a set of smart contracts on the protocol.
- *Collateral*: Unlike in traditional finance or CeFi lending, it is impossible for depositors/lenders to apply credit ratings to intermediating or borrowing counterparties. To compensate for this lack of information and to build sufficient trust, DeFi protocols generally offer only secured lending. More specifically, borrowers are required to over-collateralize their loans, that is, they need to pledge at least the loan amount in another (crypto-)currency and are not allowed to enter into net debt. This means that the initially required loan-to-value (LTV) ratio, that is, the notional value of the loan, measured against the market value of its collateral, is substantially lower than 100%. In addition, many DeFi lending protocols enforce automatic liquidation thresholds that are typically above but not far from the initial LTV requirements.[29]

29. *See* Docs.aave.com, "Risk Parameters – Risk," 2022, https://docs.aave.com/risk/asset-risk/risk-parameters.

**Example:**
*Use of collateral in DeFi crypto lending*: A DeFi borrower wants to take a loan with a face value of USD 70.00, denominated in Ethereum (ETH). Assuming a minimum initial LTV requirement of 70%, the borrower must pledge USD 100.00 in another (crypto)currency as collateral, for example, (wrapped) bitcoin cryptocurrency (BTC).[30] Assuming a liquidation threshold at a 75% LTV, the loan is automatically liquidated when the pledged BTC collateral depreciates below USD 93.33 (70.00/75%).

In such arrangements, lenders can always redeem the pledged collateral when the borrower defaults. In fact, this takes out most (if not all) of the direct counterparty risk vis-à-vis the borrower(s). In crypto lending with crypto-denominated collateral, the collateral assets can be transferred directly to the lenders' account/wallet. Therefore, collecting on default is less of an issue than in traditional collateralized lending in fiat currency. Traditional collateral is only pledged, but not transferred which can make collecting on default a slow, uncertain, and costly process. Moreover, most crypto assets are more liquid than other types of common collateral such as real estate. Cryptocurrencies can be sold relatively easily if the LTV deteriorates. As a result, crypto-backed crypto or cash lending can be compared to some extent to traditional repurchase agreements (repos).[31]

In the repo market, treasury securities or other typically highly liquid assets are sold/purchased and then resold/repurchased for cash for a fixed term at close to face value (*see* Figure 18.7). This gives the lender control over the collateral and has similar effect to the securitization via smart contracts.

*Figure 18.7 Repurchase Agreement*

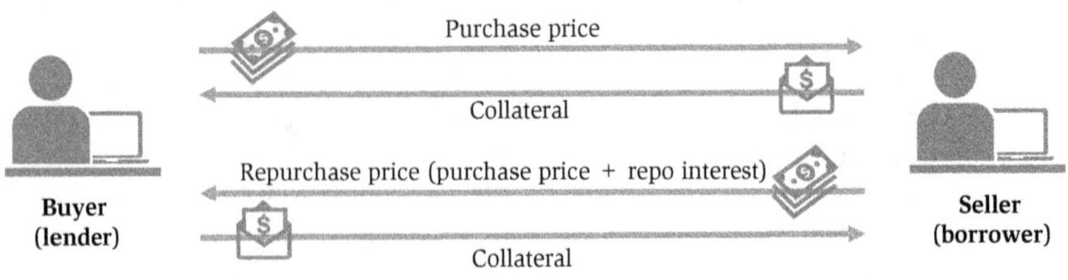


- *Lockup/maturity*: Loans on DeFi protocols generally have unlimited maturities but are redeemable at any time. This redemption feature often leads to short-term effective maturities. Moreover, maturity is directly related to

30. Wrapped BTC is a digital token that has the same value as one bitcoin but is based on ERC-20 (Ethereum Request for Comments 20), the standard used for creating and issuing smart contracts on the Ethereum blockchain. This makes it usable on the DeFi ecosystem.
31. *See* Medium, "A Comparison Between the Collateralized Crypto Lending and the Repo Market (pt 3)," 2022, https://medium.com/woonetwork/a-comparison-between-the-collateralized-crypto-lending-and-the-repo-market-pt-3-f958be37ceb3.

collateralization (due to the collateral features discussed already). Even for loans with indefinite maturity that are not redeemed proactively by the lender, the loan is automatically liquidated should the LTV meet a fixed liquidation threshold. In such an event, the lending protocol liquidates the locked collateral to cover the underlying debt. The liquidation thresholds vary across different protocols and can be adapted to the volatility of the corresponding currencies.

- *Interest/yield*: Unlike in CeFi crypto lending platforms, the interest rate is typically completely variable. It is recalculated continuously according to market conditions. More specifically, the interest rate is a direct function of the available liquidity, that is, the ratio of funds supplied and borrowed in the given market/protocol. The mechanism to set these rates is intrinsic to the protocol design.[32] There is an inverse relationship between liquidity and lending yield/interest; in periods of low liquidity, rising interest rates shall incentivize borrowers to repay their loans and vice versa.

## 2 Data Availability for Benchmarking

In DeFi crypto lending, actual staking yield depends on the ever-changing relationship between supply and demand. Yields quoted on the websites of DeFi protocols are not contractually fixed in advance. They represent projections based on estimated liquidity ratios. As described above, DeFi crypto lending is generally characterized by over-collateralization and fixed liquidation thresholds enforced via smart contracts. This can effectively neutralize credit default risk. However, some risk of technical difficulties remains such as platform error, or improper collateral liquidation.[33] The other key remaining risk relates to the volatility of the relevant underlying currencies and the risk of depreciation during the lending period. Considering these factors, DeFi lending yields typically range between 0% and 10%, but higher rates of 20% or more are also possible.[34]

In CeFi lending it is conceivable that traditional pricing methods can be relied upon to measure and price these contracts including determining the level of credit risk, taking into consideration the timing, the amount, the maturity, etc., and identifying the appropriate benchmarks. In this context, the websites of different CeFi

32. *See* L. Gudgeon et al. (2020) "DeFi Protocols for Loanable Funds: Interest Rates, Liquidity and Market Efficiency," in AFT '20: Proceedings of the 2nd ACM Conference on Advances in Financial Technologies, October 2020, 02-112; https://doi.org/10.1145/3419614.3423254.
33. This risk is not nonexistent. There have been repeated instances where hackers have been able to drain the collateral from a smart contract. *See* https://bravenewcoin.com/insights/how-to-earn-interest-and-boost-yield-with-bitcoin-and-crypto.
34. As of March 2022, minimum yield across five main lending currencies (wrapped Bitcoin Cryptocurrency (BTC), Ethereum, USDC, DAI, USDT) and seven DeFi lending platforms (Compound, Fulcrum, Cream, CAKE, AAVE, DDEX, NOTIONAL) amounts to 0.01%, the maximum amounts to 8.65%. Data based on an article published on an insights article published by BraveNewCoin. *See* https://bravenewcoin.com/insights/best-crypto-interest-rates.

lending companies present yield data that could be used for crypto yield benchmarking. In CeFi lending, there can be credit default risk vis-à-vis the CeFi company when it acts as a principal and/or the ultimate borrower when the CeFi company acts as a pure intermediary agent. Considering the additional counterparty risk, CeFi lending rates should generally be higher than DeFi lending rates. Actual CeFi lending yields typically range between 5% and 15%.[35]

## V IDENTIFIED RISK FACTORS AND PRICING IMPLICATIONS

We have detailed the economic characteristics and risk and return drivers of crypto staking and crypto lending. Crypto staking and crypto lending represent income options for (associated) companies with crypto holdings. In this sense, they can affect the opportunity costs of intercompany financing transactions in cryptocurrencies. In summary the main risks and their implications to be considered for transfer pricing purposes include:

- *Regulatory risk*: In the long term, there is significant uncertainty with regard to the effect of regulation on crypto staking and lending, especially in the DeFi space.
- *Credit risk*: Crypto staking and crypto lending through DeFi protocols come with limited credit default risk. In crypto staking, there is no credit default risk because there is no borrowing counterparty.[36] In DeFi lending, credit default risk can be neutralized through over-collateralization and liquidation thresholds. Material credit risk may only be incurred in CeFi lending.
- *Technology risks*: Crypto staking and lending are based on blockchain and other cloud infrastructure that may be hacked or fail to perform. Depending on the willingness to transfer custody to a staking or lending platform, some of the technology risks may (partially) be transferred to a third party. However, this can introduce certain counterparty risks in relation to that provider or intermediary.
- *Currency/volatility risk*: The principal risk in any crypto-denominated (intercompany) transaction is the volatility of the cryptocurrencies being staked or lent. Even with relatively short lockup/maturity periods, this risk can be material. Since their appearance in 2009, most cryptocurrencies (excluding stablecoins that are pegged to fiat currencies) have demonstrated high volatility in prices/exchange rates in fiat currencies and among each other. Figure 18.8 plots the USD prices of BTC and ETH, the largest cryptocurrencies by market capitalization, since the beginning of 2021, indexed to their all-time

35. As of March 2022, minimum yield across five main lending currencies (wrapped BTC, Ethereum, USDC, DAI, USDT) and seven CeFi lending platforms (NEXO, Block-Fi, YouHodler, CoinLoan, Celsius, Crypto.com, Hodlnaut) amounts to 4.50%, the maximum amounts to 12.73%. Data based on an article published on an insights article published by BraveNewCoin. *See* https://bravenewcoin.com/insights/best-crypto-interest-rates.
36. The only counterparty risk may be in relation to StaaS provider, especially when transferring custody of the staked tokens.

highs observed on November 8, 2021. Since then, both currencies have lost around 71 % of their value in USD.

*Figure 18.8 BTC and ETH Price in USD*

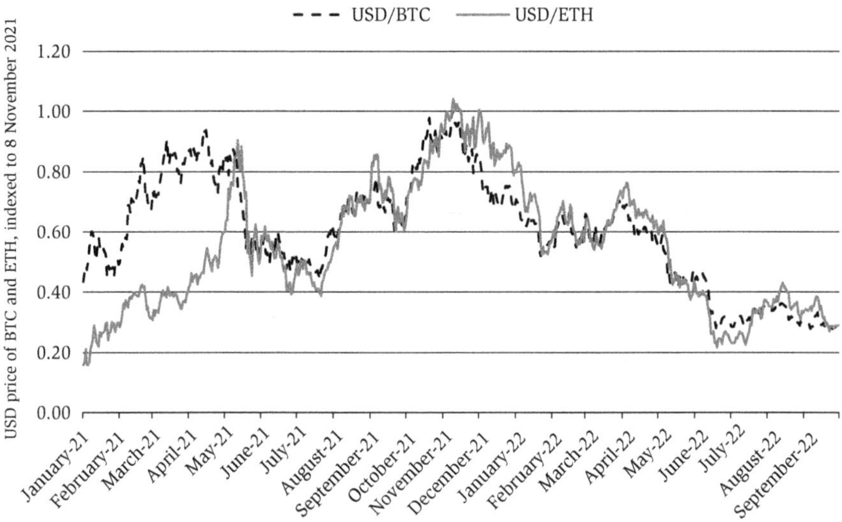


*Data source*: Investing.com.

With currency/price volatility representing the main risk factor, the (transfer) pricing of crypto-denominated transactions—or at least the quantification of opportunity costs from crypto staking and DeFi lending—can rely on general economic principles and traditional pricing approaches that rely on the relationship between volatility and yield. This relationship can be observed and estimated for financial instruments denominated in fiat currencies. In broad terms, the general approach can be broken down into two steps:

- The first step is the analysis of the yields observed for fiat instruments that are otherwise comparable to the tested cryptocurrency transaction. In practice, this relies on repo rates or risk-free sovereign rates with a short-term maturity—due to the low/algorithmically neutralized probability of default and typically short or non-existent lockup periods in crypto staking and lending.
- The second step is identifying the risk premium to account for the difference in volatility and estimated effect on yield. For this purpose, it is possible to rely on existing methodologies to quantify the price of (reduced) volatility, including option pricing models and actuarial pricing models.

As discussed, for CeFi lending more traditional loan pricing methods can be relied upon. This process involves a credit risk analysis, taking into consideration the timing, the amount, the maturity, other lending terms, and identifying the appropriate benchmarks.

## VI CONCLUSION

This chapter provides an overview of factors affecting the financial dynamics of crypto funding and considerations for transfer pricing. Due to the developing nature of the crypto market place the academic literature has not yet been developed and test case law has not been published. . Nonetheless, the approach outlined in the OECD guidance, including an accurate delineation of the transaction and analysis of the various comparability factors, provides a current indication of risk factors for crypto transactions. Once one identifies the main risks and how they compare to those in traditional fiat lending, standard pricing tools and methods can be used to adjust for differences in risk between traditional funding vis-à-vis crypto funding.

# CHAPTER 19
# The *Chevron* Case: A Detailed Analysis

*Niv Tadmore, Simon Bowden & Benjamin Lancaster**

## I INTRODUCTION

The litigation between the Australian Commissioner of Taxation (Commissioner) and the Chevron group over loan arrangements entered into by Chevron's Australian subsidiaries was a landmark in the development of transfer pricing law.

It may have been thought that the pricing of loans, which are encountered every day between arm's length parties, should have been a matter of clear and settled principle. However, the decisions of the Federal Court of Australia in *Chevron Australia Holdings Pty Ltd v. Federal Commissioner of Taxation* [2015] FCA 1092 (hereinafter '*Chevron First Instance*') and on appeal in *Chevron Australia Holdings Pty Ltd v. Federal Commissioner of Taxation* [2017] FCAFC 62 (hereinafter '*Chevron Appeal*') touched on a wide range of issues relevant to pricing of intra-group financial arrangements, including:

- whether it is appropriate in principle to price intra-group arrangements based on the whole group's cost of borrowing;
- whether the creditworthiness of a borrower should be determined having regard to the actual borrower's membership of a corporate group or as if it were a standalone entity;
- whether the transfer price needed to be determined based on the transaction entered into by the parties or whether the terms of the arrangements, such as the currency of the loan or the provision of security or credit support, could be changed by the revenue authority in determining the transfer price;

* The views and opinions set forth herein are the personal views or opinions of the author(s); they do not necessarily reflect the views or opinions of the organization with which the authors are associated.

- whether the 'associated enterprises' articles in Australia's tax treaty network provided their own source of taxing power; and
- whether the retrospective laws, which sought to ensure the 'associated enterprises' articles were given force under domestic law, were constitutionally invalid.

The apparent simplicity of pricing money itself was shown to be anything but easy. The litigation involved extensive expert evidence, most of which was determined by the Court to be irrelevant in answering the questions posed by the statute. Although the Commissioner's arguments were unsuccessful on several significant issues, the tax assessments were ultimately upheld as the taxpayer (who has the onus of proof in the Australian tax system) failed to provide sufficient evidence to persuade the Court that the assessments were excessive.

This has unfortunately left the answers to many of the questions raised in the dispute unclear. Those questions remained to be determined by other courts in future cases, some of which are now starting to emerge. However, the headline success of the Australian Taxation Office (ATO)[1] in the *Chevron* cases has undoubtedly emboldened it to pursue other multinational groups' arrangements in the meantime.

This paper explores:

- the background facts of transactions at issue in the *Chevron* cases;
- the changing legislative backdrop against which the dispute played out;
- a detailed analysis of the issues considered in the case; and
- the developments in Australian transfer pricing law and practice since the *Chevron* decisions were handed down.

## II BACKGROUND

### 1 The Financial Arrangements under Consideration

The taxpayer, Chevron Australia Holdings Pty Ltd (CAHPL), was an Australian company wholly owned by the United States (US)-based Chevron Corporation (CVX), the New York Stock Exchange (NYSE)-listed parent of the global Chevron group.

In June 2003, CAHPL entered into a Credit Facility Agreement with a US-resident subsidiary, Chevron Texaco Funding Corporation (CFC), that was wholly owned by CAHPL. The use of US-incorporated subsidiaries (like CFC) is common in Australia, due to a withholding tax exemption designed to facilitate access to US credit markets.[2]

Under that agreement, CFC lent an amount of Australian dollars equivalent to USD 2.5 billion for a term of five years at a monthly interest rate of AUD LIBOR plus 4.14% per annum. CAHPL did not provide any security for the loan and the agreement did not contain any financial covenants. Similarly, CAHPL's obligations in respect of

1. In this chapter, the terms Commissioner and ATO are used interchangeably.
2. *Income Tax Assessment Act 1936* (Cth) section 128F.

the loan were not guaranteed by any third party. CAHPL could repay the loan early, and CFC was also entitled to terminate at any time.

The funds lent by CFC were raised on the commercial paper market in US dollars at a rate close to US LIBOR. CFC's obligations in respect of this fund-raising were guaranteed by CVX, gaining the benefit of the credit rating of the whole of the Chevron group.

At the time the Credit Facility Agreement was entered into, AUD LIBOR was substantially higher than USD LIBOR. With the addition of the relevant margins, the interest rate payable by CAHPL to CFC was equivalent to approximately 9% per annum whilst the interest rate payable by CFC on its commercial borrowing was equivalent to approximately 1.2% per annum.[3]

By borrowing funds at a low-interest rate which it on-lent to CAHPL at a significantly higher interest rate, CFC made significant profits that could be paid to its parent, CAHPL, by way of dividends. Dividends of approximately AUD 1.1 billion were received by CAHPL over the audit period, which could be used to fund payment of its interest obligations to CFC or to pay dividends to its parent company. The receipt of dividends from CFC was neither subject to tax in Australia nor subject to withholding tax in the US.[4] CFC was also not subject to US or Australian tax on the interest payments it received from CAHPL.[5]

## 2 The Procedural History of the Dispute

The ATO commenced an audit of the financial arrangements which culminated, in April 2010, in the making of determinations to apply the transfer pricing provisions existing at the time in Division 13 of Australia's domestic tax laws.[6] Under those determinations, the ATO asserted that the consideration given by CAHPL exceeded the arm's length consideration for the property it had acquired under an international agreement. In essence, the adjustments were based on a position that, if the parties had been dealing at arm's length, CAHPL would have paid interest at a lower rate, as a result of borrowing in US dollars with the benefit of CVX's credit rating.[7]

In May 2010, the Commissioner issued amended tax assessments to give effect to those determinations.

---

3. *Chevron Appeal* per Pagone J at [100].
4. *See Income Tax Assessment Act 1936* (Cth) section 23A, where dividends received by an Australian resident company on a non-portfolio interest in another company were non-assessable, non-exempt income; *Convention between the Government of Australia and the Government of the United States of America for the Avoidance of Double Taxation and the Prevention of Fiscal Evasion with respect to Taxes on Income*, opened for signature 6 August 1982 (entered into force 31 October 1983), as amended by *Protocol Amending Convention with Australia Regarding Double Taxation and Prevention of Fiscal Evasion*, opened for signature 27 September 2001 (entered into force 12 May 2003) Article 10(3), where dividends paid to an Australian company by a wholly owned US subsidiary are exempt from dividend withholding tax.
5. *Chevron Appeal* per Pagone J at [101].
6. *Income Tax Assessment Act 1936* (Cth) Division 13 (former).
7. Notably, the Commissioner did not choose to also make determinations under the general anti-avoidance rules in Part IVA of Australia's tax laws, despite the arrangements allowing CFC's profits to be returned to CAHPL on a tax-free basis.

CAHPL subsequently lodged objections to the assessments. Those objections were deemed to be disallowed and, in April 2012, CAHPL instituted appeals against the disallowances to the Federal Court of Australia.[8]

Following legislative amendments which introduced further transfer pricing provisions into subdivision 815-A of the Australian tax laws, the Commissioner made determinations to apply those new provisions to the financing arrangements in October 2012. The retrospective operation of those determinations provided an alternative basis for the May 2010 assessments.

In any appeal of an objection decision to the Federal Court, the taxpayer bears the onus of proving that the relevant assessment was excessive or otherwise incorrect and what the assessment should have been.[9]

On 23 October 2015, some twelve years after the Credit Facility Agreement was entered into, the Federal Court handed down its decision that CAHPL had not met this onus of proof. The Court determined that CAHPL had not demonstrated that the consideration under the Credit Facility Agreement was an arm's length consideration or that the assessments were otherwise excessive.

CAHPL then appealed to the Full Court of the Federal Court. The Full Court's decision was handed down on 21 April 2017 and, once again, it was held that the taxpayer had failed to meet its onus of proof.

CAHPL subsequently applied for special leave to appeal the Full Court's decision to the High Court of Australia. However, the parties agreed to settle their dispute before the hearing of the application.[10] The terms of that settlement were not made public.

## III CONTINUITY THROUGH CHANGE: THE AUSTRALIAN TRANSFER PRICING REGIME

### 1 Division 13

The transfer pricing provisions that were operative in the Australian tax laws at the time the Credit Facility Agreement was entered into were contained in Division 13 of the *Income Tax Assessment Act 1936* (Cth).

Division 13, which was introduced in 1982, imposed a three-part test which would need to be met before the Commissioner could make a transfer pricing adjustment:

8. *See Taxation Administration Act 1953* (Cth) section 14ZYA, where a person may give a notice requiring the Commissioner to make a decision on an objection. If no decision is made within 60 days after the notice is given, the Commissioner is taken to have made a decision to disallow the objection.
9. *Taxation Administration Act 1953* (Cth) section 14ZZO.
10. *See, e.g.*, Eryk Bagshaw, *Multi-billion dollar tax windfall after Chevron abandons appeal*, Sydney Morning Herald (18 August 2017, 6.03 p.m. AEDT), https://www.smh.com.au/business/the-economy/multibillion-dollar-tax-windfall-after-chevron-abandons-appeal-20170818-gxz718.html; Sonali Paul, *Australia Puts Multinationals on Notice after Chevron Drops Tax Appeal*, Reuters (18 August 2017, 2:15pm AEDT), https://www.reuters.com/article/us-australia-chevron-taxavoidance-idUSKCN1AY0DV.

(1) there must be a supply or acquisition of property under an international agreement;
(2) the Commissioner, having regard to any connection between the parties to the agreement or any other relevant circumstances, must be satisfied that the parties were not dealing at arm's length in relation to the supply or acquisition; and
(3) consideration was receivable in respect of the supply which was less than the arm's length consideration in respect of the supply, or consideration was payable in respect of the acquisition which was greater than the arm's length consideration in respect of the acquisition.[11]

Where the Commissioner determined that the provisions should apply in relation to the supply or acquisition, then the arm's length consideration was deemed to be the consideration for the supply or acquisition for the purposes of the income tax laws. That is, the application of Division 13 required the making of a determination by the Commissioner that the provisions applied, rather than operating automatically.

Unlike most issues, where the Commissioner had a limited period to amend taxpayers' assessments where they had not paid the correct amount of tax, no limitation period applied to the Commissioner's power to amend assessments to give effect to Division 13 determinations.[12] Even though Division 13 was repealed in 2013, this unlimited period of review for Division 13 determinations means the Commissioner can - and does - continue to apply the provisions in relation to arrangements in income years prior to 2013.

### A Expressions Considered in the Chevron Cases

An 'international agreement' covered any agreement, arrangement, transaction, understanding or scheme, whether formal or informal, express or implied, enforceable or not, where, amongst other things, a non-resident supplied or acquired property under the agreement otherwise than in connection with a business carried on in Australia by the non-resident at or through a permanent establishment.

As the taxpayer accepted that it did not deal at arm's length in relation to the acquisition it had made and that the Credit Facility Agreement was an 'international agreement',[13] the key expressions in Division 13 that the Court considered were:

(1) 'property';
(2) 'consideration'; and
(3) 'arm's length consideration'.

11. *Income Tax Assessment Act 1936* (Cth) section 136AD (former).
12. *Ibid.*, sections 136AB, 170(9B), 170(10) (former).
13. *Chevron Appeal* per PAGONE J at [113].

'Property' was defined to include a chose in action, any estate, interest, right or power in or over property, any right to receive income, and services. In turn, relevantly to this matter, 'services' was defined as follows:

> ***Services*** includes any rights, benefits, privileges or facilities and, without limiting the generality of the foregoing, includes the rights, benefits, privileges or facilities that are, or are to be, provided, granted or conferred under:
>
> ...
>
> (d) an agreement for or in relation to the lending of moneys.[14]

Unlike other key terms, the term 'consideration' was not defined in Division 13. The Court adopted the broad construction of the word consideration' that had previously been applied by Australian courts in the context of other tax legislation. In doing so, the Court confirmed that the term 'is not to be construed narrowly and includes that given by the acquiring party so as to move the agreement whether that be in money or in money's worth'.[15] As such, the consideration was not confined only to the interest rate.

The Court also went further, stating that the relevant consideration 'is not confined to the consideration moving only between the parties to the transaction'.[16] Whilst this statement was made in the context of construing the 'arm's length consideration', there seems no reason why such a statement would not be equally accurate in the context of the consideration given by the taxpayer to a third party as part of the transaction.

Finally, 'arm's length consideration' was defined as the consideration that might reasonably be expected to have been payable or receivable as consideration in respect of the relevant supply or acquisition if the property had been supplied or acquired under an agreement between independent parties dealing wholly at arm's length with each other.[17] This definition established the hypothetical nature of the task under Division 13, as it called for 'an evaluative prediction of events and transactions that did not take place'.[18] The task was 'fundamentally a factual enquiry'.[19] The discussion of this aspect of Division 13 was the most significant legal analysis in the *Chevron* cases, and so is covered in some detail below.

The definition required the Court to identify the consideration that might have been expected to be given for the supply of the same property in a hypothetical agreement between arm's length parties dealing wholly independently.[20] That is, contrary to the taxpayer's argument, the task was not to price the transaction actually entered into,[21] though the need for reliability means that the hypothetical agreement

14. *Income Tax Assessment Act 1936* (Cth) section 136AA(1) (former).
15. *Chevron Appeal* per Pagone J at [133].
16. *Ibid.*
17. *Income Tax Assessment Act 1936* (Cth) section 136AA(3)(c), (d) (former).
18. *Chevron Appeal* per Pagone J at [127].
19. *Ibid.*, per Pagone J at [126].
20. *Ibid.*, at [119]; *Chevron First Instance* per Robertson J at [76].
21. *Chevron Appeal* per Pagone J at [120].

must be 'sufficiently like the actual agreement'.[22] The process of moving from the circumstances of the actual parties and agreement to a hypothetical agreement between hypothetical parties was referred to by the Court as 'depersonalization'.[23]

The extent to which the characteristics of the actual parties are to be imputed to the hypothetical parties remained controversial. In *Chevron Appeal*, the Court stated that the 'actual characteristics of the taxpayer must ... ordinarily serve as the basis' of the analysis because the characteristics of the purchaser must be such as to meaningfully inform an enquiry into the arm's length consideration.[24] However, the Court also observed that some features of a taxpayer may not be relevant to determining the arm's length consideration.[25]

Relevantly, the Court concluded that it was permissible to take into account the taxpayer's membership of the broader Chevron group. The Court considered that treating the borrower 'as if it were an orphan' standalone entity 'would distort the application' of the transfer pricing rules, and would 'fundamentally undermine' the purpose of identifying a 'reliably predicted amount which CAHPL might reasonably be expected to give ... by way of consideration'.[26] The Court stated that to treat the taxpayer as an orphan would lead to an analysis 'without reliable foundation in the facts or reality of the circumstances of the taxpayer in question'.[27]

As such, the Court concluded that the hypothetical borrower would be 'a company like CAHPL',[28] as 'an oil and gas exploration and production subsidiary' of a group like the Chevron group.[29] It followed from this conclusion that it was permissible, as a matter of law, to take implicit credit support from its parent company into account.[30]

It appeared accepted that, when depersonalizing the agreement, the objective characteristics of the taxpayer that affect price are to be taken into account as characteristics of the hypothetical parties.[31] However, the questions of what those features are and whether other features of the taxpayer are also to be taken into account were more controversial.

In this case, the Court justified its conclusions based on the group's policies, the requirement that the Australian subsidiary obtains approval to borrow, and the goal of obtaining 'the lowest cost of funding to the group for external borrowing'.[32] However, a subsequent decision of the Court has held that 'it would be appropriate to exclude'

22. *Ibid.*, at [128].
23. *Ibid.*, at [119], per Allsop CJ at [45]; *Chevron First Instance* per Robertson J at [76].
24. *Chevron Appeal* per Pagone J at [128].
25. *Ibid.*, at [128], citing *SNF (Australia) Pty Ltd v. Commissioner of Taxation* [2010] FCA 635.
26. *Ibid.*, per Pagone J at [130].
27. *Ibid.*
28. *Ibid.*, at [129].
29. *Ibid.*, at [128].
30. This conclusion is consistent with Chapter X of the 2022 version of the OECD Transfer Pricing Guidelines for Multinational Enterprises and Tax Administrations (2022 OECD Guidelines) at C.1.1.3.
31. *See also*, *Commissioner of Taxation v. Glencore Investment Pty Ltd* [2020] FCAFC 187 at [187]; Decision Impact Statement on *Commissioner of Taxation v. Glencore Investment Pty Ltd* [2020] FCAFC 187. These are discussed below at §V.2.
32. *Chevron Appeal* per Pagone J at [132].

circumstances that are the product of a 'non-arm's length relationship' between the taxpayer and the broader global group of which it is a member.[33] Whilst the Commissioner did not accept that this would lead to group policies being disregarded, in light of a suggestion by the Court that they 'might have been relevant' if they were in evidence, it remained a question to be resolved in future cases.[34]

### *B* *Application*

Applying the provisions in Division 13 was a four-step process:

(1) identify the property that the taxpayer acquired – this step was 'critical'[35] because the property 'serves as the reference point' for the next two steps (and cannot be altered);[36]
(2) identify 'the consideration actually given ... by the taxpayer' for that property;
(3) identify the 'arm's length consideration', being 'the consideration that may reasonably have been expected to have been given ... if the property had been acquired in the hypothetical agreement' discussed above;[37] and
(4) compare each set of considerations identified in steps two and three, to determine whether or not the consideration given by the taxpayer exceeded the arm's length consideration.

### 2 Subdivision 815-A

In November 2011, after the Commissioner had issued the first set of determinations and amended assessments to CAHPL but prior to the commencement of litigation, the Federal Government announced that it would 'modernize' Australia's transfer pricing laws.[38] These amendments followed recent case law in which the Commissioner had failed in his bid to apply Division 13 to a taxpayer whose Australian business had experienced many years of consistent losses, as that taxpayer had paid arm's length prices to its related party suppliers.[39] The amendments sought to address the Court's decision that the OECD Transfer Pricing Guidelines for Multinational Enterprises and Tax Administrations (OECD Guidelines) were not relevant, and the 'potential uncertainty' around whether Australia's tax treaties provided a standalone basis for the making of transfer pricing adjustments (in addition to the powers in Division 13).

---

33. *Commissioner of Taxation v. Glencore Investment Pty Ltd* [2020] FCAFC 187 at [180]. *See also* below at §2.05[B].
34. *See, e.g.*, Decision Impact Statement on *Commissioner of Taxation v. Glencore Investment Pty Ltd* [2020] FCAFC 187. *See also* below at §V.2.
35. *Chevron Appeal* per ALLSOP CJ at [16].
36. *Ibid.*, per PAGONE J at [112], *see also* ALLSOP CJ at [16].
37. *Ibid.*, per PAGONE J at [112].
38. 'Robust transfer pricing rules for multinationals', Media release by the Hon Bill Shorten MP, Assistant Treasurer and Minister for Financial Services and Superannuation, 1 November 2011.
39. *Federal Commissioner of Taxation v. SNF (Australia) Pty Ltd* [2011] FCAFC 74.

In announcing the amendments, the Government asserted there was a 'strong argument that tax treaty rules already operate independently of the domestic rules' and that it 'decided to put this beyond doubt to promote consistency between Australia's rules and the international approach'.[40]

The Government argued that it was the intention of Parliament that the treaties provide such an assessment power. The issue of whether the 'associated enterprises' article in a tax treaty already provided this power came to be in issue in the *Chevron* cases, primarily because of the unusual circumstance of the case that the determinations required by Division 13 had been made by a person that was not authorized to do so (though this was found not to affect the validity of the amended assessments based on those determinations).[41]

Most controversially, the Government asserted that the most recent statement to this effect had been made in 2003 and, therefore, these new rules for treaty cases would apply from 1 July 2004. Conveniently, this period of retrospectivity would cover all but the first year of operation of the Credit Facility Agreement between CAHPL and CFC. On the other hand, it would give rise to questions regarding the validity of the retrospective provisions, including whether the Commonwealth had the power to enact retrospective legislation of this nature.[42] In each of the *Chevron* cases, the Court held that the *Australian Constitution* does not prevent taxes from being imposed on a retrospective basis[43] and that there were no other constitutional barriers to the operation of the provisions.[44]

Ultimately, the broader aim of modernizing the transfer pricing rules would prove to be a more challenging task. The Government instead decided to legislate the treaty-equivalent rules separately from the broader project.

Subdivision 815-A was therefore introduced in 2012 but with effect from 1 July 2004. These new provisions were framed in wholly different terms to Division 13, despite addressing essentially the same subject matter. This reflected that Division 13 and subdivision 815-A were introduced 30 years apart, and dealt with a different range

40. 'Robust transfer pricing rules for multinationals', Media release by the Hon BILL SHORTEN MP, Assistant Treasurer and Minister for Financial Services and Superannuation, 1 November 2011.
41. *Chevron Appeal* per PAGONE J at [104].
42. The taxpayer accepted in *Chevron Appeal* that the Commonwealth had power to legislate retrospectively, but argued that subdivision 815-A amounted to an 'arbitrary exaction' or 'incontestable tax' which was beyond the Commonwealth's power. Amongst other things, CAHPL argued that subdivision 815-A relied on 'nebulous criteria' and the 'vague' OECD Guidelines. In *Chevron First Instance*, the Court held that CAHPL's constitutional validity challenge failed: the mere effect of a statute to impose tax by reference to past transactions did not 'bespeak invalidity' (per ROBERTSON J at [548]). Although the enquiry demanded by subdivision 815-A 'may be complex and the correct answer debatable, that did not deprive the applicable criteria of objectivity or generality, at least so long as the Commissioner's assessment was amendable to review and appeal' (per ROBERTSON J at [538]). In *Chevron Appeal*, the Full Court agreed, holding that the taxpayer had not demonstrated that subdivision 815-A was beyond the constitutional power of the Commonwealth because it imposed an arbitrary and incontestable tax (per PAGONE J at [144]).
43. *Ibid.*, per PAGONE J at [141], citing *The Colonial Sugar Refining Co Ltd v. Irving* [1903] St R Qd 261, 76; *Suntory (Aust) Pty Ltd v. Federal Commissioner of Taxation* (2009) 177 FCR 140; *Mutual Pools & Staff Pty Ltd v. Commonwealth* (1994) 179 CLR 155, 167-168, 209, 217-218.
44. *Ibid.*, per PAGONE J at [144].

of taxpayers (Division 13 applied to all taxpayers who entered into an 'international agreement', whereas subdivision 815-A only applied to cases governed by Australia's tax treaties).

Under subdivision 815-A, the Commissioner could make a determination for the purpose of 'negating a transfer pricing benefit an entity gets'.[45] However, this would only apply where the entity got the transfer pricing benefit 'at a time when an international tax agreement containing an associated enterprises article applies to the entity'.[46]

An 'associated enterprises article' was defined as Article 9 of the tax treaty between Australia and the United Kingdom or a corresponding provision under another tax treaty.[47] Article 9(1) of the Australia-UK tax treaty read as follows:

Where:

(a) an enterprise of a Contracting State participates directly or indirectly in the management, control or capital of an enterprise of the other Contracting State; or
(b) the same persons participate directly or indirectly in the management, control or capital of an enterprise of a Contracting State and an enterprise of the other Contracting State;
and in either case conditions operate between the two enterprises in their commercial or financial relations which differ from those which might be expected to operate between independent enterprises dealing wholly independently with one another, then any profits which might, but for those conditions, have been expected to accrue to one of the enterprises, but, by reason of those conditions, have not so accrued, may be included in the profits of that enterprise and taxed accordingly.

An Australian resident entity would get a 'transfer pricing benefit' if:

(1) an associated enterprises article applied to the entity;
(2) the amount of profits which, but for the conditions mentioned in the article, might have been expected to accrue to the entity, has, by reason of those conditions, not so accrued; and
(3) had the profits accrued, the taxable income of the entity would be greater or the amount of a loss would be less.

Whether an entity got a transfer pricing benefit was required to be worked out consistently with the OECD Model Tax Convention of Income and on Capital (which formed the basis for most of Australia's tax treaties), and its Commentaries, as well as the OECD Guidelines, but only to the extent those documents were 'relevant'.[48]

45. *Income Tax Assessment Act 1997* (Cth) section 815-10(1).
46. *Ibid.*, section 815-10(2).
47. *Ibid.*, section 815-15(5).
48. *Ibid.*, section 815-20.

Where the requirements were met, the Commissioner could determine an amount by which the taxable income of the entity is increased or an amount by which a loss of the entity is decreased.[49]

Like Division 13, an unlimited amendment period is applied to give effect to determinations under subdivision 815-A.

Subdivision 815-A was summarized by Pagone J in *Chevron Appeal* as directing 'attention to the relationship and conditions existing between two enterprises in their commercial or financial relations to determine whether "conditions operate[d]" between them in their commercial or financial relations which differed from those which might be expected to operate between 'independent enterprises dealing wholly independently with one another'.[50] Like Division 13, it is also 'a factual enquiry'.[51]

In addressing the meaning of 'conditions', the Court stated that it was to interpret Article 9(1) 'in accordance with the rules of interpretation applicable to a treaty provision'.

The Court saw the relevant task as being 'to identify those conditions existing between enterprises in two countries affecting their commercial or financial relations', which it considered 'permits a broad and wide ranging enquiry into the relations existing between the enterprises concerned'.[52] However, this would appear to reverse the operation of Article 9, which looked to the conditions that 'operate between two enterprises *in* their commercial or financial relations'.

Significantly, the Court rejected the taxpayer's argument that it was necessary to distinguish between a 'commercial or financial relation' and a 'condition' that is 'operating in respect of those relations'.[53] The Court held that 'the relations between' the borrower, lender and other members of the global group could be regarded as 'conditions' when applying subdivision 815-A.

The Court also rejected CAHPL's argument that there was no 'amount of profits which had not accrued' to it because it had received substantial tax-exempt dividends from the lender, which was its wholly owned subsidiary.[54] In rejecting this argument, the Court held that the 'focus of the provision is the tax effect of a dealing not the overall income of a taxpayer'.[55] Therefore, whilst such dividends were expected, there was nonetheless an amount of profits which had not accrued to CAHPL which might have been expected if the arm's length conditions had operated.

It is possible that the correctness of the Court's analysis of Article 9(1) may not be revisited in an Australian context, having regard to the changes to the domestic transfer pricing provisions that are discussed below.

49. *Ibid.*, section 815-30(1).
50. *Chevron Appeal* per PAGONE J at [151].
51. *Ibid.*, at [145].
52. *Ibid.*, at [153].
53. *Ibid.*, at [152]-[153]. The further elaboration on the differences between 'conditions' and 'commercial or financial relations' in the 2022 OECD Guidelines may lead to different conclusions being reached by future courts.
54. *Ibid.*, at [158].
55. *Ibid.*

## 3 Subdivision 815-B

Following a further period of consultation, the modernized transfer pricing laws were introduced in 2013, with subdivision 815-B replacing both Division 13 and subdivision 815-A with effect from 1 July 2013. The features of the new laws included:

(1) self-executing operation, not dependent on the making of any determination by the Commissioner, such that taxpayers were now required to self-assess the application of the transfer pricing rules;
(2) the automatic substitution of 'arm's length conditions' in the commercial and financial relations of two parties where the actual conditions gave rise to a transfer pricing benefit;[56]
(3) a requirement that the arm's length conditions be identified based on the commercial or financial relations between the parties in connection with which the actual conditions operated unless the form and substance of those relations were inconsistent or independent entities dealing wholly independently would not have entered into those relations;[57]
(4) a requirement that the arm's length conditions be identified so as best to achieve consistency with the OECD Guidelines;[58] and
(5) a limitation period of seven years for amending assessments.[59]

Subdivision 815-B did not affect the years in question in the *Chevron* cases and therefore the Court was not required to consider the new provisions in any detail. However, as it had been introduced into the statute books by the time *Chevron First Instance* was heard, CAHPL sought to deploy the new provisions to support its arguments in relation to the earlier laws. In particular, the taxpayer posited that the new subdivision 815-B included an express power to substitute other terms (such as a different currency, security or covenants) for the actual terms of the loan agreed between the parties.[60] The fact that neither Division 13 nor subdivision 815-A included any such express power should, CAHPL argued, allow the Court to draw a negative inference that it was impermissible to make such a substitution under those older laws, which the Commissioner was seeking to do.

In response, the Commissioner argued that he was not recharacterizing the transaction or impermissibly changing the terms of the loan between the parties in identifying consideration for a loan in a different currency and supported by security or covenants. Nevertheless, the Commissioner argued that Division 13 and subdivision 815-A could not be interpreted by reference to subsequent amendments enacted for a

56. *Income Tax Assessment Act 1997* (Cth) sections 815-115, 815-120.
57. *Ibid.*, section 815-130.
58. *Ibid.*, section 815-135. The legislation currently incorporates the 2017 version of the OECD Guidelines, and an amendment to the legislation would be required to replace this with a reference to the 2022 version of the OECD Guidelines.
59. *Ibid.*, section 815-150.
60. *Ibid.*, section 815-130. Section 815-130 is based on the 'exceptional circumstances' now set out in paras 1.142-1.145 of the 2022 OECD Guidelines.

'different purpose' and the machinery of which was 'quite different' to the earlier laws. Subdivision 815-B was therefore said to shed no light on the earlier provisions. The Court accepted the Commissioner's arguments on this point.[61]

## IV APPLYING THE LAW

The *Chevron* cases were argued on the basis that there was no difference in how Division 13 and subdivision 815-A applied to the facts, despite the differences in structure and terminology discussed above. However, at both first instance and on appeal, Division 13 was considered first by the Court (which noted that 'the need to consider the substantive application of' subdivision 815-A only arises 'in the alternative').[62] The below discussion highlights the particular issues of interest addressed by the Court across both sets of provisions.

### 1 The Actual Transaction

#### *A What Property Was Acquired by CAHPL?*

The correct identification of the relevant property which the taxpayer had acquired for the purposes of Division 13 was a 'fundamental point of difference between' the parties.[63] Chevron argued that the 'unsecured nature of the loan' formed part of the property supplied,[64] whereas the Commissioner argued that the property was confined to the 'amount of money obtained'.[65]

The Commissioner's position was readily rejected, having regard to the statutory definition specifically including the rights and benefits under the Credit Facility Agreement.[66]

The question of whether the absence of security formed part of the property supplied was more difficult, having regard to the intentionally broad way in which 'property' was defined in the legislation.[67] However, the Court ultimately concluded that 'the absence of security ... is more aptly seen as part of the consideration' for the purposes of Division 13.[68]

#### *B The Relevant 'Conditions'*

The Court's view that the identification of the relevant 'conditions' for the purposes of subdivision 815-A and Article 9 of the tax treaty between Australia and the United

61. *Chevron First Instance* per Robertson J at [597]-[598].
62. *Chevron Appeal* per Pagone J at [150]; *see also*, *Chevron First Instance* per Robertson J at [526].
63. *Chevron Appeal* per Pagone J at [115].
64. *Ibid.*, at [115].
65. *Ibid.*, at [113].
66. *Chevron First Instance* per Robertson J at [73]; *Chevron Appeal* per Pagone J at [114].
67. *Chevron Appeal* per Pagone J at [115].
68. *Ibid.*, Pagone J at [115]; *see also*, Pagone J at [117] and [131].

States was a broad enquiry led to a wide range of factors being identified as relevant. The list of conditions between CAHPL and CFC that were said to differ from those that might be expected to have operated at arm's length relevantly included that:

- CAHPL owned CFC and they both had a common parent, CVX;
- CVX Treasury decided how much debt and at what interest rate CAHPL should borrow from CFC;
- there was no bargaining or negotiation between CAHPL and CFC;
- the terms and conditions of the Credit Facility Agreement, including the terms in respect of the interest rate charged, the duration and the currency of the loan and the absence of covenants;
- the sole reason for CFC's incorporation, and the purpose of its commercial paper program, was to raise funds solely to on-lend to its parent CAHPL;
- the credit profiles of CFC and CAHPL could be controlled by decisions made by CVX;
- CFC profited from lending to CAHPL at a high-interest rate; and
- the higher the interest-bearing loan from CFC and the higher the interest rate, the more profit CAHPL stood to make.[69]

By including the 'common parent' in the list of conditions differing from those which might be expected to operate between independent enterprises dealing wholly independently with one another, the Court has essentially said that this aspect of subdivision 815-A will be satisfied in any dealing between members of corporate groups. As such, attention turns to whether any of these conditions have affected the profits that might be expected to have accrued to the taxpayer if arm's length conditions had instead operated.

### C *Currency of the Loan*

The parties were in dispute as to both the currency of the loan actually entered into and the currency of the hypothetical arm's length loan agreement. CAHPL contended that both the actual and arm's length loans were denominated in Australian dollars, whereas the Commissioner argued that United States dollars was the relevant currency. Because the prevailing interest rates for USD loans were significantly lower than those for loans denominated in AUD, the Commissioner's change to the currency of the loan made up a substantial component of the tax in dispute.[70]

The dispute over the actual currency of the Credit Facility Agreement appeared to arise from the fact that the borrowed sums were credited to a USD-denominated account, and the amount of the loan was described by the parties as the AUD

69. *Chevron First Instance* per ROBERTSON J at [582], endorsed by PAGONE J in *Chevron Appeal* at [152].
70. *Chevron First Instance* per ROBERTSON J at [629].

equivalent of a specified USD amount. Nonetheless, the Court considered it 'clearly the case, that the actual loan was in Australian dollars'.[71]

## 2 The Arm's Length Consideration

Whilst the Court provided some relevant guidance on how the transfer pricing rules are to be applied to loans, the Court ultimately found that there was insufficient evidence to support a conclusion as to the arm's length interest rate.[72] Given the taxpayer had the burden of proving the assessments made by the Commissioner were excessive, this lack of evidence was ultimately fatal to its case, even though the Commissioner was also unsuccessful in many of his arguments.

### A *The Characteristics of the Actual Borrower (but Not the Lender) Were Relevant*

The parties agreed that 'that the pricing of the loan between CAHPL and CFC must take into account the assets, risks and functions of CAHPL which informed the likelihood of CAHPL repaying both principal and interest'.[73] The Court held that the relevant characteristics of the hypothetical borrower included that it 'was to be an oil and gas exploration and production subsidiary'.

Looking to the other side of the transaction, the Court held that 'the correct perspective is that of a commercial lender'.[74] The characteristics of the actual lender (which was not a commercial lender) were not to be attributed to the hypothetical lender.[75] As such, the hypothetical transaction to be considered was between a borrower sharing the characteristics of CAHPL relevant to pricing, and a 'commercial lender' (and it was not necessary to attribute more detailed characteristics to the hypothetical lender).

### B *The (Non-) impact of Implicit Support*

Despite the Court considering implicit support as being relevant as a matter of law, it was not found to be relevant as a matter of fact. This finding reflected the expert evidence accepted by the Court that 'in the absence of a legally binding parental guarantee, implicit credit support had very little, if any, impact on pricing by a lender in the real world'.[76]

This conclusion was a consequence of finding that the arm's length consideration was to be determined from the perspective of a commercial lender. The finding was

71. *Chevron Appeal* per Pagone J at [134].
72. *Chevron First Instance* per Robertson J at [525].
73. *Ibid.*, at [484].
74. *Ibid.*, at [503].
75. *Ibid.*, at [482]. This can be contrasted with the 2022 OECD Guidelines, which may require the consideration of the lender's perspective: *see* Chapter X at C.1.1.1.
76. *Ibid.*, at [606].

based on the evidence of the taxpayer's experts as to how commercial lenders priced loans and was consistent with an article co-authored by the Commissioner's expert that reached the same conclusion.[77] That article was published after the expert had already provided two reports in this case, and contradicted the evidence that the expert had given.

Although the decision of the Tax Court of Canada in *General Electric Capital Canada Inc v. The Queen* [2009] TCC 563 was only mentioned in passing in this case, it is noteworthy that the same conclusions in relation to implicit support were reached by the courts of both Canada and Australia. In each case, the revenue authority's evidence did not support a finding that implicit support actually affected the interest rates that an independent lender would be expected to charge.

### C A Parental Guarantee Might Reasonably Have Been Expected

The Court concluded that it might reasonably be expected that, were CAHPL to have borrowed from an independent party, such a borrowing would have been supported by security in the form of a guarantee from its ultimate parent.[78] The relevance of the matters supporting this conclusion (the group's policies, the requirement that the Australian subsidiary obtains approval to borrow, and the goal of obtaining 'the lowest cost of funding to the group for external borrowing'), is discussed at §III.1.A above.

Broader questions around whether other forms of security, or financial covenants, would have been provided by the borrower are likely to have been 'of no relevant consequence'.[79] Once it was concluded that 'the reasonable expectation would be that Chevron or a company in Chevron's position would give a guarantee',[80] the arm's length interest rate would necessarily have been that which reflected the rates at which the ultimate parent could borrow.

The conclusion that a parent company guarantee might have been expected at arm's length necessarily raised the question of whether a fee for that guarantee needed to be taken into account. As set out at §III.1.A above, the Court considered that the relevant 'consideration' to be taken into account for Division 13 purposes was not limited to that moving between the parties to the transaction. It therefore could include a fee payable by the borrower to a guarantor. The Court accepted that there was 'some force' to the proposition that it would be necessary 'to assume that CAHPL had paid a fee to its parent for the provision of' the guarantee.[81] However, the taxpayer's onus of proof meant that the absence of evidence demonstrating 'that a fee might reasonably have been expected to have been paid' necessarily led to this argument being unsuccessful.[82]

77. *Ibid.*
78. *Chevron Appeal* per Pagone J at [132], per Allsop CJ at [62].
79. *Ibid.*, per Allsop CJ at [60].
80. *Ibid.*, at [60].
81. *Ibid.*, at [133].
82. *Ibid.* Further detail as to the appropriate approach to be followed in determining the arm's length terms of a financial guarantee has since been included in the 2022 OECD Guidelines in Part D of Chapter X.

It is also notable that the evidence of the taxpayer's own experts was that the loan obtained 'would not have been available to a hypothetical company with CAHPL's creditworthiness as a stand-alone company', and that the loan 'would not have been sustainable' in the absence of the interest being returned to the borrower by way of non-taxable dividends from the lender.[83] Given the need to consider what might reasonably have been expected in a dealing 'unaffected by the lack of independence and the lack of arm's length dealing',[84] this presented a further barrier to the taxpayer's argument that the Court was required to price the transaction actually entered into.

### D *Currency of the Loan*

There was significant argument regarding which currency would have been preferable for the hypothetical loan. However, the Court ultimately accepted that borrowing in AUD, which was the taxpayer's functional currency for accounting and fiscal purposes, 'would avoid or limit foreign currency gains and losses', and therefore might reasonably have been expected to have been agreed between independent parties.[85] The Court was not persuaded by expert evidence called by the Commissioner to the effect that 'the optimal loan currency was USD' for reasons including the lower interest rate, '88 % of the CAHPL group revenue' being in USD, or the 'natural hedge' resulting from sales in USD.[86]

This was perhaps an unsurprising conclusion in circumstances where the property acquired by the taxpayer cannot be altered, as it would not ordinarily be expected that the lender and borrower would agree to make a loan in one currency and repay the loan in another. Subdivision 815-A may perhaps allow for a broader consideration of the currency of the loan (were it not found that an arm's length loan would be in AUD), though the issue was unnecessary to resolve in the case.[87]

Although the taxpayer was successful in rebutting this aspect of the Commissioner's case, it had no effect on the ultimate outcome because the taxpayer had seemingly not led evidence of the costs of borrowing on a fully guaranteed basis. In the absence of this evidence, the Court was unable to reduce the assessments to take into account the higher interest rates that would have been payable on AUD-denominated debt.

### E *Credit Rating Agency Methodologies Not Relevant*

Both the taxpayer and Commissioner led evidence from expert witnesses that sought to establish how a recognized credit rating agency would have rated the taxpayer. However, such evidence was not seen as relevant by the Court,[88] having accepted

83. *Ibid.*, per Pagone J at [124]. Further guidance in relation to such situations is now provided in Chapter X of the 2022 OECD Guidelines at B.1.
84. *Ibid.*, per Pagone J at [126].
85. *Chevron First Instance* per Robertson J at [583]; *see also Chevron Appeal* per Pagone J at [134].
86. *Chevron First Instance* per Robertson J at [293].
87. *Chevron Appeal* per Pagone J at [134].
88. *Chevron First Instance* per Robertson J at [242].

evidence from an expert banker that 'lending institutions performed their own independent credit analyses when deciding whether to lend to a prospective borrower' and that they 'did not rely on' the ratings produced by rating agencies.[89]

### F Rejection of Transfer Pricing Economists' Evidence

The Commissioner sought to support his case that the arm's length interest rate was equivalent to that at which CVX could borrow by leading evidence from two transfer pricing economists (Mr John Hollas and Dr Thomas Horst, each based in the United States). The evidence of each was rejected by the Court, which described such evidence as an 'artificial' exercise not 'done by either lenders or rating agencies'.[90]

The Court also noted that comparables may not always supply the answer to the relevant question. Whilst it was accepted that 'in some cases the consideration that might reasonably be expected to be given ... may be found in comparable dealings in an open market', the Court confirmed that 'in each case the inquiry called for is a factual enquiry'.[91]

In doing so, the Court's decision highlights the importance of bringing relevant industry expertise to bear on the determination of the arm's length consideration.

### G Rejection of the Taxpayer's Experts

The taxpayer's case was based upon the view that the task was to price the loan actually entered into,[92] which was rejected as discussed in §III.1.A above. Many of the experts had been asked to opine on questions that were asked on that premise, and therefore their evidence was not considered to be relevant to the statutory task.[93]

The taxpayer's primary evidence on the pricing of the loans was led by two experienced bankers, Mr Eugene Martin (formerly of Morgan Stanley) and Mr Richard Gross (formerly of Bank of America). In the case of Mr Martin, the Court determined that he had not addressed 'what the consideration would have been if [the loan agreement] had been negotiated at arm's length'.[94] In addition, the Court did not accept his evidence as to the arm's length interest rate for the loan as he:

- 'had no relevant experience in or substantial knowledge of the' taxpayer's industry;
- disregarded specific credit metrics relevant to that industry;

89. *Ibid.*, at [181]. The relevance of credit ratings now receives significantly more detailed consideration in the 2022 version of the OECD Guidelines: *see* Chapter X at C.1.1.2.
90. *Ibid.*, per ROBERTSON J at [381], *see also*, at [407]. This suggests that an Australian court may not accept the approaches to determining the arm's length interest rate of intra-group loans set out in Chapter X of the 2022 OECD Guidelines as C.1.2.
91. *Chevron Appeal* per PAGONE J at [128].
92. *Ibid.*, per PAGONE J at [120].
93. *See, e.g.*, *Chevron First Instance* per ROBERTSON J at [506].
94. *Ibid.*, per ROBERTSON J at [182].

- inappropriately assumed that the transaction could be priced based on 'between 75 and 100 lenders';
- priced the loan based on a 'form of transaction which would not have occurred'; and
- used a method of determining the margin over LIBOR (which included making certain adjustments) which was 'unreliable'.[95]

The evidence of Mr Gross was also affected by the questions asked of him.[96] In addition, his view of the credit rating of the borrower differed from that of the other experts (and the basis on which the taxpayer ran their case),[97] and his view on the 'minimum fee' that Bank of America would accept was shown to be wrong in cross-examination.[98] Further, like Mr Martin, he 'accepted that there could not have been a single lender',[99] and gave evidence allowing the conclusion that an independent borrower 'could not have entered into the' actual loan facility.[100]

### *H Conclusion on the Arm's Length Consideration*

Despite the taxpayer's success on the currency of the loan and the acknowledgement that the AUD currency would have meant a significantly higher interest rate than was taken into account by the Commissioner when making the disputed assessments, there was no evidence before the Court that allowed this interest rate to be identified. Given the taxpayer's onus of proving the extent to which the disputed assessments were excessive, the assessments therefore stood unchanged.

## 3 Role of the OECD Guidelines

Section 815-20 called for subdivision 815-A to be applied 'consistently with' the OECD Model Tax Convention on Income and on Capital, its Commentaries, and the OECD Guidelines. Because the relevant transaction was entered into in 2003, it was the 1995 version of the OECD Guidelines that was in issue.[101]

However, the direction to apply the provisions consistently with this guidance material only applied 'to the extent they are relevant'.[102] The Court considered terms of the OECD Guidelines do not 'modify or alter the operative provisions' of the domestic law, but rather the reference to the guidance materials is 'a direction given in aid of interpretation'.[103]

95. *Ibid.*, at [182]-[183], *see also*, Robertson J at [511]-[517].
96. *Ibid.*, per Robertson J at [506].
97. *Ibid.*, at [507].
98. *Ibid.*, at [510].
99. *Ibid.*, at [508].
100. *Ibid.*, at [509].
101. *Income Tax (Transitional Provisions) Act 1997* (Cth) section 815-5.
102. *Income Tax Assessment Act 1997* (Cth) section 815-20(1).
103. *Chevron Appeal* per Pagone J at [145].

This is not to say that the OECD Guidelines were not taken into account by the Court. The Court noted that the OECD Guidelines reinforced the conclusions that it had already reached on the correct approach to applying the transfer pricing laws. In particular, the Court noted that the view that the hypothetical taxpayer is not an orphan unconnected with any group is consistent with the position in the OECD Guidelines[104] and that the 'OECD Guidelines contemplate that a cross-border guarantee by a parent to a subsidiary may require the payment of an arm's length guarantee fee'.[105]

## 4 Absence of the Required Comparison

As noted above, the application of Division 13 required a comparison between the consideration actually received (or receivable) and the arm's length consideration. A comparison was also required in the application of Article 9, being a comparison between the profits which actually accrued to an entity with those that might have been expected to accrue if arm's length conditions had instead operated (or, in the context of Division 13, a comparison between the consideration actually provided and the consideration that might be expected to have been provided between arm's length parties).

It is significant that the *Chevron* cases do not address these comparisons. Comparing the actual and arm's length consideration poses significant challenges where the arm's length consideration takes a different form to that adopted (as it did here, as the arm's length consideration included a parent company guarantee that was not present in the actual transaction).

However, this should not be regarded as a criticism of the Court's decision. In the absence of evidence as to the value of the guarantee, the amount of a fee that might have been paid for a guarantee or the consequences of pricing a different currency, it was unnecessary for the Court to directly address the statutory comparisons, as it was inevitable that the Court would have found that the taxpayer failed to discharge its onus of proof. The evidence could not support findings that the consideration actually received was at least equal in value to the arm's length consideration or the extent to which a guarantee fee might have been expected to affect CAHPL's profits.

## 5 Irrelevant Witnesses

Whilst the Court acknowledged that 'admissible, probative and reliable expert opinion' can be used to address the statutory task,[106] the Court at first instance found that most of the evidence given by 20 expert witnesses called by the parties did not assist the Court to address the relevant statutory questions.

104. *Ibid.*, per PAGONE J at [130].
105. *Ibid.*, at [133].
106. *Ibid.*, at [127].

This can be contrasted with the lay witnesses who provided the background to the relevant loans, whose evidence was accepted without a great degree of controversy.

In addition to those experts discussed above, it is useful to briefly discuss some of the other evidence that the Court did not consider to be relevant to the statutory task. This included evidence from:

- a former Chief Financial Officer of another oil and gas company (Chesapeake Energy), whose circumstances were considered by the Court to have been 'quite different from CAHPL at that time';[107]
- a former Chief Financial Officer of a listed Australian oil and gas company (Santos), whose evidence was focused on the behaviour of publicly listed corporations, rather than subsidiaries;[108]
- a former Group Treasurer of another oil and gas company (Royal Dutch Shell), who was asked questions about the prudence of entering into the Credit Facility Agreement, which was 'of very limited utility';[109]
- an economist previously employed by an airline, whose evidence about a natural hedge between oil prices and the AUD/USD exchange rate involved the impermissible use of hindsight;[110]
- a former head of the OECD Transfer Pricing Unit, whose evidence as to the interpretation of the OECD Guidelines was found inadmissible, and instead received by the Court as a submission;[111] and
- the lead negotiator of the relevant tax treaty for the United States, whose evidence did not 'cast any light on the construction of' the relevant article.[112]

## V THE LANDSCAPE AFTER THE *CHEVRON* CASES

There have been three major developments following the decisions in the *Chevron* cases, being:

(1) the issuance of a new Practical Compliance Guideline (PCG), PCG 2017/4 *ATO compliance approach to taxation issues associated with cross-border related party financing arrangements and related transactions*;
(2) the decision of the Full Court of the Federal Court of Australia in *Commissioner of Taxation v. Glencore Investment Pty Ltd* [2020] FCAFC 187 (*Glencore Appeal*); and
(3) the ongoing dispute in Singapore *Telecom Australia Investments Pty Ltd v. Commissioner of Taxation* [2021] FCA 1597 (*Singtel* case).

107. *Chevron First Instance* per Robertson J at [227].
108. *Ibid.*, at [241].
109. *Ibid.*, at [348].
110. *Ibid.*, at [314].
111. *Ibid.*, at [316].
112. *Ibid.*, at [318].

## 1 PCG 2017/4

The Commissioner issued PCG 2017/4 in draft on 16 May 2017, a little under a month after the decision in *Chevron Appeal*. Following a period of consultation on the draft, the final PCG was ultimately issued on 18 December 2017.

PCG 2017/4 sets out the Commissioner's approach to compliance in relation to taxpayers with cross-border related party financing arrangements and related transactions. It is not a legal view and does not provide advice or guidance on the technical interpretation of Australia's transfer pricing laws or other taxation provisions. It also does not provide taxpayers with a safe harbour. Rather, it is an administrative tool that is used by the Commissioner to assess risk and to aid the Commissioner in determining whether to review or audit taxpayers.

In practical terms, there are two key points that come through the PCG. First, the PCG aims to see 'in most cases, the cost of financing to align with the costs that could be achieved, on an arm's length basis, by the parent of the global group to which the borrower and lender both belong'.[113] In some respects, this aspect of the ATO's view is directly inconsistent with the arm's length principle, as it relies on the non-arm's length relationship between group members.

Second, when comparing the cost of financing, PCG 2017/4 states that it requires a comparison with the 'all in' cost of debt, which includes guarantee fees.[114] This is a particularly interesting comment for foreign-headquartered multinationals given the comments of Pagone J in *Chevron Appeal* about guarantee fees and the fact that, unlike interest, a specific guarantee fee is not subject to withholding tax under Australian law.[115]

PCG 2017/4 sets out a framework of six 'risk zones' that will influence the compliance approach that the Commissioner will take in relation to particular taxpayers. These risk zones range from 'white', for arrangements already reviewed, and 'green' for low risk through to 'red' for arrangements seen by the Commissioner as very high risk. A taxpayer's zone is determined based on their highest risk financing arrangement, the risk rating of which is determined by two sets of factors:

(1) 'pricing risk', which considers matters such as the price of the debt and broader terms (including the currency, whether the debt is secured and any collateral provided); and
(2) 'motivational risk', which considers the matters such as the borrower's leverage and ability to service the loan, the applicable tax rates and any hybrid features.

As a practical reality, the PCG has been used by the ATO in its attempts to influence multinationals to restructure their financial arrangements within the scope of

113. PCG 2017/4 at [52].
114. *Ibid.*, at [68].
115. The ATO had originally announced that PCG 2017/4 would include a specific schedule to deal with guarantees. However, as at the time of writing, no schedule has been released.

the 'green zone'. Those multinationals who have not restructured their financial arrangements have typically found themselves subject to audits, where a significant quantum of tax is often sought (based on the rates at which the ultimate parent company of the taxpayer could borrow).

## 2 *Glencore* Transfer Pricing Cases

The *Glencore* transfer pricing cases are a series of decisions relating to the application of Division 13 and subdivision 815-A to an Australian subsidiary of the Glencore group, which operated a copper mine in Australia. That company had been selling all of the mine's production to a related Swiss company under a long-term offtake agreement.

In 2007, the parties amended that agreement, so that the way in which the price was set changed. These changes were forecast to, and did, reduce the profitability of the Australian taxpayer. However, these changes also insulated the taxpayer from certain price risks and further limited the buyer's ability to terminate the agreement.

In *Glencore Appeal*, the Full Court of the Federal Court found that the 2007 agreement was within the range of agreements which an arm's length party might reasonably have been expected to enter into. The case was the Court's first consideration of the transfer pricing rules post the *Chevron* cases, and the Court's reasoning would have significant implications in relation to financing transactions:

(1) where debt is refinanced, that the new debt is on less favourable terms to the taxpayer is unlikely of itself to be a trigger for the application of the transfer pricing rules, so long as the terms of the new debt are consistent with the arm's length principle;
(2) a taxpayer should be free to choose fixed or floating interest rates, as these reflect the taxpayer's approach to risk and prudence;
(3) the arm's length range is not just about price. The decision in *Glencore Appeal* observes that there may be a range of pricing mechanisms that might reasonably be entered into by third parties. As a result, multiple forms of debt transactions may be arm's length in a particular case;
(4) the Court's approach to comparables is consistent with that in the *Chevron* cases. Looking at how comparable debt issuances are priced may not be sufficient to establish the appropriate transfer price. However, transactions which are substantially different from that undertaken by the taxpayer may still shed light on what bargain independent parties might have struck; and
(5) the decision raises questions as to how relevant the group's policies for external borrowings are to the transfer pricing hypothetical.

On 21 May 2021, the High Court of Australia declined to grant the Commissioner special leave to appeal the decision (*Commissioner of Taxation v. Glencore Investment Pty Ltd* [2021] HCATrans 98), bringing the dispute to an end.

The ATO has since issued a Decision Impact Statement in relation to the *Glencore* cases (Glencore DIS).[116] Notably, the Glencore DIS seeks to confine *Glencore Appeal* to its facts (perhaps unsurprisingly, given the decision was unfavourable to the Commissioner). In support of this approach, the Glencore DIS appears to lean on a statement made by Kiefel CJ of the High Court in refusing special leave to appeal that:

> The Commissioner seeks to overturn findings of fact upheld by the Full Court below. In our view no question of principle sufficient to warrant a grant of special leave arises.[117]

The Glencore DIS contains a number of comments relevant to the ATO's approach to transfer pricing of financing transactions, including:

(1) whilst the Commissioner had initially suggested in his application for special leave that the Court's decision meant that subdivision 815-A is limited to substituting conditions that define the price payable (which may have limited adjustments to the interest rate), he now states that 'there is no justification in the statutory language to limit the terms and conditions that can be substituted under Division 13 and subdivision 815-A to only those that "define the price"';
(2) despite arguing otherwise in its application for special leave, the ATO no longer considers that *Glencore Appeal* means that a taxpayer could succeed where 'a depersonalized market participant might possibly have adopted' the same terms, but rather that any such conclusion was factual in nature, and therefore confined to the facts of the *Glencore Appeal* decision (which is likely to mean that the ATO will continue to seek to determine what he considers was the best available financing option for the taxpayer);
(3) the ATO maintains that group policies and the taxpayer's attitudes may be relevant, such as group treasury policies or external borrowing practices, despite the relevance of such matters being subject to question following *Glencore Appeal* because they are products of non-arm's length relationships within the group; and
(4) the ATO accepts 'that it will always require a careful examination of the totality of evidence available to best establish the arm's length consideration' – in doing so, the ATO is accepting that economic analysis alone is not the answer in transfer pricing cases. The ATO is likely to consider that relevant evidence in a financing transaction might include relevant group policies, how the taxpayer and its group dealt with third parties for the same or similar transactions, prevailing contemporaneous practices in the industry, and what other independent entities in the same or similar circumstances might reasonably have been expected to have done.

116. A decision impact statement sets out the ATO's view on what a court's decision in a case stands for and how it will affect its administration of the law. A decision impact statement will usually include a summary of the case, the ATO's view of the decision, and the implications on current public rulings, determinations and law administration practice statements.
117. *Commissioner of Taxation v. Glencore Investment Pty Ltd* [2021] HCATrans 98.

## 3 *Singtel* Case

The *Singtel* case relates to the Singapore Telecommunications Limited group's acquisition of 100% of the issued shares in an Australian company, Cable & Wireless Optus Limited in 2001 (later renamed Singtel Optus Pty Ltd) (Optus), funded by debt and equity.

The *Singtel* case was heard by the Federal Court of Australia in August 2021, with a judgment largely favourable to the ATO handed down on 17 December 2021.

In contrast to the *Glencore* cases, the *Singtel* case directly concerns financing transactions. The Singtel Group acquired Optus (through its subsidiary, Singtel Australia Investment Limited (SAI), a company incorporated in the British Virgin Islands and tax resident in Singapore). An Australian wholly owned subsidiary of SAI (Singapore Telecom Australia Investments Pty Ltd (STAI)) then acquired the shares in Optus in 2002 for a price of approximately AUD 14.2 billion, funded by AUD 9 billion of equity issued by STAI to SAI, and AUD 5.2 billion of debt, by way of loan notes issued by STAI to SAI. The loan notes were initially on terms that:

(1) bore interest at a standard reference rate (the Bank Bill Swap Rate) plus 1%;
(2) allowed interest payments to be capitalized;
(3) required interest payments to be grossed up for the withholding tax incurred on payment; and
(4) were repayable on demand, with a maximum 10-year term.

The ATO did not dispute that the interest rate payable at the time the loan notes were established was an arm's length rate. However, the terms of the loan notes were then amended three times:

(1) first, approximately six months after the transaction, to reduce the term by a single day, which was uncontroversial (in Australia, the debt/equity classification rules take a different approach to instruments of less than a 10-year duration and those of a longer tenor);
(2) second, after three more months, substantial amendments stopped the accrual of interest until certain benchmarks were met – it was argued by the ATO that this was such that interest was not to be incurred until the Australian operations were profitable and accrued tax losses were utilized. To compensate the lender for the interest-free period, a premium interest rate was imposed once interest became payable; and
(3) third and finally, in March 2009 (after the end of the interest-free period, and during the Global Financial Crisis) to fix the variable component of the interest rate, whilst maintaining the premium to account for the original interest-free period (which worked out to more than 13% p.a.).

The key aspect of the decision was the Court's acceptance that the borrower would have the benefit of a parental guarantee without being required to pay a guarantee fee. This finding was reached as a factual matter, as Singtel provided a guarantee for financings by other subsidiaries, and there was no evidence that Singtel charged a guarantee fee for providing those guarantees. The Court did not consider whether independent parties in comparable circumstances might reasonably be expected to have charged such a fee. Despite the absence of an express policy to borrow externally at the lowest cost (akin to that of Chevron), the Court was satisfied that the higher interest costs to which the subsidiary would have been exposed made the parent 'likely to prefer to provide a guarantee'.

Having regard to this finding, the Court found that the arm's length interest rate was the interest rate payable on the loan notes at the time of their issuance.

Significantly, the Court was not persuaded that it was relevant to consider the terms on which the taxpayer may have raised the funds in a debt capital markets (DCM) transaction, despite it being common ground between the experts that DCM was the 'most economical, and likely only, source of debt' for this amount.[118] That aspect of the decision is likely to raise significant practical difficulties in demonstrating appropriate transfer prices, given DCM are the most liquid and transparent sources of pricing information for debt capital.

The decision also rejected the taxpayer's interpretation of key aspects of the *Glencore Appeal*, finding that:

(1) implicit support remains relevant as a matter of law (though it must be shown to be relevant on the evidence, which was not the case in the *Chevron Appeal*); and
(2) subdivision 815-A is not limited to substituting conditions that define the price payable.

At the time of writing, an appeal against the Singtel decision is currently pending before the Full Federal Court. As a result, it is likely to be some time before additional clarity around the application of the Australian transfer pricing laws in the context of financing transactions is achieved.

## 4 Summary

As recently as a few years ago, financing was a key battleground in transfer pricing in Australia, with a large number of disputes. Following the decision in *Chevron Appeal*, the ATO appears to have successfully used the views expressed in PCG 2017/4 to influence multinationals to restructure their financial arrangements, lest they be subjected to potentially intensive and costly audits. However, many taxpayers consider that the decision in *Glencore Appeal* potentially changed the legal landscape, particularly in relation to depersonalization.

At the time of writing, the appeal against the decision in the *Singtel* case has not yet concluded. Any decision on appeal is expected to be a landmark in relation to the

118. This can be contrasted with the 2022 OECD Guidelines, which include comments supporting the use of credit ratings in Chapter X at C.1.1.2.

Australian transfer pricing laws, and will hopefully provide additional clarity in relation to the application of the arm's length principle to financing transactions, particularly in relation to parental support and guarantee fees.

## VI CONCLUSION

The *Chevron* cases have had a significant effect on the transfer pricing landscape in Australia. Amongst other things, they have led to the adoption of an approach by the ATO to pricing intra-group loans on the basis of the parent entity's cost of financing in external markets. Anecdotally, the revenue authority has been very successful in persuading multinational groups to price their financial arrangements on that basis for the purposes of their Australian tax liabilities, even on issues where the Court did not find the ATO's position persuasive.

The many issues which were ultimately left unclear or undecided in the *Chevron* cases will no doubt see the light of a courtroom door in the future.

CHAPTER 20

# Transfer Pricing Aspects of Loans: Focus on German Federal Tax Court Case Law—A Detailed Analysis

*Sven-Eric Bärsch*[*]

## I INTRODUCTION

It is a typical issue on international business taxation, closely scrutinized by tax authorities and often disputed in tax audits: are transfer prices for controlled transactions between related entities set at arm's length? For German transfer pricing rules, the Federal Tax Court rendered two landmark decisions concerning transfer pricing for intra-group loans on May 18, 2021. The Federal Tax Court confirmed that the comparable uncontrolled price (CUP) method takes priority over other transfer pricing methods when determining interest on intra-group loans, in particular over the cost-of-funds approach. In addition, the Federal Tax Court has taken a view on several other aspects when determining interest on intra-group loans, which should also be relevant for other types of intercompany transactions.

Those transfer pricing cases are highly relevant because intra-group loans are currently highly contested in German tax audits. This contribution gives an overview of the Federal Tax Court's landmark decisions of May 18, 2021 (I R 4/17 and I R 62/17) on applying the arm's-length principle under German tax law. It also outlines the practical consequences of these decisions.

* The views and opinions set forth herein are the personal views or opinions of the authors; they do not necessarily reflect the views or opinions of the organization with which the authors are associated.

## II CASES ON INTERCOMPANY LOANS

### 1 Case I R 4/17

A group finance company based in the Netherlands granted several loans to a German affiliate. The annual interest was based on the Euribor reference rate and was increased by 1.25%. The loan term was between four to seven years and the borrower did not provide any collateral. The finance company used borrowed funds and equity capital while the interest rates were determined using the external CUP method using publicly available databases. For the application of this method, among others, the stand-alone rating of the German affiliate was used, obtained using a standardized rating tool by Standard & Poor's. The German tax authorities, however, denied the deduction of a significant part of the interest which was supposedly above arm's length.

The Tax Court of Münster confirmed in its decision of December 7, 2016 (first instance) that the interest deduction was to be denied (case no. 13 K 4037/13 K, F). The court rejected the application of the external CUP for the determination of arm's-length interest for intercompany loans received from a related finance company. It argued that intercompany loans granted by finance companies cannot, in principle, be sufficiently compared to third-party loans. The reasoning is that finance companies' business activities are—in the view taken by the court—not comparable to those of independent banks. Moreover, the results of the tool used by Standard & Poor's (i.e., the rating) cannot form the basis of any tax assessment due to the fact that the algorithms underlying the rating tool were not made transparent to the court. Further, the court argued that ratings are usually determined for corporate groups rather than on a stand-alone basis.

In light of these arguments, the Tax Court of Münster took the view that the external CUP cannot, in principle, be applied to intercompany loans unless the borrower had received comparable loans from independent banks (internal CUPs). Instead, the court applied a cost-oriented approach to determine the interest. Accordingly, the finance company's refinancing costs were used as the starting point. In addition, the finance company's operating costs, which were increased by a profit markup of 5%, were added to the refinancing costs.

In its decision of May 18, 2021, the Federal Tax Court overturned the initial decision taken by the Tax Court of Münster. The Federal Tax Court referred the case back for a re-assessment of the underlying facts and circumstances taking into account the principles established by the Federal Tax Court in its decision. Resultingly, the Tax Court of Münster must determine an arm's-length interest rate.

### 2 Case I R 62/17

A German subsidiary acquired the shares in another company from a third-party seller. It financed the acquisition by the means of three loans: The first (intercompany) loan was a shareholder loan with an interest rate of 8% p.a. No collateral was provided for this loan, and the term of the shareholder loan was approx. nine years and the loan took the form of a bullet loan. The second loan was granted by the third-party seller with an interest rate of 10% p.a. Again, the loan was structured as a bullet loan while the term of the seller's loan was six years. Finally, bank loans with an average interest rate of 4.8% p.a. were granted for which collaterals were provided. The term of bank loans was five years redeemed in part by annuities.

The interest of the shareholder loan was determined using the external CUP method, for which a benchmark study based on publicly available databases was used. The German tax authorities, however, denied the deduction of a significant portion of the interest due to an alleged breach of the arm's-length principle. The German tax authorities took the view that an interest rate of 5% p.a. is at arm's length because it applied an internal CUP regarding bank loans.

The Tax Court of Cologne confirmed that there has been a breach of the arm's-length principle (first instance) in its decision dated June 29, 2017 (case no. I R 62/17), with the court rejecting the application of the external CUP for the assessment of the interest amount concerning the shareholder loan at dispute. The court argued that the bank loans, as internal CUP, take priority over an external CUP. Moreover, the court dismissed the benchmark study because it was prepared only after the shareholder loan had been granted. The court further denied the application of an internal CUP based on the seller's loan. The court rejected the higher interest for the seller's loan (as compared to the bank loans) as an internal CUP because it suspected compensation in the form of a lower purchase price. As a result, the court concluded that the bank loan-based internal CUP must be applied to the shareholder loan.

In its second ruling of May 18, 2021, the Federal Tax Court rejected the initial decision and referred it back to the Tax Court of Cologne for a re-assessment of the underlying facts and circumstances, considering the principles established by the Federal Tax Court.

## III PRINCIPLES OF THE FEDERAL TAX COURT FOR THE DETERMINATION OF ARM'S-LENGTH INTEREST RATES FOR INTERCOMPANY LOANS

As a result of the decisions of May 18, 2021 (Case I R 4/17 and Case I R 62/17), the Federal Tax Court is requesting the lower tax courts to apply the arm's-length principle once again, this time in an appropriate manner. For this purpose, the lower tax courts must observe various principles for the determination of arm's-length interest rates for intercompany loans, which are very relevant in practice for intra-group loans.

### 1 Recognition of the Loan Relationship

The Federal Tax Court confirms that, in a first step, the recognition of the loan relationship as debt must be examined on its merits. In other words, the first question is whether it is equity or debt from a tax perspective. Characterizing a loan for German taxes normally follows the characterization standards in civil law. In its decision taken on May 18, 2021, the Federal Tax Court reaffirmed that the re-characterization of a loan into equity for German tax purposes should be clearly distinguished from situations in which non-arm's length conditions of such loans need to be altered without the relevant loan losing its debt character. Accordingly, not every deviation from the arm's-length principle necessarily precludes the recognition of an interest-bearing loan for tax purposes.[1] Specifically, agreements that do not comply with the arm's-length principle with respect to the interest rate or other conditions, such as the provision of collateral or the due date of the interest payments, do not necessarily preclude the recognition of the contractual relationship as debt for tax purposes. If a loan for civil law purposes must be repaid, the tax treatment of such a loan should be that of debt financing for German tax purposes.

## 2 Priority of the CUP Method

The most suitable transfer pricing method is one where the arm's-length price can be determined in the specific individual case with the greatest possible probability of accuracy. After the lower tax courts had fundamentally questioned the choice of the CUP method and favored the application of a cost-of-funds approach, the Federal Tax Court reaffirmed that the CUP method is the most direct method of comparing the arm's-length and the latter is therefore always preferable, insofar as it is applicable, in its decision of May 18, 2021. In other words, the Federal Tax Court unequivocally states that the CUP method represents the "basic method" for determining transfer prices. This particularly applies to intercompany loans.[2] The Federal Tax Court's view is to be agreed with, given that the provision of funds for a certain period of time is essentially homogeneous and objectively comparable, with there being numerous markets with information available for the taking out and granting of loans.

Moreover, no excessive requirements may be placed on the choice of the CUP method. In particular, the CUP method must not be rejected merely because the comparative values are based on deviating, albeit considerable conditions (e.g., provided collateral), or because information in this regard is not fully comprehensible for the tax authorities and tax courts (here: determination of the borrower's creditworthiness). As regards the former, the effects of any deviations in the case of intercompany loans can be determined relatively accurately and accordingly considered by means of adjustments. The second aspect can be encountered by the tax courts through further investigations.

In the view taken by the Federal Tax Court, the internal and external CUP methods are on the same level. The Federal Tax Court concluded that the internal price comparison method should not be rejected too hastily. Although uncontrolled bank loans have a significantly different risk structure for the independent lender in

1. BFH of May 18, 2021, I R 62/17, here under II.3.A.
2. Federal Tax Court of May 18, 2021, I R 4/17, recital IV.3.b) aa).

comparison to controlled loans due to the underlying shareholder relationship, it must be examined whether existing differences, such as in collateralization, can or cannot be made comparable by making appropriate adjustments when applying the internal CUP. Accordingly, the assessment of the existence of internal comparable transactions is of particular importance in the case of intra-group loans.

The Federal Tax Court refers extensively to the recently written Chapter X of the OECD Transfer Pricing Guidelines on financial transactions, according to which a cost-oriented transfer pricing determination ("cost of funds") should only be applied if no sufficient comparative values are available. If a comparative price (here: interest) can be determined based on the merits, it must be considered even if that comparative price is higher or lower than the price that would result from the costs of funds approach.

## 3 Application of the CUP Method

The Tax Court of Münster took the view that the external CUP method was not applicable. The reasons for this, *inter alia*, were because an intra-group finance company did not operate on the market, had fewer employees and its business model was less complex than that of a bank. The Federal Tax Court does not subscribe to this line of argument.

In principle, the price comparison requires the controlled transaction underlying the price to be assessed while the *uncontrolled* transaction underlying the price—which will be used as a benchmark—is based on essentially identical conditions.[3]

The application of the CUP method is, however, not subject to any requirements which ultimately end up unfulfillable. Therefore, if the intra-group loan to be assessed involves special circumstances that differ from loan agreements which actually exist with or between third parties, the CUP method may require appropriate adjustments.

Moreover, the Federal Tax Court points out that, in principle, a difference in the organizational structure alone does not prevent the use of bank loans as being generally comparable to intra-group loans. In the case at dispute, the taxpayer had not chosen bank loans as comparables, but instead corporate bonds; generally aimed at a broad spectrum of investors and are not only subscribed by banks.

The Federal Tax Court rejected the assumption made by the court of first instance that bonds are typically subordinated capital and, thus, generally riskier than loans. Therefore, the court of first instance took the general view that bonds are not comparable to intra-group loans. The Federal Tax Court now indicates a certain preference for the use of corporate bonds when applying the external CUP method, but it still does not seem to exclude the use of publicly available bank loans either.

The view that the external CUP method cannot be applied because the rating tools used operate with algorithms that cannot be verified taken by the Tax Court of Münster must be rejected. There are countless financial transactions concluded every day among third parties which make use of these ratings without being aware of the

3. Federal Tax Court of May 18, 2021, I R 62/17, recital II.3.b).

underlying algorithms. The Federal Tax Court stated that an approach for assessing the creditworthiness of companies, which is recognized and applied by market participants, may be used—even if the precise calculation rules remain secret.

## 4 Creditworthiness of the Borrower

In addition to the loan terms actually agreed upon (e.g., the term of the loan), the credit default risk and, thus, the creditworthiness of the borrower, i.e., its ability to meet its payment obligations on time in the future, is much relevant for the determination of arm's-length interest. However, there has been some dispute as to how creditworthiness is to be specifically determined in a transfer pricing context. Specifically, it is questionable whether the stand-alone rating of the borrower or a rating for the entire group should be used. Here, the Tax Court of Münster has taken the view that a group rating would be typically used to determine the creditworthiness of the affiliated borrower.[4] Such a view is regularly taken by the German tax authorities in case of inbound financing, i.e., the individual rating of the borrower shall not be relevant, but that the group rating is decisive due to the support within the group with the implication that the interest for the controlled loan corresponds ceteris paribus to the external refinancing costs of the entire group.

Yet, in the opinion of the Federal Tax Court, a lender acting in a commercially reasonable manner and outside a business group would, in principle, only include those aspects in the assessment of the creditworthiness of its contractual partner (i.e., the borrower) on which the lender could actually rely in the event of a crisis.[5] As a result, the Federal Tax Court holds a clear position in favor of the use of a stand-alone rating and against the use of a group rating.

The importance of the group affiliation (i.e., the implicit group support) can be taken into account for the determination of the relevant rating only on a case-by-case basis. However, this does not mean that the existence of implicit group support is to be assumed in all cases and always leads to the application of a uniform group rating when determining creditworthiness. Group affiliation can have an influence on creditworthiness if the borrower is of strategic importance to the entire group (e.g., an essential part of the group identity or the future strategy). This may result in an increase in the creditworthiness of the borrower. The Federal Tax Court is, however, silent on the extent of any impact of the implicit group support on the credit rating (e.g., by notching the stand-alone rating up). General publications of independent rating agencies provide appropriate indications for this. Moreover, the Federal Tax Court does not explicitly allow for the possibility to derive an appropriate credit rating from the group rating by means of downward adjustments. Finally, it should be noted that a careful determination of stand-alone ratings can involve considerable effort. This raises the question of whether this effort is justified in every case.

4. Tax Court of Münster of December 12, 2016, 13 K 4037/13 K,F, EFG 2017, 334.
5. Federal Tax Court of May 18, 2021, I R 4/17, recital IV.3.b) cc).

## 5 Application of the Cost-of-Funds Approach

### *A View Taken by the Local Tax Court*

In the absence of comparable uncontrolled transactions, the Federal Tax Court indicates that the cost-of-funds approach could still be used as an alternative to pricing intra-group loans in some circumstances. The Tax Court of Münster did reject the choice of the CUP method in the case at dispute and applied a cost-of-funds approach in order to calculate the appropriate interest. According to the view taken by the Tax Court of Münster, the cost of funds reflects the capital costs incurred by the lender in raising the funds to be lent. To this, the costs of arranging and servicing the loan would be added, plus a profit markup on the latter costs. The Tax Court of Münster considered three components and the following financial information when calculating the capital costs in the case at dispute:

| | *2001* | *2002* | *2003* | *2004* |
|---|---|---|---|---|
| Interest expenses before any adjustment | 244.083 | 304.054 | 301.774 | 197.788 |
| Refinancing share (%) | 57.66 | 56.38 | 50.81 | 50.43 |
| Deemed refinancing expenses | 140.738 | 171.425 | 153.331 | 99.744 |
| Share of equity (%) | 31.44 | 23.41 | 29.58 | 37.73 |
| Cost of equity (150%) | 96.809 | 78.595 | 96.610 | 90.654 |
| Arm's-length interest | 237.547 | 250.020 | 249.942 | 190.399 |
| Personnel expenses and profit markup | 6.549 | 12.642 | 8.823 | 9.167 |
| **Total** | **244.097** | **262.663** | **258.765** | **199.567** |
| Transfer pricing adjustments[6] | -13 | 41.391 | 43.008 | -1.779 |

First, the cost for the debt capital, which the related lender borrowed from an unrelated borrower and which the former passed to the ultimate related borrower, must be calculated. The lender's cost for the debt capital has been calculated by the Local Tax Court according to the ratio of the lender's interest expenses to its interest income. The values required for this purpose have been taken from its profit and loss accounts for the years in dispute. The values involved for the case in dispute are as follows:

| | *2001* | *2002* | *2003* | *2004* |
|---|---|---|---|---|
| Interest income from affiliated companies | 577.322 | 678.178 | 662.133 | 526.547 |
| Interest income banks | 2.344 | 31.321 | 40.095 | 58.462 |
| Subtotal | 579.666 | 709.499 | 702.228 | 585.009 |
| Interest expense affiliated companies | 0 | 1.601 | 19.737 | 264.758 |

6. The "negative" transfer pricing adjustments determined for the years 2001 and 2004 have no consequences under German transfer pricing rules.

| | 2001 | 2002 | 2003 | 2004 |
|---|---|---|---|---|
| other interest expense | 334.238 | 398.382 | 337.057 | 30.282 |
| Subtotal | 334.238 | 399.983 | 356.794 | 295.040 |
| Ratio in % | 57.66 | 56.38 | 50.81 | 50.43 |

Accordingly, the lender's cost for the debt capital shall be 57.66 % (2001), 56.38 % (2002), 50.81 % (2003) and 50.43 % (2004) of its interest income in the view taken by the Local Tax Court. In the calculation of the borrower's interest, this ratio is to be applied to the interest expense booked by the plaintiff, i.e., the borrower, in order to quantify those refinancing costs of the lender, which relate to the loans extended to the plaintiff. The refinancing expenses are thus calculated—as an example for the year 2001—as follows: EUR 244.083 × 57.66 % = EUR 140.738.

Second, the lender's cost of the equity required to support the intra-group loan must be calculated, which was not apparent from either the lender's income statements or its balance sheets. The Local Tax Court's starting point is the determination of the lender's equity ratio corresponding to the lender's ratio of equity to its balance sheet total. The Local Tax Court considered the remaining portion of the lender's capital to be debt capital. The debt ratio is therefore the difference between 100 % and the equity ratio of the lender. From the refinancing costs for the debt described above the cost of equity can be derived using a multiplicator – the court considered the factor of 150 % to be appropriate. The following ratios for calculating the equity ratio are derived from lender's balance sheets:

| | 2001 | 2002 | 2003 | 2004 |
|---|---|---|---|---|
| Equity | 3.144.289 | 2.854.509 | 3.158.821 | 3.341.257 |
| Balance sheet total | 10.000.878 | 12.192.776 | 10.678.168 | 8.855.589 |
| Ratio in % | 31.44 | 23.41 | 29.58 | 37.73 |

The cost of equity is thus calculated—as an example for the year 2001—as follows: EUR 140.738 ÷ 68.56 % × 31.44 % × 150 % = EUR 96.809. The court considered the factor of 150 % to be appropriate in its estimate, since such factor must, in any case, exceed the amount of 100 %, as a return on equity is always to be assessed higher than a return on borrowed capital in the view taken by the Local Tax Court. This shall take into account the fact that equity is associated with a higher risk than debt. With the factor of 150 %, the Local Tax Court took into account the return on equity of the entire group (8% to 9%) to which the borrower and lender belonged. The Local Tax Court determined this factor by taking into account the average interest rate on debt of the loans which the borrower had taken out from the lender. The interest on debt for the loans taken out by the plaintiff (total loan amounts: EUR 7,027,284) amounted to a total of EUR 404,981 per year (excluding repayments), which shall correspond to an average interest rate on debt of all loans of 5.763 %. Taking into account a factor of 150 %, this resulted in an estimated cost of equity of 8.644 %, which the court considered to be appropriate.

Third, the lender's personnel costs plus a profit markup were added by the Local Tax Court. The personnel costs amounted to EUR 6,237 in 2001, EUR 12,040 in 2002, EUR 8,403 in 2003 and EUR 8,731 in 2004. The profit markup was set at 5%.

### *B* *Overriding View Taken by the Federal Tax Court*

In the absence of comparable uncontrolled transactions, the Federal Tax Court indicates that the cost-of-funds approach could still be used as an alternative to pricing intra-group loans in some circumstances. However, the Federal Tax Court did not only reject the choice of the cost-of-funds approach in the case at dispute (*see* above) but also criticized the court of first instance's calculation of the interest when applying the cost-of-funds approach. Due to the priority of the CUP method, the Federal Tax Court does not explicitly comment on the question of whether the balance sheet equity ratios are an appropriate yardstick for determining the costs of equity in the first place. However, it is clear from the context that the Federal Tax Court has considerable doubts as to whether the balance sheet equity capital represents an appropriate basis.

Instead of an analysis based on the equity ratios resulting from the balance sheets of the years in dispute, the Federal Tax Court appears to favor costs of equity, at the time of the conclusion of the loan agreement, being projected for the entire term of the loan under arm's-length conditions. The Federal Tax Court's reasoning thus follows the "price-setting approach" from the OECD.[7] Furthermore, the Federal Tax Court's conclusion (that the court of first instance should consider calling in a valuation expert in the second round of proceedings) raises doubts as to whether the tax court itself can properly assess the essentially purely economic questions arising in connection with the cost-of-funds approach.

## 6 Relevance of OECD Transfer Pricing Guidelines

Whereas the lower court[8] had dismissed the OECD Transfer Pricing Guidelines on the grounds that they were based neither on national nor on intergovernmental law and were therefore irrelevant, the Federal Tax Court expressly emphasizes their importance. This is particularly noteworthy because the relevant OECD guidance on the determination of interest only dates from 2020, whereas the relevant tax treaty in the case at dispute is much older.

The OECD Transfer Pricing Guidelines are, in principle, recognized as an aid in interpreting the agreement standard reproduced in Article 9(1) OECD-MA in the specific income tax treaty. However, according to the static interpretation—which has so far been upheld by the Federal Tax Court—the guidelines fulfill this role only if and to the extent that they already existed when an income tax treaty based on the OECD model income tax treaty was concluded, and it can be assumed that the contracting states included them in their decision-making processes. In contrast, more recent

7. OECD Transfer Pricing Guidelines, paras 3.69 et seq.
8. Tax Court of Münster of December 7, 2016, 13 K 4037/13 K, F, EFG 2017, 334.

OECD commentaries (in this case: the addition to Chapter X in 2020) cannot reflect the will of the contracting parties to income tax treaties that have been concluded before those OECD commentaries had been issued.[9]

This raises the question as to whether the Federal Tax Court's ruling of May 18, 2021 represents a hidden shift towards a dynamic interpretation of the original ruling, given the Federal Tax Court considered Chapter X of the OECD Transfer Pricing Guidelines on Financial Transactions: Inclusive Framework on BEPS—Actions Points 4, 8-10 of February 2020 for the concretization of the arm's-length principle, although the years in dispute, 2002 and 2003, lie somewhat far in the past. For the current application of Chapter X of the OECD Transfer Pricing Guidelines on Financial Transactions from 2020 and the (new) recommendations contained therein, there would have been—at least according to the understanding of the previous opinion of the Federal Tax Court—no legal basis. In my view the Federal Tax Court has not changed its opinion with this decision, i.e., treaty provisions are still not to be interpreted dynamically, but statically. The Federal Tax Court's references to the most recent version of the OECD Guidelines only serve to direct one to case law for future years in dispute. Alarmingly, there is a risk that the Federal Tax Court's reference to the most recent version of the OECD Guidelines will encourage a dynamic interpretation of the arm's-length principle and be interpreted by the tax authorities as confirmation of their view that the current version of the OECD Guidelines is applicable to all open cases. At the time the loans at dispute were issued in 2002, the 1995 OECD Guidelines had already been adopted. The Federal Tax Court did not consider the 1995 OECD Guidelines, nevertheless, this would have been the more appropriate point of reference in the Federal Tax Court's reasoning.

## 7 Exercise of Risk Control Does Not Override the Loan Agreement

The Federal Tax Court also articulated its view on the considerations of the Federal Ministry of Finance, which joined in on the appeal proceedings. The Federal Ministry of Finance said that the finance company in the case at dispute does not in fact bear the usual risks of a lender, instead acts merely as a low-risk service provider and that the appropriate remuneration should therefore be determined using the cost-plus method. According to the Federal Ministry of Finance, in order for the financing company to be classified as a "true" lender (instead of a mere service provider), it would have to actually bear the economic risks resulting from the loans (i.e., the credit default risk, the refinancing risk, and the interest rate risk) and be in a position to perform the activities associated with the financing and the associated risk management tasks in a self-determined manner. These conditions would not be met if ensuring the financial stability and liquidity of the financing company was in the interest of its ultimate parent company or the group of companies, according to the position taken by the Federal Ministry of Finance.

9. Federal Tax Court of September 8, 2010, I R 6/09, Federal Tax Gazette II 2013, 186; Federal Tax Court of May 25, 2011, I R 95/10, Federal tax Gazette. II 2014, 760.

However, the Federal Tax Court has rejected the Federal Ministry of Finance's viewpoint: The fact that the finance company may have a comparatively weak functional and risk profile should not result in an outcome according to which the finance company is only entitled to a routine remuneration based on the costs of funds approach. Importantly, the performance structure concluded in the loan agreement is to be considered with primary importance. As a result, the Federal Tax Court reinforces the importance of contractual agreements in intercompany loans.

In the absence of any loan collateral from the borrower, the financing company as the lender has borne the credit default risk. Therefore, there is no reason to reduce the interest rate on the loan, even if the lender may have received financial support from the ultimate parent company. In the case of distress, this has no impact on the performance structure of the loan agreement, which has been concluded between only the lender and the borrower. At most, it should be considered whether a fee by the lender to its parent company could be conceivable, though this issue was not subject to the case at dispute and does not affect the relationship between the lender and the borrower. As a result, the lender's financial capacities do not play a role in the determination of the arm's-length nature of the intercompany loan granted by that lender. Thus, the Federal Tax Court also contradicts the new view taken by the German tax authorities, according to which a financing company should only be entitled to a remuneration up to the amount of a risk-free return to remunerate the capital's provision if it does not have the capacity and authority to control or bear risks.[10]

## 8 Cooperating Obligations and the Burden of Proof

The Federal Tax Court emphasizes a self-evident fact: The burden of establishing that the agreed interest rate is not at arm's length lies with the tax authorities if the taxpayer fulfills the requirement of sound transfer pricing documentation. Thus, it is not the taxpayer who must prove the arm's-length nature of the interest rate; rather it is first and foremost the tax authorities that have to prove a violation of the arm's-length principle, thus bearing the objective burden of proof. This regulation on burden of proof will only not apply without restriction if the taxpayer violates his duty to cooperate. The simple assertion that a third party would have granted a subordinated and unsecured loan at the same "price" as a senior and/or secured loan is not sufficient to prove arm's-length interest.

Moreover, the Tax Court of Cologne had rejected a benchmark study submitted by the plaintiff. The reason given for this was that a database study prepared only after the loan had been granted could not prove that an interest rate was at arm's length. The Federal Tax Court did not take an explicit position on this. This is likely to be understood to mean that the time at which a benchmark study is prepared to verify the arm's-length nature of the interest rate does not allow any conclusion to be drawn as to the quality of the data and that a benchmark study prepared only after the loan has been granted does not lead to any breach of obligations to cooperate.

10. Federal Ministry of Finance of July 14, 2021, para. 3.92.

In addition, the Tax Court of Münster had concluded that the borrower violates its own duty to cooperate under section 90(2) AO if the borrower does not disclose vis-à-vis its competent tax office the refinancing costs of the foreign lender. The Federal Tax Court seems to disagree with this conclusion, and correctly so. After all, from the borrower's point of view, there is no need to have the refinancing costs revealed when the loan agreements are concluded. This is because the cost-of-funds approach was not determined as the most suitable transfer pricing method. Only if the cost-of-funds approach were the most suitable method, could there be any factual clarification deficit at all as a result of the failure to disclose the refinancing costs of the lender. This clear view from the Federal Tax Court is incompatible with the excessive view taken by the German tax authorities, according to which the evidence should also include the documents and data on alternative methods that the tax authorities would like to use for verification purposes.[11] Thus, the taxpayer is not obliged to provide evidence of the calculation bases for every conceivable alternative transfer pricing method.

## IV CONCLUSION

The Federal Tax Court held in its landmark decisions rendered on May 18, 2021, that the CUP method should be given priority as compared to the costs of funds approach regarding intra-group loans. The Federal Tax Court also took the view that not every deviation from the arm's-length principle necessarily precludes the recognition of an interest-bearing loan and a stand-alone rating of the borrower should be used to determine its creditworthiness. However, it remains questionable whether the Federal Tax Court has changed its view towards a dynamic interpretation of income tax treaties or whether treaty provisions are still to be interpreted statically. In any case, the fact that the borrower, such as a finance company, may have a comparatively weak functional and risk profile should not result in an outcome according to which it is only entitled to a routine remuneration based on the costs of funds approach, according to the explicit view taken by the Federal Tax Court; instead, the court reinforces the importance of the contractual agreement in intercompany loans. Moreover, the Federal Tax Court reaffirmed that it is not the taxpayer who must prove the arm's-length nature of the interest for intra-group loans if the taxpayer fulfills the requirement of sound transfer pricing documentation. This should restrict the reach of future transfer pricing adjustments on intra-group loans, in particular.

11. Federal Ministry of Finance of December 3, 2020, IV B 5; S 1341/19/10018:001, recital 13.

## CHAPTER 21

# The Use of Safe Harbours for Intercompany Loans: Lenders' and Borrowers' Perspective

*Alessandro Turina*[*]

## I INTRODUCTORY REMARKS: THE ARM'S LENGTH STANDARD, SAFE HARBOURS AND PREDETERMINED APPROACHES

In light of the foregoing, this chapter addresses the potential offered by safe harbours providing simplification measures for testing the arm's length nature of intra-group financing transactions. In doing so, it first provides an account of the increasingly relevant role played by safe harbours based on simplifications in the application of the arm's length standard and points out to their perceived advantages and countraindications from a general policy and legal perspective. Despite such a trade-off, these trends have led to a recognition of an international consensus, expressed in particular in the OECD Transfer Pricing Guidelines, of such approaches in connection with certain categories of transactions, most notably low value- adding intra- group services. On the other hand, no analogous recognition of safe harbour approaches concerning intra-group loans has been expressed. Acknowledging such a state of the art, this chapter highlights how such approaches, despite the lack of international recommendations in their favour, are nonetheless quite prevalent across an ample pool of jurisdictions. In this respect, the chapter further provides a critical assessment, based on a desktop review, and develops a taxonomy of the most significant experiences, comparing them in light of the adopted perspective (notably the lender's or borrower's one) and

* The views and opinions set forth herein are the personal views or opinions of the authors; they do not necessarily reflect the views or opinions of the organisation with which the authors are associated.

structural features. The concluding section of the chapter envisages possible evolutionary perspectives, addressing in particular which kind of intra-group financing transactions could form the core of an internationally recognised set of simplification measures and which key terms and characteristics of these transactions should be defined in order to delimitate the perimeter of this regime. As a second-best approach, the chapter then investigates possible developments based on the reliance of a network of Memoranda of Understanding where the terms of safe harbours applicable respectively to the lender's and borrower's perspective may be laid down.

A monolithic account of the arm's length standard, in particular with regard to its asserted radical incompatibility with predetermined approaches has arguably been, if not disproved,[1] gradually become anachronistic.

Namely, a common thread running through the history of the practical application of the arm's length standard is to be found in the increasingly pervasive use of approaches based on safe harbours.

In fact, the expression 'safe harbours' has come to take on at least two different meanings:

(1) Safe harbours involving the exclusion of certain transactions (typically in accordance with a *de minimis* criterion) from the scope of application of transfer pricing regulations.
(2) Safe harbours involving the application of simplified rules for the application of the arm's length standard, typically on the basis of predeterminations by virtue of which the compliance of certain transactions with the above standard is to be considered, *ex ante*, fulfilled, where the reference profit indicators fall within a predetermined range.[2] The present contribution will focus on such second meaning of this expression.[3]

In this regard, the position of the Organisation for Economic Co-operation and Development (OECD) with regard to safe harbour regimes has evolved considerably over time. In the 1995 version of the Guidelines, in fact, there was a rather categorical recusal in this regard, although even then many Member States had already adopted approaches in practice that supported their validity in certain circumstances.[4] Such caution could be seen in the Guidelines up to the 2013 version,[5] given that the new

1. Even though there is no lack of examples going in that direction in scholarship, compare S.I. Langbein, *The Unitary Method and the Myth of Arm's Length*, Tax Notes, special report/1986, p. 653.
2. Typically expressed as gross or net margins.
3. As it has been observed, the term 'safe harbour' used in connection with transfer pricing is rather generic but, in the narrow sense, can precisely be understood as '[a]utomatic presumptions of the appropriateness of the prices and, therefore, of conformity with the arm's length principle, in the event those prices comply with predefined (...) parameters'. In this sense, G. Maisto, *DAC 6 and Transfer Pricing: The Hallmark Concerning Unilateral Safe Harbours*, Kluwer International Tax Blog, 11 June 2020, accessible at the following link: http://kluwertaxblog.com/2020/06/11/dac-6-and-transfer-pricing-the-hallmark-concerning-unilateral-safe-harbours/ (last accessed 15 April 2022).
4. Compare in particular paras 231 et seq. of the 1995 OECD Transfer Pricing Guidelines.
5. Illustrated in further detail in the sections that follow.

direction had been fostered by the results of a survey conducted by the OECD in 2011,[6] which acknowledged as a *fait accompli* the pervasive use of a safe harbour regime by many States, even members of the Organisation, thus leading to an update of the dedicated section in 2013, characterised by a qualified reconsideration comparatively more favourable to such approaches.

As already pointed out, safe harbour regimes are often the result of initiatives arising within the various legal systems and not the implementation of international recommendations.[7] At this juncture, in addition to possible convergences of a substantial nature promoted by the changed orientation of the OECD regarding the desirability of safe harbours approaches in certain specific areas, such as intra-group services,[8] an important contribution offered by the Guidelines lies in having provided a procedural framework for the adoption of safe harbours of a bilateral nature through the inclusion of memorandum of understanding models.[9] As in the case of advance pricing agreements, in this case, it is not so much the specific indicators that are the subject of the bilateral agreement but rather the methodologies and the reference framework.[10] At this juncture, as well as playing a role in the prevention of international double taxation, these memoranda of understanding configuring bilateral safe harbours lend themselves to protecting the tax bases of the countries involved from erosion phenomena with reference to recurring intra-group transactions.[11]

Most safe harbour rules are elective in nature, which implies that these rules cannot normally be used to the disadvantage of a taxpayer[12] and even where the rules are designed to be applied by default, they would typically entail the possibility for the taxpayer to rebut the underlying presumptions.[13]

The theoretical benefits of safe harbours based on predetermined approaches seem to be confirmed by recent empirical studies from which it can be seen that,

6. A Discussion Draft was released in June 2012 and subject to public consultation. On 16 May 2013 the new E section of the Guidelines was adopted.
7. For an overview of the approaches adopted by developing Countries, compare A. Turina, *Back to Grass Roots: The Arm's Length Standard, Comparability and Transparency – Some Perspectives from the Emerging World*, World Tax J. 2/2018, pp. 295 ss.
8. G. Maisto, *Transfer Pricing Aspects of Low Value Adding Services*, in *Transfer Pricing in a Post-BEPS World* (M. Lang et al. eds, Kluwer Law International 2016), 150.
9. *See* the attachment to section E of the Fourth Chapter of the OECD Transfer Pricing Guidelines where three models of Memorandum of Understanding for the establishment of bilateral safe harbours are presented following the approval by the OECD Committee on Fiscal Affairs on 26 April 2013 [CTPA/CFA(2013)23] and approved by the Council on 16 May 2013 [C(2013)69], on which further *infra*.
10. *See* Turina, *Back to Grass Roots*, *supra* n. 7, pp. 325-330.
11. *Ibid.* At the same time, the adoption of bilateral safe harbours appears to date rather uncommon and the most notable examples typically refer to somewhat unique configurations of cross-border economic activity, such as the maquiladora business practice, in relation to which the US and Mexico agreed upon a bilateral APA which contains safe harbours. The bilateral agreement (retrievable at the following link: https://www.irs.gov/pub/irs-news/ir-16-133.pdf?_ga=1.134315953.1959233956.1449872249, last accessed 15 January 2022) has recently been reconfirmed, *see* M. Hamadi, *IRS Renews US-Mexican Competent Authority Agreement on Maquiladoras*, in: IBFD News, 18 November 2020.
12. *Ibid.*
13. This is typically the approach that applies in connection to the safe harbours applicable to financing transactions.

gradually, over time, approaches based on logics consistent, ultimately, with the criterion of the profit split and based on a certain predetermined percentage designed to divide the profitability of a certain transaction between the counterparties, are accepted as appropriate by the concerned Tax Administrations;[14] in other words, there is a stratification regarding what Tax Administrations consider acceptable, such informal 'precedents' are increasingly followed and thus reinforced, in place of approaches oriented towards compliance with certain postulates that require an analysis of a 'facts-and-circumstances' nature, i.e., a calibration in light of certain facts and circumstances, which, by contrast, constitutes the core of the functional and comparability analysis that the application of the arm's length principle otherwise presupposes. In particular, again according to the above study, such approaches based on precedents informally shared with the Tax Administrations concerned are expressed in the adoption of a predetermined margin for certain types of transactions, most notably, a margin of 3% for distribution activities.[15]

In this respect, the recent developments in this area in connection with the so-called Amount B proposal within the framework of the first Pillar of the 'Two Pillar' solution may be indicative of a recognition of such prevailing practices within multinational enterprises (MNE).[16]

## II POLICY TRADE-OFFS UNDERLYING SAFE HARBOUR APPROACHES

The goals pursued through reliance on safe harbours revolve primarily around the need for greater administrability and reduction of compliance costs. On the substantive plane, the main feature associated with safe harbours is predictability: this applies to States, who can in a way demarcate *ex ante* the boundaries of their tax base in connection with the concerned cross-border transactions, as well as to taxpayers, who can more easily predict the tax implications of such transactions.[17] As such, in principle, the rationale behind safe harbours would lie primarily in the prevention of

---

14. *See* H. Rogers & L. Oats, *Emerging Perspectives on the Evolving Arm's Length Principle and Formulary Apportionment*, BTR 2/2019, p. 156.
15. *Ibid.* Thereby it is also pointed out that companies often prefer not to introduce adjustments based, for example, on different functional profiles, as this could lead to further verifications by the authorities. Certain domestic experiences are reflective of such metrics, for instance, the Israeli Tax Administration has acknowledge an analogous predetermination in its administrative guidance, foreseeing a 3%-4% (return on sales) profitability margin applies for distribution activities and a 10%-12% (return on costs) margin applies for marketing activities. *See* Israel Tax Authorities, Income Tax Circular No. 12/2018 of 5 September 2018, pp. 1-11, available at https://home.kpmg/content/dam/kpmg/xx/pdf/2018/10/tnf-israel-12-oct9-2018.pdf (unofficial translation, accessed 15 April 2022).
16. Within the Pillar One project, Amount B would aim at standardising the remuneration of related party distributors that perform 'baseline marketing and distribution activities' in a manner that is aligned. For an analysis of the policy implications, compare V. Chand, A. Turina & L. Ballivet, *Profit Allocation Within MNEs in Light of the Ongoing Digital Debate on Pillar I – A '2020 Compromise'?*, World Tax J., 12(3)/2020, p. 578 and I.F. Dykes & L.H. Keegan, The OECD Pillar 1 Blueprint: Why Amount B Matters, Bull. Intl'. Taxn., 75(3)/2021.
17. Compare in this sense the section on safe harbours in Chapter IV of the OECD Transfer Pricing Guidelines, following the update introduced back in May 2013.

(primarily domestic) disputes on transfer pricing matters which in turn would arguably carry a positive impact on investment decisions.[18] In this respect, one could observe desirable implications on both the formal/procedural and substantive plane.

More generally, it has been observed that safe harbours can contribute to greater predictability and administrability, both from the point of view of the authorities and from the point of view of the taxpayer, for whom they translate into lower compliance costs.[19]

At the same time, certain criticalities have been found in connection with safe harbour regimes for transfer pricing purposes, especially when adopted unilaterally. One of the most commonly mentioned ones is that such regimes may increase the risk of double taxation and double non-taxation.[20] The former hypothesis would arise in particular in cases where the other State were to disagree with the assertion that the defined safe harbour profit level reflects arm's length dealings, also considering that unilateral safe harbours may tend to force taxpayers into reporting higher than arm's length levels of income and to incur some resulting double taxation, as the price to be paid for administrative convenience and simplicity.[21] Conversely, unilateral safe harbours can, at times, provide a windfall to taxpayers whose specific circumstances might suggest that income above the safe harbour level would be more consistent with arm's length dealing.[22] What may exacerbate the potentially negative impact of these measures in this respect is that there may be an implicit assumption that the same would be accepted in other jurisdictions,[23] which may typically not be the case.

Certain undesirable features are then not as much associated with safe harbours as such but rather with the way they may be designed, notably their arbitrariness in the determination of the parameters on which they rely, which may lead to an outright incompatibility with the arm's length standard, which in turn would generate international double taxation or, conversely, may open up opportunities for tax planning translating into an instance of double non-taxation.[24] These risks may be exacerbated

18. It may thus be argued that such an approach may prove particularly beneficial in the perspective of developing Countries. In particular, by following safe harbours for most transactions that affect their economy, a developing country would be placed in a position collect significantly more revenue than it does at the present time. Clarity of rules would in fact diminish or help stem trade mispricing and reduce the administrative cost of audit. This, over the long run, could also provide a degree of certainty to the investor and thereby result in more foreign direct investment into the developing country.
19. Compare, in particular, paras 4.106-4.109 of the 2017 OECD Transfer Pricing Guidelines.
20. Compare paras 4.110-4.125 of the 2022 *OECD Transfer Pricing Guidelines.*
21. Compare OECD Transfer Pricing Guidelines (2022), Annex I to Chapter IV.
22. *Ibid.*
23. UN, *Practical Manual on Transfer Pricing for Developing Countries*, New York, 2021, para. B.4.5.10.
24. It is also in light of these considerations that reliance on safe harbours would constitute a relevant hallmark triggering mandatory reporting obligations under Council Directive (EU) 2018/822 of 25 May 2018 ('DAC 6'). For an analysis of the issues raised by this inclusion, *see* Maisto, DAC 6 and Transfer Pricing, *supra* n. 3 and G. Capristano Cardoso, *Balancing Tax Transparency and Tax Certainty: Reporting Obligations for Unilateral Safe Harbours Under DAC 6*, Intertax 49(8/9), 2021, p. 691.

where the safe harbours do not aim to 'track' commercially rational outcomes but are purely conventional and static.[25]

One further issue to be considered in order to ensure that the potential positive effects of safe harbours be not emptied concerns their temporal scope of application, in particular, it should be foreseen that if the safe harbours are optional for the taxpayer, no exposure should be triggered for earlier years when the safe harbour had not been opted in. Conversely, if a company opts out of a safe harbour regime, it should ideally not be subject to safe harbour markups for subsequent years.

The above general considerations can be suitably extended also to the specific area of intra-group financial transactions, on which the following section will focus in further detail.

## III A COMPARATIVE ASSESSMENT OF THE USE OF SIMPLIFICATION REGIMES IN CONNECTION WITH INTRA-GROUP FINANCING

### 1 Design and Policy Considerations

The area of financial services is paradigmatic with respect to the proliferation of unilateral safe harbours based on predetermined indicators. In fact, this circumstance can be easily explained in the light of structural reasons, since the object of predetermination in this context concerns in particular the determination of interest rates applicable to intra-group financing.

In principle, this area appears to be one of the most fertile for the use of safe harbour logic, given that, on the one hand, reference is typically made to 'spot' indicators and, on the other hand, the processes necessary to identify the measurement of such benchmarks can be particularly complex and based on approaches that require simulations and iterations, especially with regard to non-investment grade loans so that the advantages associated with the underlying trade-off may be comparatively higher than for other categories of transactions.

Despite this circumstance, International Organisations have been wary to endorse recourse to safe harbours in the area of intra-group financing. In fact, the OECD in its Transfer Pricing Guidelines simply makes no reference to such approaches while the UN in its Transfer Pricing Manual expresses considerable caution,[26] recognising that a few countries have introduced safe harbours, most of which concern interest

25. A parallel could be made in this respect with low value-adding services, in connection to which it has been observed that '[it is] doubtful that one margin for all costs would properly reflect an arm's length remuneration', *see* G. Maisto, *Transfer Pricing Aspects of Low Value Adding Services*, in *Transfer Pricing in a Post-BEPS World* (M. Lang et al. eds, Kluwer Law International 2016) at 154.

26. Under section 9.11.3 of the 2021 UN Transfer Pricing Manual, it is observed that: '[w]hen determining the arm's length compensation for an intragroup financial transaction, the use of simplification measures or safe harbour rules should be carefully considered. Furthermore, it should be considered how the simplification or safe harbour interplays with the definition and application of the arm's length principle both on a domestic and on an international level. In

rates and are meant to remove the obligation for taxpayers to prove that the compensation for those transactions is at arm's length, while also providing some assurance that the intra-group rate will not pose a risk of base erosion.[27]

Despite such lack of endorsement, there are in fact numerous examples in OECD member states and BRICS (Brazil, Russia, India, China, South Africa) countries, as well as in traditional financial centres, as will be illustrated in the following section. The proliferation of approaches based on pre-determinations may perhaps also be explained by a relative regulatory void in this area when it comes to international recommendations in the form of guidelines provided by International Organisations, granted that the formalisation of such guidance is a recent phenomenon. Yet, the ample empirical evidence suggesting that recourse to simplifications in this area is commonplace, as it will be outlined in the following sections, warrants the question of whether intra-group loans, at least those that meet certain requirements to be considered of 'modest entity' and 'low risk' and that operate in the form of a rebuttable presumption, granting the possibility to the taxpayer to rebut the outcome of the safe harbour by demonstrating that an alternative determination would be at arm's length, may receive a recognition analogous to that has been granted to low value-adding intra-group services and, prospectively, to certain distribution and marketing activities.

From a policy perspective, as recognised also in the UN Transfer Pricing Manual,[28] safe harbour rules can be an attractive option for developing countries, mainly because they can provide predictability and ease of administration of the transfer pricing regime by a simplified method of establishing taxable profit,[29] thus lowering compliance costs and providing certainty for taxpayers, as well as administrative simplicity for tax authorities.

This applies in particular to smaller transactions, as domestic experiences in the area of safe harbours for intra-group loans suggest, where there may simply be a disproportion between the magnitude of the transaction and the complexity associated with the data collection, analysis and valuation difficulties associated with establishing the arm's length price associated with these transactions.[30]

In the case of safe harbour applying to cross-border intra-group financing, the risk of international double taxation is a particularly concrete one, especially when considering that, as earlier illustrated, most safe harbours operate from the perspective of the borrower and not that of the lender so that the foreign tax authorities would be inclined to challenge the high safe harbour rule as it may lead to less taxable income reported by the foreign subsidiary. In more general terms, the unilateral nature of the safe harbour would simply run counter to the recommendations conveyed by the

some countries, taxpayers maintain the right to rebut a safe harbour or simplification rule by demonstrating that an alternative amount is at arm's length. In other countries, no such option exists'.

27. *Ibid.*
28. Compare section B.8.8.2 of the 2021 edition.
29. On the narratives surrounding transfer pricing simplification vis-à-vis the arm's length standard, *see also* G. Capristano Cardoso & R. Petruzzi, *Simplifying the Transfer Pricing Analysis: An Illusory Chimaera or a Realistic Ambition?*, World Tax J., 11(4)/2019, 531.
30. UN Transfer Pricing Manual 2021, B.8.8.4.

OECD Transfer Pricing Guidelines, according to which the accurate delineation of the transaction should be conducted in light of the canon of commercial rationality, taking into consideration both the perspective of the lender as well as that of the owner insofar as possible.[31] Both sets of concerns, however, may arguably be satisfactorily addressed by relying on predeterminations designed in such a way that, despite not entailing a full-fledged 'facts-and-circumstances' analysis, would be adaptable enough to reflect commercial rationality and would require as a pre-condition for their applicability a mutual recognition on a bilateral basis.

## 2 Intra-group Loans

### *A Borrower's Perspective*

With reference to the borrower's perspective, that is, having regard to inbound transactions, where a tax resident of the concerned jurisdiction has borrowed funds from related party resident of another tax jurisdiction, safe harbours adopted in various national experiences may fit in a fourfold taxonomy.

The first category concerns special regimes for 'small intra-group loans'. The common rationale behind this approach is to envisage a fixed rate to be applied only to loans that are perceived not to pose significant risks.

Examples of such an approach can be found in Australia, where the Income Tax Assessment Act provides for a maximum funding rate below which Australian resident debtors are not subject to assessment.[32] Similarly, New Zealand has adopted safe harbour for small intra-group loans (less than NZD 10 million), the predetermination being a fixed interest rate that is updated periodically and is currently 3 %.[33]

Another typical approach, which can be considered a variant of the former, is to be found in connection with minimum rates, that typically tend to apply across the board and thus not only to 'small loans',[34] hence the need to regularly revise the

31. Compare OECD *Transfer Pricing Guidelines for Multinational Enterprises and Tax Administrations*, Chapter X, C.1.1.1, Paris, 2022.
32. Division 820 (ITAA 1997). *See* J.P. Donga & P. Korganow, *Safe Harbour Not So Safe?*, Asia-Pac. Tax Bull. 16(4)/2010), 284, Journal Articles & Papers IBFD.
33. For more details on New Zealand's transfer pricing rules regarding financial cost, *see* New Zealand Inland Revenue, Transfer pricing practice issues, available at https://www.classic.ird.govt.nz/international/business/transfer-pricing/transfer-pricing/practice/transfer-pricing-practice-financing-costs.html#08. *See also* New Zealand's Transfer Pricing Country Profile, in OECD, Transfer Pricing Country Profile, question 24, available at https://www.oecd.org/tax/transfer-pricing/transfer-pricing-country-profile-new-zealand.pdf. The interest rate is revised on a periodical basis and reflects the following formula: 300 basis points (3 %) on top of the relevant base indicator. One of the peculiarities of the New Zealand approach is that it would apply only in the absence of a readily available market rate for a debt instrument with similar terms and risk characteristics.
34. Although an analogous approach is foreseen in Singapore, where a safe harbour interest rate margin above reference rates (e.g., LIBOR) applies to related party loans below a certain amount (i.e., SGD 15 million at the time the loan is obtained or provided). The indicative margin is published on the tax authority website and updated at the beginning of each calendar year. For example, if the indicative margin is 250 basis points or bps (i.e., 2.50 %), and the appropriate reference rate is LIBOR, this means that if a taxpayer uses LIBOR + 250 bps for its intra-group

underlying benchmark. An example of this approach is represented by Switzerland, where the Federal Tax Administration has de facto adopted safe harbours for intra-group loans, both for loans denominated in Swiss francs and for those in foreign currencies. The safe harbour interest rates are updated annually, most recently in the circulars of 28 January[35] and 29 January 2021.[36] These safe harbours operate as simple presumptions since the Circular on Foreign Currency Loans specifies that 'it is, however, possible to claim higher interest rates on the basis of comparisons with third parties' while, however, 'there is also an economic justification for not taking out a debt in Swiss francs at a lower interest rate'.[37] In Liechtenstein, the Tax Administration also issued a circular regarding safe harbour rules for interest rates[38] which closely follows the approach adopted by Switzerland.

A further configuration of the approach under review is to be found in floating safe harbour rates, typically amended at regular intervals on the basis of administrative guidelines and anchored to the interest rate fluctuations observed domestically or internationally.

The epitome of the former variant is represented by the US approach, where the Treasury has issued a 'safe haven interest rate' in its Regulations,[39] according to which a range between 100% and 130% of the applicable legal interest rate ('Federal rate') is envisaged, which effectively acts as a minimum interest rate.

On the other hand, an example of the latter approach can be found in connection with the South Korean experience, where the Ministry of Finance has introduced a floating safe harbour for intra-group financing rates based on averages of rates applied in different international financial markets.[40]

An even more articulated form of safe harbour applying to the borrower perspective is then the one introduced by India, where safe harbours anchor the interest rate to the Indian subsidiary's creditworthiness, based on certain stylised pre-determined categorisations: for instance, the safe harbour for a wholly owned

loans, it need not prepare TP documentation in relation to the loan. For further specifications, compare UN, *Practical Manual on Transfer Pricing for Developing Countries*, New York, 2021, para. 9.11. *See also* Chapter 13 of the local transfer pricing guidelines, accessible at the following link: https://www.iras.gov.sg/irashome/uploadedFiles/IRASHome/eTax_Guides/etaxguide_Income%20Tax_Transfer%20Pricing%20Guidelines_5th.pdf.

35. 2-189-DV-2021-i, on Swiss franc loans.
36. 2-190-DV-2021-i, on foreign currency loans.
37. *See* section 2 of the Circular of 29 January 2021 referred to above.
38. For more details on Liechtenstein's regulation, *see* Zinssätze für die Berechnung der geldwerten Leistungen (German only), available at https://www.llv.li. *See also* Liechtenstein's Transfer Pricing Country Profile in OECD, Transfer Pricing Country Profile, question 24, available at https://www.oecd.org/tax/transfer-pricing/transfer-pricing-country-profile-liechtenstein.pdf.
39. Enforcement Decree of the Adjustment of International Taxes Act, Treas. Reg. §§ 1.482-2(a)(2)(iii) and 1.482-9(b), accessible at the following link: https://www.irs.gov/retirement-plans/treasury-regulations
40. More specifically, in 2017, a safe-harbour rule for intercompany loan transactions was introduced by a Ministerial Regulation, introducing a rate equal to the 12-month LIBOR plus 1.5% for inbound transactions, where a Korean tax resident borrows funds from its foreign related parties. For more details, *see* KR: Enforcement Decree of the Adjustment of International Taxes Act, Article 6(7), available at https://elaw.klri.re.kr/kor_service/lawView.do?hseq=35965&lang=ENG As it will be highlighted infra, South Korea has recently revised its approach to safe harbours.

subsidiary with creditworthiness between AAA and A is 1.75% in Indian rupees (INR) and 1.5% in foreign currencies.[41]

All of the above approaches appear to feature a common structural characteristic, namely, the pursuance of an assurance function: regardless of whether the rate is a fixed or a floating one and is expressed in the form of an official interest rate or spread, such pre-determination provides a benchmark which, if complied with, typically extinguishes the obligation for the taxpayer to prove that the compensation related to those transactions is at arm's length[42] while providing some assurance that the rate applied will not pose a significant risk of base erosion.[43] This also explains why the above-illustrated predeterminations operate on a default basis, even though, the quantification of the interest rate as resulting from the predetermination may be rebutted by taxpayers provided that they substantiate their interest rate with proper economic analysis and transfer pricing documentation.[44]

### *B* *Lender's Perspective*

While most of the above-mentioned predeterminations operate from the perspective of the borrower and focus on the quantification of the interest rate (or a relevant range of rates) such as to be considered in line with arm's length results, the approach adopted by Luxembourg relates to the perspective of the lender for which a safe harbour of net profitability equal to 2% of the total assets financed applies.

This measure, introduced by Circular 56/1-56 bis/1 of 27 December 2016[45] constitutes a tightening compared to the previous regime, given that the Circular declared that the Advance Pricing Agreements (APAs) previously in place are no longer applicable. In addition, the Circular expressly requires persons making use of the safe harbour to communicate it to the tax authorities at the time of their tax return, given that such information may be exchanged with other authorities of European Union (EU) Member States or with States with which Luxembourg has concluded a double taxation agreement. Quite interestingly, data recently made available by the Council of the European Union within the framework of the Code of Conduct Group (Business Taxation) show that the entities concerned have apparently very rarely made use of the safe harbours in question.[46]

The Cypriot Tax Administration in its Interpretative Circular 3/2017 has also adopted in practice a fixed safe harbour remuneration for loans determined at a 2% rate

---

41. For a complete overview, *see* the tables in S.K. Bilaney, *New Safe Harbour Rules for Intra-Group Loans and Guarantees: How Safe Is the New Harbour?*, Derivs. & Fin. Instrums. 6/2017.
42. This does not imply that required compliance with the arm's length is waived but rather that, if certain requirements are met in connection with the determination of the rate, compliance with arm's length is presumed.
43. In the latter sense, *see also* UN, *Practical Manual on Transfer Pricing for Developing Countries*, New York, 2021, para. 9.11.
44. *Ibid.*
45. Accessible at the following link: https://impotsdirects.public.lu/content/dam/acd/fr/legislation/legi16/circulairelir561-56bis1-27122016.pdf.
46. *See* Report 14230/21 of 26 November 2021, accessible at the following link: https://data.consilium.europa.eu/doc/document/ST-14230-2021-ADD-8/en/pdf For potential criticalities

of return on assets.[47] More broadly, the Circular applies to intra-group financing activities where loans or cash advances are granted by a Cypriot tax resident company (or Cypriot permanent establishment of a non-resident company) to related parties, financed by financial means and instruments, such as debentures, private loans, cash advances, or bank loans.[48] Given these specifications, one may wonder whether the simplification measure could be opted for in cases where the company pursues a purely intermediary activity within the financing arrangements, borrowing from related parties and then lending to related parties.

It is also notable to remark to conclude this overview on simplifications concerning the lender's perspective that the Republic of Korea's approach to safe harbours in the area of intra-group loans is in fact two-sided, as, in addition to the earlier mentioned rate applicable to inbound transactions, thus from the borrower's perspective, it also foresees that a 4.6% rate, which is the overdraft lending rate, shall be applied for outbound transactions, i.e., where a Korean tax resident lends funds to its foreign related parties.[49]

Analogously, Switzerland has also adopted a two-sided approach to its interest rate safe harbours, namely these safe harbour interest rates operate from both an inbound and outbound perspective, as they can be considered as maximum allowable (on loans payable) respectively minimum required (on loans receivable) interest rates for intra-group loans which are considered by the Swiss Tax Administration as arm's length interest rates.[50]

## 3 Safe Harbours and Credit Rating

In addition to the above-outlined approaches, predetermined splits or safe harbours appear in other intra-group financing arrangements, in particular in connection to the apportionment of the positive implications deriving from group affiliation in connection with financing transactions involving third parties. The following exemplification,

---

associated with this approach, *see* H.R. HABERMACHER & D. WEDER, *Transfer Pricing: Do Swiss Safe Harbour Interest Rates Apply to All Intra-group Loans?*, in: International Tax Review, 12 March 2013.

47. *See* further https://www.ey.com/Publication/vwLUAssets/ey-its-newsletter-14-july-2017-eng/$FILE/ey-its-newsletter-14-july-2017-eng.pdf. The text of the Circular is retrievable at the following link: https://www.mof.gov.cy/mof/tax/taxdep.nsf/All/8533B85FF1404F76C22582180042152D/$file/%CE%95%CE%95%203%20%CE%A6%CF%8C%CF%81%CE%BF%CF%82%20%CE%95%CE%B9%CF%83%CE%BF%CE%B4%CE%AE%CE%BC%CE%B1%CF%84%CE%BF%CF%82.pdf?OpenElement (accessed 15 April 2022).
48. *Ibid.*
49. *See* T. KWON, S. MINHOO KIM & G. HONG, *Intercompany Loan Transactions: Recent Developments in South Korea's Transfer Pricing Regime*, Bloomberg Tax, 18 February 2022, retrievable at the following link: https://news.bloombergtax.com/daily-tax-report-international/intercompany-loan-transactions-recent-developments-in-south-koreas-transfer-pricing-regime (accessed 15 April 2022).
50. *See* H.R. HABERMACHER & D. WEDER, *Transfer Pricing: Do Swiss Safe Harbour Interest Rates Apply to All Intra-group Loans?*, International Tax Review, 12 March 2013, https://www.internationaltaxreview.com/article/b1fbsy2l755t1x/transfer-pricing-do-swiss-safe-harbour-interest-rates-apply-to-all-intra-group-loans (accessed 15 April 2022).

in the context of intra-group financial guarantees, could be illustrative of the above.[51] The parent company of Group F has an Aaa credit rating. Its subsidiary S has a credit rating of Baa. On a standalone basis, the subsidiary could acquire a loan from an independent bank at an interest rate of 6%. Due to its affiliation with the group, however, the subsidiary's credit rating would be increased up to an A rating and it can obtain an interest rate of 4%. Assuming that the parent company guarantees the loan, the subsidiary's credit rating would be raised to Aaa, which allows it to obtain a 2% interest rate. Generally, the advantage linked to the group affiliation, i.e., the drop of the interest rate from 6% to 4%, would qualify as an incidental benefit. However, the benefit derived from the drop from 4% to 2% would stem from a deliberate concerted group action. The question then arises as to how the 2% benefit should be split between the parent and subsidiary. While several approaches exist to split the fee,[52] for simplification purposes rules of thumb such as 50/50 splits appear to be very common.[53]

Such approaches undertaken as unilateral domestic initiatives also displayed influence on the international tax policy debate.[54] In particular, in its work on the transfer pricing aspects of financial transactions, the OECD considered the option to introduce a rebuttable presumption according to which the independently issued credit rating at the group level would have been considered as credit rating for each group member. Such credit rating may have also served as a starting point to establish the credit rating of the borrower and consequently price an intra-group interest rate, operating as a rebuttable presumption, so that the taxpayer may have always contended that a different credit rating should apply for a particular member of the group.[55] However, this approach was eventually not endorsed, so in the final Report on Financial Transactions as well as in the current version of the OECD Transfer Pricing Guidelines, the MNE group ratings can be used only when the facts indicate that separate-entity ratings are not reliable.[56]

By contrast, in the UN Transfer Pricing Manual, analogous simplifications for purposes of the credit rating are addressed, proposing to rely on the group rating under certain circumstances.[57] In particular, the UN Manual acknowledges that access to the credit rating of individual associated enterprises and the determination of the impact/effect of implicit support on intra-group financial transactions may be difficult and often based on judgements or determinations that can be very hard to verify for

51. *See* further on this example Chand, Turina & Ballivet, *supra* n. 16, section 3.4.
52. OECD, *Financial Transactions* (2020), at paras 10.154-10.188.
53. M. Butani, *India*, in *Transfer Pricing and Intra-Group Financing: The Entangled Worlds of Financial Markets and Transfer Pricing* p. 279 (A. Bakker & M. Levey eds., IBFD 2012). For a comparative overview of domestic experiences in this area, *see* OECD, *Financial Transactions* (2020), paras 10.154-10.188.
54. In fact, the very first core of what more recently became a dedicated section, devoted to financial transactions, within the Transfer Pricing Guidelines consisted of a compilation of brief country notes on financial transactions relevant to transfer pricing in the Transfer Pricing and Multinational Enterprises Report of 1979, repealed by the OECD's Council in 1995, and in the Thin Capitalization Report of 1987.
55. *See* OECD, *Financial Transactions* (2020), para. 67.
56. *See ibid.*, paras 10.81-10.82 and OECD Transfer Pricing Guidelines (2022), paras 10.81-10.82.
57. UN, *Practical Manual on Transfer Pricing for Developing Countries*, 2021, section 9.11.2.

Tax Administrations. In order to address such difficulties and with the goal of providing certainty and reducing the administrative burden to both tax administrations and taxpayers, the UN Manual thus envisages, as a possible simplification, the use of the MNE (or parent) credit rating as a basis if taxpayers do not provide evidence to substantiate the credit rating used.[58]

## IV EVOLUTIONARY PERSPECTIVES

### 1 Safe Harbour Approaches and Intra-group Financing: Phasing Out or (Qualified) International Recognition?

Safe harbour approaches adopted by jurisdictions on a unilateral basis are commonplace and their advantages in terms of administrability and predictability have already been illustrated. Nonetheless, their application without any further consideration of the commercial rationality concept and the two-way approach devised by the OECD has the potential to trigger issues that would outweigh their benefits if not properly designed and implemented.

It is thus perhaps not surprising that some jurisdictions that traditionally relied extensively on safe harbours in the past are in the process of reconsidering such approaches, the experience of the Republic of Korea, which, as earlier mentioned, had adopted safe harbours in connection with both the lender's and the borrower's perspective. In the review process that led to the 2022 amendment of the Decree that regulates, *inter alia*, the transfer pricing regime applicable to intra-group loans, the fundamental concerns associated with the safe harbour regime were, on the one hand, that the yardsticks embedded into the safe harbour needed updating and, on the other hand, that the safe harbours were formulated in excessively abstract terms.[59] Eventually, the 2022 amendment focused on introducing alternative analytical methods for determining intra-group interest rates; however, it is considered likely by industry commentators that a revision of the same safe harbours may also be introduced along the earlier mentioned lines, foreseeing, in particular, a modular safe harbour assuming as a basis the average funding cost without credit and liquidity risks, to which a variable risk premium would be added[60]

Perhaps a parallel with the historical developments that characterised the approach of the Republic of Korea to transfer pricing could be seen as illustrative in this respect. Before joining the OECD, the Republic of Korea's national tax authority employed a so-called "standard offer-commission rate" for import and export business taxation, relying in particular on a standard offer-commission rate based on a survey of actual commission rates. This was available as a last resort under its ruling only in

58. *Ibid.*
59. *See* T. Kwon, S. Minhoo Kim & G. Hong, *Intercompany Loan Transactions: Recent Developments in South Korea's Transfer Pricing Regime*, Bloomberg Tax, 18 February 2022, retrievable at the following link: https://news.bloombergtax.com/daily-tax-report-international/intercompany-loan-transactions-recent-developments-in-south-koreas-transfer-pricing-regime (accessed 15 April 2022).
60. *Ibid.*

cases where other methods for identifying the arm's length rate were inapplicable in determining commission rates charged by a foreign party.[61] Even though this approach was eventually repealed it could be seen as an example of an effective transitional pathway where safe harbour regimes based on predetermined approaches and facts and circumstances approaches coexist in a modular way.

While understandable, it may be wondered whether, in the case of intra-group financing, completely dismissing safe harbour approaches in favour of a full-fledged application of a facts-and-circumstances analysis as per the indications laid down in the current version of Chapter 10 of the OECD Transfer Pricing Guidelines to any type of financing transaction would be desirable. There are certain considerations that appear to militate against such an outcome and perhaps in favour of a conditional acceptance of the earlier mentioned safe harbour approaches, also in consideration of the circumstance that many of the most concrete negative implications of said simplified approaches may derive not from their actual content but, rather, from their unilateral nature.

In the view of the author, care should thus be taken not to completely dismiss safe harbour approaches in the area of intra-group financing but, rather, to re-focus their scope of application and ensure a design of such measures so that they may at once be more consistent in their underlying logic and flexible in their articulation, more suitably lending themselves at least to a bilateral implementation. In this respect, the considerations set forth in the UN Transfer Pricing Manual on this point may perhaps offer some first indications. As earlier mentioned, the UN Manual acknowledges the opportunity of adopting safe harbour approaches in situations that may pose a comparably lesser risk of base erosion and in connection with the determination of 'interest rates in respect of short-term inter-company "plain vanilla" (i.e., on standard terms) loans of moderate value'.[62]

In the following sub-sections, some suggestions would be set forth as to how such criteria may be concretely implemented.

## 2 Preliminary Considerations on the Assessment of Base-Erosion Risks

On a broader level, despite the two sets of rules operating on two different planes, there is a clear interrelation between the risk assessment process for transfer pricing and thin capitalisation purposes,[63] with the latter typically relying on a debt-to-equity safe harbour ratio. Despite the two different operational planes, a functional link may perhaps be envisaged so that such thin capitalisation rules may perhaps be considered to provide a backstop against the most severe instances of base-eroding arrangements. In other words, this circumstance may be considered to perhaps broaden the scope of intra-group financing arrangements that may be considered low-risk.

61. Compare UN Transfer Pricing Manual, 2022, B.8.8.7.
62. *See supra* note 30.
63. With regard to the crucial function of such rules in curtailing base erosion phenomena, *see* C. Burnett, *Intra-Group Debt at the Crossroads: Stand-Alone Versus Worldwide Approach*, World Tax J. 6(1)/2014, 40.

Yet, the design of safe harbours presupposes a certain degree of understanding and a categorisation of transaction types perceived to be 'low-risk' from the perspective of Tax Administrations but, in the case of financial transactions, such a categorisation may prove elusive. This applies in particular if the categorisation needs to be introduced in purely abstract terms but such difficulties may be overcome if the matter is approached through a bilateral lens: each jurisdiction would in fact be in a position to assess such elements and this may constitute the basis for ad hoc administrative agreements to be concluded on a bilateral basis. This development would not require a complete overhaul of the system or the devising of complex administrative solutions but would, instead, prove rather incremental as it would build upon administrative infrastructure that appears to be already available and relied upon, although not in a widespread way.

## 3 Terms and Value of Financing Transactions Susceptible of Being Subject to Safe Harbour Simplifications

The recommendation included in the UN Transfer Pricing Guidelines according to which safe harbour-based approaches should apply essentially to 'short-term' intra-group loans may raise certain perplexities as such categorisation is highly context dependant and widely differing perceptions can be observed, on the basis of a high-level comparative assessment, as to which loans would be considered 'short term' in different jurisdictions.[64] Moreover, any 'short-term' loan could simply be renewed ad libitum. These considerations may be conducive to discarding the 'short-term' nature of the loan to be considered as a relevant one for the purposes of determining where it would be susceptible to safe harbour-based simplification measures for transfer pricing purposes.

On the other hand, the notion of 'plain vanilla' loans, that is, displaying 'standard terms' would be something quite difficult to define in purely abstract terms. International Organisations may perhaps consider devoting further technical analysis to this issue in order to identify a common core of standard terms intra-group financing transactions, in ways analogous to what has been done for low value-adding intra-group services.

As a starting point, useful indications may in this regard be derived from a comparative survey conducted by the UN Subcommittee on Transfer Pricing, according to which safe harbour rules adopted unilaterally by jurisdictions in their domestic law and/or administrative practice respond to a variety of objectives and design policies[65] typically encompass the following elements:

---

64. In certain jurisdiction, the threshold is often represented by the one-year timeframe, however in some jurisdictions the notion of what constitutes a 'short-term' loan is considerably broader, for instance, in the US the short-term applicable federal rate is charged on loans with a maturity period of three years or less, as per the following prospectus: https://tax.thomsonreuters.com/us/en/checkpoint/afr-rates (accessed 15 April 2022).

65. For instances, they may consist in 'are rules that apply to a category of transactions, allow a defined category of taxpayers to follow a simple set of prescribed transfer pricing rules, or exempt taxpayers from the application of the general transfer pricing rules. These rules could be

- the identification of the types of transactions that fall within the scope of the safe harbour;
- the determination of the applicable fixed remuneration or of a range thereof;
- the associated documentation requirements, if applicable.

With regard to the moderate value of the concerned loans, once again this could be the subject of further technical analysis, even though the determination of a quantitative threshold would be, in the view of this author, significantly less relevant than devising suitable anti-fragmentation rules.

## 4 Implementation and Possible Legal Basis

As outlined in the previous section, international coordination expressing the outcome of an international convergence on simplified safe harbour approaches to intra-group financing, analogous to outcomes observed in the area of low value-adding services, would be the most desirable goal as this would provide for an international framework expressive of an international consensus on the matter which would entail a substantively multilateral solution to the concerned issue.[66] Yet, such an outcome would require a considerable amount of technical negotiations in order to be achieved and, to the best of the author's knowledge, it does not appear to feature prominently on the transfer pricing policy agenda of either the OECD or the UN, even though the latter has displayed a greater degree of openness on this point.

An alternative, second-best, approach in this area may then be represented by a more extensive reliance on bilateral advance pricing agreements that take these matters into consideration, or, in an even simpler fashion, Memoranda of Understanding concluded on a bilateral basis specifically devoted to this and other safe harbour-based simplifications.

Namely, bilateral safe harbours would feature several desirable characteristics so that they would lend themselves in a particularly suitable way to the earlier envisaged targets connected with the adoption of safe harbours for intra-group financing. In particular, such bilateral safe harbours could be more adequately tailored to the

limited to taxpayers with reported profits below a threshold amount, expressed as a percentage or in absolute terms. This simpler mechanism to establish tax obligations can be relied upon by a taxpayer as an alternative to a more complex and burdensome rule, such as applying the transfer pricing methodologies.' *See* UN, *Practical Manual on Transfer Pricing for Developing Countries*, New York, 2021, para. B.8.8.1. There are other types of simplified mechanism for transfer pricing that the countries concerned also categorise as safe harbours: for example, another simplified mechanism sometimes used enables a company to avoid making a transfer pricing adjustment where the ratio between international transactions and the overall transactions of a given company is smaller than a percentage stipulated in the law or regulation, compare UN, Practical Manual, *ibid.*

66. Analogous conclusions have been reached in connection with low value-adding services. Namely, this view appears to be confirmed also by the position taken by the Commission Services within Working Party IV of the European Commission, according to which safe harbours should be regarded as 'unilateral' only where they depart from the international consensus embodied in the OECD Guidelines (*see* Summary Record of 24 September 2018, reported by G. Maisto, *DAC 6 and Transfer Pricing*, *supra* n. 3).

economics of a particular market and circumstances and thus increase the chances of compatibility with the arm's length standard. Moreover, bilateral safe harbours would be conveyed through Memoranda of Understanding concluded on a mutually selective basis, so it is unlikely that jurisdictions would agree to conclude them with counterparts that harbour regimes conducive to possible instances of base erosion and profit shifting. The reliance on Memoranda of Understanding would also typically render such framework for safe harbour arrangements a flexible one, as it could be reviewed and modified from time to time by the respective Competent Authorities.

As earlier mentioned, the OECD Transfer Pricing Guidelines include an Annex[67] containing sample Memoranda of Understanding meant to be used as a basis by Competent Authorities in negotiating bilateral safe harbours for common categories of transfer pricing transactions. Currently, the model memoranda deal with low-risk distribution functions, low-risk manufacturing functions and low-risk research and development functions with the stated intent '[t]o to provide jurisdictions with a tool to adapt and use in addressing, through bilateral safe harbours, important classes of transfer pricing cases that now take up a great deal of time and effort when processed on a case-by-case basis'.[68]

Quite interestingly, in the same introduction to the model Memorandum of Understanding, it appears to be reckoned that, due to the aforementioned symmetrical double taxation and double non-taxation risks, 'few jurisdictions, if any, have developed functioning safe harbours for dealing with these common types of transfer pricing issues'.[69] The recommendation to adopt bilateral safe harbour in such areas, where unilateral predetermination appears by far the exception rather than the rule could thus perhaps be fruitfully extended to what appears to be a rather widespread practice across a diverse pool of several jurisdictions, as it is the case with intra-group financing.

The legal basis for such bilateral safe harbours is offered by the so-called interpretive Mutual Agreement Procedure laid down by treaty provisions modelled after Art. 25, Para. 3 as per the OECD or UN Model Tax Conventions. In fact, the OECD Transfer Pricing Guidelines remark that some jurisdictions have adopted such bilateral arrangements, relying on this same legal basis, which, according to the 'general view of such jurisdictions' provide sufficient authority to support a bilateral competent authority agreement on a safe harbour rule that would apply to numerous similarly situated taxpayers.[70]

In principle, the same legal basis could be multilateralised by relying on a network of bilateral Memoranda of Understanding, even though there is to date no evidence of such a practice in the concerned areas.

67. Annex I to Chapter IV.
68. *Ibid.*
69. *Ibid.*
70. *Ibid.*

## V CONCLUDING REMARKS

The area of intra-group financing displays a peculiar situation with regard to the applicable transfer pricing regime. After several years of relative regulatory void, following the adoption of the Report on Financial Transactions and its inclusion as Chapter X in the 2022 version of the OECD Transfer Pricing Guidelines, exhaustive methodological guidance has been provided in this area. Yet, there appears to be still a relative prevalence of approaches devised unilaterally by several jurisdictions which rely on safe harbours entailing simplification rules based on predeterminations, especially for what concerns the determination of the interest rates applicable to intra-group loans, in particular from the perspective of the borrower. In the aftermath of the adoption of the current OECD Guidance, the scenario is that of a bifurcation: some jurisdictions may decide to simply obliterate the safe harbour approaches adopted so far while others appear intentioned to retain them. These differing attitudes and the lack of coordination resulting therefrom may be conducive to unprecedented instances of double taxation or double non-taxation in this area. The concern is a real one as many jurisdictions may simply not be ready to relinquish their simplification regimes. At least as a transitional measure, it may thus be highly desirable that International Organisations active in the issuing of international recommendations in the area of transfer pricing include such issues on their agenda. In the lack of the emergence of an international consensus on the matter, the conclusion of the Memoranda of Understanding on a bilateral basis should be considered as an appropriate incremental solution bridging the gap between the reality of the prevailing practice and desired convergence towards the methodological consensus expressed by the OECD Guidelines. This experiment may also allow testing the resilience of such approaches once the negative connotations associated with unilateral safe harbours have been removed, so that it may perhaps be envisaged that such simplification approaches may receive international endorsement at least for intra-group loans considered to be raising lesser risks of base erosion and profit shifting, as it may be the case with 'plain vanilla' (i.e., on standard terms) loans of moderate value intra-group loans singled out in the UN Transfer Pricing Manual.

CHAPTER 22

# The Impact of Crisis Situations Such as COVID-19 on Transfer Pricing of Intercompany Financial Transactions and Comparability Considerations

*Vispi T. Patel, Anwesha Bandyopadhyay & Rhea Wadia*[*]

## I SUMMARY

The unprecedented challenges presented by the COVID-19 health crisis have made businesses rethink their existing business strategies, financial policies and even their overall business models. COVID-19 has affected all businesses, small and large. Two years into this crisis has taught companies resilience, survival and adaptability to changing market situations.

This Article dives into the impact that the pandemic has had on intra-group financial transactions such as loans and guarantees. It further attempts to analyse the measures available to mitigate the impact during and after such a crisis period. Although this chapter focuses on the health crisis, many implications identified are often observed in other crises situations.

It primarily discusses the impact of COVID-19 health crisis on transfer pricing of such intra-group financial transactions along with the approaches given by both Organisation for Economic Co-operation and Development (OECD) and the UN and the way forward for both taxpayers and tax authorities.

* The views and opinions set forth herein are the personal views or opinions of the authors; they do not necessarily reflect the views or opinions of the organization with which the authors are associated.

## II INTRODUCTION

To understand the effects caused by the novel coronavirus health crisis, it is important to understand what a crisis is and its consequences in society. A crisis is referred to an unexpected event or a situation that threatens to cause disruptions. A crisis may be financial, economic, health, social, environmental, etc. COVID-19 can be described as a health crisis that eventually escalated to an economic and social crisis affecting, business, employment, livelihood, food security and collapse of the economy world-wide.

On 11 March 2020, the World Health Organization (WHO) declared COVID-19 a global pandemic, which indicated the deadly impact of the virus worldwide. In no time, the virus had spread, widely infecting people globally.

As of 2020, COVID-19 had infected over 82 million people and killed more than 1.8 million worldwide. The year 2021 was more devastating and saw over twice as many cases and deaths. As of June 2022, the total reported cases amount to almost 544 million along with more than 6 million deaths. The actual numbers are estimated to be even higher.

The COVID-19 health crisis has confronted the global economy with the largest threat since the global financial crisis of 2008. The latter crisis has created a long-lasting impact on the global financial system due to the interconnectedness financial services sector globally.

In the case of the COVID-19 health crisis, governments around the world took rapid actions such as shutting borders, restricting movement of its citizens, introducing social distancing norms and overall shutdown of the economy for several months, stifling the gross domestic product (GDP) of the countries.

Governments and monetary institutions globally offered various fiscal and monetary measures such as reduction in bank rates, injection of liquidity into the financial system, relaxation of regulations and extension of deadlines in the payments market, provision of government lending or loan guarantee for required sectors and other such facilities to alleviate financial difficulties faced during the COVID-19 health crisis.

Small- and medium-sized businesses (SMEs) across sectors are often some of the worst-hit businesses in times of crisis. A survey across the US stated that the health crisis affected 1.7 million small businesses that employ about 20 million workers and earn almost 12% of US business revenue.[1] These companies are the most vulnerable companies that must rely on debt-based funding to conduct business during such times.

It is necessary to also mention that as private borrowing increases, public borrowings also increases. Governments around the world borrowed heavily to counter the effects of the pandemic and public debt levels have been at a record high following the health crisis.

1. *See* https://www.mckinsey.com/featured-insights/americas/which-small-businesses-are-most-vulnerable-to-covid-19-and-when.

Various countries have faced their worst recessions and have struggled to get back to normality, with growth rates improving only marginally. Economies have opened with cautionary measures as rising COVID-19 cases continued to cause disruption.

With vaccine rollouts in place, countries were finally on the path to recovery and the health and economic risks finally subsided. Nonetheless, as with all crises when considering multi-national enterprises (MNE's) and how they operate; especially with respect to intercompany financing, the implications of the crisis will be visible still for years to come.

## III IMPACT OF CRISIS SITUATIONS SUCH AS COVID-19 ON INTERCOMPANY FINANCIAL TRANSACTIONS

### 1 The Need for Intercompany Financial Transactions

Intercompany financial transactions play a pivotal role in functioning of a business. Such transactions typically include loans, guarantees, cash pooling arrangements, captive insurance, hedging and so on.

These transactions help businesses to optimize liquidity by channelling funding to affiliates within the group with liquidity constraints from other affiliates that may be more cash rich or able to raise more cost effective capital from the market e.g., from banks or other financial market participants. It helps the group and local borrowers to expand and diversify its business. More specifically, Intercompany financing may be used for purchasing assets, restructuring purposes, management of working capital and so on. The need for Intercompany financing transactions is accentuated in a crisis and plays an important role in achieving the MNE group's strategic objectives not only through navigating the crisis itself but also securing its future longevity.

All Multinational companies resort to intercompany lending and borrowing to avail funds for business purposes. Parent companies may also provide guarantees to enable a subsidiary to secure lending at more favourable rates or volumes. Based on international tax law appropriate pricing to the extent relevant of such loans and guarantees must be carried out. From a transfer pricing perspective, it is necessary to assess that the interest charged on such financing transactions are aligned with the arm's length standard (ALS).

The sudden economic downturn as a result of the global health crisis resulted in increased borrowings as companies were cash-strapped and needed instant financial help. As the effect of the crisis were not limited to a specific location or industry, in some instances even the financial institutions providing lendings/ funds were impacted. In cases where MNE's may have had existing debts, the market disruption and credit quality deterioration meant that terms and conditions in existing debt instruments had to be either modified or even refinanced. In case of new loans, third party lenders became wary of advancing long-term loans and wanted to secure themselves with appropriate covenants as to limit exposure to the increased default risk on transactions.

Some realistically available options available to companies when faced with a crisis like the COVID-19 health crisis include:

- Modifying the existing intercompany financing policies: If related parties are unable to meet their debt obligations due to a crisis, it is necessary that the existing intercompany financing terms and policies are revisited to factor in the impact of the crisis, namely to determine if the policies can be modified (and to what extent the market may have processed such changes), for example, the steps to be taken by entities who want to borrow, source of funds, amount that can be borrowed, security to be offered, covenants to be used, etc.
- Modifying the loan agreement to the extent possible: As a part of overall financing policies, existing loan agreements may need to be re-evaluated such as repayment schedules, penalties for early repayments, altering interest rates to the extent reasonable, granting of moratorium, etc.

  Re-characterization of existing debts: It should be examined whether the existing debt can also be re-characterised into equity or partly equity and the resulting consequences of the same.
- Leveraging financial guarantees: An increase in financial guarantees may be more commonly relied upon in times of a crisis. A crisis may also render these types of instruments obsolete if the guarantor no longer have the financial standing to support an affiliated company The economic benefit of a guarantee should carefully be considered.
- Equity financing: Firms that are affected by the crisis can also resort to equity financing to raise funds for their working capital needs.
- Cash pooling: Cash pooling refers to bringing together, either physically or notionally, all available cash balances of an MNE group to achieve better cash and liquidity management by transferring excess cash to offset negative cash balances of subsidiaries. Cash pooling technique becomes increasingly important during crises times as MNEs struggle with liquidity management.

### *A Role of Transfer Pricing in Intercompany Financial Transactions*

Companies entering intercompany financial transactions must ensure that such transactions follow the arm's length principle in order to avoid significant transfer pricing adjustments.

The way such transactions are structured and priced will be determined by the intent of the members of an MNE group, its business strategies, capital structure, the terms of the transactions and if any benefits are offered to the member entity in lieu of group membership.

Companies entering intercompany financial transactions should take into consideration the applicability of various transfer pricing methods and select the one most suitable for the transaction that is evaluated. Over the past few years, taxpayers have been subjected to increased scrutiny wherein the arm's length nature of the transactions is questioned, e.g., the terms and conditions of the controlled financing transaction are held to be not in line with independent agreements.

The transfer pricing inquiries and audits are only expected to increase further in the coming years. MNEs therefore need to be more vigilant in ensuring arm's length conditions involving transactions are met, especially in the light of the financial challenges brought on for many governments by the health crisis. What is critical is to have appropriate documentation, as it will act as the first line of defence in case of an audit/assessment. The available OECD Guidelines should be carefully studied and incorporated where appropriate. Risks should be evaluated at all levels. Ultimately, in many cases, the onus remains on the taxpayer to demonstrate to the tax authority the reasonableness of the transactions entered.

## *B* *Impact of Crisis Situations on Interest Determination for Intra-group Loans*

Against the backdrop of the above discussions, we will try and understand the varied degree of impact that the health crisis has had on intra-group loans and advances and discuss the specific considerations/approaches to mitigate such impact.

Crisis situations such as COVID-19 results in declining operating profits, lower turnover, etc., and pose a threat to the overall liquidity and sustainability of enterprises. High volatility of markets, along with fluctuating interest rates makes it difficult for companies to obtain funds for business purposes. The subsequent paragraphs highlight the practical challenges faced by both taxpayers as well as tax authorities while benchmarking, and also considering the impact of the health crisis on the transfer pricing aspects of such intergroup loans.

Broadly, any entity that enters intra-group loan transactions must examine it holistically with special focus on:

(1) Whether the present interest rates are to be reviewed and modified to correctly reflect the impact of the crisis?
(2) Whether current intercompany financing policies are to be re-evaluated?
(3) Analyse the financial transactions from:
    (a) Lender's perspective.
    (b) Borrower's perspective.
(4) Considering the effect that its Group membership has on such transactions.
(5) Any other specific measures that are to be taken into consideration, when evaluating the arm's length price of controlled financial transactions.

The economic disruption may result in limited availability of comparable data that can be used to benchmark intra-group loans. Further, what may be acceptable to tax authorities in one jurisdiction may not be acceptable in another jurisdiction. This places taxpayers, especially MNEs that operate globally in a tricky position and requires them to correctly adhere to the ever-changing transfer pricing landscape.

Therefore, apart from following the steps stated above, for intra-group loans, it is also critical that entities evaluate the commercial viability of the terms of the loan, the available credit ratings, the money market conditions prevalent in the market of both borrower and lender, the benchmarking for pricing of the loan and whether, the same needs to be revisited considering other options available, that better reflect the impact of a crisis.

Companies may have incurred immense losses and may be unable to service their debts. Based on the circumstances, it may be prudent to offer a moratorium, as has been a common practice in several countries by companies and governments. The European Banking Authority reported the significant use of moratoriums across the European Union (EU) banking sector.[2]

The International Monetary Fund (IMF) also published a country-wise key economic response by governments which reflected that a moratorium was offered on lending across multiple countries.[3] Further, the OECD, in its report on policy responses for SMEs, reported that debt moratoriums were provided by multiple countries across the world.[4]

Moratorium on loans can be helpful if it is determined that the impact caused by the pandemic is temporary and the loans will be repaid as the situation improves. Credit ratings will also have to be evaluated going forward and if the entity requires additional financing above the existing loan, the current lending environment along with the overall financial health of the company also needs to be studied before further loan is advanced. The creditworthiness of the borrower may also be affected due to the crisis. Credit ratings, which are one of the determinants of creditworthiness, may need to be revisited at the entity level as well as the group level. The OECD Guidance sets out a detailed analysis of how credit ratings can be useful in arm's length determination.

In terms of interest rate determination, intercompany interest rates are undergoing a major change and the generally used Interbank offered rates (IBOR) are being replaced by alternative rates, such as the Secured Overnight Financing Rate (SOFR) which is a secured interbank overnight reference rate, established as an alternative to LIBOR, published in several currencies for financial contracts all over the world. Companies need to be watchful of this changing environment and evaluate their existing arrangements if the current interest rates need some modifications.

Therefore, companies should not assume that previously applied arm's length rates can remain unchanged without additional analysis. The worldwide lending market saw historically low rates. Further, there were also a drop in credit quality of many companies with an increased default on payments. Hence, entities must evaluate facts and circumstances of each case to determine whether the arm's length intercompany interest rates need to be lower or higher than previous rates.

2. *See* https://www.eba.europa.eu/banks-report-significant-use-covid-19-moratoria-and-public-guarantees.
3. *See* https://www.imf.org/en/Topics/imf-and-covid19/Policy-Responses-to-COVID-19.
4. *See* https://www.oecd.org/coronavirus/policy-responses/coronavirus-covid-19-sme-policy-responses-04440101/.

It is, therefore, up to the taxpayer to ensure that appropriate internal controls are in place to mitigate the effects of the disruption. All options realistically available must be evaluated and it should be kept in mind, that there may not be a single approach that can be applied across sectors and industries. Each situation must be examined on a standalone basis.

## 2 Financial Guarantees

Financial Guarantees are agreements, or a promise entered into by two entities, wherein the guarantor is required to fulfil the debt obligations in case of a default by the borrower. It is a legally binding commitment that a guarantor undertakes in case of a non-payment by the borrower. In a related party transaction, one related party provides a guarantee to an unrelated lender, on the loan borrowed by a related borrower.

In a transfer pricing context, guarantees can be of two types:

(1) Financial Guarantees: Such guarantees are legal promises undertaken by the guarantor to fulfil debt obligations of the borrower. This enables the borrower to obtain funds at a lower rate of interest, in addition to larger funds and reasonable terms and conditions.
(2) Performance guarantee: Such guarantees are also legal promises that provide assurance of the completion of a contract.

### *A Impact of Crisis Situations on Interest Determination for Intra-group Guarantees*

It will be necessary to observe the actual impact on the guarantees provided, whether such impacts are temporary or have long-term effects. The guarantor's ability to service the debt in case of default may also have changed due to unprecedented situations. An adverse market is likely to impact both the guarantor as well as the borrower and thus may even render the guarantee non-fulfillable. The market conditions because of the crisis may be considered such an event.

On the other side, external lenders may increase their need for guarantees on loans that they would otherwise not require in the face of volatile market conditions. These guarantees may be temporary but may invite significant scrutiny from tax authorities going forward. It should be kept in mind that a guarantee only enhances the borrower's ability to get funds rather than acting as a replacement for capital.

Some steps that need to be undertaken when evaluating guarantees from a crisis perspective are:

(i) Parties entering into guarantee arrangements should ensure that it is able to justify the commerciality of the guarantee fee to the tax authorities.
(ii) Ability to demonstrate the arm's length price of such guarantee and if any adjustments are due as a result of the crisis.

(iii) Evaluation of the financial capacity of the guarantor should be conducted and whether the same is sustainable in the current market conditions.

(iv) A differentiation should be made between implicit and explicit support made available by the guarantor and the impact thereof.

## 3 Additional Transfer Pricing Effects of Health Crisis on Intercompany Financial Transactions

An adverse economic event such as a health crisis has varied effects on intra-group financial transactions. While some of the important ones have been discussed in the above paragraphs, we will examine how transfer pricing affects such transactions in other ways.

One primary problem with transfer pricing benchmarking will be the availability of sufficient and reasonable comparable data in the public domain. The existing data available may not correctly reflect the market conditions and lead to inappropriate determination of the arm's length price.

Correct benchmarking data will only be available at a subsequent date. For example, correct data for the year 2020 may only be available in 2021 or even 2022. The tax authorities need to be cognizant of this fact and accordingly allow reasonable adjustments to arrive at the arm's length price. The taxpayers should also carefully analyse the evolving situation and market conditions and take additional measures to ensure that the transactions being entered into can be demonstrated to be always at arm's length.

In these unpredictable times, it will not be a stretch to say that the tax authorities around the world would be closely monitoring intra-group transactions, which are otherwise also embroiled in controversies and litigations. If companies are not careful, the volatile market rates may lead the authorities to believe that the benchmarking has been done merely on a cherry-picking basis to avail lower interest rates. Robust documentation will be required at all stages to exhibit the taxpayer's bona fide intentions.

## 4 A Case Study on the Effects of the Health Crisis on Intercompany Financing

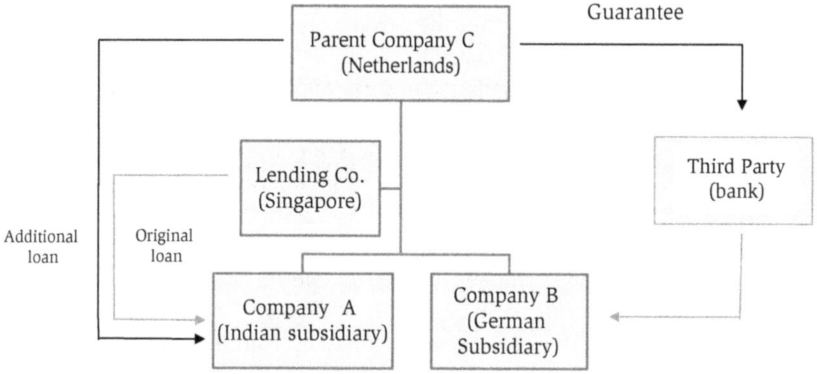


Facts of the case:

The parent company C is located in the Netherlands and is engaged in the manufacturing and distribution of automobile parts. It has a subsidiary company named Lending Co. in Singapore, and subsidiary company A and company B are located in India and Germany, respectively.

These subsidiaries are primarily engaged in marketing and distribution of auto parts to third parties and conduct other related activities under the instructions of the parent company.

The global auto industry was already facing a slowdown due to various reasons such as Brexit, increase in tariffs and so on. To boost sales globally, the lending company located in Singapore lent USD 5 million to subsidiary A located in India in November 2019. The said loan was given at an interest rate of 10.20% (SBI – The State Bank of India is India's largest bank) Marginal Cost of Lending Rate + 200 basis points as of 10 November 2019) for a period of five years. The loan was a rupee loan, whereby the lending company earned a higher rate of interest, albeit after considering the foreign exchange cost.

The sudden onset of the health crisis in March 2020 resulted in a complete shutdown of businesses worldwide as borders were shut and travel became restricted. Strict lockdowns were enforced in India which halted the movement of goods countrywide. There was a shortage of availability of labour, raw materials, and logistics.

As demand fell massively, company A in India suffered huge losses and was unable to continue its operation without the infusion of more funds. It then began to evaluate the various options available to raise more capital. As the financial position of A was weak, it was unable to obtain funds from third parties independently. Thus, it approached the parent company C, located in the Netherlands for infusion of additional funds to meet its daily working capital requirements and remain afloat. The parent company, after assessing the overall economic scenario, the importance of the Indian market and for easing the financial distress of A, agreed to lend a further USD 5 million by way of a rupee loan as a temporary measure.

This loan agreement was entered into considering that company A has presence in a large market and acted as an important distributor of various auto parts manufactured by the group. In addition to this, the parent company also considered the sudden impact of the health crisis which caused heavy operating losses, resulting in reduction of cash flow, due to which A was unable to carry on business. As a result, company C agreed to give a three-year loan in June 2020, interest-free for a period of one year, with the intention to strengthen the financial position of company A and to give it time to stabilize its business. Company C agreed to charge interest at the rate of 9.30% (SBI MCLR + 200 basis points) for the balance two years at the prevalent market rates at the time.

For the existing loan, company A was unable to make timely repayments of instalments and was suffering major losses. It evaluated the existing loan agreement and intended to invoke the force majeure clause, by considering the pandemic as a force majeure event.

It is, however, important to note that the clause cannot be invoked without appropriate evaluation of the same. For instance, it has been held in several rulings that this clause cannot be invoked if some alternate performance of the contract is possible, or if there has been a mere change in the terms like price/exchange rate that do not deem the performance of a contract impossible. The party to the contract wanting to invoke this clause would have to demonstrate that the conditions for invoking this clause are sufficient and reasonable, i.e., it has exhausted all alternate means of performing the contract and has taken all steps to mitigate the consequences of such event.

Therefore, once company A approached the Singapore entity about its intention to invoke the force majeure clause, other available alternatives were assessed.

COVID-19 significantly disrupted the financial position of company A, it was agreed to revise the terms of the loan agreement temporarily, to mitigate the economic effect of the pandemic and the various policy decisions taken by the government to enforce strict lockdowns. In view of the severe economic downturn and financial crisis, after several negotiations and analysis of the terms and conditions of the existing agreement, the overall market conditions and economic scenario by the lending entity, it was concluded that invoking the force majeure clause would not be beneficial for the lending entity, which instead offered a moratorium for a period of six months, in line with the similar moratoriums on loans that were already being offered by the banks in India as directed by the Reserve Bank of India (RBI).

However, company A demonstrated that its financial position had drastically deteriorated and therefore the moratorium offered of six months would help in decreasing the financial strain, but it would not be sufficient to sustain the business. Thus, it was agreed with the lender that a part of the loan would need to be converted into equity so that the debt burden would reduce and at the same time shore up its capital structure. Further, the evaluation of the future business prospects and the current financial position of company A, it was thought prudent by the lender to reduce interest on the balance loan to the prevalent market rates, so as to allow A to continue its business operations and also to safeguard the balance on the loan. This was all aimed to fortify A's financial position and to provide a buffer for it to survive during the crisis; this would also protect the lending company, as otherwise, it could lead company A to bankruptcy, which would not be in the interest of the group.

Company B on the other hand was comparatively better off, but its business also had suffered a downturn and it was in requirement of funds to survive the ill effects of the crisis and carry out its business operations. Thus, company B approached various financial institutions for a three-year working capital loan. It was able to secure a loan from an independent bank, only if the parent company C agreed to provide a legal guarantee for the said loan. This would allow company B to secure financial assistance from the bank at lower rates of interest, due to the financial guarantee to be provided by company C. Further, this would also be advantageous to the group, as it would conserve the financial resources of the group during the crisis.

The parent company agreed to provide the necessary support to Company B in the form of a guarantee and that too without charging any guarantee fee for the first year to support the subsidiary. For the remaining period of the loan, a guarantee fee of around 1 % was agreed to be charged considering the prevalent bank guarantee charges charged by the banks in Germany.[5]

Determination of arm's length price of the above Loan(s)/Guarantee

(1) Loan from Lending company (Singapore) to its Subsidiary Company A

The loan was obtained prior to the health crisis for a term of five years at the rate of 10.20 % based on the SBI Marginal Cost of Lending Rate (SBI MCLR + 200 basis points) at that time.

This arrangement was modified and a deferment of six months on the loan was granted. As the crisis had catastrophic impacts across sectors, many lenders agreed to waive off certain portions of the loan or modify the existing arrangements. In the present case, the moratorium offered some respite to A which was in line with the moratorium offered by RBI in India and considering the unprecedented impacts of the health crisis, such moratorium could be economically justifiable and therefore at arm's length. Additionally, as a result of a survey by the OECD Committee on Financial Markets (CMF), it was observed in 17 member countries that the main policy measure taken by governments has been the creation of partial and full guarantees, followed by moratoriums on short-term loans.

The subsidiary also rightly evaluated the force majeure clause and as the same would not be financially beneficial for the lending company and could give rise to unnecessary litigation, other alternatives were opted for.

The RBI introduced resolution plans for COVID-19-related stress wherein lending institutions were permitted to implement the resolution plan as necessary subject to

5. *See* https://corporates.db.com/files/documents/legalre-sources/company/Trade_Finance_List_of_Prices_and_Services_for_Corporate_Clients_in_Germany_E_121220.pdf.

certain conditions for individuals and small businesses. One such option permitted was to convert the portion of the debt into equity or other marketable, non-convertible debt securities issued by the borrower. It was decided that the loan would be partially converted into equity after passing a special resolution in India and a Board of Director's resolution in the Netherlands.

It should be noted that the said loan cannot be considered as a quasi-capital as the partial conversion is directly into equity capital and was carried out only as a preventive measure due to the pandemic; hence, no notional interest can be charged in the future.

Further, the RBI norms with respect to COVID-19 resolution plans can be considered as one of the appropriate barometers for demonstrating the arm's length principle in respect of the financial transaction under consideration. It can therefore be concluded that the conversion of the loan (along with the interest outstanding at the time of conversion), partially into equity is justifiable considering the present economic circumstances and hence, can be demonstrated to be at arm's length. In addition to the above, interest outstanding on the loan balance can be charged at the prevailing market rate as compared to the interest rate negotiated at the time of the agreement. This is due to the economic exigencies prevalent due to the pandemic, and it was in line with the prevalent interest rates, which were brought down by the Central Banks of various nations across the world, to protect the economies as a result of the downturn due to the pandemic. Thus, this reduction was in accordance with the lowering of interest rates by RBI and other Central banks and can be justified to be at arm's length.

(2) Additional loan from the Parent company

The purpose of the additional loan to subsidiary A was to provide it assistance in facing the financial burden created at the time of the pandemic and to safeguard against the severe economic disruption.

In order to provide financial support to subsidiary A during the testing times, the parent company decided to provide the above assistance in the form of interest-free loan for a period of the first twelve months.

The above position was taken by the parent company after considering the overall economic benefits to the group. It also evaluated infusion through equity which would have been more expensive as the repatriation of equity would be more cumbersome as compared to the repayment of loan.

Considering the unusual circumstances, it is economically justifiable to provide interest-free loan for an initial period of the first twelve months. For the balance period till the time of repayment of the loan, interest was charged at the prevalent market rates and thus the entire arrangement can be deemed to be at arm's length.

(3) Guarantee given by the parent company to the third-party lender

The bank, also located in Germany agreed to offer the loan to company B only if a guarantee was provided by the parent company C. It was considered economically justifiable to provide the said guarantee free of charge. The rationale for providing the guarantee free of charge is to enable company B to avoid a liquidity crunch and provide assistance to meet its other financial obligations on time. It has been suggested by a well-known economist and former president of the European Central Bank, Moria Draghi that guarantee costs should not be based on credit risk and should be zero regardless of the cost of funding during a crisis such as the pandemic.[6]

Therefore, such guarantee could be given free of charge for the initial one year of the loan and the same would be considered at arm's length given the unprecedented circumstances that arose during the pandemic.

## 5 The COVID-19 Era: How Were Businesses Coping?

As the health crisis progressed and the initial lockdowns were lifted, certain businesses began to slowly recover and return to almost normal levels of business operation. However, as it has been seen, the effect of the pandemic is extremely uncertain and erratic. The severity of the crisis fluctuated with multiple mutations threatening the world. Lockdowns had to be re-imposed and businesses had to be shut down more than once in various countries. This led to long periods of exceptional losses and other hardships for such businesses.

As the second round of restrictions was being slowly lifted in many parts of the world, and hugely successful vaccination drives carried out, companies were also gaining confidence to perform better in the upcoming months. As per OECD's economic outlook interim report for September 2021,[7] there has been a strong global economic recovery and the global GDP has risen above its pre-pandemic level. However, the report also states that the risk of the pandemic still remained, as 'large differences in vaccination rates between countries were adding to the unevenness of the recovery. Renewed outbreaks of the virus were forcing some countries to restrict activities, resulting in bottlenecks and pressures on supply chains'.

Even though companies begin their recovery, the long-lasting ramifications of the effects of the health crisis cannot be overlooked. While the onus is on the taxpayer to ensure that the impacts are adequately documented and existing contracts and arrangements are revisited, it is the authors view that tax authorities should also act pragmatically and fairly. Their approach should be more accommodative and understanding, in line with the present difficult business environment and not rush to impose unnecessary transfer pricing adjustments, penalties, etc.

Tax experts around the world feel that there will be an increase in scrutiny of all transactions going forward. However, inquiry into intercompany financial transactions, which were anyway comprehensively examined, will only intensify. Taxpayers should be able to demonstrate at all levels that they acted in good faith and each of their transactions entered truly reflect the market scenario at that point in time.

6. *See* https://www.ft.com/content/c6d2de3a-6ec5-11ea-89df-41bea055720b.
7. *See* https://www.oecd-ilibrary.org/sites/490d4832-en/index.html?itemId=/content/publication/490d4832-en&_ga=2.173706275.1867872413.1635190972-307308060.1615804014.

## IV CONCLUSION: THE FUTURE OF TRANSFER PRICING AND INTERCOMPANY FINANCIAL TRANSACTIONS

The pandemic has brought about some catastrophic consequences on businesses globally. Naturally, the restrictions in global trade posed a big threat to companies, impacting transfer pricing and effective determination of arm's length price. The impact of the COVID-19 health crisis on intra-group financial services has been discussed at length in the above paragraphs. However, going forward, it will be necessary to assess the overall transfer pricing policies of MNE groups in order to align the same with the acceptable transfer pricing models worldwide.

Such assessment would involve identifying the adjustments required in the transfer pricing model that correctly account for changes in global supply chains, allocation of costs, and Functions, Assets and Risk analysis of the group as a whole. Any deviation from the existing models should be justified with commercial rationale and sound economic principles.

Article 9 of the OECD Model Tax Convention clearly sets out the importance of the arm's length principles. The ALS is the universal standard for evaluating intra-group transactions and has been adopted by the comity of nations in their taxation laws, to determine whether the intra-group transactions, are reasonable taking into account the economic conditions prevalent, at the time when the controlled transactions were entered into by the related parties.

The ALS has survived amidst various periods of financial stress in the last couple of decades, due to its inherent nature of it being an impartial standard, as its goal is to equate controlled transactions, with similar juxtaposed uncontrolled transactions. Its foundation is wide enough to absorb the vicissitudes of economic change, as comparability is its footstool, which would ensure that the economically relevant characteristics of the controlled transaction, would be prevalent in the uncontrolled transactions. The OECD Transfer Pricing Guidelines (TPG) also puts stress on the importance of accurate economic comparability in paragraph 1.34: 'The application of the arm's length principle depends on determining the conditions that independent parties would have agreed in comparable transactions in comparable circumstances. Before making comparisons with uncontrolled transactions, it is therefore vital to identify the economically relevant characteristics of the commercial or financial relations as expressed in the controlled transaction'.

Under normal circumstances, it would be enough to rely on historical data of companies and it is assumed that they have reasonable stability in operations for determining comparability. With an unprecedented crisis like the COVID-19 health crisis, such historical data will prove to be unreliable for calculating the correct profits. It is therefore probable, that the arm's length principle will be required to be continually tested to develop alternative approaches that offer a better outlook of comparable companies that helps both the taxpayer and tax authorities.

Such alternate approaches could involve making adjustments to reflect the data as per pre-crisis levels. For instance, some countries like Australia have adopted the 'but for COVID-19' approach that compares the budgeted and actual results. Further, it can be seen whether multiple-year data for the tested party can be used for benchmarking and whether loss-making comparable companies can also be included. Extraordinary costs arising out of COVID-19 should be excluded as non-operating expenditures.

As the trajectory of the pandemic remains uncertain, the following factors must be kept in mind when benchmarking the restructuring of the financial transactions, caused by the actions taken by various governments to curb the spread of COVID-19. The OECD Guidelines for Multinational Enterprises and Tax Administrations states:

- In paragraph 10.32, that the 'Macroeconomic trends such as central bank lending rates or interbank reference rates, and financial market events like a credit crisis, can affect prices. In this regard, the precise timing of the issue of a financial instrument in the primary market or the selection of comparable data in the secondary market can therefore be very significant in terms of comparability.'
- In paragraph 10.33, that the 'Currency differences are another potentially important factor. Economic factors such as growth rate, inflation rate, and the volatility of exchange rates, mean that otherwise similar financial instruments issued in different currencies may have different prices. Moreover, prices for financial instruments in the same currency may vary across financial markets or countries due to regulations such as interest rate controls, exchange rate controls, foreign exchange restrictions and other legal and practical restrictions on financial market access.'
- In paragraph 10.15, that the 'MNE groups operating in different sectors may require, for example, different amounts and types of financing due to different capital intensity levels between industries, or may require different levels of short-term cash balances due to different commercial needs between industries.'
- In paragraph 10.60, that the 'Macroeconomic circumstances may lead to changes in the financing costs in the market. In such a context, a transfer pricing analysis with regard to the possibilities of the borrower or the lender to renegotiate the terms of the loan to benefit from better conditions will be informed by the options realistically available to both the borrower and the lender.'
- In benchmarking the restructuring of the financial transactions, the business strategy adopted by the related parties to ensure survival of the group in this pandemic, which has had drastic economic consequences also needs to be properly demonstrated. Business strategy is an important factor for evaluating comparable uncontrolled transactions.
- Paragraph 1.114 of the OECD TPG on Financial Transactions (February 2020) also stresses on the importance of business strategy when evaluating comparability, they state that 'Business strategies must also be examined in delineating the transaction and in determining comparability for transfer pricing purposes. Business strategies would take into account many aspects of an enterprise, such as innovation and new product development, degree of diversification, risk aversion, assessment of political changes, and input of

> existing and planned labour laws, duration of arrangements, and other factors bearing upon the daily conduct of business. Such business strategies may need to be taken into account when determining the comparability of controlled and uncontrolled transactions and enterprises.'

The impact of the COVID-19 health crisis will demonstrated in the years to come whether the ALS has inherent flexibility to absorb the economic impact of the pandemic and still remain relevant in benchmarking cross-border controlled transactions. Governments will also have to demonstrate by their policies that they have the vision to provide flexibility in their laws, so that future events can be used to benchmark and adjust data and the controlled transaction to truly reflect the economic scenario in the year of the crisis. This would be a pragmatic approach as normally comparable data would be available much later after the year-end, however, safeguards would need to be built in such an approach, as profit-making companies not affected by the pandemic, should not use an exceptionally beneficial measure to shift profits.

Further, the measures taken should also be similar by both the countries so as to harmonize the methodology to use data after the year-end, as otherwise it could lead to extreme difficulty for the companies to align their transfer pricing policies and could lead to disputes and long drawn-out litigation.

Thus, the COVID-19 health crisis (as with other crises before it) will allow the ALS to evolve and will show the path ahead for both taxpayers and tax administrators to adopt in such situations, to make transfer pricing law flexible but at the same time remain true to its central philosophy of being an impartial standard based on economic and comparability analysis to benchmark controlled transactions.

# CHAPTER 23

# Intercompany Agreements Relating to Financial Transactions

*Paul Sutton*[*]

## I INTERCOMPANY AGREEMENTS RELATING TO FINANCIAL TRANSACTIONS

This chapter sets out general considerations for the legal implementation or review of intercompany agreements relating to financial transactions, focussing on loan agreements and loan notes.

It looks at two recent cases which illustrate the interaction between transfer pricing considerations on the one hand, and legal and corporate governance issues on the other: the 2021 case of *Singapore Telecom Australia Investments Pty Ltd v. Commissioner of Taxation*,[1] and the 2022 case of *HMRC v. BlackRock Holdco 5 LLC*.[2]

The *Singapore Telecom* case demonstrates the central role which the legal terms of intercompany loans play in transfer pricing analysis and the issues which can arise when the commercial rationale for the loan (and for subsequent changes in the legal terms of the loan) is not adequately documented.

The UK case of *BlackRock* illustrates a situation where the deciding factor for determining the transfer pricing issue under consideration was the form of the legal

* The views and opinions set forth herein are the personal views or opinions of the authors; they do not necessarily reflect the views or opinions of the organization with which the authors are associated.

1. *Singapore Telecom Australia Investments Pty Ltd v. Commissioner of Taxation* [2021] Federal Court of Australia (AustLII), FCA 1597, https://www.austlii.edu.au/cgi-bin/viewdoc/au/cases/cth/FCA/2021/1597.html?context=1;query=2021%20FCA%201597%20or%20FCA%202021%201597;mask_path=, 17 December 2021.
2. *The Commissioners for HM Revenue and Customs v. Blackrock Holdco* 5 LLC [2022] UKUT 00199 (TCC), https://assets.publishing.service.gov.uk/media/62da693cd3bf7f1704a39605/HMRC_v_Blackrock_Holdco_LLC5_UT-2021-000022_-_final_decision_.pdf, 19 July 2022.

documentation of the relevant loan: only the borrower and the lender were party to the arrangements. No covenants had been provided by any parties other than the borrower. The Tribunal decided that the presence or absence of such covenants 'materially altered the economically relevant characteristics of the transaction'. An independent lender would not have made a loan in such circumstances. Therefore, HM Revenue and Customs' (HMRC) denial of the interest deduction was upheld.

## II INTRODUCTION

From a legal perspective, intercompany agreements arguably have a heightened role in relation to financial transactions, compared to other intercompany transaction types. This is for two main reasons.

First, it is arguably impossible to delineate financial transactions through an analysis of the parties' conduct alone. Fundamental terms such as repayment dates, interest rates (fixed or floating) and security or ranking cannot be deduced from merely observing the actions of the respective parties. One financial instrument cannot be compared with another for pricing purposes unless there is clarity on the associated legal rights and obligations of the respective parties in each case.

Second, from a legal entity perspective, corporate governance issues tend to be more transparent and immediate for financial transactions. For example, an intra-group lender necessarily incurs a credit risk in relation to the borrower's ability to repay the loan. (This risk may or may not be economically significant for the lender, depending on whether or not the borrower is a subsidiary of the lender.) Similarly, a borrower may be exposed to liquidity risks relating to its ability to pay the interest arising on an intra-group loan when due and to meet a demand for repayment of the loan.

It may be tempting to take a consolidated, group-wide view of financing arrangements, and to regard transfer pricing issues merely as a potential after-the-event adjustment. However, this would not meet the requirements of the arm's length principle for transfer pricing purposes or the legal duties of the directors of the respective entities. If a member of a corporate group (or the group as a whole) is subject to unforeseen liquidity issues, the legal control of individual legal entities may pass to trustees (in bankruptcy) or other officers (in similar insolvency proceedings). Those officers may have a duty to consider potential claims against directors if those directors have failed to comply with their personal duties, such as those of safeguarding the entity's employees and its creditors. This may give rise to a risk of personal liability for directors.

When considering the legal implementation of proposed intercompany financial transactions, it is therefore critical to consider the separate interests of each individual legal entity involved in the transaction. Although this review may be carried out centrally (e.g., by the group's tax, finance and legal functions), ultimately it is for the directors of each individual legal entity to approve.

## III IMPACT OF THE LEGAL AND REGULATORY ENVIRONMENT

The 2022 OECD Transfer Pricing Guidelines recognize that the regulatory and legal environment within which the parties to an intercompany loan operate must be taken into account in assessing the transfer pricing implications of the arrangements:

> The economic conditions of loans should also be viewed in the context of regulations that may affect the position of the parties. For example, insolvency law in the jurisdiction of the borrower may provide that liabilities towards associated enterprises are subordinated to liabilities towards unrelated parties (C.1.1.1, paragraph 10.61).[3]
>
> Where the relevant MNEs are regulated, such as financial services entities subject to regulations consistent with recognized industry standards (e.g. Basel requirements), due regard should be had to the constraints those regulations impose on them (B.2, paragraph 10.15).[4]

The consideration of financial services regulations is outside the scope of this chapter, but to the extent that they apply, their requirements as regards the form and content of intercompany agreements may in practice override all other considerations, including transfer pricing.

Aside from constraints affecting groups in the financial services sector, other legal considerations affecting the form and terms of intercompany debt may include:

- company law requirements regarding maintenance of capital or minimum paid-up capital;
- legal restrictions attached to government grants and government-backed loans (e.g., COVID-19 support) as regards how the proceeds of those grants or loans may be used; e.g., this may mean that those proceeds cannot be used for the purpose of loans to, or cash pooling arrangements with, associated entities overseas; and
- requirements as regards the transferability and other terms of debt which is structured in loan note form if the relevant loan notes are to be listed on a stock exchange. (*See* further section VIII below.)

The reference to insolvency risks in paragraph 10.61 of the OECD Transfer Pricing Guidelines[5] is instructive. In the event of insolvency of an entity within a multinational group, the group's transfer pricing documentation will not be the primary focus of creditors, regulators or officeholders in insolvency proceedings. Rather, they will look first at the actual transactions entered into by the insolvent entity in the period preceding the insolvency, and the actual terms of the intercompany agreements involved.

3. OECD (2022), OECD Transfer Pricing Guidelines for Multinational Enterprises and Tax Administrations 2022, OECD Publishing, Paris, https://doi.org/10.1787/0e655865-en, C.1.1.1, para. 10.61.
4. OECD (2022), OECD Transfer Pricing Guidelines for Multinational Enterprises and Tax Administrations 2022, OECD Publishing, Paris, https://doi.org/10.1787/0e655865-en, B.2, para. 10.15.
5. OECD (2022), OECD Transfer Pricing Guidelines for Multinational Enterprises and Tax Administrations 2022, OECD Publishing, Paris, https://doi.org/10.1787/0e655865-en, para. 10.61.

## IV TWO-SIDED ANALYSIS AND OPTIONS REALISTICALLY AVAILABLE TO THE PARTIES

The OECD Transfer Pricing Guidelines require a two-sided analysis of intercompany financial transactions. For example, it is stated that:

> In considering the commercial and financial relations between the associated borrower and lender, and in an analysis of the economically relevant characteristics of the transaction, both the lender's and borrower's perspectives should be taken into account, acknowledging that these perspectives may not align in every case. (C.1.1.1 paragraph 10.51).[6]

This is closely related to the transfer pricing concept of 'options realistically available to the parties':

> 10.19. Independent enterprises, when considering whether to enter into a particular financial transaction, will consider all other options realistically available to them, and will only enter into the transaction if they see no alternative that offers a clearly more attractive opportunity to meet their commercial objectives (see paragraph 1.38 of Chapter I). In considering the options realistically available, the perspective of each of the parties to the transaction must be considered (B.2 paragraph 10.19).[7]

These considerations have particular application to the borrower:

> From the borrower's perspective, the options realistically available will include broader considerations than the entity's ability to service its debt, for example, the funds it actually needs to meet its operational requirements. In some instances, although an entity may have the capacity to borrow and service an additional amount of debt, it may choose not to do so to avoid placing negative pressure on its credit rating and increasing its cost of capital, and jeopardising its access to capital markets and its market reputation (B.2 paragraph 10.19).[8]

The impact of these considerations is twofold.

First, in many cases, this form of analysis reinforces and aligns with the typical legal analysis of intercompany transactions. As discussed above, this legal analysis tends to emphasize the role of directors as 'custodians' of the interests of the relevant legal entity of which they are directors, irrespective of their roles as directors of related entities.

Second, it must be remembered that from a practical perspective, the scrutiny of intercompany loans in terms of the options available to the parties and the two-sided transfer pricing analysis of transactions is likely to take place after the event. In many cases, it will be a number of years after the event, when one or more of the relevant tax

6. OECD (2022), OECD Transfer Pricing Guidelines for Multinational Enterprises and Tax Administrations 2022, OECD Publishing, Paris, https://doi.org/10.1787/0e655865-en, C.1.1.1, para. 10.51.
7. OECD (2022), OECD Transfer Pricing Guidelines for Multinational Enterprises and Tax Administrations 2022, OECD Publishing, Paris, https://doi.org/10.1787/0e655865-en, B.2, para. 10.19.
8. OECD (2022), OECD Transfer Pricing Guidelines for Multinational Enterprises and Tax Administrations 2022, OECD Publishing, Paris, https://doi.org/10.1787/0e655865-en, B.2, para. 10.19.

administrations raises enquiries, challenges or adverse assessments. The legal agreements and associated corporate approvals - which need to be put in place in advance of the transaction - therefore have a key role to play in evidencing the commercial rationale for the arrangements from an entity-by-entity perspective, as illustrated by the case study below.

## V CASE STUDY 1: *SINGAPORE TELECOM AUSTRALIA INVESTMENTS PTY LTD V. COMMISSIONER OF TAXATION [2021] FCA 1597*[9]

In its 2021 decision involving Singapore Telecom Australia Investments Pty Ltd (STAI), the Federal Court of Appeals in Australia ruled in favour of the Commissioner of Taxation in a dispute relating to intercompany debt totalling AUD 5.2 billion (approx. USD 3.7 billion). The Commissioner of Taxation contested tax deductions claimed by STAI for interest paid on the debt in the tax years ending 31 March 2010, 2011, 2012 and 2013, on the basis of the applicable transfer pricing provisions. The Court upheld the Commissioner's assessments, resulting in increased taxable income of nearly AUD 895 million (USD 640 million). The group later announced that the resulting net tax exposure and related interest and penalties amounted to AUD 304 million (USD 217 million).

The relevant debt was in the form of loan notes issued under a loan note issuance agreement (LNIA). That agreement was entered into on 28 June 2002 and subsequently amended three times: on 31 December 2002, 31 March 2003 and 30 March 2009.

The loan notes were issued by STAI as borrower. The holder of the relevant loan notes was Singtel Australia Investment Ltd (SAI), a company incorporated in the British Virgin Islands and resident in Singapore. Both companies were wholly owned subsidiaries of Singapore Telecom.

Prior to the issuance of the loan notes, SAI had acquired a company called Cable & Wireless Optus Ltd. That company's name was later changed to Singtel Optus Ltd (SOPL). As part of an intra-group reorganization, STAI subsequently acquired the shares of SOPL from SAI, in consideration for the issuance of shares and the AUD 5.2 billion loan notes mentioned above.

The group structure immediately following that acquisition is shown in the diagram below:

9. *Singapore Telecom Australia Investments Pty Ltd v Commissioner of Taxation* [2021] Federal Court of Australia (AustLII), FCA 1597, https://www.austlii.edu.au/cgi-bin/viewdoc/au/cases/cth/FCA/2021/1597.html?context=1;query=2021%20FCA%201597%20or%20FCA%202021%201597;mask_path=, 17 December 2021.

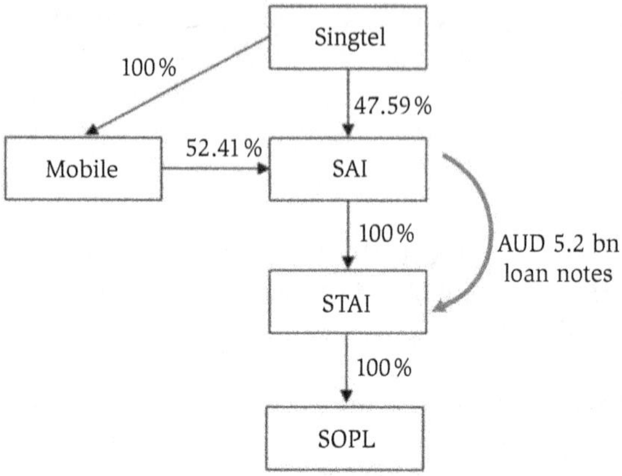


The issues considered by the Court included:

- the impact of 'implicit parent company support' on STAI's credit rating as borrower (there was no disagreement between the parties on the 'standalone' credit rating of STAI);
- whether the terms of the LNIA (as amended throughout its life) were comparable with those of debt capital markets (DCM) transactions; and
- the impact of special terms relating to accrual and payment of interest.

As regards the comparability with DCM transactions, it is clear that the starting point for the Court was the terms of the LNIA in place between the parties (the actual transaction):

> STAI relies heavily on Mr Chigas's analysis, which has been outlined above. The principal difficulty with this approach, in my respectful opinion, is that it departs too far from the actual transaction and the characteristics of the parties to that transaction, and thus departs from the approach required under Subdiv 815-A. The actual transaction involved a vendor and a purchaser of shares, and an issue of loan notes totalling approximately $5.2 billion by way of partial consideration for the acquisition of the shares. It did not involve a DCM bond issue. Further, as already indicated, *I consider there to be significant differences between the terms of the LNIA and the terms of a typical DCM bond issue.*[10] (Italics added.)

The Court seems to have been particularly struck by the absence of convincing evidence of a tenable commercial rationale for the changes in the terms of the loan notes over time, particularly in the second and third amendments. The decision contains extensive commentary that attempts to reconstruct the reasons for the changes, including reviewing extracts from emails. One has to assume that the group did not have a practice of creating briefing notes for the directors of the two legal entities involved (STAI and SAI), explaining the documents which they were being asked to approve.

10. *Ibid.*, para. 343.

In this case, it is notable that the loan notes in their original form provided for the debt of AUD 5.2 billion to be repayable on demand. The relevant clause (7.1) of the LNIA stated: 'A Holder may at any time require the Issuer to redeem all or any Notes registered in the name of the Holder by notice in writing. The date on which the Holder specifies the relevant Note is to be redeemed is the Maturity Date.'[11]

Given that the borrower, STAI, appeared to have no significant assets other than a (presumably illiquid) investment in SOPL, it is hard to see how STAI's directors could have properly approved such a financing arrangement. STAI's position was not assisted by the profit and cash flow projections for SOPL. Paragraph 170 stated:

> As at October 2001, SOPL's financial projections included the following: net profit after tax (NPAT) was projected to decrease from $425 million in the year ending 31 March 2001 to $245 million and $264 million in the years ending 31 March 2002 and 31 March 2003 respectively. Further, free cash flow was projected to continue to be negative (-$905 million and -$459 million in the years ending 31 March 2002 and 31 March 2003 respectively), with positive free cash flow projected to be generated in the year ending 31 March 2004.[12]

The Court's decision in this case highlights the clear linkage between, on the one hand, the corporate governance process for approval of transactions on behalf of legal entities, and on the other hand, the explanation of the transaction for transfer pricing purposes. The taxpayer appeared to have been unable to produce contemporaneous evidence of the commercial rationale for the debt in its original form, or for the changes in the terms of the loan notes over time, particularly in the second and third amendments. The judgment contains extensive commentary that attempts to reconstruct the reasons for the changes, including reviewing extracts from emails between the group and its tax advisers.

## VI CASE STUDY 2: *HMRC V. BLACKROCK HOLDCO 5 LLC [2022] UKUT 00199 (TCC)*[13]

On 19 July 2022, the Upper Tribunal in the UK released a judgment in the case of *HMRC v. BlackRock Holdco 5 LLC*. This overturned the previous decision of the First-tier Tribunal (FTT) and found in favour of HMRC: it disallowed an interest deduction on an intercompany loan of approximately USD 4 billion.

In the words of the Upper Tribunal judgment, the scenario was as follows:

> This appeal concerns the structure used by the BlackRock group of companies ('the BlackRock Group') to acquire the North American investment management business of Barclays Global Investors ('BGI US') from Barclays Bank plc in December 2009. The ultimate issue in this appeal is whether the Respondent, BlackRock Holdco 5, LLC ('LLC5'), which was created and used as part of the acquisition structure, was entitled to non-trading loan relationship debits in

11. *Ibid.*, Clause 7.1.
12. *Ibid.*, para. 170.
13. *The Commissioners for HM Revenue and Customs v. Blackrock Holdco 5 LLC* [2022] UKUT 00199 (TCC), https://assets.publishing.service.gov.uk/media/62da693cd3bf7f1704a39605/HMRC_v_Blackrock_Holdco_LLC5_UT-2021-000022_-_final_decision_.pdf, 19 July 2022.

respect of the interest and other expenses payable on $4 billion worth of loan notes. The loan notes ('the Loans') were issued in return for the loan LLC5 received from its parent, BlackRock Holdco 4, LLC ('LLC4'). As described in greater detail below, the Loans were part of the intra-group financing for the purchase by the BlackRock Group of BGI US.[14]

The group structure is set out in the diagram below:

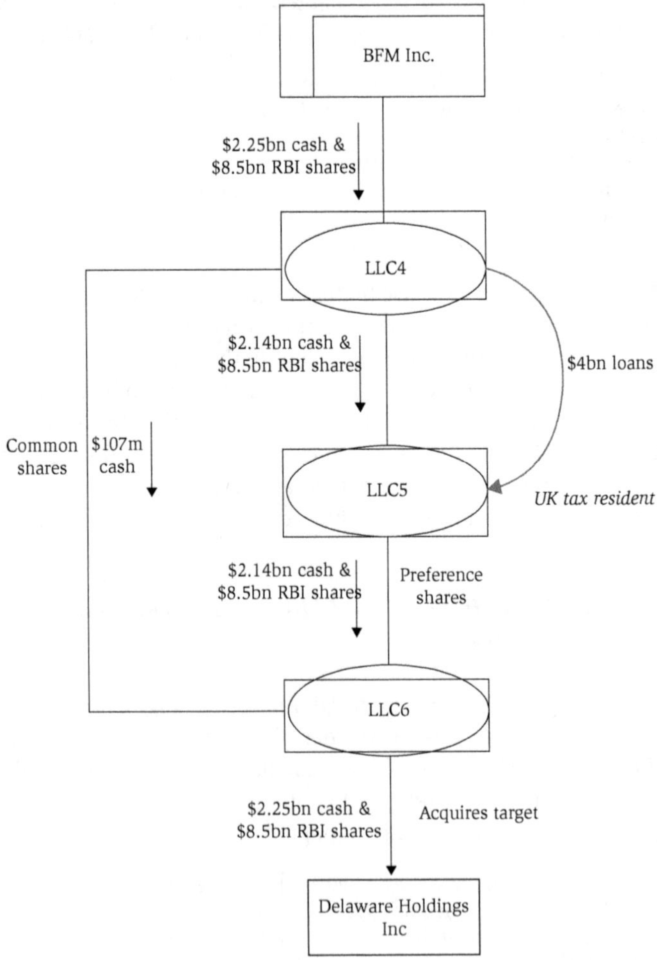


14. *Ibid.*, para. 1.

The FTT decided in favour of BlackRock: it found that an independent lender acting at arm's length would have made loans to LLC5 in the same amount and on the same terms as to interest as were actually made by LLC4 (the 'Transfer Pricing Issue'). The FTT further found that the Loans had both a commercial purpose and a tax advantage purpose, but that it would be just and reasonable to apportion all the debits to the commercial purpose and so they were fully deductible by LLC5 (the 'Unallowable Purpose Issue').

The Upper Tribunal, however, found in favour of HMRC on both the Transfer Pricing Issue and the Unallowable Purpose Issue.

It is worth noting that the experts for the respective parties both agreed that an independent lender would have entered into an arrangement subject to it being able to obtain the necessary covenants. This was therefore not a typical transfer pricing dispute relating to the pricing of loans. It was a case of 'all or nothing', in which the form of the legal documentation of the loans played a decisive role.

A central question in the Transfer Pricing Issue concerned covenants to support the USD 4 billion loan made by LLC4 to LLC5. The parties agreed that an independent arm's length lender would have required covenants from various third parties including BGI (the target) and LLC6 (the bidco), in addition to covenants from LLC5 as borrower.

The experts for HMRC and BlackRock also agreed that the main concern of an independent lender of USD 4 billion to a company like LLC5 would be the risks around the control over the dividend flow to it and so its ability to repay the loan. The FTT and the Upper Tribunal considered the following hypothetical covenants which the lender LLC4 may have required:

> (1) covenants by BGI [the target] and LLC6 [the bidco] restricting the amount of debt that could be raised by them (to prevent profits to be diverted in repaying such debt);
> (2) negative pledges by BGI [the target], LLC5 [the borrower] and LLC6 [the bidco] restricting them from granting security to other lenders;
> (3) a covenant by LLC4 [in its capacity of holder of some of the shares of the bidco] that it would not interfere with the declaration of dividends by LLC6 [the bidco] and BGI [the target];
> (4) covenants by BGI [the target] and LLC6 [the bidco] that, without prejudice to their own discretion regarding the declaration of dividends, they would not frustrate the expected dividend flows (e.g. by making loans to LLC4); and
> (5) change of control covenants by LLC4, LLC5 and LLC6 to block any sale of LLC6 or BGI.[15]

A key question was whether covenants of this nature could be imputed into the loan arrangement, for the purposes of providing a comparable transaction for transfer pricing purposes. The Upper Tribunal judgment considered the 1995 version of the OECD Transfer Pricing Guidelines (the relevant version for the case in hand), and quoted the following provisions (amongst others):

15. *Ibid.*, para. 23.90.

> Application of the arm's length principle is generally based on a comparison of the conditions in a controlled transaction with the conditions in transactions between independent enterprises. In order for such comparisons to be useful, the economically relevant characteristics of the situations being compared must be sufficiently comparable. To be comparable means that none of the differences (if any) between the situations being compared could materially affect the condition being examined in the methodology (e.g. price or margin), or that reasonably accurate adjustments can be made to eliminate the effect of any such differences.[16]

The relevant UK legislation includes the Taxation (International and Other Provisions) Act 2010 (TIOPA). Section 147(1)[17] of that Act provides as follows:

> **147 Tax calculations to be based on arm's length, not actual, provision**
>
> (1) For the purposes of this section 'the basic pre-condition' is that –
>
> (a) *provision ('the actual provision') has been made or imposed as between any two persons ('the affected persons') by means of a transaction or series of transactions,*
>
> (b) the participation condition is met (see section 148),
>
> (c) the actual provision is not within subsection (7) (oil transactions), and
>
> (d) *the actual provision differs from the provision ('the arm's length provision') which would have been made as between independent enterprises.*
>
> (Italics as added in the Upper Tribunal's judgment.)

Section 164 of TIOPA states that the relevant provisions of that Act are to be read in such manner as best secures consistency with the OECD Transfer Pricing Guidelines.

However, section 147(1)(a) of TIOPA refers only to an 'actual provision' as made between 'two persons'. The Upper Tribunal cited the 2009 UK transfer pricing case of *DSG Retail Ltd v. HMRC* [2009] STC (SCD) 397, in which the Special Commissioners said:

> [The predecessor of s.14D7(1)] speaks of provision between two persons. For the [legislation] to apply those two persons must be identified. Whilst the transaction or series of transactions by which the relevant provision is made or imposed may encompass transactions between persons other than those two persons, the identified provision must be between two persons only. There is, in our view, no scope for reading 'two' as 'two or more'.[18]

On that basis, the Upper Tribunal concluded that:

> the FTT erred in law in permitting new third-party covenants absent from the actual transaction to be taken into account when considering whether an independent lender would make a $4 billion loan to LLC5. The FTT decided that such an independent lender would not have made a $4 billion loan to LLC5 without such covenants being in place and that important finding should itself have determined that there was no comparable arm's length transaction. Having decided that, the

16. OECD (1995), Transfer Pricing Guidelines for Multinational Enterprises and Tax Administrations 1995, Transfer Pricing Guidelines for Multinational Enterprises and Tax Administrations, OECD Publishing, Paris, https://doi.org/10.1787/g2g7fa2a-en, para. 1.15.
17. Taxation (International and Other Provisions) Act 2010, section 147.
18. *DSG Retail Ltd & ORS v. Revenue & Customs*, First-tier Tribunal, 31 March 2009, https://www.casemine.com/judgement/uk/5b5055bf2c94e04d9c5ad3ee, para. 65.

> FTT would have been bound to conclude that no 'provision would have been made as between independent enterprises' (section 151(2)).[19]

This was therefore very much a binary decision on the Transfer Pricing Issue, with the reasoning running as follows:

- an independent arm's length lender would not have lent without covenants from parties in addition to the borrower;
- no such third-party covenants were present in the actual transaction;
- section 147(1)(a) TIOPA precludes the imputation of covenants from third parties;
- therefore there is no comparable transaction under which the loan would have been made at all;
- therefore no interest deduction can be allowed.

The *BlackRock* judgment therefore means that multinational groups and their advisers may need to pay more attention to the legal documentation of intercompany loans, and in particular the form and content of the 'security package' required to mitigate risk from a lender's perspective.

## VII KEY LEGAL TERMS IN TYPICAL INTERCOMPANY LOAN AGREEMENTS

As indicated above, in loan agreements between unconnected third parties, the pricing of those loans (such as the setting of interest rates) is extremely sensitive to the contractual terms involved, and not merely to the financial standing of the respective parties.

The 2022 OECD Transfer Pricing Guidelines contain the following commentary:

> **B.3.3. Characteristics of financial instruments**
>
> 10.28. There is a wide variety of financial instruments in the open market that present very different features and attributes, which may affect the pricing of those products or services. Consequently, when pricing controlled transactions, it is important to document the transactions' features and attributes.
>
> 10.29. For instance in the case of a loan, those characteristics may include but are not limited to: the amount of the loan; its maturity; the schedule of repayment; the nature or purpose of the loan (trade credit, merger/acquisition, mortgage, etc.); level of seniority and subordination, geographical location of the borrower; currency; collateral provided; presence and quality of any guarantee; and whether the interest rate is fixed or floating.[20]

19. *The Commissioners for HM Revenue and Customs v. Blackrock Holdco 5 LLC* [2022] UKUT 00199 (TCC), https://assets.publishing.service.gov.uk/media/62da693cd3bf7f1704a39605/HMRC_v_Blackrock_Holdco_LLC5_UT-2021-000022_-_final_decision_.pdf, 19 July 2022, para. 76.
20. OECD (2022), OECD Transfer Pricing Guidelines for Multinational Enterprises and Tax Administrations 2022, OECD Publishing, Paris, https://doi.org/10.1787/0e655865-en, B.3.3., paras 10.28-10.29.

In the documentation of intercompany loan facilities, as for any other intercompany agreement, the objective is not necessarily to adopt the form of legal documentation used in third-party financing arrangements. Unless long-form loan agreements and security documents are appropriate because they correspond to the way that the arrangements are actually managed, the objective is usually to evidence the essence of the risks undertaken by the parties.

Legal considerations regarding the drafting of intercompany loans include the following.

## 1 Type of Facility

The following sets out a high-level overview of some common types of intra-group loan facilities.

*Overdraft:* an arrangement where the borrower is able to draw down amounts and repay amounts at will, within a specified credit limit. The facility is uncommitted, in the sense that the lender can withdraw the facility at any time, and can demand repayment of the outstanding balance at any time.

*Term loan facility:* an arrangement whereby the lender makes one or more advances which are repayable on a specified date or dates. The lender is typically under no contractual obligation to re-advance sums which are repaid. The borrower may or may not have the option to repay the loan early, i.e., before the contractual maturity date. For the sake of simplicity, intra-group term loans are often documented on the basis of a single advance on a specified date, with repayment due on the expiry of the specified term, as opposed to multiple advances and multiple repayment dates.

*Revolving credit facility:* an arrangement whereby the borrower has the flexibility to draw down and repay amounts on multiple occasions, within the context of an overall credit limit, the conditions for the ongoing availability of the facility, and the provisions for the repayment of the outstanding balance. It therefore combines elements of an overdraft and a term loan facility.

## 2 Legal Form of Loan Facility

Alternatives include:

- bilateral loan agreements, namely a 'traditional' loan agreement between a single lender and a single borrower;
- multilateral loan agreements (such as a global framework agreement setting out the terms on which individual advances may be made from time to time between participating entities);
- loan notes issued under a loan note instrument (*see* section VIII below);
- promissory notes, which are legal instruments in which one party (the maker or issuer) promises in writing to pay a specified sum of money to the other (the payee), either at a fixed or determinable future time or on demand of the payee.

Note that the legal form of the loan documentation does not usually affect the commercial terms or the allocation of risk. However, it may affect the way in which the loan needs to be administered. For example, under a loan note structure, advances would typically be documented as the issue of loan notes, repayments as redemptions of loan notes, and assignments as transfers of stock. (More on this below.) Similarly, debt obligations documented in the form of promissory notes may be subject to the applicable rules relating to bills of exchange, with a corresponding impact on the formalities required for the assignment of that debt.

## 3 Facility Amount and Structure of Advances

Key terms include:

- the amount of the loan advance or facility;
- the structure of the loan advance(s), such as whether the facility relates to a single specified advance, or instead specifies a facility amount or credit limit within which advances may be made;
- the availability period (the period during which the borrower is entitled to draw down amounts under the loan);
- whether the loan is 'committed' (i.e., the lender is obliged to make loan advances, subject to specified 'conditions precedent' being satisfied) or 'uncommitted' (i.e., the lender has no obligation to make loan advances in the future);
- 'conditions precedent' which must be satisfied in order for the lender to be obliged to make advances/re-advances (if applicable);
- whether the lender is obliged to re-advance funds which have been repaid;
- the currency of advances and repayments.

## 4 Purpose of the Loan

From a legal perspective, specifying the purpose of a loan facility in the relevant agreement may have the effect of restricting how the borrower is permitted to use the loan proceeds (for example, for the purpose of acquiring a specific asset). In an intercompany context, an intercompany lender may not require this type of legal restriction. In line with the general desire to keep intercompany agreements as simple as possible, it is common for the purpose of the facility in intercompany loan agreements to be widely defined (e.g., general working capital) or not mentioned at all.

From a transfer pricing perspective, as mentioned above it may be helpful to document the commercial rationale for the facility, including the borrower's requirement for the loan in the first place. This should be considered on a case-by-case basis. The commercial rationale for a loan may either be documented in the intercompany loan agreement (e.g., in the recitals or purpose of the loan), in the corporate approval documents (such as board minutes), or in briefing notes or similar documents provided prior to the formal approval of the relevant documents by the boards of the entities concerned.

## 5 Interest

Key terms include:

- whether interest accrues at a fixed rate or floating rate;
- for floating interest rates, the reference rate (e.g., the Sterling Overnight Index Average (SONIA)) and the margin to be added to that rate to determine the actual rate of interest payable;
- periods for calculation of interest (e.g., one, three, six, twelve months) and the mechanism for fixing of interest rates (e.g., the applicable reference rate at a specified time on the first business day of each successive interest period);
- dates for payment of interest;
- dates for compounding of interest, if applicable;
- the 'default' rate of interest which accrues on overdue payments or in the event that the borrower is in breach of its obligations under the loan.

## 6 Repayments

- On demand, on notice, or on specified date(s).
- Amortization over the term of the facility.
- Balloon repayment (repayment is made in instalments, with the final instalment being the biggest).
- Bullet repayment (repayment is made in a single instalment at the expiry of the loan facility).
- Term or tenor of loan, at the expiry of which the loan facility must be repaid.

## 7 Voluntary Prepayment by Borrower

- Without notice (if applicable)
- Notice period (if applicable)
- Penalty for prepayment (if applicable).

## 8 Mandatory Prepayment/Events of Default

Typical events triggering mandatory prepayment in third-party loan facilities include matters such as:

- illegality in relation to the loan agreement or security documents;
- change of control;
- proceeds of disposals, subject to agreed carve-outs;

- proceeds of insurance, subject to agreed carve-outs;
- a specified percentage of excess cash flow ('excess cash flow' would need to be defined in the agreement).

## 9 Security and Ranking

- Whether the loan ranks in priority to, or is subordinated to, other debt of the borrower.
- Any security (e.g., guarantee by third party, fixed or floating charges over assets).

## 10 Covenants

These fall within two general categories.

### *A Maintenance Covenants*

These constitute promises by the borrower to maintain a certain state of affairs during the term of the loan facility, such as:

- ratio of debt to EBITDA (earnings before interest, taxes, depreciation and amortization);
- ratio of debt to tangible net assets;
- interest coverage ratio as a percentage of EBITDA;
- interest coverage ratio as a percentage of cash flow from operations;
- fixed charge coverage;
- total assets;
- tangible net assets.

### *B Incurrence Covenants*

In the words of the OECD's Transfer Pricing Guidelines, 'incurrence covenants require or prohibit certain actions by the borrower without the consent of the lender'.[21] This therefore includes both *positive covenants* (to do certain things), and *negative covenants* (not to do certain things), for so long as amounts remain outstanding under the facility.

In the context of typical arm's length loans, examples of *positive covenants* include those relating to carrying on business in accordance with applicable laws, maintaining insurance policies, and procuring security by third parties.

21. OECD (2022), OECD Transfer Pricing Guidelines for Multinational Enterprises and Tax Administrations 2022, OECD Publishing, Paris, https://doi.org/10.1787/0e655865-en, C.1.1.5 para. 10.84.

Typical *negative covenants* in third-party loan facilities include restrictions on the borrower undertaking or permitting any of the following, except with the lender's prior consent:

- payment of dividends;
- disposal of material assets;
- incurring of additional borrowing;
- granting of security ranking in priority to the loan in question;
- material acquisitions.

As acknowledged in the OECD's Transfer Pricing Guidelines, the lenders in intra-group loans may have access to more information regarding the borrower than would typically be the case in loans between unconnected parties. Intra-group lenders may therefore choose not to require contractual covenants of the types referred to above. In any event, providing for 'informational' contractual covenants of this nature in the context of intra-group loans would only be appropriate if the group is in a position to monitor compliance with those covenants and actually comply with the procedures specified in the intercompany agreements concerned.

However, a cautious approach in response to the decision in *BlackRock* may involve putting in place full 'security packages' for intercompany loans (albeit potentially using short-form documents): the Upper Tribunal in *BlackRock* suggested that the Transfer Pricing Issue would have been resolved in favour of BlackRock, if the relevant covenants from BGI [the target] and LLC6 [the bidco] and others had been put in place as part of the legal documentation of the intercompany loans.

## VIII LOAN NOTES AND LOAN NOTE INSTRUMENTS

In arrangements between third parties, loan notes are commonly used for raising funds for a wide range of purposes, including institutional investments, securitizations, property development projects, public companies, owner-managed businesses and start-ups. They are also commonly used for documenting the terms of intra-group debt.

As mentioned above, the choice of loan notes as the legal form of a debt obligation does not impact the commercial terms of the debt. In other words, any commercial terms which can be documented in a 'conventional' loan agreement can also be reflected in the terms of loan notes, and vice versa. The main differences tend to be:

- the tax treatment of the debt (which is outside the scope of this *chapter*);
- the regulatory treatment of the arrangements (which is also outside the scope of this *chapter*);
- the terminology involved; and
- the ongoing administration of the arrangements from a legal perspective.

The following is a brief description of the basic mechanics of loan notes from a legal perspective.

A loan note is essentially an instrument recording a promise to repay a loan, with or without interest, on specified terms. Loan notes may be secured or unsecured, listed on a stock exchange or unlisted, transferable or not transferable.

Loan notes are governed by a master document, often referred to as a 'loan note instrument' or 'LNIA'. This sets out the terms and conditions relating to the loan notes. It is signed by the issuer, and (in the case of a loan note instrument) is addressed to the world at large. The loan note instrument typically contains schedules which include the commercial terms of the loan and the procedures for holding meetings of note holders.

The 'issuer' of a loan note is the borrower or debtor under the loan relationship.

The 'note holders' or 'subscribers' are the lenders or creditors in relation to the debt.

The individual 'loan note certificate' operates in a way similar to a share certificate. It is usually a short document, and is signed by the issuer and delivered to the relevant note holder. It constitutes formal evidence of the debt. Each loan note certificate will set out the names of the issuer and the holder, the date of issue, the maturity date, the interest rate and the amount of loan notes held. It will also attach the terms and conditions relating to the loan notes.

'Redemption' of a loan note means repayment of a loan note – in other words, when the issuer pays all outstanding principal and interest, and the loan note is cancelled.

The treatment of security and third-party covenants in the context of loan notes is often different as compared to 'conventional' loan agreements. This is because one of the key features of loan note instruments is that they contemplate that the identity and number of loan note holders may change over time. From a legal structural perspective, if security such as a guarantee or a charge is provided, that security is often held by a separate entity known as a 'security trustee'. This entity holds the benefit of the security of trust for the noteholders collectively. In an enforcement situation, it would be the security trustee who enforces the relevant security and accounts to the noteholders for the proceeds of that enforcement.

## IX CONCLUSION

As is apparent from the above discussion, the economic substance of intercompany loan transactions is inextricably linked with the legal form. A purported transfer pricing analysis without proper consideration of the proposed legal form is therefore at best inadequate and at worst wholly misleading.

Consideration to the proposed form of the legal documentation should therefore be given alongside the intended treatment for tax, transfer pricing and purposes. Key considerations from a legal perspective therefore include:

- The purpose of the loan (and why the borrower needs the funds).
- The business strategy to be followed by the borrower, and how this affects the structure of the documentation.
- From the lender's perspective, the risks relating to the loan and assumptions as regards the cash flows and assets.

- From the borrower's perspective, its ability to service the debt and meet potential repayment obligations.
- Any legal or regulatory constraints which affect the ability of the parties to lend or borrow.
- The key terms of the debt, including whether the facility is committed or uncommitted, the repayment date/term of the loan, the ability of the borrower to prepay, the ability of the lender to require early repayment, interest rates (fixed or floating), interest payment dates and so on.
- Ranking and security (including the relevance of guarantees/covenants/ security provided by parties other than the borrower).
- The requirement (if any) for other covenants, such as negative pledges or financial covenants.

# C Intercompany Financial Guarantees

CHAPTER 24

# Setting the Arm's Length Framework for Financial Guarantees

*Marta Pankiv*[*]

## I INTRODUCTION

Financial guarantees are quite common within multinational groups, but there has always been a certain degree of uncertainty as to how they should be approached from a transfer pricing perspective. The key questions are whether a guarantor should charge a fee to a borrower for the provision of guarantees and, if so, what amount should be charged. The answers to these questions along with practical examples are provided in the new guidance on financial guarantees issued by the Organisation for Economic Co-operation and Development (OECD) in 2020 and by the United Nations (UN) in 2021.

This chapter covers the main provisions of the OECD and the UN guidance by describing the arm's length framework for financial guarantees in the first section, explaining the importance of 'implicit support' and how to differentiate it from 'active promotion' in the context of delineation of the actual transaction in the second section, as well as discussing the approaches to pricing of financial guarantees together with the relevant examples in the third section. The chapter concludes with the author's remarks.

* The views and opinions set forth herein are the personal views or opinions of the authors; they do not necessarily reflect the views or opinions of the organisation with which the authors are associated.

## II ARM'S LENGTH FRAMEWORK FOR FINANCIAL GUARANTEES

A new framework for the arm's length pricing of financial guarantees is provided by the OECD and the UN in their respective guidance. Both are largely aligned and summarise the approaches to assessing and pricing of financial guarantees within multinational enterprises (MNEs).

### 1 OECD Guidance

The guidance on the arm's length pricing of financial guarantees is provided in a separate section of the OECD's Transfer Pricing Guidance on Financial Transactions released in February 2020 ('the OECD Guidance')[1] – section D (Financial guarantees) – and incorporated into the new edition of the OECD's Transfer Pricing Guidelines for Multinational Enterprises and Tax Administrations of January 2022 ('the OECD Transfer Pricing Guidelines 2022') in Chapter X.[2] The OECD defines a guarantee as 'a legally binding commitment on the part of the guarantor to assume a specified obligation of the guaranteed debtor if the debtor defaults on that obligation'.[3] Guarantees are seen from a lender's perspective as a means to reduce the risk of the borrower's default, whereas from a borrower's perspective, they are considered as a tool to increase the borrower's rating to the level of that of the guarantor. As a result of such uplifting in the credit rating, the provision of a financial guarantee may result in better loan conditions and allow the borrower to access larger amount of funds than it would otherwise have access to if no guarantees were provided. As such, the effect of guarantees may be reflected in the reduced interest rate on borrowings and increased borrowing capacity.[4]

In its guidance, the OECD elaborates on the accurate delineation of a financial guarantee transaction and on the determination of the arm's length price of such financial guarantee. The guidance on the delineation of the actual transaction includes a discussion about the economic benefits resulting from the guaranteed debt for a borrower such as a reduction in cost of borrowing reflected in a lower interest rate as well as access to a larger amount of funds. In case of increased borrowing capacity as a result of the provided guarantee, the OECD Guidance suggests considering the additionally borrowed funds as 'a loan to the guarantor followed by an equity contribution by the guarantor to the borrower'.[5] The OECD thus recommends to re-characterise the additional funds that were provided by the lender to the borrower

1. OECD, *Transfer Pricing Guidance on Financial Transactions: Inclusive Framework on BEPS Actions 4, 8-10* (Paris: OECD, 2020), https://www.oecd.org/tax/beps/transfer-pricing-guidance-on-financial-transactions-inclusive-framework-on-beps-actions-4-8-10.pdf [OECD, *OECD Guidance*].
2. OECD, *OECD Transfer Pricing Guidelines for Multinational Enterprises and Tax Administrations 2022* (Paris: OECD, 2022), https://read.oecd-ilibrary.org/taxation/oecd-transfer-pricing-guidelines-for-multinational-enterprises-and-tax-administrations-2022_0e655865-en#page1 [OECD, *Transfer Pricing Guidelines 2022*], Chapter X.
3. *Ibid.*, para. 10.155.
4. *Ibid.*, para. 10.161.
5. *Ibid.*

because of the existing guarantee as a loan to the guarantor and not as an increased loan amount to the borrower.

The guidance further explains how the group membership can determine the arm's length price for financial guarantees by stating that no remuneration should be expected in case of passive association, also referred to in the guidance as 'implicit support'. Moreover, no remuneration may be required even if the guarantees are explicit, i.e., provided in the form of a binding legal agreement, in case the economic risk of the guarantor does not change significantly as a result of such guarantee. In order to accurately delineate the actual transaction, the financial capacity of the guarantor should be considered.[6] Following such delineation, where the guarantees are found to be appropriate, the OECD provides a number of pricing methods for such transactions. In case of other form of credit support such as a letter of comfort, which does not involve any explicit assumption of risk, the benefit should be attributable to the borrower's group membership and would be resulting from passive association with no remuneration required.[7] As is the case with any other intercompany transaction, the selection of the most appropriate transfer pricing method should be based on a functional analysis.

## 2 UN Guidance

The UN guidance on financial guarantees, which was published by the UN Committee of Experts on International Cooperation in Tax Matters ('the UN Tax Committee') as part of the third edition of the UN Practical Manual on Transfer Pricing for Developing Countries ('the UN Transfer Pricing Manual') in April 2021 ('the UN Guidance'),[8] supplements the OECD Guidance and provides the following classification of the explicit financial guarantees:

- downstream guarantees when a parent company issues a guarantee to external creditors for the benefit of one of its subsidiaries that are signing agreement with such external creditors;
- upstream guarantees when a group company issues a guarantee to external creditors for the benefit of its parent company that is signing agreement with such external creditors;
- cross guarantees when several group companies issue a guarantee to external creditors for each other benefit.[9]

6. *Ibid.*, para. 10.168.
7. *Ibid.*, para. 10.163.
8. *Transfer Pricing: The UN Practical Manual on Transfer Pricing*, UN Department of Economic and Social Affairs (6 November 2021), https://www.un.org/development/desa/financing/capacity-development/topics/transfer-pricing.
9. UN, *UN Guidance*, para. 9.13.1.2. In case of cross guarantees, the group companies would be considered as one single obligor, for example, in cash pooling. *See* Vikram Chand, *Transfer Pricing Aspects of Cash Pooling Arrangements in Light of the BEPS Action Plan*, 23 Int'l Transfer Pricing J. 1, 40 (2016) [Chand].

The UN Guidance follows the OECD Guidance by referring to such mechanisms of increasing the creditworthiness of the borrower as a letter of comfort (or intent) and keep-well agreements. Considering that no risk is transferred under such arrangements, they generally are not considered financial guarantees and should not be requiring arm's length remuneration.[10]

According to the UN Guidance, the economically relevant characteristics for the determination of the arm's length guarantee fees are the contractual terms, which should be supported by the conduct of the parties; the risk profile of the borrower, taking into account the impact of any implicit support; the risk profile and financial capacity of the guarantor; the characteristics of the financial guarantees, including the benefits they provide; the economic circumstances of the borrower and the guarantor and of the markets where they operate; the guarantor's and the borrower's business strategies.[11]

The factors that may be relevant for the determination of the arm's length guarantee fees may include the probability of the debtor's default, the guaranteed amount, and the cost of capital of the guarantor, considering that such capital would need to be treated as contingent liability in the event of the debtor's default, as well as the benefit to the borrower resulting from the received guarantees after the impact of implicit support is accounted for.[12]

## III DELINEATION OF ACTUAL TRANSACTION

The key considerations that should be taken into account for the accurate delineation of a financial guarantee transaction are the economic benefits arising from such guarantee for a borrower, the effect of group membership and the financial capacity of a guarantor.

### 1 Benefit for a Borrower

Based on the OECD Guidance, for the accurate delineation of a financial guarantee transaction, it is necessary to identify if any economic benefit is arising to the borrower beyond its passive association with an MNE group. In its guidance, the OECD refers to the passive association as implicit support, or incidental benefits resulting from a mere group affiliation, without any deliberate concerted actions of the members of an MNE group or performance of any services by such group members. Importantly, the term 'incidental' does not refer to the amount of such benefits, nor does it indicate that the benefits should be insignificant to be considered incidental. The incidental benefits do not need to be compensated or allocated within an MNE group.[13]

The OECD recognises that because of differences in local laws, such deliberate concerted action as, for example, an explicit guarantee, would constitute a transaction

10. UN, *UN Guidance,* para. 9.13.1.3.
11. *Ibid.*, para. 9.13.2.1.
12. *Ibid.*, para. 9.13.2.6.
13. OECD, *Transfer Pricing Guidelines 2022,* Chapter I, para. 1.178.

in some jurisdictions, whereas in other jurisdictions it may not be the case. However, it is generally accepted that if through deliberate concerted actions an MNE group company performs functions, uses assets and assumes risks for the benefit of one or more group members, there is a need for the arm's length remuneration of such actions.[14] The determination of whether the benefit from group synergies (or, in certain cases, not benefit but burden[15]) arises due to such deliberate concerted group actions, can be performed through a robust functional analysis as well as comparability analysis.[16]

No guarantee fees should be payable by a borrower unless there is an explicit guarantee it has received from a guarantor. In case the guarantor has a lower credit rating than the borrower, but the guarantee effectively allows the lender to access wider recourse, i.e., the lender's legal right to collect funds in case of the borrower's default, such guarantee would be justifiable from an arm's length perspective as it can also result in a benefit to the borrower in the form of a lower interest rate.

## 2 Effect of Group Membership

The effect of group membership in the context of identifying and pricing of intercompany services was addressed by the OECD well before it issued its 2020 guidance on financial guarantees. Already in its Transfer Pricing Guidelines 2017, the OECD stated that 'no service would be received where an associated enterprise by reason of its affiliation alone has a credit rating higher than it would if it were unaffiliated'.[17] This statement essentially disregards any intercompany charge in case it is in place because of the improved credit rating as a result of implicit support. However, the OECD recognises that 'an intra-group service would usually exist where the higher credit rating was due to a guarantee by another group member, or where the enterprise benefitted from deliberate concerted actions such as global marketing and public relations campaigns'.[18] As such, passive association that does not require any compensation should be distinguished from active promotion that increases the profit potential of a particular group entity and should, therefore, be compensated.[19]

The notion of implicit support and whether it should be considered when establishing a standalone credit rating of an MNE group company has been the cause of controversy in transfer pricing practice for decades. In the landmark transfer pricing

14. *Ibid.*, para. 1.179, footnote 3.
15. In certain cases, the group synergies created through such deliberate concerted actions may result in burden rather than benefit; for example, certain operations of an MNE group may lead to administrative barriers or inefficiencies within its businesses that are not faced by smaller companies. *See* OECD, *Transfer Pricing Guidelines 2022,* Chapter I, para. 1.178.
16. OECD, *Transfer Pricing Guidelines 2022,* Chapter I, para. 1.179.
17. OECD, *OECD Transfer Pricing Guidelines for Multinational Enterprises and Tax Administrations 2017* (Paris: OECD, 2017), https://www.oecd-ilibrary.org/taxation/oecd-transfer-pricing-guidelines-for-multinational-enterprises-and-tax-administrations-2017_tpg-2017-en [OECD, *Transfer Pricing Guidelines 2017*], Chapter VII, para. 7.13. *See also* OECD, *Transfer Pricing Guidelines 2022,* Chapter VII, para. 7.13.
18. OECD, *Transfer Pricing Guidelines 2022,* Chapter VII, para. 7.13.
19. *Ibid.*

case of General Electric Capital Canada Inc. ('GE Canada'),[20] the Canadian court has ruled on the issue of implicit support by confirming that such support should indeed be an indispensable part of the transfer pricing analysis.[21] The OECD Guidance as well as the UN Guidance follow the court's argumentation that implicit support should not be considered as such that is in contradiction with the arm's length principle. In particular, according to the UN Guidance, '[w]hen applying the arm's length principle, the starting point is that the related parties involved in the financial transaction should be treated as if they were entities independent of each other, but otherwise in the same circumstances. However, "the same circumstances" must include any incidental benefits and group synergies that derive from the fact that the related entities belong to an MNE. This would include the impact of any implicit support (sometimes also referred to as "passive association", "parental support", or "group support")'.[22]

By referring to 'parental support' as a synonym for passive association, the UN Guidance indicates that implicit support can be provided only top down, which is from the parent company of an MNE group to its subsidiary and thus focuses primarily on the downstream guarantees.[23] Credit ratings applied by independent credit rating agencies such as Standard & Poor's, Moody's and Fitch are usually available only for

20. *See General Electric Capital Canada Inc. v. The Queen*, 2009 TCC 563, aff'd 2010 FCA 344 (Canada). The GE Canada transfer pricing case on financial guarantees concerns an explicit financial guarantee paid by GE Canada, a Canadian commercial lending company, to its US parent. The Canadian tax authorities disallowed the deduction of the guarantee fee on the grounds that the existence of explicit guarantee cannot be justified as even without such extra guarantee the US parent would not allow GE Canada as its core subsidiary to default on its external debts. The tax authorities considered the likelihood of the US parent stepping in and supporting its subsidiary in the event of default to be high enough to assume that due to such implicit support the subsidiary should have the same credit rating as its US parent (i.e., AAA on the Standard & Poor's scale) and, therefore, the explicit guarantee would be of no value. The Court agreed with the tax authorities' position that implicit support should be taken into account when assessing the credit rating of GE Canada as well as the arm's length nature of the guarantee fee. However, the Court did not agree with the tax authorities' assessment that implicit support would be enough for the subsidiary to have the AAA rating of the parent; the Court held that in addition to implicit support the explicit guarantee would be necessary. As for the estimation of the arm's length fee for such explicit guarantee, the Court accepted the tax authorities' yield approach under which the credit ratings of GE Canada with and without the explicit guarantee were set, but instead of the tax authorities' analysis the Court preferred the credit rating analysis of one of the expert witnesses. Considering that the interest cost saving between guaranteed and unguaranteed debt estimated based on such analysis was higher than the 1% guarantee fee paid by GE Canada to its US parent, the Court concluded that the 1% fee of GE Canada was equal or below an arm's length price for financial guarantee and is therefore acceptable. The Canadian Federal Court of Appeal upheld the decision of the Court of first instance and confirmed that the yield approach is an acceptable method of estimating the arm's length price for financial guarantees.
21. *See* Wilkie, *Reflecting on the 'Arm's Length Principle': What Is the 'Principle'? Where Next?*, 137-156, 146 in: Schön & Konrad (eds), *Fundamentals of International Transfer Pricing in Law and Economics* (2012). ('Despite the deference paid to "arm's lengthedness" as a controlling limit on profit distortions, the application of the arm's length principle does not require that the "family pedigree" of a tested party be ignored in establishing the basis on which its profitability would be evaluated according to the arm's length principle and … that the so-called comparable circumstances be precisely the same'.)
22. UN, *UN Guidance*, para. 9.8.6.
23. *Ibid. See also* Birhanu T. Daba, *OECD – Valuation of Implicit Support from a Transfer Pricing Perspective*, 28 Int'l Transfer Pricing J. 2, 138 (2021) [Daba].

the parent company.[24] In case no credit rating is available for an MNE group company other than the parent, such approaches as the estimation of the parent company's credit risk and its adjustment to approximate the borrower's credit risk as well as the establishment of the borrower's credit risk by applying various credit scoring tools may be considered.[25] At the same time, the OECD Guidance does not seem to differentiate between the downstream and upstream guarantees by stating that the most common guarantees in transfer pricing practice are those in which a guarantor (with no specification of whether it is a parent company or a subsidiary) provides a guarantee on a loan taken out by its affiliated company from a third-party lender.[26]

As for the cross guarantees, both OECD and UN guidance defines them as a guarantee issued by two or more entities of an MNE group to external creditors for each other's obligations. The OECD Guidance further elaborates on the lender's and borrower's perspective of this type of guarantee. From the lender's perspective, such guarantee allows the lender to have access to the assets of guarantors in the event of a default by a guaranteed borrower. From the borrower's perspective, the cross-guarantees may be difficult to evaluate in case of a large number of guarantees where each party providing a guarantee may at the same time be guaranteed by the party receiving such guarantee. Considering that it may be impossible to determine the effect of cross-guarantees where the same risk is subject to multiple guarantees, the OECD Guidance suggests treating this arrangement as such that does not enhance the creditworthiness of an MNE group company beyond the level of passive association. The outcome of such treatment is that any support from an MNE group company in the event of default of the borrower should be considered a capital contribution.[27]

## 3 Financial Capacity of a Guarantor

The guarantor's capacity to step in and support the borrower in the event of the latter's default is another key consideration that should be evaluated as part of the accurate delineation of a financial guarantee transaction. For such evaluation, the guarantor's and borrower's credit rating should be established by taking into account the effect of implicit support.[28] If an MNE group company has a publicly available credit rating published by an independent credit rating agency, such rating can also be used in the transfer pricing analysis. However, in practice, public credit ratings are usually available for the group as a whole rather than for its companies on a standalone basis. If this is the case, the publicly available financial tools or the methodologies of independent credit rating agencies may be used to approximate the credit rating of a particular group company.[29]

24. UN, *UN Guidance*, para. 9.8.7. *See also* GEORG DETTMANN, GARY LAMBERT & AMANDA PLETZ, *Policy Forum: Implicit Support and Its Implications on Guarantee Fee Pricing: Fact or Fiction*, 47 Intertax 12, 1077 (2019) [DETTMANN, LAMBERT & PLETZ].
25. UN, *UN Guidance*, para. 9.8.7.
26. OECD, *Transfer Pricing Guidelines 2022*, Chapter X, para. 10.155.
27. *Ibid.*, para. 10.165.
28. *Ibid.*, para. 10.167.
29. *Ibid.*, para. 10.71.

For the evaluation of the credit rating of an MNE group company, the quantitative analysis of historic and forecasted company performance as well as the qualitative analysis of such characteristics as the management capabilities of the company's executives, industry-specific characteristics and the company's market share in its industry, would need to be applied.[30] The financial capacity of an MNE group company to meet its obligations as a guarantor in the event of the default of a borrower will also depend on how closely the business of the borrower correlates with that of the guarantor. If both operate in the same or similar markets, then any market event that may potentially lead to the default of the borrower can also impact the financial capacity of the guarantor to meet its obligations. In such cases, the risk of double default, i.e., the risk that in the event of default, both the borrower and the guarantor would default, should be considered when pricing the guarantee. The higher the risk of double default, the lower the value of the guarantee.[31]

## 4 Appropriateness of a Guarantee Fee

Economically a guarantee fee can be justified from the perspective of the put option theory. If a loan is supported by a warranty, then a lender has effectively purchased 'a put option on the cash flows of the outstanding debt'.[32] The owner of a put option has the right, but not the obligation, to sell the underlying (i.e., the cash flows of the guaranteed loan) at a set price within a specified time. As such, the lender can recover the collateral (i.e., the assets from the guarantor) in the event of default by the borrower. This leads to the conclusion that the guarantee has a positive value before the loan expires, which justifies the guarantor's claims for certain compensation for the issuance of the guarantee, i.e., a guarantee fee, from an economic point of view.[33]

From a transfer pricing perspective, the justification of a guarantee fee would require some additional considerations in order to account for implicit support. In particular, it may be reasonable to charge a guarantee fee if there is a binding obligation of the guarantor to step in and support its group company in the circumstances defined in the financial guarantee agreement, or when the borrower achieves better conditions such as a lower interest rate as a result of the provided explicit guarantee, or when a third-party borrower would be willing to pay for such guarantee in the similar situation.[34] If, however, a financial guarantee does not improve the creditworthiness of the guaranteed entity beyond its creditworthiness as a group entity, or it is a function performed by the parent company in its own interest instead of supporting the borrowing entity (when such parent company essentially is the borrower), or it has been requested by the creditor with the only aim to ensure that the parent company

30. *Ibid.*, para. 10.73.
31. *See* Fabio Pizzutilo & Francesco Calò, *Loan Guarantees: An Option Pricing Theory Perspective*, 5 Intl J. of Econ. and Financial Issues (IJEF) 4, 907 (2015) [Pizzutilo & Calò].
32. *Ibid.*, at 906.
33. *Ibid.*
34. UN, *UN Guidance*, para. 9.13.2.4.

does nor divert the funds of the borrower, then in such cases charging a guarantee fee would be considered inappropriate.[35]

To illustrate how the concept of implicit support applies in the transfer pricing analysis, the OECD describes the following situation. The parent company of an MNE group has a higher rating of AAA than other company of the same MNE group with BBB rating on a standalone basis. Such other affiliated company needs to borrow a certain amount of funds from a third-party lender. As a result of the accurate delineation of the actual transaction, it was identified that due to the group membership (i.e., implicit support), the credit rating of the affiliated company may rise from BBB to A. The credit rating of such company may rise even further, to the level of the parent's rating of AAA, if the parent company provides explicit guarantees to its affiliate. It is assumed in the guidance that the information on interest rates charged by independent lenders based on the credit rating of borrowers is available and that the interest rates for A and AAA credit ratings are 8 % and 6 %, respectively, giving a 200 basis points spread on interest. If in such situation the parent company charges its affiliate a fee of 3 % for the provision of guarantees, such charge would be disregarded by tax authorities as a third-party borrower would not be willing to pay such high price for a guarantee. This is because the borrower would be better off without explicit guarantees of the parent company as it would pay 8 % interest with A rating (which is its rating without explicit guarantee but taking into account implicit support) instead of 6 % interest plus 3 % guarantee fees with AAA rating (which is its rating with explicit guarantee).

Building upon the example of implicit support described above, the OECD Guidance also describes the situation in which the application of an explicit guarantee and thus of a guarantee fee would be appropriate. It is assumed that the information about the level of guarantee fees in a third-party arrangement is available and that such fees are in the range of 1 % to 1.5 %. Based on the accurate delineation of the actual transaction, it has been identified that the increase in the credit rating of the affiliated company from A (if the group membership is taken into account) to the level of the parent's rating of AAA is due to a deliberate concerted group action, i.e., provision of explicit guarantees. Considering that the interest rates charged by independent lenders are 6 % and 8 % for rating A and AAA, respectively, an independent borrower would be willing to pay a guarantee fee of up to 1.5 % to the parent company and such charge would be justifiable from an arm's length perspective. This is because the borrower would pay 6 % interest plus a 1.5 % guarantee fee with AAA rating with explicit guarantee, which is lower than the 8 % interest it would be paying with a lower credit rating of A if no explicit guarantee were provided.

## IV PRICING OF GUARANTEES

The OECD Guidance recommends five approaches for calculating the arm's length guarantee fees with certain benchmarking analyses required in each particular case. This includes the comparable uncontrolled price (CUP) method, the yield approach,

35. *Ibid.*, para. 9.13.2.5.

the cost approach, the valuation of expected loss method and the capital support method. The first three approaches are also discussed in the UN Guidance.

## 1 CUP Method

The CUP method can be applied when independent guarantors provide guarantees for comparable loans to other borrowers or where the same borrower has comparable loans for which independent guarantees are provided.[36] Both external and internal comparables can be used to establish the arm's length price of guarantees.

To establish the comparability of controlled and uncontrolled transactions, the OECD Guidance suggests considering such comparability factors as the risk profile of the borrower, terms and conditions of the guarantee and of the underlying loan, credit rating differential between guarantor and guaranteed party, market conditions, and other relevant factors.[37] However, it is difficult to apply the CUP method as the publicly available information about the guarantees of bank loans is unlikely to be found between unrelated parties. The OECD in its guidance also emphasises that the charges of independent guarantors may partly reflect costs incurred in the process of raising capital and in satisfying the regulatory requirements, whereas such costs may not be relevant for associated companies.[38]

For example, the internal CUP method can be applied if a company of an MNE group receives a financial guarantee from its affiliated company for a loan it obtained from a third-party lender and at the same time such company receives a guarantee on another loan from a third-party insurance company. Provided the characteristics of the second loan are similar to the first one, the borrowing company and its affiliated company guaranteeing the first loan should be able to estimate the guarantee fees for such loan based on the premium applied by the insurance company to the second loan. This would be possible in case the intercompany financial guarantee and the third-party insurance are comparable considering all economically relevant characteristics.[39] The external CUP method would be reliable in establishing the arm's length price of the financial guarantees between two related companies only if the information about the terms and conditions applied between unrelated parties with respect to comparable financial guarantees is available.[40]

## 2 Yield Approach

Under the yield approach, a spread is calculated between the interest rate that would have been payable by the borrower without the guarantee (but considering implicit support as a result of the group membership) and the interest rate payable with the

36. OECD, *Transfer Pricing Guidelines 2022*, Chapter X, para. 10.170.
37. *Ibid.*, para. 10.171.
38. *Ibid.*, para. 10.173.
39. UN, *UN Guidance*, para. 9.13.2.11, Example 13.
40. *Ibid.*, para. 9.13.2.12, Example 14.

guarantee.[41] The OECD Guidance suggests calculating the benefit of implicit support as the difference between the terms available to the borrowing entity based on its credit rating as a member of the group and its standalone rating that would be available if it were an independent entity. No adjustments would usually be required if the borrower has its own credit rating as in such case the effect of implicit support would already be considered in its rating.[42] As a result of such analysis, a maximum fee expected from a borrower for the obtained guarantee is calculated, which represents the maximum price that the borrower would be willing to pay. However, such maximum fee does not necessarily reflect a bargain made between the borrower and the guarantor at arm's length.[43]

For example, an MNE group company requests a five-year loan from a third-party lender. Another company of the same MNE group provides a financial guarantee to the borrowing company for this loan. The interest charged by the third-party lender on such loan is 2%. The credit rating of the guarantor is A, whereas the credit rating of the borrower considering the effect of implicit support is BBB. Based on the publicly available information, a comparable loan between two independent parties would bear interest of 3.25%. Based on the yield approach, the interest benefit received by the borrower as a result of the guarantees provided by its affiliated company, which is represented by the reduced interest rate charged by the third-party lender based on the provided guarantee, is 1.25% (i.e., 3.25%-2%). As such, 1.25% is the maximum guarantee fee that the guarantor may charge to the borrower for the provided guarantee. This amount can be reduced by considering how the benefit derived from the guarantee should be split between the guarantor and the borrower. The amount that should be split between the two can be identified based on the cost approach, however, there is no requirement to use both cost and yield approaches to determine an arm's length guarantee fee.[44]

## 3 Cost Approach

The cost could be determined in the following two ways:

(i) by quantifying additional risk for the guarantor and estimating the value of its expected loss in case of the borrower's default; or
(ii) by estimating the capital required to cover the risks assumed by the guarantor under the guarantee agreement.

The required capital can be calculated by using various pricing models where the guarantees are compared to certain financial instruments. For example, the value of the guarantee can be established as a proxy of credit default swap fees, where the

41. OECD, *Transfer Pricing Guidelines 2022*, Chapter X, para. 10.174.
42. *Ibid.*, para. 10.176.
43. *Ibid.*, para. 10.177. The yield approach was considered by the Court in the GE Canada transfer pricing case as being appropriate to determine the arm's length fee for explicit guarantees. *See General Electric Capital Canada Inc. v. The Queen*, 2009 TCC 563, aff'd 2010 FCA 344 (Canada).
44. UN, *UN Guidance*, para. 9.13.2.13, Example 15.

identification of the default event (e.g., bankruptcy) is the key consideration in the comparability analysis. Another instrument that can be used in pricing of financial guarantees is a contingent put option, which is the price that the guaranteed entity would need to pay for a hypothetical right to sell the guaranteed instrument to the guarantor at a certain price (i.e., face value) and under certain circumstances (i.e., credit event). The guarantee fees can also be estimated as the cost of additional equity capital that the guaranteed entity would hypothetically need in order to achieve the same level of creditworthiness as it has with the guarantee. The insurance premiums can also be considered in pricing the guarantees.[45]

The evaluation of the cost method under any financial model defines the minimum guarantee fee that a guarantor would expect to receive when providing a guarantee. The cost approach, as well as the yield approach, does not necessarily reflect the outcome of a bargain made at arm's length. Both borrower's and lender's perspectives, taking into account the options realistically available, should be considered in order to calculate the arm's length guarantee fee.[46]

For example, an MNE group company provides a financial guarantee to its affiliated company. The latter requests a 5-year loan from a third-party lender. The expected 5-year probability of default rate is 1.44% and its expected recovery rate, considering its fixed assets and securities, is 40%. Under the cost approach, the additional risk of the guarantor is estimated as the value of the expected loss that such guarantor may incur on the provided guarantee in the event of the borrower's default. Based on the available data, the expected cost of providing the guarantee is 0.86% (i.e., 1.44% x (1-40%)). As such, 0.86% would be the minimum guarantee fee that the guarantor may charge to the borrower for the provided guarantee. This fee can be increased by taking into account how the benefit derived from the guarantee should be split between the guarantor and the borrower. The amount that should be split between the two can be identified based on the yield approach, however, there is no requirement to use both cost and yield approaches to determine an arm's length guarantee fee.[47]

## 4 Other Pricing Methods

One of the other two methods suggested by the OECD for guarantee pricing (and which are not included in the UN Guidance) is the valuation of expected loss method.[48] Under this method, the value of guarantees is estimated based on the probability of default with subsequent adjustments to account for the expected recovery rate in the event of default. The nominal guaranteed amount would then need to be increased by the result

45. *Ibid.*, para. 9.13.2.9.
46. OECD, *Transfer Pricing Guidelines 2022*, Chapter X, paras 10.178-180.
47. UN, *UN Guidance*, para. 9.13.2.14, Example 16.
48. OECD, *Transfer Pricing Guidelines 2022*, Chapter X, para. 10.181.

of such calculation to establish the cost of providing the guarantees. The OECD Guidance suggests pricing the guarantee based on an expected return on such amount using commercial pricing models such as, for example, the Capital Asset Pricing Model (CAPM).

Another method described in the OECD Guidelines as suitable for the guarantee pricing is the capital support method.[49] The OECD suggests applying this method in the cases when the difference between the risk profiles of the guarantor and the borrower could be reduced by providing more capital to the borrower. For the application of this method, it is necessary to determine the credit rating of the borrower without any guarantee but considering its group membership (i.e., implicit support). The amount of additional notional capital would then need to be identified to increase the borrower's credit rating to the guarantor's level. The return on such additional capital would be the basis for the guarantee fee. Such expected return should appropriately reflect only the results of the guarantee provision instead of the overall activities of the guarantor.

## V CONCLUDING REMARKS

Financial guarantees are quite common in the intra-group setting; however, the necessity to recognise a financial guarantee as a separate transaction with the appropriate arm's length considerations for its pricing is often overlooked or purposively neglected by many multinational companies. This can partly be explained by the complexity of financial transactions as well as by inconsistency in how they have been treated by tax authorities. As such, an arm's length framework established by the OECD Guidance as well as the UN Guidance on financial transactions including financial guarantees is likely to bring more certainty for multinational companies in dealing with their financial affairs.

In particular, the guidance on financial guarantees is expected to resolve many controversial transfer pricing issues when it comes to implicit support. As stated in the guidance, implicit support (or passive association with an MNE group) may have significant impact on the creditworthiness of a borrower and should therefore be considered in an arm's length pricing of financial guarantees. Although the OECD's acknowledgement that the degree to which such implicit support should be taken into account in the transfer pricing analysis is a matter of judgement inevitably leaves some room for interpretation, it nevertheless is an important statement that multinational companies may now rely upon when defending their position if confronted by tax authorities.

As the countries continue updating their local transfer pricing rules on financial guarantees based on the guidance, it can reasonably be expected that this tendency would lead to more consistent treatment of such types of transactions in cross-border arrangements. This could be manifested by more precise rules on the accurate delineation of financial transactions and the pricing methodology and should thus

49. *Ibid.*, para. 10.182.

bring more certainty for multinational companies. At the same time, the new framework may carry some challenges for businesses as the companies would be required to justify their decision of either charging or not charging for financial guarantees by thoroughly documenting their analyses and arguments.

CHAPTER 25

# Accurate Delineation of Financial Guarantees

*Natassia Burkhalter-Martinez*[*]

## I INTRODUCTION

The topic of intra-group financial guarantees is of significant importance for multinational groups relying on external debt for their financing needs. The topic has also received increased attention from tax authorities around the world during the past few years. Although it is in some ways complex, especially from a transfer pricing perspective, the Organisation for Economic Co-operation and Development (OECD) was not particularly focused on it in the past. Moreover, due to the circumstances related to the COVID-19 pandemic and the economic downturn increasing multinational groups' need for financing through external debt, the attention paid to this topic is not expected to diminish. Despite this, as surprising as it may sound, before the Base Erosion and Profit Shifting (BEPS) project, only a few paragraphs of the OECD Transfer Pricing Guidelines for Multinational Enterprises and Tax Administrations[1] dealt with financial guarantees. Through a Discussion Draft, the OECD published technical guidance on intra-group financial transactions, including financial guarantees, for the first time in July 2018.[2] This Discussion Draft was part of the mandate of the BEPS Action 4 and Actions 8–10 and resulted in a report published by the OECD on 11

* The views and opinions set forth herein are the personal views or opinions of the authors; they do not necessarily reflect the views or opinions of the organisation with which the authors are associated.

1. OECD, Transfer Pricing Guidelines for Multinational Enterprises and Tax Administrations (*OECD Guidelines*).
2. OECD, Discussion draft BEPS Actions 8–10 – Financial Transactions (OECD July 2018).

February 2020.[3] The guidance contained in the report is now included in the 2022 OECD Guidelines as Chapter X.[4]

## II FINANCIAL AND PERFORMANCE GUARANTEES

Financial guarantees secure a payment by the borrower in respect of a financial obligation. More specifically, financial guarantees mean the guarantor assumes responsibility for a debt should the borrower be unable to repay it.

Non-financial guarantees provide security for non-financial obligations such as the delivery of goods or the completion of a project.[5] Performance guarantees are typical non-financial guarantees whereby the guarantor assumes liability in instances in which the contractor does not fulfil the agreed obligations. Therefore, the underlying obligation of such guarantees is not a payment but a performance from the guarantor. In an intra-group context, the pricing of such guarantees is quite complex. Performance guarantees as non-financial guarantees are beyond the scope of this chapter and will not be addressed.[6]

## III ACCURATE DELINEATION

### 1 General Concept

The concept of 'accurate delineation' is a recent one that was officially introduced in the 2017 OECD Guidelines under Chapter I Section D as a result of the Final Report on BEPS Actions 8–10.[7]

The notion of 'accurate delineation' has its origins in the initial mandate given by the OECD's BEPS Action Plan to 'clarify the circumstances in which transactions can be re-characterised'.[8] The term 're-characterisation' used in the 2010 OECD Guidelines has been replaced with the term 'non-recognition' even though it has the same

3. OECD, Transfer Pricing Guidance on Financial Transactions: Inclusive Framework on BEPS Action 4, 8-10 (OECD February 2020).
4. The UN TP Manual also includes a chapter dealing with financial guarantee (Chapter B.9.4). However, because this chapter is focusing on the OECD Guidelines it will not systematically rely on the UN TP Manual.
5. Gaurav Deshpande, *The Transfer Pricing Aspects of Cross-Border Performance Guarantees*, Bulletin for International Taxation (2017) 358; Raffaele Iervolino & Serena Picariello, *Performance Guarantee: How to Avoid Pitfalls and Overcome Hindrances in a Transfer Pricing Analysis*, International Transfer Pricing Journal, 85(2022).
6. For more details on performance guarantees, *see* Deshpande, *supra* n. 5, at 358; Iervolino & Picariello, *supra* n. 5, at 85.
7. The concept remained unchanged in the latest version of the OECD Guidelines published in 2022, *see* OECD Guidelines 2022, Chapter I, section D.
8. OECD, Action Plan on Base Erosion and Profit Shifting (OECD 2013) 20-21.

meaning according to the OECD.[9] The intricacies of these different concepts will be discussed further.

Any transfer pricing analysis, including in the context of intra-group financing transactions, should start with the accurate delineation of the transaction, which is an increasingly important stage for tax authorities and multinational enterprises but also a complex process going beyond the determination of the nature and purpose of a transaction.[10]

The accurate delineation process is a preliminary step of the comparability analysis on which the arm's length principle is based. Indeed, the comparability analysis starts with the identification of the commercial or financial relationships between the associated enterprises and the conditions and economic circumstances attached to these relationships.[11] By making this assessment, the controlled transaction should be accurately delineated and once done can be compared to similar transactions taking place between independent entities. This is due to the fiction imposed by the arm's length principle, where the transaction taking place between related parties is compared to the conditions that independent entities would have concluded for a transaction having the same factual basis.[12]

The accurate delineation of a transaction is thus broader than the analysis of the contractual agreements.[13] It also has to encompass the understanding of the economic circumstances and the market in which the parties are interacting, their business strategies and the functions performed by each of the parties to the transaction, taking into account assets used and risks assumed and the characteristics of property transferred or service provided.[14] Analysis of all of those characteristics of the transaction is even more important when they are actually inconsistent with the written agreements concluded between the related parties.[15] Thus, there is a particular emphasis on the conduct of the parties in the accurate delineation process gives.[16] It is a fact analysis requiring various qualitative and quantitative considerations.[17] Because

9. OECD, Discussion Draft on Revisions to Chapter I of the Transfer Pricing Guidelines (OECD 2014), para. 83.
10. Antonio Russo & Andre Dekker, *Accurate Delineation of Financial Intra-Group Transactions in Transfer Pricing & Intra-Group Financing*, 27-29 (IBFD 2021).
11. OECD Guidelines 2022, para. 1.33.
12. Aitor Navarro, *Transactional Adjustments in Transfer Pricing*, 119 (IBFD Doctoral Series 2018); Gabriela Capristano Cardoso & Raffaele Petruzzi, *Simplifying the Transfer Pricing Analysis: An Illusory Chimaera or a Realistic Ambition?*, World Tax J. 11, 531, 534 (2019), Journal Articles & Papers IBFD.
13. OECD Guidelines 2022, para. 1.42.
14. *Ibid.*, para. 1.36.
15. *Ibid.*, para. 1.45.
16. Russo & Dekker, *supra* n. 10, at 27; Merja Raunio & Matti Urpilainen, Case SAC 2020:35 – Supreme Administrative Court Reasserts the Prohibition to Recharacterise Transactions, Now in a Case that Deals with Group Internal Financing, Intl. Transfer Pricing J., 379, 382 (2020), Journal Articles & Papers IBFD; Capristano Cardoso/Petruzzi, *supra* n. 12, at 534. The emphasis on the conduct of the parties is actually not recent and was already mentioned in the first OECD Guidelines published in 1995 (*see* OECD Guidelines 1995, para. 1.28), for more details *see* Vikram Chand & Giovanni Lembo, Intangible-related Profit Allocation within MNEs based on Key DEMPE Functions: Selected Issues and Interaction with Pillar One and Pillar Two of the Digital Debate, 6 International Tax Studies, 2, 9-16 (2020).
17. Capristano Cardoso & Petruzzi, *supra* n. 13, at 535.

of that, some authors have wondered whether simplifying this stage of the transfer pricing analysis would be possible.[18] Given the particularities of each type of transaction or taxpayer, a thorough analysis has to be performed to deal with complexities of this process.[19] In concluding that it was not possible to simplify the accurate delineation process, it has been suggested that a step-by-step approach could be proposed by the OECD.[20]

Coming back to the initial comment made on the concept of re-characterisation and the new concept of accurate delineation, both concepts share the basic principle of substance over form although they differ in their details.[21] Under the 2010 OECD Guidelines, it was specified that a tax administration would be able to disregard a transaction if its economic substance would differ from its form or if the transaction would lack commercial rationality by differing from transactions that would have been adopted in similar circumstances by unrelated parties.[22] Nowadays, accurate delineation still relativises the importance of the contract by including its analysis in a broader process and by focusing on the conduct of the parties where the substance should be found but without ignoring the form.[23] The suggestion of the 2010 OECD Guidelines that a transaction should be re-characterised when it lacks economic substance has been removed and has been integrated into the concept of accurate delineation.[24] The form of the transaction is only disregarded, or to use 2017 OECD terminology, 'non-recognised' when the transaction lacks commercial rationality.[25] Thus, the accurate delineation process is a first step before the potential non-recognition of a transaction. However, it is unclear how to stick to the form when the conduct of the parties differs so substantially from the contract that it is necessary to rework the functions, assets and risks.[26] This is probably why some authors consider that the accurate delineation process introduced in 2017 is an important change of the OECD Guidelines, giving more power to tax administrations by going further than the re-characterisation process that was more limited to exceptional cases under the 2010 OECD Guidelines, even though Chapter I of the OECD Guidelines is inspired by the content of Chapter IX of the 2010 OECD Guidelines.[27]

18. *Ibid.*
19. *Ibid.*
20. *Ibid.*
21. Raunio & Urpilainen, *supra* n. 16, at 382; Graeme Cooper & Richard Vann, *Transfer Pricing Money bis* in *Thinker, Teacher, Traveller – Reimagining International Tax*, Chapter 12, 7, online book (IBFD 2021).
22. OECD Guidelines 2010, para. 1.65.
23. Porus F. Kaka, Transfer Pricing: History, Lessons and Experiences as a Litigator in Thinker, Teacher, Traveller – Reimagining international tax, Chapter 19, 3, online book (IBFD 2021).
24. OECD Guidelines 2010, para. 1.65; Chand & Lembo, *supra* n. 16, at 13.
25. OECD Guidelines 2022, para. 1.142.
26. Kaka, *supra* n. 23, at 3.
27. Raunio & Urpilainen, *supra* n. 16, at 382; Adolfo J. Martin Jimenez, *Value Creation: A Guiding Light for the Interpretation of Tax Treaties?*, Bull. Intl. Taxn. 197, 208 (2020); for a contrary view *see* Adnand Sulejmani, *Pricing Intercompany Financial Transactions: Loans, Guarantees and Cash-Pooling Arrangements*, Intl. Transfer Pricing J., 388, 393 (2019). For more details on the relation between the OECD Guidelines 2017 (Chapter I) and the OECD Guidelines (Chapter IX), *see* Chand & Lembo, *supra* n. 16, at 2.

## 2 Accurate Delineation of Financial Transactions

As with any other intra-group transaction, general considerations that can be found in Chapter I section D of the OECD Guidelines regarding accurate delineation also apply to intra-group financial transactions. This is now clearly stated by the OECD in Chapter X dealing with financial transactions.[28]

Thus, as stated above, the economically relevant characteristics have to be determined by analysing the industry sector, the terms and conditions of the contract, the functions performed, the assets used and the risks assumed, the characteristics of the financial instruments, the economic circumstances and the market in which the parties operate and as well the business strategies.[29] All these economically relevant characteristics are described generally by the OECD in Chapter X, sometimes through examples illustrating issues that can specifically arise in the field of financial transactions.

In addition, specific factors such as the effect of government regulations or the availability of financial resources in a given industry are also to be taken into account when delineating an intragroup financial transaction.[30] Depending on the sector in which the entity is operating, the volume and the type of financing may vary or the commercial needs may require different levels of short-term cash balances. Regulations may impose some constraints that also have to be taken into consideration.[31]

As stated in Chapter I, the options realistically available to the parties have to be considered before concluding any intragroup financial transaction, as independent entities will only enter into the transaction if they see no other better opportunity to meet their commercial needs.[32] In that context, a two-sided analysis is to be performed.[33]

Finally, the accurate delineation process in relation to intragroup financial transactions is significant when it deals with the balance of debt and equity funding. More specifically, the question of whether a loan should be re-characterised partially or totally into equity and under which circumstances is a core topic of intragroup financial transactions and is specifically addressed by the OECD.[34] A comprehensive description and analysis of the issue can be found in Chapter 10. It is noteworthy that the OECD acknowledges that other approaches may be taken in domestic legislation (e.g., thin capitalisation rules) to address capital structure and interest deductibility.[35]

28. OECD Guidelines 2022, para. 10.14.
29. *Ibid.*, para. 10.17.
30. *Ibid.*, para. 10.15.
31. *Ibid.*
32. *Ibid.*, para. 10.19.
33. *Ibid.*
34. *Ibid.*, paras 10.4-10.13.
35. *Ibid.*, para. 10.8.

## IV DELINEATION OF FINANCIAL GUARANTEES: KEY FACTORS

### 1 Introductory Comments

All the general comments that have been made so far on the delineation of an intragroup transaction are also applicable to intragroup financial guarantees. The terms and conditions of the guarantee are the starting point for delineating the transaction. Based on the contract, the guarantor is legally committed in case of default of the borrower, thus the contract will determine the risks assumed by the guarantor. In addition, the facts and circumstances analysis will enable determination of whether the commitment is legally binding or a 'soft' commitment (section 2). The accurate delineation process then requires consideration of whether the guarantee is providing an economic benefit (section 3) going beyond the benefit derived from the passive association (section 5) and will therefore have to be analysed considering the credit ratings of the parties involved (section 4).

### 2 Legally Binding Agreement

Within a group, financial support may take various forms. The most common ones are letters of comfort, keep-well agreements and formal guarantees.[36]

Letters of comfort can be issued by different entities of a group, typically by the parent company or a regional holding company, and take the form of a communication of the willingness of an entity to support a subsidiary or to refrain from undertaking actions that would affect the financial situation of a subsidiary.[37]

Keep-well agreements are declarations issued by parent companies stating that they will provide additional capital to their subsidiaries to avoid any default situation.[38]

The particularity of these tools in comparison to a formal guarantee agreement, which is legally binding, is their degree of legal enforceability. They are expressing a willingness that is not legally binding. They do not provide the same degree of certainty to the lender.[39] Thus, they have to be seen as more of a moral commitment. This has also been confirmed by the OECD stating that non-legally binding commitments such as comfort letters/letters of intent, keep-well agreements or other similar commitments lack legal enforceability and should not be viewed as financial guarantees (the OECD uses the term 'explicit guarantee').[40]

---

36. Anuschka J. Bakker, *Transfer Pricing and Intra-Group Financing: Low-Hanging Fruit?*, 15(2) Derivs & Fin. Instruments 27, 32 (2013).
37. Sunny Kishore Bilaney, Is a Letter of Comfort a Chargeable Intra-Group Service?, Intl. Transfer Pricing J. 200, 200 (2017); Omar Moerer, Georgi Mavrodiev & Sharvari Kale, *Common Types of Intragroup Financing Arrangements* in Transfer Pricing & Intra-Group Financing, 136 (IBFD 2021).
38. Moerer, Mavrodiev & Kale, *supra* n. 37, at 136.
39. *Ibid.*
40. OECD Guidelines 2022, para. 10.163.

The name given to the commitment is a first indication for determining its degree of legal enforceability. However, the facts and circumstances analysis should prevail over the name in the evaluation. Thus, the name and the content of the commitment have to be analysed but so does the conduct of the parties. Any language construed as any kind of promise can give an indication of the degree of legal enforceability. Accordingly, the conduct of the parties should be in line with their intention. At the time when they are issuing a soft commitment (not legally binding) or a legally binding agreement, the parties should be aware, in the former case, that they do not have any binding obligations while in the latter, they are subject to binding obligations.[41] More specifically, through a legally binding guarantee, the guarantor will assume the risk of default of the borrower. Thus, if the borrower is not able to pay the principal and/or the interest or is not able to meet the terms of the loan agreement, the guarantee will be called upon. In such situations, the guarantor will have to make good the loss of the lender.[42] Based on the OECD Guidelines, a formal financial guarantee: '[...] is a legally binding commitment on the part of the guarantor to assume a specified obligation of the guaranteed debtor if the debtor defaults on that obligation'.[43] In the following sections of this chapter, it is always assumed that a guarantee taking the form of a legally binding agreement is in place between the parties.

## 3 Benefit Test

Once it has been determined that a legally binding agreement has been concluded, the application of the arm's length principle will require an analysis of whether there is a service rendered through the formal guarantee. The accurate delineation process will also clarify the reasons for entering into the transaction and whether the guarantee provides a benefit. At this stage of the accurate delineation process, it is assumed that there is a legally binding agreement in place, but according to the OECD, even in this case, it does not necessarily imply that the guarantee is providing a benefit to the borrower.[44] This will be discussed in more detail below. Thus, before determining the appropriate remuneration and the level of any guarantee fee, it has to be established whether there is an economic benefit derived from the financial guarantee for the borrower.[45] The fundamental question is to analyse whether a third party would have been ready to pay for such a guarantee. In the absence of any economic benefit, it is doubtful that a third party would have been willing to pay any remuneration (i.e., a guarantee fee). However, when there is a benefit, remuneration should be paid by the

41. Bilaney, *supra* n. 37, at 201.
42. *Ibid.*
43. OECD Guidelines 2022, para. 10.155.
44. *Ibid.*, para. 10.164.
45. Moerer, Mavrodiev & Kale, *supra* n. 37, at 140.

borrowing entity to the guarantor.[46] To answer this question, it is necessary to undertake the so-called benefit test as for any other type of intragroup services.[47]

Thus, for a guarantee, an intragroup service can be specifically considered as rendered when the guarantee enables the borrowing entity to obtain a loan at a lower interest rate or with better conditions (i.e., extended debt capacity[48] or less strict covenants).[49] When such effect is provided by the guarantee it can be argued that there is a benefit for the borrower to enter into the transaction. This would also be the case if the lender would not have loaned money to the borrower without the guarantee. The perspective of both parties being considered, the guarantor should also have a benefit for entering into the transaction or providing a guarantee. From the guarantor's perspective, because the guarantee will increase the risk exposure, they will expect to receive remuneration covering the risk taken and the potential costs incurred.[50] From a transfer pricing perspective, such guarantees have to be distinguished from those where the benefit is solely a result of group affiliation (implicit guarantee).

Even if a benefit is clearly provided by a guarantee, accurate delineation of the guarantee will have to be performed, as different tax consequences may arise. For instance, consider the following example: a subsidiary of a multinational group needs to borrow EUR 8 million from a bank. Based on the financial capacity of the subsidiary, without any guarantee, the bank is willing to provide a loan of EUR 7 million. After the parent company of the group provides a guarantee, the bank agrees to increase the loan up to EUR 8 million. In this example, the effect of the guarantee is increasing the borrowing capacity. Two questions should be addressed. The subsidiary was able to attract a part of the loan (EUR 7 million) without the guarantee. Thus, it must first be analysed whether the guarantee is influencing the interest rate and whether the bank is offering a lower interest rate after the guarantee is provided by the parent company. That would probably be the case if the subsidiary can benefit from the credit rating of the parent company. If the interest rate was higher without the guarantee, it can be argued that the guarantee is providing a benefit and a guarantee fee is to be paid. In this example, there is a part of the loan that the subsidiary would not have been able to attract on a stand-alone basis. Thus, according to the OECD, this portion of the loan (EUR 1 million) could be delineated as a loan from the bank to the parent company

46. Antonio Russo & Omar Moerer, Introduction in Transfer Pricing & Intra-Group Financing, 32-33 (IBFD 2012); Alexander Haller & Vikram Chand, Application of the Arm's Length Principle to Physical Cash Pooling Arrangements in Light of the OECD Discussion Draft on Financial Transactions, 47 Intertax (2019), 349, 357; Markus R. Neuhaus & Rolf Watter, Handels- und steuerrechtliche Aspekte von Up-, Down- und Sidestream-Garantien zugunsten von Konzerngesellchaft in Festschrift für Peter Böckli zum 70. Geburtstag 174, 176 (Schulthess 2016).
47. According to the OECD Guidelines, an intra-group service will be considered to be rendered only when the activity performed provides an economic or commercial value to enhance or maintain the business position of the group company to which it is provided (so-called 'benefit test'), *see* OECD Guidelines 2022, para. 7.6. *See also*, Russo & Moerer, *supra* n. 47, at 32.
48. In this case, the OECD also mentions that, in certain circumstances, a portion of the guarantee could be re-characterised as equity.
49. OECD Guidelines 2022, para. 10.161; Moerer, Mavrodiev & Kale, *supra* n. 37, at 140; Bakker, *supra* n. 36, at 32.
50. Moerer, Mavrodiev & Kale, *supra* n. 37, at 140.

followed by an equity contribution to the subsidiary. The guarantee fee will not have to be paid on this portion of the loan.[51]

## 4 Credit Rating

As stated above, a formal guarantee will normally provide the borrowing entity with certain benefits, namely an increased capacity to borrow funds or lower interest rates on the loan. These benefits are generally due to the fact that the borrowing entity will benefit from the credit rating of the guarantor, thereby decreasing the risks assumed by the bank or financial institution.[52] According to the OECD '[...] the guarantee allows the borrower to borrow on the terms that would be applicable if it had the credit rating of the guarantor rather than the terms it could obtain based on its own, non-guaranteed, rating'.[53]

Thus, the credit rating evaluation is of significant importance.[54] It provides useful information in relation to the creditworthiness of the parties involved and is key to measuring the potential benefit provided by the guarantee. In this context, it is interesting to mention that although today there is no need to illustrate the importance of credit rating for taxpayers and tax administrations in the transfer pricing analysis of financial transactions, the use of credit ratings has not always been systematic.[55] This change is now confirmed by the OECD referring extensively to the notion and to the use of credit ratings in its Chapter X.[56]

Credit ratings are issued by credit rating agencies.[57] However, official credit ratings are determined only for certain companies and most of the time at group level, i.e., they reflect the creditworthiness of the parent company taking into account financial flows arising from subsidiaries and the value of their ownership.[58] Therefore, it might be necessary to determine the credit rating on a stand-alone basis for each party involved in the financial guarantee transaction. This evaluation can either be

51. OECD Guidelines 2022, para. 10.161.
52. Sunny Bilaney, *The Unsettled Issue of Intercompany Guarantees*, 18 Derivs & Financial Instruments 6 (2016); Russo & Moerer, *supra* n. 46, at 32.
53. OECD Guidelines 2022, para. 10.158.
54. Russo & Moerer, *supra* n. 46, at 15; Vikram Chand, Transfer Pricing Aspects of Intra-Group Loans in Light of the Base Erosion and Profit Shifting Action Plan, 44 Intertax (2016), 885, 888; Raffaello Fossati, Should Transfer Pricing Practitioners Become Credit Rating Analysts? Practical Instructions Based on Final OECD Guidance on Financial Transactions, Intl. Transfer Pricing J. 355, 355 (2021); Thomas Petrakos, Vikram Chand & Amanda Pletz, Interest Rate Benchmarking for Transfer Pricing Purposes: A Comparison between the Loan and the Bond Approach, Intl. Transfer Pricing J. 242, 246 (2021).
55. Benoît Gabelle, Credit ratings in Transfer Pricing & Intra-Group Financing, 73-74 (IBFD 2021).
56. *See* among other paragraphs dealing with credit ratings, OECD Guidelines 2022, para. 10.62 'credit ratings can serve as a useful measure of creditworthiness and therefore help to identify potential comparables or to apply economic models in the context of related party transactions'.
57. The best-known credit rating agencies are Moody's, Standard and Poor and Fitch. For more details on how credit ratings are determined by these credit rating agencies *see* Chand, *supra* n. 55, at 890.
58. OECD Guidelines 2022, para. 10.71; Petrakos, Chand & Pletz, *supra* n. 54, at 246; Gabelle, *supra* n. 55, at 80.

based on the credit rating methodologies developed by the credit rating agencies (by replicating their methodology) or on online tools (such as RiskCalc or S&P Risk Model), the former being more rigorous than the latter.[59] The credit rating on a stand-alone basis may differ from the group's credit rating.[60]

When determining the credit rating on a stand-alone basis, the OECD confirms that the group membership, and the inherent benefit that an entity will obtain due to its membership, have to be carefully assessed. This incidental benefit, which can be referred to as implicit support, will be discussed in the next section. Taking the implicit support into consideration in the evaluation of the stand-alone credit rating may lead to some upwards adjustments by a few notches.[61] If an official credit rating is available, any benefit from the implicit support will already be considered and no adjustment would be needed.[62]

## 5 Implicit Support

According to the recent OECD developments, the effect of implicit support cannot be ignored in the evaluation of the credit rating of the parties involved in an intragroup financial guarantee.[63] The notion of implicit support refers to a benefit obtained by the taxpayer based on its passive affiliation with the group and not to any specific activity that it performs. Implicit support is based on the underlying idea that a parent company of a group will not let an entity of the group go bankrupt.[64] The benefit that an entity may obtain because of its affiliation with the group will be closely influenced by its status within the group. If the entity is strategic to the group or is strongly integrated within the group, it will be more likely that this entity will be supported by other entities of the group.[65] Conversely, an entity of the group that has limited interactions with other entities of the group or that is of no strategic importance to the group will be unlikely to benefit from any support of the group.[66] In the first scenario, it may be reasonable to consider that the credit rating of a strategic entity will be notched up because of the effect of implicit support. This uplift and the related benefit would be because the group has a better credit rating than the stand-alone credit rating of the borrowing entity.[67] However, in the second scenario, the credit rating would probably

59. OECD Guidelines 2022, para. 10.71-10.75; Petrakos, Chand & Pletz, *supra* n. 54, at 246.
60. Michel E.P. van der Breggen, *Intercompany Loans: Observations from a Transfer Pricing Perspective*, Intl. Transfer Pricing J. 295, 297 (2006).
61. Chand, *supra* n. 54, at 890.
62. OECD Guidelines 2022, para. 10.176.
63. The OECD Guidelines refer to the implicit support in Chapter VII related to the intra-group services, *see* para. 7.13. The notion of implicit support was further developed by the OECD in its Chapter X, *see* paras 10.77, 10.78, 10.80, 10.81, 10.148, 10.159, 10.164, 10.167, 10.174-177 and 10.182.
64. van der Breggen, *supra* n. 60, at 298; Vera Averyanova & Jigna Sampat, *Transfer Pricing Aspects of Intra-Group Financial Guarantees in Light of the BEPS Action Plan*, Intl. Transfer Pricing J. 361, 362 (2015); Chloé Burnett, *Intra-Group Debt at the Crossroads: Stand-Alone Versus Worldwide Approach*, World Tax J. 40, 65 (2014), Journal Articles & Papers IBFD.
65. OECD Guidelines 2022, para. 10.78; Petrakos, Chand & Pletz, *supra* n. 54, at 247.
66. OECD Guidelines 2022, para. 10.78; Petrakos, Chand & Pletz, *supra* n. 54, at 247.
67. Chand, *supra* n. 55, at 890; van der Breggen, *supra* n. 60, at 298.

be equal to or close to the stand-alone credit rating of the entity. In practice, it may be difficult to evaluate the potential effect of implicit support. Credit rating agencies provide practical guidance on how to measure the effect of implicit support. For example, based on the S&P guidance, if the company is 'highly strategic', S&P recommends a rating that would be one notch lower than the group rating. For a 'non-strategic' company, S&P considers that a stand-alone rating analysis should be performed.[68]

The benefit of implicit support alone should not be remunerated. Hence, when looking at an intragroup guarantee where the borrowing entity obtains better conditions on a loan merely because of its group membership, none of the group is deemed to have procured a service.[69] Consequently, no guarantee fee should be paid.[70] According to the OECD, even an explicit guarantee (i.e., formal guarantee) will not necessarily confer a benefit on the borrower.[71] In some circumstances, entities of the group may be financially interdependent despite the fact that a formal guarantee has been issued, for example when legal, financial or operational ties mean it would not be possible to abandon the borrower if it encounters financial difficulties.[72] In such situations '[...] the formal guarantee may represent nothing more than an acknowledgement that it would be detrimental to the interests of the MNE group not to support the performance of the borrower'.[73] Accordingly, even if a formal guarantee is issued, the borrower may not benefit beyond the level of credit enhancement attributable to the implicit support, and no guarantee fee would be due.[74] However, some administrative fees may be due.[75]

Based on the 2022 OECD Guidelines, implicit support cannot be ignored.[76] However, under the former versions of the OECD Guidelines, this was a controversial issue.[77] According to some authors, implicit support is contrary to the very essence of the arm's length principle.[78] The arm's length principle reflects the separate entity approach, which assumes that associated enterprises of a multinational group should

---

68. S&P, General Criteria: Group Rating Methodology, July 2019. For another credit rating agency approach, *see* for instance, Moody's, Rating non-Guaranteed Subsidiaries: Credit Considerations in Assigning Subsidiary Ratings in the Absence of Legally Binding Parent Support, July 2021.
69. Some authors observed that there is no concrete indication given by the OECD to operate this analysis in practice, *see* MARKUS F. HUBER ET AL., *Blickpunkt BEPS*, Steuer Revue, 765, 774 (2018).
70. OECD 2022 Guidelines, para. 7.13; OECD Guidelines 2022, para. 10.164.
71. OECD Guidelines 2022, para. 10.164.
72. *Ibid.*
73. *Ibid.*
74. *Ibid.*
75. *Ibid.*, para. 10.160.
76. The notion of implicit support was already present in the 2010 OECD Guidelines under para. 7.13. Some jurisdictions had also enacted guidance on the issue before the publication of the OECD Guidance on Financial Transactions, *see* MOERER, MAVRODIEV & KALE, *supra* n. 37, at 141.
77. For an opinion in favour of taking into account the implicit support, *see* CHAND, *supra* n. 54, at 891. For a contrary opinion, *see* JENS WITTENDORFF, *The Arm's-Length Principle and Fair Value: Identical Twins or Just Close Relatives?*, Tax Notes Intl., 223, 248 (2011). *See also*, RUSSO & MOERER, *supra* n. 46, at 20-21 raising the issue of the consistency with the arm's length principle and SHAPTAMA BISWAS, *Intra-Group Services: Issues, Solutions and Issues in Solutions*, Intl. Transfer Pricing J. 393, 396 (2016) for more general considerations on incidental benefits.
78. WITTENDORFF, *supra* n. 77, at 248.

be taxed as independent enterprises.[79] Therefore, in their view, the arm's length principle ignores the benefits that a multinational group could achieve by its integration.[80] This issue was at the core of the *Canadian General Electric case* (GE case)[81] decided on 4 December 2009. In this case, the borrowing company took the view that its credit rating should be determined on a stand-alone basis, any implicit support being disregarded in interpreting the arm's length principle. The judge rejected this argument and concluded that the implicit support had to be taken into account as it turned out to be a relevant economic characteristic of the controlled transaction.[82] His conclusion is now included in the OECD Guidelines. Indeed, the OECD put an end to this controversial issue by stating in its Chapter X that any implicit support has to be taken into account by taxpayers and tax authorities when applying the arm's length principle in the context of financial transactions.[83]

## 6 Types of Guarantees

Within a group, a financial guarantee may take different forms. The financial support may be granted by a parent company to a subsidiary (downstream guarantee), by a subsidiary to its parent company (upstream guarantee) or between two subsidiaries (cross-stream guarantee). Except for some considerations on cross-stream guarantees, these different forms of guarantees are neither specifically addressed nor excluded by the OECD in its Chapter X. Therefore, it can be concluded that the OECD Guidelines are applicable to all of these forms of guarantees.

Generally, a guarantee is provided by an entity with a better financial capacity than the borrowing entity to ensure the loan granted by a third party, generally a bank, to this borrowing entity.[84] The creditworthiness of a subsidiary is usually not better than that of its parent company and it is therefore common to find downstream intragroup financial guarantees. Indeed, in case of bankruptcy, the likelihood that a parent's bankruptcy would not trigger the bankruptcy of its subsidiary (even if stronger than the parent) is highly unlikely. In addition, a parent company (even weak) always has the possibility of taking assets from its subsidiary.[85] A typical downstream guarantee can be illustrated by the following example: the subsidiary of a multinational

79. For more details on the separate entity approach, *see* BURKHALTER-MARTINEZ NATASSIA, Cohérence internationale de l'imposition des entreprises – Analyse au regard du projet de lutte contre l'érosion de la base d'imposition et le transfert de bénéfices (projet BEPS), 50-51 (Schulthess 2018).
80. ERIK KAMPHUIS, *How to Deal with Affiliation in Interpreting the Arm's Length Principle: The GE Case Reviewed*, Intl. Transfer Pricing J. 292, 292 (2010); WITTENDORFF, *supra* n. 77, at 248.
81. *General Electric Capital Canada Inc. v. The Queen*, 2009 TCC 563.
82. For more details on the case, *see* KAMPHUIS, *supra* n. 80, 292-297.
83. Before the OECD Guidance, some tax authorities already took into account the implicit support in their assessment of controlled financial transactions (mainly Australia, Canada, the Netherlands, the United Kingdom and the United States), *see* AVERYANOVA & SAMPAT, *supra* n. 64, at 368; WITTENDORFF, *supra* n. 77, at 248.
84. BILANEY, *supra* n. 52; RUSSO & MOERER, *supra* n. 46, at 32.
85. Independent finance companies, especially if they are regulated, may be in a different situation in relation to the credit rating of the parent company. For more details, *see* https://www.maalot.co.il/Publications/MT20161103180153.pdf (accessed 12 January 2022).

group with a *Baa3* (Moody's scale) credit rating needs financing and is taking out a loan from a bank. Without any guarantee, the bank is offering a five-year loan-bearing interest at 4.5%. Considering the guarantee of the parent company with a credit rating of *A3*, the bank would offer a loan-bearing interest of 3.8%. In such a case, the subsidiary is clearly benefitting from the credit rating of its parent company. This benefit results in more favourable conditions offered by the bank. Consequently, the guarantee should be remunerated.

In case of an upstream guarantee, it is less likely that the credit rating of the parent company will be increased by the effect of the guarantee because as stated previously, the credit rating of a parent company is usually better than that of its subsidiary. However, it does not necessarily imply that the guarantee is not providing any economic benefit. Where the parent company is financed by a bank, it is common to secure the loan by a pledge of assets. Without a guarantee including a pledge of assets, the bank will be subordinated to the creditors of the subsidiary in the event of default by the parent company. Even though the parent company will have access to the shares of its subsidiary, the guarantee will ensure the bank has a direct claim to the subsidiary's assets. By putting such a guarantee in place, the bank will obtain an equal ranking with the subsidiary's creditors. Thus, the structural subordination effect will be offset for the bank, which is not subordinated to the repayment of all the other creditors of the subsidiary.[86] Because of that, an upstream guarantee including a pledge of assets would generally have the effect of reducing the credit risk of the bank. This could also be reflected in the issue rating (specific-issue rating, issuance rating) and may allow the bank to offer a better interest rate taking into account the pledge. In such circumstances, when a benefit is clearly provided, remuneration should be considered. As a reminder, the issue rating is 'a forward-looking opinion about the creditworthiness of an obligor with respect to a specific financial obligation, a specific class of financial obligations, or a specific financial program (including ratings on medium-term note programs and commercial paper programs)'.

An upstream guarantee may also be required by the bank as part of its own risk management policy.[87] Here again, it is crucial to evaluate whether the guarantee is providing an economic benefit, as such guarantees (even if explicit) may merely constitute a comprehensive package of security and will not necessarily confer a benefit to the parent company borrowing funds.[88]

Thus, the accurate delineation of the guarantee is of significant importance as it will be used to evaluate whether the guarantee is providing an economic benefit.

This is also true for cross-stream guarantees that are issued by multiple entities of the group and would typically not be found between independent entities.[89] In such cross-stream guarantee structures, multiple entities will assume the same credit risk and measuring the risk assumed and the benefits provided by each guarantee would increase the difficulty. According to the OECD, it may be that such arrangements will

86. Neuhaus & Watter, *supra* n. 46, at 175; Moerer, Mavrodiev & Kale, *supra* n. 37, at 138.
87. Moerer, Mavrodiev & Kale, *supra* n. 37, at 138.
88. *Ibid.*, at 138; OECD Guidelines 2022, para. 10.164.
89. OECD Guidelines 2022, paras 10.147-10.148.

not provide a benefit beyond the one attached to the implicit support coming from the affiliation to the group.[90]

## V PRICING FINANCIAL GUARANTEES

Once the credit ratings of the borrowing entity and of the guarantor have been determined after considering implicit support, the benefit of the guarantee can be measured. Thus, if the provision of the guarantee enhances the credit rating, thereby providing a benefit (lower rate or increased borrowing capacity), a guarantee fee would be justified. As for any other intragroup services transaction, the arm's length level of a guarantee fee should be determined by taking into account the perspectives of both parties.[91] The selection of the most appropriate transfer pricing method is applicable for any other intragroup transactions and has to be consistent with the accurately delineated transaction.[92] The most appropriate method has to be selected based on the circumstances and by taking into account the respective strengths and weaknesses of the OECD-recognised methods.[93] Before the 2022 OECD Guidelines, the OECD Guidelines did not provide any guidance on how to price an intragroup financial guarantee.[94] Different approaches are now being considered by the OECD. They are briefly described below.

### 1 CUP Method

The comparable uncontrolled price (CUP) method may be used when there are some internal or external comparables. It would be possible to use internal comparables if the borrowing company has other comparable loans guaranteed by third parties for which it pays a fee. Alternatively, external comparables would provide information about comparable loans guaranteed by independent parties. However, for these kinds of transactions, publicly available information is unlikely to be found although there could be some exceptions.[95] Therefore, the CUP method may be difficult to apply in practice.

### 2 Yield Approach

The yield approach is a method for pricing a guarantee fee based on the perspective of the borrowing entity. It aims to measure the benefit that the guarantee is providing to this entity.[96] This is done by comparing the interest rate that the borrowing entity would pay in the absence of any guarantee (but taking into account the implicit

90. *Ibid.*, para. 10.165.
91. OECD 2022 Guidelines, para. 7.29; *see also* per analogy OECD Guidelines 2022, paras 10.51 ff.
92. OECD Guidelines 2022, para. 10.169.
93. *Ibid.*, para. 2.2.
94. The 2017 OECD Guidelines only referred to intra-group guarantees in para. 7.13.
95. OECD Guidelines 2022, para. 10.172.
96. *Ibid.*, para. 10.174; Russo & Moerer, *supra* n. 46, at 36.

support) and the interest rate obtained with the guarantee.[97] In practice, it is unlikely that the borrower will receive an offer for the same loan with and without the effect of the guarantee. Thus, the benefit of the guarantee will be measured by undertaking a transfer pricing benchmark searching comparables with the same or a similar credit rating as that of the borrower on a stand-alone basis (adjusted for implicit support) and comparing the range obtained with the interest rate agreed with the external lender.[98]

The spread quantifies the total benefit of the guarantee. Hence, the guarantee fee should not be equal to or higher than the spread. In such cases, the guarantee would not provide any benefit to the borrowing entity, so it would not have any incentive to engage in the transaction.[99] It is therefore expected that the spread be split between the borrowing entity and the guarantor. The division of the spread may take into account different factors such as the negotiation position of each party, the incentive to obtain an intragroup guarantee instead of a guarantee from a third party or the risk exposure for the guarantor.[100]

The yield approach used on its own may be subjective due to the lack of detailed guidance with regard to the elements that should be taken into account for the split.[101] Therefore, in practice, the yield approach may be used in conjunction with the cost approach. These two analyses combined are known as the 'cost-benefit approach'.[102]

## 3 Cost Approach

The cost approach is a method for pricing a guarantee fee based on the perspective of the guarantor. It aims to measure the additional risk borne by estimating the value of the guarantor's expected loss in case of default of the borrowing entity, or the probability that capital will need to be injected.[103]

Credit default swaps (CDS) concluded between independent parties can be used to evaluate the default risk. CDS agreements are financial agreements where: 'one party (the credit protection buyer) pays either an upfront fee or a periodic fee to a counterparty (the credit protection seller) in exchange for the credit protection seller's agreement to either (1) pay the excess notional principal amount of the CDS over its market value (cash-settled CDS) or (2) take delivery of the reference obligation from

97. OECD Guidelines 2022, para. 10.174.
98. Moerer, Mavrodiev & Kale, *supra* n. 37, at 142-143.
99. OECD Guidelines 2022, para. 10.177; Averyanova & Sampat, *supra* n. 64, at 363; Russo & Moerer, *supra* n. 46, at 37; Salim Damji, Irina Diakonova & Urs Brügger, *Transfer Pricing DNA as a Tool to Achieve the Optimal Balance of Risks and Efficiency*, 3 Der Schweizer Treuhänder (2006) 185, 188.
100. Averyanova & Sampat, *supra* n. 64, at 363; Nicolas Bonvin, Fabian Berr & Marc-Antoine Chevalley, *Pratique des prix de transfert relatifs aux transactions financières (partie 1)*, Expert Focus (2020) 390, 394.
101. Vera Averyanova & Vikram Chand, Applying the Arm's Length Principle to Intra-Group Financial Guarantee in light of the OECDs Draft Guidance on Financial Transactions, section 3.2, Kluwer International Tax Blog, http://kluwertaxblog.com/2019/02/14/applying-the-arms-length-principle-to-intra-group-financial-guarantees-in-light-of-the-oecds-draft-guidance-on-financial-transactions/ (accessed 19 December 2021).
102. Russo & Moerer, *supra* n. 46, at 37.
103. OECD Guidelines 2022, para. 10.178.

the credit protection buyer in exchange for the principal amount (physically settled CDS), in a credit event caused by a particular obligor (the reference entity) on a particular obligation (the reference obligation)'.[104] Thus, the upfront fee or the periodic fees of a CDS may be used as comparables to determine a guarantee fee as CDS agreements have similar characteristics to guarantees.[105] That being said, the OECD recognizes that each model will be sensitive to the assumptions made in the modelling process and does not of itself necessarily reflect the outcome of an arm's length situation.[106] Nevertheless, the cost approach sets the minimum fee that the guarantor would expect to receive for taking the additional risks related to the guarantee.[107]

The combination of the yield approach with the cost approach would result in a range of guarantee fees by setting a maximum and a minimum guarantee fee.[108] The guarantee fee will generally be determined within the interquartile range depending on the bargaining power of each party.[109]

### 4 Capital Support Method

The capital support method aims to calculate the additional notional capital required for the borrower to reach the same credit rating of the guarantor. Once this amount of capital has been determined, the guarantee fee is an expected return on it. The guarantee fee can be calculated using this method, to the extent that the expected return only reflects the effect of the guarantee and not the overall activities of the guarantor.[110]

### 5 Valuation of Expected Loss

Using this approach, the expected default rates and recovery rates data available in the market are considered in order to evaluate the potential costs for the guarantor to provide the guarantee. Once the capital amount that is at risk is determined, an appropriate return is calculated for the guarantor.[111] This would reflect the minimum amount that the guarantor would expect by granting the guarantee.

## VI CONCLUSION

Until recently, the pricing of intragroup financial transactions was an area without any specific guidance from the OECD. Given the complexity of this field, the OECD

---

104. Alexander F. Peter, *Characterization of Credit Default Swaps for Tax Purposes*, 8 Derivs. & Financial Instruments 3, 4 (2006).
105. Moerer, Mavrodiev & Kale, *supra* n. 37, at 143-144.
106. OECD Guidelines 2022, para. 10.180.
107. *Ibid.*, para. 10.178; Russo & Moerer, *supra* n. 46, at 36.
108. Russo & Moerer, *supra* n. 46, at 37.
109. *Ibid.*
110. OECD Guidelines 2022, para. 10.182.
111. Moerer, Mavrodiev & Kale, *supra* n. 37, at 144. *See also* OECD Guidelines 2022, para. 10.181.

Guidance on Financial Transactions was welcomed. In practice, since it was published almost two years ago, it has been the subject of much discussion between tax authorities and taxpayers. Although the OECD could not address all the issues related to financial transactions comprehensively, it has confirmed some main principles with a significant impact regarding intragroup financial transactions and more specifically intragroup financial guarantees. The impact of any potential implicit support in the transfer pricing analysis is one of them. But more generally, most of the discussions between taxpayers and tax authorities are about the accurate delineation of the guarantee, to determine whether the guarantee provides a benefit to the borrower. An important part of the transfer pricing analysis is therefore to achieve a mutual understanding of that crucial aspect before discussion of any remuneration.

CHAPTER 26

# Options Realistically Available for Financial Guarantees

*Denis Amici*[*]

## I OPTIONS REALISTICALLY AVAILABLE[1]

The concept of options realistically available (ORAs), under the Organisation for Economic Co-operation and Development Transfer Pricing Guidelines (OECD TP Guidelines), represents the framework in which the arm's length principle (ALP) finds its practical delineation.

This is based on the idea that independent enterprises, when they evaluate whether or not to arrange a new transaction, compare it to the other ORAs to them and choose to arrange a specific transaction if they do not see a clearly more attractive alternative.

Therefore, understanding, analysing and properly documenting ORAs is extremely important to demonstrate the commercial rationale under the agreements – as well as the conduct – the associated enterprises have adopted.

The concept of ORAs recurs in different areas of the OECD TP Guidelines, in particular when the same refer to the:

- assessment of comparability factors to accurately delineate intra-group transactions;[2]

* The views and opinions set forth herein are the personal views or opinions of the authors; they do not necessarily reflect the views or opinions of the organisation with which the authors are associated.

1. This paragraph is based on the article published by the author *In-Depth Analysis of the Concept of Options Realistically Available in Transfer, Pricing* International Transfer Pricing Journal, IBFD, 2020.
2. OECD TP Guidelines at para. 1.38: 'Independent enterprises, when evaluating the terms of a potential transaction, will compare the transaction to the other options realistically available to

- selection and application of the most appropriate transfer pricing method;[3]
- re-characterisation of a controlled transaction (transactional adjustments);[4]
- transactions involving intangibles;[5]
- transfer pricing aspects of business restructurings;[6]

them, and they will only enter into the transaction if they see no alternative that offers a clearly more attractive opportunity to meet their commercial objectives. In other words, independent enterprises would only enter into a transaction if it is not expected to make them worse off than their next best option.' *See also* 'identifying the economically relevant characteristics of the transaction is essential in accurately delineating the controlled transaction and in revealing the range of characteristics taken into account by the parties to the transaction in reaching the conclusion that there is not clearly more attractive opportunity realistically available to meet their commercial objectives than the transaction adopted'.

3. OECD TP Guidelines, at para. 1.40: 'All methods that apply the arm's length principle can be tied to the concept that independent enterprises consider the options realistically available to them and in comparing one option to another they consider any differences between the options that would significantly affect their value.'
4. OECD TP Guidelines, at para. 1.122: 'The transaction as accurately delineated may be disregarded, and if appropriate, replaced by an alternative transaction, where the arrangements made in relation to the transaction, viewed in their totality, differ from those which would have been adopted by independent enterprises behaving in a commercially rational manner in comparable circumstances, thereby preventing determination of a price that would be acceptable to both of the parties taking into account their respective perspectives and the options realistically available to each of them at the time of entering into the transaction.'
5. OECD Guidelines, at para. 6.52: 'Where associated enterprises other than the legal owner perform relevant functions that are anticipated to contribute to the value of the intangibles, they should be compensated on an arm's length basis for the functions they perform under the principles set out in Chapters I-III. The determination of arm's length compensation for functional contributions should consider the availability of comparable uncontrolled transactions, the importance of the functions performed to the creation of intangible value, and the realistically available options of the parties.' Paragraph 6.62: 'The contractual arrangements will generally determine the terms of the funding transaction, as clarified or supplemented by the economic characteristics of the transaction as reflected in the conduct of the parties. The return that would generally be expected by the funder should equal an appropriate risk-adjusted return. Such return can be determined, for example, based on the cost of capital or the return of a realistic alternative investment with comparable economic characteristics. In determining an appropriate return for the funding activities, it is important to consider the financing options realistically available to the party receiving the funds.' Para. 6.111: 'In applying the principles of the Guidelines related to the content and process of a comparability analysis to a transaction involving intangibles, a transfer pricing analysis must consider the options realistically available to each of the parties to the transaction.' *See also* para. 6.113: 'While it is important to consider the perspectives of both parties to the transaction in conducting a comparability analysis, the specific business circumstances of one of the parties should not be used to dictate an outcome contrary to the realistically available options of the other party.'
6. OECD TP Guidelines, at para. 9.27: 'Independent enterprises, when evaluating the terms of a potential transaction, will compare the transaction to the other options realistically available to them, and they will only enter into the transaction if they see no alternative that offers a clearly more attractive opportunity to meet their commercial objective [...] Consideration of the other options realistically available may be relevant to comparability analysis, to understand the respective positions of the parties.' *See also* para. 9.31: 'The reference to the notion of options realistically available is not intended to create a requirement for taxpayers to document all possible hypothetical options realistically available. Rather, the intention is to provide an indication that, if there is a realistically available option that is clearly more attractive, it should be considered in the analysis of the conditions of the restructuring.'

- transfer pricing aspects of financial transactions.[7]

Independent parties, when they are thinking about whether or not to enter into a specific financial transaction, normally consider ORAs available to them, and will only enter into a transaction if they see no one that offers a more attractive opportunity to meet their commercial objectives.

In particular, the borrower and the lender, when they belong to the same Multinational Enterprises Group (MNE Group), in considering their financial relations as well as in analysing the economically relevant characteristics of the transaction, have essentially to take into account both their own perspectives, also acknowledging that these perspectives may not be always aligned.[8]

The lender's/guarantor's perspective, in the decision of whether or not to grant a loan or a guarantee, typically involves the evaluation of various factors relating to: (i) the associated borrower, (ii) the corresponding market and business strategies of both lender and borrower and (iii) the other ORAs to the lender in order to better employ its own funds.

The borrower's/guaranteed's perspective, instead, in the decision of whether or not to ask for financial support, usually involves the optimisation of its weighted average cost of capital and the correct evaluation of the different funding resources available in the financial market in order to meet its short-term (boost the liquidity) as well as long-term financial needs (pursue new business opportunities, develop new projects).[9]

In fact, an independent enterprise, in seeking funds for its own commercial purposes, first considers its ORAs and will implement only the most cost-effective solution with reference to the market and business strategy it has adopted.

For transfer pricing purposes, intercompany financial transactions need to be tailored to the specific needs of the parties involved (lender and borrower).

In order to strengthen the position of the associated lender and borrower in front of the tax authorities it is necessary to properly structure and document the financial transaction policies, such as lending or guarantying facilities, of the MNE Group.

7. OECD Transfer Pricing Guidance on Financial Transactions 2020, which will result in the new Chapter 10 of the OECD TP Guidelines, at para. 10.19: 'Independent enterprises, when considering whether to enter into a particular financial transaction, will consider all other options realistically available to them, and will only enter into the transaction if they see no alternative that offers a clearly more attractive opportunity to meet their commercial objectives (see paragraph 1.38 of Chapter I). In considering the options realistically available, the perspective of each of the parties to the transaction must be considered. For instance, in the case of an entity that advances funds, other investment opportunities may be contemplated, taking account of the specific business objectives of the lender and the context in which the transaction takes place. From the borrower's perspective, the options realistically available will include broader considerations than the entity's ability to service its debt, for example, the funds it actually needs to meet its operational requirements. In some instances, although an entity may have the capacity to borrow and service an additional amount of debt, it may choose not to do so to avoid placing negative pressure on its credit rating and increasing its cost of capital and jeopardising its access to capital markets and its market reputation.'
8. OECD Transfer Pricing Guidance on Financial Transactions 2020, at para. 10.51.
9. *Ibid.*, from paras 10.53-10.58.

In fact, as the Chevron Australia (2017) case[10] demonstrated, the focus of the tax authorities in intra-group financial transactions is not only based on prices effectively paid (interest rates) but also on all other different conditions of the loan.

Considering the various conditions necessary to set an arm's length transaction, it is crucial, first, to properly structure the same from a contractual standpoint and, second, to document it with all the information regarding both the lender and the borrower perspective.

In particular, clear and robust documentation allows taxpayers to demonstrate the commercial rationale under the financial transaction put in place.

However, ORAs analysis should not have the effect of switching the burden of the proof from tax authorities to taxpayer, creating an excessive burden of compliance on the latter.

Taxpayer, in fact, should not be obliged to document all the ORAs at the time of the transaction but should instead have to be able to refer only to those he examined at that time in order to: (i) prove that the analysis was effectively performed and (ii) defend their choice in a reliable manner.[11]

In the author's opinion, the use of ORAs analysis should be regarded as an advanced evaluation framework, strongly reaffirmed at international level and required to maintain and preserve the ALP as the fundamental standard for allocating profits between associated enterprises.[12]

---

10. AU: Australian Federal Court of Appeal, 21 April 2017, *Chevron Australia Holdings Pty Ltd (CAHPL) v. Commissioner of Taxation*, [2017] FCAFC 62, available at https://www.taxinstitute.com.au/news/chevron-case-ato-wins-landmark-transfer-pricing-case.
11. R. Petruzzi et al., Comments Received on the BEPS Public Discussion Draft on Financial Transactions – Part III by WU Transfer Pricing Center (OECD 2018). *See also* A. Lobb, Comments Received on the BEPS Public Discussion Draft on Financial Transactions – Part I by Deloitte UK (OECD 2018): 'The options available to a subsidiary are heavily influenced by its ultimate parent and the benefit to the group as a whole. In practice the subsidiary is often faced with a binary choice of realistic options: (i) accept additional funding from the group, on the understanding it will put the funding to the use the group intended (subject to evaluation of the commerciality of such an arrangement and negotiating the terms of the debt) or (ii) refusing the additional funding. It would not be a realistic proposition for the subsidiary to proceed with other options for investing the funds offered: such as lending the money out on the markets, or lending the money to subsidiaries in other groups, notwithstanding the possibility that these options could result in a slightly higher return on investment. In many cases, the most likely realistic option would be for a company to put money on deposit with a bank. It would be helpful if the Discussion Draft could expand on the meaning of "realistically", acknowledging the limitations in the context of group companies. In circumstances where there is a wider range of other realistic options, an independent party would make best effort to evaluate many different realistic options, but would stop once they are confident, they have a sufficient understanding of the range of potential outcomes. It would be inappropriate if the draft guidance gave rise to an onerous requirement to consider and document all other realistic options – reasonable endeavour to evaluate the range of options should be sufficient.'
12. OECD, OECD Transfer Pricing Guidelines for Multinational Enterprises and Tax Administrations (Paris: OECD 2017), para. 1.1: 'the arm's length principle … is the international transfer pricing standard that OECD member countries have agreed should be used for tax purposes by MNE groups and tax administrations'. *See also* United Nations, Practical Manual on Transfer Pricing for Developing Countries (UN 2017), Part A, para. 4.6: 'The arm's length principle allows national tax authorities to make an adjustment to the profits of one enterprise where the terms of transactions between associated enterprises differ from terms that would be agreed between unrelated enterprises in similar circumstances' and Part B, para. 1.1.6: 'These transactions are

In this framework, the quality of transfer pricing documentation assumes a pivotal role in demonstrating the compliance of the transfer pricing policy of the MNE Group to ALP[13] and eases the relationships with the different tax authorities in which the same MNE Group operates.[14]

Dealing with intra-group financing (lending and/or guaranteeing activities) requires also:

- to formalise an analysis of the debt capacity of the associated company which needs financial assistance; this analysis could be very complex and time-consuming too since it involves the projection of cash flows during the time horizon of the loan's duration as well as the consideration of ORAs of both the lender/guarantor entity and the borrower/guaranteed ones;
- to place the financial transactions within the tax risk control framework.

## II INTRA-GROUP FINANCIAL GUARANTEES

A financial guarantee is a promise made by one entity, usually, the parent company of an MNE Group which acts as the guarantor, in favour of another unrelated entity, usually a third-party bank or financial intermediary, to cover the debt assumed by a related entity, usually a subsidiary, which is the borrower as well as the guaranteed entity, in case the latter may eventually not be able to pay back its obligation in the future.

In other words, on the basis of the financial guarantee, the guarantor has to meet specific financial obligations (i.e., guarantee commitment) in the event the guaranteed entity is not able to do so.

The financial guarantee basically allows:

- the borrower to have a loan on the same (or equivalent) terms and conditions as those applicable to the guarantor and/or a larger amount of loan;
- the lender to take into account the stronger financial capacity of the guarantor since the guarantee commitment received effectively gives him access to wider financial resources; and, finally,
- the MNE Group to decrease its overall cost of funding.

---

also referred to as 'controlled' transactions, as distinct from 'uncontrolled' transactions between companies that are not associated and can be assumed to operate independently ('on an arm's length basis') in setting terms for such transactions' and R.S. Collier & J.L. Andrus, Transfer Pricing and the Arm's Length Principle after BEPS (Oxford University Press 2017).

13. On the BEPS Action 13 subsection of its website (http://www.oecd.org/tax/beps/beps-actions/action13/), OECD states that 'the lack of quality data on corporate taxation has been a major limitation to measuring the fiscal and economic effects of tax avoidance, making it difficult for authorities to carry out transfer pricing assessments on transactions between linked companies and even more difficult to carry out audits'.

14. OECD, Study into the Role of Tax Intermediaries (OECD 2008), available at http://www.oecd.org/tax/administration/39882938.pdf. It constitutes the seminal work on the matter in which basic relationships start to be distinguished from enhanced relationships.

In the context of intra-group financial guarantees, the following are the most common:[15]

- Downstream guarantee: the subsidiary receives the guarantee from the parent company.
- Upstream guarantee: the parent company receives a guarantee from the subsidiary.
- Cross guarantee: two or more companies, belonging to the same MNE Group provide a guarantee to each other.

As far as cross guarantees are concerned, each party could provide a guarantee and be guaranteed by the party for whom it is acting as guarantor at the same time. In fact, when entities are part of an MNE Group, it might be easier and cheaper to borrow money if a financial guarantee from related parties is put in place.

In this case, the complexity increases not only because a large number of guarantees is put in place but also because an associated borrower could have multiple guarantees on its borrowings and may stand as guarantor for multiple borrowings itself.

However, due to the cross-guarantee scenario, all the financial guarantees put in place could not enhance the credit rating of the entity of an MNE Group beyond the level of passive association.[16]

From a transfer pricing perspective, only the guarantees that constitute a legally binding commitment on the guarantor's part are considered. In fact, according to the OECD, anything less than a legally binding commitment – such as a comfort letter, a letter of intent or a keep-well agreement – should not lead to the payment of a commission fee since it does not involve an explicit assumption of risk.[17]

---

15. Nicolas Gillet, https://www.ey.com/en_lu/tax/new-challenges-on-pricing-intragroup-financial-guarantees.
16. OECD Transfer Pricing Guidance on Financial Transactions 2020, at para. 10.76: 'The effect of group membership is relevant for informing the conditions under which an MNE would have borrowed from an independent lender at arm's length in two ways in particular. Firstly, the external funding policies and practices of group management will assist in informing the form and terms and conditions of the debt the MNE would have entered into with an independent lender, including the pricing (i.e., interest rate paid), and all economically relevant characteristics such as the type of loan, its term, currency, security, covenants, business strategies, and so forth. Secondly, the MNE may receive support from the group to meet its financial obligations in the event of the borrower getting into financial difficulty. Paragraph 1.158 of Chapter I of these Guidelines is relevant to analyse the effect of group membership on the terms and conditions of a borrowing when the borrowing MNE obtains an incidental benefit arising solely by virtue of group affiliation, i.e., passive association.' For further details regarding cross-guarantee scenarios, reference could be made to V. Chand, *Transfer Pricing Aspects of Cash Pooling Arrangements in Light of the BEPS Action Plan* (International Transfer Pricing Journal, IBFD, 2016) and A. Heller & V. Chand, *Application of the Arm's Length Principle to Physical Cash Pooling Arrangements in Light of the OECD Discussion Draft on Financial Transaction* (Intertax, Kluwer Law International, 2019). The cross guarantees put in place are nothing more than an acknowledgement that it would be harmful to the global interest of the group not to support the related entity so basically, there should not be any charge for these guarantees.
17. OECD Transfer Pricing Guidance on Financial Transactions 2020, at para. 10.163.

While financial guarantees are commonly used in the MNE Group context, less attention has been paid to their correct structuring and documentation so far.

As for the other intra-group transactions, from a transfer pricing perspective, the accurate delineation of a financial guarantee granted between related entities is essential to gain full understanding of the characteristics and the scope of the guaranteed's obligations as well as the real impact of the guarantee commitment for all parties of the MNE Group involved.

Moreover, in order to consider the payment of a commission fee for the financial guarantee granted, it is necessary to identify the nature and the extent of the obligations assumed for all the parties of the MNE Group involved.

Such a process mainly focuses on:

- the economic benefits created by the guarantee to the borrower (i.e., enhancement of the terms of the borrowing and/or access to a larger amount of borrowing);
- the availability of the guarantor to provide support to the associated guaranteed; and
- the commercial rationality of the intra-group guarantee structure put in place.

Furthermore, the commission fee the guaranteed entity is willing to pay should reflect, at the maximum, an amount equal to the reduction of the interest rate applied to the loan due to the guarantee commitment put in place.

This amount, in fact, must be adjusted in order to take into consideration:

- the effects of the passive association;
- the effects of the notional equity contribution in case the guaranteed entity, due to the guarantee commitment put in place, has access to a larger amount of funds;[18] and
- any other costs related to the issuance of the financial guarantee (i.e., transactional as well as negotiation costs).[19]

It is essential to properly structure and document the intra-group financial guarantee in order to demonstrate its commercial rationality.[20]

18. *Ibid.*, at para. 10.161: 'Where the effect of a guarantee is to permit a borrower to borrow a greater amount of debt than it could in the absence of the guarantee, the guarantee is not simply supporting the credit rating of the borrower but could be acting both to increase the borrowing capacity and to reduce the interest rate on any existing borrowing capacity of the borrower. In such a situation there may be two issues – whether a portion of the loan from the lender to the borrower is accurately delineated as a loan from the lender to the guarantor (followed by an equity contribution from the guarantor to the borrower), and whether the guarantee fee paid with respect to the portion of the loan that is respected as a loan from the lender to the borrower is arm's length. The conclusion of an analysis of such transactions may be, taking into account the full facts and circumstances, that the evaluation of the guarantee fee should be limited to a fee on the portion that has been accurately delineated as a loan, and the remainder of the loan granted should be regarded as effectively a loan to the guarantor followed by an equity contribution by the guarantor to the borrower.'
19. OECD Transfer Pricing Guidance on Financial Transactions 2020, at para. 10.177.
20. OECD TP Guidelines, at para. 1.123: 'The key question in the analysis is whether the actual transaction possesses the commercial rationality of arrangements that would be agreed between

As we have already seen in the preceding paragraph, evaluating whether the guarantee constitutes an arm's length transaction within the MNE Group implies considering both the perspectives of the guarantor and the guaranteed entity.

From the guarantor's perspective, granting a financial guarantee may worsen his creditworthiness due to the indirect exposure at risk related to the financial guarantee issued.

So, the guarantor would never agree to enter into a guarantee commitment without obtaining an arm's length compensation for the aforesaid exposure.

In the MNE Group context, ORAs analysis for the guarantor, as a viable alternative of assuming a direct guarantee commitment, may take into consideration the option to (i) inject the funds directly to the associated entity as debt or equity, (ii) require another bank or financial intermediary, different from the lending bank which is evaluating whether to finance or not the associated entity, to provide a financial guarantee by totally or partially pledging the funds, maintained therein but not readily available since invested, as a counter-guarantee, (iii) structure an intra-group cash pooling arrangement, and let the associated entity get into it in order to minimise, to the maximum extent possible, its working capital needs,[21] (iv) make a year-end transfer pricing adjustment,[22] if and to extent the contracts in force by and between them allow to do it, in order to move up the profitability of the associated entity and, consequently, improve its credit rating or, as last resort, (v) not grant any financial assistance to the associated entity with the full awareness that the latter could not be able to autonomously meet its funding needs.

From the guaranteed entity's perspective, receiving a financial guarantee will surely let the same achieve both its short and long-term financial needs.

The guaranteed entity could pay lower interests on funds borrowed and/or borrow a greater amount of funds too.

---

unrelated parties under comparable economic circumstances, not whether the same transaction can be observed between independent parties. The non-recognition of a transaction that possesses the commercial rationality of an arm's length arrangement is not an appropriate application of the arm's length principle. Restructuring of legitimate business transactions would be a wholly arbitrary exercise the inequity of which could be compounded by double taxation created where the other tax administration does not share the same views as to how the transaction should be structured. It should again be noted that the mere fact that the transaction may not be seen between independent parties does not mean that it does not have characteristics of an arm's length arrangement.'

21. In the author's opinion, such an option could face the associated entity's short terms financial needs only since long terms ones should normally rely on determined and specific credit facilities.
22. Year-end transfer pricing adjustments typically recur when Parent Company wants to ensure that actual financial results of an associated entity, usually a subsidiary with a specific characterisation in terms of Functions performed/Assets used/Risks borne, match what is defined in transfer pricing policies and intercompany agreements within the MNE Group. However, year-end adjustments could be challenged from tax authorities when the profitability of an associated entity is not affected by transfer prices but rather local mismanagement. So, MNE Groups should therefore properly review the extent to which year-end adjustments are made and use this instrument carefully. In any case, it is recommended to clearly document the reason for any year-end adjustment.

In any case, the guaranteed entity should never agree to pay a commission, higher than the benefits resulting from the financial guarantee.

Correspondingly, ORAs analysis for the guaranteed entity, as a viable alternative of receiving a financial guarantee from the parent company guarantor, may take into consideration the option to (i) pay a higher interest rate to a third-party bank for its debt, (ii) borrow a lower amount of debt from a third-party bank, (iii) reconsider, to the maximum extent possible, its own working capital strategies[23] or, as a last resort, (iv) abandon its long-term investment plans.

## III ORAS IN PRACTICE WITH A FOCUS ON NON-RECOGNITION

The strategic importance of the guaranteed entity within the MNE Group, including any potential negative impacts deriving from its default to the rest of the MNE Group, defines the effective feasibility of a specific ORA.

In most cases, internal intra-group reasons may influence the decisions to grant financial support.

Whether the consequences of not supporting an associated entity:

- may create negative impacts on the MNE Group due to the increased operational risks; or even;
- may anyhow affect reputation damages related to the default of the associated entity, then the number of ORAs to the parent company (prospect lender/guarantor) may narrow further.

However, in some cases, external reasons could lead to the decision to grant financial support.

For instance, when the financial guarantee is expressly required to access the local loan market where the subsidiary operates,[24] the parent company called upon to provide financial assistance by issuing the guarantee, does not have to immediately and directly inject its own funds (as debt and/or equity) to the subsidiary, and, consequently, may pursue the ORA of using the funds for its own purposes.

But if the guaranteed entity has accessed the local loan market and received the funds based only on the guarantee commitment of the parent company, instead on its own credit rating, tax authorities may disregard the transaction and, consequently, (re)qualify, for tax purposes, the financial guarantee put in place as an equity injection.[25]

23. For example, shortening the terms of collection and/or lengthening those of payment from, respectively, its clients and suppliers depending on the bargaining power position of the parties under reference.
24. Since for wholly foreign-owned small, medium and/or start-up enterprises, local banks, the biggest ones too, usually request the financial guarantee of the parent company to assess its credit worthiness and, consequently, to offer any financial support.
25. S. Palestini, 'Finanziamenti infragruppo superiori alla capacità di indebitamento e garanzie del gruppo rilasciate a terzi finanziatori', in Fiscalità & Commercio Internazionale (Italian Monthly Journal edited by Wolters Kluwer Italia) n.1/2021.

In this case, even if there is a third subject (i.e., the bank or other financial intermediary), external to – and independent from – the MNE Group, tax authorities may consider the loan from the said third-party bank as granted directly in favour of the parent company which, at the same time, transfers the funds to its subsidiary as an equity injection.

The rationale of such a requalification is considering the loan, even if the same is formally contracted by the subsidiary with a third-party bank, as an advance payment made by the aforesaid bank to the subsidiary on behalf of the parent company (which has issued the financial guarantee) for an equity injection that the latter would make in order to financially support the said subsidiary, which has no debt capacity, if and to the extent the financial guarantee will be enforced by the bank in the future.

The issue above could be better understood by making reference to the following Figures 26.1 and 26.2, where a parent company, resident in Country A, has issued a financial guarantee to a third-party bank, resident in Country B, in order to facilitate the granting of a loan to its subsidiary, also resident in Country B.

Regardless of the fact that the amount of the guarantee fee could be deemed or not at arm's length, the tax authorities of Country B may (i) requalify the transaction, since the same does not reflect the debt capacity of the subsidiary, and, consequently, (ii) consider the loan – for transfer pricing purposes only – as a loan granted from the bank first to the parent company which, in the light of the requalification, has then made an equity injection to its subsidiary.

*Figure 26.1 Original Intra-group Transaction*

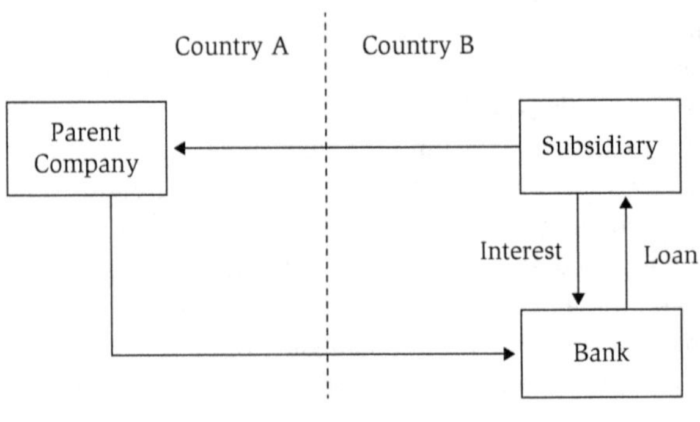

*Figure 26.2 Requalified Intra-group Transaction for Transfer Pricing Purposes*

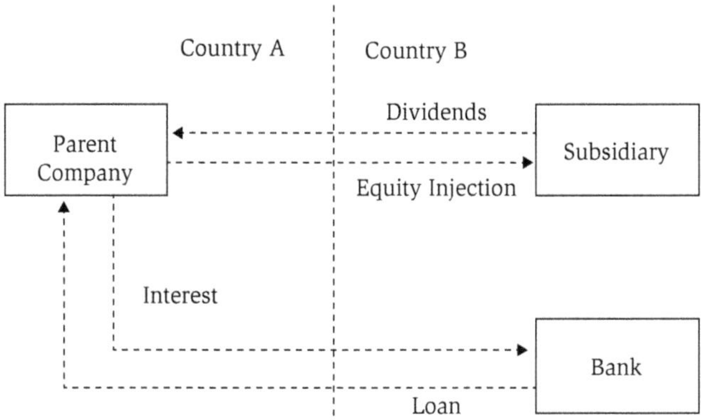


The requalification above may have an impact on profits and losses accounts of both the parent company and subsidiary and could lead to a different distribution of the taxable income among the aforesaid enterprises between Country A and Country B.

An additional example of how external reasons may lead to the decision to provide the associated entity with financial support is when a financial guarantee is required in order to prevent moral hazard issues.[26]

This further issue could be better understood making still reference to the above-mentioned figures.

Assume that the corporate laws of Country B require wholly foreign-owned start-up enterprises to have a minimum level of equity in order to operate in a specific sector. So, when incorporated, the subsidiary was adequately capitalised by the parent company and, consequently, it has, now, an autonomous debt capacity, and it would be able to take out the loan on its own.

Nevertheless, the third-party bank expressly requests, in order to finance the subsidiary, the issuance of the financial guarantee from the parent company as it intends to prevent the risk that the same may somehow use for its own purposes the funds granted to its subsidiary.

The parent company, from one side, is willing to issue the aforesaid financial guarantee since it would like to avoid pumping further cash into the subsidiary and the latter, from the other, is willing to pay the commission fee since it would like to avoid further delays for implementing its projects.

All the counterparties of the financial transaction under reference seem to have a sound business reason and there are not any other ORAs to them.

We would like to bring to the attention of the reader that the borderline between analysing the transaction under the 'accurate delineation' umbrella and the 'commercially irrational' umbrella is not crystal clear. Thus, in case of intra-group financial

26. In case the parent company could somehow divert for its own purposes the funds granted to its subsidiary by the third-party bank.

guarantees, it would be opportune also to check and analyse the commercial rationality of the overall transaction put in place, even if accurately delineated.

In fact, even if accurately delineated, the tax authorities of Country B may disregard the financial transaction by challenging the commercial rationality of the overall transaction put in place, and, in particular, the payment of the commission fee from the subsidiary to the parent company, since unrelated parties are not usually willing to pay for a financial guarantee which does not provide a specific and measurable benefit to the guaranteed entity.

The relevant question here is whether a compensation (i.e., commission fee) for the financial guarantee could be charged or not.

An independent party is willing to pay a compensation, for the financial guarantee received, only if and to the extent such a compensation does not exceed the benefit deriving from the same.

If the compensation is higher than the benefit, as reported in Table 26.1, then the difference between the two amounts may trigger exceptional circumstances[27] which allow tax authorities to adjust the transaction accurately delineated as well as the terms and conditions agreed upon by the associated enterprises.

*Table 26.1 Benefit of/Compensation for Guarantee*

| | |
|---|---|
| interest rate w/out guarantee (A) | 5% |
| interest rate w/guarantee (B) | 4% |
| benefit of guarantee (A – B = C) | 1% |
| compensation for guarantee (D) | 1.25% |
| difference between (D) and (C) | 0.25% |

Tax authorities should, first, calculate the amounts under letters A and B above and, second, verify if there are any other ORAs to the counterparties in order to demonstrate whether or not the transaction under reference has any sound business reasons.

The calculation will imply performing financial analyses and/or using multifactor modelling in order to determine the debt capacity, the arm's length price (i.e., interest rate) with or without the financial guarantee and, consequently, its compensation.

These analyses, usually performed by professional operators of the financial sector, may also lead to different results from one operator to another.

In addition, the verification of the existence of any other ORAs to the counterparties should be carried out at the time of the transaction when the relevant agreements were put in place and not at the time of the tax audit.

So, financial transactions and intra-group financial guarantees, in particular, remarkably increase the burden of complexity for both MNE groups and tax authorities in performing the convenience calculations and the verifications to support, respectively, financial decisions made, and tax audits to be carried out.

27. OECD Transfer Pricing Guidelines, at para. 1.121

Regardless of how the different tax authorities, involved in the countries where an MNE Group operates, will apply (i) the new OECD approach to the financial transactions in close connection with their domestic tax Laws and double tax treaties provisions, if any, and (ii) the outcomes of the financial analyses/modelling required by said approach, it will be of interest to understand how specific internal/external intra-group reasons may affect ORAs analysis, from one side, as well as tax authorities' conduct, from the other, and, most important, how the aforesaid reasons may be compliant with the ALP.[28]

Therefore, having a robust contractual structure as well as maintaining a solid documentation framework to support the intra-group financial guarantees put in place is strongly recommended to face – and cooperate with – tax authorities of the different countries involved in the MNE group financial transactions. In particular, it is necessary to properly detail financial analyses performed, including cash flow projections and the relevant ORAs analyses performed and pursued.

---

28. *See*, Italian Supreme Court no. 13850 of 12 May 2021, which ruled that it is not excluded that free intra-group financing may exist where it is demonstrable that the deviation from the ALP is due to internal commercial reasons related to the market in which the MNE Group operates. In the case under reference, it seems the ALP is due to commercial reasons within the MNE Group and it is somehow linked to the role played by the parent company in supporting the other companies belonging to the same MNE Group.

    In the author's opinion, it would be possible, for instance, that a parent company may decide to give financial support to one of its foreign subsidiaries without requiring any payment of interest, for example by showing an ORAs analysis in which the parent gives evidence of the fact that the purpose of the intra-group transaction is to invest the available resources in order to: (i) aid the subsidiary in its start-up phase, (ii) maintain the MNE Group market share in a foreign country, or (iii) avoid the excessive exposure of the subsidiary to third parties (i.e., banks, other financial intermediaries).

CHAPTER 27

# Using the Market Approach to Price Guarantees: A Case Study

*Rachit Agarwal*[*]

## I INTRODUCTION

As covered in the previous chapters, the main principles in relation to financial guarantees are: (a) the assessment of the commercial rationality of the transaction; (b) the concept of implicit support; and (c) the consideration of the two-sided perspective. The theoretical aspects regarding the approaches and the methods for pricing guarantees have also been explained in detail in prior chapters. The focus of this chapter is to apply those principles and theories in a practical case study.

## II CASE STUDY: BACKGROUND

(a) A multinational organisation, Perfect Sneakers Inc. (PSI or 'the Group'), is headquartered in the United States (US) with subsidiaries all around the world.
(b) PSI is engaged in the business of designing, manufacturing and selling sneakers to retailers and customers globally. Their global revenue for the previous financial year (FY) was US Dollars (USD) 20 billion.

* The views and opinions set forth herein are the personal views or opinions of the authors; they do not necessarily reflect the views or opinions of the organisation with which the authors are associated.

(c) The Group sources its raw materials from a few countries in Latin America namely Argentina, Brazil and Peru with manufacturing facilities in China, Indonesia and Vietnam. Once the sneakers are manufactured, they are distributed through related limited-risk distributors situated across the globe.
(d) The Group has a central treasury division based in the US which deals with all of its financing needs. This division employs 15 people and is headed by a Vice President, Finance who reports to the Chief Financial Officer.
(e) This division is involved in the following activities:
  - negotiating financing arrangements with external banks;
  - issuing bonds in the market;
  - operating an in-house cash pool;
  - setting strategy for cash management within the Group;
  - providing access to funding to other operating entities when required;
  - managing all finance-related exposures such as foreign exchange risks; and
  - investing excess funds in the market.
(f) The credit rating agencies, such as Moody's Corporation ('Moody's') and Standard & Poor's ('S&P'), have assigned the Group a credit rating of 'Baa1' and 'BBB+', on the Moody's and S&P scale respectively.
(g) PSI has an operating entity in the United Kingdom, Perfect Sneakers UK Ltd ('PKUK'), which acts as a Principal distributor for Europe and is considered a critical entity in the Group's European supply chain.

PSI is considering expanding its presence in Europe and has been surveying opportunities to acquire companies. A new opportunity to acquire Best Shoes B.V., a Netherlands-based group valued at USD 300 million, has arisen with PSI needing to arrange financing swiftly if acquisition is pursued as there are multiple bidders for this group. The Group, in consultation with PKUK, has decided to acquire Best Shoes B.V. through debt financing and in that respect, PKUK would have to borrow funds from external banks.

PKUK has been facing some headwinds in the market due to current state of the European shoe industry with factors such as supply chain issues due to Brexit, inflationary pressures leading to decreasing buying power of the customers and the lack of a steady cash flow for the company in recent years. Although PKUK has not been assigned a standalone credit rating, its financial statements were used in conjunction with a credit ratings model to determine a standalone rating. It was determined that PKUK has a standalone credit rating of 'B1' and 'B+' on Moody's and S&P scales respectively to PKUK.

Based on the interest rate environment prevalent in the market, a bank loan of any amount between USD 100 million and 300 million for a period of five years has been attracting the following interest rates (*see* Table 27.1).

*Table 27.1 Interest Rates Overview*

| *Moody's* | *S&P Global Ratings* | *Fitch Ratings* | *Interest Rates*[1] *(%)* |
|---|---|---|---|
| Aaa | AAA | AAA | 0.25 |
| Aa1 | AA + | AA + | 0.50 |
| Aa2 | AA | AA | 0.75 |
| Aa3 | AA– | AA– | 1.00 |
| A1 | A + | A + | 1.25 |
| A2 | A | A | 1.50 |
| A3 | A– | A– | 1.75 |
| Baa1 | BBB + | BBB + | 2.00 |
| Baa2 | BBB | BBB | 2.25 |
| Baa3 | BBB– | BBB– | 2.50 |
| Ba1 | BB + | BB + | 2.75 |
| Ba2 | BB | BB | 3.00 |
| Ba3 | BB– | BB– | 3.25 |
| B1 | B + | B + | 3.50 |
| B2 | B | B | 3.75 |
| B3 | B– | B– | 4.00 |
| Caa | CCC | CCC | 4.25 |

1. The interest rates provided here are only for illustrative purposes and not fact based.

Based on Table 27.1, the financing cost for acquiring Best Shoes B.V by PKUK would be significantly high, with an interest rate of 3.50% based on its standalone credit rating of 'B1' and 'B + ' on Moody's and S&P scale. In light of this, the Group and PKUK conducted several rounds of discussions with the third-party banks where it was agreed that PSI would enter into a legally binding commitment with these banks and 'guarantee' the loan of USD 300 million from the banks to PKUK. Without this guarantee, the banks would have only lent USD 150 million to PKUK. From the bank's perspective (with the guarantee), they are now lending funds to PSI and therefore the risk profile of this investment is considerably lower. As such, the banks will now apply the credit rating of the Group, i.e., 'Baa1'/'BBB + ', to the loan to PKUK rather than the standalone credit rating of 'B1' / 'B + '. As a result, PKUK can now borrow the funds at an interest rate of 2.00% rather than 3.50% in addition to an increased funding of USD 150 million.

## III TRANSFER PRICING ISSUES TO CONSIDER

The facts presented in the above case highlight a few transfer pricing issues that need to be identified and dealt with. In this section, we will identify those issues and consider the possible approaches to analyse them from an arm's length perspective.

Before we dive into it, it is essential to ascertain whether there is an actual or deemed intra-group guarantee transaction or not and which entities are on either side of the transaction. Once that question has been answered one can move to the next task of estimating the risk borne by the guarantor and the benefits obtained by the guaranteed entity before finally pricing the arm's length guarantee fee, taking into account the perspectives of both parties to the transaction. All of these steps can essentially be combined into an arm's length framework on guarantees as discussed in the earlier chapters which are:

(a) accurate delineation of financial guarantees; and
(b) determining arm's length price of guarantees.

With regards to the case study, the guarantor has been identified as PSI with the guaranteed entity being PKUK. Applying the above framework would require careful deliberation of the aspects listed below. With respect to the first aspect of accurate delineation of the financial guarantee, one would have to analyse the following:

(a) What are the economic benefits derived from the guarantee from PKUK's perspective:
   - Is there an enhancement in terms of PKUK's borrowing from third-party banks?
   - Does PKUK have access to a larger amount of debt than prior to the guarantee being provided?
(b) What is the strategic importance and the level of support PKUK enjoys within the Group?
(c) Does PSI have the financial capacity to provide the guarantee to third-party banks?

Once these points have been analysed and the transaction has been accurately delineated, the question of the arm's length price of the guarantee arises, which is:

- What should be an arm's length guarantee fee that rewards PSI appropriately for the risks it bears and that PKUK would be willing to pay for the benefit it receives?

The application of the arm's length framework to the case including the issues raised above has been discussed in the sections below.

## 1 Accurate Delineation of a Financial Guarantee

With respect to the accurate delineation of a financial guarantee, the same principles as advocated in Chapter 1 of the OECD Guidelines apply and are examined with respect to the case study below. The first issue deals with determining the economic benefits accruing to PKUK from the financial guarantee. Two assessments need to be undertaken to ascertain the economic benefits:

(a) *Whether the terms of the borrowing after the guarantee are better in comparison to the terms when there was no guarantee.* The terms here could refer to variables such as interest rates or lighter covenants. If the borrower is now better off, it is certainly benefiting from the guarantee. In this case, in the absence of the guarantee PKUK would be able to access funds from third-party banks at an interest rate of 3.50% whereas with the guarantee the interest rate is 2.00% due to the credit rating enhancement from 'B1' / 'B+' to 'Baa1' / 'BBB+'. From this perspective, PKUK has certainly benefitted from the guarantee.

(b) *Whether PKUK is able to access a larger amount of funds with the guarantee compared to the absence of guarantee.* PKUK would have been able to borrow USD 150 million on a standalone basis, i.e., based on its own financial standing within the current economic environment. However, because of the financial guarantee, it can now borrow USD 300 million, which is an additional USD 150 million. Therefore, PKUK has benefitted from the guarantee.

Based on the above, it is clear that PKUK has economically benefitted from the guarantee provided by PSI when considering the terms of the loan and the amount of the loan. It is important to note that to establish the benefit both the above tests need not be met; either one should be acceptable to conclude on the benefit depending on the facts and circumstances.

It has been recognised that PKUK has benefitted from the financial guarantee. The next question is whether all of this benefit can be attributed to the legally binding commitment from the guarantee or whether a portion of it can also be ascribed to 'passive association' or 'implicit support' emanating from PKUK being part of the Group. If PKUK is determined to be an important entity for the Group, PSI will provide support to PKUK to meet its financial obligations. Therefore to fully assess the benefit from the financial guarantee one needs to substantiate the advantage from passive association. In order to analyse that, it is essential to understand the importance of PKUK within the Group.

Given the information we have, it can be said that PKUK is a significant member of the Group due to its strategic importance in the European supply chain and that the Group is planning to expand its presence in Europe. One of the approaches used by the practitioners to quantify the impact of passive association is the application of guidance provided by credit rating agencies who recognize the parent-subsidiary relationship and the level of support expected from the parent when determining the credit rating of the subsidiary. One of the papers in this regard has been published by S&P which provides Table 27.2.

*Table 27.2 Group Status*

| *Group Status* | *Brief Definition* | *Potential Long-Term Credit Rating of the Subsidiary* |
|---|---|---|
| Core | Integral to the group's current identity and future strategy. The rest of the group is likely to support these entities under any foreseeable circumstances | Credit Rating equal to Group credit rating profile (GCP). |
| Highly strategic | Almost integral to the group's current identity and future strategy. The rest of the group is likely to support these group members under almost all foreseeable circumstances. | One notch lower than the GCP unless the standalone credit rating profile (SACP)[1] is equal to, or higher than, the GCP. In such a case, the potential credit rating is equal to the GCP. |
| Strategically important | Less integral to the group than "highly strategic" group members. The rest of the group is likely to provide support in most foreseeable circumstances. However, some factors raise doubts about the extent of group support. | Three notches above SACP. This is subject to a cap of one notch below the GCP, unless the SACP is at least equal to the GCP, in which case the potential credit rating is equal to the GCP |
| Moderately strategic | Not important enough to warrant support from the rest of the group in some foreseeable circumstances. Nevertheless, there is potential for some support from the group. | One notch above SACP. This is subject to a cap of one notch below the GCP, unless the SACP is at least equal to the GCP, in which case, the potential credit rating is equal to the GCP. |
| Nonstrategic | No strategic importance to the group. | SACP, subject to a cap defined by the GCP. |

*Source*: General Criteria: Group Rating Methodology, S&P Global Ratings, July 2019.

1. The SACP refers to the credit rating of the entity without the implicit support

The above table is an example of a framework that can be used to measure the impact on the credit rating from 'implicit support'. There are similar tools provided by other credit rating agencies too. From this table, the subsidiary can be characterised in one of the five categories (based on the first column) using certain specific criteria that are detailed in the methodology paper. Once the category has been identified, an adjustment to the SACP can be made with reference to that category.

For the purpose of this case, let us assume that PKUK meets the listed criteria of a 'Strategically Important Entity' and as a result, its SACP would require adjustment. This would result in an upward adjustment of three notches to a credit rating of 'Ba1'/'BB+' to account for its importance within the Group or 'passive association' or 'implicit support'. Quantitatively this means that PKUK would be able to borrow at an interest rate of 2.75% rather than at an interest rate of 3.50%, which is a benefit of 0.75%.

The two aspects detailed above were from the guaranteed entity's perspective, whereas for accurate delineation of the transaction, one should also analyse the perspective of the guarantor entity, i.e., PSI. It is evident that PKUK receives benefit from the guarantee however does the guarantor, PSI, has the financial capacity to provide the financial guarantee? To answer this question, one would require an evaluation of the guarantor's and the borrower's credit rating including an assessment of the business correlations between them.[1]

The credit rating of PSI is much stronger than PKUK (even after accounting for implicit support), which is reflected in a three-notch difference in the credit rating of PSI at 'Baa1'/'BBB+' and the adjusted credit rating of PKUK at 'Ba1'/'BB+'. This highlights the view from the credit rating agencies that in their opinion the probability of default for PSI is lower than PKUK and it would be able to withstand financial difficulties and challenges better than PKUK. With respect to the business dependency between PSI and PKUK, if the same economic factors impact both PSI and PKUK with equal force during adverse market conditions then PSI's ability to support PKUK might be limited and it may be argued that PSI does not have the adequate financial capacity to provide the guarantee. However, based on the facts it seems that supply chain and political issues around Brexit are specific to Europe and PKUK. In this regard, one can assume that the impact of a potential economic downturn on PSI and PKUK would be in different directions and the two are decoupled. Do note that such an analysis depends on the specific facts and circumstances, which would need to be analysed accordingly.

In this section, the perspectives of both parties to the transaction, PKUK and PSI, have been observed. From PKUK's standpoint, there is a definite economic benefit from the guarantee and as it is an important entity within the Group it also has advantages from being part of the Group. Whereas from PSI's perspective, it has a stronger credit rating than PKUK (after adjusting for implicit support) and does have the financial capacity to provide financial guarantee. Therefore from an arm's length perspective one has accurately delineated this transaction as a provision of a guarantee from PSI to third-party banks on behalf of PKUK and this warrants a determination of an arm's length guarantee fee.

## IV DETERMINING ARM'S LENGTH PRICE OF GUARANTEE

Once the transaction has been accurately delineated, the next step is to determine an arm's length fee for the guarantee taking into account the risk of default borne by the guarantor and the benefit provided to the guaranteed entity. There are a number of methods and approaches that have been detailed in the OECD Guidelines such as:[2]

(a) CUP method
(b) Yield Approach

1. OECD Transfer Pricing Guidelines, *Transfer Pricing Aspects of Financial Transactions*, 10.166 (2022).
2. *Ibid.*, D.2.

(c) Cost Approach
(d) Valuation of Expected Loss Approach
(e) Capital Support Method.

The above list should not be considered an exhaustive list as there may be other methods which could be applied to determine an arm's length guarantee fee. It is however important to highlight that application of any method depends on the information available and the facts and circumstances of the transaction. For the purpose of this section, the focus is on showcasing the practical application of some methods to account for the two perspectives, i.e., guarantor and guaranteed entity.

The borrower/guaranteed entity can apply the Yield Approach to quantify the benefit that it receives from the guarantee in terms of lower interest rates. This method calculates the spread between the interest rate that would have been payable by the borrower without the guarantee and the interest rate payable with the guarantee.[3] The Yield Approach is akin to a CUP-based approach as comparable market data is generally utilised. The first step requires one to determine the interest rates that would have been paid by the guaranteed entity based on its SACP (without the financial guarantee) but including the impact of implicit support. The second step would be to calculate the interest rate that the borrower would be charged with the benefit of the financial guarantee. The difference between the two is determined as the maximum guarantee fee payable by the borrower. In other words, the resulting interest rate spread can be considered as the ceiling for the guarantee fee and the borrower would ideally not be willing to pay anything higher as it would be commercially unreasonable.

Application of the Yield Approach to the case study quantifies the benefit accruing to PKUK from implicit support and the benefit related to the financial guarantee. This is represented in Table 27.3.

*Table 27.3 Application of the Yield Approach*

| *Credit Rating of PKUK* | *At What Instance?* | *Interest Rate (%)* |
|---|---|---|
| **B1 / B+** | Standalone Credit Rating without implicit support | 3.50 |
| **Ba1 / BB+** | Standalone Credit Rating with implicit support | 2.75 |
| **Baa1 / BBB+** | Credit Rating with guarantee | 2.00 |

As PKUK's credit rating increased from 'B1'/'B+' to 'Ba1' / 'BB+' on account of implicit support, it has benefitted from a 0.75% decrease in the interest rate (3.50% – 2.75%). The data used in this case study are arbitrary numbers, however, in practice, publicly available databases are utilised to identify comparable third-party loan transactions or bonds issued in the market to determine a range of arm's length interest

3. *Ibid.*, 10.174.

rates. In order to ensure comparability of potential transactions to the tested transaction, certain characteristics such as the credit rating, maturity, purpose, industry, amount, ranking, etc., are usually considered.

The reduction of 0.75% in the interest rate is attributable to the synergy derived from PKUK's affiliation with the Group and not through any intra-group service or any activity being performed for which PKUK would be willing to pay. To calculate the maximum guarantee fee, one needs to consider the credit enhancement from the guarantee after accounting for implicit support, i.e., credit rating increment from 'Ba1'/'BB+' to 'Baa1'/'BBB+' which is a three-notch adjustment, resulting in a decrease in applicable interest rates by 0.75% (2.75% - 2.00%). As such, PKUK will not a pay guarantee fee in excess of 0.75% or 75 bps.

Once the borrower's perspective has been taken into account, it may be prudent for the guarantor's viewpoint to also be accounted for from an arm's length perspective, which would also allow for a range of guarantee fees to be determined. For the guarantor, it is about quantifying the default risk that it bears with respect to the guarantee. One of the possible methods is the Cost Approach which aims to quantify the additional risk borne by the guarantor, by estimating the value of the expected loss that the guarantor incurs by providing the guarantee (loss given default). Alternatively, the expected cost could be determined by reference to the capital required to support the risks assumed by the guarantor.[4] There are several possible models for estimating the expected loss and capital requirement. Popular pricing models for this approach work on the premise that financial guarantees are equivalent to another financial instrument and pricing the alternative, for example, treating the guarantee as a put option and using option pricing models, credit default swap pricing models, etc. For instance, publicly available data on credit default swap spreads may be used to approximate the default risk associated with the borrowing and, therefore, the guarantee fee.[5] Some of the pricing models of the Cost Approach are explained in detail in the following chapters of this book.

One of the other methods for determining the guarantee fee is the Valuation of Expected Loss Method, which estimates the value of a guarantee on the basis of calculating the probability of default and making adjustments to account for the expected recovery rate in the event of default. This would then be applied to the nominal amount guaranteed to arrive at a cost of providing the guarantee. The guarantee could then be priced based on an expected return on this amount of capital using commercial pricing models such as the Capital Asset Pricing Model (CAPM).[6] The results from such an analysis could potentially serve as the floor as it reflects the minimum that the guarantor would want to receive for assuming the credit risk.

The above analyses consider the viewpoints of both parties to the guarantee transaction, PKUK and PSI. Any guarantee fee higher than the ceiling or lower than the floor could be deemed commercially unreasonable and potentially considered non-arm's length. An arm's length guarantee fee would ideally make both PKUK and PSI

4. *Ibid.*, 10.178.
5. Ibid., 10.179.
6. *Ibid.*, 10.181.

better off as it would be lower than the ceiling and higher than the floor. Where the arm's length guarantee fee ends up between the two ends (floor or ceiling) generally depends on the bargaining power of the parties involved and the facts and circumstances of the case.

## V CONCLUSION

In this chapter, the main principles and theoretical aspects regarding the approaches and methods for pricing guarantees have been applied to a practical case study. As showcased in the case study, there are a few transfer pricing issues that are to be addressed, with the initial question of whether there is an actual or deemed intra-group guarantee transaction or not including the analysis of risks borne by the guarantor and the benefits obtained by the guaranteed entity. Once this is complete, the next step is to determine the arm's length guarantee fee.

There are several methods which can be applied to determine an arm's length guarantee fee, with the application of any method dependent on the facts of the case and the information available. It may be relevant to perform the analysis considering both perspectives, i.e., guaranteed entity and guarantor as this will allow determining a range of arm's length guarantee fees. The analysis from the guaranteed entity's perspective would determine a ceiling (one end of the range) whilst the analysis from the guarantor's perspective may determine a floor (other end of the range) and an arm's length guarantee fee accounting for both perspectives would potentially fall within this range.

## CHAPTER 28

# Using the Actuarial Approach to Price Guarantees

*Gary Lambert**

## I INTRODUCTION

The main advantage of market methods is that they are easy to implement. For this reason, they are the most commonly used methods amongst market participants. They may also form the most direct method to price the guarantee, in particular where market data are not available.[1] However, getting relevant data for market pricing methods may be difficult: they need to be sufficiently comparable to the transaction, or required adjustments can be performed, which might not always be possible.

An alternative is the actuarial approach, which offers the advantage that it can be applied in almost all cases, because it does not rely on financial market data to get results. This method has been highlighted by the Organisation for Economic Co-operation and Development (OECD) in its latest guidance on financial transactions. In fact, variations of this method are described in the OECD guidance as a valuation of expected loss approach and a cost approach.[2] In simple terms, this approach assesses the losses a guarantor will have to face in the context of a binding guarantee agreement. In this method, the price of the guarantee is estimated by calculating the cost of

---

* The views and opinions set forth herein are the personal views or opinions of the authors; they do not necessarily reflect the views or opinions of the organisation with which the authors are associated.

1. Market data include bonds yields and Credit Default Swaps (CDS) the latter being financial derivative OTC contract that allows an investor to offset his credit risk with another investor. Depending on the underlying reference entity, this market can be deep, and one can therefore rely on CDSs for information on its credit quality).
2. OECD, *Transfer Pricing Guidelines for Multinational Enterprises and Tax Administrations* (January 2022), Chapter X, sections D.2.4 (p. 440) and D.2.3 (p. 439).

earmarking capital to cover expected and unexpected losses linked to the guarantee arrangement.[3]

## II APPLICATION OF THE METHODOLOGY

To apply the actuarial method, two models can be relied on. Both consist of two components: expected and unexpected losses. The models are the default model and the mark-to-market model.[4] The terms of the guarantee agreement (including the definition of the credit event) dictate which model is most appropriate.

Unlike other approaches, the actuarial approach can easily be adjusted to determine the marginal benefit achieved from a guarantee transaction. More specifically, the aim is to estimate the added protection received by the creditors of the subsidiary through the additional guarantee of the parent (or related) company. This added protection corresponds to the economic value of the guarantee and protects the lenders from scenarios where the guaranteed entity was to face bankruptcy, without bringing the parent into extreme financial difficulties (joint bankruptcies).[5]

Under the actuarial approach, one can estimate the probability that the parent (or related company) does not default after the default of the subsidiary by calculating the joint probability of default of both entities. This hinges on the correlation of their default, that is, the interconnectedness of their respective default probability. This approach ties into measuring the ability of providing support, as described by Moody's.[6] The importance of measuring this correlation was also highlighted in the recent OECD guidance that states:[7]

> the examination of financial guarantees under accurate delineation needs also to consider the financial capacity of the guarantor to fulfil its obligations in case of default of the borrower. This requires an evaluation of the credit rating of the guarantor and the borrower and of the business correlations between them.

The next section describes this approach in more detail.

### 1 Default Model

The default model is suitable for contracts that guarantee default on an obligation during a specified period under predefined conditions. The guarantor makes payment

3. Or opportunity cost, as capital could be deployed elsewhere but for the fact that it is needed to provide the guarantee.
4. A. Saunders & L. Allen, *Credit Risk Measurement: New Approaches to Value at Risk and Other Paradigms* 84-106 (2nd ed., Wiley Finance, 2002).
5. This method is even more useful if the guarantor has the same or a lower credit rating than that of the subsidiary.
6. Moody's, *Incorporation of Joint-Default Analysis into Moody's Bank Ratings: A Refined Methodology*, March 2005, p. 5.
7. OECD, *Transfer Pricing Guidelines for Multinational Enterprises and Tax Administrations* (January 2022), Chapter X, section D.1.3 (p. 437).

only if the subsidiary fails to meet its financial commitments (default). The model consists of two main components: the expected losses and the unexpected losses.

## A Expected Losses

In this method, the expected losses are a function of the probability of default of the guaranteed entity, while the parent (related party) does not default, and the loss given default (LGD, or 1 minus the recovery rate following a default). This model is more commonly relied on when assessing intercompany guarantees. Under this model, the expected losses can be computed by the following formula:

Expected losses = probability of default × nominal amount × (1 - recovery rate),

where:

- nominal amount is the total amount of the credit facility;
- probability of default is the likelihood that the subsidiary (or entity guaranteed) will default, whilst the guarantor will not default; and
- recovery rate is the amount that the creditor would receive in final satisfaction in an event of a default.

The goal is to assess the cost of the marginal advantage conferred by the guarantee, or the probability that the parent (related party) does not default following a default of the subsidiary. If we define $P(P)$ and $P(S)$ as the probabilities of default of the parent and the subsidiary, respectively, and $P(P|S)$ as the probability of default of the parent after a default of the subsidiary, then the probability of the parent not defaulting following a default of the subsidiary can be written as 1 - (P|S).

The effective reduction of expected losses is then $1 - P(P|S) \times P(S)$, or marginal benefit. This measures the additional benefit of having the parent (or related party) guarantee the subsidiary compared with a situation where no such guarantee exists.

According to the theory of conditional probabilities, $P(P|S)$, or the probability of default of the parent following a default of the subsidiary, can be written as:

$$P(P|S) = P(P \cap S)/P(S),$$

where $P(P \cap S)$ is the joint probability of default of the parent and the subsidiary.

Following Moody's approach,[8] we can specify a correlation $W$, to further explain the joint probability of default, $P(P \cap S)$ as:

$$P(P \cap S) = W \times P(S) + (1 - W) \times P(P) \times P(S).$$

8. Moody's Investors Services, *Incorporation of Joint-Default Analysis for Systemic Support into Moody's Bank Rating Methodology*, Moody's (October 2005). http://www.Moodys.com/research/Incorporation-of-Joint-Default-Analysis-for-Systemic-Support-into-Moodys--PBC_94781

- $W = 1$ implies a perfect correlation between the defaults of the two entities: the default of one of the entities implies a default of the other, in all cases.
- $W = 0$ entails perfect independence of the defaults of the two entities.

In summary, one calculates the joint probability of default $[P(P \cap S)]$ based on a correlation assumption $[W]$ between the two entities, followed by the default probability of the parent following the default of the subsidiary $[P(P|S)]$. This enables the marginal benefit to be computed, followed by the expected losses.

Often from a transfer pricing perspective, determining the correlation $(W)$ between related parties can be a difficult and subjective matter. One approach is to base correlation estimations for this purpose on an analysis of price returns: of interest-bearing securities, from both entities or, if not available, comparable companies or equity price returns from both entities or, if not available, of comparable entities. Equity data is at times the only data source that can be relied on for correlation estimations.[9] Box 1 shows how to estimate the expected losses.

**Box 1: Default Model: Expected Losses Example**

A parent company, with a rating of A- (A3), extends a guarantee to one of its AA-rated (Aa2) subsidiaries for a period of 10 years, for a notional amount of GBP 10 million. What should the subsidiary pay upfront for this guarantee?

Moody's Investors Service and Standard and Poor Global Ratings publish historical cumulative default probabilities by rating and duration. For this example, I rely on hypothetical data. The default probabilities are 2.21% and 0.83% for A- and AA-rated companies, respectively, for that duration.[10] Next, I calculate the joint probability of default, which is in turn a function of the correlation between the entities. In Table 28.1, using recovery rates of 34%,[11] prices of the guarantee are shown for varying levels of assumed correlation between guarantor and guaranteed entity.

*Table 28.1 Expected Losses under the Default Model*

| *Correlation (%)* | *Joint Probability of Default (%)* | *Probability P\|S (%)* | *Marginal Benefit (%)* | *Expected Losses (£)* |
|---|---|---|---|---|
| **(1)** | **(2)** | **(3)** | **(4)** | **(5)** |
| 15 | 0.14 | 16.88 | 0.69 | 45,533.96 |
| 50 | 0.42 | 51.11 | 0.41 | 26,784.68 |
| 85 | 0.71 | 85.33 | 0.12 | 8,035.40 |

The results show that for increasing levels of assumed correlation (column 1), the price of the guarantee decreases (columns 5 and 6) because of an increased probability of joint default (column 3) and hence a decreasing marginal benefit (column 4). In

9. Correlation can also be estimated with structural models, such as the one developed by J. HULL & A. WHITE, *Valuing Credit Default Swaps II: Modelling Default Correlations*, 80020 NYU Working Paper (2000).
10. Hypothetical data that can be sourced from the rating agencies
11. Senior unsecured bond recovery rates can be sourced from the rating agencies

simple terms, the economic benefit attained by the subsidiary reduces as the default correlation increases. Thus at 100% correlation, there will be very limited or no benefit,[12] whereas, at 0% correlation, there will be potentially significant economic benefit from the guarantee.[13]

Please note that unexpected losses and the opportunity cost of the guarantee are not yet included in these calculations. As a next step, one should determine the effect of unexpected losses.

### *B Unexpected Losses*

The unexpected losses represent the losses above and beyond what might be expected that can arise due to the guarantee being called.

The unexpected losses can be estimated as the difference between a value-at-risk (VaR) estimate and the expected losses. The VaR represents the losses the guarantor can suffer over a given time period and for a given level of confidence. This will determine the amount of capital to be set aside by the guarantor to prepare for such situations. Because this capital could have been deployed to other ends, the price of the guarantee includes the cost of setting aside this capital to face unexpected losses. For this reason, one references 'opportunity cost' when describing unexpected losses.

Figure 28.1 shows schematically the difference between expected losses and unexpected losses under a normal loss distribution curve.

12. There is no benefit under this correlation assumption, because when one entity defaults, the other does as well.
13. There is a large benefit under this correlation assumption because the defaults of the two entities are independent of each other.

*Figure 28.1 Loss Distribution*

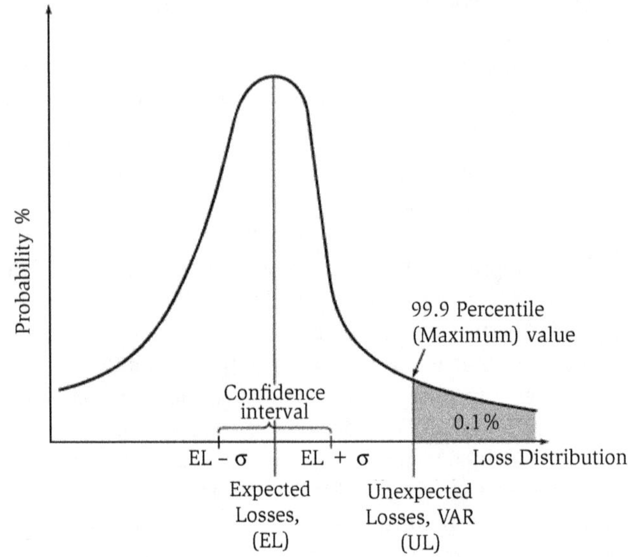


*Source*: A. Saunders & L. Allen, Credit Risk Measurement: New Approaches to Value at Risk and Other Paradigms, p. 6 (2nd ed., Wiley Finance 2002).

**Box 2: The Default Model: Unexpected Losses Example**

Revisiting the example of Box 1, the price of guarantee will also have to include unexpected losses, or more precisely the cost of capital linked to earmarking additional capital to face unexpected losses in the event the guarantee is called. One models the unexpected losses as an amount given a certain confidence (e.g., 95%) interval, assuming a normal distribution of these losses.[14]

*Table 28.2 Unexpected Losses under the Default Model*

| *Correlation (%)* | *Joint Probability of Default (%)* | *Probability P\|S (%)* | *Marginal Benefit (%)* | *Expected Losses (£)* |
|---|---|---|---|---|
| **(1)** | **(2)** | **(3)** | **(4)** | **(5)** |
| 15 | 0.14 | 16.88 | 0.69 | 45,533.96 |
| 50 | 0.42 | 51.11 | 0.41 | 26,784.68 |
| 85 | 0.71 | 85.33 | 0.12 | 8,035.40 |

14. 1.65 × the standard deviation is used in this example.

One sees that the additional need to cover unexpected losses can add a relatively high cost to the guarantee (compared with the cost of insuring expected losses).[15]

## 2 Mark-to-Market Model

As described already, the default model triggers a payment only in case of a default of the subsidiary. The mark-to-market model is suitable for contracts that guarantee the market value of the obligation: payments could be made prior to default because of the changing risk profile of the guaranteed entity. For example, if the market value for a loan decreases due to a rating downgrade of the subsidiary, the guarantor will make a payment corresponding to the capital loss associated with the downgrade.

The mark-to-market model considers the potential credit quality migration of the subsidiary guaranteed to assess the expected and unexpected losses. The main difference from the previous model is that the mark-to-market model considers both the upside and downside of the loan guaranteed. Indeed, this model considers the fact that, for instance, an A-rated debt can be downgraded into a BBB-rated security or upgraded to an AA-rated asset.

### *A Expected Losses*

The first step is to compute the expected value of the loan by summing the product of the probabilities of the 'rating state' and the present value of the cash flow of the loan associated with the rating state. Let's assume that the credit rating of the subsidiary is BBB, the formula of the expected value E(loan) will be:

$$P_{BBB}\,(AAA) \times NPV_{AAA} + P_{BBB}(AA) \times NPV_{AA} + \ldots + P_{BBB}\,(CCC) \times NPV_{CCC} + P_{BBB}\,(Default) \times NPV_{Default}$$

Where

$P_i(j)$ probability that the subsidiary is $j$-rated at the next period given that it is currently $i$-rated;[16]
$NPV_j$ present value of the coupons and principal using the $j$-rated yield curve as a discount factor;
$NPV_{Default}$ value of the loan in case of default.

The expected losses are the difference between the current market value of the loan and its expected value.

15. Please note that the calculation of unexpected losses under the market model follows the same method.
16. Commonly called migration rates. Recent ones can be found in Moody's, *Default Trends – Global*, 42-43, ex. 32-37.

### *B Unexpected Losses*

The default model and the mark-to-market model assess the unexpected losses in the same way.

## 3 Implications of Implicit Support

Implicit support affects the estimation of the expected and unexpected losses of the subsidiary, the former by decreasing the probability of default or increasing recovery rates associated with a higher credit rating and the latter by potentially decreasing the variability of the VaR calculations and hence the potential level of unexpected losses. This implication is considered part of the credit rating analyses relied on for applying the methodology.

## 4 Final Computation for Both Models

Once the expected and unexpected losses are computed based on one of the methods already described, the guarantee fee can be estimated by the sum of the expected losses and the opportunity cost associated with the guarantee. The capital asset pricing model (CAPM) can proxy the cost of capital associated with unexpected losses.

$$\text{Guarantee fee} = \text{expected losses} + \text{cost of opportunity (unexpected losses)}$$

**Box 3: The Default Model: Total Price of the Guarantee Example**

Bringing our calculations together from Box 1 (expected losses) and Box 2 (unexpected losses), one can compute the total cost of the guarantee. We use a cost of capital of 8%.

*Table 28.3 Total Price of the Guarantee under the Default Model*

| *Correlation (%)* | *Expected Losses (£)* | *Cost of Capital (£)* | *Total Cost of Guarantee (%)* |
|---|---|---|---|
| (1) | (2) | (3) | (4) |
| 15 | 45,533.96 | 72,112.46 | 1.18 |
| 50 | 26,784.68 | 55,386.78 | 0.82 |
| 85 | 8,035.40 | 55,386.78 | 0.38 |

Based on the calculations, the guarantee fee is 0.38% of the notional outstanding amount if the joint-default probability or correlation is determined to be 85% and 1.18% if the correlation is determined to be 15%. To this guarantee fee, one can add an administration fee for functional costs incurred in managing the guarantee. Unlike insurance companies or banks that incur large functional costs, which they need to factor in when extending guarantees, such a cost could be negligible in most intercompany situations. This latter element should nevertheless be considered on a case-by-case basis.

## III CONCLUSION

The main advantage of the actuarial method is that it can be relied on in almost all cases where market methods cannot be applied. However, this approach is rather academic (i.e., technical) and might be difficult to apply for market participants in practice. Being based on historical (default) probability and recovery rate data, comparability to current market conditions might prove problematic, and adjustments might have to be performed.

Even so, the marginal benefit and potential losses estimations of the actuarial approach are especially useful when credit rating differentials would lead to nonsensical results under the market approach, for example, when both entities have the same credit rating or in some isolated instances when the guarantor has a lower credit rating than the guaranteed entity, which may occur in the context of performance (operational) guarantees.

Given the foregoing considerations and the specific limitations of the different pricing approaches, it is often advisable to rely on multiple approaches when performing a pricing study, if possible.

CHAPTER 29

# The Use of CDSs When Pricing Debt Guarantees

*Timothy McKenna*[*]

The arm's length price of a company's debt guarantee for its subsidiary's debt can be assessed using data from the credit default swap (CDS) market. In general terms, a CDS contract can be viewed as insurance against a company's default. The following approach uses market prices for CDS contracts to estimate the arm's length price of a debt guarantee. The price is estimated as the difference between two CDS contracts: a CDS contract on the subsidiary as a standalone entity and a CDS contract on the parent. The recently released Organisation for Economic Co-operation and Development (OECD) Transfer Pricing Guidance on financial transactions refer to using CDS data in the context of loans.[1] In fact, this type of data is one of the most directly comparable data sources for pricing guarantees available in the open market.

CDS contracts are over-the-counter derivative contracts that reference the debt (the reference obligation) of a third party, often a corporate or sovereign entity (the reference entity). In a CDS contract, one counterparty (the protection buyer) agrees to pay a regular fee to the other counterparty in the swap (the protection seller).[2] In return, the protection seller agrees to make a payment to the protection buyer if a credit event is triggered. Although the specific credit events that apply to a given CDS contract

* The views and opinions set forth herein are the personal views or opinions of the authors; they do not necessarily reflect the views or opinions of the organization with which the authors are associated.

1. OECD, 'Transfer Pricing Guidance for Multinational Enterprises and Tax Administrations', January 2022, para. 10.101, p. 424, https://read.oecd-ilibrary.org/taxation/oecd-transfer-pricing-guidelines-for-multinational-enterprises-and-tax-administrations-2022_0e655865-en. (hereinafter 'OECD Guidelines').Transfer Pricing Guidance on Financial Transactions, Inclusive Framework on BEPS Actions 4, 8-10, para. 10.101, 22.
2. An over-the-counter (OTC) financial contract generally refers to a contract where the terms of the trade are negotiated between two parties and the trade does not take place on an exchange. CDS contracts are typically done using the standardized terms set forth by the International Swaps and

are defined ahead of time by the parties, in rough terms, a credit event can be thought of as a default by the reference entity. Events such as missed interest or principal payments, debt restructuring, or a change of control may be included as credit events. The regular fee is commonly referred to as the spread and is paid on a periodic basis, often quarterly. The total amount insured in the contract is referred to as the notional value, and the spread is a fraction of this amount. CDS contracts are for set time spans, with five years being a common choice.[3]

In the case study, CDS contracts on the subsidiary and the parent are not publicly traded. Instead, the price of CDS for the parent and the subsidiary are estimated using a set of relationships between measures of credit quality and CDS spreads for firms that are similar to the parent and subsidiary. The predicted CDS spreads for the parent and subsidiary are used to estimate the benefit of the guarantee. The measures of credit quality are earnings before interest, taxes, depreciation, and amortization (EBITDA) to net debt, EBITDA to interest expense, assets to net debt, and the volatility of the value of the firm's equity.[4] The particular relationships chosen should not be read as being set in stone. Rather, what is important is that the metrics reflect the determinants of the price of credit risk for the industry in question, are readily available for peer companies, and can be estimated for both the parent and subsidiary.

## I DISCUSSION OF THE CDS METHODOLOGY

### 1 Transfer Pricing Method

The CDS methodology described here is based on the realistic alternatives of the subsidiary. I assume that the subsidiary, as a substantial entity in its own right, could have borrowed on a standalone basis for the amount being guaranteed. The benefit of the guarantee to the subsidiary is measured by the reduction in borrowing cost to the subsidiary because of the guarantee.

A CDS contract can be viewed as measuring the cost of a credit risk guarantee, so the use of CDS data discussed in this chapter falls into the Comparable Uncontrolled Services Price Method under US Internal Revenue Service regulations[5] and the

Derivatives Association (ISDA). ISDA is an industry group composed of derivative market participants. As part of their work, ISDA creates and encourages the use of standardized contracts for OTC derivative transactions.

3. For more details, *see* John C. Hull, *Options, Futures, and Other Derivatives* Ch. 25 (10th ed. Pearson 2018). Note that the potential for different recovery rates at the parent or subsidiary should be considered and, if necessary, modelled directly when predicting spreads for the parent or subsidiary.
4. Ideally, one would use expected future volatility of each firm's stock price, a measure that is obtainable from options data. However, it may be difficult to obtain options data for the parent, subsidiary, and comparable peer companies. Measures of equity volatility that are derived from past stock price returns can still have a relationship with CDS spreads and are used in the following analysis.
5. US Treas. Reg. §1.482-9(c)(1).

Comparable Uncontrolled Price Method under OECD guidelines.[6] These guidelines allow for uncontrolled transactions to measure the benefit of the guarantee.

A CDS contract can also be viewed as a synthetic corporate bond. This can be seen by comparing the returns of two portfolios, one consisting of a five-year corporate bond and the other a five-year risk-free bond plus a CDS contract where you sell protection for five years on same corporation.[7] In this sense, the CDS method can also be thought of as a variant of the yield approach in OECD guidelines.[8] Rather than using bond data to estimate the effect of the guarantee, one can use CDS data. Ultimately the availability and ease of use of the data may dictate which source is better.

### 2 Suitability of Method

The spread in a CDS contract is a measure of a company's credit risk.[9] The difference between the estimated CDS spread of the subsidiary and the CDS spread of the parent measures how much less credit risk the market perceives the parent to have. Thus, the reduction in borrowing cost, measured by the difference in predicted CDS spreads, represents the benefit to the subsidiary and thus should be the maximum that the subsidiary would be willing to pay for the guarantee.

## II CDS DATA CONSIDERATIONS

CDS spread data is commonly available for larger firms with existing debt. Whether there are publicly traded CDS contracts for the parent or subsidiary is not critical. It is enough that the parent and subsidiary are similar to those firms with traded CDS. This implies that both the parent and subsidiary will likely need to be relatively large firms. If the parent and/or subsidiary are not comparable with those firms with traded CDS, one should be cognizant of the fact that the methods described below, where one essentially predicts what the CDS spread would be for the parent and the subsidiary, may not be appropriate.

As of the end of June 2021, there was approximately USD 8.8 trillion in notional value of CDSs outstanding. Single-name CDS (where the CDS contract references just

6. OECD Guidelines, p. 97, section B. OECD, 'Transfer Pricing Guidance for Multinational Enterprises and Tax Administrations', July 2017, p. 101, section B.
7. One can rewrite the comparison of the portfolios as 'a risk-free bond = corporate bond + buying CDS protection'. Note that these comparisons are only heuristics, and the two portfolios will only exactly equal each other under certain conditions.
8. OECD Guidelines, p. 285, section D.2.2. Transfer Pricing Guidance, section D.2.2, p. 32.
9. As noted by Hull (2018), 'the spread of the yield on an $n$-year bond issued by a company over the risk-free rate should approximately equal the company's $n$-year CDS spread', p. 573. Note that this relationship does not always hold and the CDS spread for a particular corporation can be influenced by technical factors such as the price of the cheapest-to-deliver bond for the CDS and the exact rules for a credit event.

one firm) represent USD 3.4 trillion of this amount.[10] Index CDS are more popular, with USD 4.3 trillion notional outstanding.[11]

Although it is substantial, the CDS market is still smaller than the overall corporate debt market. As of June 2021, in just the United States (US) there was USD 11 trillion in corporate debt for nonfinancial firms outstanding.[12] CDS data certainly can be useful, but one should consider whether bond data will allow for more reliable inferences.

The relationship between CDS spreads and measures of credit quality commonly varies by industry. In particular, firms in some industries may tolerate higher debt loads than those in other industries. Consistency of demand, operating margins, and financing needs may all play into this. For these reasons, it is important to consider the industry when choosing comparable firms for analysing guarantee fees.

The data required for the methodology described here is generally publicly available. Each step of the analysis can be replicated by a third party given the underlying data. In particular, analysing the cost of credit does not rely on obtaining bond ratings for the subsidiary and parent. The cost of credit risk is modelled directly using market prices.

## III CASE STUDY OUTLINE

### 1 Overview of Case

In the case study, a US subsidiary issues debt that is guaranteed by its parent, a non-US domiciled corporation. The subsidiary, on a standalone basis, is a large firm. The corporate parent has substantial operations beyond its US subsidiary and is larger than the subsidiary. The parent and the subsidiary are assumed to be electrical equipment manufacturing companies.

The analysis assumes that the guarantee fee was negotiated at the start of the fiscal year and the parent committed to the guarantee for a five-year period. Extensions of this framework to multiple fiscal years and arrangements where the value of the guarantee is recomputed periodically can be accommodated by replicating the analysis at different points in time.

10. Bank of International Settlements, 'OTC Derivatives Outstanding', 15 November 2021, https://www.bis.org/statistics/derstats.htm (accessed 13 December 2021).
11. Index CDS are contracts in which one can buy or sell protection on multiple firms all at once. For example, the CDX North American Investment Grade Index CDS contract allows one to buy or sell protection on 125 different investment-grade companies with one contract. Other non-index multiname CDS contracts (such as basket CDS contracts) make up the remaining USD 1.1 trillion in notional outstanding.
12. Board of Governors of the Federal Reserve System (US), Nonfinancial Corporate Business, Debt Securities and Loans, Liability, Level [BCNSDODNS], retrieved from FRED, Federal Reserve Bank of St. Louis; https://fred.stlouisfed.org/series/BCNSDODNS (accessed 13 December 2021).

## 2 Financial and Market Data for Parent and Subsidiary

The analysis requires financial and market data for the parent and the subsidiary as a standalone entity. It is often necessary to adjust the financials of the parent and subsidiary. For example, published financials may include the guarantee fees in them. The analysis of the subsidiary as a standalone entity should be done as if these guarantee fees had not been paid, so these payments should be removed from the available financial data.

It may also be necessary to adjust the financial statement of the subsidiary to reflect a higher interest expense without the guarantee in place. If the interest expense is put into the financial ratios used to estimate the arm's length price of the guarantee (as it is in the case study), one should account for the fact that the subsidiary would have had higher interest expenses without the guarantee. An approximation for this effect can be done by estimating the guarantee fee once using the following methodology to estimate the additional interest cost the subsidiary would incur without the guarantee. Using this additional cost, one can adjust the subsidiary's financial statements to reflect the additional interest expense and rerun the guarantee fee computation. It is usually not necessary to repeat this process, as the additional increase in interest expense from another round of estimation of the guarantee fee is typically minimal.

Stock price data for the subsidiary (or the parent) may be difficult to obtain. In such cases, one may need to rely on measures of credit quality other than equity volatility.

Table 29.1 shows the measures of credit quality used in the example. Unlike the other three measures, equity volatility needs to be estimated using market data, not financial data.

*Table 29.1 Parent and Subsidiary Financial Ratios*

| *Parent* | | *Subsidiary (Stand-Alone Basis)* | |
|---|---|---|---|
| ***(MM USD)*** | **2020** | ***(MM USD)*** | **2020** |
| *Income Statement Items* | | *Income Statement Items* | |
| Revenue | 13,000 | Revenue | 5,000 |
| EBITDA | 7,800 | EBITDA | 1,800 |
| Interest Expense | 2,050 | Interest Expense | 1,750 |
| Depreciation | 1,600 | Depreciation | 700 |
| Taxes | 390 | Taxes | 90 |
| Net Income | 3,760 | Net Income | -740 |
| *Balance Sheet Items* | | *Balance Sheet Items* | |
| Assets | 1,60,000 | Assets | 70,000 |
| Net Debt | 50,000 | Net Debt | 35,000 |
| Net Debt/EBITDA | 6.41 | Net Debt/EBITDA | 19.44 |
| EBITDA/Interest Expense | 3.80 | EBITDA/Interest Expense | 1.03 |

| Parent | | Subsidiary (Stand-Alone Basis) | |
|---|---|---|---|
| *(MM USD)* | **2020** | *(MM USD)* | **2020** |
| *Income Statement Items* | | *Income Statement Items* | |
| Net Debt/Assets | 0.31 | Net Debt/Assets | 0.50 |
| Equity Volatility | 0.14 | Equity Volatility | 0.17 |

## 3 Relationship Between Credit Quality and CDS Spreads

Comparable companies are used to estimate the relationship between the cost of credit (measured by CDS spreads) and the four measures of credit quality. When selecting comparable companies, factors such as industry and firm size should be considered. The guarantee was made for five years, so one should consider five-year CDS spreads for comparable companies.

The relationship between the measures of credit quality and five-year CDS spreads are first examined using the non-parametric LOESS methodology (*see* Figure 29.1).[13] This allows one to capture non-linear effects in the relationship.

Due to licensing limitations, the financial data shown here are hypothetical data. Actual CDS spreads can be obtained from data providers, such as Bloomberg, FactSet, and IHS Markit.

13. LOESS (Locally Estimated Scatterplot Smoothing) refers to the technique of local regression. *See* Eric Falkenstein, *DefProb: A Corporate Probability of Default Model*, SSRN (15 July 2008), https://ssrn.com/abstract=1103404 or http://dx.doi.org/10.2139/ssrn.1103404.

*Figure 29.1 Relationship Between Credit Quality Measures and CDS Spreads*

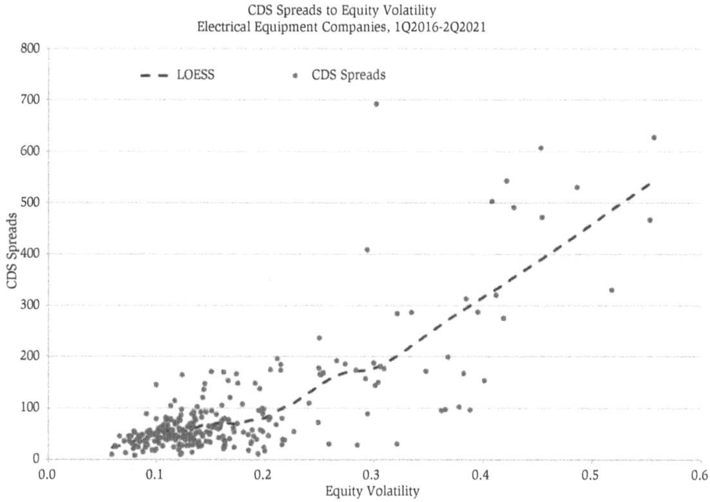


*Notes and Sources*:

Company financial data are from FactSet Research Systems.

Electrical Equipment companies are firms included in the Dow Jones US Industrials Index with GICS code 201040

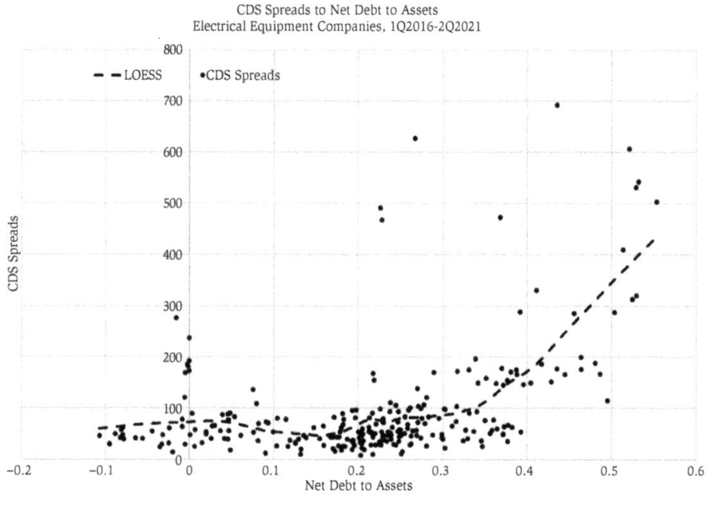


*Notes and Sources*:

Company financial data are from FactSet Research Systems.

Electrical Equipment companies are firms included in the Dow Jones US Industrials Index with GICS code 201040

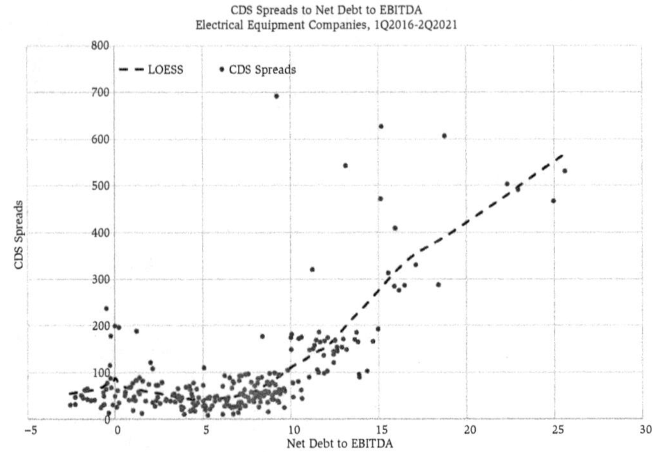


*Notes and Sources*:

Company financial data are from FactSet Research Systems.

Electrical Equipment companies are firms included in the Dow Jones US Industrials Index with GICS code 201040

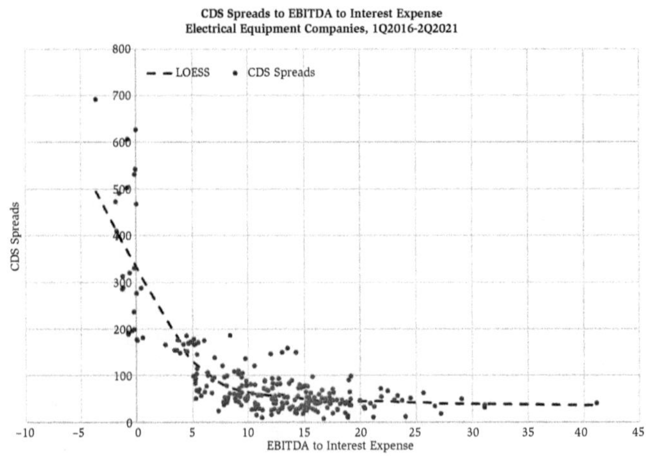


*Notes and Sources*:

Company financial data are from FactSet Research Systems.

Electrical Equipment companies are firms included in the Dow Jones US Industrials Index with GICS code 201040

These measures of quality reflect an important feature of credit risk – that the risk can be non-linear. For example, EBITDA to interest expense ratios above 10 are generally associated with a low level of CDS spreads, rising from around 50 basis points at high levels of the ratio to around 70 basis points at 10. As the ratio declines, the associated CDS spreads start to increase much more rapidly. This nonlinearity is an important feature in credit risk and can be captured directly using this methodology.

Given one of the measures of credit quality, one can compute a predicted CDS spread by referencing the level of the LOESS line. For example, an EBITDA to interest expense ratio of around 15 results in a predicted CDS spread of about 50 basis points (i.e., finding 15 on the $x$-axis and then seeing the level on the $y$-axis of the LOESS line for that value of $x$). An EBITDA to interest expense of 2.5 results in a predicted CDS spread of approximately 200 basis points.

## 4 Predicted CDS Spreads for Parent and Subsidiary

The effect of the guarantee can be seen visually by examining the predictions for the subsidiary and the parent. Although the exact estimate will be made using the combined prediction based on the regression equation, one can get a sense of the benefit visually. The guarantee grants the subsidiary the credit quality of the parent, and that benefit can be seen by looking at the predicted CDS spreads for the parent and the subsidiary (*see* Figure 29.2).

*Figure 29.2 Predictions for Parent and Subsidiary*

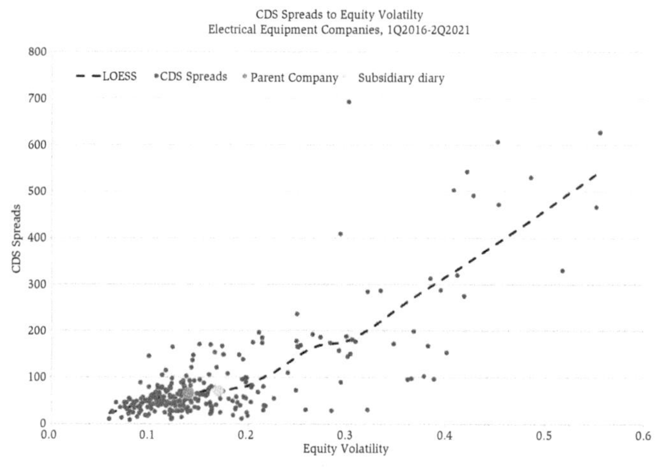


*Notes and Sources:*

Company financial data are from FactSet Research Systems.

Electrical Equipment companies are firms included in the Dow Jones US Industrials Index with GICS code 201040.

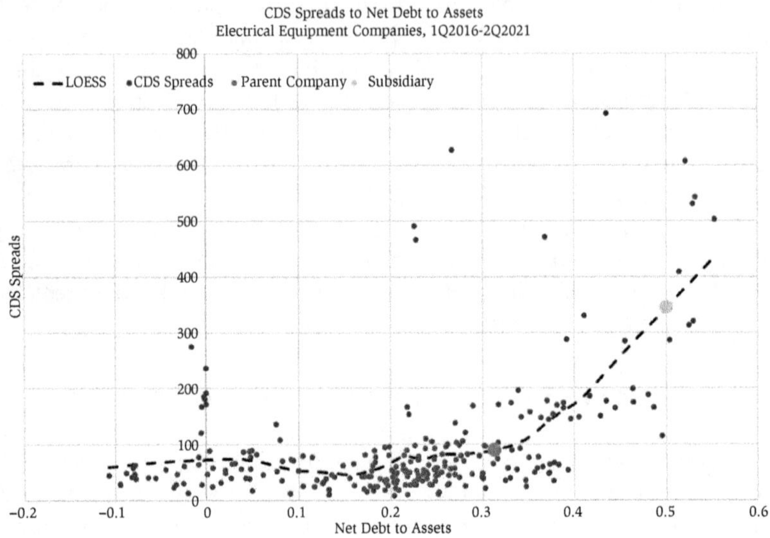


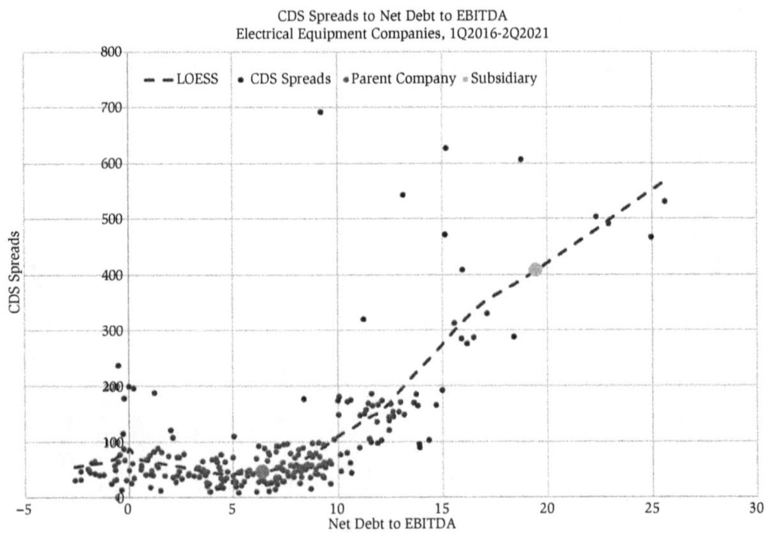


*Notes and Sources:*

Company financial data are from FactSet Research Systems.

Electrical Equipment companies are firms included in the Dow Jones US Industrials Index with GICS code 201040.

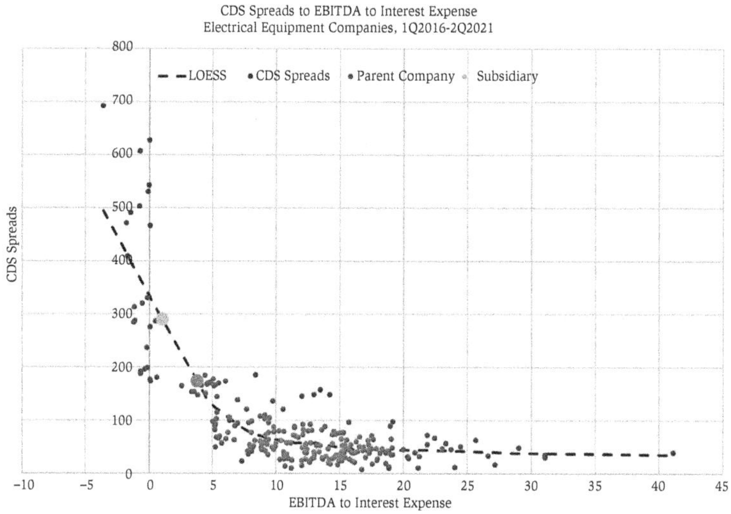


*Notes and Sources:*

Company financial data are from FactSet Research Systems.

Electrical Equipment companies are firms included in the Dow Jones US Industrials Index with GICS code 201040.

The predictions for the parent and the subsidiary are shown as dots on the LOESS line. The parent and subsidiary had relatively similar equity volatility measures, so it is not surprising that the guarantee is predicted to have minimal effect using that measure of credit quality. The other measures show greater effects from the guarantee. The EBITDA to interest expense ratio predicts a 100 basis point lower CDS spread, net debt to assets predicts a roughly 250-point difference, and the net debt to EBITDA ratio predicts an approximately 350-point difference.

To make a single prediction for either the parent or subsidiary, one must combine the four predictions. To do this, I use a multivariate regression.[14] The actual CDS spread of each comparable company observation is the dependent variable, and the four predicted spreads for the company (as predicted using the LOESS lines) are the independent variables. Essentially the regression model is used to estimate the 'weight' for each independent variable to use when making an estimate of the actual CDS spread

14. Regression is a statistical technique that measures the association between a dependent variable and an independent variable. A multivariate regression measures the relationships between a dependent variable and more than one independent variable. It can be used to assess which, if any, of the independent variables have a strong relationship with the dependent variable. For more details, *see* Daniel Rubinfeld, 'Reference Guide on Multiple Regression', in *Reference Manual on Scientific Evidence* 303-358 (3d ed. National Academies Press 2011).

for an observation. An alternative methodology is to simply take an average of the four independent variables. *See* Table 29.2 for coefficient estimates.

*Table 29.2 Coefficient Estimates*

| | *Coefficients* | *Standard Error* |
|---|---|---|
| Intercept | −22.57 | 4.78 |
| LOESS Net Debt to EBITDA | 0.27 | 0.06 |
| LOESS Net Debt to Assets | 0.04 | 0.06 |
| LOESS EBITDA to Int. Expense | 0.62 | 0.04 |
| LOESS Equity Volatility | 0.30 | 0.05 |

In this example, the coefficient for EBITDA to interest expense has the highest coefficient (0.62), with equity volatility (0.30) and net debt to EBITDA (0.27) also having sizable coefficients.[15]

The four single predicted spreads are combined using the regression coefficients (including the constant) as well as using a simple average in Table 29.3.

*Table 29.3 Predicted CDS Spreads for Parent and Subsidiary*

| | *LOESS Predictions* | | | | | |
|---|---|---|---|---|---|---|
| | *Net Debt to EBITDA* | *Net Debt to Assets* | *EBITDA to Interest Expense* | *Equity Volatility* | *Simple Average Estimate* | *Regression Weights Estimate* |
| | *(1)* | *(2)* | *(3)* | *(4)* | *(5)* | *(6)* |
| Parent | 46 | 89 | 174 | 65 | 93 | 120 |
| Subsidiary | 407 | 344 | 290 | 70 | 278 | 300 |
| Difference | | | | | 184 | 180 |

## 5 Estimated Arm's Length Benefit of Guarantee

The foregoing calculations estimate how much more expensive, in basis points, the market would view a CDS contract for the subsidiary than for the parent. This difference, which can also be thought of as the additional amount the subsidiary would pay in interest costs, is an estimate of the benefit of the guarantee. Focusing on column

15. All of the independent variables have the same scale, as the regression uses the LOESS transformations as the numerical values in the regression, so one can make this comparison directly from the coefficients.

6 in Table 29.3, the subsidiary benefits by 180 basis points a year due to the guarantee.[16]

To estimate the arm's length benefit of the guarantee in dollars, one multiplies the value of the guaranteed debt by the estimated basis point benefit. This is an estimate of how much less the subsidiary paid in interest expenses over the course of the period at issue, in this case, assumed to be one year. The calculations for our example firm are in Table 29.4.[17]

*Table 29.4 Estimated Value of the Benefit*

| *Benefit (Basis Points)* | *Guaranteed Debt (MM USD)* | *Length of Guarantee (Days)* | *Benefit (MM USD)* |
|---|---|---|---|
| *-1* | *-2* | *-3* | *-4* |
| | | | *= (1)/10000 * (2) * (3)/365* |
| 180 | 35,000 | 365 | 631 |

In this case, the benefit of the guarantee is estimated at USD 631 million per year.

Computing a range of acceptable arm's length estimates is commonly accepted by tax authorities.[18] For example, the OECD states 'statistical tools that take account of central tendency to narrow the range . . . might help to enhance the reliability of the analysis'.[19]

For the methodology outlined here, one can use the regression model to compute an interquartile range around the benefit of the guarantee in basis points.[20] Using these high and low estimates of the benefit, one can compute the top and bottom of the interquartile range for the arm's length fee. To obtain the range in dollars, one would use the top and bottom of the basis points range in place of the estimated benefit in column 1 of Table 29.4.

In this estimate of the benefit of the guarantee, implicit support can be incorporated by estimating the effect of implicit support in terms of basis points.[21] This estimate is used to reduce the predicted CDS spread of the subsidiary. It is possible that certain methods for predicting the CDS spread of the subsidiary may already reflect

16. The question of how to weight the univariate predictions using a regression or using a simple average is not straightforward. If one believes each univariate prediction is equally valid, then a simple average may be useful to look at because it does not risk poor out-of-sample predictions due to overfitting. On the other hand, the regression weights may capture that some of the univariate predictions are not as valid predictors as others, so the regression may improve predictions.
17. This calculation can be extended to cover partial years by multiplying by the fraction of the year that the agreement is in place.
18. For example, *see* https://www.dlapiper.com/en/us/insights/publications/2019/11/the-use-of-the-interquartile-range-in-transfer-pricing/ (accessed 22 December 2021).
19. OECD Guidelines [1], para. 3.57. Also *see* Treas. Reg. 1.482-1(e)(2)(iii)(B), (C).
20. Naturally, the specific rules of the relevant tax authorities should be considered when constructing such a range.
21. *See* OECD Guidelines, para. 1.167, example 2, and para. 7.13; Treas. Reg. 1.482-9(l)(3)(v).

implicit support from the parent. If so, it is possible that no further adjustment for implicit support is needed.

Perhaps the more difficult part of this exercise may be determining how much an adjustment for passive association should be. In addition to using already published estimates of the size of the benefit, one could directly estimate the effect using CDS data for similar firms with known corporate parents. This line of analysis is complicated by the fact that one needs financial data for the subsidiary, which may not be available if the subsidiary is consolidated into the parent's financial statements. If enough firms are available, one could perform analyses that estimate how much lower the CDS spread is for firms with corporate parents similar to the tested case. Such an analysis should be treated with caution, because similar firms may have varying business strategies and therefore different positions on the extent to which a parent or group entity may support a subsidiary. Other methods, such as those outlined by rating agencies, are available and can be used as a basis for adjusting the analysis. For this case study, we assumed that both entities were able to borrow in their own capacity and that there was limited need for any further adjustments for passive association to the predictions.

## IV ALTERNATIVES TO CDS DATA

Corporate bond data is typically more easily accessed than CDS data. The methodology outlined in this chapter could be applied using bond data instead of CDS data with some adjustments. The primary difficulty with using bond data lies in the fact that many bonds have features that need to be adjusted for before one can compare them.

A full accounting of the various factors that one needs to adjust for is outside of the scope of this chapter, but some major differences that do not appear when using CDS data are:

- Bonds price data should be converted to yield-to-maturity (YTM).
- YTMs should be expressed as the yield over the risk-free rate (often referred to as the z-spread).
- The influence of embedded options, such as issuer call options, on the YTM should be removed from the YTM.
- Like the CDS contracts, maturities of bonds should match the length of the guarantee. To do this, one could use only bonds with a maturity similar to the guarantee, or one could estimate bond yields at the desired maturity using techniques, such as interpolation.

Adjustments like these are nontrivial, but they are certainly feasible. In addition, although CDS data may appear easier to use because it comes in standardized maturities for each firm, a researcher needs to take care that analyses done with CDS data, especially when comparing CDS spreads across firms, is valid.

## V CONCLUDING REMARKS

Using CDS data, one can access a relatively well-standardized data set of credit risk measures. The methodology outlined here lets one measure the difference in credit risk between a subsidiary and its parent, and this difference is a measure of the benefit a subsidiary enjoys from its parent guaranteeing its debt.

The method is transparent and can easily be replicated by third parties, which is often useful when presenting analyses to tax authorities around the world. The methodology can be validated using bond-level data as well. Although it is not always suitable, in particular for smaller companies where CDS data may be scarce, it can be a useful alternative to other methods.

# D Special Consideration for Performance Guarantees

Chapter 30

# Transfer Pricing Aspects of Performance Guarantees

*Adam Kosmala*[*]

## I INTRODUCTION

A performance guarantee is an arrangement between three parties: a client, a contractor and a guarantor. The first two conclude a contract under which the contractor undertakes to perform certain actions, e.g., deliver goods or provide services to the client. Meanwhile, the guarantor promises that, in case the contractor does not deliver, it will take over the underlying obligations, effectively replacing the contractor. A primary difference between a performance and a financial guarantee is that the underlying obligations of the former always include a non-financial component (completion of work), either exclusively or in combination with a compensation payment.

Performance guarantees benefit both the contractor and the clients. Thanks to a performance guarantee, the contractor may, e.g., secure access to a market or obtain better terms in relations with the client. On the other hand, clients often require performance guarantees to limit their risk, e.g., if:

- the contractor lacks experience and/or a proven track record; or
- the contract covers a long period and/or has significant value.

Performance guarantees can be found in many industries, often where contracts tend to be long-term and large. The increasing capital intensity of modern economy further widens their area of application.

---

* The views and opinions set forth herein are the personal views or opinions of the authors; they do not necessarily reflect the views or opinions of the organization with which the authors are associated.

Transfer pricing (TP) issues with respect to performance guarantees arise when the contractor and the guarantor are related parties (intra-group performance guarantee). Depending on the relation between them, the intra-group performance guarantee can be downstream (contractor = subsidiary, guarantor = parent company), upstream (contractor = parent company, guarantor = subsidiary) and cross-stream (contractor and guarantor = sister companies).[1] In practice, downstream intra-group performance guarantees are most common as the parent company usually pools resources of the whole multinational enterprise (MNE) group (funds, reputation, technical capabilities, etc.).

Intra-group performance guarantees used to receive relatively little attention – they are not as common as intra-group financial guarantees and require a time-consuming, case-by-case approach. However, in 2013, the Organisation for Economic Co-operation and Development (OECD) included them in its *Action Plan on Base Erosion and Profit Shifting*, under Action 4: Limit base erosion via interest deductions and other financial payments. Subsequently, Annex II to Chapter V of the revised OECD TP Guidelines listed intra-group performance guarantees as one of material controlled transactions to be included in TP documentation – local file. Since the need for performance guarantees by customers of the MNE groups will likely rise in the post-COVID-19 world,[2] the purpose of this chapter is to provide an overview of various approaches to applying the arm's length principle to them.

## II INTRA-GROUP PERFORMANCE GUARANTEES: DELINEATING THE TRANSACTION

Under the OECD TP Guidelines, the first step in analysing any intra-group transaction is to accurately delineate it, i.e., to identify the actual relations between the parties as well as their conditions and economically relevant circumstances.[3]

Despite a clear mandate to address 'the pricing of related party financial transactions, including … performance guarantees',[4] the revised OECD TP Guidelines do not refer to performance guarantees at all. In particular, they do not provide any recommendations on how to delineate such transactions. However, delineation of financial guarantees is discussed quite extensively. Therefore, this chapter will analyse (i) OECD's guidance on delineating financial guarantees and (ii) feasibility of applying it in the context of performance guarantees.

### 1 Economic Benefit for the Borrower (Contractor)

Under the OECD TP Guidelines, delineation of financial guarantees requires identifying economic benefits for the borrower beyond the ones coming from passive association.[5] This, in turn, determines whether a fee is due.

1. Megan Lapwood & Mark Atkinson, *Group Guarantees Remain a Tax Minefield*, p. 1.
2. Anshu Khanna, *Cross Border Intragroup Financing – Increased TP Focus Post COVID-19*, p. 5.
3. OECD TP Guidelines (2022), para. 1.33.
4. OECD *Action Plan on Base Erosion and Profit Shifting* (2013), p. 17.
5. OECD TP Guidelines (2022), para. 10.156.

The logic behind financial and performance guarantees is the same – a 'stronger' entity pledges to replace a 'weaker' one when needed. Accordingly, economic benefit for the 'weaker' company comes from a difference in 'strength'.

In the case of financial guarantees, this difference is expressed through credit ratings. Namely, credit rating of a guarantor must be at least equal (usually higher) than that of a borrower.

The core underlying obligations of performance guarantees are non-financial. Therefore, 'strength' of a guarantor does not come from its credit rating but rather from certain specific competences. In other words, a guarantor does not need to have an equal or higher credit rating than a contractor but it must employ human, technical or intangible (knowledge) assets that the contractor does not have. These assets will allow it to step in when a trigger event occurs.

Bearing in mind the above, OECD's guidance on delineating financial guarantees can generally be applied to performance guarantees (as they share the same business logic) but not always directly (as key factors impacting the guarantor's ability to act differ).

## 2 Benefit from Passive Association

Economic benefit coming from passive association arises only because an entity is a part of the MNE group, not in relation to any specific activity (deliberate concerted action).[6] The OECD TP Guidelines illustrate the difference with respect to financial guarantees using examples of a parent company with an AAA credit rating that has a subsidiary with a stand-alone credit rating of Baa.

In Example 1,[7] the parent does not take any action but lenders still assume it will support the subsidiary when necessary and therefore treat the subsidiary similarly to companies with a credit rating of A. The subsidiary does not need to pay any fee to the parent. This is because all benefit comes from lenders' expectations.

In Example 2,[8] the parent issues a formal guarantee to the subsidiary, explicitly assuming the risk of borrower's default. As a result, the borrower has the strength of the parent's balance sheet behind it and thus effectively assumes the parent's credit rating (AAA). In this case, paying a fee to the parent is justified[9] because it is a result of deliberate concerted action.

Similar distinction explicitly in the context of performance guarantees can be found in the United States (US) TP regulations.[10]

In practice, apart from formal guarantees, some lesser forms of credit support exist that involve no explicit assumption of risk, e.g., letters of comfort.

6. OECD TP Guidelines (2022), para. 7.13.
7. *Ibid.*, para. 1.184-1.186.
8. *Ibid.*, para. 1.187.
9. However, only to cover the difference between A and AAA; the increase from Baa to A is considered a result of passive association.
10. Code of Federal Regulations, 1.482-9(l)(5) – Example 15 (passive association), Example 16 (explicit guarantee).

A letter of comfort is 'a letter, esp. from a parent corporation on behalf of a subsidiary, stating its support (but short of a guarantee) for the activities and commitments of another corporation'.[11] The simplest ones just confirm certain facts, e.g., that the MNE group knows about the (planned) transaction between its member and a third party or that it has and/or intends to keep a share in this member.[12] The more complex also declare the MNE group's general intention to support its member but usually using vague language that avoids binding obligations.[13]

In the past, the approach to letters of comfort and similar instruments was not clear, However, the revised OECD TP Guidelines clarified that any respective benefit should be treated as arising from passive association. This is because letters of comfort and similar instruments involve no explicit assumption of risk and thus 'any expectation by any of the parties that other members of the MNE group will provide support to an associated enterprise in respect of its borrowings will be derived from the borrower's status as a member of the MNE group'.[14] As a result, no fee is due.

The above clarifications aligned the OECD approach with US TP regulations.[15]

## 3 Benefit Beyond Passive Association

When an explicit financial guarantee is issued, economic benefit of the borrower reflects the fact that, as a result, 'the lender's risk would be expected to be reduced by having access to the assets of the guarantor(s) in the event of the borrower's default'.[16] This, in turn, improves the situation of the borrower.

However, the OECD TP Guidelines note that not every explicit financial guarantee provides this benefit and that not every improvement of the borrower's situation warrants a fee. For example:[17]

- if, due to other circumstances (e.g., terms of banking covenants), default of a subsidiary would cause serious adverse consequences for the whole MNE group, this subsidiary may in practice already have group rating through passive association. In this case, an explicit financial guarantee would just confirm it without providing additional economic benefit;
- if members of the MNE group provide explicit financial guarantees mutually (e.g., in the cash pool structures), all benefits a company receives when other entities guarantee its obligations may be negated by risk assumed when it becomes a guarantor. As a result, only benefit from passive association remains;

11. *Black's Law Dictionary*.
12. *Letters of Comfort: A Practical Guide*, p. 15.
13. *Comments and Recommendations for Guidance Pertaining to the Transfer Pricing of Related Party Guarantees*, p. 11.
14. OECD TP Guidelines (2022), para. 10.163.
15. Code of Federal Regulations, 1.482-9(l)(5) – Example 18.
16. OECD TP Guidelines (2022), para. 10.158.
17. Vera Averyanova & Vikram Chand, *Applying the Arm's Length Principle to Intra-Group Financial Guarantees in light of the OECD's Draft Guidance on Financial Transactions*, pp. 2-3. Final wording of the revised OECD TP Guidelines does not differ from the draft in this respect.

- if an explicit financial guarantee not only reduces interest rate on the borrower's existing debt capacity but also provides it with new debt capacity, these effects may need to be decoupled and considered individually;
- finally, the OECD TP Guidelines recommend that the actual financial capacity of the guarantor should be analysed. In order for benefit to arise for the borrower, the guarantor must be actually able to fulfil its obligations in case of a default.[18]

Some of the above considerations do not apply to performance guarantees. In particular, they typically are not provided on a mutual basis or linked to the contractor's debt capacity. In the same vein, the guarantor usually has abilities to step in (otherwise, the client would likely not accept the guarantee). Other factors play a role only in very specific cases like strategic projects of key importance for the whole MNE group. However, the conceptual question of whether intra-group performance guarantees fall under shareholder activities still requires analysis.

According to the OECD TP Guidelines, a shareholder activity is performed 'even though ... group members do not need [it] (and would not be willing to pay for it were they independent enterprises'.[19] In other words, the parent should be its sole or at least main beneficiary. Common examples include preparing consolidated reports, rising funds for acquisitions, corporate governance, etc.[20] Shareholder activities do not warrant a fee.

The MNE groups provide performance guarantees so that their subsidiaries can compete for contracts.[21] In other words, the contractors clearly need them. For example, countries granting licences for extraction of minerals often require that the contractors present parent guarantees regarding performance of the exploration and development contract.[22] This is because such contracts typically cover a long period, have significant value and are relatively risky (the contractor may try to withdraw if initial results of research are not promising, the MNE found a better field in another country, etc.).

In Cyprus, any successful applicant for a licence must enter into a special agreement in a form published by the country's Ministry of Commerce, Industry and Tourism.[23] Under this agreement, 'each entity comprising the Contractor shall provide adequate security for the performance of the Contractor's obligations under this Contract throughout the term thereof. The adequate security shall be in the form of an irrevocable guarantee as provided in Annex F to this Contract, from the ultimate parent company of such entity or from a wholly owned subsidiary of the ultimate parent of such entity that meets financial standards acceptable to the Minister. Such guarantee

18. OECD TP Guidelines (2022), para. 10.166.
19. *Ibid.*, para. 7.9.
20. *Ibid.*, para. 7.10.
21. *Comments and Recommendations for Guidance Pertaining to the Transfer Pricing of Related Party Guarantees*, p. 15.
22. UN Handbook on Taxation of Extractive Industries, p. 223.
23. Michalis Kyriakides & Penelope-Alex Giosa, *Oil and Gas Regulation in Cyprus: Overview*, p. 3.

shall be provided simultaneously with the execution of this Contract'.[24] Moreover, should the contractor want to assign the *Exploration and Production Sharing Contract* to another entity, this entity must provide a similar parent company performance guarantee.[25]

Similar requirements are imposed on holders of licences for extraction of minerals in many other countries, e.g., India[26] or Tanzania.[27] National oil companies often request parent company performance guarantees from traders that participate in their tenders, developers – from construction and engineering companies, and governments – from suppliers of military equipment. Each time there is a risk the local contractor lacks resources, experience or proven record of accomplishment; the client can make signing of the contract conditional upon presentation of an intra-group performance guarantee.

## 4 Conclusion

Just as in the case of financial guarantees, delineation of performance guarantees requires analysing whether thanks to the guarantee the contractor achieved a clear economic benefit that it could not achieve otherwise. If yes, the intra-group performance guarantee warrants a fee. This, in particular, happens where:

- the performance guarantee is explicit and enforceable for the client;
- the guarantor is actually capable of stepping in and taking over obligations of the contractor;
- other factors (e.g., group strategy) do not make the explicit performance guarantee redundant;
- the performance guarantee is actually necessary, not a mere formal requirement.

The above conclusions, derived from the OECD works, potentially contradict explicit position of the UN. The UN Handbook on Taxation of Extractive Industries notes that third parties (e.g., banks) do not provide performance guarantees or similar instruments for free and consider using prices in these transactions as comparables when valuing intra-group performance guarantees. However, later on, it claims that, in real-life situations, the MNE groups usually do not charge for intra-group performance guarantees because the parents benefit from them as much as the subsidiaries. An alternative reason is that, supposedly, intra-group performance guarantees are often considered an equivalent of a promise to increase the affiliate's capital if needed and thus fall under shareholder activities.[28]

In most cases, intra-group performance guarantees are provided by a parent to a subsidiary (i.e., downstream). More often than not, parents have a seat in developed

24. Republic of Cyprus, *Model Exploration and Production Sharing Contract* (2016), Article 35.
25. *Ibid.*, Article 18.2.
26. Republic of India *Model Production Sharing Contract* (2010), Article 29.1(b) and 28.1.1(b).
27. United Republic of Tanzania *Model Production Sharing Agreement* (2013), Article 3(g)(xi)(e).
28. UN Handbook on Taxation of Extractive Industries, pp. 279-280.

countries, while subsidiaries – in developing ones. The inconsistency of approaches may reflect the fact that the OECD usually takes the perspective of the former, while the UN – the latter. This is illustrated, e.g., by the main difference between respective Model Double Taxation Conventions: 'the United Nations Model Convention imposes fewer restrictions on the taxing rights of the source country; source countries, therefore, have greater taxing rights under it compared to the OECD Model Convention'.[29]

## III TP VALUATION OF PERFORMANCE GUARANTEES

TP valuation of an intra-group performance guarantee means analysing the arm's length nature of a fee paid by a contractor to a guarantor. Terms and conditions of the guarantee itself do not require examination because they were agreed upon by independent parties, i.e., the contractor and the guarantor from one side and the client from the other. That being said, the valuation process must consider them[30] (in particular, events that trigger the contractor's failure to fulfil its obligations and compensation due) as factors directly affecting risk assumed by the guarantor.

This chapter will analyse applicability of OECD TP methods (and other approaches) to various components of performance guarantee fees.

### 1 Performance Guarantee Fees

A typical performance guarantee fee is a product of:

- a guarantee fee rate (e.g., 1 %);
- a guarantee base (e.g., the total cost of contract).[31]

The guarantee base represents the amount at risk and therefore depends on (i) events that trigger the contractor's failure to fulfil its obligations and (ii) probability that they occur.[32] At the same time, just as in the case of financial guarantees, probability of the contractor's default affects the guarantee fee rate.

### 2 The CUP Method

The comparable uncontrolled price (CUP) method[33] compares (i) a price between two members of the MNE group with (ii) prices charged by independent enterprises in comparable transactions and circumstances. In practice, internal and external comparables can be used. Internal comparables are transactions between one of the above

29. Brian J. Arnold, *An Introduction to Tax Treaties*, p. 5.
30. Benjamin Koch & Srini Lalapet, *Valuing Cross-Border Intercompany Performance Guarantees*, p. 1.
31. *Ibid.*, p. 2.
32. *Ibid.*, p. 1.
33. OECD TP Guidelines (2022), paras 2.14-2.26.

members of the MNE group and a third party, while external – between two other third parties.

The OECD TP Guidelines recognize that no method is applicable to every case and that the analysis must take into account facts and circumstances. However, all other things equal, the CUP method should be applied first.[34]

Application of the CUP method relies on identifying comparable transactions between independent enterprises. In the case of performance guarantees, potential comparables include:

- other performance guarantees;
- surety bonds and standby letters of credit;
- financial guarantees;
- competitive offers.

The CUP method requires a high level of comparability, in terms of not only the functional profile of the parties and market conditions but also the transaction subject.[35] Therefore, factors affecting the guarantee fee rate and the guarantee base in all the above cases must be analysed in detail.

### A Other Performance Guarantees

Apart from the analysed intra-group performance guarantee, the related guarantor may provide performance guarantees that cover obligations of third-party contractors in other projects.

The guarantee base always depends on the nature and scope of the contractor's primary obligations (i.e., is case specific), and therefore will differ by definition. The same applies to the guarantee fee rate as it is affected by probability of the contractor's default. In view of the above, even if the related contractor provides performance guarantees outside the MNE group, they will most like be incomparable to the intra-group performance guarantee.

In practice, MNE groups rarely guarantee performance of third parties.[36] However, a third party may provide a guarantee to additionally secure obligations of the related contractor in the same project. Countries granting licences for mining and extraction of minerals often require that the contractors present not only parent performance guarantees but also bank guarantees. For example, under the Tanzania *Model Production Sharing Agreement* (2013), 'Contractor shall provide the Minister with an unconditional, irrevocable on-demand guarantee from a bank acceptable to the Minister.'[37] Similar requirements are imposed by many other countries.

34. *Ibid.*, paras 2.2 and 2.3.
35. *Ibid.*, paras 2.16-2.17.
36. Gaurav Deshpande, *The Transfer Pricing Aspects of Cross-Border Performance Guarantees*, Bulletin for International Taxation, no. 7, 2017 (vol. 71), p. 6.
37. United Republic of Tanzania *Model Production Sharing Agreement* (2013), Article 3(g)(xi)(a).

The fact that the additional guarantee regards the same project (i.e., covers the same primary obligations) removes a large incomparability factor. However, responsibility of the additional guarantor is usually limited. For example, India *Model Production Sharing Contract* (2010) caps the amount of the bank guarantee at '7½% of [the contractor's share in] total estimated expenditure'.[38] Meanwhile, there are no explicit limits to the value of the respective parent performance guarantee.[39] In view of the above, the guarantee bases will still differ.

Finally, external comparables may exist. Most European companies do not publish data on performance guarantees but this information sometimes falls under disclosure requirements for entities with securities listed in the US.

Primary obligations covered by performance guarantees found in the public sources are not the same as for the intra-group performance guarantee. Therefore, the main issue with this kind of data is the same as with performance guarantees provided by the MNE group with respect to obligations of third-party contractors. Namely, finding at least broadly comparable agreements may prove very difficult.[40]

### *B Surety Bonds and Standby Letters of Credit*

A third party may also provide other instruments to additionally secure obligations of the related contractor in the same project. The most common ones include surety bonds and standby letters of credit.

Surety bond is '*a bond* [promise] *given to ensure the timely performance of a contract*'.[41] Surety bonds warrant that if the contractor fails to complete the project, the client will receive an upfront-agreed compensation. The issuer of a surety bond receives a fee from the contractor.[42]

Surety bonds may be used to give the client certainty that the winner of tender procedure will conclude the contract (bid bonds), that it will perform its obligations (performance bonds), that it will pay its personnel, suppliers and subcontractors (labour and material payment bonds),[43] etc. They are issued by specialized insurers or banks and are particularly common in the construction industry.

Standby letter of credit is 'a letter of credit used to guarantee either a monetary or a nonmonetary obligation (such as the performance of construction work), whereby the issuing bank agrees to pay the beneficiary if the bank customer defaults on its obligation'.[44] It plays a similar role to a surety bond.

---

38. Republic of India, *Model Production Sharing Contract* (2010), Article 29.3(a).
39. *Ibid.*, Appendix E-1, para. 3.
40. Benjamin Koch & Srini Lalapet, *Valuing Cross-Border Intercompany Performance Guarantees*, p. 2.
41. *Black's Law Dictionary*.
42. J. Riedy, N. Anwar & D. Wright, *Pricing of a Guarantee Fee in a Related-Party Context*, p. 4.
43. R. Jenkins & A. Wallace, *Construction Bonds: What Every Contractor and Owner Should Know*, pp. 2, 6 and 16.
44. *Black's Law Dictionary*.

If a surety bond or a standby letter of credit accompanies an intra-group performance guarantee, its terms and conditions need to be examined to assess comparability.[45] A different guarantee base poses the most common problem because surety bonds[46] are limited in time and amount. The same applies to standby letters of credit.

Moreover, they play a slightly different economic role: under a negative scenario, when the contractor fails to perform its obligations, a surety bond or a letter of credit allows the client to recover costs borne and complete the project another way. Meanwhile, an intra-group performance guarantee is rather a way of ensuring a positive outcome, i.e., making sure that the contractor does not fail.[47]

Publicly available information on surety bonds and standby letters of credit is scarce.

### *C* *Financial Guarantees*

For practical reasons, financial guarantees are sometimes used as comparables when valuing intra-group performance guarantees.

In the Indian tax authorities versus Bilcare Limited case, the taxpayer provided three free-of-charge intra-group performance guarantees. They covered:

- a sale and lease back of some assets by a Bilcare entity in Singapore;
- a sale of 100% shares in a subsidiary by the same company;
- a sale of business by a Bilcare entity in the US.

Indian tax authorities challenged the lack of fees and used market data on financial guarantees to assess the arm's length performance guarantee fee rate. The court shared this view and concluded that 'if performance guarantee entails financial consequences, that is, on the failure of the other party to perform his obligation and the guarantor becoming liable to pay some amount, then it cannot be placed at a pedestal different from the regular corporate [financial] guarantee given for obtaining loan. In that sense, performance guarantees … are a specie of the genus of corporate [financial] guarantees and cannot be given a treatment different from the corporate [financial] guarantees'.[48]

This approach seems to ignore key differences between financial and performance guarantees. The basic one (difference in factors affecting the guarantor's ability to act) was discussed in section II.1 above.

Moreover, unlike financial guarantees, performance guarantees often do not specify the amount at risk (i.e., the guarantee base). For example, under the India *Model Production Sharing Contract* (2010), 'the Guarantor shall fulfil or cause to be fulfilled the said obligations … and will indemnify the Government against all losses,

45. Benjamin Koch & Srini Lalapet, *Valuing Cross-Border Intercompany Performance Guarantees*, p. 2.
46. Karen Mackay, *Parent Company Guarantees and Performance Bonds*, p. 2.
47. *General Principles for the Use of Parent Company Guarantees and Performance Bonds*, p. 1.
48. *Assistant Commissioner of Income Tax v. Bilcare Limited*, p. 5.

damages, costs, expenses or otherwise which may result directly from such failure to perform or breach'.[49] The 'said obligations' include numerous tasks to be completed in accordance with agreed schedule and the 'losses, damages, costs, expenses or otherwise' were not listed.

Furthermore, probability that the contractor fails to fulfil its obligations depends on many specific factors. In the above example, they include geological situation, availability of personnel and equipment, weather conditions, etc. – not just availability of free cash flow. As a result, there is no universal methodology to assess the default probability as is the case for financial guarantees.

This view was shared by another court in the Indian tax authorities versus Mastek Limited case. The taxpayer provided a performance guarantee covering provision of software services by a United Kingdom (UK) Mastek entity to a third-party client. Indian tax authorities challenged the level of performance guarantee fee rate and used market data on financial guarantees to adjust it. The court disagreed, arguing that 'the criteria for giving the performance guarantee for a particular product would be entirely different than that of the financial guaranty for a particular loan or credit. The performance guarantee would depend on the technical expertise and the skills of the company and the historical performance data of the product'.[50]

Finally, in the case of performance guarantees, probability that the contractor fails to fulfil its obligations affects both the guarantee fee rate and the amount at risk.

In view of the above, fees for financial guarantees should not generally be relied upon when valuing intra-group performance guarantees. At best, they can provide a sanity check of information obtained from other sources.

### *D Competitive Offers*

The MNE group may seek offers on the market, e.g.:

- from unrelated financial institutions for performance guarantees exactly as requested by the client in the project;
- from unrelated service providers to act as backup for the contractor (i.e., be ready to take over the project)[51] for the so-called standby fees.

This approach reflects the concept of options realistically available to a taxpayer, endorsed by the OECD TP Guidelines, both in the general part[52] and specifically with respect to guarantees.[53] Moreover, this concept is also explicitly supported by the US tax regulation as a base for the so-called unspecified methods.[54]

Third parties approached by the MNE group will assess probability of default in accordance with their knowledge and procedures. In the best-case scenario, this will

49. Republic of India, *Model Production Sharing Contract* (2010), Appendix E1, para. 3.
50. *Assistant Commissioner of Income Tax v. Mastek Limited*, p. 10.
51. Gaurav Deshpande, *The Transfer Pricing Aspects of Cross-Border Performance Guarantees*, p. 8.
52. OECD TP Guidelines (2022), paras 1.38, 1.40.
53. *Ibid.*, paras 10.19, 10.180.
54. Code of Federal Regulations, 1.482-3(e)(1), 1.482-4(d)(1) and 1.482-9(h).

produce strong comparables as long as all vital information about the project (scope and schedule of work, operating capacity, risk factors, trigger events, etc.) is provided. In particular, the guarantee fee base will be similar, even when presented as, e.g., a lump sum.

Both taxpayers and tax authorities apply this approach in practice. In the latter case, not all information about the project is often provided and thus answers received may be less useful.[55]

Using competitive offers to verify whether related party prices comply with the arm's length principle has one significant disadvantage. Conditions proposed may differ from conditions finally agreed; in other words, an offer is not a transaction, especially if a party making it realizes that a deal will not follow. As a result, the third party can consider the contractor's request not genuine and thus perform the valuation without due diligence.[56] Moreover, guarantees of the financial institutions do not necessarily mirror intra-group performance guarantees,[57] while unrelated contractors on standby do not commit to cover all losses of the client.

The OECD Guidelines do not explicitly disallow this approach. However, when discussing comparables, they consistently refer to prices and profitability in 'transactions'. Moreover, in the chapter on loans, they question usefulness of competitive offers in a form of written bank opinions stating a hypothetical interest rate because they do not constitute actual transactions.[58]

### *E Conclusion*

All potential comparables have serious drawbacks:

- performance guarantees or similar instruments in other projects cover different primary obligations and therefore have an incomparable amount at risk and probability of default. The same applies to financial guarantees;
- performance guarantees or similar instruments provided by third parties in the same project (in parallel with the intra-group performance guarantee) typically limit responsibility of the additional guarantor;
- competitive offers can be highly comparable in terms of amount at risk and probability of default but legislation and approach of the tax authorities to this kind of data vary from country to country, and the latter even within one country.[59]

In view of the above, application of the CUP method to intra-group performance guarantees is difficult and probably requires combining data from various sources. Under this approach, fees for performance guarantees or similar instruments in other

55. Sunny Bilaney, *The Unsettled Issue of Intercompany Guarantees*, p. 5.
56. *Comments and Recommendations for Guidance Pertaining to the Transfer Pricing of Related Party Guarantees*, p. 34.
57. Gaurav Deshpande, *The Transfer Pricing Aspects of Cross-Border Performance Guarantees*, p. 8.
58. OECD TP Guidelines (2022), para. 10.108.
59. Ashutosh Rastogi, *Bonafide Quotations – Possible Panacea for Transfer Pricing dilemma?*, p. 2.

projects could broadly indicate whether the fee rate of the intra-group performance guarantee corresponds with the market. At the same time, fees for performance guarantees or similar instruments provided by third parties in the same project would serve as an arm's length 'floor' to it. The resulting range will be crosschecked against fees for financial guarantees and competitive offers collected from third parties.

## 3 Other OECD TP Methods

Other OECD TP methods are not applicable to intra-group performance guarantees.

The Resale Price method by definition requires that goods be purchased from a related supplier and resold to the market. Therefore, its typical area of application includes marketing operations.[60] Intra-group performance guarantees may cover supply of goods to the client but no goods are sold by the guarantor to the contractor. Consequently, the Resale Price method cannot be used to verify whether the intra-group performance guarantee fees are at arm's length.

The Cost Plus method, in turn, starts with costs incurred by the supplier and is probably most useful for sales of semi-finished products, long-term supplies of goods and for provision of services.[61] Intra-group performance guarantees can be considered services but the guarantor does not incur many costs when issuing them - the guarantee fee constitutes compensation for risk it assumes[62] rather than for functions it performs. Consequently, the Cost Plus method does not apply except maybe for situations where the guarantor 'subcontracts' intra-group performance guarantee to a third party.

Taking into account that the Transactional Net Margin method operates in a manner similar to the Cost Plus and the Resale Price methods,[63] it cannot be used to verify whether the intra-group performance guarantee fees are at arm's length, either.

The Profit Split method is often appropriate for highly integrated operations and when both MNEs make unique and valuable contributions (e.g., unique intangibles),[64] and therefore both claim a part of residual income. Intra-group performance guarantees typically do not involve such situations.

## 4 Other Approaches

Using the CUP method to value intra-group performance guarantees for TP purposes is difficult. Other OECD TP methods cannot be applied at all. In such situations, the OECD TP Guidelines allow MNE groups to establish prices in transactions between affiliates using other approaches as long as the results of applying them comply with the arm's

60. OECD TP Guidelines (2022), para. 2.27.
61. *Ibid.*, para. 2.45.
62. James A. Riedy, Nabeel Anwar & Deloris Wright, *Pricing of a Guarantee Fee in a Related-Party Context*, p. 4.
63. OECD TP Guidelines (2022), para. 2.64.
64. *Ibid.*, para. 2.119.

length principle and the method selection process is properly documented.[65] Similarly, the US TP regulations provide for the so-called unspecified methods.

Two additional methods that might work for intra-group performance guarantees include:

(i) compensation payment approach;
(ii) expected loss approach.

### A Compensation Payment Approach

The compensation payment approach can be used to determine arm's length level of the guarantee fee rate. It assumes that the taxpayer already knows arm's length guarantee base.

Under this approach, arm's length level of the guarantee fee rate is considered equal to the cost of funds the guarantor needs to compensate the client:

- interest (and additional costs, if any) on a hypothetical loan the guarantor would need to take in order to pay the compensation – if it does not have cash or liquid reserves;
- the guarantor's Weighted Average Cost of Capital – if it can use all available sources of funds (equity, returned earnings and debt) and does it in exactly the same proportion as in its balance sheet (Table 30.1).[66]

*Table 30.1 Compensation Payment Approach*

<table>
<tr><th colspan="3"></th><th colspan="2">Cost of Capital</th><th>Weighted Average Cost of Capital</th></tr>
<tr><td rowspan="3">Liabilities</td><td>Equity</td><td>USD 4,000,000</td><td>7.0%</td><td>USD 280,000</td><td rowspan="3">(280,000 + 0 + 150,000) / 10,000,000 = 4.3%</td></tr>
<tr><td>Retained earnings</td><td>USD 3,000,000</td><td>0.0%</td><td>USD 0</td></tr>
<tr><td>Debt</td><td>USD 3,000,000</td><td>5.0%</td><td>USD 150,000</td></tr>
<tr><td colspan="3">Guarantee fee rate</td><td colspan="3"></td></tr>
<tr><td colspan="3">No cash or liquid reserves</td><td colspan="3">5.0%</td></tr>
<tr><td colspan="3">All sources of funds available</td><td colspan="3">4.3%</td></tr>
<tr><td colspan="3">Guarantee base (known or determined separately)</td><td colspan="3">USD 1,000,000</td></tr>
<tr><td colspan="3">Guarantee fee</td><td colspan="3"></td></tr>
<tr><td colspan="3">No cash or liquid reserves</td><td colspan="3">5.0% * 1,000,000 = USD 50,000</td></tr>
<tr><td colspan="3">All sources of funds available</td><td colspan="3">4.3% * 1,000,000 = USD 43,000</td></tr>
</table>

65. *Ibid.*, para. 2.9.
66. Gaurav Deshpande, *The Transfer Pricing Aspects of Cross-Border Performance Guarantees*, p. 8.

Depending on availability of data, interest on the hypothetical loan (cost of debt) can be determined with reference to existing third-party financing of the guarantor or using 'standard' benchmarking tools. The guarantor's Weighted Average Cost of Capital is usually known as companies often use it for planning or budgeting purposes.

### *B* *Expected Loss Approach*

Expected loss is a product of (i) value of a potential loss and (ii) probability that this loss will occur.[67] For example, a 2% chance of incurring a USD 1,000 loss gives an expected loss of USD 20. Total expected loss for a project is a sum of expected losses for all exposure levels (Table 30.2).

*Table 30.2 Calculation of Expected Loss*

| *Value of a Potential Loss* | *Probability That This Loss Will Occur (%)* | *Expected Loss* |
|---|---|---|
| USD 10,000,000 | 1.5 | USD 150,000 |
| USD 5,000,000 | 2.5 | USD 125,000 |
| USD 1,000,000 | 4.0 | USD 40,000 |
| | **Total expected loss** | **USD 315,000** |

In the context of performance guarantees, it requires identifying all major trigger events over the duration of the contract and assessing (i) probability that they will occur as well as (ii) expected losses (compensation payments, costs of hiring alternative contractors, additional financial costs, etc., less recoverable expenses, if any) in each case. To this end, industry experience, historic data or plans can be used.

In the next step, total expected loss for a project without a performance guarantee is compared to total expected loss if a performance guarantee is issued, taking into account that it might decrease value of some potential losses, probability that they will occur or both (Table 30.3).

*Table 30.3 Calculation of Expected Loss with Performance Guarantee*

| *Value of a Potential Loss [with Performance Guarantee]* | *Probability That This Loss Will Occur [with Performance Guarantee] (%)* | *Expected Loss [with Performance Guarantee]* |
|---|---|---|
| USD 7,000,000 | 1.0 | USD 70,000 |
| USD 4,000,000 | 2.5 | USD 100,000 |
| USD 1,000,000 | 3.0 | USD 30,000 |
| | **Total expected loss** | **USD 200,000** |

67. Gary L. Wolfram & D. Joseph Olson, *Basics of Insurance*, p. 1.

The difference between expected loss with and without performance guarantee (USD 115,000 in the above example) sets the cap for the performance guarantee fee. Conceptually, this approach resembles determining the fee for a financial guarantee by comparing the interest rate with and without it.

For a limited number of parameters, the above calculations can be performed manually. However, when there are multiple trigger events with uncertain probabilities and value of losses, a taxpayer may need to employ a statistical tool – Monte Carlo simulations.

A Monte Carlo simulation takes a random combination of parameters that affect a certain process, calculates the process' outcome for this combination and repeats both steps many times. In the end, it produces a ranking of all outcomes by probability.[68]

Taxpayers may also use the expected loss approach only to determine the worst-case scenario, i.e., the maximum possible loss at a certain level of probability without a performance guarantee (USD 315,000 in the above example). This value may then serve as an arm's length guarantee base[69] to which a guarantee fee rate determined otherwise (e.g., with the compensation payment approach) is applied.

### C *Conclusion*

Similarly to the OECD TP methods, other approaches have disadvantages, too. The compensation payment approach treats performance guarantees as ordinary debt, ignoring that probability of the contractor's default depends on factors other than the guarantor's financial situation. On the other hand, the expected loss approach relies on subjective assumptions and – if Monte Carlo simulations were used – requires knowledge of relatively advanced statistical tools.

## IV SUMMARY

Intra-group performance guarantees that legally bind the guarantor and allow the contractor to compete usually warrant a fee.

Performance guarantee fees depend on probability of the contractor's default. Unlike in the case of financial guarantees, this probability differs case by case. In view of the above, 'there is no standard way to value a performance guarantee'.[70]

From a TP perspective, neither the OECD methods nor other approaches can provide a definitive answer to the question of whether a fee for an intra-group performance guarantee is at arm's length. The OECD TP Guidelines generally discourage the use of more than one method[71] but in this case, it may be inevitable.

68. *Monte Carlo 101: Understanding Monte Carlo Simulation and Risk Analysis*, p. 1.
69. Benjamin Koch & Srini Lalapet, *Valuing Cross-border Intercompany Performance Guarantees*, p. 3.
70. *Ibid.*, p. 1.
71. OECD TP Guidelines (2022), para. 2.12.

# E Cash Pooling

CHAPTER 31

# Setting the ALP for Cash Pooling

*Rani Peffer*[*]

## I INTRODUCTION

In February 2020, the Organisation for Economic Co-operation and Development (OECD) published long-awaited guidelines on transfer pricing for financial transactions, including corporate treasury activities such as cash pooling. The OECD guidance on cash pooling opens with the following brief description of cash pooling activities: "The use of a cash pool is popular among multinational enterprises as a way of achieving more efficient cash management by bringing together, either physically or notionally, the balances on a number of separate bank accounts."[1] The document then notes potential benefits that cash pooling may provide to a multinational enterprise (MNE). These benefits include more effective liquidity management, including reduced reliance on external borrowing and enhanced returns on aggregated cash balances, and lower costs from spreads and fees paid to external financial institutions.

After these introductory comments and a short section outlining the differences between physical and notional cash pooling, the OECD document transitions to a discussion of accurate delineation and appropriate arm's length pricing for cash pooling activities. As a treasury practitioner with over 20 years of experience in corporate finance for a large, global enterprise, I can affirm that the OECD's description of cash pooling and its benefits is well articulated. However, before any taxation specialist can use the OECD's guidelines to appropriately evaluate the transfer pricing applied to an entity's cash pool, they must first develop a deeper understanding of the

---

* The views and opinions set forth herein are the personal views or opinions of the authors; they do not necessarily reflect the views or opinions of the organization with which the authors are associated.

1. OECD (2020), *Transfer Pricing Guidance on Financial Transactions: Inclusive Framework on BEPS Actions 4, 8-10,* OECD, Paris, www.oecd.org/tax/beps/transfer-pricing-guidance-on-financial-transactions-inclusive-framework-on-beps-actions-4-8-10.htm.

underlying business activities being performed. What specific functions does the cash pool perform? Why would a multinational enterprise (and/or its affiliates) choose to engage in these cash pooling activities rather than using external banks to meet its financing needs? And what factors drive the benefits of cash pooling that are briefly outlined in the OECD document?

The following section will answer these questions, describing the business and commercial rationale for cash pooling to lay the groundwork for more technical discussions on transfer pricing later in this book. This section will not address the income tax treatment of cash pooling operations. However, it should be noted that in many cases, cash pooling provides little or no income tax benefit to the MNE. Rather, MNEs engage in cash pooling to realize the significant operational, risk management, and cost-saving benefits described below.

## II GLOBAL CASH-POOLING ACTIVITIES AND BENEFITS

As previously noted, this chapter is written from the perspective of a longtime Treasury manager experienced in managing cash pooling operations for a large, global enterprise (the 'Company'). This Company has a significant geographic footprint and cash flows around the world. The size, scope, and complexity of the Company's operations present significant treasury and financial management challenges: each day, the Company must control and account for the operational cash flows of hundreds of affiliates, finance local operations in many markets across the globe, invest net excess cash generated from commercial transactions, and manage foreign exchange and third-party credit risks. The Company's global cash pool was created in the mid-1990s to manage these aspects of its global business, and today it operates as an in-house bank providing financial intermediation and risk management services to the Company's affiliates (the "cash pool members"). The Company operates a physical cash pool, as opposed to a notional cash pool, and this pooling structure is at the center of the enterprise's financing operations, providing cash management services to members in over 50 different markets and over 30 different currencies. A large majority of the Company's high-value external and related-party transactions are executed and controlled via the cash pool's liquidity management mechanisms, and the cash pool is one of the most critical tools for executing the Company's financing strategy.

To illustrate the commercial rationale for cash pooling, this section will examine several key functions commonly performed by MNE cash pools. The section will then describe the benefits these activities provide to both the cash pool members and the overall MNE, as well as the alternative third-party activities the MNE would need to engage in absent a cash pool structure. Examples shared will focus on physical cash pooling rather than notional cash pooling, although many of the same activities and benefits apply to notional cash pooling arrangements as well.

An effective cash pooling arrangement may perform some or all of the following activities for the benefit of the MNE and its member entities:

- *manage daily cash positions for cash pool members*, including acting as a safe counterparty for cash deposits of members with surplus cash and providing reliable and fast access to liquidity for members with cash deficits;
- *invest the MNE's net excess cash externally* for the benefit of both cash pool members and the overall MNE;
- *settle related-party receivable and payable positions among cash pool members* without transacting with external financial institutions; and
- *manage foreign exchange positions* for the cash pool members and the overall MNE.

## III DAILY CASH MANAGEMENT

MNEs typically establish cash pools with the primary goal of improving daily global liquidity management. As noted in the OECD's introduction to the subject, cash pooling leads to more efficient cash management for the cash pool members and the MNE overall. Consider a hypothetical cash pool with 100 member entities in 30 different countries. Each member may have daily cash inflows and outflows. Some members will consistently operate with surplus cash balances, others may occasionally or habitually need to borrow cash to fund obligations such as payroll or working capital investments, and still others may fluctuate between surplus and deficit positions.

### 1 Daily Cash Management Without Cash Pooling

In the absence of a cash pool, all individual entities' daily depositing and borrowing activities must take place with external financial institutions. This requires first identifying appropriate local financial institutions with which to conduct business in each market. In developed markets with robust and well-regulated banking systems, finding a safe and reliable local banking partner should not present a problem. However, in less developed markets, finding an acceptable banking partner may be more difficult, and the resulting banking relationship may carry a higher level of counterparty credit risk, regulatory risk, and sovereign risk. If the hypothetical MNE's 100 entities successfully identify banking partners in 30 local markets, the result will be many banking relationships to manage and maintain. Personnel will be needed to manage banking service contracts and reconcile external accounts, and each of the external bank accounts will bear associated fees.

Many of the MNE's 100 entities will habitually have surplus cash to deposit. Without a cash pool, each of these entities will deposit excess cash overnight with its chosen local banking partner. Because of the general lack of scale and negotiating power at a local entity level, these local bank accounts may carry unfavorable terms, such as low-interest rates and high fees. If the depositor entity has consistent levels of surplus cash and is unsatisfied with the rate of return on its overnight local bank account, it may decide to seek a more attractive local investment option for its structural excess cash. In this case, though, the depositor must allocate resources to manage an additional investment account and pay additional fees to the bank or fund manager associated with the investments. The depositor will still need to leave a small amount of operating cash in its local bank account to mitigate the risk of overdrawing the account if surprise cash outflows occur. This small amount of operating cash sitting in a local bank account may not be significant for one entity, but when these small balances are held locally by dozens or hundreds of entities in different local bank accounts, the result is a large aggregate amount of cash that is likely not being efficiently managed and invested by the MNE. In summary, managing the entities' local deposit balances without a cash pooling system can lead to inefficient management of cash, high bank fees, and required investment in resources to manage bank accounts and local investment accounts.

Some entities in the MNE may periodically need to borrow funds to cover operating cash shortages. Without a cash pool, each of these entities must finance its deficits by establishing a borrowing arrangement with a third-party financial institution. An external bank may agree to finance the entity via overdraft privileges on the bank account or by extending a separate facility or term loan, but any external financing option will require administrative and regulatory obligations and bank fees in addition to charging standard market rates of interest. Further, third-party financing is likely to be inflexible in terms of currency options and repayment schedules, and an individual entity will not have the same bargaining power as the overall MNE, leading to excessive fees, costs, and spreads.

Entities that fluctuate between deposit and borrowing positions are in the worst situation of all. Without a cash pool, they must be prepared to deposit excess cash overnight with their local bank or invest in local investment options on one day, while obtaining local overdraft or facility financing to cover short cash positions on the next day. These entities are forced to invest significant resources to manage these positions and pay significant bank fees associated with their transactions whether they are depositing or borrowing on a given day.

Without cash pooling, the result for each of these types of entities and the overall MNE is the same: inefficient management of cash balances, significant resources required to manage banking relationships and transactions, and costs associated with bank fees and spreads.

## 2 Daily Cash Management With Cash Pooling

If these one hundred entities are members of the MNE's cash pool, daily liquidity management is very different. Each cash pool member enters a service agreement with the MNE's cash pool that governs the depositing and borrowing transactions between the member and the cash pool, as well as other activities performed by the cash pool for the benefit of the member. Most of the cash pool members' cash transactions take place with the cash pool instead of with local banks. An MNE's cash pool can be centrally managed and controlled by a highly trained small group of specialists, so individual members need not invest human resources and funds in managing banking relationships. Further, effective MNE cash pools are well capitalized, with robust risk management policies and principles in place, helping to protect the MNE and its member entities from certain market risks, credit risks, and operational risks. Even with a cash pooling arrangement in place, some local banking relationships must still be maintained, but these relationships are fewer in number and manage fewer and smaller transactions. These banking relationships therefore require fewer resources and lower costs to maintain and can represent lower risk to the individual member entities and the MNE as a whole.

For cash pool members that are habitual depositors, all excess cash can be swept to the cash pool daily. Many physical cash pools are established with "zero-balancing accounts," (ZBAs), which means that all cash is automatically swept out of local bank accounts at the end of each day, leaving a zero balance in local banks and one hundred per cent of the member's excess cash in the accounts controlled by the cash pool. Zero-balancing leads to efficient cash management, with all excess cash available for central management and investment instead of fragmented across many different bank accounts and markets (with associated credit exposure) and potentially earning little or no return. The cash pool consolidates funds from all depositors across the MNE and centrally invests all surplus funds, with associated economies of scale and scope. Aggregation of cash in this central location benefits the overall MNE as well as the individual member entities: centralizing excess cash and making it available to the MNE and its affiliates improves visibility and access to cash, reduces the need to borrow funds externally, and reduces credit risk, therefore improving the MNE's ability to maintain a solid credit rating.

For members that need to borrow cash on a regular basis, the cash pool provides an immediate source of liquidity. Like an external bank, the cash pool can provide funds at an arm's length rate of interest, but without the additional external fees, bank spreads, and administrative requirements associated with third-party borrowing. Further, the cash pool can easily provide members with customized borrowing options to meet their needs for currency of borrowing and repayment timeline.

Last, for members that fluctuate between depositing and borrowing positions, the cash pool can meet their depositing or borrowing needs with little effort and no additional administrative cost to the member entity. A member can sweep funds from its local ZBA account to deposit into its account with the cash pool on one day, then borrow funds from the cash pool the next day to meet payroll requirements. Transactions for all member entities can be efficiently managed by one central group of highly trained professionals.

This is the simplest and most powerful function of the MNE's cash pool: efficient liquidity management for member entities and the overall MNE, delivered with the benefits of significantly lower cost, complexity, and risk compared to cash management executed by individual entities working with external financial institutions. Additional cash pooling functions and benefits are detailed below, but the cash management function just described is at the heart of the business and commercial rationale for MNE cash pooling.

## IV EXTERNAL INVESTMENT MANAGEMENT

At any given time, some of an MNE's affiliate entities have surplus cash, while others have a cash deficit. If these positions net to a cash surplus, then the MNE or its entities likely choose to invest the cash in external investment vehicles, both to maximize the return on investment and to minimize counterparty credit risk exposure to individual financial institutions. External investment practices are guided by the MNE's investment and credit policies, which differ across MNEs based on their priorities and risk profile. Potential investments include short-term instruments such as money market funds or certificates of deposit, longer-term vehicles such as government securities or corporate bonds, or any other instruments the MNE deems appropriate for its portfolio.

### 1 Investment Management Without Cash Pooling

Without a cash-pooling structure, each member entity must independently identify and invest in external investment vehicles. Because of their size or local jurisdiction, the individual entities may struggle to access attractive investment opportunities that conform to the MNE's priorities and policies. Without cash pooling, the external investments must be managed by the individual entities, which requires both resources and additional fees.

### 2 Investment Management With Cash Pooling

With a cash pooling structure, all members' cash deposits can be consolidated and centrally managed, and the cash pool can externally invest the MNE's aggregate funds. Participation in this aggregated investment portfolio enables members to access a wide variety of external investments, providing them with a diversification benefit and access to investment opportunities that may not be available to them on a standalone basis. Further, because the MNE's funds can be pooled centrally for external investment, the cash invested may yield economies of scale for transaction costs and management fees, as well as economies of scope via the cash pool's ability to invest in a more diversified portfolio.

## V SETTLEMENT OF INTERCOMPANY PAYABLES

In any MNE, a large number of related-party transactions take place among the MNE's individual entities. These intercompany transactions include payments to or from affiliates for provision of products, fees for services, royalty payments, principal and interest related to intercompany loans, payments related to foreign exchange transactions, and intercompany dividends. These intercompany transactions among the MNE's entities must be processed and settled on a regular basis.

### 1 Settling Intercompany Payables Without Cash Pooling

Without a cash-pooling structure, each of an MNE's individual entities must settle its related-party receivables and payables via physical transfer of cash to and from external bank accounts. In the hypothetical example of 100 entities in 30 different markets, this results in thousands of transactions between the MNE's affiliates and third-party banks. These transactions incur significant banking fees and require company resources to manage the cash flows. From a risk standpoint, when funds leave the MNE's control via transfer to a third party, there is risk of transaction errors and risk that the transaction will fail to be settled with the external bank in an accurate and timely fashion. Significant settlement risk is created by the execution of thousands of related-party payments with third-party banks.

### 2 Settling Intercompany Payables With Cash Pooling

In a cash-pooling structure, the MNE's related-party payments can be managed and settled without transferring funds outside the MNE's control. First, receivable and payable transactions among all cash pool members can be netted against one another. If Member A owes USD 100 to Member B for product sales, while Member B owes USD 25 to Member A for services, those two obligations can be netted together so that Member A pays USD 75 to Member B to settle both transactions. This netting process significantly reduces the number of transactions necessary to settle the thousands of intercompany receivables and payables. Once affiliate payable and receivable positions have been netted, then the remaining cash flows (the USD 75 from Member A to Member B in the example above) can be settled without sending cash outside the control of the MNE—the cash pool simply credits Member B's cash pool account and debits Member A's account. By netting and then settling affiliate payables through the cash pool instead of through external financial institutions, the individual members and the overall MNE realize a dramatic reduction in bank fees and transaction risks.

In addition to providing settlement of intercompany payables, cash pools typically also add value to members by providing a variety of additional administrative services. These may include accounting services, maintenance of foreign exchange and interest rates within information systems, confirmation of trades transacted with outside parties, execution of payments, verification of external bank accounts, and monitoring of transactions to ensure compliance with internal controls. By centralizing these activities with the cash pool instead of dispersing them across multiple individual entities, these administrative functions can be performed with the support of sophisticated information systems, complex infrastructure technology, and a highly trained and professional cash pool staff.

## VI MANAGEMENT OF FOREIGN EXCHANGE

The MNE's management of cash inflows and outflows across multiple individual entities is made significantly more complex by foreign exchange. In any MNE, entities often receive and pay cash in currencies other than their base functional currency. In these cases, a cash pool can perform foreign exchange management activities to provide additional reduction of cost, complexity, and risk.

### 1 Foreign Exchange Management Without Cash Pooling

Without cash pooling, the MNE's individual entities must satisfy their foreign exchange needs by using external banks, which can be inefficient and expensive. Assume that Entity A and Entity B both use the US Dollar as their functional currency. Entity A receives a cash inflow of EUR 100, while Entity B needs to make a payment of EUR 60. Without a cash-pooling structure, Entity A uses an external bank to sell its EUR 100 and receive US Dollars in the foreign exchange spot market. Separately, Entity B uses a bank to sell US Dollars in the foreign exchange spot market and purchase the EUR 60 needed to make its payment. Thus, the MNE's two individual entities execute two separate spot foreign exchange transactions with external banks, incurring bank fees, suffering the bank bid-ask spread, and incurring settlement risk by exchanging currency with a third party on both transactions.

### 2 Foreign Exchange Management With Cash Pooling

Cash pooling provides a mechanism for the MNE's member entities to net their foreign exchange needs against one another and limit risk from the MNE's external foreign exchange transactions. In the example above, Member A needs to sell EUR 100, while Member B needs to purchase EUR 60. The MNE's cash pool can net these two transactions against one another within its own system—Member A can sell EUR 100 to the cash pool, which then uses those funds to pay EUR 60 to Member B so that it can meet its obligation. The cash pool then has EUR 40 remaining, which it can exchange for US Dollars on the external spot market. Instead of executing two transactions with a total value of EUR 160 and paying fees and the bid-ask spread on both transactions, the cash pool can execute one external transaction for only EUR 40, dramatically reducing fees, spreads, and settlement risk. With thousands of foreign currency transactions occurring across a large number of entities, the cash pool's ability to internally net foreign currency payments and externally trade only the residual amount can save the MNE millions of dollars in bank fees and spreads while also reducing settlement risk and counterparty credit risk.

## VII CONCLUSION

From a business and commercial perspective, cash pooling provides an elegant mechanism for managing an MNE's liquidity, optimizing external investments, settling related-party payables, and managing foreign exchange. Effective cash pooling requires thoughtful design and a highly trained team of resources to optimize execution, but can yield huge benefits via improved operations and dramatically reduced cost, complexity, and risk. With an enhanced understanding of the activities performed and benefits provided by the MNE's cash pooling structure, you should now be ready to delve into the complexities surrounding the cash pool's appropriate taxation and transfer pricing.

# CHAPTER 32

# Transfer Pricing of Cash-Pooling Transactions in the Post-BEPS Era

*Melanie Appuhn-Schneider & Alexander Haller*[*]

## I INTRODUCTION

The relevance of (internal) liquidity management (within an multinational enterprise (MNE) group) is most notable in times of crises such as the COVID-19 pandemic. However, financial transactions entered into between associated enterprises to facilitate (internal) liquidity management such as cash pool arrangements are (also) subject to intense scrutiny by tax authorities. The reason could be that financial transactions (including cash pooling transactions) are perceived to be more vulnerable to base erosion and profit-shifting strategies applied by MNEs groups since capital and linked functional activities and income flows can potentially quite easily be transferred between companies (and countries). Additionally, some types of financial transactions entered into by associated enterprises such as cash pooling transactions are commonly not found between independent enterprises so the pricing of these transactions within the framework of the arm's length principle (ALP) may even be more complex (than the pricing of other types of transactions such as the delivery of physical goods between associated enterprises).

The BEPS Action Plan (2013) identified that the existing transfer pricing rules could be misapplied resulting in outcomes not aligned with the (economic) substance of the transaction. Consequently, the Organisation for Economic Co-operation and

[*] The views and opinions set forth herein are the personal views or opinions of the authors; they do not necessarily reflect the views or opinions of the organization with which the authors are associated.

Development (OECD) developed a framework (Actions 8-10) to tackle such a (perceived) misapplication of the transfer pricing rules. As a result, the transfer prices applied must accurately reflect the economic substance of the transaction and the contribution of the parties to the value creation in the MNE group rather than the 'paper reality'. The BEPS Action Plan report on Action 4 (Limiting base erosion involving interest deduction and other financial payments) and Actions 8-10 (Aligning Transfer Pricing Outcomes with Value Creation) mandated follow-up work on the transfer pricing aspects of financial transactions. This follow-up work resulted in the Transfer Pricing Guidance on Financial Transactions released in February 2020 which has been included in the OECD Transfer Pricing (TP) Guidelines as new Chapter 10. This guidance provides a more detailed framework for the transfer pricing of financial transactions including cash pooling transactions (based on the general ALP methodology as contained in Chapters 1-3 of the OECD TP Guidelines). However, the content of this guidance enables a certain interpretative leeway on how the ALP should actually be applied to cash pooling transactions.

Against this background, this contribution focuses on important practical questions and issues related to the transfer pricing of cash pooling transactions in the post-base erosion and profit shifting (BEPS) era (such as the appropriate interpretation and application of the ALP standard after BEPS on cash pooling transactions, the practical implementation of the OECD guidance and the implications of the COVID-19 pandemic on the transfer pricing of cash pools). Specifically, after an introduction to the fundamentals of liquidity management and cash pooling (section II) and the ALP standard after BEPS (section III), this contribution introduces and critically discusses the limited guidance of the OECD on the (transfer) pricing of cash pooling transactions (section IV) and provides practical considerations and suggestions to the application of the ALP on cash pooling transactions facilitated by case studies (derived from the practice of the authors) by taking into account the (theoretical) framework as provided by the OECD (section V). This contribution also examines the general implications of the COVID-19 pandemic on the transfer pricing of cash pools and provides practical suggestions on how to cope with these challenges (section VI).

## II CASH POOLING

### 1 Fundamentals of Liquidity Management and Cash Pooling

The ready access to liquidity (i.e., cash) is essential for a company to cover current expenses (e.g., salaries, short-term liabilities) and make short-term investments.[1] A low level of liquidity could result in financial constraints and even in a bankruptcy of the company.[2] However, also a significant amount of liquidity surplus is commonly not desired by a business since it could negatively impact its profitability.[3]

1. M. Hill, J. Zietlow & T. Maness, *Short-Term Financial Management*, Sixth Edition, at 5 (2021).
2. Y. Hristozov, *How to Manage The Liquidity and Fight The Firm Debt*, 2 International Business and Accounting Research Journal 24 (2018); Fabiano Schivardi & Guido Romano, *A Simple Method to*

In times of an economic downturn, managing liquidity becomes even more critical and challenging for businesses.[4] The COVID-19 pandemic led to a global economic downturn.[5] The pandemic significantly hurts the revenues of companies in various business sectors.[6] The companies (facing declining revenues and profits) nevertheless need to timely fulfil their (short-term) debt obligations (e.g., payment of salaries, taxes, etc.). Access to (external) cash (e.g., from banks, and governments) could not be readily available.[7] Additionally, some business sectors or business models are more affected by the crisis than others.[8] Also within an MNE group with a heterogeneous product portfolio and a global market reach, one group company may suffer more than another group company from the crisis (e.g., depending on the products produced and distributed and/or markets penetrated by the group company). Thus, in times of an economic downturn, the proper management and allocation of internal liquidity of the group may become even more important.[9]

Nearly all multinational groups have established cash pools among their group companies to facilitate their liquidity management along the group's value chain.[10] The OECD generally defines cash pooling as the pooling of cash balances as part of a short-term liquidity management arrangement.[11] Cash pools can make (internal) liquidity more visible and better accessible to group companies with (short-term) liquidity needs.[12] Cash pools can however also enhance the effectiveness of liquidity management. For instance, the establishment of cash pools between group companies can significantly reduce the external funding costs (of the group). In addition, better interest rates can potentially be obtained on the aggregated cash amount (of the master account) due to economies of scale (e.g., improved bargaining power).[13]

From an operational viewpoint, cash pooling brings together (either physically or notionally) the balances of several separate bank accounts (of the various group

---

*Estimate Firms' Liquidity Needs During the COVID-19 Crisis with an Application to Italy*, CEPR Press, COVID Economics, vol. 35, at 52 (2020).

3. Liquidity management is an old topic. It has already been discussed at least since Keynes' (1936) General Theory of Employment, Interest and Money.
4. For instance, the 2008-2009 Financial Crisis has renewed interest in the way in which firms manage liquidity, given firms' access to external financing was a major challenge of firms' survival during this period (*see* H. ALMEIDA ET AL., *Corporate Liquidity Management: A Conceptual Framework and Survey*, 6 Annual Review of Financial Economics 135 ss. (December 2014).
5. J. JACKSON ET AL., *Global Economic Effects of COVID-19*, Congressional Research Service (2020).
6. M. GUERINI ET AL., *Firm Liquidity and Solvency under the COVID-19 Lockdown in France*, OFCE policy brief, vol. 76, at 10 (2020).
7. N. MCGEEVER, J. MCQUINN & S. MYERS, *SME liquidity needs during the COVID-19 shock*, Central Bank of Ireland Financial Stability Note, No. 2, at 7 (2020).
8. H. ALMEIDA, *Liquidity Management During the COVID-19 Pandemic*, 50 Asia-Pacific Journal of Financial Studies 8 (2020); GUERINI ET AL., *supra* n. 6, at 10 (2020).
9. HILL ET AL., *supra* n. 1, at 5.
10. PwC, Clarifying the Rules: Sustainable Transfer Pricing in the Financial Services Sector 137 (PwC Apr. 2012).
11. OECD, OECD Transfer Pricing Guidelines for Multinational Enterprises and Tax Administrations 2022, at 10.110 (OECD Publishing January 2022).
12. UK: Her Majesty Revenue and Customs (HMRC), *Cash Pooling: Introduction to Cash Pooling*, INTM 503110.
13. OECD, *supra* n. 11, at 10.109; PwC, Clarifying the Rules: Sustainable Transfer Pricing in the Financial Services Sector 137 (PwC April 2012).

companies participating in the cash pool, 'cash pool participants' (CPPs)). The cash surpluses of the CPPs are thus concentrated in the master account held by the cash pool master (CPM). This function is typically assumed by the parent company or a financing company of the group. Negative balances (of CPPs) are eliminated by the same master account. Thus, each (positive or negative) cash balance of the participating group companies (on their individual bank account) is periodically (usually daily) brought to a target level (usually '0'). The master account shows the resulting net cash amount (from the cash concentration). Only this net amount of the master account is subject to (external) interest payments. The CPM may receive interest payments from the (external) bank on the surplus cash. In times of low or even negative (short-term) interest rate environment, the bank could even decide to apply negative interest rates on surplus cash of the master account (resulting in an interest payment obligation of the CPM) or to floor the interest rate at zero. The CPM may however also be required to pay (i) a fee to the bank for running the cash pool and (ii) interest to the bank if the balance of the master account is negative. The task of the treasury department usually is to optimize cash management such that no overdraft occurs at the level of the master account and to minimize interest payable for maintaining sufficient liquidity for the cash pool.

**Example 1**

A group consists of the parent company (PCo) and three subsidiaries, namely SCo 1, SCo 2 and SCo 3 which have differing funding requirements: SCo 1 and SCo 2 have surplus cash in the amount of EUR 300 and EUR 50, respectively, whereas SCo3 has a negative balance of EUR 350. The interest rates offered by the external banks are 5 % on deposits (SCo 1 and SCo 2) and 10 % on withdrawals (SCo 3). It is assumed that these amounts do not fluctuate.

The total savings from the establishment of a cash pool are calculated as follows:

| | *Without Cash Pooling* | | | | *Cash Pooling* | *Total Savings* |
|---|---|---|---|---|---|---|
| | *SCo1* | *SCo2* | *SCo3* | *Total* | | |
| Balance | 300 | 50 | −350 | 0 | 0 | |
| Interest Rate (%) | 5 | 5 | 10 | | | |
| Interest | 15 | 2.5 | −35 | −17.5 | 0 | + 17.5 |

In this example, if no cash pool is established, the group's net interest payable to the bank is EUR 17.5 while the aggregate cash amount of the group was nil. If a cash pool was in place with the parent company (as CPM), the bank would only apply interest on the net amount, which is nil. Thus, there would not be any external funding costs with a cash pool. The group would save interest expenses in the amount of EUR 17.5. This is the saving from the netting effect of the cash pool ('netting benefit'). A cash pool may potentially also entail certain other quantifiable advantages such as 'volume discount' (if any), i.e., better interest rates on the master account of the CPM due to economies of scale. In practice, there are usually significant complexities in calculating the benefit such as, for instance, fluctuating balances in different currencies. Further, in this example, without a proper transfer pricing analysis, the entire savings (from the netting of the accounts) could flow to the cash pool borrower, namely SCo 3, whereas the cash pool depositors (SCo 1 and SCo 2) and the CPM (PCo) could not receive an adequate compensation (for the cash provided to the pool or the services rendered). Accordingly, the major challenge from the transfer pricing perspective is the quantification and allocation of these savings to the various group companies according to their contribution to the creation of the benefit.

## 2 Types of Cash-Pooling Arrangements

There are generally two basic types of cash pooling arrangements. The group could either decide to establish a physical or a notional cash pool. Also, variations and combinations of both types can be arranged to take specific business needs into account. Furthermore, a CPM may perform different types of functions and may bear different types of risks depending on the underlying setup.

In a physical cash pool, the surplus cash of the CPPs is physically transferred to the master account whereas liabilities are physically balanced by the same master account. Thus, physical pooling enables the group to concentrate the cash in one place, namely in the master account of the CPM. If the netting of the accounts results in a debit balance of the master account, the CPM may borrow funds from the bank. Any surplus cash (from the netting) could be invested by the CPM (by taking into account, for instance, liquidity risks). Thus, within a physical cash pool, only the master account of the CPM is subject to risk from the perspective of the bank. The bank could however ask the parent company to issue a guarantee (if the cash pool is headed by a separate financing company) or all CPPs to issue a joint guarantee for the CPM.[14] By issuing a joint guarantee, the CPPs would become jointly and severally liable for a default of the CPM. Further, due to the physical cash transfer, the ownership in cash changes with the effect of creating (intercompany) financial transactions between the CPM and the CPPs.[15] A cash deposit (or borrowing) on the master account creates a liability (or receivable) of the CPM and a receivable (or liability) of the CPP which transferred the cash (or vice versa).[16] In addition, within a physical pool, a CPM could perform a broad set of functions[17] and possibly act as an 'internal bank'.[18] Alternatively, the CPM could have low-level functionality, such as a coordination or agency function. A CPM with a

14. V. Chand, *Transfer Pricing Aspects of Cash Pooling Arrangements in Light of the BEPS Action Plan*, 23 Intl. Transfer Pricing J. 1, at 40 (2016).
15. A.J. Bakker, *Transfer Pricing and Intra-group Financing: Low Hanging Fruit?*, 15 Derivatives & Fin. Instruments 2, at 30 (2013).
16. The German Federal Tax Court classified the financial arrangements between the CPM and the cash pool participants as loan arrangements for domestic (tax) law purposes (DE: BFH, 16 January 2006, II RZ 75/04, GmbHR 2006, 477).
17. R. Petruzzi, *Transfer Pricing Aspects of Intra-Group Financing*, at 145, 146 (Wolters Kluwer 2016); Chand, *supra* n. 14, at 39.
18. J. Hollas & G. Hands, Transfer Pricing and Intra Group Cash Pooling, 19 Tax Mgmt. Transfer Pricing Rep. 20, at 4 (Feb. 2011); A. Haller & V. Chand, *Application of the Arm's Length Principle*

high level of functionality could, for instance, take over the (centralized) liquidity planning and controlling (for the whole group), decide about investment and portfolio strategies and could completely internalize the cash accounts of the CPPs.[19] It is imperative that the level of the functionality of the CPM is an essential criterion for the allocation of savings (benefits) from the establishment of a physical cash pool. Thus, within a physical pool, the savings should be shared among the CPPs by taking into account the functions performed (assets used and risks assumed) by the CPM and the (relative) contribution to creation of the saving.[20]

By contrast, in a notional cash pool, the bank accounts of the CPPs are not physically balanced by the master account. The cash balances of the CPPs are rather only notionally (i.e., virtually) consolidated (in a virtual master account).[21] Accordingly, the (external) bank calculates the interest on this virtual net position and pays or charges this interest respectively. A notional cash pooling arrangement may therefore be regarded as simple interest rate compensation.[22] As the cash positions (deposits or borrowings) of the single CPPs towards the bank remain unaffected by a virtual cash pool, the bank will generally bear the (credit) risk of every single participant. Thus, within a notional cash pool, it can often be observed that the bank asks the participants of a virtual cash pool to issue cross guarantees among each other to reduce credit risks.[23] A CPM in the narrow sense is commonly not present as the bank takes over the main functions (and risks).[24] The net interest (from the virtual consolidation) after deduction of the bank charges would commonly be transferred from the bank by applying certain apportionment factors agreed upon beforehand with the group to the CPPs. Thus, within a virtual cash pool, the savings (from the virtual consolidation) must be determined and shared between the participants by taking into account (only) the contribution of each CPP to the creation of the saving.

## III THE ALP AFTER BEPS AS AN ANTI-AVOIDANCE MEASURE?

The ALP is widely regarded as the cornerstone of transfer pricing.[25] It is embedded in domestic laws as well as treaties. It appears as Article 9 paragraph 1 of the OECD and UN Model Tax Conventions.[26] The principle requires comparing transactions between

*to Physical Cash Pooling Arrangements in Light of the OECD Discussion Draft on Financial Transactions*, 47 Intertax 350 (2019).

19. Petruzzi, *supra* n. 17, at 146 & 147; Chand, *supra* n. 14, at 39; Hollas & Hands, *supra* n. 18, at 4.
20. Haller & Chand, *supra* n. 18, at 362.
21. S. Hillman, *Notional vs. Physical Cash Pooling Revisited*, Intl. Treasurer (February 2011).
22. HMRC *supra* n. 12, INTM 503120.
23. OECD, *supra* n. 11, at 10.113.
24. *Ibid.*, para. 10.114.
25. For an in-depth analysis of the arm's length principle, *see* J. Wittendorff, *Transfer Pricing and the Arm's Length Principle in International Tax Law, Series on International Taxation* (Kluwer Tax Law International 2010). For a critical discussion on the arm's length principle, *see* L. Schoueri, Arm's Length: Beyond the Guidelines of the OECD, 69 Bull. Intl. Taxn. 12, at 690-716 (2015).
26. Article 9 para. 1 provides: '[Where] conditions are made or imposed between the two [associated] enterprises in their commercial or financial relations which differ from those which

associated enterprises with comparable transactions of independent enterprises under similar conditions and economic circumstances and pricing the transactions between associated enterprises accordingly.[27] Consequently, if the (transfer) prices applied on the transactions between the associated enterprises differ from those which would be agreed between independent enterprises (under comparable conditions and economic circumstances), adjustments to the profits may be imposed.[28] Overall, the underlying idea behind the ALP is the attempt to place transactions, both uncontrolled and controlled, on equal terms with respect to the tax advantages (or disadvantages) that they create.[29] Thus, the ALP generally is an objective standard.[30] This means that it is not affected by the taxpayer's motive (e.g., shifting of profits to 'tax heavens') for a controlled transaction.[31] Considering the nature and mechanism of the ALP, Wittendorf even concludes that it 'goes hand in hand with tax planning, which may undermine national tax bases. The arm's length principle is like a Trojan horse, and contains the seeds of the problem it is intended to resolve'.[32]

A particular area of concern (and disputes) is the transfer pricing of financial transactions including cash pooling transactions between associated enterprises. Financial transactions (including cash pooling) are perceived to be more vulnerable to base erosion and profit-shifting strategies applied by MNE groups as capital and linked functional activities and income flows can potentially quite easily be transferred between companies (and countries).[33] Additionally, some types of financial transactions entered into by associated enterprises such as cash pooling transactions are commonly not found between independent enterprises so the pricing of these transactions (within the framework of the ALP) may even be more complex (than the pricing of other types of transactions).[34] Even though tax authorities generally acknowledge

would be made between independent enterprises, then any profits which would, but for those conditions, have accrued to one of the enterprises, but, by reason of those conditions, have not so accrued, may be included in the profits of that enterprise and taxed accordingly.'

27. OECD, *supra* n. 11, at 1.6.
28. OECD, *Model Tax Convention on Income and on Capital*, Article 9, at para. 2 (OECD Publishing 21 November 2017).
29. OECD, *supra* n. 11, at 1.8; UN, *United Nations Practical Manual on Transfer Pricing for Developing Countries*, at 2.4.2.7 (UN 2021).
30. The OECD TP Guidelines emphasize that the consideration of transfer pricing should not be confused with the consideration of problems of tax fraud or tax avoidance (*Ibid.*, para. 1.2).
31. Collier and Andrus discuss the capability of the ALP (after BEPS) to tackle tax planning by MNE groups. They conclude that the ALP (even after BEPS) will not prevent the realization of tax advantages by MNE group since MNE groups can just facilitate the contractual allocation of functions, assets and risks with an 'appropriate' economic substance. Given that, they suggest to introduce some form of subjective test (i.e., motive test) in the ALP system to eliminate tax planning. R.S. Collier & J.L. Andrus, *Transfer Pricing and the Arm's Length Principle after BEPS*, at 265-267, 274-276 (Oxford U. Press 2017).
32. Wittendorff, *supra* n. 25, at 786.
33. S. Greil & D. Schilling, *Cross-Border Intra-Group Financial Transactions: Evidence from Germany*, 24 Intl. Transfer Pricing J. 6, at 503 (2017).
34. H.M. Andresen, N. Pearson-Wood & H.-M. Jørgensen, *ConocoPhillips Case: Implications in Norway and Beyond*, 17 Intl. Transfer Pricing J. 6, at 464 (2010); E. Vistisen, Bombardier Case: First Published Cash Pool Decision, 21 Intl. Transfer Pricing J. 3, at 189 (2014).

that the reasons for the establishment of cash pooling arrangements can be commercially justified,[35] they nevertheless perform intense tax audits to determine the transfer pricing aspects of cash pools.[36]

The BEPS Action Plan (2013)[37] identified that the existing transfer pricing rules could be misapplied resulting in outcomes not aligned with the (economic) substance of the transaction. Consequently, the OECD developed a framework (Actions 8-10) to tackle such a (perceived) misapplication of the transfer pricing rules.[38] As a result, the transfer prices applied must accurately reflect the economic substance of the transaction and the contribution of the parties to the value creation in the MNE group rather than the 'paper reality'.[39] The 'substance' of the transaction can be derived from an accurate delineation (i.e., analysis) of the (actual) transaction by taking into account the economically relevant characteristics of the transaction (i.e., the contractual terms, the functions performed, risks assumed and assets used by the parties, the characteristics of the property transferred or services provided, the broader economic circumstances and the business strategies pursued by the parties).[40] If the written contracts significantly differ from the economic substance (i.e., actual conduct of the parties), the economic substance (i.e., actual conduct) will prevail.[41] Consequently, the actual conduct of the parties (and not the contractual allocation of functions, assets, risks) will be subject to the comparison in the second step of the comparability analysis to determine arm's length transfer prices.

However, according to the OECD, tax administrations should only disregard the actual transaction (derived from the delineation of the transaction) or substitute other transactions in exceptional circumstances.[42] The key question from the OECD's perspective would be whether the actual transaction possesses the commercial rationality of arrangements that would be agreed between unrelated parties under comparable circumstances, not whether the same transaction can be observed between independent parties.[43] Thus, even if certain transactions entered into between associated enterprises cannot be found between independent enterprises, they should not be disregarded given that the commercial rationale of the transaction can be demonstrated. In other words, only if the transaction viewed in its totality differs from that

35. HMRC *supra* n. 12, INTM 503110.
36. K. Łukosz, A. Ursu & M. Druga, *Transfer Pricing of Intra-Group Cash-Pooling Arrangements Through the Lens of Business and Economic Reality*, 25 Intl. Transfer Pricing J. 3, at 208 (2018); Chand, *supra* n. 14, at 38-47 (2016).
37. OECD, *Action Plan on Base Erosion and Profit* Shifting *(OECD Publishing 19 Jul. 2013).*
38. The work of the OECD resulted in final reports to BEPS Actions 8-10 published in October 2015. The amendments proposed by these reports were incorporated in the OECD Transfer Pricing Guidelines in 2017.
39. OECD, *Aligning Transfer Pricing Outcomes with Value Creation – Actions 8–10 Final Reports*, OECD/G20 Base Erosion and Profit Shifting Project, e.g., at 13-14 (OECD Publishing 5 October 2015).
40. OECD, *supra* n. 11, paras 1.36, 1.43.
41. For example, *ibid.*, at 1.45.
42. *Ibid.*, e.g., at para. 1.141.
43. *Ibid.*, at para. 1.143.

which would be agreed upon by independent enterprises, tax administrations may obtain a mandate to disregard the transaction.[44]

The BEPS Action Plan reports on Action 4 (Limiting base erosion involving interest deduction and other financial payments) and Actions 8-10 (Aligning Transfer Pricing Outcomes with Value Creation) mandated follow-up work on the transfer pricing of financial transactions. This follow-up work resulted in a final Transfer Pricing Guidance on Financial Transactions in February 2020 which has been included in the OECD TP Guidelines as new Chapter 10.[45] Essentially, similar to other controlled transactions, the transfer pricing of financial transactions must concentrate on the economic substance of the (single) transaction (i.e., actual conduct of the parties) by taking into account the special facts and circumstances of each individual case.[46] Consequently, the limited availability of third-party evidence does not mean that cash pooling transactions are not at arm's length at all. In particular, if the commercial rationale of entering into such transactions (e.g., improvement of internal liquidity management, reduction of funding costs) can be demonstrated, cash pooling transactions should not be disregarded.[47]

In a nutshell, in the BEPS project (including the follow-up work on financial transactions), the OECD developed and defined measures within the framework of the ALP (not outside the ALP).[48] By concentrating the BEPS project on the economic substance and the development and provision of concrete concepts and tests (such as the six-step process for the allocation of risks) to determine the substance, the OECD has confirmed and enhanced the (existing) economic approach of transfer pricing.[49] In our view, the measures in their totality (including the enhanced transparency obligations) build an effective framework (by maintaining the ALP) against BEPS (based on a contractual allocation of function, assets and risks without proper economic substance). Additionally, the OECD has arguably decided not to include a subjective test (i.e., motive test) in the ALP system even if some authors would consider the inclusion of some form of subjective test as a more effective measure to tackle tax planning.[50]

44. *Ibid.*, at para. 1.142.
45. Besides the OECD, the United Nations has also included new guidance on financial transactions in Chapter 9 of Part B of the latest edition of the UN TP Manual). While the chapter also discusses cash pooling practices, it does not go into any further detail on the delineation and arm's length pricing of those specific transactions.
46. OECD, *supra* n. 11, para. 10.14.
47. HALLER & CHAND, *supra* n. 18, at 351.
48. '(...), the goals set by the BEPS Action Plan in relation to the development of transfer pricing rules have been achieved without the need to develop special measures outside the arm's length principle.' (OECD, *supra* n. 39, at 12).
49. The 'people functions' (rather than the terms and conditions as fixed in 'written' contracts) may be seen as the deciding factor for the allocation of returns to an entity (M. HEGGMAIR, *The New Interpretation of the Arm's Length Principle: A Post-BEPS Evaluation*, 24 Intl. Transfer Pricing J. 4, at 2 et seq. (2017). The (new) economic approach to the transfer pricing of transactions between group companies seem to be inspired by the (authorized) OECD approach on the attribution of profits to a permanent establishments. *See* W. SCHÖN, *International Taxation of Risk*, 68 Bull. Intl. Taxn. 6/7, at 290 (2014); J. WITTENDORFF, *BEPS Actions 8–10: Birth of a New Arm's Length Principle*, 81 Tax Notes Intl. 4, at 331-332 (2016).
50. For instance, Collier and Andrus suggest the introduction of a subjective test (i.e., motive test) in the ALP system after BEPS: 'Attempts in the BEPS project to develop an objective approach or

Thus, the OECD maintained the ALP as an objective standard.[51] Consequently, the realization of any tax advantages by MNE groups could not be prevented by the ALP (after BEPS).[52] However, if the realization of a tax advantage is facilitated by sufficient economic substance, the execution of such transaction (resulting in the tax advantage) could, in our view, unlikely be regarded as (aggressive) tax planning that should be tackled by the ALP. It would rather be a policy issue (resulting from the tax competition between countries) which should not be solved within the ALP system.[53]

**Example 2**

ParCo (resident in Germany) has a subsidiary, SubCo, in country X. Country X has significantly lower tax rates in place than the applicable tax rates in Germany. SubCo functions as a treasury centre within the group. It inter alia provides loans to other group companies and assumes a CPM function. SubCo has offices, employees, equipment, etc. It is assumed that credit and liquidity risks are economically significant risks. Based on the TP analysis, SubCo performs risk control functions and also has the financial capacity to bear those credit risks. Under the ALP, SubCo should receive compensation similar to that of an independent enterprise (under comparable conditions and economic circumstances). The amount of the compensation correlates with the functions (actually) performed, risks (actually) assumed and assets (actually) used. This (arm's length) compensation should be earned by SubCo even if the group realizes tax advantage (from the establishment of SubCo in country X). In this respect, it should be noted that also an independent enterprise could decide to establish its business (e.g., provision of loans to third parties) in country X. The independent enterprise would obtain the same tax advantage as the MNE group (i.e., lower tax rates). Attempts to determine consequences within the ALP system (e.g., non-recognition of the transactions or the adjustment of the income of SubCo) just because an MNE group realized the tax advantage could distort the (tax) neutrality of the ALP system and, as an effect, could also create (relative) economic imbalances.[54]

test based on specific functional activities pursuant to the substance theme and specifically targeting the alignment of value-generating activity and profits have been only partially successful. (...) Given that, some form of subjective test, i.e. motive test, seems a more plausible route to pursue.' Collier & Andrus, *supra* n. 31, at 274-276.

51. The (new) economic approach of transfer pricing requires an in depth-analysis of the facts and circumstances of each transaction (based on the concepts provided by the OECD). The application of the (new) economic approach can however involve subjective interpretations of these facts and circumstances. The risk of double taxation and disputes may increase. This increased risk of double taxation was considered by the OECD under Action 14 aimed to improve the effectiveness of dispute resolution mechanisms.
52. R.S. Collier & J.L. Andrus, *Transfer Pricing and the Arm's Length Principle after BEPS*, at 265-267, 274-276 (Oxford U. Press 2017); a critical position against risk premiums within MNE groups (as a possible source of tax planning) is taken by Schön, *see* W. Schön, *International Taxation of Risk*, 68 Bull. Intl. Taxn. 6/7, at 290 ss (2014).
53. Wittendorf concludes that 'BEPS action 5 on harmful tax competition is arguably of greater importance if an end should be put to cross-border tax planning because the primary driver of tax planning is the difference in effective tax rates among countries' (J. Wittendorff, *supra* n. 42 at 333).
54. 'There are several reasons why OECD participant countries and other countries have adopted the arm's length principle. A major reason is that the arm's length principle provides broad

## IV OECD GUIDANCE ON THE TRANSFER PRICING OF CASH POOLING TRANSACTIONS

According to the OECD, the transfer prices applied must properly reflect the economic substance of the transaction. The substance of the transaction can be derived from an accurate delineation (i.e., analysis) of the (actual) transaction by taking into account the economically relevant characteristics. In the context of cash pooling, the accurate delineation of the (actual) cash pooling transactions (based on objective criteria) can thus be regarded as the key task within the transfer pricing analysis of cash pooling transactions. Consequently, paragraphs 10.4-10.38 of the new Chapter 10 of the OECD TP Guidelines provide guidance on the application of the general methodology contained in Chapters 1-3 on financial transactions including a concept to test whether a purported loan should be regarded as loan (or infusion of equity). This guidance is supplemented by paragraphs 10.109-10.148 which provide more specific considerations on the accurate delineation and the pricing of cash pooling transactions (including some limited guidance on the treatment of cash pool guarantees).

The most important considerations of the OECD in the guidance referring to the transfer pricing of cash pooling transactions can be summarized as follows:

(i) Delineation/characterization:
- A CPP will likely participate in the pool as a part of a broader group strategy which may include a range of benefits that can only be achieved as part of a collective strategy of the pool participants.[55] The benefits must be established through a thorough functional analysis. Accordingly, in the context of cash pooling, it is necessary to determine (i) the nature of the advantage, (ii) the amount of the benefit provided, and (iii) how that benefit should be divided among the participants of the MNE group.[56]
- No participant in the pooling arrangement would expect to participate if it made them worse than its next best option.[57]
- CPPs could maintain debit and credit positions which, rather than functioning as part of a short-term liquidity arrangement, become more long term. It would be necessary to consider whether it would be correct to treat them as something other than a short-term cash pool balance (e.g., longer-term deposit or a term loan).[58]

parity of tax treatment for participants of MNE groups and independent enterprises. Because the arm's length principle puts associated and independent enterprises on a more equal footing for tax purposes, it avoids the creation of tax advantages or disadvantages that would otherwise distort the relative competitive positions of either type of entity. In so removing these tax considerations from economic decisions, the arm's length principle promotes the growth of international trade and investment', OECD, *supra* n. 11, at 1.8.

55. *Ibid.*, para. 10.117.
56. *Ibid.*, para. 10.120.
57. *Ibid.*, para. 10.118.
58. *Ibid.*, para. 10.122.

(ii) **Reward of the CPM:** The appropriate reward of the CPM will depend on the facts and circumstances of the individual case.[59] Even if a CPM typically performs no more than coordination or agency function, a thorough functional analysis may nevertheless establish that it has a higher functionality.[60] In case of a higher level of functionality, the CPM would be entitled to a higher return.[61]

(iii) **Reward of the CPPs:** The remuneration of the CPPs will be calculated through the determination of the arm's length interest rates applicable to the debit and credit positions within the pool. This mechanism will allocate the synergy benefits to the CPPs after deduction of the reward of the CPM.[62] Additionally, considering the lack of comparable arrangements, banking arrangements involving the CPM, taking into account functional differences (between the bank and the CPM), and the options realistically available to the CPPs may inform about comparable interest rates in the transfer pricing analysis.[63]

(iv) **Cash pool guarantees:** As part of the cash pool agreement, cross-guarantees and rights of set-off between participants may be required (by the bank). Such guarantees (or set-off rights) would not occur between independent parties. In this context, the OECD concludes that the result of such guarantees could be nothing more than an acknowledgement that it would be detrimental to the interests of the group not to support the performance of the CPM (and the borrower) and that the guaranteed borrower could not be benefitting beyond the level of credit enhancement attributable to the implicit support of other group participants. Consequently, under such circumstances, a guarantee fee could not be payable.[64]

In summary, the guidance provides important clarifications, such as for instance the acknowledgement that the CPM – depending on the particular facts and circumstances of the single case – could be more like a simple financial service provider and that the issuance of cash pool guarantees (especially cross-guarantees) could potentially be explained by the shareholder relationship not subject to a separate (guarantee) fee.[65] However, the guidance does not sufficiently discuss and explain other important

59. *Ibid.*, para. 10.129.
60. *Ibid.*, paras 10.130-10.142.
61. *Ibid.*, para. at 10.141.
62. *Ibid.*, para. 10.143.
63. *Ibid.*, para. 10.145.
64. *Ibid.*, paras 10.147 & 10.148.
65. The OECD acknowledges that a CPM – even if it typically not assumes more than a (low-risk) service provider function – could (actually) perform additional functions (and actually assume risks). It should then be remunerated accordingly. A CPM (with a high level of functionality and risk assumption) could even be entitled to earn a part or all of the interest spread between the borrowing and lending positions which it adopts. Consequently, according to the OECD, a CPM should consistently be remunerated on the basis of the functions it (actually) performs, the risks it (actually) assumes and the assets it (actually) uses. Even if the prior scholarly literature on this topic supports the approach as published by the OECD, some (local) tax authorities have applied a different treatment in the past, wanting to characterize the CPM as (low-risk) service provider

features of cash pooling arrangements such as the determination of appropriate cash pool interest rates. Specifically, the explanations on the determination and allocation of any cash pool advantages were not significantly enhanced in the final OECD guidance (compared to the public discussion draft). By contrast, the public discussion draft outlined (three) potential allocation mechanisms and the factors (i.e., criteria) that could lead to a certain allocation mechanism (such as the similarity of credit profiles).[66] The OECD has decided to remove this discussion from the (final) guidance. In addition, the two examples (as contained in paras 10.133-10.142 of the final guidance) give a greater emphasis on the remuneration of the CPM and less so on how the benefits of the CPPs could be shared. Thus, the (final) guidance (only) concludes that each CPP would expect enhanced interest rates (by taking into account options realistically available to them). Consequently, in this regard, it is not substantially clear which economically significant characteristics (i.e., factors or determinants) should be taken into account and analysed properly (in order to derive an appropriate allocation mechanism for the sharing of the cash pool benefits). Further, considering the lack of more detailed guidance and examples on the practical implementation, the existing guidance, while being helpful in providing a certain (theoretical) framework, has also created a significant level of uncertainty on how it shall be implemented in practice. It can thus be questioned if the guidance (actually) facilitates a consistent application of the ALP on cash pooling transactions (by taxpayers, tax authorities or among tax authorities).

## V PRACTICAL CONSIDERATIONS FOR THE TRANSFER PRICING OF CASH-POOLING TRANSACTIONS EXPLAINED ON THE BASIS OF CASE STUDIES

### 1 Introduction: Basic Facts and Circumstances of the Case

Abstracting from the (theoretical) background as discussed in the previous chapter, it can be concluded that the ALP in synthesis requires the review and analysis of three different aspects pertaining to cash pool transactions:

- the CPM needs to be accurately remunerated considering the functions performed, risks borne and assets held;
- the interest rate charged for deposits and borrowings to/from the pool has to be arm's length; and
- the cash pool advantages have to be allocated appropriately among parties participating in the cash pool considering the facts and circumstances of the single case.

in general (without accurately delineating the functions including risk assumption of the CPM in the single case). In our view, such an approach would clearly indicate a departure from the general methodology as provided by the OECD TP Guidelines (e.g., the risk and return framework as contained in chapter I) and would thus not be consistent with the ALP system of the OECD.

66. OECD, Discussion Draft, *BEPS Actions 8-10: Financial Transactions, OECD/G20 Base Erosion and Profit Shifting Project*, paras 124-129 (OECD Publishing 3 July 2018).

The following section aims at making suggestions for possible practical considerations for the transfer pricing of cash pools on the basis of case studies.

In the underlying case, let us assume that an MNE group decided to establish a financial hub (FinCo), a direct subsidiary of the parent company. In its function as FinCo, FinCo also acts as CPM for the cash pool.

FinCo and the CPPs entered into a zero balance agreement (ZBA) with bank A. FinCo as CPM and the CPPs each maintain a ZBA account. FinCo as CPM is the owner of the concentration account. The daily target balance of the CPP's ZBA account is zero. The function of bank A is to transfer excess funds from the CPPs' ZBA accounts to the CPM's concentration account and vice versa. The daily sweeping is run in an automated manner by bank A.

No fee is charged by bank A on the sweeps or the cash pool transactions. However, an overdraft rate of Euribor + 4% is charged to the CPM in case of a negative balance at the master account level. Due to the current low-interest rate environment, there is no interest rate margin for deposits such that the interest rate for positive balances is Euribor + 0%, where Euribor is floored at zero.

In addition to the ZBA and concentration account in place with bank A, the CPM and the CPPs maintain intercompany current account/-s. The ZBA accounts are bank accounts held by the CPPs. On a daily basis, (positive or negative) cash balances of the CPPs in this Zero Balance Account are brought to a target level of 0. The net balance of all the CPPs is concentrated in the concentration//master account held by the CPM. While the ZBA and concentration accounts record all transactions carried out by bank A, the intercompany current accounts record all transactions between the CPM and the CPPs resulting from the cash pooling transactions.

In order to ensure sufficient liquidity for the cash pool, the CPM entered into a revolving credit facility (RCF) with bank B, which allows the CPM to draw on the RCF in cases where more funds are borrowed from the pool than deposited into the pool by the CPPs. The bank required a guarantee from the parent company. The revolving nature of the RCF allows FinCo to withdraw, repay, and withdraw again depending on its funding needs.

## 2 Case Study 1: CPM as Service Provider

### *A Additional Facts*

Let us assume that the parent company, located in Germany, decided to set up the CPM as a service provider in Luxembourg. The cash pool is a EUR-denominated cash pool for affiliated entities located in the Euro area. Therefore, all participants have the same functional currency (Euro) and this is the only currency in the pool.[67]

The netting of the cash pool accounts is automatically carried out on a daily basis by bank A. The functions of the CPM in relation to the cash pool are limited to routine treasury and related administrative functions. The treasury department monitors the

67. OECD, *supra* n. 11, at 10.133.

bank balances of the master cash pool account by daily cash disposition and bank account reconciliation. Every month end, the treasury department provides the interest calculation to the CPM account holder and CPPs such that the accounting department of the MNE can make the respective entries. These cash pool-related tasks take on average not more than 15 to 30 minutes a day.

Strategic funding decisions are made by the parent company. Decisions include bond issuances (at the level of the parent company), entering into external financing arrangements, issuance of new intercompany loans and drawdowns from the external bank facilities to increase cash needs for the cash pool. The parent company also provided an explicit guarantee to bank B for the RCF. Therefore, credit and structural market risks are first and foremost borne by the parent company.

Bank A required that the cash pool arrangement is jointly and severally guaranteed by the CPPs. To avoid the CPM would bear any credit risks towards the CPPs, the parent company also provided a guarantee towards the CPM in the internal relationship, thereby guaranteeing to pay to the CPM any amount due and not paid by the CPPs in relation to the cash pool arrangement.

Additionally, the following specifics apply to the RCF: the RCF has a one-year term. The interest rate granted by bank B to the CPM is Euribor + 1%, whereby Euribor is floored at 0%.

The following diagram provides an overview of the key set-up relevant to the I/C cash pool and the key questions to be analysed:

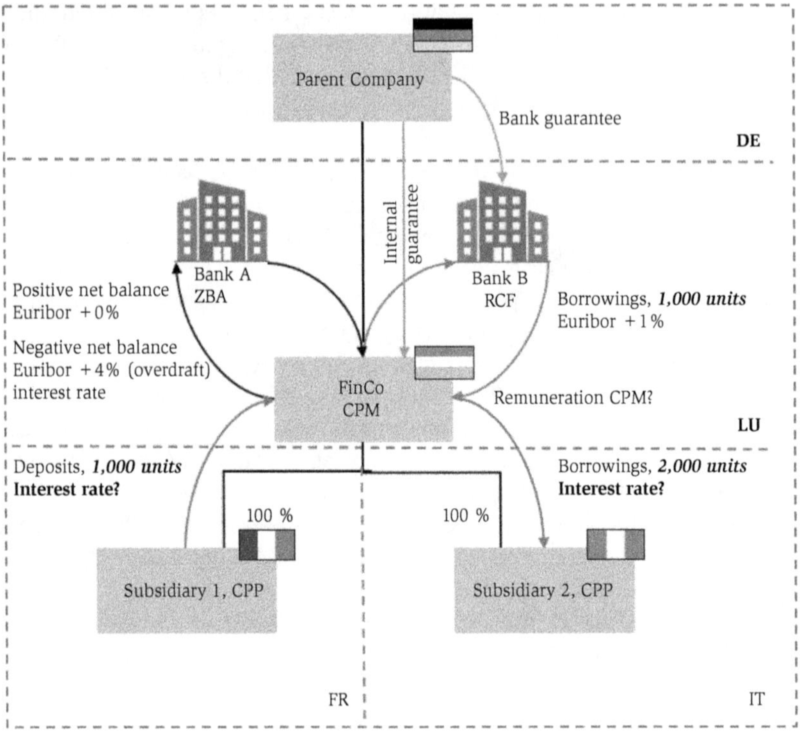


## B Determining an Arm's Length Remuneration for the CPM

According to the OECD, the appropriate reward of the CPM will depend on the functions performed, assets used and the risks assumed. That said, the OECD highlights that frequently a CPM only performs a coordination or agency function with the master account being a centralized point for a series of book entries to meet the pre-determined target. Based on the facts and circumstances described above, the functions of the CPM are actually limited to performing administrative coordination and supporting treasury functions. Due to (i) the external guarantee granted by the parent company to bank B, (ii) the internal payment guarantee provided by parent company to the CPM covering the default risk of the CPPs and (iii) the fact that the cash pool arrangement is jointly and severally guaranteed by the CPPs towards bank A, the CPM does not bear any significant risks and does not own or use any significant assets in connection with the cash pool. Consequently, the CPM in this case study 1 example should generally (only) earn a reward commensurate with the service provider functions it provides to the pool.[68]

68. OECD, *supra* n. 11, at 10.137.

Simple (low-risk) service providers are often remunerated on a full markup on a cost basis, whereby the cost base frequently consists of any direct and indirect non-interest-bearing operating costs incurred by the service provider for the relevant activity.[69] According to the German tax authorities, finance costs shall not be included in the cost basis where a CPM is remunerated on a cost plus basis.[70] The OECD methodology on low value-adding services enables MNEs to apply a markup of 5% for low value-adding services without the need of performing a benchmarking analysis.[71] Within this context, the OECD TP Guidelines provide a non-exhaustive list of possible low value-adding services.[72] Low value-adding services are defined to be of supportive nature, not relating to the core business of the MNE.[73] The OECD guidance on cash pooling emphasizes that treasury and the CPM activity may qualify as a support activity.[74] Therefore, a markup of 5% could constitute an appropriate cost plus markup for the limited risk activities of the CPM in connection with the cash pool. Further guidance is provided by the German tax authorities, which note that a cost plus markup between 5% and 10% could be appropriate.[75] Consequently, by taking into account the particular facts of the case, the appropriate reward of FinCo for its CPM function could be a markup (of 5%-10%) on the non-interest-bearing operating costs.

### C Determining Arm's Length Interest Rates for Deposits to and Borrowings from the Pool

In the following, two exemplary alternatives are discussed to set the interest rate for deposits and borrowings of the cash pool.[76] These two scenarios rely on the premise that (i) the CPM, where characterized as a service provider, would generally not be expected to bear any significant risks in connection with the cash pool and hence should not bear associated costs, and (ii) the CPPs should derive a benefit from participating in the cash pool, meaning that participating in the cash pooling arrangement should not make them any worse off than their next best option.[77] Where the CPM acts as a service provider, the cash pool benefits should be passed on to CPP as far as possible. The way the interest rate is set and/or re-allocated affects the allocation of benefits among the CPPs, as will be shown in the following two examples.[78]

69. OECD, *supra* n. 11, e.g., at para. 2.99.
70. DE: BMF, *Verwaltungsgrundsätze Verrechnungspreise 2021*, para. 3.98.
71. OECD, *supra* n. 11, at para. 7.46.
72. *Ibid.*, at para. 7.49.
73. *Ibid.*, at para. 7.45.
74. OECD, *supra* n. 11, at 10.45.
75. DE: BMF, *supra* n. 70, para. 3.98.
76. The case studies represent two possible options to set the interest rate. This does not imply that there are not different options to derive an arm's length (range of) interest rate(s).
77. OECD, *supra* n. 11, para. 10.118.
78. In theory, the question arises if the remuneration and/or allocation should differentiate between a benefit attributable to economies of scale and a benefit attributable to netting positions within

### a Alt. A: Applying the RCF Interest Rate to Deposits and Borrowings by Relying on the Internal Comparable Uncontrolled Price (CUP) Method

One alternative to set the deposit and borrowing rate would be to apply the RCF interest rate to deposits and borrowings to//from the pool as demonstrated in the following diagram:

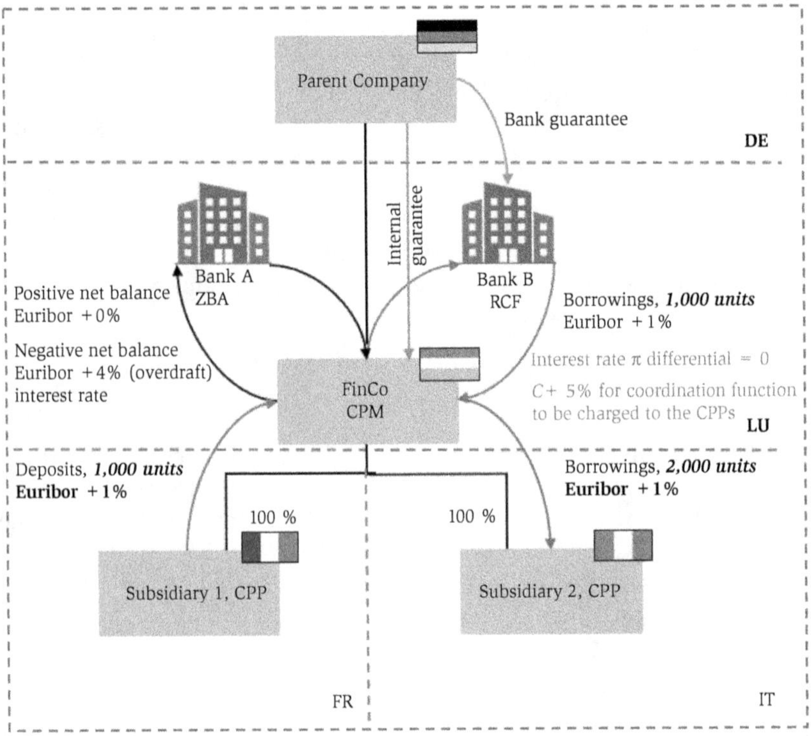


Where the actual functions of the CPM consist of a mere coordination function, applying the same interest rate conditions to deposits and borrowings from the pool ensures that theoretically, no residual income accumulates at the level of the CPM. Any benefits generated by the cash pool would be automatically attributed to the CPPs. Consequently, the question is whether the equalization of the (cash pool) interest rate (by applying the RCF interest rate on cash pool deposits and borrowings) provides arm's length results (from the perspective of the CPPs):

- **Arm's length nature of the borrowing rate:** Given the external and internal guarantees provided by the parent company as well as the fact that the cash

the pool. That said, there is no detailed OECD guidance on this point. Therefore, reference is made to one conglomerate benefit within the remainder of this paper.

pool is jointly and severally guaranteed by the CPPs,[79] the credit rating of the CPPs is lifted to the credit rating of group in accordance with the OECD TP Guidelines.[80] Based on the rating nomenclature published by for instance Standard & Poor Global Ratings, the group crediting rating generally sets the ceiling credit rating.[81] From this perspective, the interest rate margin provided by bank B as part of the RCF at the group conditions reflects the best interest rate conditions that could be achieved by the MNE/the individual CPPs considering the terms and conditions of the RCF. Therefore, the CPPs receive a benefit in terms of the differential between their standalone credit rating after considering implicit support and the group credit rating, representing the maximum achievable interest rate benefit. Given that any other benefits such as a volume discount would equally be maintained in this interest rate and considering that the RCF has a one-year term and thereby being reflective of an arm's length short-term interest rate, it seems reasonable to conclude that there should be no other options making any of the CPPs better off or at least not worse off.

- **Arm's length nature of the deposit rate**: By applying the same interest rate to deposits to and borrowings from the pool (i.e., the RCF interest rate),[82] the entities making advances to the pool might be economically thought of as acting as lenders of funds to the affiliated CPPs borrowing from the pool. The CPM would accordingly (only) act as intermediary of the funds. Consequently, the depositors (not the CPM) would earn the (residual) interest income (from the borrowers). The current low-interest rate environment and associated low to negative interest rates especially for short-term investments may imply that independent parties would not make short-term investments and would rather use their excess funds to lend to other market participants. This would further support treating both cash advances to and from the pool as a short-term lending subject to the same short-term lending/borrowing interest rate.

79. Assuming that all key affiliated group entities participate in the cash pooling arrangement.
80. OECD, *supra* n. 11, paras 1.166-1.167.
81. Standard & Poor Global Ratings, *General Criteria: Group Rating Methodology* (1 July 2019).
82. The Public Discussion Draft on Financial Transactions, which was published by OECD on 3 July 2018 and preceded the OECD Transfer Pricing Guidance on Financial Transactions, described three approaches that could be applied for allocating benefits among the participating cash pool members. In a situation where all cash pool members share the same or similar credit profile, the OECD discussion draft noted that applying the same interest rate for both deposits and borrowings may be an option. OECD, *supra* n. 66, para. 128. This is also an approach that can be found in German literature. D. Schilling & S. Greil, *Cash Pool Vereinbarungen. Darstellung einer fremdvergleichskonformen Behandlung anhand eines Fallbeispiels*, IStR, at 201-206 (2020).

### b Alt. B: Reflecting the External Short-Term Deposit and Borrowing Conditions by Relying on the Internal CUP Method

Another option to set the deposit and borrowing rate could be to (initially) mirror the external deposit and borrowing conditions connected with the cash pool as demonstrated in the following diagram:

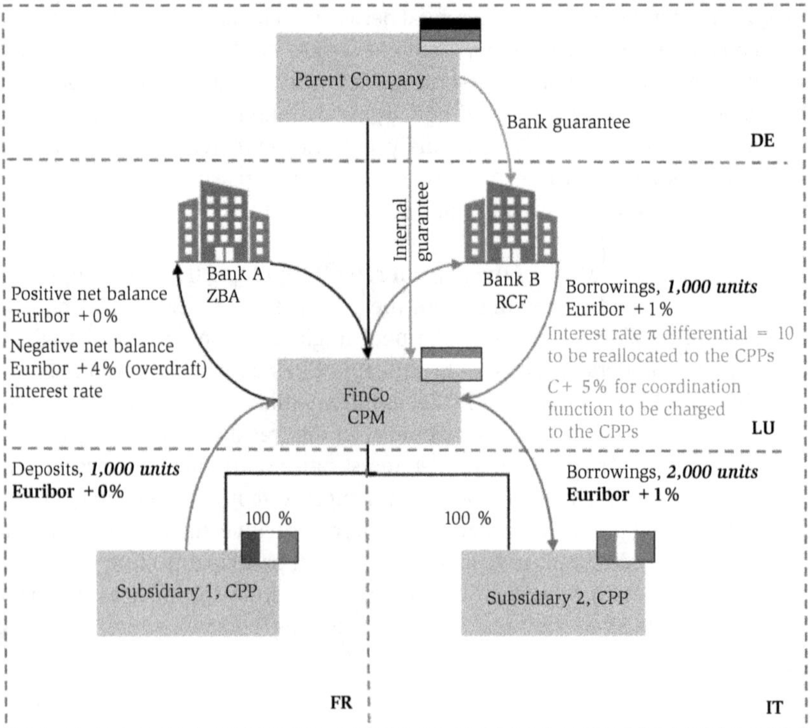


If there are only deposits, the CPM would not receive any interest income from borrowing entities, but also would not have to pay any interest rate to the cash pool depositors, considering that the interest rate is (initially) set at 0% in line with the external interest rate conditions for short-term deposits offered to the CPM. If there are only borrowings from the pool and no deposits to the pool, the CPM would have to finance the whole borrowing amount by drawing on the RCF. Given that the interest rate margin for borrowing positions from the pool is equal to the external refinancing interest rate conditions, the CPM would not bear any interest costs. Whenever there is a mixture of deposit and borrowing positions within the cash pool and these positions are netted, an interest rate profit differential would arise at the level of the CPM. In the following, a calculation example is provided:

| | *Units* | *Interest Rate (%)* | *Interest Income/Cost at CPM Level* |
|---|---|---|---|
| Deposits | 1.000 | 0 | 0 |
| Borrowings | 2.000 | 1 | 20 |
| Required external financing | 1.000 | 1 | -10 |
| Interest income | | | 10 |

Considering the characterization of the CPM as a (limited risk) service provider entitled to not more than a limited (cost plus) return, it seems reasonable to conclude that the residual profit should be allocated to the CPPs. Thus, the question arises of how this residual income (of EUR 10) should be allocated to the CPPs. There could be various options, such as for instance the allocation of the benefit to the depositors or the enhancement of the interest rates for all participants:[83]

- **Allocating the (residual) cash pool benefits to the depositors:** If the complete residual income was allocated to the depositors, the effective interest rate received by the CPPs making deposits would be 1%. The borrowing rate would remain at 1%.[84] Therefore, this allocation mechanism would result in an approach where the same interest rate was applied to all CPPs, thereby leading to an outcome similar to alternative A above.
- **Enhancing the interest rates for all participants:** If the residual income was allocated to both depositors and borrowers to/from the pool, the depositors would experience an interest increase above the initial Euribor + 0% interest rate and borrowers would experience an interest rate decrease down from Euribor + 1%. The effect of such an increase//decrease is dependent on the allocation mechanism chosen. Such approach, while leading to an approximation between deposit and lending positions, would in many instances lead to different interest rates for deposits and borrowings, thereby financially differentiating between returns on short-term investments (lower) and returns on short-term borrowings (higher). The following provides a possible example for allocating the benefit both to depositors and borrowers based on their proportionate deposit and borrowing positions:

83. The OECD Public Discussion Draft on Financial Transactions described three (non-mutually exclusive) approaches that could be applied for allocating benefits among the participating cash pool members: (i) enhancing the interest rate for all participants, (ii) applying the same interest rate for all participants, (iii) allocating the cash pooling benefit to the depositors. OECD, *supra* n. 66, paras 124-129.
84. Technically, the deposit and borrowing interest rate would be Euribor + 1%. Given that the base rate is floored at 0, the effective interest rate is equal to the interest rate margin of 1%.

| | Units | *(Initial) Interest Rate* | *Interest Income (+)/Cost (-) at CPM Level* | *Proportionate Cash Pool Participation of CPPs (%)* | *Resulting Proportionate Interest Income Allocation from CPM to CPPs* | *Net Interest Income (+)/Expense (-) Considering Initial Interest Rate and Cash Balance of CPPs* | *Resulting Effective Interest Rate of CPPs* |
|---|---|---|---|---|---|---|---|
| **Depositors** | 1,000 | 0.00% | 0 | 0.33 | 3.33 | 3.33 | 0.33 |
| **Borrowers** | 2,000 | 1.00% | 20 | 0.67 | 6.67 | −13.33 | 0.67 |
| **Required external financing** | 1.000 | 1,00% | -10 | | | | |
| **Net interest income (to be reallocated)** | | | 10 | | 10 | 10 | |

A proportionate reallocation of the net interest rate income from the CPM to the CPPs would lead to an allocation of one-third to the depositor and two-thirds to the borrower. Interest income of the depositor would increase from 0 to 3.33, while interest expense of the borrower would decrease from previously 20 to 13.33. Considering this interest income and expense post-reallocation, the effective interest rate of both the depositor and borrower would be further enhanced. Specifically, the reallocation of the net income at the CPM level would result in an effective interest rate of 0.33% (up from 0%) for the depositor and 0.66% (down from 1%) for the borrower. Therewith, both the depositor and lender should be better off compared to the options realistically available at group level, considering the parameters of this case study.

In summary, the OECD guidance on financial transactions does not specify any detailed way how the benefits could be allocated to the CPPs and which CPPs (depositors, borrowers or both) should primarily receive the benefits. Alternatives A and B serve to show that the decision on how the benefits shall be shared among the CPPs could nevertheless have a considerable impact on the returns realized by the CPPs, with the CPM continuously earning a routine cost plus return. Therefore, special care should be given to the selection and appropriateness of the chosen allocation mechanism considering the underlying facts and circumstances of the case. Valid arguments should be made to allocate the residual cash pool advantages either to the cash pool depositors only (by applying the external RCF interest rate on the cash pool deposits as well) or to both, to the depositors and borrowers (by enhancing the interest rates of both depositors and borrowers compared to the options realistically available). Thus, within this framework, there could (potentially) be a range of arm's length results providing a certain (limited) flexibility in the setting (appropriate) interest rates for the cash pool.

However, there could also be some additional challenges (in practice) which must be taken into account, such as for example:

- In the example relied upon above, the RCF had a one-year term and, therefore, qualified as a short-term facility agreement in line with the operating needs of the cash pool. Often, RCFs are medium-term financing vehicles, granted over a three to five-year time horizon. Therefore, the RCF usually does not reflect pure short-term (one year or less) interest rate conditions. Consequently, depending on the facts and circumstances, term adjustments may be necessary if the RCF interest rate is relied upon as an internal CUP. Additionally, bank B, providing the RCF, would likely charge a commitment fee on any non-drawn portion of the RCF, meaning that the CPM would be charged with lending associated costs even if it did not draw on the RCF.
- Considering the relatively high overdraft interest rate associated with any negative balance, the treasury department will generally ensure that the CPM maintains a certain cash buffer available at the level of the concentration account, which – while much lower than any overdraft interest rate charges – might come at a (small) cost due to negative Euro deposit rates that banks might in the current times decide to pass on to the CPM.
- Depending on whether or not the guarantees granted provide a credit-enhancing effect, the question arises if the parent company should charge a guarantee fee for providing the guarantee. In situations where the parent guarantee merely represents a pro forma guarantee, no guarantee fee would generally be due.[85] In situations where the guarantee provides a credit-enhancing effect, a guarantee fee should generally be applied.[86] The individual facts and circumstances as well as the strategic importance of FinCo as CPM would also be a decisive factor.

Consequently, depending on the facts of the case, there might be further bank and other finance-related costs, which – in addition to any benefits – might need to be allocated among the participants of the cash pool arrangements under a cost plus CPM service arrangement, assuming that ultimately linked to the cash pooling arrangement and hence to benefit of the CPPs and not of the group//shareholder.

## 3 Case Study 2: CPM as 'In-House Bank'

### *A Additional Facts*

Contrary to the case discussed above, let us assume that the parent company decided to set up the CPM as an in-house bank. The necessary prerequisites have been taken to

85. OECD, *supra* n. 11, para. 10.160.
86. *Ibid.*, para. 10.159.

ensure that FinCo employs the appropriate personnel, carries out the risk control functions and is in a position to bear the corresponding risks.

More specifically, with regard to the cash pool arrangement, FinCo is responsible for deciding how to invest surplus funds or fund any shortfall. FinCo sets the intra-group interest rates and is at risk for any differences between the rates it sets with other group participants and the rates at which it transacts with independent lenders.

In addition to serving as CPM for the cash pool, FinCo also raises bonds on the financial market, makes strategic financial decisions and manages the group's overall liquidity. FinCo also bears credit risk, liquidity risk and currency risk for intra-group finance and decides on how or whether to hedge such risks.[87] In addition to acting as CPM, FinCo also grants medium and long-term loans to the operating entities of the MNE group.

FinCo is a direct subsidiary of the parent company, located in the same country as the parent company and shareholder of all key affiliated entities of the MNE Group.

Additionally, the following specifics apply to the RCF with bank B and the ZBA with bank A: the RCF has a three-year medium term. The interest rate granted by bank B to FinCo is Euribor + 2%, whereby Euribor is floored at 0%. The parent guarantee required by the bank does not result in any interest benefit to FinCo and essentially represents a pro forma guarantee. While the RCF in theory serves as a backup financing instrument for the cash pool, it is assumed that the cash pool is usually generating a cash surplus, so that FinCo usually does not have to draw from the RCF to fund the cash pool. The main purpose of the RCF is to fund medium or long-term loans to affiliated group entities. Given the current negative nature of inter-bank rates denominated in Euros, the negative base rate is passed on by bank A to the CPM, such that a small fee is charged to the CPM on any net surplus in the concentration account, equal to the prevailing negative EUR deposit rate (assumed to be about 30 bps).

The CPPs have different functional currencies, such as Euro, British Pounds and US Dollars. Consequently, the CPM bears exchange rate risk.

The following diagram provides an overview of the key set-up relevant to the cash pool and the key questions to be analysed:

87. *Ibid.*, 10.138-10.139.

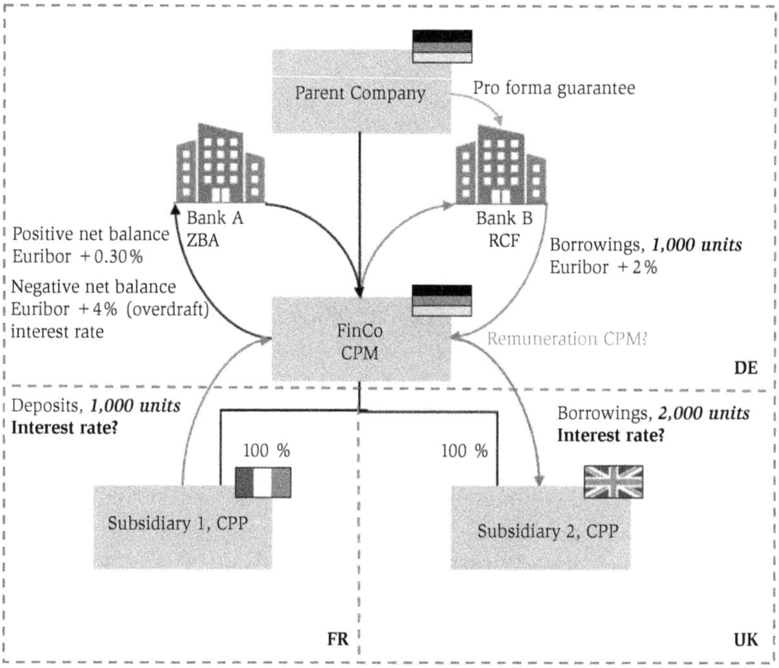


### B *Determining an Arm's Length Remuneration for the CPM*

According to the OECD, the appropriate reward of the CPM will depend on the functions performed, assets used and the risks assumed. Even if a CPM typically performs no more than coordination or agency function, a thorough functional analysis may nevertheless establish that it has a higher functionality. Considering that the CPM has concluded the key agreements in place with bank, performs the key treasury functions and bears the associated risks, FinCo can be characterized as a CPM with a high level of functionality, i.e., in-house bank. Accordingly, FinCo should be entitled to earn part or all of the interest rate spread between the borrowing and lending positions which it adopts. This includes earning the difference in interest rate spreads between the deposit and borrowing rates of the cash pool.[88] This spread should allow FinCo to cover the financing cost incurred in connection with the cash pool to realize a profit.[89] In cases where the interest rate spread earned by FinCo with the cash pool is not sufficient to cover its external financing cost, FinCo would have to bear the associated loss and would not be entitled to receive a compensation payment.[90] While the cash

88. *Ibid.*, paras 10.140-10.141.
89. It could be advisable that the resulting spread should be verified by a combination of a routine and risk adjusted return analysis so that the effective margin realized by the CPM can be supported by means of a separate corroborative analysis.
90. OECD, *supra* n. 11, paras 1.56 & 1.63.

pool benefits and drawbacks remain largely with the CPM under such a setup, the cash pool should not be disadvantageous for the CPPs.[91]

### C Determining Arm's Length Interest Rates for Deposits to and Borrowings from the Pool by Relying on the External CUP Method

On the premise that FinCo acts as in-house bank, one way to determine an arm's length short-term interest rate for deposits and borrowings could be by relying on the price observable for short-term finance transactions that can be identified between independent parties on the financial market, possibly plus/minus a certain bps spread.

#### *a Determining an (Arm's Length) Range of Borrowing Rates*

**Step 1: Determining a credit rating**

The first step is usually to estimate the credit default risk associated with a borrower since the credit default risk represents an important comparability factor within the search for potentially comparable transactions.

A commonly used approach in defining credit default risk is the use of credit ratings. A credit rating is the result of an assessment of the creditworthiness of a borrower in general terms or with respect to a particular debt or financial obligation. A credit rating can be assigned to entities that seek to borrow money, an individual, corporation, state or provincial authority, or sovereign government. Credit assessment and evaluation for companies and governments are generally done by credit rating agencies such as Standard & Poor's, Moody's or Fitch.

The credit rating has an inverse relationship with the credit default risk/probability of default. According to the rating agencies, a high credit rating indicates that the borrower has a low credit default risk/probability of default; conversely, a low credit rating suggests a high credit default risk/probability of default.

If and to what extent the group credit rating should be applied for deriving a range of arm's length bond yields for cash pooling transactions could be subject to a paper on its own. On the one hand, considering that in this case study 2 the cash pool is not jointly and severally guaranteed by CPPs, the standalone credit rating of the CPPs after considering the effect of implicit support should in theory be applied, which might lead to different credit ratings for individual CPPs.[92] According to the rating nomenclature published by for instance Standard & Poor's, the group credit rating may be applied if the CPPs are core and/or strategic entities to the MNE.[93]

Let us assume that a rating agency recently assigned a credit rating of BB to the parent company. In the underlying case, considering that FinCo is a direct subsidiary of the parent company and acts as the main shareholding entity of the affiliated operating companies, it seems reasonable to conclude that there should not be much difference

91. *Ibid.*, para. 10.146.
92. Schilling & Greil, *supra* n. 82, pp. 201-206.
93. Standard & Poor Global Ratings, *supra* n. 81.

between the credit rating assigned to the MNE group by the credit rating agency and a credit rating derived at the level of FinCo. Furthermore, all affiliated entities participating in the cash pooling arrangement are considered to be core or strategically important. Further, it might reasonable to conclude that all CPPs could be deemed to have a similar credit rating if transacting on a short-term basis. Therefore, a credit rating in the BB range is relied upon for purposes of deriving arm's length borrowing rates.[94]

**Step 2: Deriving an arm's length range of short-term bond spreads**

Once the credit rating has been determined, an arm's length range of comparable interest margins or proxies thereof can be derived. As there are practically no cash pool transactions between independent parties, no public data on a transactional basis is generally available. Therefore, an alternative approach could be to rely on yields//spreads of tradable bonds, e.g., corporate bonds with similar characteristics since such information is usually publicly available. Tradeable bonds are debt securities issued by a corporation or government with a stated interest rate and fixed due dates by when interest and principal of debt amount must be paid. Bondholders have a right to repayment of the principal of debt amount and payment of interest.

Short-term bond yields can be identified by searching for comparable bonds in a financial database such as for instance the Bloomberg database, the S&P credit analytics module or Refinitiv Eikon. Key comparability factors usually include among others the credit rating, term to maturity, the currency, asset classes (usually corporates), coupon type (fixed versus floating), collateral/rank and country/region. Further screenings may be applied based on availability.

The application of these screening steps results in a set of identified bonds. In order to acknowledge possible differences between controlled transactions and the identified financial transactions, an interquartile range of results, which is supposed to reduce the likelihood of over- or underestimation of the arm's length range, is usually calculated over the yields of the identified bonds once they have been subject to a manual screening process.

Let us assume that the bond yield analysis sufficiently reliably met the comparability factors above and the EUR-denominated bond spreads identified are the following:[95]

94. Alternatively, a credit rating could also be derived with the help of a credit rating tool. Based on certain general input parameters as well as certain financial income statements and balance statement information, the credit rating tools calculate the resulting credit rating.
95. In case of multicurrency cash-pools such as in case study 2, a bond search would generally have to be performed for each major currency in order to determine currency specific spreads and interest rates for borrowings from the cash pool.

| *Range of Results for EUR-Denominated Bond Spreads* | |
|---|---|
| *Calculation method* | *Quartile method* |
| Minimum | 0.43 |
| **Lower Quartile** | **1.20** |
| Median | 1.63 |
| **Upper Quartile** | **2.10** |
| Maximum | 2.47 |
| Number of observations | 12 |

In general, every value within the interquartile range of results should be in line with the arm's length principles. Therefore, a return for borrowing rates should be selected within the interquartile range of results. Assuming that a variable interest rate is applied for the I/C cash pooling set-up, the benchmarked return should then be added to the relevant currency-specific short-term base rate, such as Euribor in the underlying case, in order to derive a currency-specific variable interest rate to be applied for cash pool borrowings.

In line with the arguments made in section V.2, the group credit rating reflects the ceiling credit rating that can be achieved by affiliated entities of the MNE group in line with the rating nomenclature as published by rating agencies. Therefore, from the perspective of the CPPs, the interest rate paid for short-term cash pool borrowings derived based on comparable short-term bond yields having the same credit rating as the group credit rating should not make the CPPs worse off than alternative borrowing options.

### b *Determining an (Arm's Length) Range of Deposit Rates*

Historically, under the banking approach, one way to determine deposit rates was to rely on currency-specific deposit rates as a proxy for short-term investment returns. Deposit rates can be benchmarked by reference to central bank statistics or by reference to currency-specific deposit rates as provided for instance by the S&P database.

Triggered by the low-interest rate environment, these deposit rates, depending on the currency involved, have been exhibiting low to negative returns. While representing third-party market returns, the question arises if in low-interest times, an independent party would be willing to pay an interest rate for all of its excess liquidity or if it would rather decide to maintain only a minimum savings cushion in order to keep the associated interest expense at a minimum and look at alternative investment options in order to maximize its interest rate return.

One option to derive an arm's length interest margin for deposits could be to benchmark returns offered by money market funds. Money market funds are low-risk mutual funds. Financial service firms essentially pool money from many different individuals and invest the money in low-risk, short-term securities. Money market funds may be characterized as serving a similar purpose to saving accounts in the sense that money is readily accessible, but providing a higher return compared to regular saving accounts, yet lower compared to investing in the stock market.[96] Consequently, from a CPP perspective participating in a cash pool under an in-house banking approach, achieving a return derived based on money market fund investments could represent one of the best short-term investment options realistically available to the CPPs similar to a low-risk deposit nature, with returns in the one to two digit basis point spread range. That said, also money market funds have exhibited quite low returns towards the end of 2021 so that there might not be that big of a difference between deposit rates and yields on money market funds.

Assuming that a variable interest rate is applied for the I/C cash pooling set-up, the benchmarked return should then be added to the relevant currency-specific short-term base rate, such as Euribor, Euro Short Term Rate (ESTR) or the relevant currency equivalent in order to derive a currency-specific variable interest rate to be applied for cash pool deposits. In times of negative returns or negative deposit interest rates, another option could be to floor the deposit rate at zero depending on the facts of the case.

From the perspective of the CPPs, setting interest rates in line with short-term returns observable in the financial market between independent parties should in theory result in arm's length interest rates. Any advantages or disadvantages in relation to the cash pool would be maintained by the CPM under such an approach. The OECD recognizes that a CPM with a more comprehensive functional, asset and risk profile might earn all or part of the spread between the borrowing and lending positions it adopts depending on the functions it performs and the risks it assumes.[97] Therefore, depending on the facts of the case, it could be appropriate to allocate further benefits to the CPPs. This would result in (i) the CPM earning not all but part of the residual interest rate spread and (ii) the CPPs being slightly better off compared to the options realistically available at the group level. Such a profit sharing between the CPM and the CPPs could be achieved by the application of the profit split method to the residual interest income (or loss) at the CPM level. The more of this residual income (or loss) is shared with the CPPs, the more the overall remuneration would move away from a CPM as a fully fledged entity to a routine entity (with a cost plus entity allocating most to all benefits to the CPPs as shown in case study 1).

## VI COVID-19 AND CASH-POOLING ARRANGEMENTS

### 1 Effect of COVID-19 on the Interest Rate Environment

During the first surge of the COVID-19 pandemic in March 2020, the financial market exhibited an increase in interest rates in most rating categories and across all

96. Andrew Beattie, *Money Market Fund vs. Savings Account: What's the Difference?*, Investopedia (3 November 2021), https://www.investopedia.com/articles/mutualfund/07/money_market_savings.asp.
97. OECD, *supra* n. 11, para. 10.140.

industries, with certain industries being hit harder than others and lower rating categories experiencing higher interest rate increases:

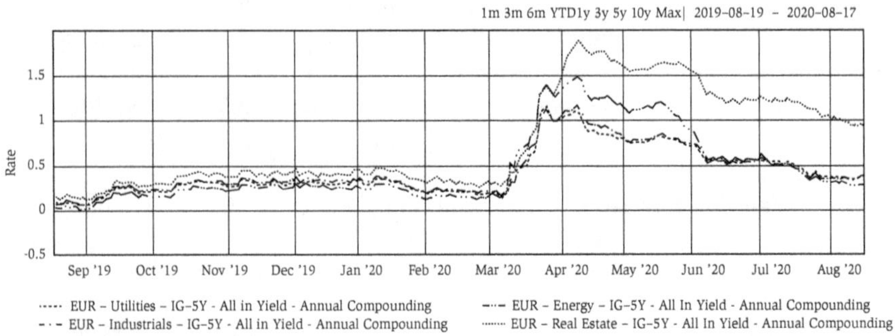


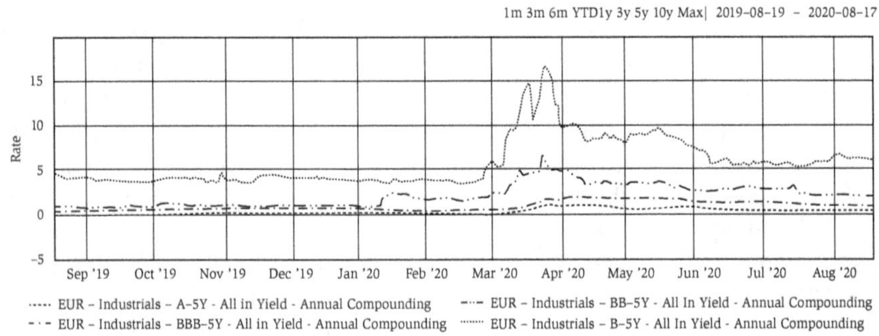


*Source*: Standard & Poor's Capital IQ Database (18 August 2020).

When the COVID-19 pandemic hit globally at the beginning of 2020, various MNEs were faced with supply and/or demand shocks and had to stop production for an interim period of time. To ensure sufficient liquidity and to provide a safety cushion during uncertain times, various MNEs drew down on existing credit facilities or had to apply for additional funding at higher interest costs. Additionally, many MNEs applied for state aid loans, also caused by supply restrictions imposed by the banking industry. Depending on the cash centralization system in place within the group, some MNEs put (a portion of) the external funding into the cash pool for use of the CPPs. This led to increased interest expenses and bank fees in connection with the operations of the cash pool, especially in situations where not all external bank funds drawn were immediately used by the CPPs. While the COVID 19 pandemic initially led to a surge of interest rates at the beginning of 2020, interest rates started decreasing again in the second half of 2020. Within this context, the question arises: which entity//entities should bear the extraordinary costs that may be arising in connection with the operation of I/C cash pools?

## 2 OECD Guidance on the Transfer Pricing Implications of the COVID-19 Pandemic

On 18 December 2020, the OECD released Guidance on the transfer pricing implications of the COVID-19 pandemic ('OECD COVID-19 Guidance'). The publication provides guidance on the practical application of the arm's length principle on four topics: (i) comparability analysis, (ii) losses and the allocation of COVID-19-specific costs, (iii) government assistance programs, and (iv) advance pricing agreements. On the one side, the OECD COVID-19 Guidance notes that the COVID-19 pandemic has created conditions in which associated parties may consider whether they have the option to apply force majeure clauses, revoke or otherwise revise their intercompany agreements, which may impact the allocation of losses and COVID-19 specific costs between associated parties.[98] On the other side, the OECD COVID-19 Guidance also considers that limited risk entities that do not assume any credit risk should not bear losses derived from playing out the credit risk.[99] Furthermore, the OECD COVID-19 Guidance also provide that the availability, duration and utilization of government assistance programs may have an impact on controlled transactions and transfer prices, regardless of whether such government assistance is provided to a member of a multinational group directly or to third parties in the market, where the multinational group is active. Since government assistance may influence the (economic) behaviour of parties that are engaged in potentially comparable transactions, the effect of such government assistance is to be considered for purposes of determining arm's length outcomes.[100]

Only a few countries have released separate national guidance on transfer pricing considerations in connection with COVID-19.[101] Consequently, careful consideration should be given to the underlying facts of the case, the functional and risk allocation and the contractual arrangements in place as the special circumstances tied to the COVID-19 pandemic might lead to increased scrutiny and dispute in tax audits. The following section aims at making suggestions for possible practical considerations on the basis of a case study, by relying on the facts and circumstances of case studies 1 and 2 in sections V.2 and V.3.

## 3 Case Study 3: Practical Implications of COVID-19 on Cash-Pooling Arrangements on the Basis of a Case Study

Let us assume that an MNE group was hit by the COVID-19 pandemic. Plants had to shut down for several weeks at the beginning of the year 2020 and sales plummeted. The available external funding is fully used and the MNE requires additional external

98. OECD, *Guidance on the transfer pricing implications of the COVID-19 pandemic*, para. 42 (OECD Publishing December 2020).
99. *Ibid.*, para. 40.
100. BDI, *Rundschreiben Nr. 2020-003*, at 4.
101. K. Dorner & D. Treidler, *Die COVID-19-Pandemie und Verrechnungspreise, Die OECD-Position und ausgewählte Beispiele aus Deutschland, den Niederlanden und Polen*, 18 IWB at 738-745 (2021).

funds. Considering the overall market situation and the industry in which the MNE is active, the credit rating of the group is put on a negative outlook from the end of the first quarter of 2020 onwards by the major global rating agencies. As a consequence of the COVID-19 pandemic, the industry in which the MNE is active and the weakened credit profile of the MNE Group, banks are no longer willing to lend funds at the previously prevailing interest rate of Euribor + 1% for short-term financing but instead demand an (annual) interest rate of Euribor + 3% for a one-year bank loan. To ensure liquidity for the group, it is decided to enter into this one-year bank loan for an amount of MEUR 30 at an interest rate of Euribor + 3%. The loan is entered into by the CPM and guaranteed by the parent company. In light of the uncertainty, the decision is made at the first height of the COVID-19 pandemic at the beginning of April 2020 to draw the full amount of MEUR 30 and to make these funds available for the I/C cash pool considering that all key affiliated entities participate in the group cash pooling arrangement.

Additionally, access to state aid loans is explored at different entity levels. State aid loans are concluded with two affiliated entities mid of 2020, which are also CPPs.

While MEUR 20 of the MEUR 30 of the external bank funds made available to the cash pool are relatively quickly used by the pool, MEUR 10 are not, leading to interest expense at the level of the CPM in the amount of MEUR 10 times Euribor + 3% times number of days drawn and not used by the pool over 360 days. If the amount of MEUR 10 had not been drawn, the CPM would have been charged with commitment fees by the bank instead. Commitment fees are often a fraction of the applicable interest rate and are charged on the undisbursed loan amount. Assuming that the commitment fee amounts to 30 bps, the additional interest expense accumulated at the CPM for maintaining a COVID-19 safety cushion of MEUR 10 amounts to Euribor + 2.7% on a 360-day basis.

In line with theoretical background and the practical considerations developed in the last chapters, the following questions arise:

- how the CPM should be remunerated considering the functions performed, risks borne and assets held;
- if and how any changes to the interest rate charged for deposits and borrowings to/from the pool should be made; and
- if and how the cash pool advantages and associated COVID-19-related costs should be allocated among parties participating in the cash pool arrangement.

## A Remuneration of the Cash Pool Master

### CPM as a service provider

The OECD COVID-19 Guidance states that for purposes of determining whether or not a limited risk entity may incur losses, the risks assumed by an entity will be particularly important. This reflects the fact that at arm's length, the allocation of risks between the parties to an arrangement affects how profits or losses resulting from the transaction are allocated.[102]

Let us take as a base case the CPM service provider of case study 1. In case study 1, the CPM only performs a coordination function and does not bear any significant risks. Credit risk is assumed by the parent company in the external and internal relations, as well as by the CPPs which are jointly and severally liable towards the bank managing the ZBA cash pooling arrangement. The new external bank facility in the amount of MEUR 30 is again guaranteed by the parent company and the CPM still benefits from the internal guarantee from the parent company as well as from the joint and several liability of the CPPs. Consequently, the characterization of the CPM has not changed in light of the COVID-19 pandemic. Therefore, it seems reasonable to conclude that the CPM should continue to be remunerated on a cost plus basis. Where empirical evidence suggests that also independent service providers would accept a reduction in markup or even incur losses, a short-time adjustment of the cost plus remuneration of the CPM might be possible. In practice, the overall effect of such short-term remuneration adjustment is often limited in terms of overall value, with larger effects usually tied to extraordinary costs and losses.

**CPM as an in-house bank**

In line with the suggested proceedings in case study 2; where the CPM acts as a fully fledged in-house bank, it might be reasonable to concentrate the arm's length analysis on the arm's length nature of interest rates, where the interest rates should allow the CPPs to not make them worse off than comparable options available. In consideration of the fully fledged profile, the CPM should theoretically be entitled to earn the residual income or loss. In the underlying case, this should be followed by an analysis if the benefits and extraordinary interest expenses due to COVID-19 are to be fully assumed by the CPM or are to be (partially) shared with the CPPs in a second step.

### *B Interest Rates to Be Applied to the Cash Pool*

**CPM as a service provider**

The OECD COVID-19 Guidance remarks that 'it will not be appropriate for a "limited risk" distributor that does not assume any marketplace risk or another specific risk to bear a portion of the loss associated with the playing out of that risk. For instance, a limited risk distributor that does not assume any credit risk should not bear losses derived from the playing out of the credit risk'.[103]

Based on the facts and circumstances of case study 1, the CPM acts as a service provider performing coordination activities and does not bear any significant risks. Therefore, the CPM would generally be expected to not bear any interest rate risk in connection with the cash pool. Due to the risk-free profile, the borrowing rate in case study 1 was pegged to the short-term external funding rate of 1% tied to the cash pool.

102. OECD, *supra* n. 98, para. 40.
103. OECD, *supra* n. 98, para. 40.

The new short-term bank facility is again guaranteed by the parent company. Consequently, the new external funding rate of Euribor + 3% reflects the group interest rate conditions that can be achieved in the financial market in light of the COVID-19 pandemic. Based on the rating nomenclature published by for instance Standard & Poor's, the group credit rating sets the ceiling credit rating.[104] Therefore, the CPPs receive a benefit in terms of the differential between their standalone credit rating after considering implicit support and the group credit rating, representing the maximum achievable interest rate benefit. Especially during the first height of the COVID-19 pandemic, external funding at the consolidated group level might have been preferential considering that individual operating entities experienced significant cuts in production and/or sales.

Elaborating on case study 1, by applying the new short-term interest rate conditions of Euribor + 3% as borrowing rate (and possibly also as deposit rate), the synergies that can be realized by the joint cash pooling efforts at the group financing conditions are thereby directly passed on to the CPPs, while at the same time relieving the CPM service provider from interest rate risk. As such, it seems reasonable to conclude that the updated interest rate conditions should be passed on to the CPPs.

**CPM as an in-house bank**

As demonstrated in section VI.1, the COVID-19 pandemic led to a surge in interest rates in most rating categories and across all industries on the financial market at the beginning of the year 2020. While there may have been less of a change to the return for deposits, the price for short-term borrowings between independent parties on the financial market increased significantly. On this premise, it seems reasonable to verify and amend the interest rate margin applicable to deposits and borrowings that can be observed on the financial market in April 2020 in line with the methodology described in section V.3, since also the CPPs would face higher interest rate conditions if they were to borrow locally.

**Contractual arrangements**

No matter if the CPM acts as a service provider or as an in-house bank, cash pool agreements frequently contain a clause stating that the interest rate margin applicable to deposits and borrowings shall be revisited and adjusted in certain time intervals or in light of extraordinary events having an impact on the interest rate margins. But even in instances where no such clause is contained in the I/C cash pool agreement, the OECD provides that the COVID-19 pandemic has created conditions in which associated parties may consider whether they have the option to apply force majeure clauses, revoke or otherwise revise their intercompany agreements. This may impact the allocation of losses and COVID-19 specific costs between associated parties, and therefore also requires specific consideration in the current economic environment.[105] Whether or not the revision of the intercompany agreements is consistent with the behaviour of unrelated parties operating under comparable circumstances has to be

104. Standard & Poor's, *supra* n. 81.
105. OECD, *supra* n. 98, para. 37.

based on the accurate delineation of the controlled transaction.[106] Therefore, where the facts and circumstances support an increase in interest rates due to (i) new banking conditions provided to the MNE, (ii) changes in the group credit rating, and/or (iii) changes in the financial market due to for instance COVID-19 related effects, it seems reasonable to conclude that also independent parties would have amended the interest rate conditions applicable to the I/C cash pool.

That said, independent parties would in such case likely also agree in writing that the interest rate conditions should equally be reduced again once the external bank conditions tied to cash pool and/or the financial market conditions have recovered again. Therefore, careful monitoring of the financial market developments and associated adjustments to the I/C conditions is necessary in such case.

## C Allocation of COVID-19 Related Advantages and Disadvantages

The OECD COVID-19 Guidance points out that '[...] the party initially incurring an exceptional cost may not be the party assuming risks associated to that cost at arm's length, and consequently such costs may need to be passed on to parties that do assume such risks'.[107]

**CPM as service provider**

The CPM only performs a coordination function; the CPM does not use any of the funds. The funds are only used by the CPPs. Given its risk-free profile and following the benefits test, the CPM was not entitled to receive any of the cash pool advantages in case study 1. Therefore, it should in theory also not be burdened with COVID-19-related external interest rate expenses accumulated at the level of the CPM due to the fact that not all funds initially drawn were not immediately used. As such, it seems reasonable to conclude that the interest rate expenses arising at the CPM due to the COVID-19 safety cushion should not be borne by the CPM.

**Analysis from a CPP perspective**

As outlined above, two CPPs obtained state aid loans in July 2019. Let us assume that for the French CPP, the state aid loan was tied to the condition that the French CPP leaves the cash pooling arrangement such that the state aid loans cannot be passed on to finance any affiliated entities. In such case, the French CPP could only be allocated the proportionate excess interest rate expense for the three-month period from April through June 2019. For the other CPP receiving a state aid loan, an allocation of the excess interest rate expense could be appropriate to the extent that the state aid loan does not cover the full financing needs of the CPP.

A recharge of the excess interest rate expense to the CPPs might be appropriate as long as it appears reasonable to conclude based on the fact of the case that also independent parties – including the CPPs on a stand-alone basis – would have

106. *Ibid.*, para. 42.
107. *Ibid.*, para. 48.

maintained a safety cushion during uncertain COVID-19 times and would have been willing to pay the associated costs. CPMs usually always maintain a certain cash buffer. Triggered by increased default probabilities and presumably the need to diversify their customer and risk profile, certain banks imposed supply restrictions during the heights of the COVID-19 pandemic, freezing available (remaining) bank loan funds. From this perspective, it appears appropriate to maintain a larger cash buffer during uncertain pandemic times. If recharged to the CPPs, the resulting cost recharge should be reasonable from the perspective of the CPPs and should not lead to a burden significantly larger than the CPPs would have been willing to bear on a standalone basis. In practice, factors such as if the cash pool is jointly and severally guaranteed by the CPPs and if the CPPs are fully fledged or limited risk entities may also play a role in determining the appropriate level of proportionality. In instances where the same interest rate is applied to deposits to and draws from the pool and/or all CPPs are similarly affected by COVID-19, a proportionate recharge to both depositors and borrowers to the pool could be appropriate. In other circumstances, an allocation based on the CPPs' proportionate borrowings might be more appropriate. Also, other allocation keys might be appropriate.

#### CPM as an in-house bank and analysis from a shareholder perspective

Where the CPM acts as an in-house bank and has decided to fully draw all external available funds in its capacity as a risk-taking FinCo, it could also be appropriate that the portion of the non-required external funding made available to the pool may qualify as shareholding type expenses[108] that should not be recharged to the CPPs but instead maintained by FinCo or, to the extent that decisions to draw the funds were made by the ultimate parent company in its capacity of shareholder and in its own interest, by the ultimate parent company.

## VII CONCLUSIONS

Intercompany financing transactions, including cash pool transactions, have increasingly been subject to review in tax audits. The recent publications at the level of the OECD and at different national levels combined with additional liquidity needs in the beginning and throughout the COVID-19 pandemic have increased the spotlight on this transfer pricing area.

The ALP generally is an objective standard. This means that it is not affected by the taxpayer's motive (e.g., shifting of profits to 'tax heavens') for a controlled transaction. By concentrating the BEPS project on the economic substance and the development and provision of concrete concepts and tests (such as the six-step process for the allocation of risks) to determine the substance, the OECD has confirmed and enhanced the (existing) economic approach of transfer pricing. In our view, the

108. Shareholding services are described by the OECD TP Guidelines as services that do not provide a benefit for the receiving entities and independent enterprises would not be willing to pay for these services. Shareholder services are solely performed due to the ownership interest in one or more other group members. *See* OECD, *supra* n. 11, para. 7.9.

measures in their totality (including the enhanced transparency obligations) build an effective framework (by maintaining the ALP) against BEPS (based on a contractual allocation of function, assets and risks without proper economic substance). Additionally, the OECD has arguably decided not to include a subjective test (i.e., motive test) in the ALP system even if some authors would consider the inclusion of some form of subjective test as a more effective measure to tackle tax planning. Thus, the OECD maintained the ALP as an objective standard even if this approach may not always prevent the realization of tax advantages by MNE groups.

Similar to other controlled transactions, the transfer pricing of financial transactions must concentrate on the economic substance of the (single) transaction (i.e., actual conduct of the parties) by taking into account the specific facts and circumstances of each individual case. The OECD provides a certain (theoretical) framework for the transfer pricing of cash pooling transactions. However, important aspects remain unclear.

In light of the limited guidance available on the practical implications for cash pooling transactions, this paper provides remuneration examples for cash pooling transactions under consideration of the following aspects:

- the CPM needs to be accurately remunerated considering the functions performed, risks borne and assets held;
- the interest rate charged for deposits and borrowings to/from the pool has to be arm's length; and
- the cash pool advantages have to be allocated appropriately among parties participating in the cash pool considering the facts and circumstances.

Considering the limited guidance on the practical implications, the arm's length behaviour has to be determined by approximating how third parties would behave by relying on general transfer pricing principles and data availability:

- In line with the OECD's guidance to benchmarking the least complex party since returns are identifiable, the authors suggest a two-step process for the accurate delineation of the CPM where the CPM acts as a service provider: (i) deriving a routine return for the CPM and (ii) re-allocating any residual profit and/or cost to the CPPs under consideration of the benefits test. Different alternatives exist to set arm's length interest rates. Once the interest rate has been determined, an allocation mechanism for the sharing of benefits and related expenses has to be chosen. The decision on how the benefits shall be shared among the CPPs could have a considerable impact on the returns realized by the CPPs, with the CPM continuously earning a routine cost plus return. Therefore, special care should be given to the selection and appropriateness of the allocation mechanism considering the underlying facts and circumstances of the case.
- Where the CPM acts as a fully fledged in-house bank, it might be reasonable to concentrate the arm's length analysis on the arm's length nature of interest rates, where the interest rates should allow the CPPs to not make them worse off than comparable options available. In line with a fully fledged profile, the

CPM should theoretically be entitled to earn the residual income or loss. At the same time, it could be appropriate to verify the resulting spread by a combination of a routine and risk-adjusted return analysis so that the effective margin realized by the CPM can be supported by means of a separate corroborative analysis, where suitable.

This approach also sets the framework for dealing with the effects of COVID-19 on cash pool arrangements, whereby one key area represents the allocation of COVID-19-related extraordinary costs and/or losses.

In practice, the differentiation between a CPM performing a mere coordination function and a fully fledged in-house bank-type FinCo which is also running the cash pool might not be that clear. Additionally, both the OECD Guidance on Financial Transactions as well as the German administrative principles suggest that a CPM usually only performs routine functions such that it is currently not entirely clear under which exact facts and circumstances a CPM - if at all – might actually represent an 'in-house bank' entitled to more than a routine return. Therefore, further guidance on a service provider versus a more comprehensive CPM functional, asset and risk profile, associated remuneration options of the CPM, interest rate determination and the sharing of benefits would be welcome in order to decrease potential disputes arising due to diverging national views on how the arm's length principles should be implemented in practice.

# CHAPTER 33

# Options Realistically Available with Respect to Cash-Pooling Transactions

*Ulf Andresen*[*]

## I THE ARM'S LENGTH PRINCIPLE AFTER 2017

The arm's length principle essentially requires the comparison of the (commercial) conditions including the consideration in an uncontrolled transaction between independent parties with those in a related party transaction or so-called 'controlled transaction'. In order for such comparison to be meaningful in the context of the correct assessment of taxes, it is important to determine the economically relevant characteristics or comparability factors[1] of the two to-be-compared transactions. Whereas the *2010* Organisation for Economic Co-operation and Development (OECD) Transfer Pricing Guidelines focused only on the five comparability factors mentioned in no. 1.36,[2] the *2017* Guidelines put a higher emphasis on economic aspects and introduce the concept of other options realistically available in no. 1.38,[3] and thus complement the five comparability factors previously known.

The evaluation of financial transactions under the arm's length principle has been a controversial topic throughout the entire base erosion and profit shifting (BEPS) process.[4] The considerable time period it has taken to issue a joint publication is document of the different opinions and perceptions across the globe when it comes to

* The views and opinions set forth herein are the personal views or opinions of the authors; they do not necessarily reflect views or opinions of the organisation with which the authors are associated.
1. *See*, OECD, Transfer Pricing Guidelines, 44 (2017), Chapter I, No. 1.36.
2. *See*, *ibid.*, 43.
3. *See*, *ibid.*, 45, 1.38.
4. This is reflected in the fact that 'the Committee on Fiscal Affairs produced a non-consensus discussion draft on financial transactions in July 2018'; OECD, Transfer Pricing Guidance on Financial Transactions, 3 (2020).

the accurate delineation analysis in relation to financial transactions. An important aspect in this context is the perception that financial transactions are, among other transactions, a main instrument of tax planning, and, at the same time, a type of transactions that is often not found between independent third parties, either at all, or in the ways such transactions are structured. The Transfer Pricing Guidance (paper) on Financial Transactions, now Chapter X of the OECD Transfer Pricing Guidelines 2022, provides, for the first time in history, guidance for the application of Article 9 OECD-MTC to financial transactions with the aim of reducing double taxation that might be triggered by any deviating application of the arm's length principle to cross-border financial transactions in different jurisdictions.

## II THE CONCEPT OF 'OPTIONS REALISTICALLY AVAILABLE'

The OECD suggests in no. 1.38 that:

> independent enterprises, when evaluating the terms of a potential transaction, will compare the transaction to the other options realistically available to them, and they will only enter into the transaction if they see no alternative [option] that offers a clearly more attractive opportunity to meet their commercial objectives. In other words, independent enterprises would only enter into a transaction if it is not expected to make them worse off than their next best option.[5]

The new Chapter X in the OECD Transfer Pricing Guidelines 2022 builds on this concept and refines it for financial transactions:

### 1 The OECD Concept in Relation to Financial Transactions

For a taxpayer who plans to conclude a financial transaction with a related party, the OECD takes the view that independent enterprises will 'consider all other options realistically available to them'[6] and would only enter the related party transaction if it offers the comparatively best opportunity to meet its own commercial objectives.

In contrast to non-financial transactions, the OECD requires a double-sided approach in applying the concept of other options realistically available to the evaluation of financial transactions, i.e., the options of both, the supplier and the recipient, in the controlled financial transaction must be considered. In the context of a cash pool transaction, this would mean that the options available to the ultimate parent company[7] of a group of multinational enterprises would have to be evaluated and similarly those of, for example, the cash pool leader and of all cash pool participants in the bilateral transactions, these stakeholders would be concluding in the cash pool setting.

5. OECD, Transfer Pricing Guidelines, 41 (2022), Chapter I, No. 1.38.
6. *Ibid.*, 406-407, Chapter X, No. 10.19.
7. It is assumed that the ultimate parent company is very often the cash pool leader where all cash pool accounts are being consolidated for cash-management purposes.

In identifying these options of all relevant stakeholders, i.e., parties to any cash pool transaction, tax administrations and taxpayers, when applying Article 9 OECD-MTC or any of its derivatives in bilateral tax treaties should pay attention to a few aspects outlined by the OECD. In the context of a functional analysis, they should keep in mind that the contributions, capabilities and other features of the related parties involved in the cash pool may influence their available options, e.g., the number of treasury personnel in particular locations.[8] As far as the analysis of risk is concerned, the OECD emphasises that the access to funding similarly influences the options realistically available to both parties to the cash pool transaction, e.g., suggesting that individual access to liquidity may only be available to the strong members of a cash pool.[9] The OECD further suggests that the taking on or laying off of risk would be seen as economically neutral as long as the adopted decision with respect to the level of assumed risk is made in return for higher or lower anticipated nominal income that results in an equal net present value of both options.[10] It does not seem to be entirely clear what practical relevance this economic textbook phrase may develop. It is certainly not in the interest of taxpayers to perform multi-period analyses based on a large variety of assumptions in choosing one option over another and to develop a financial model for every simple business decision. Hence, the absence of such financial models should not be taken as a non-fulfilment of the new duty of considering other options realistically available. All the above considerations would have to be made at least twice, for the supplier and for the recipient in a financial transaction (double-sided approach).

While the double-sided approach is generally not meant to be leading to any disregarding of a controlled transaction for which the OECD has very high standards,[11] it may require the (significant) adjustment to the terms and conditions of a potentially comparable uncontrolled transaction or the finding of a new uncontrolled transaction that is matching the controlled transaction better in terms of comparability.

Depending on how it is being applied in practice, the actual documentation on the options available to independent third parties for purposes of the arm's length comparison may develop into a nightmare. A taxpayer, for example, may feel that a wealth of options exist that would need to be compared and documented to arrive at a decision for the best option, potentially with a financial model behind every single option. If such options translate into anticipated payment streams in the future, the performance and documentation of this concept may prove to involve a lengthy and costly exercise for a taxpayer because it would have to cover a long time period in the future involving assumptions and the associated need to plausibly and credibly support them for a later discussion with the tax administration. Conversely, if the tax administration comes up with new options it believes would have been available at the point in time the decision had been made about concluding a controlled transaction, a similar discussion about hypothetical events may evolve. Hence, it would be fair to say

8. *See* OECD, Transfer Pricing Guidelines, 46 (2022), Chapter I, No. 1.52.
9. *See ibid.*, 50, No. 1.64.
10. *See ibid.*, 57-58, No. 1.79.
11. *See ibid.*, 75-76, No. 1.142.

that the introduction of economic concepts rather increases the time and cost burden of multinational enterprises and likely increases the time it takes to find the correct transfer price in a controversial setting. With this scenario on the horizon, one is inclined to appeal to the tax administrations to apply this concept with a sense of proportion. This is supported by paragraph 9.31 of OECD Transfer Pricing Guidelines 2022 which suggests in the context of business restructurings, that there is no intention to require the documentation of 'all possible hypothetical options realistically available'.[12]

## 2 Lack of Actual Cash-Pooling Transactions Between Independent Enterprises

The new concept of options realistically available requires the consideration of other options or alternatives that have been available to one or more independent enterprise(s) at the decision-making point in time. Further, the concept requires an evaluation as to why such independent enterprises would not have opted for such an alternative. Independent enterprises, however, do not group together and approach a bank to form a cash pool and be part of such a cash pool between unrelated entities. Thus, it would seem that independent enterprises are not available as a testing ground for the desired behaviour under the arm's length principle when it comes to cash-pooling transactions.[13]

If this was indeed the final answer to the question, the underlying concept of options realistically available would never be applicable to transactions that exclusively exist within multinational groups of companies, including cash-pooling transactions. Paragraphs 10.117 to 10.119 of the OECD Transfer Pricing Guidelines 2022, however, suggest that the behaviour of an independent enterprise in cash-pooling transactions would have to be evaluated by taking into account the wider context of the pooling arrangement as a whole and by considering the entire range of benefits that would become available to the pool member as a result of a collective (group) strategy where group synergies may be achieved through deliberate concerted action of all or selected members of the multinational group of companies.[14]

In other words, what is required to make the concept applicable, is to hypothesise the situation around the controlled transactions and to use a hypothetical uncontrolled transaction in which context the available options are being evaluated. In Germany, this approach is commonly referred to as the hypothetical arm's length test[15] and is contrasted with the actual arm's length test that can be applied if uncontrolled transactions have occurred with or between independent enterprises as a matter of fact. The hypothetical arm's length test mirrors a decision-making situation and aims

12. *See ibid.*, 369, Chapter IX, No. 9.31.
13. *See also ibid.*, 426-427, Chapter X, No. 10.115.
14. *See ibid.*, 427, Chapter X, No. 10.116-10.119.
15. *See* section 1 para. 3 sentence 5 Foreign Tax Act up to and including 2021 ('Aussensteuergesetz' (AStG)); section 1 para. 3 sentence 7 Foreign Tax Act from 2022. *See* BAUMHOFF & LIEBCHEN, in WASSERMEYER & BAUMHOFF, Verrechnungspreise international verbundener Unternehmen, 246, 250-267 (2020) Nos 3.125, 3.132-3.160.

at balancing the pros and cons of the different decisions (options) a decision-maker could take (chose).

## 3 The Prudent Business Manager Approach of the German Federal Tax Court

The hypothetical arm's length test or comparison is inextricably linked with the so-called prudent business manager approach. That approach has been developed by the Federal Tax Court in Germany in case law over decades.[16] It resembles the similar approach in German company law, namely sections 93 paragraph 1 sentence 1 Corporation Act ('Aktiengesetz') and 43 paragraph 1 Company Act ('GmbH-Gesetz'), which can be traced back to Roman law ('pater diligens familiae') and is known in many European jurisdictions.[17] It is used to evaluate whether a business decision of the managing director or employee was made in the interest of their company, or rather in the interest of the shareholders of that company in which case the judges of the Federal Tax Court would have seen and decided for the existence of a hidden profit distribution within the meaning of section 8 paragraph 3 sentence 2 Corporation Tax Act ('Körperschaftsteuergesetz'). An assessment of a hidden profit distribution would have resulted in an increase of the taxable income of the company, equivalent to a transfer pricing adjustment, and, in a second step, would have resulted in deeming a profit distribution to the shareholders if they themselves or people in their sphere of influence would have benefited from the underlying business decision by receiving a monetary advantage, or an advantage in kind:

> If, for example, the managing director of Manufacturing GmbH, a company resident in Germany, would have deposited EUR 40 million excess liquidity in a cash pool in year $t_1$ and would continue depositing a portion of the cash generated by the company's annual profits in the years $t_2$ through $t_5$ in that cash pool totalling additional EUR 56 million, for a deposit interest of 0.15% only, this decision may trigger the assessment of a hidden profit distribution of Manufacturing GmbH to its shareholder, if that shareholder was the cash pool leader and, at the same time, was lending EUR 90 million to Logistics GmbH, a German sister company of Manufacturing GmbH, for it to finance the construction of a new logistics centre (10-year term loan), and the interest rate for the agreed loan would have been 2.76%.

In this example, the rationale of the Federal Tax Court would be that the prudent business manager of Manufacturing GmbH would have taken the excess liquidity out of the cash pool and would have lent it to Logistics GmbH at an interest rate that would have reflected the terms and conditions of the then to-be-concluded loan agreement between these two entities. Foregoing a higher interest income and leaving the excess liquidity at a comparatively lower interest rate in the cash pool would have been a

16. *See* German Federal Tax Court, judgment dated 16 March 1967 case no. I 261/63 Federal Tax Gazette III 1967 p. 626.
17. *See* BECKER, in KNOBBE-KEUK, KLEIN & MOXTER: Handelsrecht und Steuerrecht: Festschrift für Dr. Dr. h.c. Georg Döllerer, 19 (1988).

business decision or other option independent enterprises would only take or choose under very specific circumstances, if at all. It appears that this example describes the behaviour in relation to laying off risk which is described in the OECD Transfer Pricing Guidelines.[18] Entering into a riskier transaction at an appropriate higher return is an acceptable option realistically available. One would think that the onus of proof for less probable behaviour, i.e., foregoing a higher interest rate, would be with the taxpayer and not with the tax administration.[19]

In this context, the German Federal Tax Court would usually differentiate between two levels in the decision-making process. On the first level, the Federal Tax Court would evaluate whether a prudent business manager would have concluded the transaction at all ('dem Grunde nach'), i.e., depositing EUR 96 million in the cash pool for years in exchange for 0.15% interest income per annum. When the court concludes that the prudent business manager would enter the transaction in principle, on the second level, it would evaluate whether the prudent business manager would have agreed on the consideration (here: the interest rate; 'der Höhe nach'), i.e., does the interest rate agreed reflect the risk inherent in the transaction, e.g., by taking into account the credit rating of the cash pool leader, the term of the deposit and other relevant factors.[20] It would be important to note though, in this context, that the answer to that question may vary depending on how long such depositing takes place.

In 1995, the German Federal Tax Court introduced the duplication of the prudent business manager and thus incorporated the considerations of both contractual parties of a controlled transaction into the hypothetical arm's length test.[21] Today, the duplicated prudent business manager is settled case law[22] that applies to all types of controlled transactions and is not limited to financial transactions. The applied yardstick in this context is the plausible decision-making behaviour of the two business managers transacting with each other. Usually, this implies the economically sensible behaviour in a one-off transaction. If the controlled transaction forms part of a series of transactions, however, it may be economically plausible to test the behaviour with respect to such series of transactions or package deals covering even a certain or defined time period.[23] Similarly, a business manager may accept a disadvantage in one

18. *See* OECD, Transfer Pricing Guidelines, 57-58 (2022), Chapter I, No. 1.79.
19. *See for general comments on the burden of proof rules in different jurisdictions* OECD, Transfer Pricing Guidelines, 15 (2022), Preface, No. 18.
20. *See, ibid.*, 409-410, Nos 10.28-10.33.
21. *See* German Federal Tax Court, judgment dated 17 May 1995 case no. I R 147/93 Federal Tax Gazette II 1996 p. 204.
22. *See* German Federal Tax Court, judgment dated 6 December 1995 case no. I R 88/94 Federal Tax Gazette II 1996 p. 383; judgment dated 19 May 1998 case no. I R 36/97 Federal Tax Gazette II 1998 p. 689; judgment dated 27 March 2001 case no. I R 27/99 Federal Tax Gazette II 2002, p. 111; judgment dated 17 October 2001 case no. I R 103/00 Federal Tax Gazette II 2004, p. 171; judgment dated 24 April 2002 case no. I R 18/01 Federal Tax Gazette II 2002 p. 670; judgment dated 28 January 2004 case no. I R 87/02 Federal Tax Court/unpublished judgments 2004, p. 736; judgment dated 6 April 2005 case no. I R 15/04 Federal Tax Gazette II 2006, p. 196 and case no. 22/04 Federal Tax Gazette II 2007, p. 658; judgment dated 21 August 2007 case no. I R 27/07 HFR 2008, p. 367; judgment dated 17 February 2010 case no. I R 97/08 Federal Tax Court/unpublished judgments 2010, p. 1307.
23. *See* OECD, Transfer Pricing Guidelines, 152-153 (2022), Chapter III, Nos 3.11-3.12.

transaction against an advantage in another transaction (intentional set-off) if the mutual benefits are sufficiently accurately quantified and agreed upon in advance, preferably in writing.[24]

## 4 Applying the Prudent Business Manager Approach (Hypothetical Arm's Length Test) to the Options Realistically Available in Cash-Pooling Transactions

In the absence of actual cash-pooling transactions between independent enterprises, Article 9 OECD-MTC and its derivatives require that the hypothetical arm's length test is used to establish a benchmark against which cash-pooling transactions can be tested. Concretely, this would mean that the cash-pooling transaction would be the option to be chosen under the arm's length principle if it places the relevant tested party or parties (double-sided approach) in a more advantageous position than it (they) would be if it (they) had not been a member to the cash pool, and consequently would:

(a) have needed a credit facility from a bank or other outside party at the spot market interest rate if such tested party would have a shortage of liquidity;
(b) have had to place an investment of excess funds, potentially on a short-term basis, into any kind of financial instrument at the associated risk; and/or
(c) have needed to acquire outside financial advice to assist in the financial decision making including the transaction cost associated with a single customer as opposed to a multinational group of enterprises with volume discounts based on the scale of activity with the cash pool bank.

The three examples above illustrate already that the decision-making situation likely involves a fair amount of parameters the prudent business manager would (have to) consider when comparing the participation in a cash pool and the entering into a cash pool transaction with other options outside of the cash pool. Ronald Coase's '*The Nature of the Firm*'[25] suggests that the efficiencies within a group of companies, the reduction of risk and the cost savings provide a compelling argument for the grouping of companies. The same rationale is applicable to the entering into cash-pooling arrangements. Hence, the working assumption for the application of the arm's length principle to cash-pooling transactions is that the benefit for the entire group would become a self-fulfilling prophecy[26] in that a controlled transaction within a cash pool should always be the better realistically available option compared to other options outside of the cash pool. One would expect that the interest rates for borrowing are

24. *See ibid.*, 154, Chapter III, No. 3.14.
25. *See* RONALD COASE, The Nature of the Firm, Economica Vol. IV, 386-405 (1937); RONALD COASE, The Institutional Structure of Production, in American Economic Review Vol. 82 (1992) No. 4 pp. 713-719.
26. *See* ANDRESEN, Comments on Professor SCHOUERI's Lecture 'Arm's Length: Beyond the Guidelines of the OECD' (Dr ULF ANDRESEN comments on Professor SCHOUERI's Klaus Vogel Lecture of 25 September 2015, hosted by the Institute for Austrian and International Tax Law (WU), Vienna), in: Bulletin for International Taxation, December 2015, pp. 717-721.

lower in the cash pool as for the individual cash pool member vis-à vis outside parties.[27] One would expect that the return on an investment would be higher in a cash pool with lower banking fees because of the larger scale of investments being made by the group through the bank. And finally, one would assume that the consolidation of supply and demand in relation to liquidity would generate group synergies from which every single member of the cash pool would invariably benefit, and thus place itself better than in an independent enterprise transaction setting.

## III DESCRIPTION OF RELATED-PARTY CASH-POOLING TRANSACTIONS

A cash pool is essentially a financial instrument by which multinational groups of companies manage their liquidity across different legal entities and jurisdictions potentially in a multitude of different currencies. Such a cash pool usually forms part of a group's cash management and is meant to ensure that the excess liquidity in some legal entities in a group is transferred into the cash pool and made available to other group companies, which may need liquidity, e.g., in the form of short-term loans. Thus, the overall interest expenses of a multinational group of companies are reduced because only the net amount of liquidity requirements would be taken out as a loan from a third-party bank. Conversely, a net excess cash position may command more beneficial terms and conditions vis-à-vis the cash pool running bank. Technically, the balancing of accounts is achieved through a master account into which all defined cash pool accounts are cleared every night, either physically by actual money transfer (physical cash-pooling) or notionally in some form of shadow accounting (notional cash-pooling).[28]

In this context, two questions would have to be answered:

(1) Would an independent enterprise have joined the cash pool, i.e., would it have signed the contractual framework with a third-party bank that makes it part of the cash pool and which has an influence on the terms and conditions of the cash-pooling transactions between the cash pool members?
(2) Would an independent enterprise have accepted the terms and conditions for the on-going cash-pooling transactions, e.g., deposit-making conditions including interest rates, short-term borrowing conditions including interest rates, etc.

Both questions would have to be analysed separately whereas entering into a cash pool may also raise questions as to whether it would qualify as a business

27. This would be the case because the ultimate parent company or cash pool leader usually would have a better credit rating than other group companies.
28. *See*, for a description for example, European Central Bank, Analytical Credit Datasets ('AnaCredit'), Questions in relation to the credits to be reported, https://www.ecb.europa.eu/stats/money_credit_banking/anacredit/questions/html/ecb.anaq.200131.0014.en.html (on 30 January 2022).

restructuring within the meaning of Chapter IX of the OECD Transfer Pricing Guidelines 2022.

It is important to note in this context that a cash pool is meant to be a cash management instrument for the short term, i.e., for liquidity needs in a twelve-month period. This fact is a parameter that has to be considered in the context of applying the arm's length principle to cash-pooling transactions, similar to government policies[29] which confine the options realistically available to all parties in a defined market setting, related parties and independent third parties alike.

## 1 Entering a Cash Pool

Becoming a party to a long-term contract such as a cash-pooling agreement with a third-party bank together with other group companies qualifies as a related-party transaction because the contractual framework creates a contractual relationship between group companies, and it fixes the consideration paid for the provision of liquidity between the group companies. Entering the cash pool may also be perceived as a business restructuring depending on the circumstances.

The conclusion or amendment of long-term contracts qualifies as extraordinary business event ('außergewöhnlicher Geschäftsvorfall') in section 3 paragraph 2 of the German Transfer Pricing Documentation Regulations ('Gewinnabgrenzungsaufzeichnungsverordnung') if such conclusion or amendment has a significant impact on the amount of taxable income of the taxpayer. Such qualification triggers the requirement to create contemporaneous documentation, i.e., the documentation must be produced or be ready for review by the tax administration by 30 June of the calendar year following the year such extraordinary transaction took place.

This qualification does not necessarily mean that entering a cash pool is a business restructuring, though.

In the absence of a legal or universally accepted definition, the OECD Transfer Pricing Guidelines 2022 describe a business restructuring as a 'cross-border reorganisation of the commercial or financial relations between associated enterprises, including the termination or substantial renegotiation of existing arrangements'.[30] Based on this broad definition, one would have to subsume the entering of a cash pool as being a business restructuring. According to the OECD, however, a business restructuring that triggers exit taxation would require a reallocation of profit potential, or that something of value,[31] e.g., intangible assets, leaves a country[32] without any consideration paid in return or an inappropriately small consideration.

In the financial services industry, a straight sale of a financial asset, e.g., a loan portfolio, will clearly not qualify as a business restructuring but as a sale of an asset. This is the case irrespective of whether a financial asset, e.g., a loan portfolio, may be hard to value when a large number of derivatives are sold within the scope of such loan

---

29. *See* OECD, Transfer Pricing Guidelines, 78-80 (2022), Chapter I, Nos 1.152 following.
30. *Ibid.*, 357, Chapter IX, No. 9.1.
31. *See* OECD, Transfer Pricing Guidelines, 371 (2022), Chapter IX, No. 9.39.
32. *See ibid.*, 358, Chapter IX, No. 9.6.

portfolio. A business restructuring in the financial services industry requires that a people function or that people move to a different location in another country.

Hence, if no people move to the central treasury department that may be situated geographically at the place of residence of the ultimate shareholder or the cash pool leader of a multinational group of companies (centralisation of functions),[33] entering a cash pool does not qualify as business restructuring. This is further supported by the fact that there would be no intangible asset involved on the part of the multinational group of companies in consolidating supply of and demand for liquidity. All relevant know-how would be with the people performing the relevant activity as this is the norm in a service industry comprising banks and other financial institutions.

At the same time, the terms and conditions of the cash pool arrangements, and here in particular, those between the participating group companies, largely determine whether entering the cash pool on such terms and conditions is the best option for each group company that is foreseen to participate in the cash pool. The OECD Transfer Pricing Guidelines 2022 are very clear on this:

> It is important to note though that '*it is not sufficient from a transfer pricing perspective that a restructuring arrangement makes commercial sense for the group as a whole: the arrangement must be arm's length at the level of each individual taxpayer, taking account of its rights and other assets, expected benefits from the arrangement […], and realistically available options.*'[34]

Hence, the decision to enter a cash pool is inextricably linked to the conditions with respect to one or even a bundle of different controlled transactions. For ease of understanding, the following examples describe only one transaction in such a cash pool setting. In this context, Nos 9.27, 9.28 and 10.118 OECD Transfer Pricing Guidelines describe very well the rationale to be applied by the cash pool participants, for example:

(a) a cash poor entity;
(b) a cash rich entity.

Example A

- *Pre-cash pool situation*: A cash poor entity A Ltd. has a credit line with third-party Bank A in country A with an interest rate on drawn-down funds of 2.3%. Bank A has insisted on a mortgage on the property of A Ltd. as a security for the credit line itself and for a long-term loan taken out from Bank A for a period of 8 years at an interest rate of 3.4%.
- *Cash pool situation*: Under the cash pool agreement, A Ltd. may draw short-term liquidity from the cash pool at an interest rate of 2.3%. The mortgage on the property of A Ltd. is no longer linked to the credit line but limited to the long-term loan from Bank A.

33. *See* the fourth example in *ibid.*, 357-358, Chapter IX, No. 9.2.
34. *Ibid.*, 370-371, No. 9.37; less precise with respect to financial transactions or cash-pooling transactions *ibid.*, 427, Chapter X, No. 10.116 and/or No. 10.118.

With all other things being equal, A Ltd would enter the cash pool because it would not be worse off compared to the situation before. Moreover, the mortgage may be available for further financing needs or investments if perceived necessary.

Example B

- *Pre-cash pool situation*: A cash rich entity B S.à.r.l. has a shares and derivatives portfolio of EUR 25 million with third-party Bank B in country B and, in addition, maintains an average deposit of EUR 14 million in cash with the bank, for which it pays interest of -0.24%. The fees Bank B charges for handling any share and derivative transactions are 0.05% of the respective transaction value.
- *Cash pool situation*: Under the new cash pool agreement B-Group enters into with Bank C headquartered in state C, B S.à.r.l. reduces the deposit amount to EUR 8 million and, thus, reduces, the annual interest payment by EUR 14,400. In addition, B S.à.r.l. receives interest income on the balance of EUR 6 million which it has placed in the cash pool for an interest of 0.33%. Moreover, B S.à.r.l. benefits from better conditions for its share and derivatives transactions because Bank C, the new cash pool bank, is prepared to reduce the charges for such transactions to 0.038% given the higher number of transactions now being channelled through Bank C.

With all other things being equal, B S.á.r.l. has an incentive to enter the cash pool because it would be better off compared to the situation before.

The decision to enter a cash pool based on such comparisons as has been described above should be easy to substantiate and document under the arm's length principle and the other options realistically available. The simple reason is that the consolidation of supply and demand of several legal entities of the same group of multinational companies generates synergies, for example, by saving transaction costs or other banking costs, which manifest themselves in more favourable conditions. Therefore, it is almost by definition that entering a cash pool provides a benefit to each participant.

The more difficult question under the arm's length principle is, whether the synergies, as they are reflected in the consideration or mix of considerations in the various cash pool transactions, are appropriately attributed between the cash pool participants.

This question may only be answered appropriately in a two-step process, taking a two-sided look at the different participants in the respective transactions individually, and for the entire group.[35]

35. *Ibid.*, 427, No. 10.116 and/or No. 10.118.

## 2 Ongoing Transactions in the Cash Pool

Applying the arm's length principle to the ongoing transactions in the cash pool to explore the other options realistically available requires a clear delineation of the specific transaction. The following transactions are examples of the transactions that may be entered into by the cash pool participants. The first step in applying the arm's length test is the identification of comparable transactions the independent party (e.g., a third-party bank) has – as a matter of fact – entered into *with* the tested cash pool party (*internal* arm's length comparison). Alternatively, resort may be had to a comparable transaction *between* the bank as an independent third party and another independent third party (*external* arm's length comparison).

### *A Depositing Short-Term Liquidity into the Cash Pool*

A cash pool participant who wants to deposit short-term liquidity into a cash pool would have to compare the cash pool conditions with the conditions that are available from other alternative suppliers of the same product or service.

If, for example, a third-party bank would offer the tested party an interest rate of 0.09 % for a three-month deposit whereas, in the cash pool, the tested party would only receive 0.03 %, the tested party would have to ask for 0.09 % deposit interest rate in order to be able to deposit its excess liquidity in the cash pool unless there are other reasons or factors of comparability that require adjustments to the third-party interest rate used in performing the arm's length comparison. A comparison with the deposit rates offered by the major banks in a particular country that are being published by the country's central bank in the form of an average rate may serve as an indicator for calibrating the deposit interest rates in the cash pool for transfer pricing purposes.

The same applies if such short-term liquidity would be placed into the cash pool as a whole or with a particular cash pool participant, not in the form of a deposit but as a short-term loan or as an amount for investment in shares or derivatives.

In the case of a loan, the tested party would expect an interest rate that is at least equal to the interest rate it would receive in comparable transactions with a third party, or that would have been agreed between independent third parties, for example, in the form of interest rate information available in publicly accessible databases.

In the case of an investment amount, the tested party would expect that the transaction fees for the buy and sell transactions of shares and derivatives are the same or lower than the equivalent fees it would have to pay to any of the local banks, for example. The same holds true for the deposit fees for the tested party's portfolio of shares and derivatives.

All these examples, however, only identify the lower bound of the decision of the tested party, i.e., determines whether the tested party would stay in the cash pool.

### B Borrowing Short-Term Liquidity from the Cash Pool

A cash pool participant who wants to borrow short-term liquidity from the cash pool would have to compare the cash pool conditions with the conditions that are available from other alternative suppliers, e.g., from a bank for a short-term loan.

If, for example, a third-party bank would offer the tested party an interest rate of 1.3% for a short-term loan (bridge loan) for 2 months to finance, for example, the value-added tax in a large investment, and in the cash pool, the tested party would have to pay 2.1%, the tested party would have to ask for a reduction of the interest rate to 1.3% in order to be able to borrow from the cash pool unless there are other reasons or factors of comparability that require adjustments to the interest rates. A comparison with the loan interest rates offered by the major banks in a particular country that are being published by the country's central bank may serve as an indicator for calibrating the loan interest rates in the cash pool for transfer pricing purposes.

The loan example above only identifies the lower bound of the decision of the tested party, i.e., determines whether the tested party should stay in the cash pool with the respective related-party transaction.

### C The Other Side of the Cash Pool: How to Allocate Synergies?

The rationale described in the previous two sub-sections is not sufficient to determine whether the consideration offered in the cash pool is at arm's length. Usually, one would think that the terms and conditions available from the central bank reflect the uncertainty and risk that exists between third-party market participants including banks. This data does not reflect the synergies that are available in a multinational group of companies. Hence, the tested party should – by definition – be able to opt for the offer the cash pool can make. The critical question, therefore, is, how much more deposit interest, how much less fees and how much lesser loan interest the cash pool (leader) should offer to pass on group synergies to other cash pool participants and to what extent. The concept of other options realistically available does not provide an answer to this question.

What is clear though is, that the cash pool leader may not keep the residual profit from the pooling of supply and demand for liquidity but would have to pass it on to the sources of such supply and demand[36] by adjusting the interest rates for short-term liquidity for both depositing and borrowing transactions in the cash pool. This flows from the fact that the cash pool leader is essentially a service provider with respect to the bundling of supply and demand for liquidity. A more differentiated view needs to be applied to other aspect of investment and finance that involve decision-making that involves the assumption of risk and the possibility of achieving extra returns. There, the question is whether the cash pool leader in isolation owns the amount of capital to assume significant risk.

36. *Ibid.*, 86/367, Chapter I, Nos 1.177 following and Chapter IX No. 9.25.

If one would be able to segregate the profit and loss account of the cash pool leader and allocate the treasury personnel's total cost for the management of short-term liquidity (deposit and cash pool borrowing) to the segment which shows these expense and income items only, the deposit and borrowing interest rates should be adjusted so that the cash pool leader, i.e., the treasury department, received an arm's length profit mark-up on the total costs for the (service) activity of coordinating supply and demand of excess short-term liquidity. If transaction and deposit fees from the bank are passed on from the cash pool leader to the cash pool participants, no inappropriate advantage should stick with the cash pool leader because it usually does not take any risk and essentially provides a service. Conversely, if and to the extent the treasury department increases investment returns, for example, by beating certain benchmarks in certain asset classes, this may be a reason why the treasury department should receive extra remuneration for asset picking or an asset management fee similar to portfolio managers for which external market data on profitability is also available and can be used for transfer pricing purposes.

## IV CONSIDERATIONS BASED ON THE CJEU-DECISION IN HORNBACH

The Court of Justice of the European Union (CJEU), in its Hornbach-decision, has held that there may be 'commercial reasons' for a parent company to agree to provide capital on non-arm's length terms to a foreign subsidiary.[37] It further held that a transfer pricing adjustment provision would not be violating the freedom of establishment within the meaning of Article 43 EC (today: Article 267 Treaty on the Functioning of the European Union (TFEU)) if 'the authorities responsible for the enforcement of that legislation afford the resident taxpayer the opportunity to prove that the terms were agreed on for commercial reasons'.[38]

The judges at the CJEU had to deal with a situation that would not have happened between independent third parties because an independent third party, for example, a bank, would not have granted a loan to an ailing company without any guarantee from a sound guarantor or any other kind of security.

In the absence of a comparable transaction, the term 'commercial reasons' points in a similar direction as the OECD concept of other options realistically available. It may be commercially sensible, for example, to grant an interest-free loan to an ailing subsidiary to allow it to restructure and not be burdened with high-interest rates, which would have been asked for given the bad credit rating an ailing company usually has. In the context of a multinational group of companies, the ultimate parent company or some other company would grant such support even though it may not be remunerated appropriately on the level of the transaction itself. The CJEU approves such behaviour

37. *See* CJEU, Judgment dated 31 May 2018, case C-382/16 Hornbach Baumarkt, No. 54.
38. *See ibid.*, No. 58.

and requires that tax administrations listen to arguments which explain and document the commercial rationale for the decision that was taken in the group.

## V IS THE ARM'S LENGTH PRINCIPLE BECOMING A BEHAVIOURAL STANDARD?

One of the flaws of the arm's length principle is and has always been the perceived lack of comparable transactions, companies, etc. While the lack of comparable transactions and companies in practice does not appear to be as bad as one might think, it is one of the reasons why the arm's length principle has been developed or extended to include economic concepts more than in the past, such as the other options realistically available.

It would be fair to say, though, that the perceived deficit is primarily a deficit in the tax administrations that creates an obstacle for the desired application of the arm's length standard when trying to argue for adjustments. Whether this shortcoming of applying the arm's length test may be overcome by the concept of other options realistically available remains to be seen.

At the same time, it appears that this concept may be an introduction of a behavioural standard that is built on an understanding of what people do or would do in certain situations. As such information influences the taxable income as a reflection of a taxpayer's ability to pay, three questions come to mind:

- Who determines arm's length behaviour?
- Who determines the available options?
- Who determines what is realistically available?

Recent case law from the German Federal Tax Court suggests that the tax administration, the tax auditors and even the Lower Tax Courts often replace the comparison with actual or hypothetical third-party situations with assumptions about what market participants would do or would have done in a particular situation.[39] This holds particularly true in the context of financial transactions. The Federal Tax Court has dismissed quite a few of these assumptions as unrealistic and has passed most cases back to the Lower Tax Courts with clear instructions as to what they need to do in relation to the fact finding around these cases and how they have to do so.[40]

In light of these judgments, taxpayers are well advised to invest time in carefully analysing other options meant to be realistically available and put forward by the tax administrations to argue their case. Expert witnesses may be a helpful instrument to confine discussions to actual behaviour that would be found in the market.

39. *See* German Federal Tax Court, judgments dated 18 May 2021 case no. I R 4/17 GmbHRundschau 2021 p. 107 and case no. I R 62/17 Zeitschrift für Wirtschaftsrecht [und Insolvenzpraxis] 2021 p. 2445; judgment dated 9 June 2021 case no. I R 32/17 Der Betrieb, p. 2673.
40. *See* German Federal Tax Court, judgments dated 18 May 2021 case no. I R 4/17 GmbHRundschau 2021 p. 107 and case no. I R 62/17 Zeitschrift für Wirtschaftsrecht [und Insolvenzpraxis] 2021 p. 2445; judgment dated 9 June 2021 case no. I R 32/17 Der Betrieb, p. 2673.

## VI ARM'S LENGTH FRAMEWORK FOR CASH-POOLING TRANSACTIONS

The analysis above has shown that the concept of other options realistically available to independent enterprises needs to be modified for the application to cash-pooling transactions in that the complete absence or lack of actual cash-pooling transactions between independent third parties calls for a replacement by hypothetical transactions. Such hypothetical transactions, though, must be evaluated in the context of the collective strategy applied by MNCs in generating group synergies by saving costs through entering into a cash-pooling arrangement with an outside bank.

Entering into such a group-wide transaction should generate enough benefit for the group as a whole that the allocation of such benefit should allow every single cash pool member to be better off entering the cash-pooling and participating in any kind of cash-pooling transaction that fits its needs compared to the alternative situation of depositing funds in a bank, making individual investment decisions and not benefiting from favourable terms and conditions in dealing with the third-party bank because of the scale of demand the multinational group of enterprises places with that bank.

As long as the benefit from bundling supply and demand for liquidity is channelled back to the source of such supply and demand, i.e., every single cash pool member, and is not kept by the cash pool leader for no compelling reason, it should be fairly easy to comply with the arm's length test when evaluating cash-pooling transactions. It would even seem feasible to agree on a comparatively higher interest rate for short-term loans and a comparatively lower interest rate on deposits. These interest rates should be more favourable than those under the hypothetical arm's length test, though. Time should be taken, however, to document such rationale carefully. Taxpayers should be aware that tax administrations will challenge any kind of financial transaction specifically in the current decade and, hence, should prepare for such a scenario.

One aspect that requires specific attention is the building up of a structural deposit and/or lending positions over time in the cash pool without any decision-making activity on the part of the cash pool participants in order to change that situation. If a cash pool member foregoes opportunities because it does not shift deposits into financial instruments with a higher return or lends at comparatively higher interest rates, and if other options realistically available would render better commercial results for such cash pool member, transfer pricing adjustment may be the consequence.

Economic behaviour may be difficult to prove in court proceedings. Hence, the other options realistically available may turn out to have the same shortcomings as the arm's length standard when being put to the test in court.

# Part IV ALP Framework for Treasury Activities

CHAPTER 34

# General Overview of Financing Operations Including Different Types of Structures Used Within an MNE

*Alessandro Bucchieri & Benedetta Veneziano*[*]

## I FINANCIAL MODEL: CENTRALIZED VERSUS DECENTRALIZED

For multinational groups, the management of finances and liquidity is a highly strategic and potentially very complex activity. Every business needs capital for day-to-day management and to support investments and business decisions.

The larger the size of the activity and the organizational structure of the entity carrying it out, especially in the case of a Multinational Enterprise (MNE) Group, the more the need to structure and rationalize financial management emerges, for example, by coordinating or centralizing the operational and/or strategic finance of the subsidiaries.

All business decisions will be determined by the definition of the financial model and, therefore, it can only be linked to the structure of the Group itself, to the commercial strategy adopted, to the cycle of products and/or services provided, to the sector to which it belongs and to the geographical locations on which the currencies of operation depend.

Treasury structures can therefore be set up with a different degree of centralization depending on the willingness of the subsidiaries to limit their financial autonomy by referring their management to another entity within the group. In the most *decentralized* form, each company within the group has full autonomy over financial transactions. This type of structure is often adopted in multinational groups with

* The views and opinions set forth herein are the personal views or opinions of the authors; they do not necessarily reflect views or opinions of the organization with which the authors are associated.

several divisions operating in different sectors or with regional structures, or in the case of multinational groups that must comply with specific local regulations.

In the opposite case, by opting for a *centralized* treasury model, the financial center in charge of this activity has full control over the group's financial transactions, while the Group's operational entities remain responsible for specific non-financial business issues.

The main advantage of having a centralized finance is that it allows the Group to globally manage its cash position and exposure to interest rate and currency risk (if any) in a timely manner.

Indeed, by centralizing operations in one company, it's possible to benefit from economies of scale, achieve efficiencies in the management of internal cash flows, improve group financial planning, optimize over-the-country cash flows and the use of cash, reduce external bank fees and lower operating costs.

Decisions on the most appropriate degree of centralization will depend on a number of variables including, for example, the volume and nature of payments, the type of payment, the geographical spread of the Group, banking relationships, types of information technology systems and their integrability, and the presence of highly specialized staff.

In fact, there are different models of centralization of finance, ranging from "Central" to "Central-In-house bank" models.

In the "Central" models, treasury is structured at the level of the holding company, which enters transactions for the Group companies or organizes them on their behalf. In this model, the parent company operates with specialized staff and a sufficient amount of equity to be able to assume and manage the financial risks resulting from the transactions.

In the "Central-Captive bank" models, centralization is concentrated on a Group financing entity which acts as the Group's bank, normally with highly specialized staff, which proceeds to structure all intragroup transactions with the various subsidiaries, with support from the central treasury team.

## II "CENTRAL-CAPTIVE BANK": FINANCIAL MODEL

A financial model generally found within multinational groups is precisely the model just described, i.e., a "central-captive bank" model in which a legal entity operates as an internal captive bank.

Often, such a financial entity is located in the most efficient financial centers in terms of greater operational simplicity, certainty, stability and international view of the regulatory and tax system.

In such a centralized structure, the *parent* company defines the strategic objectives in its role of guidance and coordination. Within the *strategic plan*, the business areas are identified in terms of product portfolio and country of reference. The strategic plan, therefore, defines the areas in which the group intends to invest while defining the expected return on investment.

From the strategic plan directives, the *Industrial Plan* is drawn up, the implementation of which is reflected in a *financial plan* that establishes the methods for covering requirements at a centralized level and for all the subsidiaries in line with the reference targets assigned to the business units (i.e., growth in technical assets and working capital).

Once the financial plan has been defined, the holding company defines the *guidelines* to guarantee the achievement of the objectives in terms of capital structure, financial charges/dividends ratio, thus defining the level of leverage with respect to the group's own means.

Based on the above-mentioned objectives, the captive bank, taking into account the evolution of the capital and financial markets and the expectations of those in financial surplus, implements *funding programs* by choosing a time composition consistent with the return prospects of the industrial business.

For example, in the case of the need to finance investments in fixed assets, it will be more efficient to structure the investment with long-term debt, which allows the recovery horizon of the investment to be correlated with the maturity of the debt. It would, therefore, not be logical to finance a long-term investment with short-term financial sources.

At the same time, working capital dynamics are satisfied with short-term financial sources. In fact, every industrial enterprise not only needs financial requirements to invest in long-term fixed assets but also requires short-term support to compensate for the temporary asynchrony of the cost-revenue dynamics linked to the evolution of working capital. The main factors involved in a short-term requirement can be easily summarized as the temporary mismatch in the cycle of payments and receipts of trade payables and receivables resulting from the postponement of the collection of sales against the advance payment of costs for the purchase of production factors. The financial indebtedness resulting from the dynamics of the working capital, as for the best market practices, is therefore satisfied through short-term financial operations to be sized year by year in relation to the forecast evolution of the business.

In this context, the captive bank's mission is to act as a financial partner to the Group's business activities, supporting the subsidiaries in the process of value generation and long-term growth, providing sustainable and competitive financial resources, structures, and services. The captive bank's strategy is to optimize the management of assets and liabilities by concentrating on financial needs and risks, approaching financial markets to seize the best financing opportunities.

## III RELEVANT ACTIVITIES AND FUNCTIONS PERFORMED IN THE CENTRALIZED FINANCIAL MODEL

The activities that characterize a centralized financial model are typically focused on the management of funding activities on the market and on financing activities for the Holding Company as well as for the operating subsidiaries.

In the creation of a new financial asset, the main functions performed by the Group's finance company consist of examining the companies' requests for the needs and implementing all the front/middle office activities for the granting of the loan(s). In particular, the finance company is responsible for (i) assessing the creditworthiness of the Group companies; (ii) assessing the credit, exchange rate and market risks related to the loan(s) requested; (iii) deciding the level of acceptance of the exposure to credit, exchange rate and market risks; (iv) negotiating the contractual terms and amount of the loan(s) with the requesting parties; (v) considering guarantees or credit enhancement with respect to the loan(s) under analysis; and (vi) pricing the loan(s) under analysis.

Consequently, another important function performed within a centralized financial model is aimed at raising funds and capital to finance the loan(s) under analysis, typically all those trading/treasury activities to make the corresponding funds available to the Group companies.

Finally, the finance company performs back-office activities which ensure (i) the definition of the corresponding draft loan contract; (ii) the contractual formalities; (iii) the resolution of any outstanding legal issues; (iv) the checking of any guarantees offered; (v) the signing of the contract and (vi) the recording of the loan(s) under analysis in the books.

Once the appropriate instrument for ensuring the financial needs of the subsidiary has been defined and finalized, the captive bank must perform a series of activities as part of its *risk monitoring and control functions,* in order to ultimately provide the parent company with an overview of the performance of financial assets, outstanding capital balances, expectations of market developments (interest rates, country risks, exchange rate risks) and any other information that may be relevant to the established financial plan.

These monitoring and control activities range from *Loan Support* Activities, e.g., managing the loan disbursed or interest payments, to *Monitoring and Risk Management,* e.g., deciding whether (and, if so, to what extent) the various risks should continue to be borne or transferring most of the loan and all residual risks (including market and liquidity risks) to the holding company or writing off bad loans, or finally to Sales/Marketing Activities, e.g., deciding whether to renew or extend a loan and, if so, under what conditions.

In fact, the captive bank assumes the following risks during its daily business:

- *Default risk*: actively manages and monitors credit risk in relation to financial transactions entered through origination and credit management activities.
- *Currency risk*: (i) the risk that a particular transaction may be settled at a different exchange rate from that prevailing at the time the transaction was negotiated; (ii) the risk that changes in exchange rates may affect the underlying economic circumstances of an enterprise.
- *Interest rate risk*: the main source of exposure to interest rate risk is the variability of funding costs and loan portfolio yields, linked to the uncertainty of the interest paid on variable-rate debt and received on variable-rate debt. The captive bank manages the risk by reducing the amount of debt exposed to interest rate fluctuations through derivative hedging transactions, containing borrowing costs over time and limiting the volatility of results.

- *Withholding tax risk*: An entity may incur a withholding tax risk if a withholding tax is levied on interest payments received and the entity cannot recover it in full.
- *Operational risk*: risk of loss arising from inadequate internal processes, people and systems or from external events. This definition includes legal risk but excludes strategic and reputational risk.

In carrying out its activities, the assets employed by the captive bank generally consist of routine tangible assets (e.g., real estate and equipment/furniture, stationery, computer hardware), but also financial software such as Bloomberg/Reuters and necessary for carrying out financial analysis.

## IV TOOLS FOR IMPLEMENTING THE CENTRALIZED FINANCE PROCESS

As mentioned, the activities that characterize a centralized financial model are typically focused on the management of funding activities on the market and on financing activities for the Holding Company as well as for the operating subsidiaries.

### 1 Funding Process

The captive bank serves as the primary point of reference for the management of the financial needs and surpluses, foreign exchange and interest rate risks generated by the Group's operating subsidiaries. It operates by raising funds in the market through (i) bond issues (EUR, GBP, USD and JPY), loans, commercial papers and other financial transactions.

*Bond issues* (so-called Corporate Bonds) respond to generally long-term hedging needs (CAPEX with a long-term return on investment) as the ability to repay the capital raised in the market, and the payment of the return by the company are generally linked to the cash flow that will be generated through the realization of future operations. In some cases, the company's own physical assets can be used as collateral for corporate bonds offered in the market.

The same needs can also be covered by *bank loans or commercial paper*, which are financing instruments generally used for needs related to investments whose return is expected to be shorter.

### 2 Lending Process

Based on the activity carried out by the counterparty, the captive bank assesses the risk profile and financial needs of the operating companies by providing specific financial instruments with the aim of meeting both treasury and financial needs, to support the financial structure of the operating business.

The financial instruments available to meet the needs of group entities can be identified as treasury instruments and/or financing instruments.

Treasury instruments aim to ensure the liquidity concentration process to optimize cash flows through the concentration of available liquidity at country level and to reduce short-term financial needs at group level. In this context, time deposit instruments and/or Intercompany Current Accounts are used, respectively, to optimize liquidity from operating companies – with the aim of centralizing liquidity at group level to minimize bank balances – and to support payments to third parties and intercompany. Treasury instruments generally also include all financial services aimed at concentrating foreign exchange and interest rate risks by providing foreign exchange and interest rate derivative transactions to hedge the risk incurred by the operating companies.

However, financing instruments can be differentiated into:

- *Term loan*: This type of transaction should be required for General Purposes activities or for investments in fixed assets, depending on the need for structural financing of liabilities or refinancing of short-term exposure, or for financing investment projects.
- *Revolving credit lines*, to cover financial needs related to working capital; generally, these are multi-year credit lines for cash elasticity that could temporarily finance long-term needs pending the definition of a long-term loan.
- *Club Deals*, generally put in place to integrate financial partners (banks or other investors) into business projects.
- *Project Financing*, mainly used to support new corporate initiatives/projects.

## V PRICING OF INTRA-GROUP FINANCING AND MAIN CHALLENGES[1]

In performing the above functions, it is of considerable importance, also following the new recommendations provided by the Organisation for Economic Co-operation and

1. OECD, *OECD Transfer Pricing Guidelines for Multinational Enterprises and Tax Administrations 2022*, OECD Publishing, Paris, 2022, https://doi.org/10.1787/0e655865-en. R. Petruzzi, *Transfer Pricing Aspect of Intra-Group Financing*, Wolters Kluwer (2016); T. Petrakos, V. Chand & A. Pletz, *Interest Rate Benchmarking for Transfer Pricing Purposes: A Comparison Between the Loan and the Bond Approach*, International Transfer Pricing Journal (2021); U. Chwała & K. Łukosz, *6. How to Take Intra-Group Financing Forward in Your Organization in Transfer Pricing & Intra-Group Financing: The Entangled Worlds of Financial Markets and Transfer Pricing*, IBFD (2021); B.T. Daba, *Valuation of Implicit Support from a Transfer Pricing Perspective*, International Transfer Pricing Journal (2021); R. Fossati, *Should Transfer Pricing Practitioners Become Credit Rating Analysts? Practical Instructions Based on Final OECD Guidance on Financial Transactions*, International Transfer Pricing Journal (2020); S. Greil & D. Schilling, *The Determination and Assessment of the Appropriateness of Interest Rates in the Case of Cross-Border Financial Transactions between Related Parties – A Case Study*, International Transfer Pricing Journal (2020); D. Amici, *In-Depth Analysis of the Concept of Options Realistically Available in Transfer Pricing*, International Transfer Pricing Journal (2020); A. Sulejmani, *Pricing Intercompany Financial Transactions: Loans, Guarantees and Cash-Pooling Arrangements*, International Transfer Pricing Journal (2019); A. Storck, *The Financing of Multinational Companies and Taxes: An Overview of the Issues and Suggestions for Solutions and Improvements*, Bulletin for International Taxation (2011).

Development (OECD) with the publication of Chapter X, to monitor and verify the existence of certain specific characteristics that will correctly delineate the financed party as well as the transaction that the captive bank intends to implement, even before defining the terms of the financing and the relative pricing.

In particular, the captive bank verifies and assesses the *borrower's borrowing capacity, creditworthiness,* and *realistic options.*

About the *borrowing capacity,* even before determining the correct rate to be applied to the transaction, the captive bank verifies whether the amount of the financing itself is adequate or whether it could potentially be subject to (total or partial) re-qualification as a capital contribution.

The verification of these capital adequacy parameters, which are also necessary to guarantee the soundness and stability of the company, should be constantly monitored through the business plans as well as through the financial plans to demonstrate that the borrower is able to service the debt throughout its duration.

The captive bank also checks for the presence of an explicit guarantee provided by the parent company. In such a case, it must be verified that the guarantee granted is not intended to allow the borrower to increase its borrowing capacity, but rather to allow the borrower to discount a lower interest rate. In other words, the guarantee granted must be necessary to increase the creditworthiness of the company and not to increase the principal of the debt.

The *creditworthiness* of the borrower represents another central, unavoidable, and fundamentally important element in the process of determining the interest rate applicable to a financing transaction. The credit rating, in fact, represents an assessment of the solvency of the company requesting the financing. The higher the credit rating, the lower its default risk, and consequently the interest rate applicable to the loan. In fact, an independent investor who has to provide financing will tend to prioritize the repayment capacity of the debt, i.e., its risk profile.

In this regard, the lender, in determining the creditworthiness of a company - in line with the new guidance provided by the OECD in Chapter X - also considers the effect of the entity's membership in the multinational group. In fact, in analysing the riskiness of the borrower, not only is the stand-alone capacity of the financed entity to repay the obligation considered but also the possibility of the latter receiving financial support from the parent company regardless of the explicit presence of a legal obligation (i.e., guarantee). The passive association, therefore, leads to a decrease in the risk perceived by the lender and consequently to a decrease in the return expected from the transaction. The implicit support is all the greater the strategic relevance of the subsidiary within the Group. This relevance is assessed through some specific qualitative factors (as also used by the rating agencies) such as, among other things, the use of the same brand, the level of integration of the business, the reputational impacts deriving from the possible failure of the borrower company.

Once the borrower's borrowing capacity and creditworthiness have been ascertained, the lender then determines the correct instrument to be offered as well as its pricing.

Therefore, both in the creation phase and, as mentioned in the previous paragraphs, in the management phase of the financial asset, a verification of the *options realistically available* is carried out, aimed at achieving the greatest degree of reliability of the price of the instrument with respect to the market parameters. In fact, a lender might consider alternative investment opportunities, or the borrower might not find the transaction convenient because it would involve an excessive increase in the cost of capital.

More specifically, in the asset creation phase, the captive bank verifies the underlying for which the financing is required (investment, refinancing, capital injection and the like) and proposes the best instrument to the borrower, also in consideration of the latter's ability to repay the debt.

The analysis of realistically available options is necessarily also carried out by the borrower who may, for example, choose not to subscribe to a large financial instrument despite being able to service it to avoid creating potential credit stress, avoid increasing the cost of capital or jeopardizing the possibility of access to the capital market.

This analysis is also carried out throughout the life of the loan. For example, in situations of macroeconomic imbalances, the counterparties to the transaction check whether it is better to close the instrument in advance or to renegotiate it. In such situations, a cost-benefit analysis is also carried out in light of the contractual clauses, and the type of interest rate agreed (fixed or variable rate).

In this regard, the possible presence of clauses related to the so-called "break-up costs" would lead to an early repayment of principal and interest by the borrower at maturity. Breaking costs take the form of "Make-Whole" payments, i.e., payments which ensure that investors, in the event of early repayment, receive the flows they would have received had their investment (i.e., loan) been repaid on the originally agreed maturity date. The Make-Whole clause can also be understood as a partial compensation, where it considers any profits from the reinvestment of the prepayment (discounted to net value) until the maturity of the contract.

Once the complete framework underlying the granting of a loan has been established, one of the main activities carried out by the captive bank is to set the remuneration, implementing best market practices if no comparable external transactions exist.

One of the most used methodologies, typically in cases where bonds have been issued by the Group, can be identified in the following steps:

(a) Observe the yield-to-maturity of a relevant sample of bonds issued by the Group, listed on the secondary financial market (so-called yield-to-maturity). This rate incorporates the risk-free rate and the remuneration expected by third-party investors for assuming the Group's credit risk.
(b) Apply any reasonable adjustment to the primary benchmark in accordance with the terms and conditions of the relevant financing transaction to properly remunerate all the risk assumed by the lender with respect to the risk-free rate, depending on both the borrower's profile (creditworthiness) and the specific terms of the financing transaction (liquidity, size, subordination, currency and similar).

For example, consider a multinational group with its registered office in Country A. The group's captive bank is based in Country B and is directly controlled by the latter.

With the aim of financing its subsidiaries through capital injections, the Holding Company has requested a loan from the Captive Bank whose terms and conditions are (*see* Table 34.1).

*Table 34.1 Captive Bank: Terms and Conditions*

| | |
|---|---|
| Notional Amount | 3 billion |
| Currency | EUR |
| Repayment structure | Bullet |
| Tenure | 10 years |
| Interest Rate | Floating (EURIBOR 6M + spread) |
| Ranking | Senior Unsecured |
| Signing Date | 2019/06/28 |

Both companies have equal creditworthiness (BBB+), and the search for comparable contracts and/or individual bond issues did not return any evidence that could be used to determine the pricing of the above loan.

Considering that the Group's captive bank bases its funding strategy mainly on the issuance of bonds, sources such as the Bloomberg BVAL[2] function can be used to identify the 10-year yield-to-maturity of the captive bank's issues on the secondary market, which is the best proxy for the issuer's credit spread.

Given the daily data series observable in the period preceding the transaction, it was possible to determine a range of values representative of the market situation (*see* Table 34.2).

*Table 34.2 Arm's Length Range Resulting from the Primary Benchmark Daily Observation*

| | *EUR Yield Curve 10 Year*[3] |
|---|---|
| | *Period 04/29/2019-05/29/2019* |
| First Quartile | 1.56% |
| Median | 1.58% |
| Third Quartile | 1.61% |

An intercompany loan (like a bank loan between independent parties) is by definition an illiquid instrument, characterized, moreover, by the exposure of a single lender to a single borrower for the entire amount financed, which therefore generates a concentration of risks on a single entity.

2. Bloomberg Valuation Service.
3. Data included in the table is hypothetical and not from any data source provider.

Therefore, an adjustment was applied to the rate thus identified through the bond yield search which, through a research process characterized by qualitative and quantitative screening, identified a liquidity risk premium of 30 bps.[4]

Considering this adjustment, the range of values emerging from the bond yield search plus the liquidity premium is composed as follows (*see* Table 34.3).

*Table 34.3 Arm's Length Range Resulting from the Primary Benchmark Daily Observation Adjusted with Liquidity Risk Premium*

| | *EUR Yield Curve 10 Year + Liquidity Adjustment* |
|---|---|
| | *Period 04/29/2019-05/29/2019* |
| First Quartile | 1.86% |
| Median | 1.87% |
| Third Quartile | 1.91% |

Finally, considering that the adjusted primary benchmark (i.e., bond yield search results + Liquidity Adjustment) expresses a fixed interest rate while the intercompany loan was agreed at a variable rate, an interest swap has to be simulated.

## VI CONCLUSIONS

With the publication by the OECD, in February 2020, of the Transfer Pricing Guidance on Financial Transactions, included in the new chapter X of the OECD Transfer Pricing Guidelines for Multinational Enterprises and Tax Administrations 2022 version, a deep knowledge of financial phenomena, their operational management and business dynamics within multinational groups becomes the key element to ensure the construction of pricing models and processes consistent with market principles.

Understanding the financial model (centralized vs. decentralized), the role played by the funding companies within the group (e.g., in house banks) and the relative strategic importance of the operating companies receiving the funding has become as important as, if not more important than, carrying out a solid benchmark analysis.

In this context, typically tax-related skills need to be appropriately combined with an in-depth knowledge not only of financial instruments but also of the strategic choices and organizational models of the finance function.

4. In this respect, the illiquidity premium was estimated as the average of the difference between the spreads of illiquid and liquid bonds of the same issuer, in order to take into account the premium an investor would seek to receive for investing in financial instruments characterized by a liquidity risk comparable to that of the intercompany transaction. Such a search can be carried out through the Bloomberg Fixed Income Search (SRCH) function.

CHAPTER 35

# Allocation of Risks and Returns: Critical Issues for Financial Transactions

*Andrew Hickman*[*]

Allocation of risks and returns is part of the process of accurately delineating the transaction described in Chapter I of the Organisation for Economic Co-operation and Development Transfer Pricing Guidelines (OECD TPG). The process applies to all transactions, including financial transactions, and depends on allocating risk returns to capability and performance of defined functional control over risk. The provision of capital itself does not generate a risk return if the provider lacks the defined standard of capability and performance. Thus the link between capital and risk is contingent on a functional standard. New Chapter X of the TPG is devoted to financial transactions, and it follows the guidance on control over risk without developing additional, specific illustrations of its application. Financial transactions have different features from non-financial transactions, and riskiness is systemic and influenced by the capital allocation in the controlled relationship. The guidance on non-recognition of transactions is afforded higher priority in financial transactions. Policymakers are confronted by competing pressures under the arm's length principle to price the transaction as structured and also to challenge the allocation of capital in financial transactions. The solution to use control of risk to reallocate the return to risk without reallocating capital carries a heavy burden and is incomplete without considering borrower's risk.

## I INTRODUCTION

This chapter examines the guidance provided in the OECD *Transfer Pricing Guidelines*[1] (TPG or 'Guidelines') on how to determine in a transfer pricing analysis which party to

* The views and opinions set forth herein are the personal views or opinions of the authors; they do not necessarily reflect views or opinions of the organisation with which the authors are associated.

1. OECD, *Transfer Pricing Guidelines for Multinational Enterprises and Tax Administrations* (OECD 2022).

the transaction assumes economically significant risks arising from the transaction and consequently should be allocated the returns associated with risk-bearing. The identification and allocation of risk is vital in a transfer pricing analysis since risk assumption affects pricing in the open market and determines the allocation of unanticipated profits or losses. Similar guidance is also found in the revised *UN Practical Manual on Transfer Pricing for Developing Countries* (2021) ('UN Manual').[2]

Guidance on the allocation of risks is found in Chapter I of the TPG. The way in which the TPG is organised is to provide general principles in the opening chapters, followed by guidance on pricing methods and on specific categories of transaction and other matters in subsequent chapters. There are, for example, chapters devoted to transactions involving intangibles, services, cost contribution arrangements, business restructuring, and on financial transactions. These subsequent chapters acknowledge the principles of the opening chapters but provide additional guidance specific to the type of transaction.

Following the revisions to Chapter I under the Base Erosion and Profit Shifting (BEPS) project, and in particular the revised guidance on risk allocation, some chapters required consequential amendment. This was particularly the case in the guidance on cost contribution arrangements, business restructuring, the transactional profit split method, and the concurrent revision of the chapter on intangibles. An essential theme running throughout these revisions is the emphasis on allocating risk returns to the party that has the capability to perform and actually does perform the evaluation of risk, and has the capacity to bear the associated outcomes. An important consequence is that the provision of capital itself does not generate a risk return if the provider lacks the defined standard of capability and performance in relation to the risk generating the return. Thus the link between capital and risk is contingent on a functional standard. Several examples illustrate this principle in the revised Guidelines, including Examples 6 and 16 in the Annex to Chapter VI, Example 5 in the Annex to Chapter VIII, and Example 3 in Chapter I which is discussed in depth later in this chapter.

The chapter on financial transactions did not have to be revised because there was no chapter on financial transactions in the TPG prior to 2022. Therefore, the new chapter on financial transactions, which becomes Chapter X of the TPG, released in February 2020,[3] is the first one which, from the outset, has been drafted with the benefit of the approaches developed in the revised Chapter I. The drafters of Chapter X take the opportunity to clarify what is meant in Chapter I by risk-free and risk-adjusted rates of return but do not develop any sustained illustration of control of risk as it applies to the specific circumstances of financial transactions. Verification of risk assumption in financial transactions through the test of control depends explicitly on the guidance and illustrations in Chapter I.

2. *See* the UN Model on Transfer Pricing for Developing Countries (2021) https://www.un.org/development/desa/financing/sites/www.un.org.development.desa.financing/files/2021-04/TP_2021_final_web%20%281%29.pdf.
3. OECD (2020), *Transfer Pricing Guidance on Financial Transactions: Inclusive Framework on BEPS Actions 4, 8-10*, OECD, Paris, www.oecd.org/tax/beps/transfer-pricing-guidance-on-financial-transactions-inclusive-framework-on-beps-actions-4-8-10.htm.

This chapter is organised by first examining in section II the approaches in Chapter I to the allocation of risks and returns. Section III discusses how aspects of risk in financial transactions, including cash boxes and allocation of capital, are treated in Chapter I, together with the guidance on non-recognition of transactions. These concepts set the boundaries of the guidance in Chapter X on allocating risks and returns in financial transactions, presented in section IV. This section includes consideration of the borrower's risk and leads to the suggestion of a complete solution to risk allocation than that specifically illustrated in the Guidelines. Section V provides concluding comments.

## II CHAPTER I GUIDANCE

### 1 Allocation of Risks and Comparability

The arm's length principle described in the Guidelines depends on comparing the pricing of controlled transactions, once accurately delineated, with the pricing of similar uncontrolled transactions. That will usually involve finding uncontrolled transactions with a similar allocation of assets, functions, and risks to the party or parties being examined. How economically significant risks are assumed by the parties under the terms of the transaction will tend to affect the pricing of the transaction. Therefore, determining the assumption of risk by the parties to a transaction can be critically important in making reliable comparisons with transactions involving a similar risk assumption so that appropriate pricing can be identified under the arm's length principle.

Determining the allocation of risk to the parties in a transaction is embedded in the wider process of accurately delineating the transaction. The bulk of Chapter I is devoted to providing guidance on how accurately to delineate the actual transaction, a process which 'requires analysis of the economically relevant characteristics of the transaction'.[4] Those characteristics include contractual terms, functions, assets, and risks, characteristics of the property transferred or services provided, economic circumstances, and business strategies. Risks are consistently identified as an important aspect of understanding the transaction: 'Identifying risks goes hand in hand with identifying functions and assets and is integral to the process of identifying the commercial or financial relations between the associated enterprises and of accurately delineating the transaction or transactions.'[5] In turn, risks are important in making comparisons between transactions: 'in making comparisons between controlled and uncontrolled transactions and between controlled and uncontrolled parties it is necessary to analyse what risks have been assumed, what functions are performed that relate to or affect the assumption or impact of these risks and which party or parties to the transaction assume these risks.'[6]

4. OECD TPG, 1.35.
5. *Ibid.*, 1.57.
6. *Ibid.*, 1.58.

Therefore, application of the arm's length principle requires examination of which parties to the transaction assume specific economically significant risks that would affect the pricing of the transaction at arm's length in order that reliable comparisons can be made. But it does not require the identification of all possible risks and risk outcomes that could be encountered by the parties to the transaction if they would not affect the pricing at arm's length.

## 2 Verifying Assumption of Risk in a Transaction

Once economically significant risks in a transaction have been identified and evidence assessed as to how those risks have been assigned to the parties, the Guidelines provide for the concept of control over risk as the means of verifying assumption of risks in a transaction. Control specifically does not mean influencing or modifying risk (*see* 1.67). Instead, control is a defined term in the guidance that is derived from its definition of risk management. 'Risk management comprises three elements: (i) the capability to make decisions to take on, lay off, or decline a risk-bearing opportunity, together with the actual performance of that decision-making function, (ii) the capability to make decisions on whether and how to respond to the risks associated with the opportunity, together with the actual performance of that decision-making function, and (iii) the capability to mitigate risk, that is the capability to take measures that affect risk outcomes, together with the actual performance of such risk mitigation.'[7] Control over risk involves the first two elements of risk management and it 'is not necessary for a party to perform the day-to-day mitigation, as described in (iii) in order to have control of the risks.'[8] The guidance recognises that these day-to-day risk mitigation activities may be outsourced. 'However, where these day-to-day mitigation activities are outsourced, control of the risk would require capability to determine the objectives of the outsourced activities, to decide to hire the provider of the risk mitigation functions, to assess whether the objectives are being adequately met, and, where necessary, to decide to adapt or terminate the contract with that provider, together with the performance of such assessment and decision-making.'[9]

The concept of control of risk is not new to the Guidelines and its references to control parallel changes in United States (US) Treasury regulations.[10] The connection between risk allocation and control was made in the 1995 version at 1.27 and repeated in the 2010 version at 1.49: 'In arm's length dealings it generally makes sense for parties to be allocated a greater share of those risks over which they have relatively more control.' The 2010 version included a new chapter, Chapter IX, on business restructurings which further developed the connection. It defined control in 9.23 and

7. *Ibid.*, 1.61.
8. *Ibid.*, 1.65.
9. *Ibid.*, 1.65.
10. For an account of the development of the concept in international guidance *see* Vikram Chand & Giovanni Lembo, *Intangible-Related Profit Allocation Within MNEs Based on Key DEMPE Functions: Selected Issues and Interaction with Pillar One and Pillar Two of the Digital Debate,* International Tax Studies, 6-2020, p. 9, and Fabian Arnold, *In-Depth Analysis of the Concept of Control over Risk,* International Transfer Pricing Journal, January/February 2021, pp. 37-38.

9.24 in similar terms to how it appears in the revised Guidelines and reverse-engineered in 9.22 what was meant in 1.49 and, therefore, what had been meant in 1995: 'The question of the relationship between risk allocation and control as a factor relevant to economic substance is addressed at paragraph 1.49.' Chapter IX has been revised in the 2022 TPG to be aligned with the detailed guidance on control in Chapter I.

In those earlier versions of control, somewhat clumsy attempts were made to validate as an arm's length test the connection between risk assumption and control of risk. In the 2022 Guidelines, it is left implicit that independent parties assuming in a transaction an economically significant risk that affects the pricing of the transaction would have the capability to evaluate the assumption of that risk, either by themselves or by appropriately commissioning expert advice, in order to conclude the pricing and other terms of that transaction.

The guidance is framed in terms of a binary test: if the party assuming risk based on a contract or other evidence exercises control, then that party's assumption of risk is confirmed. The control test under the transactional approach in the revised Guidelines seeks to determine the legal entity assuming risk and does not allocate risk to every party that might have an involvement in control. It is, therefore, unlike the approach adopted under the OECD Authorised OECD Approach (AOA)[11] for attributing profits to different parts of a legal entity based on certain people functions relevant to the economic ownership of assets and to the assumption of risk. The AOA envisages situations in which the risk is economically jointly owned by different parts of the same enterprise because functions leading to the assumption of risk are performed in more than one location within the single enterprise.[12]

The effect of the control test is to challenge the purported assumption of risk based on a contract or other evidence by a party to the transaction that is not involved in the control of that risk. There is no concept of partial control or a certain level of control that needs to be reached to justify the assumption of risk.

If a party to the transaction contractually assuming risk exercises control over that risk, then the risk remains with that party and no further analysis is required (*see* 1.87). The fact that other parties are capable of contributing to control does not complicate the analysis if the party contractually assuming risk is the only party that actually exercises control through capability and functional performance (*see* 1.93). Importantly, where the associated enterprise assuming risk controls that risk, no further analysis is required even if other enterprises also exercise control over the risk (*see* 1.94).

These statements recognise that in an multinational enterprise (MNE) group several associated enterprises may have involvement in risk management and may participate in the exercise of control (*see*, e.g., 1.76 where various parties in the MNE group may be involved in managing the inventory risk used as an illustration). Notwithstanding management and control by several associated enterprises, if control

11. *2010 Report on the attribution of profits to permanent establishments*, OECD, 22 July 2010 [AOA].
12. *See* the discussion of split functions in the AOA, p. 195.

is demonstrated by the enterprise contractually assuming risk, then there is no need to consider reallocation of that risk. Two or more parties to the transaction would only share an assumption of risks under the guidance if those parties contractually agree to do so, and that joint assumption of risk is borne out in their conduct (a matter relevant to the transactional profit split method, as discussed further below) (*see* 1.95).

There is no concept of relative control determining which party to the transaction assumes risk except in one defined, and probably unusual, circumstance. That circumstance is where the party contractually assuming risk, does not control the risk and multiple associated enterprises do control the risk. In that case, 'the risk should be allocated to the associated enterprise or group of associated enterprises exercising the most control'.[13] There is no other circumstance in the guidance where risk is allocated on the basis of relative contribution to control. In all other circumstances, the test is a simple one: does the party to the transaction contractually assuming risk control the risk? If it does, the existence of other parties exercising control through their decision-making is irrelevant to the assumption of risk.

To misread the guidance as referring to relative contribution to control leads to a further misconception[14]. The guidance provides that compensation to a party that controls risk will usually derive from the consequences of being allocated risk since that party 'will be entitled to receive the upside benefits and to incur the downside costs'.[15] Where a party contributes to the control of risk but does not assume the risk, the Guidelines state: 'compensation which takes the form of a sharing in the potential upside and downside, commensurate with that contribution to control, may be appropriate'.[16] That guidance was intended, I believe, to be interpreted as referring to incentivised pricing structures that may be seen between independent parties under which a party might be entitled to an additional fee (or suffer a penalty) when it meets (or fails to meet) certain pre-determined targets that may impact the risk consequences of the principal party assuming the underlying risk; those targets might relate to, for examples, time taken, cost variability, or the quality and effectiveness of the delivered product or service. It is precisely because risks are not shared that a measure of alignment of different interests can be achieved through incentivised pricing. A typical example of an incentivised pricing structure is that of a gain share in procurement contracts.[17] These typically adjust the fee by reference to a predefined share of upside

13. OECD TPG, 1.98.
14. For a fuller account of some of the misconceptions observed in practical application of the guidance *see* ANDREW HICKMAN, *Arm's Length Principle Mutations: Control of Risk in the OECD Guidelines and Variations in Practice,* MNE Tax, 13 January 2021, https://mnetax.com/arms-length-principle-mutations-control-of-risk-in-the-oecd-guidelines-and-variations-in-practice-42047.
15. OECD TPG, 1.105.
16. *Ibid.*
17. 'There are many different versions of the gain-sharing model. However, they will often stipulate that the service provider's fee is determined based on reached cost savings by the customer against a pre-defined baseline. The benefit of a gain-sharing model is that the service provider is incentivised to focus on the customer's cost savings or revenue realisation, thereby aligning a common interest and reduce the risk for the customer that the payment of fees in an outsourcing agreement are wasted.' *See Pricing models in outsourcing agreements: alternatives, adjustments and the need for transparency,* OLE HORSFELDT, *Outsourcing Global Guide,* Thomson Reuters

benefit arising directly from the procurement activity, such as cost savings. The UN Manual discusses incentivised procurement fee structures and indicates: 'In practice hybrid fee structures may be seen, combining a commission on managed spend with a gain-share element.'[18] In such a pricing structure, the party providing procurement services does not assume the principal's risk associated with the goods or services procured but does contribute to the control of the principal's risk. As the UN Manual states: 'recipient associated enterprises would be prepared to pay more for a procurement service that reduces or eliminates their risks, but care needs to be taken to ascertain that risks have in fact been mitigated for the recipient associated enterprises, and that the group procurement company contributes to such mitigation by performing risk control functions'.[19]

Unhappily, the guidance in 1.105 seems to be interpreted as meaning a transactional profit split method may be applied. However, this erroneous interpretation[20] has been corrected by the guidance on profit splits released in 2018[21] which revises Chapter II of the TPG: 'the mere fact that an entity performs control functions in relation to a risk will not necessarily lead to the conclusion that the transactional profit split is the most appropriate method in the case'.[22] References to 1.105 in Chapter VI of the Guidelines are consistent with the interpretation that contribution to control of economically significant risks does not lead to the application of a profit split method. Rather, contribution to control may lead to the further determination that 'arm's length remuneration of these functions would include a profit sharing element'.[23] Remuneration that includes a profit-sharing element does not denote the application of a profit split but describes incentivised pricing structures. It is noted that the equivalent to 1.105 of the TPG is worded as follows in the UN Manual: 'Similarly, where a party is performing control functions, this should be taken into account even if it does not assume the risk relating to those control functions. The form of this compensation will depend on the arrangements between the enterprises and the nature of the contribution: it may be appropriate for such a party to share in the potential upside and downside consequences resulting from the playing out of the underlying risk. Alternatively, the contribution might be compensated in a manner that is not contingent on the underlying risk.'[24] This wording emphasises that contingent pricing based on the underlying risk may in some circumstances be appropriate, but the guidance does not mandate or describe the profit split method.

---

Practical Law https://uk.practicallaw.thomsonreuters.com/w-010 9726?transitionType=Default&contextData=(sc.Default)&firstPage=true#co_anchor_a975706.

18. UN Manual, 5.14.1.2.
19. *Ibid.*, 5.12.6.
20. The error in this interpretation has been extensively analysed in Eyal Gonen, Leonid Karasik & Michael McDonald, *Control over Risk, DEMPE Functions, and the Remuneration of R&D Service Providers*, Tax Notes International. Volume 102, June 21, 2021, pp. 1625-1627.
21. OECD (2018), *Revised Guidance on the Application of the Transactional Profit Split Method: Inclusive Framework on BEPS: Action 10*, OECD/G20 Base Erosion and Profit Shifting Project, OECD Paris. www.oecd.org/tax/beps/revised-guidance-on-the-application-of-the-transactional-profit- split-method-beps-action-10.pdf.
22. OECD TPG, 2.137.
23. *Ibid.*, 6.70 and 6.72.
24. UN Manual, 3.4.4.43.

The misreading of 1.105 to support profit splits contains a logical inconsistency. The purpose of the control test is to identify the party to a transaction assuming risk, and an important consequence for transfer pricing flows from the finding. The important consequence is that the profits or losses arising from risk outcomes rest with the party assuming the risk (*see* 1.106) and that a party not assuming risk will not be entitled to returns or bear losses associated with that risk. Having spent the effort in applying the control of risk framework to identify the party assuming risk, it is logically inconsistent to read 1.105 as saying, despite that analysis, if there is a party that does not assume risk it can nevertheless share in the risk outcomes. It seems inconceivable that this paragraph could be taken to mean that a party which does not assume risk should have a pricing mechanism which reflects the outcome of assuming risk that it has been determined it does not assume.

The revised guidance on profit splits is consistent with the view that profits which reflect the playing out of risks should be split only between the parties assuming those risks. The guidance endorses the application of a profit split where both parties share the assumption of risks in relation to the transaction, as envisaged in 1.95, and where the split of actual profits arising from the transaction will reflect the playing out of the risks assumed by each party.[25] The guidance on profit splits is unequivocal on this point: the splitting of profits 'would only be appropriate where the accurate delineation of the transaction shows that the parties either share the assumption of the same economically significant risks associated with the business opportunity or separately assume closely related, economically significant risks associated with the business opportunity and consequently should share in the resulting profits or losses'.[26] The guidance in 1.105 cannot properly be read to mean that a party not assuming a risk should share in a split of the profits which incorporate risk outcomes, or to signify an endorsement of profit splits that is contrary to the extensive qualification of profit splits in the revised Chapter II of the Guidelines.

It is worth pointing out that in the discussion of group treasury companies in the guidance on financial transactions, it is acknowledged that treasury companies contribute to the management of cash and liquidity and make the financing of the MNE group as efficient as possible (*see* 10.39-10.50). They are likely, therefore, to make some contribution to the control of risks, but it is strongly implied in the guidance that they are unlikely to control risk (*see* 10.49). The guidance suggests that a treasury function will usually be a support service (*see* 10.45), even though it is acknowledged it may perform complex functions (*see* 10.47). Notwithstanding the contribution of a treasury company to cash and liquidity risk, and to the meeting of financial performance targets, there is no suggestion in the guidance that a treasury company should typically participate in a profit split.[27]

25. OECD TPG, 2.139-142.
26. *Ibid.*, 2.159.
27. I am characterising a treasury company as a facilitator not as an investor with the result that the guidance on the return to the funder of development of intangibles in 6.64 does not apply.

## III CHAPTER I GUIDANCE

### 1 Financial Transactions, Cash-Boxes, and Allocation of Capital

The previous section outlined the framework for allocating risks that had been agreed when the attention of the OECD drafting process returned to focus on providing tailored guidance on financial transactions. However, financial transactions were not far from the drafters' thoughts in revising Chapter I since attempts, that were eventually delayed, had been made to meet the original BEPS timetable of producing transfer pricing guidance on financial transactions concurrently with the Chapter I revisions. In addition, the BEPS transfer pricing initiative was somewhat overshadowed by concerns caused by profit shifting to so-called cash-boxes, capital-rich group companies that are the vehicles for asset ownership or intra-group funding. The Executive Summary to the Report accompanying the release of what is now the revised guidance in Chapter I highlighted how the problem of cash-boxes had been addressed:

> The revised guidance also addresses the situation where a capital-rich member of the group provides funding but performs few activities. If this associated enterprise does not in fact control the financial risks associated with its funding (for example because it just provides the money when it is asked to do so, without any assessment of whether the party receiving the money is creditworthy), then it will not be allocated the profits associated with the financial risks and will be entitled to no more than a risk-free return, or less if, for example, the transaction is not commercially rational and therefore the guidance on non-recognition applies.[28]

The solution presented in Chapter I is one of pricing and allocation of profits, not one involving challenges to the allocation of capital. It reflects concerns on the part of countries involved in the BEPS process to continue to direct the application of the arm's length principle to issues of pricing, and not to extend further its application to changing the structure of the transaction. The allocation of capital was not directly challenged under the revisions to the transfer pricing rules, but the party entitled to any risk premium associated with the use of capital was challenged.[29]

An extreme illustration of the impact of the reallocation of risk is Example 3 in Chapter I. In that illustration, the legal owner of an asset, Company A, is found not to have control over the economically significant risks associated with the investment in and exploitation of the asset:

> The functional contribution of the legal owner of the asset is limited to providing financing for an amount equating to the cost of the asset. However, the functional analysis also provides evidence that Company A has no capability and authority to control the risk of investing in a financial asset. Company A does not have the capability to make decisions to take on or decline the financing opportunity, or the

28. OECD (2015), *Aligning Transfer Pricing Outcomes with Value Creation, Actions 8-10 – 2015 Final Reports*, OECD/G20 Base Erosion and Profit Shifting Project, OECD Publishing, Paris, p. 11, http://dx.doi.org/10.1787/9789264241244-en.
29. For a critical evaluation of the approach adopted in the Guidelines *see* Richard S. Collier & Joseph L. Andrus, *Transfer Pricing and the Arm's Length Principle after BEPS*, Oxford, 2017, 7.22-42 in particular.

> capability to make decisions on whether and how to respond to the risks associated with the financing opportunity. Company A does not perform functions to evaluate the financing opportunity, does not consider the appropriate risk premium and other issues to determine the appropriate pricing of the financing opportunity, and does not evaluate the appropriate protection of its financial investment.[30]

Two consequences flow from this illustration. The first is that Company A does not meet the control test to verify its assumption of risk:

> However, the functional analysis also provides evidence that Company A has no capability and authority to control the risk of investing in a financial asset. Company A does not have the capability to make decisions to take on or decline the financing opportunity, or the capability to make decisions on whether and how to respond to the risks associated with the financing opportunity. Company A does not perform functions to evaluate the financing opportunity, does not consider the appropriate risk premium and other issues to determine the appropriate pricing of the financing opportunity, and does not evaluate the appropriate protection of its financial investment. In the circumstances of Example 3, Company A would not be entitled to any more than a risk-free return as an appropriate measure of the profits it is entitled to retain, since it lacks the capability to control the risk associated with investing in a riskier financial asset. The risk will be allocated to the enterprise which has control and the financial capacity to assume the risk associated with the financial asset.[31]

This conclusion suggests that Company A remains the nominal provider of capital, but the return to capital is reallocated in accordance with the reallocation of risk.

The second consequence is that unanticipated profits or losses would not be allocated to Company A since it is not allocated the risk associated with unanticipated returns: 'Accordingly, if the asset in Example 3 were unexpectedly destroyed, resulting in an unanticipated loss, that loss would be allocated for transfer pricing purposes to the company or companies that control the investment risk, contribute to the control of that risk and have the financial capacity to assume that risk, and that would be entitled to unanticipated profits or losses with respect to the asset.'[32] The example has already stated that Company A is treated in substance as having a financial asset, and so the example seems to postulate two assets, one financial and one physical. The destruction of the physical asset could in other circumstances give rise to a possible write-down of the financial asset, but this is not envisaged in the example. Instead, it is explicitly stated that Company A continues to be paid its risk-free return by the party or parties allocated the unanticipated losses (*see* final sentence of 1.106). Company A thus appears to be deemed to hold a completely secure and enduring financial investment that continues to generate a return commensurate with its risk-free status notwithstanding the destruction of the physical asset that was acquired through that investment.

30. OECD TPG, 1.85.
31. *Ibid.*, 1.103.
32. *Ibid.*, 1.106.

The guidance has little room for manoeuvre given the principles the example seeks to illustrate. In acknowledging that Company A remains the capital provider, and in determining that it is entitled to a risk-free return, Company A's deemed financial asset must be one with no risk of loss. It seems, therefore, that Company A will continue to be compensated with a risk-free return in periods after the destruction of the asset and cessation of its ability to generate income, and potentially *ad infinitum*. The outcome flows logically from the constraints caused by unwillingness to contemplate that the application of the arm's length principle could reallocate capital from Company A and ignore for transfer pricing purposes the transaction involving Company A.

## 2 Non-recognition

Nevertheless, the discussion of Example 3 in the Guidelines does hint at a way potentially to reallocate capital and ignore Company A for transfer pricing purposes. The hint lies in a footnote in 1.103 and in the reference at the end of 1.103 to making an assessment of the commercial rationality of the transaction based on the guidance on recognition of the accurately delineated transaction in section D.2 of Chapter I. It is noteworthy that the same reference was deemed important enough to appear in the Executive Summary, quoted above. Treating Company A as permanently entitled to a risk-free return on a deemed financial investment equivalent to the cost of the physical asset and simultaneously positing the destruction of that physical asset is starting to look commercially irrational, particularly from the perspective of Company B that is deemed to have incurred an obligation to pay an indefinite risk-free return out of highly-risky and finite anticipated earnings. Looking at the totality of the arrangements, for one party to be entitled to a risk-free return when the funds are invested in a depreciating and risky asset appears commercially unrealistic. But if Company A were no longer to be paid a risk-free return, perhaps because of the destruction of the physical asset, then it would have assumed risk contrary to the principles of control and would have required more than a risk-free return. Funding the acquisition of a physical asset subject to risk of capital loss through a deemed risk-free financial investment seems to raise the potential application of the non-recognition criteria of commercial irrationality and ability to reach prices acceptable to the parties (*see* 1.122). If a fundamental principle underlying Example 3 is that Company B is allocated all relevant risks of investment and all the associated risk return, then there is no place for another party operating as a commercially rational funder. A rational outcome would be to deem that Company B, in keeping with the risk return it is required to be allocated, is reallocated capital with the effect that it is using its own capital to acquire its own asset, and Company A is ignored. Such an outcome may meet the requirements in the guidance that the replacement structure 'should comport as closely as possible with the facts of the actual transaction undertaken whilst achieving a commercially rational expected result that would have enabled the parties to come to a price acceptable to both of them at the time the arrangement was entered into.'[33]

33. *Ibid.*, 1.124.

My view is that it would have been unacceptable to some countries when the revised guidance was being debated to have explicitly provided that the arm's length principle could reallocate capital for transfer pricing purposes. In the 2014 Discussion Draft, various solutions were presented for public comment that sought to address the issue of inappropriate allocation of capital, including the concept of 'independent investor' under which the capital would be deemed to have been contributed to the company providing the more rational investment opportunity to an independent investor.[34] This, and other ideas, attracted little support. It was more acceptable to suggest that the capital flows as structured should be respected, but the returns to capital could be priced in a way that reallocated the risk return to a party that did not provide capital. Nevertheless, the guidance on non-recognition is explicitly flagged as having relevance, opening the possibility that application of the carefully circumscribed non-recognition guidance could reallocate capital under the arm's length principle.

This framework of verifying contractual assumption of risk by reference to control, reallocating risk, determining whether a party is entitled to any risk premium associated with the use of its capital, and potentially re-drawing the structure of the transaction is one which determined the scope and boundaries of the guidance on financial transactions. Some of the implications for financial transactions are discussed in the following section.

## IV CHAPTER X GUIDANCE

### 1 Allocation of Risks for Financial Transactions

The guidance on financial transactions in what is new Chapter X of the 2022 Guidelines, promptly references the principles of Chapter I, and endorses the conclusions about risk allocation and returns in that Chapter and illustrated in Example 3:

> When, under accurate delineation, the lender is not exercising control over the risks associated to an advance of funds, or does not have the financial capacity to assume the risks, such risks should be allocated to the enterprise exercising control and having the financial capacity to assume the risk (see paragraph 1.98 of Chapter I). For instance, consider a situation where Company A advances funds to Company B. Consider further that the accurate delineation of the actual transaction indicates that Company A does not exercise control functions related to the advance of funds but that Company P, the parent company of the MNE group, is exercising control over those risks, and has the financial capacity to assume such risks. Under Chapter I analysis, Company P will bear the consequences of the playing out of such risks and Company A will be entitled to no more than a risk-free return (*see* section D.1.2.1 in Chapter I).[35]

34. Public Discussion Draft BEPS Actions 8, 9 and 10: Discussion Draft on Revisions to Chapter I of the Transfer Pricing Guidelines (including risk, recharacterisation, and special measures), OECD, 19 December 2014, p. 42, https://www.oecd.org/ctp/transfer-pricing/discussion-draft-actions-8-9-10-chapter-1-TP-Guidelines-risk-recharacterisation-special-measures.pdf.
35. OECD TPG, 10.25.

The guidance also gives prompt emphasis to the principles of non-recognition in 10.7 and signals a higher priority to this mechanism than given to it in Chapter I. Some of the reasons for this are discussed in the following section.

## 2 Riskiness of Financial Transactions and Non-recognition

Given the timing of its drafting, there should be no inconsistency between the guidance on financial transactions in Chapter X and the principles of risk allocation already published in Chapter I. However, there are some differences which arise from the differences between financial transactions and non-financial transactions. At the risk of over-generalisation, when analysing a transaction involving, for instance, the supply of laptops, the arm's length price will need to consider which party bears risks such as obsolescence or supply chain disruption, but the analysis of risk in such a case will likely involve incremental changes to the price and will rarely be systemic such that there might be a basis for determining that the transaction itself is too risky and requires structural modification to be compatible with arm's length terms. Indeed, an important principle of Chapter I is that in a transfer pricing analysis one should seek to price the accurately delineated transaction as actually structured by the parties, and that the obligation to find a price does not depend on observation of the same transaction with similar riskiness between independent parties. The emphasis on that principle changes in the guidance on financial transactions.

There are two mechanisms in Chapter I that bring riskiness into consideration under an arm's length test. One is the requirement that the party supposedly assuming risk should have financial capacity to bear the anticipated risk. Financial capacity is defined as 'access to funding to take on the risk or to lay off the risk, to pay for the risk mitigation functions and to bear the consequences of the risk if the risk materialises. Access to funding by the party assuming the risk takes into account the available assets and the options realistically available to access additional liquidity, if needed, to cover the costs anticipated to arise should the risk materialise.'[36] Subsequent examples state as an assumed fact whether financial capacity is satisfied or not satisfied, and do not turn on examining whether riskiness is too high for financial capacity. The guidance gives the impression that the financial capacity test in Chapter I is not regarded as a sensitive one involving precise calibrations of riskiness and capacity.

The second mechanism involves non-recognition as discussed in section D.2 of Chapter I. That section is headed 'Recognition of the accurately delineated transaction' reflecting the positive emphasis in the guidance that the accurately delineated transaction should be recognised and priced accordingly (*see* 1.121). Cautionary guidance appears several times in the short section that the mere fact that the transaction may not be seen between independent parties does not mean that it does not have characteristics of an arm's length arrangement. The criteria for non-recognition focuses on commercial irrationality inherent in the controlled transaction as accurately delineated that prevents determination of a price acceptable to both parties (*see* 1.122). Both

36. OECD TPG, 1.64.

illustrations of the criteria in the guidance involve excessive risks that prevent a price being determined, with the emphasis in Example 1 (*see* 1.126-1.127) being on the commercial irrationality of the transaction resulting in the impossibility of finding an acceptable price, and the emphasis in Example 2 (*see* 1.128) being on the entirely speculative nature of valuation arising from the manner in which the transaction is structured. Thus riskiness tends to appear in Chapter I as something exceptional, associated with commercial irrationality rather than with the fundamental nature of the commercial transaction as it is in the case of financial transactions.

Another difference between risks in non-financial and financial controlled transactions is that in non-financial controlled transactions the risks can be allocated by virtue of the controlled relationship, but the riskiness tends not to be determined or influenced by the controlled relationship but by external factors affecting controlled and uncontrolled parties alike. As a result, Chapter I tends to focus on the means to test whether the assumption of risk is affected by the controlled relationship. Once the party assuming risk is verified, for example once the party assuming obsolescence risk in the case of supply of laptops is determined, then consequences flow to controlled and uncontrolled parties alike in accordance with market conditions. In contrast, in the case of financial transactions both the allocation of risks and the consequences of risk assumption – the riskiness of the transaction – can be determined or influenced by the controlled relationship. This is because risk is systemic in a financial transaction and a significant source of risk and its consequences involve the financial structure of the transacting party. The financial structure of a controlled borrower can be determined and changed by the controlling shareholder and so there is capability for both the risk itself and also the consequences of assumption of that risk to be influenced by the controlled relationship.

As a result, the guidance on financial transactions focusses not only on whether the allocation of risk is affected by the controlled relationship, but also on whether the riskiness is affected by the controlled relationship and whether the risks require to be modified so that the transaction conforms to what can be observed between independent parties. Consideration of risk in financial transactions not only involves the verification of the controlled party assuming risk, for example credit risk in a loan transaction, but also needs to consider whether the credit risk itself is different in its riskiness to what would be assumed by an uncontrolled party. In non-financial transactions covered by Chapter I, therefore, the emphasis is on understanding the risks arising from the transaction that affect arm's length pricing and in determining which party should be allocated those risks. In financial transactions, that element is present, but is supplemented by consideration of whether the riskiness associated with the transaction as structured by the taxpayer is compatible with arm's length terms. In a nutshell, in a financial transaction equivalent to the supply of laptops, consideration can be given to whether the controlled transaction should be for 100 laptops, for 60, or for none at all.

These differences lead to the mechanism of non-recognition being given a more prominent position in the guidance on financial transactions. The connection between non-recognition and financial transactions is long-standing and signified desire on the part of some OECD members to place thin-capitalisation rules within the scope of

Article 9. Thus, the early articulation of the guidance on non-recognition in the 1995 version of the Guidelines at 1.37 included as the first example authorisation to treat a loan as a subscription of capital based on, it was claimed, an economic substance test which has now been replaced in the current guidance.[37]

In the case of non-financial transactions non-recognition is exceptional. The plain message is that you should always try to price the accurately delineated transaction as structured. In contrast the guidance on financial transactions opens with a section that specifically addresses whether the transaction as structured by the taxpayer should be respected, and whether the balance of debt and equity and the consequential riskiness of the transaction conform to observable parameters in transactions between independent parties. To return to the laptops, it would be rare to determine that the supply of 100 laptops should be for only 60, whereas consideration of a financial transaction appears to begin with consideration of whether the loan of 100 should be recognised and substituted with a loan of 60 and equity of 40. Therefore, the guidance on financial transactions seeks not only to follow the principles of risk allocation under Chapter I, but also to verify the quantum of risk and limit it by reference to observations of the quantum of risk reflected in transactions between independent parties.

The way in which the guidance achieves the limitation of risk under the arm's length standard is a mixture of principles found in Chapter I – accurate delineation (10.6 and 10.12) and non-recognition (10.7). The guidance is rather sparse, reflecting the different policy and technical interpretations that countries may espouse, but the example that concludes the opening section at 10.13 seems drafted to persuade the reader that the solution is reached under the process of accurate delineation, whereas logically the solution can be reached only by invoking the principles of non-recognition. The conflating of the process of accurate delineation of the transaction with the process of non-recognition perhaps reflects the difficulty in reconciling different views among the OECD participants. Nevertheless, conflation is contrary to the guidance in Chapter I. In that guidance the two processes are distinct and sequential; it is only after the transaction has been accurately delineated that considerations of non-recognition may be relevant (*see* 1.120).

The example in 10.13 depends on the factual findings that the advance of funds is denominated as a 10-year loan and that the borrower is projected to be unable to service the loan. The first finding suggests that the advance has the characteristics of a loan. The second finding of fact suggests that the advance is too risky to be a loan that would be seen between unrelated parties. The process of accurate delineation cannot reconcile the contradictory facts without additional observations of the circumstances. In a different example, such additional evidence might include the specific purpose of the borrowing, any other commercial arrangements between the parties, and the potential availability of collateral including any assets in development. Accurate delineation depends on evidence that can be observed. Thus, accurate delineation can

37. For a fascinating exploration of the treatment of capital under Article 9 and the relevance of the non-recognition guidance before the BEPS revisions *see* COLLIER & ANDRUS, *supra* n. 29, Chapter 5.

observe excessive riskiness, but it cannot be an arbiter on riskiness or change it.[38] Nevertheless, the guidance goes on to suggest that the process of accurate delineation can determine the amount of funding that might be regarded as being within the parameters of risk for unrelated parties in order for the transaction to be acceptable as a loan for transfer pricing purposes. Thus, it is implied, a loan of, say, 100, becomes accurately delineated as a loan of, say, 60. But such transformation is not accurate delineation; instead it involves comparing what unrelated parties might have done, conforming the observed transaction to one which meets standards of arm's length behaviour, and substituting a different transaction to the one observed.

The proper process to arrive at the solution presented in the example would seem to involve reaching the conclusion under the first stage that the transaction as accurately delineated reveals commercial contradictions such that the process cannot move to pricing based on uncontrolled commercial transactions, but instead moves to a second stage of considering the application of the guidance on non-recognition. It is commercially irrational for one party to take on a loan that it cannot service, and for the other party to advance a loan for which it will receive no return; in addition, the inability of the purported borrower to service the loan indicates the impossibility of identifying a price for the transaction as accurately delineated that would be acceptable to each party. The principles of non-recognition seem applicable to this example, and would extend to the consideration of a replacement structure for the transaction that comports 'as closely as possible with the facts of the actual transaction undertaken whilst achieving a commercially rational expected result that would have enabled the parties to come to a price acceptable to both of them at the time the arrangement was entered into.'[39] Following this guidance, the replacement structure might be a loan that could be priced at an acceptable level by reducing the level of risk assumed or, if this proved impossible, the replacement structure would be regarded in its entirety as an advance of gifted capital.

It does a disservice to the guidance on accurate delineation to suggest that accurate delineation extends beyond identifying observable characteristics and can be used to correct observations of excessive riskiness and replace the transaction with something that is deemed to conform to a commercial standard of risk. Such a suggestion comes close to second-guessing what the transaction should have been and is removed from the process of delineating the characteristics of the actual transaction. The sole sanction for substitution of transactions is found in the guidance on non-recognition, and is accompanied by tight conditions.

Useful clarification of the distinction between accurate delineation and non-recognition is found in the Chapter 9, 'Intragroup Financial Transactions,' of the UN Manual. There are several illustrations of accurate delineation (*see* Examples 4, 5, and 6 at 9.12.2.11-9.12.2.13), and a helpful analysis is provided in Example 1 of the distinct and sequential nature of the two processes of accurate delineation and non-recognition

38. Chand & Lembo, *supra* n. 10, p. 22, observe a blurred boundary between accurate delineation and non-recognition, but the distinction presented in the Guidelines is that of changing what is observed under accurate delineation and substituting something else.
39. OECD TPG, 1.124.

at 9.7.2.7. Example 1 notes that 'some features of the arrangements suggest hallmarks of equity rather than debt' (there is no maturity date for the loan, no security, interest is contingent on profits, and the borrower uses the funds to develop a new business concept) and 'may lead to a determination that for transfer pricing purposes the arrangement might not be delineated as a loan'. This is an important difference compared with the OECD example since it highlights that there are observable characteristics of the funding that provide evidence that it might not be a loan. Example 1 goes on to note the possible application of the non-recognition guidance: 'Moreover, even if the arrangement is delineated on the evidence as a loan, the commercial rationality of the transaction might be questioned and may prevent determination of a mutually acceptable price. In particular, it is doubtful that BCo and a third-party lender would have been able to agree terms for a loan given the very high level of risk to the lender.' The UN Manual is clear that it is the test presented by the guidance on non-recognition that can deal with excessive riskiness and may lead to the determination that the loan transaction could be substituted: 'This evidence may lead to the determination under the guidance of sections 3.3.2.1 to 3.3.2.6 [the non-recognition guidance similar to that in the OECD Guidelines] that the loan arrangement might not be recognized as an interest-bearing loan for transfer pricing purposes.'[40]

## 3 The Borrower's Risk

The second mechanism that addresses excessive riskiness in Chapter I of the OECD Guidelines - financial capacity to bear risk - is not emphasised in the guidance on financial transactions. It is acknowledged that the borrower assumes risks related to the acceptance and use of the funds (*see* 10.52), but the borrower's financial capacity to bear that risk is not illustrated. The financial capacity test in the various examples in the Guidelines is seen only from the lender's perspective. Since debt capacity is linked to financial capacity to take on the risk associated with debt, and since there is significant attention paid in the guidance to determining whether a purported loan should be regarded as a loan, it seems odd that the test established in Chapter I of whether the risk assumed exceeds financial capacity is not given more prominence in the guidance on financial transactions.

The examples of risk allocation and delineation of the transaction as one of funding in Chapter I (and in the guidance on intangibles in Chapter VI and the accompanying examples) tends to be from the perspective of the capital provider: the cash-box nominal legal owner is awarded a financing return, which may be a risk-free return depending on control of risk. There are no examples of control of risk from the perspective of the recipient of funds. This seems surprising given the description of the sources of risk in Chapter I that specifically includes financial capacity, and represents a missed opportunity in the dedicated chapter on financial transactions.

Risk is broadly considered in the Guidelines as 'the effect of uncertainty on the objectives of the business'[41]. The guidance points out that all risks are likely to affect

40. UN Manual, 9.7.2.7.
41. OECD TPG, 1.71.

a company's financial performance, but identifies specific financial risks 'related to the company's ability to manage liquidity and cash flow, financial capacity, and credit-worthiness'.[42] This list seems clearly to envisage risks associated with a company's capital structure and its financing. In a financial transaction such as a loan, the borrower takes on risk; it takes on the obligation to pay interest and repay the principal, and places limitations on available cash flows; it risks its ability to raise additional funds, and may put its assets at risk through the provision of collateral for the loan. Its performance under the loan contract risks its credit-rating and its cost of debt; there will also be further risks associated with the terms of the debt instrument itself, such as fluctuation in interest rates. The new guidance on financial transactions specifically acknowledges the general guidance on considering the perspectives of each party to the transaction (*see* 6.113), and discusses both the lender's and the borrower's perspectives. From the lender's perspective, the guidance discusses credit risk, but the guidance also discusses a range of risks from the borrower's perspective:

> 10.58. Borrowers seek to optimise their weighted average cost of capital and to have the right funding available to meet both short-term needs and long-term objectives. When considering the options realistically available to it, an independent business seeking funding operating in its own commercial interests will seek the most cost-effective solution, with regard to the business strategy it has adopted. For example, in respect of collateral, in some circumstances, assuming that the business has suitable collateral to offer, this would usually be secured funding, ahead of unsecured funding, recognising that a business's collateral assets and its funding requirements may differ over time, e.g. because collateral is finite, the decision to pledge collateral on a particular borrowing precludes the borrower from pledging that same collateral on a subsequent borrowing. Therefore, an MNE pledging collateral would take into account its options realistically available regarding its overall financing (e.g. possible subsequent loan transactions).
>
> 10.59. Borrowers will also consider the potential impact of changes in economic conditions such as interest rates and exchange rates, as well as the risk of not being able to make timely payments of interest and principal on the loan if the borrower's business encounters unexpected difficulties, and the risk of not being able to raise more capital (either debt or equity) if necessary.

Having made this relevant observation about the borrower's risk the guidance fails, however, to link the borrower's perspective of risks and the borrower's assumption of risk with the risk control framework. The risk control framework requires that the contractual assumption of risk by the borrower is verified through capability and performance. The test posed by control applies to the borrower: does the borrower make decisions to take on the debt risk and decide how to respond to the risk assumed? In the same way that the lender may not have controlled the credit risk through capability and performance, as described in 10.25, with the result that it is not allocated the risk return but only a risk-free return from the investment, so it is possible that a borrower may not have controlled the debt risk through capability and performance.

42. *Ibid.*, 1.72c.

The effect should be similar in that the borrower is not allocated the risk element of the payments but only a risk-free element associated with funds deposited with it.

For example, assume that Company A is lent 100 by its Parent under contractual terms which include a five-year loan period at a fixed interest rate of 8% and without any security. Company A has therefore assumed debtor risk associated with the obligations taken on under the loan. The risk control framework requires consideration of how Company A evaluated that risk, and in particular its capability to decide to take on the risk and its performance of that decision-making. That process may involve considering how a borrower determined its need for a capital injection, the determination of the amount required, whether alternative financing arrangements were considered, how it determined the lowest-cost or most flexible options, how it considered options for pledging collateral, and how it evaluated the impact of interest payments on cashflow and its ability to repay the principal. In the case of Company A it is found on the evidence that its Board was offered the loan by the Parent and the Board formally accepted the offer, without identifying any specific purpose for the funds, without evaluating different terms or other options, and without evaluating the impact on cashflow. In such a case, Company A does not exhibit control over the debtor risk with the conclusion that Company A is not allocated the risk element of the interest payments but only a risk-free element commensurate with receiving a deposit.

## 4 Completing the Solution to Risk Allocation

The conclusion in the preceding paragraph regarding the assumption of the borrower's risks flows from the treatment of risks under the control test, but the implications have not been developed in the Guidelines. One implication is that the application of the control test to the borrower's risk assumption could challenge the supposed assumption of debt risk when the loan can be priced, but the borrower does not control the risk. A further implication is that the movement of capital around an MNE group in which the nominal creditor does not assume risk under the control test and the nominal borrower does not assume risks under the control test would result in risk-free receipts and payments. As illustrated in the following example, adoption of this concept would offer a more complete solution to practical issues raised by the current scope of the examples in the guidance.

The following example builds on the elements of Example 3 in Chapter I discussed in III.1 above but continues to a more complete solution.

Company A is funded by its Parent with an appropriate balance of debt and equity. It has a loan from its Parent of 100 that has an arm's length interest rate of 10%. Company A makes a loan of 100 to an affiliated party, Company B; the loan has an arm's length interest rate of 10%. Company B has an appropriate balance of debt and equity. The accounts of Company A show interest income (from Company B) of 10 and interest expense (payable to Parent) of 10. For the purposes of the example, there is full support for the arm's length nature of the loan to Company B and for Company B's ability to control its risk. For the purposes of the example, a risk-free rate of return is 1%.

Under the principles of control of risk as illustrated in Chapter I, Company A does not meet the conditions for control of its risk when investing in a loan to Company B. Control is exercised by Parent. Therefore, Chapter I and the guidance on financial transactions explicitly endorse a reallocation of investment risk from Company A to Parent. This means that the investment income of Company A is reduced to a risk-free return of 1, and the parent is allocated the risk element of the return of 9.

This is as far as the explicit illustrations extend in Chapter I and in the guidance on financial transactions, unless the guidance on non-recognition is relevant. However, in this example, the situation as described is not complete. In this first stage Company A is left with a tax loss of 9, since its investment income is reduced to 1 but its costs remain at 10. The Parent is left doubly taxed since it retains its original interest income of 10 and is allocated income from Company A of 9 which relates to the loan interest payable by Company B.

Possible completion of the situation of the parties in this example is not explicitly illustrated by the current guidance. One way, as illustrated in the discussion of Example 3 above, would be to invoke non-recognition since Company A can no longer service its loan from the Parent and the commercial rationality of the loan is brought into question. The replacement structure under non-recognition guidance may be to consider the loan flowing from the Parent to Company B. This may be a simpler solution, and it is a pity that the guidance in Chapter X is not clearer on the application of non-recognition.

However, another option that is consistent with the principles of the guidance on control of risk but which is not mentioned, is to consider the debtor risk. Let us assume that Company A, in addition to not meeting the conditions for control of its investment risk, additionally does not meet the conditions for control in assuming its debtor risk on its loan from Parent. According to the principles of control of risk, this would mean that Company A in substance has been the depository of funds in a risk-free arrangement and would pay no more than a risk-free return on the funds that have been deposited with it. It follows, therefore that the guidance does not endorse the assumption of debtor risk by Company A and would exclude the risk element from payments made. This means that the payment made by Company A to Parent is reduced to a risk-free return of 1.

In this completed solution, Company A no longer has a tax loss, but has income of 1, as determined in the first stage, and costs reduced to 1, representing a risk-free return payable to Parent on the funds deposited by Parent. Parent no longer has interest income of 10 on its loan to Company A since Company A does not assume debtor risk, but has a risk-free return of 1 on its deposit. Thus the Parent has reallocated income of 9 under the first stage, which relates to the loan interest payable by Company B, and a risk-free return on its deposit in Company A of 1.

The outcome is correct for the Parent since it exercises control of the loan of 100 ultimately invested in Company B and should receive the interest income. The outcome for Company A is correct since, on the assumptions in the example, it is a passive vehicle with no control over its investment risk or over its debtor risk. Table 35.1 provides a summary of the example, illustrating how the Chapter I guidance is extended to provide a complete solution.

*Table 35.1 Summary of Example*

| *Facts of Example* | *Profits Originally Presented* | | *Chapter I Explicit Solution Where Company A Does Not Meet Control Test on Its Investment Risk (Unless Non-recognition Applies)* | | *Complete Solution Where Company A Does Not Meet Control Test on Its Borrowing Risk* | |
|---|---|---|---|---|---|---|
| **Parent Company** | Income | 10 | Income | 10 | Reduced income on its risk-free deposit in Company A | 1 |
| | Profits | 10 | Reallocated risk income from Company A | 9 | Reallocated risk income from Company A | 9 |
| | | | Profits | 19 | Profits | 10 |
| *Parent lends 100 at 10%* | | | | | | |
| **Company A** | Income | 10 | Risk-free income | 1 | Risk-free income | 1 |
| | Costs | –10 | Costs | –10 | Risk-free costs | –1 |
| | Profits | 0 | Losses | –9 | Profits | 0 |
| *Company A lends 100 at 10%* | | | | | | |
| **Company B** | Costs | –10 | Costs | –10 | Costs | –10 |

Readers will note that in this contrived example, in which Company A's income and expenditure are in the same amounts and on the same terms, the complete solution leaves the parties with the same profits as they had before any adjustments. However, the practical point is that the partial Chapter I explicit solution may create problems of double taxation if the tax authority of the Parent seeks to tax the reallocated risk income on top of its originally returned income. The taxpayer would likely need to invoke the Mutual Agreement Procedure (MAP) to eliminate double taxation, but even then the correct outcome should not leave Company A with losses since it does not assume risk. The lack of explicit guidance in the TPG on control of debtor risk may make reaching agreement under MAP in line with the principles of this example unnecessarily hard.

## V CONCLUDING REMARKS

The illustration discussed in the preceding section assists in drawing some conclusions about allocation of risk and return in the revised Guidelines.

The first is that the risk control framework can be applied in ways not explicitly illustrated either by Chapter I or in the guidance on financial transactions but which are consistent with the principles of that guidance, and which could provide logical completion to financial arrangements which would otherwise produce incomplete solutions. It seems a missed opportunity to rely entirely on the guidance on risk allocation in Chapter I without illustrating the application of the principles more completely by reference to the situation of financial transactions in the new Chapter X. In particular, clearer illustration of the application to financial transactions of the principles of non-recognition would be helpful given the greater prominence afforded to that mechanism. The missed opportunity is heightened since a thorough grounding of the principles in illustrations is essential in interpreting and applying those principles in practice when the evidence may not be as clear as the necessarily assumed facts of examples.

The challenges in applying the risk control framework in practice reflect the heavy burden of complexity placed on it, which stems from the continuing theoretical difficulty encountered in dealing with capital under transfer pricing rules based on Article 9. On the one hand the Guidelines advocate encouragement to recognise in most cases the adopted structure of transactions and to find a price; the Guidelines do not consider the allocation of capital as part of the financial relations between associated enterprises which can be examined and adjusted under the assumption that the parties were independent. On the other hand, considerable efforts are made by the drafters of the Guidelines to use the pricing rules to inhibit the effect on profits of capital allocations which are deemed to offend a standard. The reallocation of risk return to capital depending on capability and performance of functional control proved the central way in which risk return is reallocated without directly challenging the allocation of capital.

CHAPTER 36

# The Allocation of Risks and Returns to Treasury Entities

*Richard Collier & Dan Pybus*[*]

## I INTRODUCTION

This chapter is concerned with the allocation of risks and returns to treasury entities. In referring to treasury entities, we mean group treasury entities whose operations normally include the funding of group companies. The activities of such group treasury operations may vary materially from one multinational enterprise (MNE) group to another. At a minimum, the business operations may include entering into, and monitoring, a small number of related party loans (in an extreme case, the provision and monitoring of a single loan), possibly with some limited hedging activity relating to the hedging of interest rate and currency risk and the investment of surplus cash. At the other end of the scale, the larger, and more sophisticated group treasury operations may have responsibilities to manage the long- and short-term funding of the group coupled with a large portfolio of group loans and significant hedging activity. This may also include managing cash and liquidity in the group, including operating cash pooling and netting arrangements, investing surplus cash, and entering into financial guarantee arrangements. They may also manage regional or group banking relationships.

Given the mobility of capital and the historical effectiveness of offshore funding structures in international tax planning, offshore group treasury companies have been commonly used by MNEs. Indeed, such treasury entities have been a staple of

* The views and opinions set forth herein are the personal views or opinions of the authors; they do not necessarily reflect views or opinions of the organisation with which the authors are associated.

international tax planning by MNE groups for several decades.[1] This is because, at least until the changes made by the Base Erosion and Profit Shifting (BEPS) project, the treasury entity could normally be created in a low- or no-tax jurisdiction and capitalised without adverse tax implications, with the capital then lent out in the form of intra-group loans to other subsidiaries in the group, typically in high-tax jurisdictions. This delivered the ability to strip profits (in the form of deductible interest, paid in respect of the loan funding) from the higher-tax jurisdictions where business operations were carried on, to the lower-tax jurisdiction of the treasury entity.[2]

Not surprisingly, group treasury entities were identified as a key target in the BEPS project,[3] with several of the BEPS Action points intended to help nullify or at least reduce their effectiveness in delivering tax planning advantages. These BEPS Actions include a number of specific transfer pricing measures discussed in the following section, but also other action points such as those concerned with restricting the deductibility of interest in the borrowing companies,[4] improving the effectiveness of controlled foreign company regimes,[5] and increased transparency and reporting measures.[6]

Treasury entities and group funding arrangements typically raise a wide number of tax issues, including, for example, issues relating to controlled foreign company rules and treaty issues such as the beneficial owner test. However, the discussion in this chapter is restricted to the income allocation issues[7] raised by treasury vehicles. The general treatment in the Transfer Pricing Guidelines of risks and returns is comprehensively addressed in the chapter in this book, *Allocation of Risks and Returns: Critical Issues for Financial Transactions* by Andrew Hickman. The material covered in that chapter is not repeated here but rather the discussion in this chapter is intended to complement that discussion by addressing a number of practical aspects of applying the transfer pricing rules in the context of group treasury operations, as well as by dealing with some additional matters not covered in that chapter.

In practice, the income allocation issues relating to group treasury entities commonly include both transfer pricing and permanent establishment (PE) issues. It is

1. In the mid-1980s, the OECD's discussion of what it described as the 'extensive use of "classical" tax havens' included the identification of base companies used to finance international operations – *see* OECD (1987) Issues in International Taxation, No. 1, International Tax Avoidance and Evasion, Four Related Studies, Tax Havens: Measures to Prevent Abuse by Taxpayers, at pp. 24-25. However, though often motivated by tax concerns, there are also many commercial reasons why treasury functions are centralised – e.g., management efficiencies, better financial risk management, economies of scale, etc.
2. A fuller discussion is contained in R.S. Collier & J.L. Andrus, *Transfer Pricing and the ALP after BEPS*, Oxford University Press, 2017, Chapter 5.
3. OECD (2013) Addressing Base Erosion and Profit Shifting, OECD Publishing, pp. 44, 48, 53.
4. OECD (2015), Limiting Base Erosion Involving Interest Deductions and Other Financial Payments, Action 4 – 2015 Final Report.
5. OECD (2015), Designing Effective Controlled Foreign Company Rules, Action 3 – 2015 Final Report.
6. OECD (2015) Transfer Pricing Documentation and Country-by-Country Reporting, Action 13 – 2015 Final Report.
7. References in this chapter to the 'income allocation rules', are intended to encompass the transfer pricing rules (OECD Model Tax Convention on Income and on Capital, Article 9) and the rules on the attribution of profits to PEs (Article 7 of the OECD Model).

also common for issues to arise concerning the relationship between the transfer pricing and PE profit attribution rules. We, therefore, deal with all these issues in the discussion below.

## II TRANSFER PRICING ISSUES

From a treasury transfer pricing perspective, there are two fundamental areas that need to be addressed: first, what are the appropriate arm's length returns from financing activities and, second, to whom are those returns allocable? We address each of these issues in turn below.

### 1 Returns from Financing

For many years groups have faced the issue of determining the appropriate arm's length remuneration for funding activity. In its most basic form, for example, for a single vanilla loan instrument, this would typically require the following:

(a) some form of credit assessment of the underlying borrower (to create a proxy credit rating corresponding to that which an external bank would typically perform when lending);
(b) a search for comparable loan instruments in the market; and
(c) the making of adjustments to those instruments (e.g., to adjust for the effect of a different maturity (duration) of the loan or for the impact of a different currency in which the loan is denominated, or to convert floating rate comparable instruments into fixed rate instruments).

With respect to the assessment of the credit rating of the borrower, a common starting point for many MNE groups is to look at the external credit rating produced for the group as a whole[8] and then utilise guidance which is available from the external rating agencies as to the extent to which that external credit rating may need to be adjusted (to reflect the creditworthiness of a subsidiary within the group).[9] The primary adjustment required would normally be in respect of what is known as 'implicit support'.

In the context of financing, the reference to implicit support relates to the expectation that a parent company will step in with financial assistance to support a subsidiary in the event of it encountering financial difficulties, notwithstanding the absence of any legal obligation to do so (such an obligation might arise where there is a legally enforceable guarantee arrangement involving the parent company).

8. This approach aligns with commentary in OECD (2022) Transfer Pricing Guidelines, OECD Publishing, C.1.1.4 'Use of MNE group credit rating', at p. 420.
9. This guidance, often referred to as notching guidance, is published by the rating agencies in order to take account of the presence or lack of extraordinary support (otherwise referred to as implicit support) that might be anticipated to be provided to a subsidiary by the wider group.

Following the leading case on this issue,[10] there has been much discussion of the issue and its treatment for transfer pricing purposes.[11] It is now clarified that the Organisation for Economic Co-operation and Development (OECD) takes the view that the effect of potential group support on the credit rating of an entity and any effect on that entity's ability to borrow or the interest rate paid on those borrowings would not require any payment or comparability adjustment, but should be taken into account when determining a subsidiary's creditworthiness.[12] This reflects a relaxation of a strict functionally separate enterprise approach to the interpretation of the arm's length principle (ALP) in favour of an approach which takes account of how a third-party lender would approach the pricing of a loan (such third-party lenders would normally appraise a subsidiary on the basis of it being part of the wider MNE group).

It follows from the above discussion that when using the external group credit rating as a starting point (which essentially reflects 100% implicit support from the group) for a subsidiary credit rating, a downward implicit support adjustment to the credit rating may be needed as it may not be the case (and it will often not be) that the subsidiary has the same credit rating as the wider group (e.g., given the size, market and product diversity of the group as a whole). As such, an adjustment to reflect the fact that the subsidiary does not receive 100% implicit support from the group would likely cause the subsidiary credit rating to be lowered below (i.e., made weaker than) that of the wider group.

In the absence of an external group credit rating, the credit rating agencies also publish methodology papers for each industry sector providing guidance on how they typically go about a credit assessment process relating to companies or MNE groups operating in that sector. These methodology papers are written so as to allow the user to determine a standalone credit rating for an entity (i.e., absent any form of implicit support). Many MNE groups utilise these methodology papers as a means of determining a standalone credit rating for a subsidiary, but like the use of the external group credit rating as a starting point, an adjustment for implicit support is again needed. The difference here is, as the starting point is the standalone credit rating of the subsidiary (reflecting, therefore, 0% implicit support), an upward adjustment may be required to the established standalone credit rating to reflect the financial support the subsidiary could expect from the wider group. As such, an adjustment to apply the effect of implicit support to the standalone credit rating would likely cause the subsidiary credit rating to be increased/strengthened and notched towards the group credit rating.

A third possible approach is to rely on the quantitative models that are available from third-party providers and which, through the input of certain financial inputs and

---

10. *General Electric Capital Canada, Inc. v. The Queen* (2009). The Canadian Tax Court's 2009 opinion was upheld by the Canadian Federal Court of Appeals in December 2010 – *see* 2010 FCA 344.
11. *See, e.g.*, B.T. Daba, OECD: Valuation of Implicit Support from a Transfer Pricing Perspective, 28(2) International Transfer Pricing Journal (2021).
12. *See* further OECD (2022) Transfer Pricing Guidelines, OECD Publishing, at 10.76-10.80.

data relating to a specific subsidiary, can produce a proxy credit rating.[13] However, it should be noted that the OECD has expressed some criticisms of this third approach.[14]

The task of identifying suitable comparable loan instruments in the market and making appropriate adjustments to reflect maturity and currency, etc. is materially simplified by the fact that traded debt instruments are observable in the market for a vast array of durations, credit ratings and currencies. This normally allows ready real-time pricing on a day-to-day basis. This in turn means that the comparability analysis in respect of financing returns is often significantly more straightforward than in the case of non-treasury-related transfer pricing analysis (where suitable comparable data may not be as readily available).

It may be seen from the above discussion that the pricing of the return from group loans is usually one of the more straightforward transfer pricing tasks. It is true that there has been a lack of clear guidance on how to price intercompany financing transactions, a matter that has been the subject of some criticism of the OECD, for example, by Vann and Cooper.[15] However, the OECD Guidance on Financial Transactions published in 2020 (which now forms Chapter X of the 2022 OECD Transfer Pricing Guidelines) has sought to address a number of the basic elements of the transfer pricing exercise relating to the transfer pricing of loans (drawing, in large part, from established practices across multiple territories over the past 10-15 years).

Despite the conclusion that the transfer pricing issues for the most basic form of financing are not normally especially problematic, there is an important caveat to be made. The discussion so far addresses only the most basic form of financing (a single, vanilla loan). However, the reality is that in-house treasury functions will often be responsible for a multitude of financing transactions (which will likely include a number of simple loan transactions, alongside some more complex loans, cash pooling arrangements, guarantees and other foreign exchange (FX)/netting arrangements). The operations of such a multifaceted treasury vehicle present much greater complexity for transfer pricing purposes. Broadly, the taxpayer is left with a choice - namely, whether to analyse the proper transfer pricing return on an individual transaction by individual transaction approach or alternatively to assess the overall return to the treasury vehicle in the light of the aggregate or portfolio of risks that it bears.

An individual transactional-based approach is probably more commonly seen in practice. However, it is time consuming, costly and may over/understate the return to the treasury entity by not accounting for the multiplicity and linkage of transactions passing through the entity at any one time. For example, if one were to look at the returns the treasury entity generates from loans that it makes, without considering the

13. Examples of such models are S&P's CreditModel and Moody's RiskCalc.
14. The OECD has expressed concern over the use of such models on the basis that "the results are not based on a direct comparison with transactions between independent parties but are subject to the accuracy of the input parameters, a tendency to rely more on quantitative inputs at the expense of qualitative factors, and a lack of clarity in the processes (i.e., the workings of the underlying algorithms and processes may not be transparent)'. *See* OECD (2022) Transfer Pricing Guidelines, OECD Publishing, p. 417.
15. Richard Vann & Graeme Cooper, 'Transfer Pricing Money: The Chevron Case', Sydney law School, Legal Studies Research Paper No. 16/72, August 2016.

fact that some of these loans simply mirror the terms and conditions of corresponding borrowings entered into by the treasury entity, it could lead to a materially higher amount of profit being retained in the treasury company than would be the case if an aggregate view had been taken. For this reason, it is also common for MNE groups to identify the overall treasury return to the treasury company (in some instances as a back-test or corroboration to a transaction-by-transaction approach and in others as a primary testing/pricing mechanism). As might be expected, identifying suitable comparables to size the overall return to the treasury vehicle can present additional challenges, given that a group treasury vehicle cannot normally be compared to a fully-fledged commercial bank (which is likely to have a different scale and range of risks for example). Equally, neither would it normally be appropriate to simply characterise a group treasury vehicle as fulfilling a mere administrative function, a matter which the OECD has acknowledged in the context of assessing the applicability of service returns to cash pool leaders that do more than a basic administrative function.[16]

In order to determine an appropriate overall return to the treasury vehicle, it is generally necessary to determine the level of equity capital that might be required to support the risks borne by the treasury vehicle. This might be achieved by resorting to reference material such as the Basel framework and determining a return on that identified equity using tools such as the Capital Asset Pricing Model (CAPM) which seeks to identify an appropriate return on equity using a market risk factor (a Beta) applied to a market risk premium (the difference between the market portfolio return and a risk-free return). Care is needed in applying this approach – *see, e.g.*, the European Commission's state aid assessment of Fiat's financing arrangements, whereby the Commission disagreed with the determination of the hypothetical regulatory capital according to the treasury vehicle in that case, noting that the amount of required capital had been understated due to a number of assumptions being made which deviated from what could have been anticipated had arm's length terms been applied.[17] This included the use of the minimum equity level rather than the published equity capital of the entity in the first place, but then noting that, even if this were appropriate, the taxpayer had also incorrectly applied the risk weighting of assets and misapplied the capital requirement ratios. The assessment further noted that financial institutions will rarely retain only the minimum equity prescribed under Basel and the return generated through the CAPM approach was also observed to be lower than what is typically achieved in the financial sector (more than 10%).[18]

It may be concluded that whilst the determination of basic funding returns for transfer pricing purposes can be relatively straightforward, where an in-house treasury

16. OECD (2022) Transfer Pricing Guidelines, OECD Publishing, p. 429.
17. European Commission (2015), Commission Decision of 21.10.2015 On State Aid SA.38375 (2014/C ex 2014/NN) which Luxembourg granted to Fiat.
18. The *Fiat* case has been the subject of an appeal to the European Court of Justice, leading to the judgment of that court in November 2022 – *see* Judgment of the Court (Grand Chamber) of 8 November 2022, *Fiat Chrysler Finance Europe and Ireland v. European Commission*, joined cases C-885/19 P and C-898/19 P, Document 62019CJ0885. The judgment did not expand in detail on the issues discussed here.

vehicle performs a diverse mix of activities, the transfer pricing analysis becomes more complicated.[19] Also, the comments made so far focus largely on the pricing aspects of a loan transaction, whereas there is also a range of other tax issues that will usually need to be considered in relation to any potential funding exercise from the borrower's perspective (e.g., withholding tax, restrictions on the overall amount of deductible interest that may be claimed by the borrower, thin capitalisation issues, etc.). While any deductible interest limitation and/or any thin capitalisation restriction is immediately an issue for the borrower, an assessment of whether a borrower can really sustain the levels of debt being advanced is a key aspect of risk control that must be demonstrated by the lender.

## 2 The Allocation of Funding Returns

In common with the treatment of non-financial transactions, it is not permitted under the OECD Guidelines to simply allocate the entire funding return established in the prior section to the treasury entity if it cannot be demonstrated that the treasury entity has the ability to control the funding risks associated with the underlying instrument. More specifically:

> When, under accurate delineation, the lender is not exercising control over the risks associated to an advance of funds or does not have the financial capacity to assume the risks, such risks should be allocated to the enterprise exercising control and having the financial capacity to assume the risk.[20]

A large portion of the guidance included in the OECD Financial Transactions Paper, and in particular the narrative in section F of that paper on 'Risk Free and Risk Adjusted rates of return', was written in response to the proliferation of 'cash-box' structures whereby entities set up to conduct group lending activities were considered to lack the substance to manage the risks associated with the underlying loan instruments. It is worth noting that several territories have introduced their own substance requirements (e.g., Luxembourg, Cyprus) which broadly align with, but offer more specificity than, the requirements outlined in the OECD Financial Transactions Paper.

It is made clear in Chapter 1 of the OECD Guidelines that:

> Where, in accordance with the guidance in this Chapter, the accurate delineation of the actual transaction shows that a funder lacks the capability, or does not perform the decision-making functions, to control the risk associated with investing in a financial asset, it will be entitled to no more than a risk-free return as an appropriate measure of the profits it is entitled to retain. In this context, the funder's costs related to the borrowing associated with the funding should be taken into account in determining the risk-free rate of return, and subject to other

19. Certain treasury transactions, such as entering into financial guarantees, may also raise complex transfer pricing issues, though these more complex transactions are outside the scope of the discussion in this chapter.
20. OECD (2022) Transfer Pricing Guidelines, OECD Publishing, p. 408. *See also* Transfer Pricing Guidelines at 1.98.

> constraints, the funded party would still be entitled to a deduction up to an arm's length amount in respect of the funding. The difference between those amounts would be allocable to the party exercising control over the investment risk in accordance with the guidance in this chapter.[21]

In simpler terms, if the lending entity lacks the requisite 'people substance' to support the lending arrangement (as reflected primarily in the decision-making which leads to the creation and management of the loan) then only a risk-free return should be allocated to the lending entity (after account is taken of the lending entity's own cost of funds). The remainder of any return from the funding activity is allocated to the vehicle that is in reality making the real decisions that create and manage the loan.

For example, assume a simple vanilla loan is made to a group borrower by a treasury vehicle in Country Y (with the loan funded through an equity injection in the lending entity). Assume also that the relevant decision-making relating to the loan (including whether to make a loan at all and on what terms) was exercised by a different group entity in Country X. In such a case, the OECD guidance requires that no more than a risk-free return would remain with the 'legal' lender (being the treasury vehicle in Country Y). Such a risk-free return might be determined by reference to the return on government security in the same currency as the functional currency of the lender. The risk premium element that is reflected in return on loan (most commonly accounting for most of the overall interest cost) would flow to the entity in Country X. The nature or character of the payment or allocation to the entity in Country X is not addressed by the OECD guidance, and this presents its own separate technical challenges. For example, which entity is treated as making the payment to the entity in Country X? What is the character of such payment for withholding tax purposes? Does this additional flow have consequential beneficial ownership impacts? etc. These difficulties would be magnified in the event there is an overall loss on the lending arrangement (e.g., where the loan is not repaid) as in such a case the loss would, on the same principles, presumably be allocated to the entity in Country Y – *see* further below.

In addition to the characterisation issue discussed above, there are various more detailed practical concerns in the application of this approach in a treasury context.[22] A number of these practical issues are discussed below.

For a tax authority in Country X to seek a return for the functions performed by the entity in that country (given the absence of substance in Country Y), it would need to have some visibility of the local functional activity and its linkage to the loans being made by the lending entity in Country Y. This makes the practical application of the rule very difficult even in an extreme case where there is no functionality in the lending entity. The issues will be much more complicated where there is a functional contribution to the creation and management of the loan by both the entity in Country X and the treasury entity in Country Y.

21. OECD (2022) Transfer Pricing Guidelines, OECD Publishing, D.1.2.2.1.
22. The practical experience of the OECD risk framework rules is surveyed in detail in R.S. Collier & I.F. Dykes, *The Virus in the ALP: Critique of the Transfer Pricing Guidance on Risk and Capital in the Light of the COVID-19 Pandemic*, 74 Bull. Intl. Taxn. 12 (2020).

If the lending entity (here the treasury vehicle in Country Y) was funded by a loan rather than by funds representing its equity base, and the terms of that loan mirror the terms of the loan made by the treasury vehicle to the group borrower, then the normal transfer pricing treatment would likely be to leave only a relatively modest spread in the treasury vehicle (probably determined as a number of basis points). In some instances, this spread might be lower than the return implied by leaving a risk-free return in the lending location. This would obviously be an incongruous result.

The OECD rules also raise some fundamental questions about what it is to control risk and how this is to be evidenced. The ability - or inability - to control risk is easier to evidence in the more extreme (but extremely rare) situations where the treasury entity wholly lacks people's substance. This would be especially true in situations involving a fully-fledged treasury operation (making simple and complex loans, operating cash pooling arrangements, entering into FX and interest rate hedging contracts, etc.) and it is clear that the relevant decision-making relating to those activities is not being performed in the treasury vehicle location. However, such a situation is not commonly encountered. As noted, difficulties arise in practice in the more common situation where participation in the relevant decision-making relating to treasury transactions is split between one or more group entities. In such cases, it is necessary to determine whether the joint participation prevents the treasury vehicle from being recognised as controlling the relevant financing risk.[23]

Issues may also arise in practice from the fact that treasury activities may be limited, particularly as the required people substance/decision-making for group lending may be very limited. The practical difficulty in such cases is that tax authorities may challenge treasury arrangements on substance grounds reflecting their unease with the low substance threshold that may apply in any particular case. For example, if a board meeting is convened to make a decision on single, vanilla loan, and the board is supplied with supporting materials (which may deal with rudimentary financing and commercial issues) to make a decision as to whether to lend or not, (and the board is qualified to make such a decision and makes the decision in the course of the meeting) then it would be expected that the relevant control of risk threshold (evidenced by the decision-making process) has been met. Ongoing control of the underlying risks may be limited to simply ensuring the underlying borrower remains solvent, makes its payments on time and is able to repay the debts when they fall due - and this might be achieved through appropriate outsourcing as permitted by the Transfer Pricing Guidelines,[24] with those outsourcing activities controlled through annual board meetings. However, notwithstanding that in this example, the relevant control of risk/decision-making requirements are arguably properly satisfied, the relatively modest functional activity that is required to achieve this result, coupled with the significant financial

23. The technical position is that the lending entity would be required to play at least some role in the decision-making relating to the control of risk and have the financial capacity to assume the risk - Transfer Pricing Guidelines at 1.65. However, there is some uncertainty as to the level of participation that is required to fulfil the test. *See*, e.g., R.S. Collier & I.F. Dykes, *On the Apparent Widespread Misapplication of the OECD Transfer Pricing Guidelines*, 76(1) Bull. Intl. Taxn. (2022), at section 3.3.2.
24. OECD, Transfer Pricing Guidelines at 1.65 and 1.66.

effects arising from the allocation of financing returns, means that in practice such arrangements involving limited treasury activity are frequently challenged by tax authorities.

A final practical point concerns what happens if there is a loss on loan. If, as in the example discussed earlier, the risk premium relating to a loan from a treasury vehicle in Country Y has been paid away to a related entity in Country X, what is the consequence of the loan going into default? At that point, the legal lender (here, the treasury vehicle in Country Y) would normally seek recourse for the outstanding capital. However, in this scenario, assume the legal lender does not control the risks associated with the lending for the purposes of the transfer pricing analysis. This means that in principle the return to the legal lender is limited – and in turn this must also mean that it should not bear the risk of the loan defaulting. The entity in Country X has received the risk premium which accounts for the underlying possibility of default of the borrower, so any bad debt write off should be borne in the books of that entity in Country X. That may be straightforward in technical terms, but mechanically it is difficult to see how this could be achieved as there is no loan in the books of the entity in Country X.[25] This means that a bad debt writes off would have to be somehow imputed in Country X, most likely by a special adjustment reflected in the tax computation of that entity.[26] The same arises in the event that the loan is transferred prior to maturity by the legal lender to another party as upon transfer, a gain or loss could be triggered, but again the legal lender would not be regarded as controlling such a risk and therefore entitled to neither gain nor loss beyond imputation of the risk-free amount.

It may be seen from this discussion of transfer pricing issues that whilst Chapter X of the OECD 2022 guidelines goes some way to assisting taxpayers in determining the appropriate allocation of funding returns in a transfer pricing context, a number of questions remain. This inevitably makes the practical application of the guidance difficult for both taxpayers and tax administrations.

## III PERMANENT ESTABLISHMENT ISSUES

### 1 The Relevance of PE Issues

PE issues are commonly relevant to cases involving separate legal entities which function within an MNE as treasury centres providing loans (and related services and facilities) to group entities. The reasons for the relevance of PE issues are largely concerned with concerns on the part of the tax authorities about the long-standing use of group treasury vehicles in MNE international tax planning.

As discussed further below, the work on one of the more important (in the present context) BEPS Action points lowered the PE threshold tests in Article 5 of the

25. The difficulty is not dissimilar to the inability to create a balance sheet intangible where DEMPE functions lie but where there is no legal ownership of any intangible or other asset.
26. This scenario raises doubts as to whether such a loss would be accepted by the tax authorities in Country X.

OECD Model. The effect, *inter alia*, is to widen the circumstances in which the operations of a group treasury entity may be vulnerable to a challenge based on the PE rules in states other than the one in which the treasury entity is resident for tax purposes. This is relevant to the discussion here because tax authorities will often wish to pursue PE issues in addition to any transfer pricing issues in relation to group lending arrangements. Such PE challenges may arise in the country of a group entity that is borrowing from a group treasury entity or in a country where a services or holding company or the ultimate parent company is located. The nature of such challenges is discussed further below. Underlying this PE challenges normally is the assumption that it may be possible to tax a greater return under the PE rules than is possible under the transfer pricing rules. This is a controversial point that is also discussed further below.

The impact of the above comments is that it is usually important to consider the relevant PE issues in addition to the relevant transfer pricing issues in analysing the tax position of group treasury entities. Specifically, this means addressing whether the arrangements under consideration involve the creation of any PE under the threshold tests of Article 5 of the OECD Model – and, if they do, it is necessary to address the quantum of attributable profit to that PE under the rules of Article 7 of the OECD Model. The third issue that normally needs to be addressed concerns the interactions between, and the differences in the result of applying, the transfer pricing rules and the PE attribution rules. All three matters are addressed below.

## 2 The PE Threshold Tests

The immediate relevance of the PE threshold issue is not that it necessarily affects the return to the treasury company but rather that it affects the state where that return is allocated and taxed.

The main practical concern stems from the inadvertent (unintended) creation of a PE. This is less commonly a matter concerning the fixed place of business test of Article 5(1) of the OECD Model as it would be unusual for the operations of a group treasury vehicle to create one or more branches in other states (though some treasury operations have in the past sometimes been structured as finance branches and it is also possible that unstructured activities in a group company on behalf of the treasury vehicle may create a fixed place of business PE).[27] It is in practice more likely that any issue would arise under the dependent agent PE rule of Article 5(5) of the OECD Model, for example, in the situation where there is some participation in the operations of a low-tax treasury vehicle by the employees of the group parent, or of another group subsidiary company, such as a regional services company or an intermediate holding company, acting under some form of services arrangement.[28] The nature of such participation could vary from,

27. Post-COVID, there is arguably an increased risk of employees working in different states to that in which the treasury vehicle is resident also creating a fixed place of business PE of the treasury entity.
28. Where a company acts on behalf of an enterprise the actions of the employees and directors of that company are considered together for the purposes of determining whether and to what extent the company acts on behalf of the enterprise – *see* para. 86 of the Commentary to Article 5 in the OECD Model.

at the one extreme, making all relevant operational decisions (such as whether to enter into a lending arrangement and on what terms) and then simply booking loans into the treasury vehicle or, at the other, simply providing information on the opportunity for, or information in connection with, a group loan to the employees of that vehicle. It follows that, correspondingly, the level of substance in the treasury vehicle may vary materially from one case to another. The position is arguably not helped by the relatively limited functionality or substance that is needed to support group treasury operations (especially if the number of loans and the accompanying hedging transactions, if any, is low). This is because, as discussed earlier, the level of substance required to conduct the operations of small-scale treasury vehicle may be quite limited.

The task of applying the dependent agent PE tests across this spectrum of situations is complicated by the vagueness of the relevant tests and the accompanying guidance. A further issue is that the terms of Article 5(5) were altered by the BEPS project, though there has been a mixed enthusiasm toward implementing the new measures in double tax treaties. The following comments, therefore, deal with the position before and after the BEPS changes.

The dependent agent PE test prior to the BEPS changes (which will remain the current test in those cases where the BEPS modifications have not been incorporated into the terms of an existing Article 5),[29] is concerned with whether a dependent agent has and habitually exercises an authority to conclude contracts on behalf of the enterprise (here, the treasury vehicle).[30] The test is likely to be relevant in those situations where a treasury entity is operationally not fully autonomous, such as where decisions on the making of group loans, or decisions on interest rate and foreign currency hedging, etc. are not made in the treasury entity but instead are determined by personnel in, say, the parent entity or in another subsidiary, with the loan then booked in the treasury vehicle. This raises the question of what level of participation in any decision is decisive to trigger the dependent agent test.

The description in the OECD Commentary to Article 5 of what is intended by the reference to concluding contracts is somewhat vague. It clearly includes actions that have the effect of concluding a contract at law, but in some instances, it might also include participation in the contracting process, such as in the negotiation of the contract.[31] It might be thought that the requirement for 'habitual' contracting might lessen the relevance of the test in cases of intra-group lending activity where the number of loans made is modest. However, the test of what is habitual is to be assessed on the basis of the commercial realities of the situation and depends on 'the nature of the contracts and the business of the principal'.[32] Where a dependent agent PE exists by virtue of this rule, the PE exists to the extent of the relevant activities of the dependent agent.[33]

29. It is of course also true that there may be no applicable double tax treaty meaning that the threshold issue will be settled by a domestic law test.
30. The contracts must relate to 'operations which constitute the business proper of the enterprise' - Commentary to Article 5 at para. 97.
31. OECD Model, Commentary to Article 7, para. 87.
32. *Ibid.*, para. 98.
33. *Ibid.*, para. 99.

Under Article 5(6) of the OECD Model, the dependent agent rule does not apply to an agent of independent status. The guidance in the OECD Commentary on the requirement for such independence is again somewhat vague. However, the issue is not usually relevant in cases involving group treasury activity because, whether or not the various other tests of an independent agent are met (i.e., the requirements to be legally and economically independent), the additional requirement to be acting in the 'ordinary course of business' when acting on behalf of the treasury vehicle would not commonly be met.[34]

As noted above, the output from the BEPS project led to changes to Article 5(5) and significantly expanded the accompanying commentary.[35] The main change made for present purposes is the addition of a new alternative test, namely whether the agent 'habitually plays the principal role leading to the conclusion of contracts that are routinely concluded without material modification by the enterprise'. Although designed to deal with commissionaire arrangements and the like,[36] the test is also relevant in the case of group treasury operations, particularly in those situations referred to above where there is some activity in the parent company or other group subsidiary but with treasury transactions such as loans and hedging transactions booked into the treasury entity. The question to be asked under this new test is whether the conclusion of contracts is the direct result of the activities in question. Unfortunately, this may be quite a subjective matter. The main problem is with the vagueness of the test and, therefore, what is to count as the 'principal role'. For example, if loan opportunities are introduced to the treasury entity through a treasury function in the parent or if services are routinely provided to the treasury vehicle by the parent or another subsidiary in the group there may be uncertainty as to whether the test is met. Not surprisingly, concerns have been voiced about the uncertainty surrounding the test and the possible range of different standards applied by tax authorities.[37] In practice, it will help to mitigate these dependent agent issues by tight constraints on any activity outside the treasury vehicle.

## 3 The Attribution of Profits to PEs

If the dependent agent (or fixed place of business) threshold PE test is fulfilled, then it is necessary to determine the amount of profits that are attributable to the PE.[38] In this

34. Article 5(6) and para. 111 of the 2017 Commentary. The BEPS changes to Article 5(6) have in any event made it impossible for a person to be an 'independent' agent where it acts exclusively or almost exclusively on behalf of one or more enterprises to which it is closely related.
35. The revised Article and Commentary were included for the first time in the 2017 version of the OECD Model.
36. *See* OECD (2015) *Preventing the Artificial Avoidance of Permanent Establishment Status, Action 7 – 2015 Final Report*, at pp. 9-10 and 15-16 and also para. 92 of the Commentary to Article 7 in the 2017 version of the OECD Model.
37. For a discussion of several difficulties raised by the new test, *see* the discussion in R. Collier, *More Guidance Needed on PE Threshold Issues*, 80 Tax Notes Int'l 249, p. 249 (19 October 2015); and G. Sprague, *Playing the Principal Role in Creating a Permanent Establishment*, Tax Management International Journal (8 January 2016).
38. The following discussion assumes that the attribution of profits will be made by reference to the provisions of Article 7 of the OECD Model. It is of course possible that a different approach may

regard, a common problem arising is the widespread variation in approaches by states to the attribution of profits. The OECD tried to address this issue with the introduction of its 'approved OECD approach' (AOA),[39] but this approach to the interpretation of Article 7 has fallen a long way short of being globally adopted by states, meaning that the problem of varying approaches by states remains.[40] Nonetheless, the AOA remains the approach that is adopted under the OECD Model.[41]

The AOA requires that assets and risks are allocated between any PE and the head office of a treasury vehicle by reference to the location of the 'significant people functions' (SPFs) that relate to those assets and to the assumption and management of those risks. The application of this approach in the extreme case referred to (where all relevant functions are in the dependent agent PE and the transaction – say, a loan – is simply booked into the treasury vehicle) is relatively straightforward – the loan and the return from loan would be wholly attributable to the dependent agent permanent establishment (DAPE). In this case, where there is no functional contribution from the head office, there is nothing under the PE attribution rules to justify any allocation to the head office that is analogous to the approach under the Transfer Pricing Guidelines

---

be required – as where, for example, the relevant Article 7 in an applicable double tax treaty is not interpreted in a manner that is consistent with the OECD approach or where there is no tax treaty, and the matter is determined by domestic law provisions.

39. The AOA was partially introduced by the amendments made to the Commentary to Article 7 in the 2008 version of the OECD Model, but it was fully applied by the revised version of Article 7 and accompanying Commentary in the 2010 version of the OECD Model.

40. Several OECD Member States have entered reservations on the 2010 version of Article 7 on the basis that they reserve the right to use the former (pre-2010) version of the Article. Outside the OECD, there has been even less appetite to embrace the AOA. The approach was rejected by the UN Committee of Experts in 2009, even before the release of the final version of the PE Report and revised Article 7 in 2010. For a fuller discussion of these issues, *see* Richard Collier & John Vella, *Five Core Problems in the Attribution of Profits to Permanent Establishments*, 11(2) World Tax Journal 163-168 (May 2019).

41. It is assumed the reader is familiar with the operation of the AOA but for completeness a summary of the AOA is included in this footnote. The AOA involves a two-step approach to Article 7(2). Under the first step, the PE concerned is 'hypothesised' as a separate and independent enterprise. This is achieved by allocating the economic ownership of assets within the legal entity according to the location of the 'SPFs' relating to the asset concerned. Risks are similarly allocated within the enterprise according to the location of the 'SPFs' relevant to the assumption and management of risk. A different approach is taken to capital allocation. On the basis that a PE should have sufficient capital to support the functions it undertakes, the assets it economically owns, and the risks it assumes, capital is allocated as necessary to support the assets and risks of the PE. Lastly, under this first step to hypothesise the PE as a separate and independent enterprise, it is necessary to recognise (or not recognise) the 'dealings' between the PE and the rest of the enterprise of which it is part. This is done by reference to the existence of real functional activity carried on in the PE that is consistent with the purported dealing. The second step is more familiar. Once, under step one, the assets, risk and capital have been allocated to the PE, and once the dealings have been identified, step two requires that the profits of the PE are determined based upon a comparability exercise, with arm's length pricing applied on the basis of the assets, risk and capital of the PE, taking into account the dealings to be recognised. This is achieved by applying the OECD Transfer Pricing Guidelines by analogy, in other words comparing the dealings between the PE and the rest of the enterprise of which it is part with transactions between independent enterprises. *See* Report on the Attribution of Profits to Permanent Establishments, 17 July 2008, OECD, Paris and 2010 Report on the Attribution of Profits to Permanent Establishments, 22 July 2010, OECD, Paris (hereafter the '2010 PE Report') at pp. 14-20, 24-57.

of allocating a risk-free return to the lender of record.[42] The calculation of the return to the loan would, following the second step of the AOA, normally simply replicate the transfer pricing approach explained above (i.e., through identifying market returns for similar instruments). However, under the AOA, the dependent agent PE would also need to have an appropriate capital base including some free capital (because lending is not normally financed *wholly* by a corresponding borrowing). This may be more problematic as there may be different views on the appropriate level of free capital required in such a situation and the impact on the amount of tax-deductible loan capital. In the case of a PE carrying on treasury activities, difficult issues may also arise in connection with the currency of the imputed capital, and the interest rate - or blended interest rate - attaching to the imputed loan capital. Both issues may affect the calculation of profits of the dependent agent PE.

The attribution exercise is more complicated in the less extreme cases, such as where there is a functional contribution from both the treasury vehicle head office and from one or more dependent agent PEs. In such a case, disputes will often arise on the character, and value, of the role of the dependent agent PE - for example, on whether the dependent agent PE is originating transactions or merely assisting with the execution of transactions which have already been agreed by the head office of the treasury vehicle - or, for example, on the intrinsic importance to the generation of profits of a function/service exercised in the dependent agent PE. Where there are such 'joint' functional contributions to the relevant SPFs, they may in some cases give rise to 'split assets' under the AOA rules, meaning that loans (and the accompanying interest receipts) are attributable partly to the head office of the treasury entity and partly to a dependent agent PE.[43] The practical problems stem from the fact that in many situations it is difficult to isolate and value the functional contribution made by the dependent agent PE or head office.[44] These are the sort of difficulties that arise in cases of the global trading of financial instruments, with a central problem being that of determining to what functions the profit or return from a single pool of profits should properly be split between two or more parties (in this case, the 'parties' being the head office of the treasury entity and any PEs). However, though the task raises similar issues to those arising in the transfer pricing situation, it must of course be addressed by a different set of rules, namely those comprised in Article 7, the accompanying Commentary, and the AOA (rather than Article 9 and the Transfer Pricing Guidelines).[45] This naturally leads to the wider question of how, in the case of a dependent agent PE, the result of any Article 7 attribution to the DAPE differs from the amount allocated to the dependent agent PE enterprise (i.e., the enterprise whose activities on

42. The transfer pricing position is discussed above and dealt with in Transfer Pricing Guidelines at 1.85 and 1.103.
43. OECD, *2010 Report on the Attribution of Profits to Permanent Establishments* (OECD 2010), Part II, at para. 75.
44. For a critique of the use of functions as the anchor point in the income allocation rules, *see* R.S. Collier & I.F. Dykes, *On the Apparent Widespread Misapplication of the OECD Transfer Pricing Guidelines*, Bull. Intl. Taxn. (2022), (volume 76), No. 1.
45. *See supra* n. 38.

behalf of the treasury entity create the dependent agent PE) under the transfer pricing rules. This issue is explored below.

## 4 The Interaction of the Transfer Pricing Rules and the PE Attribution Rules[46]

As a practical matter, the need to address the interaction of the transfer pricing rules and the PE attribution rules has become much more common in recent years, largely as a result of the perception in some quarters that tax authorities may be able to use the PE attribution rules to yield incremental revenues over any transfer pricing return.[47] Consequently, there are now many more cases where a group entity that is allocated a return under Article 9 of the OECD Model is challenged by the tax authorities on the basis it is a dependent agent PE, to which a return under Article 7 should be allocated. The most important question in these cases is usually whether the return to the legal entity under Article 9 of the OECD Model is in fact the same as the return that is accorded to the dependent agent PE under Article 7.

Addressing the interaction of these two sets of rules raises several complex issues. In cases involving financial transactions (and more generally too), the analysis often hinges on whether the return due under Article 9 of the OECD Model, taking account of the control of risk framework, is the same as the return to the dependent agent PE based on the relevant SPFs exercised by the dependent agent PE.[48] For example, reverting to the illustration used earlier, assume an entity in Country X participates in the conduct of treasury business and the relevant transactions (assumed here to be loans) are booked in the group treasury entity in Country Y. If the activities of the entity in Country X create in Country X a dependent agent PE of the treasury vehicle, it will be necessary to address both the Article 9 and Article 7 returns to Country X, the former being due to the dependent agent enterprise (the entity in Country X) and the latter due to the dependent agent PE itself in Country X. For Article 9 purposes a critical question in determining the return under Article 9 is whether the dependent agent enterprise controls the financial risks in the transactions (this is tested by, broadly, an examination of the relevant decision-making relating to the creation and management of the loans).[49] If it does, then, as the earlier discussion demonstrated, the risk premium is allocated to that entity, and the treasury vehicle is limited

46. This is a particularly complex issue and space constraints mean that the discussion and analysis here is necessarily truncated.
47. This is partly fuelled by the lowering of the dependent agent PE threshold as a result of the BEPS project (discussed earlier in this chapter) but arguably a much greater impact stems from the comments made by the OECD several years before the OECD/G20 BEPS initiative on dependent agent PEs and the 'two taxpayer approach'. *See* OECD, *2010 Report on the Attribution of Profits to Permanent Establishments* (OECD 2010), Part III, at paras 274-285 which have in practice led to many allegations of dependent agent PEs.
48. In such cases, it is notable that the same functional activity of decision-making carried out by the same person/ entity gives rise simultaneously to two different sets of tax rules that are applied to that activity to determine the respective Article 9 and Article 7 consequences of the OECD Model.
49. The detailed tests are contained in Transfer Pricing Guidelines at 1.61 and 1.65 and explained in some detail in the chapter in this book by ANDREW HICKMAN.

to the risk-free return. For Article 7 purposes, the return to the dependent agent PE turns on the degree to which it discharges the relevant SPFs (again, tested largely by the degree to which the dependent agent PE is making the decisions relating to the creation and management of the loans). As noted, the critical question is whether the two separate analyses under Articles 9 and 7 lead to the same result.[50]

The task of explaining and clarifying this interaction between Article 9 and Article 7 of the OECD Model in this situation was part of the OECD's scheduled work following the OECD/G20 BEPS Project. Unfortunately, after a first draft of a paper which did engage with the relevant technical difficulties (which are significant), the subsequent work on the detailed technical interaction of the two measures subsequently largely ignored those technical difficulties, meaning that a clarification of the position by the OECD was not forthcoming.[51] This remains the current situation.

In the absence of relevant OECD guidance on the matter, the practical experience of the authors is that there can be some wide (and sometimes wild) variations in the interpretation of this issue. Arguments that more profits arise under Article 7 in comparison to under Article 9 seem to be commonly based on the 2010 PE Report and its commentary on the 'two taxpayer' approach.[52] At the time this was written, the differences in the effect of the rules could be wide. In a dependent agent PE context, the main reason for this was that, as the transfer pricing guidance was interpreted at the time, it was in practice relatively difficult to allocate to an entity providing services (i.e., the dependent agent enterprise) an Article 9 return in respect of assets and risks that are not legally owned by that entity.[53] However, this position has now changed materially. Deference under the transfer pricing guidance to the *legal* owners of assets and risks has been subsequently eroded over the last decade by an appreciable shift in

50. The dependent agent PE would normally be entitled to a deduction for the Article 9 payment to the dependent agent enterprise or service provider (here, the dependent agent enterprise in Country X) meaning that if the amount of allocable profits under Articles 9 and 7 is the same there are no net profits to be attributed to the dependent agent PE.
51. The work of the OECD following the OECD/G20 BEPS initiative on additional guidance on profit attribution led to three versions of guidance produced by the OECD. These are the discussion drafts of July 2016 and June 2017 and a finalised paper of March 2018. (*See* OECD, *Public Discussion Draft: BEPS Action 7 – Additional Guidance on the Attribution of Profits to Permanent Establishments*, OECD/G20 Base Erosion and Profit Shifting (OECD 2016), Primary Sources IBFD [hereinafter the *July 2016 Discussion Draft*]; OECD, *Public Discussion Draft: BEPS Action 7 – Additional Guidance on Attribution of Profits to Permanent Establishments*, OECD/G20 Base Erosion and Profit Shifting (OECD 2017), Primary Sources IBFD [hereinafter the *July 2017 Discussion Draft*]; and OECD, *Additional Guidance on the Attribution of Profits to Permanent Establishments: BEPS Action 7*, OECD/G20 Base Erosion and Profit Shifting Project (OECD 2018), Primary Sources IBFD.) The OECD, *July 2016 Discussion Draft*, *supra*, attempts to explore in detail the relationship between Article 7 and Article 9 of the *OECD Model* (2017) in the light of the transfer pricing guidance on risk. However, the public response to the OECD, *July 2016 Discussion Draft*, *supra*, was hostile due to its complexity (which was inevitable given the underlying technical material), and this led subsequently to a complete reversal of the approach with a much-simplified text in the next version of the document. (*See* the OECD, *July 2017 Discussion Draft*, *supra*.) This action followed 'a different approach' of setting out 'high-level general principles'. It made the guidance of much less practical use, given that it contained no effort to engage with the relevant technical difficulties in the manner of the OECD, *July 2016 Discussion Draft*, *supra*.
52. *See supra* n. 44.
53. Indeed, this point is reflected in the 2010 PE Report, Part III at para. 281.

favour of a functional analysis approach based particularly on the conduct of the parties. The transfer pricing work on business restructurings and particularly the work in BEPS has now put appreciably more emphasis on the need to ensure an appropriate return for the *functional contribution* of the parties, and it materially reduces the deference to legal contracts and legal booking arrangements. This inevitably brings returns under Article 9 and returns under Article 7 closer together.[54]

On the specific relationship between control of risk functions and SPFs, it is true that the concepts are not identical or exactly aligned, though some decision-making functions relating to the assumption and management of risks will usually rank simultaneously as being both control of risk functions and SPFs.[55] However, based on the experience of the authors, it is considered that differences resulting from the application of these concepts in practice are usually likely to be relatively marginal.[56]

Given the nature of the interaction issues and their practical relevance, there is an urgent need for further technical work by the OECD on this matter. In the absence of any such technical clarification, the consequences of crystallising dependent agent PEs may be hard to identify with confidence.

## IV CONCLUSION

From this discussion of issues relating to the income allocation rules as applied to group treasury activities, it may be concluded that the key practical issues are generally less about calculating the proper return from treasury activities (such as the return from lending activities) and more about the difficulties in determining how that return is to be allocated (e.g., as between different group entities, or as between a head office and a dependent agent PE). This is because the calculation of returns from treasury transactions will often be aided by the availability of a significant depth of information and data relating to instruments that are traded in the market (including in relation to different terms, maturities, and currencies, etc.). As the above discussion has noted, there can be situations in which the calculation of returns from treasury activities is more complex, but the overall picture is that the calculation of returns from treasury

54. Notwithstanding these comments there is no complete alignment. For example, there is no notion of attributing a risk-free return under Article 7 that is equivalent to the approach adopted under Article 9.
55. *See* OECD, *Additional Guidance on the Attribution of Profits to Permanent Establishments: BEPS Action 7*, OECD/G20 Base Erosion and Profit Shifting Project (OECD 2018), at para. 40.
56. This conclusion is drawn for a number of reasons. For instance, if a risk is found to be assumed by the dependent agent enterprise for the purposes of the transfer pricing rules, it cannot also be attributed to the dependent agent PE itself under Article 7 – *see* OECD, *Additional Guidance on the Attribution of Profits to Permanent Establishments: BEPS Action 7*, OECD/G20 Base Erosion and Profit Shifting Project (OECD 2018), at para. 41. This implies a degree of alignment of the SPF concept and the risk control concept. There are also obvious policy reasons why it is necessary for Article 7 to align, at least in broad terms, with Article 9 in relation to the return given to the same functional activity given the otherwise absurd position that would result from having two different versions of the ALP (which should not be possible given the single principle that the ALP represents) and the policy goal of the AOA to align the approach to income allocation for a PE and a legally distinct and separate enterprise to the extent possible – *see* 2010 PE Report, Part I, paras 3, 9.

instruments (and specifically loans and routine hedging transactions) is generally not especially problematic. Materially greater difficulties arise in the allocation of those returns. This is especially true where the treasury operation is not completely autonomous, such as where it is supported by group services arrangements, or where it is a small-scale operation. A consequence of this is that, though many MNE group treasury activities are relatively straightforward, the current position under the OECD's income allocation rules is not. The technical and practical complexities identified in this chapter would benefit from further work by the OECD in clarifying the rules, and this includes in particular dealing with the interaction between the Transfer Pricing Guidelines and the AOA as outlined above.

CHAPTER 37

# Hedging Options in Multinationals

*Meindert de Vreeze, Robin Deutsch & Niraja Srinivasan**

## I INTRODUCTION

This chapter provides an overview of the nature of financial risks multinational enterprises (MNEs) face and of hedging as a strategy used by MNEs to mitigate that risk.[1] We explore various interconnected themes, such as the need MNEs have for hedging, the typical financial instruments used in hedging operations by MNEs, what responsible hedging looks like, and how MNE corporate treasury departments are organized to use these instruments. The chapter reflects on how third-party transactions and market-based practices of an MNE's treasury operations are linked to intercompany hedging transactions and the MNE's transfer pricing (TP) policies, especially in light of the Organisation for Economic Co-operation and Development (OECD) 2020 guidance on financial transactions and the OECD TP Guidance issued in 2022 (collectively, OECD Guidance)[2] and the public commentary solicited by the OECD in the months following the draft publication of the 2020 guidance.[3]

* The views and opinions set forth herein are the personal views or opinions of the authors; they do not necessarily reflect views or opinions of the organization with which the authors are associated.

1. This chapter focuses on MNEs that are nonfinancial institutions, although we discuss the role that financial institutions play in providing hedging solutions to those nonfinancial MNEs.
2. OECD, *Transfer Pricing Guidance on Financial Transactions: Inclusive Framework on BEPS Actions 4, 8-10*, OECD, Paris, 2020, www.oecd.org/tax/beps/transfer-pricing-guidance-on-financial-transactions-inclusive-framework-on-beps-actions-4-8-10.htm; OECD, *OECD Transfer Pricing Guidelines for Multinational Enterprises and Tax Administrations 2022*, OECD, Paris, 2022 https://doi.org/10.1787/0e655865-en.
3. In September 2018, the OECD issued *Comments Received on the Public Discussion* Draft, a three-part compilation of public comments on the draft version of OECD (2020) cited above. Specific questions on TP and offsetting hedging were raised in Box C.11. We examine the public comments in section 4 using case illustrations.

The chapter is organized as follows. Section II explains the fundamentals of financial risks and how hedges work to offset or mitigate these risks. Section III explores the challenges and key ingredients of a responsible hedging operation, including how MNEs must deal with residual risks. Section IV brings an "inside-out" perspective of hedging functions in MNEs and the ways corporate treasury functions can be set up with varying degrees of centralization and as profit centres or cost centres. Section V then highlights the practical aspects of an MNE's hedging operations that drive the allocation of risk between the MNE's affiliated entities and affect their intercompany pricing. We conclude with a short summary of the chapter's main points.

## II FINANCIAL RISK AND THE NEED FOR HEDGING

Everywhere in life, risks need to be appropriately and continually measured, calibrated and managed to generate consistent and foreseeable upsides by managing potential downsides. This is also true for MNEs as they conduct their business. Like an individual who calibrates the amount of risk they are willing to take for a given reward and the mitigating action required (e.g., wearing a seat belt to partially mitigate the risk of driving), MNEs are willing to expose themselves to different types of risks to varying degrees.

### 1 What Is Hedging?

Firms are exposed to two fundamental categories of risks: nonfinancial risks and financial risks:

(i) Nonfinancial risks are often operational or reputational in nature, arising from procedures, people, and systems. These risks could have an effect on the company's financials if they materialize, but they are not primarily driven by financial exposures.

(ii) Financial risks are directly related to the financial exposures of the company. There are a broad range of financial risk types, ranging from risks that relate to operating profit and loss (P&L), cash flow, and liquidity, to those relating to balance sheet solvency (*see* Figure 37.1).

*Figure 37.1 Financial Risks*

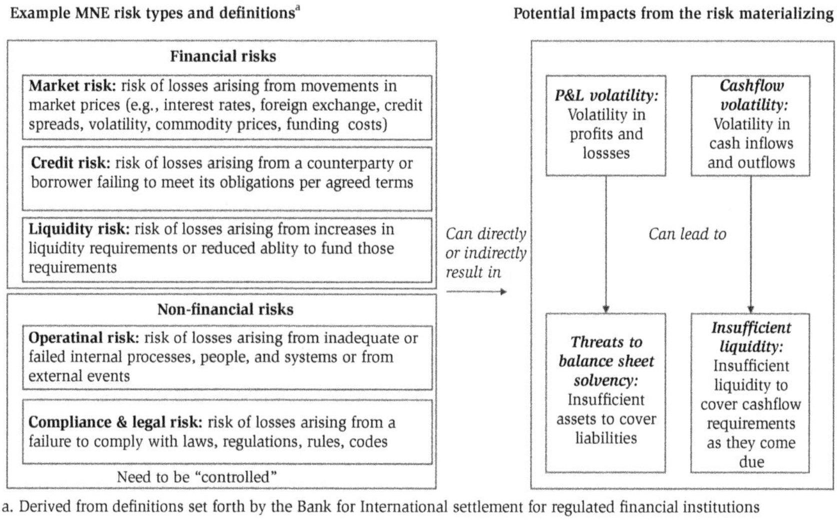


a. Derived from definitions set forth by the Bank for International Settlements for regulated financial institutions.

## 2 Why Hedge?

MNEs are most focused on hedging market-related risks, as MNEs—with the exception of those providing financial services—are not generally in the business of exposing themselves to volatility in financial markets. Some prominent examples of such hedgeable risks are:

- *Interest rate risk*: Losses that could result from changes in interest rates. For example, an MNE may have borrowed funds at a floating rate, meaning the interest payment fluctuates based on an underlying reference rate. If left unhedged, the MNE's borrowing costs could increase substantially if the underlying reference rate increases because of market factors.
- *Currency or foreign exchange (FX) risk*: Losses that could result from changes in exchange rates. For example, an MNE may have borrowed funds in a currency that differs from the currency needed to meet its own cash flow obligations. Should the currency needed to make payments strengthen relative to the one from which the MNE has borrowed, the firm's ability to make payments would be reduced, and losses could be incurred.
- *Commodity risk*: Losses that could result from changes in the price of commodities. For example, an MNE may depend on specific energy sources, such as oil or natural gas, to maintain its operations. If the price of these energy sources increases, the MNE will have higher expenses.

- *Funding risk*: Losses that could result from loss of funding or changes in funding costs. For example, an MNE may be exposed to increases in its funding costs if it is perceived to be a riskier borrower or if the external market environment has changed the broader credit environment (such as during an economic crisis).
- *Credit risk*: Losses that could result from a counterparty or borrower failing to meet an agreed-on financial obligation. For example, an MNE could be faced with clients with extended payment terms or clients whose payments are in arrears. In the period between delivery of the service or good and the payment, the MNE is exposed to counterparty credit risk. Similarly, the MNE could be exposed to the credit risk of the counterparties in which it invests excess cash or the financial institutions providing hedges to the MNE.

The financial risks an MNE faces depend heavily on the nature of the business activities it engages in, as well as the jurisdictions and currencies it conducts them in. MNEs are willing to expose themselves to many financial risks that arise in their business-as-usual activities and in special situations like mergers and acquisitions. After all, some financial risks may be inherent to the business model of a company, and risks can generate rewards. Mitigating risks usually means giving up some upside, too.

However, not all financial risks are appropriate for all firms to be exposed to, and thus some are hedged.

For example, imagine an MNE engaged in international wholesale imports of a good—say, clothing. Let us call it Proto-MNE. Proto-MNE is innately exposed to international prices, and its profits are essentially driven by two factors:

(1) buying the clothing for a lower price in the country of origin (e.g., Vietnam) than it can sell them for in the destination country (e.g., the United States); and
(2) adding economic value at various points across the supply chain by engaging global shippers, brokers, and vendors.

Let us focus on the first of these factors. The financial exposure to the lower cost of production in the origin country (Vietnam)—a key input to the import price—and to the higher purchasing price for this good in the destination country (the United States) is part of the firm's innate profit equation. How volatile or exposed to changes are these underlying factors, and how much risk does that pose to the company? Proto-MNE could view the financial risk of increased production costs in Vietnam or macroeconomic challenges in the United States in one of several ways:

- as a financial risk, that is an acceptable part of the business equation. For example, the firm may think there are only very remote scenarios that would fundamentally alter the underlying factors; or
- as a financial risk that is acceptable in normal scenarios, but that one needs to pre-emptively mitigate against extreme scenarios, that is, prolonged or sudden and extreme changes in the factors; or

- as a financial risk that needs to be eliminated, with the driver of profit being more on the supply chain value-add than the price arbitrage.

Which of these options would one choose? The answer very much depends on the raison d'être of the company as well as its risk appetite. The actions a firm will take to hedge the financial risks described above, that is, the hedging activities and the instruments, will vary depending on the answer to these questions.

Some financial risks are at the core of the company's mission and setting the risk appetite for these is more difficult. Companies also face a set of unwanted financial risks that are by-products of their core business. A common example of this is currency or FX risk. In the example of our Proto-MNE clothes importer, the price of clothes in the origin country may be denominated in Vietnamese dong, while the sale of clothes in the destination country may be in US dollars. If the exchange rate between the currencies changes materially, the company is exposed to financial losses or gains.

This is not a risk most MNEs would be comfortable being exposed to without at least some mitigation. The underlying factor (exchange rates) is volatile, and any profit generated from moves in the factor is outside the businesses' core purpose. Incurring losses due to the same factor is hence unacceptable. In this case, the company will seek to eliminate the risk to the fullest extent possible via hedging arrangements.

## 3 How to Hedge?

Financial risks can be mitigated by transferring them elsewhere or offsetting them by generating new and inverse financial risks.

Some financial risks can be hedged internally within the company, for example, by offsetting an exposure in one country to another, or inverted exposure in another country. Other financial risks are hedged by financial firms, such as banks and insurance companies. These are often takers of financial risk and intermediaries in the transfer of risk; they distribute it into the broader financial system.

One way to hedge financial risk with third parties is through so-called cash instruments, that is, securities or loans that derive their value directly from their own cash flow characteristics. For example, an MNE may have a line of credit with a financial institution at pre-set terms to hedge its funding risk. Or it may take a long position in a security to offset a position of a client receipt that needs to be paid to a vendor at a later date. More often than not, MNEs combine these cash instruments with derivatives instruments, which derive their value from the value of other instruments or market rates (*see* Figure 37.2).

*Figure 37.2 Hedging Instruments*

**Examples of common third-party derivatives-based hedging instruments available to MNEs**

**Swaps (forward claim)**

- Agreement to exchange future cashflows between parties based on pre-set terms, usually for a recurring periods of time
- Usually OTC[a], but increasingly standardized and cleared
- Contracts are usually settled in cash

*Illustration: floating to fixed interest rate swap hedging an MNE's floating rate exposure*

**Futures (forward claim)**

- Agreement to buy, sell or exchange assets or cashflows a future data based on pre-set terms and price
- Futures are usually exchange-traded and cleared, while forwards are OTC[a]
- Can be settled in cash or for physical delivery of asset

*Illustration: physically delivered oil future to hedge cost of oil*

**Options (contingent claim)**

- Agreement giving the right to buy ("call") or sell ("put") an asset or cashflow on or before a given date[b], based on pre-set terms and price
- Can be exchange-traded ("listed" ), or OTC[a]
- Can be settled in cash or for physical delivery or asset

*Illustration: vanilla FX option to hedge FX risk*

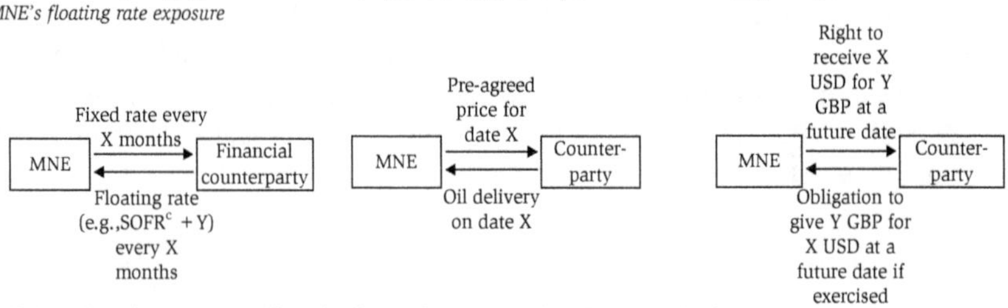


a. OTC = Over the counter, usually with a financial institution taking the other side of the position
b. American options give the right to exercise any point before the expiration data of the option; European options can be exercised only on the expiration date
c. SOFR = Secured Overnight Financing Rate

*Source*: Authors' analysis.

To visualize this, let us turn to Proto-MNE again. Proto-MNE requires funding to purchase goods. To raise funds, it can either borrow money or sell equity in the business. Proto-MNE issues short-term debt to generate funding that will be used to purchase clothing in Vietnam. The debt has the following characteristics:

- pays a floating coupon, that is, the interest rate Proto-MNE pays fluctuates based on an underlying reference rate;
- is denominated in US dollars, that is, the funding Pro-MNE receives will be in US dollars;
- matures in six months, that is, Proto-MNE will repay the debt fully in six months; and
- is issued by Proto-MNE United States LLC, a legal subsidiary entity of Proto-MNE geographically located in the United States.

Which main financial risks does this transaction create for Proto-MNE?

- *Interest rate risk*: given that the debt is based on a floating interest rate, increases in the reference rate would increase Proto-MNE's cost of funding and affect its P&L, balance sheet, and cash flow position.

- *Currency or FX risk*: the debt is denominated in US dollars, but the purchases will be made in Vietnamese dong. A material strengthening of Vietnamese dong versus US dollars would make purchases more expensive, affecting margins.
- *Funding risk*: given that the debt already matures in six months, Proto-MNE could face cash shortfalls when the debt comes due. For example, if cash is still required thereafter for additional purchases, Proto-MNE will need to issue new debt at the market rate that prevails at this future point.

How might one hedge these risks by leveraging the broader financial system and its financial intermediaries? Here are some examples:

- *Interest rate risk*: Proto-MNE could enter into an interest rate swap with a financial counterparty, thereby swapping its floating-rate obligations for a fixed-rate obligation to the financial counterparty.
- *Currency or FX risk*: Proto-MNE could enter into an FX forward contract with a financial institution, whereby they agree to exchange Vietnamese dong and US dollars at a set rate in the future.
- *Funding risk*: Proto-MNE could arrange a line of credit with a financial institution at pre-set terms, such that should it be unable to issue debt, it can still access funding at predictable rates. It could also ladder additional debt issuances such that the funding maturities are more spread out over time or complement larger benchmark bonds with smaller private placements to space out the maturity profile of debt.

In addition to these solutions in the financial system, Proto-MNE has the opportunity to enter offsetting transactions between its subsidiaries to hedge some of its risks. For example, it is possible Proto-MNE has a second legal entity in Vietnam called Proto-MNE Vietnam Ltd. Maybe Proto-MNE Vietnam Ltd has taken out a fixed-rate loan in Vietnamese dong or even has excess liquidity that it could provide to or pool with Proto-MNE United States LLC to supplement its own debt funding. Could the two entities enter an intercompany swap or loan arrangement, thereby avoiding the need to use third-party financial counterparties to hedge their respective currency risks? In many circumstances, this is exactly what the MNE's corporate treasury function will choose to do.

## III HEDGING RESPONSIBLY: THE KEY INGREDIENTS

As we have discussed, companies seek to hedge unwanted financial risks to a level where residual risks are minimized to an acceptable range. However, financial markets are unpredictable, and there are challenges to perfectly hedging each type of financial risk a company faces. Residual risks are common and sometimes difficult to understand. For example:

- An MNE may decide to hedge its entire portfolio in aggregate, rather than each financial position. If the MNE's funding sources are based on different types of reference interest rates, the MNE may either choose to hedge against increases in each one or instead macro-hedge all exposures only using the most common interest rate in the portfolio (assuming they generally behave similarly to each other). The risk that remains should the behaviour of underlying reference interest rates differ from each other is called basis risk and may be acceptable in most circumstances.

- An MNE may decide that the FX risk it faces is acceptable under most circumstances. For example, it may buy products in a currency that is generally pegged to the currency it sells in. There is historical precedent for such pegs to be removed, but the MNE may determine that this is a remote risk that can be hedged if it ever materializes.
- An MNE may find that it has multiple potential sources of energy and that an increase in the cost of one (e.g., oil and gas) may be offset by switching to another (e.g., renewable energy). The MNE may choose not to hedge the price of its energy sources directly.

Each of these examples exposes an MNE to a financial risk. How does the MNE determine how much of a risk is acceptable? In other words, what is its risk appetite? The approach to setting this risk appetite is generally as shown in Figure 37.3.

*Figure 37.3 Steps to Determining the Right Level of Hedging*

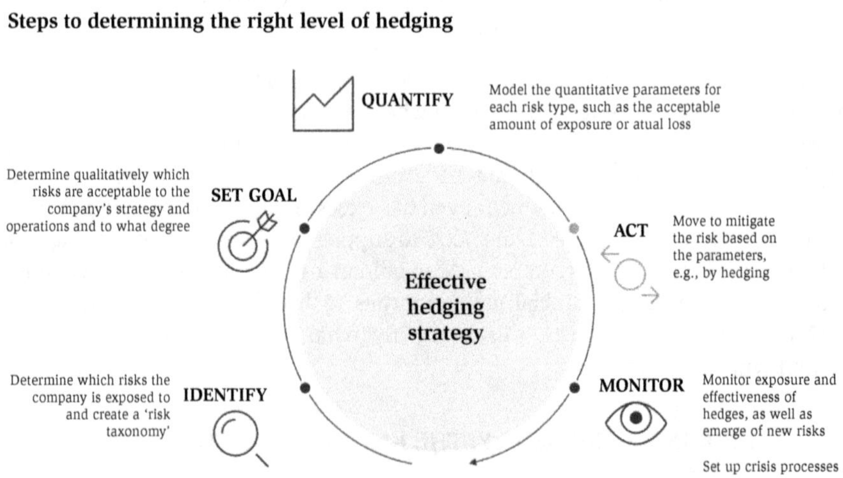


It is important for companies to have certain capabilities for successfully managing financial risks and enabling appropriate hedging. In MNEs following best practices, for example, you may find the following:

- a risk identification process that is based on a coherent risk taxonomy, that is, a list of potential risks that the company could face under different circumstances;

- an institutionalized governance process by which the types and levels of acceptable risks are discussed regularly and agreed upon with the board and senior management;
- a risk appetite statement that documents the level of acceptable risk (qualitatively and quantitatively) that ties this back to the strategy and operational requirements of the firm;
- data and analytical capabilities to estimate how the MNE's exposure might change under different scenarios;
- policies and procedures to drive adherence to the goals of the risk appetite statement;
- documented roles and responsibilities for hedging and monitoring different types of risks the firm is exposed to; and
- a crisis plan or playbook provides emergency options and clarifies the process to mitigate risks should they materialize beyond acceptable levels.

Let us again take the example of our Proto-MNE. Through its risk identification process and discussion of its institutionalized governance processes, the firm realizes that it is exposed to the potential risk of its funding becoming more expensive or an inability to fund itself once its current funding matures. In an ideal world, Proto-MNE will want to have a way to quantify the amount and duration of funding it wants to have at all times in its risk appetite statement and the relative cost it is comfortable with to lock this in.

To estimate this, Proto-MNE needs the data and analytical capabilities to understand its cash needs in business-as-usual and in adverse scenarios it could face. From a data perspective, this requires accurate views of existing cash and funding positions across all of the MNE's entities and banking relationships. It also requires a view of contractual cash flow expectations (e.g., interest due on existing debt) as well as working capital estimates. In addition, the MNE will want to be able to estimate incremental cash flows that could materialize under unexpected circumstances. For example, the price of goods in Vietnam or the level of customs duties between Vietnam and the United States could increase and require additional funding to meet cash needs. A ship may break down and require repair or replacement. MNEs will often have treasury management systems in their corporate treasury teams, which will help forecast cash requirements and other potential risks. However, only recently have these become more dynamic and able to forecast potential scenarios in a flexible and customizable way. An MNE following best practices will have ways to project potential cash flow stress scenarios based on historical experiences and forward-looking variable modelling.

These best practices help the firm plan for potential crises, but they also help TP practitioners, by providing written records and capabilities that clarify how financial risks are managed by an MNE's various entities and how the entities are remunerated for their risk management (and hedging) services. Furthermore, they support the corporate treasury team in directing the MNE's hedging activities to address those scenarios that reflect situations it deems to be possible, commensurate with the objectives of the firm.

## IV HEDGING FUNCTIONS IN MNES

Within an MNE, the Board of Directors (BoD) in principle has ultimate authority over decisions with regard to financial risk management. Following the identification of the financial risks, the BoD may decide to delegate the management of certain risks to various teams in the MNE. Financial risks that are not business-specific are often delegated via the Chief Financial Officer (CFO) to the corporate treasury function.

The activities that the corporate treasury will perform are linked to the strategy of the MNE or its business lines and will thus follow the vision, direction, and policies set out by the MNE's management team(s). Accordingly, the approach of the corporate treasury function to risk management and associated hedging activities will depend on and should reflect the objectives of the firm. The degree to which firms aim to hedge financial risks is often expressed as the company's risk appetite and is captured in a risk appetite statement, as discussed in section III.

The actions of the corporate treasury team will ideally follow the parameters in the risk appetite statement (and/or other policies) set out by the firm. This will inform how various trade-offs are made by the corporate treasury function. Most notably, it will inform the extent to which a corporate treasury function will seek to completely eliminate centralized financial risks, such as interest rate and FX risks, versus maintaining some exposure.

In an MNE that operates across borders, the corporate treasury team can be organized according to different levels of centralization (organizationally and legally), as well as with a profit motive or as a cost centre. This section explores a number of approaches and the rationale for:

- *Organizational models*: centralizing or decentralizing risk management and hedging responsibilities (*see* Figure 37.4).
- *Legal entity models*: centralizing risk management and hedging in one legal entity or federating it across entities.
- *Profit versus cost centre models*: incentivizing corporate treasury effectiveness.

*Figure 37.4 Approaches to Centralizing Corporate Treasury Activities in MNEs*

Approaches to centralizing Corporate Treasury activities in MNEs

| Hedging entities \ Treasury responsibilities | *Decentralized*<br>Entity Treasury functions drive decisions and actions on financial hedging for their entity | *Centralized*<br>A group Treasury function drives decisions and actions on most financial hedging across entities |
|---|---|---|
| *Centralized*<br>A central entity is used for consolidated risk management and hedging | *Rare*<br>*Entity Treasury functions book third party hedges into a centralized hedging entity, pooling risk management but without central – oversight* | *Common*<br>*A central Group Treasury function books third party hedges in a centralized hedging entity, facing off against local entities via intracompany arrangement* |
| *Decentralized*<br>Hedging activity mostly takes place in local entities directly | *Somewhat common*<br>*Entity Treasury functions book third party hedges into their own legal entities, transacting with other entities and third parties directly* | *Somewhat common*<br>*A central Group Treasury function books third party hedges in local entities, and manages the intracompany arrangements between entities* |

*Note*: Centralization can occur at different levels, and in practice, firms may have hybrid versions of the above.

## 1 Centralized Versus Decentralized Risk Management and Hedging Responsibilities

To implement its financial risk management strategy, an MNE may need to enter hedging transactions with financial institutions or offsetting exposures in the MNE's various entities. How these hedging arrangements are managed, and who is responsible for them, can differ from firm to firm.

In the most decentralized form of corporate treasury organization, each entity in the MNE group has autonomy over the financial transactions related to its own financial risk management and hedging. A local finance or treasury function manages the entity's financial exposures independently from broader group considerations (likely with some exceptions). In this model, regional or local treasury teams enter into hedging arrangements that allow mitigating risks faced specifically by the entity or region the team is responsible for. For example, a specific entity may face currency risks on a stand-alone basis, which at the group level may net out against inverse exposures in other entities. In a fully decentralized treasury structure, such trans-entity netting considerations would not be a material factor in hedging decisions made by each local entity. Decentralized corporate treasuries may be present, to varying degrees, in MNE groups with multiple operating divisions in different industries or in MNE groups that are required to comply with specific local regulations or capital controls.

At the opposite end of the spectrum, a centralized group corporate treasury function has control over the financial transactions, consolidated risk management, and hedging activities of all parts of the MNE group and across all entities. In this model, hedging for risks that have been delegated to corporate treasury would take place centrally in the group corporate treasury team, which would act in the consolidated interest of the group while considering the nuanced needs of specific entities. For example, although a specific entity may face currency risks on a stand-alone basis, this may net out at the group level against inverse exposures in other entities. Group corporate treasury would take this into consideration, as long as local regulations permit it. Such a centralized corporate treasury structure could exist in MNE groups where activities are concentrated in specific jurisdictions, or the financial risks are comparable across entities. They are more common where more financial interdependencies naturally exist between business lines and entities.

An intermediate form between decentralized and centralized models is one where a global treasury centre exists, and various regional treasury centres cover each region. Certain risks may be managed in the region.

One of the main arguments for centralization of corporate treasury activities is the existence of economies of scale through centralized expertise and management of group-wide constraints. This can lead to improved effectiveness and efficiency, as there is less duplication of activities and redundant headcount. However, centralization can also bear risks should local considerations not receive sufficient attention.

## 2 Centralized Legal Entity Models for Hedging Responsibilities

Centralized corporate treasury responsibilities are often coupled with a mirroring in terms of legal entity set-up. In a centralized model, individual entities generally might not contractually enter hedging arrangements with third parties, as their risk is hedged through a centralized treasury entity, which consolidates risk management and hedging for the MNE group. This centralized treasury entity also contracts intercompany hedges with other MNE group entities, to then hedge remaining exposures with third-party financial institutions.

Intragroup financial transactions may include instruments by which risk is transferred within the MNE group. For example, hedging arrangements are frequently used in the ordinary course of business as a means of mitigating exposure to risks such as interest rate, FX, or commodity price movements. An entity managed by a centralized corporate treasury function may assume such risks and/or hedge against them according to its own policies.

The OECD (2020) Guidance mentions a number of possible arrangements by which an MNE may centralize the hedging of risk:[4]

- Delegating responsibility for hedging to an MNE group treasury entity, with the hedging contracts arranged for and in the name of the relevant operating companies.
- Delegating responsibility for hedging to an MNE group treasury entity, with the hedging contracts made by and in the name of another MNE group entity.

4. OECD (2020), *Transfer Pricing Guidance on Financial Transactions: Inclusive Framework on BEPS Actions 4, 8-10*, section 10.151, p. 28.

- Identifying the existence of natural hedges in the MNE group, in which case no formal hedging contracts are made.

Let us use the Proto-MNE example to illustrate some of these intercompany hedging instruments and options when a centralized hedging entity exists. Proto-MNE has a Hungarian subsidiary, Proto-MNE Hungary Kft, which sells clothing to the local Hungarian market in euros. The entity was incorporated as a Hungarian forint (HUF) functional entity. To avoid any impact of a material swing from the euro to HUF, Proto-MNE Hungary Kft enters into an intercompany hedge with the Proto-MNE's centralized treasury entity, based in the US. The contract allows Proto-MNE Hungary Kft to forward sell euros and buy HUF, thus neutralizing the entity's currency risk. The centralized treasury entity in turn will offset this intercompany hedge with other exposures in the group or hedge them externally with third parties.

Second, let us illustrate an example whereby the Proto-MNE considers options to hedge its equity investment in a UK subsidiary. Let us assume that the main functional currency of Proto-MNE is USD and that Proto-MNE has invested a certain amount of equity in its 100% owned UK subsidiary. In this case, to hedge the movement of a GBP depreciation versus USD, Proto-MNE's central treasury entity entered into an agreement to sell GBP forward against USD with one of its banking counterparts. The result of this hedge is that if GBP depreciates versus the USD, central treasury would receive a net pay-out from the banking counterpart offsetting the depreciation of the equity investment, whereas if GBP appreciates, it would pay-out to the banking counterpart offsetting the appreciation of its investment.

Not all MNEs have centralized treasury entities, and often risk management and hedging consolidation take place only in each legal entity. In some industries, there may be regulatory reasons for this. In other cases, it may be that the MNE would be exposed to unacceptable cross-jurisdictional risks (such as capital controls) if it were to rely on a centralized treasury entity to hedge risks in each operating entity. In the end, the decision is a trade-off between risk appetite, business needs, and complexity of operations.

## 3 Corporate Treasury as a Cost Centre or a Profit Centre

Corporate treasury functions can be philosophically seen as playing one of two main roles:

(i) as a service centre that determines and performs certain tasks (e.g., mitigating risk) on behalf of the MNE group's entities and businesses; or
(ii) as a profit centre that manages and mitigates financial risk and enhances return on residual risk.

It is often the case that the MNE applies the service provider model for certain treasury functions and a profit centre model for others. It may operate a hybrid model between the two approaches for different jurisdictions.

The corporate treasury function of an MNE is normally part of a corporate function that does not have a direct link to the client-facing business activities of the firm. Given this, many MNEs naturally treat corporate treasury as a cost centre, that is, without an explicit profit objective. In this construct, corporate treasury would charge the businesses and entities it provides services to (such as risk management, hedging, and analytics) in a similar way as other corporate functions. It would also need to charge out to the various businesses and functions any residual risk it is unable to hedge centrally, as well as the cost of hedging. This is generally a conservative and risk-averse approach to corporate treasury activities.

However, a corporate treasury function is fundamentally in the business of managing financial risk. Because risks can also generate returns, there could be arguments for corporate treasury functions to manage their own P&L account, whereby they translate any unhedged risks into financial returns for the company. For example, financial income could be derived from investing the group's excess cash in low-risk financial instruments or by not fully hedging interest rate risk to take a directional view on the evolution of the rate environment.

A profit-enhancing corporate treasury function is often perceived as a higher-risk approach to financial risk management that requires careful controls, as the profit-enhancing motive of the function needs to be balanced against the firm's risk appetite. Errors in this equilibrium could otherwise result in overly aggressive financial risk-taking. Given that the core business of a nonfinancial MNE is typically not to take directional bets on financial markets, this approach is not appropriate for all firms. In some ways, an MNE with a profit-enhancing corporate treasury function has at least partly, more similarities with financial institutions.

## V HEDGING AND ITS EFFECT ON TRANSFER PRICING ANALYSIS

The previous sections have provided an overview of the varied nature of hedging different types of financial risks in an MNE and how this is typically done. Among other observations, we noted that MNEs can sometimes transfer financial risks and their respective hedging activity across multiple entities in the MNE group by engaging in complex offsetting transactions. What does this mean for the TP practitioner setting prices for intercompany transactions?

From a TP perspective, it is important to understand what intercompany hedges are in place and how those affect the level of financial risk assumed by a controlled legal entity whose prices and profits are subject to arm's-length scrutiny. This is not as simple as it appears. Sophisticated MNE treasury groups have deep expertise and experience in hedging activities. They continually monitor and manage financial risk with multiple offsetting internal hedges using different instruments (e.g., interest rate swaps, forward contracts, and options) and hedge residual risk with external financial institutions. Whether the MNE treasury function operates in a centralized or decentralized manner, one of its major functions is to mitigate risk as defined by the MNE's governance framework and risk appetite. This makes the TP practitioner's job—setting arm's-length compensation for intercompany hedging operations —anything but straightforward.

The OECD Guidance recognizes this difficulty, stating:[5]

> More difficult transfer pricing issues may arise, however, if the contract instrument is entered into by the treasury entity or another MNE group entity, with the result that the positions are not matched within the same entity, although the MNE group position is protected. Where off-setting hedging contract instruments exist within the MNE group but not within the same entity, or where contract instruments do not exist within the MNE group but the MNE group position is protected (as may be the case with a natural hedge, for example), it would be inappropriate to match the hedges within the same entity or recognise hedging transactions where written contracts do not exist without a comprehensive analysis of the accurate delineation of the actual transactions ... (for example, the existence of a deliberate concerted action to engage in a hedge of a specific risk) and the commercial rationality of the transactions ... .

The above statement suggests that there are two main considerations:

(1) *How to compensate group corporate treasury for its services*: First, where there is a centralized group corporate treasury function that arranges hedging contracts for an operating entity, the group corporate treasury function should receive compensation on arm's-length basis for services rendered.
(2) *How to accurately delineate intercompany hedging transactions*: Second, where a centralized treasury entity (or another MNE group entity) enters into multiple offsetting internal and external hedging transactions on behalf of member entities of the MNE group, there should reasonably be a TP framework to evaluate whether every participating entity of the MNE group is compensated on an arm's-length basis.

To illustrate these points, let us consider a few case studies to see how various hedging arrangements might affect transfer prices.

## 1 Hedging Services Model

In the simplest case, let's assume that our Proto-MNE has a single affiliate, Proto-MNE Hungary Kft, a distributor of clothing for the local Hungarian market. According to the global TP policy of the MNE, this entity buys goods from a related party in euros and sells to local customers in HUF. Proto-MNE has a centralized corporate treasury group, housed in its US entity, that arranges to hedge for all group subsidiaries. Anticipating a material depreciation of the HUF, Proto-MNE's central treasury group arranges for Proto-MNE Hungary Kft to enter into a forward FX contract with a third-party Hungarian bank to buy euros and sell HUF at a future date (*see* Figure 37.5). We can

5. OECD (2020), *Transfer Pricing Guidance on Financial Transactions: Inclusive Framework on BEPS Actions 4, 8-10,* section 10.153, p. 28.

also assume that all terms of the forward contract are decided by Proto-MNE's central treasury group.

*Figure 37.5 Case 1: Centralized Hedging Services Model*

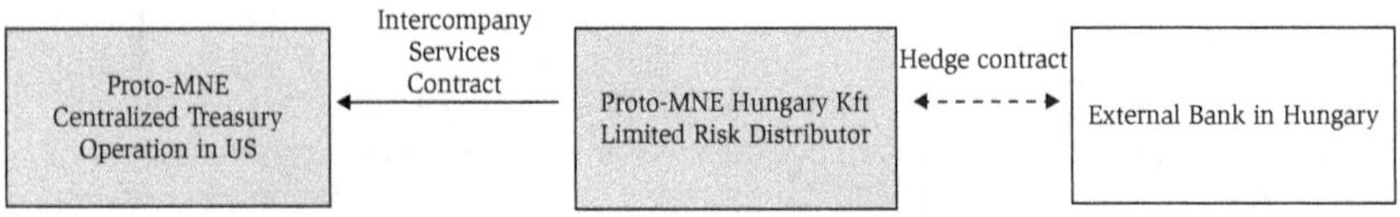


**Transfer Pricing Analysis:** A functional analysis of the related parties is performed, and it reveals that substantially all the financial risk is held by Proto-MNE Hungary Kft, the entity holding the contract. As the entity that holds of the hedge contract, all residual FX gains/losses are recorded on Proto-MNE Hungary Kft's P&L statement. Since Proto-MNE's corporate treasury group arranged the hedge on behalf of and for the benefit of the Hungarian affiliate, the latter entity will pay an arm's-length fee for services rendered.

The MNE's TP manager would evaluate all applicable TP methods and based on reliability and availability of data, might select the Transactional Net Margin Method (TNMM), under which the appropriate profit level indicator is the return on total costs (operating income/total cost). This is used to determine an arm's-length profit markup to apply to the cost of Proto-MNE's centralized hedging services. Comparable companies selected for applying the TNMM may be standalone FX brokerage houses and hedging divisions of financial institutions. Let us say the median of the range of markups is 7% and the Proto-MNE's central hedging group incurs USD $5 million of administrative cost of which 50% is attributable to the euro-HUF hedging operations. The TP manager might then estimate an arm's-length remuneration for Proto-MNE's hedging service at USD 175,000 or 7% of USD 2.5 million (50% of USD 5 million).

## 2 Back-to-Back Hedging and Risk Sharing

A second, more complex, and perhaps more realistic scenario is where the centralized corporate treasury entity enters back-to-back hedges with an external bank on the one hand and several operating subsidiaries on the other.[6] To illustrate this, let us consider a second case in Figure 37.6, where we use the same functional facts for our Proto-MNE and its Hungarian affiliate from Case 1 (i.e., buying goods in euro and selling them in HUF) but add a second related party, Proto-MNE Ireland, a distributor of clothing to customers in the UK and Ireland. The Irish distributor entity buys goods in USD and sells them to local customers in euro. The FX exposure for the Hungarian entity arises from a depreciation of the HUF against the euro, but in the case of the Irish entity, the

6. This scenario was described in more detail in section III.1.

exposure arises from the USD appreciating against the euro. To keep the illustration simple, we assume that all three entities are USD-functional.[7]

*Figure 37.6 Case 2: Back-to-Back Hedging*

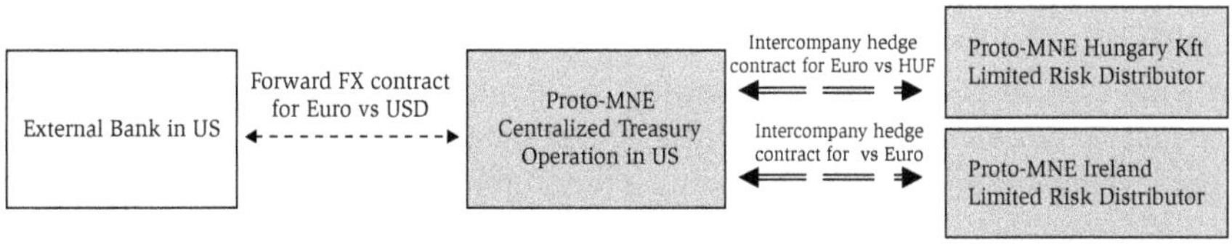


As shown in Figure 37.6, in Case 2, Proto-MNE's central treasury entity faces the external US bank and provides back-to-back intercompany hedges to multiple participating subsidiaries. Based on the cash balances and working capital needs of the distributors, Proto-MNE's central treasury group sees a natural financial risk offset opportunity within the group and decides to sell Proto-MNE Hungary Kft the amount of EUR 1,000 versus HUF and buy EUR 400 versus USD from Proto-MNE Ireland. The central treasury entity then nets the two amounts and enters into a forward contract for EUR 600 versus USD with an external bank. This is an example where the central treasury has proactively and efficiently reduced the FX exposure and the hedging costs for the MNE group as a whole. Proto-MNE then books intercompany hedges with the Hungarian and Irish affiliates at prevailing market rates, which can help support the arm's-length nature of the intercompany hedges in that their contract terms are similar to the terms that the distribution entities may have entered into with third-party banks. In terms of TP documentation, the intercompany hedge contract terms may be system generated and perhaps included as an appendix in a lengthier intercompany agreement that describes the entities and purpose of the hedge.

*Transfer Pricing Analysis*: The fundamental TP principle is that every entity must pay a market rate for a benefit conferred by the actions performed or services provided by another member of the controlled group. According to the OECD (2020) Guidelines,[8] '[b]y identifying and taking action to address financial risk, treasury can help to optimise the cost of capital to the advantage of the users of the MNE group's treasury services'.

As we observed in section III, an MNE that operates in numerous countries and across multiple business divisions is offered an opportunity to hedge risks in the consolidated interests of the group while still meeting the needs of specific entities. But when there are multiple offsetting hedge contracts with different legal entities, a TP

7. Functional currency can be an important driver of hedging. When an MNE registers and incorporates a new legal entity, it selects the functional currency the entity will use to file its local financial statements. Barring any regulatory restrictions, the entity's functional currency will be aligned to its primary economic environment, i.e., the currency in which the entity is expected to conduct its major market transactions and generate cash. To the extent that the entity then transacts in a non-functional currency, it creates a real financial exposure that potentially needs to be hedged.
8. OECD (2020) *supra* at section 10.42, p. 13.

functional and financial analysis of all the related parties does not necessarily reveal the nuances of where the financial risk is ultimately being borne, whether there ought to be some form of intercompany payment, and how to determine that payment. There is no clear-cut answer. In Case 2, all three entities could be facing some level of financial risk or all residual risk may be on the shoulders of the central treasury entity.

Should the Hungarian and Irish subsidiaries compensate Proto-MNE for netting and offsetting the financial risk to the company as a whole? Alternatively, should—and can—the cost of the external hedge (a true financial cost to the MNE group) be allocated to the two distribution entities?[9] What allocation key would be the best proxy of the level of benefit conveyed? Should a markup be applied to this cost?

In September 2018, the OECD published the public commentary it had received on various aspects of the (then) draft guidance on financial transactions TP. In the context of hedging, the OECD solicited comments on what type of TP analysis would help identify and accurately delineate the actual transactions underlying offsetting hedge positions within an MNE group. The thoughtful views expressed by over thirty different accounting and law firms, industry and trade associations and universities presented many divergent approaches and ultimately provided no consensus on a 'standard' TP framework that could be deployed for all company facts and circumstances. To illustrate the variety of suggestions, we grouped the majority of the comments into the four approaches listed below:

(1) *Booking entity should bear financial impact*: When the hedge is booked in a different entity than the one with the underlying risk-bearing assets or transactions, it is appropriate to allocate profits or losses from the booking entity to the entity that generated the underlying risk-bearing transaction. The booking entity should be bearing the financial risk and resultant financial impact.

(2) *Offsetting natural internal risk is corporate treasury's function as fiduciary*: If there exists a natural hedge across multiple counteracting positions within the MNE group, then a central treasury group or entity is merely consolidating these positions to minimize the group's cost of entering into multiple external hedges. It acts as a "passive manager" of risk that is akin to the protection of the MNE shareholder's interest. The centralized hedging function is, therefore, non-compensable via an intercompany service agreement. Any gains and losses impacting the operating entities should be transferred to the central treasury or headquarter entity via an intercompany accounting entry.

(3) *It is still a service*: When an MNE group corporate treasury entity is interposed between individual MNE group members and external counterparties, it is exposed to the credit risk of multiple member entities. It bears the risk of a

9. Depending on the historical volatility of exchange rate movements hedged or the degree of economic uncertainty in which the MNE operates, the costs of hedging may be substantial or immaterial. If the macroeconomic environment is highly unpredictable (due to political or social conflicts, natural disasters, etc.), the hedging costs will be very high and have a meaningful effect on the MNE or its constituent entities' profitability.

potential default by any one group member. The fact that the group treasury entity has entered into the external hedge is an indicator that it also has control over and the financial capacity to bear the risk of default by any one group member. The centralized hedging function can be viewed as providing an inter-group service and remunerating via an intercompany hedging service fee.

(4) *No TP analysis necessary*: There is no reason to assume that the group affiliate has entered into a hedge just because the hedge relates to the currency that it trades in. It is the party who enters into the hedge with an external party that subjects itself to the risk of profit or loss. There is no non-arm's-length transaction or imputation of an intercompany transaction that is necessary, nor is it possible or practical to try and continuously monitor setoffs between entities. The central hedging functions may be viewed the same as group membership synergies and would not require a TP analysis.

It is apparent even from the simple illustration in Case 2 that there is no 'one size fits all' on TP arrangements for complex multi-country hedging operations. A forced recharacterization of the actual transaction - by either the taxpayer or tax authority - could at its worst, create more controversy with respect to double taxation. Furthermore, any complicated financial modelling to determine the allocable costs of hedging to each participating member of the group would be overly burdensome relative to the risk and magnitude of perceived tax avoidance. The OECD (2020 and 2022) guidance points to the fundamental importance of identifying who bears the risk and who performs the risk management function when delineating intercompany transactions in relation to hedging. Beyond that, not much more has been published and therefore represents an area where future research and additional commentary from TP practitioners is a desired next step to define a TP framework for hedging.

## VI CONCLUSION

MNEs hedge their financial risks in a variety of ways to avoid potential losses that fall outside the risk appetite of the firm. This chapter provided an in-depth look at the fundamentals of financial risks and how hedges operate to offset or mitigate these risks. We discussed what residual risks may remain even in an MNE with the most proactive and efficient treasury function and what this residual means for the capabilities an MNE needs to confidently hedge unwanted financial risks. We linked the ideas of effective mitigation of risk to how the treasury function in an MNE is organized—the degree of centralization and profit versus cost orientation. This has implications for how intercompany hedges are designed and implemented and, in turn, how a TP practitioner investigates the sharing of financial risk mitigation costs between related parties in an intercompany transaction.

# Part V ALP Framework for Other Types of Activities

## A Factoring

CHAPTER 38

# Assessing Factoring Transactions Within the Arm's Length Principle Framework

*Emmanuel Llinares & Bernardo Danesi*[*]

## I INTRODUCTION

Factoring, or accounts receivable financing, is a financial transaction involving three parties: a supplier (or seller) of products or services, who is typically seeking to secure its accounts receivable; a buyer of the products or services; and a financial intermediary, generally called a factor. In typical factoring arrangements, suppliers sell or assign accounts receivable to the factor for immediate cash at a price below the aggregate face value of those accounts.[1] The difference between the face value of the receivables and the price negotiated between the factor and supplier is the factor's remuneration.

Suppliers may recognize several benefits from factoring transactions (these are not always present, but they are features commonly bundled in these arrangements):

- credit to fund working capital requirements, which is particularly important in settings where long payment delays are the norm;
- outsourced credit collection offered by specialized providers, potentially creating efficiencies in the supply chain; and
- foreign exchange coverage is when suppliers hold accounts receivable in several currencies.

* The views and opinions set forth herein are the personal views or opinions of the authors; they do not necessarily reflect views or opinions of the organization with which the authors are associated.

1. 'Factoring Agreements, Finance, Document Description – Factoring Agreements', Bloomberg Law, accessed December 2021, 1.

Factoring transactions differ from simple financing transactions. In the former, a creditor (i.e., the factor) evaluates the creditworthiness of the buyer (i.e., the client of the financing recipient, the supplier), whereas, in the latter, a creditor (i.e., a traditional lender or a subscriber of corporate debt) evaluates the creditworthiness of the financing recipient that acts as a supplier. In addition, in factoring arrangements, the supplier/client of the factoring company immediately receive cash for its accounts receivable and has no obligation to pay interest or repay principal. Finally, unless the factoring agreement provides for recourse, a factoring arrangement appears on the supplier's balance sheet as a sale of assets rather than a debt liability.

A number of variables should be considered when analysing a factoring arrangement. These include features such as recourse and nonrecourse arrangements. The most appropriate pricing approach depends on these characteristics.

We present a review of the main types of factoring and their relative characteristics to contextualize our conclusions. After this review, we discuss how to characterize and price factoring transactions in a transfer pricing context. The rest of the chapter is structured as follows:

(i) In section II, we provide more information about the role of factoring arrangements and trade finance in global supply chains:
   - We focus on the most common features of factoring agreements and the benefits of factoring agreements.
   - We also review the transfer pricing literature on factoring. Note that the sources on this topic are not particularly numerous, potentially because factoring is not the most common transaction in intragroup settings.

(ii) In section III, we examine the difficulties of applying the arm's length principle to factoring transactions and we look at relevant court cases.

(iii) In section IV, we discuss how to properly and accurately characterize and price factoring transactions.

(iv) In section V, we present our conclusions.

## II FACTORING IN A MARKET ECONOMY

In 2008, Frances Williams estimated that 80%-90% of world trade is facilitated by trade credit.[2] In addition, as of 1992, accounts receivable used to make up 20%-25% of the total assets of firms in the manufacturing sector.[3] Leora Klapper reports that the volume of factoring transactions grew by 88% between 1998 and 2004 in the United States (US), further signalling the importance of these agreements in modern economies.[4] The

2. *See* Frances Williams, 'Article Title', *Financial Times*, 11 November 2008, ft.com/content/9ebcdfaa-b012-11dd-a795-0000779fd18c.
3. Kasper van der Vliet, Matthew J. Reindorp & Jan C. Fransoo, 'The Price of Reverse Factoring: Financing Rates vs. Payment Delays', *European Journal of Operational Research* 242, no. 3 (2015): 842.
4. Leora Klapper, 'The Role of Factoring for Financing Small and Medium Enterprises', *Journal of Banking & Finance* 30, no. 11 (2006): 3113.

above suggests that the role of trade financing, including factoring in modern supply chains, is significant and multifaceted.

## 1 Types of Factoring

Factoring agreements vary substantially based on their characteristics.

The transfer of accounts receivable can be made on a recourse or nonrecourse basis. In the former, the factor has a claim against the supplier for payment deficiencies, and in the latter case, it does not. In other words, nonrecourse factoring removes accounts receivable from the supplier's balance sheet, whereas recourse factoring does not and is generally classified as borrowing.[5] The majority of factoring arrangements performed in developed economies are carried out on a nonrecourse basis.[6] However, suppliers with poorer quality receivables and suppliers who had stronger credit ratings were more likely to factor with recourse to reduce the cost of factoring.[7]

Reverse factoring, or supply chain financing, has become increasingly common due to payment delays progressively increasing in many industries in recent years.[8] Reverse factoring is a scheme whereby buyers offer a guarantee on the accounts receivable to which they are counterparties. Because suppliers are often smaller than buyers,[9] this type of scheme can lower the cost of funding for small and medium enterprises and similar types of suppliers.

Factors also disburse cash to the suppliers at different points depending on the specific agreement stipulations.[10] These include:

- *Advance* factoring schemes pay suppliers once the goods have shipped or the once the account receivable is generated (in advance of delivery).
- In *maturity* factoring, the factor pays the client when the purchased accounts reach their average maturity date.
- In *collection* factoring, the factor pays the client when the purchased accounts are collected.[11]

Last, we distinguish between *notification* and *non-notification* factoring. In a notification factoring arrangement, the factor collects accounts receivable and directly

5. PANOS KOUVELIS & FASHENG XU, *A Supply Chain Theory of Factoring and Reverse Factoring*, SSRN (2018), 2, https://papers.ssrn.com/sol3/papers.cfm?abstract_id=3241484.
6. MARC AUBOIN, HARRY SMYTHE & ROBERT TEH, 'Supply Chain Finance and SMEs: Evidence from International Factoring Data', CESifo Working Paper series no. 6039, 3.
7. KLAPPER, 'The Role of Factoring', 3133.
8. VAN DER VLIET, REINDORP & FRANSOO, 'The Price of Reverse Factoring', 842.
9. RUMAYSA BILGIN & YUSUF DINC, 'Factoring as a Determinant of Capital Structure for Large Firms: Theoretical and Empirical Analysis', *Borsa Istanbul Review* 19, no. 3 (2019): 275.
10. 'Factoring Agreements, Finance, Document Description', 2.
11. Collection factoring can be either nonrecourse or recourse. In nonrecourse collection factoring, if the factor is unable to collect an approved account receivable after it has matured, before the factor pays the client for the receivable, it must make a determination that the account debtor is financially unable to pay. Collection factoring is also known as retail factoring because the factor's client is typically a retailer. *See* 'Practice Note, Issues in Factoring: Collection Factoring', Practical Law, Thomson Reuters https://uk.practicallaw.thomsonreuters.com/w-018-8652.

communicates with the debtor. In contrast, interactions between the factor and the debtor are almost non-existent in a non-notification factoring.[12]

These features have significant implications for the characterization and pricing of a factoring transaction. For example, recourse and nonrecourse arrangements require different approaches to pricing as the former shares similarities with a loan backed up by collateral while the second can be viewed as a sale of assets (receivables). For another example, in a reverse factoring transaction, the implicit guarantee offered by the buyer should be considered when evaluating the credit rating of the tested receivables (issuer credit rating).

## 2 The Benefits of Factoring and Trade Finance

Factoring arrangements allow suppliers to fund working capital requirements, especially in environments where payment terms are dictated by buyers.[13]

Buyers may opt for longer payment terms, although such terms may increase the cost of goods. In the literature, three explanations have been offered for this phenomenon:[14]

(1) 'Financing advantage' arguments, which posit that trade credit contributes to easing problems of asymmetric information in the supply chain. For example, a supplier may be better positioned than a bank to obtain information regarding its clients (e.g., creditworthiness). At the same time, trade finance can limit supplier moral hazard using delayed payments, an effective way to control suppliers' incentives to shirk on product quality.[15]
(2) 'Price discrimination' arguments are presented in the context of a model whereby a supplier offers trade credit or early payment discounts. Buyers choose to take advantage of early payment discounts or accept trade credit based on their type (i.e., preferences, characteristics of the business).[16]
(3) The 'transaction cost' reasoning proposes that accumulating all invoices so that all payments are made at the same time reduces costs for an enterprise.

Factoring arrangements may be particularly beneficial for 'informationally opaque sellers', that is small or medium companies, which may not have developed a sufficient reputation. Factoring may also be attractive to suppliers in financial systems

---

12. *See* Balazs Karancsi, 'Transfer Pricing and Factoring', KPMG Switzerland Blog, 18 November 2021, https://home.kpmg/ch/en/blogs/home/posts/2021/11/transfer-pricing-and-factoring.html.
13. Sripad K. Devalkar & Karish Krishnan, 'The Impact of Working Capital Financing Costs on the Efficiency of Trade Credit', *Production and Operations Management* 28, no. 4 (2019): 881.
14. Mitchell A. Petersen & Raghuram G. Rajan, 'Trade Credit: Theories and Evidence', NBER Working Paper no. 5602, 1996.
15. Volodymyr Babich & Christopher S. Tang, 'Managing Opportunistic Supplier Product Adulteration: Deferred Payments, Inspection, and Combined Mechanisms', *Manufacturing & Service Operations Management* 14, no. 2 (2012): 301-315.
16. Michael J. Brennan, Vojislav Maksimovics & Josef Zechner, 'Vendor Financing', *Journal of Finance* 43, no. 5 (1988): 1127-1141.

with weak commercial laws and enforcement. By tying risk of default to its accounts receivable, the supplier can improve its ability to raise funds (accounts receivable are relative to sales achieved with counterparty firms that may be more established and potentially associated with better credit ratings).

For a variety of these reasons, local suppliers that are part of multinational organization may be in a position where their major clients request trade finance in the form of dilated payment terms. In this case, it may be optimal for a supplier to seek factoring finance rather than traditional finance instruments, such as loans. In case a supplier is part of a multinational organization, factoring services may be rendered by an affiliate with an adequate profile.

Generally speaking, when the creditworthiness of the accounts receivable (i.e., the creditworthiness of the buyers) is higher than the creditworthiness of the supplier, factoring is likely to lower the cost of financing working capital, making it a more attractive option than loans. It may speed up the ability to obtain the necessary working capital for the supplier's business to operate effectively. It is important to assess the benefits that an intragroup factoring transaction brings to a distributor to correctly characterize the transaction.

The next subsection looks at how factoring transactions have been characterized and priced in transfer pricing terms.

## III TRANSFER PRICING PRECEDENTS AND CONSIDERATIONS

In most cases of intragroup factoring transactions, a transfer pricing practitioner is tasked with determining the arm's-length discount factor charged by the factor to the supplier. The arm's-length discount or factoring price on the receivables can be estimated directly when sufficiently robust comparable transactions are available, thus using a comparable uncontrolled price (CUP) method. Alternatively, the discount can be computed by deriving the factoring costs of operations and applying an appropriate return, based on a transaction net margin method (TNMM) analyses.[17] In a TNMM framework, practitioners may use a comparable company search to determine returns, if sufficient comparability in the type of customers, industry, and types of receivables serviced is achieved. A more synthetic approach can be used in cases where no such comparables are available. An example of this kind of analysis is presented in a next chapter.[18] Alternatively, one can make direct comparisons with third-party transactions to the extent that these are available.[19]

When reviewing previous factoring literature and precedents in a transfer pricing context, we should mention the case of McKesson versus the Canadian authorities.[20]

17. Chapter 1, Introduction, Antonio Russo & Omar Moerer, in *Transfer Pricing and Intra-Group Financing*, edited by Anuschka Bakker & Marc M. Levey (Amsterdam: IBFD, 2012), 48.
18. *See* Chapter 40 of this book for a more in-depth description of a case study in the area of factoring.
19. Chapter 1, Introduction, Antonio Russo & Omar Moerer, in *Transfer Pricing and Intra-Group Financing*, 48.
20. McKesson Canada Corporation and Her Majesty the Queen, Docket: 2008-2949(IT)G.

This case highlights many of the issues that a practitioner should consider when assessing a factoring transaction.

McKesson Canada Corporation (MCC) was the main operating entity of the US-headquartered McKesson Group in Canada as a distributor of over-the-counter and prescription medicines. In 2002 (FY 2003), MCC became a party to a receivables sales agreement (RSA) and a servicing agreement with a related entity, McKesson International Holdings III S.à.R.L (MIH; based in Luxembourg). According to the arrangement, MIH purchased all of MCC's current receivables (approximately CAD 460 million) and continued accumulating receivables daily up to a CAD 900 million cap. The discount applied was 2.206% of face value, calculated to be equivalent to an annual financing rate of about 27%.

The RSA contained a provision allowing MIH to sell back the nonperforming receivables to MCC at 75% of face value, which was later adjusted to the amount collected by MCC. This resulted in any liquidity risk related to the nonperforming receivables ultimately remaining with MCC. There was also no recourse for MIH for unpaid purchased receivables and, as such, no protection in the event of defaults.

Last, under the servicing agreement, MIH paid MCC a fixed annual fee of CAD 9.6 million to continue servicing the receivables.

The Canada Revenue Authority (CRA) took the position that the discount rate applied was greater than the arm's-length rate. Under the RSA, the overall discount rate was calculated using three different components. These were the yield rate, a loss discount, and a discount spread. The latter two were challenged by the CRA, which reasoned that the arm's-length discount rate would be 1.0127% for FY 2003, resulting in a very different annualized effective rate of 13%. The difference between the two discount rates resulted in a transfer pricing adjustment of CAD 26.6 million.

The CRA did not challenge the CAD 9.6 million servicing agreement between MCC and MIH. However, the fact that the Canadian operating company continued servicing the receivables after the sale may have raised doubts about MIH's ability to assume and manage the credit risk. There were questions regarding whether the risk of collecting payment of receivables was effectively shifted from MCC to MIH. This is a case where there may be material differences between the contractual terms and the conduct of the parties. The functions performed and risks assumed should ultimately determine the factual substance of the services rendered as part of the actual transaction.[21] In the McKesson case, the CRA may have had doubts about the actual substance relative to the factoring activities performed by MIH.

MCC replied using an analysis undertaken by a third-party expert with experience in securitizing receivables. Ultimately, the judge did not agree with some aspects of the analyses from both parties and found that there were issues with critical assumptions and calculations. Some of these included differing opinions on the use of the days sales outstanding (DSO) input, which should have been floating rather than fixed, but more importantly, that the DSO for the original receivables amount (CAD 480

21. OECD Transfer Pricing Guidelines for Multinational Enterprises and Tax Administrations, January 2022, para. 1.46; available at https://www.oecd.org/tax/transfer-pricing/oecd-transfer-pricing-guidelines-for-multinational-enterprises-and-tax-administrations-20769717.htm.

million) was more appropriately determined using a 30-day term on a four-month rolling average over the five-year term. The court also did not agree with MCC's loss discount, which should have been between 0.06% and 0.08%, in contrast with MCC's 0.23% rate. The discount spread was calculated to be much lower than the applied rate. Finally, the total factoring discount rate range was estimated to contain the CRA's estimated rate. However, MCC's rate was materially above this range.

From a technical point of view, the McKesson case highlights that the comparability of factoring transaction characteristics should be carefully considered when determining the most appropriate transfer pricing method, as using a parameter (in this case, the loss discount) deemed inappropriate may trigger large differences in the final arm's-length range. As we will see next, this is due to the difficulty in identifying directly comparable transactions or companies. At the same time, practitioners should be aware that the parameters chosen for these types of analysis may significantly drive results and should thus be chosen carefully. The McKesson case illustrates the importance of conducting a detailed value chain analysis that frames the context in which the factoring transaction can be understood; a functional, assets, and risks analysis; and economic analyses that consider the various components of the pricing precisely. These include understanding the transaction terms and their implications on the pricing of the transaction.

## IV CHARACTERIZING AND PRICING FACTORING TRANSACTIONS: RECOMMENDATIONS

### 1 OECD Framework

The Organisation for Economic Co-operation and Development (OECD) instructs practitioners to consider the following economically relevant characteristics to provide an accurate delineation of the assessed financial transaction:[22]

(1) Contractual terms
(2) Characteristics of financial instruments
(3) Functional, asset, and risk analysis
(4) Economic circumstances
(5) Business strategies.

The factoring arrangement in the tested arrangement should be considered in terms of its contractual terms and its financial characteristics ((1) and (2) above). In this context, one should evaluate what type of factoring the tested arrangement falls under. The categorization of factoring transactions in section II.1 provides a useful framework for assessing an arrangement.

22. OECD Transfer Pricing Guidance on Financial Transactions, Inclusive Framework on BEPS, 10-12.

Thorough value chain, functional, asset, and risk analyses are key to properly delineating a financial transaction. Factors need to ensure that they have the appropriate functions to manage risks in relation to collecting payment. In a nonrecourse factoring arrangement, factors should be equipped to manage the credit risk associated with the acquired receivables. Certain arrangements may require factors to control foreign exchange risk stemming from receivables in different currencies. As highlighted by the McKesson case, an agreement in which the factor does not have the functions to perform core factoring activities and manage key risks may raise concerns with tax authorities.

Finally, economic circumstances and business strategies are important for understanding the rationale of the transaction. Performing a detailed value chain analysis allows practitioners to identify options realistically available to the supplier and weigh the respective benefits of each option against factoring arrangements. The nature of intragroup factoring transactions might be scrutinized by tax authorities, which may require an analysis of the options realistically available to the taxpayer to avoid reclassifying the transaction. As mentioned in section II.1, factoring transactions presents business advantages when the creditworthiness of the buyer exceeds that of the supplier.

## 2 Pricing Considerations

Once a factoring transaction has been accurately delineated according to the framework presented by the OECD, practitioners are tasked with performing economic analyses to establish the arm's-length range of applicable discount factors.

As usual, the first step of this process involves assessing whether the taxpayer entered any potentially comparable arrangement with a third party. If any potential internal CUP agreements exist, they should be evaluated carefully to determine their level of comparability with the tested transaction. Often, credit institutions such as banks or specialized factoring providers are only interested in working with receivables with high creditworthiness. As a result, a firm may sell its highly rated receivables to third parties while the remainder is serviced internally by the group treasury. In such a situation, a practitioner should carefully consider whether any economically sound adjustment can be applied to the data to reach sufficient comparability. This can be done, for example, by estimating the difference in yields between debt rated similar to the internal CUPs and debt rated similar to the tested transaction.

If no internal CUP is available, identifying alternative sources for market transactions is difficult in our experience. Factoring transactions are private arrangements rarely reported in public regulatory filings, databases, or annual reports. In the rare cases that such transactions can be identified in annual reports, full details of the risk profile of the factored receivables are generally not available, and therefore it is difficult to produce a like-for-like comparison. As a result, it is usually more realistic to apply a transactional profit method.

A simple comparable company search may be performed to identify a sample of comparable firms in the same space (i.e., factoring) and seek to identify a suitable measure of their financial performance. There are two main difficulties with this approach:

(1) First, there are very few independent firms that operate primarily as factors and do not have significant unrelated businesses. Most players in the market are large financial institutions with very diverse activities. The returns of such financial institutions are not indicative of a factoring arrangement.
(2) Second, even when independent factoring companies are identified, it is possible that they focus on a mix of receivables that is not comparable to the tested transaction. In addition, the common terms of the factoring offered by the independent companies should be compared to the tested transaction (e.g., advance/in maturity/in collection, notification/non-notification).

Cases of recourse factoring where credit risk is shared between the factor and suppliers and where the information visibility granted by the factoring agreement plays a role in the conduction of core business activities may be candidates for profit split methods.

In most cases, a synthetic application of the TNMM may be considered to price a factoring transaction. The methodology requires a practitioner to section the factoring remuneration into the following components:

- *The costs incurred for credit collection services*: the servicing costs of the factor should be reflected in the pricing policy. This cost may include administrative, legal, bookkeeping, and dunning expenses.
- *The expected loss resulting from clients' defaults*: the pricing of the discount should reflect the risk profile of the factor, the supplier, and the buyer.
- *The opportunity cost of capital*: the factor's remuneration should contain a profit margin that reflects returns on the costs/expenses of the factor. Sometimes the remuneration for the time value of money may be disaggregated from this item.

## V CONCLUSIONS

This chapter aims to provide an account of the considerations a transfer pricing practitioner should make in relation to factoring transactions. Characterizing and benchmarking a factoring transaction is complex for a variety of reasons:

- First, these arrangements are multilayered and entail significant credit risk as well as credit collection activities being performed by the factor for a remuneration. Factoring transactions may bundle other activities (e.g., foreign exchange management), which may have to be priced separately. As explained in Section 1, it is important to establish what benefits a supplier enjoys as part of a factoring agreement.

- Second, the characteristics of the specific factoring agreement are very important for determining the correct pricing strategy for this transaction (e.g., recourse/nonrecourse, reverse factoring, timing of cash disbursement).
- Third, these characteristics should be considered in the broader context of the role the parties play in the value chain of the multinational enterprise; their functional, asset, and risk profiles; the economic circumstances they operate in; and their business strategies. These factors influence the options that are realistically available to the parties.
- Finally, the data available to benchmark these transactions are likely not abundant, especially because a practitioner should aim to match the creditworthiness of the receivables ceded as part of the tested transaction with the creditworthiness of the comparable data.

The McKesson case exemplifies several of these issues, while highlighting the importance of using accurate assumptions in the models.

One approach to benchmark factoring transactions involves dividing the arrangements into constituent components and then benchmarking each one independently. This is described in the next chapter.

CHAPTER 39

# Factoring: Focus on Accurate Delineation

*Vikram Chand, Aitor Navarro & Camille Vilaseca**

## I INTRODUCTION

In 2020, the Organisation for Economic Co-operation and Development (OECD) released a guidance on the transfer pricing aspects of financial transactions[1] which has been integrated in the 2022 OECD Transfer Pricing Guidance (TPG) under Chapter X.[2] The chapter includes guidance on the transfer pricing aspects of intra-group loans, guarantees, cash pooling arrangements, hedging and other activities such as captive insurance. This being said the chapter does not comment on transfer pricing aspects of factoring arrangements. In fact, in the public comments to the discussion draft of the report released in 2018,[3] several commentators highlighted the necessity to provide guidance on such transactions,[4] nonetheless, this position has not been reflected in the said 2022 update of the TPG. Accordingly, the contribution aims at providing guidance on the application of the arm's length principle (ALP) to factoring arrangements, in particular, at the accurate delineation stage.

* Some parts of the contribution were inspired from an unpublished contribution of Prof. Chand which was co-written with Aline Waeber, a former alumnus of the Executive Program in Transfer Pricing in 2018. The views and opinions set forth herein are the personal views or opinions of the authors; they do not necessarily reflect views or opinions of the organization with which the authors are associated.

1. OECD, *Transfer Pricing Guidance on Financial Transactions: Inclusive Framework on BEPS Actions 4, 8-10* (OECD Publishing, 2020).
2. OECD, *OECD Transfer Pricing Guidelines for Multinational Enterprises and Tax Administrations 2022* (OECD Publishing, 2022).
3. OECD/G20, *BEPS Action 8-10, Discussion Draft on Financial Transactions* (OECD Publishing, 2018).
4. OECD, *Comments on Public Discussion Draft BEPS Actions 8-10, Part I* (OECD Publishing, 2018), e.g., CAJETAN FIEDLER, Ludovici Piccone & Partners, A. DE FRANCESCHI & M. FONTANA.

In order to do so, the contribution will be structured as follows. Section II will provide an overview of factoring transactions and will analyze the different types of factoring arrangements. Section III will introduce the arm's length standard and discuss its application to factoring arrangements. Specifically, the section will further be divided into three parts. The first part will investigate how the ALP is applied to factoring arrangements. In the second part, the authors will present and critically discuss the Canadian *McKesson case*. Similarly, in the third part, the Spanish *Acer case* will be scrutinized. Finally, section IV will conclude.

## II CONCEPT OF FACTORING AND INTRA-GROUP FINANCING

Factoring is a financial transaction in which a business (the client) sells its accounts receivable to another entity, which can be a bank or a company established specifically for this purpose (the factor[5]), at a discount price[6] (i.e., factoring fee). Thus, three different types of economic agents are usually involved in the set up: the client firm (i.e., the company selling the receivables to the factor), the customer firm (i.e., the customer of the client firm), and the factor.[7]

The sale transfers all rights and duties associated with the receivables. The factor thus obtains the right to receive the payments made by the debtor for the invoice amount.[8] Factoring can provide a useful tool to deal with short-term cash requirements.[9] In addition, the administrative tasks related to the management of the account receivables are transferred to the factoring entity.[10] In order to diversify potential risks (specifically, the credit default risk), the client firm could sell all of its receivables to the factor. This is intended to prevent the client firm from mainly selling bad debts.[11]

A factoring arrangement can be carried out on a non-recourse or recourse basis. In non-recourse factoring, the factor takes title to the accounts and bears the default risk associated with the non-payment of the accounts receivable it purchases. In a recourse factoring arrangement, the default risk remains with the client and is not sold to the factor. In practice, within Multinational Groups, non-recourse factoring occurs more frequently.

5. The factor may provide the following services, such as analysis of the credit risk of the debtor, administrative services with respect to the management and collection of the receivables, including recording and monitoring of invoices, etc., *see* ANUSCHKA BAKKER & MARC LEVEY, *Transfer Pricing and Intra-Group Financing* (IBFD Publishing, 1st ed., 2012), 46 (2nd ed., 2021).
6. In the United States, factoring fees can be 0.35% of the face value of the accounts receivable if the factoring entity is not responsible for collection, *see* J. HAROLD MCCLURE, *A Model for Intercompany Factoring Arrangements*, 3 Transfer Pricing Insider 1, 2 (2009).
7. SOUFANI KHALED, *The Decision to Finance Account Receivables: The Factoring Option*, 23 Managerial and Decision Economics 21 (2002).
8. BAKKER & LEVEY, *supra* n. 5, 45 ff.
9. SOUFANI KHALED, *On the Determinants of Factoring as a Finance Choice: Evidence from the UK*, 54 Journal of Economics and Business 239, 240 (2002).
10. HORST GRÄFER ET AL., *Finanzierung: Grundlagen, Institutionen, Instrumente und Kapitalmarkttheorie* (Erich Schmidt Verlag, 2001).
11. HANS PAUL BECKER, *Investition und Finanzierung*, 260 (Springer Fachmedien Wiesbaden, 2012).

In addition, factoring can be done on either a notification or a non-notification basis.[12] In a notification basis factoring, the client firm notifies the account debtors that their accounts have been sold to a factor.[13] The debtors can make their payments only to the factor. Most factoring arrangements are based on a notification basis. However, non-notification factoring, where the client firm does not inform the account debtors about the transaction, also occurs. In this case, the client firm collects the payments on behalf of the factor.[14]

The following example illustrates the mechanism of an intra-group factoring arrangement. Company A, located in Switzerland, sells its products to customers located in Luxembourg (Company B) for a total amount of EUR 100 million. Company A then sells its accounts receivable to a related entity (Company C) at an arm's length discount of 3 % and receives EUR 97 million from Company C (alternatively, Company C could pay EUR 100 million to Company A and Company A would then pay Euro 3 million as commission to Company C). The ownership of the receivables has thus been transferred to Company C, which obtains the right to receive the payments made by Company B for the amount due. The factoring agreement is carried out on a non-recourse basis, which means that Company C bears the default risk associated with the non-payment of the accounts receivable it purchases. Company C's overall profit is the difference between the price it paid for the receivables and the money received from Company B, less the amount lost due in case of default.

From a transfer pricing perspective, the factor needs to receive remuneration for its factoring services that are in line with the value it creates, i.e., based on its functions performed, risks assumed and assets employed. In general, the factor is remunerated in consideration of:[15] (i) the costs incurred for credit collection services; (ii) the expected loss resulting from the clients default (i.e., default risk); (iii) the opportunity cost of capital (i.e., the time value of money).[16] Section III will provide a more elaborate discussion on the arm's length remuneration of a factoring activity.

## III APPLICATION OF THE ALP TO FACTORING ARRANGEMENTS: OVERVIEW AND CASE LAW

### 1 Application of the ALP to Factoring Arrangements

#### *A Accurate Delineation of the Transaction*

When dealing with factoring arrangements, as a first step, it is important to analyze whether the factors "relevant economic circumstances" or "economically relevant

12. Cristoph Braunschweig, *Unternehmensfinanzierung*, 119 (De Gruyter Oldenbourg, 1999).
13. Bakker & Levey, *supra* n. 5, 45-46.
14. Becker, *supra* n. 11, 258.
15. Bakker & Levey, *supra* n. 5, 47.
16. Marta Pankiv, *Contemporary Application of the Arm's Length Principle in Transfer Pricing*, 46 (WU - Tax Law and Policy Series, IBFD Publishing, 2017).

characteristics" would indicate that it is actually carrying out factoring activities.[17] If the facts and circumstances indicate that the factor's functional profile (functions performed, assets employed and risks assumed) would not support its qualification as a factor, then the tax authorities may delineate the related party arrangement based on the actual conduct of the parties.[18]

The question then arises as to under which situations can the factor be entitled to its core income, i.e., debtor-related income. Essentially, the OECD TPG state that the risks and returns should be allocated to the entity that controls the risk and has the financial capacity to bear the risk.[19]

The economically significant risk for a factor, in a non-recourse factoring arrangement, is the assumption of the credit risk associated with the non-payment of the accounts receivables.[20] The most active decision-making function that constitutes assumption of the credit risk pertains to an analysis of the creditworthiness of the trade receivables prior to and after entering into the factoring arrangement (e.g., analysis of the data provided by the selling entity vis-à-vis its customers by the factor in order to determine the default probability).[21] In other words, this would also imply that the factoring company has the necessary personnel who could evaluate the risk of taking on the receivables. Moreover, the other key functions of the factor generally relate to the operational aspects of the factoring arrangement such as the management of the accounts receivable, invoicing and dunning processes and cash management activities.[22] Also, the factor performs the financing activity in the sense that it advances the amounts of the trade receivables prior to the payment of the invoices. Accordingly, following OECD guidance in this regard, the argument can be made that the factor should be entitled to its core income when it employs appropriate personnel and these personnel's functions demonstrate that they have the capability to make decisions with respect to (i) taking on, laying off or declining the credit risk as well as the risks associated with other key activities; and (ii) deciding whether and how to respond to the credit risk as well as other risks associated with the decisions making opportunity. Moreover, the entity should also demonstrate that it can perform the decision-making activity associated with the risks. Furthermore, even if the management of risks is outsourced, the personnel in the factoring entity must be able to demonstrate that they can oversee and manage the outsourced risks.[23]

Additionally, the factor needs to have the financial capacity to bear the credit risk.[24] This would be the case when the factor is adequately capitalized (e.g., it has substantial equity funding) to meet its financial obligations or when the factor has the necessary funds to assume and mitigate this risk by entering into arrangements to hedge its risks.

17. OECD TPG 2022, *supra* n. 2, para. 1.36.
18. *Ibid.*, para. 1.45.
19. *Ibid.*, para. 1.60.
20. Bakker & Levey, *supra* n. 5, 45.
21. Becker, *supra* n. 11.
22. Bakker & Levey, *supra* n. 5, 46.
23. OECD TPG 2022, *supra* n. 2, para. 1.63.
24. *Ibid.*, para. 1.64. *See also* Bakker & Levey, *supra* n. 5, 48.

However, the factor should not be entitled to core income when it acts on behalf of the members of the multinational group. Thus, even if the directors of the factor formalize the decisions in the state where the factor is set up by holding local meetings, documenting minutes and signing documents, although the credit risk (other risks) related decisions were made in another state (for instance, the state of the parent company), then it is clear that the decision-making function exercised by the directors does not qualify as an exercise that demonstrates control over the risks. Therefore, if one follows the OECD parameters on risk attribution, this could result in a reduction in the allocation of risk-related returns, or ultimately a reallocation of the risk to the entity where the control is asserted.[25]

For example, assume that Company A, located in Country A, sells its products to customers located in Country B (Company B) for a total amount of EUR 100 million. Company A then enters into a "factoring arrangement" with a related entity (Company C) in Country C and sells its accounts receivable at a discount rate of 5% and receives EUR 95 million from Company C. Company A then claims EUR 5 million as a deduction for tax purposes. However, the accurate delineation process shows that Company C does not have the appropriate decision makers who could "control" the default risk but rather Company C has personnel who only provide administrative services associated with the factoring activity. In this case, most likely, the factor would only be remunerated on a cost-plus basis (assume this is EUR 1 million). Consequently, Company A would be denied a deduction of EUR 1 million.

Furthermore, under fairly exceptional circumstances,[26] the OECD asserts that a controlled transaction may be disregarded, and if appropriate, replaced by an alternative transaction, where the arrangements made in relation to the transaction, viewed in their totality, differ from those which would have been adopted by independent enterprises behaving in a commercially rational manner in comparable circumstances, thereby preventing determination of a price that would be acceptable to both of the parties taking into account their respective perspectives and the options realistically available to each of them at the time of entering into the transaction.[27] A factoring arrangement thus needs to have the commercial rationality of an arrangement that third parties would agree to under similar economic circumstances.

### *B* *Determining Arm's Length Pricing*

In the next step, an adequate compensation for the factoring activity and the risks assumed by the factor needs to be determined. As outlined in chapter (Chapter 40),

25. OECD TPG 2022, *supra* n. 2, para. 1.66.
26. *See ibid.*, para. 1.143: "Restructuring of legitimate business transactions would be a wholly arbitrary exercise the inequity of which could be compounded by double taxation created where the other tax administration does not share the same views as to how the transaction should be structured." For a detailed analysis of the limits of recharacterization in transfer pricing, *see* Andreas Bullen, *Arm's Length Transaction Structures: Recognizing and Restructuring Controlled Transactions in Transfer Pricing* (IBFD Doctoral Series, 2011), and Aitor Navarro, *Transactional Adjustments in Transfer Pricing* (IBFD Doctoral Series, 2018).
27. *Ibid.*, para. 1.142.

more often than not, it may be difficult to apply the traditional or transactional-based methods. Thus, other methods may need to be applied. In this regard, the discount rate (or the commission) is often calculated as the sum of several components,[28] such as an administrative fee, the risk of default assumed by the factoring entity (which is higher in the case of non-recourse factoring), the opportunity cost of capital and a remuneration for time value of the money.[29] Other factors may also be considered.

*Factoring services/Administrative fee:* Within an multinational enterprise (MNE) Group, factoring activities are often provided centrally by a factoring entity for economic reasons (such as a more efficient management of liquidity and debt risks). The administrative operations (management of the accounts receivable, invoicing processes, and cash management activities) with respect to the factoring activity can be regarded as an intra-group service. For the provision of such a service, the factoring entity should receive an arm's length remuneration. This is clearly mentioned in 2022 OECD TPG under Chapter VII in paragraphs 7.14 and 7.39 and this could most likely be determined by using the comparable uncontrolled price (CUP) or the transactional net margin method (TNMM). However, specific pricing formulas have to be adopted for the default risk and the opportunity cost of capital.

*Default risk:* The default risk can be defined as the "risk of loss arising from the risk of a counterparty's failure to perform on its contractual obligations."[30] This loss can be estimated by using the probability of default of the trade receivables. The probabilities of default can be obtained from Credit rating agencies.[31] Generally speaking, companies with a lower credit rating have a higher risk of default, which leads to a higher required return.

*The opportunity cost of capital and a remuneration for time value of money*: The equity engaged by investors in the factoring company should be remunerated in light of the opportunity cost. Additionally, irrespective of the expected return of the factoring entity, a remuneration for time value of money should be added (most likely, a risk-free rate).

Some of these components were also discussed in the *McKesson*[32] case which we now turn too.

## 2 Canadian McKesson Judgement

### *A Facts*

In December 2002, McKesson Canada Corporation (MCC)[33] entered into a factoring arrangement with a related party located in Luxembourg, McKesson International

28. Bakker & Levey, *supra* n. 5, 264.
29. The arm's length pricing of each component can be assessed using different methods.
30. *Default Risk*, Erik Banks, *The Palgrave Macmillan Dictionary of Finance, Investment and Banking* (Palgrave Macmillan, 2010).
31. Pierre Vernimmen et al., *Corporate Finance: Theory and Practice* (John Wiley and Sons Ltd, 6th ed., 2014).
32. *McKesson Canada Corporation v. The Queen*, 2013 TCC 404, para. 22.
33. MCC is a wholly owned subsidiary of McKesson Corporation, the largest US public health company. They are mainly involved in the distribution of pharmaceutical products.

Holdings III (MIH). More specifically, the company sold its trade receivables to MIH in the amount of CAD 460 million. In addition, MIH agreed to continue to purchase new receivables on a daily basis for a period of five years (with a maximum limit of CAD 900 million).[34]

The terms and conditions of the sale of receivables were governed by a contractual arrangement consisting of a Receivables Sales Arrangement (RSA) and a Servicing Agreement. These receivables were mainly traded account receivables from third-party customers of MCC whose receivables did not exceed 2% of MCC's outstanding receivables pool.[35] Under the RSA, the receivables were sold at a discount rate of 2.206% from their face amount.[36] The discount rate was intended to compensate MIH for the potential risk that some receivables may not be collected. It was calculated as the sum of three components; a yield rate, a loss discount (reflecting the risk of default of the trade receivables), and a discount spread (the largest element of the discount spread). Under the Servicing Agreement, MCC agreed to continue to act as a service provider for MIH with respect to these receivables for a yearly fee of CAD 9.6 million.[37]

*The Yield Rate:* The Yield Rate reflected the risk-free market rate of return to consider the time value of money. The risk-free rate was based on the Canadian 30 Day Overnight Rate (CDOR).[38]

*The Loss Discount:* The Loss Discount captured the risk of default that may arise from the trade receivables failing to meet their payment obligations (i.e., credit risk). It was calculated as the sum of the weighted Individual Loss Discount for all debtors.[39]

*The Discount Spread:* The RSA fixed the discount spread at 1.7305%. It was composed of four elements:[40]

(i) a servicing discount to cover the expected cost of finding a new service provider in case the servicing arrangement was terminated;
(ii) a prompt payment dilution discount to reflect the risk that MCC's customers might increase the amount of the prompt payment discount that is available to them;
(iii) an accrued rebate dilution discount to compensate for the possibility that any of the receivables might offset its liabilities to MCC using accrued rebates;
(iv) an interest discount to compensate MIH (the factor) for its cost of capital.

At the time of the receivables transfer, MCC had sales of CAD 3 billion, profits of CAD 40 million, 2,400 employees and the largest share of the Canadian market.[41]

34. David L.P. Francescucci & Sophie Larochelle, *Is the Canadian Statutory Transfer Pricing Adjustment Formula in Need of an Adjustment?*, 21 Int'l Transfer Pricing J. 241, 241 (2014).
35. *McKesson* case, *supra* n. 32, para. 22.
36. *Ibid.*, para. 14.
37. *Ibid.*, para. 27.
38. *Ibid.*, para. 37.
39. *Ibid.*, para. 40.
40. Danny Beeton et al., *The McKesson Canada Decision: Further Guidance on the Transfer Pricing of Debt Factoring Arrangements*, 21(1) Int'l Transfer Pricing J. 1-5 (2014); *McKesson* case, *supra* n. 32, para. 45.
41. *McKesson* case, *supra* n. 32, para. 6.

Furthermore, it was successfully managing its receivables pool, having a roughly 30-day payment average and a 0.043% bad debt experience. MCC had a large credit and collections department, headed by accountants, and managed to collect 99.96% of its receivables.[42]

In fact, the Court pointed out that MCC did not have any business need for a cash infusion or borrowing and did not approach its commercial banks (nor any other lender) before entering into the RSA.[43] It added that "the predominant purpose of McKesson Canada entering into the transactions was the reduction of its Canadian tax on its profits. McKesson Canada's predominant purpose was not to raise or free up capital, reduce the credit risk of its customers or improve its balance sheet; they were results of the transactions."[44] Throughout the years of the factoring arrangement, MIH had a single employee.[45] Unfortunately, the functions carried out by the employee are not developed or described in the decision.

In order to finance the receivables purchase, MIH entered into a loan agreement with an Irish-related company. The repayment of the loan was fully guaranteed by another related company in Luxembourg (MIH2). In addition, MIH was granted an indemnity in case of any defaults of MCC's receivables.[46] Both the guarantee as well as the indemnity thus reduced MIH's credit risk significantly.[47]

As a result of the discounts upon the purchase of the receivables, the Canadian entity MCC was no longer able to operate profitably in the tax year following the sale of receivables to the factor.[48] Subsequently, the Canada Revenue Agency (CRA) analyzed the arm's length nature of the applied discount rate in a transfer pricing audit. The CRA came to the conclusion that it was greater than the rate that would have been agreed between independent parties dealing at arm's length.[49] The CRA assessed whether third parties bearing similar risks and performing similar functions would agree upon the same discount rate.[50] According to calculations of the CRA, the arm's length discount rate would be equal to 1.0127%. The CRA thus made a transfer pricing adjustment for the year of CAD 26.6 million.

42. *Ibid.*, para. 7.
43. *Ibid.*, para. 9.
44. *Ibid.*, para. 18. The Court ulteriorly adds: "The purpose was to reduce McKesson Canada's Canadian tax liability (and therefore McKesson Group's worldwide tax liability) by paying the maximum discount under the RSA that McKesson Group believed it could reasonably justify. For the McKesson Group this appears to have been much more of a tax avoidance plan than a structured finance product. No reason as ever given for wanting to transfer risk to Luxembourg" para. 274.
45. *Ibid.*, para. 173. There is no mention of what were the functions of this single employee.
46. *Ibid.*, para. 34.
47. *Ibid.*, para. 14.
48. FRANCESCUCCI & LAROCHELLE, *supra* n. 34, 241.
49. *Ibid.*
50. *Ibid.*

### B The Judgement of the Court

Nearly two years after the conclusion of a 32-day trial heard over a period of five months, and in consideration of many expert reports and evidence, the Tax Court of Canada (through Justice Patrick Boyle)[51] made its long-anticipated decision.[52]

The Court stated that "the predominant purpose and intention of McKesson Canada participating in the RSA and related transactions with the other McKesson Group members was not to access capital or to lay off credit risk. Those were results of the transactions but did not motivate them. The purpose was to reduce McKesson Canada's Canadian tax liability (and therefore McKesson Group's worldwide tax liability) by paying the maximum discount under the RSA that McKesson Group believed it could reasonably justify. For the McKesson Group this appears to have been much more of a tax avoidance plan than a structured finance product. No reason was ever given for wanting to transfer risk to Luxembourg."[53] Nonetheless, because the Crown did not rely upon Article 247(2)(b) and (d) and did not demand the recharacterization of the transaction, the Court did not examine the commercial rationale of the transaction and whether arm's length parties would enter or not into similar factoring arrangement.[54] It concludes that "In this case the Court is able to limit itself to a consideration of terms and conditions which it finds to not be on arm's length terms and that directly relate to pricing."[55] Consequently, the Court performed a transfer pricing adjustment based on Article 247(2)(a) and (c).

The Court accepted MCC's transfer pricing approach to calculate the discount rate formula and rejected the recalculation proposed by the CRA. However, the Court recalculated each component of the discount rate applied by MCC (i.e., yield rate, rate, loss discount as well as the discount spread) and concluded that the range of the final arm's length discount rate is between 0.959% and 1.17%[56] (*see* Table 39.1).

*Table 39.1 Reassessment of the Discount Spread by the Court*[57]

| *Components* | *Sub-components* | *MCC* | *Court* |
|---|---|---|---|
| Yield rate | | 0.2375% | 0.2293% |
| Loss discount | | 0.2380% | 0.06%-0.08% |
| Discount spread | | 1.7305% | 0.67%-0.86% |
| | Servicing Discount | 0.65% | 0.17%-0.25% |
| | Prompt Payment Dilutions Discount | | 0.50%-0.53% |

51. *McKesson* case, *supra* n. 32, paras 184-215.
52. *Ibid.*, para. 19.
53. *Ibid.*, para. 274.
54. *Ibid.*, para. 125.
55. *Ibid.*, para. 127.
56. *Ibid.*, para. 350.
57. Francescucci & Larochelle, *supra* n. 34, 242.

| *Components* | *Sub-components* | *MCC* | *Court* |
|---|---|---|---|
| | Accrued Rebate Dilutions Discount | 0.244% | 0.00% |
| | Interest discount | 0.4564% | 0.00%-0.08% |
| *Total Discount rate* | | *2.206%* | *0.959%-1.17%* |
| Rate calculated by CRA | | 1.10127% | |

As the overall discount rate calculated by the CRA was within the range estimated by the Court, and the discount rate applied by the taxpayer was outside the range, the Court ruled in favour of the CRA.[58] The Court further argued that MCC did not properly demonstrate that the calculation of the discount rate of 2.206% was in line with the ALP.[59]

### C Critical Comments on Accurate Delineation of the Arrangement and Its Recognition in Light with the Recent Developments in Canada

As shown in Table 39.1, the Court recognized the factoring transaction as a whole but emphasized that its pricing was not at arm's length based on Article 247(2)(a) and (c). The Court, therefore, rejected many elements of the discount rate that MCC and MIH agreed to.[60] The Court argued that a recharacterization of the transaction is only allowed under paragraphs 247(2)(b) and (d) of the Income Tax Act (ITA), which the CRA did not rely upon.[61] The Court further stated that under paragraphs (2)(a) and (c) of the ITA, the CRA is authorized to adjust both the nature and the quantum of an amount used by the taxpayer to reflect the quantum or nature of that amount that would have been used had the "terms and conditions" been at arm's length.[62] In its decision, the Court varied some of the terms of the discount rate. The question arises as to whether these adjustments could already be classified as a recharacterization of the transaction. The Court provided that there may come a point at which changes to the terms and conditions of a transaction are so fundamental that they could constitute in effect a recharacterization.[63] However, no further elaboration on the limits of the scope of adjustments that may be performed in this situation was done.

Another issue at stake that should have deserved more scrutiny is the functional profile of MIH. Indeed, the facts have shown that the entity had a single employee during the years under review. This could probably indicate that the entity did not have control over the risks related to the RSA (e.g., all debtor-related risks pre and post RSA). One may also argue that MIH did not bear financial risks. Indeed, the Court asserted

58. *Ibid.*, para. 358; Pankiv, *supra* n. 16, para. 4.4.3.4.
59. *McKesson* case, *supra* n. 32, para. 353.
60. Pankiv, *supra* n. 16, para. 4.4.4.
61. *McKesson* case, *supra* n. 32, para. 125.
62. *Ibid.*, para. 126.
63. *Ibid.*, para. 127.

that "MIH, McKesson Canada's counter-party to the RSA and the Servicing Agreement, did not take any financial risk under this group of contemporaneous, inter-woven agreements all of which were financially and legally linked and related. All such risk was borne by other entities in the McKesson Group. That risk ultimately remained economically with McKesson U.S., everyone's ultimate parent company, both before and after the RSA transactions."[64] Hence, based on the current OECD TPG, it may be argued that MIH should not have been entitled to any return as it did not take on any significant risk in relation to the RSA.

This said, in the Canadian legal system, the trend for not re characterizing transactions is also witnessed in the recent *Cameco* and *AgraCity* cases. We briefly discuss these cases and then return to the *McKesson* case.

The *Cameco* case dealt with the application of the Canadian transfer pricing rules to a commodity trading structure. At the core and on the basis of a highly simplified fact pattern, a Canadian parent (taxpayer) had shifted its Uranium trading business to European establishments. Specifically, to the Swiss branch of a Luxembourg Subsidiary (CESA) which was later converted to a Swiss subsidiary (CEL). CESA/CEL had a few employees who were involved in carrying out the core trading operations. Essentially, the European establishments entered into contracts with third parties and the taxpayer (and its other associated enterprises). According to the contracts, CESA/CEL bought Uranium mostly from independent parties and then sold the Uranium to their related parties which then sold the items to independent clients.

By doing so, the related parties received compensation from the clients and then after retaining a commission fee, passed on bulk of the income to the European establishments. Consequently, profits were accumulated in the European establishments (in particular, Swiss subsidiary). In this case, price risk was identified as an economically significant risk. The question arose as to which party bore this risk, that is, the taxpayer or the Swiss subsidiary?

The tax administration argued that this risk was borne by the taxpayer (parent) and should be entitled to residual profit. Correspondingly, the Swiss subsidiary should be characterized as a limited risk entity and thus be entitled to lower profits. In this regard, the Canadian Tax Court (CTC) taking into consideration the Swiss subsidiary functional profile states in paragraph 838 "Of course, contractual terms may not always reflect the economic substance of an arrangement, which may in turn warrant a transfer pricing adjustment. In this case, CESA/CEL entered into a number of contracts for the purchase of uranium. In doing so, CESA/CEL took on the price risk associated with its ownership of the uranium acquired under those contracts." Although it is not clear, it seems that the CTC focuses on which party bears the risk from a legal and contractual standpoint as the functional profile of the Swiss subsidiary was not deliberated upon extensively. This could be at odds with the six-step framework contained in Chapter I of the OECD TPG.

Additionally, under section 247(2)(b) of the Canadian Income Tax Act, a structural adjustment can be made if the transaction or series of transactions (i) "would

64. *Ibid.*, para. 34.

not have been entered into by persons dealing at arm's length" and if it (ii) "can reasonably be considered not to have been entered into primarily for bona fide purposes other than to obtain a tax benefit." The tax administration applied this two-prong provision to the taxpayer (Canadian parent) and argued that the profits of the Swiss subsidiary should be reallocated to the taxpayer as independent enterprises would never enter into such agreements. However, the CTC ruled against the tax administration. Specifically, it stated that while the conditions of section 247(2)(b)(ii) seem to be satisfied as the main purpose of the arrangement was to obtain a tax saving,[65] the provisions of section 247(2)(b)(i) are not satisfied. Only key points of the judgment will be discussed henceforth.

With respect to the provision, as a start, the CTC remarked in paragraph 696 that "Paragraph 247(2)(d) is sometimes referred to as a recharacterization rule ... However, strictly speaking, paragraph 247(2)(d) does not authorize the Minister to recharacterize the transaction or series identified in the preamble. Rather, paragraph 247(2)(d) authorizes the Minister to identify an alternative transaction or series that in the same circumstances would be entered into by arm's length parties in place of the transaction or series and then to make an adjustment that reflects arm's length terms and conditions for that alternative transaction or series. Because the adjustment is based on the arm's length terms and conditions of an alternative transaction or series, the adjustment may alter the quantum or the nature of an amount."

Thereafter, in paragraph 714, the CTC analyses section 247(2)(b)(i) and states that "... the subparagraph is asking whether the transaction or series under scrutiny would have been entered into by arm's length persons acting in a commercially rational manner. The focus of the test is the commercial rationality (or irrationality) of the transaction or series, taking into consideration all relevant circumstances... The determination of whether a transaction or a series is commercially rational requires an objective assessment of the transaction or series."

With respect to section 247(2)(b)(i), the key question analyzed was whether it is commercially rational for the taxpayer to transfer its Uranium trading business (business opportunity) to the Swiss subsidiary?[66] In response, the Court highlighted in Para 719 that "I ... conclude that it is commercially rational for a person to give up a business opportunity and that the correct focus in such a situation is the compensation received for doing so. The issue of arm's length compensation is addressed by paragraphs 247(2)(a) and (c)." Moreover, the Court remarked in paragraph 722 that "... the behaviour of the parent corporation in establishing subsidiaries and placing business opportunities in those subsidiaries is not commercially irrational. I would go so far as to suggest that such behaviour is a core function of the parent of a multinational enterprise." Thus, the fact that the taxpayer transferred its business opportunity to a subsidiary cannot be considered to be commercially irrational as independent parties would do the same if they were compensated adequately. While delivering its judgment, the CTC referred to the exceptional circumstances contained in the 1995 and 2010 OECD TPG (discussed in Chapter 10 of this book).

65. *Cameco Corporation v. The Queen*, 2018 TCC 195, paras. 739-743.
66. *Ibid.*, para. 717.

The decision of the CTC was appealed by the tax administration before the Canadian Federal Court of Appeals (CFCA).[67] As a start, in paragraph 43, it was remarked that "subparagraph 247(2)(b)(i) of the Act does not refer to whether the particular taxpayer would not have entered into the particular transaction with the non-resident if that taxpayer had been dealing with the non-resident at arm's length or what other options may have been available to that particular taxpayer. Rather, this subparagraph raises the issue of whether the transaction or series of transactions would have been entered into between persons dealing with each other at arm's length (an objective test based on hypothetical persons)—not whether the particular taxpayer would have entered into the transaction or series of transactions in issue with an arm's length party (a subjective test). A test based on what a hypothetical person (or persons) would have done is not foreign to the law as the standard of care in a negligence case is a 'hypothetical 'reasonable person'."

The underlined statement somehow indicates that the key question analyzed by both the CTC and CFCA was whether the same transaction can be observed between independent parties as opposed to whether the actual transaction (undertaken by the particular taxpayer) possesses the commercial rationality of arrangements that would be agreed between unrelated parties under comparable economic circumstances. This is at odds with the guidance included in paragraph 1.123 of the 2017 Guidance which states "The key question in the analysis is whether the actual transaction possesses the commercial rationality of arrangements that would be agreed between unrelated parties under comparable economic circumstances, not whether the same transaction can be observed between independent parties." As a result, both Courts did not engage in a detailed discussion on options realistically available.

The CFCA in paragraphs 66-68 also referred to the two exceptions contained in the 1995/2010 OECD guidelines but made specific references to the commercially irrational exception. To reiterate, in order for this exception to apply, the 1995/2010 OECD guidelines state that two cumulative criteria need to be fulfilled. Keeping this in mind, regarding the second criterion, the CFCA states "in this case, there is no indication that the structure, as implemented, impeded the determination of an appropriate transfer price. There is nothing to indicate or suggest that the structure impeded either the Canada Revenue Agency's or the Tax Court Judge's ability to determine the appropriate transfer price." As a result, the commercial rationality exception is not triggered, and the income cannot be reallocated to the parent.

As the Courts did not enter into a detailed discussion on options realistically available, the judgment indicates the power given to the tax administration under domestic law could be narrower than that provided in the guidelines. As a result, depending on the country, the scope of the national rule could be far more restrictive than the scope of Article 9 (and the guidelines). Accordingly, depending on the country, Courts may reject the application of structural adjustments if the wording of the law does not provide that power.

67. *Cameco Corporation v. The Queen*, 2020 FCA 112.

Another example of a recent decision in Canada that witnessed the refusal of the Tax Court to recharacterize a transactions is enshrined in the 2020 *AgraCity* case.

AgraCity is a company located in Canada and is owned by Jason Mann. AgraCity is part of the Farmers of North America group of companies (FNA Group). The FNA Group wanted to make available to the Canadian farmers a glyphosate-based herbicide, ClearOut, nonetheless, the sale of this product was not allowed in Canada based on the Pest Management Control Act. Therefore, James Mann, Jason's brother, decided to set up a company in the United States (US), US NewAgCo to purchase and store ClearOut in the US to, later on, sell it to the Canadian farmers, as a result of the Own User Import (OUI) program. Consequently, US NewAgCo made profits out of the sales of ClearOut to AgraCity and other FNA Group members. Accordingly, AgraCity entered into a service agreement with US NewAgCo whereby AgraCity had to attend to the logistical and related activities of the sales and deliveries to the Canadian buyers. Therefore, AgraCity was paid by US NewAgCo an amount per litre of ClearOut sold to perform these services.[68]

In March 2006 NewAgCo Barbados is incorporated to take on the role of US NewAgCo. Agra City, US NewAgCo and NewAgCo Barbados are deemed as associated enterprises. The handover also covered inventory and rights on ClearOut, which were transferred to NewAgCo Barbados in 2006. It followed that AgraCity entered into a Services Agreement with NewAgCo Barbados to carry on the activities of selling ClearOut to members of the FNA Group in Canada.[69]

In assessing AgraCity for its 2007 and 2008 fiscal tax years, the Canadian Revenue Agency (CRA) performed a transfer pricing adjustment and reallocated all profits derived from NewAgCo Barbados to the income of AgraCity. The latter appealed the decision. In the Court, the Respondent, the Crown, supported the CRA position and suggested three legal alternatives: first, the transactions are a sham; second, a recharacterization of the controlled transactions under Article 247(2)(b) and (d) should be carried out; finally, a pricing adjustment under Article 247(2)(a) and (c) should be performed. Following is the argumentation and response of the Court to the Respondent's demands.

First, the CTC relied on the definition of a sham provided in *Snook*,[70] according to which it "means acts done or documents executed by the parties to the 'sham' which are intended by them to give to third parties or to the court the appearance of creating between the parties legal rights and obligations different from the actual legal rights and obligations (if any) which the parties intend to create."[71] It also relied on the most recent definition laid out in Cameco[72] and *Palletta v. The Queen*.[73] The Court insisted on the fact that to determine whether the transaction was a sham or not, it must be analyzed whether the parties misrepresented the nature of their arrangements to the

68. *AgraCity v. The Queen*, 2020 TCC 91, para. 50.
69. *Ibid.*, para. 88.
70. *Snook v. London & West Riding Investments*, Ltd [1967] 1 All E.R. 518.
71. *Ibid.*, 528.
72. *Cameco* case, *supra* nn. 65 & 67.
73. *Paletta v. The Queen*, 2019 TCC 205.

tax authorities. It also stated the difference between a sham and abuse and that a sham is a serious allegation that requires the presentation of convincing evidence.

It concluded that no convincing evidence could lead to the consideration of a sham because it cannot be established "i) that the parties to the transactions sought to present to anyone that the legal rights and obligations of the parties were different than what they knew or understood them to be, or ii) that any of those parties sought to deceive anyone about their purpose or intention or reasons for entering into any of the transactions."[74] The CTC justified its position asserting that the transactions between NewAgCo Barbados and AgraCity were similar to the one carried out between US NewAgCo and AgraCity in the previous year. Indeed, it asserted that the "basic structure involving a non-Canadian company to source and sell the ClearOut was done for bona fide non-tax reasons with no reason to, or intention to, to deceive anyone."[75]

Subsequently, the Court took position on whether the controlled transaction should be recharacterized under Article 247 (2)(b) and (d) due to a lack of commercial rationality.

Regarding the difference between Article 247 paragraphs (c) and (d), the CTC highlighted that "The difference [...] is that income amounts are redetermined as to quantum and/or nature under paragraph (c) by reference to revised terms and/or conditions of the parties' transactions, whereas under paragraph (d) it is by reference to substituted notional transactions. That distinction is clear from the text of the provisions. The nature and/or the quantum of income amounts can be redetermined under either sets of provisions."[76]

The Court's argumentation on the denial of recharacterization is rather brief. It is stated that due to an absence of evidence to support the position that arm's length parties would not enter into transactions similar to the controlled transactions presented in the case, and due to the fact that NewAgCo Barbados had assets and resources, and took real risks regarding the transactions, the CTC cannot decide in favour of the Respondent. Therefore, no recharacterization should be carried out based on Article 247(2)(b) and (d).[77]

Finally, the Court went on to determine whether Article 247(2)(a) and (c), resulting in a transfer pricing adjustment, is applicable to the controlled transactions. Against the functional analysis of NewAgCo Barbados presented by the Respondent, which stated that the entity did not have the necessary profile in terms of functions and risks to be allocated returns, the Court asserted that the evidence provided could in fact not prove that "if NewAgco Barbados and AgraCity were arm's length parties, they would have entered into a Services Agreement on terms and conditions that gave 100% of the ClearOut sales profits to AgraCity and no share whatsoever of those profits to NewAgco Barbados."[78] For the CTC, the Respondent was not able either to support the position that the service fees received by AgraCity were not at arm's length. Therefore,

74. *AgraCity* case, *supra* n. 68, para. 77.
75. *Ibid.*, para. 78 (i).
76. *Ibid.*, para. 24.
77. *Ibid.*, para. 83.
78. *Ibid.*, para. 99.

the Court rejected the application of Article 247(2)(a) and (c) and did not grant the defendant's request to make a transfer pricing adjustment. Indeed, it based its decision on the Appellant's report which stated that the result of a comparable analysis using the CUP method led to the conclusion that the transaction was at arm's length and supported this position.

The *AgraCity* case, like the *Cameco* case, are example of how difficult it is for the CRA and the Crown to demand the recharacterization of transactions based on Article 247(2)(b) and (d) and to succeed in the Canadian courts. However, it also proves that the CRA still needs to enhance its argumentation to convince the CTC that Article 247(2)(b) and (d) should apply, as the latter concluded that the Respondent was not able to bring evidence to demonstrate that the transaction would not be entered into between arm's length parties. Indeed, the Appellant was the only party to provide a comparable analysis using a transfer pricing method and leading to the determination of an arm's length range.

One of the critical aspects of the CTC decision is that it does not clearly discuss the commercial rationale of the structure while asserting that the transactions should not be recharacterized. Indeed, the only mention of the rationale of the initial transactions between the US and Canadian entities can be found in a different section of the decision where the Court states that these transactions have been carried out for bona fide non-tax reasons.[79] The initial structure was commercially rational because it aimed at making accessible a product for the Canadian entities that would otherwise not be able to buy such product. The rationale for the transactions between the Barbadian and Canadian entities seems to be to replicate the one previously taking place between US NewAgCo and AgraCity. Nonetheless, the CTC asserted in the facts that the incorporation of a new entity in Barbados "was done primarily to minimize the US tax payable on the sales profits."[80] Hence, the commercial rationale of the controlled transactions under review appears to be in fact more than debatable. Moreover, the Respondent defended that "it is obvious that arm's length commercial parties would never agree to let NewAgco Barbados have any of the profits if it served no function in the transactions given that it had no assets, employees, resources, or other role or value to contribute to the profit making enterprise or to bring thereto."[81] Finally, no mention is made by the parties of the options realistically available.

Furthermore, our second critical remark revolves around the functional profile of NewAgCo Barbados. As stated in the OECD TPG, the functional analysis is crucial to determine whether an entity should be allocated returns. The Court asserts that NewAgCo Barbados had the necessary functions and risks to be allocated returns, nonetheless, the Respondent alleged the exact opposite. Indeed, according to the latter, NewAgCo Barbados was a shell company with no employees, and its functional profile proved that it did not perform functions, used assets and assumed risks necessary to be allocated any profits. That is why the Respondent was advocating for the reallocation of 100% of the profits derived by NewAgCo Barbados to the income of AgraCity

79. *Ibid.*, para. 78.
80. *Ibid.*, para. 57.
81. *Ibid.*, para. 82.

through a transfer pricing adjustment based on Article 247(2)(a) and (c). The CTC did not follow the Respondent position and affirmed that the Barbadian entity, based on its functional profile, should be allocated returns. Therefore, the Court position seems to be not aligned with the OECD position implying that to be allocated return, an entity must perform functions, bear assets and assume risks.

In light of the above discussion, it is relevant to return to the *McKesson* case and comment on two issues. First, should MIH be allocated the risks and returns? Second, does the entire set up of MIH make commercial sense?

As already highlighted, it appears that MIH should not be allocated risks and consequently neither should it be allocated returns. Put differently, it could be argued that MIH did not perform any significant function and did not have the control over the risks which consist in "(i) the capability to make decisions to take on, lay off, or decline a risk-bearing opportunity, together with the actual performance of that decision-making function and (ii) the capability to make decisions on whether and how to respond to the risks associated with the opportunity, together with the actual performance of that decision-making function."[82]

With respect to whether the entire structure involving MIH has commercial rationality, it must first be noted that if an arrangement lacks commercial rationality, it could potentially be disregarded and recharacterized for transfer pricing purposes according to the OECD TPG.

To ascertain the commercial rationality of an arrangement, first, it must be established whether the arrangement, in its totality, differs from an arrangement that would have been entered into by independent parties behaving in a rational manner and in comparable circumstances. Second, it must be determined whether such difference between the intra-group arrangement and an arrangement between independent parties would subsequently prevent the determination of a price that would be acceptable for both parties. Such analysis of the arrangement must be performed based on the respective perspectives of both parties and on their options realistically available at the time of entering into the transaction.

In the *McKesson* case, because MCC "had no identified business need for a cash infusion or borrowing, nor did McKesson Group need McKesson Canada to raise funds for another member of the group"[83] when entering into the RSA and because the structure appeared to have been established "to reduce McKesson Canada's Canadian tax liability (and therefore McKesson Group's worldwide tax liability) by paying the maximum discount,"[84] it could be argued that no independent parties would have accepted to sell their receivables and to purchase them through an RSA, implying the payment of a fee. In fact, the buyer (MIH) added no value to the transaction. Moreover, no independent party would have agreed to such a discount price as it is not at arm's length. Furthermore, because MIH borrowed funds to finance the purchase of receivables, it means that the entity did not have its own capital in case of default of payment. Therefore, the controlled transaction, i.e., sale/purchase of receivables, could differ

82. OECD TPG 2022, *supra* n. 2, para. 1.65.
83. *McKesson* case, *supra* n. 32, para. 9.
84. *Ibid.*, para. 274.

from an arrangement that would have been entered into by independent parties behaving in a rational manner and in comparable circumstances.

Furthermore, MCC had no business need for cash and consequently, as an option realistically available, it could have simply not entered into the RSA. Actually, a similar conclusion can be drawn for MIH. Indeed, the latter had to borrow funds to finance the purchase of MCC receivables, and hence (most likely) had to pay interest to another entity of the group. Therefore, an option realistically available to MIH would also have been not to enter into such an arrangement with MCC to avoid more transaction and funding-related costs. Hence, it can be derived from this analysis that the difference between the intra-group arrangement and an arrangement independent parties would have agreed on would subsequently prevent the determination of a price that would be acceptable for both parties.

## 3 The *Acer* Case: Detailed Analysis

The Spanish *Acer* case is also a great example of the challenges that potential mismatches between contracts and the conduct of the parties pose within transfer pricing, even under relatively standardized structures such as limited risk distribution agreements. In short, the case revolves around the liquidity constraints of Acer Spain –a limited risk distributor– caused due to mismatches between the payment terms of its customers vis-à-vis the remuneration terms arranged with its principal, Acer Europe, tax resident in Switzerland. Specifically, the tax authorities consider that the latter—instead of Acer Spain—should bear the consequences of the said mismatch. Such approach results in a denial of the deductibility of financial expenses resulting from factoring agreements that Acer Spain subscribed with unrelated financial institutions to manage its liquidity (the factoring arrangement discussed here is different from the one seen in the *McKesson* case).

The *Acer* case is relevant for the analysis of the transfer pricing implications of factoring agreements because the liquidity constraints that were covered somehow derive from the conduct of the related parties, as it will be shown below. Therefore, the main issue at stake is whether the conduct of controlled parties and their contractual arrangements should be assessed when determining the existence and impact of the liquidity constraints that are covered through factoring agreements.

### *A Facts of the Case and Appeals Before the TEAC and the National Court*

The facts of the case are as follows:[85] Acer Inc is a Taiwanese hardware and electronics multinational corporation. Acer Europe AG (Acer Europe), tax resident in Switzerland, is the entity that acts as a principal and coordinates the operations of the Acer Group in the Europe, Middle East and Africa (EMEA) region. In Spain, a subsidiary named

85. The description follows that of Aitor Navarro, *Contractual Allocation of Risks and Substance: The Acer Case*, 28 International Transfer Pricing Journal 203, 203-204 (2021).

Acer Computer Ibérica S.A. (Acer Spain) acts as a wholesale distributor of electronic goods in Spain and Portugal and provides technical services to customers. These two entities signed a limited risk distribution agreement, under which Acer Spain would act as a stripped buy-sell distributor, and Acer Europe would accordingly guarantee arm's length remuneration on the distribution of products by Acer Spain in Spain and Portugal. Acer Spain holds title to goods sold, albeit only immediately prior to the sale to the customer (flash title) once the product has been transported to the final customer. It deals in its own account and negotiates the terms of the sale to local customers, although following those previously established by Acer Europe. Orders bind the supplier, Acer Europe, only when this entity accepts them through an explicit confirmation or when the items are shipped, whatever comes first. In addition, Acer Spain performs functions referred to (1) invoicing and collection, (2) the implementation of marketing and advertising strategies designed by Acer Europe, (3) the provision of sales support services, (4) the provision of technical support to customers and (5) the management of equipment returns.

The adjustment performed by the tax authorities relates to the payment terms agreed upon by the involved parties. Specifically, the terms settled by Acer Spain with its customers establish that the payment deadline takes place on the delivery date. Nonetheless, Acer Spain agreed to a payment deadline with Acer Europe that expires 55 days after the order date, instead of taking the delivery date as reference. As the dates did not match, collection and liquidity tensions were generated at the level of Acer Spain. Thus, the entity entered into factoring agreements with unrelated banks that covered the financial consequences of the said time difference in collection, as well as those of cancelled purchases.

The tax authorities considered that the liquidity issues generated by the said timing mismatch should not be borne by Acer Spain, as its functional profile is that of a limited risk distributor. Plus, the flash title clause agreed by the parties would lead to allocate the ownership risk to Acer Europe. Specifically, fact that the cancellation of client orders was not followed by a cancellation by Acer Spain of the purchase from Acer Europe is what triggered the adjustment proposed by the tax authorities. In fact, client cancellations were not reflected in the accounting records of Acer Spain at the moment they were communicated, but at the moment, the product was reallocated to another client. Thus, the tax authorities considered that the financial costs derived from the cancellation risk and the timing mismatch risks due to a delay in the delivery should not be assumed by a limited risk distributor.

The adjustment was based on article 16 of the 2004 Corporate Income Tax Act,[86] in combination with Article 9(1) of the Spain-Switzerland Income and Capital Tax Treaty (1966),[87] both encapsulating transfer pricing regulations based on the OECD

86. Real Decreto Legislativo 4/2004, de 5 de marzo, por el que se aprueba el texto refundido de la Ley del Impuesto sobre Sociedades, Article 16 (amended 2006) [Spanish Corporate Income Tax Act 2004]. Currently, the transfer pricing regime in Spain is mainly regulated in Ley 27/2014, de 27 de noviembre, del Impuesto sobre Sociedades [Spanish Corporate Income Tax Act 2015], Article 18, generally in line with OECD standards.
87. Convention between Spain and the Swiss Confederation for the Avoidance of Double Taxation with Respect to Taxes on Income and Capital, Article 9(1) (26 April 1966).

standard. The applicability of these rules was not discussed by the parties. The recourse to the Transfer Pricing Guidelines also remained uncontroversial. The taxpayer confronted the said arguments by highlighting that the tax authorities obviated the content of the distribution agreement signed between the parties and that the rise in financial costs of Acer Spain was compensated with a higher remuneration by Acer Europe.

The case was first reviewed by the Spanish Central Economic-Administrative Court (Tribunal Económico-Administrativo Central (TEAC)). This body is a permanent panel with the power to either confirm or overturn tax assessments performed by the tax authorities. It is not an independent panel—hence the "Court" denomination is very unfortunate—: its members are tax officials, and organically, the TEAC forms part of the Ministry of Finance. Appealing the tax assessment is a mandatory step previous to accessing judicial remedies, i.e., prior to an appeal before the National Court. The TEAC upheld the tax authorities' assessment and validated all the arguments mentioned in the previous section. The core of its reasoning referred to the fact that the "flash title" clause of the contract was not honored, as demonstrated by the fact that the annulment of client orders was not followed by the cancellation of the purchase of the product from Acer Europe. In its reasoning, the TEAC generally followed the reasonings presented by the tax authorities.

The taxpayer appealed before the National Court—a judiciary body—although without success. The National Court upheld both the views of the TEAC and those of the tax authorities without adding any substantial arguments aside from those already mentioned.

### *B Critical Comments: The Relevance of the Accurate Delineation of Transactions for a Sound Comparability Analysis*

The decision to uphold the tax authorities' assessment may be criticized due to a number of reasons, namely: (1) the inappropriateness of applying transfer pricing regulations to neglect the deductibility of expenses vis-à-vis independent parties (i.e., the financial institutions with which the factoring agreements were concluded); (2) the disregard of the risk allocation parameters posed in the TPG that led to the attribution of the risk to Acer Spain; (3) the arbitrary disregard of the analyzed transactions, in a manner not consistent with the TPG or the rationale of the comparability analysis; and (4) the inevitable economic double taxation outcome resulting from the adjustment, as the outcome of the case entails the non-deductibility of the financial payments at the level of Acer Spain and the taxation of this income at the level of the unrelated financial institutions.[88]

Notwithstanding, in this section, the analysis will focus on a very specific aspect that lies at the heart of the comparability analysis, namely the delineation of the actual transaction in accordance with the contractual terms agreed by their parties and their conduct. The identification of the commercial or financial relations between the

88. All these criticism points were examined in depth in Navarro, *supra* n. 85, 204-209.

associated enterprises and the conditions and economically relevant circumstances attaching to those relations constitutes the first step of the comparability analysis.[89] It condenses a fact-finding process to determine the nature and features of the controlled transaction and all elements surrounding it. The outcome constitutes the departure point to undertake the benchmark stage of the comparability analysis, namely the search for comparable uncontrolled references replicating the agreement of independent parties under identical circumstances. In other words, the benchmark analysis—the comparison of the controlled transaction and independent uncontrolled references—will depend on its outcome.[90] An incorrect delineation of the controlled transaction would result in a misguided benchmark process and ultimately in a primary adjustment that does not reflect an arm's length outcome. Therefore, deviating from the facts that actually occurred would imply the breach of the arm's length rationale and thus the applicable transfer pricing rules based on such standard, both at a domestic and a treaty level. In fact, the OECD firmly establishes that a tax administration should not disregard the actual transaction or substitute other transactions for it unless exceptional circumstances exist.[91] The whole TPG section on the delineation of the actual transaction should be read taking this specific guidance point in mind.

Among the economically relevant characteristics or comparability factors that need to be identified, the contractual terms of the transaction and the conduct of the parties are the most relevant ones.[92] The formalization of controlled transactions in written contracts constitutes the starting point in the delineation of the transaction.[93] Between independent parties, the divergence of interests between the parties ensures that contractual terms are concluded that reflect the interests of both parties, that they will ordinarily seek to hold each other to the terms of the contract, and that contractual terms will be ignored or modified after the fact generally only if it is in the interests of both parties.[94] Such divergence of interest does not exist between controlled parties, as they pursue common interests. In fact, the *raison d'être* of transfer pricing rules based on the arm's length standard lies in levelling the taxable base resulting from both controlled and uncontrolled transactions, to pursue neutrality in the tax treatment of both scenarios and prevent profit shifting.[95] Hence, at arm's length, it must be examined whether the parties have concluded a balanced contract that properly reflects the incidence of the economically relevant characteristics of the transaction in the duties agreed by each party. The arm's length range lies between the minimum

89. OECD TPG 2022, *supra* n. 2, para. 1.33.
90. *Ibid.*, paras 1.35, 1.37, 1.39.
91. *Ibid.*, para. 1.121. Bullen labels this notion as the 'as-structured' principle. *See* BULLEN, *supra* n. 26, Ch. 4 (IBFD Doctoral Series, 2011).
92. The other comparability factors pinpointed by the OECD are highly dependent of the contractual terms and the conduct of the parties, namely characteristics of property transferred, or services provided, the economic circumstances of the parties and of the market in which the parties operate and the business strategies pursued by the parties. *See* OECD TPG 2022, *supra* n. 2, paras 1.107-1.118.
93. OECD TPG 2022, *supra* n. 2, para. 1.42.
94. *Ibid.*, para. 1.46.
95. *See* WOLFGANG SCHÖN, *International Tax Coordination for a Second-Best World (Part III)*, 2 World Tax Journal 227, 230 (2010). *See also* LUIS E. SCHOUERI, *Arm's Length: Beyond the Guidelines of the OECD*, 69 Bull. Int'l Tax'n 690, 695 (2015).

price acceptable to the transferor and the maximum price acceptable to the transferee, in line with their bargaining positions.[96] The remuneration that an independent operator is obtaining must be in line with the terms of the agreement it has decided to honor.

As determined by the OECD, the functions the parties actually perform, the assets they use, and the risks they assume, considered in the context of the contractual terms, should ultimately determine the factual substance and accurately delineate the actual transaction.[97] But one must never forget that in this stage, facts are to be discovered, not established. In other words, references to substance should not lead to a discretionary power to alter the facts that actually occurred.[98] Otherwise, the aforementioned prohibition to disregard the actual transaction would be vulnerated. In short, the assessment of contracts and the conduct of the parties cannot be undertaken discretionarily. The limitations posed on the recharacterization of transactions exist to prevent arbitrariness and thus are an essential component of this first stage of the comparability analysis.

In the *Acer* case, the configuration of the clauses of the agreement is clearly unsatisfactory to provide an answer to which party should bear the consequences of mismatches between accounts payable and accounts receivable. This is because the contract does not provide parameters to define the computation of payment deadlines. Notwithstanding, the tax authorities inferred payment term conditions from the clauses regarding ownership and risk assumption. Here is the wording of the clauses:

- 2.4 Risk assumption. Unless otherwise stated in this agreement, Supplier shall substantially assume all risks relating to the sale and distribution of the products, including, but not limited to, currency gains and losses, collection risk, inventory risk, warranty or extended warranty repair obligations and similar contingencies that may arise in the course of Distributor's purchase and sale of the products from Supplier.
- 5.4 Ownership and risk. Distributor shall purchase the products from Supplier in its own name and at its own expense. The ownership rights and the risk of loss as well as the risk of damage to the products shall be transferred to Distributor immediately before delivery of the products to the customer [...].

These clauses are silent regarding payment terms, yet the tax authorities somehow inferred from them the need that the payment terms match the moment of ownership transmission of the product by Acer Spain, which takes place on a flash title basis, right before the product is delivered to the customer. The tax authorities considered that adopting the purchase order as a payment term reference—as the parties effectively did—generates liquidity tensions, the consequences of which Acer

96. OECD TPG 2022, *supra* n. 2, para. 6.114 and UN TP Manual 2021, para. 2.1.3.1. *See* David Ledure et al., *Financial Transactions in Today's World: Observations from a Transfer Pricing Perspective,* 38 Intertax 350, 357-358 (2010). *See also* Vera Averyanova & Jigna Sampat, *Transfer Pricing Aspects of Intra-Group Financial Guarantees in Light of the BEPS Action Plan,* 22 Int'l Transfer Pricing J. 361, 363 (2015); Vikram Chand, *Transfer Pricing Aspects of Cash Pooling Arrangements in Light of the BEPS Action Plan,* 23 Int'l Transfer Pricing J. 38, 44 (2016).
97. OECD TPG 2022, *supra* n. 2, para. 1.46.
98. Navarro, *supra* n. 26, section 3.1.

Spain, as a limited risk distributor, should not assume. The emphasis was placed on cancelled orders, as the cancellation by a client was not followed by a corresponding cancellation of the order by Acer Spain. Instead, the product was reallocated to another client and in the meantime, Acer Spain was burdened with the liquidity constraint derived from having paid Acer Europe in due time, i.e., 55 days after the purchase order, even if the order was cancelled. Due to this, the tax authorities affirmed that, instead of being a limited risk distributor, Acer Spain turns out to be a hedger, guaranteeing price collection even if the sale takes place with a significant delay. The tax authorities also affirmed that such advancement of funds cannot be derived from the terms of the contract.

The conflict lies, therefore, in the assessment of the contract, the conduct of the parties and the functional profile of Acer Spain. According to the TPG, it is particularly important in considering the commercial or financial relations between associated enterprises to examine whether the arrangements reflected in the actual conduct of the parties substantially conform to the terms of the written contract, or whether the actual conduct indicates that the contractual terms have not been followed, does not reflect a complete picture of the transactions, have been incorrectly characterized, or are a sham.[99] If the characteristics of the transaction are inconsistent with the written contract, the actual transaction should generally be delineated for purposes of the transfer pricing analysis in accordance with the conduct of the parties.[100] Likewise, if no written terms exist, the actual transaction would need to be deduced from the evidence of actual conduct.[101] Hence, as it is logical, the TPG solves both conflictive scenarios by giving prevalence to the conduct of the parties. Moreover, only when the contractual terms and the conduct of the parties are firmly assessed, one may infer the functional profile of each related party, an aspect that is critical to undertake a sound comparability analysis.

Notwithstanding, in the *Acer* case, the tax authorities ignored the described course of action. The actual conduct of the parties clearly reflected the fact that the liquidity constraints generated by the mismatch between accounts receivable and accounts payable lied in Acer Spain. Nonetheless, the authorities claimed that, due to the functional profile of Acer Spain, such risk should have been assumed by Acer Europe, the principal. In other words, the tax authorities first drew the functional profile and only then, in accordance with their conception of what a limited risk distributor is, allocated the risk to the principal. Thus, the authorities wrongly inverted the terms of the examination.

---

99. OECD TPG 2022, *supra* n. 2, para. 1.46. *See*, in the context of risk allocation, SUNNY K. BILANEY, *Understanding Risk in the Era of the OECD/G20 Base Erosion and Profit Shifting Initiative*, 70 Bull. Int'l Tax'n 576, 579 (2016). *See also*, ISABEL VERLINDEN ET AL., *The Risky Side of Transfer Pricing: The OECD Base Erosion and Profit Shifting Reports Sharpen the Rules on Risk Allocation under the Arm's Length Standard*, 23 International Transfer Pricing Journal 109, 110 (2016); RICHARD S. COLLIER & JOSEPH L. ANDRUS, *Transfer Pricing and the Arm's Length Principle after BEPS*, para. 7.18 (Oxford University Press, 2017).
100. OECD TPG 2022, *supra* n. 2, para. 1.45. *See* JENS WITTENDORFF, *BEPS Actions 8-10: Birth of a New Arm's-Length Principle*, 81 Tax Notes Int'l 331, 336 (2016); RUTGER HAFKENSCHEID, *The BEPS Report on Risk Allocation: Not so Functional*, 24 Int'l Transfer Pricing J. 19, 20 (2017).
101. OECD TPG 2022, *supra* n. 2, para. 1.49.

At a different level, one may wonder whether the agreed contractual risk allocation effectively would allocate such liquidity risk to Acer Europe. It might seem so because clause 2.4. stipulates that "Unless otherwise stated in this agreement, Supplier (i.e. Acer Europe) shall substantially assume all risks relating to the sale and distribution of the products." Yet, as stated, when contractual terms and the conduct of the parties are contradictory, the latter should prevail. Meanwhile, in the *Acer* case, the conduct of the parties is displaced in some sort of a "form over substance" approach that goes against the rationale of the comparability analysis, as the content of the contract—wrongly interpreted by the tax authorities—would replace the facts—the conduct of the parties—as they actually occurred.

The assumption of the liquidity risk by Acer Spain is a fact and, as such, it should not be neglected. Therefore, an appropriate examination of the issue would consist in ascertaining whether Acer Europe is obliged to compensate Acer Spain due to such liquidity tensions. If the answer is affirmative, then the discussion would be whether such compensation has taken place and whether it was calculated at arm's length. In fact, such claim was posed by the taxpayer, as it stated that "the increase of financial expenses of Acer Spain was compensated with a higher remuneration reflected in an increase of its net profitability that allowed the absorption of the said expenses." The issue of the arm's length character of the compensation was utterly ignored; hence it remains unknown whether Acer Spain was sufficiently remunerated in this regard.

## IV CONCLUSION

To conclude, the contribution pursued the ambition to provide guidance on the application of the ALP to factoring arrangements, in particular, at the accurate delineation stage, due to the lack of discussion on this type of financial arrangement in the OECD 2022 TPG.

First, the concept of factoring has been briefly analyzed, and it has been highlighted that from a transfer pricing perspective, the factor needs to receive a remuneration for its factoring services that are in line with the value it creates based on its functions performed, risks assumed and assets employed. Second, it has been demonstrated that regarding the application of the ALP to factoring agreements, it is crucial as a first step to analyze the functional profile of the factor to determine whether the factoring arrangement has been accurately delineated from a transfer pricing standpoint. As a second step, the arm's length price for the factoring arrangement must be determined.

Regarding the selected case law, on the one hand, the Canadian decisions indicate that, in light of Canadian law, Courts may have a restrictive approach towards recharacterizing transactions. However, these cases should not be considered global benchmarks as Courts in other jurisdictions follow the OECD TPG to a great extent. Accordingly, alignment with OECD guidelines is recommended to prevent disputes.

However, in the *Acer* case, the factoring arrangement agreed by Acer Spain—a limited risk distributor—with unrelated banks was disregarded because it was considered that the underlying liquidity tensions should have been assumed by Acer

Europe—the principal—instead of Acer Spain and consequently the deductibility of resulting financial expenses was denied. Therefore, it is important to review not only the factoring agreement as such but also the nature of the underlying risks it is referring to. More specifically, it is critical that the conduct of the parties is aligned with the contracts—which should be as exhaustive as possible in the delineation of risks—and their resulting functional profile.

Therefore, from an accurate delineation and recognition standpoint, in light of the case law discussed, we believe that tensions could arise between taxpayers and tax administrations when (i) the contractual arrangements are not drafted properly and/or are open to different interpretations; (ii) the factor (a related party) does not have the appropriate functional profile to bear key risks; (iii) the factoring transaction does not have any commercial rationale and has been entered into with the main purpose of generating a tax benefit. These tensions could ultimately lead to recharacterizations or to the disregard of the controlled transaction.

CHAPTER 40

# Pricing Factoring Transactions: A Case Study

*Emmanuel Llinares & Bernardo Danesi*[*]

This chapter provides an example situation where transactions related to factoring were analysed. This case study is inspired by a variety of real cases but is not representative of any specific situation.

The chapter is structured as follows:

- Section I provides a description of the facts of the case.
- Section II provides the method selection process.
- Section III details the approach to evaluate the arm's-length nature of the transaction.
- Section IV concludes.

## I FACTS OF THE CASE

A multinational enterprise (MNE) operating in manufacturing of mechanical components is headquartered in Germany and has affiliates across world. The group treasury company (FactorCo) is also based in Germany and is a direct subsidiary of the group's head company. FactorCo manages group liquidity and funding requirements, centralizing most treasury activities.

The group operates a number of local subsidiaries worldwide. The local subsidiaries' main activity is sales and management of relationships with third-party dealers in local jurisdictions. Each subsidiary (local entities: LocEnt1, LocEnt2, LocEnt3, and

* The views and opinions set forth herein are the personal views or opinions of the authors; they do not necessarily reflect views or opinions of the organization with which the authors are associated.

so on) are paid by their customers 90 days after the shipment of the goods. FactorCo and the local entities have an active service factoring agreement setting out the terms of the arrangement.

The group established the factoring system between FactorCo, the local entities, and their customers to:

- Better manage transactions.
- Ensure payment to the operating entities, which act as distribution entities.
- Minimize the costs related to the payment flows by allowing participating entities to net the amounts receivable and payable.
- Ensure better visibility on payment flows and provide a simple reporting of the flows to each participating entity.

The factoring is without recourse,[1] that is, the credit risk of the clients defaulting on payment (or paying late) is borne by FactorCo. Essentially, non-recourse factoring transactions can be seen as a sale of account receivables from the local entity to the factor. The supplier accessing the factoring service is shielded from non-payment or late payment from the client.

## 1 Characteristics of the Transaction

In practice, a local entity issues an invoice to its client (the purchaser). The invoice is transferred to FactorCo as the goods are shipped to the client. FactorCo pays the local entity in one to three working days. The local entity pays the factoring commission to FactorCo in the form of the discount.[2]

The client of the local entity (a local business, not a related party) pays the full amount of the invoice to FactorCo before or at the date specified on the invoice, which is 90 days after shipment of the goods. In case the invoice is not paid in full, FactorCo is responsible for a potential loss.

Figure 40.1 provides a visualization of the transaction used as an illustration in this chapter.

*Figure 40.1 Example of Factoring Transaction*

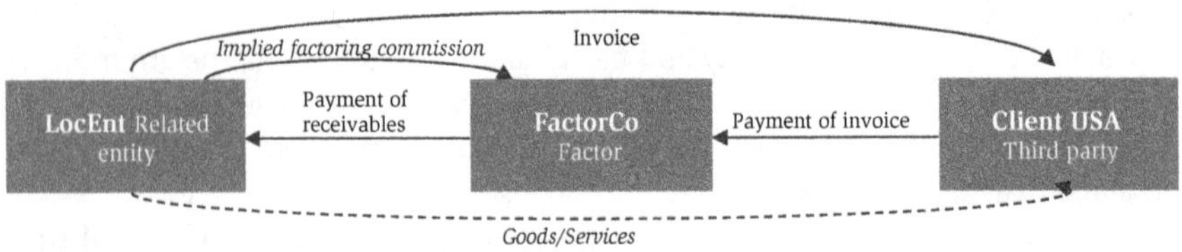


1. Factoring without recourse is explained in PANOS KOUVELIS & FASHENG XU, *A Supply Chain Theory of Factoring and Reverse Factoring*, SSRN (2018), 2, https://papers.ssrn.com/sol3/papers.cfm?abstract_id=3241484.
2. The factoring commission is represented by the difference between the face value of the receivables and the payment made by FactorCo.

FactorCo charges a factoring commission to local entities in the form of a discount on the face value of the receivables. This factoring commission is intended to remunerate FactorCo for the functions it performs and the risks it assumes. The factoring commission charged to local entities is a related party transaction, which needs to be priced in accordance with the arm's-length principle.

To do so, it is important to understand the functions, assets, and risks of FactorCo and the local entities in the context of the broader value chain of the group.

## 2 Value Chain Analysis of the Group

Before looking at the roles and responsibilities of FactorCo and the local entities, we provide an overview of the group's overall value chain analysis. A value chain analysis aims at setting the groundwork for understanding the functions, assets, and risks of the transacting parties in the context of their relationship.

The value chain of the group is represented in Figure 40.2.

*Figure 40.2 Group Value Chain*

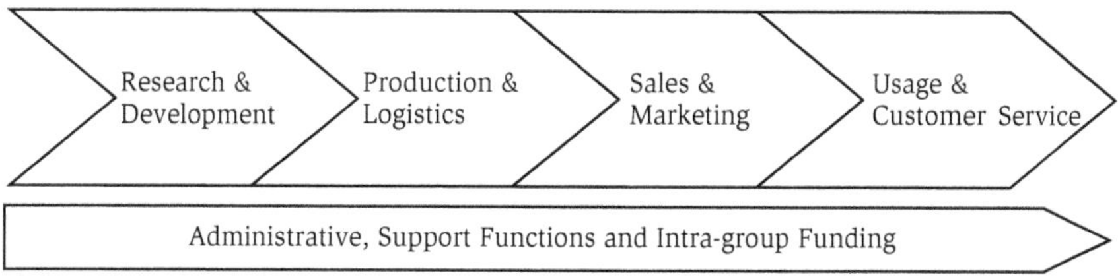


### *A Research & Development*

The group supplies mechanical components and devices to its clients, which operate in a variety of industries, such as car manufacturing, aerospace, and industrial machinery. The company works with its clients to create bespoke solutions to address their design problems. Competition to supply these types of products always hinges on providing the best technical solutions. As a result, the value driver of research and development is among the most significant for the MNE.

### *B Production and Logistics*

The group operates in markets where there is intense competition, especially in mature markets. As a result, the ability to supply its products at a competitive price point is fundamental to the success of the business.

### *C Sales and Marketing*

This value driver pertains to the group's ability to formulate adequate pricing given the competition and the capabilities of its clients. In addition, it relates to the ability of the group sales teams to build lasting relationships with their clients, win long-term contracts, and produce satisfactory results. The suppliers, we have mentioned earlier in this chapter (the local entities) engage with this value driver.

### D *Usage and Customer Service*

The products manufactured by the group usually need to be integrated with products built by clients. Due to this high level of integration between the technologies, it is very important that the group engineers work closely with the clients to ensure that the proposed solutions are functional and relatively easy to implement. Engineers and salespeople work together to ensure customer satisfaction and maintain the best possible relationships with them. Again, it is a duty of the local entities to aid clients by integrating the group solutions in their processes.

### E *Administrative and Support Services*

In addition to the foregoing value drivers, the enterprise relies on a number of administrative and support functions. The financing activities of the MNE are part of these activities.

### F *Role of Factoring in the Value Chain*

Whilst financing is not a core activity of the group, the ability to effectively manage receivables contributes to managing the financial risks of the MNE as a whole and can secure the credit position of the local entities.

## 3 Functional, Asset, and Risk Profile

The Organisation for Economic Co-operation and Development (OECD) underscores the importance of the functional analysis in the Transfer Pricing Guidelines for Multinational Enterprises and Tax Administrations 2022 version (OECD TP Guidelines 2022), as well as in its previous Transfer Pricing Guidance on Financial Transactions. The Transfer Pricing Guidance on Financial Transactions states in Chapter B, paragraph 10.23, that functional analysis seeks to identify 'the functions performed, the assets used, and the risks assumed by the parties', in order to accurately delineate the actual financial transaction.

The current section focuses on providing a description of the functional profile of FactorCo, and the functions it performs in relation to the factoring activities in particular. In addition, the functions performed by the operational entities, as well as the risks faced by both parties in relation to the factoring transaction, are also discussed.

### A Functional Profile of FactorCo

In addition to its factoring functions, FactorCo acts as the central treasury company of the Group and provides financial services to its related entities. The company fits the profile of the treasury function described in section C of the 2020 Transfer Pricing Guidance on Financial Transactions by the OECD, as it is involved in, for example, optimizing liquidity across the group,[3] managing the relations with external bankers and independent credit rating agencies,[4] and serving as a contact point to centralize external borrowing of the group.[5]

FactorCo has significant equity (nearly EUR 3.8 billion in 2020), which ensures the financial stability of the company and confirms that it is capable of assuming the economic risks linked to its activities.

With highly qualified staff on its payroll, the company ensures that all functions can be performed internally at FactorCo. FactorCo employs the financial analysis team, the treasurer of the group, and a front, middle, and back office, which host the factoring team. The Chief Financial Officer (CFO) is not employed by FactorCo but by another entity of the group. In 2021, the salary and other costs incurred by FactorCo corresponded to EUR 4.3 million. This cost base notably includes the costs of dedicated Information Technology (IT) solutions and costs of third-party suppliers and contractors FactorCo may rely on as part of its activities (including providers that focus on following up on unpaid invoices).

### B FactorCo Functions in Relation to Factoring

FactorCo operates as a standard factor with respect to the local entities in the group. In the context of the factoring transactions, FactorCo:

- provides delegated management of accounts receivables (managing internal transaction flows, dealing with outstanding net positions and client management, ensuring payments are made in a timely manner);
- provides a currency exchange service by hedging against any foreign exchange risk;
- Allows the participating companies to diminish cost of financial flows by netting the amounts receivable and payable;
- allows suppliers to have efficient and risk-free payment flows for payments; and
- produces credit analysis services to the local entities, determining the credit ratings of the clients and estimating the global exposure of FactorCo with the different external clients, including the commercial relationships.

3. OECD Transfer Pricing Guidelines for Multinational Enterprises and Tax Administrations, January 2022, para. 10.41. Available at: https://www.oecd.org/tax/transfer-pricing/oecd-transfer-pricing-guidelines-for-multinational-enterprises-and-tax-administrations-20769717.htm
4. *Ibid.*, para. 10.43.
5. *Ibid.*, para. 10.46.

In FactorCo, five full-time employees ensure the smooth functioning of the factoring activities. These employees work in finance, and administrative functions, including monitoring the invoices issued by the local entities, dealing with specific requests from local entities (e.g., approval to extend terms of payment), and managing and coordinating the activities of the third-party suppliers FactorCo relies on as part of its factoring activities.

The team receives support from the treasury's cash management team, also based in FactorCo. This business unit analyses flows and new clients (especially in terms of their creditworthiness), performs market analyses, prepares the factoring calendar, and coordinates fiscal matters.

FactorCo has the ability to decide which receivables are taken on and which are not. These decisions are made by the factoring team as a day-to-day activity. However, the criteria are set ex ante by the treasurer with the approval of the CFO. Common cases when receivables are not acquired by FactorCo include clients that have defaulted on similar obligations previously or unrated customers with no previous history of commercial relationships with a group entity. In certain cases, FactorCo may reevaluate its guidelines on receivable purchasing.

In 2020, for example, during the thick of the COVID-19 crisis, many clients (especially in the aerospace industry) asked the local entities for more time to pay their invoices. Local entities negotiated with their clients, agreeing to a partial extension of terms. As production slowed or halted in March and April, a higher proportion of those invoices were not purchased by FactorCo.

As mentioned already, FactorCo also hosts the more traditional treasury activities of the group. This allows the company to retain a full view of the working capital and funding necessities of the local entities without needing to coordinate with an affiliate (and as a result without any internal transaction). This also means that FactorCo hosts all the necessary human capital to evaluate the risk of taking on receivables of a certain quality. The treasurer, aided by the factoring team, draws up the guidelines determining which receivables should be purchased and which should be left with the local entities based on the level of credit risk they are comfortable with.

### *C Risks Assumed by the Parties in Relation to Factoring*

The factoring transaction entails a transfer of economic risk. FactorCo prefunds the receivables of its internal clients. Hence, it bears the associated credit risks in line with the clients' payment dates. In addition, FactorCo fully guarantees the receivables of the local entities. It bears the associated default risks in line with clients' non-payment.

FactorCo tiers the factoring charged to the local entities to the credit rating of the receivables it takes on. Most customers of the group are publicly listed companies with a credit rating. As a result, the group is capable of charging implied factoring fees that reflect the underlying risk of the assets purchased.

## 4 Summary of the Facts

To effectively assess the pricing structure proposed by the group, it is necessary to fully and accurately delineate and recognize the transaction as outlined in Chapter D.1 of the OECD Transfer Pricing Guidance. Thus, understanding the value chain and the functional, asset, and risk profiles of the transacting parties provides important insights. We summarize the key features of this transaction:

(i) The factoring agreement has no recourse, that is, it is akin to the sale of account receivables from the local entity to FactorCo.
(ii) Local entities issue an invoice in the functional currency of the purchaser and transfer it to FactorCo.
(iii) FactorCo is responsible for collecting the payment from the third-party clients.
(iv) The local entities pay a commission to FactorCo, which is meant to remunerate:
   - the administration activities performed by FactorCo;
   - the credit risk incurred by FactorCo when buying the receivables.

As part of the factoring transaction, the local entities of the group benefit from:

- Better management of sales transactions, which ensures good cash flow management for the local entities and guarantees better visibility to the local businesses' operations for the group (akin to administrative activities).
- Minimized costs related to payment flows by allowing participating entities to net the amounts receivable and payable, as well as an improvement of the balance sheet of the local entities.

We laid out the primary features of the transaction: the functional, asset, and risk profile of the parties involved in the transaction, the terms of the agreement, and the value chain of the industry, including the role of financing in overall value creation.

We move to present our approach to benchmark the arm's-length remuneration for this factoring transaction.

# II METHOD SELECTION

In this section, we present a review of the appropriateness of the main transfer pricing methods mentioned by the OECD Transfer Pricing Guidelines 2022.

The arm's-length principle is the international transfer pricing standard that OECD member countries have agreed should be used for tax purposes by MNE groups and tax administrations. When transfer pricing does not reflect market forces and the arm's-length principle, the tax liabilities of the associated enterprises and the tax revenues of the host countries could be distorted.

The arm's-length principle treats the members of an MNE as separate entities operating independently, rather than inseparable parts of a single unified business, by adjusting profits using the conditions that would have been obtained between independent enterprises in comparable transactions and comparable circumstances as reference (i.e., in 'comparable uncontrolled transactions').

The OECD Guidelines provide detailed descriptions of methods that can be used to establish whether the conditions imposed in the commercial or financial relations between associated enterprises are consistent with the arm's-length principle.

## 1 Comparable Uncontrolled Price Method

The comparable uncontrolled price (CUP) method compares the price charged for property or services transferred in a controlled transaction to the price charged for property or services transferred in a comparable uncontrolled transaction in similar circumstances.

The OECD Guidelines recognize that 'Where it is possible to locate comparable uncontrolled transactions, the CUP method is the most direct and reliable way to apply the arm's length principle. Consequently, in such cases the CUP method is preferable over all other methods' (paragraph 2.15).

From a theoretical point of view, the CUP method is the preferred OECD method.

In the case of the providing of factoring services by FactorCo to related industrial entities, no internal CUP transactions were identified. Indeed, FactorCo does not provide factoring or other services to independent companies outside the group (nor does any outside factor provide factoring services to FactorCo's affiliates). In addition, we were not able to identify sufficiently comparable transactions between third parties to apply the CUP method.

## 2 Resale Price Method

The resale price method compares the gross margins earned on the resale of products or services by the controlled party with the gross margins earned by similar uncontrolled parties selling similar products in similar conditions.

This method is typically applied to evaluate the remuneration associated with distribution-related functions. Given that the transaction being evaluated does not relate to distribution-related activities, this method was not relied on in this case.

## 3 Cost-Plus Method

The OECD Guidelines state:

> The cost plus method begins with the costs incurred by the supplier of property (or services) in a controlled transaction for property transferred or services provided to an associated purchaser. An appropriate cost plus mark-up is then added to this cost, to make an appropriate profit in light of the functions performed and the market conditions. What is arrived at after adding the cost plus mark up to the above costs may be regarded as an arm's length price of the original controlled transaction. This method probably is most useful where semi-finished goods are

> sold between associated parties, where associated parties have concluded joint facility agreements or long-term buy-and-supply arrangements, or where the controlled transaction is the provision of services. (paragraph 2.45)

This method is typically used to evaluate the remuneration associated with simple manufacturing or provision of services functions. Given the transaction being evaluated, the nature of risks it assumes, and that FactorCo does not provide factoring services to third parties (which could have potentially served as a source of comparison for applying this method), it is unlikely that the application of this method could reliably capture the complexity of the role of FactorCo.

## 4 Profit Split Method

The OECD Guidelines describe the profit split as a method which:

> seeks to eliminate the effect on profits of special conditions made or imposed in a controlled transaction ... by determining the division of profits that independent enterprises would have expected to realise from engaging in the transaction or transactions. (paragraph 2.114)
>
> The transactional profit split method first identifies the profits to be split for the associated enterprises from the controlled transactions in which the associated enterprises are engaged (the 'combined profits'). References to 'profits' should be taken as applying equally to losses ... It then splits those combined profits between the associated enterprises on an economically valid basis that approximates the division of profits that would have been anticipated and reflected in an agreement made at arm's length. (paragraph 2.114)

As indicated in the OECD Transfer Pricing Guidelines, a transactional profit split method can offer a solution for highly integrated operations and may be the most appropriate method in cases where both parties make unique and valuable contributions (e.g., contribute unique intangibles) to the transaction, share economically significant risks, or separately assume closely related risks. In this case, there is no contribution to unique intangibles, the transactions are not reflective of highly integrated operations, and, given the no recourse condition, there is no joint assumption of economically significant risks or separate assumption of closely related risks. Thus, we conclude that the conditions for the profit split method are not met. Hence, this method was not selected in this case.[6]

## 5 Transactional Net Margin Method

This method compares the controlled company's net profitability on a transaction to the net profit obtained by broadly similar companies on similar transactions. The OECD Guidelines state that the transactional net margin method (TNMM) may afford a practical solution to otherwise insoluble transfer pricing problems if it is used sensibly and with appropriate adjustments to account for differences.

6. *Ibid.*, paras\ 2.130-2.142.

The TNMM assesses the arm's-length nature of the transfer price in a controlled transaction by testing the profit results of one of the parties. The OECD Guidelines state, 'The transactional net margin method examines the net profit relative to an appropriate base (e.g., costs, sales, assets) that a taxpayer realises from a controlled transaction.'[7]

First, a search for independent factoring companies was conducted. We call this approach traditional TNMM for ease of use. In this case, it was not possible to identify independent comparable companies with a functional profile that was sufficiently comparable for using the TNMM. This is not unusual – a significant challenge in benchmarking factoring transactions is represented by obtaining comparable, reliable data for the analysis. Independent companies operating mostly as factoring providers are relatively rare in mature markets, and this poses a significant challenge to applying the TNMM using a simple comparable search.

In case no sufficiently comparable companies can be identified, a different approach should be used. Next we describe a way to analyse the transaction that enables us to benchmark it. For simplicity, we refer to this approach as the synthetic TNMM. In practice, we consider that it fits the description of the TNMM.

## III PROPOSED APPROACH: SYNTHETIC TNMM

### 1 Overview of Proposed Approach

With the inability to identify comparable transactions or directly comparable companies, and to reflect the complexity of factoring transactions analysed here, it can be useful to segment the remuneration into its basic components. FactorCo's total factoring revenues in the context of the intragroup factoring arrangements should include the following four elements:

(1) The costs incurred for credit collection services. Such costs are incurred by FactorCo in performing its services and should be covered by its remuneration. Local entities should be able to save some costs by not having to hire or retain resources for these activities.[8]
(2) The expected loss was resulting from clients' defaults. Expected losses resulting from client defaults constitute a likely cash outflow that should be covered by the remuneration of FactorCo.
(3) The opportunity cost of capital. The equity engaged by investors in FactorCo should be remunerated in light of the opportunity cost. In essence, this is the profit element of FactorCo's remuneration.

7. *Ibid.*, para. 2.64.
8. Factoring agreements involve the factor managing the sales ledger relative to the sold receivables. As a result, it is reasonable to expect that factors incur significant costs as part of their activities. In the case of an invoice discounting transaction, where the credit collection remains with the supplier, these costs may not be a significant component of the analysis.

(4) Remuneration for the time value of money. Regardless of the expected return of FactorCo, a remuneration for time value of money should be added. This corresponds to the remuneration of a risk-free short-term loan: the loan made to prefund receivables should be remunerated at the risk-free rate to account for the time value of money (remuneration of default risk is accounted for in items (2) and (3)).

This breakdown of FactorCo's remuneration is useful because it allows us to potentially benchmark each segment of its revenues individually. This breakdown of remuneration is particularly useful when no directly comparable data can be relied on to price the factoring agreement accurately.

A breakdown of the elements that should be covered by FactorCo's remuneration is presented in Figure 40.3.

*Figure 40.3 Breakdown of Factoring Transaction*

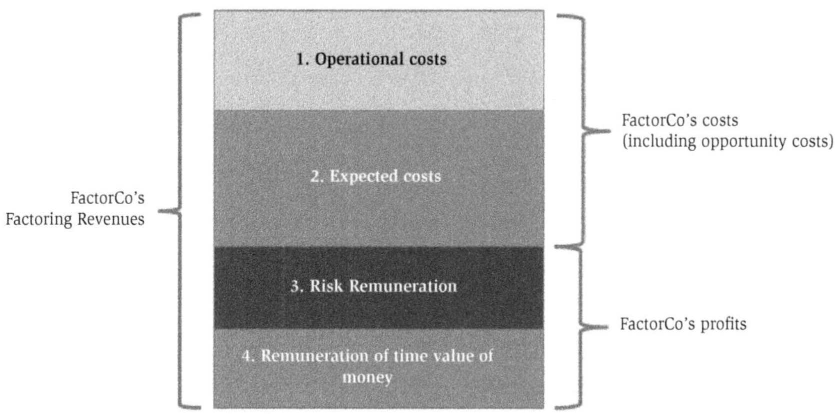


The idea behind the synthetic TNMM is to first calculate the cost elements (parts 1 and 2 in Figure 40.3) of FactorCo's revenues using internal data and then estimate its arm's-length profits (sections 3 and 4 in Figure 40.3) using a framework such as the Basel banking regulation one, which stipulates FactorCo's required equity, as well as a custom comparable company search to identify the appropriate return to equity.

## 2 Application of the Synthetic TNMM Method

As explained, the objective of this methodology is to benchmark each portion of FactorCo's total revenues individually to derive its arm's-length remuneration. This section is organized by focusing on each revenue portion individually.

### A Operational Costs

FactorCo performs several activities on behalf of the group. As a result, it is necessary to segment the P&L of the group to obtain the costs incurred in the context of factoring activities. Fortunately, the group's accounting practices allow for a full disaggregation of its costs by activities. These costs, incurred as part of the factoring activities, were approximately EUR 4.2 million in 2018, EUR 4.3 million in 2019, and EUR 4.3 million in 2020.

FactorCo factored EUR 7.1 billion, EUR 7.2 billion, and EUR 6.6 billion of third-party receivables in 2018, 2019, and 2020, respectively. Hence, the operating costs represent 0.062% of the factored turnover, on average. The details on factoring costs and factoring turnover are presented in Table 40.1.

*Table 40.1 Costs for Factoring Function at FactorCo by Year*

| | | | *2018* | *2019* | *2020* | *Average* |
|---|---|---|---|---|---|---|
| Factoring costs (€) | [a] | M. EUR | 4,240 | 4,340 | 4,260 | 4,280 |
| Factoring turnover (€) | [b] | M. EUR | 7,080,000 | 7,180,000 | 6,560,000 | 6,940,000 |
| Average yearly factoring Costs as % of turnover | [c] = [a]/[b] | % | 0.060 | 0.060 | 0.065 | 0.062 |

*Source*: FactorCo Internal Data, NERA calculations.

In 2018-2020, the costs incurred by FactorCo in performing its credit collection services ranged between 0.060% and 0.065% of the factored third-party turnover. The average yearly factoring costs as percentage of turnover represents portion 1 of FactorCo's revenues, as presented in Figure 3.

### B Expected Losses

Losses on customer receivables happen mostly due to the default of the end customer. Because of defaults on receivables, on average, FactorCo is expected to collect less than the face value of the receivables it factored.

From a theoretical perspective, the expected losses incurred by FactorCo on its portfolio of receivables depend on:

- the receivables face value;
- final customers' probability of default; and
- recovery rate (the percentage of the receivables amounts paid by the external client or the insurances in case of default).

Mathematically, FactorCo's expected loss can be written as:

$$Expected\ losses = Turnover \times \left(\frac{DSO}{365}\right) \times Default\ Probability \times (1 - Recovery\ rate)$$

where DSO is Days Sales Outstanding. The group primarily sells to listed corporations, whose creditworthiness is assessed by at least one of the three main rating agencies. In 2020, 61% of the group's receivables were with a rated counterparty. For these receivables, it is possible to estimate their probability of default and recovery rate based on historical data, published by several credit rating agencies.

For the remaining 39% of receivables relative to unrated customers, we have looked at the historical performance of these receivables within the group. In other words, we used the group's historical default and recovery rates connected with unrated receivables to estimate the default probability and recovery rate going forward. The group provided 15 years of data regarding the solvency of its customers.

Using these sources, we can calculate the expected loss relative to receivables with all credit ratings as well as with the unrated entities (*see* Table 40.2).

*Table 40.2 Expected Loss Estimation*

| *Rating (Moody's Categories)* | *DSO* | *Annual Default Rates (%)* | *Recovery Rates (%)* | *Expected Loss (%)* |
|---|---|---|---|---|
| | [a] | [b] | [c] | [d] = [a] / 365 × [b] × (1 – [c]) |
| A | 90 | 0.03 | 35.13 | 0.005 |
| Baa | 90 | 0.10 | 42.35 | 0.014 |
| Ba | 90 | 0.52 | 43.46 | 0.072 |
| B | 90 | 2.00 | 37.13 | 0.310 |
| Unrated | 90 | 2.37 | 29.52 | 0.412 |

*Source*: Credit Rating Agency Estimation, NERA Calculations.

*Note*: For annual default rates and recovery rates, the underlying data ranges from 1983 to 2020.

Thus, the expected loss element of FactorCo's revenues has been estimated to range between 0.005% for A-rated customers and 0.412% for unrated customers.

### C *Credit Risk Remuneration*

As mentioned already, we used international banking requirements set by the Basel III accords to calculate the minimum equity that the FactorCo must hold to carry out the lending activity implicit in the factoring agreement. The remuneration of equity was estimated based on the associated risks.

According to the Basel banking regulation framework, the amount of equity FactorCo needs to hold can be determined using the following formula for each layer of FactorCo's portfolio of receivables.

$$\textbf{Capital required} = \textbf{Turnover} \times \left(\frac{\textbf{DSO}}{\textbf{365}}\right) \times \textbf{Weighting Ratio} \times \textbf{Solvency Ratio}$$

Weighting ratios are used to construct a risk-weighted balance sheet, which represents the risk in the portfolio. They depend on the credit rating of the receivables factored. Weighting ratios used in the analysis are based on the Basel banking regulation. Weighting ratios per credit rating are provided in Table 40.3.

*Table 40.3 Prescribed Weighting Ratios*

| *Corresponding Rating (Moody's Categories)* | *Weighting Ratio (%)* |
|---|---|
| A | 50 |
| Baa | 100 |
| Ba | 100 |
| B | 150 |
| Caa-C | 150 |

*Source*: Basel long-term banking regulation.

A range of solvency ratios for European Banks have been retained based on the first and the third quartile of the solvency ratio observed for European Banks in 2021. These solvency ratios are 15.3% and 17.4%.[9]

Element 3 of FactorCo's remuneration can be calculated by multiplying the capital required, which we estimated using the formula above, by the expected return to equity for a financing company operating in similar circumstances to FactorCo:

$$\textit{Nominal Remuneration of Capital} = \textit{Capital Required} \times \textit{Equity Risk Premium}$$

To estimate the appropriate return to equity, we launched a peer search on a commercial database. Such databases collect extensive amounts of financial and economic information.[10] We restricted our search to target companies operating primarily in Europe that are publicly listed and whose activities are limited to financing. We isolated 12 peers. The database in question reports an equity risk premium (ERP) for these peers. We used the average ERP for these entities for our analysis. This was calculated to be 13.2% in 2020.

9. The European Central Bank publishes aggregated supervisory banking statistics on the following aspects of banks designated as significant institutions: general statistics, balance sheet composition and profitability, capital adequacy and leverage, asset quality, funding, liquidity, and data quality. We used the statistical release relative to 2021 Q3 in this analysis.
10. There are several examples of these databases, including Bloomberg, FactSet, and Capital IQ.

Given what we know, we can calculate the percent remuneration of capital using the formula:

$$\text{Remuneration of capital}(\%) = (\frac{\text{DSO}}{365}) \times \text{Weighting Ratio} \times \text{Solvency Ratio} \times \text{ERP}$$

The results of our estimation, as usual by credit rating, are presented in Table 40.4.

*Table 40.4 Credit Risk Remuneration Estimation*

| *Rating (Moody's Categories)* | *DSO* | *Weight. Ratio (%)* | *Solvency Ratio (%) (Lower Bound)* | *Solvency Ratio (%) (Upper Bound)* | *ERP (%)* | *Opportunity Cost of Capital (%) (Lower Bound)* | *Opportunity Cost of Capital (%) (Upper Bound)* |
|---|---|---|---|---|---|---|---|
| | [a] | [b] | [c] | [d] | [e] | [g] = ([a] / 365) × [b] × [c] × [e] | [g] = ([a] / 365) × [b] × [d] × [e] |
| A | 90 | 50 | 15.3 | 17.3 | 13.2 | 0.25 | 0.28 |
| Baa | 90 | 100 | 15.3 | 17.3 | 13.2 | 0.50 | 0.56 |
| Ba | 90 | 100 | 15.3 | 17.3 | 13.2 | 0.50 | 0.56 |
| B | 90 | 150 | 15.3 | 17.3 | 13.2 | 0.75 | 0.85 |
| Unrated | 90 | 150 | 15.3 | 17.3 | 13.2 | 0.75 | 0.85 |

*Source*: Basel Long-term banking regulation, NERA calculations.

The opportunity cost of capital ranges from 25 basis points for an A-rated receivable (lower bound) to 85 basis points for an unrated receivable (upper bound). We now estimate the risk-free return to be assigned to the factor.

### D Remuneration for Time Value of Money

Finally, in addition to the credit risk remuneration estimated in the previous two sections, FactorCo should receive a remuneration to prefund its clients' receivables.

Because no credit risk should be attributed to this element, the risk-free rate should be added to the remuneration of FactorCo for prefunding services.

A risk-free loan is a loan without any related default risk. Risk-free rates remunerate the time value of money. The risk-free rate is estimated using the interbank money market rate.

Because the receivables have a duration of 90 days, we used the Euribor three-month rate to estimate the risk-free rate for an entity such as FactorCo. We took the average of the 2020 yields for this index at market close, obtaining an annual rate of –0.48%. Converting this rate into a rate that is representative for three months aligned with the duration of FactorCo receivables is approximately –0.12%.

### E Final Results

Finally, we sum all results of the benchmarks for individual elements to obtain the arm's-length remuneration for the factoring transactions (*see* Table 40.5).

*Table 40.5 Factoring Fee Estimation by Client Rating*

| *Rating (Moody's Categorization)* | *Internal Cost (%)* | *Expected Loss (%)* | *Cost of Equity Required (%) (Lower Bound)* | *Cost of Equity Required (%) (Upper Bound)* | *Financing (%) (Euribor)* | *Factoring Rate (%) (Lower Bound)* | *Factoring Rate (%) (Upper Bound)* |
|---|---|---|---|---|---|---|---|
| | [a] | [b] | [c] | [d] | [e] | [f] = [a] + [b] + [c] + [e] | [g] = [a] + [b] + [d] + [e] |
| A | 0.062 | 0.005 | 0.25 | 0.28 | –0.12 | 0.20 | 0.23 |
| Baa | 0.062 | 0.014 | 0.50 | 0.56 | –0.12 | 0.45 | 0.52 |
| Ba | 0.062 | 0.072 | 0.50 | 0.56 | –0.12 | 0.51 | 0.58 |
| B | 0.062 | 0.310 | 0.75 | 0.85 | –0.12 | 1.00 | 1.10 |
| Unrated | 0.062 | 0.412 | 0.75 | 0.85 | –0.12 | 1.10 | 1.20 |

*Source*: NERA calculations.

Finally, we compare the fee charged internally with the results of our benchmark. We do so by producing a weighted average of the arm's-length fees calculated for each credit rating (*see* Table 40.6).

*Table 40.6 Overall Factoring Fee Estimation*

| *Rating (Moody's Categorization)* | *Factored Volumes for 2020 (EUR)* | *Arm's-Length Fee (%) (Lower Bound)* | *Arm's-Length Fee (%) (Upper Bound)* |
|---|---|---|---|
| A | 588,260,870 | 0.20 | 0.23 |
| Baa | 1,568,695,652 | 0.45 | 0.52 |
| Ba | 1,408,260,870 | 0.51 | 0.58 |
| B | 1,105,217,391 | 1.00 | 1.10 |
| Unrated | 1,889,565,217 | 1.10 | 1.20 |
| Total | 6,560,000,000 | 0.72 | 0.80 |

*Source*: Client data, NERA calculations.

We conclude that the fee charged ranges from 0.72% to 0.80%.

### 3 Comparability Analysis

The OECD states that the comparability between the tested transaction and the chosen comparables should be evaluated considering:

- Contractual terms
- Functional analysis
- Characteristics of the instruments
- Economic circumstances
- Business strategies of the parties.

The contractual and economic characteristics of the arrangement were provided so that any differences with the comparables may be taken into account as adjustments. Notably, we determined that the type of factoring adopted by the group does not involve any recourse for FactorCo, which means that the disposal of receivables is akin to a sale. We established that receivables are sold when goods are shipped, and FactorCo makes a payment to the local entity concurrently. This represents an average financing term of three months for the local entities.

The value chain analysis has enabled us to contextualize the respective value contributions of the entities involved in the transaction. In this case, the local entities mainly contribute to the sales and marketing efforts of the group, in addition to building long-lasting relationships with customers, which they help on-site by integrating the solutions. On the other hand, FactorCo is part of the transversal support functions of the group. Its main responsibility is to contribute to helping the organization run more efficiently and effectively with regard to its receivables.

The functions performed and risks managed by FactorCo and the local entities show that the local entities act as distributors and client support providers while FactorCo hosts the group treasury and many of its back and middle office functions. This means that FactorCo has the resources to extend credit and the capabilities to evaluate the relative financial positions of the local entities and the group as a whole.

FactorCo assumes the credit risk related to the receivables it acquires because of the non-recourse feature of the agreement. Our benchmarking analysis uses this fact as we use probabilities of defaults on the receivables to assess what return FactorCo should require.

The conclusions to the value chain, functional, and risk analysis help us determine the business rationale of the transaction and its economic circumstances.

## IV CONCLUDING REMARKS

In this chapter, we provided a practical example of a factoring arrangement and used it to engage with typical considerations that should be made when evaluating its conformity to the arm's-length principle. We outlined the facts of the case and the factoring arrangement in question, then we proposed an approach to price the transaction. This structure is consistent with the OECD's newly published guidance on benchmarking financial transactions.[11]

Having established the characteristics of the transaction, we moved on to detailing our proposed approach to benchmarking the implied factoring fee. In principle, internal CUP transactions can be relied on to do this and should always be analysed when available. However, the group does not sell receivables to any third-party provider, which renders this approach not viable. Again, in principle, external CUP transactions can be used for this purpose, but to our knowledge, no independent databases collecting factoring data currently exist.

Another route that we explore is a standard TNMM using a comparable company search. We find that independent companies providing pure factoring services are very rare. In practice, it may be challenging to find a large enough set of comparables to carry out such a study.

We decided to use a different TNMM approach, which relies on segmenting the factoring transaction into its base components and benchmarking these components individually. These components are:

(1) The costs incurred for credit collection services: such costs are incurred by FactorCo in performing its services and should be covered by its remuneration.
(2) The expected loss resulting from clients' defaults: expected losses resulting from client defaults constitute a likely cash outflow that should be covered by the remuneration of FactorCo.
(3) The opportunity cost of capital: the equity engaged by investors in FactorCo should be remunerated in light of the opportunity cost. This is the profit element of FactorCo's remuneration.
(4) The remuneration of time value of money (risk-free short-term loan): the loan made to prefund receivables should be remunerated at the risk-free rate to account for the time value of money

In the end, the benchmarks for these segments are added to obtain the total remuneration for FactorCo.

The advantage of this method is that it can be used in a majority of cases because it mostly relies on information published by independent databases and research organizations. This application of the TNMM, however, requires a particularly in-depth knowledge of the transaction. The specific characteristics of the four components need to be clear for the professional who is undertaking the benchmarking.

In summary, we stress the importance of carrying out an accurate value chain and functional, asset, and risk analyses prior to getting into the exercise of selecting and applying a transfer pricing method. This may sound obvious from a transfer pricing perspective, but our experience is that such analyses are too often overlooked when it comes to ad hoc financing transactions such as factoring. Performing qualitative

11. OECD, Transfer Pricing Guidance on Financial Transactions, Inclusive Framework on BEPS.

analyses enables the practitioner to establish the level of substance that resides at the factoring entity, in addition to the corporate and business dynamics that exist between factors, suppliers, and clients. We expect a factor to have the capability of extending credit from a balance sheet perspective and have access to the human capital to make complex decisions on which receivables should be purchased. On the pricing front, the main challenge is data availability. When CUP transactions are not available or when it is impossible to adjust them, practitioners will often turn to TNMM. Independent factoring companies that do not operate in other businesses are rare, so an alternative synthetic approach is presented here. This approach enables us to fit the specific facts of the case.

# B Captive Insurance

CHAPTER 41

# The Use of Captives and How They Are Normally Organized

*Stephen Hawkes*[*]

Before considering captives, it is important to recognize the wider concept of risk financing and how a risk-financing strategy should be developed in any organization. The traditional strategy tends to focus on an insurance purchase, either direct with an insurance company or with the assistance of an insurance intermediary, such as a broker. Before contemplating such a transaction, an organization might want to evaluate the true economic value it will gain from it. The purchase of an insurance policy has become common both professionally and privately to such an extent that it is arguable that we no longer actively assess the true economic value of the transaction. For instance, how would a commercial enterprise bear the cost of a large event if it were not insured? What would be considered a large event? What are the sources of capital available to finance a large event and how would they be affected after the event? What is the enterprise's tolerance (capacity) and appetite (desire) to retain risk in general and insurable risk specifically? Answering these questions might lead to a greater understanding of where and when an insurance transaction (being the reliance on a third party's balance sheet should a named peril occur) would be beneficial.

## I SOURCES OF CAPITAL

An insurance transaction is only one option to finance an unexpected event. There are other sources of capital, and each option has advantages and disadvantages. The list below is not exhaustive, but some of the options and associated considerations.

* The views and opinions set forth herein are the personal views or opinions of the authors; they do not necessarily reflect views or opinions of the organization with which the authors are associated.

### 1 Debt

A company could rely on a debt facility to finance an unexpected event. This would have the advantage of being prearranged and without any requirements to prove a specific peril had occurred. However, the cost and availability of the debt may change over time, and at the time it is actually required, the company may have many calls on the debt facility. In addition, the full debt will need to be paid back.

### 2 Equity

Another option might be to raise additional equity. This has the advantage of limited parameters for use (subject to the prospectus document) but might be unsuccessful with insufficient investors at the time of greatest need. Furthermore, like debt, the desired priorities for usage may change at the time of need.

### 3 Insurance

Insurance is another form of contingent capital. It has the benefit of being fixed cost (at least for every policy year) but comes with detailed terms and conditions that must be complied with to achieve indemnity.

### 4 Summary

When considering the appropriateness of a specific action, it is desirable that a detailed risk-financing strategy is developed to understand how the company could finance an event if it were to occur. This should include a detailed review of the company's tolerance and appetite for financial volatility and identify what indicators should be monitored to suggest that the strategy requires modification. It should also be remembered that this strategy should encompass all forms of risk, not just insurable risk, as there are likely to be differing strategies for each type of risk. As an example, is the same strategy used for treasury risks (such as currency fluctuations) as for insurable risks? If not, then why not? In conclusion, there are many dynamics to an insurable risk-financing strategy, and these require consideration and evaluation before executing any form of insurance purchasing.

## II RISK RETENTION

A risk-financing strategy should start with contemplating appropriate retention levels. When would risk transfer be required to generate financial value for the company? To conduct such a retention analysis, it is useful to contemplate the corporate tolerance to financial volatility. It is also likely that this tolerance will differ between the corporate level and any internal profit centers. For evaluating a captive strategy, the corporate level tolerance remains of primary concern, as any profit center differences can be catered for within the structure or via internal reimbursement mechanisms.

The risk tolerance might be defined as the corporate ability to finance risks (should they occur) from existing resources. Such tolerance encompasses all risks, not just insurable risks and therefore, the corporate appetite to accept such risks will vary depending on a range of competing pressures. When considering risk retention for insurable risks, it is helpful to refine the corporate risk tolerance to a risk appetite for insurable risk. Once an evaluation of risk appetite has been concluded and a financial quantification agreed on, some consideration for the structure of that retention can be considered. There are perhaps three possible structures to finance this retention.

## 1 Pay as You Go

Under a pay-as-you-go structure, retained losses are paid by the company (at corporate or division level) from operating cash flows as and when they arise. There is no formal pre-loss funding or income statement protection. This has the advantage of requiring no administration time or cost and no exposure to insurance premium tax. It also encourages basic risk-management practices at operational level. However, it does not provide cash flow or income statement protection, which may become challenging if expenses become exceptional. Furthermore, there is likely to be limited reporting of events and, therefore, no central learning regarding risk management or the capture of management information. This structure works best for low financial levels where the cost associated with financing and managing the event are low.

## 2 Formal Internal Fund

Structuring risk retention with a formal internal fund requires the creation of a central fund managed and operated at a group level. Contributions to the fund can either come from the central finance function or can be collected from each profit center protected by the fund. The fund reimburses each profit center for any predefined losses in the defined retention. This creates centralized funding of retained risk and effectively mutualizes the defined risk(s) across all profit centres. It has the advantage of minimal administration (time and cost) and does not incur insurance premium tax on contributions. Furthermore, it allows some budget certainty for the profit centres, although the group might be exposed to volatility if total losses exceed the fund value. It also allows the capture of lost data and management information. However, such a fund cannot be used for compulsory insurance classes or where evidence of insurance is required under law, regulation, or contractual relationship. It is also likely to increase the risk of inspection from tax authorities, especially if profit centres in other tax jurisdictions have taken a tax deduction for their contribution to fund. Tax and accounting treatment can be uncertain and will require input from finance and/or an auditor, and the fund can easily be raided for other business purposes or to fund events not contemplated when the fund was created. This structure can be efficient when applied to low-severity, high-frequency events that are predictable in nature although their legal, accounting, and tax treatment would require validating for each territory and corporate circumstance.

## 3 Captive Structure

A captive structure is a more formalized version of the internal fund. There are two main recognized captive structures: either a wholly owned captive insurer or a cell in a protected cell company (PCC). Other group risk retention vehicles, such as group captives or mutuals, do exist, but these are complex structures involving multiple parties. For the purposes of this discussion, these have been ignored. Either a wholly owned captive or a PCC cell bring formality to risk-financing arrangements and the risk financing is structured in the same way as any other formal insurance contract. The generally accepted definition of a captive is "a bona fide licensed insurance or reinsurance company owned by a non-insurance company and which insurers or reinsures the risks of its parent and/or affiliated companies." It is a regulated entity, and hence the assets and liabilities of the insurance company are protected by the legislation in the country that issued the insurance licence.

The captive insurer will issue an insurance policy in exchange for an agreed premium to any entity in the same economic family as its shareholder, being any sister or affiliated company. This creates a centralized fund for the insured risks and provides budget certainty to each of the insured entities.

Many benefits are generated from this structure depending on the goals and objectives for its original creation. These might include the capture of detailed underwriting and loss data that previously may not have been collated centrally. These data can be used to highlight risk-management opportunities. A captive insurer is a legal and compliant means of retaining and pooling business unit risk across borders, and the legal, tax, and accounting treatment of these transactions has been established over many years. The captive insurer will issue a formal insurance policy, which can be used to provide evidence of insurance to third parties, although it might also be open to challenge as the captive insurer is not likely to hold a credit rating.

A captive insurer comes with the requirements of adequate solvency, as defined by the territory in which it is licenced. These requirements can be substantial and although the subsidiary's assets and liabilities are likely to be included in its parent on consolidation, they may result in some cash being trapped in the captive insurer. The captive will also incur operating expenses to comply with the regulatory requirements of its domicile. Further, there will be day-to-day operational expenses as well as insurance premium tax in each jurisdiction of the insured parties.

A PCC will also benefit from the above-mentioned benefits and implications. A PCC structure is created, usually by a captive management company, to allow any entity to benefit from most of the risk-financing benefits of a captive structure while limiting the operating costs. As an illustrative example, a captive manager might incorporate a PCC in a jurisdiction that has specific PCC legislation and allow third parties to create individual cells (effectively experience accounts) with which to finance specified risks. The scope (both types and quantum of specified risks) will be defined by the PCC owner, but each cell is legally separated under the legislation to ensure that the financial performance of any cell owner will not affect any other cell owner. The main difference between a wholly owned captive and a protected cell are that the cell owner has no ownership and limited management control over the operation of the PCC. This control is exerted by the PCC owner. Because the cell owner has no ownership, they will be unable to elect directors to the board of the PCC, will not be involved in the day-to-day management or governance of the PCC, and will not appoint auditors. A PCC cell does bring the benefit of financing the defined risks with lower operating costs attributed to each individual cell. This is because each cell only pays a portion of the operating expenses of the whole PCC. PCCs can have many cells, and hence the operational overhead costs can be minimized for each individual cell.

## III REASONS FOR FORMING A CAPTIVE

Organizations have many reasons for forming a captive insurance vehicle, and the below summarizes the main drivers:

- *Cost*: To reduce reliance on third parties and capture the profits made by commercial insurers. Irrespective of the annual claims performance, commercial insurers expect to make a profit over an extended period (perhaps 5 or 10 years) from the majority of their policyholders. The core principle is "the premiums of the many pay for the losses of the few." Accepting the volatility of claims performance at non-catastrophic levels will generate cost savings, as the expenses incurred at this level of risk retention financed through a captive structure are less than those of commercial insurers.
- *Capacity*: A captive insurance vehicle might be able to access international reinsurers and speciality insurers directly, which can introduce new capacity, greater competition, and better pricing for insured risks.
- *Control*: As the primary insurer, a captive insurance vehicle can tailor its cover (policy language), manage claims, and direct subsequent reinsurance to make sure that the parent organization enjoys the widest possible coverage, at the best price, in a fully transparent way. This may create a difference in conditions between the primary (captive) policy and any excess placement, but it allows the organization to finance the risks that are of most concern.
- *Compliance*: A captive insurance vehicle provides a legal basis for subsidiaries to pool retained risk across borders and different tax systems. The accounting, tax, and legal treatment is well known and understood in most jurisdictions.
- *Cover*: A captive insurance company can issue proof of insurance (cover note or an insurance policy) to comply with contractual obligations. The group may prefer to retain certain risks it is contractually obliged to insure, for example, professional liability insurance for customers or leased property insurance to a landlord. A captive insurance vehicle can evidence insurance and capture premium that otherwise would be leaked to third parties. It should be remembered that depending on the jurisdiction of the captive licence and any

rating obtained, third parties may challenge the security offered by an insurance policy issued by a captive.
- *Commercial*: A captive insurance vehicle can participate in third-party insurance offered to customers, vendors, or other-related parties, such as customer warranty insurance or subcontractors under an owner-controlled insurance program.

## IV OPTIMAL INSURANCE STRUCTURES

The actual insurance structure involving a captive depends entirely on the parent organization's wants and needs, the class of risk being underwritten, and the interaction with commercial insurers.

For instance, a traditional risk for a captive insurer would be property material damage. It would be sensible from a cost-effectiveness viewpoint to self-insure (either directly or through a captive structure) the expected level of claims activity. The captive might find that their owner's appetite to retain the property risk actually extends beyond this level of expected claims activity, and therefore the captive may underwrite to a higher limit. This limit could be on an each-loss basis or could be aggregated over a policy year but would usually be the level of risk immediately in excess of a policy deductible. This is because the level of premium attributable to each tranche of risk reduces as you move towards the policy limit. Furthermore, an aggregated limit allows for greater certainty in the captive but will depend on either commercial insurers providing the aggregate stop loss protection or the owner accepting the exposure in excess of the defined aggregate.

Another structure that might be considered would be a quota share, where the captive takes a proportional element of the risk to the full policy limit (or the full layer if the placement is organized on a layered basis). These structures tend to be used when the commercial placement is difficult to execute at the desired pricing, and the captive structure is used to complete a particular structure.

Although reference has been made to property insurance for the purpose of explanation, these structures can apply to other classes of risk. The actual structure implemented in each case will be driven by the specific circumstances.

## V DIRECT OR REINSURANCE

Captives can underwrite on a direct basis where the insurance policy is issued directly to the ultimate insured or on a reinsurance basis where a commercial insurer issues the policy to the ultimate insured and reinsures part of all the risk with the captive reinsurer.

The drivers for these structures will depend on the overall structure of the placement and the regulatory and commercial requirements of the insured and captive owner. For instance, it is possible that insurance policies issued by an insurer licenced outside of the country where the risk exists are either illegal in accordance with the local insurance legislation or permitted in certain circumstances. Placements involving insurers licenced outside where the risk is located are classed as non-admitted insurance. It is important to establish the legal requirements in all territories where the captive might be required to issue a policy. If non-admitted insurance is not permitted, then a commercial insurer who is appropriately licenced will be required to issue the local policy and reinsure the whole or part of the risk to the captive reinsurer. Commercial insurers will charge for these services, so this has a cost effect on the captive premium.

However, a reinsurance arrangement might also bring other benefits. For instance, commercial insurers have developed extensive expertise in supporting claims settlements, engineering and loss preventions services, payment of local insurance taxes, and other risk-related consulting services that could be considered beneficial to the insured organization.

Conversely, a direct relationship between the captive insurer and the parent organization will tend to provide the lowest cost overhead to the actual transaction as there will not be a fronting charge levied by the fronting insurer.

## VI CAPTIVE MANAGEMENT

A captive insurance or reinsurance company is a formally regulated entity that will be licenced in its chosen jurisdiction. The insurance licence will require the formation of a local company with a board of directors, suitably knowledgeable and qualified to manage an insurance company. These directors should be prepared to meet periodically in the domicile of the company to provide proper oversight of all aspects of the captive company's operation. This includes setting underwriting parameters, monitoring the financial performance, and maintaining suitable levels of corporate governance in accordance with best practice standards.

The captive insurance company directors will need to consider how the day-to-day operations of the company will be carried out. There might be various requirements for actual physical substance imposed by the licencing authority. These can range from the employment of staff and physical premises to a fully outsourced model allowing the operational functions to be contracted to a specialist management company. Most recognized captive domiciles will allow many functions to be outsourced, although the directors remain ultimately responsible for the company. Specialist management companies can provide all the underwriting, accounting, corporate secretarial, treasury, and compliance functions, reporting to the directors when required. However, there is no requirement to outsource any or all of these functions, and the directors may choose to undertake them themselves or employ staff to perform these functions. The choice between an in-source or outsource model will likely depend on the costs and availability of suitable staff. However, the outsource model is adopted by the vast majority of captives because the parent organization and the local regulatory authority take comfort from the expertise available from the management companies.

## VII CAPTIVE DOMICILE

The choice of a domicile for a captive venture is driven by the domicile of the parent organization, the location of the risks to be underwritten, and the tax and regulatory implications for the parent organization and the captive insurer.

There are over 70 recognized captive insurance jurisdictions around the world. Each domicile has unique features and virtues that make it attractive to certain geographies or industries. The primary choice is between an onshore and an offshore domicile.

An onshore domicile is located in a major country or region, such as the European Union or the United States. The key benefit of an onshore domicile is the ability to issue direct policies and avoid procurement taxes or fronting fees that may apply otherwise. For instance, an EU captive insurance company can underwrite risks in any other European Economic Area Member State on a direct and admitted basis under EU passporting rights for insurance.

All EU onshore domiciles are governed by the same European regulations, known as Solvency II.[1] These regulations have increased the amount of capital and governance required to operate a captive insurance company. Because the same pan-European regulations apply to all Member States captive owners usually select the most convenient (proximity) or tax-efficient domicile for their captive.

An offshore domicile is located outside a major country, but the term generally refers to the UK overseas territories and Crown dependencies, such as Bermuda, the Cayman Islands, Guernsey, and the Isle of Man.

Offshore domiciles tend to have similar corporate tax rates (none or 0%), regulatory and governance requirements (based on International Association of Insurance Supervisors core principles), and operating costs and have mature captive (re)insurance industries and infrastructure. As a result, there is very little to differentiate between offshore domiciles other than their proximity and familiarity with the organization.

## VIII CAPTIVE RATING

As mentioned already, captive insurance companies do not tend to seek a commercial credit rating. However, some captives seek a rating by a recognized commercial rating agency. This provides the benefits of an independent, third-party assessment of the captive, its financial strength, and its operation, which adds to the overall perception of the captive. It can also assist in negotiating collateral requirements with fronting insurers. Where a captive has assumed a longer tail exposure (an exposure that might not be known or quantified for a number of years), commercial fronting insurers might request that collateral is posted to secure their financial position regarding the captive

1. Directive 2009/138/EC of the European Parliament and of the Council of 25 November 2009 on the taking-up and pursuit of the business of Insurance and Reinsurance (Solvency II).

reinsurance arrangements. This might be minimized if the captive insurer can demonstrate a commercial credit rating. The other main benefit of a commercial rating is to demonstrate to third parties the overall financial strength of the captive insurer. This can be helpful if the captive insurance policy is used to demonstrate to an interested third party that insurance has been purchased.

## IX FEASIBILITY ASSESSMENT

Before considering if a captive structure will generate a benefit, most organizations use a specialist consultant to conduct a feasibility study and assess the options based on the specific goals and objectives of the organization. These studies are best conducted in conjunction with the team who will actually place any commercial insurance to make sure that the captive proposal will sit comfortably alongside the commercial insurance without causing any conflicts. The study should cover the structure of the insurance placement, compare the appropriate domiciles, and evaluate the financial benefits that might be achieved from implementing a captive insurance company.

## X CONCLUSION

Captive insurance companies have been formed for many reasons and across many jurisdictions; there are currently well over 6,000 captives in the world, and captive formations continue to grow even at times when commercial insurance is widely available. Companies who use captives tend to have adopted a more sophisticated approach to risk financing. The main driver for captive formation is almost always financial efficiency, but the actual implementation and financial structures vary widely, so it is important to give consideration to all of these elements before creating a captive.

Chapter 42
# Overview into Captive Structures

*Andrea Grainger & Emilia Siravo*[*]

## I INTRODUCTION

Captives are a powerful financial tool. If used appropriately for managing a corporation's risks, captives provide a plethora of benefits beyond tax savings. In this article, the authors provide an overview of captive insurance, outline typical captive structures and plans used, and highlight the commercial rationale for establishing a captive.

## II CAPTIVES DEFINED

Simply defined, a captive is a form of corporate self-insurance. A captive is an insurance company protecting the risks of its 'affiliated' operating companies belonging to a commonly shared parent.[1] The Organisation for Economic Co-operation and Development (OECD) defines captives as 'an insurance undertaking or entity substantially all of whose insurance business is to provide insurance policies for risks of entities of the MNE [multinational enterprise] group to which it belongs'.[2] By self-insuring with captives, corporations utilize an efficient financial planning tool that allows the enterprise to manage its risk in a cost-effective manner.

Like traditional insurance companies, captives receive a payment of premium in return for risk coverage in the event of a loss.[3] Captive insurers are regulated by local

* The views and opinions set forth herein are the personal views or opinions of the authors; they do not necessarily reflect views or opinions of the organization with which the authors are associated.
1. Jay D. Adkisson, Captive Insurance Company, p. 1.
2. OECD Transfer Pricing Guidance on Financial Transactions, p. 35.
3. Jay D. Adkisson, Captive Insurance, intro xiii.

financial regulators and must adhere to appropriate actuarial, reserving, accounting and other capital and solvency requirements of insurance.[4] Different to traditional insurance companies, captives generally obtain most of their premiums from insuring affiliated operating companies' risks. Notwithstanding, in recent years, captives have experienced growth in third-party exposure risks including, for example, voluntary benefits and extended warranty risks.[5]

*Figure 42.1 Simplified Overview of an Insurance Captive*

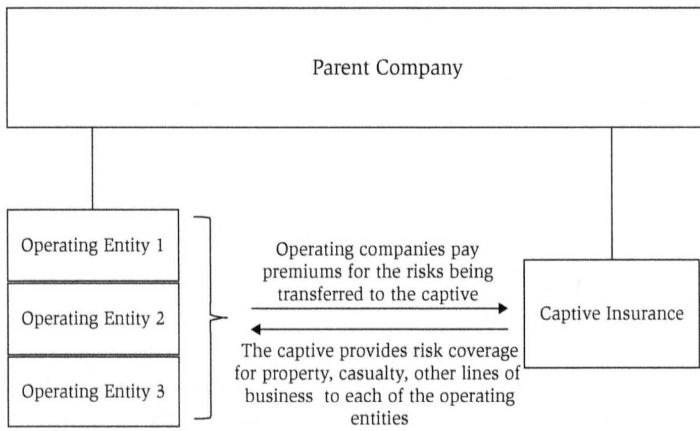


## III SCOPE AND COVERAGE

Captives provide multinational companies flexibility on what lines of business to cover and on how to devise the organizations overall insurance coverage.[6] Captive companies insure both traditional Property and Casualty (P&C) non-life lines of business (e.g., property, general liability, and motor risks), offer coverage on non-standard risks (e.g., cyber, intellectual property or complex engineering or energy facilities)[7] and cover risks that are difficult to insure.[8] These include: risks that traditional insurance companies lack appetite for (e.g., contingent business liability due to cyber-attacks), risks that third-party insurers are limited in writing due to internal capacity restraints (e.g., risks with excessive North Atlantic Hurricane exposures) or risks that face

4. OECD Transfer Pricing Guidance on Financial Transactions, 10.192.
5. Marsh, Captive Insurance Report, *The Captive Landscape: Global Growth Affirms Captives' Value in Solving Business Challenges*, 2021, slide 9.
6. Jay D. Adkisson, Captive Insurance Company, p. 56.
7. PwC, Captive Insurance Brochure. Retrieved from https://www.pwc.com/us/en/industries/insurance/assets/pwc-captive-insurance-brochure.pdf.
8. Marsh, Captive Insurance Report, *The Captive Landscape: Global Growth Affirms Captives' Value in Solving Business Challenges*, 2021, p. 5.

mounting reputational concerns (e.g., environmental damage caused during oil exploration activities).

Captive insurance solutions are often used for bespoke structures and are increasingly used to support newer industries that struggle to obtain insurance otherwise. One recent example includes the newly established Cannabis Captive Solution established to support qualifying cannabis companies to obtain insurance that is otherwise deemed too expensive or unavailable in the traditional (re)insurance market.[9]

## IV HISTORICAL OVERVIEW

Historically, captive insurance companies were developed out of economic need.[10] Evidence of early captive structures is found in the US starting in the early 1920s, but the concept further developed in the late 1950s thanks to Fred Reiss's work with Youngstown Sheet and Tube Company.[11] When Youngstown faced increasingly high insurance costs, Reiss worked together with Lloyd's of London to set up Youngstown's own insurance company, Ohio Steel Insurance Company of America,[12] to mitigate rising insurance costs.[13] Reiss coined the term 'captive' using the name Youngstown executives gave various mines ('captive mines') that supplied Youngstown's steel mills at the time.[14]

Since the early 1920s, the number of captives has continuously grown.[15] In 1985, there were an estimated 1,200[16] captives registered worldwide but by year-end 2020, there were over 7,000 captives licensed in 71 jurisdictions.[17] Ninety per cent of Fortune 500 companies have at least one captive.[18] Bermuda, Cayman Islands and Vermont are the top three jurisdictional domiciles for worldwide captives[19] but, in recent years,

---

9. Captive Insurance Times magazine issue number 277, retrieved from: https://www.captiveinsurancetimes.com/citimes/issue.php?issuelink=https://www.captiveinsurancetimes.com/citimes/CITimes_issue_227.pdf&issueNo=227&year=2021.
10. Hale, Steward and Cantley, Beckett: US Captive Insurance Law, Second Edition, 2015, p. 67.
11. Peter J. Strauss, *The Business Owner's Definitive Guide to Captive Insurance Companies*, 2017, p. 3.
12. *Ibid.*, p. 6.
13. Jay D. Adkisson, Captive Insurance Company, intro xiii.
14. Peter Strauss, The Business Owner's Definitive Guide to Captive Insurance Companies. 2017, p. 6.
15. Swiss Re. Integrating Corporate Risk Management, p. 99 (referencing the Tillinghast Towers Perrin Captive Insurance Company Directory).
16. *Ibid.*
17. Retrieved from https://captivereview.com/news/world-domicile-update-reveals-surge-in-captive-insurance-cell-formations/, also in https://content.naic.org/cipr_topics/topic_captive_insurance_companies.htm.
18. PwC, Captive Insurance Brochure. Retrieved from https://www.pwc.com/us/en/industries/insurance/assets/pwc-captive-insurance-brochure.pdf.
19. Retrieved from:https://www.statista.com/statistics/217535/leading-global-captive-domiciles/.

European and Asian jurisdictions (e.g., Guernsey and Singapore) have experienced an increase in both numbers of captive domiciles and captive premium volumes.[20]

## V BENEFITS AND RISKS

Historically tax was seen as a motivation for forming a captive. Captives were particularly beneficial in jurisdictions like the US, where the tax code did not allow ordinary companies to set contingencies against potential future losses. By self-insuring with a captive, corporations could manage their risk and set reserves towards future claims[21] while achieving a tax deduction for these expenses. Worldwide, tax authorities challenged captives because they felt captives aided aggressive tax planning and allowed for manipulation of corporate earnings.[22] Nevertheless, despite the tax challenges, captive benefits (beyond tax) trumped the risks. As a result, the captive industry has continually grown.[23]

Captives remain an important financial tool for multinationals today. Captive benefits include, but are not limited to:[24,25,26]

- stabilizing the cost of insurance[27] and reducing insurance pricing market volatilities;[28]
- improving the terms and flexibility of insurance coverage;[29]
- providing added claims control;[30]
- managing the overall company's risk retention levels;[31,32]

20. Marsh, Captive Insurance Report, *The Captive Landscape: Global Growth Affirms Captives' Value in Solving Business Challenges*, 2021, p. 12. Guernsey has had 79% increase in premium volumes in 2020 and Singapore 30% increase in premium volume.
21. Jay D. Adkisson, Captive Insurance Company, p. 13.
22. Hale, Steward and Cantley, Beckett: US Captive Insurance Law, Second Edition, 2015, p. 65. US IRS had over 40 years of litigating captives in court.
23. Steward F. Hale, Captive Insurance in Plain English, 2017, p. 5.
24. Petronas management provides various benefits to captives in their video: Retrieved from: https://www.mondaq.com/insurance-laws-and-products/632206/panel-discussion-why-and-how-did-petronas-manage-its-risks-via-captive-insurance-video.
25. Raziah Zahya (Petronas) indicates that for every five years of premium paid in insurance premiums, in terms of cost savings, one year is free using the captive mechanism. She adds that captive insurance is a powerful risk financing tool for any large multinational. Retrieved from: https://www.mondaq.com/insurance-laws-and-products/632206/panel-discussion-why-and-how-did-petronas-manage-its-risks-via-captive-insurance-video.
26. OECD Transfer Pricing Guidance on Financial Transactions, Part E, 10.193.
27. Jay D. Adkisson, Captive Insurance Company, p. 2.
28. Zurich Insurance Company, Our Guide to Captives. Retrieved from: https://www.zurich.com/en/products-and-services/protect-your-business/commercial-insurance-risk-insights/our-guide-to-captives.
29. Jay D. Adkisson, Captive Insurance Company, pp. 5-8.
30. *Ibid.*, p. 5.
31. *Ibid.*, p. 7. Captive company can be used to insurance the deductibles of commercially obtained insurance.
32. Steward F. Hale, Captive Insurance in Plain English, pp. 4-5.

- enhancing company loss prevention management;[33] and
- obtaining access to the reinsurance market directly.[34]

During the COVID-19 pandemic, captives witnessed historic growth formations motivated by the hardening (re)insurance market.[35] Enterprises faced with increasingly high and volatile insurance costs embraced the captive concept. During this time, captives offered the perfect solution to multinationals who feared having to 'going naked'[36] (having no insurance coverage at all) because of reduced insurance company appetite and limited supply of certain types of risk coverage. Additionally, during the recent hard market, captives offered corporations access to more competitive (re)insurance pricing in cases where market quotes were punitive.

Despite the benefits, there are risks to captives. Because captives are self-insurance, one of the biggest disadvantages (especially for captives who keep all risks net and do not use additional reinsurance) is that the risk is retained within the organization.[37] In the event of a severe loss, the organization will have to bear the loss without potential for external relief. Additionally, there are potential tax risks and administrative costs associated with the captive.[38] In cases where captives are less stringently regulated, or where captives employ a lean business model with little risk diversification or substance and key staff to take the risk and run the business, there is the potential for the captive structure to be abused. This can lead to both tax disputes and reputational risk for the organization.

## VI CAPTIVE STRUCTURES AND PLANS

The term 'captive' can refer to a wide spectrum of entities, from very small entities insuring one risk of just one group company to very large entities insuring many risks for many group entities. Different captive setups will lead to different functional analysis impacting the captive's remuneration.

Captives may broadly be classified by (1) *Ownership*: *single-parent* (single owner/wholly owned) versus *multiple-parent/group captives or associate captives*[39] (2) *Customer base*: *Pure captive* (only insurer risks of its owners) versus *diversified captive* (insurers third-party risks and reinsures part of their risk in the open market)[40] and by (3) *Insurer plan*:[41] *insurance* captive, and *reinsurance* captive.

33. JAY D. ADKISSON, Captive Insurance Company, p. 9.
34. JAY D. ADKISSON, Captive Insurance Company, p. 7.
35. Marsh Captive Insurance Guide Video retrieved from: https://www.marsh.com/us/services/captive-insurance/insights/captive-trends-and-data.html.
36. Steward F. HALL, Captive Insurance in Plain English, p. 5.
37. Wiening, Foundations of Risk Management and Insurance, 1st Edition, 7.5.
38. *Ibid.*
39. Jay D. Adkisson, Captive Insurance Company, p. 29.
40. *Ibid.*
41. Elliott: Fundamentals of Risk Financing, 3.17.

Additionally, captive types can be summarized to include:[42]

| *Type* | *Ownership* | *Base* | *Insurer Plan* | *Examples* |
|---|---|---|---|---|
| Pure[43] | Single Parent | Write mostly insurance policies of affiliated brother-sister operating companies owned by the multinational group of which they are a member.[44] Represent the most common captive type.[45] | Insurance and Reinsurance.[46] | *Corporate Captive*: owned by large multinational.[47] *Mini-captives/831 (b) captives*:[48] US captive companies making less than USD 2.2 billion annually (adjusted for inflation).[49] *CHIC (closely held insurance companies)*:[50] owned by family members (often children or grandchildren) but used to insure the business. Often considered a means of wealth management and planning.[51] |
| Group[52]/ Associated | Multiple Parents | Diversified to include affiliated and non-affiliated company risk | Insurance and Reinsurance | *Associative/Affiliate Captives*: offers insurance to companies within the same group types[53] *Industry Captives*: offers insurance to |

42. Jay D. Adkisson, Captive Insurance Company, pp. 29-36.
43. Insurance/Reinsurance. Only cover the risks of that multinational group/typical no risks are from outside the economic family except if reinsurance is purchased.
44. Marsh Captive Insurance Report, *The Captive Landscape: Global Growth Affirms Captives' Value in Solving Business Challenges*, 2021, slide 8.
45. Marsh Captive Insurance Report, *The Captive Landscape: Global Growth Affirms Captives' Value in Solving Business Challenges*, 2021, slide 8 – 74% of captives are single parent.
46. *Retrieved from* https://selfinsurancemarket.com/articles/different-types-of-captive-insurance-company.
47. Jay D. Adkisson, Captive Insurance Company, p. 29.
48. In both Syzygy and in *Avrahami v. Commissioner*: Have recently been challenged by the IRS in cases where they lacked economic substance, failed to evidence bona fide insurance operations by lacking appropriate risk distribution, or lacked adequate actuarial pricing review as is necessary in standard insurance companies.
49. Jay D. Adkisson, Captive Insurance Company, p. 30.
50. *Ibid.*
51. *Ibid.*
52. *Ibid.*, p. 31.
53. *Ibid.*

| Type | Ownership | Base | Insurer Plan | Examples |
|---|---|---|---|---|
| | | | | organizations within the same industry[54,55] (e.g., Steel Captives) |
| Other/ Sponsored Captives/ Protected Cell Captives | Multiple Parent | Diversified to include affiliated and non-affiliated company risk and represent a fast-growing type of captives.[56] | Various structures | *Agency Captives*: typical owned by insurance broker or agent.[57] *Rent-a-captives*: third party uses existing captive base; often used by small companies to avoid set up costs of establishing a captive.[58] *Risk Retention Groups*: established by businesses to pooling and share similar business risks.[59] |

## VII CAPTIVES IN THE (RE)INSURANCE SPECTRUM[60]

### 1 The (Re)insurance Spectrum

Insurance is a communal venture – many need to pool together to support the misfortunes of a few.[61] However, to ascertain this concerted sharing works, insurance

54. *Ibid.*
55. Retrieved from: https://selfinsurancemarket.com/articles/different-types-of-captive-insurance-company.
56. Marsh Captive Insurance Report, *The Captive Landscape: Global Growth Affirms Captives' Value in Solving Business Challenges*, 2021, slide 8.
57. Jay D. Adkisson, Captive Insurance Company, p. 32.
58. *Retrieved from* https://selfinsurancemarket.com/articles/different-types-of-captive-insurance-company.
59. Jay D. Adkisson, Captive Insurance Company, p. 34.
60. Article 13 of Solvency II defines captive insurance and reinsurance undertakings as follows:

    (2) 'captive insurance undertaking' means an insurance undertaking, owned either by a financial undertaking other than an insurance or reinsurance undertaking or a group of insurance or reinsurance undertakings within the meaning of Article 212(1)(c)11 or by a non-financial undertaking, the purpose of which is to provide insurance cover exclusively for the risks of the undertaking or undertakings to which it belongs or of an undertaking or undertakings of the group of which it is a member;

    (5) 'captive reinsurance undertaking' means a reinsurance undertaking, owned either by a financial undertaking other than an insurance or reinsurance undertaking or a group of insurance or reinsurance undertakings within the meaning of Article 212(1)(c) or by a non-financial undertaking, the purpose of which is to provide reinsurance cover exclusively for the risks of the undertaking or undertakings to which it belongs or of an undertaking or undertakings of the group of which it is a member.

61. Robert Strain et al., Reinsurance: Indemnifying Insurers for Insurance Losses, 1997, p. 3. The authors write, 'the workings of insurance can be disarmingly simple: many pay for the loss of a few'.

companies need to properly manage their offerings, assets and investments in a capital-effective way to safeguard the long-term sustainability of the protective offering.

Insurance is broadly defined as the transfer of risk with a real possibility of loss,[62] between two parties (insurer and insured), where the insurer promises to pay the insured an amount of money for a potential loss sustained in the set period.[63] The premium payment (from the insured) transfers the probability of risk (to the insurer). The insurer then allocates these many individual uncertainties together and through pooling manages the predictability of the overall group portfolio future losses.[64]

Within the insurance spectrum, reinsurance is defined as insurance for insurance companies[65] and serves as a vital financial management tool available to insurers.[66] It enables insurers to more manage their risk appetites and to limit annual loss fluctuations that insurers would otherwise need to bear on their own account.[67] Through reinsurance, insurance companies cede off-peak risks that stem from major catastrophe events, including hurricanes, earthquakes or even from man-made events, for example, acts of terrorism.

Reinsurance also provides financial relief to insurers. Risks that require capital are removed from a company's balance sheet through reinsurance arrangements. Some reinsurance products reduce local capacity requirements allowing for acceptance of more risks and improved solvency margins.[68] Furthermore, because of the capital relief and volatility protection reinsurance provides, reinsurance purchasing may translate to less expensive insurance for individuals and corporations.[69]

Ultimately, reinsurance allows insurers to tap into the diversification benefits by pooling risks into a central entity.[70] Diversification obtained by reinsurance ultimately

62. Downs, Rob *Reinsurance Risk Management Testing: Methods and Management of Process.* available at: https://www.casact.org/community/affiliates/maf/0906/downs.ppt (accessed 1 November 2020). Downs cites the Reinsurance Attestation Supplement 20-1 stating, 'It is reasonably possible that the reinsurer may realize a significant loss from the transaction.' The author indicates that reasonability can be measured using the 10/10 rule, Tail Value at Risk (TVAR) or the Expected Reinsurer Deficit (ERD).
63. Robert Strain et al., Reinsurance: Indemnifying Insurers for Insurance Losses, 1997, p. 67.
64. Joseph Mangan et al., *Underwriting Principles.* American Institute for Chartered Property Casualty Underwriters Insurance Institute of America (1995) at p. 162; Also *see* Robert Strain et al., Reinsurance: Indemnifying Insurers for Insurance Losses, 1997, at p. 6; Also in Vikram Chand. *Transfer Pricing Aspects of Captive Insurance Arrangements: Recommendations to the OECD.* IFF-HSG (2017).
65. Joseph Mangan et al., *Underwriting Principles.* American Institute for Chartered Property Casualty Underwriters Insurance Institute of America (1995) at p. 162.
66. Robert Strain et al., Reinsurance: Indemnifying Insurers for Insurance Losses, 1997, p. 67.
67. *Ibid.*, 67.
68. OECD Transfer Pricing Guidance on Financial Transactions, at p. 172. The OECD states, 'Through reinsurance, insurers can manage their insurance and investment risk. By buying reinsurance, insurers can "free up" surplus (reduce the amount of surplus needed to support reinsured business) and reduce reserves, which allows insurers to write more insurance contracts.'
69. Maurus Rischatsch, Swiss Re: The Benefits of Global Diversification: How Reinsurers Create Value and Manage Risk, 2006, pp. 6-8.
70. *Ibid.*

leads to lower capital requirements which translate into potentially lower-priced reinsurance coverage and overall, more protection.[71]

## 2 Where Do Captives Fit into the (Re)insurance Sector?

Captives are a form of self-insurance and are a growing part of the insurance sector. In 2021, worldwide, the insurance industry underwrote over USD 7 trillion[72] in gross premiums written,[73] and of that, captives wrote USD 60.7 billion[74] of gross written premiums which represents a 30% increase in premium volumes in the past three years.[75]

Captive solutions are found along various points in the insurance-reinsurance spectrum. Corporates may consider using captives as a form of *direct self-insurance*[76] providing insurance for their own group's risks. Corporate could use captives to protect themselves from emerging risks, for example, Cyber or D&O broad covers that may not be available in the insurance market[77] or reduce insurance pricing volatility swings due to hard market cycles. Corporates might also use *reinsurance captives*[78] which cede risks into the captive via fronting companies for easier access to the reinsurance market.

## 3 Direct Insurance Captive

Direct insurance captive companies are fully licensed and provide their operating entities with primary insurance coverage. To maintain an insurance license, a captive insurer must comply with the rules of the financial regulator typically covering governance, accounting, and capital requirements. Although a captive insurer needs to be licensed by a local regulator, many captives often have only limited authorization (e.g., only being allowed to insure group risks and not those of unrelated parties[79]). In exchange for limited authorization, the regulation of a captive is generally less stringent[80] than the regulation of a fully licensed insurance or reinsurance company.[81]

71. *Ibid.*, pp. 6-8.
72. Swiss Re Institute, Sigma Series (2021), available at https://www.sigma-explorer.com (accessed on 1 November 2020).
73. *Ibid.*, according to Swiss Re Institute, worldwide life and non-life insurance premiums represent about 7.0% of GDP for both 2018 and 2019. The OECD, however, indicates insurance spending (Gross Written Premium/GDP) to be at 8.918% for 2018, available at https://data.oecd.org/insurance/insurance-spending.htm#indicator-chart (accessed on 01 November 2020).
74. Marsh Captive Insurance Report, *The Captive Landscape: Global Growth Affirms Captives' Value in Solving Business Challenges*, 2021, slide 4.
75. Marsh*Ibid*.
76. *Retrieved from* https://www.captive.com/articles/how-do-captive-insurers-use-reinsurance.
77. *Retrieved from* https://www.captiveinternational.com/contributed-article/revisiting-your-captive-strategy-maximising-the-efficiency-of-existing-captives-and-building-out-their-use.
78. *Retrieved from* https://www.captive.com/articles/how-do-captive-insurers-use-reinsurance.
79. Jay D. Adkisson, Captive Insurance Company, p. 23.
80. OECD Transfer Pricing Guidance on Financial Transactions, 10.221.
81. Also in Jay D. Adkisson, Captive Insurance Company, p. 21.

## 4 Fronting to Reinsurance Captives

Given potential complexities and costs of obtaining and maintaining insurance licenses in various jurisdictions,[82] captives who are not licensed in a particular jurisdiction, or captives whose risks are not big enough to justify creating their own insurance company, may use unrelated insurance companies as a risk transfer mechanism to write or 'front' the underlying operating companies' risks to the captive (re)insurer.[83] The independent fronting company keeps limited and sometimes no underwriting risk;[84] instead, it 'fronts' the risks to the multinational's captive.

The fronting insurer is remunerated with a fronting fee/commission. This commission typically includes administrative fees to cover the fronter's costs which may include premium collection fees, network partner fees, credit risk charges, any additional profit margins the fronter may require along, with any additional internal or external expenses associated with the transaction. Generally, fronting fees range anywhere from 1% to 10% of premiums, but this will vary based on the business, geographic location, and other transactional considerations.

The captive reinsurer can create economic efficiency by pooling risks from affiliated companies, and then packaging them into an attractive package to sell to in the retrocession market. Buying coverage from the reinsurance/retrocession market will protect the captive's overall balance sheet and smooth profitability from peak events. In this way, the multinational group may achieve a better price for its insurance needs, to the extent that it does not want to fully self-insure. In many cases, larger captives use a mix of both fronting companies and unrelated reinsurance companies to maximize the jurisdictions and lines they can cover, at the optimal price for the group.

Although transactions between captives and fronters, or between captives and retrocessionaires, are between unrelated parties, under the tax rules of most jurisdictions, these transactions would often be considered together as one transaction. The fronter may well be indifferent to the price (i.e., premiums paid), since virtually all premiums received, and risks assumed may be shifted to the captive-leaving the fronter with a commission (and a small credit risk). In some cases, the risks reinsured may not even be ones the fronter would normally cover. Therefore, the fronter's premiums cannot necessarily be taken as evidence of an arm's length price, especially where no risk is retained.

In contrast, where a retrocessionaire is used, this would be considered a transaction between unrelated parties, given that the retrocessionaire is accepting the risk and has no incentive to use anything other than an arm's length price.

---

82. Michael Elliott, Fundamentals of Risk Financing, 2002., 3.17.
83. Steward Hale, Captives in Plain English, p. 12. The importance of risk distribution as outlined in *Helvering v. LeGierse*.
84. 'Fronting companies issue fronting policies, which are "a risk management technique in which an insurer underwrites a policy to cover a specific risk but then cedes the risk to a reinsurer." Hanover Ins. Co. v. Urban Outfitters, Inc., 806 F.3d 761, 764 n.3 (3d Cir. 2015).' *Syzygy Ins. Co. v. Comm'r*, T.C. Memo. 2019-34, 9 n.8 (U.S.T.C. 10 April 2019).

*Figure 42.2 Exemplary Use of Fronting and Reinsurance in Captive Setup*

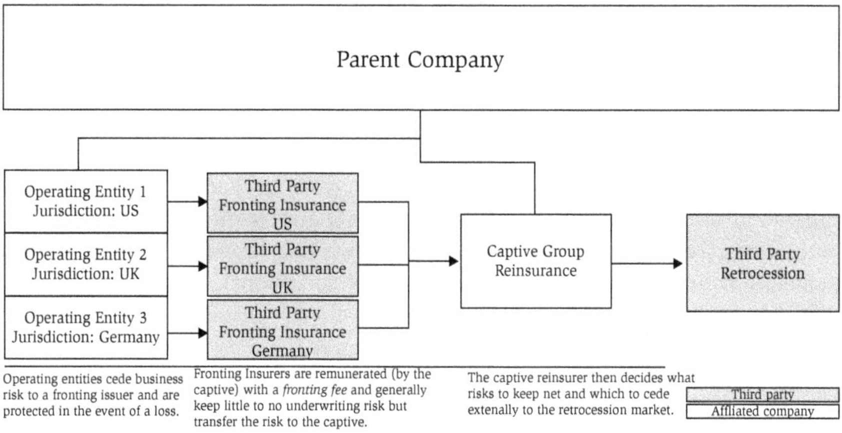


## 5 Structural Arrangements for Captives: Proportional Versus Non-proportional (Re)insurance

Insurance and reinsurance risks are generally structured into two main agreement types including: *proportional agreements* or *non-proportional agreements*.[85] The main difference between proportional and non-proportional arrangements includes how the premium, claims and costs are shared and the rationale for sharing the risk.

In proportional reinsurance, premiums, claims and commissions are shared based on a cession amount. Proportional programmes include quota shares (where premiums, claims and commissions are shared based on a fixed cession amount) and surplus programmes (reinsured caps risks to a given amount (retained line).[86] Insureds received many benefits from purchasing proportional reinsurance; however, one key benefit and rationale for using proportional reinsurance is improved solvency ratios.[87]

In contrast, in non-proportional reinsurance arrangements, the insured pays a premium to the reinsurer based on the overall costs for the programme and in return the reinsurer indemnifies the insured for a loss after a pre-defined deductible has been met.[88] Non-proportional programmes may include per risk, per event and aggregated covers. Unlike proportional arrangements, there is no sharing of premiums or costs in

85. *Mangan, Joseph and Harrison, Connor. Advanced Underwriting Techniques*, at 1.10.
86. DAVID CLARK, Basics of Reinsurance Pricing: Actuarial Study Note, p. 3.
87. JOSEPH MANGAN and CONNOR HARRISON. *Advanced Underwriting Techniques*, at 1.10.
88. *Ibid.*

**Non-Proportional Reinsurance Example:**

Assume the reinsurance non-proportional program covers a portfolio for losses (stemming from an event) for a reinsurance program of USD 20 million (limit) excess of USD 10 million (deductible). For this coverage, total losses from an event must exceed the USD 10 million deductible before the reinsurer starts paying. However, the reinsurer will only pay up to a maximum USD 20 million limit.

non-proportional arrangements. The reinsurer will charge the insurer a premium amount for the risk transfer based on the portfolio's expected loss.

Corporates will typically use either proportional or non-proportional structures to cede risks into their captives. Proportional structures may be used to uniformly cede a large portion of corporate risks to the captive. Non-proportional structures could be used to cede peak risks into the captive. For example, if a corporation wants to protect its entities from peak catastrophe losses including hurricane and earthquake perils, it could establish catastrophe event non-proportional programmes the protects legal entities in the event of a catastrophe loss. Overall, corporates will likely use a combination of proportional and non-proportional arrangements optimize their risk into their captives depending on their risk appetite, risk strategy and other economic considerations (like the current insurance market conditions).

## VIII CONCLUSION

Simply defined captives are as a form of corporate self-insurance that can provide corporate a multitude of benefits. Captives, when carefully managed, are a powerful financial tool enabling multinational companies to optimize their insurance coverings, stabilize the cost of insurance and reduce insurance pricing market volatilities. As a result, since being first established in the early 1920s, captives have since witnessed exponential global growth.

Captive structures take many shapes and forms, but can be broadly categorized by ownership, customer base and where they are on the insurance-reinsurance spectrum. Furthermore, corporations can use proportional or non-proportional (re)insurance) structures to optimally cede risks into the captive.

---

**Example A**: If an event with total losses of USD 45 million happened, the reinsurer would pay USD 20 million. This is the minimum between the USD 20 million total limit and the difference between the USD 45 million loss and the USD 10 million deductible.

**Example B**: If an event with total loss of USD 15 million happened, the reinsurer would pay USD 5 million. This is the minimum between the USD 20 million total limit and the difference between the USD 15 million loss and the USD 10 million deductible.

CHAPTER 43

# Setting the ALP Framework for Captive Insurance

*Louise Sykes, Amanda Pletz & Diana Kabir*[*]

Captive insurance companies and their transfer pricing arrangements are complex topics and are often misunderstood. A captive (re)insurance company is a (re)insurance entity or undertaking that has been created or is owned by an industrial, commercial, or financial group, to (re)insure exclusively all or part of the risks of the group it belongs to.[1]

In the context of the arm's-length principle (ALP), there is a multitude of intercompany transactions a captive (re)insurance company may undertake in its role as a (re)insurer. Furthermore, many functions of captive (re)insurance companies may be outsourced, or staff may be located in head office or other affiliated entities that service the captive (re)insurance undertaking. Typical intercompany transactions between a captive company and other group entities can include services-based transactions for support services, (re)insurance premiums, asset management-related fees in the context of the asset and liability management (ALM) of the captive (re)insurance company's' balance sheet, and finally, loan transactions involving related parties. The relevant transactions to be evaluated may also be dependent on the role that the captive (re)insurance company fulfils for the multinational enterprise (MNE) it is a part of.[2]

The relational dynamic and particularly the commercial and financial relations between the captive (re)insurance company and the MNE is, therefore, an important

* The views and opinions set forth herein are the personal views or opinions of the authors; they do not necessarily reflect views or opinions of the organization with which the authors are associated.

1. OECD, 'Transfer Pricing Guidance for Multinational Enterprises and Tax Administrations', January 2020, Chapter X, para. 10.190.
2. 'MNE' and 'group' represent the same concepts and these terms are used interchangeably throughout the chapter.

consideration when evaluating the arm's-length nature of transactions involving captive (re)insurance companies.[3] Another complexity when dealing with transfer pricing issues for captive (re)insurance companies is the fact that they are subject to varying levels of regulations depending on industry, purpose, and country of residence. The questions arise: what are the arm's-length conditions for a captive (re)insurance provider, and how does one determine if the undertaking adheres to the ALP?

To answer these questions, one should revert to the basic framework and definition of the ALP as set out in Article 9 of the Organisation for Economic Co-operation and Development (OECD) Model Tax Convention. The ALP seeks to adjust profits by reference to the conditions that would have been obtained between independent enterprises in comparable transactions and comparable circumstances.[4]

To apply this principle in the context of captive (re)insurance undertakings, it is necessary to understand how they operate as part of a larger MNE and how captive (re)insurance companies compare with other operators providing similar products and services in the wider insurance sector.

## I ESTABLISHING COMMERCIAL AND FINANCIAL RELATIONS

In broad terms, captive insurance companies can be divided globally between 'pure' captive (re)insurance companies and 'sponsored' captive (re)insurance companies.[5] A pure captive insures related party liabilities, while a sponsored captive mimics the structure described in the *UK v. DSG Retail* case (Dixon case) where the captive is potentially unrelated to the insured.[6] Furthermore, where an MNE first insures its risks with an unrelated insurance company, captives are often used as reinsurance companies to which a large portion of the MNE's risk may be reinsured.

The value contributions of these captive (re)insurance companies to the MNE are very different. Moreover, the rationale for creating a captive (re)insurance company could be driven by a variety of factors, including but not limited to enhancing efficiency in the group, commercial reasons driven by supply and demand of the commercial insurance market, or having a stronger level of control over the MNE's insurance programme. For pure captives, including those used by insurance companies for reinsurance, many of these reasons may be cost and capital driven, whereas, for sponsored captives, the decision to establish such a captive may be more commercially oriented.

Thus, it is not surprising that given the varying benefits that an MNE may achieve from the captive (re)insurance undertaking,[7] the commercial and financial relations between the undertaking and across various MNEs are very different.

---

3. OECD, 'Transfer Pricing Guidance for Multinational Enterprises and Tax Administrations', January 2020, Chapter I, para. B.1, 1.6.
4. *Ibid.*, para. D.1, 1.34.
5. K. Westover, *Captives and the Management of Risk* (International Risk Management Institute 2014).
6. *UK v. DSG Retail (Dixon)*, Tax Tribunal Case No. UKFT 31.
7. OECD, 'Transfer Pricing Guidance for Multinational Enterprises and Tax Administrations', January 2020, Chapter X, para. 10.193.

Because transactions are typically expressions of these relationships that influence the setting of arm's-length prices, when performing a comparability analysis, it is necessary to understand the value contribution of a captive insurance company to the MNE, including the economic benefit achieved.[8] Moreover, as stipulated in the OECD guidance, a 'broad-based understanding of the industry sector in which the MNE group operates (e.g., mining, pharmaceutical, luxury goods) and of the factors affecting the performance of any business operating in that sector' is required.[9] The OECD guidance further clarifies that such an understanding is achieved from an overview of the particular MNE group that outlines how the group responds to the factors affecting performance in the sector, including its business strategies, markets, products, supply chain, key functions performed, material assets used, and important risks assumed.[10]

In the context of a captive (re)insurance company, such an overview would not just relate to the wider MNE and how the captive is used by the MNE but would also consider the internal insurance business on its own. This means that one has to deeply understand the industry and value chain of the group and that of the captive (re)insurance company as an insurance operation.

As a next step, one should establish the economically relevant characteristics, which include understanding the conditions of the transaction and the economically relevant circumstances in which the transaction takes place.[11] As stipulated by the OECD, 'The application of the arm's-length principle depends on determining the conditions that independent parties would have agreed in comparable transactions in comparable circumstances. Before making comparisons with uncontrolled transactions, it is therefore vital to identify the economically relevant characteristics of the commercial or financial relations as expressed in the controlled transaction.'[12] To achieve this, a detailed examination of the contractual agreements, functional analysis, characteristics of insurance arrangements or other transactions, economic circumstances, and business strategies are required.[13]

An analysis of the foregoing factors establishes an arm's-length framework to accurately delineate a transaction. The remainder of this chapter offers more detail on how to establish an arm's-length framework for a captive insurance company. It does not cover all possible factors that could be analysed to accurately delineate an insurance transaction nor all the options realistically available.

## II INSURANCE COMPANIES' VALUE CHAIN VERSUS A CAPTIVE INSURER

The captive (re)insurance company's role and responsibilities in the MNE is only one part of the information matrix to be considered when evaluating arm's-length

8. *Ibid.*, Chapter 1, para. D.1.
9. *Ibid.*, 1.34.
10. *Ibid.*
11. *Ibid.*, 1.35.
12. *Ibid.*
13. *Ibid.*, 1.36.

conditions. It is important to recognize that a captive insurance company is similar to a (re)insurance operation, also with its own inherent value-creation process.

In this respect, one should understand not only the relationship between the MNE and the captive (i.e., understanding the group value chain and the captive's role in this respect) but also how a captive (re)insurance undertaking operates and how this compares to the wider insurance industry. In some cases, a captive insurance company may choose to reinsure or insure some or all of the risks of the MNE through a third-party insurance company. Thus, understanding how a captive (re)insurance company interacts with other third-party insurance operations that may support it should also be considered. It is also inherently important to be aware that business models and value chains can vary even among captives. Most will implement a hybrid model based on specific strengths, strategy, and risk appetite, which can vary over time to adapt to market or business changes.[14]

The remainder of this section provides a summary of an insurance operation's value chain and outlines how captive (re)insurance companies typically compare in this respect:

## 1 Product Development and Management

- This value driver entails the commercial decision-making process that involves defining coverage (policies) offered by a (re)insurer and the management thereof.[15] This value driver typically includes functions such as market research, product design and definition, actuarial processes involved in establishing and pricing anticipated premiums and profitability, product testing, and maintenance.
- Compared with a general insurer, a captive generally has fewer functions that would contribute to this value driver. In fact, because a captive offers coverage that is driven by business needs rather than its competitive position in the market, functions such as market research, product design and definition, and product testing are less relevant. The functions that remain may be outsourced to third parties, such as insurance brokers, that support the process of structuring and managing the captive undertakings.

14. B.M. O'Hara, 'Additional Remarks and Comments on Global Expansion and the Impact on the Insurance Value Chain: The Reassessment of Business Models and the Revisiting of the Value Proposition', International Association for the Study of Insurance Economics, 2003.
15. This section based on OECD, '2010 Report on the Attribution of Profits to Permanent Establishments', 22 July 2010, section B-2, paras 26-28.

## 2 Sales and Distribution

- This value driver typically involves functions such as marketing, distribution, or sales of insurance policies to the market.[16] For pure captives, this value driver is not relevant. However, there may be some sales, marketing, and distribution functions performed by sponsored captives. Where this function may be relevant, these activities may be hosted by various group entities in the local markets where coverage is sold. In the wider insurance market, this value driver may be shared between an insurance group and an insurance broker or agent and depends on the type of insurance products sold.

## 3 Underwriting

(i) This value driver involves the 'process of classifying, selecting and pricing the insured risks to be accepted'.[17] There are numerous activities that can be seen as being part of this value driver. Some examples include:

- *Setting underwriting policy*: This function includes setting the (re)insurance company's level of risk appetite and capacity limits. Although some advice may be obtained from third parties, the key decision-making in this respect is driven by the risk financing needs and appetite of the MNE, including realistically available risk funding options available to the wider group. Thus, the main decision-making considerations for this function would typically be internalized in the MNE, in particular in the captive insurance company.
- *Risk analysis, classification, and selection*: This function could be partially outsourced to underwriters/actuaries to provide analysis and proposals, but the final selection decision would be driven by the underwriting policy set by the captive company.
- *Risk pricing*: This function is normally performed by the underwriter supported by an actuarial team. Third-party underwriters and actuaries can usually be relied on, but the final price and any negotiations concerning the terms and conditions must be approved by the captive in line with the underwriting policy.
- *Risk-retention analysis*: Although analysing a risk-retention policy can be outsourced to third parties, the final decision relating to laying off or taking on the risk must be made by the captive. This decision would be driven by the objective of the captive insurance company in the context of the MNE it services, the risk appetite of the group and the captive,

16. OECD, '2010 Report on the Attribution of Profits to Permanent Establishments', section B-2, paras 29-30.
17. This section is based on OECD, '2010 Report on the Attribution of Profits to Permanent Establishments', section B-2, paras 34-37.

and any cost savings to be achieved. Moreover, it is important for a captive to evidence any assessments done in relation to its own risk appetite and it should not simply just take on the risk appetite of the MNE.

- *Acceptance of insured risk*: This function entails the decision on whether to take on a particular insurance risk. Although this function may be supported by underwriters, actuaries, and in some cases, the sales teams, the key decision-making lies with the captive company and must be based on the defined underwriting policy.

(ii) The extent to which the underwriting and actuarial functions supporting the underwriting value driver are outsourced to third parties will vary across captive companies. Considering the facts and circumstances of each case based on a functional analysis is an important step in a comparability analysis for arm's-length pricing. Furthermore, the extent to which insurance risk is accepted will depend on the financial capacity of the captive (re)insurance company, the availability of reinsurance and the business strategies of the MNE and the captive insurer.

## 4 Risk Management (Including Asset and Liability Management)

This value driver includes functions involved in the retention and monitoring of risk and the assets used to support that risk.[18] This would entail an assessment of risk related to coverage offered and whether an insurance company or captive has appropriate reserves in place or other risk mitigation strategies, such as effective ALM or reinsurance strategies. In this context, it is not possible for a captive to control insurance risk; rather, a captive (re)insurance business is involved in managing the downside risk. The insurer can reduce their exposure by:

- Selecting appropriate risks, that is, only underwriting risks within the risk appetite of the insurer (which will take into account the portfolio of risks the insurer is exposed to and the consequent diversification achieved).
- Rating (pricing) adequacy (i.e., appropriate pricing). The insurer must verify that the rating methodology used to determine the levels of premiums is in accordance with the estimated potential claims (expected losses).
- Deciding whether to retain risk or lay off (transfer) risk to a reinsurer. Decisions on which risks to transfer can be influenced by the business's strengths and weaknesses in managing certain risks, organizational structure, availability of alternate entities to take on the transferred risk, and preferred or established strategies determining the optimal risk mix.[19]

18. This section is based on OECD, '2010 Report on the Attribution of Profits to Permanent Establishments', section B-2, paras 38-41.
19. A. Rossum, *The Debate on the Insurance Value Chain*, 27 Gen. Pap. Risk Ins. No. 1 (2002).

Because of the inherent uncertainty associated with the total cost of claims, it is important for any (re)insurer to set aside funds to pay the ultimate value of claims, which depend on various influencing factors, such as exposure, coverage, location, and regulatory considerations. This type of analysis involves consistently reviewing claim information to reflect the most recent information and adjusting ultimate claim values (and thus loss reserves) accordingly. The monies received from premiums are retained and reinvested via an asset manager in liquid or short-term securities (or other investment assets that match the duration of the underlying insurance policy) to ensure that a level of return is achieved to enable the insurer to meet claims as they are due.

Similar to insurance companies, this value driver plays a key role in captive undertakings. However, arm's-length pricing will be driven not only by the necessary loss reserves but also by other functions that may support the risk management of captives, such as the risk appetite or asset management practices. For example, in some MNEs, captive undertakings would include a captive insurance company, a captive asset management company, and a captive reinsurance company. The asset management company acts as a captive to the MNE operations, and the monies retained for ALM may be partly reinvested into the MNE in the form of loans. In such circumstances, consideration should be given to what extent such a relationship may influence the captive insurance undertaking's ability to honour its obligations under the policy in case of a claim associated with the borrowing entity.

We demonstrate this point by means of an example. On initial review, it may appear that a captive insurance company is operating independently from other group entities and that a risk transfer has in fact occurred. However, when analysing the insurance company's ALM policy, the pooled capital from premiums earned may be reinvested into the group companies, perhaps as loans or other financial instruments. This may lead to a situation where, if a loss event occurs, the captive may not be able to obtain access to the capital needed to honour its financial obligation without support from the parent company or other group subsidiaries in the insurance pool. In this example, there is a direct correlation between the captive's ability to honour its obligation in case of a significant event and the financial position of the related parties it insures. Therefore, there will be reduced or limited benefit from the insurance policy being issued by the captive. This lower level of benefit would have direct implications on the arm's-length premium to be paid, which needs to be reflected as part of a comparability analysis.

## 5 Claims Management and Client Care

The final value driver analysed in this chapter is claims management and client care.[20] This value driver includes functions such as claims review and processing, management of payment flows, claims to report, and general client care. A pure captive provider will not typically have general client care functions but will exhibit the other

20. This section is based on OECD, '2010 Report on the Attribution of Profits to Permanent Establishments', section B-2, paras 42-43.

functions supporting this value driver. Even so, many of these functions are outsourced in the context of captive insurance companies, although the final decision to settle a claim lies with the captive.

### 6 Summary of Value Drivers

Many of the functions supporting the value drivers described here are often outsourced by captive (re)insurance providers or provided by related party entities, such as the head office of an MNE. Key decision-making activities or key entrepreneurial risk-taking functions involve a high level of governance functions (e.g., setting the underwriting policy), and therefore these decisions related to the acceptance of particular risks and their management must be performed by the captive insurance company.

In addition to these value drivers, captive insurance undertakings may benefit from some general administrative support. These functions may be outsourced or typically provided by other group entities.

## III ASSETS RELIED ON BY A CAPTIVE COMPANY

Assets relied on by a captive insurance company typically include the financial assets held as part of its regulatory solvency obligations, tangible assets such as properties and equipment, and know-how of any significant people functions hosted by the captive. In particular, financial assets are important to consider for various reasons:

- Insurance operations are typically regulated and have a regulatory license. Regulation places certain obligations on an entity and also drives the minimum solvency (and level of assets required to be held). An entity that does not have an insurance license (i.e., is not regulated) is not comparable with a third-party insurer. The regulatory environment has introduced more stringent measures over the years, and these can vary across national or regional levels. If an entity is subject to certain financial regulations, due to possibly wide variations, it would also have to be determined that the regulations imposed are comparable between that of the captive entity and the third-party insurer.[21]
- Regardless of the minimum regulatory requirements, an insurance operation must be adequately capitalized considering its insured risks. This means that an insurer must have the financial capacity to assume the insurance risk inherent in the contracts it has entered into, as also stated by the OECD Transfer Pricing Guidance.[22]

21. K. Pauli, *Optimizing the Value Chain: Collaborative Customer Knowledge in Global Insurance* (TowerGroup 2009).
22. OECD, 'Transfer Pricing Guidance for Multinational Enterprises and Tax Administrations', January 2022, Chapter X, para. 10.202.

## IV RISK FRAMEWORK FOR CAPTIVE COMPANIES

Understanding the value drivers – including who does what and where – are key considerations for analysing related party captive transactions. However, such an analysis also needs to consider where, in the MNE, responsibility for different risks lies. Although the risk profile of the entities will likely become obvious following the above-described approach, it is still important to consider the extent to which various risk factors are borne by the entities supporting the captives and the captive itself and which risks can be deemed economically significant risks in the relevant relational context.

The OECD Transfer Pricing Guidance section D1 considers control of risk and assigns rewards to the entity that controls risk.[23] The question now arises: how does this apply to a captive insurance company? In this context, it is important to note that a captive insurance company is not in the business of controlling risk but managing downside risk via a contractual arrangement that has been transferred to it. That said, using the framework as outlined in the OECD Transfer Pricing Guidance and given that risk is the effect of volatility, the responsibilities of group entities for different risks drive the dynamic in establishing the final arm's-length remuneration for those entities. For evaluating contractual arrangements of the captive in taking on risk, for the insurance policy to be a contract of insurance, it must transfer insurance risk from the holder of the contract to the issuer. More specifically, International Financial Reporting Standard (IFRS) 4 notes that a contract that exposes the issuer to financial risk without significant insurance risk is not an insurance contract.[24]

When applying the OECD framework, typical risk factors that may need to be considered for a captive insurance company include:

(i) *Market or strategic risk*: In the context of a captive insurance company, this would relate to the risk affecting the value of investments, for example, investments made and held via ALM may not generate sufficient income or may fall below the value needed if a claim materializes. By means of various actuarial analyses, captive insurance companies would typically analyse the extent to which losses may materialize and the relevant solvency ratios to honour their obligations. This is an important risk factor and goes hand in hand with assessing the financial capacity of the captive insurance company to assume the downside risks (insured risks) it has contractually agreed to take on. In certain cases, some of this risk may be reinsured to other providers. Fully identifying the main bearers of the risk contractually assumed by the captive is a fundamental step in establishing arm's-length conditions.

(ii) *Infrastructure or operational risk*: This is likely to include uncertainties associated with the captive's processes and operations. Moreover, a captive insurance company's processes and systems may include technology or

23. *Ibid.*, Chapter I, paras D.1.2.1.1, 1.71-1.73.
24. Note that IFRS 4 will be replaced by IFRS 17 with effect from 1 January 2023.

other processes for risk management. With the increasing digitalization of the insurance industry, the extent to which captives continue their investment in current technology will likely affect their ability to efficiently mitigate not only infrastructure (e.g., cyber security) and operational risks but other risks as well, including strategic risks (through better-informed risk assessments) or financial risks (automated underwriting based on data analytics and artificial intelligence).[25] Human or technological errors can lead to unwanted liabilities for the captive insurance company.

(iii) *Financial risks*: As stated in the OECD Transfer Pricing Guidance, all risk factors are likely to affect a company's financial performance to some extent. Nonetheless, specific financial risks are related to the company's (in this case, the captive insurance company's) ability to manage liquidity and cash flow, financial capacity, and creditworthiness. This is no different for a captive insurance company and is in fact an even more important risk factor to consider. Examples of this risk factor include:
   - Credit risk with the policyholder and with any reinsurers the captive may have dealings with.
   - Liquidity risk to the extent that imperfect correlation between actual losses and investment returns leads to a situation where a captive does not have sufficient cash and short-term financial resources to meet its obligations as they fall due, or meaning it can only secure such resources at excessive cost.

(iv) *Transactional risks*: This is a difficult item to fully identify and is separate from financial risk items. For the insurance sector, it includes factors concerning difficult-to-value risks, such as climate change and the risk of an increase in natural catastrophes that exceeds modelling predictions. This may lead to a situation in which the premiums charged are not in line with the potential losses the captive may become responsible for. Insurance risk in particular gives rise to the potential for the amount or timing of actual claims cash flows to differ from expected cash flows.[26] The extent to which this latter risk influences an insurance company's financial performance depends heavily on the type of insurance issued (e.g., car insurance versus life insurance).

(v) *Hazard risk*: This refers to adverse external events that may cause damages or losses, including accidents and natural disasters, which can be mitigated by insurance. This risk factor goes hand in hand with the core operations of a captive insurance company. In some cases, some of these risks transferred to the captive may be offloaded to third-party reinsurance companies.

25. M. Eling & M. Lehmann, *The Impact of Digitalization on the Insurance Value Chain and the Insurability of Risks*, Gen. Pap. Risk Ins. (2018).
26. OECD, '2010 Report on the Attribution of Profits to Permanent Establishments', section B-2, para. 56.

## V TERMS AND CONDITIONS

Once a comprehensive view of the industry, group value chain, functional, asset, and risk analyses is complete, the types of insurance cover offered by the captive, including contractual terms and conduct, should be closely considered. Thus, if a loss event occurs, the captive insurer must reimburse and be in a position to reimburse in line with the contract.[27] The contractual roles and responsibilities of the insured and the insurer should be comparable to those of third parties. Moreover, contract conditions will dictate the appropriate level of capital required in light of the insured risk the captive takes on via the contractual arrangement. Furthermore, in situations where some of the risks may be laid off to a reinsurance provider, the extent to which this may have occurred and the level of insured risk that remains at the captive is a key factor in establishing arm's-length conditions.

## VI CONCLUSION

Captive insurance operations are often used by MNEs for various purposes. To fully understand how a captive operates in the context of the MNE and whether its conduct is aligned with that of an insurance company, conducting an analysis of the MNE and the captive insurance company's value chains and performing an industry analysis (including understanding the regulatory framework) is necessary. This provides insight on the benefits achieved by the MNE and more specifically how the captive (re)insurance operation is organized.

The value chains and industry analysis should be supported with a complete review and an analysis of the functions undertaken, assets used, and risks assumed by the captive and other entities on behalf of the captive. These components come together to provide a more complete information matrix, acting as a valuable starting point for determining the arm's-length conditions.

This should be followed with a detailed analysis of the contractual arrangements and conduct between the relevant parties. Such analysis provides sufficient information allowing careful consideration of all the relevant comparability criteria, including (1) contractual terms; (2) functional analysis; (3) characteristics of transaction or policies, including limits, capitalization ratios, and the insured risk; (4) economic circumstances between the controlled and uncontrolled transaction, including the bargaining position; and (5) business strategies between the controlled and uncontrolled parties such as different objectives of various stakeholders. This comparability analysis needs to be done in accordance with relevant and suitable market observations.

Overall, the aforementioned factors need to be considered in light of each other and are critical components in understanding the business operations of the captive

27. OECD, 'Transfer Pricing Guidance for Multinational Enterprises and Tax Administrations', Chapter I, paras D.1.1, 1.43.

undertaking. Each step represents a piece of the ALP framework that can be used when reviewing captive insurance companies and assists with determining the arm's-length nature of the relevant transactions under review.

CHAPTER 44

# Accurate Delineation of Captive Insurance Transactions Including Options Realistically Available

*Louise Sykes, Vikram Chand, Amanda Pletz & Camille Vilaseca*[*]

## I INTRODUCTION

As with other intercompany financing transactions, understanding the value chain and the functions, assets and risks analysis is an important step before one can then focus on the actual transaction.[1] Such an analysis, including analyzing the industry, regulation and terms and conditions, are important steps needed to analyze a transaction. It is important to have a detailed understanding of the transaction so that the eventual comparability analysis used to test the arm's length nature of the pricing is accurately applied and any differences between the controlled and the uncontrolled transactions can be identified, and appropriate pricing adjustments can be made.

In delineating a captive insurance transaction, it is necessary to examine not only the contractual basis and characteristics of the transaction itself but also how the captive insurance company interacts with other members of the multinational enterprise (MNE) group and how the commercial and financial relationships with other group members influence the captive's business strategy.

Captive insurers, by their nature, are in the business of managing downside risk, whether that is solely for an MNE group or for the group together with its clients. A detailed analysis using the risk framework as outlined in Chapter 1 of the Organisation

---

* The views and opinions set forth herein are the personal views or opinions of the authors; they do not necessarily reflect views or opinions of the organization with which the authors are associated.

1. OECD, *Transfer Pricing Guidelines for Multinational Enterprises and Tax Administrations 2022* (OECD Publishing 2022), para. 10.195.

for Economic Co-operation and Development (OECD) Guidelines 2022[2] is, therefore, a fundamental component of the delineation.

However, this is not necessarily sufficient. The first step is to consider whether the captive insurance company actually undertakes genuine insurance business.[3]

As captive insurers and insurance arrangements continue to grow in complexity, it is crucial for captives to operate in the same manner and under similar conditions as independent insurance companies, particularly in the management of the risks they underwrite. This may be difficult to discern as captives may have complex structures, including instances of transactions involving multiple group entities and numerous financial flows between the captive insurance company, related party entities and third-party insurers and reinsurers.

## II INDICATORS OF A GENUINE INSURANCE BUSINESS

Paragraph 10.199 of the OECD Guidelines 2022 considers the need for all, or substantially all, of the following indicators to exist if a captive insurer is to be regarded as a genuine insurance business.[4]

### 1 There Is Diversification and Pooling of Risk in the Captive Insurer

Pooling risks to create diversification is the essence of insurance.[5] Insurers are able to accept risk in exchange for premium because they pool multiple risks of different types and/or from different geographies which are not highly correlated, thus allowing them to spread the risk of loss.[6]

In this respect, captive insurers are no different from independent insurers, they accept risks in return for premium. For diversification to occur, the captive insurer needs to take on a sufficient quantum and variety of risks.

When examining diversification, an important factor to consider is risk distribution.[7,8] Generally speaking, risk distribution seeks to evaluate whether the number of parties being insured, the relative size of each party's risk to the overall collective risk insured by the captive insurer and the extent of correlation between claims that may

2. *Ibid.*, para. 1.60.
3. *Ibid.*, paras. 10.199 and 10.200.
4. *Ibid.*, para. 10.199.
5. The OECD TPG 2022 defines risk diversification as "the pooling of a portfolio of risks by which the insurer achieves an efficient use of capital," para. 10.203.
6. US Court of Appeals, Ninth Circuit 3.3.1987, *Clougherty Packing Co. v. Commissioner*, 812 F.2d 1297, para. 10: "Insuring many independent risks in return for numerous premiums serves to distribute risk. By assuming numerous relatively small, independent risks that occur randomly over time, the insurer smoothes out losses to match more closely its receipt of premiums."
7. Risk distribution has been identified by the US Supreme Court as a common characteristics of insurance in *Helvering v. Le Gierse*, 312 U.S. 531 (1941), at 539.
8. Vikram Chand, *Transfer Pricing Aspects of Captive Insurance Arrangements : Recommendations to the OECD*, IFF Forum Für Steuerrecht 154 (2017).

arise are such that the underwritten risks are reasonably predictable. Hence, risk distribution is assessed from the perspective of the insurer through his actions.[9]

There are no generally accepted tests and/or analytics to address risk distribution. As such, significant judgment is necessary to address these items through quantitative and qualitative efforts. Analysis of the following factors will help to determine whether risk distribution exists in a captive insurer:

(i) Are there a sufficient number of risks for the law of large numbers to apply?[10]
(ii) Are the risks statistically independent (i.e. they are not highly correlated)?

Diversification can be achieved solely by insuring risks from MNE group members, provided there is a sufficient number of risks and those risks cover different exposures and/or different geographies.[11] Diversification may be further enhanced if the captive insures third-party risks,[12] but the presence of third-party risk is not a requirement for a captive insurance portfolio to be considered to be diversified.

Some sort of diversification is fundamental to the establishment of a transaction as bona fide insurance, and its absence would suggest the captive is not operating as an insurance company, even if it were regulated as such.[13]

This would be the case, for example, if an insurance company offers insurance against flood damage, but only insures clients in one specific location. If it only issues flood policies in this one location, it is heavily exposed to the risk of flooding in that location. If there is a flood event, it will likely be required to pay back all premiums it has received and more as claims compensation. If it had also insured against fire damage and had insured against flood damage in other locations, then the statistical probability of all three events happening (flood damage in two locations, plus fire

9. *See* US Tax Court 29.10.2014, *Securitas Holding, Inc. and Subsidiaries v. Commissioner of Internal Revenue*, TC Memo. 2014-225, Docket No. 21206-10, at 25. *See also*: US Tax Court 14.1.2014, *Rent A Center v. Commissioner*, 142 TC 1, at 24; US Tax Court 21.08.2017, *Avrahami v. Commissioner*, 149 T.C. 7, at 60: risk distribution occurs "occurs when the insurer pools a large enough collection of unrelated risks."
10. In insurance, the law of large numbers is a statistical principle that states that the larger the number of exposure units independently exposed to loss, the greater the probability that the actual loss experience will equal the expected loss experience (www.irmi.com). Additionally, this theory has been described by Professor Cummins in the *Amerco* judgment to mean that *[a]s the size of the pool increases, the chance that the loss per policy during any given period will deviate from the expected loss by a given amount (or proportion) declines. See* US Tax Court: 5.11.1992, *Amerco Inc. v. Commissioner of Internal Revenue*, Docket No. 91-70732. *See also*, US Court of Appeals, Ninth Circuit 3.3.1987, *Clougherty Packing Co. v. Commissioner*, 812 F.2d 1297, para. 10: "Distributing risk allows the insurer to reduce the possibility that a single costly claim will exceed the amount taken in as a premium and set aside for the payment of such a claim. Insuring many independent risks in return for numerous premiums serves to distribute risk. By assuming numerous relatively small, independent risks that occur randomly over time, the insurer smoothes out losses to match more closely its receipt of premiums." *See also*, US Tax Court 29.10.2014, *Securitas Holding, Inc. and Subsidiaries v. Commissioner of Internal Revenue*, TC Memo. 2014-225, Docket No. 21206-10, p. 25: "The insurer achieves risk distribution when it pools a large enough collection of unrelated risks, those that are not generally affected by the same circumstance or event."
11. OECD TPG 2022, *supra* n. 1, para. 10.204.
12. *Ibid.*, para. 10.205.
13. *Ibid.*, para. 10.208.

damage) is less likely (i.e., the insurance portfolio is diversified), and it would be able to use premiums from the other policies to help settle the flood claims from the first location.

## 2 The Economic Capital Position of the Entities Within the MNE Group Has Improved as a Result of Diversification and There Is Therefore a Real Economic Impact for the MNE Group as a Whole

The question here is not necessarily one of an improved capital position (as the group requires capital to be held in the captive insurer, which it would not do if it had insured externally), but whether economic benefits are achieved through use of a captive. One important benefit, in addition to those discussed in paragraph 10.193, is that captive insurance companies are often able to offer lower premiums than third-party insurers. This can be for several reasons:

- First, third-party insurance companies cover risks across multiple sectors and markets (countries). The consequence of this is that a policyholder in Europe may effectively be cross subsidizing an unrelated policyholder in the United States because the level of risk in the United States is higher than the same risk in Europe (e.g., hurricane risk). Using a captive means that only the MNE group's own specific risk experience for the markets it operates in is taken into account when pricing the risk, rather than the whole of the market. If the group has a low level of loss experience,[14] then they may pay lower premiums to the captive than they would to a third party which may rely on pricing in line with an insurer's wider market experiences and exposures.
- Second, using a captive allows MNE groups to gain a deeper understanding of the nature of the insured risk and the likelihood of losses. A captive can capture and record the MNE's loss experience data in detail and build a comprehensive picture over time specific to the insured risk, which allows it to price on a more informed basis and can lead to reduced premiums compared to a third-party insurer, which may not have access to such insightful data as its clients may be unwilling to share market sensitive or proprietary data regarding specific losses.
- Third, captives tend to have a lower expense ratio (expenses/premiums) than third-party insurance companies. Generally, they are in the 15% range or lower whereas independent insurance companies are around 25%-30%. Unlike third-party companies, pure captive insurance companies do not need to maintain a large infrastructure or a sales team or a presence in multiple countries.
- Finally, if the group has a good loss record (i.e., has not experienced many loss events over time) then profits that would otherwise have been made by third-party insurance companies are retained in the group. (Conversely, if

14. Loss experience refers to the actual number of claims events (losses) that have occurred. A low level of loss experience means the policyholder has made very few claims.

there are large losses, these are borne by the group and the economic benefit of insuring with a captive is potentially reduced.)

## 3 Both the Captive Insurer and Any Reinsurer Are Regulated Entities with Broadly Similar Regulatory Regimes and Regulators That Require Evidence of Risk Assumption and Appropriate Capital Levels

Insurers and reinsurers are regulated to protect their policyholders, by ensuring they hold sufficient capital and have sufficient solvency to meet claims as they fall due. Regulatory regimes, as indicated in paragraph 10.192 of the OECD Transfer Pricing Guidelines (TPG) 2022, may vary depending on the type and extent of risk the insurer takes on and whether the entity taking the risk is an insurer with primary liability to the policyholder or a reinsurer which has liability to an insurer, rather than to the underlying policyholder. In particular, under the Solvency II regulatory regime, the proportionality principle plays a key role, requiring the regulator to assess the risk profile of the individual insurance undertaking.[15] The principle requires that the regulations are proportionate to the nature, scale and complexity of the risks inherent in the business of an insurance undertaking: a lower risk profile can result in exemptions from requirements, a more pronounced risk profile will lead to tighter implementation requirements. The absence of any regulation would suggest the captive is not operating as an insurance company. However, different levels of regulation must be considered in the context of the insurance business being written rather than requiring a 'one size fits all' standard of regulation.

## 4 The Insured Risk Would Otherwise Be Insurable Outside the MNE Group

The term 'insurable' is taken to mean a risk that satisfies the following conditions: there must exist an eventuality for loss or damage that is (1) definable; (2) fortuitous; (3) part of a similar group of risks, so as to make the loss reasonably predictable; and (4) pays a premium that is commensurate with the potential loss.[16]

'Insurable' could, however, also be interpreted as whether the group is able to find a third-party insurance company (or group of companies) willing to take on the particular risk. In this context, it is worth considering the following scenarios in which a third party may not be willing to accept risk.

Indeed, insurance companies, in particular, generally do not want to insure what is known as the bottom layer of coverage (in the context of car insurance, this would

15. European Parliament and Council, *Directive 2009/138/EC on the taking-up and pursuit of the business of Insurance and Reinsurance (Solvency II)*, (OJ L 335, 25 November 2009), Article 29 al. 4.
16. OECD, *Comments Received on the Public Discussion Draft on Financial Transactions, Part III*, NERA Economic Consulting Comment at 62 (OECD Publishing, 2018).

be known as the 'excess' or the 'deductible', i.e., the amount of loss claim that the insurance company will not cover). This bottom layer is where most claims are experienced because the majority of claims tend to be small. The administration costs and staff resources associated with processing a high volume of small claims amounts mean this is not commercially attractive for an insurer. Therefore, to obtain insurance for this layer and remove expense volatility for the policyholder, the only option is often to use a captive insurance company.

For example, a group with a large fleet of commercial vehicles wishes to insure the fleet against all types of damage, including accidental fire, flood, theft, etc. Given the comprehensive nature of the insurance, there are likely to be hundreds or thousands of small claims for accidental damage. Each claim must be assessed and processed, resulting in a significant amount of administration cost, which may outweigh the value of the claim. It is not commercially viable for a third-party insurer to take on the cost of processing these multiple claims, so it sets a limit below which it will not accept claims. The policyholder likely already has an administration team looking after the maintenance and other aspects of the fleet and this team could liaise with the captive insurer at a lower cost than the third-party insurer would incur. However, if there was a significant claim event, perhaps several vehicles were destroyed in a storage facility fire, that would be a single event for a large claim with a single set of administration costs. The insurer would be willing to take on such a risk, and the policyholder would want to be insured against such a potentially large amount of damages.

Furthermore, there may be a market for that type of risk, but it may already be saturated. Insurance companies look to run balanced portfolios; if their portfolio already holds the allotted amount of risk for that line of business, they will not be able to accept additional risk.

Finally, the risk in question may be new and therefore not sufficiently understood, or an understanding may still be developing (e.g., cyber risk is arguably still not sufficiently understood), and therefore, there may be a reluctance amongst market participants to take on a novel risk.

In these circumstances, the risk in question satisfies the four criteria set out above as insurable, but the insurance market is not willing to accept this type of risk. Such a non-acceptance does not mean that this indicator is not met, but simply that at a particular point in time, for varying reasons, the insurance market does not have the capacity, appetite or tolerance for such a risk. These factors should be taken into account when considering paragraph 10.194 of the OECD TPG 2022, which suggests that where it is difficult or impossible to obtain insurance coverage for such risks, this may raise questions as to whether the arrangement is commercially rational and whether it is possible to determine an arm's length price. On this point, an example is discussed in the OECD TPG 2022 Chapter 1 in paragraph 1.127 which we will discuss later in this chapter.

## 5 The Captive Insurer Has the Requisite Skills, Including Investment Skills, and Experience at Its Disposal

It is common in the insurance industry, as in other areas of the financial services sector, for certain functions to be outsourced to either internal or external service companies. Where functions are outsourced, the scope of the service to be provided and the parameters within which the outsourced provider operates must be formalized and clearly defined under a contract, and remunerated appropriately. Where the outsourced provider is part of the same MNE group, there must be a clear segregation of duties.

Investment management is commonly outsourced by both independent and captive insurers, it is rare for investment management to be performed by the insurance company itself. The outsourced provider may be a third-party asset manager or an internal investment group that either has the investment management skills itself or wholly or partially delegates the investment management to third parties. As stated above, the requirement is for the captive to have 'investment skills' at its disposal, it does not necessarily have to employ investment managers. At this point, it may be pertinent to consider the guidance in paragraph 1.70 of the OECD TPG 2022, which sets out the relationship between an investor and a fund manager.[17] While the captive insurer (investor) may not have specific investment skills, it is still required to: establish its investment strategy and risk appetite; carry out regular and credible oversight of the investments; take decisions on the appointment or removal of the investment manager; decide what level of authority it delegates to the investment manager; and decide what amount of investments will be managed.

The performance of these functions indicates the captive is operating in the same manner as an independent insurer, even if it does not employ an investment specialist.

A captive insurer will often use a third-party captive manager to provide actuarial modelling, handle claims processing and payments, prepare regulatory returns and provide back office services such as finance and information technology. As noted in Part IV of the OECD's 2010 Report on the Attribution of Profits to Permanent Establishments, these are not Key Entrepreneurial Risk Taking (KERT) functions and, therefore, may be outsourced, provided the captive insurer actively makes the decision to outsource, clearly defines the responsibilities and monitors the performance of the outsource provider.[18] In this respect, the captive is operating in a similar manner to independent insurers who will often establish an internal service company to provide these services to multiple other group insurance companies.

Furthermore, as noted in paragraph 10.213 of the OECD TPG 2022, the insurance market has a business model known as Managing General Agent or authorized insurance intermediary, under which an independent insurer delegates most aspects of the underwriting function to third parties, for example, insurance brokers.

---

17. OECD TPG 2022, *supra* n. 1, para. 1.70.
18. OECD, *Report on the Attribution of Profits to Permanent Establishments* (OECD Publishing, 2010), para. 94.

The delegation is made by the insurance company board in line with the underwriting policy it has established and is formalized in a contract giving the third party the authority to bind the insurance company within strict parameters such as type and amount of risk that may be accepted, policy wording, limits on liability, territorial restrictions etc. The third party is then authorized to select, price and accept insurance risk within the terms of its delegated authority, in return for an arm's length remuneration. Where such a delegation is made, the importance of other aspects of the underwriting process, in particular setting the underwriting policy, including the risk appetite and capacity limits, is increased. Where a captive insurer has followed this market model, it must be able to demonstrate that it has a strictly defined underwriting policy and it has the ability to monitor and take necessary action if the terms of the delegated authority are breached by the authorized underwriter.

Given the responsibilities of the captive insurer set out in the preceding paragraphs, it is important that the board of directors of the captive collectively have the skills and experience necessary to manage effectively all outsourced operations, including outsourced insurance management functions and delegated underwriting authorities.

If a captive insurer has delegated all aspects of the underwriting process and does not have adequate control, oversight and management of the process (governance), then it is likely to have breached its regulatory standards and may not be considered to be carrying on insurance business.

## 6 The Captive Insurer Has a Real Possibility of Suffering Losses

There are two points to consider here: first has a risk transfer occurred, such that the captive insurer is liable for the loss and second does the captive insurer evidence that liability by holding sufficient reserves to support the expected level of loss?

Chapter 1 of the OECD Guidelines 2022 commences the delineation of a transaction with the contract, in this case, the insurance policy.[19] An insurance policy issued by the captive will clearly define the risks covered, the limits of coverage, any deductibles, territory, time period and other relevant details. Under international accounting standards,[20] an insurance contract is defined as a "contract under which one party (the insurer) accepts significant insurance risk from another party (the policyholder) by agreeing to compensate the policyholder if a specified uncertain future event (the insured event) adversely affects the policyholder."[21] Where a policy exposes the issuing company to financial risk without significant insurance risk, the standard notes that this is not an insurance contract. Therefore, for a transaction to be accounted for as insurance, the captive insurer must assume significant insurance risk (downside risk) and be exposed to the reasonable possibility of a significant loss.

Insurance risk gives rise to variability in both the amount and timing of loss reimbursement payments. This means a claim of potentially unknown magnitude (up

19. OECD TPG 2022, *supra* n. 1, paras. 1.42-1.50.
20. IFRS 4, to be superseded by IFRS 17 with effect from January 1, 2023.
21. International Accounting Standards Board, *IFRS 4 Insurance Contracts* (2004), Appendix A.

to the agreed limit specified in the insurance contract) can occur at different undefined intervals. Any contractual provisions that limit the timely reimbursement of the policyholder (e.g., an insurance company spreading its obligations by limiting the timings at which a claim is paid), would prevent this condition from being met.

If a captive insurer is exposed to downside risk and is exposed to the possibility of significant loss, a risk transfer has potentially occurred. Evaluation of whether it is reasonably possible for the insurance entity to realize a significant loss is based on the present value of all cash flows between the insured party (policyholder) and the insurer under reasonably possible outcomes.

Historically, the insurance industry tested risk transfer primarily using what is referred to as the "10-10 Rule." Under this test, for the amount of risk transferred between the insured and insurer to be considered significant, there must be at least a 10% probability of the insurer incurring a 10% present value loss. In other words, there must be at least a 10% probability that the present value of losses incurred by the insurer is at least 10% greater than the present value of premium. While the 10-10 Rule can be insightful for many insurance transactions, it has been criticized in the insurance industry for its focus on a single point of the loss distribution (the 90th percentile) and its inapplicability of the rule for insurance transactions with a less than a 10% probability of loss. As such, an alternative method referred to as "The Expected Reinsurance Deficit Test" (ERD Test) should also be considered.[22]

The ERD Test has gained acceptance in the insurance industry for use as a measure of risk transfer as it measures the risk across the entire loss distribution rather than focusing on a single point of the distribution. The deficit associated with the ERD Test is measured as the product of two terms: (1) the probability that the insurer is exposed to a present value underwriting loss; and (2) the average present value underwriting loss across all present value underwriting loss scenarios expressed as a percentage of the present value of premium. A deficit greater than 1% is commonly accepted as evidence of a significant transfer of risk between the insured and insurer.

As there is no definitive test to determine whether a risk transfer has taken place, this question must be satisfied based on the judgment of individual facts and circumstances, although if a policy has been accounted for as an insurance contract that will be persuasive.

In this regard, we would like to highlight that the U.S. tax authorities, by relying on the economic family doctrine,[23] have tried to argue that risk shifting does not occur in a multinational group context[24], as it amounts to self-insurance.[25] However, Courts

22. David L. Ruhm & Paul J. Brehm, *Risk Transfer Testing of Reinsurance Contracts: A Summary of the Report by the CAS Research Working Party on Risk Transfer Testing*, 1 Casualty Actuarial Society 10, section 3 (2005).
23. The doctrine provides that members of a multinational group constitute an economic family, and when the loss of a member is made good by another member of the family – risk shifting and risk distribution do not take place. For instance, *see* Internal Revenue Service, Revenue Rulings, 77-316, 1977-2, CB 53; 78-338, 1978-2 CB 107; 2001-31, 2001-26 IRB 1348.
24. Oscar Grisales-Racini, *Offshore Captive Insurance Companies under BEPS Attack*, 82 Tax Notes Int'l 1103 (2016), 1103.
25. William P. Elliott, *Captive Insurance Arrangements: A Comprehensive Update*, Tax Notes Int'l (2004), 297.

have rejected this argument and have subsequently developed a balance sheet and net worth analysis test to ascertain the economic consequences of the captive insurance arrangement. Essentially, the tests look at the insured's assets to understand whether the insured has *divested itself of the adverse economic consequences* of a claim covered by the insurance policy. Typically, in parent-subsidiary arrangements (captive providing insurance to its parent), the courts have denied a deduction of the insurance premium, as it is argued that the parent bears the economic loss of the captive insurance arrangement. This is because, when a parent suffers an insured loss that its captive subsidiary has to pay, the assets of the captive will be reduced by the amount of payment, thereby reducing the value of the captive's shares held by the parent as an asset. The depletion in the value of the shares held in the captive affects the balance sheet and net worth of the insured, i.e., the parent.[26] Nevertheless, if the captive has sufficient third-party risks, the insurance payments may be allowed as a deduction even if the deduction of the payment would be denied under the balance sheet test. This is because, based on the law of large numbers, risks are considered to be shifted from the insured to the captive.[27] However, in brother-sister arrangements (captive providing insurance to the members of the multinational group that do not have any ownership interest in it), the courts have allowed a deduction of the insurance expense to the extent that the captive is not a sham.[28] In such arrangements, the payments by the captive on insured losses do not impact the balance sheet and net worth of the insured, as the latter does not have any ownership interests in the former.[29] Accordingly, a deduction of the insurance premium is allowed as long as the captive is formed for a valid business purpose; it is a separate, independent and viable entity; it is financially capable of meeting its obligations; and it reimburses the insured losses when the claim arises.[30]

It should be noted that, if the captive is not sufficiently capitalized for the risks it has agreed to cover, the U.S. Courts in some situations have held that risk shifting has not taken place.[31] Put differently, where a risk transfer has occurred, the captive should have an appropriate asset and liability management policy to ensure it has the right

26. US Court of Appeals, Ninth Circuit 6.3.1981, *Carnation Company v. Commissioner of Internal Revenue*, 640 F.2d 1010; US Court of Appeals, Ninth Circuit 3.3.1987, *Clougherty Packing Co v. Commissioner*, 812 F.2d 1297.
27. For instance, *see* US Tax Court 5.11.1992, *Amerco Inc. v. Commissioner of Internal Revenue*, Docket No. 91-70732.
28. A sham can either be a sham in fact or a sham in substance. A factual sham arises where the transactions reported by the taxpayer never occurred or were only created on paper but never actually took place. If the doctrine applies, then the transactions reported by the taxpayer will be considered non-existent for tax purposes. However, a sham in substance arises when the purported transaction does not have any underlying economic substance and is undertaken solely for achieving a reduction in tax. *See* US Supreme Court 14.11.1960, *Knetsch v. United States*, 364 US 361 (1960).
29. *See* US Court of Appeals, Sixth Circuit 7.7.1989, *Humana Inc. v. Commissioner*, 881 F.2d 247.
30. *See* US Tax Court 14.1.2014, *Rent A Center v. Commissioner*, 142 TC 1.
31. For instance, *see* US Court of Appeals, Ninth Circuit 6.3.1981, *Carnation Company v. Commissioner of Internal Revenue*, 640 F.2d 1010.

amount of liquidity of invested assets (premiums and capital) based on the underwritten risks and subsequent liabilities, including the need to pay claims when they are due.

By its nature, insurance is an uncertain business: it is impossible to predict either the exact amount of claims that will arise from any one policy, or the timing of those claims, some of which may only be settled many years after the policy was written. Due to this inherent uncertainty, it is important and, indeed, a regulatory requirement, for insurers, including captive insurers, to ensure their capitalization is commensurate with the risks they have underwritten and to set aside funds to ensure that monies will be available to pay the ultimate value of claims as and when they fall due. These funds are held in the balance sheet as reserves, and the calculations supporting them are constantly reviewed and adjusted to reflect the most recent claims information available. Consideration, therefore, needs to be given as to whether the captive insurer holds an adequate level of reserves to cover the risk transfers it has accepted.

Both a risk transfer and appropriate reserving must be present in a genuine insurance business.

In addition to the six indicators listed above, paragraph 10.214 refers to fronting arrangements.[32] Under a fronting arrangement, a local insurance company writes a policy for a client located in that country. The local insurer then reinsures all, or substantially all, of the risk to an insurance company (which may be an independent insurer or a captive insurer) in another country. Fronting is commonly used by independent insurers where they have an MNE client that wishes to have global insurance coverage for all its subsidiaries from one insurer. It is rare for an insurance group to have a regulated local presence in every country, local insurers are therefore used to 'front' for the global insurance group. Similarly, captive insurers may also use fronting, as they do not have a presence in every country. In this respect (the use of fronting), captive and independent insurers are the same. For reasons that are not clear, Para 10.214 implies that "traditional insurance companies" do not use fronting and that it is the preserve of captives: "captive insurance may not be able to underwrite insurance policies in the same way as traditional insurance companies... This may lead to the use of a fronting arrangement."[33] Independent insurance companies make frequent use of fronting arrangements, and therefore, their use by captives is more a point of comparison than an indication the captive is not a genuine insurance business.

## III ACCURATE DELINEATION: CONTROL OVER RISK AND FINANCIAL CAPACITY TO BEAR THE RISKS

Having determined that the captive insurer is in fact carrying on a genuine insurance business, the next step is to examine, within the MNE group that owns the captive, where the control of the captive's risks is exercised (whether by the captive itself or another group entity). At this point, it is important to note that control over risk,

32. OECD TPG 2022, *supra* n. 1, para. 10.214.
33. *Ibid.*, para. 10.214.

defined in paragraphs 1.61 and 1.65 of the OECD Guidelines 2022, involves "(i) the capability to make decisions to take on, lay off, or decline a risk-bearing opportunity, together with the actual performance of that decision making function and (ii) the capability to make decisions on whether and how to respond to the risks associated with the opportunity, together with the actual performance of that decision making function."[34]

Control of risk is a key aspect of delineating a transaction: the most significant risks arising from insurance business are:

- *Insurance risk* – this is the primary risk for an insurer. It arises from the risk of loss or adverse change in the value of insurance liabilities due to inadequate premium pricing and reserving assumptions. Examples include unexpected losses arising from fluctuations in the timing, frequency and severity of claims compared to expectations.
- *Market-based risk* – the potential for loss in the value of investments or investment income due to adverse changes in the fair value of financial and other instruments. Market risk includes: interest rate risk, foreign exchange risk, equity price risk.
- *Liquidity risk* – the risk that the insurer either does not have sufficient cash and short-term financial resources available to enable it to meet its obligations as they fall due or can secure such resources only at excessive cost. The primary liquidity risk is the obligation to pay claims to policyholders as they fall due.
- *Credit risk* – the risk of loss due to an unexpected default, or deterioration in the credit standing of counterparties and debtors, including amounts due from reinsurers in respect of claims already paid and premium amounts due from insurance policyholders.

Control over these types of risks involves the following activities:

- Setting the risk appetite for the captive – the quantum and type of risk it is prepared and able to take on.
- Establishing a risk retention policy to supplement the risk appetite – the proportion of risk that will be retained and the proportion that might be reinsured (i.e., laid off to another party).
- Establishing the underwriting policy in the context of the risk appetite – policy limits, exclusions and wordings, geographic location and detailed specification of acceptable risk types.
- Establishing an investment policy and asset/liability management policy.
- Establishing the terms and conditions of any outsourcing arrangements.
- Appointing, removing, and monitoring outsource providers to ensure they are acting within the terms of their remit.

34. OECD TPG 2022, *supra* n. 1, paras. 1.61 and 1.65.

- Monitoring the risk portfolio, solvency, liquidity, capital and reserve adequacy, investment performance and profitability of the captive. Taking action to remediate or improve these items as required.

In a regulated insurance entity, it is expected that these activities will be carried out by the board of directors and senior management. The regulator requires the board to have control, where this cannot be evidenced, the license to write insurance business may be withdrawn. If the captive carry out these functions and can evidence that, it should be regarded as controlling the insurance and other risks arising from the insurance business.

Additionally, where a captive does not outsource to an insurance manager, board members and senior management must have the required skills and experience to carry out their roles effectively, including underwriting and accounting skills.

In the context of a captive, it may be unclear in practice as to who sets the risk appetite (i.e., how much and what type of risk the captive is prepared and able to accept). The risk appetite for an independent insurer is dependent on how much capital it can raise from investors and the state of the commercial insurance market. A captive insurer is dependent on the MNE parent for its capital, although once it has been allotted capital it should be able to set its own risk appetite and to decide which risks it accepts and under what terms and conditions. If it is not able to do this, for example, if it never rejects, challenges or analyses insurance risks, but merely formalizes a decision to issue a policy, it is not controlling the risk.

A second element to consider, alongside control of risk, is financial capacity. Paragraph 1.60 of the OECD TPG 2022 requires not only that an entity controls risk but also that it has the financial capacity to assume that risk. Paragraph 10.202 of the OECD Guidelines 2022 points out that the "assumption of risk can only take place if the insurer has a realistic prospect of being able to satisfy a claim in the event of the risk materialising."[35] When considering this from a captive insurer perspective this needs to be analyzed further: the captive needs to be able to satisfy a claim without any financial implications on other related parties in the group. A captive insurance company may prima facie appear to be operating independently from other group entities, and risk transfers may have genuinely taken place. However, when analyzing its asset and liability management policy, the pooled capital from premiums earned may be reinvested back into the group companies which it insures, perhaps in the form of loans or other financial instruments. This may lead to a situation where, if a loss event were to occur, the captive may not be able to obtain access to the capital needed to honor its financial obligation without support from the parent company or other group subsidiaries participating in the insurance pool. There is, therefore, a direct "correlation" between the captive's ability to honor its obligation when a significant loss event occurs, and the financial position of the related parties. In this scenario, the ability of the captive to manage its assets to match expected liabilities is constrained.

To summarize, the captive should be entitled to the premiums and investment returns when it employs appropriate personnel, for instance, but not exclusively

35. OECD TPG 2022, *supra* n. 1, para. 10.202.

underwriters, and these personnel's functions should demonstrate that they have the capability to make decisions with respect to (i) taking on, laying off or declining the insurance risk; and (ii) deciding whether and how to respond to the insurance risk associated with the decisions making opportunity. The underwriting function typically involves (i) setting the underwriting policy; (ii) risk classification and selection; (iii) pricing the policy; (iv) risk retention analysis; and (v) acceptance of the insured risk.[36] The captive insurance is not required to take all listed decisions, they are indicative. Moreover, the entity also should demonstrate that it can perform the decision-making activity associated with the risks, especially the insurance risk. Furthermore, even if the management of risks is outsourced, the personnel in the captive are able to demonstrate that they can oversee and manage the outsourced risks. To the contrary, "a captive insurance that outsources all aspects of the underwriting process without performing control functions would not assume the insurance risk."[37] Hence, the retention of the control functions by the captive insurance should be thoroughly analyzed.[38] Additionally, if the captive exercises the control functions and has the financial capacity to bear the insurance risk, it should be allocated risks.[39]

## IV NON-RECOGNITION OF THE DELINEATED TRANSACTION

As a start, as noted in paragraph 1.38 of the OECD Guidelines 2022, when evaluating a transaction, an entity will consider the other Options Realistically Available (ORA) to it and will enter into the transaction that offers the best opportunity to meet its commercial objectives. Price may be a significant factor in evaluating the best opportunity, but for insurance transactions other considerations will also be taken into account, for example:

- Depth of coverage – independent insurers set a minimum limit on claims, below which they will not offer insurance. As the majority of claims are low value, high frequency, this would mean the insured party would have to allocate resources to resolving, administering and settling multiple small loss events. A captive insurer will offer this coverage and thus, in addition to reimbursing the claim, it will save administrative resources for the insured party. An example of this would be the multiplicity of small claims for accidental damage to a commercial motor vehicle fleet, which would be unlikely to be covered by an independent insurer due to the costs involved in administering many small claims.
- With regard to low frequency, high-value claims, funds to cover such losses are separated and clearly ring fenced in a captive balance sheet, which relieves

36. OECD, *Report on the Attribution of Profits to Permanent Establishments* (OECD Publishing, 2010), part IV, para. 34.
37. OECD TPG 2022, *supra* n. 1, para. 10.213.
38. *Ibid.*, para. 10.213.
39. *Ibid.*, para. 10.211.

potential pressure from shareholders to pay out such funds as dividends, if the funds had remained on the balance sheet of the operating company.
- The captive may be willing to take on risks when the supply and demand in the commercial insurance market mean it is either saturated or has no appetite for such risk.
- Speed and efficiency of claims processing and settlement is a key factor in choosing an insurer. A captive insurer may settle claims more quickly with less disruption than an independent insurer.
- Using a captive can drive changes in behavior in the policyholder company. If the risk is retained within the group more attention may be given to managing and mitigating risks than if the risk was insured externally.
- Retaining premiums within the group allows groups to centralize all their investment assets for more effective and efficient investment management.
- If the group wishes to reinsure some risk externally, it will obtain lower premium rates from external reinsurers if it first centralizes the risk into a captive, which can then offer a diversified risk pool to the market.

A captive insurer is able to provide all the benefits above and, as noted earlier, may also be able to offer lower premiums than an independent alternative because it has detailed experience of the risks it is accepting and has fewer infrastructure requirements and, therefore, a lower cost base than external insurers. Furthermore, if there are no significant loss events and the insurance transaction results in a profit, that profit is retained within the group.

Against this backdrop, we now turn to the issue of non-recognition. Paragraph 1.122 of the OECD TPG 2022 states: "[t]he transaction as accurately delineated may be disregarded, and if appropriate, replaced by an alternative transaction, where the:

1) arrangements made in relation to the transaction, viewed in their totality, differ from those which would have been adopted by independent enterprises behaving in a commercially rational manner in comparable circumstances,
2) thereby preventing determination of a price that would be acceptable to both of the parties taking into account
   a) their respective perspectives; and
   b) the options realistically available to each of them at the time of entering into the transaction."

Specific to the insurance industry, the revised Guidelines discuss an example wherein a manufacturing company (S1 – the insured) pays an insurance premium to a related party (S2 – the insurer) to protect its assets (plant and machinery and inventory) from frequent natural disaster (flooding) related risks. The premium amounts to 80% of the value of its assets. It is stated that third parties will never enter into insurance contracts given that significant uncertainty exists toward large claims. In other words, this is a case where there is a high-frequency and high-value claim. As a result, there is no active market for the insurance of properties in the area where S1 has its manufacturing business.

First, the OECD TPG 2022 provide that the arrangement is irrational for S1 from a commercial standpoint as third parties would never enter into such agreements (there is no active market for such high-value claims). Second, it is stated that since the transaction is irrational, there is not a price that is acceptable to both S1 and S2 from their individual perspectives. Third, it is argued that either relocation or not insuring could be more attractive and realistic alternatives. Consequently, the premium paid by S1 should not be allowed as a deduction, and S2 should not be liable for any claim that arises from the insurance contract.[40]

The authors share the OECD position, although the argumentation adopted can be challenged. To determine whether the arrangement is commercially irrational or not, special consideration must be given to whether the controlled transaction, i.e., the insurance arrangement, differs from those which would have been adopted by independent enterprises behaving in a commercially rational manner in comparable circumstances. To this end, the ORAs to both the insurer and the insured must be analyzed. In the example, given that the claims would be high due to the frequency of the risk, i.e., floods, independent parties would not enter into such an agreement.

In the case an independent insurer would insure such risk, the insured would pay costly premiums and not being insured would be an option realistically available that would be preferable (the price of the premiums would potentially be higher than the cost of the damages). From the insurer's perspective, an ORA would be not to insure because the value of the claims would be too significant, although the insurer has risk diversification.

Therefore, taking into account the respective perspectives of the insurer and the insured, and their respective ORA, no price that would be acceptable to both of the parties could be determined, and the insurance arrangement should be disregarded for transfer pricing purposes.

To justify its position, the OECD advocates that there is no market for this type of insurance given the likelihood of significant claims due to the high frequency of the risk.[41] However, the OECD Guidelines 2022 provide that "The key question in the analysis is whether the actual transaction possesses the commercial rationality of arrangements that would be agreed between unrelated parties under comparable economic circumstances, not whether the same transaction can be observed between independent parties."[42] Therefore, the lack of comparables, i.e., the inexistence of a market for such insurance, should not automatically lead to the conclusion that the controlled transaction lacks commercial rationality. It is not because there is no existing market that the arrangement is commercially irrational, but rather because independent parties in similar circumstances and behaving in a commercial manner would not enter into such an arrangement. Moreover, the OECD suggests relocation as an ORA for the insured. Nonetheless, this option is not realistic because it solely takes into consideration the flood risk and the subsequent insurance, without taking into

40. *Ibid.*, paras. 1.126 and 1.127.
41. *Ibid.*, para. 1.126.
42. *Ibid.*, para. 1.123.

account the whole business of the entity and the reasons and benefits derived from the chosen location of the operation of its activities.

## V CONCLUSION

The delineation of the transaction requires an initial assessment as to whether the captive is genuinely undertaking insurance business, as indicated by the six hallmarks listed above, although it should be noted that not all hallmarks must be met, nor in some cases, do they need to be met in full.

The next step is to examine the risk control exercised by the captive and the financial capacity of the captive. To be allocated the risks (and consequent financial results) from the insurance business, it must perform the risk control activities and must have sufficient financial capacity to bear losses arising from the policies it has issued.

Finally, consideration must be given to whether the captive arrangement should be disregarded for transfer pricing purposes because it lacks commercial rationality. To this end, ORAs for both the insurer and the insured parties to the captive arrangement must be analyzed. The ORAs would either be not to insure and to retain the risk in the operating company, an option that is likely to be unrealistic given the level of capital the group would require in each operating entity's balance sheet or to insure with an independent insurer who may not offer the required amount of coverage, the desired level of premium or the necessary speed and standard of claims services.

CHAPTER 45

# Transfer Pricing Considerations on Captive (Re)insurance Companies: Overview and Case Studies Using CUP and TNMM

*Andrea Grainger & Emilia Siravo*[*]

## I INTRODUCTION

Captives are a powerful financial tool that provides a plethora of corporate benefits. In this chapter, the authors present key case law on captive insurance, discuss general (re)insurance concepts relevant to captives and tie these points to the recent guidance regarding how captive transactions should be delineated and priced.

Additionally, in two case studies, the authors illustrate important considerations and potential challenges captives may face regarding pricing remuneration based on each case's respective facts and circumstances. Lastly, the authors conclude by providing a practical checklist pinpointing the key hallmarks to consider with captive transactions.

## II NOTABLE CASE LAW ON CAPTIVES

This chapter does not intend to give a complete overview of case law relating to captives but rather to outline how international case law influenced and shaped Organisation for Economic Co-operation and Development (OECD) guidance on captives.[1]

* The views and opinions set forth herein are the personal views or opinions of the authors; they do not necessarily reflect views or opinions of the organization with which the authors are associated.

1. A more complete overview of case law relating to captives is available in *see* Dr VIKRAM CHAND, Transfer Pricing Aspects of Captive Insurance Arrangements: Recommendations to the OECD, 2017.

Captive insurance was originally developed in the US because corporations needed protection for *hard to place risks*[2] but also in response to the US tax code provisions regarding noninsurance company handling of reserves.[3] As captive formation and usage increased, the Internal Revenue Service (IRS) spent decades[4] challenging US company use (and abuse) of captives; in doing so, it set precedent for the handling of captives. As captives expanded internationally, other tax offices also posed challenges to captives. The guidance provided in various international jurisdictional case law helped shape (and is reflected in) the current OECD guidance[5] on captives. Notably, the rulings in *Helvering v. LeGierse*[6] set the stage on how courts view captive governance and how insurance is defined, while case law from Humana[7] and Harper[8] (among others) crystalized how risk shifting and risk distribution in captives should be considered.

## 1 Early 1900s: US "Reserve Cases"

In the early 1900s, the IRS challenged several multinationals who set reserves for potential losses and then deducted those amounts in their tax filings.[9] Notable cases included *Pan-American Hide,*[10] *Spring Canyon Coal*[11] and *Lucas v. American Code Co.*[12] The IRS challenged the deductions on the basis that (1) the tax code did not allow for internal reserve deductions to be considered expenses or deductions; (2) the movements of funds internally did not constitute any risk shifting; and (3) allowing for such internal reserve deductions would encourage earning manipulations.[13] In the US, unfavorable rulings against captives continued until the mid-1980s.[14]

## 2 *Helvering v. LeGierse*[15] (1941): Insurance Defined

Helvering is important in insurance case law because it defines insurance to include "risk shifting and risk distribution."[16] Risk shifting was viewed from both the insured's

2. CARTER, ROBERT, LUCAS, LESLIE and RALPH, NIGEL. Reinsurance, 2000, p. 38.
3. HALE, STEWARD and CANTLEY, BECKETT. *US Captive Insurance Law*, 2nd ed., 2015, p. 66.
4. STEWARD, F. HALE. *Captive Insurance in Plain English*, 2017, p. 1.
5. OECD Transfer Pricing Guidelines for Multinational Enterprises and Tax Administrations 2022.
6. *Helvering v. Le Gierse*, 312 U.S. 531 (1941).
7. *Humana Inc. and Subsidiaries, Petitioner v. Commissioner of Internal Revenue.*
8. *The Harper Group, and Includible Subsidiaries, Petitioners-Appellees, v. Commissioner Internal Revenue Service.*
9. HALE, STEWARD and CANTLEY, BECKETT. US Captive Insurance Law, 2nd ed., 2015, p. 72.
10. Pan-American Hide: taxpayer set aside money for fidelity insurance that it self-insured and claimed this amount was similar to depreciation. The courts ruled that there was a difference between deductions for depreciations and reserves. In STEWARD, p. 73.
11. In Spring Canyon the courts referred again to Pan-American Hide (depreciation versus reserves) and added that payments to the taxpayer itself are not the same as premiums paid in the case of external insurance. In STEWARD, p. 74.
12. HALE, STEWARD and CANTLEY, BECKETT. US Captive Insurance Law, 2nd ed., 2015, pp. 72-80.
13. *Ibid.*, pp. 79-80.
14. Humana case marked a turning point where the court started considering the taxpayer's economic rationale for having a captive.
15. *Herlvering v. LeGierse*, 312 US 531, 532 (1941).
16. HALE, STEWARD and CANTLEY, BECKETT. US Captive Insurance Law, 2nd ed., 2015, p. 80.

and insurer's perspectives and was defined as the movement of a particular risk from the insured to the insurer so that in the event of a loss the insurer would reimburse the insured that loss amount. In contrast, risk distribution was viewed more from the insurer's perspective,[17] and consists of the insurer pooling multiple, independent risks together "risks are combined in a pool with other independently insured risks."[18] This pooling of diverse risks is a fundamental tenant of insurance economics (law of large numbers) and is essential for any insurer.

The concepts of risk shifting and risk distribution as originally defined in *Helvering v. LeGierse* and later clarified in *Harper*[19] and *Kiddie*,[20] among others, are carried over to current OECD guidelines on captives, including the OECD Guidelines on Financial Transactions, paragraphs 10.203 ("insurance also requires risk diversification") and 10.204 ("risk diversification is at the core of insurance business").[21]

## 3 Humana[22] and Gulf Oil[23]

Although Humana and Gulf Oil have similar facts and circumstances, their differences, specifically their differences regarding how their respective captives were initial capitalization, and differences in each captive's risk distribution led the US courts to distinct rulings.[24]

Humana, a health care company, established a captive (Health Care Indemnity) because it could not find insurance otherwise in the market.[25] Although Humana lost in the trial case,[26] it won on appeal as the courts recognized Humana's Health Care Indemnity captive as a separate company.[27] Notably, Humana won because it could prove that (1) it acted as a bona fide insurance company; (2) it was adequately capitalized so that it could independently pay claims (i.e., could stand on its own[28]); (3) it was formed for genuine business purposes and not simply for tax avoidance; (4) the captive issued insurance policies that were priced following market standards and would be commonly recognized as such in the market.[29]

The *Humana* case was the first case that marked a turnaround in the US courts' perceptions on captives and established some tenants (that were later fortified in Harper) regarding captive insurance companies.

17. *Ibid.*, p. 82.
18. *Ibid.*
19. *Harper v. CIR* 96 T.C 45, 58-59 (1991).
20. Hale, Steward and Cantley, Beckett. US Captive Insurance Law, 2nd ed., 2015, p. 82.
21. OECD Transfer Pricing Guidelines for Multinational Enterprises and Tax Administrations 2022.
22. *Humana v. Commissioner*, 88 T.C 197 (1987).
23. *Gulf Oil v. CIR*, 914. *See* Steward, p. 134.
24. Hale, Steward and Cantley, Beckett. US Captive Insurance Law, 2nd ed., 2015, p. 134.
25. *Ibid.*, p. 122.
26. *Ibid.*, p. 123.
27. *Ibid.*, p. 132.
28. In contrast in Gulf Oil where the taxpayer was not adequately capitalized and would potentially need the parent to provide additional capital. *See ibid.*, p. 136.
29. *Ibid.*, p. 133.

Similar to Humana, Gulf Oil had also established its captive (Insco) because insurance market conditions at the time led to increasingly high and uneconomical insurance costs. However, the courts rejected the Insco captive as a bona fide insurance company because, different to Humana, it (1) lacked appropriate initial capitalization (it could not operate without the support of the parent group[30]), and (2) did not have sufficient risk diversification.[31]

Recent rulings, like *Avrahami v. Commissioner*,[32] reiterate the importance of evidence of risk distribution in captive insurance. If the captive fails to provide evidence of adequate diversification of risks (risks of different independent lines of business, different geographic regions and varied perils) the captive may be seen as lacking adequate risk diversification, therefore, not achieving the fundamental insurance goal of pooling risk.

In combination, the Humana and Gulf cases set key principles needed in captive insurers to be recognized as bona fide; namely, *adequate capitalization, economic intent, appropriate evidence of risk diversification and providing coverage that is commonly accepted as such in the open market.*

## 4 Establishment of the Harper[33] Test

1. The *Humana* case marked the US courts' shift in captive rulings while Harper crystalized the standard tests and benchmarked captives would need to follow to prove they were acting as bona fide insurance companies. In Harper, the court noted that it would "consider all the facts and circumstances to determine whether a transaction nominally labeled insurance should be self-insurance."[34] The Harper ruling serves as roadmap for proving a captive is legitimate[35] providing a three-prong test to check the viability of a captive including:

1. if the transaction involves insurance risk: specific to this point the court noted that "basic to any insurance transaction must be risk."[36]

   if transactions to the captive involved both risk shifting and risk distribution; and
2. whether the arrangement was for insurance in a commonly accepted sense:[37] this included checking if the insurance was organized and operated as an insurance company, whether it was regulated and capitalized accordingly, if policies were valid and binding and if pricing was at arm's length.[38]

30. *Ibid.*, p. 135.
31. In the case of Gulf Oil only 2% of the risks came from a non-parent. The courts found this to be *de minimus*. *See ibid.*, pp. 135-139.
32. *Avrahami v. Commissioner*, 149 TC No. 7. (2017).
33. *The Harper Group v. CIR*, 96 T.C, 45, 47 (1991).
34. HALE, STEWARD & CANTLEY, BECKETT. US Captive Insurance Law, 2nd ed., 2015, p. 153.
35. *Ibid.*, p. 190.
36. *Ibid.*, p. 143.
37. *The Harper Group v. CIR* (*see* Steward, p. 71).
38. HALE, STEWARD and CANTLEY, BECKETT. US Captive Insurance Law, 2nd ed., 2015, p. 144.

The principles set out initially in Humana and crystalized in Harper shape current OECD guidance on captives. With these cases, the courts began considering more facts and circumstances around captives considering specifically if the organization, governance and capitalization of the captive were indeed like a bona fide insurance company and if the policies issued would be considered insurance in a commonly accepted manner.[39]

### 5 BEPS 2.0

The economic benefits of an effective captive insurance program (e.g., cost-effective protection for the business) generally far outweigh any tax advantages which could be generated. Additionally, today's captives are not motivated primarily by tax, but by the many other benefits captives provide.[40] Although the case law and OECD guidance described above emphasizes looking at the substance and economic circumstances of captive transactions to determine the appropriate remuneration for the captive, there has been continued criticism that captives (along with many other corporate structures and entities) enable multinational groups to avoid paying their fair share of tax, especially when they make use of offshore tax havens.

The OECD and the Inclusive Framework of countries have worked together during the past years to devise a set of rules which will establish a global minimum tax of 15% (Pillar 2 of the Base Erosion and Profit Shifting project). These rules are designed to ensure that multinational enterprises (MNEs) pay at least 15% tax on all profits, regardless of which jurisdiction in which they arise. This will mean that any captives which were set up primarily for tax avoidance, and which fail to achieve the other objectives of risk transfer and economic savings, will no longer be effective and it may be more efficient to wind these down.

## III 2022 OECD TRANSFER PRICING GUIDANCE ON FINANCIAL TRANSACTIONS

OECD Transfer Pricing Guidance on Financial Transactions[41] provides guidance on Captive Insurance (section E) including how to delineate captive transactions and how to establish whether the transaction is genuinely one of insurance. The OECD's hallmarks of an insurance transaction as outlined in paragraph 10.199 have similarities to case law established in the US. For example, similar to the Harper Test, OECD guidance on captives outlines key principles for captives including: (1) evidence that the captive is a bona fide insurance company;[42] (2) evidence that the risk has been assumed including proof that the captive has the possibility of loss and has been

39. *Ibid.*, p. 207.
40. Marsh Captive Insurance Guide Video retrieved from: https://www.marsh.com/us/services/captive-insurance/insights/captive-trends-and-data.html.
41. OECD (2022).
42. OECD TPG, para. 10.199.

adequately capitalized to pay claims;[43] and (3) evidence that risk diversification has been achieved.[44]

Like US court precedent, OECD guidance indicates that captive must provide evidence of "diversification and pooling of risk" and, "the economic capital position of the entities within the MNE group has improved resulting from risk diversification and there is therefore a real economic impact for the MNE group as a whole."[45]

Furthermore, in terms of governance, the captive should be regulated to ensure that captive is taking on a risk assumption function and is capitalized at appropriate levels in accordance with regulatory requirements.[46] Additionally, the captive must have substance and employ a team with, "requisite skills, including investment skills, and experience at its disposal."[47] Additionally, the captive must evidence the "real possibility of suffering losses."[48]

Further, the OECD focuses on the function of underwriting (which is generally regarded as the key entrepreneurial risk-taking function) and elaborates that this includes setting underwriting policies, classifying ad selecting insured risk, setting premiums, analysis of risk retention and the acceptance of the insured risk.[49] *A captive must carry out these functions in order to demonstrate that it exercises control over its risks (and therefore economically owns that risk under paragraph 1.65 of the 2022 guidelines). In the absence of this control, the captive is only entitled to a risk-free return on its capital.*

## 1 General Guidance

Like other intra-group transfers, the transfer pricing analysis includes two main steps: (1) accurately delineating the facts and circumstances of a transaction through a functional and factual analysis, and (2) appropriately remunerating the parties to the transaction at arm's length on the basis of recognized dealing. The OECD Guidance on Captive insurance outlines the main considerations for following both steps.

## 2 Accurate Delineation of Facts and Circumstances and Appropriate Remuneration

Vital to both (re)insurance in general and for captive insurance transactions is establishing whether risk sharing and risk diversification exists.[50,51] Once the facts and

43. *Ibid.*, para. 10.201.
44. *Ibid.*, paras 10.202-10.207.
45. *Ibid.*, para. 10.199.
46. *Ibid.*
47. *Ibid.*, para. 10.213.
48. *Ibid.*, para. 10.199.
49. OECD (2022), para. 10.211.
50. Rischatsch, Maurus, *The Benefit of Global Diversification: How Reinsurers Create Value and Manage Risk*. Swiss Re Ltd Economic Research & Consulting (2016). In this article, Rischatsch

circumstances have been accurately delineated, OECD Guidance provides factors to consider when determining the arm's length remuneration on captive transactions. These include: (1) pricing of premiums either using the comparable uncontrolled pricing (CUP) or actuarial approach; (2) considering remuneration based on a combined ratio and return on capital benchmark; (3) potentially applying the benefits obtained from group synergies to the transaction; and (4) adjusting remuneration in the event the captive benefits from agency sales.[52]

## 3 Pricing of Premiums

### *A Comparable Uncontrolled Pricing*

The CUP method (using CUP, either internal or external), is one method that can be used to price captive (re)insurance transactions. The OECD highlights potential issues with finding appropriate comparables for captive transactions nothing that considerations for different functional analysis, business volumes or level of capital required by a captive should be considered.[53] Additionally, in the authors' opinion, when selecting comparables, considerations should be made for the transaction's insurance structure, underlying business scope and general program features.

The insurance program's structure should include considerations on the type of (re)insurance provided (e.g., if the transaction is proportional[54] or non-proportional[55]). In proportional structures, comparables should have similar key features, like cession amount, annual limit or deductible provided or other common contractual terms typical in proportional quota share arrangements. In non-proportional structures, comparables should consider including layer width,[56] reinstatement provisions, annual aggregate limits or deductibles and other important contractual terms that impact the price.

notes that global risk diversification is a key principle in (re)insurance, and it is well established that, "A well-diversified portfolio is the cornerstone of the long-term success of a (re)insurer," at p. 15.

51. As originally defined as defined in Helvering and crystalized in Harper.
52. OECD (2022) section E, E.3.
53. *Ibid.*, 10.218.
54. *See* Overview Chapter: In proportional reinsurance, premiums, claims, and commissions are shared based on a cession amount. Proportional programs include quota shares (where premiums, claims and commissions are shared based on a fixed cession amount) and surplus programs (reinsured caps risks to a given amount (retained line).
55. *See* Overview Chapter: In non-proportional reinsurance arrangements, the insured pays a premium to the reinsurer based on the overall costs for the program and in return the reinsurer indemnifies the insured for a loss after a pre-defined deductible has been met. Non-Proportional programs may include per risk, per event and aggregated covers.
56. The layer width is defined as the difference between the total cover provided and the attachment point of a cover. For example, if a non-proportional cover is a USD 100 million xs USD 10 million, the layer width is USD 90 million (100 million minus the 10 million attachment point).

Additionally, when selecting comparables, the underlying program risk scope and characteristics need to be considered. That is, comparables should consider programs with similar lines of business, in similar geographic locations and similar peril exposures (e.g., Hurricane, Fire, Earthquake). Lastly, it is also important to consider a program's expected loss and how it compares to the overall line in the program (RRoL[57]). The RRoL is comparable and is sometimes used in insurance market studies (e.g., Lloyds[58]). Failure to consider these features may lead to rejection of the comparables selected.

While industry studies on pricing and general market benchmarks exist, prices for individual transactions are not published, effectively in many instances ruling out external CUPs as an option. Given that captives typically do not conduct insurance with external parties (with the exception of some retrocession), it is unlikely that internal CUPs will be available either. Therefore, in practice, finding and selecting defendable comparables can be difficult.

### *B Actuarial Analysis*

As an alternative to using CUP, the OECD Guidance on Financial Transactions discusses the use of actuarial analysis in determining appropriate remuneration for captive (re)insurance.[59] This approach essentially simulates a (re)insurance transaction using commonly accepted parameters and assumptions.

#### *a Note on (Re)insurance Market Pricing*

In general, (re)insurance market prices are set to cover the *expected losses* estimated to arise from the risk transfer along with *expenses* (internal, external, other) and additional *profit margins* for the reinsurer.[60] In (re)insurance market pricing, underwriters and actuaries determine the expected loss[61] of a program using various actuarial methods and approaches. Once the expected loss is determined, additional loadings for internal expenses, capital costs, tax and other expenses are added to the expected loss to determine final pricing.

57. RRoL or Risk Rate on Line is defined as the expected loss of a program over the total cover of the program. For example, if the expected loss of a program is USD 10 million and the cover provided is USD 100 million, the RRoL equals 10% (10 million divided by 100 million).
58. Lloyds provides annual TCNA (Tropical Cyclone North Atlantic) RRoL (Risk Rates on Line) and RoL (Rates on Line) benchmarks annual, for example.
59. OECD, para. 10.219.
60. Mangan, Joseph and Harrison, Connor, Advanced Underwriting Techniques. 2002. Chapter 2.2. Similar components are also defined in Bugmann, Christoph, *Proportional and Non-proportional Reinsurance*, Swiss Re. 1997, at p. 19.
61. Expected loss is generally defined as probable average of claims expected to be paid (based on various probability components) for a risk portfolio over a period of time (generally defined annually).

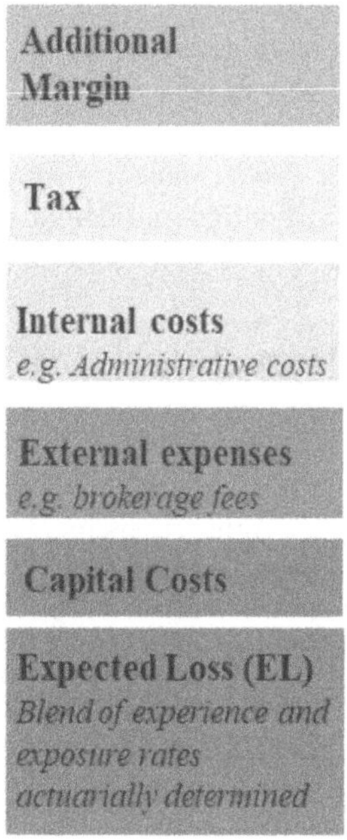


The expected loss is what the reinsurer expects to lose on average per year (or contract period) on the assumed business from covered losses (e.g., fires, natural catastrophes, liability claims as defined in the contract). This is generally a composite ratio based on a blend of past historical losses/past claims in the reinsurance portfolio (*experience*[62]) and current exposure risk profile and characteristics (*exposure*[63]).[64] The expected loss must consider the contractual terms of the transaction and be adjusted to reflect and contract features that impact the overall loss to the program.

Expenses in a reinsurance transaction typically include any general expenses (overhead), underwriting expenses (tax, license, fees) and other acquisition expenses (costs with processing the accounts, for example, brokerage) that are associated with the risk transfer.[65] Additionally (re)insurance premiums will need to include an additional margin to ensure a return to shareholders.[66]

The OECD notes that the actuarial analysis is not for an "actual transaction," therefore, adjustments should be made considering the facts and circumstances in the case. In the event appropriate adjustments cannot be made, the approach may be rejected.

Although using the actuarial approach will require more resources, it offers benefits. Firstly, although each transaction is bespoke, actuaries may rely on generally

62. Stettler, Heinz, et al. Reinsurance Matters: A Manual of the Non-life Branches, Swiss Re, 2005.
63. Michael, Cass R., et al. Reinsurance Practices, 1997, pp. 105-109.
64. *Ibid.*
65. Mangan, Joseph & Harrison, Connor. Advanced Underwriting Techniques, 2002, Chapter 2.8.
66. *Ibid.*

accepted actuarial models and principles when pricing a transaction that can be reasoned and defended. Additionally, for some types of (re)insurance programs, there are standard models a captive can draw upon. For example, when pricing natural catastrophe non-proportional programs, industry tools like AIR or RMS could be used to determine the expected loss. These tools are robust and of standard use in the market, therefore, may offer a structured and defendable approach to pricing certain types of catastrophe programs.

### C Transactional Net Margin Method (TNMM), Using Combined Ratio and Return on Capital

In addition to the CUP and Actuarial approach outlined, the OECD outlines the possibility of remunerating captive transactions in a two-step approach that considers both profitabilities of claims and return on capital.[67] The steps include:[68]

Step 1

- Determine the captive's *combined ratio* which according to the OECD equals "claims and expenses payable as a percentage of premium receivable."
- Determine a *benchmarked combined* ratio using comparable unrelated insurance company combined ratios.
- The *benchmarked combined ratio* is applied to the tested party's premiums, claims and expenses to determine "underwriting profit."

Step 2:

- Assess the investment return of the captive by looking at the capital held by the captive and the rate of return on those investments.
- Further, the level of capital held should be assessed for comparability with other insurers (on the assumption that a captive would have less stringent capital requirements).
- Finally, though not mentioned by the OECD, the type of assets held as capital should be considered for comparability with insurers as well, as many regulators require insurers to hold low-risk assets which also yield a lower return

The sum of steps 1 and 2 gives the total *operating profit* applicable to the transaction.

67. OECD TPG, para. 10.220.
68. *Ibid.*, paras. 10.220 ss.

**Example**

| Step 1 | | |
|---|---|---|
| | Captive | Benchmark |
| Claims | 60 | 65 |
| Expenses | 20 | 25 |
| Premium | 100 | 100 |
| Combined Ratio | 80% | 90% |
| **Adjusted Underwriting Profit** | **90% × 100 = 9** | |

| Step 2 | | |
|---|---|---|
| | Captive | Benchmark |
| Capital held | 60 | 80 |
| Investment Return | 3% | 2% |
| Investment Income | 1.8 | 1.6 |
| Adjusted investment income | 1.6 | |
| **Adjusted Operating Profit** | **9 + 1.6 = 10.6** | |

*Potential Challenges with the suggested approach:*[69]

Regarding Step 1, the OECD defines the Combined Ratio as "claims and expenses payable as a percentage of premiums receivable."[70] However, the OECD does not provide guidance into either the definition of claims (it is unclear if this includes claims incurred, incurred but not reported, other reserve movements, or if other considerations should be made for claims) or expenses (it is unclear if expenses include allocated loss adjustment expenses, unallocated loss adjustment expenses, internal/external or other). In particular, reserve movements are a key element of insurance accounting, which take into account the multi-year nature of insurance contracts.

Furthermore, while the OECD provides the reader reference to Chapter III, B.5 on the use of multiple-year data, the OECD provides no guidance as to what time period should be considered for the combined ratio determination. The OECD notes, "it would

69. OECD notes: "No two insurers have the same pricing policy or risk profile. Differences in individual insurers pricing policy and their claims experience will result in very different combined ratios across insurers writing insurance in similar classes of business. These differences make it impossible to identify an arm's length combined ratio to benchmark against the results of the captive. Given the sensitivity of combined ratios to pricing policy and risk profile, we consider that combined ratios are too sensitive to market factors to provide a reliable method for determining the arm's length price."
70. OECD TPG, para. 10.220.

not be appropriate to set prescriptive guidance as to the number of years to be covered by multiple year analyses."[71]

In market practice, company combined ratios will vary by line of business, geography and over time. Rarely should underwriters or actuaries in any line consider one-year Combined Ratio in isolation given the long-term nature of insurance. Certain lines of business typically consider 5-7 years, while others only consider 20-50-year time periods. In other cases, where a company has recently pruned their business, historical combined ratios are not relevant and cannot be used. For other insurance lines, for example, Life and Health business, the combined ratio is not considered appropriate, and measures like benefits ratios are more adequate.

Benchmarking combined ratios of captives with unrelated insurance companies insuring similar risks will also present challenges. First, it will be difficult to ascertain if the companies insure similar risks—even if the lines of business are the same, the terms of how an insurer accepts those risks are different, weakening the comparability.

Lastly, the OECD does not provide guidance for considerations to be made in severe loss-making years when the combined ratio and investment returns are negative (i.e., the benchmark ratio is above 100% and there is no positive investment return or income to offset the high-combined ratio).

### *D Group Synergies*

The OECD notes that in the event a captive arrangement is used to obtain reinsurance and because of the collective pooling of various operating entities obtains costs savings, any residual group synergies (savings obtained minus the appropriate remuneration for the services provided the captive receives) should be reallocated back to the operating entities.[72]

The OECD outlines group synergies with an example of an MNE with 50 subsidiaries (each with earthquake exposure) that pool their risk through the captive and then cede their earthquake risk out to the independent reinsurance market[73]. The OECD states:

> By bringing together a portfolio of insurance risks across different geographical zones, the MNE group already represents diversified risk to the market. The synergy benefit arises from the collective purchasing arrangement, not from value added by the captive insurance.[74] However, there are potential challenges for captives using this approach.

Firstly, it will be difficult for the captive to ascertain what the exact group synergies are. In the example provided, the captive would either need (a) to provide the market pricing of each individual subsidiary purchasing reinsurance on a standalone

71. OECD guidelines, Chapter III, B.5.
72. OECD TPG, para. 10.222.
73. *Ibid.*, para. 10.223.
74. *Ibid.*

and compare that cumulative cost against the cost of the reinsurance obtained or (b) to provide benchmarked pricing for each of the subsidiaries alone versus together.

If the captive provides market pricing (a), the market prices given would be theoretical. If the captive provides benchmarked pricing (b), the benchmarks may be challenged for comparability. Additionally, the skill of the captive in selecting and pricing risks for insurance and/or retrocession does add value to the arrangement.

Second, in the example provided by the OECD, "each (subsidiary) insurers against earthquake damage at its manufacturing plant, with each plan in a different location."[75] Synergies would only be obtained if the different locations' earthquake perils are not correlated with one another. So, the group synergy would need to prove that the geographic locations and perils therein are not correlated. In the example provided by the OECD, earthquake is assumed to be non-correlative. However, dynamic stress transfer/triggering[76] a large earthquake in one location may trigger another in a different region. This peril correlation, which is not easy to determine, would need to be reflected in the reinsurance pricing and would potentially reduce group synergies.

Lastly, the OECD suggests that group synergies, if obtained, should be reallocated back to the operating entities based on "level of premium contributed."[77] However, this approach is potentially problematic because premium volumes may not reflect an operating entity's contribution to the group synergies. A better allocation key could be the use of expected loss because the expected loss is reflective of the nature of the portfolio's risk.

## IV CASE STUDY A: GIANT OIL ENERGY CAPTIVE

### 1 Energy Captive Overview: Substance and Governance

Giant Oil is a multinational energy conglomerate active in oil and gas exploration, drilling, manufacturing, and distribution and headquartered in the United States. Worldwide, Giant Oil has 10 operating entities in multiple jurisdictions and employs 90,000 people. Giant owns 10,000 oil fields, 3,000 exploration wells, over 1,000 refineries and 30 major operating vessels.

Recently, Giant Oil suffered a major oil leak in the North Sea. Repairs from that cleanup were over USD 20 billion. Since then, Giant Oil has not been able to obtain commercially viable priced insurance either because prices offered are prohibitive or in many cases insurance companies have no appetite to take on Giant Oil's risks. Environmental Social Governance (ESG) pressures on energy and gas companies have exacerbated the issue as insurance companies are increasingly reluctant to offer coverage to $CO_2$-intensive organizations. Giant Oil remains unable to obtain commercial insurance for its risks. As a result, Giant Oil has established an insurance captive company, named *Energy Captive*.

75. *Ibid.*
76. *See* https://www.usgs.gov/faqs/can-large-earthquake-trigger-earthquakes-distant-locations-or-other-faults.
77. OECD TPG, para. 10.223.

Energy Captive has 100 full-time local employees, including teams of underwriters, actuaries and reserving specialists. The company's main segments include Actuarial and Underwriting, Risk Management, Finance (including Asset and Liability Management (ALM) and Treasury) in addition to the executive team.

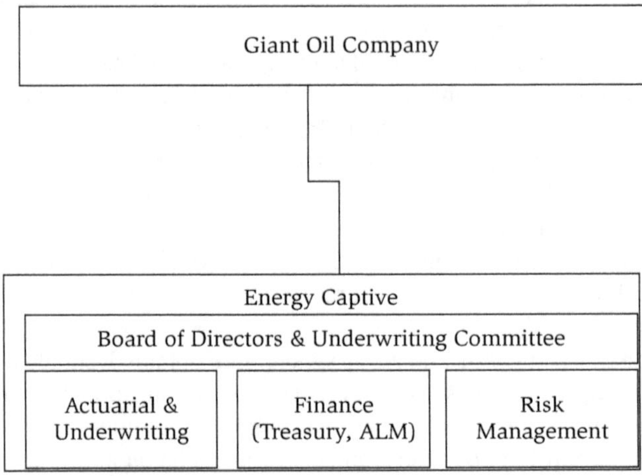


Energy Captive has a Board of Directors comprising of seven members, all located in Bermuda. The Energy Captive Board works closely with Energy Captive Underwriting Committee who is responsible for setting the underwriting policy, setting the overall risk appetite and risk retention policy and monitoring underwriting performance. The Energy Captive Board of Directors reports to Giant Oil Executive committee (EC). Although Giant Oil has delegated the entire group's risk-taking and risk-management functions to Energy Captive, Energy Captive must review the risk strategy with the Board annually and the Board has the right to require amendments to the strategy.

Overall, Energy Captive's main functions include risk management, actuarial analysis, actuarial reporting and risk underwriting, overall company compliance and review. All key decisions on its capital allocation, overall underwriting policy, and line of business risk appetite (regarding what Energy keeps internally vs cedes to reinsurance) are made by Energy Captive's Underwriting Committee based on various actuarial and risk management studies Energy Captive's teams perform.

Most underwriting tools with a focus on determining the expected loss on the underlying risks are made by Energy Captive actuarial and underwriting staff or purchased from third-party vendors (like RMS[78]). Additionally, Energy Captive's Finance Team is responsible for management of assets and investments and other financial risks.

78. RMS, AIR and EQCAT are standard market tools used worldwide for natural catastrophe pricing. According to the Lloyd's market study, "Catastrophe modelling technology is now used extensively by insurers, reinsurers, governments, capital markets and other financial entities": Catastrophe modelling and climate change (Lloyds.com).

Energy Captive offers several insurance programs to Giant Oil's operating entities. This includes Groupwide Employee Benefits cover (protecting Giant Oil employees short-term and long-term disability and medical health insurance), Property Per Risk covers (protecting various entities' physical assets in the event of loss from fire), Special Lines Engineering covers (protecting operating entities in the event a facility is under construction or under repair) and Natural Catastrophe Protection (covering operating entities in the event of a loss from a natural event named peril, like Earthquake or Hurricane).

Energy Captive actuaries and risk management teams are also responsible for completing a Risk and Solvency Assessment Report that details any underwriting risks the captive may have. Energy Captive has a small claims management team that oversees the company's overall claims management but also employs an external claims management service to support routine claims management processes.

Energy Captive is based in Bermuda but, for tax purposes, is registered in the United States. Energy Captive is regulated under Bermuda insurance law and capitalized following Bermuda capital solvency requirements. Energy Captive is licensed in most of Giant's jurisdictions. However, in jurisdictions where Energy is not licensed, it uses fronting external insurers to transfer risks to Energy.

## 2 Selected Transaction

*Natural Catastrophe Program: 3 billion USD excess 10 million USD, with an Annual Aggregate Limit of 9 billion USD*

The Energy Captive Board together with Energy Captive Underwriting Team have conducted a detailed risk analysis review and determined that Giant Oil operating companies should not keep more than USD 10 million in total annual risk exposures stemming from natural catastrophes. This includes exposure to events including, Earthquake, Hurricanes and Hail, Wind and Flood.

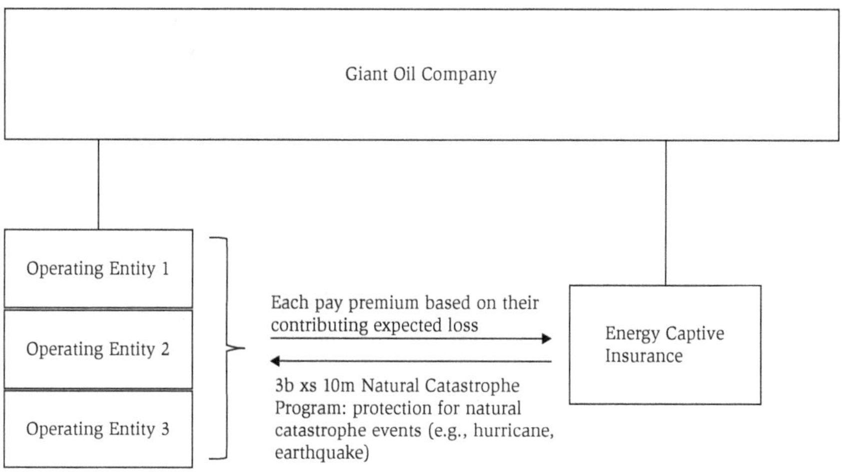

Energy Captive has structured a program for all worldwide operating entities as annual non-proportional natural catastrophe cover of USD 3 billion excess 10 million.[79] This cover protects the operating entities' risks per event and is subject to an annual aggregated limit of USD 9 billion. For the natural catastrophe cover, Energy Captive has licenses in the jurisdictions involved, therefore, a fronting insurer was not used.

The Natural Catastrophe (Nat Cat) cover indemnifies local operating entities for each loss occurrence as defined in the insurance contract up to USD 3 billion. As an example, if the program experienced three events in the calendar year, the Nat Cat cover would pay as follows:

| *Event, All Figures (in USD)* | *Total Loss* | *Attachment* | *Limit* | *Payment for Event* |
|---|---|---|---|---|
| Event 1: North Atlantic Hurricane | 35000,00,000 | 100,00,000 | 30000,00,000 | 30000,00,000 |
| Event 2: China Flooding | 3000,00,000 | 100,00,000 | 30000,00,000 | 2900,00,000 |
| Event 3: Canada Wildfires | 7000,00,000 | 100,00,000 | 30000,00,000 | 6900,00,000 |
| **Total** | | | | **39800,00,000** |

Once the total sum of payments during the calendar year reaches the annual aggregate limit of USD 9 billion, the cover is fully exhausted and will not pay for future events in that year.

## 3 Natural Catastrophe Contract Terms

Energy Captive issues the USD 3 billion excess USD 10 million natural catastrophe policy which follows standard industry contract wording for natural catastrophe event covers. The contract includes standard insurance clauses, including the parties to the agreement, applicable law, termination clauses, key definitions, and standard industry loss occurrence hours clause.[80] The contract is for one calendar year running from January 1 to December 31. Contracts are signed by each of the operating entity's Chief Financial Officers and the Chief Risk Underwriter of Energy Captive.

79. In reinsurance per event or per risk covers the program is usually labeled as the *cover excess (xs.) the attachment point*. A USD 3 billion excess of 10 million per event cover, would cover the aggregate of losses from a named event above USD 10 million up until the cap of USD 3 billion. For example, if a hurricane happened with a total loss of USD 1.5 billion, Energy Captive would pay USD 1,490,000,000 in claims (1.5 billion minus 10 million).
80. Defined as "a provision in a reinsurance contract requiring the time at which a loss occurs to be reported, and, sometimes, restricting coverage to a certain time frame" taken from https://www.investopedia.com/terms/h/hourly-clauses.asp.

## 4 Transfer Pricing Analysis

In the Transfer Pricing Analysis for captives, one must distinguish (1) whether a captive is a bona fide insurance company looking at, for example, the captive's governance, regulation, and substance including if there is appropriate staffing of insurance functions; (2) whether the risk has been assumed by the insurer (e.g., is the transaction considered insurance in a commonly accepted sense); and (3) if risk diversification exists (e.g., number of independent risks insured, type and correlation of risks and perils). Based on the facts and circumstances of the case, appropriate arm's length remunerations can be determined.

## 5 Accurate Delineation of Captive Insurance and Reinsurance

OECD guidance on delineating transactions includes analyzing (i) the contractual terms of a transaction; (ii) functions performed by the parties to the transaction (iii) characteristics of product; (iv) economic circumstances that may be relevant; and (v) the overall business strategies followed by the parties.[81]

### *A Contractual Terms & Characteristics of Property Transferred (D1.1, D1.3)*

Energy Captive program is a natural catastrophe per event cover attaching at 10 million USD with a total limit of 3 billion USD and with an annual aggregated limit of 9 billion USD. Based on their analysis, Energy Captive actuaries determined that there is more than a 10% chance of loss to the program (following Risk Transfer Test principles[82]). Overall, natural catastrophe per event covers are common in the reinsurance market typically offered with annual aggregated limits on an annual basis like the program Energy Captive provides the operating entities. The contract uses standard market-wording terms and conditions and is signed by both parties to the agreement.

### *B Functions, Assets and Risks*

Energy Captive is regulated under Bermuda law, has teams dedicated to specific insurance functions (underwriting, actuarial and underwriting committees). Additionally, Energy has extensive staffing (actuarial and underwriting staff, relevant risk management staff), clear pricing processes and documents (including the use of standard actuarial methods for pricing, external models for the determination of the expected loss), contract and policy validity, claims management and evidence of appropriate capitalization.

81. OECD TPG, Chapter 1.36.
82. More information on the risk transfer testing principles can be found on Risk Transfer Testing of Reinsurance Contracts A Summary of the Report by the CAS Research Working Party on Risk Transfer Testing (casact.org)

The 2010 OECD report on Allocation of Profits to Permanent Establishment notes, "One area of particular significance for types of insurers that focus on accepting complex insured risks is the identification of the functions which create the greatest value and risks. Such functions require a key decision: the decision as to what insured risks to accept and on what terms."[83]

Current OECD Guidance reiterates the key underwriting activities described in the Allocation of Profits to Permanent Establishments Part IV section B-2, I, c, namely as: (i) setting the underwriting policy; (ii) risk classification and selection; (iii) pricing; (iv) Risk Retention Analysis; and (v) ultimate acceptance of the insured risk.[84] In the case of Energy Captive, the actions carried on by the Underwriting Committee in determining Giant's overall risk framework, retention levels, and pricing can be summarized as follows:

*Functions, Assets and Risks: Summary Table*

| | *Functional Analysis* | |
|---|---|---|
| *Function* | *Operating Entities* | *Energy Captive* |
| Product Development | – | x |
| Sales & Marketing | – | – |
| Underwriting | – | x |
| Risk Management & Reinsurance | – | x |
| Contract & Claims Management | – | x[85] |
| **Assets** | **Operating Entities** | **Energy Captive** |
| Investment Assets | – | x |
| Asset and Liability Management | – | x |
| Physical Assets | x | x |
| **Risks** | **Operating Entities** | **Energy Captive** |
| Insurance Risks | – | x |
| Investment Risks | – | x |
| Risk Management | – | x |
| Regulatory and other risks | – | x |

### C Economic Circumstances and Business Strategies

Economic circumstances indicate that it is difficult to purchase insurance in the external market. Without the captive, the operating entities would need to keep significant risk net which would increase their overall volatility. As an alternative, Giant Oil could try to obtain insurance through Insurance Linked Security structures or

83. *Ibid.*
84. Allocation of Profits to Permanent establishments *ibid.*, at pp. 176 and 192.
85. Partially outsourced to third party.

other forms of Alternative Risk Transfer. However, these vehicles may also not be available, nor would they provide the additional benefits a captive does.

## 6 Arm's Length Pricing Consideration on the Natural Catastrophe USD 3 Billion Excess 10 Million Program

### A *Option 1: CUPs*

Underwriters from Energy Captive worked with third-party brokerage agents to obtain benchmarked Rates on Line (RoL) for global catastrophe business.[86] The RoL is defined as the premium paid over the total limit for the coverage. Energy Captive's Natural Catastrophe Program's Rate on Line[87] is 9% (270 million/USD 3 billion).

Third-party brokers provided 10 natural catastrophe global programs to Energy. The programs were brokered and provided natural catastrophe coverage for global natural catastrophe programs. Given the sensitivity of providing contract data, the third-party brokers could only provide the following data:

| *All Figures in USD in Millions* | | | | | |
|---|---|---|---|---|---|
| *Program* | *Limit* | *Attachment* | *Annual Aggregate* | *Rate on Line* | *Premium* |
| 1 | 6,000 | 1,000 | 18,000 | 1.5% | 90 |
| 2 | 1,000 | 500 | 2,000 | 7.0% | 70 |
| 3 | 3,000 | 300 | 6,000 | 15.0% | 450 |
| 4 | 2,500 | 1,000 | 5,000 | 5.0% | 125 |
| 5 | 1,750 | 1,000 | 3,500 | 3.5% | 61.25 |
| 6 | 250 | 250 | 500 | 7.0% | 17.5 |
| 7 | 200 | 50 | 400 | 9.0% | 18 |
| 8 | 150 | 150 | 300 | 15.0% | 22.5 |
| 9 | 75 | 75 | 150 | 10.0% | 7.5 |
| 10 | 50 | 50 | 100 | 5.0% | 2.5 |

According to the benchmarks provided, the average RoL on these programs is 7.5% with the following ranges:

| | |
|---|---|
| Total Range | 1.5% to 15% |
| Quartile 1 | 5.0% |
| Quartile 2 | 7.0% |
| Quartile 3 | 9.8% |

86. Market data is not always available however.
87. Rate on Line (RoL) is defined as the premium over the cover.

### *a* *Pros and Cons of the CUP Approach*

The CUP approach provides third-party external pricing ranges and therefore is very useful. However, without having the specific contract terms and conditions for each of the comparables, defending their use may be difficult.

For example, although all comparables are external pricings, the exact peril distribution, geographic exposure distribution and risk profiles for each contract are unknown. Some of the deals may be heavily exposed to one type of risk or peril or may have special features which impact the pricing. To have a better set of comparables, the data set would also need to include factors like Risk Rate on Line (RRoL) which provides the expected loss of a program over the cover.

## *B* *Option 2: Actuarial Approach*

To corroborate the CUP, underwriters and catastrophe specialists at Energy Captive priced the natural catastrophe program as follows:

(1) *Expected Loss*: Typical in the market Energy underwriters used the local operating entities' exposure data to analyze the expected loss for each peril. The catastrophe model specialist used the RMS[88] market took to determine the expected loss for the program. Based on the multiple perils included from the various operating entities, *Energy Captive determined the expected loss for the program to be USD 180 million.*

(2) *Added additional loadings to cover expenses*: Energy Captive actuaries added a 1.5 loading of the expected loss. This additional loading was added to cover their Energy's internal costs including administrative loadings, cost of capital and any additional margins they would need to fund themselves accordingly. *With the additional 1.5 loading, the pricing of the Natural Catastrophe Program totals 270m USD at a 9% RoL.*[89]

Of the total program cost (USD 270 million), the various operating entities will be charged based on the portion of their expected loss. For example, the US operating entity contributes USD 100 million of expected loss out of the 180 million total expected loss (55.5%). Therefore, of the 270 million total costs, the US entity will have to pay USD 149.85 million.

(3) To verify the accuracy of the loadings applied, actuaries use market data of similar comparables (based on the same perils covered, geographic scope and risk and expected loss features) to determined comparable loadings in the

88. RMS, AIR and EQCAT are standard market tools used worldwide for natural catastrophe pricing. According to the Lloyd's market study, "Catastrophe modelling technology is now used extensively by insurers, reinsurers, governments, capital markets and other financial entities": https://assets.lloyds.com/assets/pdf-modelling-and-climate-change-cc-and-modelling-template-v6/2/pdf-modelling-and-climate-change-CC-and-modelling-template-V6.pdf.
89. RoL is defined as the Rate on Line (premium charged over total cover).

market. They determine market benchmarks to be between 1.3 and 1.7 loading of the expected loss.

*a* *Pros and Cons of Actuarial Approach*

The approach is sound because it uses RMS to determine the natural catastrophe program's expected loss. RMS is a standard external tool for natural catastrophe pricing and is recognized and used by all major market insurance and reinsurance players.

Energy Captive also applied loadings to cover their costs similar to what a third-party (re)insurer would do. Energy Captive corroborated the loadings with external benchmarks. However, Energy Captive will need to provide additional rationale on how the benchmarks were selected.

### C Option 3: TNMM Using Combined Ratio Approach

The OECD allows for the use of a Combined Ratio and Return on Capital for potential remuneration (see above). In the case of Energy Captive, this would include:

| Step 1 | | |
|---|---|---|
| | Energy | Benchmark |
| Claims | 55 | 75 |
| Expenses | 15 | 20 |
| Premium | 100 | 100 |
| Combined Ratio | 70% | 95% |
| **Adjusted Underwriting Profit** | **95% × 100 = 9.5** | |

| Step 2 | | |
|---|---|---|
| | Captive | Benchmark |
| Capital held | 60 | 80 |
| Investment Return | 5% | 3% |
| Investment Income | 3.0 | 2.4 |
| Adjusted investment income | 2.4 | |
| **Operating Profit** | **9.5 + 2.4 = 11.9** | |

### D Pros and Cons of the TNMM Approach

Overall, assuming benchmarks are readily available, this approach is easier to complete. However, availability of benchmarks that are comparable can be problematic and each comparable may have limitations. Furthermore, as established above, this approach assumes the combined ratio and investment return are always positive. In cases of loss[90], it is unclear how remuneration would work.

## V CASE STUDY B: GRASS ROOTS

### 1 General Overview: Substance and Governance

Grassroots is a US-based cannabis grower, manufacturer and distributor operating through multiple subsidiaries in three jurisdictions. Grass Roots owns over 50 processing sites, 25 cultivation farms, 100 dispensaries and employs 5,000 people.

Although the cultivation, sale, and use of cannabis is legal in each jurisdiction, various legal and reputational hurdles relating to this new and controversial industry mean that Grass Roots faces numerous risks including (i) transactions are generally in cash, increasing the risk of theft to Grass Roots; (ii) products are novel/not well researched and are subject to product liability and safety recalls in a developing market; and (iii) crops and processing plants are subject to the same weather, fire and other perils as any other crop.

Grass Roots wishes to purchase insurance cover for these risks, however very few insurers will cover cannabis-related risks, and those that do will only offer very limited coverage (even for standard lines of risk, for example, property fire risk). Therefore, Grass Roots has created a captive insurer "*Capsure*" to both manage Grass Roots' overall risk profile and various insurance protection for these risks. Capsure is located in Vermont, US, and is regulated by the Vermont Insurance Regulator.

Capsure has five employees which include two underwriters, an actuary, a risk manager and a finance person. Capsure's underwriting risk manager manages the overall risk appetite and risk retention policy and monitors underwriting performance and cedes out risks (when possible) to reinsurers in the event of poor underwriting results. In addition, they have an outsourcing arrangement with a broker ("Savvy"), to provide support on contracts, underwriting, reserving, accounting, and claims management.

Capsure has developed the following policies to cover Grass Root's risks: (i) Property Per Risk covers to protect the processing sites and dispensaries from risks including fire and theft; (ii) Agriculture Natural Catastrophe Program to protect the farms from loss of crop due to weather events; (iii) Employee Benefits cover offering Grass Root employee Life and Health benefits; and (iv) Products Liability cover, protecting Grass Roots overall for potential from various product liability claims including medical costs and settlement costs due to bodily harm caused by a product.

90. Since 2017, (re)insurance market has experienced high-combined ratios given the various natural catastrophe and more recently COVID-19 events.

## 2 Transaction: Products Liability Cover: 10m xs 500k Excess of Loss[91]

Capsure offers Grass Roots subsidiaries a 10m xs 500k USD Casualty Excess of Loss cover. The cover is on a claims-made policy basis[92] covering multiple coverages involved in a single occurrence.[93] The cover is subject to an aggregate limit[94] of USD 40 million providing immediate reinstatements.[95] For example, in a particular year, the program would cover as follows:[96]

| 10m xs 500k USD<br>*Event, all Figures in USD* | *Total Loss* | *Attachment* | *Limit* | *Payment for Event* |
|---|---|---|---|---|
| Event 1: Product pipe malfunction, leading to burns | 2,000,000 | 500,000 | 10,000,000 | 1,500,000 |
| Event 2: Stroke induced by product intake, medical and settlement costs | 15,000,000 | 500,000 | 10,000,000 | 10,000,000 |
| Event 3: Marijuana overdose from edible cannabis treat, leading to panic attacks and psychosis in claimants | 25,000,000 | 500,000 | 10,000,000 | 10,000,000 |
| Event 4: Failure to warn against injestion: leading to stomach ulcers | 1,000,000 | 500,000 | 10,000,000 | 500,000 |
| Event 5: Improper dose recommendations on label leading to sickness | 30,00,000 | 5,00,000 | 100,00,000 | 25,00,000 |
| **Total** | | | | **245,00,000** |

Additionally, the contract terms follow general market standards for casualty excess programs and include standard clauses, including (i) retention and limit clause; (ii) key definitions clause; (iii) sunset and sunrise clauses; and (iv) claims and claims handling clauses.[97]

Capsure assesses and prices the risks to be insured in the Grass Roots operating entities agrees with the premium and then issues the insurance policies to those entities. The operating entities pay the insurance premium to purchase the insurance cover for these risks. The insurance premium is tax deductible as a business expense for the operating entities. Capsure must hold capital to cover all risks.

91. This case study will focus on the Products Liability Excess cover.
92. Cass, Kensicki et al., Reinsurance Practices, Volume 2, p. 119. "Claims-made policies are primary policies covering only those claims first made against the insured during the term of the policy."
93. *Ibid.*, p. 123. "Occurrence is defined as an accident or occurrence or series of accidents arising out of or caused by one event."
94. Maximum liability for the year.
95. Reinstates the cover after an event.
96. Examples adapted from: https://frostbrowntodd.com/growing-products-liability-claims-against-the-marijuana/.
97. Cass, Kensicki et al., Reinsurance Practices, Volume 2, p. 145.

## 3 Delineation of the Transaction

As a threshold matter, the first concern is whether the transaction was "commercially rational" or, in other words, whether the parties had any more attractive commercial options realistically available.[98]

Here, the options for risk protection open to Grass Roots were to (i) go "bare" (absorb losses locally without any protection); (ii) purchase whatever cover might be available in the market, even if it was not adequate; and (iii) provide cover internally through a captive, with extra protection through reinsurance.

Going bare or being underinsured were not attractive options given that the risks it is exposed to are low frequency but high exposure-meaning that a single event could potentially bankrupt the affected entity. Therefore, the final option of using the captive insurer to pool risks as much as possible internally, with additional cover from a reinsurer where possible.

OECD guidance suggests that where there is no active market for insurance of a particular risk,[99] then there may be a question around the commercial rationality of a transaction, however in this case, product liability coverage is a commonly offered protection and the only novelty is the industry; therefore a price can reasonably be calculated, as discussed below.

### A *Contractual Terms of the Transaction*

The insurance contracts provide all relevant legal terms for the transaction, including scope, duration and limits of coverage, premium amounts, how payments should be made, and termination provisions.

### B *Functions*

Key functions in an insurance transaction have been outlined by the OECD (as discussed in Case Study A) and can serve here as a starting point for analysis. Key functions in this transaction include product development, underwriting, risk management and contracts and claims management.

Insurance product development[100] is managed by Capsure's underwriting and risk management team. Given that the cannabis market is newly legal in many jurisdictions, relevant insurance products are still in the development stage, but input on the nature, frequency, and severity of the risks is provided by client operating entities and modelled by Capsure's underwriting team in conjunction with Savvy's market brokers.

The risks at issue in this transaction are a combination of well-established and understood (e.g., frequency of fire or natural catastrophe) and newer risks (e.g.,

98. OECD TPG, Chapter 1.38.
99. *Ibid.*, Chapter 1.126.
100. The structuring of the risk cover offered.

frequency of theft of cannabis-carrying transportation or cannabis dispensaries, or cannabis product liability). In this transaction, Capsure provides underwriting expertise on cannabis products[101] and is supported by Savvy when it comes to general product liability knowledge.

Additionally, Capsure is responsible for managing insurance risks[102] by either retaining them or ceding them to a reinsurer, along with capital management and investment risk on retained business. Importantly, even with a small staff, Capsure has both the capability to make underwriting and risk decisions, and the financial capacity to bear risk, therefore, it can be said to have control over the risk, and the transaction should not be recharacterized as something other than insurance. With regard to claims management[103] in this transaction and for Grass Root, this function is completely outsourced to Savvy. However, this does not diminish Capsure's control over the risks.

The parties perform the following functions in relation to Product Liability Excess of Loss Cover:

| *Transaction 1: Initial insurance to Capsure* | | | |
|---|---|---|---|
| *Function* | *Operating Entity* | *Capsure* | *Savvy* |
| Product Development | – | x | x |
| Underwriting | – | x | (support) |
| Risk Management | – | x | |
| Contract & Claims Management | – | – | x |

### C Risks and Assets

Unique to re/insurance transactions, risk and capital cannot be separated—due to regulatory rules, no risk can be assumed without appropriate capital. Here, the Vermont regulator will ensure that Capsure has sufficient financial resources to manage the risks it assumes. Along with financial capital, assets commonly used in reinsurance transactions are underwriting tools (e.g., loss models) and know-how (e.g., experience of a particular market or risk).

Insurance risks assumed by Capsure cover a number of jurisdictions and business lines, therefore, they are able to achieve benefits from the diversification of risk- in other words, since all of the risks covered are not likely to happen at the same time Capsure can use the same financial capital to cover a number of risks. Risks typically associated with re/insurance transactions the risks are borne as follows:

101. The process of classifying, selecting and pricing risks to be accepted.
102. The management of overall risks (especially insurance risk).
103. Includes managing premiums, claims, commissions.

| *Risk*[104] | *Savvy* | *Capsure* | *Reinsurer* |
|---|---|---|---|
| Insurance Risk | – | On retained risks | On reinsured risks |
| Investment Risk | – | On retained risks | On reinsured risks |
| Credit Risk | – | (with Reinsurer) | – |
| Liquidity risk | – | On retained risks | On reinsured risks |

### *D Characteristics of the Transaction/Economic Circumstances/Business Strategies*

This transaction provides insurance for a combination of risks, some of which are well established and some of which are relatively new and, therefore, not well modelled or understood. Therefore, premium pricing and loss modelling may not be very accurate on the newer risks as there is little market data or experience available on these risks. Although external insurers are hesitant to provide cover for these newer risks, there is no legal or moral reason that they should not be insurable.

The functions performed by Capsure (either itself or outsourced to Savvy), the risks assumed, and the assets are comparable to those which would be performed, assumed, and used by an external insurer in the same transaction.

## 4 Arm's Length Pricing Consideration

### *A Option 1: Actuarial Analysis/CUP*

Given that no market data on transactions of this type is publicly available to use as a CUP, there are no external CUPs available. Furthermore, Capsure does not insure any external clients, therefore, it does not have access to internal CUPs. However, Capsure's actuary can use commonly used actuarial principles to help determine a market price. Underwriters at Capsure price the insurance program as follows:

(1) Expected Loss: The Capsure underwriters and actuary use existing actuarial methods based on experience and exposure rating for product liability to analyze expected loss for the 10m xs 500k cover. The experience and exposure rates are blended using a credibility approach and the overall assumptions are taken following standard actuarial principles for product liability lines. Actuaries, therefore, determine the *expected loss for the 10m excess 500k program 2.5m USD.*

104. Insurance risk: the risk that the re/insurer's liability on a particular contract is higher than expected, resulting in a loss on a contract. Investment risk: the risk that investment performance on assets held as capital is not as high as expected. Credit risk – the risk that a counterparty fails to fulfill its obligations. Liquidity risk: the risk that an entity cannot access cash quickly to meet large claims.

(2) Add additional loadings to cover Capsure expenses: the actuary added a 1.3 loading to the expected loss to cover their internal costs, including administrative loadings, cost of capital and any additional margins they would need to fund themselves accordingly. Using the 1.3 loading, the total pricing for the program totaled *3.25m USD*.
(3) To verify the accuracy of the loadings applied, actuaries at Savvy could use market data of similar comparables where available to determine comparable loadings in the market. Savvy comparables indicated loadings to be in the range of 1.3-2.

#### *a Pros and Cons of Actuarial Approach*

The actuarial approach is sound here because it uses all available market data and makes estimates of the risks not covered by market data. This is consistent with what an external insurer would do in the same circumstances.

In this case, the lack of data on some risks is not evidence that the risks are not insurable, but rather that the market is too new to have reliable loss data. In this case, working closely with the teams in the operating companies can have an impact on losses (e.g., extra security can be provided for deliveries of cannabis or transportation of cash from dispensaries). This could also be factored into the risk modelling.

### *B Option 2: TNMM/Combined Ratio*

In addition to the CUP/Actuarial approach outlined, the OECD outlines the possibility of remunerating captive transactions by benchmarking combined ratio as a profit level indicator against other similar businesses.

Here, Capsure could determine its combined ratio by taking claims and expenses as a percentage of premium. It could compare this to a benchmarked ratio using unrelated party combined ratios, and in this way, determine whether underwriting profits are in line with those expected at arm's length. As a second step, Capsure would assess its investment return by looking at its capital and applying a rate of return on its investment. Looking at these items together would give Capsure an indication of whether its return was in line with third-party transactions.

#### *a Pros and Cons of TNMM/Combined Ratio Approach*

As with the CUP/Actuarial Analysis method, in this transaction, we lack market data for some of the risks insured, although this method would work well with the more traditional risks. In the case of newer risks, or even for some existing risks, this factor would point towards using a longer time horizon for multi-year data, in order to take account of slow-developing risks (e.g., product liability) or quickly changing risks (e.g., the cash nature of the business could change if banks are authorized to do business with cannabis groups).

Even with well-understood risks, it should be noted that there are challenges in using the range generated by transactions with published combined ratio data, as the coverage and terms can vary considerably by transaction. Any range derived from transactions which have not been published should be used with caution.

## VI CONCLUDING REMARKS

Captives are an important financial tool that company could use to effectively manage risks while garnering substantial cost savings. When establishing captives, corporations should consider the key points[105] to ensure the captive qualifies as bona fide insurance company including:

- The company is regulated.
- The company is adequately capitalized to take on risk.
- The company has substance—staffing, including actuaries, underwriters and appropriate risk management personnel to make appropriate insurance risk decisions.
- The transactions have the potential for loss following either actuarial verified risk transfer testing or expected reinsurance deficit (ERD) testing.
- The company has substantial risk diversification—taking multiple, diversified (noncorrelated) risks from different geographical regions or different lines of business.
- If the transactional pricing includes the actuarial approach, the assumptions must follow similar actuarial assumptions that would be made for external transactions of similar nature.
- If the transaction follows the CUP approach, the comparables must be sound and match in terms and conditions to the tested transaction.

Appropriate governance, substance and pricing will provide the captive with a strong foundation and ensure it benefits accordingly.

105. As outlined in 10.199.

CHAPTER 46

# Determining Arm's Length Premium Rates Using Insurance Approach: A Case Study

*Daniel F. Gibson*[*]

## I INTRODUCTION

Businesses around the world are facing unprecedented challenges resulting from the still unknown economic impacts of the COVID-19 global pandemic, new and increasingly complex risks (e.g., natural catastrophes, terrorism, cyber, etc.), and a hardening insurance market that is driving increases in exclusions, reductions in capacity, and rising prices. Perhaps more than at any time in history, businesses are facing uncertain conditions and are seeking alternative solutions to help manage their insurance risks. One such solution that is seeing significant growth is the formation of captive insurance companies.[1]

As captives have grown and become more complex, they have also come under increased scrutiny from various governmental entities, including insurance regulators and tax authorities. One area facing this enhanced scrutiny relates to the price a captive charge for the insurance policies it provides to its insureds. While it is important that a captive charges a reasonable price for the underwritten risk – i.e., a price that is sufficient to cover losses when they occur – regulators want to ensure the price is not so high that it creates unfair tax savings for the captive.

To help address this concern, in February 2020, Organisation for Economic Co-operation and Development (OECD)/G20 Base Erosion and Profit Shifting (BEPS)

---

* The views and opinions set forth herein are the personal views or opinions of the authors; they do not necessarily reflect views or opinions of the organization with which the authors are associated.

1. We acknowledge that there are different captive structures (e.g., single parent, group, etc.). While this chapter was written with a single parent captive in mind, the actuarial pricing techniques are relevant and could be deployed for other captive structures.

Project provided, among other items, "transfer pricing guidance … regarding the pricing of related party financial transactions, including … captive and other insurance arrangements." This guidance has now been incorporated into the OECD Transfer Pricing Guidelines.[2] We note section E.3.1. Pricing of Premiums:

> 10.217. Comparable uncontrolled prices (CUP) may be available from comparable arrangements between unrelated parties. These may be internal comparables if the captive insurance has suitably similar business with unrelated customers, or there may be external comparables.
>
> 10.218. The application of the CUP method to a transaction involving a captive insurance may encounter practical difficulties to determine the need for a quantification of comparability adjustments. In particular, account should be taken of potential differences between the controlled and uncontrolled transactions that may affect the reliability of the comparables. Those differences may refer, for instance, to situations where the functional analysis indicates that a captive insurance performs less functions than a commercial insurer (e.g., a captive insurance that only insures internal risks within the MNE group may not need to perform distribution and sales functions). Similarly, differences between the captive insurance and the potential comparables in business volume or in the level of capital between the captive insurance and unrelated parties may require comparability adjustments.[3]

For a captive management team to utilize the CUP method, it will often rely on market pricing based on quota share pricing or insights from its insurance broker. As noted above, this approach may encounter challenges in quantifying necessary adjustments for the comparability pricing. In addition, such pricing approaches that reflect insurance market pricing will see instability in the year-to-year pricing as the approach is subject to supply and demand economic conditions of the insurance market. To account for these challenges, the guidance offers an alternative approach:

> 10.219. Alternatively, actuarial analysis may be an appropriate method to independently determine the premium likely to be required at arm's length for insurance of a particular risk. In setting prices for an insurance premium, an insurer will seek to cover its expected losses on claims, its costs associated with writing and administering policies and dealing with claims, plus a profit to provide a return on capital, taking into account any investment income it expects to receive on the excess of premiums received less claims and expenses paid.[4]

Leveraging this alternative option, we present in this chapter an actuarial pricing approach that eliminates the need for insurance market pricing adjustments and provides more stability in annual pricing as it seeks to quantify the risk based on long-term averages exclusive of insurance market economic conditions.

---

2. The OECD Transfer Pricing Guidance for Multinational Enterprises and Tax Administrations, released January 2022, Chapter 10, section E.
3. Transfer Pricing Guidance on Financial Transactions: Inclusive Framework on BEPS: Actions 4, 8-10 (February 2020), https://www.oecd.org/tax/beps/transfer-pricing-guidance-on-financial-transactions-inclusive-framework-on-beps-actions-4-8-10.pdf. *See also*: The OECD Transfer Pricing Guidance for Multinational Enterprises and Tax Administrations, released January 2022 Chapter 10, section E.3.1, p. 448.
4. *Ibid.*

## II THE ACTUARIAL PROFESSION

Before we dive into the approach, we should first start with some understanding of the actuarial profession and why these professionals have the skillset required to provide a reasonable estimate of a captive's premium. An actuary is defined as "a person who compiles and analyses statistics and uses them to calculate insurance risks and premiums."[5] Becoming a credentialed actuary requires rigorous training, both on the job and through examinations. In addition, an actuary must meet annual continuing education requirements both to remain credentialed and to continue practicing in the actuarial profession.

In addition to significant training, actuaries must adhere to standards established by the Actuarial Standards Board[6] (www.actuarialstandardsboard.org) to maintain their credentials and meet the qualifications standards to render actuarial opinions, which includes such actions as implementing an actuarial pricing approach to estimate premiums for a captive. Precept 1 of the Code of Professional Conduct lays the foundation upon which the rest of the Precepts that describe the structure of the actuarial professionalism are built: "An actuary shall act honestly, with integrity and competence, and in a manner to fulfil the profession's responsibility to the public and to uphold the reputation of the actuarial profession."[7]

The actuarial standards specifically address four key principles around ratemaking, noting that estimating premium is "prospective because the property and casualty insurance rate must be developed prior to the transfer of risk":

(1) *Principle 1: A rate is an estimate of the expected value of future costs. Ratemaking should provide for all costs so that the insurance system is financially sound.*
(2) *Principle 2: A rate provides for all costs associated with the transfer of risk. Ratemaking should provide for the costs of an individual risk transfer so that equity among insureds is maintained. When the experience of an individual risk does not provide a credible basis for estimating these costs, it is appropriate to consider the aggregate experience of similar risks. A rate estimated from such experience is an estimate of the costs of the risk transfer for each individual in the class.*
(3) *Principle 3: A rate provides for the costs associated with an individual risk transfer. Ratemaking produces cost estimates that are actuarially sound if the estimation is based on Principles 1, 2, and 3. Such rates comply with four criteria commonly used by actuaries: reasonable, not excessive, not inadequate, and not unfairly discriminatory.*

---

5. *See* https://www.lexico.com/definition/actuary.
6. *See* https://www.actuarialstandardsboard.org.
7. Actuarial Standards Board: Precept 1: Honesty, Integrity, and Competence, https://www.actuarialstandardsboard.org/profcounts/precept-1-honesty-integrity-and-competence/.

(4) *Principle 4: A rate is reasonable and not excessive, inadequate, or unfairly discriminatory if it is an actuarially sound estimate of the expected value of all future costs associated with an individual risk transfer.*[8]

An actuary's training, coupled with the standards of the profession, allow for the development and incorporation of a reasonable approach to estimate the premiums charged by a captive. The ratemaking Principles noted above make it clear that an actuarially sound estimate should be reasonable and not inadequate, excessive or unfairly discriminatory. This provision supports the notion that a captive can leverage an actuary to provide premium estimates based on an actuarial approach.

Offering additional support for this approach, we note the below Actuarial Standards of Practice regarding actuarial communications:

> Actuarial Report—The actuary should complete an actuarial report if the actuary intends the actuarial findings to be relied upon by any intended user. The actuary should consider the needs of the intended user in communicating the actuarial findings in the actuarial report.
>
> An actuarial report may comprise one or several documents. The report may be in several different formats (such as formal documents produced on word processing, presentation or publishing software, e-mail, paper, or web sites). Where an actuarial report for a specific intended user comprises multiple documents, the actuary should communicate which documents comprise the report.
>
> In the actuarial report, the actuary should state the actuarial findings, and identify the methods, procedures, assumptions, and data used by the actuary with sufficient clarity that another actuary qualified in the same practice area could make an objective appraisal of the reasonableness of the actuary's work as presented in the actuarial report.[9]

As noted earlier, captives have found themselves facing scrutiny by various governmental entities, including regulatory and tax. One of these key areas of scrutiny is around the premium being charged by the captive. An actuary, deploying her training, adhering to the standards of the profession, and providing robust documentation through an actuarial report should be an avenue captives can leverage to help address challenges from various entities. An actuarial report, signed by a credentialed actuary, should be provided that explains the data, methods and assumptions such that another actuary qualified in the same practice areas could review for reasonableness. In many instances, a captive will have an independent actuary provide an annual opinion regarding the reasonableness of the unpaid liabilities on its financial statements. Similarly, a captive management team may suggest that its independent actuary provide a report around the reasonableness of the premium being charged.

8. Statement of Principles Regarding Property and Casualty Insurance Ratemaking (May 2021), https:// www.casact.org/sites/default/files/2021-05/Statement-Of-Principles-Ratemaking.pdf.
9. Actuarial Standards Board: Actuarial Standards of Practice Number 41: Actuarial Communications, https://www.actuarialstandardsboard.org/asops/actuarial-communications/.

## III AN ACTUARIAL PRICING APPROACH

Noting the benefit of being able to provide a group entity with consistent pricing, the acknowledgement from the OECD of the reasonability of an actuarial pricing approach, and the professional standards adhered to by the actuarial profession, we are now ready to provide a more detailed look at an actuarial pricing approach. This chapter provides insights into the three key components of an actuarial pricing approach: (1) expected loss; (2) uncertainty load; and (3) expense load.

### 1 Expected Loss

The first key component associated with the premium charged for a policy should account for the losses for the underwritten risk during the period of the insurance policy. In other words, for a policy covering underwritten exposure from January 1, 20XX to December 31, 20XX, one must estimate the losses that will occur during this time. Due to the inherent nature of insurance, i.e., providing coverage for unknown future events, an estimate must be made to approximate the projected losses to be covered by an insurance policy. We look at three key items actuaries consider in an analysis to estimate losses: (a) data credibility; (b) data adjustments; and (c) forecasting techniques.

#### *A Data Credibility*

An actuarial forecast leverages historical experience to the fullest extent credible and supplement with industry information. For high-frequency and low-severity risks (e.g., automobile liability), an actuary will typically be able to rely predominantly on a company's own loss experience. However, for low-frequency and high-severity risk (e.g., property losses resulting from catastrophes), an actuary will need to rely more on industry information. The key to determining the right mix of company experience versus industry information is ensuring that there is enough historical experience to adequately capture the volatility of losses from one year to the next. While actuarial judgment will be necessary, below we provide examples[10] of one way to assess the amount of weight given to a company's data versus industry information:

- High-frequency Example: If forecasting a coverage where a company averages 1,000 claims per year, we would give credit of 96.1% (= square root of 1,000/1,082) to the company's own experience and 3.9% (= 100% - 96.1%) to industry information.

10. These examples rely on the Classical Credibility Approach ("Basic Ratemaking" by GEOFF WERNER, FCAS, MAAA and CLAUDINE MODLIN, FCAS, MAAA). The estimated number of claims for full credibility is 1,082, which is based on the assumption that the loss experience is fully credible if there is a 90% probability that the observed experience is within 5% of its expected value.

- Low-frequency Example: If forecasting a coverage where a company averages 10 claims per year, we would give credit of 9.6% (= square root of 10/1,082) to the company's own experience and 90.4% (=100% - 9.6%) to industry information.

### *B Data Adjustments*

Regardless of whether we are relying on company-specific or industry historical loss information for our loss forecasting, it is imperative to adjust the data to reflect the forecasted underwritten exposures. We note here a few key data adjustments that should be considered.

- Loss Development: Because an insurance policy covers the entirety of a loss event (subject to policy limits), but the full value of a loss is often not known for many years after the date of loss, an actuary needs to estimate the full value of historical losses. For historical losses that remain open, an actuary will estimate the ultimate value of losses by applying actuarial methodologies to the historical losses.
- Loss Trend: Because the insurance policy is covering future losses, it is necessary to trend all historical losses to the mid-point of the future policy period.[11] An actuary should apply trend factors such that the dollar value of the historical loss event is adjusted to reflect the cost should that event occur in the projected policy period.
- Loss Removal: If changes in policy terms, conditions or exclusions have taken place such that historical losses would no longer be covered by the future policy, these losses should be removed for forecasting purposes.[12]

### *C Forecasting Techniques*

For most captives, an actuary will perform a reserve analysis at least once per year. As noted above, the full value of a loss is not known immediately at the time the loss occurs. In addition, there may be lags in reporting loss events. As such, actuarial estimates are needed to determine a reasonable estimate of the unpaid liabilities associated with historical policy periods for financial statements. As a result of these reserve analyses developing losses to ultimate, actuaries can rely on the ultimate loss estimates for historical policy periods to forecast the projected policy period.[13]

11. Such a trend assumes uniform loss dispersion and no seasonality. One should consider alternative trend points when seasonality is present, or when policies are unevenly written through the year, or when other factors exist that might contradict the assumption of uniformity.
12. Caution should be taken when removing large loss events that one may argue are unlikely to occur again. While this exact event may never occur again, other large events that have not occurred historically may occur in the future and thus removal of large events as "outliers" may result in unreasonably low estimates.
13. For forecasting, adjustments are needed to reflect differences such as trend and changes in exposure.

Leveraging a reserve analysis for forecasting works well for high-frequency and low-severity risks.

For low-frequency and high-severity exposures, an actuarial reserve analysis is likely to be insufficient for forecasting purposes. In such cases, a modeling approach may be considered. One such approach is to create a frequency-severity Monte Carlo simulation model. These models will require separate frequency and severity estimates, described below.

- Frequency: An estimate of the number of losses needs to be determined for the underwritten risks of the policy period being priced. An actuary will rely on historical claim count information in addition to industry information. A frequency distribution will need to be leveraged to reflect the volatility in the number of losses each year. Typically, the Poisson or Negative Binomial distribution is selected.
- Severity: After losses have been developed to ultimate and trended to the projected policy period, one will fit multiple distributions. Several goodness-of-fit tests should be applied to evaluate the quality of the fit of the distribution on the underlying data. In addition, one should evaluate the quality of the fit of the distribution on the underlying data for the layer of coverage being estimated. Following these various considerations, the actuary will use judgment to select the most reasonable severity distribution and its associated parameters.

Once the frequency and severity distributions with respective relevant parameters have been selected, the Monte Carlo simulation model can be created. The model will simulate the number of losses in a given year from the frequency distribution applied to a severity for each of the simulated losses based on the severity distribution and aggregate these together. The result of the model will be tens of thousands of simulated loss years for the underwritten risks in the projected policy period. (*Note*: In many cases, modeling software is beneficial in building simulation models.)

For high-frequency and low-severity exposures, we noted previously that the reserve analysis may be sufficient to determine a reasonably expected loss estimate. However, as we will explain in more detail in a later section of the chapter, part of the premium charged for underwritten risk is associated with the volatility or uncertainty of the losses. A frequency-severity Monte Carlo simulation will generate tens of thousands of projected loss years and thus will provide insights regarding volatility that is unlikely to be captured through the actuarial reserve analysis. Therefore, actuaries may rely on a model approach for high-frequency and low-severity risks as well.

Regardless of high-frequency and low-severity or low-frequency and high-severity underwritten risks, an actuarial reserve analysis is a good reasonability check of the modeled results—for both the expected loss estimate and the volatility. For example, if the expected loss estimate results in a total that is lower or higher than all historical loss years, an actuary will want to review the reasonability of the estimate and may consider adjusting. In addition, if we have 10 years of historical loss experience, one should look at the 1-in-10-year (or 90th percentile) simulated output as an additional reasonability check. Assuming that the coverage and underwritten risks are consistent, it is important that the pricing and reserve analyses are also consistent.

### D Estimating Different Types of Losses Differently

Throughout the Expected Loss section, we have referenced high-frequency and low-severity and low-frequency and high-severity loss exposures. Additionally, one should consider if there are different types of losses within the underwritten risk that should be estimated differently. Below we offer a few examples of these other losses to consider.

- Attritional: Losses typically seen from one year to the next and are thus less uncertain and less volatile. An actuary may be able to rely more on the company's own experience due to the predictable nature of these losses.
- Large (Catastrophic): Large loss events that do not occur with regularity, such as a fire, explosion, or multi-car accident. The uncertainty associated with the frequency, severity, and timing of these losses makes their predictability challenging. A company's loss experience will likely not be credible, and thus industry information will need to be leveraged. Furthermore, frequency-severity modeling may be useful in estimating the expected loss and volatility.
- Natural Catastrophe: Similar to the prior example, these types are sizeable loss events that do not occur with regularity. However, the difference is that these types of losses are the result of natural events, such as hurricanes, earthquakes, and floods. Due to the nature of these losses, historical loss events may be insufficient to reasonably estimate the expected loss and volatility. Robust modeling software that relies on information beyond historical losses reflecting various expertise from professionals such as meteorologists, economists, and climatologists, is often leveraged for underwritten risks with exposure to natural catastrophe risks.

The additional level of sophistication and robustness associated with separating different types of losses and estimating them differently in the expected loss forecasting approach may improve the accuracy of the expected loss estimate and the defensibility and ability to explain the approach and results, as well as possibly allowing for more credibility to be given to a company's own loss experience.

## 2 Uncertainty Load

The second key component associated with the premium charged for a policy accounts for the uncertainty of the underwritten risk. While an actuarial technical pricing approach is designed to estimate a premium based on long-term averages, insurance risk is uncertain, and thus an additional charge needs to be applied to account for this uncertainty.

We start with a simple example for illustrative purposes. Assume we have a risk that averages USD 1 of loss every year. If the risk incurs USD 1 of loss every year, then there is no uncertainty as we know there will be USD 1 of loss each year. Now instead assume we have a risk that will have one USD 5 loss event every five years. Like the first risk, this risk also averages USD 1 of loss every year (USD 5 / 5 years = USD 1 per year). However, unlike the first risk, there is additional uncertainty. If the premium only accounted for the expected loss of USD 1, then there would be insufficient funds to pay for the loss if it occurred in years 1 through 4. What is hopefully clear through this simple example is that even though the expected losses of these two risks are identical, the uncertainty is very different. As such, it is reasonable to expect that the cost of the second risk should be more than the cost of the first risk to account for this uncertainty.

As the example explains, a captive must ensure that it has an adequate amount of capital to pay for the losses when they are incurred. Said another way, a captive must retain capital to pay for loss years that are worse than expected. In the simple example of the second risk, a captive would need to have USD 4 of additional capital in excess of the USD 1 of expected loss to ensure payment could be made for the USD 5 loss event occurring in the first year.

A key question for a captive management's team is the level of capital it should look to retain for its underwritten risks. Phrased another way, what level of insolvency risk is the management's team willing to take based on the entity's risk appetite and tolerance? Let's look at some extreme examples for illustrative purposes.

If a captive wants to operate at the expected loss level, then it would be accepting that it will go insolvent approximately one year out of every two years. Most, if not all, captive managers would find operating at such a high-risk tolerance to be unreasonable, as it would require the need to regularly infuse additional capital into the captive to maintain solvency. Taking another extreme, if a captive wanted to maintain capital to ensure solvency at 1-in-10,000-year loss year, then this kind of risk would likely require such a sizeable amount of capital that it would be an inefficient use of capital. In short, a captive management's team needs to balance capital carefully. It needs to ensure there is enough capital to operate at solvency levels that align with its risk appetite and tolerance, but not so much that it creates challenges from a capital efficiency perspective.

An advantage of taking a modeling approach to determine the expected loss (as outlined above) is that outputs can include different confidence levels, which can then be considered for the solvency level to operate the captive. For example, the outputs can look at various confidence levels based on insolvency expectations by year and Value-at-Risk (VaR) percentiles: 1-in-10-year (90.0th percentile), 1-in-25-year (96.0th percentile), 1-in-50-year (98.0th percentile), 1-in-100-year (99.0th percentile) and 1-in-200-year (99.5th percentile). Additional values such as Tail-Value-at-Risk (TVaR) could also be considered. For certain highly volatile risks that are low frequency and high severity in nature, full-limit losses may be considered. Ultimately, we believe that it is a captive management team's responsibility to determine the right capital level to operate within and, since no two captives are the same, we believe it is reasonable that captives will operate at different solvency thresholds.

Once the captive management team has determined the appropriate capital to hold to meet solvency expectations, we can determine a reasonable amount of additional premium to charge. Because the additional capital needs to be held to protect against adverse loss years, and thus cannot be used for other purposes, a reasonable return should be charged for this opportunity cost. To determine a reasonable return on this capital, one should consider rates of return for the insurance industry, rates of return for the captive industry, and hurdle rates of the parent company. Table 46.1 provides one source for industry information that may be considered when determining reasonability associated with the charge for uncertainty.

*Table 46.1 Industry Returns*[14]

| *Year* | *CIC (%)* | *SPC (%)* | *RRG (%)* | *Average (%)* |
|---|---|---|---|---|
| 2016 | 6.6 | 7.1 | 6.1 | 6.6 |
| 2017 | 7.4 | 7.5 | 8.1 | 7.7 |
| 2018 | 2.0 | 6.5 | 0.6 | 3.0 |
| 2019 | 8.1 | 8.3 | 11.5 | 9.3 |
| 2020 | 5.6 | 7.5 | 9.2 | 7.4 |
| 5-year Average | 5.9 | 7.4 | 7.1 | 6.8 |

CIC: Captive Insurance Composite.

CCC: Commercial Casualty Composite.

RRG: Risk Retention Groups.

In addition, if the capital being held is being invested, then the expected return of this investment portfolio should also be reflected in determining the reasonable rate. Reflecting on these considerations, we note the following formula for the volatility load of the premium:

Volatility Load = (Required Capital – Expected Loss) × (Opportunity Cost – Expected Investment Portfolio Return)

Ultimately, we believe it is the captive management's responsibility to select a reasonable confidence level and return on capital to reflect in premium estimates. As consideration for a reasonable confidence level to operate a captive, we note Solvency II:

> The Solvency Capital Requirement shall be calibrated so as to ensure that all quantifiable risks to which an insurance or reinsurance undertaking is exposed are taken into account. It shall cover existing business, as well as the new business expected to be written over the following 12 months. With respect to existing business, it shall cover only unexpected losses. It shall correspond to the Value-at-Risk of the basic own funds of an insurance or reinsurance undertaking subject to a confidence level of 99.5% over a one-year period.[15]

14. Single-Parent and Group Captives, Risk Retention Groups and Protected Cell Captives, AM Best (August 2021), https://www. www.ambest.com/captive/captivereviewbook.pdf.
15. Directive 2009/138/EC of the European Parliament and of the Council (November 25, 2009).

As consideration for a reasonable return, we again note Solvency II:

> The Cost-of-Capital rate referred to in Article 77(5) of Directive 2009/138/EC shall be assumed to equal 6%.[16]

## 3 Expense Load

The final key component associated with the premium charged for a policy accounts for the expenses of the underwritten risk. One of the key differences between an insurance company and a captive is that a captive will most likely have a lower cost of operation and thus have lower expenses to issue and maintain policies. It is reasonable and appropriate to include an expense load to account for this cost, and one should look to reflect the actual expense of the captive. However, as a captive has a lower cost than an insurance company, reliance on insurance industry expense loads may result in overstating the premium estimate.

There are two types of expenses, Fixed and Variable, and both should be reflected in the premium estimate:

(1) Fixed Expenses: As the name implies, these expenses are fixed regardless of the number of policies written. Therefore, one can simply allocate the fixed expenses to the number of policies by adding to the Expected Loss and Volatility Load.
(2) Variable Expenses: These expenses differ based on the number of policies written. One can apply by dividing the Expected Loss and Volatility Load by (1 - Variable Expense Load %).

As an additional consideration, the expense load should reflect the expenses associated with an underwritten policy. As such, different policies may not have the same expense load. For example, if a captive is writing a property policy with natural catastrophe exposure, it may consider running a natural catastrophe model to reflect this risk. It would be appropriate to account for this expense within the property premium. However, if the captive also writes automobile policies, then it would be optimal not to have the natural catastrophe modeling expense be allocated to the automobile policies.

As a final consideration, one should review prior annual financial statements and compare the expense amount, in both dollars and percent of premium, to determine the reasonability of the Expense Load for the underwritten risks.

## 4 Putting the Pieces Together: A Numerical Example

A captive is underwriting a risk that averages less than two claims per year with an average severity between USD 45 million and USD 55 million. The captive management team has decided to hold capital at a 1-in-200-year solvency level or 99.5% VaR, which

16. European Insurance and Occupational Authority, www.eiopa.europa.eu/rulebook/article-6377_en.

is USD 500 million from modeling outputs. The captive's investment portfolio is relatively low risk with a subsequently low expected return. Thus, the range of returns net of investment return is 5%-7%. The captive's expenses are fixed at USD 5 million.

Table 46.2 displays the actuarial pricing approach for estimating a reasonable range of indicated premiums for a low-frequency and high-severity exposure. Like other actuarial opinions that rely on judgmental selections, we provide a range of reasonable indications to offer pricing defensibility.

*Table 46.2 Range of Reasonable Premium Indications*[17]

| | | *Low* | *Middle* | *High* | *Unit* |
|---|---|---|---|---|---|
| Expected Loss | Frequency | 1.70 | 1.75 | 1.80 | Claims |
| | × Severity | 45 | 50 | 55 | USD MM |
| | Expected Loss | 77 | 88 | 99 | USD MM |
| Volatility Load | Capital | | | | |
| | (Net of Expected Loss) | 424 | 413 | 401 | USD MM |
| | × Return | 5% | 6% | 7% | % |
| | (Net of Investment Return) | | | | |
| | Volatility Load | 21 | 25 | 28 | USD MM |
| Expense Load | | 5 | 5 | 5 | $MM |
| Indicated Premium | Expected Loss | 77 | 88 | 99 | USD MM |
| | + Volatility Load | 21 | 25 | 28 | USD MM |
| | + Expense Load | 5 | 5 | 5 | USD MM |
| | Premium | 103 | 117 | 132 | USD MM |

Numbers for Illustrative purposes only

## IV ADDITIONAL CONSIDERATIONS

### 1 Capital Modeling

As noted above, a key consideration in the premium estimate is determining a charge for volatility. As outlined, we suggest an approach that determines a reasonable return for the additional capital that should be held to ensure the captive can operate within a reasonable solvency expectation. If a frequency and severity model has been

17. Amanda Pletz & Daniel F. Gibson, OW Experts Suggest OECD Discussion Draft on Financial Transactions Covering Insurance Captives Needs to Address Captive Insurance Companies Using a More Holistic Approach (12 September 2018), https:// www.nera.com/publications/archive/2018/ow-experts-suggest-oecd-discussion-draft-on-financial-transactio.html.

developed, then it is fairly straightforward to identify the simulated output at a given confidence level – for example, the 1-in-200/99.5th VaR percentile. While such an approach is reasonable for pricing an individual line of coverage, more robust capital modeling should be considered if a captive is writing multiple lines of coverage.

While capital modeling is beyond the scope of this chapter, we note that robust capital modeling should be considered as an enhancement to the actuarial pricing approach noted above. Capital modeling can entail analytics that varies significantly in levels of sophistication. A bespoke capital model can be created to reflect the various risks of an individual captive. In addition, there are various capital modeling software solutions that can help in the creation and development of a capital model for a captive. A few items that a capital model can help with are described below.

- *Diversification*: The impact of underwriting risks that are not 100% correlated and thus resulting in the confidence level of the two risks combined being less than the sum. This approach will result in a reduction in required capital compared to modeling the individual risks.
- *Correlation*: The impact of underwriting risks where having a loss in one line of coverage will result in a loss to another line of coverage. Correlation will result in an increase in required capital compared to modeling individual risks and assuming independence.
- *Asset Risk*: Should a captive look to invest its capital, there will be volatility and uncertainty around the expected return. In determining the confidence level, a capital model can help reflect the asset risk associated with an investment portfolio and the diversification and correlation compared with the underwritten risks.
- *Other Risks*: Depending on the level of sophistication of the capital model, additional risks can be estimated to help determine the volatility around the results of a given year. A couple of additional risks include model risks, such as process and parameter risks, along with operational risks. As a captive grows in complexity, a capital model can be leveraged to include additional risks into its capital modeling to estimate its solvency confidence level more accurately.

While a capital model will be beneficial to modeling the risks of a captive on a combined basis, it will create a challenge when leveraging for pricing purposes – namely, the total capital will need to be allocated to the individual lines of coverage being priced. There are multiple capital allocation approaches, each with pros and cons. While such an evaluation is beyond the scope of this chapter, we note a reasonable approach for consideration. Assuming a confidence level of 99.5th percentile, one would run the entire capital model and seek the 1-in-200-year output. Then, one would remove one of the lines of coverage and re-run the capital model and seek the 1-in-200-year output. The difference between the 1-in-200 of the total and the 1-in-200 of the model excluding the line of coverage would be the assumed capital for the individual line of coverage. This exercise would then be completed for each line of coverage underwritten in the captive. To ensure that the capital associated with an individual line sum to the total of the capital model run with all lines, actuarial judgement will need to be implemented. One approach may be to calculate the percentage of a given line according to the summation of the individual capital estimates and then to apply the percentage to the total capital output.

### 2 Duration

For many types of underwritten risks, it takes many years to know the full value of a loss. As such, it is reasonable to anticipate that a captive will need to hold capital for multiple years following a policy period to ensure that there is adequate capital to pay for the development of claims, late reporting of claims and closed claims that reopen. In the above section, we noted the charge for volatility. One may consider reflecting an estimate for the time required to hold capital and the additional opportunity cost.

We note that reflecting duration in premium estimates is contrary to Solvency II guidance. As referenced above, Solvency II notes "a confidence level of 99.5% *over a one-year period*." As with all aspects of estimating premiums for a captive, consideration should be given to regulatory and tax authority requirements prior to implementation.

## V ALTERNATIVE PRICING APPROACHES

There are several alternative approaches that actuaries may consider in their analysis of the reasonability of the premium charged for the underwritten risks in a captive. This chapter focuses on an actuarial pricing approach that is centered on the need for capital. While additional methodologies are outside the scope of this chapter, we note a few additional approaches[18] for consideration, described below.

> *Market Based Methods*
>
> Market based methods essentially amount to industry comparisons of commonly used market benchmarks, such as combined ratios from publicly available information.
>
> The principal advantage of these types of methods is simplicity.
>
> A disadvantage to these methods is that they may not reflect the nuances of a particular contract, and as such the more uncertainty and/or the longer the payout of claims, the less reasonable these methods are for transfer pricing.
>
> *Contract Comparison Methods*
>
> In determining an arms-length price, an actuary may leverage insights gained from the pricing of contracts with unrelated parties. This may include directly comparing the pricing for similarly reinsured business, indirect comparisons, and an approach we refer to as "the rate-on-line method." Rate-on-line is defined as the price of a layer divided by the width of the layer. In application, this method leverages information regarding rates-on-line from externally placed reinsurance

18. Lynne Bloom & Marc Oberholtzer, The Actuary's Role in Transfer Pricing (Casualty Actuarial Society E-Forum, Spring 2015).

to estimate rates-on-line on other layers being reinsured between related parties for the same underlying business.

An important advantage to these methods is that they directly or indirectly provide evidence that the pricing is consistent with actual contracts between unrelated parties.

A disadvantage to these methods might be that they don't consider a broader market or economic perspective or unique contract features because they are focused on just a few contracts.

*Expected Profit Methods*

The expected profit method is used for straight quota share contracts only, and it compares the expected profit of the assuming company to the expected profit of the ceding company. All else being equal, taxing authorities may expect that the ceding and assuming companies share profits consistent with their proportional share as contractually set under the contract.

An advantage of this method is its logical appeal and simplicity.

However, there are several disadvantages. One, apart from acquisition expenses, it is not clear how the assuming company's operating expenses are considered. Two, it is not clear if the equivalence of profit is performed before or after income taxes. The application of this method can yield significantly different results depending on how these assumptions are set.

## VI CASE STUDIES

We present three examples to show the value of an actuarial approach. While the names of the captives, their parent companies, and certain details have been removed and/or changed to protect privacy and to avoid disclosing any proprietary information, the details provided are based on actual captive experiences.

### 1 Example I: A Lack of Capital in Captive Leads to Disruption for Business Operations

Following several years of significant growth, a company sought to invest in its risk management program with the hiring of a risk manager who would be dedicated to lowering the cost of its current insurance program. One of the risk manager's first observations was that the company was purchasing guaranteed cost policies—insurance policies that provide coverage for the first dollar of loss. As such, the risk manager presented to management that there would be savings in premiums if the company retained some of its own risk. Working with the company's insurance broker, the company received premium quotes from the market for large-dollar deductible plans. The premium savings were fairly significant, and thus the risk manager presented a recommendation to move from a guaranteed cost to a large-dollar deductible program to management.

While the risk manager was pleased with the immediate savings to the company's insurance program, he also saw added benefit in the company's retaining some of its own losses. The risk manager was rolling out various risk management efforts throughout the company and knew that he would be able to reflect loss experience into the overall performance of the different business units. He believed their being able to allocate actual losses to the business units incurring the losses would provide the incentive for business unit leaders to enact and adhere to these new risk management processes. In the long run, the risk manager believed this action would ultimately drive further insurance savings to the company by lowering its insurance losses, and thus the spend on its retained deductible layers.

As the risk manager continued to work with the company's insurance broker and shared more of his risk management strategies, the insurance broker suggested that the company consider starting a captive and place its retained layers into the captive. A captive feasibility study was performed and presented to the company's management team. The study conveyed the various advantages of a captive along with how the broker's team could help manage the captive at a relatively low expense. Management agreed to move forward with starting a captive and selected a domicile with minimal capital requirements to further lower the start-up cost.[19]

Because the company was primarily focused on cost savings for its insurance program, it operated the captive at the minimal capital level. In addition, the captive chose to simply charge a premium based on the expected loss with the rationale that any additional premium charged would be profit, which was not part of its business strategy.

With such a heavy focus on cost savings, the company did not fully appreciate the uncertainty associated with the underwritten risks. The company is not in the business of insurance and previously purchased guaranteed cost coverage. As a result, it did not have a full understanding of the uncertainty around its insurance cost following premium payment to its captive. By changing to a large dollar deductible program, the company was now retaining the first layer of all losses, and thus there was added uncertainty for both the frequency of losses.

Unfortunately, the company experienced poor loss experience in the early years of the captive's operation and the premium paid proved insufficient to cover the actual loss experience. Because the captive was operating at the minimum capital requirement level, there was insufficient capital within the captive to pay for the losses. This deficiency resulted in the company's having to provide additional funds to the captive to address these shortages.

To address these funding needs, the company's management team had to delay several strategic initiatives, which caused disruption in the company's operations. As a result, the company determined that its captive created too much uncertainty for its day-to-day operations and sought to close the captive. To add further frustration, the company came to understand that these losses would take several years to fully develop and payout. As such, and although the company ceased underwriting risks through its captive, the captive's regulator required it to maintain significant funds in the captive for many years until all claims were paid.

19. The OECD Transfer Pricing Guidance for Multinational Enterprises and Tax Administrations, released January 2022 para. 10.213, p. 447 further highlight that it is necessary to provide "special consideration of the retention by the captive insurance of the control functions would be required in order to conclude whether the risk is allocated to the captive insurance."

What should be understood is that the payments for this self-insured layer would have required payment by the company regardless of whether it started a captive. However, a key takeaway is that the company's management team did not fully appreciate either the impact of the uncertainty or the potential disruption this strategy could impose on the operations of its company. Its business continued to operate in the same way it did before it entered the large dollar deductible program by treating the premium paid to the captive in the same way it treated the premium paid to the commercial insurance market for its previous guaranteed cost program.

As outlined above, an analysis performed using the actuarial principles on the large-dollar deductible layer being underwritten through its captive would have helped this company make more fully informed decisions. Had a model been created, outputs would have been shown around the solvency at various confidence levels and would have thus identified the importance of charging for this uncertainty. In addition, having management work with an actuary to reflect the company's risk appetite and tolerance to determine the right capital to hold, thus going beyond minimal capital requirements, would have further helped the company understand the risk and be prepared to address years of poor performing loss experience.

## 2 Example II: Hard Insurance Market Leads to Underwriting Highly Uncertain Risks

A company has a captive that has been successfully operating for many years. The company started the captive for the primary purpose of underwriting its large-dollar deductible programs. The company leveraged independent actuarial insights coupled with market premium quotes from its insurance broker to determine a reasonable premium. In addition, the captive set aside capital to ensure solvency with a confidence that was consistent with its risk appetite and tolerance thresholds.

The company operated in an industry that was seeing a rise in natural catastrophe loss events. Historically, the company purchased an insurance policy from the commercial market to address these loss events. In addition, the company made significant risk management investments to reduce the impact of these loss events. While the insurance industry underwriting these risks was making significant loss payments at an industry level, the company's risk management efforts resulted in minimal losses and thus minimal insurance policy payments.

As the insurance industry continued to see a rise in both frequency and severity of these loss events, premiums rose to reflect this added level of uncertainty. In addition, several commercial market insurers reduced the capacity they offered to the market by lowering limits and increasing exclusions. As a result, the company saw a significant rise in its premium coupled with a policy that offered less coverage - in both capacity and covered events. When the risk manager presented the information to the management of the company, management suggested that the coverage simply be underwritten through its captive. Management believed that the company would be able to charge its operating units a lower premium, offer consistent limits from prior years and provide coverage without the newly added exclusions.

An analogue can be drawn to text from the OECD Transfer Pricing Guidance paragraph 1.42 which states that, "every effort should be made to determine the actual nature of the transaction and apply arm's length pricing to the accurately delineated transaction, and to ensure that non-recognition is not used simply because determining an arm's length price is difficult." [20]

This guidance paragraph further states that "the mere fact that the transaction may not be seen between independent parties does not mean that it should not be recognised. Associated enterprises may have the ability to enter into a much greater variety of arrangements than can independent enterprises, and may conclude transactions of a specific nature that are not encountered, or are only very rarely encountered, between independent parties, and may do so for sound business reasons." [21]

In this case, the risk manager wanted to be responsive to management's decision but was concerned about the increase in volatility associated with underwriting a low-frequency, high-severity exposure into the captive. An actuarial analysis was consequently performed to determine the impact of underwriting this new coverage. The first step started by modeling the current underwritten risks to determine the current capital position. The company's management team had previously decided to operate the captive at the 1-in-100-year confidence level. The actuary therefore compared the 99.0% VaR with the current capital to determine if there was any excess surplus and found that the excess was minimal. She then created a frequency and severity model that leveraged the company's own experience and supplemented it with available industry data to determine the expected loss and various confidence level outputs. From there, the actuary modeled the current underwritten risks with the new potential exposure to determine the combined 1-in-100-year confidence level.

With these modeled outputs, the risk manager and the actuary were able to craft a message to the company's management team that facilitated a strategic discussion and helped it make a sound decision. They outlined that they had previously decided to operate the captive at a 1-in-100-year confidence level. They noted the additional capital that the parent company would need to commit to the captive if it wanted to maintain operations at that same level. In addition, they provided actuarial premium estimates for the new coverage that quantified a charge for the volatility of the underwritten risks. The risk manager worked with the company's insurance broker to obtain additional market quotes from the commercial market that looked at retaining different amounts of coverage, such as different limits and quota share arrangements. With this added information, the risk manager and the actuary were able to utilize the model and actuarial pricing approach to display to management the additional capital required to continue operating at 1-in-100-year confidence level for various coverage amounts, along with the premium based on the actuarial approach compared with the commercial market premium quote for each of these options.

The company's management team was surprised to see the results of the additional capital required to operate at a 1-in-100-year confidence level. The company

20. The OECD Transfer Pricing Guidance for Multinational Enterprises and Tax Administrations, released January 2022, Chapter 1, para. 1.142, p. 75.
21. *Ibid.*

had several strategic initiatives and the additional capital to retain the entirety of this new exposure would have caused delays in these initiatives. Also, management was pleased with the success of the captive and was not interested in taking additional insurance risk by lowering the 1-in-100-year confidence level. It was therefore determined that the right course of action for the company would be to underwrite a portion of the risk in the captive and to purchase an insurance policy from the commercial market for the remainder of the coverage. Because of the low-frequency and high-severity nature of the newly underwritten risk, management understood that the capital position could increase beyond 1-in-100 should the company not have losses. As such, management decided to reevaluate the retained portion each year based on capital position of the captive, pricing of the commercial market, and strategic initiatives of the company to determine the most optimal use of their capital.

## 3 Example III: Addressing a Challenge from a Tax Authority

A captive had been in operation for many years. It was originally established to provide its operating companies with additional capacity as well as to receive the tax benefit of underwriting the risks through a captive. The captive engaged in a quota share arrangement with a commercial market insurance company so, the captive simply relied on the same rates as the commercial market insurance company for the premium it charged to the operating units.

In recent years, the company had exceptional loss experiences. While this loss experience was not entirely unexpected, due to the low-frequency and high-severity nature of the underwritten risk, it generated a challenge from the tax authority where the underwritten risks were located when it was observed that the premiums charged in recent years were significantly higher than the loss payments. The captive management team initially responded to the challenge by explaining that it used the same rates from the commercial market insurance company participating in the quota share for the same underwritten risks and thus the premium should be deemed reasonable. The tax authority responded with three key arguments associated with its challenge:

(1) The commercial market insurer had a different operating and cost structure, such as underwriting and marketing expenses, and thus adjustments should have been made to the commercial market rate.
(2) Both the company and the commercial market insurance company had incentive towards charging a high premium. The company received a larger reduction in tax liability and the commercial market insurance company received a higher profit.
(3) Premiums from other commercial market insurance companies had decreased in recent years more than the decreases in premiums generated from rates from their quota share insurance company partner.

The captive management team sought an actuarial analysis to review the reasonability of the premium charged by the captive to the parent company over the past several years. The actuary applied the pricing approach outlined in this chapter to determine a reasonable range of the premium charged over the past several years.

The actuary utilized the company's loss experience to the fullest extent credible and supplemented with industry information. In addition, the actuary estimated each of the premium components separately (expected loss, uncertainty load, and expense load) and provided robust documentation about the underlying approach, assumptions, and judgmental selections. The actuary's analysis concluded that the results of the premium charged over the recent years were reasonable.

The actuary's analysis and report were helpful in outlining an approach to evaluate the reasonability of pricing. In addition, the actuary answered questions from the tax authority to address some of the challenges that were based on the differences in the commercial market pricing. The actuary was able to explain that the pricing approach was not influenced by the economic conditions of the commercial insurance market. At the time of the tax authority's challenge, the insurance market had seen a rise in capacity (an increase in supply) while the demand for coverage had decreased with the increase in self-insurance and creation of captives. This environment was driving the reduction in market rates, as opposed to a reduction in the risk of the underwritten exposure. The actuary was able to explain that one could reasonably expect actuarial pricing to be higher during soft market conditions (when capacity was high) and lower during hard market conditions (when capacity was low). The actuary further explained that his independence and professional standards were such that his approach and results would be consistent regardless of what entity was looking to leverage the results. For example, a tax authority may want a low premium for higher tax revenue, but an insurance regulator may want a higher premium for lower insolvency risk. An actuarial approach will provide a consistent result that will be helpful and beneficial to ensure reasonability in premium estimates that can be leveraged by all entities impacted by the premium.

Over the next several years, additional losses throughout the industry took place. In addition, insurance companies withdrew some of their capacity from the industry as they did not feel the return for the risk was adequate. These compounding items drove the market to increase premiums and ultimately rates that were higher than the more consistent rates being charged by the captive. These actions provided further credibility to the reasonability of the actuarial pricing approach as a pricing method for the underwritten risk.

## VII CONCLUSION

As outlined above, an actuarial pricing approach based on capital has several advantages from a defensibility perspective, including being based on long-term historical averages that will typically produce less volatile results. In addition, having an independent actuary perform the analytics helps to avoid bias and ensure reasonability in premium estimates, regardless of the entity looking to utilize the premium estimate. An actuary's on-the-job and academic training required to attain the actuarial credentials, coupled with the actuarial standards of practice to which all actuaries must adhere, will further enhance the level of quality and sophistication associated with the estimates. Finally, an actuarial report will provide ample documentation to support the various components of a premium estimate (Expected Loss, Uncertainty Load and Expense Load) such that another actuary could review for reasonableness.

With that said, the key disadvantage of the actuarial pricing approach is that it will not reflect insurance market conditions driven by supply and demand factors. As such, one can reasonably expect that during certain times of the insurance market cycle, the premium estimates resulting from the actuarial pricing approach above will be higher or lower than the premiums being charged in the commercial market. While we believe that the consistency in premium estimates from one year to the next is a key advantage of the actuarial approach, we acknowledge that it may generate challenges from government authorities. To proactively address these potential challenges, it may be beneficial to consider including multiple pricing approaches in a captive's pricing strategy. For example, having an approach that leverages an actuarial pricing approach coupled with an approach that will compare premium estimates with commercial market estimates, such as the CUP Method, should allow a captive to benefit from the actuarial approach while still reflecting the insurance market conditions in its premium estimates. Additional detail about these methods[22] is outside the scope of this chapter.

We note that there are additional analyses and reports beyond pricing that a captive may want support with and for which actuarial science may be helpful, described below.

- Reserve Analysis: An estimate of unpaid loss and loss adjustment expense reserves for financial reporting.
- Risk Transfer Analysis: An analysis to test if there is a reasonable chance of significant loss, thus allowing the transaction to be viewed as insurance.
- Risk Distribution Analysis: An analysis to determine if the insurance coverage has a sufficient spreading of risk by answering three key questions: (1) Are there a sufficient number of risks for the law of large numbers to apply? (2) Are the risks statistically independent? and (3) Is this transaction viewed as insurance in the commonly accepted sense?

Having an independent actuary involved in the operations of a captive should be strongly considered by captive management teams to support more fully data-driven, sound decision-making that advances the parent company's priorities.

22. Amanda Pletz & Daniel F. Gibson, OW Experts Suggest OECD Discussion Draft on Financial Transactions Covering Insurance Captives Needs to Address Captive Insurance Companies Using a More Holistic Approach (September 12, 2018), https://www.nera.com/publications/archive/2018/ow-experts-suggest-oecd-discussion-draft-on-financial-transactio.html.

# PART VI Special Considerations for Transactions with Permanent Establishments

CHAPTER 47

# Allocation of Profits to a Permanent Establishment with Treasury Activities: General Considerations

*Céline Martin**

## I PRELIMINARY REMARKS

Treasury activities include liquidity management, intra-group financing, investment decisions and risk management, as well as various financial services. This management of a group's finances is an important, if not to say crucial activity for the continuation and prosperity of an enterprise. In the past, treasury activities have often been allocated to permanent establishments (PEs) in preferential tax jurisdictions. While this becomes ever less decisive due to Base Erosion and Profit Shifting (BEPS) and the latest Organisation for Economic Co-operation and Development (OECD) developments, as well as an increased awareness towards corporate social responsibility, treasury activities remain very mobile and independent from the organizational setting of a group. With the need for highly qualified and trained staff as well as legal (and tax) certainty and predictability, treasury activities are likely to continue being allocated to separate legal entities or PEs in stable jurisdictions.

This chapter first discusses the general principles regarding the legal and accounting aspects of a treasury PE. It then provides an overview of the relevant profit allocation rules for the attribution of profit (and capital related thereto) between the head offices and the PE, in particular the Authorised OECD Approach (AOA) and the separate entity approach respectively, and the recognition of internal dealings. Special consideration is given to specific topics in the context of a treasury PE, such as the

* The views and opinions set forth herein are the personal views or opinions of the authors; they do not necessarily reflect views or opinions of the organization with which the authors are associated.

allocation of capital and minimum capitalization requirements, as well as the deductibility of interest expenses by the PE.

In the second part of the chapter, a detailed case study is developed to illustrate the allocation of the balance sheet and income statement positions between the head offices and the PE with both external transactions and internal dealings and potential corrections for tax purposes.

As Switzerland remains a common jurisdiction for treasury PEs[1] and is the author's country of origin, examples and the case study refer to Swiss law. However, unless indicated otherwise, the general principles discussed remain valid for any jurisdiction applying the AOA in profit allocation cases, with country-specific variations at the unilateral level.

## II GENERAL PRINCIPLES

### 1 Treasury Activities

Treasury typically includes a wide range of finance-related intra-group management activities. The approach adopted by different industries will depend on the business strategy, the structure of the business, the stage in the business cycle, financing instruments and currencies used etc.[2] They may include group liquidity management and cash pooling as well as transactions (*see* section D), intra-group financing, such as the providing of loans, bonds or notes in any form (*see* section B), intra-group financial guarantees as well as implicit support (*see* section C), advise in and implementation of investment decisions, group (financial) risk management and risk hedging and so on.

Having said that, the scale of centralization is widespread. While in multinational enterprises (MNE) with several operational divisions operating in discrete industries or being subject to specific local regulations, the centralization of treasury functions can be very limited. Where this is not the case, an MNE can centralize almost all finance management and administration activities on a regional or even global scale.

With such centralization of activities, the functions, assets and risks involved in these activities must be properly delineated and attributed from a legal and tax perspective, in particular where a PE of an enterprise is concerned.

### 2 Legal Basis (Civil Law)

As far as treasury activities are not bundled in a separate legal entity but rather attributed to the branch[3] of the parent or another group company, they are directly linked to the legal entity of the head offices. In contrast to a subsidiary, a branch forms a legal entity together with the head offices and is for itself neither capable of being a

1. R.Ökten & M. Drenth, The Treasury Functions, in: Bakker/Kale (eds), Transfer Pricing and Intra-Group Financing, IBFD (2021), 19 ff.
2. *See also* description in OECD, TP Guidelines 2022, 10.39 ff.; Ökten & Drenth, 2 ff.
3. While tax law uses the term '*permanent establishment*', civil law usually refers to a local business with a certain economic and organizational independence as '*branch*' ('*Zweigniederlassung*';

contracting nor a litigation party. From a civil law perspective, a branch cannot legally be separated from its head offices, i.e., all parts of the enterprise belong to the same legal subject.[4] External contracts are concluded and fulfilled between the enterprise entity and the third party and become part of the financial statements of the legal entity according to the commercial law in the state of residence.

### 3 Accounting Rules

All transactions of a PE are part of the legal entity of its head offices and are included in the entity's financial statements which are established according to the accounting standards of the head offices (e.g., International Financial Reporting Standard (IFRS)). Unilateral civil and commercial law can, however, provide for additional (separate) accounting rules, in particular for registered PE (*'Zweigniederlassung'*, *'branch'*) and in regulated industries.[5]

For example, in Switzerland, according to Article 160(1) of the Federal Act on Private International Law (IPRG),[6] Swiss law is applicable to PE's of foreign companies.[7] Hence, based on Article 160 IPRG, the accounting of the PE is not to be governed by the company statute of the head offices' location but rather by Articles 957 ff. of the Swiss Code of Obligations.[8]

Such accounting rules pave the way for the profit allocation to the PE for tax purposes. The accounting forms the basis for the commercial law financial statements. They record the business transactions and facts that are necessary for the presentation of the branch's net assets, financial status and results of operations (economic position).[9] Therewith, they imply a fictional independence of the branch in order to attribute the relevant transactions, assets and liabilities (*see* section IV.1 below).

## III PROFIT ALLOCATION RULES

### 1 Separate Entity Approach

The international profit allocation follows a dual system. The profit of an enterprise (separate legal entity or PE) is primarily determined from a unilateral view based on

*'succursale'*); M. Vogelsang, Der Begriff der Betriebsstätte im schweizerischen und internationalen Steuerrecht (2015), 61 ff.; K. Albrecht et al. (Eds), Handbuch Schweizer Aktienrecht, Basel 2014, 12.24.

4. Swiss Federal Supreme Court: decision 4A_129/2014, cons. 2.5; Articles 109 ff. Swiss HRegV regarding branches of legal entities; on international level OECD PE Report, e.g., Part I at 33 ss.
5. *See, e.g.*, FINMA Guidance Branch Financials.
6. Swiss Federal Act on Private International Law.
7. While Swiss international private law (Article 160(3) PILA) implicitly provides for a duty to register a qualified PE as a branch in Switzerland (*'Zweigniederlassung'*; *'succursale'*; also stated in Article 931 CO), the accounting rules are linked to the qualitative characteristic of the branch rather than the actual formal registration in the Commercial Register; *see* further details regarding the qualification as branch in R. Rodriguez, Art. 160 PILA, in Grolimund/Loacker/Schnyder (eds), Internationales Privatrecht (2021), 3.
8. *See also* Rodriguez, 15 with further reference; FINMA Guidance Branch Financials.
9. Article 957a CO.

national law. Treaty provisions aim at avoiding international double taxation[10] and, if necessary, restrict unilateral taxation.[11]

While Article 5 of the OECD Model Convention (OECD MC) defines the PE as such,[12] Article 7 deals with the attribution of business profits to a PE. Article 7(2) of the OECD MC (2017) reflects the separate entity approach stating that the profits that are attributable to the PE are 'the profits it might be expected to make, in particular in its dealings with other parts of the enterprise, if it were a separate and independent enterprise engaged in the same or similar activities under the same or similar conditions, taking into account the functions performed, assets used and risks assumed'. Guidance on interpreting Article 7 can be found in the OECD Commentary and in the AOA reports of 2008[13] and 2010,[14] as well as in the additional guidance for the allocation of profits to new (post-multilateral instrument (MLI)) PEs issued in 2018.[15,16] The separate entity approach under the AOA allocates functions, assets and risks between the head offices and a PE according to economic ownership, i.e., 'the equivalent of ownership for income tax purposes'.[17] In the context of treasury activities, this means the allocation of the financial assets and liabilities (risks) as well as the income and expenses to the PE as far as it performs the corresponding treasury functions. Particular attention is paid to the separate accounting of the PE as the basis for the profit allocation.[18]

## 2 Recognition of Internal Dealings

With the PE lacking independence under civil law, the allocation of treasury activities to the PE for tax purposes requires a fictional approach deviating from the civil law approach.[19] This is even more so as the assets and liabilities underlying the treasury

10. Tax treaties allocate the right to tax to one of the contracting states, but do not obligate them to actually use their right to tax (so-called negative effect of double tax treaties; *see, e.g.*, Swiss Federal Supreme Court 2C/606/2016, 2C_607/2016, cons. 3.5 and Swiss Federal Supreme Court, 2C_436/2011, cons. 4.1.1; X. Oberson, Droit Fiscal Suisse (2020), 79-81).
11. For this common view, *see, e.g.*, J. Wittendorf, Transfer Pricing and the Arm's Length Principle in International Tax Law (2010), 190 (with further references); P. Eisenring, Art. 9 of the OECD Model Tax Convention, in: Zweifel/Beusch/Matteotti (eds), Kommentar zum internationalen Steuerrecht (2015), 2; differences in the profit adjustments between two countries are to be resolved through bilateral MAP, Article 25 of the OECD Model Tax Convention (2017).
12. Updated as a result of the MLI, *see* OECD Commentary, Article 5, section 4, also on intertemporal application.
13. OECD PE Report 2008.
14. OECD PE Report.
15. *See* BEPS Guidance.
16. Nonbinding interpretation aid for Article 7(2) in the respective version, with the AOA reports (in particular OECD PE report and the OECD PE Report 2008) ranking at the same level as the OECD Commentary.
17. OECD PE Report, Part I, section 14 (fn. 4).
18. This separate accounting also becomes relevant for the determination of the financial accounting net income (or loss) relevant for the purpose of the minimum taxation rules as laid out in the OECD Pillar II Report (*see* in particular section 3.4.1).
19. *See* A. Marantelli, 'Dealing' statt Vertrag im internationalen Steuerrecht – ein Streiflicht auf die grenzüberschreitende Betriebsstättenbesteuerung, in: Emmenegger/Hrubesch-Millauer/Kraus kopf/Wolf (eds), Brücken bauen, Festschrift für Thomas Koller (2018), 541.

activities are typically mobile and not bound to a certain location (as opposed to, e.g., machines and goods of a manufacturing PE).

For a PE and its head offices to be recognized as separate businesses for profit and capital allocation purposes in the first place, each needs to have sufficient substance. From a Swiss point of view, this implies financial and functional substance as well as infrastructure and personnel. With treasury activities usually not needing much infrastructure or personnel, the financial substance, i.e., an adequate equity financing of the PE or the (mostly) foreign head offices respectively are of particular importance, as are the people functions.[20]

More often than not, a treasury PE will not only be engaged in transactions with other legal entities but also in internal dealings with its head offices. While it is possible that a jurisdiction does not treat different parts of the same legal entity as 'separate entities' and rather considers the whole enterprise as one taxpayer for domestic taxation,[21] this cannot be maintained in a cross-border context. With the 2010 version of Article 7(2) of the OECD MC, such internal dealings (including profit mark-ups) have been explicitly recognized in the wording of the model convention.[22] As internal dealings lack legal consequences, there is greater scrutiny for a dealing to be accepted, and a certain threshold needs to be passed before it is accepted as an equivalent to a 'real' legal transaction that would have taken place between separate legal entities.[23,24] A dealing is qualified as relevant for the purpose of profit allocation if it meets a certain threshold of economic significance, i.e., it must be based on an identifiable event and properly documented.[25] This can be the case for, e.g., the internal granting of loans or rendering of services (*see* Case Study in section V below) where a functional analysis will show that the internal dealing entails the transfer of responsibilities and risks as well as the corresponding remuneration. Services or any other performances rendered by the PE to its head offices must be remunerated at cost with an additional profit

---

20. *See* e.g., T. STIEGLER, Substanzerfordernis im Zusammenhang mit der Rückerstattung der Verrechnungssteuer im internationalen Konzernverhältnis, StR I/2016, 4 ff. (regarding refund of Swiss dividend withholding tax between separate legal entities, but substance principles also apply for the determination of tax liability in the head offices and PE context).
21. In Switzerland, e.g., the entire company as one legal entity is considered to be one taxpayer. As a result, there cannot be any legal transactions (internal dealings) between the head office and a PE or vice versa. Accordingly, the AOA principles may not be applied, and it is not possible to account for 'hypothesized' internal interest payments or service fees, or any related cost-plus mark-up for tax purposes (*see* C. MARTIN, V. CHAND & N. BURKHALTER, Arm's Length Principle from a Swiss Perspective: Profit Allocation to Inbound and Outbound Permanent Establishments, Intertax (2022), REF with further details and references).
22. *See* OECD Commentary 2010, Article 7, section 40; however, the German text, e.g., remains quite broad with a general mentioning of relationships to other parts of the enterprise ('*Beziehungen zu anderen Teilen des Unternehmens*').
23. OECD PE Report Part I, sections 33 ss., 55 ss.
24. For Swiss dividend withholding tax, dealings within the same entity cannot be subject to taxation due to the lack of a distribution or a dividend income respectively (concept of limitation of the Swiss dividend withholding tax to domestic companies [Inländerbegriff], Article 9(1) VStG; *see* C. MARTIN & P. RIEDWEG, Emigration, in: Zweifel/BEUSCH/RIEDWEG/OESTERHELT (eds), Kommentar Umstrukturierungen (2021), 147 ff. with details).
25. OECD PE Report, Part I, section 158; P. LOCHER, A. MARANTELLI & A. OPEL, Einführung in das internationale Steuerrecht der Schweiz (2019), 390 with further references.

component.[26] Having said that, while Article 7(2) OECD MC requires domestic law to recognize dealings for the purpose of determining the profits which are attributable to a PE as well as the deduction of expenses related therewith, the taxation of the profits so attributed to the PE is for the domestic law of each jurisdiction. Domestic law may subject the deduction of expenses to certain conditions, e.g., thin cap rules,[27] or prevent certain categories of expenses from being deducted.[28] Tax administration may require appropriate third-party transactions realized in the commercial P&L of the enterprise as a basis for accepting related costs charged to the PE.[29] However, as far as internal dealings are concerned, when applying any domestic law restrictions requiring an actual civil law transfer or payment between two different legal entities, in order to be in accordance with Article 7(2) OECD, such internal dealings ought to be treated as if such transfer or payment had been effected.[30]

## 3 AOA: Functional and Factual Analysis of a Treasury PE

In the context of the AOA, the functional and factual analysis used to define the PE as a hypothesized separate and independent enterprise will take into account the assets used and risks assumed as a result of the functions performed. The determination of the key entrepreneurial risk-taking functions of the enterprise and the extent to which the PE undertakes those functions will be of particular importance in the process of accurately delineating the transactions between head offices and PEs.[31] The following elements are decisive for such delineation:

- allocation of the rights and obligations arising out of transactions between the enterprise of which the PE is a part and separate legal entities;
- identification of the key entrepreneurial risk-taking functions relevant to the economic ownership of financial assets and related risks and allocation to the PE;
- identification of significant people functions as decisive for the attribution of economic ownership of other assets and allocation to the PE;
- identification of significant people functions relevant to the assumption of other risks and allocation to the PE;
- identification of other functions of the PE;

26. Depending on the specific case, this requirement may derive from the OECD principles regarding the remuneration of services (*see*, discussion in OECD Commentary 2008, Article 7, section 35 s.; for Swiss practice *see* Martin, Chand & Burkhalter, 2.2.3 with further references).
27. *See* IV.1 below.
28. *See* OECD Commentary, Article 7 section 30 s.
29. *See* for Switzerland S. Oesterhelt & M. Mühlemann & M. Bertschinger, Art. 58, in: Zweifel/Beusch (eds), Bundesgesetz über die direkte Bundessteuer (DBG) (2022), 225 (also on the interdependency of taxation in relation to external dealings).
30. *See* OECD Commentary, Article 7 section 30 s.
31. OECD PE Report Part I, sections 48, 60 (step One, functional and factual analysis; the determination of the at arm's length pricing is not discussed in this chapter, please *see, e.g.*, § 10).

- identification and characterization of dealings between the PE and its head offices (threshold test).
- allocation of capital based on the assets and risks attributed to the PE.

Based on this functional and factual analysis, the assets and liabilities of the enterprise and the corresponding profits will be allocated to the PE.

For a treasury PE, relevant financial assets are, e.g., loans receivable in its books which have been granted to other group companies and related risks. The PE may be attributed key entrepreneurial risk-taking functions in relation to these loans by having them in its books, managed and – if necessary – hedged or further secured by its employees. Other functions include the rendering of liquidity management services, administrative services etc., by employees of the PE to other group companies or the head offices.[32]

Having said that, even if a functional and factual analysis concludes that a certain portion of the profit of a legal entity is attributable to its PE under the AOA, the resulting profit allocation needs to be revisited where profit attributed to a PE is exempt from taxation or taxed at a substantially lower rate and hence may be scrutinized due to domestic or hybrid mismatch and anti-abuse rules.[33] Rules regarding so-called hybrid financial instruments may need to be taken into account, particularly in the context of treasury activities.[34]

## IV SPECIAL CONSIDERATIONS FOR TREASURY PE

### 1 Allocation of Capital

A PE as part of the legal entity of its head offices by definition cannot have 'equity' or capital in the regular meaning. Next to the assets and liabilities directly attributed to the PE under the functional and factual analysis,[35] its balance sheet will contain a residual amount position in the form of 'retained earnings' of the PE, a 'loan' of the head offices or a 'branch capital' mirroring a balancing current account position in the head offices' balance sheet.

The commercial balance sheet of the PE is decisive for taxation in Switzerland. This follows from the definition of the scope of the tax liability in the cantonal tax rules: 'Persons liable to tax with their domicile or actual administration abroad must pay tax on the profit generated in the canton and the capital located in the canton.'[36] This

32. *See* section IV.
33. Jurisdictions with former preferential tax regimes, e.g., for foreign finance branches have started to abolish such special tax status, e.g., Switzerland with its latest tax reform 2020 (*see, e.g.*, www.efd.admin.ch/efd/en/home/the-fdf/legislation/votes/tax-reform-ahv-financing/fb-steue rvorlage17.html). Minimum taxation rules will also contribute to the alignment of tax status and the avoidance of hybrid mismatch arrangements (OECD Pillar II Report).
34. OECD, Report BEPS Action 2; PSD, ATAD and ATAD 2; OECD, Report BEPS Action 2, section 125; OECD, Report BEPS Action 6, sections 49 ff.; for a critical review *see* Martínez Laguna.
35. *See* section III.3 above.
36. § 53 para. 4 StG ZG (English translation of original wording, exemplary; as capital tax is levied on cantonal level only and not on federal level, only the cantonal tax rules explicitly mention the

results in a direct (object-based) capital allocation based on the independence fiction of the PE under AOA rules, which is manifested in the form of the balance sheet of the PE. Such PE balance sheet must be established according to commercial law accounting rules, i.e., for Switzerland Articles 957ff., and will contain any relevant internal dealings with the head offices. The equity ('free capital') attributable to the PE is in principle derived from the difference between the assets and liabilities.

However, the capital allocation is not discretionary. There are correction mechanisms in place which aim at a minimum 'equity' capitalization of the PE with 'free capital' which may not be subject to (tax-deductible) interest payments to the head offices.[37] This free capital serves as a puffer to capture losses, if any, related to the risks assumed by the PE.[38] In this context, it is important to note that the starting point for the attribution of capital under the AOA is the fact that such capital must support the risks assumed by the PE through its granting of loans (or continuous commitments to make loans). Such risks follow the assets owned, which in turn follow the functions performed. The capital allocation should therefore rely on the significant people functions identified within the PE. Different jurisdictions may have different views on how the AOA ought to be applied to determine the free capital attributable to a PE. The OECD Transfer Pricing (TP) Guidelines in the newly integrated Chapter 10 on financial transactions aim at providing guidance in this regard, i.e., to determine whether a 'loan' may be regarded as a loan for tax purposes or rather as a contribution to 'equity capital'.[39] To draw up a 'tax balance sheet' for the PE, the OECD recognizes several methods:[40]

- *Capital Allocation Method:* Total equity of the legal entity is allocated to the head offices and the PE based on a functional and factual analysis.[41] In the context of a treasury PE, the attribution of the external assets and liabilities connected to the specific treasury activities will in many cases be rather clear. From a Swiss accounting point of view, the financials should constitute a complete, truthful and systematic recording of the business transactions and facts in connection with the PE's activities[42] which will already imply an allocation based on a functional and factual analysis. However, the free capital attributed to the PE may remain blurred due to the internal dealings with the

capital; profit correction mechanism in connection with capital allocation on federal level follows general principles; SFTA Circular no. 6 regarding thin capitalization (*Verdecktes Eigenkapital*) is applicable for separate legal entities and PE alike.)

37. OECD PE Report, Part I, section 28; while the international standards primarily aim at ensuring an at arm's length attribution of profits to the PE, in Switzerland, such minimum 'equity' of a PE will also be relevant for capital tax.
38. OECD PE Report, Part I, section 105; also *see* T. Schwaerzler, Using the Capital Allocation Approach to Attribute Capital to a Permanent Establishment, in International Transfer Pricing Journal (2017), pp. 97 ff., 97.
39. OECD TP Guidelines 2022, section 10.10; *see* section IV.2 below regarding the recognition of interest payments on internal loans for tax purposes.
40. OECD PE Report, Part I, sections 99 ff.; *see* [Chapter Thomas Hug, III.2] for a detailed discussion and examples for the different methods.
41. OECD PE Report, Part I sections 121 ff.
42. Article 957a(2)(1.) CO.

head offices, in particular 'receivables' or 'loans' from the head offices to the PE which 'finance' the PE's treasury activities, and a proper delineation may be difficult due to the treasury PE performing very different functions from the rest of the enterprise, or when the entity as a whole is undercapitalized while the PE based on its activities should not be so.[43] This is where the Thin Capitalization Method or domestic safe haven methods provide an adequate correction mechanism (*see* below).

- *Economic Capital Allocation Method:* This approach measures risks and attributes an economic capital; it might be useful where a PE has substantial risks inherent in its business, such as developmental risks,[44] or in the regulated finance industry (e.g., risk-weighted assets under the Basel III international regulatory framework for banks). For a treasury PE, this method seems to hold several challenges, including the lack of risk measurement systems in place and the implicit support in the intercompany (IC) financing context, which may render a differentiation of risks unrealistic or even impossible.
- *Thin Capitalization Method:* By allocating the necessary amount of funding for the functions. Assets and risks of the PE and determining the arm's length debt-to-equity ratio, the thin capitalization method seeks to get the same result as for an independent comparable enterprise.[45] The application of this method does not come without problems. It requires comparable data and may lead to a greater amount of (aggregated) capital being allocated to the head offices and the PE than actually exists in the enterprise as a whole. However, it constitutes an accurate application of the AOA in determining the relevant amount of free capital an independent enterprise would have to maintain.
- *Domestic Safe Haven Rules (minimum capital approach):* While such safe haven rules are not considered an authorized OECD approach, and it may be difficult to find adequate benchmarking, such safe haven rules are nevertheless considered acceptable if they do not result in the attribution of more profit to the PE than under one of the methods above.[46] In practice, for PE of foreign enterprises in Switzerland, the domestic thin capitalization rules as laid out in the Swiss Federal Tax Authority's (SFTA) Circular no. 6 are very often the only reliable basis to determine the attribution of capital to a treasury PE. Rather than looking at sector benchmarks or individual creditworthiness, these rules lay down the maximum amount of external debt an enterprise may obtain. According to this circular, the different categories of assets of a business are attributed a certain percentage of their value to be considered as the maximum amount of outside funds obtainable by the Company from its own resources. The debt ratio in the detailed list of asset categories published by the SFTA goes from cash and liquid assets (100%), Swiss Franc (CHF)-denominated bonds (90%), loans in general (85%) to participations (70%) and other

43. OECD PE Report, Part I section 124 f.
44. *Ibid.*, section 128.
45. *Ibid.*, section 130.
46. *Ibid.*, section 135 f.

assets.[47] For financial companies or treasury PE respectively, rather than calculating the debt ratio for each category of assets, it rather allows a debt financing of six-seventh of the overall assets allocated to the PE.[48] The limits established in Circular no. 6 should be applied to the book value with a possibility for the taxpayer to apply them to the market value if the latter is higher than the book value of its assets (however, for finance activities, book values usually correspond to nominal and market values).[49]

In the case of excessive financing coming from a related party or the head offices, part of the liabilities (debt) in the balance sheet of the PE may be requalified as equity for tax purposes under domestic thin capitalization rules. Hence, such 'hidden equity' will become subject to domestic capital tax, if applicable. Furthermore, and of interest in the context of profit allocation, interest payments related to such hidden equity debt may not be accepted as tax deductible expense and lead to an increase in the taxable profit of the PE.[50] In certain cases, it could also be treated as a hidden dividend distribution, potentially leading to additional tax consequences.[51]

Last, it is possible that a PE with activities in regulated business areas such as finance is subject to certain capital adequacy or other regulatory requirements. In general, a capital allocation for tax purposes must ensure that an appropriate amount of profits is attributed to the PE. The key aim remains to allocate profits to a PE, according to the AOA. A PE in a regulated sector should have sufficient capital to support the functions it undertakes, the assets it uses and the risks it assumes, just like any other PE.[52] However, it is recognized that due to the possible Economic Capital Allocation Method under the AOA, regulatory capital provisions must take precedence over any tax-related thin capitalization rules and as such may serve as arm's length standard.[53]

47. SFTA Circular no. 6 regarding thin capitalization (*Verdecktes Eigenkapital*), providing a safe haven list of maximum amounts of debt per type of asset. The limits established in Circular no. 6 should be applied on the book value with a possibility for the taxpayer to apply them on the market value if the latter is higher than the book value of its assets; *see* R. STOCKER, Chapter 21: Switzerland, in: BAKKER/KALE (eds), Transfer Pricing and Intra-Group Financing, IBFD (2021), 790 for details.
48. The six-seventh rules has its roots in the taxation of finance corporations operating under rules for banking, P. BRÜLISAUER & M. DIETSCHI, Art. 65, in: ZWEIFEL/BEUSCH (eds), Bundesgesetz über die direkte Bundessteuer (DBG) (2022), 59.
49. SFTA Circular no. 6 regarding thin capitalization (*Verdecktes Eigenkapital*) allows the taxpayer to demonstrate that financing exceeding the maximum amounts provided is at arm's length. For more details, *see* N. BURKHALTER, Transfer Pricing Aspects of Intragroup Financial Guarantees, FStR 2020, 356.
50. *See* for Switzerland Article 65 DBG: 'The taxable profit of corporations and cooperatives also includes the debt interest attributable to that part of the borrowed capital which has the economic significance of equity capital.' (English translation of original wording).
51. For Switzerland, corporate or income tax at the level of the PE as well as withholding tax at the level of the receiving entity; *see* SFTA Circular no. 6 regarding thin capitalization (*Verdecktes Eigenkapital*); Articles 20(1)(c) and 58(1)(b) DBG; Article 65 DBG; Article 4(1)(b) VStG; for the practice of the SFTA *see* BURKHALTER, 356 with references; *see also* section III.
52. *See* OECD PE Report, Part I, sections 47 ss. with detailed analysis.
53. *See also* BRÜLISAUER & DIETSCHI, 61/74 with further references.

### 2 Interest Rates for Loans from the Head Offices

Interest paid on internal 'loans' between the head offices and the PE will not appear in the legal entity's overall commercial financials. However, as internal dealings, they will be reflected in the separate accounts of the head offices and the PE. As far as they are accepted as debt for tax purposes, i.e., according to the OECD's practice, when connected with fully-fledged treasury functions actually performed by the PE,[54] interest payments ought to be accepted as tax-deductible expenses in the PE's accounts. If the internal loans exceed the admissible debt under domestic thin capitalization rules, the deduction and the taxable profit respectively might be corrected for tax purposes.[55] In addition, domestic practice based on unilateral law might impose further requirements such as only allowing internal interest payments for internal 'loans' (dealings) insofar as they correspond to external loans.[56]

Any interest paid will have to be at arm's length. While tax administrations may provide for domestic safe haven rules,[57] the taxpayer must be allowed to demonstrate that interest rates deriving from such safe haven rules are at arm's length based on internal or external benchmarks.[58] However, these must be thoroughly documented, comparable and up-to-date. Neither is it sufficient to rely on average group financing costs or examples from some years ago nor is a tax administration likely to accept a general confirmation by the head offices financing bank.[59]

Against this background, we now discuss a case study.

## V CASE STUDY

### 1 Facts of the Case

*Preliminary remark: Please note that all financials shown, and amounts used only serve for illustrating the attribution and a possible calculation mechanism for the balance sheet positions and profits of the head offices and the Swiss PE from a Swiss point of view. They do not take into account any business or other considerations, i.e., whether the chosen attribution of functions, external loans or dealings is suitable in a certain setting.*

The company in our case study is part of a worldwide group manufacturing industrial goods. We will call it 'EuropeCo'. It is headquartered in a European country. On the one hand, it holds some participations and intellectual property (IP). On the other hand, it maintains a finance branch in Switzerland as a PE (the 'Finance Branch' or 'PE'). As provided for by the civil law rules of Switzerland, the Finance Branch is

54. OECD PE Report, Part I, section 158.
55. *See* case study below with an example calculation.
56. As is the case for Switzerland, *see* LOCHER, MARANTELLI & OPEL, 396 f. with further references.
57. *See, e.g.*, for Switzerland SFTA Circular Letter Interest Rates CHF, and SFTA Circular Letter Interest Rates FCR.
58. *See also* STOCKER, 793.
59. R. GÄCHTER & M. WALT, Internationale Finanzierungen, In- und Outbound Themen, IFF 23 November 2021, 17 ff.

registered in the Swiss register of commerce as a foreign branch ('Zweigniederlassung', 'succursale'). Switzerland and the residence country of the head offices have entered into a tax treaty based on the 2008 version of the OECD Model Convention.[60] The Finance Branch provides various treasury and cash pooling services to the other group companies as well as to its head offices abroad. It has a rented office in Switzerland and currently has six employees (480% full-time equivalents (FTE)). For our profit allocation case study, the following areas of activity are of further interest:

- granting of loans to different group companies (remuneration: interest payments on outstanding amounts);
- cash pooling and financial administration services to different group companies (remuneration: based on amounts managed and costs incurred);
- financial administration services for its head offices (remuneration: cost-based).

The employees are responsible for the day-to-day cash management of the group companies as well as the management of the intra-group financial relationships with longer maturities, granting loans and aligning maturities. They cover the whole spectrum of risk management adhering to the intra-group financing, in particular, currency risks and interest rate risk and effect hedging transactions where required. They maintain relationships and contracts with external service providers and financial institutions. They also effect internal and external payments, salary payments, intra-group clearing and provide for the liquidity management throughout the group. They record the relevant accounting entries in the information technology (IT) system of the group companies and their cost centres, where applicable. They continuously work on intra-group financing policy issues and eventually report to the Chief Financial Officer of the group located in a third country.

## 2 Possible Solution from a Swiss Perspective

### *A Allocation of Assets and Liabilities (Balance Sheet)*

While EuropeCo is one legal entity, its taxable profits are divided between its head offices abroad and the Finance Branch PE. In particular, EuropeCo is subject to taxation in Switzerland for the profits of the Finance Branch, as well as for the capital attributed thereto.

The legal basis for the taxation of the profits of the Finance Branch in Switzerland lies in Swiss unilateral law, in particular, the tax liability for foreign enterprises carrying out business activities in Switzerland through a PE – the law states that the profit earned in Switzerland is the profit to be taxed.[61] Having said that, regardless of a statutory obligation to maintain a certain accounting standard, the basis for the

60. In particular Article 7 OECD MC; *see* section III.1 above regarding the separate entity approach.
61. Articles 52(2) and (4), 51(1)(b) and (2) DBG.

taxable profit in Switzerland will be the financials of Finance Branch established according to Swiss commercial law (accounting) rules.[62]

To establish a balance sheet and the corresponding P&L for the Finance Branch, in a *first step*, the balance sheet of EuropeCo as legal entity will be taken as the basis. The positions in EuropeCo's basic balance sheet are based on transactions with third parties. To maintain comparable figures, the balance sheet of the head offices is shown according to Swiss statutory accounting standards and in CHF (*see* Table 47.1).

*Table 47.1 Basic Balance Sheet of EuropeCo (in CHF)*

| | | | |
|---|---|---|---|
| Cash | 220,000,000 | 10,000 | Accrued Expenses |
| Receivables (Cash Pooling Fees) | 500,000 | 1,410,000 | Bank Liabilities |
| Receivables(Cash Pooling) | 30,000,000 | 405,000,000 | Liabilities (Cash Pooling) |
| Loans Receivable | 1,600,000,000 | 600,000,000 | Loans (Bank) |
| Foreign Exchange (FX) Transactions | 459,999 | 380,000 | FX Transactions |
| Various Receivables | 40,000 | 1,200,000 | Various Liabilities |
| Participations | 49,000,000 | | |
| Intangibles | 1 | | |
| | | 892,000,000 | Equity |
| Total Assets | 1,900,000,000 | 1,900,000,000 | Total Liabilities and Equity |

In a *second step*, all assets and liabilities will be allocated to the head offices and to the branch. In the example at hand, the head offices have taken out the external loans necessary to finance the group's activities (in a life setting, the external debt will not always but often be raised directly by the Finance Branch PE), while the cash pooling and the IC receivables are attributed to the PE. The delta in the assets and liabilities resulting from this allocation is shown as '*PE Account*' and '*Head Offices Account*' respectively. In principle, even though there is no actual transaction, from an AOA perspective, these positions would constitute a loan receivable/payable position from the head offices to the branch and vice-versa (*see* Tables 47.2 and 47.3).

*Table 47.2 Separated Balance Sheet of EuropeCo Head Offices (in CHF)*

| | | | |
|---|---|---|---|
| Cash | 20,000,000 | 2,000 | Accrued Expenses |
| Various Receivables | 10,000 | 600,000,000 | Loans (Bank) |
| Participations | 49,000,000 | 1,000,000 | Various Liabilities |
| Intangibles | 1 | | |

62. *See* section II.3 above.

| | | | |
|---|---|---|---|
| PE Account | 1,423,991,999 | 892,000,000 | Equity |
| Total Assets | 1,493,002,000 | 1,493,002,000 | Total Liabilities and Equity |

*Table 47.3 Separated Balance Sheet of Swiss Finance Branch PE (in CHF)*

| | | | |
|---|---|---|---|
| Cash | 200,000,000 | 8,000 | Accrued Expenses |
| Receivables (Cash Pooling Fees) | 500,000 | 1,410,000 | Bank Liabilities |
| Receivables (Cash Pooling) | 30,000,000 | 405,000,000 | Liabilities (Cash Pooling) |
| Loans Receivable | 1,600,000,000 | 380,000 | FX Transactions |
| FX Transactions | 459,999 | 200,000 | Various Liabilities |
| Various Receivables | 30,000 | 1,423,991,999 | Head Offices Account |
| Total Assets | 1,830,989,999 | 1,830,989,999 | Total Liabilities and Equity |

In a *third step*, internal dealings between the head offices and the Finance Branch need to be taken into account in order to establish complete accounts of the PE. For the establishment of the balance sheet, it needs to be determined which portion of the delta between the head offices' and the PE's external positions needs to be allocated to the PE as adequate free equity from a stand-alone perspective. This allocation needs to be based on the methods described above.[63] From a Swiss perspective, the PE needs to be attributed a minimum capital which may be determined based on the thin capitalization rules, in particular, a minimum one-seventh (14%) equity for finance companies.[64] From the head offices' jurisdiction's perspective, there will be a maximum equity which may be carved-out from domestic taxation for the deemed capitalization of the foreign PE. Furthermore, any applicable hybrid mismatch and anti-avoidance provisions need to be taken into account. For the example at hand, it is assumed that the PE shall be attributed a free capital ('*Branch Capital*') of CHF 400,000,000, corresponding to 23 % of the assets allocated to the PE. This is more than the minimum equity required by the Swiss thin capitalization rules (14%) and leaves the head offices with a presumably sufficient 45% equity financing of CHF 492,000,000.[65] The '*PE Account*' position and the '*Head Offices Account*' position are reduced accordingly.

*Table 47.4 Separated Balance Sheet of EuropeCo Head Offices (in CHF, Corrected)*

| | | | |
|---|---|---|---|
| Cash | 20,000,000 | 2,000 | Accrued Expenses |
| Various Receivables | 10,000 | 600,000,000 | Loans (Bank) |

63. *See* section IV.1 above.
64. SFTA Circular no. 6 regarding thin capitalization (*Verdecktes Eigenkapital*).
65. This attribution is of course subject to the individual functional and factual analysis of the enterprise involved and subject to the criteria of the capital allocation method applied. For the purpose of this basic case study, this question is not pursued here.

| | | | |
|---|---|---|---|
| Participations | 49,000,000 | 1,000,000 | Various Liabilities |
| Intangibles | 1 | | |
| PE Account | 1,023,991,999 | 492,000,000 | Equity |
| Total Assets | 1,093,002,000 | 1,093,002,000 | Total Liabilities and Equity |

*Table 47.5 Separated Balance sheet of Swiss Finance Branch PE (in CHF, Corrected)*

| | | | |
|---|---|---|---|
| Cash | 200,000,000 | 8,000 | Accrued Expenses |
| Receivables (Cash Pooling Fees) | 500,000 | 1,410,000 | Bank Liabilities |
| Receivables (Cash Pooling) | 30,000,000 | 405,000,000 | Liabilities (Cash Pooling) |
| Loans Receivable | 1,600,000,000 | 380,000 | FX Transactions |
| FX Transactions | 459,999 | 200,000 | Various Liabilities |
| Various Receivables | 30,000 | 1,023,991,999 | Head Offices Account |
| | | 400,000,000 | Branch Capital |
| Total Assets | 1,830,989,999 | 1,830,989,999 | Total Liabilities and Equity |

## B Establishment of P&L

Based on the allocation of the balance sheet positions, a corresponding allocation may then be effected for the P&L positions connected with the balance sheet positions and the according functions attributed to the head offices and the PE.

Established in a *first step*, the P&L of EuropeCo without any internal dealings looks as follows (*see* Table 47.6).

*Table 47.6 P&L of EuropeCo (in CHF)*

| | |
|---|---|
| Interest Income Short Term | 0 |
| Interest Income Loans | 16,000,000 |
| Guarantee Commissions | 150,000 |
| Cash Pooling and Service Fees | 1,300,000 |
| Other Financial Income | 2,000 |
| Participation Income | 100,000,000 |
| Royalties | 20,000,000 |
| Interest Expenses | -3,000,000 |
| Other Financial Expenses | -2,000 |
| Salary Costs | -1,250,000 |
| Social Security | -300,000 |
| Other Personnel Costs | -10,000 |

| | |
|---|---|
| Travel & Expenses | -20,000 |
| Rent (Offices) | -200,000 |
| Various Operating Expenses | -400,000 |
| Currency Result | -420,000 |
| Profit before Taxes | 131,850,000 |

In a *second step*, based on the allocation of the balance sheet positions, the external P&L positions will then be attributed to each of the head offices and the Finance Branch (*see* Table 47.4).

*Table 47.7 P&L of EuropeCo with Allocation of External Positions to Head Offices and Swiss Finance Branch PE (in CHF)*

| | *Overall* | *Head Offices* | *PE* |
|---|---|---|---|
| Interest Income Short Term | 0 | 0 | 0 |
| Interest Income Loans | 16,000,000 | 0 | 16,000,000 |
| Guarantee Commissions | 150,000 | 0 | 150,000 |
| Cash Pooling and Service Fees | 2,300,000 | 0 | 2,300,000 |
| Other Financial Income | 2,000 | 0 | 2,000 |
| Participation Income | 100,000,000 | 100,000,000 | 0 |
| Royalties | 20,000,000 | 20,000,000 | |
| Interest Expenses | -3,000,000 | -3,000,000 | |
| Other Financial Expenses | -2,000 | 0 | -2,000 |
| Salary Costs | -1,250,000 | -350,000 | -900,000 |
| Social Security | -300,000 | -90,000 | -210,000 |
| Other Personnel Costs | -10,000 | -2,000 | -8,000 |
| Travel & Expenses | -20,000 | -2,000 | -18,000 |
| Rent (Offices) | -200,000 | -120,000 | -80,000 |
| Various Operating Expenses | -400,000 | -100,000 | -300,000 |
| Currency Result | -420,000 | 0 | -420,000 |
| Profit before Taxes | 132,850,000 | 116,336,000 | 16,514,000 |

In a *third step*, the earnings and expenses corresponding to the internal dealings between head offices and branch need to be taken into account and added to the separated P&L calculations.

In particular, the following positions are relevant (*see* shaded positions in Table 47.8).

### *a* *Loans and 'Financing' of PE*

(1) While the 'Branch Capital' is treated as deemed equity for the PE, the remaining head offices account is treated as a 'loan' from the head offices to

the PE of CHF 1,023,991,999, leading to interest expenses of CHF 7,679,940 for the PE (at 0.75% p.a.).

(2) Accordingly, at the level of the head offices, a position of interest income in the same amount of CHF 7,679,940 is recorded as an earnings position.

(3) The loans granted by the Finance Branch to other group companies of CHF 1,600,000,000 (external transaction) lead to an interest income of CHF 16,000,000 ('Interest Income Loans', at 1% p.a.).

(4) The interest expenses of the head offices of CHF 3,000,000 are connected to the bank loans of CHF 600,000,000 (external transaction) the head offices have taken out at 0.5% p.a.

(5) When comparing the different interest rates paid, the figures show that each of the head offices and the PE retains an interest margin as remuneration for the risks attached to the transactions and as may be required by tax administrations. In Switzerland, the Swiss Federal Tax Administration Circular Letters provides safe haven interest rates for loans to and from related parties with a minimum interest spread margin to be retained in the branch:[66]
   - head offices retain 0.25% (0.5% paid for bank loans, 0.75% received for internal loans to Finance Branch);
   - Finance Branch retains 0.25% (0.75% paid for internal loans from head offices, 1% received for loans to group companies).

### b *Cash Pooling Management and Financial Administration Services to Different Group Companies and Between Head Offices and Finance Branch*

The cash pooling management and financial administration services are remunerated at an arm's length price to be determined according to the OECD TP Guidelines.[67] In the case study at hand, the cash pooling services are remunerated with a 0.5% fee on the relevant amounts. The remuneration for the administrative and further financial services is based on the costs of the PE (cost-plus). The earnings are shown in the position 'Cash Pooling and Service Fees' of the P&L of EuropeCo and the PE respectively. The remuneration based on external transactions with other legal entities amounts to CHF 2,300,000 and is fully attributed to the PE.

In addition, the services from the PE to the head offices with a corresponding remuneration of CHF 200,000 need to be taken into account as internal dealings. Hence, the PE generates stand-alone earnings of a total of CHF 2,500,000 in said Cash Pooling and Service Fees, while the head offices, on a stand-alone basis, booking an expense of CHF 200,000. This example shows the importance of the acceptance of internal dealings to avoid not only double taxation but also over taxation – while the branch 'earns' a total of CHF 2,500,000 from its 'Cash Pooling and Service Fees', the

66. *See* section IV.1 above; SFTA Circular Letter Interest Rates CHF, and SFTA Circular Letter Interest Rates FCR.
67. *See* LOCHER, MARANTELLI & OPEL, 393 s. regarding the permissibility to charge for specific services.

external net earnings of EuropeCo under this position only amount to CHF 2,300,000. After the correction of the internal dealings, the profit before taxes of the head offices is increased to CHF 123,815,940 (without internal dealings: CHF 116,336,000, *see* Table 47.7) and the profit before taxes of the PE is reduced to CHF 9,034,060 (without internal dealings: CHF 16,514,000, *see* Table 47.7). Added up, this again gives CHF 132,850,000.

*Table 47.8 P&L of EuropeCo with Allocation of External and Internal Dealings' Positions to Head Offices and Swiss Finance Branch PE (in CHF)*

| | *Overall* | *Head Offices* | *PE* |
|---|---|---|---|
| Interest Income Short Term | 0 | 0 | 0 |
| Interest Income Loans | 16,000,000 | 0 | 16,000,000 |
| Interest Income PE Account | | 7,679,940 | |
| Guarantee Commissions | 150,000 | 0 | 150,000 |
| Cash Pooling and Service Fees | 2,300,000 | -200,0000 | 2,500,000 |
| Other Financial Income | 2,000 | 0 | 2,000 |
| Participation Income | 100,000,000 | 100,000,000 | 0 |
| Royalties | 20,000,000 | 20,000,000 | |
| Interest Expenses | -3,000,000 | -3,000,000 | |
| Interest Expenses Head Offices Account | | | -7,679,940 |
| Other Financial Expenses | -2,000 | 0 | -2,000 |
| Salary Costs | -1,250,000 | -350,000 | -900,000 |
| Social Security | -300,000 | -90,000 | -210,000 |
| Other Personnel Costs | -10,000 | -2,000 | -8,000 |
| Travel & Expenses | -20,000 | -2,000 | -18,000 |
| Rent (Offices) | -200,000 | -120,000 | -80,000 |
| Various Operating Expenses | -400,000 | -100,000 | -300,000 |
| Currency Result | -420,000 | 0 | -420,000 |
| Profit before Taxes | 132,850,000 | 123,815,940 | 9,034,060 |

As the relevant free equity of the PE is assumed to meet the requirements of the capital allocation methods for tax purposes,[68] no further correction is needed or imposed by a domestic tax administration.[69]

68. *See* sections IV.1 and IV.2.A above.
69. For an example of a correction calculation by a Swiss tax administration, *see* Swiss Federal Supreme Court Decision 2C_560/2014, 2C_561/2014, C.

## VI CONCLUSIONS

When treasury activities are attributed to a PE, special consideration needs to be given to the allocation of free capital and profit to such PE. In contrast to a subsidiary, a PE is part of the same legal entity as its head offices, and the two parts of the enterprise cannot legally be separated. A treasury PE may partially or fully rely on its head offices for the internal financing of its activities, in particular, the granting of loans to other group companies. Internal dealings are, therefore, an integrated part of the PE's stand-alone accounting which is the basis for its commercial law financial statements.

With the path for the allocation of profit and capital to the PE set in the accounting of the PE, an assessment of such accounts for tax purposes will:

- start with the AOA separate entity approach, i.e., a functional and factual analysis of the PE and its activities with a particular focus on significant people functions;
- verify the attribution of the assets and liabilities of the enterprise belonging to the PE based on its functions performed;
- examine the 'free capital' to be attributed to the PE based on the risks taken on by the PE in connection with the functions performed and the assets used;
- establish the P&L of the PE for tax purposes based on the commercial law P&L;
- take into account any internal dealings, in particular loans and other financial transactions as well as services between head offices and the PE;
- make sure that the attribution so effected does result in neither a double taxation or an over taxation, nor a hybrid mismatch or similar based on any applicable anti-abuse rules.

CHAPTER 48

# The Recognition of Financial Dealings Between Head Office and Permanent Establishments under the AOA: Focus on External and Internal Dealings

*Xaver Ditz*[*]

## I PRINCIPLES OF THE AOA

### 1 Development and Approach

It is now almost 30 years since the Organisation for Economic Co-operation and Development (OECD) published a report focusing on the attribution of profits between a head office and permanent establishments (PEs) in the context of the service relationships within a company, and thus also the scope of the deemed independence of a PE.[1] The question at the heart of the 1994 report was the extent to which a market-oriented price or a mere reimbursement of expenses for services between the head office and the PE should be charged. The OECD found that the arm's length principle codified in Article 7 paragraph 2 OECD-MC fundamentally corresponds to the principle under Article 9 OECD-MC for associated enterprises.[2] Despite this finding, however, the application of the arm's length principle in respect of the treatment of individual intra-company supply and service relationships remained limited, which meant that this methodological maxim was not stringently implemented.

* The views and opinions set forth herein are the personal views or opinions of the authors; they do not necessarily reflect views or opinions of the organisation with which the authors are associated.

1. OECD, Attribution of Income to Permanent Establishments, Paris 1994.
2. DITZ, Internationale Gewinnabgrenzung bei Betriebsstätten, 114 ff.

The OECD soon returned to the issue of attribution of profits to PEs. On 17 July 2008, it published a new report: the Report on the Attribution of Profits to Permanent Establishments (the 'OECD Permanent Establishment Report 2008').[3] This report defined the functionally separate entity approach as the Authorised OECD Approach (AOA).[4] The AOA marked the first comprehensive OECD concept for interpreting the deemed independence of a PE for the purposes of profit attribution, going beyond the analysis of PE profit attribution in the OECD Permanent Establishment Report of 1994. The functionally separate entity approach presented in detail in the OECD Permanent Establishment Report 2008 was subsequently applied without restriction in the OECD Model Commentary of 2010. Following editorial revision and alignment to the OECD Transfer Pricing Guidelines 2010, the principles developed were finally published in a new OECD report on 22 July 2010 (the 'OECD Permanent Establishment Report 2010'). The core proposition of the AOA is that the PE is regarded as an independent enterprise that performs its own functions, owns or uses its own assets, and bears its own risks. Accordingly, the deemed independence of the PE pursuant to Article 7 paragraph 2 OECD-MC is implemented without restriction, with the PE's profit being attributed in two stages.[5]

### *A* *AOA Stage 1*

In the first stage, a comprehensive functional analysis is carried out. Here, the functions performed by the head office and the PE, the risks they assume, the assets they use, and their capital resources are analysed in detail, and the resulting intra-company supply and service relationships (dealings) are identified.[6]

#### *a* *Functional Analysis*

The functional analysis treats the parts of the enterprise involved as independent and autonomous enterprises. As a result, the principles set out for the functional analysis of associated enterprises in the OECD Guidelines 2022 should be applied.[7] The objective is a thorough and detailed[8] analysis of the functions performed by the individual parts of the enterprise. It must also be determined whether these parts bear the hallmarks of routine companies or strategic companies.[9] The decisive question in this context is whether a PE performs functions largely autonomously and independently of its head office (in which case it plays a strategic role) or merely acts as a service provider for another part of the enterprise (in which case it carries out routine functions). Whether

3. OECD, Report on the Attribution of Profits to Permanent Establishments of 17 July 2008, Paris 2008. *See also* BENNET, ET 2008, 467 ff.
4. On the development of the Authorised OECD Approach *see also* BENNET & DUNAHOU, Intertax 2005, 51 ff.; RUSSO, ITPJ 2005, 7 ff.; *Ditz*, ISR 2012, 48 ff.
5. Part I OECD Permanent Establishment Report 2010, marginal no. 10.
6. *Ibid.*, marginal nos 60 ff.
7. *Ibid.*, marginal no. 60.
8. *Ibid.*, marginal no. 67.
9. *Ibid.*, marginal no. 60.

a PE is classed as dependent or independent has a direct impact on the identification and valuation of intra-company supply and service relationships.[10] Consequently, the functional analysis also needs to examine what effects the performance of the function by the PE has on the generation of profits, i.e., whether the function in question is a main function or a secondary or supporting one. Another key aspect of the functional analysis is the identification of the significant people functions.[11] This is because, according to the OECD, it is these functions that form the basis of the allocation of assets and risks to the various parts of the enterprise. The analysis of the people functions takes account of which people perform which activities in which parts of the enterprise or assume which areas of responsibility. People functions can range from support or ancillary functions to significant functions that imply the assumption of risk.[12]

### *b* *Attribution of Risks*

Whereas risks can be attributed between associated enterprises by means of contractual agreements, this is not possible for PEs because the head office and the PE are treated as a unity under civil law. As a result, the risks of the enterprise as a whole (e.g., inventory, credit, currency, interest rate, market, product and warranty risks) are attributed by taking into account the significant people functions.[13] If, for example, products manufactured by the head office are delivered to the PE for distribution, the inventory risks resulting from stockpiling and the collection risk resulting from possible bad debts are generally attributable to the PE.[14]

### *c* *Attribution of Assets*

Assets are attributed on the basis of a functional relationship. The attribution of tangible assets generally depends on the place of use. For intangible assets, however, the attribution depends on the part of the enterprise in which the significant people functions are performed in relation to the intangible asset in question. Decisions on the development risk and its management are key in this respect.[15]

### *d* *Attribution of Free Capital*

With regard to the capital resources of the PE, the OECD assumes in principle that the PE has an appropriate amount of capital in order to support the functions it performs, the assets it uses, and the risks it assumes.[16] The endowment of a PE with free capital

10. *Ibid.*, marginal no. 61.
11. *Ibid.*, marginal no. 62.
12. *Ibid.*
13. *Ibid.*, marginal no. 70.
14. *Ibid.*, marginal nos 23-25.
15. *Ibid.*, marginal nos 72 ff.
16. *Ibid.*, marginal no. 107.

is, therefore, necessarily subsequent to the attribution of assets and risks. This also means that it is essentially based on the functional analysis, with the result that the attribution of significant people functions to the PE also has a direct effect on the amount of its free capital.

### *B* *AOA Stage 2*

The AOA recognises the intra-company supply and service relationships identified in the functional analysis.[17] This applies not only to intra-company supplies of goods but also to all conceivable service relationships between unrelated third parties (such as services and the transfer of use of tangible and intangible assets). Intra-company dealings are priced using the standard transfer pricing methods, i.e., the comparable uncontrolled price method, the resale price method, the cost-plus method, and the transaction-based profit methods. This applies both to the transfer of tangible and intangible assets and to the provision of intra-company services. The restriction of the arm's length principle to the transfer of assets, which was provided for in the OECD Permanent Establishment Report 1994 and in the OECD-MC of 1994 and 2008, was thus rejected by the OECD from 2010 onwards. For the purposes of profit attribution, the deemed independence of the PE is therefore applied without restriction.

## 2 The AOA Transposed into German Law

The AOA was transposed into German law in section 1 of the Foreign Tax Act (*Außensteuergesetz* (AStG)) in 2013.[18] From the very beginning of the legislative procedure, the German legislature intended to extend the scope of application of section 1 AStG to include the attribution of profits to PEs.[19] To this end, for financial years beginning after 31 December 2012, the deemed business relationships between the head office and the PE in section 1(4) sentence 1 no. 2 AStG ('assumed contractual business relationships') laid the foundation for section 1(5) sentence 1 AStG. Section 1(5) AStG provides for an income adjustment if the arm's length principle is not observed for intra-company supply and service relationships between the head office and the PE. In this context, the PE is treated as a separate and independent enterprise, unless its affiliation to the enterprise as a whole requires a different treatment. Section 1(5) AStG applies only to legally dependent PEs, regardless of the legal form of the enterprise, whereby the provision refers to both PEs and permanent representatives (section 1(5) sentence 5 AStG).[20] The profit attribution to PEs is again carried out in two stages, in line with the approach described above. Detailed and specific requirements

17. *Ibid.*, marginal no. 172.
18. The AOA was transposed into German law with the Administrative Cooperation Directive Implementation Act (AmtshilfeRLUmsG) of 5 June 2013, Federal Law Gazette I 2013, 1809. Given that the AOA is also a profit determination provision, its systematic placement in section 1 AStG is sometimes rightly criticised because section 1 AStG is an adjustment provision.
19. *Wassermeyer*, IStR 2012, 277 ff.
20. Bundestag printed paper 17/13722 of 5 June 2013.

for transposing the AOA into German law can be found in particular in the Ordinance on the Allocation of Profits of Permanent Establishments (*Betriebsstättengewinnaufteilungsverordnung* (BsGaV)).[21] In particular, section 3 BsGaV establishes the obligation to prepare auxiliary and ancillary accounts, wherein the financial statements must contain the net profit or loss for the PE.

## II CAPITAL RESOURCES OF THE PE

### 1 Attribution of Liability Items under the AOA

The OECD Permanent Establishment Report 2010 devotes an extensive chapter to the determination of the PE's free capital.[22] As a principle, the OECD treats the PE as having an appropriate amount of capital in order to support the functions it performs, the assets it uses, and the risks it assumes.[23] The endowment of a PE with 'free capital' is, therefore, subsequent to the attribution of assets and risks. Thus, it is essentially based on the functional analysis. For determining the capital resources of the PE, the OECD assumes that all parts of the enterprise enjoy the same creditworthiness as the enterprise of which they are a part.[24] This follows from the immutable legal unity of the enterprise as a whole and forms an important distinguishing feature in comparison to enterprises with legally independent parts.

The OECD does not stipulate any one particular method for determining free capital (understood as endowment capital of the PE). Rather, it describes various methods with their advantages and disadvantages.[25] The following methods are presented in detail.

*Capital allocation method*:[26] Under the capital allocation method, the equity of the enterprise as a whole is allocated between the head office and the PE in proportion to the assets allocated and the risks assumed. If the functional analysis shows, for example, that 10% of the assets and/or risks of the enterprise as a whole are attributable to the PE, the PE must be attributed 10% of the total equity of the enterprise as a whole. If certain amounts of equity are reserved (say, for acquisitions or dividend distributions), it is permissible to reduce the attributable equity.[27] However, the OECD largely leaves aside the question of the valuation of assets and (above all) risks, which is extremely relevant in practice.[28]

21. Federal Law Gazette I 2014, 1603. In addition, the German tax authorities issued a circular setting out their view on the attribution of profits to PEs; cf. Federal Ministry of 22 December 2016, Federal Tax Gazette I 2017, 182.
22. Part I OECD Permanent Establishment Report 2010, marginal nos 99 ff.
23. *Ibid.*, marginal no. 107.
24. *Ibid.*, marginal no. 99.
25. In Part I OECD Permanent Establishment Report 2010, marginal no. 147, the OECD openly admits in this context that it was not possible to develop a single internationally accepted approach for attributing the necessary free capital.
26. Part I OECD Permanent Establishment Report 2010, marginal nos 121 ff.
27. *Ibid.*, marginal no. 126.
28. In principle, it should be possible to recognise the book values, the market values or the historical acquisition costs. Since enterprises outside the financial industry use equity mainly for

*Economic capital allocation method:*[29] Under the economic capital allocation method, the capital resources of the PE are determined on the basis of internal risk models. In the OECD's view, this method corresponds to the AOA, although the OECD (rightly) sees practical application difficulties.

*Arm's length method:*[30] Under this method, the equity attributable to the PE corresponds to the equity it would show as an independent enterprise under comparable conditions. However, the absolute amount of the comparable enterprise's equity receives less weighting than a relative value, such as the ratio of equity to debt. Nevertheless, even the OECD Permanent Establishment Report 2010 acknowledges problems that arise in connection with determining 'arm's length' equity in this way.[31] The OECD fails to recognise that the determination of appropriate free capital of the PE is not amenable to an arm's length comparison.

*Safe haven method:*[32] Under this method, the appropriate endowment of a PE with equity is derived from the minimum capital resources of a comparable enterprise (in particular, taking into account regulatory requirements in the banking sector).

*Thinly capitalised enterprises:*[33] Finally, with respect to capital allocation, the OECD addresses the problem of thinly capitalised enterprises. In this case, the mere allocation of the equity of the enterprise as a whole would not lead to appropriate results. Therefore, the OECD suggests first adjusting the equity of the whole enterprise to an arm's length level and then allocating it to the PEs.[34]

These principles apply to the allocation of both equity and debt.

## 2 Attribution of Liability Items under German Law

The German legislature has cherry-picked from the above methods proposed by the OECD for determining free capital and has created differentiating rules for domestic and foreign PEs. Under section 12(1) BsGaV, which generally stipulates the application of the capital allocation method, for example, a domestic PE of a foreign enterprise is attributed such portion of the enterprise's equity capital as, at the beginning of the fiscal year, equates to the domestic PE's portion of the assets and of the opportunities and risks in proportion to the rest of the enterprise. Under section 12(4) BsGaV, however, the capital allocation method is not applied if the free capital calculated for the domestic PE using that method permanently produces results that a prudent and conscientious manager would not be willing to accept. This is the case, for example, if the domestic PE consistently generates losses due to high-interest expenses. The free capital of the domestic PE must then be recognised with the share in the equity of the consolidated group resulting from the proportion of the assets of the domestic PE to the

the acquisition of assets, equity is, in many cases, likely to be attributed on the basis of the acquisition costs or the book values of the assets shown in the balance sheet.

29. Part I OECD Permanent Establishment Report 2010, marginal no. 128.
30. *Ibid.*, marginal nos 129 ff.
31. *Ibid.*, marginal no. 132.
32. *Ibid.*, marginal nos 135 ff.
33. *Ibid.*, marginal no. 140.
34. *Ibid.*, marginal no. 143.

assets of the consolidated group. Finally, section 12(5) BsGaV stipulates that the minimum amount of free capital that must be attributed to a domestic PE is the capital actually shown in domestic commercial accounts of the domestic PE. Overall, this shows that the determination of the free capital for domestic PEs is complex and difficult to handle in practice.

*Example:*

Facts of the case: The domestic PE B produces and sells to third parties. B belongs to the foreign company T, which in turn belongs to the foreign group X. T reports an equity of 40. According to the capital allocation method, B would be allocated an endowment capital of 10. Due to the high interest expense, B shows permanent losses of 20 per year despite the positive operating results. The consolidated equity of X is 1,000. The capital ratio of B in relation to the equity of X is 10%.

Outcome: Since permanent losses occur due to the undercapitalisation of T, which a prudent and conscientious manager would not accept, the endowment capital is not determined according to the capital allocation method, but on the basis of the consolidated equity of X. B is, therefore, to be allocated endowment capital of 100 (10% of 1,000).

Unlike domestic PEs, foreign PEs are not subject to the application of the capital allocation method, but to the application of the minimum capital method. Under this method, at the beginning of a fiscal year, free capital must be attributed to a foreign PE of a domestic enterprise only if the enterprise provides evidence that the relevant amount of free capital is required for commercial reasons (section 13(1) BsGaV). Free capital exceeding that amount may be recognised only if, in the case in question, this higher amount produces a result for the PE that is more in line with the arm's length principle. However, the free capital must not exceed the amount that results from the application of the capital allocation method (section 13(2) BsGaV).

*Example:*

Facts of the case: The foreign PE A is part of the domestic enterprise M. A provides simple services to the rest of the enterprise. No assets are attributable to A, and A does not bear any significant risks.

Outcome: According to the minimum capital method, no endowment capital is attributable to A. There are no apparent business reasons for a higher endowment capital.

Modification: A is assigned assets intended for the provision of the service.

Outcome: According to the minimum capital method, no endowment capital is to be allocated to A. Insofar as business reasons are credibly shown (e.g., risks from the allocated assets), an appropriate endowment capital is to be allocated to A.

These rules – i.e., the application of the capital allocation method for domestic PEs and the application of the minimum capital method for foreign PEs – apply to all cases covered or not covered by a double taxation treaty (DTT), even if the relevant DTT does not contain a provision corresponding to Article 7 OECD-MC 2010. The distinction between domestic and foreign PEs provided for in German law is not based on the AOA but is centred around fiscal interests. This is because with a maximum allocation in the outbound case or a minimum allocation in the inbound case, the financing expense attributable to a domestic part of the enterprise is minimised.[35] Not uncommonly, this distinction results in double taxation and should therefore be viewed critically.

In addition to the free capital, the remaining liability items that are directly related to the assets and to the opportunities and risks attributed to the PE must also be attributed to the PE (section 14(1) BsGaV). However, this direct attribution of liabilities (mainly in the form of liabilities of the enterprise) is limited to the amount that remains after deducting the free capital from the balance sheet total of the PE, with the result that the other liabilities are regularly a residual. Any exceeding amount must be reduced pro rata and attributed to the head office or the management PE (section 14(2) sentence 2 BsGaV). Finally, a further indirect allocation of liability items to the PE is provided if the total of the free capital and the directly attributed liability items of this PE amounts to less than the balance sheet total (section 14(3) BsGaV).

## III ATTRIBUTION OF EXTERNAL FINANCING EXPENSES

The AOA recognises that the PE has certain financing needs, which are covered by both free capital and debt.[36] To take an example: The enterprise as a whole could take out a bank loan that is intended to contribute to the PE's funding needs. The interest payable on this bank loan is referred to as an external financing expense. In the OECD's view, such expenses must be allocated between the several parts of the enterprise. Various methods can be considered for allocating both the external financing expenses and the free capital, but they all pursue the same goal: to attribute interest expenses to the PE that are at arm's length.[37] First, the OECD mentions the tracing approach, in which borrowed funds are traced back to the third-party lender, and the interest expense is allocated to the PE for which the amount was borrowed. If and to the extent that the head office or another part of the enterprise has taken out a loan for another PE, the interest expense is therefore allocated internally in line with this origination.

*Example: Tracing approach*

Facts of the case: A-GmbH, a German limited liability company, develops, manufactures and sells cars and motorcycles. Its registered office is in Germany. It maintains a legally dependent (fixed place) PE in the Czech Republic, where spare parts are produced. At the beginning of financial year 01, it takes out a loan of EUR 1 million with X-Bank. With the money, it plans to purchase machinery that will be used for production in the foreign PE. The loan bears interest at 5% p.a., which means that A-GmbH pays interest in the amount of EUR 50,000 in 01.

Outcome: The interest expense of EUR 50,000 is attributable to the foreign PE.

However, it is not always possible to attribute expenses to this simply. This is where the fungibility approach, also mentioned by the OECD, can come into play. It

35. Cf. Kraft & Dombrowski, FR 2014, 1110 ff.
36. Cf. Part I OECD Permanent Establishment Report 2010, marginal no. 150.
37. Cf. *Ibid.*, marginal nos 151, 154.

can be used alone or alongside the tracing approach.[38] Under the fungibility approach, the actual interest expense incurred by the enterprise as a whole during an accounting period is allocated to the respective parts of the enterprise according to a certain key. The OECD does not give any examples of such an allocation key. However, it is obviously helpful to choose a key that is similar to the key used in allocating the free capital, to ensure that the balance sheet of the PE or the rest of the enterprise does not become unbalanced simply because different allocation keys are in use.

*Example: Fungibility approach*

A-GmbH (see above) had interest expenses totalling EUR 2 million in financial year 01, but at the end of the financial year, it can no longer be plausibly assessed what proportion of this amount is attributable to which of the numerous parts of the enterprise. The functional analysis showed that 20% of the assets of the enterprise as a whole are attributable to the Czech PE. As a result, 20% of the total equity was also attributed to the PE. With regard to the external financing expenses, it would be appropriate under the fungibility approach to attribute 20% of the interest expenses (EUR 400,000) to the Czech PE.

Under German law, the attribution of financing expenses (especially in the form of interest on borrowed capital) follows the attribution of directly attributed liability items.[39] Where the directly attributable liability items must be reduced on a pro rata basis,[40] this also applies to the financing expenses that are directly related to these directly attributable liability items. Finally, financing expenses of a foreign enterprise must be attributed to a domestic PE of this foreign enterprise only if these financing expenses are directly related to the PE's business activities.[41] The same applies to a foreign PE. In this case, the minimum portion of financing expenses attributable to it is the portion that equates to its portion of the domestic enterprise's external sales. The attribution of financing expenses must take into account that only the actually incurred (external) financing expenses, without a profit markup, are attributed. The charging of deemed interest is not permitted – including in respect of the free capital.

## IV RECOGNITION OF INTERNAL DEALINGS

### 1 Recognition of Internal Dealings in the General Exchange of Services

One of the key points of the AOA is that for the purposes of profit attribution, intra-company supply and service relationships between the head office and a PE must be recognised and remunerated at an arm's length price, even if the head office and the PE cannot enter into contracts with each other under civil law.[42] In this respect, the

38. *Ibid.*, marginal nos 154 ff.
39. Section 15(1) BsGaV.
40. Section 14(2) *ibid.*
41. Section 15(4) *ibid.*
42. For details on the recognition of dealings, *see* Part I OECD Permanent Establishment Report 2010, marginal no. 172.

OECD speaks of 'dealings' between the head office and the PE;[43] in German law, section 1(4) sentence 1 no. 2 AStG speaks of 'deemed contractual relationships'. The OECD acknowledges that there may be an exchange of supplies and services between the head office and its PE in the same way as between separate and independent enterprises. Internal dealings are, therefore, a direct consequence of the hypothetical independence of the PE.[44] However, the recognition of internal supply and service relationships is limited to the application of Articles 7 and 23A/B OECD-MC; it has no effect on the other provisions of the OECD-MC.[45] The OECD, therefore, takes the view that it is not possible to levy withholding taxes on internal service relationships (in particular on notional royalties).[46] Moreover, in the absence of contracts under the law of obligations,[47] recognising the service relationships for tax purposes is subject to more stringent requirements. For example, economically significant risks, responsibilities and benefits in respect of a dealing must be transferred between the parts of the enterprise.[48] Internal dealings must also be documented in the accounts, whereby, according to the OECD Permanent Establishment Report 2010, internal correspondence or other communication may be used for documentation purposes.[49] The aim is to ensure that the tax authorities of the Contracting States recognise internal dealings where the documentation of the internal dealing is consistent with the results of the functional analysis, where the documentation does not deviate from what independent enterprises would have reasonably agreed in a comparable situation, and the documented internal dealing does not violate the principles of the OECD Permanent Establishment Report 2010, for example, by transferring a risk independently of the underlying function.[50] In light of these requirements, not every internal transaction is automatically a dealing within the meaning of the AOA.

## 2 Dealings Not Recognised in Internal Financing Transactions

### A *Principle*

Although internal dealings are recognised in principle, the OECD does not recognise the intra-company transfer of money and the remuneration for guarantees,[51] unlike in the allocation of profits between associated enterprises. This corresponds to German national law under section 16(3) BsGaV. A PE using financial resources of the rest of the enterprise, therefore, represents an exception to the principle that economic transactions which would be regulated by agreements under the law of obligations

43. *Ibid.*, marginal no. 14.
44. *Ibid.*, marginal no. 172.
45. OECD-MC, Article 7 marginal no. 28 f.
46. Part I OECD Permanent Establishment Report 2010, marginal no. 203.
47. *Ibid.*, marginal no. 279.
48. *Ibid.*, marginal no. 178.
49. *Ibid.*, marginal no. 179.
50. OECD-MC, Article 7 marginal no. 26. According to Part I OECD Permanent Establishment Report 2010, marginal no. 181, marginal nos 1.48-1.54 and 1.64-1.69 of the OECD Guidelines 2010 should be applied.
51. Part I OECD Permanent Establishment Report 2010, marginal nos 101, 103.

between independent enterprises must be regarded as dealings or deemed contractual relationships between a PE and the head office.[52]

The OECD reasons that an enterprise as a whole generally enjoys the same creditworthiness. It states, for example, that equal creditworthiness precludes guarantee payments between the head office and the PE since it is not clear why one part of the enterprise, such as the head office, would have the higher creditworthiness necessary to enable it to guarantee the transactions undertaken by the PE.[53] This deviates from the treatment of associated enterprises, which, however, can be justified by the different legal forms involved. For such a guarantee to have substance, the capital needed to support the risks assumed would necessarily reside in a separate enterprise from that in which the risk of default occurs. However, capital and risks are not segregated from each other within a single legal enterprise.[54]

The German legislature also justifies this view with the fact that the equity and the other liabilities of the enterprise as a whole have already been attributed to the PE by way of apportionment. Recognising dealings would break with the principle that the equity and debt capital that the enterprise as a whole has raised externally or created in the balance sheet by way of a commitment is attributed by way of apportionment between the PE and the head office. In principle, this apportionment results in a balanced account. The German legislature takes the view that a subsequent intervention would make taxation more complicated, especially since, in addition, the effects from interest rate differentials assumed by the legislature as the primary motivation of the taxpayers cannot come into play due to the equal creditworthiness.

*Example:*

Facts of the case: Corporation A with its registered office and place of management in State A has a production plant D in Germany. A has 100% equity capital. D shows an appropriate endowment capital. For its own business activities, D acquires a machine from a third party. D does not have a sufficient amount of money to pay the purchase price. Therefore, A transfers the required amount to the bank account used by D for its business. Subsequently, D transfers the purchase price to the seller of the machine.

Outcome: The payment transaction does not establish a deal between A and D (no fictitious loan). There is no offsetting of fictitious interest.

In this way, however, the principle of freedom of financing (also with the same interest rates) is not sufficiently taken into account, which is why a ban on intra-company loans seems disproportionate.

## B Exception: Remuneration of the Treasury Function

Financing relationships between the head office and the PE are generally not recognised as dealings. An exception is made, however, where a part of the enterprise (the treasury centre) performs a financing function within the enterprise. In this case, the

52. For German law, *see* section 16(3) BsGaV.
53. Part I OECD Permanent Establishment Report 2010, marginal no. 101.
54. *Ibid.*, marginal no. 104.

OECD regards the treasury function as a service that must be remunerated accordingly by the service recipient.[55] Remuneration is based on the cost-plus method, with the cost base comprising the personnel and material expenses associated with the service, but not the actual interest expense. However, under the AOA, a fee may be charged only if there is clear evidence that the treasury centre provides services that go beyond the mere pooling of demand for liquidity. The greater the extent to which the treasury centre makes investment decisions and deals with complex financing issues, for which it may also call on external advisors (banks, corporate finance advisors and so on), the more likely it is to consider charging a service fee, as is the case with asset or portfolio managers. This applies not only to capitalisation services in the narrow sense but also to other treasury services such as hedging transactions. However, in order for such dealings to be recognised as remunerable, the part of the enterprise to which the risk is transferred must have the expertise to manage the risk and to perform the significant people functions in respect of those risks.[56] The performance of the treasury function must be regarded as a service even if it is performed not only for a specific PE but also for other enterprises of the group such as subsidiaries. In this case, the other enterprises would have to be included in the attribution of the services supplied by the treasury function. Moreover, if the enterprise as a whole has raised little or no outside capital, the OECD assumes that no people function is performed in the sense that it would lead to the recognition of treasury dealings.[57]

German law contains a regulation that is largely comparable with the OECD's explanations; it likewise considers the performance of the financing function within the enterprise as a service.[58] Under German law, the financing function comprises liquidity management, which includes in particular the raising of funds, the allocation of funds, and the external investment of liquidity surpluses.[59] If a part of an enterprise performs a function of this kind, the function is regarded as a service that must be remunerated at arm's length under German law by applying the cost-plus method or the transactional net margin method.[60]

## V CONCLUSION

The AOA treats a PE as a separate and independent enterprise for the purposes of profit attribution. In principle, profits are attributed in two stages. First, a detailed functional analysis is carried out, on the basis of which certain assets and risks are allocated to the PE depending on the people functions it performs, and the PE is allocated its free capital. Second, it is generally recognised that there may be internal supply and service relationships between the head office and the PE that must be priced at arm's length. However, financial dealings between the head office and the PE give rise to certain

55. *Ibid.*, marginal no. 159.
56. *Ibid.*, marginal no. 161.
57. *Ibid.*, marginal nos 153, 157.
58. Section 17(2) BsGaV.
59. Section 17(1) *ibid.*
60. Section 17(2) *ibid.*

special aspects that must be observed. One of these is that the external financing expenses of the enterprise as a whole must be attributed to the individual parts of the enterprise according to their cause or origin. Another is that for internal financing dealings, an exception is made to the principle that internal dealings between the head office and the PE are generally recognised. Although such internal dealings are recognised in principle, the offsetting of intra-group loans and guarantees is not permitted by the OECD, with the result that the AOA has not been fully or consistently implemented in this area. For treasury services, however, there is a reverse exception.

# CHAPTER 49
# Allocating Financial Assets to a PE and Corresponding Income Using the AOA

*Thomas Hug*[*]

## I PRELIMINARY REMARKS

This chapter is aimed at addressing how the arm's length remuneration for financial dealings within the same enterprise (intra-enterprise financial dealings) shall be determined if the enterprise has one or several permanent establishments (PEs) in other tax jurisdictions. According to Article 5 Organisation for Economic Co-operation and Development (OECD) Model Tax Convention, the term 'permanent establishment' means a 'fixed place of business through which the business of an enterprise is wholly or partly carried out'.

The remuneration for intra-enterprise dealings between head offices and PE is not covered under the heading of transfer pricing according to Article 9 OECD Model Tax Convention (Associated Enterprises). This article has the purpose of avoiding economic double taxation[1] within a multinational enterprise (MNE) by allocating profits on a transactional basis to the various group entities which are *legally separate enterprises*, but economically under the control of another enterprise by means of a direct or indirect participation in the management, control, or capital (associated enterprise, Article 9 paragraph 1 OECD Model Tax Convention). The profit allocation follows the internationally accepted, transactional arm's length principle (ALP)

* The views and opinions set forth herein are the personal views or opinions of the authors; they do not necessarily reflect views or opinions of the organization with which the authors are associated.

1. S. Buriak & R. Holzinger, Introduction, in Lang / Storck / Petruzzi (eds), Attribution of Profits to Permanent Establishments (2020), 7; R. Holzinger, Art. 7 AOA vs Art. 9 OECD/UN Models, in Lang, Storck & Petruzzi (eds), Attribution of Profits to Permanent Establishments (2020), 31; Definition of economic double taxation: 'Taxation of the same income of different persons in the same period.'

whereas contractual relationships between associated enterprises shall be compensated as if the condition had been those between independent enterprises.

Head offices and PE, however, are in fact *not legally separate from the rest of the enterprise* and thus not having their own legal personality.[2] Consequently, there are no contractual relationships between head offices and PE which are to be compensated as between related enterprises of an MNE according to Article 9 OECD Model Tax Convention. While for accounting purposes, assets may be allocated to a PE or services provided between the head office and the PE may be charged, this has no legal force. The intra-enterprise profit allocation follows the principles of Article 7 OECD Model Tax Convention (Business Profits), especially the underlying Authorised OECD Approach (AOA). According to Article 7 paragraph 2 OECD Model Tax Convention, both the head office and the PE shall be hypothesized as functionally separate enterprises and any dealings between them shall be compensated using the transfer pricing tools. Contrary to Article 9 OECD Model Tax Convention, the purpose of Article 7 is not to avoid economic, but juridical double taxation.[3]

One could argue that from a practical perspective, both the profit allocation between separate enterprises on one side (Article 9 OECD Model Tax Convention) and between head offices and PE (Article 7 OECD Model Tax Convention) on the other side are ultimately based on the same transfer pricing principles and tools. However, whereas the entire rationale for the interpretation of Article 9 OECD Model Tax Convention is footed on the notion of '*significant functions and risks*',[4] Article 7 OECD Model Tax Convention is footed on the notion of '*significant people functions*' (SPF)[5] which might lead to interpretational differences.[6] Nevertheless, it can be added that the base erosion and profit shifting (BEPS) project also focused on the control functions exercised by persons, especially with regard to the allocation of risks according to Article 9, with the results that Articles 7 and 9 have certain similarities (*see* Table 49.1). Additionally, there are other practical variances which are further analysed in this chapter.

*Table 49.1 Article 7 Versus Article 9 OECD Model Tax Convention*

| | *Article 7* | *Article 9* |
|---|---|---|
| **Title** | Business Profits | Associated Enterprises |
| **Purpose** | Avoidance of *juridical* double taxation | Avoidance of *economic* double taxation |
| **Scope** | Profit allocation between head office and PE of an enterprise | Profit allocation between legally separate, but economically controlled enterprises of an MNE ('associated enterprises') |

2. HOLZINGER, 33.
3. BURIAK & HOLZINGER, 7; HOLZINGER, 31; Definition of juridical double taxation: 'Taxation of the same income of the same person in the same period.'
4. OECD TP Guidelines 2022, paras 1.60 ff.
5. OECD PE Report, Part I, section 16.
6. HOLZINGER, 33.

| | *Article 7* | *Article 9* |
|---|---|---|
| **Methodology** | Authorized OECD Approach: Transactional profit allocation via arm's length compensation (transfer pricing tools) for dealings between parts of the enterprise hypnotized as functionally separate entities | Arm's length-principle: Transactional profit allocation via arm's length compensation of contractual transactions between associated enterprises |
| **Rationale** | Profit allocation driven by 'SPFs' | Profit allocation is driven by 'significant functions and risks' |
| **Additional Guidance** | Report on the Attribution of Profits to Permanent Establishments (2010, OECD PE Report) | OECD Transfer Pricing (TP) Guidelines for Multinational Enterprises and Tax Administrations (2022, OECD Transfer Pricing Guidelines) |

## II AUTHORISED OECD APPROACH

The technical workings of the profit allocation between head offices and PE in light of Article 7 OECD Model Tax Convention already started in 1993/1994 and eventually resulted in a step-wise implementation of the Authorized OECD Approach (AOA) in 2008 and 2010, respectively.[7] As part of the BEPS project, the profit allocation principles were further discussed under action point 7 with a strong focus on specific aspects in view of the enlarged PE definition under Article 5 OECD Model Tax Convention (Permanent Establishment).

The AOA according to Article 7 paragraph 2 OECD Model Tax Convention anticipates that the profits to be attributed to a PE (and the head office) of an enterprise are the profits that the PE (and the head office) would 'have earned at arm's length, in particular in its dealings with other parts of the enterprise, if it were *a separate and independent enterprise* engaged in the same or similar activities under the same or similar conditions, taking into account the functions performed, assets used and risks assumed by the enterprise through the PE and through the other parts of the enterprise'.[8] This concept of hypothesizing the PE (and the head office) as a separate enterprise is known as the 'functionally separate entity approach' or 'separate and independent enterprise fiction'.[9]

It does not seek to allocate the overall profits of the whole enterprise to the PE and the head office (indirect method, based on allocation keys like revenues or full-time equivalent of employees) but, instead, requires that the profits attributable to a PE and head office be determined as if it were a separate enterprise. Profits may therefore be attributed to a PE or the head office even though the enterprise as a whole has never

7. Buriak & Holzinger, 4.
8. OECD PE Report, Part I, section 8; OECD Commentary, Article 7, section 2.
9. OECD Commentary, Article 7, section 28.

made profits or that no profits being attributed to a PE or head office even though the entire enterprise as a whole has made profits.[10]

The 'arm's length profit allocation'[11] based on the AOA requires a two-step analysis:

- *Step 1*: Performance of a functional and factual analysis based on the hypothesis that both the head office and the PE are separate and independent enterprises. This is carried out based on an analysis of the SPFs which dictate the allocation of functions, risks, and assets (including free capital). The functional and factual analysis performs the same role in the comparability analysis in a PE context under Article 7 OECD Model Tax Convention as it does in situations with associated enterprises under Article 9 OECD Model Tax Convention.[12] Nonetheless, the analysis is more complex in an Article 7 context as both the head office and the PE do not have an own legal personality[13] and hence cannot legally own the assets, assume the risks, possess the capital or contract with separate enterprises.[14] In the absence of a legal analysis, the AOA allocates the *economic ownership* of the assets and risks to the head office and/or PE for which *SPFs* were performed (mnemonic: 'assets and risks follow SPFs'[15]).[16]
- *Step 2*: Determination of the remuneration of any dealings between the hypothesized enterprises by applying the transfer pricing tools according to Article 9 OECD Model Tax Convention (i.e., comparability analysis, selection of the most appropriate transfer pricing method). Dealings between a PE and the head office (or between PEs) have no legal consequences for the enterprise as a whole. This implies a need for a greater scrutiny of dealings than of transactions between two associated enterprises, especially greater scrutiny of documentation (in the inevitable absence, for example, of legally binding contracts) that might otherwise exist, and considering the uniqueness of this issue, countries would wish to require taxpayers to demonstrate clearly that it would be appropriate to recognise the dealing.[17] The AOA is to undertake a comparison of *dealings* between the PE and head office, with *transactions* between independent enterprises. This comparison is to be made by following, by analogy, the comparability analysis described in the OECD Transfer Pricing Guidelines.[18] Additionally, for the purpose of determining the arm's length remuneration of dealings, the most appropriate method to the circumstances of the case should be selected and applied by analogy.[19]

10. *Ibid.*, section 17.
11. Buriak & Holzinger, 10.
12. OECD PE Report, Part I, section 13.
13. Holzinger, 33.
14. OECD PE Report, Part I, section 13.
15. Holzinger, 33.
16. OECD PE Report, Part I, section 15.
17. *Ibid.*, section 175.
18. *Ibid.*, section 183.
19. *Ibid.*, section 184.

## III ATTRIBUTION OF CAPITAL

### 1 Fundamentals

The OECD states that a PE (as well as the head office) must have a minimum level of free capital for tax purposes, regardless of whether the capital is actually allocated to the PE or not. The term 'free capital' is consistently used by the OECD and defined as 'funding that does not give rise to a tax-deductible return in the nature of interest'.[20] By hypnotizing the PE (and the head office) as a separate entity, the free capital can be seen as the fictional entity's equity.[21] The attribution of capital is a pivotal step in the process of allocating profit[22] to a PE.[23] In essence, it involves the question of allocating financing cost ('funding costs'[24]) associated with borrowed debt (as the difference between total assets of the PE[25] minus free capital attributed) to the PE.[26] Where the amount of free capital attributed to the PE is less than the amount determined, an appropriate adjustment should be made in order to reduce the amount of interest expense claimed by the PE.[27]

> ***Example****: A PE has total assets of USD 100 million. If no free capital is attributed to the PE, the interest expense (assumed arm's length interest rate of 5%) associated with attributed debt is USD 5 million (100 million × 5%). If free capital of USD 60 million is attributed, the interest expense is only USD 2 million ([100 million – 60 million] × 5%).*

The starting point for the attribution of free capital to a PE is that under the ALP, a PE should have sufficient capital to support the functions it undertakes, the assets it economically owns and the risks it assumes. In other words, the role of capital is to provide a cushion against the crystallization of risks into actual losses.[28] Since according to the AOA 'assets and risks follow SPFs',[29] the capital ultimately also follows those SPFs. Conversely, however, this also means that it is not within the enterprise's competence to allocate capital to the PE at its own discretion.[30] It will

20. *Ibid.*, section 28.
21. P. Brulisauer, Art. 7 OECD Model Tax Convention, in Zweifel/Beusch/Matteotti (eds), Kommentar zum internationalen Steuerrecht (2015), Article 7, section 452; A. Oestreicher, Dotationskapital, Finanzierungsaufwendungen und die Verrechnung der Finanzierungsfunktion, in Oestreicher/Schnitger/Wellens (e), Gewinnabgrenzung nach dem Authorized OECD Approach (AOA) (2020), section 8.7.
22. In tax jurisdictions that have a capital/net asset tax in addition to a corporate income tax (e.g., Switzerland), the allocation of capital is not merely a preparatory step for the determination of profit.
23. T. Sehwaerzler, Using the Capital Allocation Approach to Attribute Capital to a Permanent Establishment, in International Transfer Pricing Journal (2017), 97.
24. Oestreicher, section 8.44.
25. Allocation on the basis of the economic ownership using the significant people functions.
26. Oestreicher, section 8.1.
27. Sehwaerzler, 100.
28. *Ibid.*, 99.
29. Holzinger, 33.
30. OECD PE Report, Part I, section 116; Brulisauer, Article 7, section 468.

become apparent that the capital allocation approach matches the BEPS project, which focuses on where economic activities take place and where value is created.[31]

The OECD PE Report recognizes a range of acceptable approaches for attributing capital that are capable of giving an arm's length result (*see* following pages), each with its own strengths and weaknesses, which become more or less material depending on the facts and circumstances of particular cases.[32] Experience shows that there is no consensus among tax administrations for a single internationally accepted approach as no approach is capable of dealing with all circumstances.[33] Additionally, simplified approaches ('safe harbour approach') are refused by the OECD.[34]

The OECD PE Report is silent on the date at which the allocation of capital must be conducted. The tax administrations of different countries follow different approaches, for example:

- *Germany* is of the opinion that the allocation is to be conducted at the beginning of each fiscal year.[35] However, if economic conditions change within a fiscal year, the capital must be adjusted.[36]
- *Hong Kong SAR* takes the position that the capital allocation is 'purely a computational one for tax purposes'[37] and hence must be performed as part of the annual tax return of the PE at the end of the tax year.[38]

If the actual amount of free capital attributed by the enterprise to the PE (or the head office) is less than the arm's length required amount as determined by one of the acceptable approaches, an appropriate adjustment would be needed to be made to reduce the amount of interest expenses claimed by the PE (of the head office).

## 2 Approaches

### *A Capital Allocation Approach*

Under the *Capital Allocation Approach*, the total statutory equity of the entire enterprise is allocated on the basis of the portion of assets and risks attributed to the PE and the head office by the functional and factual analysis (step 1).[39] The capital allocation approach attributes assets and risks by relating to SPFs, which is in line with the BEPS

31. SEHWAERZLER, 97.
32. OECD PE Report, Part I, section 31; OESTREICHER, section 8.47.
33. OECD PE Report, Part I, section 147.
34. OESTREICHER, section 8.47.
35. *Ibid.*, section 8.9.
36. *Ibid.*, section 8.22.
37. Notes No. 60, section 71.
38. *Ibid.*
39. OECD PE Report, Part I, section 121; N. HARBEKE, T. HUG & P. SCHERRER, Verrechnungspreisrecht der Schweiz – Grundlagen und Praxis (2022), N 1603.

Action 8 – 10 Final Reports seeking to ensure that profits are taxed where economic activities take place and value is created.[40]

> ***Example****: A legal entity domiciled in country A with a PE in country B has a total statutory capital of USD 5 million (share capital USD 1 million, capital reserves USD 2 million, retained earning reserves USD 2 million). According to the functional and factual analysis, the PE 'owns' 10% of the enterprise's assets and risks. Following the Capital Allocation Approach, the free capital to be attributed to the PE for tax purposes shall be USD 0.5 million (USD 5 million × 10%).*

The advantage of the *Capital Allocation Approach* is that it is easy to apply and that both the head office and the PE can benefit from the synergy effects of the financing policy of the whole enterprise.[41]

While the assets can be measured relatively straightforward by using, for example, fair market values, accounting/tax values or historical acquisition costs,[42] the disadvantage of this method is the challenge of measuring risks. The OECD PE Reports (2008) and (2010) do not include any concrete proposals on how to measure the risk of a non-financial institution.[43] The OECD emphasizes that an approach only using assets to attribute capital would seem unlikely to lead to an arm's length result in situations where significant risks are assumed by the PE (e.g., development risks, entrepreneurial risks).[44] The OECD expects the business to value those risks by using its own measurement tools.[45] In general, it may be said that risk is the impact of an event weighed against the probability that the event will happen.[46] It should be noted, however, that risks are often already taken into account in the balance sheet by depreciating assets or the recognition of provisions.[47]

Additionally, the OECD PE Reports leave the regulation of further details to the OECD member countries, such as the influence of foreign exchange and how to time recalculate of capital.[48]

The OECD draws attention to the fact that the allocation of total equity can lead to inappropriate results if the enterprise as a whole is undercapitalized. In such case, the OECD suggest that, in a first step, the enterprise's equity (as a whole) must be increased to an arm's length level and then, in a second step, must be allocated according to the asset and risks using the *Capital Allocation Approach*.[49]

---

40. SEHWAERZLER, 102.
41. BRULISAUER, Article 7, section 487.
42. OECD PE Report, Part I, sections 109 ff. and 116; BRULISAUER, Article 7, section 478; OESTREICHER, section 8.46; according to the author's opinion, fair market values or value according to international accounting standards (e.g., IFRS) are to be preferred over tax values, since tax values are determined differently depending on the country.
43. SEHWAERZLER, 103.
44. OECD PE Report, Part I, section 111; BRULISAUER, Article 7, section 484; OESTREICHER, section 8.46.
45. OECD PE Report, Part I, section 112.
46. SEHWAERZLER, 103.
47. OESTREICHER, section 8.12.
48. H. PIJL, Interpretation of Article 7 of the OECD Model, Permanent Establishment Financing and Other Dealings, in Bulletin For International Taxation (2011), 306.
49. OECD PE Report, Part I, sections 140 ff.

### B Economic Capital Allocation Approach

Under the *Economic Capital Allocation Approach*, the total statutory capital of the entire enterprise is not allocated on the basis of assets and risks, but on external or internal risk valuation models.[50] This model is widely applied in the banking industry, which has to compute its risk-weighted assets (RWA) on the basis of the international Basel III standard for determining the minimum amount of capital to be held. In simple terms, RWA are calculated by multiplying the exposed amount by the corresponding risk weight for the respective type of asset class.[51] While government bonds, for example, have a low-risk weight, unsecured loans granted to clients have a higher one.

> ***Example***: *A legal entity domiciled in country A is active in the private banking sector and has a total regulatory capital of USD 4 billion. The business activities in country B are structure via a branch.*[52] *Whereas the head office in country A holds RWA (calculated based on Basel III standards) of USD 9 billion, the branch holds USD 3 billion. Following the Economic Capital Allocation Approach, the free capital to be attributed to the branch for tax purposes shall be USD 1 billion (USD 4 billion × USD 3 billion / [USD 9 billion + USD 3 billion]).*

### C Thin Capitalization Approach

Under the *Thin Capitalization Approach*, the head office and the PE shall have the same amount of capital as would an independent enterprise carrying on the same or similar activities under the same or similar conditions in the host country by undertaking a comparability analysis of such independent enterprises on the basis of the functional and factual analysis (step 1).[53] This approach is basically equal to the comparable uncontrolled price method (CUP method) in traditional transfer pricing whereas the arm's length amount of free capital is determined based on the capital of comparable companies (*see* example hereafter). In the author's opinion, the term 'Thin Capitalization Approach' is misleading as it makes reference to domestic thin capitalization rules; the term 'Comparable Capitalization Approach' would be more appropriate.

> ***Example***: *A legal entity domiciled in country A has a PE in country B which acts as a distributor of products produced by the head office in country A. The revenues of the branch amount to USD 10 million. According to the functional and factual analysis performed, the PE is comparable to a low-risk distributor. An independent low-risk distributor in country B typically has a revenue-to-capital ratio of 5% (fictional figure). By applying the Thin Capitalization Approach, the free capital to be attributed to the PE shall be USD 0.5 million (USD 10 million revenue × 5% revenue-to-capital ratio).*

50. *Ibid.*, section 128; HARBEKE, HUG & SCHERRER, N 1603.
51. HUG, 244.
52. Qualifying as a permanent establishment (Article 5 para. 1(b) OECD Model Tax Convention).
53. OECD PE Report, Part I, section 129; HARBEKE, HUG & SCHERRER, N 1603.

*Table 49.2 Overview Methodologies for Capital Attribution*

| | *Capital Allocation Approach* | *Economic Capital Allocation Approach* | *Thin Capitalization Approach* |
|---|---|---|---|
| **Methodology** | Indirect method: Allocation of total statutory equity of the entire enterprise based on the portion of assets and risks | Indirect method: Allocation of total statutory equity of the entire enterprise based on risk valuation methods | Direct method: Allocation of the same capital amount as an independent enterprise would have |
| **Advantage** | Easy mode of operation | Proper reflection of risks assumed within business | Accurate application of arm's length-principle |
| **Disadvantage** | Measurement of risks in the absence of regulatory risks valuation method | Requirement of risk valuation method (e.g., Basel III), only commonly used in banking industry | Search for comparables |

**Excurses: Application of AOA to Interpret Treaties Concluded before 2008/2010?**

The profit allocation is based on the AOA, which is the basis for the interpretation of Article 7 OECD Model Tax Convention, has its origins in 2008 and 2010, respectively.[54] The OECD PE Reports (2008) and (2010) provided the conceptual basis for the revised Article 7 OECD Model Tax Convention and the revised OECD Commentary were both released in July 2010.[55] Whereas the OECD PE Report (2008) discussed the principles of capital attribution in general, the OECD PE Report (2010) provided detailed comments on how to attribute free capital.

The question may arise whether free capital must also be attributed to a PE under double tax treaties concluded before 2010, i.e. which are based on an older version of the OECD Model Tax Convention and the OECD Commentaries than 2010. This question is especially relevant because the OECD Commentaries (1963) and (1997) did not discuss the attribution of capital and only claimed that relevant interest may be allocated to the PE, without any limitations based on the allocation of free capital.[56] Moreover, when the Commentary (1994) discussed the attribution of capital to banks, no international consensus of a preceding capital attribution was reached. It follows that, prior to the Commentary (2008), no attribution of capital was reflected in the earlier Commentaries.[57]

In a 2020 court decision, the *Court of Appeal of the United Kingdom (Civil Division)* had to deal with the question of whether free capital must be allocated to an inbound branch of a bank domiciled in the Republic of Ireland, under the double tax treaty

54. Buriak & Holzinger, 4.
55. Pijl, 294.
56. *Ibid.*, 305.
57. *Ibid.*, 306.

between the United Kingdom (UK) and the Republic of Ireland signed in 1976.[58] Her Majesty's Revenue & Customs (HMRC), the tax authority of the UK, disallowed an amount of interest expenses in the years 2002–2007 on an intra-enterprise loan from the head office to the PE arguing no arm's length amount of free capital was attributed to the PE (among others with reference to section 21(2)(b) of the domestic UK Corporation Tax Act 2009). The denial of interest deductions created higher taxable profits in the UK. The taxpayer, however, referred to the double tax treaty of 1976 and argued that the OECD PE Reports (2008) and (2010), as well as the OECD Commentaries (2010), could not be 'read backwards' into the wording of the 1976 treaty (dynamic treaty interpretation). The Court of Appeal admitted that the wording of the OECD Model Tax Convention (2010) was more specific than the wording of the 1976 treaty. However, the judges held in essence that the 2010 Model Convention did not result in a real change in the method of attributing profits to the PE. Instead, it was considered that this merely reflected the OECD's desire for greater consistency between jurisdictions.

The Spanish *Audencia Nacional* had to deal in 2015 with a similar case under the 1971 double tax treaty between Spain and the Netherlands with respect to capital allocation to a Spanish PE of the Dutch bank *ING*. Interestingly, the Spanish judges argued that it could not construe Article 7 with the assistance of what was said in the OECD Commentary (2008) because in their view that some of the earlier commentaries in articulating the development of the principles of attribution had made substantive changes to the framework of the model conventions which could not be applied retrospectively.[59]

For the sake of completeness, it should be noted that the courts in the U.S. (*National Westminster Bank*)[60] and France (*Bayerische Hypo and Vereinsbank*)[61] have also had to deal with similar cases. Opposite to the cases in Spain and the UK, however, the rulings revolved around the question of whether the domestic PEs of foreign banks should be treated as separate registered banks. Nevertheless, the courts expressed in their rulings also the opinion that more recent OECD documents should not necessarily be used to interpret older double tax treaties.

Based on the above jurisprudence, it must be stated that the question discussed cannot be definitively answered and that the courts may take a different view depending on the tax jurisdiction. According to the author, this is due to the fact that the OECD has no legislative competence, and the various documents (e.g., OECD Commentaries, OECD PE Reports) only have the character of soft law.

## IV ATTRIBUTION OF DEBT

### 1 Fundamentals

In allocating debt to the PE and the head office, a distinction must be made between external debt transactions and internal debt dealings:

58. Court of Appeal, *Irish Bank Resolution Corporation Ltd v. HMRC*, A3/2019/3060-1 (28.08.2020).
59. *Audencia Nacional, ING DIRECT v. Central Court for Economic and Administrative*, 18 ITLR 680 (10.07.2015).
60. *United States Court of Federal Claims, National Westminster Bank plc v. The United States.*
61. *Conseil d'État, Bayerische Hypo and Vereinsbank AG*, 18 ITLR 1.

- *External debt transactions* involve 'real' debt granted to the whole enterprise either by independent third parties (e.g., banks, bondholders) or related parties (according to the definition of Article 9 OECD Model Tax Convention) at arm's length conditions. The question is how the debt and the corresponding interest expenses are properly attributed to the head office and/or the PE. According to the OECD, the term 'debt' is to be defined broadly and does not only include traditional interest-bearing loans[62] but also, for example, receivables from clients.
- In contradistinction, *internal debt dealings* ('treasury dealings') involve 'fictitious' debt granted by the head office to the PE or vice versa. With respect to such fictitious debt, the question is whether interest expenses are reflected in the arm's length profit allocation by considering tax deductible interest expenses in the PE's tax computation and taxable interest income in the head office's computation (or vice versa).

The allocation of free capital to the PE and the head office has priority over the allocation of (externally or internally) borrowed debt. Borrowed debt can only be allocated to the PE or the head office to the extent that it has a funding need greater than that covered by the free capital.[63] Similar to the attribution of free capital, the (subsidiarity) attribution of debt is a preparatory step for the profit allocation. The attributed debt determines the amount of interest income or expense in the tax computation of the head office and the PE.

## 2 Approaches

### *A External Debt Transactions*

According to the AOA, there are in principle two methods to allocate extern debt and the corresponding interest expenses to the head office and the PE, the *Tracing Approach* and the *Fungibility Approach*.[64]

#### *a Tracing Approach*

The *Tracing Approach* is based on the concept of the purpose for which external debt was borrowed.[65] If, for example, a loan is borrowed from an independent third-party bank to fund business activities conducted by the PE, the loan and the interests paid are to be attributed to the PE. The interest rate on the funds provided to the PE are determined to be the same as the actual rate incurred by the enterprise to the (third-party) provider of funds.[66] The debt is traced back to the original purpose (hence named *Tracing Approach*).

62. Oestreicher, section 8.48.
63. *Ibid.*, section 8.59.
64. OECD PE Report, Part I, section 154.
65. *Ibid.*; Oestreicher, 8.73; Harbeke, Hug & Scherrer, N 1605.
66. OECD PE Report, Part I, section 154.

> ***Example**: A legal entity with its registered office in country A is active in the construction industry. Due to a construction project in country B, the entity has a PE (Article 5 paragraph 3 OECD Model Tax Convention) in that country. To finance the project in country B, the entity obtains a loan of USD 500 million from a third-party bank at an interest rate of 5%. The loan of USD 500 million and the annual interests paid of USD 25 million (USD 500 million × 5%) are attributable to the PE.*

### b *Fungibility Approach*

Under the *Fungibility Approach*, however, money borrowed by a PE (or head office) of an enterprise is regarded as contributing to the whole enterprise's funding need, and not simply to that particular PE's (or head office's) funding needs. This approach ignores the actual movements of funds within the enterprise and any payments of head office/PE interests. Each PE is allocated a portion of the whole enterprise's actual interest expense paid on some pre-determined basis (e.g., on the basis of the portion of assets and risks attributed to the PE and the head office by the functional and factual analysis, *see Capital Allocation Approach*).[67] This approach is based on the hypothesis that the PE and the entire enterprise have the same creditworthiness and capital structure and that the financial resources in the company are fungible[68] (hence named *Fungibility Approach*).

> ***Example**: A legal entity with its registered office in country A is active in the construction industry. Due to a construction project in country B, the entity has a PE (Article 5 paragraph 3 OECD Model Tax Convention) in that country. To finance that project, the entity obtains a loan of USD 500 million from a third-party bank at an interest rate of 5%. According to the functional and factual analysis, the head office economically owns 75% and the PE 25% of the assets and risks. USD 125 million (USD 500 million × 25%) loan and annual interest paid of USD 6.25 million (USD 500 million × 5% × 25%) are attributable to the PE.*

*Table 49.3 Overview Methodologies for External Debt Transaction Allocation*

| | *Tracing Approach* | *Fungibility Approach* |
|---|---|---|
| **Methodology** | Direct method: Allocation of external debt based on the purpose for which external debt was borrowed | Indirect method: Allocation of external debt based on pre-determined basis (e.g., same basis as for Capital Allocation Approach) |
| **Rationale** | Separate funding of PE and head office as hypothesized separate enterprises | Funding of whole enterprise |

There is no international consensus on which of these two methods should be used preferentially. Some countries favour the *Fungibility Approach*, whilst others want to retain tracing of funds, especially for non-financial institutions. Others want a

67. *Ibid.*; OESTREICHER, 8.73; HARBEKE, HUG & SCHERRER, N 1605.
68. BRULISAUER, Article 7, section 490.

more flexible approach, perhaps by using the *Tracing Approach* for 'big-ticket' items and a *Fungibility Approach* for the rest of the items.[69] The OECD is silent on the question of how these approaches should be combined with free capital attribution methods. The author is of the opinion that for both the free capital and debt, either only direct methods or indirect methods should be used and no combination of direct and indirect methods. It would lead to an inconsistent result if, for example, the free capital was allocated indirectly using the *Capital Allocation Approach* (based on the economic ownership of assets and risks), but external debt was allocated directly using the *Tracing Approach*. This combination would contradict the concept of a uniform financing structure for the enterprise as a whole.

### *B* *Internal Debt Dealings*

#### *a* *Step 1: Recognition of Internal Debt Dealings*

According to the OECD, internal debt dealings ('treasury dealings') between the head office and the PE (or between PEs) – in addition to the free capital primarily attributed (*see* above) – are only recognized for the purpose of rewarding 'fully-fledged treasury functions' performed.[70] Exceptions apply to the financial services industry (e.g., banks). The OECD grounds this view with reference to the AOA, according to which assets are 'owned' by the part of the enterprise which performs the SPFs. If the head office or a PE is performing fully-fledged treasury functions, the functional analysis may determine that the treasury centre is the economic owner of the internal financial assets as it has been performing the SPFs relevant to determining economic ownership of those assets and so is entitled to the return on those assets (i.e., attribution of interest-bearing, internal debt).[71] In the situation where the treasury head office or treasury PE is doing nothing more than acting as a conduit (borrowing funds and immediate on-lending), the functional analysis is unlikely to show that the head office or PE has been performing the SPFs relevant to determining the economic ownership of assets, and so should be treated as the economic owner of those funds and entitled to the associated return.[72]

> ***Example****: A legal entity with its registered office in country A has, among others, a PE in country B with a funding need of USD 100 million (in addition to the free capital already attributed). As financing capabilities are a key value driver in the industry concerned, a treasury team is employed at the head office. The provision of funding in the amount of USD 100 million is recognized as an internal debt dealing.*

The OECD doctrine, according to which internal debt dealings are only recognized under narrow conditions (as an instrument to allocate profit to the treasury function), is partially criticized. It must be within the competence of the enterprise – within the limits of the minimum free capital (*see* above) – to decide how the financing

69. OECD PE Report, Part I, section 156.
70. OECD PE Report, Part I, section 158.
71. *Ibid.*, section 160.
72. *Ibid.*, section 159.

of the PE is structured. Since both Article 7 paragraph 2 OECD Model Tax Convention (Business Profits) and Article 9 paragraph 1 OECD Model Tax Convention (Associated Enterprises) are ultimately based on the ALP, interest-bearing loans should not only be recognized between associated enterprises but also between head offices and PEs (within an enterprise).[73] Moreover, in the OECD Transfer Pricing Guidance on Financial Transactions, which were published in 2020 (around 10 years after the PE Report) and meanwhile integrated as a separate Chapter X in the 2022 version of the OECD TP Guidelines, the OECD also addresses the issue of group finance companies with a low function and risk profile (i.e., not performing 'fully-fledged treasury functions') that grant loans to associated enterprises. According to the OECD such low-profiled finance companies shall only be entitled to a risk-free compensation.[74] The intercompany loans are thus recognized *in principle,* but the compensation is adjusted, whereas internal debts between head offices and PEs are *not recognized at all.* In the author's opinion, therefore, both cases (i.e., loans between related parties and between the head office and PEs) should be equally treated for tax purposes.

### *b* *Step 2: Pricing of Internal Debt Dealings*

Since the internal debt dealings under the AOA are basically priced by applying the transfer pricing tools according to Article 9 OECD Model Tax Convention (i.e., comparability analysis, selection of the most appropriate transfer pricing method), reference is made to the previous remarks in this book.

However, the OECD's premise is that no fictitious credit rating is to be determined for the head office and the PE although hypothesized as separate enterprises; instead, the same credit rating as for the whole legal entity is assumed for both the head office and the PEs. An exception is to apply if the free capital allocated to the PE may not be used to cover liabilities of other parts of the legal entity due to regulatory reasons. The OECD admits that the credit rating of the company as a whole may be higher than the isolated credit rating of the PE or the head office. This synergy effect cannot be attributed to just one part of the enterprise – for example, the head office – [75] as the PE or the head office does not have its own legal personality (form-over-substance view).

At first glance, this approach of the OECD may not be consistent with the functionally separate entity approach since individual stand-alone credit ratings must be taken into account for loans between related enterprises in the context of Article 9 OECD Model Tax Convention.[76] However, in the Transfer Pricing Guidance on Financial Transactions published by the OECD in 2020 (about 10 years after the publication of the PE Report), the OECD foresees that stand-alone credit ratings of group companies may nevertheless converge due to the effect of group membership (implicit group support).[77] Among the criteria for implicit group support, a shared

73. BRULISAUER, Article 7, section 470.
74. OECD TP Guidelines 2022, para. 10.11.
75. OECD PE Report, Part I, section 99 f; BRULISAUER, Article 7, section 465.
76. OECD TP Guidelines 2022, section 10.62.
77. *Ibid.*, section 10.76-10.80.

name or a high level of operational integration are mentioned,[78] which is particularly distinctive in the case of PEs of an enterprise. In the author's opinion, the AOA of 2010 is justifiable in the light of the latest Transfer Pricing Guidance for Financial Transactions in individual cases as illustrated in the following example.

> ***Example****: A legal entity with its registered office in country A has further business operations in country B which is of high strategic importance. The business operations in both countries have a high level of interdependency and cooperation and the products are distributed to clients in both countries under the same (group) brand. Legally spoken, the operations in country B can be structured either via a branch of the legal entity (PE) or a subsidiary (legally separate entity). The question arises to what extent a separate rating must be considered when determining the interest rate of a loan from the head office (or parent company) to its PE (or subsidiary).*
>
> *In the branch structuring option, the AOA does not allow the consideration of a fictitious separate credit rating for the branch. Instead, the same credit rating as for the whole legal entity must be assumed for both the head office and the PE.*
>
> *In the option of a legally separate subsidiary in country B, the subsidiary is generally to be treated as an independent enterprise in accordance with Article 9 OECD Model Tax Convention (Associated Enterprises), with the consequence that its separate credit rating is to be considered when determining the interest rates. However, since both the parent company and its subsidiary operate under the same brand, have a high level of operational integration and the subsidiary's business if of strategic importance for the whole group, the OECD assumes an implicit support of the parent company vis-à-vis its subsidiary. That said, the subsidiary has the same (or a similar) credit rating as its parent company.*

## V CASE STUDY

### 1 Facts of the Case

A legal entity with its registered office in country A and a PE in country B produces weaving machines. Whereas the development and production capabilities are located in the head office in country A, the sale and distribution functions are performed by the PE in country B. Two banks have each granted the legal entity a long-term loan, one in country A at an interest rate of 3% (exclusively for financing the head office) and one in country B at an interest rate of 5% (exclusively for financing the PE). As the PE has an additional liquidity requirement of USD 100 million, the head office granted a loan to the PE at an interest rate of 9% (considering the lower stand-alone credit rating vis-à-vis the head office). The company keeps separate accounts in country A and country B, resulting in the following internal balance sheet.

78. *Ibid.*, section 10.79.

*Table 49.4 Balance Sheet*

| *(in mUSD, International Financial Reporting Standard (IFRS) Figures)* | *Head Office (Country A)* | *PE (Country B)* | *Total (Aggregated)* |
|---|---|---|---|
| Current Assets | 200 | 100 | 300 |
| Property & Equipment | 1,200 | 100 | 1,300 |
| Internal Long Term Loan (9%) | 100 | 0 | 100 |
| Other Assets | 100 | 0 | 100 |
| **Total Assets**<br>(portion) | **1,600**<br>(89%) | **200**<br>(11%) | **1,800**<br>(100%) |
| Current Liabilities | 400 | 0 | 400 |
| Internal Long Term Loan (9%) | 0 | 100 | 100 |
| Long Term Loan Bank A (3%) | 300 | 0 | 300 |
| Long Term Loan Bank B (5%) | 0 | 100 | 100 |
| Capital | 900 | 0 | 900 |
| **Total Liabilities & Capital** | **1,600** | **200** | **1,800** |

The weaving machines are purchased at an arm's length price of USD 850 million from the head office and sold to customers for USD 1,000 million. The Earnings Before Interest and Taxes (EBIT) margins of the head office and the PE are at arm's length. Due to the separate accounting, the internal income statement is as follows.

*Table 49.5 Profit & Loss Statement*

| *(in mUSD, IFRS Figures)* | *Head Office (Country A)* | *PE (Country B)* | *Total (Aggregated)* |
|---|---|---|---|
| External Revenues | | 1,000 | 1,000 |
| Internal Purchase Price | | -850 | -850 |
| Internal Sale Price | 850 | | 850 |
| Operational Expenses | -700 | -100 | -800 |
| **EBIT**<br>(EBIT Margin) | **150**<br>(17.6%) | **50**<br>(5%) | **200** |
| | Interest Expenses | | |
| *Internal Long Term Loan (9%)* | | *-9* | *-9* |
| *Long Term Loan Bank A (3%)* | *-9* | | *-9* |
| *Long Term Loan Bank B (5%)* | | *-5* | *-5* |
| | Interest Income | | |
| *Internal Long Term Loan (9%)* | *9* | | *9* |
| **Earnings Before Taxes** | **150** | **36** | **186** |

## 2 Suggested Solution

The profit attribution to the head office and the permanent established prepared on the basis of internal accounting must be adjusted for tax purposes in several steps on the basis of the AOA. The following suggested solution is limited to the financing structure.

### *A Step 1: Attribution of Free Capital*

Due to the priority of free capital over (internal or external) debt,[79] the capital of the PE must be reviewed in a first step. Only if, after the allocation of free capital, the PE still has a funding need, debt must be attributed.

According to the enterprise's internal accounting, the PE is fully funded by (external and internal) interest-bearing debt. However, in accordance with the AOA, both the PE and the head office must have a minimum of free capital that does not give rise to a tax-deductible return in the nature of interest.[80] The assumption is made that the tax administrations of both countries apply the *Capital Allocation Approach*, according to which the enterprise's total statutory equity is allocated on the basis of the portion of assets and risks economically attributed to the PE and the head office. The additional assumption is made that the assets (and any risks) are already allocated in line with the SPFs.

Since the assets are valuated according to the international accounting standard IFRS, they should be accepted as a basis in both countries A and B. If these were valuated according to country A's tax rules, they could possibly not be accepted by country B. In case of different currencies in both countries involved, the question of the exchange rate used may also arise. The internal loan is ignored for the *Capital Allocation Approach*.

*Table 49.6 Attribution of Capital (Capital Allocation Approach)*

| *(in mUSD, IFRS Figures)* | *Head Office (Country A)* | *PE (Country B)* | *Total (Aggregated)* |
|---|---|---|---|
| Current Assets | 200 | 100 | 300 |
| Property & Equipment | 1,200 | 100 | 1,300 |
| Other Assets | 100 | 0 | 100 |
| **Total Assets** | **1,500** | **200** | **1,700** |
| (portion) | (88%) | (12%) | (100%) |
| Free Capital | 792 | 108 | 900 |
| (portion) | (88%) | (12%) | (100%) |

79. OESTREICHER, section 8.59.
80. OECD PE Report, Part I, section 28.

## B Step 2: Attribution of External Debt Transactions

In a next step, the external bank loans must be (re-)attributed to the head office and the PE. The assumption is made that both countries apply the *Fungibility Approach*. By applying this approach, money borrowed by a PE of an enterprise is regarded as contributing to the whole enterprise's funding need, and not simply to that particular PE's funding needs. This (indirect) approach disregards the fact that the loans were granted exclusively to finance the head office and the PE, respectively.

*Table 49.7 Attribution of External Debt Transactions (Fungibility Approach)*

| *(in mUSD, IFRS Figures)* | *Head Office (Country A)* | *PE (Country B)* | *Total (Aggregated)* |
|---|---|---|---|
| Current Assets | 200 | 100 | 300 |
| Property & Equipment | 1,200 | 100 | 1,300 |
| Other Assets | 100 | 0 | 100 |
| **Total Assets** | **1,500** | **200** | **1,700** |
| (portion) | (88%) | (12%) | (100%) |
| Long Term Loan Bank A (3%) | 264<br>(88%) | 36<br>(12%) | 300<br>(100%) |
| Long Term Loan Bank B (5%) | 88<br>(88%) | 12<br>(12%) | 100<br>(100%) |

For the sake of completeness, the following table illustrates the consequences if the *Tracing Approach* were applied instead of *Fungibility Approach*, considering the fact that the loans were granted exclusively to finance the head office and the PE, respectively.

*Table 49.8 Attribution of External Debt Transactions (Tracing Approach)*

| *(in mUSD, IFRS Figures)* | *Head Office (Country A)* | *PE (Country B)* | *Total (Aggregated)* |
|---|---|---|---|
| Long Term Loan Bank A (3%) | 300<br>(100%) | 0<br>(0%) | 300<br>(100%) |
| Long Term Loan Bank B (5%) | 0<br>(0%) | 100<br>(100%) | 100<br>(100%) |

## C Step 3: Attribution of Internal Debt Dealings

In the last step, any internal debt dealings must be reviewed under the AOA. The assumption is made that the head office performs fully-fledged treasury functions with the result that the economic ownership of the excess funds (raised via shareholder capital and external debt transactions) is with the head office. This said, the internal loan between the head office and the PE is recognized for tax purposes, however, only to the extent that the PE's financing need is not already covered by free capital (step 1) and external debt transactions (re-)attributed (step 2).

*Table 49.9 Attribution of Internal Debt Dealings*

| *(in mUSD, IFRS Figures)* | *PE (Country B)* |
|---|---|
| Current Assets | 100 |
| Property & Equipment | 100 |
| Other Assets | 0 |
| **Total Assets** | **200** |
| Free Capital | -108 |
| Long Term Loan Bank A (3%) | -36 |
| Long Term Loan Bank B (5%) | -12 |
| **Internal Long Term Loan** | **44** |

As a next step, the interest rate for the internal loan must be determined using the transfer pricing tools according to Article 9 OECD Model Tax Convention (i.e., comparability analysis, selection of the most appropriate transfer pricing method[81]), assuming that the head office and the PE have the same credit rating. Reference is made to the previous remarks in this book on the pricing of intercompany loans. An arm's length interest rate of 4% is assumed.

For the sake of completeness, the following table illustrates the consequences if the Tracing Approach had been applied in step 2. The specific example results in the fact that – taking into account the allocated free capital of USD 108 million (step 1) and the long-term bank loan of USD 100 million (step 2) – the PE is even 'overfinanced' in the amount of USD 8 million.

*Table 49.10 Attribution of Internal Debt Dealings (Tracing Approach in Step 2)*

| *(in mUSD, IFRS Figures)* | *PE (Country B)* |
|---|---|
| Current Assets | 100 |
| Property & Equipment | 100 |
| Other Assets | 0 |
| **Total Assets** | **200** |
| Capital | -108 |
| Long Term Loan Bank A (3%) | 0 |
| Long Term Loan Bank B (5%) | -92 |
| **Internal Long Term Loan** | **0** |

81. OECD TP Guidelines 2022, paras 10.88-10.108.

Assuming that the PE does not perform fully-fledged treasury functions, the author is of the opinion that the excess amount of USD 8 million is not qualified as an internal long-term loan granted by the PE to its head office (with an arm's length interest rate to be determined). Since the attribution of free capital (step 1) takes precedence over the attribution of external debt (step 2),[82] the attributed long-term bank loan of USD 100 million must be re-attributed in the amount to the head office in the amount of USD 8 million.

*Table 49.11 Revised Attribution of External Debt Transactions*

| *(in mUSD, IFRS Figures)* | *Head Office (Country A)* | *PE (Country B)* | *Total (Aggregated)* |
|---|---|---|---|
| Long Term Loan Bank A (3%) | 300<br>(100%) | 0<br>(0%) | 300<br>(100%) |
| Long Term Loan Bank B (5%) | 8<br>(8%) | 92<br>(92%) | 100<br>(100%) |

## D Step 4: Revised Profit Allocation

Considering the adjusted capital structure of both the PE and the parent company, the profit allocation under the AOA is as follows.

*Table 49.12 Revised Profit Allocation*

| *(in mUSD, IFRS Figures)* | *Head Office (Country A)* | *PE (Country B)* | *Total (Aggregated)* |
|---|---|---|---|
| **EBIT** | **150** | **50** | **200** |
| | Interest Expenses | | |
| *Internal Long Term Loan (4%)* | | *-2* 1) | -2 |
| *Long Term Loan Bank A (3%)* | *-8* 2) | *-1* 3) | -9 |
| *Long Term Loan Bank B (5%)* | *-4* 4) | *-1* 5) | -5 |
| Interest Income | | | |
| *Internal Long Term Loan (4%)* | +2 1) | | +2 |
| Earnings Before Taxes (**EBT**) – **Revised AOA** | **140** | **46** | **186** |
| EBT – Internal Accounting | 150 | 36 | 186 |
| **Tax Adjustments** | **-10** | **+10** | |

1) 44 × 4% = 2 2) 264 × 3% = 8 3) 36 × 3% = 1 4) 88 × 5% = 4 5) 12 × 5% = 1

82. Oestreicher, section 8.59.

In the example above, notional interest income of USD 2 million is attributed to the country A for taxation. One could argue that according to Article 11 paragraph 2 OECD Model Tax Convention, country B also has a right to levy a (withholding) tax on the interest income arising in country B. However, the OECD takes the position that separate and independent enterprise fiction does not extend to Article 11 and, for the purposes of that article, one part of an enterprise cannot be considered to have made an interest payment to another part of the same enterprise. Clearly, however, if interest paid by an enterprise to a different person is paid on indebtedness incurred in connection with a PE of the enterprise and is borne by that PE, this real interest payment may, under Article 11 paragraph 2, be taxed by the state in which the PE is located.[83]

For the sake of completeness, the following table illustrates the consequences if the *Tracing Approach* had been applied in step 2 (including a partial re-attribution of the long-term bank loan in step 3).

*Table 49.13 Revised Profit Allocation (Tracing Approach in Step 2)*

| *(in mUSD, IFRS figures)* | *Head Office (Country A)* | *PE (Country B)* | *Total (Aggregated)* |
|---|---|---|---|
| **EBIT** | **150** | **50** | **200** |
| | *Interest Expenses* | | |
| Long Term Loan Bank A (3%) | -9 [1)] | | -9 |
| Long Term Loan Bank B (5%) | -0 [2)] | -5 [3)] | -5 |
| **EBT – Revised AOA** | **141** | **45** | **186** |
| EBT – Internal Accounting | 150 | 36 | 186 |
| **Tax Adjustments** | **-9** | **+9** | |

[1)] 300 × 3% = 2 [2)] 8 × 5% = 0 (rounded-down) [3)] 92 × 5% = 5

## VI CONCLUSIONS

The determination of the remuneration for financial transactions *within* an enterprise (i.e., between the head office and the foreign PE or vice versa) are generally based on the arm's length-principle in the same manner as *between* related enterprises. Due to the different legal provisions (Article 7 versus Article 9 OECD Model Tax Convention) and the fact that the head office and the PEs do not have their own legal personality, there are nevertheless material variations to be considered:

- Due to the missing legal personality of the head office/PE, it is not possible to base the entire profit allocation predominantly on the legal circumstances, in

83. OECD Commentary, Article 7, section 28.

contrast to associated enterprises (e.g., share capital, contractual financial transaction). Depending on the approach used, free capital and debt are allocated either directly or indirectly based on auxiliary factors (e.g., allocation based on assets and risks under the *Capital Allocation Approach* and *Fungibility Approach*, respectively).

- Despite the concept of hypothesizing the PE and head office as separate enterprises, internal debt dealings are only recognized as a means to reward treasury functions in the international profit allocation. Intra-enterprise loans without treasury functions are disregarded.
- To the extent that internal debt dealings are accepted, no separate credit rating for the PE may be taken into account when determining an arm's length interest rate. This is to a certain extent in conflict with the separate entity approach.

# Part VII The EU Perspective

CHAPTER 50

# The Impact of the State Aid Rules on the Transfer Pricing Aspects of Intercompany Loans: An Analysis of the Landmark Ruling of the CJEU in the *Fiat* Case

*Jérôme Monsenego*[*]

## I INTRODUCTION

This book chapter analyses the *Fiat* case and its impact on the transfer pricing aspects of intercompany loans. The analysis focuses solely on the main issues of principle raised in the *Fiat* case and is based on the decision of the European Commission, the ruling issued by the General Court, the Opinions of Advocate General Pikamäe, and the final judgement of the Grand Chamber of the Court of Justice issued on 8 November 2022. This contribution is divided into three parts. First, the facts of the *Fiat* case are presented, together with the transfer pricing model applied. Second, the State aid assessment of the APA granted by the Luxembourg tax administration is analysed. Third, certain of the consequences of the *Fiat* case on the transfer pricing aspects of intercompany loans are considered.

## II PRESENTATION OF THE *FIAT* CASE

The *Fiat* case concerns the transfer pricing aspects of certain of the intragroup treasury activities of the Fiat group. This function was performed at the European level by a company resident of Luxembourg, Fiat Finance and Trade (FFT). Other companies of

* The views and opinions set forth herein are the personal views or opinions of the authors; they do not necessarily reflect views or opinions of the organisation with which the authors are associated.

the Fiat group performed additional treasury functions, or were responsible for the financing of other geographical markets. The State aid issue relates to a unilateral advance pricing agreement (APA) granted to FFT by the Luxembourg tax administration, in which the transfer pricing model suggested by the tax advisor of the Fiat group was accepted: the tax authorities found that the transfer pricing analysis was in accordance with Luxembourg tax law[1] and consistent with the arm's length principle. Accordingly, a unilateral APA was granted for these transactions and was binding on the Luxembourg tax administration for a period of five years, i.e., for the tax years 2012 to 2016.

FFT was involved in financial transactions both with certain of the treasury companies of the group, and with companies performing other types of functions within the group. FFT provided treasury services and financing to the Fiat/Chrysler group companies established in Europe, excluding those established in Italy. FFT was involved, in particular, in market funding and liquidity investments, relations with financial markets, financial coordination and consultancy services to the group companies, cash management, short-term or medium-term intercompany funding, and coordination with the other treasury companies.[2]

Since FFT was involved in treasury functions, the transfer pricing model had to remunerate its financing activities. As the main activity consisted of lending funds, the transfer pricing model started from the premise that capital was being put at risk. The transfer pricing method chosen was the transactional net margin method (TNMM). The remuneration of the capital put at risk was determined by using the capital asset pricing model (CAPM). The CAPM is normally used to determine a rate of return on assets, in this case, a return on equity. This return is estimated based on the variations in the price of shares, which is used to measure risk. In this respect, the '*beta*' is used as a parameter to determine the return on equity by multiplying it by a risk premium,[3] which is defined as the difference between the market return and the risk-free return. The *beta* is, accordingly, a measure of the volatility of a stock in comparison to the market that is added to the risk-free rate.[4] This transfer pricing model implied that the profit attributed to FFT based on TNMM and CAPM was determined by reference to the capital needed by FFT to perform its functions and bear its risks, in relation to the assets in use.

The transfer pricing methodology to determine the profits of FFT implied several steps. First, one would estimate the capital at risk of FFT, which was made by analogy

1. Luxembourg law consisted in the Circular 164/2 dated 28 January 2011.
2. *See Commission Decision (EU) 2016/2326 on State aid SA.38375 (2014/C ex 2014/NN) which Luxembourg granted to Fiat* (OJ 2016 L 351, p. 1), para. 42.
3. Identifying a risk premium is a difficult task. In this respect, it has been observed that '(i)n theory, using a capital asset pricing model (CAPM), it would be possible to identify a firm's market risk premium. Identifying a market risk premium is not administratively feasible due to, inter alia, a lack of ready information for non-public firms and the need to rely on data for comparable public firms. Moreover, this risk premium is not a good fit as it takes account of risks for infra-marginal returns': *see* Stephen E. Shay, *The Deceptive Allure of Taxing 'Residual Profits'*, 75 Bulletin for International Taxation, 2021-11/12, p. 529, footnote 13.
4. *See Commission Decision (EU) 2016/2326 on State aid SA.38375 (2014/C ex 2014/NN) which Luxembourg granted to Fiat* (OJ 2016 L 351, p. 1), para. 41.

with the minimum capital requirement under the Basel II framework. Then one would identify FFT's capital used to perform its functions and support its financial investments. The next step would consist in estimating the expected remuneration of FFT's capital at risk by using the CAPM, and identifying the return on the capital used to perform the functions. Finally, one would calculate the overall profitability left to FFT to remunerate the risks borne and the functions performed by combining the previous steps.[5]

The Luxembourg tax administration found that the transfer pricing study presented by the tax advisor of the Fiat group implied an appropriate remuneration of the functions performed, and the risks borne by FFT. Eventually, the APA accepted an application of the CAPM with a risk-free rate of 2.85%, a *beta* of 0.29, and an equity risk premium of 5%.[6] This transfer pricing model would result in attributing a net profit to FFT which amounted to approximately EUR 2.5 million per year with a margin of +/-10%.[7] That profit would then be subject to corporate income tax in Luxembourg at the normal rate.[8]

Shortly after the issuance of the APA by the Luxembourg tax administration, the European Commission started to examine the compatibility of this APA with the State aid rules, and a formal investigation procedure was initiated under Article 108(2) TFEU. The final decision of the Commission was issued on 21 October 2015.[9] The Commission considered that the transfer pricing model suggested by the Fiat group, and accepted by the Luxembourg tax administration, constituted a State aid within the meaning of Article 107(1) TFEU that was incompatible with the internal market and unlawfully put into effect in breach of Article 108(3) TFEU. Therefore, Luxembourg was required to recover the incompatible and unlawful aid.[10]

The decision issued by the European Commission on 21 October 2015 was challenged before the General Court of the European Union, which on 24 September 2019 upheld the decision of the Commission.[11] Fiat and Ireland then lodged an appeal to the Court of Justice, and two opinions of Advocate General Pikamäe were issued on 16 December 2021.[12] The case was finally ruled on 8 November 2022 by the Grand Chamber of the Court of Justice, which set aside the judgment of the General Court and

5. *See ibid.*, paras 57 et seq.
6. *See ibid.*, para. 64.
7. *See ibid.*, para. 54.
8. For the years covered by the APA (2012-2016), the standard corporate income tax rate was 28.80%.
9. *See Commission Decision (EU) 2016/2326 on State aid SA.38375 (2014/C ex 2014/NN) which Luxembourg granted to Fiat* (OJ 2016 L 351, p. 1).
10. The obligation to recover illegal and unlawful State aid was prescribed by Article 16 of Regulation No. 2015/1589.
11. *See* Cases T-755/15 and T-759/15, *Grand Duchy of Luxembourg and Fiat Chrysler Finance Europe v. European Commission*. For a comment *see* Ivan Lazarov & Svitlana Buriak, *Is Fiat's Tank Half-Full or Half Empty? The General Court's Decision in Luxembourg v. Commission (T-755/15)*, 27 International Transfer Pricing Journal, 2020-1, pp. 71-77.
12. *See* Opinion of Advocate General Pikamäe delivered on 16 December 2021, Case C-898/19 P, *Ireland v. European Commission*; Opinion of Advocate General Pikamäe delivered on 16 December 2021, Case C-885/19 P, *Fiat Chrysler Finance Europe v. European Commission*.

annulled the Commission decision of 21 October 2015.[13] The next part of this contribution analyses the State aid assessment of the APA granted by the Luxembourg tax administration.

## III STATE AID ASSESSMENT OF THE APA GRANTED BY THE LUXEMBOURG TAX ADMINISTRATION

### 1 Introduction and Methodological Precisions

The Commission relied on several types of arguments to support the conclusion that the APA implied an aid incompatible with the internal market. Certain of these arguments concerned the transfer pricing consequences of the facts pattern, similarly to a regular transfer pricing dispute. It can in particular be observed that the Commission disagreed with Fiat as to the amount of capital to be remunerated and the rate of return to be applied, with respect to – for example – the application of the Basel II framework to calculate the capital at risk,[14] or the determination of the *beta*.[15] These practical considerations are not analysed here, given the impossibility of making an objective and comprehensive transfer pricing assessment based on the information available from the case,[16] and with regard to the fact that the Court of Justice did not need to consider the transfer pricing aspects of the case as it solved it on the sole ground of the determination of the reference system. Therefore, the analysis focuses on the theoretical issues raised in the *Fiat* case, which are also the most interesting for determining the consequences of State aid law on the pricing of intercompany loans, and more generally on transfer pricing rules.

In the *Fiat* decision, the European Commission applied the presumption of selectivity developed in the *MOL* case.[17] Thus, the Commission analysed together the advantage and selectivity criteria under the broader concept of 'selective advantage'.[18] This approach, according to the Commission, would be justified by the fact that certain

---

13. *See* Joined Cases C-885/19 P and C-898/19 P, *Fiat Chrysler Finance Europe v. Commission*.
14. *See Commission Decision (EU) 2016/2326 on State aid SA.38375 (2014/C ex 2014/NN) which Luxembourg granted to Fiat* (OJ 2016 L 351, p. 1), para. 276.
15. *See ibid.*, para. 301.
16. It can also be observed that factual transfer pricing issues are not easily dealt with in Court. Issues of proof may also prevent a correct assessment. In this respect, the Advocate General found that the premiss of certain transfer pricing arguments had 'not been proved to the required legal standard': *see* Opinion of Advocate General Pikamäe delivered on 16 December 2021, Case C-885/19 P, *Fiat Chrysler Finance Europe v. European Commission*, para. 122. Similarly, certain of the arguments of the European Commission in the *Apple* case failed before the General Court because of the difficulties to bring evidence of deviations from market conditions: *see* Cases T-778/16 and T-892/16, *Ireland and Others v. European Commission*, e.g., at para. 448. *See also* Peter Wattel, *Starbucks and Fiat: Arm's Length Competition Law*, 48 Intertax, 2020-1, pp. 119-121.
17. *See* Case C-15/14 P, *European Commission v. MOL Magyar Olaj- és Gázipari Nyrt.*
18. *See Commission Decision (EU) 2016/2326 on State aid SA.38375 (2014/C ex 2014/NN) which Luxembourg granted to Fiat* (OJ 2016 L 351, p. 1), p. 46, section 7.2: 'Existence of a selective advantage'. This was also observed by the General Court (*see* Cases T-755/15 and T-759/15, *Grand Duchy of Luxembourg and Fiat Chrysler Finance Europe v. European Commission*, para. 119).

parts of the selectivity analysis would 'generally coincide with the identification of the advantage'.[19] The General Court found that although this joint examination was 'not in itself incorrect', it would be more appropriate to distinguish these criteria.[20] However, the General Court and the Advocate General did not reject the application of the presumption of selectivity given that the State aid assessment of the APA concerned an individual measure, as opposed to a scheme.[21] This view is not unreasonable: in the case of an APA – which indeed is an individual measure – the existence of an advantage can only be fully appreciated by comparing taxation in a particular case with the normal tax regime. Therefore, as emphasised by Advocate General Pikamäe, there is clearly 'a link between the concept of advantage and the concept of selectivity'.[22] At the same time, the two criteria may very well be analysed separately. The two analyses would then partly overlap, as for both criteria, one has to compare taxation in the actual case with the normal tax regime. In addition, as pointed out by Advocate General Pikamäe, if the combined analysis of a 'selective advantage' is to be ruled out, the whole State aid analysis may be invalidated. Therefore, it makes sense to formally distinguish between these criteria. In any case, one needs to consider two of the three-step analysis developed by the CJEU for the selectivity test, i.e., the determination of the reference system and the investigation of a possible deviation from that reference system for comparable undertakings. It is this methodological framework that is applied here.

The method to assess the selectivity of a tax measure has since long been defined by the CJEU. This method supposes a three-step analysis, which the CJEU also recalled in the *Fiat* case.[23] First, one has to identify the reference system applicable to the Member State concerned. Second, it is examined if the tax measure at issue derogates from that common regime, in so far as it differentiates between operators who are, in the light of the objective pursued by the reference system, in a comparable factual and legal situation, in which case the measure is *a priori* selective. Third, if a tax measure is a priori selective, it is assessed if the derogation is justified by the nature and general scheme of the tax system. Only the two first steps of this analytical framework are considered below, as they encompass the most important State aid issues of the *Fiat*

19. *See Commission Decision (EU) 2016/2326 on State aid SA.38375 (2014/C ex 2014/NN) which Luxembourg granted to Fiat* (OJ 2016 L 351, p. 1), para. 217.
20. *See* Cases T-755/15 and T-759/15, *Grand Duchy of Luxembourg and Fiat Chrysler Finance Europe v. European Commission*, para. 122.
21. *See* Opinion of Advocate General Pikamäe delivered on 16 December 2021, Case C-898/19 P, *Ireland v. European Commission*, para. 193: 'the General Court committed no error of law in holding that the Commission correctly established the selective nature of the tax ruling at issue by applying the presumption of selectivity'.
22. *See* Opinion of Advocate General Pikamäe delivered on 16 December 2021, Case C-898/19 P, *Ireland v. European Commission*, para. 54; *see also* para. 102 of that Opinion: 'the fact that the concept of "normal" taxation, used in the assessment of the existence of an economic advantage, is essentially equated with the concept of "reference framework", used in the analysis of selectivity, leads me to consider that the criteria used by the case-law to determine the content of the latter concept may indeed be applied to the former'.
23. *See* Joined Cases C-885/19 P and C-898/19 P, *Fiat Chrysler Finance Europe v. Commission*, para. 68.

case.[24] It is also with respect to these two steps that the advantage and selectivity criteria coincide.

## 2 The Determination of the Reference System

The determination of the reference system turned out to be the most important issue in the *Fiat* case, as the CJEU found that the Commission and the General Court had made an error in that determination, something that vitiated the whole selectivity analysis.[25]

It is settled case law that for the purposes of assessing the selective nature of a tax measure, it is necessary that the reference system be correctly identified in the Commission decision. Since the determination of the reference system constitutes the starting point for the State aid analysis and the benchmark in view of which a potential deviation is assessed, the CJEU had already in previous cases made clear that an error in that determination vitiates the whole selectivity analysis.[26]

The Commission, consistently with its practice in the area of fiscal State aid, adopted a broad definition of the reference system. It found that the reference system was made of the general Luxembourg corporate income tax rules and rejected the view that a narrower reference system could apply, such as the rules for the taxation of groups or the circular applicable in the area of intragroup financing.[27] The theoretical ground for a broad definition of the reference system is the idea that the reference system should be made of a 'consistent set of rules that apply on the basis of objective criteria to all undertakings falling within its scope as defined by its objective'.[28] A similar idea would later be developed in the 2016 Commission notice on the notion of State aid.[29] The General Court agreed with this approach, considering that the Commission could compare the tax burden of a group of companies with that of independent enterprises taxed according to the general corporate income tax system. In other words, the taxation of multinational enterprises, and in particular the transfer pricing rules, did not – according to the General Court – constitute a reference system on its own, separate from the general corporate income tax system.[30]

As I have already argued elsewhere, there are good reasons for not isolating the transfer pricing rules as a separate reference system. Instead, in cases relating to the application of the State aid rules to measures that form part of the corporate income tax, the reference system should be made of the whole corporate income tax system, which

24. There was no debate on the justification of an *a priori* selective measure in the *Fiat* case.
25. For a detailed analysis of this issue see Jérôme Monsenego, *Aides d'État et droit fiscal: les apports de l'arrêt Fiat du 8 novembre 2022 quant à la détermination du cadre de référence*, Revue Fiscalité Internationale, 2023-1, pp. 159-166.
26. *See* Joined Cases C-51/19 P and C-64/19 P, *World Duty Free Group and Kingdom of Spain v. European Commission*, para. 61.
27. *See Commission Decision (EU) 2016/2326 on State aid SA.38375 (2014/C ex 2014/NN) which Luxembourg granted to Fiat* (OJ 2016 L 351, p. 1), para. 209.
28. *See ibid.*, para. 193.
29. *See Commission Notice on the notion of State aid as referred to in Article 107(1) of the Treaty on the Functioning of the European Union*, C/2016/2946 (OJ C 262, 19.7.2016, p. 1), para. 133.
30. *See* Cases T-755/15 and T-759/15, *Grand Duchy of Luxembourg and Fiat Chrysler Finance Europe v. European Commission*, para. 141.

includes the method for the allocation of income to multinational enterprises - in this case the arm's length principle.[31] Advocate General Pikamäe adopted a similar view,[32] referring to the case law of the CJEU where it was held that 'the selectivity of a tax measure cannot be assessed on the basis of a reference framework consisting of some provisions of the national law of the Member State concerned that have been artificially taken from a broader legislative framework'.[33] A contrary view, whereby the reference system would be made of solely the transfer pricing rules (or other types of rules that fulfil a limited function within a tax system) would allow a Member State to implement differentiated tax rules, in this case, different rules for multinational and independent enterprises. As I see it, this would reveal either a discriminatory objective of the tax system, or a tax measure that is inconsistent with the objective of the tax system in which it operates. The design of a tax rule has already been found inconsistent in the light of the objective of a tax system.[34]

Although the Commission defined the reference system as the whole corporate income tax system, it also considered that the arm's length principle 'necessarily forms part of the Commission's assessment under Article 107(1) of the TFEU', 'independently of whether a Member State has incorporated this principle into its national legal system'.[35] This would mean that even if Luxembourg had not implemented the arm's length principle in its domestic law, it would nevertheless need to apply it as a consequence of Article 107(1) of the TFEU. This innovative way of reasoning, perhaps motivated by considering the effects on competition of an incorrectly designed reference system, supposes disregarding the domestic law and replacing it with what would best meet the objectives of Article 107(1) of the TFEU. The General Court seems to have validated this approach - although the formulation of the ruling of the General Court is not easily understood, considering that the arm's length principle was a 'benchmark' for establishing whether an integrated company has received an advantage.[36] Advocate General Pikamäe interpreted the General Court's position as meaning that the arm's length principle is applicable irrespective of whether it has been expressly codified in national law, provided it can be seen that the national system of corporate taxation seeks to treat integrated companies, for tax purposes, in the same way as stand-alone companies.[37] This would mean, according to the interpretation

31. *See* Jérôme Monsenego, *Selectivity in State Aid Law and the Methods for the Allocation of the Corporate Tax Base* (Kluwer Law International 2018), pp. 45 and following.
32. *See* Opinion of Advocate General Pikamäe delivered on 16 December 2021, Case C-898/19 P, *Ireland v. European Commission*, para. 58: 'the reference framework must be complete; in that it must include all the rules and principles which affect the tax burden on undertakings'.
33. *See* Joined Cases C-51/19 P and C-64/19 P, *World Duty Free Group and Kingdom of Spain v. European Commission*, para. 62.
34. *See* Case C-562/19 P, *European Commission v. Republic of Poland*, para. 43. For a comment *see* Jérôme Monsenego, *Taxes sur le chiffre d'affaires – Taux d'imposition progressif*, Revue Fiscalité Internationale, 2021-2, pp. 50-52.
35. *See Commission Decision (EU) 2016/2326 on State aid SA.38375 (2014/C ex 2014/NN) which Luxembourg granted to Fiat* (OJ 2016 L 351, p. 1), para. 228.
36. *See* Cases T-755/15 and T-759/15, *Grand Duchy of Luxembourg and Fiat Chrysler Finance Europe v. European Commission*, paras 143, 151, 153, and 159.
37. *See* Opinion of Advocate General Pikamäe delivered on 16 December 2021, Case C-885/19 P, *Fiat Chrysler Finance Europe v. European Commission*, para. 64.

made by the Advocate General of paragraph 141 of the General Court's ruling, that the sole objective of a reference system would suffice to confer it a material content, in this case the application of the arm's length principle.

While the General Court seems to have admitted at least partly the analysis of the Commission,[38] the Advocate General took a different view, considering that 'the approach adopted by the Commission in the decision at issue and endorsed by the General Court in the judgment under appeal ultimately amounts to introducing into the national tax system constituting "normal" taxation a rule, namely the arm's length principle, which is extraneous to that system'.[39] In other words, the Advocate General – in my view correctly – found that the reference system comprises only rules and principles intrinsic to the national legal system,[40] which excludes determining the material content of the reference system on the basis of Article 107(1) of the TFEU alone, or on the basis of the objective of the tax system.[41]

The Court of Justice followed the Advocate General and found that 'only the national law applicable in the Member State concerned must be taken into account in order to identify the reference system for direct taxation, that identification being itself an essential prerequisite for assessing not only the existence of an advantage, but also whether it is selective in nature'.[42] Therefore, the Court took the view that 'in dismissing the relevance of Article 164(3) of the Tax Code and Circular No 164/2, the Commission applied an arm's length principle different from that defined by Luxembourg law',[43] thus making an error that vitiated the whole selectivity analysis.

This finding is in line with the case law of the CJEU recognising the fiscal sovereignty of the Member States,[44] the consequence of which being that outside the harmonised areas it is the Member States that determine, by exercising their competence in the field of direct taxation, the characteristics constituting a tax and thus the normal tax regime. I have argued elsewhere in favour of a similar position, this view

38. *See* the interpretation of the ruling of the General Court by the Advocate General: Opinion of Advocate General PIKAMÄE delivered on 16 December 2021, Case C-898/19 P, *Ireland v. European Commission*, para. 84: 'interpreting Section 7.2.2.1 of the decision at issue, and in particular recital 228 thereof, is extremely difficult because of the infelicitous wording of certain passages of the Commission's reasoning. In those circumstances, it is all the more regrettable that the General Court decided to approve the last sentence of that recital by referring in general terms to the "context" in which such wording was used, without providing any further clarification'. For a similar view, *see* JÉRÔME MONSENEGO, *Some Observations on Starbucks, Fiat, and Their Potential Impact on Future Amendments to the Arm's Length Principle*, Kluwer Competition Law Blog, 26 September 2019, available at http://competitionlawblog.kluwercompetitionlaw.com/2019/09/26/some-observations-on-starbucks-fiat-and-their-potential-impact-on-future-amendments-to-the-arms-length-principle/ (accessed 16 November 2022).
39. *See* Opinion of Advocate General PIKAMÄE delivered on 16 December 2021, Case C-898/19 P, *Ireland v. European Commission*, para. 107.
40. *See ibid.*, paras 64 and 94.
41. *See ibid.*, para. 107 last sentence, as well as para. 111. It can also be observed that the Advocate General at para. 121 of the Opinion, and the CJEU at para. 104 of the ruling, considered that the *Forum 187* case did not imply an obligation to apply the arm's length principle.
42. *See* Joined Cases C-885/19 P and C-898/19 P, *Fiat Chrysler Finance Europe v. Commission*, para. 74.
43. *See ibid.*, para. 91.
44. *See* in particular Case C-562/19 P, *European Commission v. Republic of Poland*.

being supported by, among others, the principle of legality,[45] as also emphasised by the Court.[46] Moreover, it can be considered that only deviations from binding legal measures can imply an economic advantage,[47] and that determining remedies and quantifying an aid that must be recovered on grounds extraneous to the domestic tax system would be hazardous. The findings of the Court were deemed sufficient to set aside the ruling of the General Court.[48]

Finally, because the reference system was found to be incorrect, the Court did not need to proceed with the comparability analysis. It may nevertheless be mentioned that the comparability analysis was a key element for the success of the position of the Commission, which needed to argue that multinational enterprises and independent enterprises were in a comparable situation to have the former taxed as the latter. The General Court, in my view correctly,[49] found that these two categories of taxpayers were comparable from a legal and factual perspective.[50] This was mainly due to the scope of the reference system: since the reference system was made of the whole corporate income tax, it was also the objective pursued by that system that was used for the comparability analysis. If one assumes that the general objective of the corporate income tax is the taxation of the net income of all persons subject to that tax,[51] associated and independent enterprises indeed appear as being in a comparable situation. While not analysing this issue in depth, the Court seems to have adopted a similar view, as it considered that the Commission must 'be able to establish that the parameters laid down by national law are manifestly inconsistent with the objective of non-discriminatory taxation of *all resident companies, whether integrated or not*, pursued by the national tax system'[52] (my emphasis).

## IV CONSEQUENCES OF THE *FIAT* CASE ON THE TRANSFER PRICING ASPECTS OF INTERCOMPANY LOANS

First, the Court in the *Fiat* case confirmed that the reference system for the purpose of a State aid analysis can only be made of the domestic law. This excludes a State aid control of the pricing of intercompany loans based on Chapter 10 of the 2022 OECD Guidelines alone, unless that chapter has been included in the domestic law and given

45. *See* Jérôme Monsenego, *Selectivity in State Aid Law and the Methods for the Allocation of the Corporate Tax Base* (Kluwer Law International 2018), pp. 53 and 55.
46. Joined Cases C-885/19 P and C-898/19 P, *Fiat Chrysler Finance Europe v. Commission*, para. 97.
47. *See* Jérôme Monsenego, *Selectivity in State Aid Law and the Methods for the Allocation of the Corporate Tax Base* (Kluwer Law International 2018), pp. 52 and following.
48. Joined Cases C-885/19 P and C-898/19 P, *Fiat Chrysler Finance Europe v. Commission*, para. 113.
49. *See* Jérôme Monsenego, *Selectivity in State Aid Law and the Methods for the Allocation of the Corporate Tax Base* (Kluwer Law International 2018), pp. 82-101.
50. *See* Cases T-755/15 and T-759/15, *Grand Duchy of Luxembourg and Fiat Chrysler Finance Europe v. European Commission*, para. 141.
51. *See* Jérôme Monsenego, *Selectivity in State Aid Law and the Methods for the Allocation of the Corporate Tax Base* (Kluwer Law International 2018), p. 81.
52. *See* Joined Cases C-885/19 P and C-898/19 P, *Fiat Chrysler Finance Europe v. Commission*, para. 122.

a binding value.[53] At the same time, the Court confirmed that tax measures, including in the field of transfer pricing, are subject to the State aid control: 'action by Member States in areas that are not subject to harmonisation by EU law is not excluded from the scope of the provisions of the FEU Treaty on monitoring State aid. The Member States must thus refrain from adopting any tax measure liable to constitute State aid that is incompatible with the internal market'.[54] When performing a State aid control of a transfer pricing measure, the *Fiat* case does not seem to necessarily preclude referring to the recommendations included in Chapter 10, as the OECD Guidelines are viewed by the General Court,[55] and somewhat to a lesser extent also by the Court of Justice,[56] as a relevant interpretative source. However, since the reference system needs to be made of the domestic law alone, one needs to take into consideration the limitations that domestic law may imply for the use of Chapter 10 of the OECD Guidelines as an interpretative source, especially if the Guidelines are to be used in a retroactive manner.[57] Obviously if the domestic law does not interpret the arm's length principle in the same manner as the OECD Guidelines, the Guidelines cannot be used as a tool to perform the State aid control of transfer pricing measures; in contrast, if the two sources are compatible and that the domestic law does not preclude an interpretation based on the Guidelines, one should be able to use Chapter 10 for the purpose of the State aid control of intercompany financial transactions.

Second, assuming that a domestic arm's length rule is interpreted in the light of Chapter 10 of the OECD Guidelines, the recommendations included in that chapter in terms of substance could, in my view, be followed without infringing on State aid law. In particular, the reference in Chapter 10 to the general principles contained in Chapter 1 of the OECD Guidelines makes clear that a certain level of substance is necessary to support the pricing of financial transactions, especially the performance of appropriate

53. *See ibid.*, para. 96 where the Court expects that a national tax system makes 'explicit reference' to a soft law instrument for it to be legally binding, and thus form part of the reference system. It can be observed that certain countries, including in the European Union, have included explicit references to the OECD Guidelines in their domestic laws, thereby granting them a legally binding nature.
54. *See* Joined Cases C-885/19 P and C-898/19 P, *Fiat Chrysler Finance Europe v. Commission*, para. 65; see also para. 122.
55. *See* Cases T-755/15 and T-759/15, *Grand Duchy of Luxembourg and Fiat Chrysler Finance Europe v. European Commission*, para. 147: 'Even though the Commission correctly observed that it cannot be formally bound by the OECD Guidelines, the fact remains that those guidelines are based on important work carried out by groups of renowned experts, that they reflect the international consensus achieved with regard to transfer pricing and that they thus have a real practical significance in the interpretation of issues relating to transfer pricing.'
56. *See* Joined Cases C-885/19 P and C-898/19 P, *Fiat Chrysler Finance Europe v. Commission*, para. 96, where the Court mentioned that 'many national tax authorities are guided by the OECD Guidelines in the preparation and control of transfer prices'.
57. Indeed, there are certain provisions of the Guidelines that may not be compatible with a country's domestic law, even when that country has implemented an arm's length rule. For example, the recommendations included in the 2022 OECD Guidelines with respect to the non-recognition of certain transactions or the hard-to-value intangibles approach may not be compliant with certain domestic principles, such as the principle of legality or the principle of legal certainty.

functions, the control of risks, and the financial capacity to assume these risks.[58] In this respect, the substance requirement described in the OECD Guidelines is not inconsistent with certain principles recognised in the case law of the CJEU relating to both State aid and the fundamental freedoms, especially the territoriality principle,[59] the need to preserve a balanced allocation of the power to tax, and the prevention of tax avoidance. In other words, the reinforcement of the substance requirement in the OECD Guidelines is in harmony with the recognition in the case law of the CJEU of the Member States' need to prevent the erosion of their tax base and ensure a connection between taxation and economic activities.

Last, the Court in the *Fiat* case did not follow the approach suggested by the Commission consisting of conferring to Article 107(1) of the TFEU a material content on its own implying an obligation to apply the arm's length principle. Article 107(1) of the TFEU has not been found to infer a general obligation of equal treatment, nor does the *Forum 187* case[60] oblige the Member States to tax multinational enterprises based on the arm's length principle. This finding, combined with the domestic nature of the reference system, points to the possibility for the Member States to apply other measures than the arm's length principle in relation to intercompany financial transactions (provided such measures are not discriminatory[61]), as there is no general obligation stemming from State aid law to apply the arm's length principle as an anti-abuse measure. In this respect, Article 4 of the ATAD contains a general interest limitation rule, and the preamble to the ATAD enables the Member States to implement targeted rules (e.g., thin capitalisation rules) that supplement the general interest limitation rule. The *Fiat* case does not threaten the legality of such rules.

58. *See* the examples provided in the 2022 OECD Guidelines with respect to different intercompany financial transactions, such as para. 10.24 with respect to advances of funds.
59. *See* Opinion of Advocate General Pikamäe delivered on 16 December 2021, Case C-898/19 P, *Ireland v. European Commission*, para. 73.
60. *See* Joined Cases C-182/03 and C-217/03, *Kingdom of Belgium (C-182/03) and Forum 187 ASBL (C-217/03) v. Commission of the European Communities.*
61. *See* in particular Case C-484/19, *Lexel AB v. Skatteverket.*

# PART VIII Dispute Resolution under the OECD, UN and EU Framework

CHAPTER 51

# MAP and Arbitration for Financial Transactions under the Current Tax Treaty Framework: OECD and UN Perspective

*Jonathan Schwarz*[*]

## I INTRODUCTION

Transfer pricing constitutes the single biggest contributor to the mutual agreement procedure caseload. The inexact nature of the arm's-length principle means that there is scope for disagreement on the application of the arm's-length principle embodied in Articles 7, 9, 11 and 12 of the model treaties.[1] Little data is publicly available on the breakdown of map cases by reference to the subject matter of transfer pricing disputes.[2]

In principle, with publicly available information on interest rates and relatively transparent capital markets, the availability of useful data should mean that disputes involving the pricing of financial transactions would be less common than in other areas.

Risk areas of concern to tax administrations in relation to financial transactions are highlighted in the Base Erosion and Profit Shifting (BEPS) Action plan. These include excessive deductible payments such as interest and other financial payments.

---

* The views and opinions set forth herein are the personal views or opinions of the authors; they do not necessarily reflect views or opinions of the organisation with which the authors are associated.

1. OECD Model Tax Convention on Income and on Capital 2017 (the OECD Model); United Nations Model Double Taxation Convention between Developed and Developing Countries 2021 (the 'UN Model'). Article 24(4) (non-discrimination based on the residence of the payee) permits the arm's-length principle to apply to cross-border situations only without constituting discrimination.
2. OECD Commentary to Article 25 of the OECD Model Convention (the 'OECD Commentary'), para. 9. *See also* generally Mutual Agreement Procedure Statistics for 2019, https://www.oecd.org/ctp/dispute/mutual-agreement-procedure-statistics.htm accessed 21 November 2021.

Related transfer pricing concerns identified were deductible payments for other financial transactions, such as financial and performance guarantees, derivatives (including internal derivatives used in intra-bank dealings), and captive and other insurance arrangements.[3]

Domestic case law indicates that the most common transfer pricing issue concerning financial transactions is the recharacterisation of debt as equity and the related recharacterisation of interest as a distribution.[4] Cases before domestic courts on interest rates, currency and other benchmarks are usually less frequent.[5] However, the complex nature of modern financial transactions, including intragroup transactions, is such that pricing may be only one of several issues in contention.

Treaty provisions for resolution of cross-border disputes have evolved slowly since the introduction of the mutual agreement procedure embodied in all modern instruments namely Article 25 of the Organisation for Economic Co-operation and Development (OECD) and UN Model double taxation conventions Article 16 of the BEPS Multilateral Instrument (MLI), the European Union (EU) Arbitration Convention and the EU international tax dispute resolution directive.[6]

Minimum standards for dispute resolution set out in the OECD/G20 Base Erosion and Profit Shifting Project Final Report on Action 14[7] are supervised by peer review process undertaken by members of the countries participating in the OECD-G20 BEPS Project (the 'FTA MAP Forum') as agreed by countries participating in the BEPS Project.[8] This should give taxpayers a high degree of expectation that they will have access to the MAP process, that the competent authorities will undertake the process diligently and that any resulting agreement will be properly implemented.

## II ACCESS TO MAP

Presentation of a case for MAP is a right granted to taxpayers by Article 25(1) of the model treaties. The only requirement is that the taxpayer 'considers that the actions of

3. ACTION 4 Limit base erosion via interest deductions and other financial payments OECD (2013), *Action Plan on Base Erosion and Profit Shifting*, OECD Publishing, http://dx.doi.org/10.1787/9789264202719-en, p. 16-17.
4. *See, e.g.*, *Tribune Media Co. v. CIR*, T.C. Memo 2021-122 (United States Tax Court); *Kelly v. CIR*, TC Memo 2021-76 (United States Tax Court); A Oy, Vuosikirjapäätökset (Finnish Supreme Administrative Court) 2 April 2020, ECLI: FI: KHO: 2020: 35; *Perot Systems TSI (India) Ltd. v. DCIT* (India Income Tax Appellate Tribunal) (2010-TIOL-51-ITAT-DEL); *Knauf Insulation LLC* Russian Eighth Arbitration Court of Appeal, A70-8087/2018.
5. *See, e.g.*, *Chevron Australia Holdings Pty Ltd v. Commissioner of Taxation* [2017] FCAFC 62 (Federal Court of Australia Full court); *Blackrock Holdco 5 LLC v. HMRC* [2020] UKFTT 443 (TC) (United Kingdom First-tier Tribunal); *CIT v. Cotton Naturals India Private Limited* [ITA No. 233/2014 (AY 2007-08)] (India, Delhi High Court); *Singapore Telecom Australia Investments Pty Ltd v. Commissioner of Taxation* [2021] FCA 1597(Federal Court of Australia).
6. These instruments are discussed in detail in J. Schwarz, *Schwarz on Tax Treaties* 6th Edition (Wolters Kluwer 2021) Chapters 18, 20 and 21 to which the reader is directed.
7. OECD (2015), *Making Dispute Resolution Mechanisms More Effective, Action 14 - 2015 Final Report*, OECD/G20 Base Erosion and Profit Shifting Project, OECD Publishing, Paris (the 'Action 14 Final Report'), http://dx.doi.org/10.1787/9789264241633-en.
8. Action 14 Final Report, Annex A. Membership of the FTA MAP Forum is minimum standard 1.4. *See also*, minimum standards 1.5 and 1.6 on participation in the FTA MAP Forum.

one or both of the Contracting States results or will result for [that taxpayer] in taxation not in accordance with the provisions of [the applicable treaty]'. Any difference of opinion between the taxpayer and the tax authority of a Contracting State is sufficient to meet this standard. The relevant competent authorities have no discretion to refuse to accept a case presented by a taxpayer.

Explicit reference to financial relations in Article 9(1) of the model treaties makes clear that, in the context of financial transactions between associated enterprises, a difference of opinion about the debt-to-equity ratio of a financial debtor or any other element of the transaction that may result in the adjustment of profits of an enterprise of a contracting state will result in taxation not in accordance with the provisions of the treaty.

Where taxation of interest potentially engages Article 11, then any difference of opinion about whether the amount of the interest paid is excessive for purposes of Article 11(6) or is to be treated as dividend within Article 10(3), likewise triggers the right to present a case pursuant to Article 25(1).

By extension, where the attribution of profits to a permanent establishment in accordance with Article 7(2) of the OECD Model raises the prospect of any financial dealings between the permanent establishment and other parts of the same enterprise,[9] a difference in opinion about the recognition or of the nature of those dealings or the attribution of capital[10] will result in taxation not in accordance with the provisions of the treaty. The same is true in the attribution of profits under Article 7(2) of the UN Model[11] as well as for the specific denial of deduction of interest expense on moneys lent to or by the permanent establishment (except in the case of a banking enterprise) pursuant to Article 7(3) of the UN Model.

The 2017 OECD Model permits the case to be presented to the competent authority in either contracting state. The 2021 UN Model continues the policy of requiring the case to be presented in the state of residence (or nationality) of the taxpayer. The BEPS Action 14 minimum standard, however, requires that both competent authorities are made aware of MAP cases being presented.[12] This will enable them both to give their views on whether the case is to be accepted or rejected.[13] In those treaties where the case must be presented in the state of residence, the minimum standard requires the competent authorities to implement a bilateral notification or consultation process. This consultation process is not a consultation on resolution of the case.[14]

The only restriction on the right to present case is the time limit in Article 25(1) which requires the case must be presented within three years from the first notification of the action resulting in taxation not in accordance with the treaty.

9. OECD Commentary to Article 7, paras 22 and 23.
10. *Ibid.*, para. 21.
11. UN Commentary to Article 7 of the UN Model (the 'UN Commentary'), para. 19.
12. Action 14 Final Report, minimum standard 3.1.
13. *Ibid.*, para. 35.
14. *Ibid.*, minimum standard 3.1, 2nd bullet point.

Exceptionally, the EU Arbitration Convention gives Contracting States the discretion to deny access to MAP where there is a final ruling, whether legal or administrative, imposing penalties in relation to the actions giving rise to a transfer pricing adjustment of one of the associated enterprises.[15] The EU Arbitration Convention also gives competent authorities the discretion to stay the MAP until the penalty proceedings have concluded.[16] The modern approach as set out in the BEPS Action 14 minimum standard is that such discretion should not be exercised against the taxpayer to deny access in such cases.[17] In the absence of treaty provisions such as Article 8 of the EU Arbitration Convention, Competent Authorities have no discretion in deciding whether or not to admit a case.[18]

Article 25(3) permits the competent authorities to endeavour to resolve difficulties or doubts as to the interpretation or application of a treaty by mutual agreement. While the provision imposes a positive obligation on the competent authorities to do so, no procedure analogous to the presentation of a case by a taxpayer as permitted by Article 25(1) exists.[19] The same is true for the discretionary authority that permits the competent authorities to consult each other for the elimination of double taxation in cases not provided for in the Treaty.

## III RESOLUTION OF MAP CASES

The competent authority to which a case has been presented may unilaterally arrive at a satisfactory solution if the objection appears to it to be justified. If that competent authority is not itself able, to resolve the case, then it must endeavour to do so by mutual agreement with the competent authority of the other Contracting State.[20]

Action 14 Final Report, minimum standard 1 requires Contracting States to ensure that treaty obligations related to the mutual agreement procedure are fully implemented in good faith and that MAP cases are resolved in a timely manner. This requirement is, in effect a restatement of the obligations imposed by Article 26 of the Vienna Convention on the Law of Treaties.

The Action 14 Final Report discussion of the minimum standard specifically observes that economic double taxation that may result from the upwards adjustment of profits of associated enterprises under Article 9(1) (Associated Enterprises) is not in taxation accordance with the object and purpose of the treaty, which is to eliminate double taxation. The report emphasised that a failure to allow MAP with respect to a

15. EU Arbitration Convention, Article 8(1).
16. *Ibid.*, Article 8(2).
17. Action 14 Final Report, minimum standard 1.2.
18. Bundesfinanzhof (German Federal Financial Court), Case IR 82/17, 19 March 2020. Cf. *SGL Carbon Holding* (ECLI:ES:TS:2021:3572), where the Tribunal Supremo, Sala de lo Contencioso-Administrativo (Spanish Supreme Court) denied access to MAP in a case concerning deductibility of related party debt in respect of a transaction the court regarded as abusive. In the author's view, the Spanish Supreme Court's decision and reasoning is flawed.
19. Whether domestic law remedies such as judicial review for a failure to undertake a statutory obligation apply, is a question of domestic administrative law.
20. OECD Model, Article 25(2), UN Model, Article 25(2).

treaty partner's transfer pricing adjustments will, therefore, frustrate a primary objective of tax treaties.[21]

The relationship between Article 25 and corresponding adjustments pursuant to Article 9(2) is not entirely clear. The OECD Transfer Pricing Guidelines[22] indicate that tax administrations may consider requests for corresponding adjustments pursuant to Article 9(2) or corresponding adjustments may be made pursuant to a MAP in response to a primary adjustment under Article 9(1).[23] Article 9(2) requires the competent authorities to consult each other if necessary in making corresponding adjustments, which indicates that these adjustments may be made without presentation of a case by a taxpayer under Article 25(1). Paragraphs 11 and 12 of the OECD Commentary on Article 25 expresses the view that most OECD member countries consider that Article 25 applies both to primary adjustments under Article 9(1) and corresponding adjustments under Article 9(2).

Even where Article 9(2) is not included in a treaty, Article 9(1) reflect the inclusion of economic double taxation within the scope of the treaty with the result that transfer pricing adjustments may be made through MAP under Article 25.[24]

The burden of proof in establishing that the primary adjustment is justified in principle and amount is on the competent authority of the Contracting State that made the primary adjustment.[25] That competent authority accordingly submits its position paper to the competent authority of the other Contracting State which is then in a position to respond with its position.[26]

MAP discussions are a government-to-government process in which the taxpayer has no right to participate in negotiations. OECD Best practice recommends that in fact intensive, unusual, or complex cases it may be valuable for the taxpayer to make a presentation for the purpose of clarifying issues to both competent authorities at the same time, typically prior to the commencement of discussions between them.[27]

The UN Manual[28] emphasises the need for competent authorities to apply a consistent and principled approach in resolving cases, including treating inbound and outbound transactions in the same manner.[29]

Article 25(2) requires that any agreement reached must be implemented notwithstanding any time limits in the domestic law of the Contracting States. This requirement is an Action 14 minimum standard.[30] The purpose of the rule is to ensure that domestic law time limits do not prevent the implementation of MAP agreements and

21. Action 14 Final Report, para. 11. *See also*, OECD Transfer Pricing Guidelines 2022, para. 4.30.
22. OECD Transfer Pricing Guidelines for Multinational Enterprises and Tax Administrations 2022 (the 'OECD Transfer Pricing Guidelines').
23. OECD Transfer Pricing Guidelines 2022, para. 4.32.
24. UN Commentary to Article 25, para. 2.
25. Model treaties, Article 9(2).
26. UN Manual, para. 15.5.3.6.
27. OECD Manual on Effective Mutual Agreement Procedures (MEMAP), Best Practice 13, https://www.oecd.org/ctp/transfer-pricing/3howmap-33roleofthetaxpayer-332.htm, accessed 22 November 2021.
28. United Nations Practical Manual on Transfer Pricing for Developing Countries 2021 (the 'UN Manual').
29. UN Manual para. 15.5.3.1.
30. Action 14, minimum standard 3.3.

thereby frustrate the objective of resolving cases of taxation not in accordance with the Convention.[31] States that cannot include such a provision in their treaties must at least accept treaty provisions that limit the time during which a primary adjustment can be made pursuant to Article 9(1) or (2), in order to avoid late adjustments for which MAP relief will not be available.

## IV ARBITRATION

Resolution of MAP cases in a timely manner is an essential element of the Action 14 minimum standard.[32] This is a response to taxpayer concerns that the utility of MAP is undermined by the time taken to achieve agreement. One response to this is the adoption of mandatory binding arbitration to provide a deadline for resolution, failing which, the case is put into the hands of arbitrators.

While MAP arbitration is now standard within the EU, despite appearing in Article 25(5) of the 2017 OECD Model and as an alternative in Article 25 (alternative B), only a few non-EU countries have indicated interest in arbitration.[33] Part VI of the MLI builds on the basic arbitration framework in Article 25(5) by providing detailed rules and procedures.

Last best offer arbitration is the default choice of procedure in the MLI.[34] This is of significance in transfer pricing cases generally and to the pricing of financial transactions in particular. A simple choice between the positions presented by the two competent authorities, without the need for a reasoned opinion by the arbitrators,[35] means fewer steps that are required to reach resolution and a speedier conclusion to the dispute. Last best offer arbitration also encourages competent authorities to take a reasonable and proportionate approach in formulating their position.

## V ALTERNATIVE DISPUTE RESOLUTION

Slow take up of arbitration, especially among developing countries,[36] means that other methods of dispute resolution may need to be considered where agreement between competent authorities is difficult to achieve. In South Africa and the United Kingdom, for example, alternative dispute resolution is dealt with as an alternative, or precursor, to the normal appeal process to courts and tribunals.[37]

Mediation is the primary method of alternative dispute resolution and is specifically identified as having shown success in disputes within developed and developed

31. *Ibid.*, Final Report, paragraph 38.
32. *Ibid.*, minimum standard 1.
33. Australia, Canada, Japan, New Zealand, Switzerland, the United Kingdom and the United States, *see* Action 14 Final Report, para. 62.
34. MLI, Article 23(1).
35. For example, MLI, Article 23(1)(c).
36. Reasons for reluctance to include Article 25(5) in treaties is explained in the UN Commentary to Article 25, para. 4.
37. South Africa, of the Tax Administration Act No. 28 of 2011, section 103(2); United Kingdom, Tribunal Procedure (First-tier Tribunal) (Tax Chamber) Rules 2009 (SI 2009/273), rule 3.

economies.[38] Mediation can assist where there are difficult relationships or other issues, such as lack of experience of competent authorities, that make states reluctant to agree to arbitration, both of which may inhibit the parties from reaching an agreement.[39] Mediation helps the parties to the dispute to understand their own and the other party's position through communication with a mediator clarifies issues and communicates a view of the strengths and weaknesses of each party to the other.[40] Mediators will not normally express their own opinions or assessment of the merits of the case. Conciliation is a variation of this theme. Conciliation differs from mediation in that the conciliator will form a view as to the merits. Neither produces a legally binding decision which means that the process may or may not result in agreement between the parties. Expert determination may permit the issue or aspects to be resolved by an independent third party. In tax cases, arbitration is normally more acceptable to the parties where resolution by an independent third party is appropriate.

## VI CONCLUSION

Transfer pricing only ever aims to achieve an approximation of what would happen in transactions between independent enterprises. Consequently, it is perhaps the area of tax law most subject to disputes between taxpayers and tax administrations as well as among tax administrations. The fungibility and mobility of money, combined with a multiplicity of legal forms by which capital is provided, has also meant that there is often flexibility in related party transactions which have the effect of shifting profit from one entity to another across international boundaries. Legal mechanisms to resolve the inevitable disputes in this area are relatively primitive compared with well-established domestic judicial and administrative procedures. The EU has taken the lead towards definitive transfer pricing dispute resolution, starting with the 1990 Arbitration Convention, with the OECD and UN following at rather more measured rates.

38. UN Manual, para. 15.4.2.1. OECD Commentary on Article 25, para. 86.
39. UN Manual, para. 15.4.2.2.
40. OECD Commentary on Article 25, para. 86.

CHAPTER 52

# Application of the EU Dispute Resolution Mechanisms to Financial Transactions

*Guglielmo Maisto*[*]

## I INTRODUCTION

This chapter analyses the areas of application of the instruments available within the European Union (EU) to deal with tax disputes concerning financial transactions. The two key dispute resolution mechanisms currently available to taxpayers in the EU are the *Council Directive (EU) 2017/1852 on tax dispute resolution mechanisms in the European Union* (hereinafter, the 'Dispute Resolution Directive') and the *Convention on the elimination of double taxation in connection with the adjustment of profits of associated enterprises 90/436/EEC* (hereinafter the 'Arbitration Convention'). The Dispute Resolution Directive aims to cover a larger set of tax disputes as compared to those covered under the Arbitration Convention. Disputes falling within the Dispute Resolution Directive are indeed disputes pertaining both to the interpretation and application of bilateral tax treaties and to cases covered by the Arbitration Convention (i.e., transfer pricing cases only).[1]

* The views and opinions set forth herein are the personal views or opinions of the authors; they do not necessarily reflect views or opinions of the organization with which the authors are associated.

1. For an in-depth analysis of the scope of the Dispute Resolution Directive *see*: G. MAISTO, *Oggetto e ambito della Direttiva*, in *La risoluzione delle controversie fiscali internazionali nell'Unione Europea*, L. DEL FEDERICO, P. PISTONE & M. TRIVELLIN, Pisa, 2021, 91-119; M. LEHNER, *Neue Regelungsehenen und Kompetenzen im Internationalen Steuerrecht*, IStR, 2019, 283; G. GROEN, *Why the Revised EU Arbitration Directive Is a Big Step in the Right Direction*, in Tax Notes International, 2017, 477; S.P. GOVIND, *The New Face of International Tax Dispute Resolution: Comparing the OECD Multilateral Instrument with the EU Dispute Resolution Directive*, in EC Tax Review, 2018, issue 6, 310; A. MAMMEN, T. JANSEN & S. RASCHE, *Instrumente der Verständigung im internationalen Steuerrecht*, IStR, 2019, 375-376; P. PISTONE, *The Settlement of Cross-Border Tax Disputes in the European Union*, in P. WATTEL, O. MARRES & H. VERMEULEN (eds), *European Tax*

## II RECHARACTERIZATION OF INTERCOMPANY FINANCIAL TRANSACTIONS

The first question to be addressed is whether EU taxpayers may resort to the Dispute Resolution Directive and to the Arbitration Convention for cases involving double taxation stemming from the recharacterization of intercompany financial transactions (such as the recharacterization of a loan into an equity contribution) where such recharacterization is not based on ordinary domestic transfer pricing provisions but, for example, on domestic anti-abuse rules. In principle, adjustments which are based on domestic transfer pricing provisions rely on the application of the arm's length principle as set forth by Article 9 of the *OECD Model Tax Convention on Income and on Capital* (hereinafter, the 'OECD Model') and as implemented in double tax treaties. Any double taxation issues stemming from such adjustments thus in principle fall within the scope of application of the Dispute Resolution Directive and of the Arbitration Convention.

However, the wording of the Commentary on Article 9, which is explicitly recalled by the *OECD Transfer Pricing Guidelines for Multinational Enterprises and Tax Administrations* (hereinafter, the 'TP Guidelines'), seems to allow contracting states to rely on the arm's length principle not only for determining the quantum of a transfer pricing adjustment concerning a financial transaction but also to assess whether the characterization of a financial transaction is that which independent parties would have agreed upon. The Commentary includes the example of interest payments connected to a purported loan and indicates that such interest payments may assume a different nature where such loan is recharacterized as a contribution to equity capital.[2] The possibility of recharacterization is provided by the Commentary on Article 9 should be read alongside paragraph 10.9 of Chapter X of the TP Guidelines, which expressly limits the scope of Article 9 by maintaining that the latter is not intended to prevent countries from implementing under their domestic legislation rules aimed at addressing the balance of debt and equity of an entity and the relevant interest deductibility. Nor does it seek to mandate the accurate delineation under Chapter I of the TP Guidelines as the only approach for determining whether purported debt should be characterized as such. The TP Guidelines rather seem to acknowledge that the recharacterization of a financial transaction may not be based on transfer pricing rules only but also on other domestic provisions aimed at tackling excessive interest deductions, such as anti-avoidance thin capitalization rules.[3] Double taxation issues arising from recharacterizations of financial transactions based on such domestic

---

*Law*, Deventer, 2018, 350; G. Kofler, *EU Tax Dispute Resolution Directive: The Deathblow to Double Taxation in the European Union*, cit., 267-268.

2. Cf. para. 10.5 of Chapter X of the TP Guidelines, which reads as follows: 'Commentary to Article 9 of the OECD Model Tax Convention notes at paragraph 3(b) that Article 9 is relevant "not only in determining whether the rate of interest provided for in a loan contract is an arm's length rate, but also whether a prima facie loan can be regarded as a loan or should be regarded as some other kind of payment, in particular a contribution to equity capital"'.
3. For further considerations on this topic, *see* C. Burnett, Intra-group Debt at the Crossroads: Stand-Alone Versus Worldwide Approach, in World Tax J., 6, 2014, 1, Journal Articles & Papers IBFD.

anti-avoidance provisions may thus not automatically fall within the scope of the Dispute Resolution Directive and of the Arbitration Convention since they would not concern the interpretation and application of Article 9 of the OECD Model. Any double taxation issues arising from such recharacterizations should thus be assessed on a case-by-case basis to assess whether a transfer pricing provision or a domestic anti-abuse provision was actually employed for the purposes of the challenge.

With reference to thin capitalization rules, the OECD Council adopted in 1986 an *ad hoc* report (hereinafter, the 'OECD 1986 Report')[4] whereby it provided its views on tax treaty aspects of recharacterization of interest payments into dividend payments and debt into equity. The Organisation for Economic Co-operation and Development (OECD) concluded that if the recharacterization of interest under domestic thin capitalization rules has the effect of including in the profits of a domestic enterprise only profits which would have accrued at arm's length, Article 9 does not prevent the operation of those rules.[5] No common view was, however, reached on whether Article 9 may inhibit the operation of domestic thin capitalization rules where the application of such rules leads to attribution to the enterprise of an amount of profits which exceeds the arm's length amount.[6] The Committee agreed that, in principle, the application of rules designed to deal with thin capitalization should not increase the taxable profits of the relevant domestic enterprise to any amount greater than the arm's length profit. This principle should be followed either in applying existing tax treaties – in particular, in the operation of the mutual agreement procedure (MAP) under the equivalent of Article 25 of the OECD Model – and in the negotiation of bilateral treaties. In this respect, the Committee also agreed that MAPs under Article 25 of the OECD Model provide an appropriate framework to address double taxation issues stemming from the application of domestic thin capitalization rules to the extent that the relevant adjustment is based on the application of a substantive provision of the OECD Model (such as Article 9).[7]

Issues which may arise from the application of domestic thin capitalization rules and the possible recourse to the Arbitration Convention have also been addressed at the EU level.[8] Article 4(1) of the Arbitration Convention does not specify whether thin

4. OECD, *Report on thin capitalization,* adopted by the OECD Council on 26 November 1986.
5. *See* para. 49 of the OECD 1986 Report.
6. *See* para. 50 of the OECD 1986 Report, according to which: 'There is some diversity of opinion about this. One group of countries takes the view that where a provision similar to Article 9(1) is included in the convention, it simply prohibits an adjustment of the profits of the resident company to any amount exceeding the arm's length profit. Another group of countries takes the view that while Article 9(1) permits the adjustment of profits up to the arm's length amount it does not go beyond that to prohibit the taxation of a higher amount in appropriate circumstances. A third group, while accepting that there is an absence of such a prohibition in the language used, nevertheless takes the view that the practical effect of Article 9 must often be to impose such a restraint.'
7. *See* paras 67 to 69 of the OECD 1986 Report.
8. *See* Communication from the commission to the council, the European Parliament and the European Economic and Social Committee on the work of the EU Joint Transfer Pricing Forum in the period March 2007 to March 2009 and a related proposal for a revised Code of Conduct for the effective implementation of the Arbitration Convention (90/436/EEC of 23 July 1990) COM(2009) 472 final and Commission staff working document accompanying the communication from the Commission to the Council, the European Parliament and the European Economic and Social

capitalization cases fall within its scope of application. It only generally refers to cases where 'conditions are made or imposed between the two enterprises in their commercial or *financial relations* which differ from those which would be made between independent enterprises [...]' (Emphasis added). The expression 'financial relations' is not defined elsewhere in the Arbitration Convention. The 2009 Revised Code of Conduct for the effective implementation of the Arbitration Convention (hereinafter the 'Code of Conduct') provides that the Arbitration Convention 'makes clear reference to profits arising from commercial and financial relations but does not seek to differentiate between these specific profit types. *Therefore, profit adjustments arising from financial relations, including a loan and its terms, and based on the arm's length principle are to be considered within the scope of the Arbitration Convention*' (Emphasis added).[9] The EU Commission thereby encouraged Member States to interpret the words 'financial relations' in Article 4(1) of the Arbitration Convention in a broad manner to give the widest possible access to the benefits of the Arbitration Convention. Moreover, with respect to thin capitalization legislation based on a (fixed) debt/equity ratio, the Commission argued that, since Article 4(1) includes the words 'financial relations', the scope of application of the Arbitration Convention is sufficiently broad so as to cover all types of thin capitalization rules.[10] The Commission, therefore, invited Member States to permit access to the Arbitration Convention for all thin capitalization cases (based either on the arm's length principle or on fixed debt/equity ratios). Moreover, the Commission subsequently included the recommendation adopted by the EU Joint Transfer Pricing Forum (hereinafter, the 'EU JTPF') in its proposal for the revision of the Code of Conduct.[11] Nevertheless, a significant number of Member States made reservations aimed at restricting the scope of application of the Arbitration Convention to cases concerning the adjustments on the interest rate applied to loans rather than adjustments on the amount of the loan.[12] Such reservations actually stem from the work carried out by the JTPF between 2007 and 2009 to analyse whether or not the scope of application of the Arbitration Convention should also include thin capitalization cases.[13] In this regard, the EU JTPF's secretariat issued a questionnaire to

---

Committee on the work of the EU Joint Transfer Pricing Forum in the period march 2007 to march 2009 and a related proposal for a revised code of conduct for the effective implementation of the Arbitration Convention (90/436/EEC of 23 July 1990), final report of the EU Joint Transfer Pricing Forum on the interpretation of some provisions of the arbitration convention, SEC(2009)1169 final.

9. *See* Revised Code of Conduct for the effective implementation of the Convention on the elimination of double taxation in connection with the adjustment of profits of associated enterprises (2009/C 322/01), para. 1.2, footnote 1.
10. On the basis of the European Court of Justice's (ECJ) ruling in the thin cap case, the Commission concluded that thin capitalization rules have a relation to the arm's length principle, and for that reason, these cases are included in the scope of application of the EU Arbitration Convention. *See* European Commission, COM(2009) 472 final, para. 2.2. For the ECJ's ruling, *see* ECJ, Judgment of 13 March 2007 in Case C-524/04 Test Claimants in the Thin Cap Group Litigation v. Commissioners of Inland Revenue [2007] ECR I-2107.
11. *See* European Commission, COM (2009)472 final, paras 2.2 and 5.
12. *See* footnote 1 at p. 2 of the Code of Conduct.
13. EU JTPF, JTPF/030/REV2/BACK/2006/EN, p. 4. *See also* EU JTPF, JTPF/009/BACK/2007/EN; and EU JTPF, JTPF/020/BACK/2007/EN, p. 3. The representatives argued that thin capitalization cases have a clear link with the arm's length principle. Nevertheless, there was uncertainty

discover how Member States' thin capitalization rules were construed in their domestic legislations and whether they were willing to apply the Arbitration Convention to cases concerning capitalization rules based on the arm's length principle and on a debt/equity ratio.[14] Upon such questionnaire, all 27 interviewed Member States declared to be willing to apply the Arbitration Convention to cases concerning thin capitalization rules based on the arm's length principle. Nevertheless, Bulgaria, Cyprus, the Czech Republic, Finland, Italy, Latvia, Lithuania, the Netherlands, Poland and Portugal declared to be reluctant to apply the Arbitration Convention to thin capitalization cases concerning thin capitalization rules based on fixed debt/equity ratios. The discussions within the EU JTPF thus pointed out the lack of consensus among Member States regarding whether (o to what extent) thin capitalization cases fall within the scope of application of the Arbitration Convention. In particular, the lack of definitions of the words 'financial relations', together with the significant number of reservations made by Member States to the Code of Conduct, left open the question of whether the Arbitration Convention actually covers only cases concerning the arm's length nature of the pricing of a loan rather also cases concerning adjustments of its amount.

Based on the above, it is possible to conclude that adjustments concerning the denial of deductibility of costs for interest payments due to the application of domestic thin capitalization rules which conform to the arm's length principle should fall within the scope of application of the Dispute Resolution Directive and of the Arbitration Convention. Such double taxation issues indeed concern the correct interpretation of either (i) Article 9 of the OECD Model, as implemented in the applicable double tax treaty; or (ii) Article 4(1) of the Arbitration Convention. On the other hand, uncertainties remain on whether adjustments of financial transactions based on thin capitalization rules which rely on fixed debt/equity ratios may fall within the scope of application of the Dispute Resolution Directive and of the Arbitration Convention. Such adjustments could indeed be viewed as arising from purely domestic provisions, thus falling outside the scope of both Article 9 of the OECD Model and Article 4(1) of the Arbitration Convention.

## III SECONDARY ADJUSTMENTS

As known, with a secondary adjustment, the tax Authorities identify, and subject to tax, a constructive transaction with the aim of making the actual allocation of profits between the involved taxpayers consistent with the primary adjustment. This constructive transaction may take the form of a constructive dividend payment, an equity contribution or, in many cases, a constructive interest-bearing loan.

as to whether the Arbitration Convention applies to such cases, as not all Member States' thin capitalization legislation was based on or had a link with the arm's length principle.

14. *See* EU JTPF, JTPF/012/2007/EN, and European Commission, SEC (2009) 1169 final, annex II.

Several criticisms have been raised about the possible application of the Arbitration Convention to cases of double taxation arising from secondary adjustments.[15] In this respect, it has been pointed out that the literal interpretation of the provision of the Arbitration Convention dealing with its scope of application would rule out this possibility. This is because it only refers to primary and corresponding adjustments, without making any explicit reference to secondary adjustments.[16] The same conclusion may also be drawn considering the statements released by several Member States in the Final Report on Secondary Adjustments published by the EU JTPF in 2013.[17] In particular, most of the interviewed Member States that have declared to make secondary adjustments have also stated that they consider that cases of double taxation arising from such secondary adjustments fall outside the scope of the Arbitration Convention.[18]

As regards the possible application of the Dispute Resolution Directive to cases of double taxation arising from secondary adjustments, reference should be made to whether such cases might fall within the MAPs set forth by Article 25, paragraphs 1-3, of the OECD Model. This is because, the Dispute Resolution Directive concerns cases which 'arise from the interpretation and application of agreements and conventions that provide for the elimination of double taxation of income and, where applicable, capital'.[19] In this respect, with the term 'double taxation' the Dispute Resolution Directive refers to the application of taxes (by two or more Member States) on the same income or capital 'when it gives rise to either: (i) an additional tax charge; (ii) an increase in tax liabilities; or (iii) the cancellation or reduction of losses that could be used to offset taxable profits'.[20]

The MAPs set forth by Article 25, paragraphs 1 and 2, of the OECD Model could be deemed suitable, at first sight, for dealing with double taxation issues arising from secondary adjustments. However, these MAPs are special procedures which go beyond the scope of application of domestic rules of contracting states and may be activated only in cases of taxation not in accordance with the provisions of the convention.[21] In this respect, it must be pointed out that secondary adjustments are not governed by

---

15. *See, inter alia,* H.M. Pit, *Dispute Resolution in the EU,* Alphen aan den Rijn, 2018, 391; R.R. Texeira, Tax Treaty Consequences of Secondary Transfer Pricing Adjustments, in Intertax, 37(8/9), 2009 470 and T.J.J. Ghislain, Transfer Pricing: The EC Arbitration Convention as a Dispute Resolution Mechanism, in International Tax Journal, 28, 2002, n. 2.
16. *See* Article 1 of the Arbitration Convention: "This Convention shall apply where, for the purposes of taxation, profits which are included in the profits of an enterprise of a Contracting State are also included or are also likely to be included in the profits of an enterprise of another Contracting State on the grounds that the principles set out in Article 4 and applied either directly or in corresponding provisions of the law of the State concerned have not been observed."
17. *See* Doc. JTPF/017/FINAL/2012/EN "EU Joint Transfer Pricing Forum, Final Report on Secondary Adjustments - Meeting of 25 October 2012").
18. *See* para. 22 of Doc. JTPF/017/FINAL/2012/EN "EU Joint Transfer Pricing Forum, Final Report on Secondary Adjustments - Meeting of 25 October 2012".
19. Cf. Article 1 of the Dispute Resolution Directive (Subject matter and scope).
20. *See* Article 2 of the Dispute Resolution Directive (Definitions).
21. *See* para. 8 of the OECD Commentary on Article 25. This paragraph specifies, however, that when a levy has been imposed contrary to both the Convention and domestic law, the case can only be the subject of a MAP if the latter concerns the application of the Convention rules, unless there is a link between them and the rules of domestic law which have been incorrectly applied.

Article 9 of the OECD Model[22] and, thus, they would not expressly give rise to taxation not in accordance with such provision which could be dealt with under the MAPs of Article 25, paragraphs 1 and 2. In the author's view, however, cases of double taxation arising from secondary adjustments might fall within the scope of those MAPs if such secondary adjustments entailed an inconsistent application of the distributive rules of the OECD Model. This would be the case, for instance, if the taxation of constructive interest payments connect to a secondary adjustment were inconsistent with the provision of Article 11 of the OECD Model (as implemented in the applicable double tax treaty).

Finally, in the author's view, cases of double taxation arising from secondary adjustments should nevertheless be dealt within the MAP provided by Article 25, paragraph 3, of the OECD Model, according to which competent Authorities are also entitled to consult each other to eliminate double taxation in cases not provided for in the OECD Model.[23] This conclusion seems to be consistent with the work carried out at the OECD level, which expressed several times the need to provide comprehensive guidelines on the relationship between secondary adjustments and MAP.[24] In this respect, the OECD Secretariat has pointed out that despite secondary adjustments are not explicitly governed by Article 9 of the OECD Model, these adjustments are not excluded from the scope of application of double tax treaties and, therefore, they may fall within the scope of the relevant MAPs set forth by the OECD Model.[25]

## IV WITHHOLDING TAX ISSUES

Article 11, paragraph 6, of the OECD Model enshrines a specific provision governing cases where, by reason of special relationships between the payer and the beneficial owner or between both and some other persons, interest paid exceeds those which

22. *See* para. 8 of the OECD Commentary on Article 9 of the OECD Model. Paragraph 9 of the Commentary on Article 9 only clarifies that such provision neither recommends nor prevents contracting states from making secondary adjustments based on their domestic law.
23. *See* Article 25, para. 3 of the OECD Model, according to which: "The competent authorities of the Contracting States shall endeavour to resolve by mutual agreement any difficulties or doubts arising as to the interpretation or application of the Convention. They may also consult together for the elimination of double taxation in cases not provided for in the Convention."
24. *See* p. 26 of the OECD paper "Improving the Process for Resolving International Tax Disputes" of 27 July 2004 and p. 41 of the OECD document "Improving the Resolution of Tax Treaty Disputes" of February 2007, which suggest the following: "The relationship between secondary adjustments and the MAP process could be reviewed with a view toward greater emphasis on the desirability, but not the requirement, that such issues be considered in the MAP process."
25. *See* para. 111 of the OECD document '*Improving the Process for Resolving International Tax Disputes*' of 27 July 2004, according to which "Paragraph 4.70 of the OECD Transfer Pricing Guidelines [...] appears to be saying that Article 9 does not specifically deal with secondary adjustments, neither forbidding nor requiring them. They are not totally outside the Convention framework, so that it appears that MAP *can* apply in respect of them if the relevant conditions are met.' The possibility of access to the MAPs in the case of secondary adjustments seems, moreover, to have been confirmed by the OECD also in the 'Manual on Effective Mutual Agreement Procedures' of 2007 (*see* para. 4.6). and in the Commentary to Article 11 of the Model (*see* para. 36). However, no reference is made in either document which paragraph of Article 25 of the OECD Model is suitable to address such cases.

would have been agreed had no such relationships occurred. This provision denies treaty benefits of Article 11 with respect to the excess part of the interest, which remains taxable according to the laws of the two contracting states involved, due regard being had to the other provisions of the OECD Model.[26] As for the tax treatment of the exceeding interest, the nature of the latter must be ascertained according to the circumstances of each case, in order to determine the category of income in which it should be classified for the purposes of applying the provisions of the tax laws of the contracting states concerned and the provisions of the relevant double tax treaty.[27] Article 11, paragraph 6 nevertheless does not allow the reclassification of the loan in such a way as to give it the character of a contribution to equity capital, since it only permits the adjustment of the rate at which interest is charged.[28] Considering that 'special relationships' may be found in cases similar or analogous to those contemplated by Article 9 of the OECD Model,[29] the limitations provided by Article 11, paragraph 6 clearly apply to interest exceeding the arm's length amount in the context of intercompany loans.[30]

Against this context, questions arise as to whether double taxation issues deriving from the tax treatment applied to the portion of interest exceeding the arm's length amount may be dealt with in the context of MAPs. In this regard, the key issue is whether the determination of the applicable tax treatment of the exceeding interest is a purely domestic law matter (ruling out the possibility of resorting to MAPs) rather than a matter of application or interpretation of the relevant double tax treaty. In this respect, the Commentary on Article 11, paragraph 6, does not provide significant explanations, since it only maintains that the exact nature of such excess will need to be ascertained according to the circumstances of each case, in order to determine the

---

26. Paragraph 6 of Art. 11 of the OECD Model provides that: "Where, by reason of a special relationship between the payer and the beneficial owner or between both of them and some other person, the amount of the interest, having regard to the debt-claim for which it is paid, exceeds the amount which would have been agreed upon by the payer and the beneficial owner in the absence of such relationship, the provisions of this Article shall apply only to the last-mentioned amount. In such case, the excess part of the payments shall remain taxable according to the laws of each Contracting State, due regard being had to the other provisions of this Convention."
27. Cf. para. 35 of the Commentary on Article 11.
28. Cf. *ibid*. This is also consistent with the wording of para. 6 of Article 11, according to which the assessment of the amount of interest must be carried out 'having regard to the debt-claim for which it is paid'.
29. Cf. para. 33 of the Commentary on Article 11, which reads as follows: 'It is clear from the text that for this clause to apply the interest held excessive must be due to a special relationship between the payer and the beneficial owner or between both of them and some other person. There may be cited as examples cases where interest is paid to an individual or legal person who directly or indirectly controls the payer, or who is directly or indirectly controlled by him or is subordinate to a group having common interest with him. These examples, moreover, are similar or analogous to the cases contemplated by Article 9.'
30. This is confirmed by the wording of para. 32 of the Commentary on Article 11, which reads as follows: 'The purpose of this paragraph is to restrict the operation of the provisions concerning the taxation of interest in cases where, by reason of a special relationship between the payer and the beneficial owner or between both of them and some other person, the amount of the interest paid exceeds the amount which would have been agreed upon by the payer and the beneficial owner *had they stipulated at arm's length*.' (Emphasis added)

category of income in which it be classified 'for the purposes of applying the provisions of the tax laws of the States concerned *and* the provisions of the Convention' (emphasis added).[31] Based on such wording, it could be argued that Article 11, paragraph 6, requires first to verify the existence of domestic law provisions of Contracting States suitable for characterizing the 'excess' interest and secondly, also in the light of such classification, to assess the applicability of any other provision of the relevant double tax treaty which may govern taxing rights of Contracting States over such exceeding amount (e.g., Article 7 or 21 of the OECD Model).

Hence, it could be argued that the assessment of the tax treatment applicable to the portion of interest exceeding the arm's length does not seem to be a purely domestic law matter, since any domestic tax treatment applied should nevertheless be consistent with the other provisions of applicable double tax treaty. Consequently, one may conclude that any double taxation issue deriving from a tax treatment of the exceeding interest which is inconsistent with the provisions of the applicable double tax treaty might in principle fall within the scope of the MAP provided by such treaty and, consequently, within the scope of the Dispute Resolution Directive.

## V THE CJEU CASE LAW AND THE DISPUTE RESOLUTION DIRECTIVE

The Court of Justice of the European Union (CJEU) has many times addressed cases concerning the compatibility of domestic transfer pricing provisions with the fundamental freedoms enshrined in the Treaty of Functioning of the European Union (TFEU), whereby it developed, *inter alia*, principles dealing with the application of the arm's length principle to financial transactions. In this respect, for instance, the CJEU dealt with the arm's length principle in the context of interest-free loans and guarantees in its decisions C-311/08, of 21 January 2010 (SGI),[32] and C-382/16, of 31 May 2018 (Hornback).[33] The CJEU maintained that transfer pricing domestic rules can be considered compatible with the TFEU insofar as, *inter alia*, the taxpayer is given an

31. *See* para. 35 of the Commentary to Art. 11 of the OECD Model.
32. Cf. case C-311/08, *Société de Gestion Industrielle SA (SGI) v. Belgian State.* SGI was a holding company incorporated under Belgian law and active in the metallurgical industry. It owned a 65% shareholding in Recydem SA, a French company, and was one of the directors of that company. A Luxembourg company, SA Cobelpin, owned a 34% shareholding in SGI and was a director and managing director of SGI. The Belgian tax authorities made an upward adjustment to SGI's profits for notional interest (calculated at an annual rate of 5%) on an interest-free loan granted to Recydem and denied SGI a deduction, for corporate income tax purposes, of management fees paid to Cobelpin, arguing that these were not at arm's length.
33. Cf. case C-382/16 *Hornbach-Baumarkt.* The case concerned a parent company tax resident of Germany, which provided – free of any remuneration – guarantees and comfort letters in favour of its foreign subsidiaries. The German tax authorities, by applying the transfer pricing legislation, adjusted upwards the profits of the parent company under the assumption that unrelated parties would have agreed on a remuneration in a similar situation. The CJEU relied on its previous decision in the SGI case in which it held that transfer pricing legislations can be considered proportionate insofar as, *inter alia*, the taxpayer is given an opportunity, without being subject to undue administrative constraints, to provide evidence of any commercial justification that there may have been for that transaction.

opportunity, without being subject to undue administrative constraints, to provide evidence of any commercial justification[34] that there may have been for that transaction. In a nutshell, in the CJEU's view, there could be cases where intercompany interest-free loans or guarantees, granted free of any remuneration, may nevertheless be consistent with the arm's length principle. This principle has also been reiterated in the latest CJEU's judgment in case C-558/19 (Impresa Pizzarotti),[35] whereby the Court confirmed that there could be objective reasons for concluding intercompany transactions at prices other than the market prices. As regards interest-free loans, the CJEU went even further in its recent judgment C-257/20, of 24 February 2022 (Viva Telecom Bulgaria)[36] whereby it held that the TFEU does not preclude a Member State imposing withholding tax on notional arm's length interest under its anti-avoidance tax rules. In particular, in the Court's view, this notional amount is not eligible for the exemption provided by the Interest – Royalty Directive 2003/49/EC nor by the Parent-Subsidiary Directive 2011/96/EU as there have been no actual payment among the parties.

Against this context, questions arise as to whether the abovementioned principles developed by the CJEU's case law could be relied on by taxpayers, competent Authorities or arbitrators within disputes on financial transactions addressed through the Dispute Resolution Directive. However, in the author's view the answer is negative.

---

34. In this respect, the CJEU went on to clarify the meaning of the concept of '*commercial justification*' by stating that in a situation where the expansion of the business operations of a subsidiary requires additional capital, due to the fact that the latter lacks sufficient equity capital, there may be commercial reasons for a parent company to agree to provide capital on non-arm's-length terms (cf. para. 54). Hence, the CJEU concluded that the gratuitous granting of comfort letters containing a guarantee statement could be explained by the economic interest of the shareholder in the financial success of the foreign group subsidiaries (cf. para. 56).
35. Cf. case C-558/19, *Impresa Pizzarotti & C SPA Italia Sucursala Cluj v. Agenția Națională de Administrare Fiscală – Direcția Generală de Administrare a Marilor Contribuabili*. The case concerns the compatibility with the freedom of establishment of the Romanian transfer pricing legislation, based on which the Romanian tax Authorities challenged the interest-free nature of two loans between an Italian company (borrower) and its Romanian permanent establishment (lender). The CJEU found, *inter alia*, that the transfer pricing adjustments were justified by overriding reasons in the public interest, as they ensured the balanced allocation of taxing rights between Member States by preventing profits generated in the Member State concerned from being transferred outside the tax jurisdiction of that Member State via transactions not in accordance with market conditions. The Court also found, subject to verification by the national court, that the domestic legislation at stake did not exceed what is necessary to attain the legitimate objective underlying that legislation since, *inter alia*, the taxpayer is given the opportunity, without being subject to undue administrative constraints, to provide evidence of any commercial justification for the relevant transactions (*see* CJEU, 21 January 2010, case C-311/08, SGI, paras 71-72).
36. Cf. case C-257/20 *Viva Telekom Bulgaria EOOD v. Direktor na Direktsia Obzhalvane i danachno-osiguritelna praktika*. The case concern Viva Telekom Bulgaria EAD (Viva Telekom), a Bulgarian resident company, which entered into a loan agreement with its sole shareholder InterV Investment S.a.r.l., a company resident in Luxembourg. The agreement stipulated that the loan was interest free and would mature in 60 years from the date of entry into force (the loan could be converted to a contribution in kind in Viva Telekom's equity at any time after the date of granting the loan). Viva Telekom was subject to a tax audit and, at that time, the loan had not been converted into capital. Nor Viva Telekom had made reimbursement payments of the loan nor paid interest. The tax Authorities concluded that the performance of the loan agreement had resulted in tax avoidance as no instalments or no interest on the loan had been paid. Thus, they assessed notional interest on the loan together with a withholding tax of 10%.

This is because, notwithstanding such principles deal with the application of the arm's length principle, it must be borne in mind that they only concern the interpretation of the provisions of the TFEU, which fall outside the scope of the Dispute Resolution Directive, i.e., the interpretation and application of agreements and conventions that provide for the elimination of double taxation of income or capital.

# Part IX A Developing Countries Perspective on Financial Transactions: Selected Issues

CHAPTER 53

# Transfer Pricing Aspects of Financial Transactions: A South African Perspective

*Michael Hewson*[*]

## I INTRODUCTION

Financial transactions taking place cross border with a South African entity require careful consideration from a tax and regulatory perspective. Legislation was implemented as far back as 1995 to regulate the arm's length nature of cross-border related party transactions. These regulations have evolved over time and now focus on various different aspects of financial transactions including the arm's length level of debt, the price paid and the deductibility of interest. At the same time, there are other provisions that apply to cross-border financial transactions, including withholding taxes and exchange controls.

The topic is of particular interest in South Africa for two reasons. First, the country is a high importer of capital (compared to the capital outflows). Second, the corporate income tax (CIT) rate is relatively high. Third, it is generally more beneficial from a tax perspective to fund an entity through debt rather than equity. Accordingly, there is an incentive for South African entities to be more highly geared.

In addressing these considerations, and the risk of base erosion and profit shifting (BEPS) that arises through the use of cross-border financial transactions, policymakers in South Africa acknowledge the work of the Organisation for Economic Co-operation and Development (OECD). In particular, the OECD proposed Action 4 in response to

[*] The views and opinions set forth herein are the personal views or opinions of the authors; they do not necessarily reflect views or opinions of the organisation with which the authors are associated.

the risk of BEPS which pertains to interest limitations. It has also incorporated a new chapter on financial assistance in the 2022 version of the OECD Guidelines.[1]

According to the South African National Treasury, the 'current interest limitation rules (in South Africa) have similar design features to the fixed ratio rule recommended by the OECD, but there are differences. The existing rules are comparatively less strict than the OECD recommendations and narrower in application'.[2]

At the same time, National Treasury acknowledges that there are other rules that mitigate the risk from excessive interest deductions, specifically the transfer pricing and exchange control regulations.

This chapter provides an overview of the transfer pricing principles applying to cross-border related party transactions pertaining to financial transactions. It also highlights factors affecting interest deductions for financial transactions. Please note that it is not an exhaustive source of all the tax principles relating to financial transactions.

The chapter is set out as follows:

- Context of the legislation and guidance on transfer pricing in South Africa
- The arm's length principle
- Financial transactions in scope of the South African transfer pricing provisions
- Types of transactions
- Approach to testing the arm's length nature of financial assistance
- Order of application of income tax provisions
- Compliance requirements
- Court cases
- Conclusion.

## II CONTEXT OF THE LEGISLATION AND GUIDANCE ON TRANSFER PRICING IN SOUTH AFRICA

### 1 Brief History

South Africa and Namibia were the first two countries in Africa to introduce transfer pricing legislation in 1995. South Africa published its provisions in section 31 of the Income Tax Act no. 58 of 1962 (SA Income Tax Act). The regulations granted the Commissioner of South African Revenue Service (SARS) discretion to make a transfer pricing adjustment if he/she determined that the prices of a transaction were non-arm's length.

In 1999, a practice note was released (PN 7[3]) which contains guiding principles for the application of transfer pricing provisions in South Africa. In 2002, a second

1. OECD Guidelines, Chapter X, January 2022.
2. South African National Treasury, 'Reviewing the Tax Treatment of Excessive Debt Financing, Interest Deductions and Other Financial Payments', 26 February 2020.
3. SARS Practice Note 7: Determination of the taxable income of certain persons from international transactions: Transfer pricing, 6 August 1999.

practice note on transfer pricing (PN 2[4]) was released, and it contained guidance on transfer pricing and thin capitalisation aspects of financial transactions.

Specifically, in terms of the acceptable level of debt, PN 2 contained the thin capitalisation provisions which stipulated that the maximum Debt: Equity ratio was set at 3:1.

PN 2 also provided a safe harbour for interest rates for inbound loans set at the prime lending rate plus two percentage points in the case of Rand-denominated loans and the relevant interbank rate plus two percentage points in the case of foreign currency-denominated loans.

For years of assessment commencing on or after 1 April 2012, section 31 was amended, and the responsibility was placed on the taxpayer to ensure that transactions were arm's length and to make adjustments in the event that they were non-arm's length. The consequence of a non-arm's length amount was that it gave rise to a deemed loan that accrued deemed interest. Under the changes that were introduced, thin capitalisation and the requirement for the price of debt to be arm's length were no longer governed under a separate sub-section of section 31. Rather, the arm's length test was introduced to evaluate both the level of debt and the price of the debt with effect for years of assessment commencing on or after 1 April 2012.

PN 2 was repealed for years of assessment commencing on or after 1 April 2012 since the legislation had changed and the principles of PN 2 on financial transactions were no longer valid.

A draft interpretation note (Old Draft IN)[5] was released in March 2013, and it set out principles for considering financial transactions. In many regards, the Old Draft IN contained principles that ultimately were incorporated in the 2022 version of the OECD Guidance on financial transactions,[6] such as, the need to consider transactions from the perspective of the lender and the borrower, and the need for a full evaluation of the arm's length nature of the arrangement.

The Old Draft IN also contained a 'risk harbour rate' for inbound loans which stipulated that inbound loans are more likely to be audited if the company's Debt: EBITDA ratio exceeded 3:1. Furthermore, it stated that an inbound related party debt denominated in Rand would be of higher risk if the interest rate applied exceeds the weighted average of the Johannesburg interbank average rate (JIBAR) plus 2%. Likewise, inbound debt denominated in foreign currencies would be considered of higher risk if the interest rate exceeded the relevant interbank rate plus 2%.

The Old Draft IN was never finalised.

In February 2022, SARS released a new draft interpretation note on financial transactions (New Draft IN).[7] This New Draft IN was finalised in January 2023[8] (New IN) is discussed in more detail below.

---

4. SARS Practice Note 7: Determination of the taxable income where financial assistance has been granted by a non-resident of the Republic to a resident of the Republic, 14 May 1996.
5. SARS Draft Interpretation Note: Determination of the taxable income of certain persons from international transactions: This capitalisation, March 2013.
6. OECD Guidelines, 2022 Version, Chapter X.
7. SARS Draft Interpretation Note: Determination of the taxable income of certain persons from international transactions: Intra-group loans, February 2022.

The timeline of the South African transfer pricing regulations pertaining to financial transactions is illustrated in Figure 53.1.

*Figure 53.1 Timeline of South African Transfer Pricing Provisions on Financial Transactions*

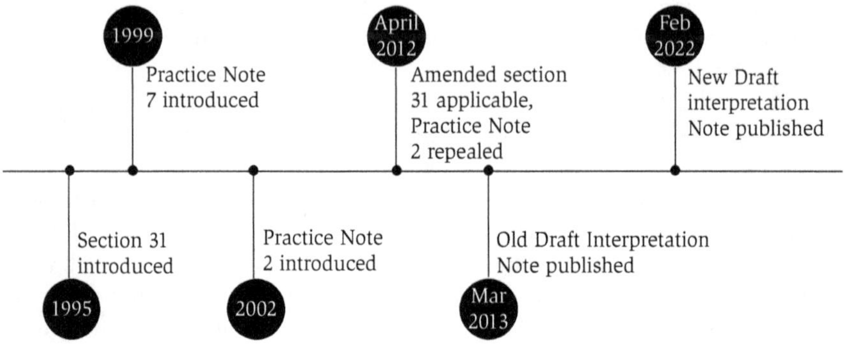


## 2 Status of Various Regulations and Guidance in South Africa

SARS issued PN 7 which sets out further guidance for performing a transfer pricing analysis. While PN 7 does not contain detailed guidance on how to analyse and evaluate transfer pricing aspects of intercompany financial arrangements, it states the following in paragraph 3.2.1:

> Because of the international importance of the Organisation for Economic Cooperation and Development's ('OECD') Transfer Pricing Guidelines for Multinational Enterprises and Tax Administrations ('OECD TP Guidelines'), this Practice Note is based on, *inter alia*, those guidelines. Although South Africa is not a member country of the OECD, the OECD Guidelines are acknowledged as an important, influential document that reflects unanimous agreement amongst the member countries, reached after an extensive process of consultation with industry and tax practitioners in many countries. The OECD Guidelines are also followed by many countries which are not OECD members and are therefore becoming a globally accepted standard.

Furthermore, paragraph 3.2.3 states that, 'The OECD Guidelines should be followed in the absence of specific guidance in terms of this Practice Note, the provisions of section 31 or the tax treaties entered into by South Africa.'

The use of guidance from the OECD and other international sources was further enhanced in a tax court ruling[9] in South Africa in December 2020 whereby the court referred to the OECD TP Guidelines and relevant international court cases.

8. Interpretation Note 127: Determination of the taxable income of certain persons from international transactions: Intra-group loans.
9. IT 14305: *ABC (Pty) Ltd v. CSARS*, 3 December 2020.

Accordingly, due to the limit of specific guidance in South Africa on the transfer pricing considerations to be applied in relation to financial transactions, it is appropriate to consider the guidance available from the OECD and other international best practices.

### 3 New IN

The stated purpose of the New IN is to provide 'taxpayers with guidance on the application of the arm's length principle in the context of the pricing of intra-group loans'. This includes consideration of the level of debt and the price of the debt.

It should be noted that interpretation notes are not law in South Africa, but they provide an indication of SARS' interpretation of the law.

The New IN covers a variety of different topics, many of which align with what was indicated in the OECD Guidelines.

Additional topics that have been specifically covered (and which align with the principles set out in the OECD Guidelines) include:

- Direct versus indirect funding.
- The wide application of the legislation.
- The need to consider the nature of the loan and accurate delineation of the transaction.
- The need to consider the lender and borrower's perspective.
- Treatment of the effect of group membership.
- Use of bank quotes.

The New IN provides guidance with respect to the timing of evaluating the arm's length nature of the transaction. In particular, it states that taxpayers should consider their ability to have obtained the funding, and the price that they would have paid, at the time when the transaction was entered into. Furthermore, it indicates that the evaluation of the arm's length nature of the transaction should be updated from time to time depending on the nature of the taxpayer's business and the extent of change that it experiences.

## III THE ARM'S LENGTH PRINCIPLE

Cross-border-related party financial transactions in South Africa are subject to the arm's length principle. Essentially this means that 'a transaction should have the substantive financial characteristics of a transaction between independent parties, where each party will strive to get the utmost possible benefit from the transaction'.[10]

Article 9 of the OECD Model Tax Convention provides further clarity in stating that:

10. PN 7, para. 7.1.

> [Where] conditions are made or imposed between the two [associated] enterprises in their commercial or financial relations which differ from those which would be made between independent enterprises, then any profits which would - but for those conditions - have accrued to one of the enterprises, but, by reason of those conditions, have not so accrued, may be included in the profits of that enterprise and taxed accordingly.

Accordingly, it is necessary to ensure that financial transactions between a South African entity and a foreign-connected person take place at arm's length prices.

## IV FINANCIAL TRANSACTIONS IN SCOPE OF THE SOUTH AFRICAN TRANSFER PRICING PROVISIONS

The starting point is to determine whether the entities and transactions are in scope of the transfer pricing provisions. This involves first determining if it falls within the requirements of section 31. Second, it is necessary to consider whether any exclusions apply. These steps are discussed below.

### 1 Entities and Transactions Affected

The application of transfer pricing provisions in South Africa is very broad, and it applies to 'affected transactions'[11] which are defined as: 'any transaction, operation, scheme, agreement or understanding' between a resident and non-resident that are 'connected persons' [12] or 'associated enterprises'[13]. It also applies where either the resident or non-resident transacts with a permanent establishment of another entity in the other country or a controlled foreign company (CFC) of a South African resident.[14]

A person is defined to include a company, an individual or a South African trust, an insolvent estate, the estate of a deceased person, any trust, any portfolio of a collective investment scheme but excludes a foreign partnership.[15]

A connected person with respect to a company is a person or company where 20% or more of the equity and voting rights are held is held by that person or company, and no holder of shares holds the majority voting rights in the company.[16]

In the case of financial transactions, there are no requirements that there not be a majority shareholder (*see* Figure 53.2).

11. SA Income Tax Act, section 31(1).
12. *Connected Persons* is defined in the SA Income Tax Act, section 1.
13. *Associated enterprises* was introduced with effect from years of assessment commencing on or after 1 January 2020. The definition applied in section 31 is as contemplated in Article 9 of the OECD Model Tax Convention.
14. SA Income Tax Act, section 31(a).
15. *Ibid.*, section 1.
16. Please refer to SA Income Tax Act, section 1 for further details of entities or persons that would be regarded as 'connected persons'.

*Figure 53.2 Example of the Application of the 'Connected Persons' Definition*

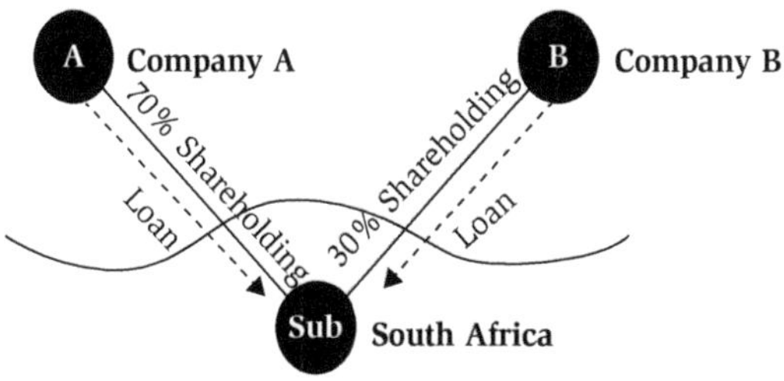


For general transactions (other than financial transactions or intellectual property-related transactions), Company A and Sub would be *"connected persons"*. However, for the loan transactions, Company A and Sub are connected persons and Company B and Sub are also *"connected persons"*.

The applicability of the transfer pricing provisions is very broad. It should be noted that they can even be applied to indirect arrangements between parties.

The definition of 'affected transaction' needs to take into account the chain of borrowing entities, including the ultimate borrower,[17] and not only the arrangement between connected persons. In particular, indirect financial transactions includes, *inter alia*:

- back-to-back transactions with banks or other financial institutions;
- guarantees by a non-resident multinational enterprise (MNE) to a bank or other financial institution in connection with funding given by that institution to a resident;
- other arrangements provided by a foreign-connected person to a local resident indirectly through other entities.

The funding will generally be treated, for transfer pricing purposes, as if it was provided directly between the connected persons. Figures 53.3 and 53.4 illustrate the broad application.

*Figure 53.3 Example of Indirect Financial Assistance*

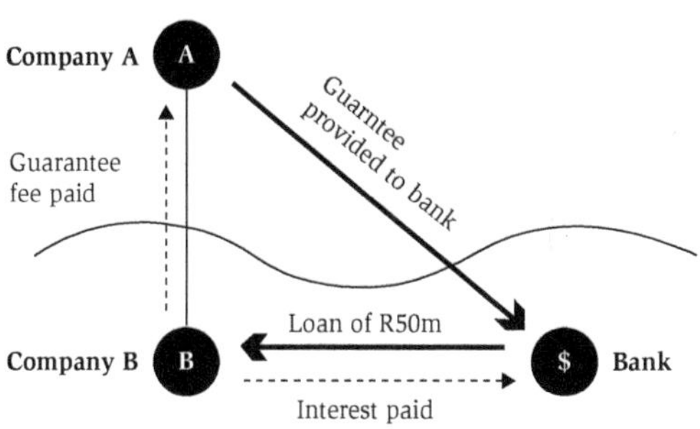


Co A is a foreign parent of Co B, resident in South Africa. An independent bank in South Africa provides a loan to Co B on condition that it receives a guarantee from Co A.

Section 31(a) requires that the whole arrangement needs to be evaluated. As a result, the following points need to be considered:

- Is the level of debt that Co B is taking on from the independent bank arm's length?
- Is the interest rate arm's length?
- Is the guarantee fee arm's length?

17. New Draft IN, section 4.1.1.

*Figure 53.4 Example of Back-to-Back Arrangements*

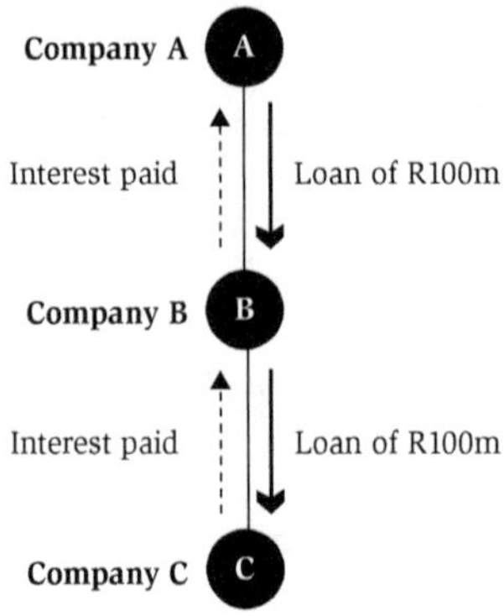


Co A is a foreign parent of Co B., which owns Co C. Co B and Co C are both resident in South Africa.

Co A provides a loan to Co B. Co B provides a loan to Co C.

The question that arises is whether to test the thin capitalisation at the level of Co B or Co C?

This requires consideration of whether the arrangement is back-to-back or not. A detailed review of the facts is required to delineate the arrangement and determine whether the loans truly are back-to-back. Features such as the timing, duration, interest rates, repayment terms etc. should all be considered to evaluate this.

The New Draft IN indicates that the test of whether a transaction is back-to-back should be whether the first leg of the transaction is sufficiently closely linked to the second leg.

## 2 Permanent Establishments

With respect to loans provided between a foreign head office and a South African branch, it is necessary to consider how to treat the interest expense. In evaluating the profit to be attributed to the permanent establishment, actual costs need to be distinguished from notional costs. Actual costs include amounts actually incurred by the head office (i.e., amounts paid or payable to another entity) whereas notional costs might include an internal amount that is charged by the head office but not a third-party charge.

Accordingly, if the interest rate charged by the head office was initially incurred by the head office, it can be recharged to the South African branch and claimed as a deduction. However, if the interest was not an amount actually incurred by the head office, it cannot be claimed as a deduction in South Africa.

## 3 Specific Exclusions

### *A Headquarter Company Exclusion*[18]

Where a South African company is structured as a 'headquarter company' and complies with the specific requirements, there are two situations where they are excluded from transfer pricing provisions.

18. SA Income Tax Act, section 31(5).

First, where a financial transaction has been provided to a South African headquarter company by any foreign person, any portion of that transaction which is provided by the headquarter company to a foreign-related party will not be subject to transfer pricing provisions. A provisor is that the headquarter company must hold at least 10% of the equity shares and voting rights in the entity that it is lending to.

Second, where a headquarter company provides financial assistance to a foreign-related party in which it holds at least 10% of the equity shares and voting rights, that transaction will not be subject to transfer pricing provisions (*see* Figure 53.5).

*Figure 53.5 Example of Back-to-Back Arrangements*

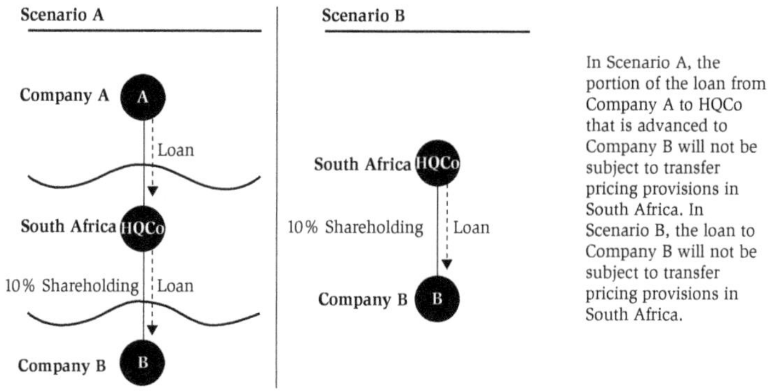


## B CFC Exclusion[19]

To encourage South African residents to invest in the continent, certain provisions were introduced to make it easier to finance subsidiaries. In particular, the transfer pricing provisions will be excluded for transactions involving financial assistance provided by a 'person that is a resident' to a CFC in relation to that person if the CFC meets certain requirements. These requirements are depicted in the following Figure 53.6.

*Figure 53.6 CFC Exclusion*

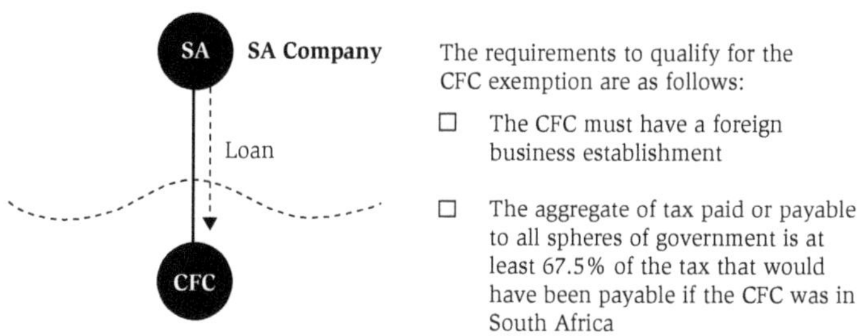


19. *Ibid.*, section 31(6).

## C Shareholder Loan Exclusion[20]

Where a South African resident (or another resident company that is part of the same group of companies) enters into a transaction to provide financial assistance to a company where it owns (on its own or together with other members of the group of companies), at least 10% of the equity and voting rights, if certain conditions are met, then the transfer pricing provisions do not apply.[21] These conditions are:

- The debt does not need to be repaid within 30 years.
- The redemption of the debt is subject to the borrower being solvent.
- No interest accrues on the debt.

It is essential that all conditions are met to apply this exclusion (refer to *Crooks Brothers v. CSARS*[22] below).

*Figure 53.7 Shareholder Loan Exclusion*

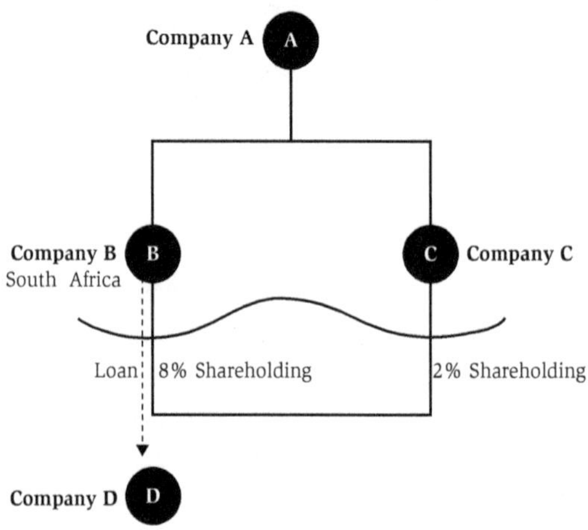


Company B and Company C form part of the same group of companies. Together, they hold at least 10% of the equity shares and voting rights in Company D. Accordingly, if the loan from Company B to Company C meets the requirements listed above, it will not be subject to South African transfer pricing provisions.

20. *Ibid.*, section 31(7).
21. The Explanatory Memorandum on the Taxation Laws Amendment Bill, 2013, indicates that the rationale for this exclusion is to provide relief to outbound loans that clearly resemble equity. 'A loan that meets the [relevant] criteria is in substance exposed to the same economic risk as equity and thus poses little or no risk to the South African tax base if interest is under-charged (because interest should not be charged at all as an economic matter).'
22. IT 14179/ 2017: *Crookes Brothers v. CSARS*, 2018.

## V TYPES OF TRANSACTIONS

For transfer pricing purposes, 'financial transactions' include 'any debt or security or guarantee'.[23] Therefore, the application to the type of instruments is very wide. This is particularly relevant given the way that businesses are increasingly operating across different industries, and finding new innovative ways of engaging with suppliers, partners and customers. The need to manage and improve liquidity and risk levels has also meant that companies increasingly have to consider certain financial instruments (for example use of loans rather than equity, or the provision of guarantees). In addition, with the evolution of technology, certain new non-traditional financial arrangements continue to appear (i.e., crypto[24]).

From a practical perspective, the types of transactions that are commonly considered are as follows.

### 1 Inbound and Outbound Loans

Companies are either funded by way of equity or debt (generally in the form of a loan). Debt funding has lower risk for the shareholder as the funds can be structured so that they can be repaid in the event of financial difficulty.

From a tax perspective, debt funding is generally advantageous because a tax deduction will usually be allowed for the recipient to the extent that the amount of the interest charged is arm's length. In contrast, the return generated from equity in the form of dividends is taxable.

In South Africa, substance over form is an important concept which means that it is necessary to consider the nature of the arrangement and not merely how it is labelled. Accordingly, in evaluating whether a transaction is equity or debt, consideration must be given to the nature of the funding, as well as the relevant terms and conditions. For example, in certain instances, a loan may be regarded as akin to equity (an equity loan) if it exhibits the features of equity, and the tax principles would then follow.

Loans may include term loans, extended payment terms or outstanding amounts. Inbound term loans need to be registered with the South African Reserve Bank (SARB) while outbound term loans require approval from the SARB. To the extent that the commercial rationale of these loans can be demonstrated, they are generally permitted by the SARB.

Historically, SARS challenged outbound equity loans that were interest free. As noted above, section 31(6) is now intended to cater for outbound loans that possess features that are akin to equity.

23. SA Income Tax Act, section 31(1).
24. Note that Crypto has not been addressed in this chapter as only limited guidance has been provided by SARS. In the SARS Media Release dated 6 April 2018, SARS noted that the taxation of crypto should follow normal taxing principles.

## 2 Guarantees

A guarantee is a form of security provided by one party to another. The guarantor would provide it to the recipient for the benefit of another party which is related to the guarantor.

The two broad categories of guarantees include financial and performance guarantees. There is no specific guidance in South Africa on the transfer pricing analysis of guarantee fees. Accordingly, the OECD Guidance should be applied.

The context in which a guarantee is provided should be carefully considered from an arm's length perspective in South Africa. For example, if an independent financial institution provides a loan to a South African resident on condition that it receives a parent company guarantee, it is necessary to consider whether the borrowing entity has the appropriate interest-bearing capacity to cover the debt interest and that there is not a situation where in fact the debt should have aspired in the head office or guarantor.

## 3 Cash Pooling

Cash pooling is a mechanism whereby entities combine their balances to obtain various benefits. These may include:

- Improved daily cash management.
- Reduction in banking costs.
- Reduced bank charges.
- Reduced need for third-party facilities by the various entities.

There are two main types:

(1) Notional cash pooling

This involves no actual sweeping of bank accounts. Rather, the net position of the various bank accounts is taken.

(2) Physical cash pooling

Amounts are swept on a daily basis to ensure the targeted balances are left in the respective accounts.

Cash pooling for South African companies is only permitted within the common monetary area (CMA) comprising South Africa, Namibia, Lesotho, Eswatini. The Reserve Bank regulations prohibit cash pooling beyond the CMA.

To create the potential for cash pooling, the concept of a Domestic Treasury Management Company was established. Companies that are established in South Africa and that qualify for this are able to enter into cross-border cash pooling arrangements subject to certain conditions.

## 4 Factoring

One way that entities can improve their liquidity is to transfer or sell their debtor's book. This is referred to as factoring. A business may choose to do this to meet its current or future cash requirements. The debtor's book is sold at a discount because the entity acquiring it (namely the factor), is assuming the credit risk.

When the factor is a foreign-related party, it is necessary to ensure that the discount is market related.

In South Africa, it is possible for a company to enter into a cross-border factoring arrangement with related parties provided that the arrangement is concluded at arm's length. However, it is necessary to obtain exchange control approval to do so. Invariably it is necessary to consider the options realistically available to the parties when considering a factoring arrangement to ensure that the arrangement can be concluded to be at arm's length prices.

## VI APPROACH TO TESTING THE ARM'S LENGTH NATURE OF FINANCIAL ASSISTANCE

There are several tax provisions to consider in terms of the cross-border financial transactions between a South African entity and a foreign-connected person. Figure 53.8 suggests an approach that can be applied to evaluate these.

*Figure 53.8 Suggested Approach to Testing the Arm's Length Nature of Financial Assistance*

## 1 Nature of the Arrangement

The first step is to accurately delineate[25] the financial transaction (in accordance with the guidance in paragraph 1.33 of the OECD Guidelines). This entails an analysis of the economically relevant characteristics of the transaction[26] which includes:

- the contractual terms of the transaction;
- the functional analysis;
- the characteristics of the transaction;
- the economic circumstances of the parties and of the market in which the parties operate; and
- the business strategies pursued by the parties.

This will enable determination of whether the transaction is appropriately characterised as debt, or whether it should be treated as a form of equity. Furthermore, as discussed below, there are certain instances where in fact it may be more appropriately characterised as a hybrid debt or equity instrument and be subject to different tax considerations.

## 2 Exchange Control

The exchange control restrictions are very important in South Africa because they govern the cross-border flow of funds. As a result, they should be considered even before the various tax implications.

### *A Overview*

South Africa's exchange control regulations are set by the SARB. The regulations that are applicable to cross border financial transactions are contained in the Currency and Exchanges Manual for Authorised Dealers.[27]

Inbound loans need to be registered on the Loan Reporting System of the Financial Surveillance Department and this can be done by commercial banks who operate as authorised dealers of the SARB. These loans are subject to the following restrictions:

- The minimum duration of each loan must me at least one month.
- The interest rate cannot exceed:
  - in the case of loans from a foreign third party;

25. The guidance in Chapter X of the OECD Guidelines, together with section D1 of the OECD Guidelines is an instructive starting point for an analysis of financial transaction in South Africa. Substance over form is a guiding principle in South African tax and is aligned with the principles of those respective sections of the OECD Guidelines. Furthermore, the New IN also supports this as the starting point of an analysis.
26. OECD Guidelines, sections 1.36 and 1.38.
27. South African Reserve Bank, Currency and Exchanges: Manual for Authorised Dealers (2019-07-02).

  - if the loan is denominated in a foreign currency, the respective base lending rate plus 3 percentage points;
  - if the loan is denominated in Rand, the South African prime lending rate plus 5 percentage points.
- In the case of a loan from a foreign shareholder:
  - if the loan is denominated in a foreign currency, the respective base lending rate;
  - if the loan is denominated in Rand, the South African prime lending rate.

It should be noted that for purposes of the Exchange Control regulations, the definition of Related Party is broader than the definition of 'Connected Person' under the Income Tax Act. It includes 'a party to a transaction that has a direct or indirect interest in the other party and has the ability to control the other party or exercise significant influence over the other party'. It also applies where both parties are under common control:

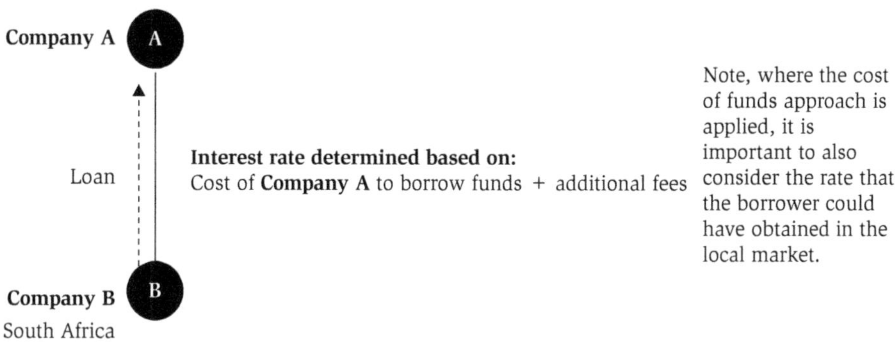


### *B* *Outbound Loans*

Where a resident is seeking to advance an outbound loan, approval is required from the SARB. Approval is generally granted where it can be demonstrated that there is commercial benefit for advancing the loan.

## 3 Level of Debt

An entity can either be funded by way of debt or equity. Generally, funding by way of debt has tax advantages as a deduction can be claimed for the interest expense, while the interest income may be exempt in the hands of the foreign lender. Accordingly, there is an inherent incentive for multinational groups to maximise their level of debt with minimal equity. However, in an arm's length setting, this would not be possible, as an independent lender would limit the extent to which it would provide funding to an entity to protect itself. The need to evaluate the acceptable level of debt (often referred to as thin capitalisation) is considered under the transfer pricing provisions in South Africa.

The question that arises is, 'What is the level of debt that the entity would have obtained in an arm's length scenario?'

Historically this was addressed in South Africa through a fixed Debt: Equity ratio of 3:1 that was applied. However, since years of assessment commencing on or after 1 April 2012, the test of the level of debt has been an arm's length test.

Taxpayers need to ensure that, where the value of the loan is material that they do not rely on the previous 3:1 Debt: Equity safe harbour because, often, that level of gearing is more generous than what would have been provided by independent third parties. In this regard, it is necessary to consider the industry that the taxpayer operates in because the capital structure of companies operating in certain industries differs from that of companies in other industries.

There are two aspects that need to be considered. A taxpayer should consider the amount of debt that an independent third party 'could' have borrowed and the amount that it 'would' have borrowed. This infers that the analysis should involve - to a degree - a consideration of the options realistically available to the parties. In other words, the transactions should be considered from both the perspective of the lender and the borrower. It should be noted that the facts and circumstances of each case are critical.

For example, if the borrower had adequate cash on hand for its operations and future objectives, it would not, under ordinary circumstances, take on additional debt. In such a scenario - if additional debt is taken - it could be considered to be excessive. In such a scenario, the borrower would need to demonstrate the commercial rationale for taking on the additional debt.

Lenders typically consider the creditworthiness of a borrower when determining whether or not to advance funding. Such an approach should be followed when considering what a third party could have been able to borrow.

The guidance from the OECD regarding the various considerations of debt capacity is helpful. Often a benchmarking analysis can be used to compare the level of debt obtained by comparable independent third parties. It is necessary to take into account any material differences that may exist between the tested party and the set of comparable companies. The appropriate means of comparing the debt capacity of the borrower to that of comparable companies may include using various financial ratios. The Old Draft IN suggested three potential financial ratios. These ratios, plus one additional ratio, were subsequently included in the South African annual CIT return in the transfer pricing disclosure section. Accordingly, these ratios may provide a useful framework for considering the level of debt of a South African borrower. The ratios include:

- Debt: Fixed Capital
- Debt: EBITDA
- EBITDA: Finance Cost
- Debt: Tangible Assets.

These are not exhaustive and are not prescribed in law. Therefore, careful consideration should be given as to which ones may be appropriate given the type of company and the industry it is operating in. Similar ratios also commonly appear in third-party bank covenants which is a further indication that independent banks consider them to be an important indicator of the ability of a borrower to service or repay the debt. It should be noted that there is no formal safe harbour or formal guidance for the acceptable value of any of these ratios.

Finally, certain industries are subject to specific regulations regarding the levels of gearing that are permitted. Where that is the case, the relevant regulations need to be taken into account and adhered to from a transfer pricing perspective.

## 4 Price

The second component of the transfer pricing analysis of financial transactions involves consideration of the price charged. The price can include any amount arising in response to the provision of the financial transactions including, *inter alia*, interest, capital raising fees, facility fees, etc.

The arm's length price may be determined through a few different methods. Commonly used methods include.

### *A Internal Comparable Uncontrolled Price (CUP)*

This may occur where an entity, such as the borrower or another entity in the group in a similar position, borrows from an independent third party and the price can be compared to that of the related party transaction. As with any CUP analysis, it is important to ensure a high degree of comparability. In particular, features like the commencement date and duration, currency, materiality, level of security, seniority, are all important considerations.

### *B External CUP*

An external CUP may arise where the price in the affected transaction can be compared to the price in an independent third-party arrangement. For example, loans entered into by companies with a similar credit rating to that of the related party borrower may be used to determine a range of arm's length interest rates.

The starting point for the application of this method is usually to determine the credit rating of the borrower. This can be performed using various different financial tools or methodologies. It is relevant to note that the New IN stipulates that, when determining the credit rating of the borrower, implicit support from the Group should be taken into account. Paragraph 10.77 of the OECD Guidelines defines implicit support in the case of intra-group loans to be the 'incidental benefit that the MNE is assumed to receive solely by virtue of group affiliation'. In other words, where the borrower is expected to receive support from the Group, the benefit that this support has on its credit rating should be taken into account. Certain companies have independently determined credit ratings that can be used. In other cases, a synthetic credit rating can be determined by taking into account various factors including, the industry, the financial position of the entity, the relative importance of the entity in the Group.

The next step when applying this method involves identifying comparable loans or other financial instruments for companies that have comparable credit ratings. The results can be analysed to determine a range of arm's length interest rates. Sources of this information include, *inter alia*, Refinitiv LoanConnector or Bloomberg.

A practical difficulty that arises when benchmarking interest rates for companies operating in Africa is the availability of third-party data. Challenges arise in two particular areas. Firstly, obtaining comparable data for a loan with a particular credit rating. Where the credit rating is lower, the availability of third-party data is significantly reduced. This is especially the case when benchmarking outbound loans into certain other countries in Africa that have much lower sovereign credit ratings. In these instances, there may not be sufficient number of traded instruments in order to enable a CUP analysis. One option to address this is to consider including a slightly wider range of credit ratings when searching for comparable loan agreements. Alternatively, a different method may be required altogether.

The second challenge that arises due to the lack of data relates to the currency of the loans. While Rand-denominated loans are available in certain databases, the low number of such agreements makes it difficult to find a sufficient number of agreements for a specific date range. It may be necessary to perform currency and interest rate swaps if the loan to be tested is denominated in Rand or, in the case of outbound loans to other countries in Africa, if it is denominated in the respective local currency.

### C Cost of Funds Approach

In certain instances, it is simpler to consider the cost that the lender incurred in obtaining funds and add to that appropriate premiums and risk spreads to determine the price to the borrower. What is important here is that the rate is considered from both the perspective of the borrower and lender to ensure that it would not in fact have been possible for the borrower to access the funds at a lower rate in its local market.[28]

*Figure 53.9 Cost of Funds*

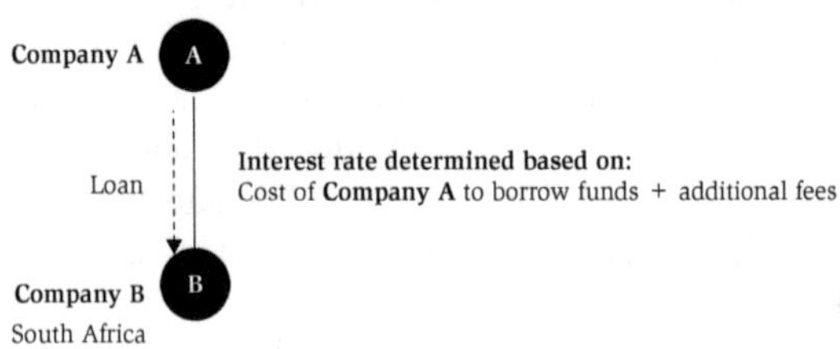


28. OECD Guidelines, paras 10.98 and 10.99.

Additional guidance is provided for these different methods in Chapter X of the OECD Guidelines.

It must be noted that the New IN is closely aligned with the OECD Guidelines on two additional considerations in terms of price. First, it is clear that bank opinions or quotes generally do not constitute an 'actual offer to lend' and, therefore, would generally not be adequate substantiation of the arm's length price.

Second, where a funder 'lacks the capability, or does not perform the decision-making functions, to control the risk associated with investing in a financial asset, it will be entitled to no more than a risk-free return as an appropriate measure of the profits'. Accordingly, the ability of the management of the entity to manage the associated risks and make the relevant decisions needs to be considered when evaluating the compensation the entity should achieve.

## 5 Consequence of Non-arms' Length Transactions (Excludes Understatement Penalties and Interest)

Cross-border transactions with related parties need to take place at arm's length prices. Therefore, during the year, if a price between a South African taxpayer and a foreign-connected person has not been at arm's length, and if a 'tax benefit'[29] has been derived by one of the parties to the transaction, taxpayers are required to make adjustments to the transaction to ensure that by the end of the financial year, the prices for that year are arm's length. Where this does not happen, there are two transfer pricing adjustments that are required. These are discussed below.[30]

### *A Primary Adjustment*

The first consequence of a non-arm's length price for a transaction is the primary adjustment. The non-arm's length amount is added back as a deduction or imputed as additional income. The statutory corporate tax rate (28% until years of assessment commencing on or after 1 April 2022 and then 27%) is applied to this primary adjustment.

### *B Secondary Adjustment*

For years of assessment commencing on or after 1 January 2015, the consequence of a non-arm's length transaction was amended. As per section 31(3), the value of the non-arm's length amount is now a deemed dividend *in specie* or a deemed donation.

The deemed dividend or deemed donation will be subject to dividends withholding tax which is currently at a rate of 20%.

29. South African Income Tax Act, section 31(2).
30. *Ibid.*, section 31(3).

*Figure 53.10 Consequence of Non-arm's Length Transactions*

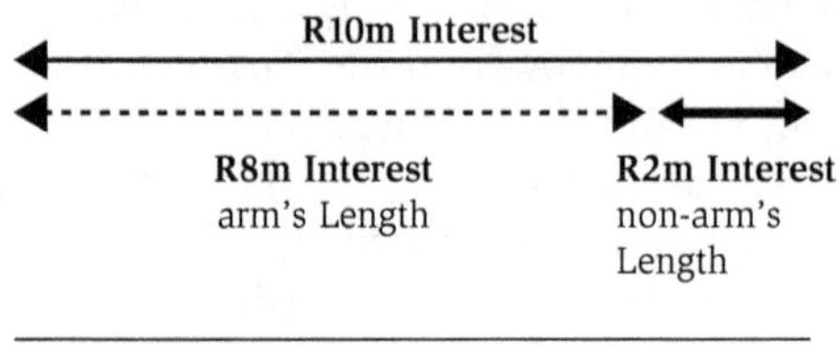


**Primary tax adjustment:**
The transfer pricing adjustment will be
R 2m × 27% = R 540 000

**Secondary tax adjustment:**
R 2m × 20% = R 400 000

The deemed dividend or deemed donation is deemed to have arisen on the last day of the sixth month following the end of the financial year. The withholding tax is required to be paid within one month of that date.

It should be noted that the withholding tax rate is not reduced under either a double taxation agreement[31] or by section 64FA[32] which deals with exemptions from and reduction of tax in respect of dividends *in specie.*

Importantly, the New IN states that section 31 requires that a transaction that was not at arm's length needs to be calculated as if it was at arm's length. It does not deem the transaction to have occurred at arm's length. Accordingly, to the extent that a transaction did not occur at arm's length, the withholding tax applicable on the interest that is payable is to be calculated based on the interest actually due and payable, not the amount calculated under section 31.

Finally, it should be noted that, where the primary and secondary adjustments are not made, there are potential penalties and interest due on the non-arm's length amounts.

## 6 Domestic Interest Limitation Rules

Notwithstanding the transfer pricing considerations set out above, several domestic interest limitation rules apply in the South African context. These are briefly discussed below.

31. *Volkswagen of South Africa (Pty) Ltd v. C*: SARS 70 SATC 195 concluded that the dividends article in a double taxation treaty does not account for dividend in specie or deemed dividend in specie.
32. Refer to section 9.2 of the New SARS IN which sets out the reasons for the non-relief of this section in the case of a section 31 adjustment.

### *A Section 23M*

Effective 1 January 2015, section 23M was introduced to limit excessive interest deductions in respect of debts owed to persons that are not subject to tax in South Africa, where the debtor and the creditor are in a controlling relationship.

Where, for example, a South African resident has received a loan from a foreign-connected person that has a controlling relationship with the resident (i.e., 50% or more), or where the resident had received funds from a creditor that is not in a controlling relationship, but the creditor received the funds from an entity in a controlling relationship with the debtor, section 23M will apply if certain conditions are met.

These conditions are that:

- the amount of interest earned by the creditor is not subject to tax in that year of assessment;
- the interest earned is not included in the net income of a CFC; and
- the interest is not disallowed under section 23N.

If these conditions are met, then there is a limit on the deductibility of the interest, with the disallowed portion being rolled forward to the immediate succeeding year. In particular, the amount of interest that can be deducted is formula based, expressed as a percentage of the tax equivalent of earnings before interest, taxes, depreciation and amortisation (EBITDA) that is adjusted up and downwards based on the average repo rate for the year. Any change to the average repo rate for the year of assessment (together with a 400-basis point addition to the average repo rate) is captured to allow for a balanced reflection of market conditions on the interest deduction limitation. A cap on the interest deduction limitation ratio of 60 per cent was inserted to protect the fiscus and tax base in periods of high-interest rates.

Please note that there are certain other exclusions that apply and they should be carefully evaluated.

In many regards, section 23M seeks to fulfil the role of a stand-alone thin capitalisation analysis.

As to the interaction between section 31 and section 23M, the South African Revenue Service is of the opinion in the New N that insofar as order is concerned, section 31 applies prior to considering the impact, if any, of sections 23M and 23N.

In 2020 the South African National Treasury published a discussion document titled 'Reviewing the Tax Treatment of Excessive Debt Financing, Interest Deductions and Other Financial Payments'. The document was aimed at conducting a review of the interest limitation rules in line with the OECD/G20 BEPS Action 4 recommendations on interest deductions.

Section 23M was redrafted to be more aligned with BEPS Action 4. The section 23M 'interest' definition was widened, for example, to include foreign exchange differences, interest rate swaps, the finance cost element included in finance lease payments, and amounts deemed to be interest under Sharia compliant financing arrangements. The formula-based calculation was further reduced to 30% of adjusted taxable income, and the adjustment based on the repo rate was deleted. Other notable amendments include catering for back-to-back loans and inserting a new formula where section 23M can proportionately apply in instances where South Africa retains a level of taxing rights say under an applicable double taxation agreement.

The amendments to section 23M will come into effect from the date on which the rate of tax in respect of the taxable income of a company is first reduced after announcement by the Minister of Finance in the annual National Budget and will be applicable in respect of years of assessment commencing on or after that date.

### *B* *Section 23N*

Whilst section 23M is an interest limitation section focusing on debts owed to persons not subject to tax in South Africa, section 23N is an interest limitation section focusing on certain reorganisation transactions (in the form of sections 45 and 47) and share acquisition transactions (in the form of section 24O).

The two sections are not mutually exclusive, and section 23M can apply to the extent that section 23N is not applicable. It follows that where section 23N applies, for example, in a typical debt push-down transaction, and the amount of interest incurred by that debtor is limited under section 23N, the interest amount that is allowed to be deducted after the application of section 23N is then subject to section 23M (e.g., a debt push-down transaction in a South African group context is funded via an offshore parent loan).

The interest incurred in respect of the acquisition debt is subject to an annual limitation pursuant to a defined formula, up to a maximum of 60% of the tax EBITDA.

Silke states in paragraph 13.398 in respect of section 23N, 'Section 23N reflects the intent on the part of the legislature to ensure that, in transactions relating to corporate reorganisation and acquisition, excessive debt it not used to achieve tax savings that are central to the viability of the deal. It establishes an objective test – a statutory ceiling in respect of the amount of deductible interest incurred by an acquiring company in relation to specified categories of debt, if a taxpayer meets the qualifying criteria, the interest incurred is taxable, subject to the stipulated deductibility thresholds … .'

## 7 Specific Anti-avoidance Provisions

Specific anti-avoidance provisions apply in the form of sections 8F and 8FA, briefly discussed below.

### *A* *Section 8F*

Section 8F, a specific anti-avoidance rule, seeks to reclassify interest incurred on a hybrid debt instrument, that is, a debt instrument with certain equity-type features, as a dividend *in specie*, thereby denying the issuer an interest deduction. The in specie dividend is deemed to be declared and paid on the last day of the year of assessment of the company. It is similarly treated as a dividend in specie for the holder, that is, the holder is not taxable on the interest.

### *B Section 8FA*

Whilst section 8F focuses on the equity-like nature of a debt instrument, section 8FA focuses on the equity-like nature of interest in relation to a debt instrument.

If section 8FA applies, the hybrid interest is reclassified as a dividend *in specie*, thereby denying the issuer an interest deduction. The *in specie* dividend is deemed to be declared and paid on the last day of the year of assessment of the company. It is similarly treated as a dividend in specie for the holder, that is, the holder is not taxable on the interest.

Examples of hybrid interest include any interest where the amount of interest is:

- not determined with reference to a specified rate of interest; or
- not determined with reference to the time value of money.
- another example of hybrid interest is a profit participation loan, that is, the rate of interest has in terms of that instrument been raised by reason of an increase in the profits of the company, so much of the amount of interest has been determined with reference to the raised rate of interest as exceeds the amount of interest that would have been determined with reference to the lowest rate of interest in terms of that instrument during the current year of assessment and the previous five years of assessment.

## 8 Withholding Tax on Interest

Withholding tax on interest was introduced on 1 March 2015.

Section 50B(1) of the Income Tax Act provides that, where interest is paid by any person to, or for the benefit of a foreign person, to the extent that the amount is paid from a source in South Africa, a withholding tax of 15% must be levied on the interest.

Interest is deemed to be paid on the earlier of the date on which the interest is paid or becomes due and payable.

Please note that there are certain exemptions to the interest withholding tax as stipulated in section 50D. The withholding tax can also be reduced under an applicable Double Tax Agreement (DTA). It should be noted that the reduced rate of withholding tax only applies to arms' length interest – that is, any excessive interest is denied DTA relief.

## 9 Outbound Loans: Double Taxation

Where a South African taxpayer receives interest income on its outbound loan, to the extent that there is withholding tax applied by the country of the recipient of the loan, the South African holder may potentially claim tax relief in relation to any foreign taxes suffered either in terms of an applicable DTA or under section 6quat.

## VII ORDER OF APPLICATION OF INCOME TAX PROVISIONS

There are several provisions in the Income Tax Act that apply to inbound financial transactions. It is proposed in the National Treasury report on 'Reviewing the tax treatment of excessive debt financing, interest deductions and other financial payments' that the order of application of the provisions is that companies should first apply the arm's length test and follow this with interest limitation rules. In other words, the interest limitation provisions would only apply to net interest expense that is considered to be arm's length.

This is supported by the New IN. Therefore, the order of application of the provisions is as displayed in Figure 53.11.

*Figure 53.11 Order of Application*

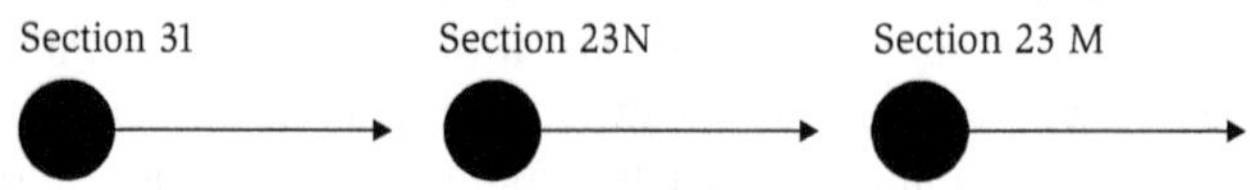


## VIII COMPLIANCE REQUIREMENTS

### 1 Burden of Proof

In South Africa, the onus of burden of proof is on the taxpayer. Therefore, it is the taxpayer that is required to have sufficient evidence to substantiate the position taken in its tax declarations of financial transactions. Nevertheless, SARS has provided certain guidance with respect to the level of detail required indicating that the cost of compliance should not outweigh the potential benefit.[33]

Accordingly, in evaluating the approach to analysing a financial transaction, regard should be given to the materiality of the transaction and the potential transfer pricing risk. A more material transaction (from a quantum and risk perspective) would warrant greater levels of analysis.

### 2 Specific Guidance

Cross-border related party loans require various declarations and submissions from a transfer pricing perspective, depending on the size of the business, as well as the nature and scale of the transaction.

33. PN 7, para. 10.2.6 and OECD Guidelines para. 5.28.

Basic thresholds for consideration are the following:

- Taxpayers that are required to submit a country-by-country report in South Africa (i.e., total consolidated revenue exceeds EUR 750 million or ZAR 10 billion) or that have more than ZAR 100 million of affected transactions are required to submit a master file and local file in South Africa.[34]
- Taxpayers that have less than ZAR 100 million of affected transactions in a year of assessment are not required to submit transfer pricing documentation but are required to retain adequate evidence to substantiate the position taken in their tax return.[35]
- For any affected transaction exceeding ZAR 5 million in a given year, specific information needs to be retained.

In addition, taxpayers are required to indicate in their tax return whether they entered into cross-border related party transactions during the year. Where they did, various information is required including, values of the transaction and country of the counterparties, as well as various financial ratios achieved by the taxpayer which are ultimately used for thin capitalisation risk assessment purposes.

The information that needs to be retained by taxpayers in support of financial transactions that exceed R 5m (over and above what ordinarily is required in a transfer pricing local file) includes:[36]

(i) Summary of financial forecasts which are contemporaneous with the financial assistance transactions in question, projected as far as is meaningful in relation to the period of the funding transactions, including a clear picture of the expected levels of interest cover, gearing or other relevant measures over the forecast period.

(ii) An analysis of the financial strategy of the business, including how capital is allocated and the relationship between capital and cash flows from operations and any changes relating to the financial assistance transactions and details regarding principal cash flows and the sources of repayment of debt.

(iii) Where the term of the funding exceeds 12 months additional records include:
   - A description of the funding structure which has been or is in the process of being put in place, including the dates of transactions, a clear statement of the source of the funds (immediate and ultimate), reasons for obtaining the funds, how the funds were or will be applied (the purpose of the financial assistance) and the repayment terms.
   - A group structure covering all relevant companies and clearly setting out any changes to the structure taking place over the course of the financial assistance transactions.

34. SARS Public Notice, 'Return to be submitted by persons in terms of section 25 of the Tax Administration Act, 2011 (Act No. 28 of 2011)', 20 October 2017.
35. Government Gazette No. 1334, 'Duty to keep records, books of account or documents in terms of section 29 of the Tax Administration Act, 2011 (Act No. 28 of 2011)', 28 October 2016.
36. *Ibid.*

- Copies of the financial statements and management accounts prepared most recently before the point in time the financial assistance is obtained and after the financial assistance has been granted.

## IX COURT CASES

There is limited jurisprudence in transfer pricing matters in South Africa. Arguably the first transfer pricing court case was delivered on 8 May 2018, and it related to the application of section 31(7) dealing with what, in nature, was considered to be a shareholder loan.

*Crookes Brothers Ltd v. CSARS* [2018] ZAGPHC 311 (*Crookes Brothers*)[37] involved a case where an interest-free loan had been provided by the South African taxpayer to a non-resident subsidiary (Sub) in Mozambique. Initially, the taxpayer had considered that the amount of interest was non-arm's length, and that interest should have been levied. Accordingly, the taxpayer had initially made a primary and secondary adjustment in their tax return for the 2015 year-off assessment.

Subsequently, on consideration of section 31(7), the taxpayer requested a reduced assessment from SARS. SARS rejected the reduced assessment.

Section 31(7) states transfer pricing provisions do not apply where:

- an interest-free loan is granted by a taxpayer to a non-resident connected person;
- the non-resident is not obliged to repay the loan within 30 years; and
- the repayment of the loan is conditional on the market value of the assets exceeding the liabilities.

In *Crookes Brothers*, SARS disputed the application of section 31(7) by the taxpayer on the following grounds:

- Clause 7 of the loan agreement stated that, in the event that the Sub was to go into business rescue, or bankruptcy, the loan would be due and payable immediately. This clause could be triggered within a 30-year period, and so the Sub would have an obligation to repay the loan within 30 years.
- Clause 7 meant that the debt would be repayable regardless of whether the market value of the assets of Sub exceeded its liabilities.
- The subordination agreement entered into by the parties did not make it equity in nature rather it merely had the effect of changing the ranking of the taxpayer's debt compared to other creditors.

The court agreed with SARS.

There are several important takeaways from this court case that are insightful when considering financial transactions in South Africa. These include:

37. IT 14179/ 2017: *Crookes Brothers v. CSARS*, 2018.

- Loan agreements are an important starting point in understanding the nature and terms of the agreements. These should be set out carefully and accurately.
- The specific terms and conditions need to be evaluated when determining if a provision or an exclusion may apply. Likewise, it can be expected that terms and conditions are to be appropriately considered when determining whether one loan agreement is sufficiently comparable to another.

## X CONCLUSION

Cross-border financial transactions entered into between a South African entity and a foreign-connected person require careful consideration from a transfer pricing perspective. The provisions are very broad, and the arm's length principle needs to be applied to take into account all relevant facts from the perspective of both the borrower and the lender.

CHAPTER 54

# Transfer Pricing Aspects of Financial Transactions: An Indian Perspective

*Mukesh Butani & Seema Kerijwal*[*]

## I INTRODUCTION

Steven Wright, the comedian, had once famously joked 'Why is it a penny for your thoughts but you have to put your two cents in? Somebody's making a penny.' This is an apt representation to justify the detailed transfer pricing scrutiny intra-group financial transactions undergo in India, from both a tax and regulatory perspective, where the statute is interpreted in India according to the 'Literal Rule',[1] but contracts, agreements, transactions, etc., are subject to a substance over form test.

In this chapter, we will attempt to decode the Indian transfer pricing landscape in the context of intra-group financial transactions. We will discuss the regulatory framework in which intra-group financial transactions are undertaken, the controversies around routinely witnessed transactions, the transfer pricing legislation around benchmarking & reporting of intra-group financial transactions. We will also analyse important Court rulings on intra-group financial transactions and discuss how the Indian legislation intersects with the Organisation for Economic Co-operation and Development (OECD) & UN Guidelines on transfer pricing and conclude with our view on the future of intra-group financial transactions.

---

* The views and opinions set forth herein are the personal views or opinions of the authors; they do not necessarily reflect views or opinions of the organisation with which the authors are associated.

1. The literal rule means that a judge has to consider what the statute says 'literally', i.e., its simple plain meaning without any ambiguity. It is said that the words themselves best declare the intention of the law-givers.

## II INDIAN BACKDROP

### 1 Growing Attention to Intra-group Financial Transactions in the Indian Context

Intra-group financial transactions are largely driven either around investing in India for business operations, expanding functions of multinational enterprises (MNEs) in India (or out of India), or around investments to expand an MNEs Indian customer base and tap the Indian market, or by large Indian MNEs expanding in offshore jurisdictions. Moreover, lending rates in India are on the higher side – in a 2021 global survey, India ranked 36 in a list of 95 countries with average lending rate to private sector at 8.70%[2] – the lowest being San Marino at 1.68% and the highest being Madagascar at 48.28%. With high lending rates in India, intra-group financing seems a more viable option for multinationals as they can leverage on lower offshore interest rates. COVID has additionally compelled multinationals to revisit their treasury operations to maximise efficient utilisation of the treasury pool – in the Indian context, revisiting of supply chains by MNEs, additional investments in remote working for back-office support teams, and similar COVID-related changes have additionally contributed to the increased focus on treasury operations.

### 2 International Transactions with Associated Enterprises Which Need Benchmarking under the Law

International transaction is defined under the transfer pricing law[3] to mean a transaction between two or more associated enterprises, either or both of whom are non-residents, in the nature of purchase, sale or lease of tangible or intangible property, or provision of services, or lending or borrowing money, or any other transaction having a bearing on the profits, income, losses or assets of such enterprises. This includes a mutual agreement or arrangement between two or more associated enterprises for the allocation or apportionment of, or any contribution to, any cost or expense incurred or to be incurred in connection with a benefit, service or facility provided or to be provided to any one or more of such enterprises.

The law specifically[4] provides that capital financing, including any type of long-term or short-term borrowing, lending or guarantee, purchase or sale of marketable securities or any type of advance, payments or deferred payment or receivable or any other debt arising during the course of business shall be included in the definition of international transaction.

The law mandates reporting of outstanding inter-company receivables as an international transaction in the statutory annual form.[5] The tax administration tends to

2. *See* https://www.theglobaleconomy.com/rankings/lending_interest_rate/.
3. Section 92B(1) of the Income-tax Act, 1961.
4. Section 92B (1)(i)(c) of the Income-tax Act, 1961.
5. Form 3CEB.

treat delayed payments of receivables as unsecured loans and impute an interest income in the hands of the taxpayer.

The law provides for deemed international transactions wherein a transaction entered into between a third party and a taxpayer is considered to be an international transaction between associated enterprises when the terms of the relevant transaction are determined in substance between the third party and an associated enterprise of the taxpayer. While this was introduced to prevent situations where a dummy third party is interposed to circumvent transfer pricing, in practice, this has led to several compliance-related challenges on unrelated transactions coming into the ambit of deemed international transaction. One such instance is where a favourable financial condition is negotiated by a regional entity with banks/financial institutions for all group entities in the region.

### 3 Litigation Landscape in India

As noted by the UN Transfer Pricing (TP) Guidelines,[6] the fact that money is mobile and fungible makes it relatively simple for an MNE to shift or locate debt in a particular MNE entity, and along with that debt, the ability to deduct associated interest. This can have the effect of reducing taxable profits of the borrowing entity, and, can, depending on the situation of other MNE members, reduce the MNE's overall tax liability. This is a factor which makes intra-group financial transactions important for taxpayers and tax administrators alike.

In the past two decades, since transfer pricing law was introduced in India, intra-group financial arrangements have witnessed their fair share of litigation, resulting in evolution of rich jurisprudence due to use of sophisticated means of raising intra-group finance. Certain vexed issues such as correct characterisation of a hybrid instrument as a loan or equity, determination of whether a corporate guarantee falls within the contours of an international transaction, debate on interest-free loans, financial arrangements characterised as shareholder activity, benchmarking of interest rates on loans, etc. are matters of extensive debate. The domestic law does not contain specific guidance other than safe harbour limits[7] on intra-group financial transactions, and therefore, the jurisprudence that has evolved over the years serves as guidance to the taxpayers and tax administration alike. Significant tax rulings have been discussed in this chapter.

## III ROUTINELY SEEN INTRA-GROUP FINANCIAL TRANSACTIONS IN INDIA

In an intra-group context, more common financial transactions include intra-group loans, financial guarantees by a parent or group financing company for third-party loans to subsidiaries, cash pooling arrangements, hybrid financing, derivatives, and

6. UN Transfer Pricing Guidelines 2021, para. 9.1.5.
7. *See* rules 10TD, Income Tax Rules.

treasury services (e.g., foreign exchange risk management, factoring and forfeiting, netting arrangements, payment factories, commodity risk management, captive insurance, asset management, carbon trading, etc.).[8] The most routinely seen forms of intra-group financial arrangements observed in India are.

## 1 Intra-group Loans

An intra-group loan is the provision of financial resources from one related party (the lender) to another (borrower) to be repaid later. With an intra-group loan, the borrower will obtain the financial resources; the lender will generally assume the credit risk related to the intra-group loan and need to be compensated for the liquidity provided and the risk taken on by an arm's length payment, i.e., an interest payment.[9] Typically, a loan instrument would include characteristics but not be limited to: the amount of loan, maturity, schedule of repayment, nature or purpose of loan, level of seniority, geographical location of the borrower, currency, collateral provided, presence and quality of any guarantee, and whether the interest rate is fixed or floating.[10] The OECD guidance is broad in its scope to cover guidance on both loans denominated in Indian as well as foreign currency. However, the safe harbour rules[11] defines 'intra-group loan' to mean a loan that is sourced in Indian rupees; is not advanced by an enterprise being a financial company including a bank or a financial institution or an enterprise engaged in lending or borrowing in the normal course of business and does not include credit line or any other loan facility which has no fixed term of repayment. It is evident that scope of an intra-group loan covered under the safe harbour is a restricted category of loans.

## 2 Corporate Guarantee

A corporate guarantee can be classified into two broad categories:

(1) *Performance Guarantee*: A guarantee to its related party in connection with the latter's non-financial obligations. Hence, under the contract, the guarantor might have to complete the task of the contractor[12] and/or compensate the client in case of a default. A performance guarantee is a non-financial guarantee and has not been covered in this chapter.

8. Paragraph 9.3.2 of the UN TP Guidelines.
9. Committee of Experts on International Cooperation in tax Matters, 18th session, Update of the United Nations Practical Manual on Transfer Pricing for Developing Countries, p. 17, para. B.9.3.1.1.
10. OECD (2020), Transfer Pricing Guidance on Financial Transactions: Inclusive Framework on BEPS Actions 4, 8-10, OECD, Paris.
11. Rule 10TA, Income Tax Rules.
12. The associated enterprise primarily responsible for completing the obligations towards the Client.

(2) *Financial Guarantee*: A financial guarantee provides for the guarantor to meet specified financial obligations in the event of a failure to do so by the guaranteed party.[13]

## 3 Hybrid Financial Instruments

Hybrid instruments are unique financial instruments having characteristics of both debt and equity. Examples of hybrid financial instruments include compulsory convertible debentures, optionally convertible debentures (OCDs), and convertible notes. These instruments enjoy an advantage due to varying degree of characterisation across jurisdictions as they may be treated as debt in one jurisdiction while equity in the other.

For instance, there are hybrid debt instruments, such as compulsorily convertible debentures (CCDs), convertible notes and OCD that are considered a loan under the Income-Tax Act and equity as per the foreign direct investment standards and the Indian Accounting Standard. However, for transfer pricing purposes, these instruments may be classified as 'Quasi Capital' or 'Debt' depending upon an examination of the characteristics of the instrument and surrounding circumstances under which the instrument was issued. Hybrid instruments are commonly seen in India due to the flexibility they offer from an exchange control perspective.

## 4 Other

Routinely seen financial transactions not very common in India are hedging arrangements and cash pool arrangements. Intra-group financial transactions include hedging arrangements to mitigate risk exposures such as foreign exchange or commodity price movements. Often an MNE group would centralise its treasury functions and implement risk mitigation techniques on behalf of independent enterprises within the MNE group. OECD notes that an MNE group may adopt the following techniques:

- Delegation of responsibility for hedging to an MNE group treasury entity, with the hedging contracts arranged for and in the name of the relevant operating companies.
- Delegation of responsibility for hedging to an MNE group treasury entity, with the hedging contracts made by and in the name of another MNE group entity.
- Identification of the existence of natural hedges within the MNE group, in which case no formal hedging contracts are made.

It is noteworthy to mention that cash pooling though popular among multinational enterprises operating in different parts of the World, however, exchange control regulations in India do not specifically provide for participation in cash pool arrangements, and therefore, it is difficult to carry out cross-border cash pooling in India.

13. OECD (2020), Transfer Pricing Guidance on Financial Transactions: Inclusive Framework on BEPS Actions 4, 8-10, OECD, Paris.

## IV APPLICATION OF ARM'S LENGTH PRINCIPLE

### 1 Accurate Delineation: OECD Perspective

OECD Transfer Pricing Guidelines for Multinational Enterprises and Tax Administrations 2022 ('OECD TPG 2022') contains general guidance at paragraph 10.17 on accurate delineation of a financial transaction.

The accurate delineation of the actual transaction should begin with a thorough identification of the economically relevant characteristics of the transaction – consisting of the commercial or financial relations between the parties and the conditions and economically relevant circumstances attaching to those relations – including: an examination of the contractual terms of the transaction, the functions performed, assets used, and risks assumed, the characteristics of the financial instruments, the economic circumstances of the parties and the market, and the business strategies pursued by the parties.

The Guidelines provide an example to state that in the context of loans, the accurately delineated amount for transfer pricing purposes would be a function of the maximum amount that an unrelated lender would have been willing to advance to a company and the maximum amount that an unrelated borrower in comparable circumstances would have been willing to borrow from the associated enterprise lending the money. This includes the possibilities of not lending or borrowing any amount, and consequently, the remainder of the loan would not be delineated as a loan for the purposes of determining the amount of interest which the company would have paid at arm's length.[14]

Further, OECD Transfer Pricing Guidelines 2022 provide that in accurately delineating an advance of funds, the following economically relevant characteristics may be useful indicators, depending on the facts and circumstances:

- the presence or absence of a fixed repayment date;
- the obligation to pay interest;
- the right to enforce payment of principal and interest;
- the status of the funder in comparison to regular corporate creditors;
- the existence of financial covenants and security;
- the source of interest payments;
- the ability of the recipient of the funds to obtain loans from unrelated lending institutions;
- the extent to which the advance is used to acquire capital assets; and
- the failure of the purported debtor to repay on the due date or to seek a postponement.

14. Paragraph 10.13 of the 2020 TPG in Chapter 1. The Guidelines do not seek to mandate accurate delineation under Chapter I as the only approach for determining whether purported debt should be respected as debt. However, the purpose of Chapter I is to provide guidance for countries that use the accurate delineation under Chapter I to determine whether a purported loan should be regarded as a loan for tax purposes (or should be regarded as some other kind of payment, in particular a contribution to equity capital) (paras 10.9 and 10.10).

For guarantees, the accurate delineation of financial guarantees requires initial consideration of the economic benefit arising to the borrower beyond the one that the borrower derives from passive association. Where a guarantee permits a borrower to borrow a greater amount of debt than it could, in the absence of the guarantee, the guarantee is not merely supporting the credit rating of the borrower. The guarantee both increases borrowing capacity and reduces interest rates on any existing borrowing capacity. The Guidelines note that in such a situation, there may be two issues - whether a portion of the loan from the lender to the borrower is accurately delineated as a loan from the lender to the guarantor (followed by an equity contribution from the guarantor to the borrower), and whether the guarantee fee paid with respect to the portion of the loan that is respected as a loan from the lender to the borrower is arm's length. The conclusion of an analysis of such transactions may be, considering the full facts and circumstances, that the evaluation of the guarantee fee should be limited to a fee on the portion that has been accurately delineated as a loan, and the remainder of the loan granted should be regarded as effectively a loan to the guarantor followed by an equity contribution by the guarantor to the borrower.[15]

The Guidelines also suggest effects of a group membership have to be taken, and a mere letter of comfort involves no explicit assumption of risk and should be attributable to passive association.[16]

## 2 Accurate Delineation: Indian Perspective

Indian transfer pricing laws are codified in the Income-tax Act of 1961, and the OECD Guidelines are usually treated as having persuasive value unless they come in friction with the domestic law. It is noteworthy that in the OECD's Country Profile, India has stated that it does not have any specific guidance for financial transactions and stipulates the adoption of the Most Appropriate Method considering all relevant facts and circumstances of the case. The Country Profile also states India's position as 'OECD Transfer Pricing Guidelines (and the UN TP Manual) are useful references for carrying out transfer pricing studies by taxpayers and audits by Indian transfer pricing officers (TPO). Indian transfer pricing law does not explicitly recognise the direct applicability of the OECD TPG (or the UN TP Manual). However, India has framed its own rules and guidance on transfer pricing, which are broadly in line with the OECD TPG as well as the UN TP Manual.'[17]

Pertinently, in a ruling of August 2021, the Mumbai Tribunal in *Bennett Coleman*[18] delved into the issue of whether interest-free advance granted by the parent to an offshore Special Purpose Vehicle (SPV) for an identified acquisition of a target company abroad, can be compared with a loan simplicitor, and be, subjected to an arm's length price adjustment on the basis of comparable uncontrolled price (CUP). The Income Tax Appellate Tribunal (ITAT) referred to a specific provision in the Indian

15. Paragraph 10.161 of the OECD TPG.
16. Paragraph 10.163 of the OECD Guidelines.
17. *See* https://www.oecd.org/tax/transfer-pricing/transfer-pricing-country-profile-india.pdf.
18. [2021] 129 taxmann.com 397 (Mumbai – Trib.).

transfer pricing rules[19] and observed that not only the transaction has to be between independent enterprises but also in uncontrolled conditions. The ITAT observed that when a strict condition about end-use, and that too end-use being decided by the owner of the SPV so much in advance that the SPV was not even in existence when the end-use decision was taken, is an inherent part of the transaction of funds being remitted, this is anything but an uncontrolled condition.

This ruling closely approximates the accurate delineation concept envisaged in the OECD Guidance on Financial Transactions released in 2020 and incorporated in the 2022 Guidelines. The Guidelines recognise that consistent with the analysis of other transactions between associated enterprises, in applying the arm's length principle (ALP) to a financial transaction, it is necessary to consider conditions that an independent enterprise would have agreed to in comparable circumstances.[20]

## 3 Benchmarking and Jurisprudence Around Intra-group Financial Transactions in India

The determination of ALP by a taxpayer in India for any international transaction must be undertaken under one of the six prescribed methods in law – the comparable uncontrolled price (CUP) method, the resale price method (RPM), the cost plus method (CPM), the profit split method (PSM), the transactional net margin method (TNMM) or Other Method which provides for a wider latitude for benchmarking. Comparability factors are also set out in law and include:

(a) the specific characteristics of the property transferred, or services provided in either transaction;
(b) the functions performed, taking into account assets employed or to be employed and the risks assumed, by the respective parties to the transactions;
(c) the contractual terms (whether or not such terms are formal or in writing) of the transactions which lay down explicitly or implicitly how the responsibilities, risks and benefits are to be divided between the respective parties to the transactions;
(d) conditions prevailing in the markets in which the respective parties to the transactions operate, including the geographical location and size of the markets, the laws and Government orders in force, costs of labour and capital in the markets, overall economic development and level of competition and whether the markets are wholesale or retail.

The regulations further provide that transactions shall be comparable only if none of the differences is likely to materially affect the price in the open market or reasonably accurate adjustments can be made to eliminate the material effects of such differences.

19. Section 92F(ii) 'arm's length price' means a price which is applied or proposed to be applied in a transaction between persons other than associated enterprises, in uncontrolled conditions.
20. Paragraph 10.18, of OECD TPG 2020.

Some of the currently debated topics and transactions in India in the context of intra-group financial transactions are.

### A Intra-group Guarantees

Under the Indian regulatory framework,[21] an Indian party may have financial commitment to its overseas Joint Venture (JV)/Wholly Owned Subsidiary (WOS) to the limit, as prescribed by the Reserve bank from time to time, of the net worth of the Indian party as on the date of the last audited balance sheet. The financial commitment may be in the form of:

(i) capital contribution and loan to the JV/WOS;
(ii) corporate guarantee (only 50% value in case of performance guarantee) and/or bank guarantee (which is backed by a counter guarantee/collateral by the Indian party) on behalf of the JV/WOS; and
(iii) charge on immovable/movable property and other financial assets of the Indian party (including group company) on behalf of JV/WOS.

The Reserve Bank of India (RBI) observed in 2014[22] that banks were extending non-fund-based credit facilities like guarantees/stand-by letter of credits/letter of comforts etc. on behalf of JV/ WOS/Wholly Owned Step-Down Subsidiaries (WOSDS) for purposes which are not connected with their business, rather, in certain cases, these facilities were used to avail foreign currency loans for repayment of Rupee loans. The RBI then clarified that banks, including overseas branches/subsidiaries of Indian banks, shall not issue standby letters of credit/guarantees/letters of comfort etc., on behalf of overseas JV/WOS/WOSDS of Indian companies for the purpose of raising loans/advances of any kind from other entities except in connection with the ordinary course of overseas business.

Also, while issuing guarantees by banks to Indian subsidiaries, the RBI stipulates the guarantee of parent companies may be obtained in the case of subsidiaries whose own financial condition is not considered satisfactory.

Both these stipulations by the RBI have led to significant intra-group guarantee transactions in India.

#### a Benchmarking of Guarantees

There is synchronisation between the OECD, UN and India on the use of CUP for benchmarking of guarantee fee. If comparable uncontrolled transactions in comparable circumstances are identified, CUP could be applied in the following ways:

21. RBI Master Circular on Guarantees and co-acceptances dated 9 November 2021, https://rbi.org.in/scripts/NotificationUser.aspx?Mode=0&Id=12189#AN2.
22. *See* https://www.rbi.org.in/Scripts/NotificationUser.aspx?Id=8846&Mode=0.

- Internal CUP: Reference shall be made to guarantee fee applied to similar transactions in similar circumstances between associated enterprise (AE) and an unrelated party.
- External CUP: Reference shall be made to guarantee fee applied to similar transactions in similar circumstances between unrelated parties.

Information from third-party financial guarantees, bankers' acceptances, credit default swap fees, letter of credit fees, commitment fees, various types of insurance and put options may be useful. It is important that the resulting guarantee fee may need to be adjusted by means of adjustments for better comparability analysis.

Indian courts have consistently preferred internal CUP as the most preferred method for determining the ALP for a guarantee fee.[23] Though internal CUP is ideal and has been upheld as most preferred method followed by external CUPs, in the absence of an internal CUP, finding an appropriate external CUP is a practical challenge.

Accordingly, taxpayers may need to resort to other methods for benchmarking corporate guarantee as prescribed by OECD such as yield approach,[24] cost approach,[25] valuation of expected loss approach[26] and capital support method.[27]

The above-mentioned methods prescribe alternative approaches; however, they pose an inherent limitation since they largely work with estimates and do not provide concrete underlying incomparable data. They are additionally not specifically recognised under Indian TP regulations, and presently there is very little jurisprudence on the same. It is perceived that the above-mentioned methods, on account of great intricacies, mandate a complex analysis. Moreover, their inherent complexity may serve as a major impediment while justifying the approach before the Indian tax authorities and invite prolonged litigation.

### *b* *Judicial Precedents on Guarantees*

With nearly 400 reported cases adjudicated by various Indian courts, including Tribunals, the issue of corporate guarantee is a highly vexed issue.

Prior to the 2012 amendment to Indian Regulations, the main issue on corporate guarantee was whether it could be brought within the definition of 'international transaction' under section 92B of the Act. The erstwhile section (prior to the 2012 retrospective amendment) did not specifically cover 'corporate guarantee' in the definition of international transaction. Taxpayers took recourse under the erstwhile

23. *CIT v. Everest Kento Cylinders Ltd* [2015] 58 taxmann.com 254 (Bombay), Asian Paints [2014] 41 taxmann.com 71 (Mumbai Tribunal), Britannia Industries Ltd [TS-359-ITAT-2018(Kol)-TP].
24. Applying the Arm's Length Principle to Intra Group Financial Guarantees in light of the OECD's Draft Guidance on Financial Transactions, Vera Averyanova & Vikram Chand, Kluwer International Tax Blog, para. 3.2. The yield approach has been adopted in the Mumbai Tribunal in KEC International 132 taxmann.com 75.
25. Transfer Pricing Guidance on Financial Transactions, Inclusive Framework on BEPS, Actions 4, 8-10, para. 10.178.
26. *Ibid.*, para. 10.181.
27. *Ibid.*, para. 10.182.

definition to strengthen their position that corporate guarantee is not an international transaction.

While in some cases,[28] the Tribunal held that corporate guarantee was not an international transaction and hence the Indian parent was not required to charge any fee, there were others[29] where the Tribunal held otherwise. Retrospective amendment to section 92B vide Finance Act, 2012. Explanation (i) to section 92B was inserted with effect from 1 April 2002, wherein the term 'international transaction' specifically included corporate guarantee within its scope.

It is important to note that section 92B(1) sets a condition to qualify as an international transaction, i.e., 'bearing on profits, income, losses, or assets' of the business. This was the position prior to the 2012 amendment. Hence, post amendment to section 92B, the question revolved around whether a transaction would be subject to ALP adjustment if it did not comply with the conditions set out in section 92B(1).

If the parent entity extended guarantee to its associated enterprise for which no fee was charged, there was no bearing on profits, income or assets of the business, and hence, not an international transaction.[30] Further, since the guarantee obligation may or may not arise in the future date depending on the default by the borrower, it cannot fall within the purview of an international transaction. It is important to note that this decision was taken by the Delhi Tribunal in *Bharti Airtel Ltd*[31] post retrospective amendment by the Finance Act, 2012 relating to the definition of 'international transaction'. It is noteworthy to mention that the facts in this case were peculiar since it was factually demonstrated that ultimately no borrowings were obtained by the associated enterprise and therefore there were no costs incurred for the extended corporate guarantee.

Another noteworthy ruling is that of the Mumbai Tribunal in the case of Siro Clinpharm[32] which delivered post amendment decision. The Tribunal held that when a taxpayer extends assistance to the associated enterprise, which does not cost anything and particularly for which the taxpayer could not have realised money by giving it to someone else in the course of its normal business, such assistance or accommodation does not have any bearing on its profits, income, losses or assets, and, therefore, outside the ambit of international transaction under section 92B(1) of the Act.

### *c* *Intra-group Corporate Guarantee: Whether a 'Shareholder Activity'?*

There have also been occasions where the taxpayers have contended that a corporate guarantee qualifies as a shareholder activity and hence does not require any charge of

28. Four Soft Limited [TS-518-ITAT-2011(HYD)-TP]. This case was decided before the amendment to the definition of International Transaction made by the Finance Act, 2012.
29. Nimbus Communications Limited [TS-167-ITAT-2013(MUM)-TP].
30. Bharti Airtel Limited [TS-76-ITAT-2014(DEL)-TP].
31. *Ibid.*
32. SIRO Clinpharm (P.) Ltd. [2017] 88 taxmann.com 338 (Mumbai – Trib).

a corporate guarantee fee/commission. In case the inter-corporate guarantee is construed as a shareholder activity, it would not require any charge as it is understood that there is no provision of service as the Parent performs such function solely because of its ownership interest. On the contrary, in case the function of issuing a corporate guarantee is considered as an intra-group service, the same would justify a charge and hence shall be subjected to ALP determination. The determination of the appropriate classification shall *inter-alia* involve an examination of factors such as purpose of the loan, the terms and conditions under which guarantee has been issued, whether a loan would have been issued had no guarantee been extended etc. The classification issue is a fact-intensive exercise.

It is noteworthy to mention that the Ahmedabad Tribunal in *Micro Ink Limited*[33] while deciding whether corporate guarantee could be construed as a shareholder activity relied upon OECD Guidelines[34] to answer the question. It examined circumstances where the corporate guarantee would qualify as shareholder activity or otherwise. The Tribunal while placing reliance on OECD observed that when the corporate guarantees are issued for the purpose of subsidiaries raising funds for acquisitions, such guarantees will be deemed to be services, and, as a corollary, when corporate guarantees are issued to raise funds for their own needs, such guarantees are to be treated as shareholder activity. There are various other Tribunals in India that have followed the *ratio decendi* laid out in the given case.

### *d* *Bank Guarantee Versus Corporate Guarantee Fees*

CUP method is used where there is external or internal comparable, i.e., independent guarantors extending guarantees in respect of comparable loans to other borrowers or where same borrower has extended other comparable loans which are independently guaranteed. In most cases, the tax authorities in the absence of internal comparable, adopt interest rates quote, and guarantee rate quotes available from banking companies as benchmarks. However, such an approach has had its fair share of controversies as the taxpayers have consistently disputed this approach on account of incomparability or lack of availability of comparable data

In *Glenmark Pharmaceuticals Limited,*[35] the Mumbai Tribunal, explaining the difference between bank guarantee and corporate guarantee, held that Transfer Pricing Officer's bank guarantee rates were 'IUP's', i.e., incomparable uncontrolled prices and could not be used to benchmark purposes. The Tribunal rejected bank guarantee rates noting that these were 'naked quotes of bank guarantee rates as given on the website for public as CUP unless they are adjusted to comparability factors mentioned in Rule 10B of the Rules. ITAT also observed that bank guarantee and corporate guarantee are conceptually different.

33. ITA No. 2873/Ahd/10.
34. Paragraphs 7.6 to 7.10, Chapter VII OECD Transfer Pricing Guidelines for Multinational Enterprises and Tax Administrations (2010).
35. ITA No. 5031/M/2012, ITA No. 5488/M/2012.

Mumbai Tribunal, in the case of Everest Kanto Cylinders Limited,[36] held that in view of the amendment brought by the Finance Act, 2012 by way of Explanation added in section 92B, payment of guarantee fee is included in the expression 'international transaction' in view of the Explanation i(c) of section 92B. Once the guarantee fee falls within the meaning of 'international transaction', then the methodology provided in the rules also becomes applicable.

The above decision of the ITAT has been approved by Bombay High Court[37] wherein the High Court has not questioned the ITAT's decision with respect to the transaction being an international transaction since in the given case, the taxpayer was charging guarantee fees of 0.5% as commission, and the High Court affirmed the Tribunal's view that it cannot be said there is no impact on 'profits, incomes, losses or assets of such enterprise'. Accordingly, the transaction was held to be an international transaction. Further, the High Court held that the only point to see was whether the commission was at ALP. The High Court held that bank guarantee issued by commercial bank cannot be compared with the corporate guarantee issued by the holding company for the benefit of computing ALP of guarantee commission and relied upon the internal CUP as suitable comparable to determine ALP.

### *B Benchmarking of Hybrid Instruments*

The characterisation of a loan instrument as quasi-equity or in fact loan is often perceived as a moot question. It is noteworthy to mention that Article 9 of the OECD Model Tax Convention states, 'not only in determining whether the rate of interest provided for in a loan contract is an arm's length rate, but also whether a prima facie loan can be regarded as a loan or should be regarded as some other kind of payment, in particular a contribution to equity capital'.[38]

It becomes essential to first identify the nature/characterisation of the purported loan between AEs for accurately delineating advancement of funds and in pursuance, thereto, the following economically relevant characteristics may be useful indicators, depending on the facts and circumstances of each case:

- Presence or absence of a fixed repayment date.
- Obligation to pay interest.
- The right to enforce payment of principal and interest.
- Status of the funder in comparison to regular corporate creditors.
- Existence of financial covenants and security.
- Source of interest payments.
- Ability of the recipient of the funds to obtain loans from unrelated lending institutions.
- Failure of the purported debtor to repay on the due date or to seek a postponement.

36. 34 Taxmann.com 19 (Mumbai - Trib.).
37. [2015] 58 taxmann.com 254.
38. Paragraph 1 Clause 3(b) of Article 9 of the OECD Model Tax Convention.

Also, it is important to identify the commercial or financial relations between AEs by analysing the following economically significant characteristics or comparability factors:

- Contractual terms of the tested loan.
- Functions performed, assets used, and risks assumed by both parties of the loan agreement involving an assessment of the purpose of loan and any interaction with other intra-group transactions.
- Economic circumstances of the borrower, the lender, the industry and the market in which they operate.
- Business strategies and circumstances of the MNE.
- Actual conduct of the parties with respect to the transaction.

An independent enterprise, when considering whether to enter into a financial transaction will consider all other options realistically available to them and enter into the transaction only if they see no alternative that offers a clearly more attractive opportunity to meet their commercial objectives. In considering the options realistically available, the perspective of each of the parties to the transaction must be considered, i.e., a two-sided perspective from the buyer and the lender is imperative.

The lender's perspective on whether to make a loan, how much to lend and on what terms, will involve evaluation of various factors relating to the borrower's creditworthiness, wider economic factors affecting both the borrower and the lender and other options realistically available to the lender for the use of the funds.

From the borrower's perspective, the options available will include broader considerations than the entity's ability to service its debt, for example, the funds it needs to meet its financing requirements. In some instances, although an entity may have the capacity to borrow and service the debt, it may choose not to do so to avoid placing negative pressure on its credit rating, increasing its cost of capital and jeopardising its access to capital markets and its market reputation. Borrowers will also consider the potential impact of changes in economic conditions such as interest rates and exchange rates, as well as the risk of not being able to make timely payments of interest and principal on the loan if the borrower's business encounters an expected difficulty and the risk of not being able to raise more capital (either debt or equity), if necessary.

Conventionally, loan transactions in India are benchmarked based on applicable interest rates for simplicitor loan transactions. However, the same benchmarking methodology would not be relevant for hybrid transactions as they are materially different than a loan simplicitor, and therefore, what needs to be assessed is the loan document, including actions of parties to the agreement. For instance, a non-refundable loan which is to be converted into equity shall not be directly comparable to a vanilla loan transaction on account of an equity component embedded into the instrument. It, therefore, becomes essential to first identify the nature/ characterisation of the purported loan between associate enterprises for accurately delineating advancement of funds.

Indian TP regulations are silent on the recharacterisation of an intra-group financial transaction unlike the General Anti-Avoidance Rule (GAAR) provisions where the instrument can be recharacterised. However, the Delhi High Court in a landmark ruling in EKL appliances[39] relied upon the guidance under Article 9 of the OECD Model Tax Convention to hold that ordinary tax administration should not disregard the actual transaction or substitute other transactions for them, and the examination of a controlled transaction should ordinarily be based on the transaction as it has been undertaken and structured by the associated enterprises. It is pertinent to note that the OECD Transfer Pricing Guidelines under Chapter 1, after referring to Article 9 of the model convention and stating the ALP the guidelines recognise that barring the exceptional cases, the tax administration should not disregard the actual transaction. The reason for characterisation of such restructuring as an arbitrary exercise, as given in the guidelines, is that it has the potential to create double taxation if the other tax administration does not share the same view as to how the transaction should be structured. However, the High Court noted that in some exceptional circumstances, the tax administration may be well justified to recharacterise an international transaction. The High Court laid out the following exceptions:

(i) where the economic substance of a transaction differs from its form; and
(ii) where the form and substance of the transaction are the same, but arrangements made in relation to the transaction, viewed in their totality, differ from those which would have been adopted by independent enterprises behaving in a commercially rational manner.

Based on the above jurisprudence, a Transfer Pricing Officer upon satisfaction of the exception may proceed to adjust the structure of an intra-group financial transaction.

It is noteworthy to mention that the Ahmedabad Tribunal in Cadila Healthcare Limited[40] examined the issue of whether an optionally convertible loan could be regarded as a loan simplicitor. The Tribunal expounded on the expression 'quasi capital' to hold that the substantive reward for such a loan transaction is not interest but opportunity to own capital. The reward for time value of money in these cases was opportunity to subscribe to the capital, unlike in a normal loan transaction where reward is interesting, which is measured as a percentage of the money loaned or advanced. It was further observed that the considerations for extending a loan simplicitor are materially distinct and different from extending a loan which is given in consideration for, or mainly in consideration for, option to convert the same into capital on certain terms which are favourable. The Tribunal finally held that optionally convertible loan is a quasi-capital transaction which cannot be compared with a simple loan transaction.

In our view, the decision of the Tribunal while deciphering the characteristics of an optionally convertible loan provided significant guidance on qualifying conditions

39. I.T.A. Nos 1068/2011 and 1070/2011.
40. IT (TP) No. 898/Ahd/2014, 694/Ahd/2015, IT (TP) No. 519/Ahd/2014 and 747/Ahd/15.

for classification of a hybrid instrument such as an optionally convertible loan to be considered 'quasi-capital'.[41]

## C Constructive Loans

Another contentious issue which is debated is on delayed allotment of shares to an associated enterprise. On various occasions, Indian tax authorities have proceeded to recharacterise share application money pending allotment as an interest-free loan. The rationale adopted is that an independent enterprise would have converted the amount into equity within a reasonable period, i.e., would not have left the amount pending in the hands of another entity. Further, an independent enterprise would have also received interest on the same construed as the opportunity cost of capital. Though such forms of recharacterisation will require the Indian tax authorities to look beyond the form and focus on the substance, it is noteworthy to mention that interest-free loan disguised as equity, may also be subject matter of scrutiny under the GAAR law, to ensure that the transaction is non-abusive and does not confer any undue tax benefit resulting in shifting of profits.

The explanation provided by the Delhi Tribunal in Bharti Airtel Limited's case is worth noting. Transfer Pricing Officer in *Bharti Airtel Limited*[42] treated share application money not converted into equity as advancement of interest-free loan and imposed adjustment on account of notional interest. However, Tribunal, deleting the adjustment, held that there is no finding of the tax authorities on what the reasonable and permissible time for allotment of shares should be. The Tribunal went on to hold that even if ALP determination was to be done in respect of such deemed interest-free loan on allotment of shares under the CUP method, as has been claimed to have been done in this case, it was to be done on the basis as to what would have been interest payable to an unrelated share applicant if, despite having made the payment of share application money, the applicant is not allotted the shares. That aspect of the matter is determined by the relevant statute. This situation is not in pari materia with an interest-free loan on a commercial basis between the share applicant and the company to which capital contribution is being made.

In another case of the Mumbai Tribunal in *Aditya Birla Minacs Worldwide Limited*,[43] that since the delay was due to obtaining necessary approval from the Securities and Exchange Commission, Philippines, it could not support the tax authorities' approach for recharacterisation of share application money as an interest-free loan.

The Mumbai Tribunal in *Sterling Oil Resources Private Limited*,[44] the Tribunal went a step further to hold that a delay in allotment of shares would not cause any prejudice to the applicant in case it was the sole shareholder of the associated enterprise. The Tribunal held that ultimately the fruits of the investment would belong

41. Paragraphs 10.4 & 10.5, OECD TPG 2020.
42. ITA No. 5816/Del/2012.
43. ITA No. 7033/Mum/2012, ITA No. 7142/Mum/2012.
44. ITA No. 1791/Mum/2014, ITA No. 1970/Mum/2014.

to the taxpayer only and in its entirety. Further, the Tribunal noted that none of the conditions for recharacterisation of transactions specified in decision of the Delhi Tribunal in *EKL Appliances*[45] was satisfied, and accordingly held that it was 'wrong to even allege that an assessee does not behave in a commercially rational manner'.

The Indian courts have time and again intervened on the purported approach of the tax authorities to recharacterise pending share application money as an interest-free loan. The Courts have examined in detail the facts of each case and surrounding circumstances to ascertain whether the reason for any delay in allotment was beyond the control of the taxpayer and at the same time factored whether hypothetically any loss would arise in case of delay in allotment of shares to the taxpayer. Such court rulings are significant jurisprudence on the subject issue as they provide ample guidance towards accurate delineation of a share application transaction to ensure that the test of Arm's length condition is fully met.

## *D Interest on Loans*

### OECD Transfer Pricing Guidelines

To effectively benchmark the interest rate pursuant to an intra-group loan transaction, it seems important for a borrower to obtain credit rating. Information is readily available in many lending markets on the different rates of interest charged for differently rated enterprises, and such information may usefully contribute to performing comparability analyses.[46] However, as a credit rating depends on a combination of quantitative and qualitative factors, there is still likely to be some variance in creditworthiness between borrowers with the same credit rating. Financing transactions undertaken by the borrowing MNE or another entity in the MNE group, for example, the MNE group parent, will be reliable comparables only where the differences between the controlled and uncontrolled transactions do not materially affect the interest rate or reasonably accurate adjustments can be made.

In a scenario where no credit rating is available, companies may consider obtaining the same from credit rating agencies such as ICRA, CRISIL, etc. (for Indian companies) or from S&P, Moody's, etc. (in case of overseas companies).

However, where obtaining such credit ratings from a renowned credit rating agency is not possible, a synthetic credit rating may be arrived at using the guidance and tools provided by rating agencies such as Moody's and S&P for determination of credit rating of companies, specific to the industries.

Examples of determining the synthetic credit ratings are as follows:

- Moody's Methodology paper, which can be used to determine the credit rating based on qualitative and quantitative parameters (this method is largely used to determine the credit rating for the real estate industry);

45. [TS-395-ITAT-2011(DEL)-TP].
46. Transfer Pricing Guidance on Financial Transactions, Inclusive Framework on BEPS, Actions 4, 8-10, p. 16, para. 10.65.

- Moody's RiskCalc, which is a quantitative method used to derive the credit rating of the company based on its financial statements; and
- the notching approach, which can be used to derive the credit rating of a subsidiary based on the rating of the parent company and the number of operating entities in the group structure of the multinational enterprise (MNE).

It is important to note that the synthetic credit rating derived using commercial tools differs significantly from the credit rating methodologies applied by independent credit rating agencies to determine official credit ratings. For instance, such tools generally use only a limited sample of quantitative data to determine a credit rating. Official credit ratings published by independent credit rating agencies are derived because of a much more rigorous analysis which includes a quantitative analysis of historic and forecast company performance, as well as a detailed qualitative analysis of the management's ability to manage the company, industry-specific features and the company's market share in its industry.

Considering the credit rating obtained or synthetically derived, a benchmarking analysis may be conducted in databases such as Bloomberg, Loan connector, ICON, etc., by applying the relevant criteria. Examples of such criteria are as follows:

- the region of the borrower;
- the region of the lender;
- the currency of the borrower;
- the terms (secured/unsecured);
- the type of instrument;
- the tenure of the loan; and
- the credit rating of the borrower.

Particular considerations should be borne in mind when determining a credit rating for a specific MNE within an MNE group for the purpose of assessing controlled transactions. Where an MNE has a publicly available credit rating published by an independent credit rating agency, that rating may be informative for an arm's length analysis of the MNE's controlled financing transactions.

Further, publicly available financial tools are also designed to calculate credit ratings. Broadly, these tools depend on approaches such as calculating the probability of default and of the likely loss should default occur to arrive at an implied rating for the borrowing. This can then be compared to a market database in a search for comparables to arrive at a price or price range for the borrowing.[47]

**Indian Perspective**

Another debatable issue has been in respect of the appropriate benchmark for rate of interest charged on outbound loans advanced by Indian entities. It is generally seen that an outbound loan denominated in foreign currency is usually benchmarked using London Interbank Offered Rate (LIBOR). However, in the past, the Indian TPO have

47. Transfer Pricing Guidance on Financial Transactions, Inclusive Framework on BEPS, Actions 4, 8-10, p. 17, para. 10.72.

taken the view that any loan advanced by an Indian entity to its associated enterprise should be benchmarked using prevalent domestic lending rates while ignoring the currency denomination for the repayment of loans. Interestingly, domestic lending rates in India are usually higher than LIBOR or any comparable international lending rates and which led to transfer pricing adjustments in the hands of the Indian Parent Co. This approach of the tax officer was challenged by the taxpayers at various appellate forums.

The controversy around domestic or foreign interest rates was put to rest by the Delhi High Court in a landmark ruling in *Cotton Naturals India Private Limited.*[48] The ruling laid out significant guidance on foreign currency-denominated loans and held that Indian prime lending rate cannot be considered a suitable comparable to benchmark foreign currency loans. The High Court in its judgment relied upon Klaus Vogel Double Taxation Conventions (Third Edition) to hold that the question of whether the interest rate prevailing in India should be applied, for the lender was an Indian company, or the lending rate prevalent in the United States should be applied, for the borrower was a resident of the said country, must be answered by adopting and applying a common sensical and pragmatic reasoning. The interest rate should be the market-determined interest rate applicable to the currency concerned in which the loan has to be repaid. The currency in which the loan is to be repaid normally determines the rate of return on the money lent, i.e., the rate of interest. It is pertinent to note that the said ruling has gained finality and has become a settled law in India.

## E *Interest-Free Loans*

The tax authorities generally perceive interest-free outbound loans from an Indian parent to its overseas subsidiary as an activity which should result in an arm's length consideration. An Expert Group established by the Indian government in April 2002 that noted that 'borrowing or lending on an interest-free basis or at a rate of interest significantly above or below market rates prevailing at the time of the transaction is an undesirable corporate practice related to transfer pricing'.[49]

The Indian tax tribunals have consistently rejected 'nil interest rate' or 'interest-free' loans advanced by an Indian entity to its overseas associated enterprise and disregarded taxpayer's contention of the provision of a loan on account of commercial expediency and dismissed the arguments on the real income theory.[50]

Conversely, the Tax Tribunal, in an old divergent ruling in *Mascon Global Ltd*,[51] stated that loans made to overseas subsidiaries were made for developing the markets

48. ITA No. 233/2014.
49. Export Group of the Indian government, report, Annexure 4 (April 2002), available at https://faculty.iima.ac.in/~jrvarma/reports/Transfer_Price/expert_group_report.htm (accessed 1 October 2020).
50. IN: ITAT Mumbai, 29 April 2016, ITA No. 641/Mum/2007, *Strides Shasun Ltd. v. ACIT*, TS-260-ITAT-2017-Mum; IN: *VVF Ltd. v. DCIT*, 2010-TIOL-55-ITAT-Mum; IN: *Perot Systems TSI (India) v. DCIT*, ITA No. 2320, 2321 & 2322/Del/2008; and IN: Delhi Tribunal, *Aithent Technologies Pvt. Ltd.* ((ITA No. 3647/Del/2007).
51. *Mascon Global Limited*, TS-482-ITAT-2011(CHNY).

and hence were based on the principle of commercial expediency. Accordingly, in one such isolated case, the Tax Tribunal held that the interest-free loans made by the taxpayer were at arm's length.

Given the overall consistent stand of Indian courts in subjecting interest-free loans to the ALP and to avoid any transfer pricing adjustment exposure, it is prudent, to ensure that parties entering financial arrangements with associated enterprises satisfy ALP principles under section 92(1) of the Act.

### *F Transition from LIBOR*

Indian MNEs that extend outbound loans rely upon LIBOR interest rates to benchmark intra-group loan transactions which are denominated in foreign currency. This approach is also vindicated by a High Court ruling[52] which prescribes LIBOR as a suitable interest rate for outbound foreign currency loans. Pursuant to the 2017 announcement, The Financial Conduct Authority (FCA), UK announced on 5 March 2021, that LIBOR will either cease to be provided by any administrator or no longer be a representative rate:

(a) immediately after 31 December 2021, in the case of all Pound sterling, Euro, Swiss Franc and Japanese yen settings, and the 1-week and 2-month US dollar settings; and
(b) immediately after 30 June 2023, in the case of the remaining US dollar settings.

Guidance[53] provided by the Reserve Bank of India on 8 July 2021, encourages banks to cease use of LIBOR and instead use any widely accepted Alternate Reference Rate. On 22 July 2021, the World Bank recognised[54] Alternate Reference Rates as under:

- Secured Overnight Financing Rate (SOFR) for USD-denominated loans
- Sterling Overnight Index Average (SONIA) for GBP-denominated loans
- Tokyo Overnight Average Rate (TONA) for JPY-denominated loans
- EURIBOR will remain the reference rate for EUR-denominated loans.

For Swiss Franc Reference Rates, SARON, which stands for Swiss Average Rate Overnight and represents the overnight interest rate of the secured money market for Swiss francs (CHF) has been recommended by the National Working Group on Swiss Franc Reference Rates. It is based on transactions and quotes posted in the Swiss repo market, a pivotal part of the Swiss Value Chain.[55] However, forward-looking term rates are not being developed by the administrators of SARON.

---

52. *CIT v. Cotton Naturals (I) (P.) Ltd* [2015] 55 taxmann.com 523 (Delhi).
53. *See* https://www.rbi.org.in/Scripts/NotificationUser.aspx?Id = 12128&Mode = 0.
54. *See* https://www.worldbank.org/en/news/press-release/2021/07/22/world-bank-approves-new-reference-rates-for-existing-and-new-loans-in-preparation-for-end-of-libor.
55. *See* https://www.six-group.com/en/products-services/the-swiss-stock-exchange/market-data/indices/swiss-reference-rates.html.

The LIBOR rate is computed using a 'trimmed arithmetic mean' approach (simple average of rates[56] submitted by a panel of contributing banks after removing outliers) for five currencies (USD, EUR, GBP, CHF and JPY) across seven maturities (overnight, one-week, one month, two months, three months, six months, and twelve months) resulting in a total of 35 rates each business day. The Swiss Franc was thus one of the five currencies considered for LIBOR; however, term rates are not being developed under SARON, which explains why it was left out by the World Bank.

The discontinuance of LIBOR necessitates a need for Indian MNEs to consider modifying existing agreements to replace LIBOR with a substitute risk-free interest rate. The substituted interest rate may not provide the same financial result as was achieved by the borrower and lender upon execution of the original agreement. However, given that Indian transfer pricing law requires maintenance of contemporaneous documentation, at the time of transaction, it should be possible to adopt a position that any change in the spread would lead to the same result as the original intent of the parties entering into the agreement.

The impact of transition from LIBOR will also require a revisit of the safe harbour rules which prescribe LIBOR for foreign currency-denominated loans for financial year 2020-2021. Given that the LIBOR rate shall cease to exist from 1 January 2022, Revenue department will need to amend safe harbour rules.

The discontinuance of LIBOR would also impact the secondary adjustment provisions under income tax act (ITA)[57] as the provisions mandate use of LIBOR for computation of imputed interest on deemed advances not repatriated to India within the prescribed time limits in case the international transaction is denominated in foreign currency.

The phase out for LIBOR would require a re-examination of concluded Advanced Pricing Agreements (APAs) on intra-group loans since one of the critical assumptions agreed upon may include LIBOR plus basis points as the appropriate interest rate for foreign currency-denominated loans.

## V IMPACT OF COVID

COVID led to a contraction of the global economy. Estimates indicate the virus reduced global economic growth in 2020 to an annualised rate of around –3.2%.[58]

Economic contraction results in decreasing revenues, constraints on cash repatriation, disproportionate fixed costs, shortages of bridge finance and uncertain covenants surrounding debt agreements.[59] Economic crises significantly alter capital

56. Before 1100 hours GMT every London business day, the Intercontinental Exchange (ICE), i.e., the administrator of LIBOR asks a panel of contributing Banks to answer the following question: 'At what rate could you borrow funds, were you to do so by asking for and then accepting interbank offers, in a reasonable market size just prior to 11 a.m.?'
57. Section 92CE.
58. *See* https://sgp.fas.org/crs/row/R46270.pdf.
59. Paragraph 10.32 *OECD Guidelines* (2017). *See also* P. Carlsson-Szlezak, M. Reeves & P. Swartz, *What Coronavirus Could Mean for the Global Economy*, Harvard Business Review (3 March 2020). Also *see* S. Prasanna & G. Capristano Cardoso, Developing a Transfer Pricing Policy

structures. During the 2007-2008 crisis, market debt ratios increased, on average, by 5.5% and were reversed by 2010.[60] The difference between the 2007-2008 financial crisis and the COVID-19-induced economic distress is that the latter is not centred on the failure of banks or financial institutions, and banks may be better positioned to service debt requirements.[61]

According to the Reserve Bank of India's report for 2020-2021,[62] monetary policy and liquidity operations during 2020-2021 were geared towards mitigating the adverse impact of the unprecedented economic devastation brought by the COVID-19 pandemic on the Indian economy.

Arm's length behaviour of related parties may include the refinancing of existing inter-company loans to avail themselves of lower interest rate terms that prevail in the short term.

However, more recent international tax regulations have mandated that related parties should maintain arm's length capital structures and comply with thin capitalisation rules, limiting the liberty to use excessive debt in the capital structure. The relatively high sensitivity of debt composition as a response to thin capitalisation rules over the past decades has been empirically proven. Further, a fall in Earnings Before Interest and Taxes (EBIT) levels during the crisis has exacerbated the risk of ratios breaching both the thin capitalisation limits and arm's length conditions.[63]

As part of the benefit test, a subsidiary could re-evaluate its ability to obtain external borrowings with or without an explicit guarantee (yield approach) and analyse whether implicit support would suffice to achieve the desired credit terms. Therefore, guarantee fees payable during the downturn are expected to be minimised if the incremental benefit of an explicit guarantee converges with the benefits of implicit support.[64] Accordingly, subsidiaries could independently assess the value of benefit and seek to renegotiate terms if the value of the benefit reduces due to reduction in credit rating of its associated enterprise.

It is also worth noting that India has not issued any guidelines for treatment of COVID-related adjustments, however, the OECD guidance[65] states it's the consensus view of the then-137 members of the Inclusive framework.[66] Hence, Indian taxpayers

Framework for the Current Economic Crisis and Beyond, 27 Intl. Transfer Pricing J. 5 (2020), Journal Articles & Opinion Pieces IBFD.

60. https://www.aabri.com/manuscripts/121213.pdf.
61. N. Mora, *Can Banks Provide Liquidity in a Financial Crisis?*, 95 Federal Reserve Bank of Kansas City Economic Review 3, pp. 31-67 (2010), available at https://www.kansascityfed.org/publicat/econrev/pdf/10q3Mora.pdf (accessed 3 July 2020).
62. *See* https://rbi.org.in/scripts/AnnualReportPublications.aspx?Id = 1316.
63. S. Prasanna & G. Capristano Cardoso, Developing a Transfer Pricing Policy Framework for the Current Economic Crisis and Beyond, 27 Intl. Transfer Pricing J. 5 (2020), Journal Articles & Opinion Pieces IBFD.
64. Paragraph 10.87 of OECD TP Guidelines.
65. Guidance on the transfer pricing implications of the COVID-19 pandemic.
66. 'The "Guidance on the transfer pricing implications of the COVID-19 pandemic" represents the consensus view of the 137 members of the Inclusive Framework on BEPS regarding the application of the arm's length principle and the OECD Transfer Pricing Guidelines to issues that may arise or be exacerbated in the context of the COVID-19 pandemic.' https://www.oecd.org/coronavirus/policy-responses/guidance-on-the-transfer-pricing-implications-of-the-covid-19-pandemic-731a59b0/.

and tax administrators could look at the OECD Guidelines as reference when factoring COVID-related adjustments.

## VI CONCLUSION

While India continues to progress in discovering the inexact science of transfer pricing, the OECD 2022 guidance (which incorporates the 2020 Guidance on Financial Transactions) provides much-needed comprehensive guidance on intra-group financial transactions. The guidance should be welcomed both by judiciary and tax administration for interpretation of ALPs. It is undeniable that the Indian courts have, time and again, interpreted OECD documents as eligible soft law. This position also stands affirmed by a recent decision in the context of income from software licensing the Supreme Court has categorically stated that for the interpretation of provisions of Indian treaties based on the OECD MC or United Nation MC, the Commentaries have persuasive value.[67]

MNEs should vigilantly document the circumstances surrounding intra-group financial transactions, apart from transfer pricing-related documentation. As an example, the role of failures on the part of credit rating agencies (CRAs) in causing losses and wider financial turmoil has been under scrutiny in recent decades. In an unprecedented move, in October 2021, the Securities & Exchange Board of India issued a show-cause as to why the licence of a credit rating agency should not be cancelled. Credit ratings of comparables are an important factor in determining arm's length spreads and guarantee commission rates – MNEs should be aware of and document similar developments that can impact their intra-group financing, especially in a heavily financially-regulated economy like India. That's our two cents!

67. *Engineering Analysis Centre of Excellence Private Limited v. CIT* TS-106-SC-2021.

CHAPTER 55

# Transfer Pricing Aspects of Financial Transactions: A Brazilian Perspective

*Luís Eduardo Schoueri & Daniel Teixeira Prates**

## I INTRODUCTION

The Brazilian Transfer Pricing system is well-known for its simplicity and also for the deviation from international practice. The legislation is geared towards achieving simplicity and providing legal certainty. However, it contains strict and inaccurate elements that create difficulties, particularly in dealing with more complex transactions and mismatches with the international practice, thus increasing the risk of economic double-taxation or non-taxation. This pattern is also observed when it comes to the discipline of financial transactions.

After a quick overview of the Brazilian transfer pricing framework (section II), this article discusses the application of domestic legislation to intra-group loans (IV), intra-group financial guarantees (section V), and cash pooling arrangement (section VI). The article focuses on a technical analysis of the Brazilian approach to dealing with such transactions also making a comparison with the international standard.

## II BRAZILIAN TRANSFER PRICING FRAMEWORK: OVERVIEW

The system was introduced in 1996 being inspired by the work of the 1979 OECD Report.[1] When it comes to the methodologies for the determination of an arm's length

* The views and opinions set forth herein are the personal views or opinions of the authors; they do not necessarily reflect views or opinions of the organization with which the authors are associated.

1. OECD & Receita Federal do Brasil, Transfer Pricing in Brazil: Towards Convergence with the OECD Standard 16 (2020).

price, Brazil adopts methods that are inspired by the traditional transaction methods foreseen in the OECD Transfer Pricing Guidelines: Comparable Uncontrolled Price Method, Resale Price Method (RPM), and Cost Plus Method.[2]

The correspondent version of the comparable uncontrolled price (CUP) method is broadly in line with the Organisation for Economic Co-operation and Development (OECD) Transfer Pricing Guidelines,[3] except for the fact that the secondary legislation imposes some limitations on the possibilities of comparability adjustments that can be performed.

The other traditional methods inspired by the OECD Transfer Pricing Guidelines (Cost Plus Method and RPM) rely on a formulaic approach that incorporates fixed margins. The fixed margins provided by the legislation vary depending on whether the control transaction is an import or an export.[4] To illustrate, the variation of Cost Plus applicable to exports requires a fixed mark-up of 15% while the correspondent version of the method used for imports demands a 20% mark-up. For the version of the Resale Price applicable to import transactions, the legislation contemplates different margins per industrial sector. However, no consideration is made to the functional profile of the enterprise – the margins are 40%, 30%, or 20% depending on the industrial sector but are applicable irrespective of the functional profile of the taxpayer.

The fixed margins as provided by the Law are subject to critics in respect of their inaccuracy and lack of adherence to the economic reality of the business sectors. Under justified circumstances, taxpayers may request the application of different profit margins from those provided by the Law[5] but to date, there is not even a single case of success, which is mainly explained due to the extensive (and not reasonable) list of documents that are required to substantiate the request.[6]

The formulaic approach as adopted by such methods eliminates most of the comparability analysis and significantly reduces the role of the accurate delineation of the actual transaction in the Brazilian transfer pricing practice.

For commodities, the legislation demands the application of specific methodologies.[7] Brazil introduced in 2012 its version of the so-called sixth method. The methodologies are broadly similar to the CUP-Commodities that were incorporated into the OECD Transfer Pricing Guidelines after the discussions taken in Actions 8-10 of the base erosion and profit shifting (BEPS) project, but their mandatory character must be considered.[8]

With respect to some financial transactions, there is also a specific and mandatory methodology that also relies on a formulaic approach for the determination of the arm's length interest rate, which will be presented and discussed in more detail in the next topics.[9]

2. Article 18 of Law n. 9,430/1996.
3. Article 9 of Normative Instruction n. 1,312/2012.
4. Articles 18 and 19 of Law n. 9,430/1996.
5. Article 21, para. 2 of Law n. 9,430/1996.
6. OECD & Receita Federal do Brasil, *supra* n. 1, at 124.
7. Articles 18-A and 19-A of Law n. 9,430/1996.
8. OECD & Receita Federal do Brasil, *supra* n. 1, at 80.
9. Article 22 of Law n. 9,430/1996.

Transactional methods (TNMM and Profit Split Method) and other methods (e.g., valuation techniques) are not foreseen in the domestic framework. The absence of the Profit Split and of 'the other methods' impose some difficulties to deal with more complex transactions.

Except for commodities and financial transactions, taxpayers have the freedom to choose any of the applicable methods. In Brazil, the selection of the transfer pricing method is not determined based on a hierarchy or on its appropriateness given the facts and circumstances of a particular case, as adopted in most OECD countries. The freedom of choice allows taxpayers to choose the method that leads to the most favourable outcome.

To complete the big picture of the Brazilian transfer pricing system, it is also valid to mention that some safe harbours are also contemplated in the legislation, especially for export transactions.[10]

## III FINANCIAL TRANSACTIONS

Brazil has a specific and mandatory methodology for the determination of the arm's length interest rate.

For other areas of financial transactions such as intra-group guarantees, hedging, captive insurance, cash pooling, and others there is no specific guidance or provision, meaning that the general framework would apply. The application of the general framework to these transactions can create difficulties to comply with the current legislation, as it would be required either identification of comparable uncontrolled transactions or use of the fixed margins in cases where such comparables are absent.[11] One may claim that the lack of comparable could lead to no adjustment since the remaining methods would not be adequate for some hard cases, however, it is unlikely that this would be recognized by tax authorities and to this moment, no case seems to have been presented before courts in such situation.

As a matter of fact, the Brazilian transfer pricing framework does not incorporate the notion of accurate delineation of the actual transaction. The most important step to perform when assessing the arm's length nature of a transaction is the comparability analysis.[12] The comparability analysis requires an assessment of whether the conditions of a transaction between related parties are similar to the conditions that would be found between unrelated. Before being able to perform the comparability analysis, it is necessary to identify the commercial or financial relations between the associated enterprises and the conditions and economically relevant circumstances attached to those relations in order that the controlled transaction is accurately delineated.[13]

10. Articles 48 and 49 of Normative Instruction n. 1,312/2012.
11. OECD & Receita Federal do Brasil, *supra* n. 1, at 192.
12. A. SULEJMANI, *Pricing Intercompany Financial Transactions: Loans, Guarantees and Cash-Pooling Arrangements,* Intl. Transfer Pricing (2019).
13. OECD, *OECD Transfer Pricing Guidelines for Multinational Enterprises and Tax Administrations 2022* item 1.33 (OECD Publishing, 2022).

In addition to the prescriptive transfer pricing method, the deduction of interest is also subject to a general deductibility test and thin capitalization rules.

By the general deductibility test, expenses and costs are deductible from Corporate Income Tax when they are necessary, usual, and normal in the enterprise activities. Based on this rule, the Administrative Tax Court did not accept the deductibility of interest when the borrower raises external funding and transfers part or all the loan to associated parties without charging any interest.[14]

Brazil has not introduced specific measures to deal with hybrid mismatches and has not implemented BEPS Action 2 recommendations.

From a tax policy perspective, the Brazilian framework has not evolved over time to deal with cross-border financial transactions. The legislation seems to have been stuck in time while this area has rapidly evolved with the creation of new forms of financing, financial instruments, and consequently, to deal adequately with the correspondent problems related to transfer pricing.

## IV INTRA-GROUP LOANS

The discipline of transfer pricing for financial transactions that involve payment or receivement of interest is ruled by Article 22 of Law 9,430/96. The determination of interest rates for intra-group loans should observe such rules.

Since the introduction of the transfer pricing system in 1996, this provision suffered several modifications, but the prescriptive approach adopted remains unchanged.

### 1 Safe Harbour

Until 2013, this provision provided a relevant safe harbour that would exclude from the application of transfer pricing rules the interests arising from intra-group loans derived from contracts registered with the Central Bank of Brazil (BACEN), regardless of the amount of the funding.

The rationale for this safe harbour, though disputable, was justified by the assumption that the Central Bank of Brazil would already have controlled the interest rate adopted in the loans agreements evaluating its suitability to the market conditions.[15] This assumption, however, is not exempt of critics given that the role of the Central Bank of Brazil has changed since the transfer pricing legislation was initially introduced and presently does not control whether interests paid or received are reasonable, but rather follows and monitors the flow of national and foreign capital[16]

The existence of this safe harbour created a significant constraint on the scope of application of transfer pricing rules, given that, generally, most of the inbound loan

14. Higher Chamber of Tax Appeals: Decision n. 01-05.423(2006) and Chamber of Tax Appeals: Decision n. 1301-002.098 (2016).
15. Article 8 of Law n. 4,131/1962.
16. C. Pelá, *Juros e Preços de Transferência. Nova Sistemática Introduzida Pela Lei n. 12.766/2012*, in S.L. Eduardo (ed.), *Tributos e Preços de Transferência* 9 (Dialética, 2013).

agreements were subject to registration within the regulatory body. Consequently, the application of transfer pricing rules was restricted only to those who failed to register their contracts with the Central Bank of Brazil[17] or to specific cases in which the registration of the contract was not required by the regulatory legislation (e.g., when the Brazilian resident had a bank account in another jurisdiction and would grant a loan to another party).[18]

The possibility of using this safe harbour for outbound loans is an issue that has been for a long time under dispute in Brazilian Courts. Tax administration argues that the scope of this measure does not include outbound loans due to the absence of a specific mechanism for registration of these contracts with the Central Bank of Brazil. In a recent case, however, the Administrative Court decided in favour of taxpayers accepting the argument that, despite those outbound loans are not subject to the same registration process with the Central Bank as inbound loans, the remittance of the funds to the borrower is also subject to the control by the regulatory body through a different mechanism of registration.[19]

It is worth highlighting that this safe harbour can still be used for loans related to contracts signed up to 2013 that remain in force. To promote tax certainty, the subsequent changes that were introduced by the Law do not modify the rules applicable to the contracts that remain in force – the rules introduced in 2012 abolished the possibility of using the safe harbour only for contracts signed after 2012 and for those that were previously signed but have been renegotiated after 2013.

## 2 Interest Rates and Spreads

Intra-group loans that are out of the scope of the aforementioned safe harbor must comply with a prescriptive approach foreseen in Article 22 of Law 9,430/1996 that is inspired on a build-up approach (adding a spread to a base rate).[20] Based on this approach, the compensation for financing is calculated based on fixed interest rates prescribed by the Law which are increased by predetermined spreads defined by the Ministry of Finance.

Until 2013, the interest deduction and the minimum income for intra-group loans were determined based on the six-month US Dollar London Interbank Offered Rate (LIBOR) increased by a 3% spread ('6-Month USD LIBOR plus 3%'). This rule is still applicable for contracts that were entered into before 2013 but are still in force.

For contracts signed up after 2013, the current wording of Article 22 of Law 9,430/1996 establishes different interest rates and delegates to the Ministry of Finance the power to define the applicable spread. The interest rates are determined based on the currency in which the loan is denominated. Accordingly, in the case of intra-group loans:

---

17. M.N. Rodriguez, *Anotações Sobre Regras de Preços de Transferência Em Contratos de Mútuo, Revista de Direito Tributário Internacional* 121 (2008).
18. Pelá, *supra* n. 16, at 07.
19. Higher Chamber of Tax Appeals: Decision n. 9101-005.666.
20. R. Petruzzi, *Transfer Pricing Aspects of Intra-Group Financing* 145-146 (Wolters Kluwer, 2016).

- in USD with a fixed interest rate, the interest rate cap will be the rate payable on the sovereign bonds of the Federative Republic of Brazil issued on the foreign market in US dollars;
- in Brazilian Reais (BRL) with a fixed interest rate, the interest rate cap will be determined as the interest rate payable on the sovereign bonds of the Federal Republic of Brazil issued on the foreign market in Brazilian reals; and
- with different terms, the six-month LIBOR.

With regard to the spread, the Ministry of Finance defined a 3.5% spread for inbound loans and a 2.5% spread for outbound loans.[21]

The Brazilian solution for determining the compensation for intra-group loans may produce outcomes that deviate from the arm's length principle. The approach eliminates most of the comparability analysis by fixing a cap for the compensation that should be provided for the financing. The spreads are fixed and prescribed without having due regard to the creditworthiness of the borrower, the characteristics of the financial instrument, and the economic circumstances of the control transaction. A third-party lender typically would only decide to advance funds after analysing the risks inherent in the loan, especially the capability of the borrower to repay the principal and the interest on the loan in due time. In addition, the prices of a financial instrument may vary substantially depending on its characteristics and based on the underlying economic circumstances (e.g., the amount of the loan; its maturity; the schedule of repayment; the geographical location of the borrower; currency; collateral provided; presence and quality of any guarantee; and whether the interest rate is fixed or floating).[22] Each term and condition in a loan agreement has an impact on the risk assumed by the lender and the borrower and, hence, also on the interest rate to be applied.[23]

The Brazilian approach does not consider those factors. The current legislation brought some improvements when abandoned the use of a single mechanism for pricing the financial instrument ('6-Month USD LIBOR plus 3%') and introduced the possibility of using different interest rates depending on the currency of the loan. However, even after this update, it is still possible to affirm that the system could easily lead to outcomes that deviate from the arm's length standard since the elements that were introduced are not sufficient to have due regard to the relevant and different factors that may affect the price of the transaction.

In fact, several flaws contained in the rule could lead to the determination of compensation that differs from what independent parties, in comparable circumstances, would have established. The use of the rate payable on the sovereign bonds of the Federative Republic of Brazil as a benchmark could at best reflect part of the risk inherent to loans when the borrower is a Brazilian. Certainly, it is unable to reflect the credit risk for the reverse situation when the borrower is a foreign entity. Besides, the fixed formula undermines the possibility of considering the relevant commercial and

21. Ordinance of the Ministry of Finance n. 427/13.
22. OECD, *supra* n. 13, at item 10.28.
23. Sulejmani, *supra* n. 12.

financial characteristics of the control transaction and eliminates most of the necessary comparability analysis that would be necessary to achieve an arm's length result.

In addition, when it comes to loans denominated in currencies different from BRL or USD, the legislation determines the use of the six-month LIBOR. The Libor rate is expressed in different currencies and comprises different maturity periods, reflecting the currency and maturity risks. Usually, long-term loans generally offer a maturity risk premium in the form of a higher built-in rate of return to compensate. At the discretion of the law, the six-month LIBOR was adopted without having any connection with the maturity of the controlled transaction.[24]

The absence of functional analysis and of the notion of the accurate delineation of the transaction could also lead to inadequate outcomes from an arm's length perspective in situations of intra-group transactions, where the capital is borrowed from third parties and passes from the original borrower through one or more associated intermediaries until it reaches the ultimate borrower. In such cases, where only agency functions are being performed by the intermediaries, an appropriate arm's length pricing could be determined based on a mark-up on the costs of the agency function.[25] In the Brazilian context, however, if the intra-group transaction is carried out as a loan, the application of the prescriptive approach would price the control taxation using the prescribed interest rates plus the fixed spreads, probably leading to a non-arm's length outcome.

The same may occur in situations in which the funder does not perform the decision-making functions to control the risk associated with the funding. In order to assume risk, a company needs to have control over the risk (so-called 'risk management functions') and the financial capacity to assume that risk. A company that would not bear any financial risk related to the intercompany loan, either because it does not perform the decision-making function or because it lacks the financial capacity, would not be entitled to more than a risk-free return.[26] While in the international practice, the creditor will probably be remunerated with no more than a risk-free rate of return in such cases, in Brazil the use of the prescriptive approach provided by the Law with the fixed rates plus the spread would lead to a different outcome, probably overcompensating the lender.

This Brazilian approach was conceived to simplify the system and ensure tax certainty. However, besides the inconsistencies with the arm's length principle, the design of the measure contains elements that often prevent the achievement of these goals. One major issue is the use of one of the standard benchmarks that are provided by the law - i.e. the sovereign bonds of the Federative Republic of Brazil. These government bonds are issued to raise funds that help the government to settle its obligations, such as the payment of salaries and investments in education and health. However, they are not frequently issued. To illustrate, from 2013, only 18 bonds were

24. M.N. Rodriguez, Nova Disciplina de Preços de Transferência Sobre Juros, in Luís Eduardo Schoueri (ed.), Tributos e Preços de Transferência 235 (Dialética, 2013).
25. OECD, *supra* n. 13, at item 10.100.
26. *Ibid.*, at item 10.25.

issued – none in BRL, 17 in USD, and only 1 in EUR.[27] This scarcity creates practical difficulties in using these bonds as a benchmark for transfer pricing purposes. To overcome such challenges, different solutions are adopted by taxpayers that are locked in such methodology but without being backed up by any administrative guidance or case law that could promote tax certainty.[28]

Another issue that will have significant implications for transfer pricing is the discontinuation of LIBOR. In March 2021, the Financial Conduct Authority (FCA) and ICE Benchmark Administration (the administrator of LIBOR) announced that GBP, EUR, CHF, and JPY LIBOR panels, as well as panels for one-week and two-month USD LIBOR, will cease at the end-2021, with the remaining USD LIBOR panels ceasing at end-June 2023.[29] As the most prevalent benchmark interest rates, USD LIBOR and EURIBOR are referenced by an estimated USD 370 trillion in financial contracts worldwide, making up approximately 80% of the total interest reference rate market exposure.[30]

As the domestic Law demands the use of these benchmarks for intra-group loans that are not denominated in USD or BRL or that are agreed with post-interest rates, without any possibility to opt-out, the cessation of LIBOR will create an issue for both tax administration and taxpayer to comply with the rules. Without any changes in the legislation, the maintenance of this benchmark will certainly raise the question of how such transactions should be priced. A possible and temporary approach to comply with the domestic Law could be to rely on the six-month USD LIBOR, regardless of the loan currency, since the cessation of this benchmark is scheduled only to end-June 2023.

To conclude, regarding intra-group loans, the domestic framework presents excessive strict rules without any possibility to opt-out. This approach tends to promote outcomes that deviate from the arm's length principle and in some cases may fail to deliver the desired simplification and certainty that drives the Brazilian tax system.

## 3 Thin Capitalization Rules

Commentary to Article 9 of the OECD Model Tax Convention provides that the arm's length principle is not only relevant 'in determining whether the rate of interest provided for in a loan contract is an arm's length rate, but also whether a prima facie loan can be regarded as a loan or should be regarded as some other kind of payment, in particular, a contribution to equity capital'.[31] Thus, where it is considered that the

27. Tesouro Nacional, 'Foreign Bond Debt' (2021), https://www.gov.br/tesouronacional/en/federal-public-debt/external-market/external-public-bonds.
28. M. Vicentini, Preços de Transferência e o Mercado Financeiro in Manual de Preço de Transferência: Beps, Brasil & OCDE 582 (Quartier Latin, 2018).
29. Financial Conduct Authority, 'About LIBOR Transition', https://www.fca.org.uk/markets/libor-transition.
30. D. Ledure et al., *The End of the LIBOR World as We Know It: A Sound Bite of Consequences Tax Professionals Should Be Aware Of*, Intl. Transfer Pricing (2019).
31. OECD, *Model Tax Convention on Income and on Capital: Condensed Version 2017* 142 (OECD Publishing, 2017).

arrangements differ from those which would have been adopted by independent enterprises in comparable circumstances, a loan can be claimed to be delineated as equity for transfer pricing purposes.[32]

In the Brazilian system, however, transfer pricing and arm's length principle are not used in the current framework to determine the amount of debt to be priced. The balance between debt and equity relies mostly on thin capitalization rules.

For related parties' debts, thin capitalization rules set a debt-to-equity ratio that may not exceed 2:1 of the net equity of the Brazilian entity. In cases where the interest is paid to a related or unrelated party in a low-tax jurisdiction or subject to a privileged tax regime, the debt-to-equity ratio may not exceed 0.3:1 (30%).[33]

Brazil has not introduced the recommended approach of BEPS Action 4 which uses a fixed ratio to limit the deductibility of an entity's net interest and financing costs to a percentage of its earnings before interest, taxes, depreciation, and amortization (EBITDA).[34]

The control of the deductibility of the interest expenses is made by the application of the general deductibility test, thin capitalization rules, and transfer pricing rules. The legislation does not guide the order of application of these rules. In the absence of such guidance, a reasonable approach is to consider that all of those rules apply together, observing the following order: first, the amount of the debt that will be the basis for the calculation of deductible interest is determined using thin capitalization rules; then, the amount of interest that will be paid on that basis is established with transfer pricing rules; finally, the amount of interest determined will only be deducted if such expenses are considered normal, usual, and necessary for the activities of the taxpayer.[35]

## V INTRA-GROUP FINANCIAL GUARANTEES

Intra-group financial guarantees are a risk transfer mechanism whereby one party agrees to assume the financial obligation of another party towards a third party in the event that the guaranteed entity defaults on its obligation.[36] Such arrangements are useful tools employed by multinational enterprises (MNEs) to obtain better conditions in the financial market.[37] The existence of a guarantee may allow the guaranteed party to obtain funding with a more favourable interest rate and to increase the amount of borrowing. Intra-group guarantees are frequently used in situations of loans, where a

32. OECD, *supra* n. 13, at item 10.4.
33. Article 24 of Law n. 12,249/2010.
34. OECD, *Limiting Base Erosion Involving Interest Deductions and Other Financial Payments, Action 4 – 2016 Update: Inclusive Framework on BEPS, OECD/G20 Base Erosion and Profit Shifting Project* (OECD Publishing, 2016).
35. L.E. Schoueri, *Preços de Transferência No Direito Tributário Brasileiro* 338 (Dialética, 3rd ed., 2013).
36. M. Lang et al., *Fundamentals of Transfer Pricing: A Practical Guide* 585 (Wolters Kluwer, 2019).
37. V. Averyanova & V. Chand, *Applying the Arm's Length Principle to Intra-Group Financial Guarantees in Light of the OECDs Draft Guidance on Financial Transactions, Kluwer International Tax Blog* (2019).

related party provides a guarantee on a loan taken by another related party from third parties.[38]

In the context of the OECD approach, two major questions are needed to be answered to determine the arm's length compensation for an intra-group guarantee. From the perspective of the borrower, the first question is whether the guarantee provides an effective economic benefit to the borrower reducing the cost of debt funding in such a way that it will be in a better position to obtain the funding if compared to a scenario without the guarantee. If the guarantee does not enhance the commercial position of the borrower, independent parties probably will not be willing to pay for it. The second question is the determination of the arm's length compensation for the guarantee. The OECD report indicates five possible pricing approaches – CUP method, Yield Approach, Cost Approach, Valuation of expected loss approach, and Capital Support Method.[39]

The CUP method could be used where there are internal or external comparable available. As recognized by OECD, the difficulty of using the CUP method is that publicly available information about comparable transactions is very unlike to be found between independent parties. To overcome such difficulties, the OECD indicates other approaches that may be used to determine the arm's length compensation for intra-group guarantees.[40]

The 'Yield Approach' consists, in short, in quantifying the benefit received by the guaranteed party from the guarantee in terms of lower interest rates. In other words, this method consists in determining the spread between the interest rate that would have been payable if the borrower was not supported by the guarantee and the interest rate payable with the guarantee.

The 'Cost Approach' aims to quantify the additional risk borne by the guarantor by estimating the value of the expected loss that the guarantor incurs by providing the guarantee (loss given default).

By the 'valuation of expected loss method', it is estimated the value of a guarantee based on calculating the probability of default and making adjustments to account for the expected recovery rate in the event of default.

Finally, the 'Capital Support Method' consists in determining the credit rating of the borrower without the guarantee but accounting for implicit support and identifying the amount of the additional notional capital required to adjust the borrower's credit rating up to the credit rating of the guarantee.

Concerning the Brazilian system, in the case of payments of guarantee, the deduction of the correspondent expense from Corporate Income Tax will also be tested by the general deductibility rule, being evaluated if such expense is necessary, usual, and normal in the Brazilian taxpayer.

Regarding the transfer pricing framework, Brazil does not have specific rules or administrative guidelines on intra-group guarantees, which means that the general framework applies to such transactions. The application of the general framework to

38. OECD, *supra* n. 13, at item 10.158.
39. *Ibid.*, at items 10.169 to 10.182.
40. *Ibid.*, at items 10.170 to 10.173.

intra-group guarantees raises potential difficulties in dealing with intra-group guarantees.

The most suitable method contained in Brazilian transfer pricing rules would be the CUP method. However, the absence of available comparable transactions for such transactions creates difficulties for the application of this method, as recognized by OECD. In addition, as previously mentioned, the secondary legislation imposes limitations on the comparability adjustments that can be performed, which may create additional complications for an adequate application of this method from an arm's length perspective.

The alternatives available in the domestic legislation would be the version of the Cost Plus and the RPM. Both methods rely on a formulaic approach that incorporates fixed margins and is not well-suitable to deal with the specificities of those transactions. Besides, the use of other approaches, as proposed by the OECD, is not feasible in the Brazilian transfer pricing practice since the application of 'other methods' is not allowed by the domestic legislation. Thus, concerning intra-group guarantees, the rigidity of the domestic framework creates difficulties in the application of the transfer pricing legislation for both tax administration and taxpayers[41].

## VI CASH POOLING

Cash pooling is an arrangement involving one or more banks that allows combining debit and credit balances in a group's separate bank accounts to derive net balances on a real or notional basis.[42]

The use of cash pooling is something usual in multinational groups. By establishing a cash pool arrangement, MNEs can better manage the liquidity requirements of the group on a consolidated basis (virtually or physically) by concentrating the cash of the group companies in one place. The general effect of cash pooling is that the MNE pays or receives interest only on the net (consolidated) cash amount of the master account.[43] With the arrangement, MNEs can obtain several benefits such as better returns from an investment of cash surplus or enhanced credit terms, including lower interest rates and charges from external funding.[44]

As cash pooling is not usually found between independent parties,[45] the application of the arm's length principle becomes challengeable to such arrangements.[46] As paragraph 1.11 notes 'Where independent enterprises seldom undertake transactions of the type entered into by associated enterprises, the arm's length principle can be

41. A.G. Oliveira & P.V. Gomes, *O Tratamento Dos Valores Remetidos a Título de Garantia a Residentes No Exterior (Guarantee-Fee) e o Seu Enquadramento Para Fins de Preços de Transferência*, in L.F.M. Castro & F.L. Moreira (eds), *Manual de Preço de Transferência: Beps, Brasil & OCDE* (Quartier Latin, 2018).
42. Lang et al., *supra* n. 36, at. 385.
43. A. Haller & V. Chand, *Application of the Arm's Length Principle to Physical Cash Pooling Arrangements in Light of the OECD Discussion Draft on Financial Transactions*, 47 *Intertax* (2019).
44. A. Russo & O. Moerer, *Introduction, in Transfer Pricing and Intra-Group Financing* (IBFD, 2012).
45. OECD, *supra* n. 13, at 10.115.
46. Haller & Chand, *supra* n. 43.

difficult to apply because there is little or no direct evidence of what conditions would have been established by independent enterprises'.[47]

As mentioned above, cash pooling can create an advantage in reducing the interest paid or increasing the interest received, which results from netting credit and debit balances. To illustrate, an arm's length interest rate for a single cash pool deposit may be 4%, while the external bank applies a 6% rate on the cash deposit in the master account due to economies of scale.[48] The amount of that group synergy benefit, calculated by reference to the results that the cash pool members would have obtained had they dealt on a stand-alone basis, should be shared by the cash pool members, provided that an appropriate reward is attributed to the cash pool leader for the functions performed.[49]

To establish an appropriate reward for the cash pool members, OECD indicates that the remuneration shall be calculated through the determination of arm's length interest rates that also allocate the synergy benefits arising from the arrangement among the members, after compensating the cash pool leader for the functions performed. Frequently, a cash pool leader performs no more than a coordination or agency function with the master account being a centralized point for a series of book entries to meet the predetermined target balances for the pool members. Given such a low level of functionality, the cash pool leader's remuneration as a service provider will generally be similarly limited.[50]

The determination of the arm's length interest rate for the cash pool loans should be made with appropriate considerations. The use of the CUP method using bank interest rate as a reference may not ensure an arm's length allocation of the synergy benefits among the members (as a matter of fact, synergy gains are a problem also for non-financial transactions[51]). By applying bank interest rates on the single loan arrangements without appropriate analysis, the cash pool leader could end up receiving the same interest income as an external bank (i.e., the interest spread between lower interest rates on cash deposits and higher interest rates on cash borrowings), which usually would not be compatible with its functional profile. Under the arm's length principle, the cash pool leader should be compensated based on the functions performed. Banks usually have a more complex business model and a cash pool leader with a low functional profile would not be entitled to earn the same compensation.[52] The Danish Administrative Tax Court and the Norwegian Court of Appeal did not accept the application of bank interest rates on physical cash pooling arrangements considering the particular facts and circumstances of the cases.[53]

47. OECD, *supra* n. 13, at item 1.11.
48. Russo & Moerer, *supra* n. 44.
49. OECD, *supra* n. 13, at 10.121.
50. *Ibid.*, at 10.130.
51. *Ibid.*, at items 1.177 to 1.193.
52. Haller & Chand, *supra* n. 43.
53. DK: LSR, 21 October 2013, Case 12-0189459; NO: LR (Court of Appeal), 11 January 2010, *ConocoPhillips Skandinavia AS & Norske ConocoPhillips AS v. Oljeskattekontoret* [*ConocoPhillips Scandinavia AS & Norwegian ConocoPhillips AS*].

The Brazilian Transfer Pricing system does not have specific rules or guidance on cash pooling arrangements. In addition, there are no tax cases about this matter.

In Brazil, cash pooling arrangements are subject to the same rules provided by intra-group loans. Thus, for transfer pricing purposes, the determination of the interest paid or received should be made on the basis of the same prescriptive approach described above. Based on this approach, the compensation for financing is calculated based on fixed interest rates prescribed by the Law which are increased by predetermined spreads defined by the Ministry of Finance.

In principle, each transaction carried out by the taxpayer will be considered as a separate loan and will be priced accordingly.[54] No consideration is made by the domestic framework with respect to the functions performed, assets used and risks assumed by the cash pool leader and the members to determine each compensation.

As mentioned, the benchmark foreseen in the Law does not take into consideration the economic circumstances underlying the financial transaction (creditworthiness, maturity of the debt, etc.), being detached in most cases from the economic reality surrounding the control transaction. Besides, when it comes to cash pooling arrangements, the use of the formulaic approach with the fixed returns could lead to additional problems by ignoring and misallocating the additional benefits that the MNE group obtain with the arrangement without sharing it adequately among the members.

## VII CONCLUSION

The Brazilian Transfer Pricing system is well-known for its simplicity and also for the deviation from international practices. The legislation is geared towards at achieving simplicity and providing legal certainty but at the same time contains strict and inaccurate elements that create difficulties, particularly in dealing with more complex transactions and mismatches with the international practice. This pattern is also observed when it comes to the discipline provided by the domestic legislation for financial transactions.

Brazil has a specific and mandatory methodology for the determination of the arm's length interest rate. Based on this approach, the compensation for financing is calculated based on fixed interest rates prescribed by the Law which are increased by predetermined spreads defined by the Ministry of Finance. This approach tends to promote outcomes that deviate from the arm's length principle and in some cases may fail to deliver the desired simplification and certainty that drives the Brazilian tax system.For other areas of financial transactions such as intra-group guarantees, hedging, captive insurance, cash pooling, and others, there is no specific guidance or provision, meaning that the general framework would apply. The application of the general framework to these transactions can create difficulties in complying with the current legislation, as it would be required either identification of comparable

54. H. Erbolato & D. Orsini, *Cash-Pooling, Inboud e Outbound: Harmonização Entre as Regras de Preços de Transferência e Subcapitalização*, in L.F.M. Castro & F.L. Moreira (eds), *Manual de Preço de Transferência: Beps, Brasil & OCDE* 732 (Quartier Latin, 2018).

uncontrolled transactions or use of the fixed margins in cases where such comparables are absent.

From a tax policy perspective, the Brazilian framework has not evolved over time to deal with cross-border financial transactions. The legislation seems to have been stuck in time while this area has rapidly evolved with the creation of new forms of financing, financial instruments, and consequently, to deal adequately with the correspondent problems related to transfer pricing.

In February 2018, the OECD and Brazil launched a joint project to examine the similarities and divergences between the Brazilian and OECD transfer pricing approaches to value cross-border transactions between associated enterprises. One of the key objectives is to eliminate the gaps between the two systems promoting the alignment of the Brazilian transfer pricing rules with the OECD Transfer Pricing Guidelines. In this context, it is expected that the Brazilian rules applicable to financial transactions will also be modified to ensure a better alignment with the arm's length principle, thus reducing the risk of economic double-taxation and double non-taxation.

# Index

**B**

**G**

**S**

www.ingramcontent.com/pod-product-compliance
Lightning Source LLC
Chambersburg PA
CBHW071234230926
51849CB00001B/98
* 9 7 8 9 4 0 3 5 4 0 2 3 8 *